Complete A+ Guide to IT Hardware and Software

A CompTIA A+ Core 1 (220-1001) &
CompTIA A+ Core 2 (220-1002) Textbook

EIGHTH EDITION

CHERYL A. SCHMIDT

FLORIDA STATE COLLEGE AT JACKSONVILLE

PEARSON IT
CERTIFICATION

Complete A+ Guide to IT Hardware and Software, Eighth Edition

Copyright © 2020 by Pearson Education, Inc.

ISBN-13: 978-0-7897-6050-0

ISBN-10: 0-7897-6050-9

Library of Congress Control Number: 2019930917

1 2019

Trademarks

All terms mentioned in this book that are known to be trademarks or service marks have been appropriately capitalized. Pearson IT Certification cannot attest to the accuracy of this information. Use of a term in this book should not be regarded as affecting the validity of any trademark or service mark.

Warning and Disclaimer

Every effort has been made to make this book as complete and as accurate as possible, but no warranty or fitness is implied. The information provided is on an "as is" basis. The author and the publisher shall have neither liability nor responsibility to any person or entity with respect to any loss or damages arising from the information contained in this book.

Special Sales

For information about buying this title in bulk quantities, or for special sales opportunities (which may include electronic versions; custom cover designs; and content particular to your business, training goals, marketing focus, or branding interests), please contact our corporate sales department at corpsales@pearsoned.com or (800) 382-3419.

For government sales inquiries, please contact governmentsales@pearsoned.com.

For questions about sales outside the U.S., please contact intlcs@pearson.com.

Editor-in-Chief
Mark Taub

Executive Editor
Mary Beth Ray

Senior Editor
James Manly

Development Editor
Ellie C. Bru

Managing Editor
Sandra Schroeder

Project Editor
Mandie Frank

Indexer
Ken Johnson

Proofreader
Debbie Williams

Technical Editor and Contributors
Chris Crayton
Jeff Burns
Melodie Schmidt
Karl Schmidt
Elizabeth Drake

Publishing Coordinator
Cindy Teeters

Cover Designer
Chuti Prasertsith

Compositor
Tricia Bronkella

Art Production
Justin Ache
Katherine Martin
Marc Durrence
Amanda McIntosh
KC Frick
Vived Graphics

Photographers
Raina Durrence
George Nichols

Contents at a Glance

Contents

About the Author

Cheryl Schmidt is a professor of Network Engineering Technology at Florida State College at Jacksonville. Prior to joining the faculty ranks, she oversaw the LAN and PC support for the college and other organizations. She started her career as an electronics technician in the U.S. Navy. She teaches computer repair and various networking topics, including CCNA, network management, and network design. She has published other works with Pearson, including *IP Telephony Using CallManager Express* and *Routing and Switching in the Enterprise Lab Guide*.

Cheryl has won awards for teaching and technology, including Outstanding Faculty of the Year, Innovative Teacher of the Year, Cisco Networking Academy Instructor Excellence Award, and Cisco Networking Academy Stand Out Instructor. She has presented at U.S. and international conferences. Cheryl keeps busy maintaining her technical certifications and teaching but also loves to travel, hike, do all types of puzzles, and read.

Dedication

A Note to Instructors:

I was a teacher long before I had the title professor. Sharing what I know has always been as natural as walking to me, but sitting still to write what I know is not as natural, so composing this text has always been one of my greatest challenges. Thank you so much for choosing this text. I thank you for sharing your knowledge and experience with your students. Your dedication to education is what makes the student experience so valuable.

A Note to Students:

Writing a textbook is really different from teaching class. I have said for years that my students are like my children, except that I don't have to pay to send them through college. I am happy to claim any of you who have this text. I wish that I could be in each classroom with you as you start your IT career. How exciting!

Another thing that I tell my students is that I am not an expert. IT support is an ever-changing field and I have been in it since PCs started being used. You have to be excited about the never-ending changes to be good in this field. You can never stop learning or you will not be very good any more. I offer one important piece of advice:

> Consistent, high-quality service boils down to two equally important things: caring and competence.
> —Chip R. Bell and Ron Zemke

I dedicate this book to you. I can help you with the competence piece, but you are going to have to work on the caring part. Do not ever forget that there are people behind those machines that you love to repair. Taking care of people is as important as taking care of the computers.

Acknowledgments

I am so thankful for the support of my family during the production of this book. My husband, Karl, daughters, Raina and Karalina, and son-in-law, Marc, were such a source of inspiration and encouragement. My grandsons, Gavin, Riley, Logan, and Liam, and my granddaughter, Brie, are a constant source of wonderment for me. They were a shining light at the end of some very long days. Thanks to my mother, Barbara Cansler, who taught me to love words and my brother Jeff Cansler for just listening. Thanks to my walking buddy, Kellie, for the miles of letting me work through knotty sections. Thanks to my colleagues, adjuncts, and students at my college who offered numerous valuable suggestions for improvement and testing the new material. Thanks to my colleagues Pamela Brauda and David Singletary for just letting me rant. Finally, I want to thank my personal technical team, Justin Ache, Raina Durrence, Marc Durrence, and Jeff Burns.

Many thanks are also due the folks at Pearson. The professionalism and support given during this edition was stellar. Thank you so much, Pearson team, especially Eleanor Bru, Mary Beth Ray, Kitty Wilson, Mandie Frank, and my favorite technical reviewer/hatchet man, Chris Crayton. A special thanks to Mary Beth Ray, my executive editor and juggler extraordinaire. I hope all of you can see the results of your contributions. I thank the whole team so much for your conscientious efforts.

Finally, thank you to the students who have taken the time to share their recommendations for improvement. You are the reason I write this book each time. Please send me any ideas and comments you may have. I love hearing from you and of your successes. I may be reached at cheryl.schmidt@fscj.edu.

Credits

Figure Number	Attribution/Credit Line	Figure Number	Attribution/Credit Line
Figure 1-1	Cheryl Schmidt	Figure 2-45	Gudellaphoto/Fotolia
Figure 1-5A	Apple Logo, Apple Inc.	Figure 2-47	Raina Durrence
Figure 1-5B	Windows Logo, Microsoft Corporation	Figure 2-49	Unkas Photo/Fotolia
Figure 1-5C	Linux Logo, Linux Inc.	Figure 2-50	Gareth Boden/Pearson Education Ltd
Figure 1-5D	Courtesy of Android Inc.	Figure 2-51a	Raina Durrence
Figure 1-7	MaverickLEE/Shutterstock	Figure 2-51b	Raina Durrence
Figure 1-10	NAN728/Shutterstock	Figure 2-52a	MRS. NUCH SRIBUANOY/Shutterstock
Figure 1-13	Unkas Photo/Fotolia	Figure 2-52b	Cheryl Schmidt
Figure 1-14	Bondarau/Fotolia	Figure 2-52c	Ericlefrancais/Shutterstock
Figure 1-15	Norikko/Fotolia	Figure 2-52d	Nata-Lia/Shutterstock
Figure 1-16	Alexlmx/Fotolia	Figure 2-52e	Ericlefrancais/Shutterstock
Figure 1-17	Scanrail/Fotolia	Figure 2-52f	Tuomas Lehtinen/Shutterstock
Figure 1-18	Bondarau/Fotolia	Figure 2-52g	1125089601/Shutterstock
Figure 1-20	Raina Durrence	Figure 2-52i	Coleman Yuen/Pearson Education Asia Ltd
Figure 1-21	Petr Malyshev/Fotolia	Figure 2-52j	Gudellaphoto/Fotolia
Figure 1-24a	Florin oprea/Shutterstock	Figure 3-1	Aleksei Lazukov/Fotolia
Figure 1-24b	Andrey_Popov/Shutterstock	Figure 3-2	Oleksandr Delyk/Fotolia
Figure 1-25	Mark Nazh/Shutterstock	Figure 3-16	Denis Dryashkin/Fotolia
Figure 1-26	ESB Professional/Shutterstock	Figure 3-17	Auran/Fotolia
Figure 1-27	Tatjana Brila/Shutterstock	Figure 3-18	Graham Kidd Zenith/Fotolia
Figure 1-36a	Vadymg/Fotolia	Figure 3-20	Timur Anikin/Fotolia
Figure 1-36b	Unkas Photo/Fotolia	Figure 3-21	Markd800/Fotolia
Figure 1-36c	zelimirzarkovic/Fotolia	Figure 3-22	Denis Dryashkin/Fotolia
Figure 2-1	Raina Durrence	Figure 3-23	Markd800/Fotolia
Figure 2-2a & c	Robootb/Fotolia	Figure 3-26	Unkas Photo /Fotolia
Figure 2-2b	Raina Durrence	Figure 3-19	Raina Durrence
Figure 2-4	Cheryl Schmidt	Figure 3-28	Raina Durrence
Figure 2-5	Ctpaep/Fotolia	Figure 3-29	Y. L. Photographies/Fotolia
Figure 2-7	Ericlefrancais/Shutterstock	Figure 3-30	Zadorozhnyi Viktor/Shutterstock
Figure 2-8	Gudellaphoto/Fotolia	Figure 3-35	BonD80/Shutterstock
Figure 2-9	Ruslan Kudrin/Fotolia	Figure 3-36	Algre/Fotolia
Figure 2-10	Raina Durrence	Figure 3-38	ASUS Workstation motherboard
Figure 2-13a	Alexey Rotanov/Fotolia	Figure 3-39	Wavebreakmedia/Shutterstock
Figure 2-13b	Yurdakul/Fotolia	Figure 4-1	Maxhalanski/Fotolia
Figure 2-14	Raina Durrence	Figure 4-6	Bondarau/Fotolia
Figure 2-15	Raina Durrence	Figure 4-8	Raina Durrence
Figure 2-16b	Cheryl Schmidt	Figure 4-15	Raina Durrence
Figure 2-18	Raina Durrence	Figure 4-17	Cheryl Schmidt
Figure 2-19	George Nichols	Figure 4-19	Cheryl Schmidt
Figure 2-21a	Raina Durrence	Figure 4-20	Cheryl Schmidt
Figure 2-21b	Raina Durrence	Figure 4-21	Cheryl Schmidt
Figure 2-22	Tuomas Lehtinen/Shutterstock	Figure 4-23	Vetkit/Fotolia
Figure 2-52h	Mikhail hoboton Popov/Shutterstock	Figure 4-24	Slyudmila/Fotolia
Figure 2-23	Shawn Hempel/Fotolia	Figure 4-26	Raina Durrence
Figure 2-26	Raina Durrence	Figure 4-27	Jiaking1/Fotolia
Figure 2-27	Raina Durrence	Figure 4-28	Jan Mika/Shutterstock
Figure 2-28	Raina Durrence	Figure 4-29	Stokkete/Fotolia
Figure 2-30	Raina Durrence	Figure 4-31	Intel Corporation
Figure 2-31	Raina Durrence	Figure 5-1	Yauhenka/Fotolia
Figure 2-34	Callum Bennetts/Fotolia	Figure 5-2	Raina Durrence
Figure 2-35	Cheryl Schmidt	Figure 5-3	Raina Durrence
Figure 2-37	Gareth Boden/Pearson Education Ltd	Figure 5-4	StockPhotosArt/Fotolia
Figure 2-39	Mau Horng/Fotolia	Figure 5-5	Cheryl Schmidt
Figure 2-40	Raina Durrence	Figure 5-6a	Raina Durrence
Figure 2-41	Anton Samsonov/123RF	Figure 5-6b	Likasiri/Fotolia
Figure 2-43	Pairoj/Fotolia	Figure 5-6c	DGMphoto/Fotolia
Figure 2-44a	Alehdats/Fotolia	Figure 5-7	Gudellaphoto/Fotolia
Figure 2-44b	Hoboton/Fotolia	Figure 5-8	LoloStock/Fotolia

Figure Number	Attribution/Credit Line	Figure Number	Attribution/Credit Line
Figure 5-9	Cristi180884/Fotolia	Figure 7-23c	Chris leachman/Fotolia
Figure 5-10	Bondarau/Fotolia	Figure 7-24a	Witthaya/Fotolia
Figure 5-12	Raina Durrence	Figure 7-24b	Milan Lipowski/Fotolia
Figure 5-13	Raina Durrence	Figure 7-25	Raina Durrence
Figure 5-14	Raina Durrence	Figure 7-28	Cheryl Schmidt
Figure 5-15	Cheryl Schmidt	Figure 7-29	CyberVam/Fotolia
Figure 5-16	Thodonal/Fotolia	Figure 7-31	PVMil/Fotolia
Figure 5-17	WavebreakmediaMicro/Fotolia	Figure 7-32	George Nichols
Figure 5-18	Raina Durrence	Figure 7-33	Igor Groshev/Fotolia
Figure 5-19	Raina Durrence	Figure 7-34	Scanrail/Fotolia
Figure 5-20	Raina Durrence	Figure 7-35	?ake78 (3D & photo)/Fotolia
Figure 5-21	Anake/Fotolia	Figure 7-44	Concept w/Fotolia
Figure 5-22	Chokmoso/Fotolia	Figure 7-46	Design56/Fotolia
Figure 5-23	RZ/Fotolia	Figure 7-50	Primzrider/Fotolia
Figure 5-24	Thodonal/Fotolia	Figure 7-52	Amy Walters/Fotolia
Figure 5-25	George Nichols	Figure 7-55	George Nichols
Figure 5-28	Raina Durrence	Figure 7-57	Giovanni Cancemi/Fotolia
Figure 5-30a	Popova Olga/Fotolia	Figure 8-1	George Nichols
Figure 5-30b	Crisit180884/Fotolia	Figure 8-5	Studio306fotolia/Fotolia
Figure 5-32	Raina Durrence	Figure 8-8	Raina Durrence
Figure 5-33	Stepan Popov/Fotolia	Figure 8-9	Denis Dryashkin/Fotolia
Figure 5-36	Yauhenka/Fotolia	Figure 8-7	Xuejun li/Fotolia
Figure 5-37	Cheryl Schmidt	Figure 8-10	Olexandr/Fotolia
Figure 5-38	Andriy Brazhnykov/Fotolia	Figure 8-12	Tommroch/Fotolia
Figure 5-39	Alexander Limbach/Fotolia	Figure 8-15	Daqota/Fotolia
Figure 5-40	House @ Brasil/Fotolia	Figure 8-18	DDRockstar/Fotolia
Figure 5-41a	Cristi180884/Fotolia	Figure 8-19	Kevma20/Fotolia
Figure 5-41b	Cheryl Schmidt	Figure 8-20	Cheryl Schmidt
Figure 5-41c	Cheryl Schmidt	Figure 8-21	Pathdoc/Fotolia
Figure 5-41d	Cheryl Schmidt	Figure 8-22	Magraphics/Fotolia
Figure 5-41e	Cheryl Schmidt	Figure 8-23	Bacho Foto/Fotolia
Figure 6-1-D	Courtesy of openoffice.org, The Apache software foundation	Figure 8-25	Grosche.nrw/Fotolia
		Figure 8-26	Raina Durrence
Figure 6-1-E	Courtesy of Angry birds,Rovio Entertainment	Figure 8-27	JcJg Photography/Fotolia
Figure 6-1-F	Coutesy of Adobe Acrobat	Figure 8-29	Wckiw /Fotolia
Figure 6-3	Cheryl Schmidt	Figure 8-30	Scanrail/Fotolia
Figure 6-4	Scanrail/Fotolia	Figure 8-31	Thomas Siepmann/Fotolia
Figure 6-11	Arudolf/Fotolia	Figure 8-32	Olya6105/Fotolia
Figure 6-14	Joseph Scott/Fotolia	Figure 8-34	Schamie/Fotolia
Figure 6-20	Pongpatpic /Fotolia	Figure 8-35	Hardheadmonster/Fotolia
Figure 6-21	Kataieva/Fotolia	Figure 8-36	Nikkytok/Fotolia
Figure 6-22	ESB Professional/Shutterstock	Figure 8-37	Piotr Pawinski/Fotolia
Figure 7-1	Photka/Fotolia Figure	Figure 8-38	Zern Liew/Shutterstock
Figure 7-2	Scanrail/Fotolia	Figure 8-39	Gustavofrazao/Fotolia
Figure 7-3	Aleksandr Lazarev /Fotolia	Figure 9-1	Burnel11/Fotolia
Figure 7-4	Raina Durrence	Figure 9-2	George Nichols
Figure 7-6	Orcea david/Fotolia	Figure 9-4	Sinisa Botas/Fotolia
Figure 7-7	Mbongo/Fotolia	Figure 9-8	Manaemedia/Fotolia
Figure 7-10	Sved Oliver/Fotolia	Figure 9-9	Mik_cz/Fotolia
Figure 7-13	Eimantas Buzas/Shutterstock	Figure 9-10	Manaemedia/Fotolia
Figure 7-15	Vetkit/Fotolia	Figure 9-11	Vetkit/Fotolia
Figure 7-16	Cheryl Schmidt	Figure 9-13	Dario Sabljak/Fotolia
Figure 7-18	Raina Durrence	Figure 9-14	Asharkyu/Shutterstock
Figure 7-19	Dcwsco/Fotolia	Figure 9-16	Cheryl Schmidt
Figure 7-20	Denis Ponkratov/Fotolia	Figure 9-24	Witthaya /Fotolia
Figure 7-21	Raina Durrence	Figure 9-25	Gareth Boden/Pearson Education Ltd
Figure 7-22a	Sergejs Katkovskis/Fotolia	Figure 9-26	Science photo/Fotolia
Figure 7-22b	Vladimir Kolesnikov/Fotolia	Figure 9-28	Dmytro Vietrov/123RF
Figure 7-23a	Artyom Rudenko/Fotolia	Figure 9-39	Sergeevspb/Fotolia
Figure 7-23b	Murat BAYSAN/Fotolia	Figure 9-44	Daniel Krason /Fotolia

Figure Number	Attribution/Credit Line	Figure Number	Attribution/Credit Line
Figure 9-48	Thor Jorgen Udvang /Fotolia	Figure 10-88	Raina Durrence
Figure 9-49	Michael Pettigrew/Fotolia	Figure 10-91	Raina Durrence
Figure 9-51	Rocketclips, Inc./Shutterstock	Figure 10-92	Violetkaipa/Fotolia
Figure 10-1	Welf Aaron/Fotolia	Figure 10-93	Ras-slava/Fotolia
Figure 10-2	Syda Productions/Fotolia	Figure 10-96	Bloomicon/Fotolia
Figure 10-3	Metamorworks/Shutterstock	Figure 10-97	Cheryl Schmidt
Figure 10-4	Nmedia/Fotolia	Figure 10-100	Tab62/Fotolia
Figure 10-5	Diego cervo/Fotolia	Figure 10-102	Ayutaroupapa/Fotolia
Figure 10-6	Goir/Fotolia	Figure 10-104	Mindscanner/Fotolia
Figure 10-7	Forest71/Fotolia	Figure 10-105	Kulyk/Fotolia
Figure 10-8	Alexey Rotanov/Fotolia	Figure 10-107	Ruslan Olinchuk/Fotolia
Figure 10-9	Riccardomojana/Fotolia	Figure 10-108	Poko42/Fotolia
Figure 10-10	3dmavr/Fotolia	Figure 10-109	Yomka/Fotolia
Figure 10-11	Renars2014/Fotolia	Figure 10-110	Mckaphoto/Fotolia
Figure 10-12	Scanrail/Fotolia	Figure 10-111	Naruedom/Fotolia
Figure 10-15	Photosaint/Fotolia	Figure 10-112	Rfvectors.com/Fotolia
Figure 10-16	Serjiunea/Fotolia	Figure 10-113	Scusi/Fotolia
Figure 10-17	Alex Ishchenko/Fotolia	Figure 10-114	Grafvision/Fotolia
Figure 10-18	Popova Olga/Fotolia	Figure 10-116	Yomka/Shutterstock
Figure 10-19	Oleksandr Kovalchuk/Fotolia	Figure 11-2	Corepics VOF/Shutterstock
Figure 10-20a	Weerapat1003/Fotolia	Figure 11-3	Dejan Stanic Micko/Shutterstock
Figure 10-20b	Popova Olga/Fotolia	Figure 11-4	Stocked House Studio/Shutterstock
Figure 10-21	Ras-slava/Fotolia	Figure 11-5	Zern Liew/Shutterstock
Figure 10-22	Alexlmx/Fotolia	Figure 11-6	Cheryl Schmidt
Figure 10-27	Kencana Studio/Fotolia	Figure 11-7	Kittichai/Shutterstock
Figure 10-28	Brian A Jackson/Shutterstock	Figure 11-8	Improvize/Shutterstock
Figure 10-31	Denys Prykhodov/Fotolia	Figure 11-9	Raj Creatiionzs/Shutterstock
Figure 10-34	Coprid/Fotolia	Figure 11-10	Tyler Olson/Shutterstock
Figure 10-35	Highwaystarz/Fotolia	Figure 11-11	Mikeledray/Shutterstock
Figure 10-37	Raina Durrence	Figure 11-12	DeSerg/Shutterstock
Figure 10-39	Raina Durrence	Figure 11-13	Natalia Siverina/Shutterstock
Figure 10-41	Albert Lozano/Shutterstock	Figure 11-14	Andrey_Popov/Shutterstock
Figure 10-42	Tyler Olson/Fotolia	Figure 11-15	Phovoir/Shutterstock
Figure 10-43	Dmitry/Fotolia	Figure 11-16	Sheelamohanachandran2010/Shutterstock
Figure 10-47	Mast3r/Fotolia	Figure 11-18	Galyna Andrushko/Shutterstock
Figure 10-48	Christos Georghiou/Fotolia	Figure 11-20	Cartoon Resource/Shutterstock
Figure 10-54	©2019, Microsoft One Drive, Microsoft Corporation	Figure 11-21	Sashkin/Shutterstock
Figure 10-55	Mathias Rosenthal/Fotolia	Figure 11-25	Pathdoc/Shutterstock
Figure 10-59	Raina Durrence	Figure 12-1	Microsoft Windows, © Microsoft Corporation
Figure 10-61	Raina Durrence	Figure 12-2	Raina Durrence; Courtesy of Vmware
Figure 10-63	Ioannis Ioannou/Shutterstock	Figure 12-3	Courtesy of Oracle Corporation; fuyi/Fotolia
Figure 10-65	Raina Durrence	Figure 12-6	Suti Stock Photo/Shutterstock
Figure 10-67	Artisticco LLC/Fotolia	Figure 12-7	rocketclips/Fotolia
Figure 10-68a	Fserega/Fotolia	Figure 12-10	Feraru Nicolae/Shutterstock
Figure 10-68b	Ratmaner/Fotolia	Figure 12-11	Evan Lorne/Shutterstock
Figure 10-69a	Ussatlantis/Fotolia	Figure 12-13	federicofoto/123RF
Figure 10-69b	Jipen/Fotoli	Figure 12-15	Roman Pyshchyk/Shutterstock
Figure 10-73	Denis_romash/Fotolia	Figure 12-17	csp_hywards/Shutterstock
Figure 10-75	Mickyso/Fotolia	Figure 12-21	© 2019, Microsoft Windows, Microsoft Corporation
Figure 10-77	Joggie Botma/Fotolia	Figure 12-47	Carlos A. Oliveras/Shutterstock
Figure 10-79	Yauhenka/Fotolia	Figure 12-48	Andrea De Martin/123RF
Figure 10-82a	Piotr Adamowicz/123RF	Figure 13-1	arka38/Shutterstock
Figure 10-82b	Raina Durrence	Figure 13-4	Alex Tihonov/Fotolia
Figure 10-82c	Vrihu/Fotolia	Figure 13-10	Georgios Alexandris/Fotolia
Figure 10-83	Raina Durrence	Figure 13-13	zhekoss/Shutterstock
Figure 10-84	Jipen/Fotolia	Figure 13-14a	SV Art/Fotolia
Figure 10-85	Jipen/Shutterstock	Figure 13-14b	SV Art/Fotolia
Figure 10-86	Blue_moon_images/Fotolia	Figure 13-15	Fotofermer/Fotolia
Figure 10-87	Cheryl Schmidt	Figure 13-16	ludodesign/Fotolia

Figure Number	Attribution/Credit Line	Figure Number	Attribution/Credit Line
Figure 13-17	nengredeye/Fotolia	Figure 18-8	PhotographyByMK/Fotolia
Figure 13-17b	Anthony O'Donnell/Shutterstock	Figure 18-9	Nokhoog/Fotolia
Figure 13-18	Plus69/Shutterstock	Figure 18-10	Alexandr Mitiuc/Fotolia
Figure 13-20	evannovostro/Fotolia	Figure 18-11	Wordley Calvo Stock/Fotolia
Figure 13-21	Scruggelgreen/Fotolia	Figure 18-12	cartoonresource/Fotolia
Figure 13-22	angelus_liam/Fotolia	Figure 18-13	BirDiGoL/Fotolia
Figure 13-23	hxdyl/Fotolia	Figure 18-15	JustAnotherPhotographer/Shutterstock
Figure 13-24	Cheryl A. Schmidt	Figure 18-35	Elemiyan01/Fotolia
Figure 13-25	Plus69/Shutterstock	Figure 18-36	Cheryl Schmidt
Figure 13-36	Don_Pomidor/Fotolia	Figure 18-36	Cheryl Schmidt
Figure 13-38	Oleksiy Mark/Shutterstock	Figure 18-38	kmls/Shutterstock
Figure 13-39	Cheryl A.Schmidt	Figure 18-40	Baur/Shutterstock
Figure 13-51	amophoto.net/Fotolia	Figure 18-42	Grasko/Fotolia
Figure 13-70	Denys Prykhodov/Shutterstock	Figure 18-53	rommma/Fotolia
Figure 13-71	MemoryMan/Shutterstock	Figure 18-54	iQoncept/Fotolia
Figure 13-72	SpeedKingz/Shutterstock	Figure 19-22	SimFan/Fotolia
Figure 13-74	©2019, command Prompt, Microsoft Corporation	Figure 19-1	Shutterstock
Figure 13-75	Denis Dryashkin/Fotolia	Figure 19-2	peefay/Shutterstock
Figure 13-76	SpeedKingz/Shutterstock	Figure 19-3	WavebreakmediaMicro/Fotolia
Figure 13-78	Jovan Nikolic/Fotolia	Figure 19-4	srki66/Fotolia
Figure 13-79	Oleksandr Delyk/Fotolia	Figure 19-5	STILLFX/Shutterstock
Figure 13-92	Peter Kotoff/Shutterstock	Figure 19-6	ninun/Fotolia
Figure 13-93a	jackykids/Fotolia	Figure 19-7	petovarga/Fotolia
Figure 13-93b	Scanrail/Fotolia	Figure 19-8	givaga/Shutterstock
Figure 13-93c	Robinson Thomas/Fotolia	Figure 19-9	petovarga/123RF
Figure 13-93d	angelus_liam/Fotolia	Figure 19-10	Sherry Young/Fotolia
Figure 13-93d	Amy Walters/Fotolia	Figure 19-11	weerapat1003/Fotolia; enterphoto/Fotolia
Figure 13-96	Justin Ache	Figure 19-13	Gareth Boden. Pearson Education Ltd
Figure 13-97	Justin Ache	Figure 19-14	evilratalex/Fotolia
Figure 14-1	©2019, Microsoft Windows, Microsoft Corporation	Figure 19-15	improvize/Fotolia
Figure 15-2	Cheryl A. Schmidt	Figure 19-16	Winai Tepsuttinun/Shutterstock
Figure 15-14	Calado/Fotolia	Figure 19-17 a	Magraphics.eu/Fotolia
Figure 15-15	Yury Zap/Fotolia	Figure 19-17 b	Vetkit/Fotolia
Figure 16-2	adrian_ilie825/Fotolia	Figure 19-19	Cheryl Schmidt
Figure 16-3	ribkhan/Fotolia	Figure 19-23	Ake1150/Fotolia
Figure 16-4	Scanrail/Fotolia	Figure 19-24	Yaaqov Tshuva/Fotolia
Figure 16-5	jijomathai/Fotolia	Figure 19-27	Oez/Shutterstock
Figure 16-31	anyaberkut/Fotolia	Figure 19-29	Benjamin Haas/Shutterstock
Figure 16-42	Thomas Jansa/Fotolia	Figure 19-30	Kheng Guan Toh/Shutterstock
Figure 16-57	© 2019, command Prompt, Microsoft Corporation	Figure 19-32	Séa/Fotolia
Figure 16-66	antimartina/Fotolia	Figure 19-33	Beatpavel/Fotolia
Figure 17-1	Africa Studio/Fotolia	Figure 19-34	Noppadol Anaporn/123 RF
Figure 17-7	Apple Inc.	Figure 19-35	Iqoncept/Fotolia
Figure 17-27	Marekuliasz/Shutterstock	Figure 19-37	Cartoonresource/Fotolia
Figure 18-1	Jürgen Fälchle/Fotolia; Microsoft Windows, ©Microsoft Corporation	Figure 19-38	Rawpixel.com/Fotolia
Figure 18-2	Patrimonio designs/Fotolia	Figure 19-39	PrettyVectors/Fotolia
Figure 18-3	JonikFoto.pl/Fotolia	Figure 19-40	Studiostoks/Fotolia
Figure 18-5	qingwa/Fotolia	Figure 19-41	Cartoonresource/Fotolia
Figure 18-6	John Tomaselli/Fotolia	Figure 19-42	Andrii Symonenko/Fotolia
Figure 18-7	dzimin/Fotolia	Figure 19-43	JanMika/Fotolia
		Figure 19-44	Jane Kelly/Fotolia

Multiple Figures: Microsoft Windows 8 & 10,© Microsoft Corporation; Microsoft Windows10,© Microsoft Corporation; © 2019, command Prompt, Microsoft Corporation; © 2019, Microsoft Analyzer, Microsoft Corporation; © 2019, Microsoft Internet Explorer, Microsoft Corporation; © 2019, Microsoft Windows File Explorer, Microsoft Corporation; © 2019, Microsoft Windows Powershell, Microsoft Corporation; © 2019, Microsoft Windows, Microsoft Corporation; Agsandrew/Shutterstock; Apple Screenshot reprinted with permission of Apple Inc.; Courtesy of Android; Courtesy of Apple Inc.; Courtesy of Canonical Ltd; Courtesy of Ubuntu; iOS screenshots are registered trademarks of Apple Inc.; UEFI screenshots

Cover: PopTika/Shutterstock

We Want to Hear from You!

As the reader of this book, *you* are our most important critic and commentator. We value your opinion and want to know what we're doing right, what we could do better, what areas you'd like to see us publish in, and any other words of wisdom you're willing to pass our way.

We welcome your comments. You can email or write to let us know what you did or didn't like about this book—as well as what we can do to make our books better.

Please note that we cannot help you with technical problems related to the topic of this book.

When you write, please be sure to include this book's title and author as well as your name and email address. We will carefully review your comments and share them with the author and editors who worked on the book.

Email: community@informit.com

Introduction

Complete A+ Guide to IT Hardware and Software, eighth edition, is a textbook and optional lab manual intended for one or more courses geared toward CompTIA A+ Certification and computer repair. It covers all the material needed for the CompTIA A+ Core 1 (220-1001) and CompTIA A+ Core 2 (220-1002) exams. The book is written so that it is easy to read and understand, with concepts presented in building-block fashion. The book focuses on hardware, software, mobile devices, virtualization, basic networking, and security.

Some of the best features of the book include the coverage of difficult subjects in a step-by-step manner, carefully developed graphics that illustrate concepts, photographs that demonstrate various technologies, reinforcement questions, critical thinking skills, soft skills, and hands-on exercises at the end of each chapter. Also, this book is written by a teacher who understands the value of a textbook from someone who has been in IT her entire career.

What's New in the Eighth Edition?

This update has been revised to include more coverage of hardware, mobile devices, and troubleshooting. There are also new sections on managed/unmanaged switches, VLANs, cloud-based network controllers, IoT device configuration, Active Directory settings, common documentation, and scripting. The following are a few of the many new features of this edition:

> This book conforms with the latest CompTIA A+ exam requirements, including those of the CompTIA A+ Core 1 (220-1001) and CompTIA A+ Core 2 (220-1002) exams.
> Chapter 2 now includes network cabling basics.
> The video chapter has been removed as the certification exam includes only Windows configuration of video, which is covered in Chapter 16.
> Chapter 12 now includes all virtualization and cloud technologies information.
> Chapter 13 includes IoT device configuration.
> The operating system–related chapters have been rearranged. Chapter 14 is an introduction to operating systems and Windows basics. Chapter 15 contains the command prompt and scripting sections. Chapter 16 contains the bulk of the information on configuring and supporting Windows 7, 8, and 10. Chapter 17 is still the macOS and Linux chapter.
> Chapters 1 through 9 focus on hardware. Chapter 10 covers mobile devices. Chapter 11 is on computer design and serves as a troubleshooting review. Chapter 12 covers Internet connectivity, virtualization, and cloud computing. Chapter 13 dives into networking. Chapters 14 through 17 cover operating systems. Chapter 18 handles security concepts. Finally, Chapter 19 contains operational procedures. Appendix A provides an introduction to subnetting.
> The book has always been filled with graphics and photos, but even more have been added to target those naturally drawn to the IT field. This edition is full color.
> There are questions at the end of each chapter, and even more questions are available in the test bank available from the Pearson Instructor Resource Center.

Organization of the Text

The text is organized to allow thorough coverage of all topics and also to be a flexible teaching tool. It is not necessary to cover all the chapters, nor do the chapters have to be covered in order.

> **Chapter 1** provides an introduction to IT and careers that need the information in this book. It identifies computer parts. Chapter 1 does not have a specific soft skills section, as do the other chapters. Instead, it focuses on common technician qualities that are explored in greater detail in the soft skills sections of later chapters. Finally, Chapter 1 has a great introduction to using Notepad, the Windows Snipping Tool, and Internet search techniques.

> **Chapter 2** is about connecting things to the computer and port identification. Details are provided on video, USB, and sound ports. The soft skills section is on using appropriate titles.

> **Chapter 3** details components, features, and concepts related to motherboards, including processors, caches, expansion slots, and chipsets. Active listening skills are the focus of the soft skills section.

> **Chapter 4** deals with system configuration basics. BIOS options, UEFI BIOS, and system resources are key topics. The soft skills section covers the importance of doing one thing at a time when replacing components.

> **Chapter 5** steps through how to disassemble and reassemble a computer. Tools, ESD, EMI, and preventive maintenance are discussed. Subsequent chapters also include preventive maintenance topics. Basic electronics and computer power concepts are also included in this chapter. The soft skills section involves written communication.

> **Chapter 6** covers memory installation, preparation, and troubleshooting. The importance of teamwork is emphasized as the soft skill.

> **Chapter 7** deals with storage devices, including PATA, SATA SCSI, SAS, and SSDs. RAID is also covered. Phone communication skills are covered in the soft skills section of this chapter.

> **Chapter 8** covers multimedia devices, including optical drives, sound cards, cameras, scanners, and speakers. The chapter ends with a section on having a positive, proactive attitude.

> **Chapter 9** provides details on printers. A discussion of work ethics finishes the chapter.

> **Chapter 10** is on mobile devices, including details on mobile device operating systems, configuration, backup, security, and troubleshooting. The soft skills section takes a brief foray into professional appearance.

> **Chapter 11** covers computer design. Not only are the specialized computers and components needed within the types of systems covered, but computer subsystem design is also included. Because design and troubleshooting are high on the academic learning progression, the chapter also includes a review of troubleshooting, including logic, error codes, and troubleshooting flowcharts. The soft skills section provides recommendations for dealing with irate customers.

> **Chapter 12** handles Internet connectivity, virtualization, and cloud technologies. Internet browser configuration is covered, along with the soft skill of mentoring

> **Chapter 13** introduces networking. Basic concepts, terminology, and exercises make this chapter a favorite. The introduction to subnetting has been moved to an appendix. The focus of the soft skills section is being proactive instead of reactive.

> **Chapter 14** provides an introduction to operating systems in general and discusses basic differences between the Windows versions and how to function in the various Windows environments. The soft skills section includes tips on how to stay current in this fast-paced field.

> **Chapter 15** is a new introduction to scripting and includes how to function from the command prompt and the basics of scripting in Python, JavaScript, shell scripting, VBScript, batch files, and PowerShell. The soft skills section discusses looking at a problem from the user's perspective and being more empathetic.

> **Chapter 16** covers Windows 7, 8, and 10. Details include how to install, configure, and troubleshoot the environment. Avoiding burnout is the soft skill discussed in this chapter.

> **Chapter 17** discusses the basics of macOS and Linux. It provides a basic introduction to these two environments to help a technician become familiar with the environment and a few tools. The soft skills section talks about being humble.

> **Chapter 18** describes computer, mobile device, and network security. The soft skills section is on building customer trust.

> **Chapter 19** guides the student through operational procedures such as workplace safety, recycling, disposal, a review of power protection, change management, and communication skills.

Features of This Book

The following key features of the book are designed to enable a better learning experience.

> **Objectives**—Each chapter begins with *both* chapter objectives and the CompTIA A+ exam objectives.

> **Graphics and photographs**—Many more full-color images and all-new graphics have been added to better illustrate the concepts.

> **Tech Tips**—The chapters are filled with Tech Tips that highlight technical issues and certification exam topics.

> **Key terms in context**— As you read the chapter, terms that appear in blue are considered key terms and are defined in the glossary.

> **Key Terms list**—At the end of the chapter, all key terms are listed, along with page numbers to which to refer for context.

> **Soft Skills**— Technology is not the only thing you must learn and practice; each chapter offers advice, activities, and examples of how to be a good tech, an ethical tech, a good work mate, a good communicator, and so on.

> **Chapter Summary**— The summary recaps the key concepts of the chapter, and you can use it for review to ensure that you've mastered the chapter's learning objectives.

> **A+ Certification Exam Tips**—Read through these tips on the CompTIA A+ exams so you aren't caught off guard when you sit for the exam.

> **Review Questions**—Hundreds of review questions, including true/false, multiple choice, matching, fill-in-the-blank, and open-ended questions, assess your knowledge of the topics taught in each chapter.

> **Applying your knowledge**—There are hundreds of Exercises and Activities by which to put into practice what you are learning. For example:

> **Exercises**—Sometimes called "paper labs," these need no lab devices to complete in the classroom or for homework.

> **Activities**—Extensive practice with Internet discovery, soft skills, and critical thinking skills round out your technical knowledge so that you can be prepared for IT work. These can be used to "Flip the Classroom;" instead of lectures, instruction is interactive and in the hands of the students.

> **Lab Exercises**—The separate companion *Complete A+ Guide to IT Hardware and Software Lab Manual* (ISBN 978-0-13-538019-2) contains more than 140 labs in total. These hands-on labs enable you to link theory to practical experience.

Companion Website

Register this book to get access to sample videos plus additional bonus content to help you succeed with this course and the certification exam. Check this site regularly for any updates or errata that might become available for this book. Be sure to check the box that you would like to hear from us to receive news of updates and exclusive discounts on related products.

To access this companion website, follow the steps below:

1. Go to www.pearsonITcertification.com/register and log in or create a new account.
2. Enter the ISBN: 978-0-7897-6050-0
3. Answer the challenge question as proof of purchase.
4. Click the "Access Bonus Content" link in the Registered Products section of your account page to be taken to the page where your downloadable content is available.

Please note that many of our companion content files can be very large, especially image and video files.

If you are unable to locate the files for this title by following the steps above, please visit www.pearsonITcertification.com/contact and select the "Site Problems/Comments" option. Our customer service representatives will assist you.

CompTIA A+ Exam Objectives

To earn CompTIA A+ certification, you must pass both the CompTIA A+ Core 1 (220-1001) and CompTIA A+ Core 2 (220-1002) certification exams.

Tables I-1 and I-2 summarize the domain content for each exam.

TABLE I-1   CompTIA A+ Core 1 (220-1001)exam

Domain	Percentage of examination
1.0 Mobile Devices	14%
2.0 Networking	20%
3.0 Hardware	27%
4.0 Virtualization and Cloud Computing	12%
5.0 Hardware and Network Troubleshooting	27%
Total	100%

TABLE I-2   CompTIA A+ Core 2 (220-1002) exam

Domain	Percentage of examination
1.0 Operating Systems	27%
2.0 Security	24%
3.0 Software Troubleshooting	26%
4.0 Operational Procedures	23%
Total	100%

Table I-3 shows a summary of the exam domains addressed in each chapter. Each chapter lists the certification objectives it covers in the chapter opener. See Appendix B on the companion website for a detailed table that identifies where you can find all the CompTIA A+ exam objectives covered in this book.

TABLE I-3   Summary of exam domains by chapter

Table of contents	220-1001 domains	220-1002 domains
Chapter 1: Introduction to the World of IT	3	4
Chapter 2: Connectivity	1, 2, 3	4
Chapter 3: On the Motherboard	3, 5	4
Chapter 4: Introduction to Configuration	3, 5	
Chapter 5: Disassembly and Power	3, 5	4
Chapter 6: Memory	3, 5	1
Chapter 7: Storage Devices	3, 5	1, 2, 3, 4
Chapter 8: Multimedia Devices	3	1, 4
Chapter 9: Printers	2, 3, 5	1, 3, 4
Chapter 10: Mobile Devices	1, 2, 3, 5	1, 2, 3

1 Introduction to the World of IT

In this chapter you will learn:

> Qualities a technician should have

> Basic skills needed to function in the Windows environment and in the technical world

> Important computer parts

> Basic computer terms

CompTIA Exam Objectives:

What CompTIA A+ exam objectives are covered in this chapter?

✓ 1001-3.6 Explain the purposes and uses of various peripheral types.

✓ 1002-4.4 Explain common safety procedures.

✓ 1002-4.7 Given a scenario, use proper communication techniques and professionalism.

Who Needs This Book?

More types of people than you would first think need this book. People who obviously need this information are those who will fix computers or work on a help desk or support desk. However, there are other types of users who might not be so obvious. Many folks who break into the information technology (IT) world do so through jobs that require the A+ certification. Consider medical electronics technicians who repair common equipment used in hospitals. These technicians need this course because many medical devices connect to a PC or have PC-based software that controls the device. Further, the medical devices commonly attach to wired and wireless networks.

Look at Figure 1.1 to see the types of jobs and people who need the information in this book. It might also give you ideas about something you might like to do for a career.

FIGURE 1.1   IT roles

Technician Qualities

Each chapter includes a small bit of space on qualities a technician should possess or strive toward. Spending a little brain power on improving what many call your "soft skills" will pay off in promotions and divergence into other IT-related fields. Three of the most important qualities of a technician are active listening skills, a good attitude, and logic. Active listening means that you truly listen to what a person (especially one who is having a problem) is saying. Active listening skills involve good eye contact, nodding your head every now and then to show that you are following the conversation, taking notes on important details, and avoiding distractions such as incoming cell phone calls or text messages. Clarify customer statements by asking pertinent questions and avoid interrupting. Allow customers to complete their sentences. Many technicians jump into a problem the moment they hear the first symptom described by the user. Listen to the entire problem. Ask open-ended questions—questions that allow the user to expand on the answer rather than answer with a single word, such as *yes* or *no*. Figure 1.2 illustrates this point.

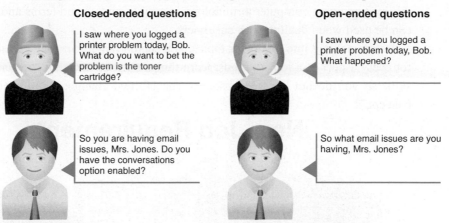

Allow the users to state the problem without leading them toward a solution.
Restate the problem to ensure understanding and ask questions for clarity
and to narrow your understanding.

FIGURE 1.2   Asking technical questions

A positive attitude is probably the best quality a technician can possess. A good attitude is helpful when a user is upset because a computer or an attached device is not working properly. A technician with a positive attitude does not diminish the customer's problem; every problem is equally important to the computer user. A positive attitude is critical for being successful in the computer service industry. Figure 1.3 shows how negative attitudes affect your success.

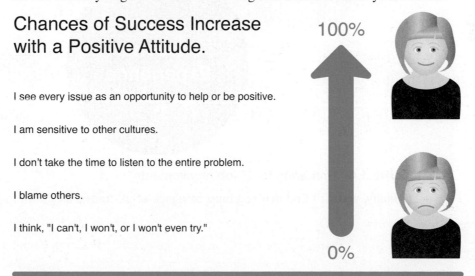

FIGURE 1.3   Have a positive attitude

A technician must be familiar with and thoroughly understand computer terminology to (1) use logic to solve problems; (2) speak intelligently to other technical support staff in clear, concise, and direct statements; (3) explain the problem to the user; and (4) be proficient in the field. Changes occur so frequently that technicians must constantly update their skills. Develop a passion for learning the latest information and searching for information that helps you solve problems.

Avoid developing tunnel vision (that is, thinking that there is only one answer to a problem). Step back and look at the problem so that all possible issues can be evaluated. Be logical in your assessment and the methods used to troubleshoot and repair. This book will help you with all of this by explaining computer terminology in easy-to-understand terms and providing analogies that can be used when dealing with customers.

Before delving into computer topics, you should remember that a class can't fully prepare you for every aspect of a job. You must learn things on your own and constantly strive to update your skills so you do not become obsolete. The IT field changes rapidly. Figure 1.4 illustrates this concept.

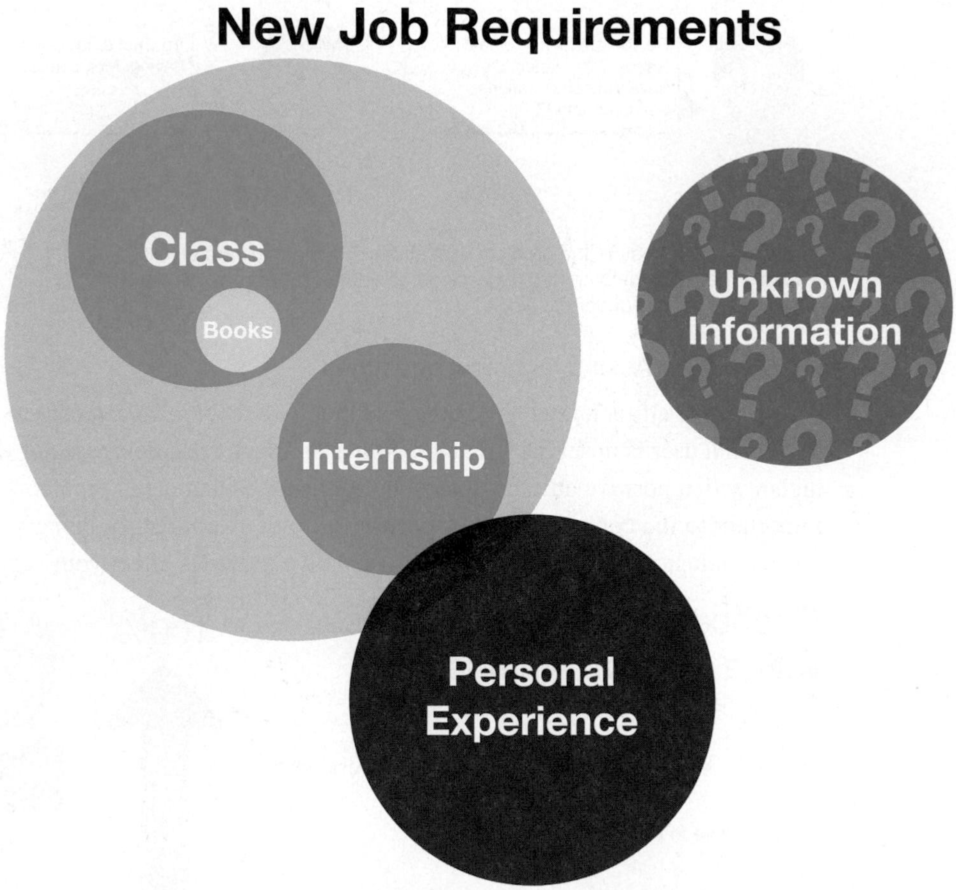

New Job Requirements

Class

Books

Internship

Unknown Information

Personal Experience

FIGURE 1.4 Preparing for IT job requirements

Finally, you will find that you must be a jack-of-all-trades, as shown in Figure 1.5.

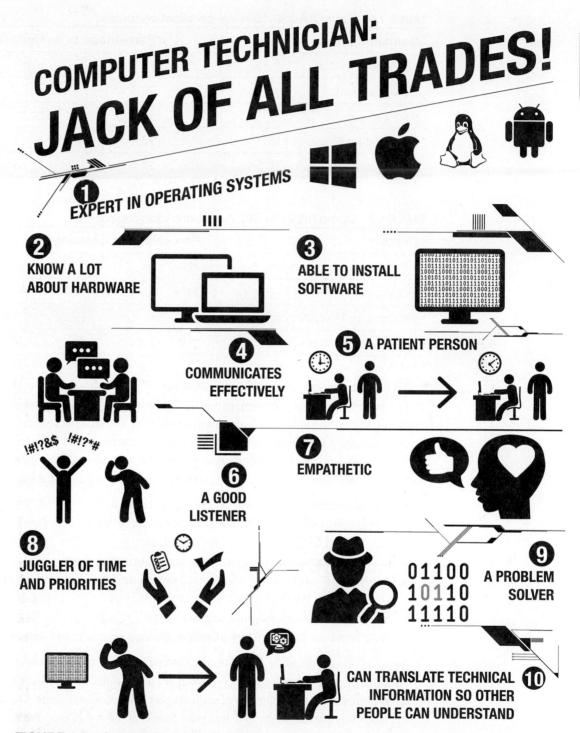

FIGURE 1.5 Computer technician skills

Breaking into IT with the CompTIA A+ Certification

Many IT-related jobs require the A+ certification. Even if not required, the certification shows that you have a good understanding of how computers work. This certification does not guarantee you a job, but it does open doors in that a company may interview you if you lack IT experience but have the A+ certification.

A+ certification requires that you take two exams (220-1001 and 220-1002). Each of these exams covers specific material. Table 1.1 shows the major categories for the 220-1001 exam and how they map to information in this book. Table 1.2 shows the same type of information for the 220-1002 exam.

TABLE 1.1 CompTIA 220-1001 A+ certification topics

Domain	Percentage of examination	Chapter(s)
1.0 Mobile Devices	14%	10
2.0 Networking	20%	12–13
3.0 Hardware	27%	1–9, 11
4.0 Virtualization and Cloud Computing	12%	12
5.0 Hardware and Network Troubleshooting	27%	1–13

TABLE 1.2 CompTIA 220-1002 A+ certification topics

Domain	Percentage of examination	Chapter(s)
1.0 Operating Systems	27%	14–17
2.0 Security	24%	18
3.0 Software Troubleshooting	26%	14–18
4.0 Operational Procedures	23%	19

"What are the exams like?" you might ask. The exams include multiple-choice and performance-based questions. Performance-based questions might be a drag-and-drop scenario or ask you to do something specific on a particular device or within a particular operating system environment. Each exam is 90 minutes long and contains a maximum of 90 questions. The testing system allows you to bookmark questions that you might want to return to at the end if you have time. Successful candidates will have the knowledge required to do the following:

> Assemble components based on customer requirements.
> Install, configure, and maintain devices including Internet of Things (IoT) devices, personal computers (PCs), and software for end users.
> Understand the basics of networking and security/forensics.
> Properly and safely diagnose, resolve, and document common hardware and software issues.
> Apply troubleshooting skills.
> Provide appropriate customer support.
> Understand the basics of virtualization, desktop imaging, and deployment.

More information can be found on the CompTIA website (www.comptia.org).

At the beginning of each chapter, you will see a list of the CompTIA A+ exam objectives that are covered in that chapter. At the end of each chapter, I've provided some A+ certification exam tips—tips to definitely pay attention to if you plan on taking the A+ exams. By the end of this course, you will have learned all the topics covered on the certification exams; however, before you actually take the exams, I recommend that you dedicate some time to review the chapters in this book thoroughly, study the objectives, and take some practice exams. Pearson IT Certification, the publisher of this book, develops many different certification exam prep resources that suit various study styles. See the back of this book for more information or go to http://pearsonitcertification.com/aplus to browse the options.

Basic Skills for This Course

In order to repair a computer, you need a few basic skills that include being familiar with the keyboard and inputting information, searching for information on the Internet, and capturing information. Just because you may not be a good typist does not mean that you will not be good in an IT-related field.

Searching for Information on the Internet

IT people need to use all available resources, including online resources. As noted, you need to be capable of searching for information online. Figure 1.6 illustrates various online resources that IT people search all the time.

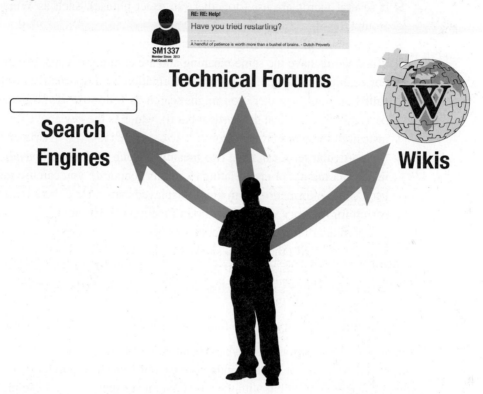

FIGURE 1.6   Search skills

Each chapter in the book has an activity at the end of it that enables you to practice searching the Internet for information relevant to the chapter. Tips for searching include the following:

> Search engines use different algorithms, so if one does not work, try another one. Examples of search engines are Google, Bing, Yahoo, AOL, Ask, and Lycos. To access a search engine, open a web browser and type one of the search engine names followed by `.com`. Figure 1.7 shows where you enter the search engine name in the address bar.

FIGURE 1.7   Web browser address bar

> Use descriptive key words.
> Do not include common words like *the*, *in*, *at*, or *for* because search engines tend to skip these words anyway. If you do want to use one of them, put a plus sign (⊞) in front of the word.
> Avoid using a complex version, plural, or past tense of a word to avoid elimination of pages that are relevant. For example, to search for how to install a Bluetooth headset, avoid using the word *installation*, *installed*, or *installing* in the search window. Simply include the word *install*.
> If several words are used together (an exact phrase), such as Windows 10, put quotations around the phrase—`"Windows 10"`.
> Use as many distinguishing words as possible.
> If two words have the same meaning and are commonly used, use the word *or* in the search. For example, to search for generic information on a dot matrix printer, which is sometimes called an impact printer, you might search as follows: `"dot matrix" or "impact printer"`. Note that the vertical bar (|), which is the key above the ⏎Enter key, can be used instead of the word *or*, as follows: `"dot matrix" | "impact printer"`.
> If a particular term can have two meanings (such as the word *memory* relating to something inside a computer or else relating to a brain function), you can use the minus sign in order to keep some information from being displayed. `memory -brain`, for example, would be a search for memory without any brain function results included.
> If a particular term (such as memory) is generic, you can add a word and use the word *AND* in order to clarify the search, such as `computer AND memory`.
> When searching for technical information, include the hardware or software manufacturer. A search for `Microsoft Windows 10` provides different results than simply a search for `Windows 10`.
> If nothing relevant is on the first page of links, change the key words used in your search.

Consider the situation of a keyboard that intermittently works on a Microsoft Surface computer. The keyboard does not come standard as part of a Surface purchase. You do not own a Surface yourself and are unfamiliar with the tablet but must support it. An example of what might be typed into a search engine is `Microsoft Surface intermittent keyboard`.

Capturing Files

Sometimes, part of technical documentation is being able to capture what is on the screen. Windows versions come with a great tool for doing just that. The Snipping Tool makes documenting problems easy. It is also easy to copy what you capture into other applications. No matter what IT job you may have when you enter the workforce, documentation is a part of all IT jobs.

Creating a Text File

Another part of documentation might involve creating or using a text file, known as a .txt file. You might need to send it as an attachment, or you might need to create a text file as part of the documentation process or as part of the job. Sometimes a text file is the easiest type of file to create, especially on a mobile device. Text files can be created using a word processor and the *Save As* process, or they can be created using specific text software or an app. Text files are popular because they can be opened by many applications or other mobile apps. Text files commonly include only text, without multiple fonts or graphics. Windows ships with a basic application called Notepad that can be used to create or open text files.

Types of Computers

The simplest place to start to learn about computer technical support is with the devices themselves. Computer devices come in many shapes and sizes. The **PC**, or personal computer, comes in desktop, tower, and all-in-one models, as well as mobile models such as laptops, smartphones, and tablets. Figure 1.8 shows some of the computing devices technical staff are expected to support.

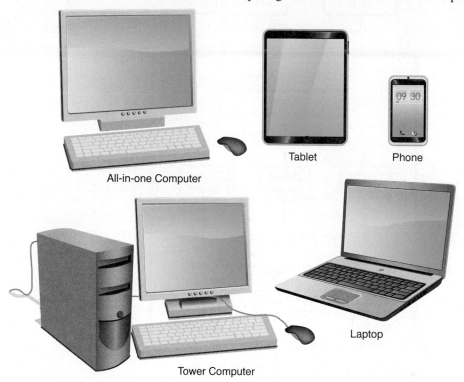

Tablet   Phone

All-in-one Computer

Laptop

Tower Computer

FIGURE 1.8   Types of computers

Basic Computer Hardware

Computer systems include hardware, software, and firmware. **Hardware** is something you can touch and feel; the physical computer and the parts inside the computer are examples of hardware. The monitor, keyboard, and mouse are hardware components. **Software** interacts with the hardware. Windows, Linux, macOS, Microsoft Office, Solitaire, Google Chrome, Adobe Acrobat Reader, and WordPerfect are examples of software.

Without software that directs the hardware to accomplish something, a computer is no more than a doorstop. Every computer needs an important piece of software called an **operating system**, which coordinates the interaction between hardware and software applications. The operating system also handles the interaction between a user and the computer. Examples of operating systems include Windows 7, 8, 8.1, and 10, macOS, and various Linux systems, such as Red Hat and Ubuntu.

A **device driver** is a special piece of software designed to enable a hardware component. The device driver enables the operating system to recognize, control, and use the hardware component. Device drivers are hardware and operating system specific. For example, a printer requires a specific device driver when connected to a computer loaded with Windows 7. The same printer will most likely require a different device driver when using Windows 8 or 10. Each piece of installed hardware requires a device driver for the operating system being used. Figure 1.9 shows how hardware and software must work together.

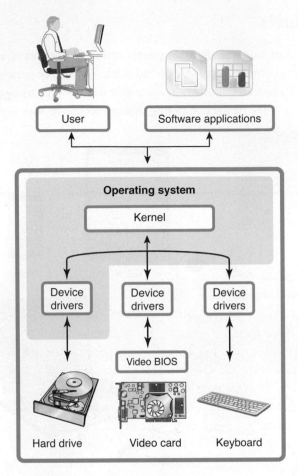

FIGURE 1.9   Hardware and software

Notice in Figure 1.9 the operating system kernel. The kernel is the central part of an operating system. The kernel is the connection between hardware and the applications being used.

Software applications are normally loaded onto the hard drive. When a user selects an application, the operating system controls the loading of the application. The operating system also controls any hardware devices (such as the mouse, keyboard, monitor through the video adapter, and printer) used with the application.

Firmware is a combination of hardware and software, such as electronic chips that contain software: The chip is physical, which is hardware, and it has software built into the chip. An example of firmware is the basic input/output system (**BIOS**) chip. The BIOS always has startup software inside it that must be present for a computer to operate. This startup software locates and loads the operating system. The BIOS also contains software instructions for communication with input/ output devices, as well as important hardware parameters that determine to some extent what hardware can be installed. For example, the system BIOS has the ability to allow other BIOS chips that are located on adapters (such as the video card) to load software that is loaded in the card's BIOS.

A PC typically consists of a case (chassis), a keyboard that allows users to provide input into the computer, a **monitor** that outputs or displays information (shown in Figure 1.10), and a mouse that allows data input or is used to select menus and options. Figure 1.10 shows a computer monitor, which may also be called a flat panel, display, or screen.

When the computer cover or side is opened or removed, the parts inside can be identified. The easiest part to identify is the **power supply**, which is the metal box normally located in a back corner of a case. A power cord connects the power supply to a wall outlet or surge strip. One purpose of the power supply is to convert the outlet AC voltage to DC voltage used internally in the

PC. The power supply distributes this DC voltage using power cables that connect to the various internal computer parts. A fan located inside the power supply keeps the computer cool to prevent damage to the components.

FIGURE 1.10   Computer monitor

A personal computer usually has a device to store software applications and files. Two examples of storage devices are the hard drive and optical drive. The **hard drive**, sometimes called the hard disk, is a rectangular box normally inside the computer's case that is sealed to keep out dust and dirt. The hard drive has no external opening. The computer must be opened in order to access a hard drive. A **DVD drive**, or **optical drive**, holds discs (compact discs, or CDs), digital versatile discs (DVDs), or Blu-ray discs (BDs) that have data, music, video, or software applications on them. The front of the optical drive has a tray that would eject outward so a disc may be inserted. Figure 1.11 shows the major components of a tower computer. Figure 1.12 shows a hard drive. Figure 1.13 shows an optical drive. Figure 1.14 shows a power supply. The hard drive in Figure 1.12, optical drive in Figure 1.13, and power supply in Figure 1.14 all are shown as they would look before being installed into the computer case. Figure 1.15 shows a tower computer case.

FIGURE 1.11   Tower computer

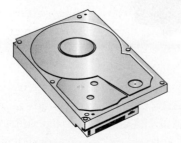

FIGURE 1.12   Hard drive

FIGURE 1.13   DVD or optical drive

FIGURE 1.14   Power supply

FIGURE 1.15   Tower case

The **motherboard** is the main circuit board inside a PC and contains the most electronics. It is normally located on the bottom of a desktop or laptop computer and mounted on the side of a tower computer. Other names for the motherboard include mainboard, planar, or system board. The motherboard is the largest electronic circuit board in the computer. External devices connect directly to the back of the motherboard or ports on the front of the computer. Figure 1.16 shows a motherboard when it is not installed inside a computer as well as memory and an adapter, which are covered next.

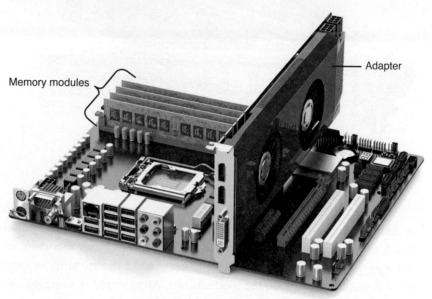

FIGURE 1.16   Computer motherboard

The motherboard holds memory modules. **Memory** is an important part of any computing device. Memory modules hold applications, part of the operating system, and user documents. Random access memory (**RAM**) is the most common type of memory and is volatile—that is, the data inside the module is lost when power is removed. When a user types a document in a word processing program, both the word processing application and the document are in RAM. If the user turns the computer off without saving the document to removable media or the hard drive, the document is lost because the information does not stay in RAM. (Note that some applications have the ability to periodically save a document, but this is not a guarantee that it has the latest information.) Figure 1.17 shows memory modules when they are not installed into the motherboard memory slots. Look back to Figure 1.16 to see the memory modules installed in the motherboard. Memory is covered in great detail in Chapter 6, "Memory."

FIGURE 1.17   Memory modules

A device may have a cable that connects the device to the motherboard. Other devices require an adapter. An **adapter** is an electronic card that plugs into an **expansion slot** on the motherboard. Other names for an adapter are controller, card, controller card, circuit card, circuit board, and adapter board. Adapters allow someone to add a functionality or enhancement that is not provided through the ports on the motherboard. An example is someone who wants better sound or video graphics, or additional ports of some type in order to connect external devices. Figure 1.18 shows an adapter. Notice how the contacts at the bottom are a particular shape. Chapter 3, "On the Motherboard," goes into more detail about the types of expansion slots and adapters. You can also look back to Figure 1.16 to see a video adapter installed into a motherboard expansion slot.

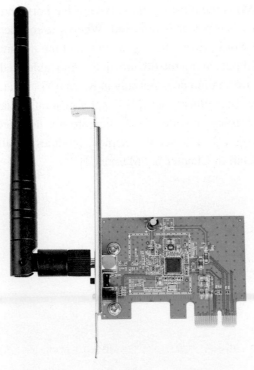

FIGURE 1.18   Adapter

TECH TIP

How to identify an adapter's function

Tracing the cable attached to an adapter or looking at the device connected to the adapter can help identify an adapter's function.

The following are the generic steps for installing adapters:

Step 1. Always follow the manufacturer's installation directions. Use an antistatic wrist strap when handling adapters. Electrostatic discharge (ESD) can damage electronic parts. (See Chapter 5, "Disassembly and Power," for more details on ESD.)

Step 2. Be sure the computer is powered off and unplugged.

Step 3. Remove any brackets from the case or plastic covers from the rear of the computer that may prevent adapter installation. Install the adapter in a free expansion slot and reattach any securing hardware.

Step 4. Attach any internal device cables that connect to the adapter, as well as any cables that go to an external port on the adapter.

Step 5. Attach any internal or external devices to the opposite ends of the cable, if necessary.

Step 6. Power on any external devices connected to the adapter, if applicable.

Step 7. Reattach the computer power cord and power on the computer.

Step 8. Load any application software or device drivers needed for the devices attached to the adapter.

Step 9. Test the device connected to the adapter.

See Figure 1.19 for an illustration of a motherboard, expansion slots, memory, and an adapter in an expansion slot.

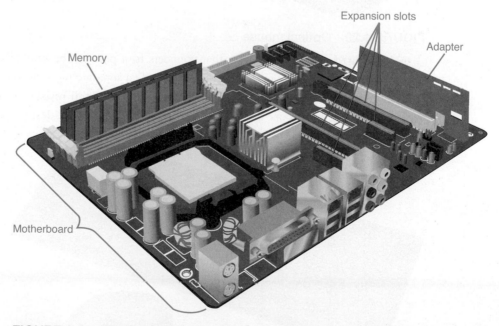

FIGURE 1.19   Motherboard with expansion slots and an adapter

Mice and Keyboards

Input devices, such as the mouse and keyboard, attach to the motherboard. The most common type of **mouse** is an optical mouse, which has optical sensors that detect the direction in which the mouse moves. It uses reflections from light-emitting diodes (LEDs) from almost any surface to detect the mouse location. Mice commonly can be adjusted for sensitivity—how far you have to move the mouse to move the cursor on the screen a desired amount. Mice are rated in dots per inch (DPI), or how many dots (pixels) on the screen the mouse moves per square inch. The higher the number, the more sensitive the mouse. Mouse sensitivity can range from 100 to 6400 DPI; mice with higher DPI numbers are typically used for gaming or design. Figure 1.20 shows a photo of the bottom of an optical mouse.

FIGURE 1.20 Optical mouse

A **keyboard** is an input device that connects to a port on the motherboard or attaches wirelessly. Features users look for in a keyboard include a separate numeric keypad for those that have to input a great deal of numbers, adjustable tilt legs, and spill resistance. Figure 1.21 shows the type of keyboard and mouse that are commonly used with a tower, desktop, or all-in-one computer.

FIGURE 1.21 Keyboard and mouse

Mouse and Keyboard Preventive Maintenance

Mouse cleaning kits are available in computer stores, but normal household supplies also work. Use the following procedures to clean an optical mouse:

> Wipe the bottom with a damp, lint-free cloth.
> Use compressed air to clean the optical sensors.

Keyboards also need periodic cleaning. Figure 1.22 shows keyboard-cleaning techniques.

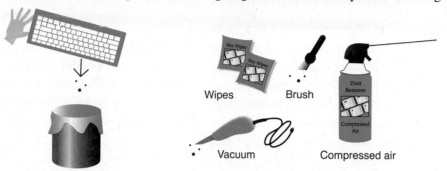

Wipes   Brush

Vacuum   Compressed air

1. Turn keyboard upside down and gently shake out debris

2. Clean the keyboard (several options shown)

FIGURE 1.22   Keyboard cleaning techniques

Keyboard/Mouse Troubleshooting

One of the easiest ways to determine whether a keyboard is working is to press the [Caps Lock] or [Num Lock] key and watch to see if the keyboard light illuminates. Sometimes an application setting may be causing what appears to be a keyboard problem. Use another application to see if the keyboard is the problem. Keyboards can have LED lights that indicate particular functions. Table 1.3 lists the most common ones. Note that different vendors label the lights in various ways.

TABLE 1.3   Common keyboard lights

Associated toggle key	Keyboard light	Description
[Num Lock]	Number lock (NUM LOCK)	Toggles the 10-key pad between digits 0 through 9 and various functions, such as HOME, PG UP, PG DOWN, END, and various arrow keys.
[Caps Lock]	Capital letters lock (CAPS LOCK)	Toggles between all uppercase and lowercase letters.
[Scroll Lock]	Scroll lock	A rarely used key used to prevent scrolling and use of the arrow keys to progress through information displayed.

TECH TIP

One key doesn't work

If a particular key is not working properly, remove the key cap. A small, flat-tipped screwdriver can assist with this. After removing the key cap, use compressed air around the sticky or malfunctioning key.

If coffee or another liquid spills into a PC keyboard, all is not lost. It is sometimes possible to clean a PC keyboard by disconnecting it, removing any batteries it might have, and soaking it in a bathtub or a flat pan of water. Distilled or boiled water cooled to room temperature works best. Afterward, the keyboard can be disassembled and/or scrubbed with lint-free swabs or cloths. However, PC keyboards and mice are normally considered throw-away technology. It is cheaper to get a new one rather than spend a lot of time trying to repair it.

Common Peripherals

Many devices connect to a computer to provide input, such as a mouse or keyboard, or output, such as a display. Some devices can be both input and output devices, such as smart TVs, set-top boxes (the boxes used to connect a TV to a cable or satellite system), Musical Instrument Digital Interface- (MIDI-) enabled devices (which are electronic musical devices), touchscreens, or printers. In the case of a printer, data is sent from a computer to the printer, and the printer can send data (information), such as an out-of-ink message, back to the computer. Figure 1.23 shows some common input and output devices.

Input Devices

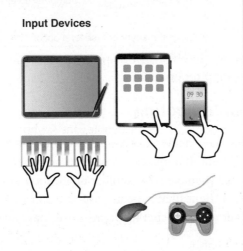

Mouse, Keyboard, Digital Pen, Digital Tablet, Finger, Signature, Pad, TouchScreen, Track Pad, TouchPad, Trackball, Track Stick, Stylus, Barcode Reader, Digitizer, Game Pad/Console, Joystick, Scanner, Camera

Output Devices

Printer, Speakers, Display Devices

FIGURE 1.23 Input and output devices

Table 1.4 lists various peripherals that you will see used and attached to computers today.

TABLE 1.4 Common peripherals

Peripheral	Description
Printer	An output device that transfers information such as text and graphics from a computer onto paper or other media.
Flatbed scanner	An input device that digitizes words or graphics and can be used as a copier. A scanner may have an automatic document feeder (**ADF**) that allows one or more documents to be fed into the scanner.
Barcode scanner/ QR scanner	A handheld device that reads a code displayed as a series of vertical lines of varying widths or a quick response (QR) code that is a square that has embedded information such as a website within the displayed pattern (see Figure 1.24).
VR headset	A virtual reality (VR) device that is worn over the eyes to see a high-definition image or situation as part of a game, demonstration, or tour (see Figure 1.25).

Peripheral	Description
Touchpad	A space on a laptop below the keyboard that is used to control the cursor.
Signature pad	A digital input device that allows users to digitally sign their names, such as when credit cards are used at a checkout register.
Game controller	An input device used with games or entertainment systems.
Camera/ webcam	An input device used to capture video images or motion. More information can be found in Chapter 8, "Multimedia Devices."
Microphone	An input device used to capture sound. More information can be found in Chapter 8.
Headset	An input/output device that commonly has a microphone and headphones, as shown in Figure 1.26.
Projector	An output device used to show an image on a screen or wall. The amount of **brightness** the projector outputs is measured in **lumens**. Common projector specifications for a business or educational environment is 2500 to 6000 lumens. Use the higher lumens projector for rooms that have windows or lights that cannot be dimmed.
External storage drive	An external hard drive, flash drive, or memory used to store data. These devices are covered in detail in Chapters 6, "Memory," and 7, "Storage Devices."
KVM	A switch that enables connectivity of devices so they can be shared between computers (see Figure 1.27). For example, one keyboard, one mouse, and one display and two computers could connect to a keyboard, video, and mouse (KVM) switch.
Magnetic reader/chip reader	A device that accepts cards that are inserted into the device in order to read data from the card or the chip on the card.
NFC device/ tap-to-pay device	A device that accepts cards that are tapped against the display (tap-to-pay) or held in close proximity (near field communication [NFC]) in order to read data from a smartphone or card.
Smart card reader	A device that can read data from a card that has a magnetic strip such as a credit card, special business card, ID card, or room access card.

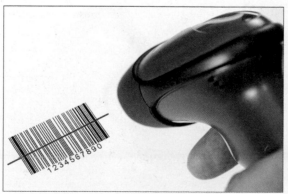

Barcode

QR code

FIGURE 1.24 Barcode and QR code

FIGURE 1.25   VR headset

FIGURE 1.26   Headset

FIGURE 1.27   KVM switch

1s and 0s

Computers are digital devices. That means they understand 1s and 0s. One 1 or one 0 is known as a **bit**. In actuality, a 1 is simply a voltage level. So, when we type characters into a word processing application, the keyboard translates those characters into voltage levels. Figure 1.28 shows this concept. Notice that each letter is represented by a combination of eight 1s and 0s. Each 1 is a voltage level sent to the motherboard (and components on it). Each 0 is simply the absence of a voltage level.

		D	E	A	R	[space]	M	O	M
What we see	👀	01000100	01000101	01000001	01010010	00100000	01001101	01010010	01001101
What a computer sees	💻	⚡ ⚡	⚡ ⚡⚡	⚡	⚡ ⚡⚡⚡	⚡	⚡ ⚡⚡⚡	⚡ ⚡ ⚡	⚡ ⚡⚡⚡

FIGURE 1.28   Binary bits

Technicians need to be able to describe capacities such as hard drive capacities and available drive space. Eight bits grouped together are a **byte**. Figure 1.29 shows a hot dog divided into eight sections (which make a big old "byte").

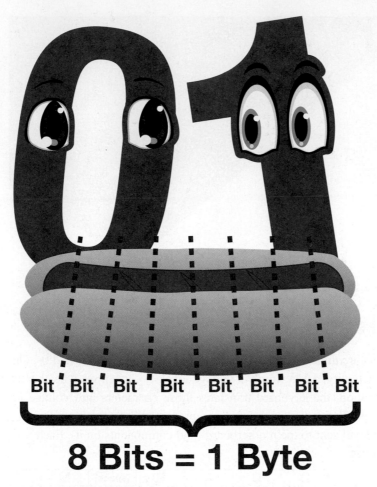

8 Bits = 1 Byte

FIGURE 1.29   A byte

Approximately 1,000 bytes is a **kilobyte** (kB), as shown in Figure 1.30. 1 kB is 1,024 bytes to be exact, but industry folks simply round off the number to the nearest thousand for ease of calculation. Approximately 1 million bytes is a **megabyte** (MB), but a true megabyte is 1,048,576 bytes. 540 megabytes is abbreviated as 540 MB, or 540 M. Notice in Figure 1.31 that a megabyte stores a lot more 1s and 0s than a kilobyte.

Approximately 1 billion bytes (1,073,741,824 bytes) is a **gigabyte** (GB), which is shown as 1 GB or 1 G. Approximately 1 trillion bytes (1,099,511,627,776 bytes) is a **terabyte**, which is shown as 1 TB or 1 T. Figures 1.32 and 1.33 show how storage capacities get larger.

FIGURE 1.30   A kilobyte

FIGURE 1.31   A megabyte

FIGURE 1.32   A gigabyte

FIGURE 1.33   A terabyte

When information needs to be expressed exactly, binary prefixes are used. For example, when describing the value 2^{10} (1,024), instead of saying this it is 1 kilobyte, which people tend to think of as approximately 1,000 bytes, the term kibibyte (KiB) is used. When describing the value 2^{20}, or 1,048,576, the term mebibyte (MiB) is used. Table 1.5 shows the terms used with computer storage capacity and binary prefixes when exact measurements are needed.

TABLE 1.5   Storage terms and binary prefixes

Term	Abbreviation	Description
Kilobyte/kibibyte	kB/KiB	~1 thousand bytes/2^{10} bytes
Megabyte/mebibyte	MB/MiB	~1 million bytes/2^{20} bytes
Gigabyte/gibibyte	GB/GiB	~1 billion bytes/2^{30} bytes
Terabyte/tebibyte	TB/TiB	~1 trillion bytes/2^{40} bytes
Petabyte/pebibyte	PB/PiB	~1,000 trillion bytes/2^{50} bytes
Exabyte/exbibyte	EB/EiB	~1 quintillion bytes/2^{60} bytes
Zettabyte/zebibyte	ZB/ZiB	~1,000 exabytes/2^{70} bytes
Yottabyte/yobibyte	YB/YiB	~1 million exabytes/2^{80} bytes

Frequencies are also important measurements in computers because people want to know how fast their computers, processors, memory, and other parts are operating. Frequencies are shown in similar measurements, but instead of bits (b) or bytes (B), speeds are shown in hertz (Hz). A hertz is a measurement of cycles per second. Something that operates at approximately 1 million cycles per second is said to operate at 1 megahertz (1 MHz). For 1 billion cycles per second, the measurement is known as 1 gigahertz, or 1 GHz. Transfer speeds are commonly shown in bits per second, such as gigabits per second, or Gb/s, or bytes per second, such as in megabytes per second, or MB/s. Notice the capital letter B to indicate bytes as compared to the lowercase b to indicate bits. These measurements are used in a lot of IT-related hardware and software.

Safety Notes

Safety is covered in each chapter, especially in Chapter 5, but no book on computer repair can begin without stating that both the technician and the computer can be harmed by poor safety habits. Before beginning any PC service, remove jewelry. To protect yourself and the computer, make sure to power off the computer and remove the power cord when disassembling, installing, or removing hardware or when doing preventive maintenance (cleaning).

TECH TIP

Some things should be left alone

Never take apart an older CRT monitor or power supply unless you have been specifically trained on these components.

Technicians can also be harmed when doing menial tasks such as lifting a computer or heavy laser printer. Lifting is a common requirement listed in IT job advertisements or explained during interviews. Technical jobs frequently specify a maximum lifting requirement of 40 to 50 pounds. Use proper safety precautions, such as those shown in Figure 1.34. The type of equipment you need and things you can do to prevent harm to the computer are covered more explicitly in Chapter 5, on power and disassembly.

Remove jewelry
before working
inside of a computer

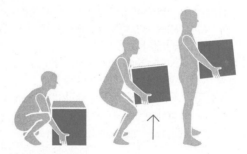

• Bend at the knees
• Use your legs to lift
• Use lifting aids when possible
• Ask for assistance when possible

FIGURE 1.34   Safety tips

Chapter Summary

> Many IT roles require detailed knowledge of PC hardware and software.
> Computer technicians should actively listen, have a positive attitude, and use logic when solving problems.
> The CompTIA A+ certification requires two exams: 220-1001 and 220-1002. Many people break into the IT field with this certification.
> IT staff must be proficient at searching for information on the Internet, capturing files, and documenting technical information.
> Computers consist of hardware (the physical parts), software (the operating system and applications), and firmware (hardware that contains software).

> A technician needs to be able to identify important computer parts installed in a computer and as standalone parts: case, keyboard, mouse, motherboard, monitor, power supply, hard drive, optical drive, adapter, and memory.

> A technician needs to know the purposes of common peripherals used in industry: printer, ADF/flatbed scanner, barcode/QR scanner, VR headset, touchpad, signature pad, game controller, camera/webcam, microphone, speakers, headset, projector, external storage device, KVM, magnetic/reader, chip reader, NFC/tap-to-pay device, and smart card reader.

> Mice, keyboards, and touchscreens are important input devices. Mice and keyboards can be wired or wireless.

> Safety is important when working on a computer. Power it down and remove the power cord before working inside it.

> Use proper lifting techniques when servicing equipment.

A+ CERTIFICATION EXAM TIPS

✓ Get a good night's rest the night before the exam.

✓ Ensure that you are knowledgeable about and proficient with all of the terms and technologies listed in the official CompTIA A+ exam objectives. Some students study for a particular exam by going through the objectives one by one and reviewing the material as they go through.

✓ Ensure that you can identify the basic parts of a computer and explain the purpose of each one. Ensure that you know the following parts: hard drive, DVD drive, power supply, motherboard, and RAM.

✓ Know the purpose of common peripherals used in the industry: printer, ADF/flatbed scanner, barcode/QR scanner, monitor, VR headset, optical drive, mouse, keyboard, touchpad, signature pad, game controller, camera/webcam, microphone, speakers, headset, projector, external storage device, KVM, magnetic/reader, chip reader, NFC/tap-to-pay device, and smart card reader.

✓ Know the following safety procedures: disconnect power, remove jewelry, lifting techniques, and weight limitations.

✓ Review the "Soft Skills" section at the end of the chapter. Make sure you know what open-ended questions are.

Key Terms

adapter 14	gigabyte 22	operating system 9
ADF 18	hard drive 11	optical drive 11
barcode scanner 18	hardware 9	PC 9
BIOS 10	headset 19	power supply 10
bit 21	keyboard 16	printer 18
brightness 19	kilobyte 22	projector 19
byte 21	KVM switch 19	QR scanner 18
camera 19	lumens 19	RAM 13
chip reader 19	magnetic reader 19	signature pad 19
device driver 9	megabyte 22	smart card reader 19
DVD drive 11	memory 13	software 9
expansion slot 14	microphone 19	tap-to-pay device 19
external storage device 19	monitor 10	terabyte 22
firmware 10	motherboard 13	touchpad 19
flatbed scanner 18	mouse 16	VR headset 18
game controller 19	NFC device 19	webcam 19

Review Questions

1. Match each part to the appropriate description.

    ____ motherboard   a. Converts AC to DC

    ____ RAM   b. Holds the most data

    ____ DVD drive   c. Has the most electronics

    ____ hard drive   d. Fits in an expansion slot

    ____ adapter   e. Contents disappear when power is off

    ____ power supply   f. Holds a disc

2. Which device would commonly be found in a laptop?
    [mouse | barcode scanner | touchpad | signature pad]

3. Which of the following are important suggested Internet search tips? (Choose two.)

    a. Try another search engine if the first one does not provide satisfactory results.

    b. Use as many common words as possible, like the, in, at, or for.

    c. Put quotation marks around two or more words that might be found consecutively in output.

    d. Use as few words as possible.

    e. Avoid using the name of the equipment manufacturer.

4. Which type of memory is commonly found on a motherboard?

    _____

5. When lifting a heavy computer, you should squat, bend at the knees, and use your legs to lift. [T | F]

6. How many tests must a person take in order to be A+ certified?
    [0 | 1 | 2 | 3 | 4]

7. Is the following question open ended or closed ended? You say your computer has been running slowly since Monday. Which applications have you installed this week? [open ended | closed ended]

8. List one example of having a positive attitude.

    _____

    _____

    _____

9. Which of the following devices are common output devices? (Select all that apply.)
    [digital piano | speakers | display | stylus | track stick | barcode reader | printer]

10. People who work with computers might be expected to lift up to how many pounds?
    [10 to 20 | 20 to 30 | 30 to 40 | 40 to 50]

11. Which Microsoft Windows application could be used to create a text file?
    [Textpad | Notepad | WriteIt | NoteIt]

12. Which Windows tool can be used to capture the screen?
    [Notepad | Bluetooth | Internet Explorer | Snipping Tool]

13. Rewrite the following conversation into an open-ended question.

    Technician: Good morning. I have a service log that states you are getting an error message whenever you access a PDF file. Have you done your Acrobat updates lately?

    _____

    _____

    _____

14. List one procedure you would do to help an erratic optical mouse.

_____

_____

15. Match the capacity to the description.

____ bit   a. 8 bits

____ kilobyte   b. a 1 or a 0

____ megabyte   c. approximately 1,000 bytes

____ byte   d. approximately 1 million bytes

____ gigabyte   e. approximately 1 trillion bytes

____ terabyte   f. approximately 1 billion bytes

16. Match the peripheral to the description.

____ flatbed scanner   a. has an ADF

____ KVM   b. might send you to a web page

____ QR scanner   c. used to capture video

____ touchpad   d. allows two computers to share multiple monitors

____ webcam   e. found on a laptop near the keyboard

17. What is a feature of an optical mouse?

    a. LEDs

    b. contacts

    c. volatility

    d. electrical conversion

18. Which device is normally found inside a computer?
    [touchpad | printer | headset | hard drive]

19. Which device normally can be seen if looking inside a desktop computer with the cover off and when normally looking at the computer?
    [hard drive | motherboard | DVD drive | RAM]

20. Where can you find RAM in a desktop computer?

    a. inside the power supply

    b. inserted into the motherboard

    c. below the keyboard

    d. in a KVM

Exercises

Exercise 1.1 Identifying Tower Computer Parts

Objective: To identify various computer parts correctly

Procedure: Identify each computer part in Figure 1.35.

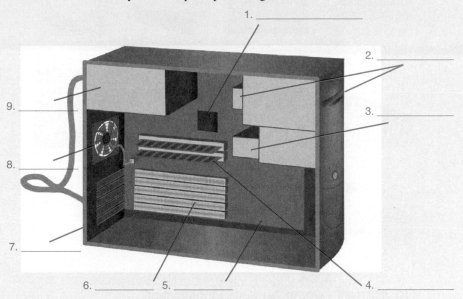

FIGURE 1.35   Tower computer parts identification

1. _____

2. _____

3. _____

4. _____

5. _____

6. _____

7. _____

8. _____

9. _____

Exercise 1.2 Identifying Computer Parts

Objective: To identify various computer parts correctly

Procedure: Identify each computer part in Figure 1.36.

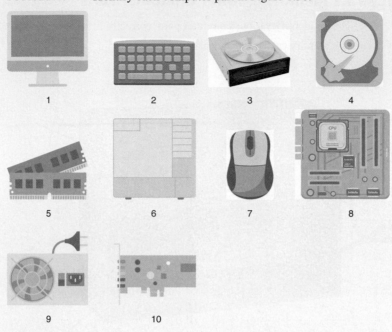

FIGURE 1.36   Computer parts identification

1. _____

2. _____

3. _____

4. _____

5. _____

6. _____

7. _____

8. _____

9. _____

10. _____

Activities

Internet Discovery

Objective: To obtain specific information from the Internet regarding a computer or its associated parts

Parts: Computer with Internet access

Procedure: Using the Internet, locate technical information about a computer. Answer the following questions based on the retrieved information. Note that you may need to open more than one document in order to answer the questions.

Questions:

1. What is the name of the computer for which you found technical information?

    _____

2. How much RAM comes with the computer?

    _____

3. Which URL did you use to find this information?

    _____

4. Which search term(s) would you use for the following scenario? An HP Windows 10 computer has a Samsung ML-2160 laser printer attached. This printer supports both wired and wireless printing. The computer that is wired to the printer can print just fine, but no wireless devices in the house can access or even see the printer.

    _____

    _____

5. Which search term(s) would you use in a search engine to help a friend who has accidentally deleted a file on a Windows 7 computer?

    _____

6. Which search terms would you use to find a video that shows you how to add an application to a Windows 8.1 desktop?

    _____

Soft Skills

Objective: To enhance and fine-tune a future technician's ability to listen, communicate in both written and oral forms, and support people who use computers in a professional manner

Procedure:

1. In a team environment, list three qualities that are important in a computer technician. Create scenarios that demonstrate these qualities. Share these findings in a clear and concise way with the class.

2. In a team environment, list three qualities that are not good practices for computer technicians. Create scenarios that demonstrate these qualities. Share these findings in a clear and concise way with the class.

Critical Thinking Skills

Objective: To analyze and evaluate information as well as apply learned information to new or different situations

Procedure:

1. Find an advertisement for a computer in a local computer flyer, in a newspaper, in a magazine, in a book, or on the Internet. List the components you know in one column and the components you do not know in another column. Select one component you do not know and research that component. On a separate piece of paper, write a description of the component, based on your research, and then share it with at least one other person. Write the name of the person with whom you shared.

2. Why do you think that many computer components are considered "throw-away" technology? List your reasoning. In groups of three or four, share your thoughts. Nominate a spokesperson to share your group reaction in two sentences or less.

3. One device touts a transfer speed of 100 Mb/s, whereas another device advertises 50 MB/s. Compare the two devices' transfer speeds and indicate which one is faster. Locate a component you have or would like to have. Compare products paying particular attention to the transfer speed. Document your findings.

2

Connectivity

In this chapter you will learn:

> The purposes of various computer ports

> What to do if you don't have a particular port

> What types of devices connect to specific ports

> Different types of connectors and cables

CompTIA Exam Objectives:

What CompTIA A+ exam objectives are covered in this chapter?

✓ 1001-2.4　Compare and contrast wireless networking protocols.

✓ 1001-3.1　Explain basic cable types, features, and their purposes.

✓ 1001-3.2　Identify common connector types.

✓ 1001-3.5　Given a scenario, install and configure motherboards, CPUs, and add-on cards.

✓ 1002-4.7　Given a scenario, use proper communication techniques and professionalism.

Introduction to Connectivity

Now that we've discussed the basic parts of a PC, we are ready to dive into the technical details. This chapter explores wired and wireless connectivity—specifically, how to connect input and output devices to specific ports. This chapter also explores what to do when things go wrong. Some of the ports may be challenging at first, but it is important that people going into the IT field know how to connect devices to PCs and mobile devices.

External Connectivity

A **port** is a connector on a motherboard or on a separate adapter that allows a device to connect to a computer. A technician must be able to identify these ports readily to ensure that (1) the correct cable plugs into a port and (2) the technician can troubleshoot problems in the right area. All IT professionals should be able to recognize and identify the common ports used today.

Many port connections are either male or female. Male ports have metal pins that protrude from the connector. A male port requires a cable with a female connector. Female ports have holes in the connector into which the male cable pins are inserted.

Some connectors on integrated motherboards are either D-shell connectors or DIN connectors. A **D-shell connector** (sometimes called a D-sub) has more pins or holes on top than on the bottom, so a cable connected to the D-shell connector can be inserted in only one direction and cannot be accidentally flipped upside down. Many documents represent a D-shell connector by using the letters DB, a hyphen, and the number of pins—for example, DB-9, DB-15, or DB-25. A DB-9 connector is also known as a serial communications D-shell connector, 9 pins.

A **mini-DIN connector** is round, has 6 small holes, and is normally keyed (which means a cable can be inserted only one way). Keyboard and mouse connectors, commonly called PS/2 ports, are examples of mini-DIN connectors. Today, a keyboard and mouse most often connect to USB ports (shown later). Figure 2.1 shows the back of a computer with a motherboard and some of the ports (DVI and VGA) covered later in this chapter. You can see a mini-DIN and two D-shell connectors on the motherboard.

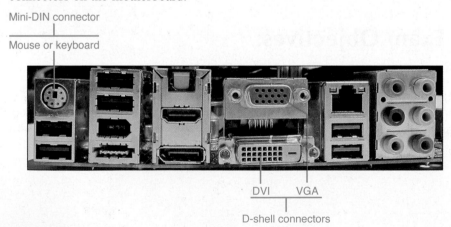

Mini-DIN connector

Mouse or keyboard

DVI   VGA

D-shell connectors

FIGURE 2.1 Mini-DIN and D-shell connectors

Mouse and Keyboard Ports

Mouse ports and **keyboard ports** were traditionally 6-pin mini-DIN ports that are sometimes called **PS/2 ports**. Today, USB ports are more commonly used for mouse and keyboard connectivity. Many manufacturers color code the PS/2 mouse port as green and the PS/2 keyboard port as purple, or they may put a small diagram of a keyboard or a mouse by each connector. Figure 2.2 shows mouse and keyboard connectivity options.

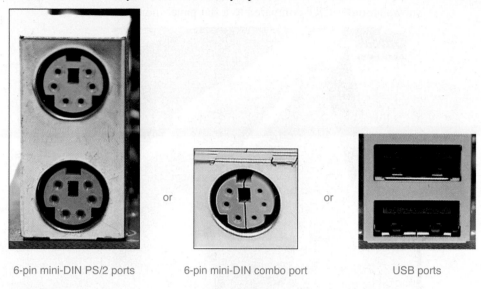

6-pin mini-DIN PS/2 ports   or   6-pin mini-DIN combo port   or   USB ports

FIGURE 2.2   **Mouse and keyboard ports**

> **TECH TIP**
>
> **Don't confuse the mouse and keyboard ports**
>
> On motherboards that have two PS/2 ports, the mouse and keyboard ports are not interchangeable, even if they use the same pin configuration (unless, of course, you have a 6-pin mini-DIN combo port).

Video Ports

A video port is used to connect a display. Video output can be the older method of an **analog signal** (varying levels, such as seen with an audio signal) or the newer output that uses a **digital signal** (1s and 0s). Because the computer uses digital signals, sending 1s and 0s is more efficient than converting an analog signal to a digital signal. This is relevant because there are still video ports around that are designed for analog signals. Figure 2.3 shows the difference between analog and digital signals.

Analog Versus Digital Signal

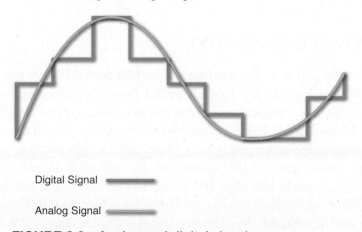

Digital Signal ⸻

Analog Signal ⸻

FIGURE 2.3   **Analog and digital signals**

Cathode ray tube (CRT) monitors were the big bulky ones that looked like old TV sets that accepted analog output from computers. Flat panel monitors accept digital signals. Figure 2.4 shows an older CRT compared to a flat panel monitor.

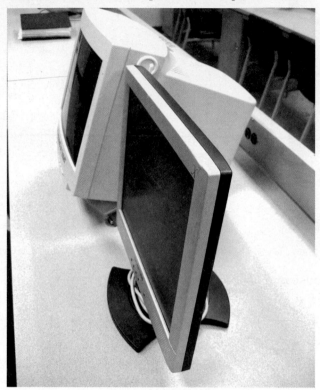

FIGURE 2.4   CRT monitor and flat panel monitor

The most common video ports used today are VGA, DVI, DisplayPort, and HDMI. These are all covered in this section. In addition, multipurpose ports such as USB-C, Thunderbolt, and Lightning are starting to be used for video. The multipurpose ports are covered separately since they can transmit more than just audio and video.

Video Graphics Array (VGA)

The video graphics array port, or **VGA port**, was designed for analog output to a CRT monitor. VGA ports are easy to identify because they have three rows of holes. The female port is sometimes advertised as an HD-15 or DE-15 port. The VGA cable has a DB-15 male end that attaches to the DE-15 female port.

Digital Visual Interface (DVI)

A newer port, the Digital Visual Interface port, or **DVI port**, has three rows of square holes. DVI ports are used to connect flat panel digital displays. Some flat panel monitors can also use the older VGA port. Some video adapters also enable you to connect a video device (such as a television) that has an **S-Video port**. Figure 2.5 shows a video adapter with all three ports. The left port is the DVI connector, the center port is for S-Video, and the right port is a VGA port.

There are several types of DVI connectors. The one used depends on the type of monitor attached. Two terms used with these DVI connectors are single link and dual link. A **single link** connection allows video resolutions up to 1920×1080. With a **dual link** connection, more pins are available to send more signals, thus allowing higher resolutions such as 2560×1600. The two major types of connectors are DVI-D and DVI-I. **DVI-D** is used for digital video connectivity only. **DVI-I** can be used for both digital and analog monitors, and it is the most common. A less common type is DVI-A, which is used for analog connectivity (and is not shown in Figure 2.6 with the other DVI connector types). Figure 2.7 shows both a DVI cable and a VGA cable.

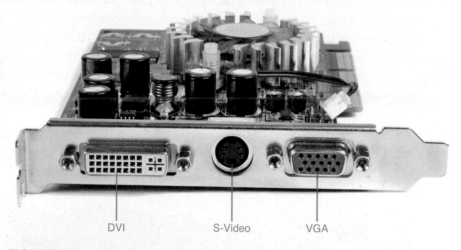

DVI   S-Video   VGA

FIGURE 2.5   DVI, S-Video, and VGA ports

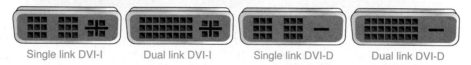

Single link DVI-I   Dual link DVI-I   Single link DVI-D   Dual link DVI-D

FIGURE 2.6   DVI connectors

FIGURE 2.7   DVI and VGA cables

TECH TIP

Match a monitor to the port type

Be careful when installing a monitor. For example, ensure that the video port matches the DVI connection type for the monitor. Converters can be purchased to adapt to a monitor with a VGA port.

DisplayPort

The **DisplayPort** developed by VESA (Video Electronics Standards Association) can send and receive video, audio, or both types of signals simultaneously. The port is designed to primarily output to display devices, such as computer monitors, televisions, and home theaters. A passive converter can be used to convert to a single link DVI or HDMI port (covered next). You use an active converter to convert to a dual link DVI.

To understand why an active converter is needed, you must understand the difference between active and passive cables. A passive cable does not contain a chip that boosts the signals, and an active cable does. An active cable allows cables to be thinner and supports sending signals further and faster than passive cables. Active and passive cables are found in computer networks and video systems.

A mini-DisplayPort is also available on mobile devices. Figure 2.8 shows the DisplayPort and a cable that would connect to this port.

FIGURE 2.8   DisplayPort

HDMI

Another upgrade over DVI is High-Definition Multimedia Interface (**HDMI**), a digital interface that can carry audio and video over the same cable. HDMI ports are found on cable TV boxes, televisions, video adapters, laptops, desktops, and tablets. Smaller **mini-HDMI** or micro-HDMI connectors are used with devices such as cameras, tablets, and smartphones. Table 2.1 describes the different HDMI ports.

TABLE 2.1   HDMI ports

HDMI connector type	Description
A	19-pin port found on a TV or PC that can have a Category 1 (standard) or Category 2 (high-speed) cable attached
B	29-pin port used with very high-resolution displays
C	19-pin mini-HDMI port (2.42 mm×10.42 mm) found on mobile devices
D	19-pin micro-HDMI port (2.8 mm×6.4 mm) found on mobile devices

Figure 2.9 shows a video card that would be used in a gaming computer (a computer primarily used for playing video games). On top is a dual link DVI-D port. On the bottom, from left to right, are a DisplayPort, an HDMI port, and a dual link DVI-I port. Figure 2.10 shows an HDMI port along with a mini-HDMI port (turned in the opposite direction). Table 2.2 summarizes important PC video ports.

Note: Thunderbolt, Lightning, and USB cables can also carry video signals; these ports and cables are covered in the "Multipurpose Ports" section, later in this chapter.

FIGURE 2.9 Video ports, including a DisplayPort, an HDMI port, and two DVI ports

DisplayPort

HDMI

DVI-I

DVI-D

FIGURE 2.10 HDMI and mini-HDMI ports

TABLE 2.2 Video port summary

Port type	Analog, digital, or both	Transfer speeds	Carries audio?	Maximum cable lengths
VGA	Analog	N/A	No	Depends on resolution
DVI-D	Digital	Dual link 7.92 Gb/s	No	Up to 15 feet (4.57 m) for display resolutions up to 1920×1200
DVI-I	Both	Single or dual link	No	Not in the standards, but a general rule of thumb is up to 15 feet (4.57 m) for display resolutions up to 1920×1200
DisplayPort	Digital	25.92 Gb/s	Yes	9.8 feet (3 m) for passive and 108 feet (32.9 m) for active
HDMI	Digital	48 Gb/s	Yes	Not in the standards, but a general rule of thumb is up to 16 feet (4.88 m) for standard cable and up to 49 feet (14.9 m) for high-speed, good quality cable and connectors

High-Bandwidth Digital Content Protection (HDCP)

In an effort to prevent piracy, some vendors implement the High-bandwidth Digital Content Protection (HDCP) feature on DVI, DisplayPort, and HDMI ports. HDCP, which is part of Intel's digital rights management (DRM) specification, is designed to protect copyrighted material. This means if you are using an Apple MacBook that has this feature, you cannot externally display a legally purchased movie unless the external display is HDCP capable.

Coaxial Cable

A type of connector you might see associated with video, but more likely with cable TV, is a Bayonet Neill–Concelman (BNC) connector. A **BNC connector** is used with a **coaxial** cable that is found in video networks such as a school where multiple TVs connect to the same distribution center or in a home that obtains TV channels through a cable provider. A BNC connector has a center conductor that pushes onto the receptacle and is surrounded by insulation. Outside the insulation is a shield of copper braid, a metallic foil, or both, to protect the center conductor from electromagnetic interference (EMI). The metal outside the conductor is twisted onto the cable to snap the connector into place, as shown in Figure 2.11. Figure 2.12 shows the front of a BNC connector already put onto the coax cable.

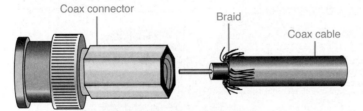

FIGURE 2.11   Coaxial cable with a BNC connector

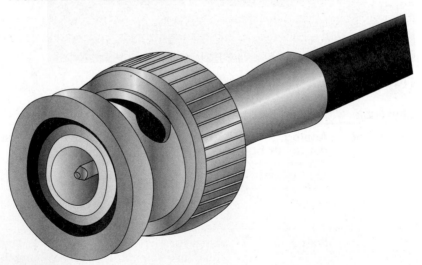

FIGURE 2.12   BNC connector

Figure 2.13 shows two popular coax connectors: BNC and F. Notice that the BNC connector has a notched side to turn and twist onto the receiving connector. The F connector simply screws onto the receiving connector. Table 2.3 lists types of coax cables.

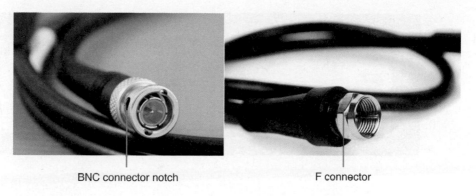

BNC connector notch   F connector

FIGURE 2.13   Coaxial BNC and F connectors

TABLE 2.3   Coax cable types

Coax cable type	Description
RG-6*	This is the type of cable least likely to be used in a network. It is a 75-ohm cable suitable for distributing signals for cable TV, satellite dish, or rooftop antenna. It has better shielding than RG-59, so it is larger in diameter. Typical distances are 1000 feet (305 m) to 1500 feet (457 m). It can carry frequencies up to 2200 MHz.
RG-59	This type of 75-ohm cable is not used in LANs but is used in video installations. Typical distances are 750 feet (225 m) to 1000 feet (305 m). It can carry frequencies up to 1000 MHz.

*RG stands for radio grade.

If a coaxial cable of different impedance attaches to another coaxial cable, signal loss results. Coaxial cable is rated according to whether it will be used in an interior or exterior space. Use the appropriate cable type for the installation. Be careful when bending the cable. When there is a problem and the right type of cable and connector are used, the most common issue is that the coax connector is not attached properly.

Video Adapters and Converters

Converters can be purchased for video ports. For example, Figure 2.14 shows a **DVI-to-HDMI adapter** (with both ends visible). Figure 2.15 shows a **DVI-to-VGA adapter**.

HDMI   DVI

FIGURE 2.14   DVI-to-HDMI adapter

FIGURE 2.15   DVI-to-VGA adapter

Multipurpose Ports

Some ports/cables can be used for multiple devices, including USB 2.0, USB 3.0, USB-C, Thunderbolt, and Lightning. The USB port is probably the one people are most familiar with, but the Thunderbolt and Lightning ports are also considered multipurpose ports. Let's explore these ports.

USB Ports

USB stands for Universal Serial Bus and is one of the most popular ports on desktop PCs and laptops. A USB port allows up to 127 connected devices to transmit at speeds up to 10 Gb/s (10 billion bits per second) or 20 Gb/s. Devices that connect to a USB port include printers, scanners, mice, keyboards, joysticks, optical drives, tape drives, game pads, cameras, modems, speakers, telephones, video phones, data gloves, and digitizers. Additional ports can sometimes be found on the front of a PC case or on the side of a mobile device. Figure 2.16 shows some USB ports.

FIGURE 2.16   USB ports

USB Versions

USB ports come in three main versions: 1.0/1.1, 2.0 (Hi-Speed), and 3.0 (SuperSpeed). USB 1.0 operates at speeds of 1.5 Mb/s and 12 Mb/s; **USB 2.0** operates at speeds up to 480 Mb/s. **USB 3.0** supports transmissions up to 5 Gb/s. The USB 3.0 port, which still accepts older devices and cables, is colored blue. USB 3.1 is available in USB Gen 1 and USB Gen 2. Whereas the Gen 1 type supports transmission speeds up to 5 Gb/s, USB 3.1 Gen 2 increases the speed to 10 Gb/s, is backward compatible with prior versions, and can deliver more power, and its ports are colored teal. The USB 3.2 standard, the newest standard at press time, can support two lanes of 5 Gb/s or two lanes of 10 Gb/s. A USB 3.2 port requires a USB Type-C (sometimes called a **USB-C**) cable and supports up to 20 Gb/s data transfer rates. Keep in mind that to achieve USB 3.x speeds, a 3.x device, 3.x port, and the USB-C cable must be used. The version 1 and 2 cables use 4 wires. Version 3.0 cables use 9 or 11 wires. Version 3.1 and 3.2 Type-C cables have 24 wires. Figure

2.17 shows the different USB versions and speed symbols. Note that the port does not have to be labeled, and sometimes looking at the technical specifications for the computer or motherboard is the only way to determine the port speed.

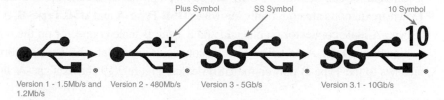

Version 1 - 1.5Mb/s and   Version 2 - 480Mb/s   Version 3 - 5Gb/s   Version 3.1 - 10Gb/s
1.2Mb/s

FIGURE 2.17   USB versions, speeds, and symbols

USB Power Delivery (USB-PD)

USB ports have been able to provide 5 V at 500 mA for 2.5 watts of power to devices since version 2.0. The newest USB standard, Power Delivery (**PD** or **USB-PD**), can provide up to 20 V at 5 A for 100 watts of power. The standard actually has five levels of power delivery: 10 W, 18 W, 36 W, 60 W, and 100 W.

USB Cables

Each USB standard has a maximum cable length:

> Version 1.0/1.1: 9.8 feet (3 m)
> Version 2.0: 16.4 feet (5 m)
> Version 3.x: 9.8 feet (3 m)

These standards are provided to ensure that devices function properly. USB cables can be longer than these specifications, but they may not work as well.

If a USB port provides power to a device, then the maximum cable length shortens. For example, if a USB 2.0 PD device is being used, the maximum cable length is less than 13 feet (4 m). If a USB 3.1 PD device is used with a USB Type-C cable, then the cable length should be less than 3.3 feet (1 m). A PD device requires a Type-C cable, but not all ports or cables support PD.

With the older ports, sometimes a USB extension cable is needed. Figure 2.18 shows a cable used to extend the length of a standard USB cable.

FIGURE 2.18   USB extension cable

USB Connectors

USB ports can be either upstream ports or downstream ports. An upstream port is used to connect to a computer or another hub. A USB device like a printer or flash drive connects to a downstream port. Downstream ports are commonly known as **USB Type-A** and **USB Type-B**. A standard USB cable has a Type-A male connector on one end and a Type-B male connector on the other end. The port on the computer is a Type-A port. The Type-A connector inserts into the Type-A port. The Type-B connector attaches to the Type-B port on the USB device. Figure 2.19 shows Type-A and Type-B connectors.

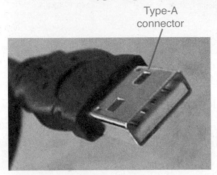

Type-A connector   Type-B connector

FIGURE 2.19   USB Type-A and Type-B connectors

The **USB Type-C** connector is the latest connector and will eventually replace the Type-A and Type-B connectors. With older devices, it is possible to use an adapter in order to attach to a Type-C connector. Many USB 3.0 ports are Type-C connectors, but they do not have to be. USB 3.1 (Gen 2) and USB 3.2 require USB Type-C connectors. Figure 2.20 shows a USB Type-C connector and cable. Notice in the photo of a USB Type-C connector in Figure 2.21 that the cable connector could be inserted into the USB-C port with either side facing up (the connector is non-directional).

Type-C USB Connector

FIGURE 2.20   USB Type-C connector and cable

TECH TIP

USB Alternate Mode

Some USB ports support other types of non-USB data, such as video and audio for DisplayPort, HDMI, Thunderbolt, Mobile High-Definition Link (MHL), and PCIe through a USB Type-C cable. Alternate Mode is enabled through the USB-PD protocol. Alternate Mode also supports sending non-USB data at the same time as USB data. For example, with Alternate Mode enabled, streaming video can be sent at the same time as USB data.

FIGURE 2.21   USB-C cable and connector

Mini-USB and Micro-USB

Two smaller USB ports used on portable devices such as hubs, external hard drives, digital cameras, and smartphones are the **mini-USB** and **micro-USB** ports. There are several types of these smaller USB ports: mini-A, mini-AB, micro-B, and micro-AB. The mini-AB and micro-AB ports accept either a mini-A/micro-A or a mini-B/micro-B cable end. Figure 2.22 shows the standard Type-A USB cable that would be inserted into a PC port compared to the mini- and micro-USB cables used with mobile devices. Figure 2.23 shows a USB 3.0 micro-B port and connector.

Micro-USB   Mini-USB   Standard Type-A USB

FIGURE 2.22   Micro-USB, mini-USB, and USB Type-A cables

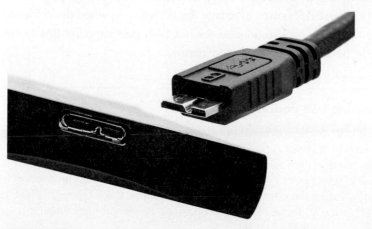

FIGURE 2.23   USB 3.0 micro-B port and connector

USB Hubs

A USB port can have more than one device attached to the port through the use of a USB hub. Many hubs can operate in two power modes—self-powered and bus-powered—and a hub may have a switch control that must be set to the appropriate mode. A **self-powered hub** has an external power supply attached. A bus-powered hub has no external power supply connected to it. Once USB devices attached to a hub are tested, the hub's power supply can be removed, and the devices can be retested. If all attached devices work properly, the hub power supply can be left disconnected. Figure 2.24 shows USB hub connectivity, and Figure 2.25 shows USB cabling rules.

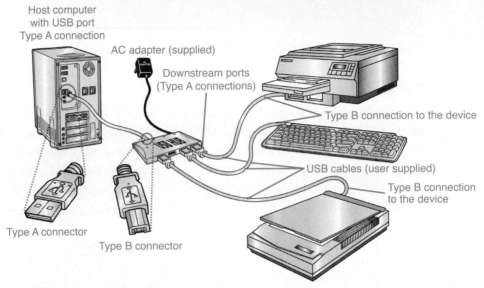

FIGURE 2.24   USB hub connectivity

USB cabling rules
- 5 hubs maximum (total max range of 88.5 feet or 27 meters)
- 127 devices maximum connected to up to 5 hubs
- Maximum distance between 2 USB hubs
    - high-speed devices – 16.4 feet or 5 meters
    - low-speed devices – 9.8 feet or 3 meters

FIGURE 2.25   USB cabling rules

USB ports have always been able to provide power to unpowered devices, such as flash drives. A **charging USB port** is a port designed to be able to provide power and charge attached devices. Note that not all USB devices can be powered on while charging. With a **sleep-and-charge USB port**, the port provides power to charge the device even when the computer is powered off. See the computing device's specifications to see if a USB port supports this feature. Table 2.4 summarizes USB speeds, port colors, and alternate names.

TECH TIP

Safely removing USB devices

To remove a USB device, do not simply unplug it from the port. Instead, click on the *Safely Remove Hardware* icon (Windows 7) or *Safely Remove Hardware and Eject Media* (Windows 8/10) from the notification area and then select the USB device to remove. On a Mac, right-click the desktop icon for the device and select *Eject x* (where *x* is the device name) or drag the desktop icon to the trash can. In Ubuntu Linux, locate the device in Files or File Explorer. Click the small eject icon or right-click the name of the device and select *Eject*. The operating system prompts when it is safe to unplug the device.

TABLE 2.4 USB port summary

Port type	Maximum transmission speed	Port color	Alternate name
USB 1.x	1.5 and 12 Mb/s	Usually white	Low speed and full speed
USB 2.0	480 Mb/s	Black	High speed
USB 3.0	5 Gb/s	Blue	SuperSpeed
USB 3.1 Gen 1	5 Gb/s	Blue	SuperSpeed
USB 3.1 Gen 2	10 Gb/s	Teal	SuperSpeed+
USB 3.2	20 Gb/s	Not available at press time	Not available at press time
USB sleep-and-charge	N/A	Yellow, orange, or red	N/A

USB Converters

Converters are available to convert a USB port to a different type of connector (or vice versa), such as PS/2 mouse and keyboard connector or mini-DIN (see Figure 2.26). Figure 2.27 shows a **USB-to-Ethernet converter** used to connect a device, such as a tablet that has a USB port, to a wired Ethernet network. Figure 2.28 shows a set of USB connectors that can be purchased as a set and that includes a **USB A-to-USB B converter**.

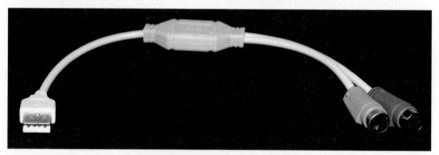

FIGURE 2.26 USB-to-PS/2 mouse and keyboard converter

FIGURE 2.27 USB-to-Ethernet converter

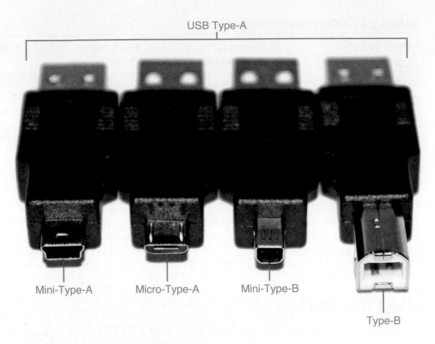

USB Type-A

Mini-Type-A   Micro-Type-A   Mini-Type-B

Type-B

FIGURE 2.28   USB converter kit

Installing Extra USB Ports

Sometimes people want more USB ports and do not want to add another hub. Many motherboards support adding two or more USB ports by using a cable that attaches to an **internal USB connector** on the motherboard, also known as a USB header. The ports mount in an expansion slot space, but they do not have a card that plugs into an expansion slot. Even if the motherboard has such pins, the ports and cable assembly might have to be purchased separately. Figure 2.29 shows sample USB ports that attach to a motherboard.

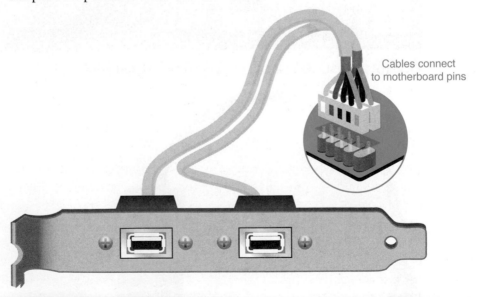

Cables connect
to motherboard pins

FIGURE 2.29   Installing extra USB ports

Thunderbolt

An updated multipurpose port that uses some of the DisplayPort video port technology is the **Thunderbolt port**. The Thunderbolt interface was developed by Intel with support from Apple.

The Thunderbolt port used on Apple computers is the same connector as the mini-DisplayPort; however, Thunderbolt 3 uses the USB Type-C connector, discussed earlier in this chapter, in the "USB Connectors" section. Thunderbolt 3 is the first Thunderbolt version to support USB. In addition to carrying video signals, a Thunderbolt cable can also be used to carry power, audio, video, and data to external storage devices at speeds up to 40 Gb/s. Figure 2.30 shows a Thunderbolt port and cable. Look back to Figures 2.20 and 2.21 to see the Type-C connector and cable that Thunderbolt 3 uses.

FIGURE 2.30   Thunderbolt cable and port

TECH TIP

Can a Thunderbolt 3 device work in a USB-C port?

Even if a Thunderbolt 3 device can attach to a USB-C port, it may not work. If the device does work, it will work at USB-C speed. However, USB-C devices can function and connect to a Thunderbolt 3 port.

Lightning

The last multipurpose port to cover is the **Lightning port** and associated cable. The Lightning port, developed by Apple, is an 8-pin port that accepts the cable with either side facing up (that is, it is reversible). The Lightning port can carry data and power from mobile devices to other devices, such as cameras, external monitors, and external storage devices. An adapter/converter can be used to allow the cable to be used with the older Apple 30-pin connector, USB, HDMI, VGA, or SD cards. The Lightning port supports USB data and USB charging, but the Lightning port or cable is not interchangeable with USB-C. Note that some MacBook computers have USB-C, not Lightning, connectors. Figure 2.31 shows a Lightning cable. Table 2.5 shows a comparison of the three multipurpose ports.

FIGURE 2.31   Lightning cable

TABLE 2.5   Multipurpose port comparison

Port type	Maximum transmission speed	Type of connector	Platforms	What it carries
USB 3.2	20 Gb/s	USB Type-C 24-pin reversible connector	Found on Apple and PCs	Data and power
Thunderbolt 3	40 Gb/s	USB Type-C 24-pin reversible connector	Intel and Apple developed	Data and power
Lightning	Speeds up to USB 3.0 with the right adapter	8-pin reversible connector	Apple-proprietary	Data and power

Audio Ports

A **sound card** converts digital computer signals to sound and sound to digital computer signals. A sound card is sometimes called an audio card. Sound ports are commonly integrated into the motherboard, but some people want better sound, and so they add a card. The most common sound ports include a port for a microphone, MP3 player, or other audio device and one or more ports for speakers. The ports can accept analog or digital signals. (Refer to Figure 2.3 to see the difference between analog and digital signals.)

The traditional analog sound ports are 3.5 mm (see Figure 2.32). The newer Sony/Phillips Digital interface (**S/PDIF**) in/out ports, on the left in Figure 2.32, are used to connect to various devices, such as digital audio tape players/recorders, DVD players/recorders, and external disc players/recorders. There are two main types of S/PDIF connectors: an **RCA** jack (last port on the left) used to connect a coaxial cable and a fiber-optic port for a **TOSLINK** cable connection (two optical ports beside the RCA jack in Figure 2.32). Sound cards are popular because people want better sound quality than what is available with the ports integrated into a motherboard.

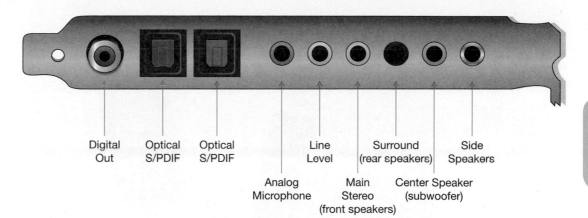

FIGURE 2.32 Sound card ports

eSATA Ports

A 7-pin nonpowered external serial AT attachment, or **eSATA**, port is used for connecting external storage devices such as hard drives or optical drives and is commonly found on laptops. eSATA can transfer data at 600 MB/s. Devices can connect at a maximum of approximately 6.6 feet (2 m). If the internal hard drive has crashed, an external drive connected to an eSATA or USB port can be used to boot and troubleshoot the system.

A variation of the eSATA port is the **eSATAp port**, which is also known as eSATA/USB, or power over eSATA. This variation can accept eSATA or USB cables and provides power when necessary. Figure 2.33 shows a standard eSATA port and an eSATAp (eSATA/USB combination) port.

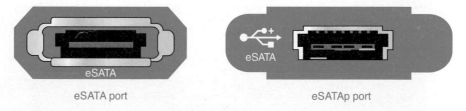

FIGURE 2.33 eSATA and eSATAp ports

Network Ports

A **network port** is used to connect a device such as a computer or printer to a network. The most common type of network port is an **Ethernet port**. A network cable inserts into the Ethernet port to connect the computing device to the wired network. A network port is commonly called a **NIC** (network interface card/controller).

Ethernet adapters or motherboards contain a Registered Jack-45, or **RJ-45**, port that looks like an **RJ-11** phone jack (see Figure 2.34). The RJ-45 connector has 8 conductors (wires) instead of 4. New technicians commonly mistake RJ-11 ports with RJ-45 network jacks or connectors. Look closely at the connectors to see the difference. The RJ-11 connector is on the left.

RJ-45 Ethernet ports can also be found on external storage devices, printers, Internet modems, and other network devices. Figure 2.35 shows an Ethernet NIC with an RJ-45 port.

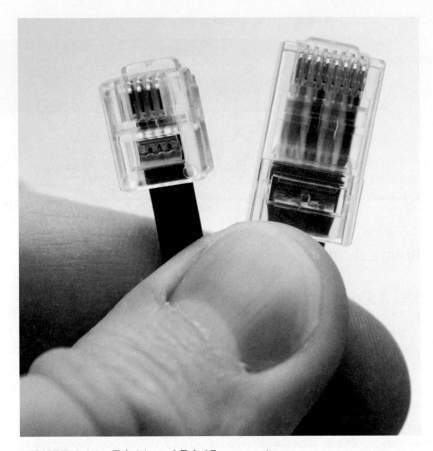

FIGURE 2.34   RJ-11 and RJ-45 connectors

FIGURE 2.35   An RJ-45 Ethernet port

Ethernet port symbols

An Ethernet port may not have any symbol above the port, or it may have one of the following:

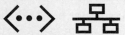

Modem and Serial Ports

A modulator/demodulator, or **modem**, connects a computer to a phone line. A modem can be internal or external. An internal modem is an adapter that has one or two RJ-11 phone jack connectors. An external modem is a separate device that sits outside the computer and connects to a 9-pin serial port or a USB port. The RJ-11 connector labeled *Line* is for the connection to the wall jack. The RJ-11 connector labeled *Phone* is for the connection to a phone, if needed. Figure 2.36 shows an internal modem with two ports.

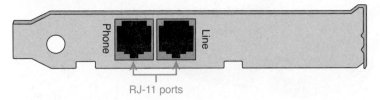

FIGURE 2.36   **An internal modem with two RJ-11 ports**

Serial ports are 9-pin male and are found on older motherboards, network equipment, and even projectors. This type of port is not seen very often today. A serial port is also called a **DB-9** or **RS-232** port. Figure 2.37 shows the DB-9 serial ports on an older computer. Figure 2.38 shows an example of a **serial cable**. The DB-9 female connector would attach to the DB-9 male connector on a device or motherboard. Figure 2.39 shows a USB-to-serial converter cable you might need to connect an external modem to a modern motherboard.

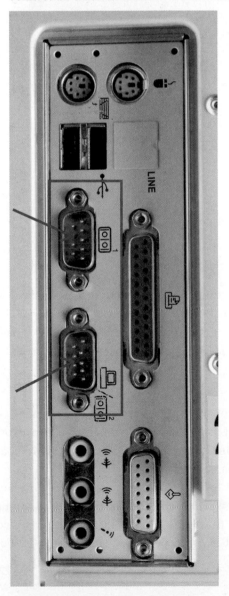

FIGURE 2.37   **DB-9 serial ports**

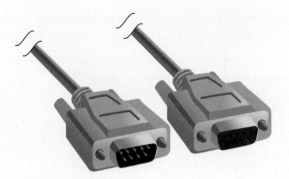

FIGURE 2.38 Serial cable ends

FIGURE 2.39 USB-to-serial port converter

Network Cabling

People who work in IT have all types of devices, including PCs, printers, servers, projectors, and displays that connect to the network. This is a good time to make sure you know what type of cable might be used. Ethernet, fiber, and coaxial cable are the types of cables commonly seen. Note that coaxial cable was covered in the Video ports section because that was its original use.

Ethernet Cable

Ethernet is the most common type of wired network seen in homes and in companies. An Ethernet cable attaches to an RJ-45 Ethernet port. The most common type of network cable is **unshielded twisted pair (UTP)**. UTP comes in three common types: **Cat 5**, **Cat 5e**, and **Cat 6**. Cat 7 is also available. The Cat in these cable names is short for category.

UTP cable has 8 wires that are twisted to prevent data that is traveling along one wire from interfering with an adjacent wire—which is called crosstalk. Figure 2.40 shows a Cat 5e cable and a Cat 6 cable. Notice that the Cat 6 cable is thinner. Table 2.6 shows a comparison of the three cable types. Cat 5e is identical to Cat 5 except for the cable twists. Cat 5e has more cable twists to reduce crosstalk.

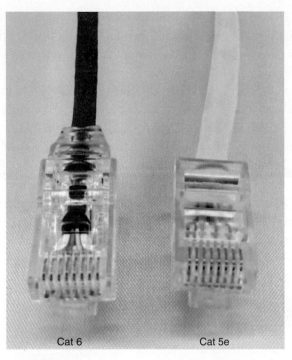

Cat 6   Cat 5e

FIGURE 2.40   Cat 6 and Cat 5e cable

TABLE 2.6   Cat 5, 5e, and 6 cable comparison

Ethernet cable type	Maximum transmission speed	Bandwidth	Distance limitation
Cat 5	100 Mb/s	100 MHz	328 feet (100 m)
Cat 5e	1000 Mb/s, or 1 Gb/s	100 MHz	328 feet (100 m)
Cat 6	1000 Mb/s, or 1 Gb/s	250 MHz	328 feet (100 m)
Cat 6a	10,000 Mb/s, or 10 Gb/s	500 MHz	328 feet (100 m)

The alternative to UTP is **shield twisted pair (STP)** cable, which is used in manufacturing and other harsh environments where the cabling needs a little more shielding to keep the data intact. The shielding is provided by a foil wrapped around all the cables as well as around each grouping of two cables, which makes STP cabling thicker than UTP.

Both UTP and STP use the RJ-45 connector, which has a tang on one side. To remove a cable from an Ethernet port, press on the tang to release the cable from the port. When inserting the cable, ensure that the cable is oriented properly and then push the cable firmly into the port until you hear a click of the tang fitting snuggly into the port. Figure 2.41 shows the top and bottom of an Ethernet cable connector.

FIGURE 2.41   Ethernet RJ-45 connector with tang

A special type of UTP or STP cable is **plenum cable**. A plenum is a building's air circulation space for heating and air conditioning systems. Plenum cable is treated with Teflon or alternative fire-retardant materials to reduce the fire risk. Plenum cable produces less smoke and is less toxic when it burns than is regular networking cable.

An alternative to plenum cable is polyvinyl chloride (**PVC**) cable that has a plastic cable insulation or jacket. PVC is cheaper than plenum cable, and it can have flame-retardant chemicals added to make it compliant with building codes. PVC is usually easier to install than plenum cable.

To avoid extra troubleshooting time, most businesses install their network cable according to the ANSI/TIA/EIA-568-A or 568-B (commonly shown as **T568A** and **T568B** or **568A/B**) standard. These standards specify how far the cable can extend, how to label it, what type of connectors to use, and so forth. Figure 2.42 shows that the colored wires within a connector must be in a particular order. Chapter 13, "Networking," shows how to make cables according to the T568A and T568B standards.

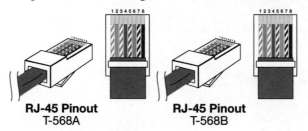

RJ-45 Pinout
T-568A

RJ-45 Pinout
T-568B

FIGURE 2.42   ANSI/TIA/EIA T568A and T568AB wiring standards

Fiber Cable

Fiber cable, also known as fiber-optic cable, is made of glass or a type of plastic fiber and is used to carry light pulses. Fiber cable can be used to connect a workstation to another device, but in industry, the most common uses of fiber-optic cable are to connect networks forming the network backbone, networks between buildings, service provider high-speed networks, and homes to a service provider. Figure 2.43 shows fiber switch connections. Notice that the fibers are grouped in pairs.

FIGURE 2.43   Fiber connections

There are many different types of fiber connectors, and some of them are proprietary. Four of the most common connectors used with fiber-optic cable are Mechanical Transfer Registered Jack, or MT-RJ (common in home installations), straight tip (ST), subscriber connector (SC), and Lucent connector (LC). Figure 2.44 shows three of these connectors.

The two major classifications of fiber are single-mode and multi-mode. **Single-mode fiber** cable has only one light beam sent down the cable. **Multi-mode fiber** allows multiple light signals to be sent along the same cable. Table 2.7 describes the characteristics of the two types. (Note that fiber's maximum speeds keep increasing as technology keeps changing.)

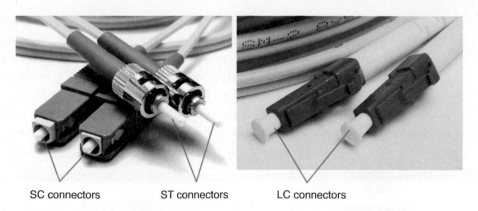

SC connectors   ST connectors   LC connectors

FIGURE 2.44   Fiber-optic connector types

TABLE 2.7   Fiber cable speed and transmission characteristics

Type	Characteristic
Single-mode	Classified by the size of the fiber core and the cladding. Common sizes include 8/125 to 10/125 microns, where the first number represents the size of the core, and the second number is the size of the cladding. Single-mode cable allows for distances more than 50 miles (80 km) at speeds more than 100 Gb/s.
Multi-mode	Sizes include 50/125 and 62.5/125 microns. Can support distances more than 1 mile (2 km) and speeds up to 10 Gb/s. ST connectors are used more with multi-mode fiber than with single-mode.

TECH TIP

Choosing the correct fiber type

Multi-mode fiber is cheaper and more commonly used than single-mode fiber and is good for shorter-distance applications; however, single-mode fiber can transmit a signal farther than multi-mode and supports the highest bandwidth.

Integrated Motherboard Ports

An integrated motherboard provides expandability because ports are built in and do not require separate adapters. If a motherboard includes USB, network, sound, keyboard, mouse, and video ports, there is more space available for other adapters. The number of available expansion slots in a system depends on the motherboard manufacturer. Figure 2.45 shows integrated motherboard ports.

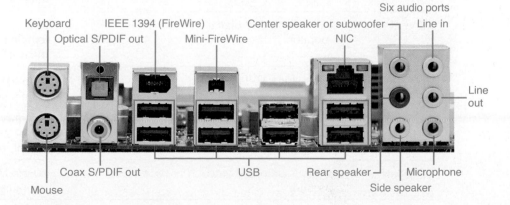

Keyboard   IEEE 1394 (FireWire)   Six audio ports
    Optical S/PDIF out   Mini-FireWire   Center speaker or subwoofer — Line in
                                            NIC

                                                    Line
                                                    out

    Coax S/PDIF out   USB   Rear speaker   Microphone
Mouse   Side speaker

FIGURE 2.45   Integrated motherboard ports

Ports built into a motherboard are faster than those on an expansion board. All adapters in expansion slots run more slowly than the motherboard components. Computers with integrated motherboards are easier to set up because you do not have to install an adapter or configure the ports. Normally, systems with integrated motherboards are easier to troubleshoot because the components are on one board. The drawback is that when one port goes bad, you have to add an adapter that has the same type of port as the one that went bad. Furthermore, ports found on an adapter might be of higher quality or might have more capabilities than an integrated port. See Figure 2.46.

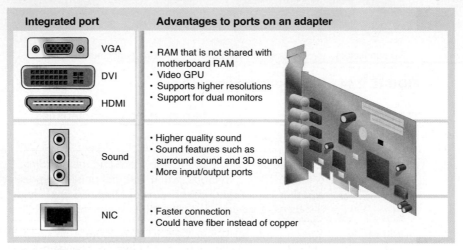

FIGURE 2.46   Advantages of adapters

Getting to Know Ports

Being able to identify ports quickly and accurately is a critical skill in computer repair. Table 2.8 lists the most common computer ports.

TABLE 2.8   Common ports

Port	Usage	Port color code	Common connector
PS/2 mouse	Mouse	Green	6-pin mini-DIN
PS/2 keyboard	Keyboard	Purple	6-pin mini-DIN
VGA	Video for an analog monitor	Blue	3-row 15-pin female D-shell or mini-VGA port
DVI	Video for a DVI digital or analog monitor	White	3-row 18- or 24-pin female DVI, mini-DVI, or micro-DVI
DVI-D	Video for a DVI digital monitor	White	3-row 18- or 24-pin female DVI, mini-DVI, or micro-DVI
DVI-A	Video for a DVI analog monitor	White	3-row 18- or 24-pin female DVI, mini-DVI, or micro-DVI
HDMI	Digital audio and video monitor	N/A	19- or 29-pin HDMI, mini-HDMI, or micro-HDMI
DisplayPort	Digital audio and video monitor	N/A	20-pin DisplayPort or mini-DisplayPort

Port	Usage	Port color code	Common connector
USB	Multipurpose port for data, video, audio, and power	Black, blue, teal, or red	USB Type-A, Type-B, Type-C, mini-USB, micro-USB
Thunderbolt	Multipurpose port that can carry data, video, audio, and power	N/A	20-pin DisplayPort, mini-DisplayPort, or USB Type-C connector
Lightning	Multipurpose port for Apple devices that can carry data and power	N/A	8-pin connector
Audio	Analog audio input	Light pink	1/8 inch (3.5 mm) jack
Audio	Analog line level audio input	Light blue	1/8 inch (3.5 mm) jack
Audio	Analog line level audio output from main stereo signal	Lime green	1/8 inch (3.5 mm) jack
Audio	Analog line level audio for right-to-left speaker	Brown	1/8 inch (3.5 mm) jack
S/PDIF	Audio input/output	Orange	RCA jack (coax) or TOSLINK (fiber)
RJ-45	UTP Ethernet network	N/A	8-conductor
RJ-11	Internal/external modem or phone	N/A	4-conductor
DB-9	RS-232 serial port found on older computers and some networking equipment	N/A	9-pin port
eSATA	External storage devices	N/A	7-pin non-powered port
eSATAp	External devices	N/A	Combination eSATA/USB port

Table 2.9 lists some older computer ports that you might still see but that are no longer on the A+ certification exam.

TABLE 2.9   Older ports

Port	Usage	Port color code	Common connector
Parallel	Printer, tape backup	Burgundy or dark pink	25-pin female D-shell
S-Video	Composite video device	Yellow	7-pin mini-DIN
Game port/MIDI	Joystick or MIDI device	Gold	15-pin female D-shell

Wireless Connectivity for Input Devices

Many input devices, such as keyboards, mice, game pads, touchpads, and headphones, have wireless connectivity. Technologies used to connect without a cord include infrared, radio, Bluetooth, and near field communication (NFC). Many computing devices, especially smartphones and other mobile devices, have cordless connectivity integrated into the device; otherwise, a transceiver is connected to a USB port to allow connectivity to the computing device. Figure 2.47 shows a wireless presenter used with a computing device and a projector.

FIGURE 2.47   Wireless presenter

Table 2.10 summarizes the various wireless technologies used with input and output devices.

TABLE 2.10   Wireless input/output technologies

Technology	Description
Infrared (**IR**)	Used for very short distances. Cheaper than other technologies.
Radio	Works in the 27 or 900 MHz, or 2.4, 5, or 60 GHz radio frequency ranges. Longer distances are supported than with infrared.
Bluetooth	Includes 128-bit security and works in the 2.4 GHz range. There are four classes of devices, with ranges up to 1.6 feet (0.5 m), 3 feet (1 m), 33 feet (10 m), and 328 feet (100 m). Note that Bluetooth 5 supports a connection between two devices up to 800 feet (242 meters) away. Up to eight devices can be connected in a master/slave relationship, with only one device being the master.
Near field communication (**NFC**)	Used to print from a phone or a camera or to transfer data between two smartphones that are positioned very close to one another (less than 6 inches [15.24 cm]). Also used in payment systems. Works in the 13.56 MHz range at transfer speeds up to 424 kb/s.

SOFT SKILLS: USING APPROPRIATE TITLES

The Internet and mobile devices have brought new methods of communication. In today's social media world, communication tends to be more casual, with people using colloquialisms, slang, and other language habits that aren't necessarily professional. In addition, some people regularly use acronyms, such as HAGD, LOL, BTW, NRN, TYVM, and YMMD, to communicate in emails, notes, text messages, and memos.

Many places of business are returning to the basics when it comes to customer service, and these businesses expect you as an IT professional to use professional communication methods. People expect the IT department to use more professional communication skills, and improved soft skills are therefore emphasized during the hiring process. For example, IT personnel are expected to use appropriate titles, such as Dr., Mr., Professor, and Ms. when talking to non-IT personnel, including external vendors. In the work environment, you should use a person's title, sir, or ma'am until the person you are addressing tells you otherwise. Figure 2.48 shows a couple of examples.

FIGURE 2.48   At work, use appropriate salutations

Chapter Summary

> A technician must be able to identify a variety of ports, including mouse and keyboard PS/2, VGA, DVI, HDMI, mini-HDMI, DisplayPort, Thunderbolt, USB, RJ-45, RJ-11, 3.5 mm sound jack, TOSLINK, RCA, DB-9, eSATA, and eSATAp ports.

> The most popular method for adding devices to desktops, laptops, and tablets is to use a USB port.

> The newest type of USB connector is USB-C (Type-C). Two additional features that may be supported through the Type-C connector are PD, so power can be distributed, and Alternate Mode, for distribution of non-USB data.

> USB 3.0/3.1/3.2 will accept USB 3.0/3.1 and older devices and provide more power. You can add additional ports by connecting a USB hub.

> Up to five USB hubs can be daisy-chained to one port. Upstream ports connect to the computer or another USB port. Devices connect to downstream ports.

> USB hubs can be self-powered or bus powered.

> Additional USB ports can be added by connecting an internal USB connector from the motherboard to a metal plate that mounts in an empty expansion slot.

> Adapters are available to convert between different types of display ports, such as DVI and VGA or DVI and HDMI.

> Converters are available for USB ports, such as USB Type-A to mini-Type-A or USB to Ethernet.

> Audio ports can be analog or digital. S/PDIF ports are digital. There are two types of S/PDIF ports: TOSLINK and fiber.

> Ethernet ports have RJ-45 connectors. RJ-11 ports are found on internal and external modems. External modems and networking equipment sometimes have DB-9 ports and use a serial cable.

> Ethernet ports commonly have a Cat 5e or Cat 6 cable attached. Ethernet cables can be unshielded twisted pair or, if additional shielding is needed, shielded twisted pair. Plenum cabling is made of fire-retardant materials. A cheaper type of cable is PVC. Ethernet cables adhere to the T568A or T568B standard.

> Fiber cabling is used to carry data over longer distances, and coaxial (coax) cabling is used for video networks.

> Input devices can connect to a computer by using four wireless technologies: IR, radio, Bluetooth, or NFC.

> When speaking with others, use appropriate professional titles when appropriate.

A+ CERTIFICATION EXAM TIPS

✓ Be able to identify the following connectors: RJ-11, RJ-45, RS-232, BNC, RG-59, RG-6, USB, micro-USB, mini-USB, USB-C, DB-9, Lightning, and eSATA. (On 3×5 cards, write the names of ports you have a hard time remembering. Put a picture of the port on one side and the name of the port on the other. Also include the type of connector each type of cable attaches to, such as RJ-11 is a connector for a phone cable; RJ-45 is a connector for a network cable; BNC, RG-59, and RG-6 are connectors for a coaxial cable; and DB-9 is used on a serial cable. Practice until you know them all.)

✓ Be able to describe the following network cables and explain the purpose of each, as well as their speeds and transmission limitations: Ethernet (Cat 5, Cat 5e, Cat 6, plenum, shielded twisted pair, unshielded twisted pair, and the T568A/B standard), fiber, and coaxial. (Make a chart of key characteristics for each of these types of cable. Have someone quiz you on them.)

✓ Be able to explain the following video cables, features, and their purposes: VGA, HDMI, mini-HDMI, DisplayPort, DVI, DVI-D, and DVI-I. (Do a web search off images for video ports and see if you can recognize these ports.)

✓ Be able to explain the features and purposes of the following multipurpose cables: Lightning, Thunderbolt, USB, USB 2.0, USB 3.0, and USB-C. (Make another chart for each of these cables and characteristics of each.)

✓ Make sure you know the features and purposes of a serial cable. Also know the characteristics of DVI-to-HDMI, USB-to-Ethernet, and DVI-to-VGA adapters.

✓ Look over how to install and configure an internal USB connector.

✓ The following communication and professionalism skills are part of the 220-1002 exam: Be culturally sensitive and use appropriate professional titles when applicable.

Key Terms

568A/B 56	digital signal 35	fiber cable 56
analog signal 35	DisplayPort 38	HDMI 38
Bluetooth 60	dual link 36	internal USB connector 48
BNC connector 40	DVI port 36	IR 60
Cat 5 54	DVI-to-HDMI adapter 41	keyboard port 34
Cat 5e 54	DVI-to-VGA adapter 41	Lightning port 49
Cat 6 54	DVI-D 36	micro-USB 45
charging USB port 46	DVI-I 36	mini-DIN connector 34
coaxial 40	eSATA 51	mini-HDMI 38
D-shell connector 34	eSATAp port 51	mini-USB 45
DB-9 53	Ethernet port 51	modem 52

CHAPTER 2

Review Questions

1. Match the port to the description.

   ____ DVI   a. Ethernet

   ____ VGA   b. TOSLINK

   ____ PS/2   c. up to 127 devices

   ____ USB   d. mouse/keyboard

   ____ NIC   e. CRT

   ____ S/PDIF   f. flat panel monitor

2. What is one visual indication that a USB port can be used to charge a mobile device?

   _____

3. What is a visual indication that a port is USB version 3.0?

   _____

4. Which port uses an RJ-45 connector?

   [modem | Ethernet | Lightning | S/PDIF]

5. How is an eSATAp port different from an eSATA port?

   _____

6. When considering VGA, HDMI, DVI, and DisplayPort, which video port can output both digital audio and video signals and is the most technologically advanced?

   [DisplayPort | DVI | HDMI | VGA]

7. What is the most common DVI port?

   [DVI-A | DVI-D | DVI-C | DVI-I]

8. Which has the faster transfer time, a USB 3.0 or 1000 Mbps Ethernet port?

   [USB 3.0 | 1000 Mbps Ethernet]

9. What is the maximum cable length for an Ethernet UTP cable?

   [100 meters | 150 meters | 200 meters | 1000 meters]

10. Describe the physical difference between an analog sound port and a digital one.

    _____

    _____

11. List two titles that might be used in the workplace that are not sir or ma'am.

    _____

12. You see a port on a computer that you have never seen before. There are no markings. How will you determine the purpose of the port?

    _____

13. What type of port uses an RJ-11 connector?

    [Ethernet | internal modem | display | keyboard]

14. Which port is more likely found on an Apple computer than any other type of PC?

    [Ethernet | RJ-45 | Lightning | USB-C]

15. Which adapter is used to convert from an analog signal to a digital one?

    [VGA to DVI-D | DVI-I to HDMI | Thunderbolt-to-DVI-I | USB to Ethernet]

16. A PC would contain the largest number of which type of USB port?

[Type-A | Type-B | Type-C | Type-A/B]

17. Which cable can carry video and audio signals and can be used to connect external storage devices?
[Type-A | DVI-I | Thunderbolt | mini-DIN]

18. In which of the following situations would Bluetooth most likely be used?

a. To connect to a corporate wireless network

b. To attach a keyboard to a PC

c. To connect a PC to a phone line

d. To connect a flash drive to a camera

19. List one advantage of having an adapter rather than an integrated motherboard port.

_____

_____

20. What are two commonly used connectors on coaxial cable used in video distribution systems? (Choose two.)

[RG-6 | RG-11 | RG-59 | RJ-11 | RJ-45]

Exercises

Exercise 2.1 Identifying Computer Ports

Objective: To identify various computer ports correctly

Procedure: Identify each computer port in Figure 2.49.

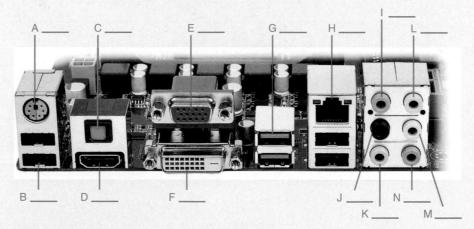

FIGURE 2.49 Identify motherboard ports

A. _____   H. _____
B. _____   I. _____
C. _____   J. _____
D. _____   K. _____
E. _____   L. _____
F. _____   M. _____
G. _____   N. _____

Exercise 2.2   Identifying More Computer Ports

Objective: To identify various computer port using graphics

Procedure: Identify each computer port in Figure 2.50.

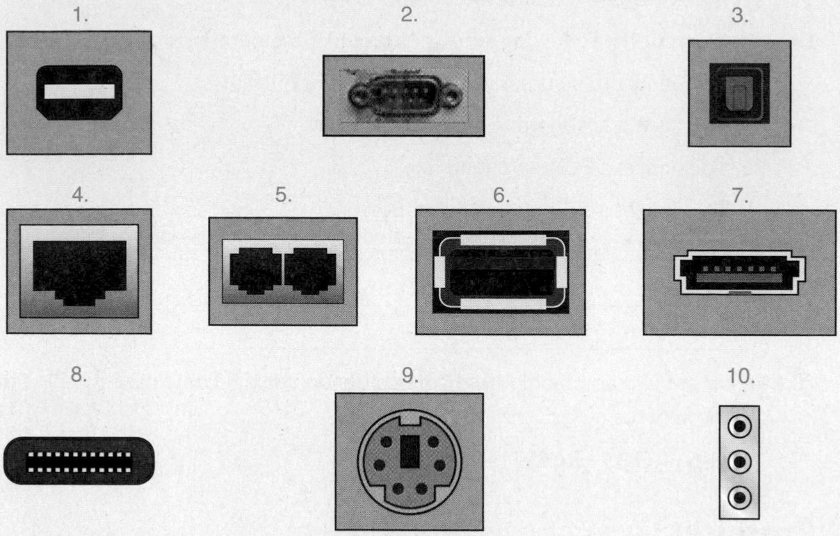

1.

2.

3.

4.

5.

6.

7.

8.

9.

10.

FIGURE 2.50   Identify computer ports

1. _____   6. _____
2. _____   7. _____
3. _____   8. _____
4. _____   9. _____
5. _____   10. _____

Exercise 2.3   Identifying Display Ports

Objective: To identify various display ports correctly

Procedure: Identify each display port in Figure 2.51.

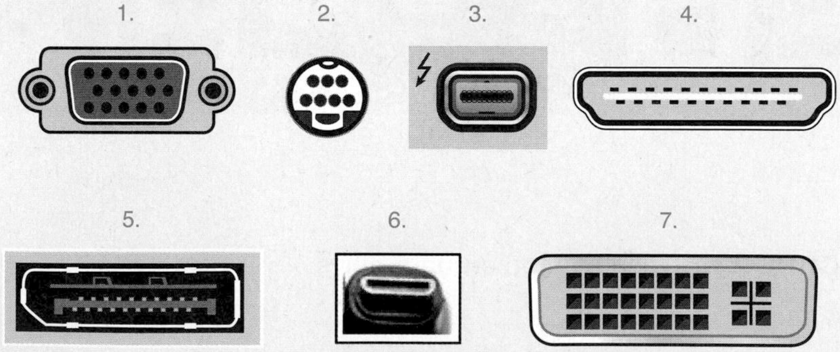

1.

2.

3.

4.

5.

6.

7.

FIGURE 2.51   Identify video ports

1. _____
2. _____
3. _____
4. _____
5. _____
6. _____
7. _____

Exercise 2.4 Identifying Cables

Objective: To identify various cables

Procedure: Identify each cable in Figure 2.52.

1.  2.  3.  4.  5.

6.  7.  8.  9.

10.

FIGURE 2.52   Identify cables

1. _____   6. _____
2. _____   7. _____
3. _____   8. _____
4. _____   9. _____
5. _____   10. _____

Activities

Internet Discovery

Objective: To obtain specific information from the Internet regarding a computer or its associated parts

Parts: Computer with Internet access

Procedure: Complete the following procedure and answer the accompanying questions.

Questions: For Questions 1–4: Obtain technical information about a particular computer (maybe your own computer or a model number given by the instructor). Answer the following questions based on the information. You may need to obtain more documents, or you may need to select a different computer model to answer questions. Please use only one computer model.

1. Which ports are available on the front of the computer?

    _____

2. Which ports are available on the back of the computer?

    _____

3. How many drive bays are available to install devices such as hard drives, optical drives, tape drives, and so on?

   _____

4. Were the photos in the documentation clear enough to differentiate between the different ports? If not, explain what is wrong.

   _____

5. List 10 Internet acronyms and what they stand for that would be appropriate in a text message to a family member but inappropriate to use when communicating (even texting) with an employee from a non-IT department who is not a close friend but a professional acquaintance. Also, provide the URL(s) where this information is found.

   _____

   _____

   _____

   _____

   _____

6. Using the Internet, list one fact about NFC that was not in the chapter and the URL where you found this information.

   _____

   _____

   _____

   _____

Soft Skills

Objective: To enhance and fine-tune a future technician's ability to listen, communicate in both written and oral forms, and support people who use computers in a professional manner

Procedure:

1. In teams of two, one student writes a professional note that contains Internet acronyms that are commonly used for texting. The other student tries to then guess what the acronyms mean. Together, rewrite the note so it is more professional.

2. Draft an email to a pretend computer customer that you just met yesterday for the first time. You did not have the part needed to repair the computer, but now the part has come in. Be sure you use professionalism in your email.

   _____

   _____

   _____

   _____

   _____

   _____

Critical Thinking Skills

Objective:　　To analyze and evaluate information as well as apply learned information to new or different situations

Procedure:

1.　Find an advertisement for a computer in a local computer flyer, in a newspaper, in a magazine, in a book, or on the Internet. List which ports you know in one column and the ports you do not know in the other column. Select one port you do not know and research that component. Write the new information and share it with at least one other person.

2.　Work in groups of three. As a group, do you think future computers will only have wireless connections or continue to have both wired and wireless connectivity? Why do you think this? What might be some hindrances to future computers having only have wireless connections?

3.　Provide five tips that might help someone identify the different computer ports. If possible, each person in the class should state a tip without duplicating someone else's tip.

_____

_____

_____

_____

_____

3 On the Motherboard

In this chapter you will learn:

> How to recognize and identify important motherboard parts

> The basics of how a processor works

> Issues to consider when upgrading or replacing a motherboard or processor

> Information regarding GPUs

> How to add cards to computers

> The differences between PCI, AGP, and PCIe adapters and slots

> Motherboard technologies such as HyperTransport, Hyperthreading, and multicore

> Symptoms of motherboard and CPU problems

> The benefits of active listening

CompTIA Exam Objectives:

What CompTIA A+ exam objectives are covered in this chapter?

✓ 1001-3.5   Given a scenario, install and configure motherboards, CPUs, and add-on cards.

✓ 1001-5.2   Given a scenario, troubleshoot problems related to motherboards, RAM, CPUs, and power.

✓ 1002-4.7   Given a scenario, use proper communication techniques and professionalism.

Introduction to the Motherboard

Chapter 1, "Introduction to the World of IT," introduces the motherboard, which holds the majority of the electronics in a computer. Chapter 2, "Connectivity," focuses on connecting devices to a motherboard port or through an adapter port. Some parts of the motherboard—including the processor and processor socket, memory or RAM slots, and the various types of expansion slots—are of specific interest to IT staff, and this chapter delves into them. Figure 3.1 points out these key motherboard components.

FIGURE 3.1   Key motherboard components

Processor Overview

At the heart of every computer is a special motherboard chip called a **processor**, which determines, to a great extent, the power of the computer. The processor is also called the central processing unit (**CPU**), or microprocessor. The processor executes instructions, performs calculations, and coordinates input/output operations. Each motherboard has electronic chips that work with the CPU and are designed to exact specifications. Whether these other electronic components can keep up with the processor depends on the individual component's specifications. The major processor manufacturers today are Intel, Motorola, VIA, Samsung, NVIDIA, Apple Inc., Qualcomm, and AMD (Advanced Micro Devices, Inc.). **Intel** and **AMD** are the predominant manufacturers for desktop and laptop processors, and the other manufacturers target the mobile/smartphone markets. A motherboard accepts the processors of one or more specific manufacturers; a motherboard that accepts an Intel processor will not support AMD processors. Figure 3.2 shows a processor.

FIGURE 3.2 Intel processor

Processor Basics

Processors come in a variety of speeds, measured in **gigahertz** (GHz). Hertz is a measurement of cycles per second. One hertz, written 1 Hz, equals 1 cycle per second. One gigahertz, or 1 GHz, is 1 billion cycles per second. The original IBM PC CPU, the 8088 processor, ran at 4.77 MHz. Today's processors can run at speeds near 5 GHz.

A processor's register size (or word size) is the number of bits the processor can process at one time. The Intel 8088 processor's register size was 16 bits, or 2 bytes. Today's CPUs have register sizes of 64 or 128 bits.

Buses

Processors operate on 1s and 0s. The 1s and 0s must travel from one place to another inside the processor, as well as outside to other chips. To move the 1s and 0s around, electronic lines called a **bus** are used. The electronic lines inside the CPU are known as the **internal data bus**, or system bus. In the Intel 8086 (from which the term x86 architecture originated), the internal data bus comprises 16 separate lines, with each line carrying a single 1 or a single 0. The word size and the number of lines for the internal data bus are equal. The 8086, for example, has a 16-bit word size, and 16 lines carry 16 bits on the internal data bus. In today's processors, 64 or 128 internal data bus lines operate concurrently.

For a CPU to communicate with devices in the outside world, such as a printer, the 1s and 0s travel on the **external data bus**. The external data bus connects the processor to adapters, the keyboard, the mouse, the hard drive, and other devices. An external data bus is also known as an external data path. You can see the external data lines by looking between the expansion slots on the motherboard. Some solder lines between the expansion slots are used to send data out along the external data bus to the expansion slots. Today's processors have 64- and 128-bit external data paths. Figure 3.3 shows the internal and external data buses.

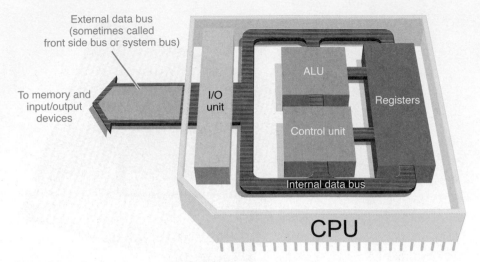

FIGURE 3.3 Internal and external data buses

ALUs

A processor has a special component called the arithmetic logic unit (ALU), which does all the calculations and comparison logic that the computer needs. Figure 3.3 shows the basic idea of how the ALU connects to the registers, control unit, and internal bus. The control unit coordinates activities inside the processor. The I/O unit manages data entering and leaving the processor. The registers in the CPU make up a high-speed storage area for 1s and 0s before the bits are processed.

Processing Data

To understand how a computer processes data, consider a letter typed on a computer that starts out *DEAR MOM*. To the computer, each letter of the alphabet is a different combination of eight 1s and 0s. For example, the letter *D* is 01000100, and the letter *E* is 01000101. Figure 3.4 demonstrates that the size of the bus greatly increases performance on a computer much the way increasing the number of lanes of a highway decreases congestion.

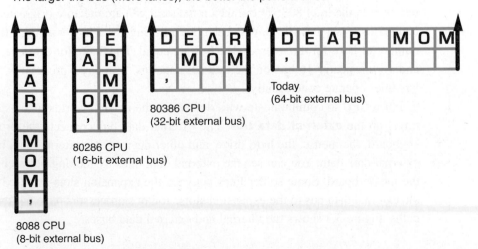

FIGURE 3.4 Bus performance

Pipelines

Processors have multiple pipelines (separate internal buses) that operate simultaneously. To understand pipelining, take the example of a fast-food restaurant. In the restaurant, assume that there are five steps (and one employee per step) involved in making a burger and giving it to the customer. First, (1) take the order and input it into the computer system; (2) brown the buns and cook the burgers; (3) add the condiments to the buns and burgers; (4) wrap the burgers, add fries, and insert them into the bag; and then (5) take the customer's money and give the bag to the customer. Keep in mind that the person taking the customer's order and inputting the order can serve another customer when he or she has completed this task for the first customer. The same is true for each other person along the line. To make this burger process go faster, you could (maybe) do one of the things shown in Figure 3.5: (1) Make your employees work faster; (2) break the tasks into smaller tasks (such as seven steps instead of five and include seven people in the process); or (3) have more lines of people doing exactly the same process tasks.

1. Make your employees work faster   2. Break the tasks into smaller tasks

3. Have more lines of people doing exactly the same process tasks

FIGURE 3.5   **Ways to get faster processes**

To relate this to processors, making the employees work faster is the same as increasing the CPU clock speed. Breaking the tasks into smaller tasks is the same as changing the structure of the CPU pipeline. Instead of performing the standard 5 tasks, the CPU might perform 6, 7, 14, 20, or even more steps. This allows each step to be acted upon more quickly, the task to be smaller, and production to be faster. Having more lines of people doing the same complete process is like having multiple pipelines.

A 32- or 64-bit CPU can have separate paths, each of which handles 32 or 64 bits. For example, if a processor has two pipelines, the Dear Mom letter can be in one pipeline, while a photo upload using a different application can be in the other pipeline.

A processor might have 12 pipelines for integers and 17 pipelines for floating-point numbers. (A floating-point number is a number that can include a decimal point.) Other processors contain anywhere from 20- to 31-stage pipelines. Debate continues about whether a longer pipeline improves performance.

Speeding Up Processor Operations Overview

You can determine the speed of a processor by looking at the model number on the chip, but processors frequently have devices attached to them for cooling, which makes it difficult to see the writing on the chip. A processor commonly does not use its maximum speed all the time in order to save power or stay cool. Also, a processor is not always functioning at its maximum potential for a lot of reasons, including coding used within an application, the user switching from application to application, inadequate bus width, or the amount of RAM installed. The processor can also operate beyond its rated specifications. Intel Turbo Boost allows a processor to operate beyond its rating in order to handle periods of increased workload.

TECH TIP

Locating processor speed

An easy way to tell processor speed with Windows is to go to Windows Explorer/File Explorer, right-click *Computer (Windows 7) or This PC (Windows 8/10),* and select *Properties.*

We have already taken a look at how increasing the CPU pipeline can, to some extent, improve processor operations, but other technologies also exist. We start by defining some of the terms that relate to this area and associating those terms with concepts and the various technologies used. Table 3.1 list some terms related to speed.

TABLE 3.1   Motherboard speed terms

Term	Explanation
Clock or **clock speed**	The speed of the processor's internal clock, measured in gigahertz.
Bus speed	The speed at which data is delivered when a particular bus on the motherboard is being used.
Front side bus (**FSB**)	The speed between the CPU and some of the motherboard components. This is what most people would term the motherboard speed. Sometimes the speed is listed in megatransfers per second, or MT/s. With MT/s, not only is the speed of the FSB considered, but also how many processor transfers occur each clock cycle. A 266 MHz FSB that can do four transfers per second could be listed as 1064 MT/s. The FSB is always being enhanced with technologies such as AMD's HyperTransport and Intel's QPI (QuickPath Interconnect) and DMI (Direct Media Interface).
Back side bus	The speed between the CPU and the L2 cache located outside the main CPU but on the same chip.
PCI bus speed	The speed at which data is delivered when the PCI bus is being used. Common speeds for the PCI bus are 33 and 66 MHz, allowing bandwidths up to 533 MB/s.
PCIe bus speed	The speed at which data is delivered when the PCIe bus is being used. The PCIe bus, which is the main bus used on the motherboard, is used for PCIe adapters. Common data transfer rates and total bandwidth for the PCIe bus are as follows: > PCIe 1.1: 2.5 GT/s (gigatransfers per second) and 8 GB/s > PCIe 2.x: 5 GT/s and 16 GB/s > PCIe 3.x: 8 GT/s and 32 GB/s > PCIe 4.x: 16 GT/s and 64 GB/s > PCIe 5.x: 32 GT/s and 128 GB/s

Term	Explanation
AGP bus speed	The speed at which data is delivered when the AGP bus is being used. The AGP bus is an older standard used for video cards.
CPU speed	The speed at which the CPU operates; it can be changed on some motherboards.
CPU throttling	Reducing the clock frequency to slow the CPU in order to reduce power consumption and heat. This is especially useful in mobile devices.

Cache

An important concept related to processor speed is keeping data flowing into the processor. Registers are a type of high-speed memory storage inside the processor. They are used to temporarily hold calculations, data, or instructions. The data or instruction on which the CPU needs to operate is usually found in one of three places: cache memory, motherboard memory (main memory), or the hard drive.

Cache memory is a very fast type of memory designed to increase the speed of processor operations. CPU efficiency is increased when data continuously flows into the CPU. Cache provides the fastest access. If the information is not in cache memory, the processor looks for the data in motherboard RAM. If the information is not there, it is retrieved from the hard drive and placed into the motherboard memory or the cache. Hard drive access is the slowest of the three. Table 3.2 lists the types of cache.

TABLE 3.2   Types of cache

Type	Explanation
L1 cache	Cache memory integrated into the processor
L2 cache	Cache in the processor packaging but not part of the CPU; also called on-die cache
L3 cache	Usually found in more powerful processors and can be located in the CPU housing (on-die) or on the motherboard

Consider an analogy: Say that you are thirsty and have access to a glass of cold lemonade, a pitcher of lemonade, and a can of frozen lemonade concentrate. If you were thirsty, you would drink from the glass because it is the fastest and most easily accessible. If the glass were empty, you would pour lemonade from the pitcher to refill the glass. If the pitcher were empty, you would go to the freezer to get the frozen concentrate to make more lemonade. Figure 3.6 shows this concept.

Usually, the more cache memory a system has, the better that system performs, but this is not always true. System performance also depends on the efficiency of the cache controller (the chip that manages the cache memory), system design, the amount of available hard drive space, and the speed of the processor. When determining memory requirements, you must consider the operating system used, applications used, and hardware installed. The Windows XP operating system takes a lot less memory than Windows 10. High-end games and desktop publishing take more RAM than word processing. Free hard drive space and video memory are often as important as RAM in improving a computer's performance. Memory is only one piece of the puzzle. All of the computer's parts must work together to provide efficient system performance. Figure 3.7 shows this hierarchy of data access for the CPU.

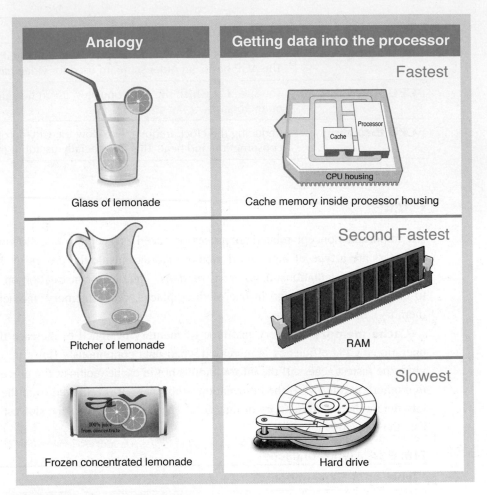

Analogy	Getting data into the processor
Glass of lemonade	Fastest — Cache memory inside processor housing
Pitcher of lemonade	Second Fastest — RAM
Frozen concentrated lemonade	Slowest — Hard drive

FIGURE 3.6   CPU data sources

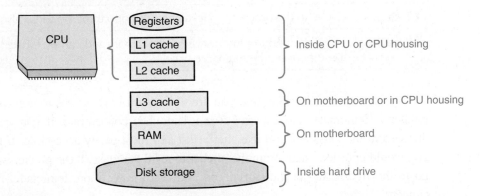

FIGURE 3.7   Data access hierarchy

Clocking

The motherboard generates a clock signal that is used to control the transfer of 1s and 0s to and from the processor. A clock signal can be illustrated as a sine wave. One clock cycle is from one point on the sine wave to the next point that is located on the same point on the sine wave later in time, as shown in Figure 3.8.

In older computers, data was sent to the CPU only once during a clock cycle. Then, newer memory technologies evolved that allowed data to be sent twice during every clock cycle. Today, data is sent four times during a single clock cycle, as shown in Figure 3.9.

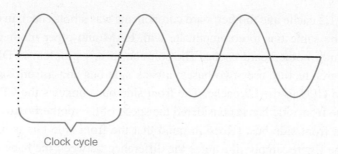

FIGURE 3.8   Clock cycle

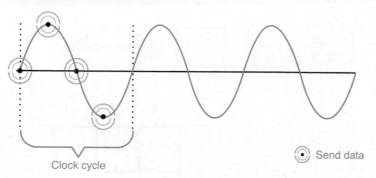

Send data

FIGURE 3.9   Clock cycle that clocks data four times per cycle

Threading Technology

Several threading techniques are used to speed up processor efficiency: multithreading and HT (Hyperthreading Technology). A **thread** is a small piece of an application process that can be handled by an operating system. An operating system such as Windows schedules and assigns resources to a thread. Each thread can share resources (such as the processor or cache memory) with other threads. A thread in the pipeline might have a delay due to waiting on data to be retrieved or access to a port or another hardware component. Multithreading keeps the line moving by letting another thread execute some code. This is like a grocery cashier taking another customer while someone goes for a forgotten loaf of bread. Figure 3.10 shows this concept.

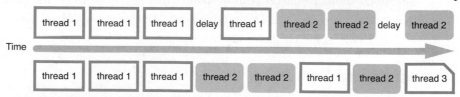

FIGURE 3.10   Multithreading

Intel's HT (**Hyperthreading**, Hyper-Threading, or HT Technology) allows a single processor to handle two separate sets of instructions simultaneously. To the operating system, HT makes the system appear as if it has multiple processors. Intel claims that the system can have up to a 30% increase in performance, but studies have shown that the increase is application dependent. If the application being used cannot take advantage of the multithreading, then HT can be disabled in the system BIOS/Unified Extensible Firmware Interface (UEFI) (covered in Chapter 4, "Introduction to Configuration").

Connecting to the Processor

We have considered various ways to speed up processor operations, including having more stages in the processor, increasing the speed of the clock, and sending more data in the same amount of time. Accessing L2 cache and motherboard components was a bottleneck in older systems because the CPU used the same bus to communicate with RAM and other motherboard components as it did with L2 and motherboard cache. The solution to this problem is DIB (Dual Independent Bus). The DIB architecture uses two buses: a back side bus and a front side bus. The back side bus connects the CPU to the L2 cache. The front side bus connects the CPU to the motherboard components. The front side bus is considered the speed of the motherboard. Figure 3.11 illustrates the concept of a front side bus. (Keep in mind that the front side bus is more detailed than this figure shows; the figure simply illustrates the difference between the back side bus and the front side bus.)

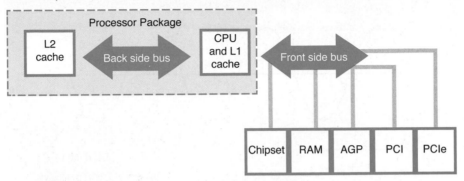

FIGURE 3.11   Front side bus and back side bus

Many people think that the higher the CPU speed, the faster the computer. This is seldom true. Several factors contribute to speed of a computer. One factor is bus speed. Bus speed describes how fast the CPU can communicate with motherboard components, such as memory, the chipset, or the PCI/PCIe bus.

Intel and AMD have technologies to replace the front side bus in some parts. AMD's solution is Direct Connect. Direct Connect allows each of the processor cores to connect directly to memory, to the other motherboard components such as the expansion slots, and to other processor cores by using a high-speed bus called **HyperTransport**. (Figure 3.13, later in this chapter, shows HyperTransport connectivity.) Intel has QuickPath Interconnect (QPI), Serial Peripheral Interface (SPI), and Direct Media Interface (DMI), which are full-duplex (that is, traffic can flow in both directions simultaneously) point-to-point connections between the processor and one or more motherboard components. This type of connectivity used with Intel-based processors and chipsets is shown later in the chapter, in Figure 3.38.

Multicore Processors

In the past, when two processors were installed, software had to be specifically written to support having multiple processors. That is no longer true. A **single-core processor** is just one CPU. A **dual-core processor** combines two CPUs in a single unit. A tri-core processor has three processors in a single unit. Both Intel and AMD have **quad-core** CPU technologies, which is either two dual-core CPUs installed on the same motherboard, two dual-core CPUs installed in a single socket, all four cores installed in one unit (which is common today). Now there are also **hexa-core** (six cores) and **octa-core** (eight cores) processors. IT professionals in the field find it easiest to just say **multicore** to describe the multiple cores contained in the same processor housing.

Single-core processors and early dual-core processors accessed memory through a memory controller, as shown in Figure 3.12. Today, the processor cores have their own memory controller built in. Figure 3.13 shows that an AMD quad-core processor has an integrated controller and interfaces with the rest of the motherboard using a high-speed bus called HyperTransport. HyperTransport is a feature of AMD's Direct Connect architecture. With Direct Connect, there are no front side buses. Instead, the memory controller and input/output functions directly connect to the CPU.

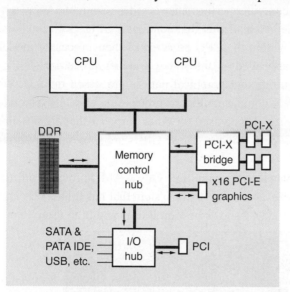

FIGURE 3.12   Older method processors used to interface with memory

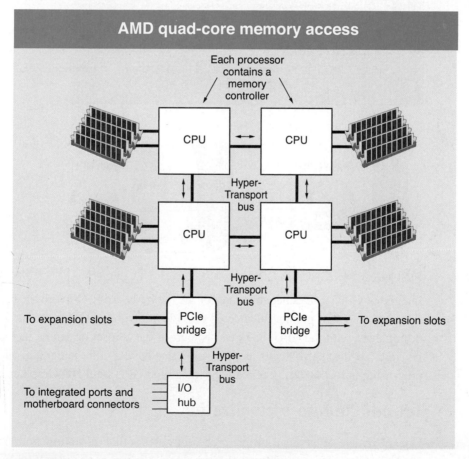

FIGURE 3.13   AMD quad-core memory access

All applications can take advantage of the multicore technology and the background processes that are associated with the operating system and applications. This improves operations when multitasking or when running powerful applications that require many instructions to be executed, such as drawing applications and games.

Graphics Processing Unit (GPU)

Another bottleneck for computer performance is video. Computer users who want better video performance buy a separate video adapter that contains a GPU. Both Intel and AMD have a graphics processing unit (**GPU**) within the CPU on some of their processor models. With an **integrated GPU** (iGPU), sometimes called an integrated graphics processor (IGP), an external video card with a GPU is not required, and graphical data is processed quickly, with reduced power consumption. Today's CPUs contain multicore processors, and GPUs contain hundreds of smaller core processors. GPUs can also be used for other purposes that are not directly related to graphics but that increase system performance. These GPUs are sometimes referred to as general-purpose GPUs (GPGPUs).

A computer system can also have multiple GPUs. AMD provides information about the number of "compute cores." For example, an AMD system that has four CPUs and two GPUs would have six compute cores. Figure 3.14 shows how an IGP is within the same housing as the CPU cores.

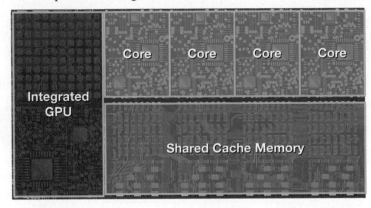

FIGURE 3.14   CPU vs. GPU

Integrated GPUs can either share part of the motherboard RAM with the rest of the system or have a separate block of memory dedicated for video. Integrated GPUs can have their own cache memory or share with the CPU. IGPs can be part of the chipset or can be included as part of the CPU housing (on-die). AMD calls its processors that have a GPU integrated with the CPU accelerated processing units (**APUs**). Intel calls its integrated GPU Intel HD Graphics and Intel Iris Graphics.

Introduction to Virtualization

One advantage of having multiple processor cores is that they allow both home and business computers to take advantage of virtual technology. **Virtual technology** (also called **virtualization**) allows you to have one or more virtual machines on the same computer. Virtualization software, such as VMware Workstation, Oracle VM VirtualBox, or Microsoft Hyper-V, enables one computer to act as if it were two or more computers. The computer can have two or more operating systems installed through the use of the virtualization software. Each operating system has no knowledge of the other operating system(s) on the computer.

Windows 7 has Virtual PC and Windows 8 and 10 have Hyper-V, which allow an application to run in a virtual environment as if an older operating system had been installed. Businesses often use virtualization so they can use legacy software on newer machines but keep it separate from the main operating system or another virtualized machine on the same computer. Reduced costs and physical space are benefits of virtualization. Home computer users can install multiple operating systems in separate VMs (virtual machines) within the same physical box, with each VM being seen as a separate computer. To prepare for the CompTIA A+ certification exam, you could install Windows 7, Windows 8, Windows 10, and Linux in order to better prepare yourself.

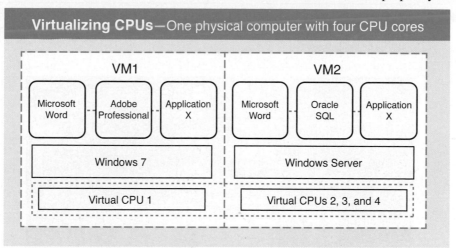

FIGURE 3.15 The concept of virtualization

Selecting a motherboard and processor is important when in a virtual environment. Not all processors were designed for virtualization. Refer to the virtualization software documentation to determine whether the CPU used is allowed to be used in a virtual environment. Another issue regarding processors and virtualization is licensing. For virtualization software that must be purchased (that is, is not freeware), the software manufacturer may charge on a per-processor or per-socket license basis or on a per-core basis.

Intel Processors

Traditionally, Intel has rated its processors by GHz, and people have compared processors based on speed alone. Now, Intel arranges its products by family numbers. In a family of processors, you can compare attributes such as speed and the amount of cache memory and other technologies. Table 3.3 shows Intel's processor families. Figure 3.16 shows a close-up of a processor installed into a motherboard.

TABLE 3.3 Intel processor families

Processor family*	Comments
Core X	18-core processor (at press time) for high performance, extreme gaming, intensive content creation, and megatasking.
Core i9	Powerful multicore processor for gaming and intensive content creation as well as megatasking.
Core i7	Multicore with cache memory shared between cores and on-board memory controller. Good for virtualization, graphic/multimedia design and creation, and gaming.
Core i5	Midrange dual- and quad-core processor. Used for video, photos, and email, and Internet access.

Processor family*	Comments
Core i3	Low-end desktop and mobile processor used for common tasks such as word processing and Internet access.
Core i7/i5 vPro	Workplace midrange and high performance with hardware-enhanced security.
Core m3	High-performance mobile devices with longer battery life and less heat than previous mobile CPUs.
Atom	Mobile Internet device processor.

*Intel is constantly upgrading processors. For more information, visit www.intel.com.

FIGURE 3.16   Installed processor

AMD Processors

AMD is Intel's largest rival in computer processors. Anyone buying a processor should research all models and vendors. Table 3.4 lists the AMD processor families.

TABLE 3.4   AMD processor families

Processor family	Comments
Ryzen Threadripper	8 to 16 cores and 20 to 40 MB cache for extremely high-end desktop processor
Ryzen 7	8 cores, 16 processing threads, 20 MB cache for gaming, high-end content creation, and megatasking
Ryzen 5	4 to 6 cores, up to 12 processing threads, and up to 20 MB cache for workplace or home computing use
Ryzen 3	4 cores and up to 10 MB cache for standard computing use
Ryzen PRO	A multicore processor that supports up to four monitors at resolution up to 4K, video conferencing, and business collaboration
FX	Multicore (4-, 6-, or 8-core) high-performance desktop processor

Processor family	Comments
A-Series	Multicore (2-, 3-, or 4-core) high-performance processor with integrated GPU
A-Series PRO	Multicore (6-, 8-, 10-, or 12- core) high-performance desktop processor for advanced productivity and content creation

CPU Sockets

A processor inserts into a socket or slot, depending on the model. In most cases today, a processor inserts into a socket. There are different types of sockets. Pin grid array (PGA), which has even rows of holes around a square socket; staggered pin grid array (SPGA), which has staggered holes so more pins can be inserted; plastic pin grid array (PPGA); micro pin grid array (μPGA); flip chip ball grid array (FCBGA); and land grid array (LGA) are all used with AMD and/or Intel processors. Figure 3.17 shows a CPU socket.

FIGURE 3.17   CPU socket

Processor sockets are also called zero insertion force sockets, or **ZIF sockets**, and they come in different sizes. A processor socket accepts one or more specific processor models. The socket has a small lever to the side that, when lifted, brings the processor slightly up and out of the socket holes. When installing a processor, you align the CPU over the holes and press the lever to bring the processor pins into the slot with equal force on all the pins. In Figure 3.17, notice the lever beside the socket that is used to lift the metal cover so the CPU can be installed into the socket. Table 3.5 lists the commonly used Intel and AMD CPU sockets.

TECH TIP

Buying the right CPU

If you buy a motherboard and processor separately, it is important to ensure that the motherboard CPU socket is the correct type for the processor.

TABLE 3.5   Desktop CPU sockets

Socket	Description
LGA 1150	1150-pin for Intel i7, i5, and i3
LGA 1151	1151-pin for Intel Core i7, i5, and i3
LGA 1155	1155-pin for Intel Core i7, i5, and i3
LGA 1156	1156-pin for Intel Core i7, i5, and i3
LGA 2011	2011-pin for Intel Core i7 and Xeon
LGA 2066	2066-pin for Intel Core i9, i7, and i5
AM3	940-pin for AMD Phenom II X3, X4, and Athlon II
AM3+	942-pin for AMD FX, Phenom II, Athlon II, and Sempron
AM4	1331-pin for Ryzen 7, 5, and 3
TR4 (sTR4)	4094-pin for Ryzen Threadripper
FM2	904-pin for AMD APUs and Trinity
FM2+	906-pin for AMD APUs, Kaveri, Godavari, and A8/A10 series

Processor Cooling

Keeping a CPU cool is critical. Both Intel and AMD have technologies that reduce processor energy consumption (and heat) by turning off unused parts of the processor or slowing down the processor when it starts to overheat. But these measures alone are not enough. Today's systems use one or more of the methods listed in Table 3.6. Figure 3.18 shows a heat sink and a fan.

TABLE 3.6   Processor cooling methods

Method	Description
Heat sink	A heat sink is a block of metal (usually aluminum or copper), metal bars, or metal fins that attach to the top of the processor or other motherboard components. Heat from the processor is transferred to the heat sink and then blown away by the air flow throughout the computer case.
Fan	Fans can be attached to the processor, beside the processor, and in the case.
Thermal paste or thermal pad	Thermal paste, compound, or grease can be applied to the top of a processor before a heat sink is attached. Some heat sinks and fans have thermal paste pre-applied. A thermal pad provides uniform heat dispersion and lies between the processor and the heat sink.
Liquid cooling	Liquid is circulated through the system, including through a heat sink that is mounted on the CPU. Heat from the processor is transferred to the cooler liquid. The now-hot liquid is transported to the back of the system, converted to heat, and released outside the case. CPU temperature remains constant, no matter the usage. Some systems require the liquid to be periodically refilled.
Phase-change cooling (vapor cooling)	This expensive option uses a technique similar to a refrigerator: A gas is converted to a liquid that is converted back to gas.
Heat pipe	A heat pipe is a metal tube used to transfer heat away from an electronic component.
Passive cooling	Passive cooling involves no fans, so a heat sink that does not have a fan attached is known as a passive heat sink.

Heat sink   Fan

FIGURE 3.18   Heat sink and fan

The largest chip on the motherboard with a fan or a heat sink attached is easily recognized as the processor. Figure 3.19 shows an Intel Core i7 that has a fan and a heat sink installed. Notice the heat pipes that are used as part of the heat sink.

FIGURE 3.19   CPU with heat sink and fan attached

Additional motherboard components can also have heat sinks attached. They are normally the chipset and/or the I/O (input/output) controller chips. Figure 3.20 shows a motherboard with these cooling elements.

FIGURE 3.20   Motherboard heat sinks

TECH TIP

When thermal paste acts like glue

Over time, thermal paste can act like glue, making a processor hard to separate from a heat sink. You can use a thermal paste cleaner, acetone, or denatured alcohol to separate the two parts. Do not pry them apart!

Installing a Processor

Processors are sold with installation instructions. In addition, motherboard manuals (or other documentation) include the steps to upgrade or install the CPU. The following are the parts and the general steps for installing a processor:

Parts: Proper processor for the motherboard (refer to motherboard documentation)

Antistatic materials

Step 1. Ensure that power to the computer is off and the computer is unplugged.

Step 2. Place an antistatic wrist strap around your wrist and attach the other end to a ground or unpainted metal part of the computer. Alternatively, use an antistatic glove.

Step 3. Push the retention lever down and outward to release the CPU retention plate. Move the handle backward until the retention plate is fully open. Do not touch the CPU socket.

Step 4. Remove the processor from packaging, taking care to hold it by the edges and never touch the bottom metal portion of the processor. Remember that a CPU fits only one way into the socket. Look at the processor and the socket before inserting the chip to ensure proper alignment. A socket and CPU normally have a triangle marking or dot to indicate pin 1, as shown in Figure 3.21. The processor also has notches on each side that align with the socket. Insert the CPU into the socket by aligning it with the socket and lowering it until it is flush with the socket, as shown in Figure 3.22. (Do not force it!)

Pin 1 triangle

Notch

FIGURE 3.21   Pin 1 and notch on a processor

FIGURE 3.22   Installing a CPU

TECH TIP

Handling the CPU

Always hold the CPU by the edges to avoid bending or touching the pins underneath. Do not touch the CPU until you are ready to install it in the socket.

TECH TIP

Cooling the CPU

Do not apply power to the computer until the CPU and the heat sink, fan, and/or cooling unit are installed. Running the CPU without installing appropriate cooling mechanisms will overheat the CPU and destroy or weaken it.

Upgrading Processors

Two common questions asked of technicians are "Can a computer be upgraded to a higher or faster processor?" and "Should a computer be upgraded to a higher or faster processor?" Whether or not a computer can be upgraded to a higher or faster processor depends on the capability of the motherboard. When a customer asks if a processor should be upgraded, the technician should ask, "What operating system and applications are you using?" The newer the operating system, the more advanced the processor should be. Some games and applications that must perform calculations, as well as graphic-oriented applications, require a faster, more advanced processor. The motherboard's documentation is very important when considering a CPU upgrade. Read this documentation to determine whether the motherboard can accept a faster processor.

TECH TIP

Upgrading a CPU

Do not upgrade a processor unless the documentation or manufacturer states that the motherboard supports a newer or faster processor.

Throttle management is the process of controlling the speed of a CPU by slowing it down when it is not being used heavily or when it is hot. Usually this feature is controlled by a system BIOS//UEFI setting and the Windows *Power Options* Control Panel. Some users may want performance to be at a maximum and so many not use CPU throttling. Laptop users, on the other hand, may want to conserve power whenever possible to extend the time the computer can be used on battery power. Manufacturers can also use automatic throttling to keep the processor from overheating.

Upgrading components other than the processor can also increase speed in a computer. Installing more memory, a faster hard drive, or a motherboard with a faster front side bus sometimes may improve a computer's performance more than installing a new processor. All devices and electronic components must work together to transfer the 1s and 0s efficiently. The processor is only one piece of the puzzle. Many people do not realize that upgrading only one computer component does not always make a computer faster or better.

Overclocking Processors

Overclocking involves changing the front side bus speed and/or multiplier to boost CPU and system speed. Overclocking has some issues:

> CPU speed ratings are conservative.
> The processor, motherboard, memory, and other components can be damaged by overclocking.
> Applications may crash, the operating system may not boot, and/or the system may hang (lock up) when overclocking.
> You may void the warranty on some CPUs if you overclock.
> When you increase the speed of the CPU, the processor's heat increases. Extra cooling, using fans and larger heat sinks, is essential.
> Input/output devices may not react well to overclocking.
> The memory chips may need to be upgraded to be able to keep up with the faster processing.
> You need to know how to reset the system BIOS/UEFI in case the computer will not boot properly after you make changes. This process is covered in Chapter 4.

TECH TIP

Being ready to cool

The primary problem with overclocking is insufficient cooling. Make sure you purchase a larger heat sink and/or extra fans before starting the overclocking process.

Many motherboard manufacturers do not allow changes to the CPU, multiplier, and clock settings. The changes to the motherboard are most often made through BIOS/UEFI Setup. However, CPU manufacturers may provide tuning tools in the form of applications installed on the computer for overclocking configuration. Keep in mind that overclocking is a trial-and-error situation. There are websites geared toward documenting specific motherboards and overclocked CPUs.

Installing CPU Thermal Solutions

A CPU may come with a thermal solution such as a heat sink and/or fan. The thermal solution commonly comes with a pre-applied thermal paste or an attached thermal pad. Heat sinks and fans attach to the processor using different methods, such as screws, thermal compound, and clips. Clips can involve retaining screws, pressure release (where you press down on them, and they release), or a retaining slot. Small screwdrivers can be used to release the clips that attach using a retaining slot. Clips for fans or heat sinks can be difficult to install. The type of heat sink and/or fan installed must fit the processor and case. Additional hardware may have to be installed on the motherboard to be able to attach a CPU thermal solution. Figure 3.23 shows a CPU cooler being installed.

FIGURE 3.23   CPU heat sink/fan installation

TECH TIP

Take a photo of the CPU

Before attaching a heat sink and/or fan to the CPU, take a picture of the markings on top. You might need to use these markings if you ever need technical support and need the exact specifications. Techs often take pictures to document motherboard replacements and wiring.

If a used thermal solution is being installed, then the thermal pad or old thermal paste should be removed and new thermal paste applied. Do not scratch the surface of a heat sink. Use a plastic scribe or tool to remove a thermal pad or old paste. A thermal paste cleaner, acetone, or denatured alcohol with a lint-free cloth can be used to remove residual paste.

When installing thermal paste, you should apply the prescribed amount in the center of the processor. Spread the compound evenly in a fine layer over the portion of the center of the CPU that comes in contact with the heat sink. When the heat sink is attached to the processor, the thermal compound will spread (hopefully not over the edges). Always follow the heat sink installation directions.

A CPU fan is likely to have a 3- or 4-pin cable that attaches to the motherboard. The motherboard might have a 3- or 4-pin connector. A 3-pin fan can be attached to a 4-pin motherboard connector, and a 4-pin fan cable can be connected to a 3-pin motherboard connector, as shown in Figure 3.24. Note that when a 3-pin cable attaches to 4-pin connector, the fan is always on and cannot be controlled, as a 4-pin cable to a 4-pin connector can.

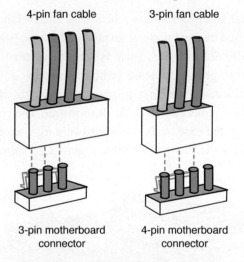

FIGURE 3.24   CPU fan connectivity

Troubleshooting Processor Issues

Processor issues can appear in different ways, as illustrated in Figure 3.25.

The following measures can help you solve CPU issues:

> The number-one issue related to processor problems is heat. Ensure that the fans work. Adding fans costs very little compared to replacing a processor or motherboard. Ensure that the computer has adequate circulation/cooling. Vacuum any dust from the motherboard/CPU. Cool the room more.

> Many BIOS/UEFI screens show the CPU temperature. (This is covered in more detail in Chapter 4.)

> Research any visual codes shown on the motherboard LEDs or listen for audio beeps as the computer beeps. Refer to the computer or motherboard manufacturer's website.

Processor issues are difficult to troubleshoot, and it is often very challenging to determine whether a problem is a CPU or motherboard issue. When a video port does not work, you can insert another video card to determine the problem. However, diagnosing processor and motherboard issues isn't so simple. If you have power to the system (that is, the power supply has power coming out of it), the hard drive works (try it in a different computer), and the monitor works (try it on a different computer), then the motherboard and/or CPU are prime suspects.

Use your senses when troubleshooting processor problems.

- Nothing on the screen (and the power supply and monitor work)
- System powers on, but turns off quickly
- BSOD (blue screen of death)
- An error code that the documentation shows as a CPU problem

- Hear the fan(s) going frantically, but the system won't boot or boots and then shuts off
- System powers on briefly, but then shuts off
- A series of beeps that the manual shows as a CPU problem

- Smell something burning (fan might be out, causing the CPU to shut down)

FIGURE 3.25 Detecting processor problems

Expansion Slots

If a computer is to be useful, the CPU must communicate with the outside world, including other motherboard components and adapters plugged into the motherboard. An expansion slot is used to add an adapter to the motherboard. It has rules that control how many bits at a time can be transferred to the adapter, what signals are sent over the adapter's gold connectors, and how the adapter is configured. Figure 3.26 shows expansion slots on a motherboard.

Expansion slots

FIGURE 3.26 Motherboard expansion slots

Expansion slots in PCs are usually some form of PCI (Peripheral Component Interconnect), AGP (Accelerated Graphics Port), or PCIe (PCI Express). Other types of expansion slots that have been included with older PCs are ISA (Industry Standard Architecture), EISA (Extended Industry Standard Architecture), MCA (Micro Channel Architecture), and VL-bus (sometimes called VESA [video electronics standards association] bus). A technician must be able to distinguish among adapters and expansion slots and be able to identify the adapters/devices that use expansion slots. A technician must also realize the abilities and limitations of each type of expansion slot when installing upgrades, replacing parts, and making recommendations.

An alternative to an adapter plugging directly into the motherboard is the use of a **riser card**, also called a riser board. A riser card plugs into the motherboard and has its own expansion slots. Adapters can plug into these expansion slots instead of directly into the motherboard. Riser cards are used with rack-mounted servers and low-profile desktop computer models. A riser card is commonly inserted into a motherboard slot or attached using screws. Figure 3.27 shows how a riser card attaches to a motherboard.

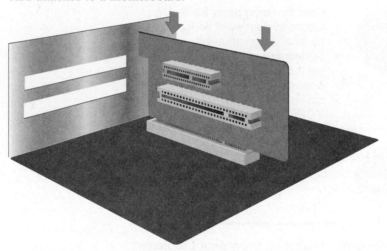

FIGURE 3.27   Installing a riser card

PCI (Peripheral Component Interconnect)

A previously popular expansion slot is Peripheral Component Interconnect (**PCI**). PCI comes in four varieties: 32-bit 33 MHz, 32-bit 66 MHz, 64-bit 33 MHz, and 64-bit 66 MHz. There was also an upgrade to the PCI bus called PCI-X that was commonly found in servers and is not covered except in comparison here. Figure 3.28 shows the most common type of PCI expansion slot.

FIGURE 3.28   PCI expansion slot

AGP (Accelerated Graphics Port)

AGP (Accelerated Graphics Port) is a bus interface for graphics adapters developed from the PCI bus. Intel provided the majority of the development for AGP, and the specification was originally designed around the Pentium II processor. AGP speeds up 3D graphics, 3D acceleration, and full-motion playback. Earlier video adapters were limited by the bottleneck caused by going through an adapter and a bus shared with other devices. With AGP, the video subsystem is isolated from the rest of the computer. Figure 3.29 shows an illustration of an AGP slot compared with PCI expansion slots. Both of these expansion slots have been replaced by PCIe (covered next).

FIGURE 3.29   AGP and PCI expansion slots

PCIe (Peripheral Component Interconnect Express)

PCI and AGP have been replaced with **PCIe** (PCI Express), which is also sometimes written PCI-E. PCIe outperforms all other types of PCI expansion slots. Figure 3.30 shows PCI expansion slots, and Table 3.7 lists the different PCIe versions.

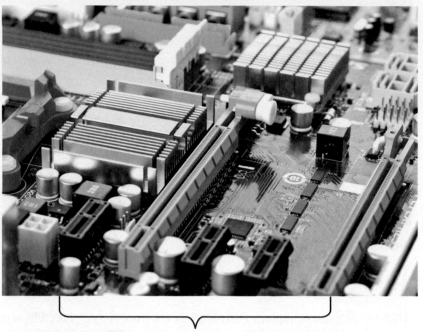

PCIe expansion slots

FIGURE 3.30   PCIe expansion slots

TABLE 3.7   PCIe versions

PCIe version	Speed (per lane per direction)
1.0	2.5 GT/s (gigatransfers per second) or 250 MB/s
2.0	5 GT/s or 500 MB/s
3.0	8 GT/s or 1 GB/s
4.0	16 GT/s or 2 GB/s
5.0	32 GT/s or 4 GB/s

The older PCI standard is half-duplex bidirectional, which means that data is sent to and from the PCI card using only one direction at a time. PCIe sends data full-duplex bidirectionally; in other words, it can send and receive at the same time. Figure 3.31 shows this concept.

TECH TIP

PCI cards in PCIe slots

Older PCI and AGP adapters will not work in any type of PCIe slots

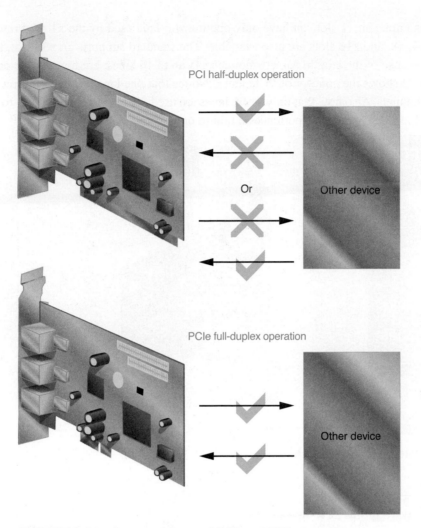

FIGURE 3.31   A comparison of PCI and PCIe transfers

The older PCI standards use a parallel bus where data is sent with multiple 1s and 0s simultaneously. PCIe is a serial bus, and data is sent 1 bit at a time. Table 3.8 shows a comparison of the PCI, AGP, and PCIe buses.

TABLE 3.8   Comparing bus bandwidth

Bus	Maximum bandwidth
PCI	133 or 266 MB/s (depending on bus speed)
AGP 2x	533 MB/s
PCIe x1	250 MB/s (in each direction)
PCIe x2	500 MB/s (in each direction)
PCIe x4	1000 MB/s (in each direction)
PCIe x8	2000 MB/s (in each direction)
PCIe x16	4000 MB/s (in each direction)
PCIe x32	8000 MB/s (in each direction)

Another difference between PCI and PCIe is that PCIe slots come in different versions, depending on the maximum number of lanes that can be assigned to the card inserted into the slot. For example, an x1 slot can have only one transfer lane used by the x1 card inserted into the slot; x2, x4, x8, and x16 slots are also available. The standard supports an x32 slot, but these slots are rare because of the length. An x16 slot accepts up to 16 lanes, but fewer lanes can be assigned. Figure 3.32 shows the concept of PCIe lanes. Notice that one lane has two unidirectional communication channels. Also note that only seven lanes are used. PCIe has the capability to use a reduced number of lanes if one lane experiences a failure or a performance issue.

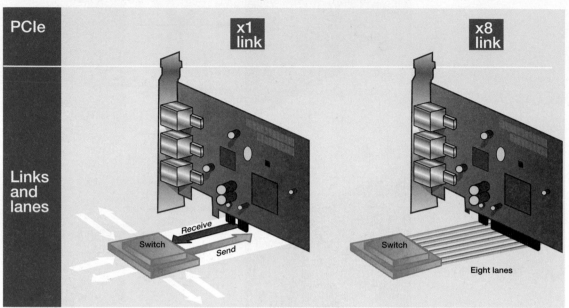

FIGURE 3.32   PCIe lanes

Beware of the PCIe fine print

Some motherboard manufacturers offer a larger slot size (such as x8), but the slot runs at a slower speed (x4, for example). This keeps the cost down. The manual would show such a slot as x8 (x4 mode) in the PCIe slot description.

A PCIe x1 adapter can fit in an x1 or higher slot. A larger card, such as a PCIe x16, cannot fit in a lower-numbered (x8, x4, x2, or x1) slot. Figure 3.33 shows this concept.

Removing an adapter is normally just a matter of removing a retaining screw or plate and lifting the adapter out of the slot. Some AGP and PCIe expansion slots have retention levers. You move the retention lever to the side in order to lift the adapter from the expansion slot. Figure 3.34 shows an example of the PCIe adapter removal process. Figure 3.35 shows a motherboard with two PCIe x1, two PCIe x16, and three PCI expansion slots. Notice that the PCIe x16 slot has a retention lever.

Removing PCIe adapters

PCIe x16 adapters commonly have release levers. You must press the lever while pulling the adapter out of the expansion slot, or you may damage the board (and possibly the motherboard).

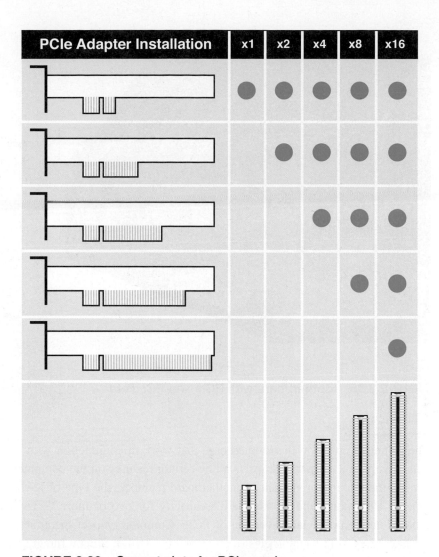

PCIe Adapter Installation	x1	x2	x4	x8	x16
	●	●	●	●	●
		●	●	●	●
			●	●	●
				●	●
					●

FIGURE 3.33   Correct slots for PCIe cards

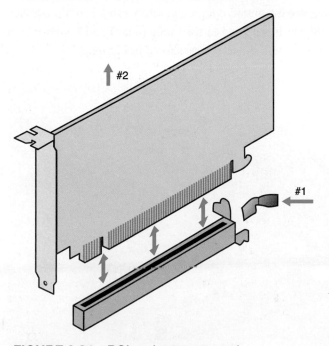

FIGURE 3.34   PCIe adapter removal

2 PCIe x16 slots

PCI slots

2 PCIe x1 slots

FIGURE 3.35   Motherboard with PCIe and PCI slots

Chipsets

The principal chips on the motherboard that work in conjunction with the processor are known collectively as a **chipset**. Chipsets allow certain features on the computer. For example, chipsets control the maximum amount of motherboard memory, the type of RAM chips, the number and type of USB ports, the motherboard's capacity for two or more CPUs, and whether the motherboard supports the latest version of PCIe. Common chipset manufacturers include Intel, VIA Technologies, ATI technologies (now owned by AMD), Silicon Integrated Systems (SiS), AMD, and NVIDIA Corporation.

A chipset is a square integrated circuit and looks similar to a processor. You normally can't see this because the chipset is soldered to the motherboard and commonly covered with a heat sink. Look for a chipset close to a processor, as shown in Figure 3.36.

FIGURE 3.36   The chipset

Types of Motherboards

Motherboards come in different sizes, known as **form factors**. The most common motherboard form factor is Advanced Technology Extended (**ATX**). Other ATX form factors include **micro-ATX** (sometimes written μATX or **mATX**), mini-ATX, FlexATX, EATX, WATX, nano-ATX, pico-ATX and mobileATX. A smaller form factor is **ITX**, which comes in **mini-ITX** (or **mITX**), nano-ITX, and pico-ITX sizes. Some motherboards, such as the NLX and LPX form factors, had a riser board that attached to the smaller motherboard. Adapters go into the slots on the riser board instead of into motherboard slots. Figure 3.37 shows some of the motherboard form factors, and Table 3.9 provides more details.

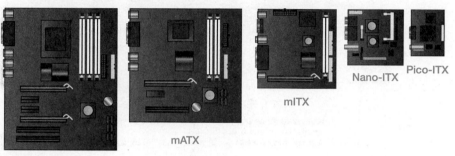

FIGURE 3.37   Motherboard form factors

TABLE 3.9   Motherboard form factor comparison

Form factor	Description	Size
ATX	Used in desktop computers	12×9.6 inches (30.5×24.4cm)
mATX	MicroATX—a smaller desktop motherboard	9.6×9.6 inches (24.4×24.4cm)
ITX or mITX	Used in very small computers and set-top boxes	6.7×6.7 inches (17×17cm)
Nano-ITX	Used in entertainment devices/computers	4.7×4.7 inches (11.94×11.94cm)
Pico-ITX	Used in very small devices	3.9×2.8 inches (3.9×7.1cm)

TECH TIP

Matching the motherboard form factor and case

The case used for a computer must match the motherboard form factor. Some cases can accommodate different form factors, but you should always check. When you are building a computer or replacing a motherboard, it is important to obtain the correct form factor.

TECH TIP

Going green with a motherboard or CPU

When upgrading or replacing a motherboard and/or processor, consider going green. Select a board that is lead free and uses a lower amount of power (wattage), one that uses a smaller form factor (such as micro-ATX), one that has integrated video, or one that has all these features.

Figure 3.38 shows an older motherboard with many of the motherboard components labeled. A technician should stay current on motherboard technologies.

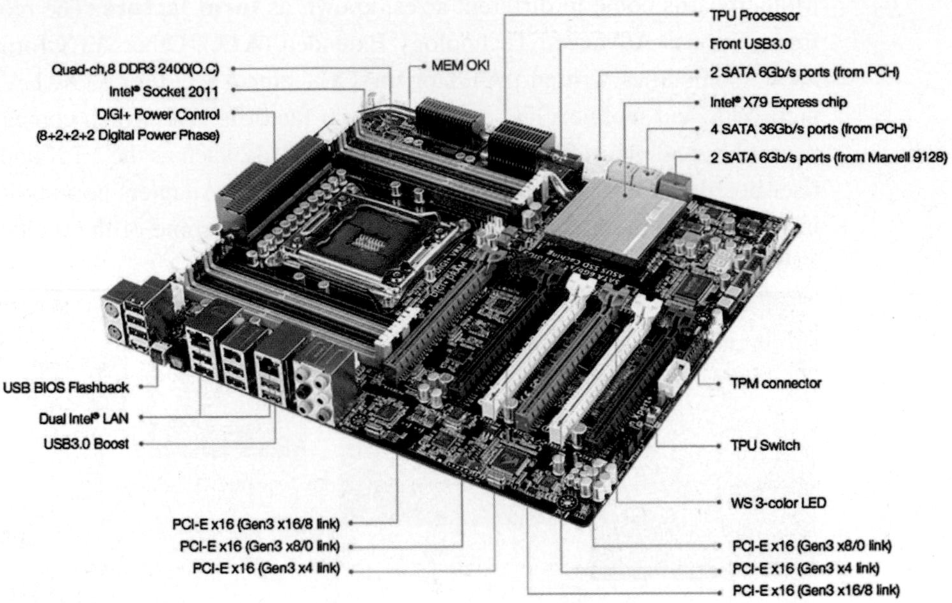

FIGURE 3.38 ASUS workstation motherboard components

Manufacturers sometimes design a case so that it requires a proprietary motherboard. With such a design, a replacement motherboard must be purchased from the original manufacturer and is usually more expensive than a generic option.

Upgrading and Replacing Motherboards

When upgrading a motherboard or processor, you must consider several issues. The following list guides you through making the decision (or helping a customer make the decision) about whether to upgrade a motherboard:

> Why is the computer being upgraded? For example, does the computer need more memory? Are more expansion slots needed? Does the computer need a bigger/faster CPU to run certain operating systems or applications? Is more space wanted in the computer area? Sometimes upgrading the motherboard does not help unless the other computer components are upgraded. The most expensive and fastest motherboard/CPU will not run applications well unless it has the proper amount of memory. Hard drives are another issue. If software access is slow, the solution might not be a new motherboard but a faster and larger hard drive or more RAM.

> Which type of expansion slot (PCI, AGP, or PCIe) and how many adapters of each type are needed from the old motherboard? Does the new motherboard have the required expansion slots?

> What type of chipsets does the new motherboard support? What features, if any, would this bring to the new motherboard?

> Will the new motherboard fit in the current computer case, or is a new one required?

> If upgrading the CPU, will the motherboard support the new type of CPU?

> Does the motherboard allow for future CPU upgrades?

> How much memory (RAM) does the motherboard allow? What memory chips are required on the new motherboard? Will the old memory chips work in the new motherboard or with the new CPU?

Before replacing a motherboard, it is important to do all the following:

> Remove the CPU and CPU fan.
> Remove adapters from expansion slots.
> Remove memory chips from expansion slots.
> Disconnect power connectors.
> Disconnect ribbon cables.
> Disconnect external devices such as mouse, keyboard, and monitor.

Replacement motherboards do not normally come with RAM, so the old modules are removed from the bad/older motherboard. A motherboard usually does not come with a CPU. Make note of the CPU orientation before removing it from the bad/older motherboard. Some retailers sell kits that include the computer case, power supply, motherboard, and CPU so that the components match, function together correctly, and are physically compatible.

TECH TIP

Use good antistatic measures when installing a motherboard

When replacing a motherboard, place the motherboard on a nonconductive surface such as an antistatic mat or the antistatic bag that came with the motherboard.

When upgrading any component or an entire computer, remember that the older part can be donated to a charity or an educational institution. Something that one person considers outdated may be an upgrade to someone else. Educational institutions are always seeking components to use in classrooms. Many stores have recycling programs for computer parts.

Motherboard Troubleshooting

Common symptoms of motherboard issues are similar to CPU problems: The system has a **blank screen on bootup** (which could mean the video cable is not attached well); an error code appears; one or more beeps occur; the system experiences **unexpected shutdowns**; a **system lockup**; the system might do **continuous reboots**; a Windows BSOD (blue screen of death) appears; or one or more of the ports, expansion slots, or memory modules fails. Note that unexpected shutdowns, system lockups, and continuous reboots can also be symptoms of a CPU or power supply problem.

Motherboard problems and power problems are probably the most difficult issues to troubleshoot. Because various components are located on the motherboard, many things can cause errors. **POST** (power-on self-test) is one of the most beneficial aids for troubleshooting a motherboard. The meaning of any code that appears on the screen should be researched. If multiple POST error codes appear, you should troubleshoot them in the order in which they are presented. The following list helps with motherboard troubleshooting:

> Is the motherboard receiving power? Check the power supply to see if the fan is turning. If the CPU or motherboard has a fan, see if it is turning. Check voltages going from the power supply to the motherboard. See Chapter 5, "Disassembly and Power," for directions.
> Check the BIOS/UEFI settings (covered in Chapter 4) for accuracy.
> Check for **overheating**, which might point to a problem with the CPU or motherboard. Power down the computer and allow the computer to cool. Power on the computer with the cover off. See if the CPU fan is turning. Is the motherboard hot to the touch?
> Check the motherboard for **distended capacitors**—small components that might appear to be bulging. If you look again at Figure 3.35, you can see the metal cylinders (which are

capacitors) in the bottom-right corner and beside the expansion slots. If you sight that such a capacitor is bulging, replace the motherboard as soon as possible.

> Reseat the CPU, adapters, and memory chips.
> Remove unnecessary adapters and devices and boot the computer.
> Plug the computer into a different power outlet and circuit, if possible.
> Check to determine whether the motherboard is shorting out on the frame.
> Check the CMOS battery (see Chapter 5 for how to take voltage readings).
> With a motherboard that has diagnostic LEDs, check the output for any error code. Refer to the motherboard documentation or online documentation for the problem and possible solution.

TECH TIP

These concepts relate to Apple computers, too

Even though this book focuses on PCs, concepts related to CPUs, motherboards, expansion slots, cache, and chipsets also apply to Apple computers. Apple computers and PCs have similar CPU and memory requirements.

SOFT SKILLS: ACTIVE LISTENING

Active listening is participating in a conversation where you focus on what the customer is saying—in other words, listening more than talking. For a technician, active listening has the following benefits:

> Enables you to gather data and symptoms quickly
> Enables you to build customer rapport
> Improves your understanding of the problem
> Enables you to solve the problem more quickly because you understand the problem better
> Provides mutual understanding between you and the customer
> Provides a means of having a positive, engaged conversation rather than having a negative, confrontational encounter
> Focuses on the customer rather than the technician
> Provides an environment in which the customer might be more forthcoming with information related to the problem

Frequently, when a technician arrives onsite or contacts a customer who has a technical problem, the technician is (1) rushed; (2) thinking of other things, including the problems that need to be solved; (3) assuming that he or she knows exactly what the problem is, even though the user has not finished explaining the problem; or (4) more interested in the technical problem than in the customer and the issues. Active listening changes the focus from the technician's problems to the customer's problems.

A common but ineffective service call involves a technician doing most of the talking and questioning, using technical jargon and acronyms and a flat or condescending tone. A customer who feels vulnerable experiences a heightened anxiety level. Active listening changes this scenario by helping you build a professional relationship with your customers. Figure 3.39 shows a technician actively listening. The list that follows outlines some measures that help you implement active listening.

FIGURE 3.39   Active listening

Have a positive, engaged professional attitude when talking and listening to customers:

> Leave your prejudices behind; be polite and aware of other cultures and customs; be open-minded and nonjudgmental.
> Have a warm and caring attitude.
> Do not fold your arms in front of your chest because doing so distances you from the problem and the customer.
> Do not blame others or talk badly about other technicians.
> Do not act as if the problem is not your responsibility.

Focus on what the customer is saying:

> Turn off or ignore your electronic devices.
> Maintain eye contact; don't let your mind wander.
> Allow the customer to finish explaining the problem; do not interrupt; avoid arguing with the customer or being defensive.
> Stop all irrelevant behaviors and activities.
> Mentally review what the customer is saying.
> Refrain from talking to coworkers unnecessarily while interacting with customers.
> Avoid personal interruptions or distractions.

Participate in the conversation in a limited but active manner:

> Maintain a professional demeanor (suspend negative emotions); do not minimize or diminish the customer's problem.
> Acknowledge that you are listening by occasionally nodding and making comments such as "I see."
> Use positive body language such as leaning slightly forward or taking notes.
> Observe the customer's behavior to determine when it is appropriate to ask questions.

Briefly talk with the customer:

> Speak using a positive tone; use a tone that is empathetic and genuine, not condescending.
> Restate or summarize points made by the customer.
> Ask nonthreatening, probing questions related to the customer's statements or questions.
> Do not jump between topics.
> Do not use technical jargon.
> Clarify the meaning of the customer's situation.
> Identify clues to help solve the problem and reduce your troubleshooting time by listening carefully to what the customer says.
> Follow up with the person at a later date to ensure that the problem is solved and to verify satisfaction.
> Offer different repair or replacement options, if possible.

Chapter Summary

> Important motherboard parts include the following: processor, RAM slots, RAM, expansion slots (PCI, PCIe, and AGP), and cooling devices.
> Processors can be multicore and can contain very fast cache memory: L1 cache inside the processor and L2 cache outside the processor but inside the chip. Processors can also support L3 cache.

> Intel processors use Hyperthreading to make efficient use of processor time by the CPU executing separate sets of instructions simultaneously.

> Processors must be kept cool with fans and/or heat sinks. A thermal paste or pad is applied between a heat sink and a processor. Never turn on a computer without some type of thermal cooling on the processor.

> The clock speed refers to the processor's internal clock. This is not the same as the FSB or bus speed.

> CPU throttling slows down the processor to prevent overheating.

> PCI is a 32- and 64-bit parallel bus. PCI and AGP have been replaced with the point-to-point serial PCIe bus.

> PCIe slots have a specific number of bidirectional lanes that are the maximum a card can use. A PCIe adapter can fit in a slot of the same number of lanes or a slot that has the ability to process a higher number of lanes.

> A chipset is one or more chips that coordinate communication between the processor and the rest of the motherboard. The chipset dictates the maximum number and type of slots and ports on a motherboard. AMD and Intel have created technologies to address the slowness of the FSB: HyperTransport, QPI, and DMI.

> An integrated GPU is on-die with the CPU and processes graphics-related functions.

> When replacing a motherboard, ensure that the CPU socket and number/types of expansion slots are appropriate.

> Use POST in troubleshooting motherboard or CPU issues. Symptoms of CPU or motherboard issues include distended capacitors, unexpected shutdowns, system lockups, blank screen on bootup, continuous reboots, and overheating.

> Active listening is an important skill for a technician. Avoid getting distracted by people or technology and do take notes, make good eye contact, and ask directed questions when appropriate.

A+ CERTIFICATION EXAM TIPS

✓ Know the following motherboard connector types: PCI, PCIe, riser card, socket types, SATA, IDE, front panel connector, and internal USB connector.

✓ Know the following CPU features: single-core, multicore, virtualization, Hyperthreading, speeds, overclocking, and integrated GPU.

✓ Review diagrams for PCI and PCIe expansion slots. Use the Internet to view motherboards to see if you can determine the type of expansion slot. The exam has graphics that are unlabeled. Do the same for other motherboard components, including the processor.

✓ Know that Intel and AMD are two prominent CPU manufacturers that require an appropriate motherboard and socket in order to install the processor.

✓ Review the types of CPU cooling methods: Fan, heat sink, liquid, and thermal paste.

✓ Be able to install a CPU and thermal cooling system. Know how and where to connect a CPU fan.

✓ Know the differences between and be able to identify ATX, mATX, ITX, and mITX motherboard form factors.

✓ Know what a distended capacitor is.

✓ Know symptoms of processor and motherboard issues: distended capacitor, unexpected shutdowns, system lockups, blank screen on bootup, continuous reboots, overheating, and a burning smell. Use POST codes to help with troubleshooting.

Key Terms

active listening 105
AGP 95
AGP bus speed 77
AMD 72
APU 82
ATX 101
back side bus 76
blank screen on bootup 103
bus 73
bus speed 76
cache memory 77
chipset 100
clock 76
clock speed 76
continuous reboot 103
CPU 72
CPU speed 77
CPU throttling 77
distended capacitor 103
dual-core processor 79
external data bus 73
fan 86

form factor 101
FSB 76
gigahertz 73
GPU 82
heat sink 86
hexa-core 79
Hyperthreading 79
HyperTransport 79
integrated GPU 82
Intel 72
internal data bus 73
ITX 101
L1 cache 77
L2 cache 77
L3 cache 77
liquid cooling 86
mATX 101
mITX 101
micro-ATX 101
mini-ITX 101
multicore 79
octa-core 79

overclocking 90
overheating 103
passive cooling 86
PCI 94
PCI bus speed 76
PCIe 96
PCIe bus speed 76
POST 103
processor 72
quad-core 79
riser card 94
single-core processor 79
system lockup 103
thermal paste 86
thread 79
throttle management 90
unexpected shutdowns 103
virtual technology 82
virtualization 82
ZIF socket 85

Review Questions

1.   Which component can be located both on a video card and on a motherboard?

[chipset | PCIe expansion slot | PCI expansion slot | GPU]

2.   Which expansion slot is *best* for a video card in a desktop computer?

[PCIe | PCI | USB | AGP]

3.   A motherboard has a PCIe x16 expansion slot. Which PCIe adapter(s) will fit in this slot? (Select any that apply.)

[x1 | x2 | x4 | x8 | x16 | x32]

4.   Match the motherboard part with its associated description.

____ L1 cache   **a.** Mounted on top of the CPU

____ CPU   **b.** Memory found in the CPU

____ FSB   **c.** Executes software instructions

____ heat sink   **d.** Bus between the CPU and motherboard components

____ HT   **e.** Slows the CPU to cool it

____ throttling   **f.** Allows one processor to handle multiple instructions simultaneously

5.   What is the front side bus?

a. The internal data bus that connects the processor core to the L1 cache

b. The internal data bus that connects the processor core to the L2 cache

c. The external data bus that connects the processor to the motherboard components

d. The external data bus that connects the processor to the L2 cache

6.   A customer wants to upgrade the L2 cache. Which of the following does this definitely require?

a. A motherboard purchase

b. A CPU purchase

c. A ROM module purchase

d. A RAM module purchase

7.   Match the expansion slot to its definition.

____ AGP   **a.** 32- or 64-bit parallel bus

____ PCI   **b.** Just for video cards

____ PCIe   **c.** Has a varying number of lanes

8.   What is the difference between Hyperthreading and HyperTransport?

_____

_____

9.   What should a technician do if a distended capacitor is found on a motherboard?

a. Replace the capacitor.

b. Replace the motherboard.

c. Check the voltages coming from the power supply.

d. Replace the power supply.

CHAPTER 3

10. Which of the following statements is true regarding PCIe?

    a. A PCIe slot will not accept a PCI card.

    b. PCIe is a parallel bus technology.

    c. PCIe is a 32- or 64-bit bus technology.

    d. PCIe is being replaced by PCI-X.

11. [T | F] A PCIe x8 adapter always transmits using eight lanes.

12. What is the significance of a motherboard specification that states the following: 1 PCIe x16 (x8 mode) slot?

    a. The slot accepts x8 or x16 cards.

    b. The slot can transmit traffic using 8 or 16 lanes.

    c. The slot can transmit in bursts of 8 or 16 bytes at a time.

    d. The slot accepts x16 cards but uses only 8 lanes.

13. What determines whether a motherboard can use a specific model of RAM or type of memory, such as DDR3 or DDR4?

    [CPU | chipset | PCIe standard | processor speed]

14. A technician for a college is going to repair a problem in another building. A professor stops the technician to talk about her slow computer. The technician gives a little eye roll but then stops and listens to the professor. The professor comments, "I can't get my email or even type my tests. The computer takes at least 20 minutes just to boot." The technician looks around, a little exasperated, and says, "Uh huh." "I logged this problem over a week ago," continues the professor, "and no one has dropped by." "Uh huh," replies the technician again. "Do you know when you folks might get to that issue or have an idea about what might be the problem?" the professor asks. The technician looks at the professor and says, "It is probably a virus that has been going around. Jim was supposed to get to those. We will get to you as soon as we can." The technician's phone rings, and he walks away to get to the phone.

    List three active listening techniques and good customer support procedures that could improve this situation.

    _____

    _____

    _____

    _____

15. Explain how a technician might be culturally insensitive.

    _____

    _____

16. Which component can be adjusted to overclock?

    [heat sink | CPU | expansion slot | chipset]

17. [T | F] When installing a CPU, orient pin 1 to pin 1 on the socket and align the other pins. Lower the ZIF socket lever and lock. Power on the computer to ensure that the CPU works. Power down the computer and install the heat sink and/or fan.

18. What is applied between a processor and a heat sink to increase heat dissipation?

    [a capacitor | thermal paste | a fan | cache memory]

19. What component is affected by the LGA 2011 specification?

    [RAM | chipset | processor | expansion slot]

20. Which method is *not* used to cool a processor?

    [CPU fan | case fan | heat sink | thermal tank]

Exercises

Exercise 3.1 Identifying ATX Motherboard Parts

Objective: To identify various motherboard parts

Parts: None

Procedure: Identify each of the ATX motherboard parts in Figure 3.40.

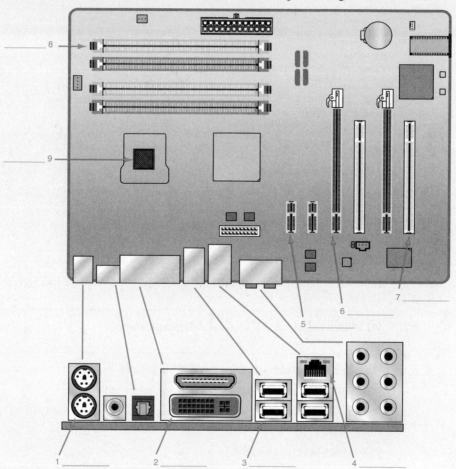

FIGURE 3.40   Motherboard ports, slots, and parts

1. _____
2. _____
3. _____
4. _____
5. _____
6. _____
7. _____
8. _____
9. _____

Exercise 3.2 Motherboard Analysis

Objective: To identify various motherboard parts

Parts: None

Procedure: Using the information you learned in this chapter and related to the specifications found in Figure 3.41, answer the questions that follow.

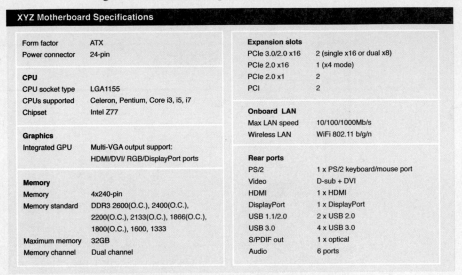

XYZ Motherboard Specifications		
Form factor	ATX	
Power connector	24-pin	
CPU		
CPU socket type	LGA1155	
CPUs supported	Celeron, Pentium, Core i3, i5, i7	
Chipset	Intel Z77	
Graphics		
Integrated GPU	Multi-VGA output support: HDMI/DVI/ RGB/DisplayPort ports	
Memory		
Memory	4x240-pin	
Memory standard	DDR3 2600(O.C.), 2400(O.C.), 2200(O.C.), 2133(O.C.), 1866(O.C.), 1800(O.C.), 1600, 1333	
Maximum memory	32GB	
Memory channel	Dual channel	

Expansion slots		
PCIe 3.0/2.0 x16	2 (single x16 or dual x8)	
PCIe 2.0 x16	1 (x4 mode)	
PCIe 2.0 x1	2	
PCI	2	
Onboard LAN		
Max LAN speed	10/100/1000Mb/s	
Wireless LAN	WiFi 802.11 b/g/n	
Rear ports		
PS/2	1 x PS/2 keyboard/mouse port	
Video	D-sub + DVI	
HDMI	1 x HDMI	
DisplayPort	1 x DisplayPort	
USB 1.1/2.0	2 x USB 2.0	
USB 3.0	4 x USB 3.0	
S/PDIF out	1 x optical	
Audio	6 ports	

FIGURE 3.41   Motherboard advertisement

1.   If you were buying this motherboard, what type of case would you need to purchase?

_____

2.   What does LGA1155 tell you about this motherboard?

_____

3.   Does this motherboard come with a CPU installed?

[Yes | No | Cannot tell from the information presented]

4.   What motherboard component controls the maximum number of USB 3.0 ports this motherboard *could* have?

[CPU | RAM | chipset | FSB]

5.   What processor(s) does this motherboard accept?

_____

6.   What do you think the letters O.C. after some of the memory chips mean in relationship to this motherboard?

_____

7.   What is the most significant difference between a version 2.0 PCIe slot and a version 3.0 PCIe expansion slot?

_____

8.   What does the PCIe 3.0/2.0 x16 line that states "2 (single x16 or dual x8)" mean?

   a.   The adapter that goes into this slot can use a single lane that goes at x16 speeds or two lanes that go at x8 speeds.

   b.   One single x16 adapter and/or one single x8 adapter can go into the expansion slots.

   c.   One x16 adapter can go into one of the version 3.0 slots and achieve 3.0 speeds, or two x16 adapters can be installed, but they can transfer only eight lanes at a time at 3.0 speeds.

   d.   A single x16 adapter can be installed in one of the version 3.0 slots, or two x8 adapters can be installed in the two version 3.0 slots.

9. What device cable can be inserted into the PS/2 port? (Select the best answer.)
    [speaker | mouse or keyboard | display | external storage]

10. Which type of video port is described as a D-sub in this documentation?
    [DisplayPort | DVI | HDMI | VGA]

11. What is an advantage of having an integrated GPU in the CPU?

    _____

12. What is the most likely reason this motherboard manufacturer chose to include two PCI expansion slots?

    _____

    _____

Activities

Internet Discovery

To obtain specific information on the Internet regarding a computer or its associated parts

Parts: A computer with Internet access

Procedure: Locate documentation on the Internet for a GIGABYTE GA-Z170-HD3 motherboard to answer Questions 1–12. Continue your Internet search to answer Questions 13 and 14.

Questions:

1. Does the motherboard support an Intel or AMD processor? _____

2. Which chipset is used? _____

3. How many expansion slots are on the motherboard? _____

4. Which form factor does this motherboard use? _____

5. Which processors can be used on this motherboard?

    _____

6. Does the motherboard support having an integrated GPU in the CPU? How can you tell whether it does or not? _____

    _____

7. Which type of CPU socket does the motherboard have? _____

8. How many and of what type of PCIe slots does it have?

    _____

    _____

    _____

9. Is there any other type of expansion slot on this motherboard? If so, what is it?

    _____

10. Does this motherboard have an integrated USB 3.1 10 Gb/s port? _____

11. What are the maximum number and type of USB ports available on the rear of the motherboard?

    _____

12. Write the URL where you found the motherboard information.

    _____

    _____

CHAPTER 3

13. Find a vendor for a motherboard that uses the A55 chipset that can support PCIe 3.0. Document the motherboard model and vendor.

_____

_____

14. Find an Internet site that describes the dimensions of the extended ATX motherboard form factor. List the dimensions and the website. _____

_____

Soft Skills

Objective: To enhance and fine-tune a future technician's ability to listen, communicate in both written and oral forms, and support people who use computers in a professional manner

Activities:

1. On a piece of paper or an index card, list three ways you can practice active listening at school. Share this information with your group. Consolidate ideas and present five of the best ideas to the class.

2. In a team environment, come up with two examples of situations you have experienced in which a support person (a PC support person, sales clerk, checkout clerk, person being asked directions, and so on) could have provided better service if he or she had been actively listening. Share your findings with the class.

3. In teams of two, have one person tell a story and the other person practice active listening skills. The person telling the story should critique the listener. The pair should then change roles.

Critical Thinking Skills

Objective: To analyze and evaluate information and to apply learned information to new or different situations

Activities:

1. Find an advertisement for a computer in a local computer flyer, newspaper, magazine, or book or on the Internet. Determine all the information about the motherboard and ports that you can from the ad. Write down any information you do not understand. Research this information and share your findings with a classmate.

_____

_____

_____

2. Your parents want to give you a new computer as a present. The one they are considering has a GPU integrated into the CPU. List at least one argument you might use for getting a different computer model.

_____

_____

_____

3. Why do you think a motherboard has different buses that operate at different speeds?

_____

_____

_____

4 Introduction to Configuration

In this chapter you will learn:

> The importance of BIOS and UEFI

> How to replace a motherboard battery

> What system resources are and how to view/change them

> Basics steps needed to install, configure, and verify common peripheral devices and USB, eSATA, video, and network cards

> How to troubleshoot configuration, video, and device issues

CompTIA Exam Objectives:

What CompTIA A+ exam objectives are covered in this chapter?

✓ 1001-3.5   Given a scenario, install and configure motherboards, CPUs, and add-on cards.

✓ 1001-5.2   Given a scenario, troubleshoot problems related to motherboards, RAM, CPUs, and power.

✓ 1001-5.4   Given a scenario, troubleshoot video, projector, and display issues.

Configuration Overview

Installing and configuring the motherboard, the processor, RAM, or other devices can involve using the system BIOS Setup program or the operating system. The system **Setup** program enables you to configure the motherboard, power, and devices. It also enables you to set performance options.

BIOS Overview

The basic input/output system (BIOS) is an important motherboard component that is commonly soldered to the motherboard, as shown in Figure 4.1. The BIOS is also known as the Unified Extensible Firmware Interface (**UEFI**) and sometimes simply as EFI, BIOS/UEFI, or UEFI/BIOS. The BIOS has the following functions:

> Holds and executes power-on self-test (**POST**)—a program that identifies, tests, and initializes basic hardware components.
> Holds a basic routine called a bootstrap program that locates an operating system and launches it, allowing the operating system to then control the system.
> Holds Setup, which is a program that allows viewing and management of settings related to the display, date/time, processor, memory, and drives. Other names used for Setup include BIOS Setup, System Setup, and CMOS Setup.
> Turns over control to an adapter's onboard BIOS so that the card can initialize during the computer boot process.

FIGURE 4.1 Motherboard BIOS

POST performs basic tests of individual hardware components, such as the motherboard, RAM modules, keyboard, optical drive, and hard drive. When a computer is powered on, BIOS executes POST. An indication that POST is running is that the **indicator lights** on the keyboard momentarily flash on and then off, or perhaps the hard drive or optical drive light momentarily flashes. Turning on the computer with the power switch is known as a cold boot. Users perform a cold boot every time they power on their computer. A technician performs a cold boot when troubleshooting a computer and needs POST to execute to check for errors. BIOS can be configured to limit the number of devices checked by POST, thus reducing boot time.

In contrast, restarting the computer is known as a warm boot. Restart a Windows 7 computer by clicking on the *Start* button > right arrow adjacent to the lock button and then selecting *Restart* or by pressing Ctrl+Alt+Del, selecting the Up arrow in the bottom-right corner, and choosing *Restart* from the menu. On Windows 8 you can press ⊞ +ⓘ to access Settings (or move the pointer to the far-right corner) > *Power* > *Restart*. In Windows 10, right-click the *Start* button > *Shut Down or Sign Out* > *Restart* or click on the *Start* button > click the power symbol > *Restart*. Warm booting causes any changes that have been made to take effect without putting as much strain on the computer as a cold boot does. A warm boot does not execute POST.

When assembling, troubleshooting, or repairing a computer, a technician must go into the Setup program to configure the system. The Setup program is held in BIOS, and through the Setup program, you can see and possibly configure such things as RAM, the type and number of drives installed, where the computer looks for its boot files, the current date and time, and so on. An error message is displayed if the information in the Setup program fails to match the hardware or if a specific device does not work properly.

> **TECH TIP**
>
> **Using Setup to disable ports and connectors**
>
> Motherboards include connectors for hard drives, optical drives, and so on. If one of these connectors fails, you can disable it through Setup and obtain a replacement adapter just as you would if an integrated port failed. Setup can also be used to disable integrated motherboard ports.

There are two main ways to configure a system or an adapter: through the Setup program held in system BIOS and through the operating system. Let's examine using the Setup program first.

> **TECH TIP**
>
> **How to access Setup**
>
> The key or keys used to access Setup are normally displayed briefly during the boot process. Otherwise, look in the motherboard documentation for the proper keystroke(s) to use.

The Setup Program

Computers have Setup software built into the system BIOS chip on the motherboard that you can access with specific keystrokes determined by the BIOS manufacturer. During the boot process, most computers display a message stating which keystroke(s) will launch the Setup program. The message shown is usually in one of the four screen corners (see Figure 4.2). The keystroke can be one or more keys pressed during startup, such as the Esc, Insert, Del, F1, F2, or F10 keys. Another key combination is Ctrl+Alt+ some other key.

> **TECH TIP**
>
> **Accessing BIOS Setup in Windows 8 and Windows 10**
>
> To access BIOS Setup in Windows 8/8.1, access *Settings* > *Update and Recovery* > *Recovery* > *Restart now* button > *Troubleshoot* > *Advanced options* > *UEFI Firmware Settings* or *Startup Settings*. To access BIOS Setup in Windows 10, access *Settings* > *Update and Security* > *Recovery* > *Restart Now*.

FIGURE 4.2   Setup keystrokes

Flash BIOS

Flash BIOS allows you to upgrade (or downgrade) the BIOS without installing a new chip or chips. Common computer BIOS manufacturers include AMI (American Megatrends, Inc.), Phoenix Technologies, Byosoft (Nanjing Byosoft Co., Ltd.), and Insyde Software. Many computer companies customize their own BIOS chips or subcontract with a BIOS manufacturer to customize them.

To determine the current BIOS version, you can do one of the following:

> Watch the computer screen as it boots. Note that you might be able to press the Pause/Break key to freeze the frame and better see the boot information.
> Enter BIOS Setup using a particular keystroke during the boot process.
> From within Windows 8 or 10, access BIOS/UEFI Setup.

An upgrade of the BIOS normally involves removing all BIOS software and settings stored in CMOS. Some manufacturers provide utilities that enable you to save the current CMOS settings before upgrading the BIOS. Two things should be done before upgrading the flash BIOS if possible: Back up current CMOS settings and back up the current BIOS.

UEFI

Unified Extensible Firmware Interface (UEFI) is the interface between the operating system and firmware, which can be the traditional BIOS, or UEFI can replace the BIOS. The traditional BIOS has roots in the original PC; the traditional BIOS always checks for certain things, such as a keyboard, before allowing the system to boot. Traditional BIOS made configuring kiosks and other touchscreen technologies difficult. UEFI fixed these issues.

With UEFI, you can boot into the environment (which includes configuration parameters), but unlike with the original BIOS environment, you can use your mouse and possibly do some of the following (depending on the manufacturer): Connect to the Internet, run applications, run a virus scan, use a GUI, execute utilities, or perform a backup or a restore—a lot more configuration options and in a much easier-to-use environment. Figure 4.3 shows an example of a UEFI environment.

FIGURE 4.3 Sample UEFI main menu

Many manufacturers have moved to the UEFI type of BIOS for the following reasons:

> It is a graphical environment that provides mouse support.
> It enables you to use a virus-scanning utility that is not operating system dependent.
> It offers more BIOS-based software that is not just configuration screens.
> It offers optional Internet access for troubleshooting or download capabilities.
> It offers better system support for cooling, voltage levels, performance, and security.
> It provides support for increased hard drive capacities and ability to divide the hard drive into sections that are not subject to the limitations of the traditional BIOS.
> It commonly has monitoring data (temperature, voltage, CPU speed, bus speed, and fan speed) prominently displayed.
> It can have a boot manager instead of relying on a boot sector. See Chapter 7, "Storage Devices," for more information on the GUID partition table (GPT) and boot sector.

From the BIOS/UEFI main menu, there might be icons you can use to access utilities or more advanced configurations, as shown in Figure 4.4.

FIGURE 4.4 Sample UEFI advanced menu

BIOS/UEFI Configuration Settings

BIOS/UEFI options vary according to manufacturer, but many options are similar. Table 4.1 shows some common settings and briefly explains each one. Most Setup programs have help that can be accessed from within the Setup program to explain the purpose of each option. Note that the key term items are on the CompTIA A+ certification exam. A technician should be familiar with these common BIOS/UEFI setup options, especially the starred **security settings**.

TABLE 4.1   Common Setup options

Setup option	Description
System Information	Displays general information, such as the processor, processor speed, amount of RAM, type and number of hard drives and optical drives installed, BIOS/UEFI manufacturer, and BIOS/UEFI date.
General Optimization	Allow faster booting through the disabling of features such as memory checking, booting to the network, and booting from removable drives.
Boot Options, Boot Sequence, Boot Drive Order, or Boot Menu	Prioritizes devices in the order in which the computer looks for an operating system. Changed when a **system attempts to boot to an incorrect device**.
CPU Configuration or Advanced CPU Settings	Contains settings such as CPU TM function, which affects CPU throttle management (slowing the CPU when overheated); clock speed, which may not be changeable; PECI (Platform Environment Control Interface), which affects how the thermal sensors report the core temperature of your CPU; Max CPUID, which is used for compatibility with older operating systems; CPU Ratio control, which sets the CPU multipliers; and Vanderpool Technology, which is used with Intel virtualization.
Fan Control	Enables the configuration of case and/or CPU fans, including the ability to place the fans in silent mode or control fan speed.
Video Options	Enables configuration such as DVMT (dynamic video memory technology) to control video memory, aperture size (the amount of system RAM dedicated for the video adapter use), and which video controller is primary or secondary.
Onboard Device Configuration	Allows modification of devices built into the motherboard, such as audio, Bluetooth wireless, network, USB, or video ports.
* **Passwords**, Power on Password, Password Options, Supervisor Password, or User Password	Allows protection of the BIOS/UEFI menu options, specifically configuration of a password to enter the Setup program, to allow the computer to boot, or to distinguish between someone who can make minor changes such as alterations to **boot options** or date and time (user password), or someone who can view and change all Setup options (supervisor password). Other vendors might have the following levels: full access (all screens except supervisor password), limited access, view-only access, or no access.
* Virus Protection	Runs a small virus-scanning application located in BIOS/UEFI. Some operating systems and software updates require this option to be disabled for the upgrade to proceed.
Numlock On/Off	Allows default setting (enabled or disabled) of the Num Lock key option after booting.
USB Configuration	Allows modification of parameters such as support for legacy devices, USB speed options, and the number of ports to enable.
Hyper-Threading	Allows enabling/disabling of Hyper-Threading technology.
Integrated Peripherals (enabling/disabling devices and ports)	Allows enabling/disabling and configuration of motherboard-controlled devices such as PATA/SATA ports and integrated ports including USB, audio, and network. Sets the amount of RAM dedicated for video use. If the computer has an ample amount of RAM, increasing this setting can increase performance, especially in applications (such as games) that use high-definition graphics.
Advanced BIOS Options	Allows configuration of options such as CPU and memory frequencies, CPU, front side bus, north bridge, south bridge, chipset, and memory voltage levels.

Setup option	Description
Interface Configurations	Either indicates a category or lists an individual interface (for example, IDE Configuration, SATA Configuration, PCI Configuration, PCIe Configuration).
IDE Configuration	Allows manual configuration of IDE devices, such as PATA, hard drives, and optical drives.
SATA Configuration	Allows viewing of Serial ATA values assigned by BIOS/UEFI and changing of some of the related options, as well as RAID configuration.
PCI/PnP Configuration	Allows viewing and changing of PCI slot configuration, including IRQ and DMA assignments.
PCIe Configuration	Allows manual configuration of the PCIe version.
Devices	Allows configuration of USB, SATA, video, onboard devices, and PCI, where the **M.2 slot** might need to be enabled so the SSD will be recognized.
Virtualization Support, Virtualization Technology, or Secure Virtual Machine Mode	Enables/disables virtualization so the virtualization software can access additional hardware capabilities.
ACPI (Advanced Configuration and Power Interface)	Determines what happens if power is lost, power options if a call comes into a modem, and power options when directed by a PCI or PCIe device or by mouse/keyboard action.
Hardware Monitor	Allows viewing of CPU and motherboard temperature monitoring as well as the status of CPU, chassis, voltages, clock speeds, fan speeds, bus speeds, chassis intrusion detection/notification, and power supply fans.
* **Disable Execute Bit**, Execute Disable, or No Execute	Prevents executable code (viruses) from being executed from a specific marked memory area.
* **Drive Encryption**	Specifies that a secret key is used to encrypt the data on the hard drive. The computer will not boot without the correct password. The drive cannot be moved to another computer unless the correct password is entered.
* Trusted Platform Module (**TPM**)	Allows initialization and setting of a password for the TPM motherboard chip that generates and stores cryptographic keys.
* **LoJack**	Allows security settings to perform tasks such as locating the device, locking the device remotely, displaying an "if lost" message, or deleting data if stolen.
* **Intrusion Detection/ Notification** or Chassis Intrusion	Allows notification if the cover has been removed.
* **Secure Boot**	Checks every driver before launching the drivers and the operating system. Prevents an unauthorized operating system or software from loading during the boot process.
iGPU	Allows configuration of how much memory is allocated for the integrated GPU.
Built-in Diagnostics	Provides access to hardware components, the hard drive, memory, the battery, and other diagnostic tests.

* Security options

CHAPTER 4

System boots from the wrong device

If the computer tries to boot from or even succeeds in booting from the wrong device, change the Boot Sequence setting in BIOS/UEFI. Examples of boot devices include USB, hard drive, optical, and PXE (network boot or image) devices. It is also possible that an optical disc is in the drive or a non-bootable USB drive is attached, and that is the first boot option currently selected.

Figure 4.5 shows a sample BIOS/UEFI screen where you can set the administrator or user password. Note that this is not a Windows or corporate network password.

FIGURE 4.5 Password security menu

You must save your changes whenever you make configuration changes. Some manufacturers allow saving screen captures to a USB flash drive. Exiting without saving changes is a common mistake. The options available when exiting BIOS/UEFI depend on the model of BIOS/UEFI being used. Table 4.2 lists sample BIOS/UEFI exit options.

TABLE 4.2 Sample configuration change options

Option	Description
Save & Exit Setup	Saves all changes and leaves the Setup program.
Exit Without Saving	Closes without saving any changes that have been made. Used when changes have been made in error or more research is needed.
Load Fail-Safe Defaults	Sets the default settings programmed by the manufacturer. Used when unpredictable results occur after changing an option.
Load Optimized Defaults	Has more aggressive settings than the Load Fail-Safe Defaults option. This option is programmed by the manufacturer.

CMOS Memory

Settings changed in system BIOS/UEFI are recorded and stored in a complementary metal-oxide semiconductor (**CMOS**) found in the motherboard chipset (south bridge or I/O controller hub). CMOS is memory that requires a small amount of power that is provided by a small coin-sized lithium battery when the system is powered off. The memory holds the settings configured through BIOS/UEFI. Part of the BIOS/UEFI software routine checks CMOS for information about what components are supposed to be installed. These components are then tested as part of the POST routine. POST knows what hardware is *supposed* to be in the computer by obtaining the settings from CMOS. If the settings do not match, an error occurs.

When working on a computer with a POST error code, ensure that the user or another technician has not changed the configuration through the Setup program or removed or installed any hardware. Correct system Setup information is crucial for proper PC operation.

> **TECH TIP**
>
> **Incorrect Setup information causes POST errors**
>
> If you incorrectly input configuration information, POST error codes or error messages that would normally indicate a hardware problem appear.

The information inside CMOS memory can be kept there for several years, thanks to a small coin-sized lithium battery known as the **CMOS battery** or motherboard battery. When the battery dies, all configuration information in CMOS is lost and must be re-entered or relearned after the battery is replaced.

Motherboard Battery

The most common CMOS battery used today is a CR2032 lithium battery, which is about the size of a nickel. Figure 4.6 shows a photo of a lithium battery installed on a motherboard. If you cannot find the motherboard battery, refer to the motherboard or computer documentation for the exact location.

FIGURE 4.6   Motherboard battery

TECH TIP

Date, time, or settings reset

A first indication that a battery is failing is the loss of the date or time on the computer.

No battery lasts forever. High temperatures shorten a battery's life span, and so does providing power to devices that use batteries. Computer motherboard batteries last three to eight years.

TECH TIP

Using a battery recycling program

Many states have environmental regulations regarding battery disposal. Many companies also have battery recycling programs. The earth911.com website provides information regarding recycling and disposing of batteries and computer components by zip code or city/state.

Firmware Updates: Flashing the BIOS/UEFI

Firmware is a combination of software and hardware: It is software inside a chip (hardware). **Firmware updates** are needed to obtain new features and address security flaws that might arise. The flash BIOS/UEFI can be upgraded. The terms used for this process are "flashing the BIOS" and "updating the firmware." A computer may need a BIOS/UEFI upgrade for a variety of reasons, including the following:

> To provide support for new or upgraded hardware such as a processor or a faster USB port
> To provide support for a higher-capacity hard drive
> For increased virus protection
> For optional password protection
> To solve problems with the current version
> To provide a security patch
> To reduce the time a computer takes to boot

Viruses can infect the BIOS/UEFI, so you should keep the BIOS write-protected until you need to update it. Refer to the computer or motherboard documentation to find the exact procedure for removing the write protection and updating the BIOS/UEFI. The following procedure is one example of how to flash the BIOS/UEFI.

Step 1. After the system BIOS/UEFI upgrade is downloaded from the Internet, execute the update by double-clicking on the filename.

Step 2. Follow the directions on the screen or from the manufacturer.

Step 3. Reboot the computer.

At times, you might need to reset the BIOS and this might require changing a jumper. A **jumper** is a small piece of plastic that fits over pins. A jumper can be used to enable or disable a particular feature, such as resetting the system Setup settings or write-protecting the BIOS/UEFI. Figure 4.7 shows an enlarged jumper; the pins and jumper are much smaller in real life than they appear here.

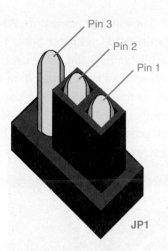

FIGURE 4.7   JP1 jumper block with pins 1 and 2 jumpered together

If flashing a laptop BIOS/UEFI, ensure that the laptop battery is fully charged or connect the laptop to AC power. If the BIOS is downloaded (and not saved locally), connect the laptop to a wired network to do the download to ensure connectivity during the download process. See Chapter 13, "Networking," for how to connect a device to a wired network.

Table 4.3 lists and describes some of the methods used to recover a BIOS/UEFI. Keep in mind that not all vendors provide a method of recovering a BIOS/UEFI if a flash update does not go well. A computer without an operational BIOS/UEFI cannot boot, and a new motherboard must be purchased. You should therefore have a good reason for flashing the BIOS/UEFI and research the method the motherboard uses before flashing the BIOS/UEFI.

TABLE 4.3   BIOS/UEFI recovery methods

Recovery method	Description
Recovery utility	A software program that can be accessed using specific keystrokes or that can be downloaded from the motherboard manufacturer's website.
Recovery jumper, switch, or push button	The recovery jumper, switch, or push button is commonly located on the motherboard.
Backup BIOS/UEFI	More expensive motherboards have a second BIOS/UEFI.
Read-only portion of the BIOS/UEFI	Some vendors have a read-only portion that is never changed. That way, if the update fails, the system can still boot to the menu.
Update to USB flash drive first	It may be possible to download a program to a USB flash drive along with the BIOS update. The computer is then booted from the USB drive to ensure that the update works.

Clearing CMOS

Sometimes BIOS/UEFI Setup settings get messed up and the best course is to start over. Resetting all settings to the factory defaults involves clearing the CMOS, which can be done through a menu option, a motherboard switch, a motherboard push button, or a back panel (where the ports are located) push button. Clearing the CMOS is not the same as flashing the BIOS/UEFI.

One specific CMOS setting that is sometimes cleared is the power-on password. Look at the computer or motherboard documentation for the exact procedure to remove the power-on password.

Some motherboards distinguish between supervisor and user passwords. Another possible security option is whether a password is needed every time the computer boots or only when someone tries to enter the Setup program. The options available in Setup and Advanced Setup are machine dependent due to the different chips and the different chipsets installed on the motherboard.

Figure 4.8 shows a jumper that is used only to reset the power-on password. If all else fails, you can try removing and then replacing the motherboard battery, but then all saved BIOS/UEFI settings stored in CMOS would be reset. Not all power-on passwords can be reset this way.

FIGURE 4.8   A CMOS password jumper

TECH TIP

Don't clear CMOS after a BIOS/UEFI update

Do not clear the CMOS immediately after upgrading the BIOS/UEFI. Power down the system and then power it back on before clearing CMOS data.

Other Configuration Parameters

Other possible parameters contained and set via the Setup program or operating system are interrupt requests (IRQs), input/output (I/O) addresses, direct memory access (DMA) channels, and memory addresses. These parameters are assigned to individual adapters and ports, such as disk controllers, and the USB, serial, parallel, and mouse ports. Sometimes these ports must be disabled through Setup in order for other devices or adapter ports to work. No matter how the parameters are assigned, collectively they are known as **system resources**. (These are not the same system resources that we refer to when we discuss Windows operating systems.) Let's take a look at three important system resources: IRQs, I/O addresses, and memory addresses. Table 4.4 briefly describes these resources.

TABLE 4.4 System resources

Type	Description
IRQ	A number assigned to an adapter, a port, or a device so that orderly communication can occur between it and the processor. For example, when a key is pressed at the same time the mouse is moved, the keyboard has the highest priority because of its IRQ number.
I/O address	A unique address that allows an adapter, a port, or a device to exchange data with a processor. These addresses enable the processor to distinguish among the devices with which it communicates.
Memory address	A unique address assigned to a memory chip installed anywhere in the system. The CPU uses these addresses when it accesses information inside the memory chip.

IRQ

Imagine being in a room of 20 students when 4 students want the teacher's attention. If all 4 students talk at once, the teacher is overloaded and unable to respond to the 4 individuals' needs. The teacher needs an orderly process to acknowledge each request, prioritize the requests (which student is first), and then answer each question. A similar situation arises when multiple devices want the attention of the CPU. For example, which device gets to go first if a key on the PS/2 keyboard is pressed and the PS/2 mouse is moved simultaneously? The answer lies in the interrupt request numbers assigned to the keyboard and the mouse. Every device requests permission to do something by interrupting the processor (which is similar to a student raising his hand). The CPU has a priority system to handle such situations.

TECH TIP

How IRQs are assigned to multiple-device ports

Ports such as USB and FireWire that support multiple devices require only one interrupt per port. For example, a single USB port can support up to 127 devices but needs only one IRQ for however many every devices connect to a USB hub.

PCI/PCIe Interrupts

When a PC first boots, the operating system discovers what AGP, PCI, and PCIe adapters and devices are present and the system resources each one needs. The operating system allocates resources such as an interrupt to each adapter/device. If the adapter or device has a ROM or flash BIOS chip installed that contains software that initializes and/or controls the device, the software is allowed to execute during the boot process.

PCI/PCIe devices use interrupts called INTA, INTB, INTC, INTD, and so on. These interrupts are commonly referred to as PCI interrupts. Some motherboard documentation uses the numbers 1, 2, 3, and 4 to replace the letters A, B, C, and D. Devices that use these interrupts are allowed to share them as necessary.

TECH TIP

What to do when a conflict occurs

If you suspect a resource conflict with a card, reboot the computer. The BIOS/UEFI and operating system will try to work things out. This may take multiple reboots. In addition, if an adapter is installed, moving it to another slot can resolve the situation.

PCI interrupts are normally assigned dynamically to the USB, PCI, PCIe, and SATA devices as the interrupts are needed. When an adapter needs an interrupt, the operating system finds an available interrupt (which may be currently used by another device that does not need it) and allows the requesting device to use it. During the boot process, the system BIOS/UEFI configures adapters. Windows examines the resources assigned by the BIOS/UEFI and uses those resources when communicating with a piece of hardware. Table 4.5 shows an example of how a motherboard might make PCI IRQ assignments.

TABLE 4.5   Sample PCI/PCIe interrupt assignments

Motherboard Component	A	B	C	D	E	F	G
PCI slot 1						used	
LAN		shared					
PCIe x16 1	shared						
PCIe x16 2	shared						
PCIe x1			shared				
USB 3.0 controller 1							shared
USB 2.0 controller 2		shared					
SATA controller 1		shared					
SATA controller 2				shared			

Starting with PCI version 2.2 and continuing on with PCIe, an adapter can use a different type of interrupt method called MSI or MSI-X. Message signaled interrupt (**MSI**) allows an interrupt to be delivered to the CPU using software and memory space. **MSI-X** supports more interrupts. This method was optional with PCI, but PCIe cards are required to support MSI and MSI-X.

Interrupts for integrated ports and some devices can be set through the BIOS/UEFI Setup program. Other adapter and device interrupts are set by using Device Manager in Windows or using various Control Panels. Technicians need to know how to use **Device Manager**, which shows the status of installed hardware. Figure 4.9 shows the various methods used to access Device Manager.

Figure 4.10 shows how IRQs appear in Device Manager after selecting *View > Resources by Type*. In Figure 4.10, notice that some interrupts have multiple entries. Multiple entries do not always indicate a resource conflict; they are allowed because devices may share IRQs. The next section goes into more detail on this issue.

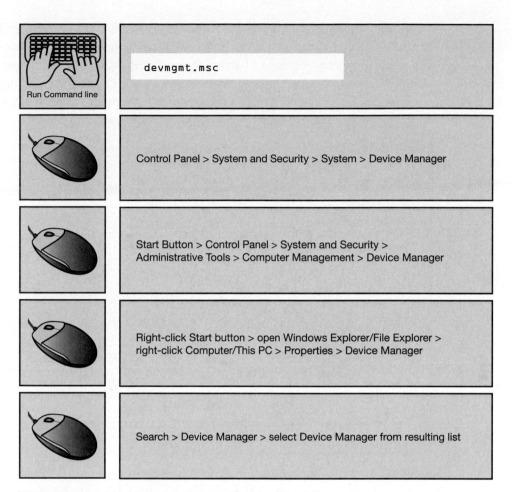

FIGURE 4.9   Methods used to access Device Manager

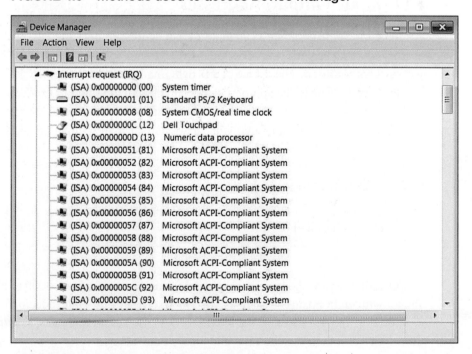

FIGURE 4.10   IRQs in Device Manager

In order to access specifics in Device Manager, use the *View > Devices by Type* option. Then expand any specific section, such as Network Adapters, right-click on a particular device or adapter and select Properties. Figure 4.11 shows an integrated network card's properties, which cannot be changed through Device Manager, as indicated by the Change Setting button being grayed out. (However, properties might be able to be modified through the system BIOS/UEFI Setup program.)

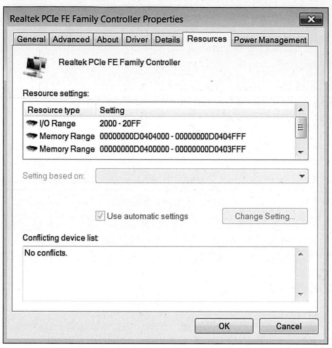

FIGURE 4.11   Resources tab in Device Manager

I/O (Input/Output) Addresses

An I/O address, also known as an input/output address or port address, enables a device and a processor to exchange data. An I/O address is like a mailbox number; it must be unique, or the postal worker gets confused. The device places data (mail) in the box for the CPU to pick up. The processor delivers the data to the appropriate device through the same I/O address (mailbox number). I/O addresses are simply addresses the processor can use to distinguish among the devices with which it communicates. Remember that you cannot deliver mail without an address.

TECH TIP

When is an I/O address needed?

Remember that every device must have a separate I/O address. Otherwise, the CPU cannot distinguish between installed devices.

I/O addresses are shown in hexadecimal format (base 16), from 0000 to FFFF. Some outputs are shown with eight positions, such as 00000000 to FFFFFFFF. Hexadecimal numbers are 0, 1, 2, 3, 4, 5, 6, 7, 8, and 9, as well as the letters A, B, C, D, E, and F. Table 4.6 shows decimal numbers 0 through 15 and their hexadecimal and binary equivalents.

TABLE 4.6 Decimal, binary, and hexadecimal numbers

Decimal	Hexadecimal	Binary	Decimal	Hexadecimal	Binary
0	0	0000	8	8	1000
1	1	0001	9	9	1001
2	2	0010	10	A	1010
3	3	0011	11	B	1011
4	4	0100	12	C	1100
5	5	0101	13	D	1101
6	6	0110	14	E	1110
7	7	0111	15	F	1111

An example of an I/O address is 390h. Normally, devices need more than one hexadecimal address location. The number of extra addresses depends on the individual device and what business it does with the processor. In manuals or documentation for a device or an adapter, a technician might see just one I/O address listed. I/O addresses can be set for some devices and ports through the BIOS/UEFI system Setup program, Device Control Panels.

Memory Addresses

A memory address is a unique address assigned to a memory chip installed anywhere in the system. The CPU uses a memory address when it accesses information inside the chip. Memory addresses are shown as a range of hexadecimal addresses in Device Manager (see Figure 4.12).

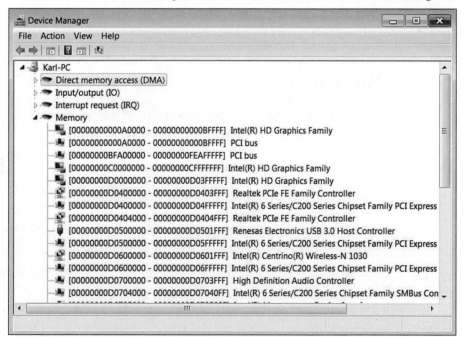

FIGURE 4.12 Memory addresses in Device Manager

Hardware Configuration Overview

Configuration of adapters and other hardware is easy if you follow the documentation and know how to obtain device drivers. Documentation for installation is frequently available on the Internet, as are many device drivers. Device drivers are also provided as part of the Windows update process.

The system BIOS/UEFI plays an important role as part of the startup routine. Not only does it check hardware for errors as part of POST, it also detects installed adapters and devices. The BIOS/UEFI, along with the operating system, determines what resources to assign to a device or an adapter. This information is stored in a part of CMOS known as the Extended System Configuration Data (**ESCD**) area. After information is configured in the ESCD area, the information stays there and does not have to be recomputed unless another device is added.

After resources are allocated, the BIOS looks in the saved settings of CMOS to determine which device it should look to first for an operating system. This part of the BIOS/UEFI routine is known as the bootstrap loader. If the BIOS/UEFI cannot locate an operating system in the first location specified in the saved settings, it tries the second device and continues on, looking to each device specified in the saved settings for an operating system. When an operating system is found, the operating system loads.

TECH TIP

What to do if the system does not recognize a new adapter

Plug and play (and sometimes a configuration utility supplied with a device) is used to configure system resources. Sometimes, a reboot is required for the changes to take effect. If the device does not work after the reboot, reboot the computer again (and possibly a third time) to allow the operating system to sort out the system resources. You can manually make changes if this does not work.

Installing Drivers

When installing hardware or an adapter in the Windows environment, a driver is required. Remember that a driver is software that allows the operating system to control hardware. The operating system detects the adapter or hardware installation and adds the device's configuration information to the registry. The **registry** is a central database in Windows that holds hardware information and other data. All software applications access the registry for configuration information instead of going to the adapter.

Windows comes with many drivers for common devices such as keyboards, mice, printers, and displays. Here are some processes used to install a driver:

> For a standard keyboard or mouse, Windows commonly includes the driver. When the device is attached, the driver loads, and the device configuration is added to the registry.
> Windows updates include updated device drivers. To determine if the latest Windows 7 or 8 updates are installed, search for and open the *Windows Update* Control Panel. Select the link to check for updates. Windows 10 does not have such a link, but you could access the *Start* button > *Settings* > *Update & Security* > *Windows Update* to update the operating system and see if there are any new device drivers not loaded, as shown in Figure 4.13, or if an operating system update is available.
> You might be prompted to install or search for the driver as part of the installation process. You may have to designate where the driver is located, such as on a CD that comes with the

hardware. You might also be required to download it and designate where the downloaded file is located.

> Use Device Manager to install a driver. Open *Device Manager* > expand the relevant particular hardware category > right-click the device > *Update Driver Software*, as shown in Figure 4.14.

> Use Windows Explorer (Windows 7) or File Explorer (Windows 8 or 10) to locate an executable file that comes with the hardware. Double-click on the Setup file provided to install software and/or a driver.

> Use the *Add a Device* (in Windows 7 or 8) or *Add Devices* (in Windows 10) link.

> Use the Add Hardware Wizard by typing `hdwwiz` in the Windows search textbox.

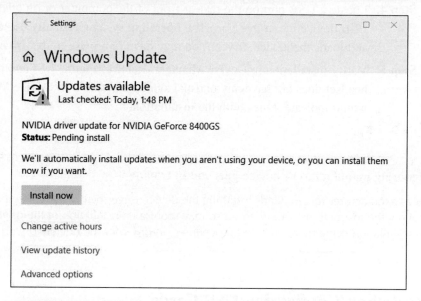

FIGURE 4.13   Windows 10 driver that needs to be updated

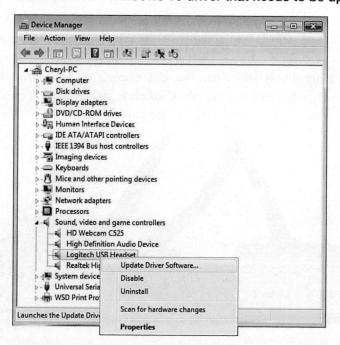

FIGURE 4.14   Update Driver Software option in Device Manager

Installing a USB Device

To install a USB device, perform the following steps:

Step 1. Power on the computer.

Step 2. Optionally, install the USB device's software. Note that some manufacturers require that software and/or device drivers be installed before the USB device is attached.

Step 3. Optionally, power on the device. Not all USB devices have external power adapters or a power button because they receive power from the USB bus.

Step 4. Locate a USB port on the rear or front of the computer or on a USB hub. Plug the USB device into a free port. The operating system normally detects the USB device and loads the device driver. You may have to browse to the driver.

Step 5. Verify installation in Device Manager. Refer to Figure 4.14 and notice that the USB headset does not have any unusual symbols beside it in Device Manager; symbols would indicate issues with the installation.

TECH TIP

Ignoring manufacturer's advice gets you in trouble

If a manufacturer recommends installing the device driver before attaching the USB device, follow the instructions! Failure to do so may require uninstallation of the driver and then reinstallation using recommended procedures, in order for the device to work properly.

Installing/Configuring USB Cards

Additional USB ports can be added by using a USB hub or connecting a **USB expansion card**, which is a metal plate that has additional USB ports that connect to motherboard pins. The plate inserts where an expansion card goes, but it does not have connectors that fit into an expansion slot. The metal plate simply slides into the spot where a card would normally go. Figure 4.15 shows one of these plates; this one has two USB ports and an eSATA port. You can also review Figure 2.29 to see how to attach the cables to the motherboard.

FIGURE 4.15   USB and eSATA bracket/ports that connect to motherboard pins

Keep in mind that if a motherboard does not have any pins, you can add more USB ports by purchasing a PCI or PCIe USB adapter with multiple ports. The adapter might not have the capability of providing power unless the adapter supports having a power cable from the power supply attached to the card.

It is possible to install a USB card to add additional USB ports to a computer. USB ports are powered; therefore, a USB card normally has a place to connect power. If the power supply does not have the appropriate power connector, a power adapter may have to be purchased. Always follow the manufacturer's instructions when installing an adapter to provide additional USB ports. Generic instructions follow:

Step 1. Power down the computer and remove the power cord.

Step 2. Remove the computer cover. Locate an empty expansion slot. You may have to remove a screw or raise a retaining bar to be able to use the expansion slot (see Figure 4.16).

Step 3. Using proper antistatic procedures (see Chapter 5, "Disassembly and Power"), ground yourself or use antistatic gloves.

Step 4. Optionally, attach a power connector to the adapter.

Step 5. Ensure that the proper expansion slot is being used and insert the card firmly into the slot (see Figure 4.17). Ensure that the card is fully inserted by pressing firmly down on the adapter and visually inspecting it afterward. The card should be at a 90-degree angle from the PC. It should not tilt at either end. Ensure that the card fits snuggly in the expansion slot.

Step 6. Lower the expansion bar or attach a screw, if needed.

Step 7. Reinstall the computer cover, reattach the power cord, and power on the computer. Install drivers as necessary.

Step 8. Test by attaching a USB device to each port.

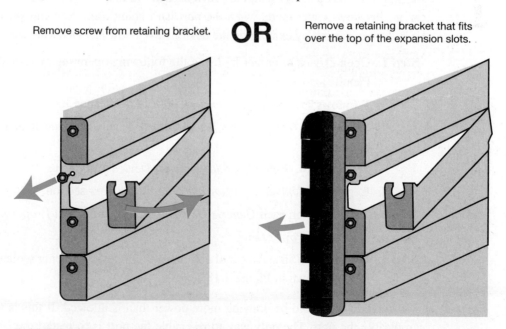

Remove screw from retaining bracket.   **OR**   Remove a retaining bracket that fits over the top of the expansion slots.

FIGURE 4.16   Adapter screw or retainer bar

FIGURE 4.17   Inserting an adapter directly into an expansion slot

Troubleshooting USB

To troubleshoot USB device problems, check the obvious first: the cabling and power. Verify whether any USB device that plugs into a USB hub works. If no devices work, swap the hub or attach to a different USB port. If some hub ports work and some do not, attach an external power source to the hub, change its configuration if necessary, and retest the devices. Restart the computer and retest the USB device.

USB 3.1 ports can provide power at different levels: 2 A at 5 V (10 W), 5 A at 12 V (60 W), and 5 A at 20 V (100 W). USB 3.0 ports can provide 900 mA (4.5 W) of 5 V power; both 3.x versions provide more power than the previous USB versions (500 mA/2.5 W). Note that a 3.x port can go into low-power mode when the port isn't being used. You can verify how much power a USB device is using by examining the device in Windows Device Manager, following these steps:

Step 1.   Open *Device Manager* by using the following operating system–dependent Control Panel:

   Windows 7: *System and Security* Control Panel. Then locate and select *Device Manager*.

   Windows 8: *Hardware and Sound* Control Panel. Then locate and select *Device Manager*.

   Windows 10: *Right-click Start button > Device Manager*.

Step 2.   Expand the *Universal Serial Bus Hub Controllers* section.

Step 3.   Right-click on each *Generic USB Hub* option and select *Properties*.

Step 4.   Access the *Power* tab.

Step 5.   Locate the USB device and note how much power is being requested of the USB port/ hub, as shown in Figure 4.18.

A USB device could be drawing more power than is allowed. If this is the case, the computer can disable the port. The only way to re-enable the port is to restart the computer. If a device is using less than 50 mA of power, the USB port never becomes active. Try plugging the USB device into a different USB port or verifying that the device works on another computer.

FIGURE 4.18   USB hub power requirements

A USB device requires a driver that may be loaded automatically. An incorrect or outdated driver could be loaded and causing problems. The following list can also help when troubleshooting USB devices:

> Use Device Manager to ensure that a hub is functioning properly.
> Ensure that the BIOS/UEFI firmware is up-to-date.
> Use Device Manager to ensure that no USB device has an IRQ assigned and shared with another non-USB device.
> USB devices sometimes do not work in Safe mode and require hardware support configured through the BIOS/UEFI.
> Sometimes a USB device stops working on a hub that has an external power source. In such a case, remove the hub's external power source and retest.
> If a self-powered USB hub gets its power disconnected, the hub becomes a bus-powered hub and outputs only lower power on each port. Reattach the power cord or remove the hub and then reattach it.
> If a newly attached USB device reports that it is attached but does not work properly, upgrade the driver.
> Do not connect USB devices to a computer that is in standby mode or sleep mode. Doing so may prevent the computer from coming out of standby mode.
> For intermittent USB device problems, disable power management to see if doing so solves the problem.
> Test a device connected to a USB hub by connecting it directly to a USB port that has nothing else attached. The problem may be caused by other USB devices or a USB hub.
> Remove the USB device's driver and reinstall it. Sometimes you must reboot the computer to give the new drivers priority over the general-purpose drivers.
> If a USB device is running slowly, try attaching it to a different port that has fewer devices connected to the same port.
> Verify that the USB port is enabled in BIOS/UEFI if integrated into the motherboard or attached to the motherboard through an adapter cable.
> Refer to the USB device manufacturer's website for specific troubleshooting details.

Installing an eSATA Card

A Serial ATA (SATA) port allows connection of a SATA storage device such as a hard drive or an optical drive. External SATA (eSATA) ports allow connectivity of storage devices outside the computer or laptop. If a computer has no eSATA ports or does not have enough of them, two options exist. The first option is that you can install an **eSATA bracket**, as shown in Figure 4.19. Notice that SATA cables are simply attached to the backs of the ports. Each SATA cable attaches to a port on the motherboard. For the bracket shown, the motherboard needs to have two available SATA ports in order to have two external ports.

FIGURE 4.19   eSATA bracket with cables

The second option is to have a PCIe **eSATA card**, as shown in Figure 4.20. Notice that this card doesn't have any cables that come with it, as an eSATA bracket does, and it has ports at the top of the card as well as external ones. You could attach a SATA cable from the top of this card to an internal device or attach an eSATA cable from one of the external ports to an external eSATA device.

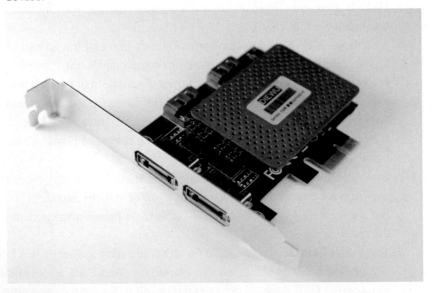

FIGURE 4.20   eSATA PCIe card

To install an eSATA card or bracket, perform the following steps:

Step 1. Power off the computer and unplug it.

Step 2. Remove the computer cover and locate an unused expansion slot. You may have to re-move a screw or raise a retaining bar to be able to use the expansion slot.

Step 3. Remove the slot cover.

Step 4. Using proper antistatic procedures (see Chapter 5), ground yourself or use antistatic gloves.

Step 5. Ensure that the proper expansion slot is being used. Insert the card firmly into the expansion slot. If only a bracket is being used, insert the bracket between the motherboard and the back of the case where there is an empty expansion slot.

Step 6. Lower the expansion bar or attach a screw to keep the card or bracket firmly in place.

Step 7. If a bracket is being used, attach each SATA cable to an available SATA motherboard port. Make note of which SATA port is being used as each one may need to be enabled within BIOS/UEFI.

Step 8. Reinstall the computer cover, reattach the power cord, and power on the computer. Go into BIOS/UEFI and enable the appropriate SATA ports as necessary. Install any software that came with the card.

Step 9. Test by attaching an eSATA device to each port.

Installing a Network Interface Card

Almost all devices connect to a wired or wireless network by using a **network interface card** (NIC). Many devices have wired and wireless NICs built into the device, but if such a NIC fails, a new NIC must be installed, such as the Ethernet NIC shown in Figure 4.21.

FIGURE 4.21   Ethernet network interface card

You must take several steps as part of the installation process before connecting to the network:

Step 1. Determine that an appropriate expansion slot is available.

Step 2. Remove the computer cover and locate an unused expansion slot. Remove the slot cover.

Step 3. Ground yourself and ensure that the proper expansion slot is being used. Insert the card firmly into the expansion slot. Secure the card.

Step 4. Reinstall the computer cover, reattach power, and power on the computer. Download and install the latest driver.

Step 5. Give the computer a unique name and optionally join a workgroup or domain.

Step 6. Configure TCP/IP addressing information, as described in Chapter 13.

Video Overview

Video quality is very important to computer users. A display is one of the most expensive computer components. Technicians must look at video as a subsystem that consists of the display, the electronic circuits that send the display instructions, and the cable that connects them. Note that the video electronics can also be an **onboard video card** (built into the motherboard). Figure 4.22 illustrates a computer video subsystem.

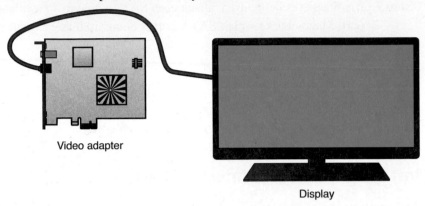

Video adapter

Display

FIGURE 4.22   Video subsystem

Video Cards

Using millions of colors, motion, sound, and video combined, computer video subsystems have made dramatic technological advances. The **video card** (also known as a video adapter) controls most of the display output. Video cards are commonly installed into PCIe expansion slots.

A PCIe video card may require either a 6- or 8-pin connector from the power supply. A 6-pin cable can provide an additional 75 W of power, while an 8-pin cable can provide an additional 150 W. A PCIe video card could require multiple power cables.

> **TECH TIP**
>
> **Add a video card**
>
> Even if a motherboard has an onboard video card, the integrated port can be disabled through BIOS/UEFI and an **add-on video card** can still be installed in order to have higher quality video output.

On the motherboard, the processor and the chipset are responsible for the speed at which data travels to and from the video adapter. It is possible to speed up video transfer to the monitor by upgrading the chipset (motherboard), the processor, or the video adapter to a faster interface. In addition, special features on the video adapter can also speed up video transfer.

A video adapter has its own processor, called the graphics processing unit (**GPU**). Other names include video processor, video coprocessor, or video accelerator. The GPU assists in video communication between the video adapter and the system processor. GPUs are also found in gaming systems, smartphones, tablets, and laptops. Figure 4.23 shows a video adapter with a video processor. GPUs commonly have fans and/or heat sinks attached.

FIGURE 4.23   Video card with GPU

The video processor controls many video functions on the video adapter that would otherwise be handled by the motherboard processor. Any time information is processed on the adapter rather than on the motherboard processor, performance increases. When signals pass to the motherboard processor through an expansion slot, performance is hampered. Most video cards today contain GPUs because video is one of the biggest bottlenecks in a computer system.

Video Memory

One of the most important functions of a video processor is to transfer data to and from a video adapter's memory. Memory on a video adapter can be just like motherboard memory, including DDR2, DDR3, and DDR4, as well as specialized video graphics double data rate (**GDDR**) modules, such as GDDR2, GDDR3, GDDR4, GDDR5, and GDDR6.

TECH TIP

How much video memory?

The amount of video adapter memory determines the number of colors available at a specific resolution.

The objective is to get data in and out of the video card memory chips as quickly as possible for a reasonable cost. An adapter must handle a large amount of data due to the increasing number of pixels and colors displayed. Ample, fast memory on a video card allows higher resolutions and more colors to appear on the screen, without the screen appearing to flicker.

Video memory can be integrated into the card as rectangular chips located around or very close to the GPU (see Figure 4.24). Video memory can also be installed into memory expansion slots on the card.

FIGURE 4.24   Video memory close to (along the side and top) the GPU

Video RAM is RAM that is used for video exclusively. When this RAM is insufficient, motherboard RAM is used. When motherboard RAM is being used in addition to video card RAM, the amount of motherboard RAM being used is known as **shared system memory**, or shared video memory. You see this when you examine the video display properties. Some systems allow customization through system BIOS/UEFI or a special Control Panel provided by the video adapter manufacturer. Common system BIOS/UEFI options to control shared system memory include AGP Aperture Size and Onboard Video Memory Size. Figure 4.25 shows the properties of a video card that has 512 MB of RAM installed (listed next to Dedicated Video Memory). The Shared System Memory amount is how much motherboard RAM is allowed to be used by the video card (and the operating system and the applications).

FIGURE 4.25   Shared system memory for video

TECH TIP

Checking how much video memory you have

The `dxdiag` command can be used to examine video properties. Otherwise, for Windows 7/8, in the *Display* Control Panel, select *Change Display Settings* link > *Advanced Settings* > *Adapter* tab. For Windows 10, use the *Start* button > *Settings* > *System* > *Display* > *Advanced Display Settings* link > *Display Adapter Properties* > *Adapter* tab.

Installing a Video Adapter

Before installing a video adapter, do your homework:

> Make sure you have the correct interface type and an available motherboard slot. PCIe is the most common, but AGP can still be found.
> Gather tools, if needed. Use an antistatic strap or grounding techniques. You may need a screwdriver to remove the slot-retaining bracket and to re-insert the screw that holds the adapter.
> Download the latest drivers for the video adapter. Make sure the adapter has a driver for the operating system you are using.
> Ensure that the power supply can supply enough power when the adapter is added. Some high-end video adapters require a PCIe 6- or 8-pin or AGP Molex power connector. Some PCIe cards can use a power cable adapter that converts two Molex power connectors to the PCIe power connector. Other video cards can receive adequate power (up to 75 W) through the PCIe expansion slot.

TECH TIP

Installing a new video adapter

When you install a new video adapter, if it does not work, disable the onboard video port by accessing system BIOS/UEFI Setup.

Before installing the adapter, power off the computer and unplug it. For best results and to prevent component damage, use an antistatic wrist strap. Access the motherboard and remove any previously installed video adapters (if performing an upgrade). If no video adapters are installed, access the expansion slot.

Sometimes with a tower computer, it is best to lay the computer on its side to insert the video adapter properly. Line up the video adapter's metal connectors with the interface slot. Push the adapter into the expansion slot. Make sure the adapter is flush with the expansion slot. Figure 4.26 shows a video adapter being installed in a tower. Notice that a cable from the motherboard S/PDIF out connector attaches to this video card for audio output. Make sure sections of the adapter's gold connectors are not showing and that the card is not skewed. Re-install the retaining screw, if necessary. Connect the monitor to the external video connector. Power on the monitor and computer.

A video card has a set of drivers or software to enable the adapter to work to its full potential. Individual software drivers from the manufacturer provide system compatibility and performance boosts. The Internet is used to obtain current video drivers from adapter manufacturers. Be sure to use the proper video driver for the operating system. Always follow the adapter manufacturer's instructions for installing drivers.

FIGURE 4.26   Video card installation

Troubleshooting Video

As with other troubleshooting, when troubleshooting a video problem, check simple solutions first. Do not assume anything! Verify that the monitor's power light is on. If it is not, check the power cable connectors, surge strip, and wall outlet. Verify that the brightness and contrast settings have not been changed. Check or disable power-saving features while you're troubleshooting. Double-check the monitor cable connected to the video port. Use the built-in diagnostics that some monitors have. Ask the user if any new or upgraded software or hardware has recently been installed, including an operating system automatic update.

> **TECH TIP**
>
> **Keep in mind the video system**
>
> If a piece of video hardware is defective, then it is the display, adapter, motherboard port, or cable. If replacement is necessary, always attempt the easiest solution first.

Many video problems involve a software driver or improperly configured settings. Anything that is problematic on the display can be a result of a bad video driver, an incompatible driver, an incorrect driver, or an incompatible system BIOS/UEFI version. The best way to be sure is to download the exact driver for the monitor and the display adapter/port from the Internet or obtain it from the manufacturer. Some troubleshooting tips related to video follow. Remember that these are only suggestions. Research and, if necessary, contact the manufacturer of the monitor, motherboard, or video adapter for specific instructions on troubleshooting the equipment.

Common video problems include the following:

> Bent or broken video pins can cause **incorrect color patterns** and/or **distorted images**. Carefully examine the monitor's cable ends. The cable may appear to correctly plug into the connector, even when the pins are bent and do not fit properly into the connector. If you find one or more bent pins, carefully use needle-nose pliers to gently straighten the pins.

> If you suspect a video driver problem, expand the *Display Adapters* section of *Device Manager*. Locate the video card and look for any visual indications of problems. Right-click (or press and momentarily hold) on the video adapter > *Properties*. On the *General* tab, check the Device status section to see whether Windows believes the device to be working properly. Check with the video card manufacturer to see whether there is a video driver update for the Windows version being used.

> If you suspect a video driver problem in Windows 7, boot to safe mode, which uses a standard generic video driver to see if the problem is resolved and to determine whether it is a software driver problem. In Window 8/10, hold down (⬆Shift) while restarting and select the *Enable Low-Resolution Video* option.

> In Windows 7, if the computer boots in **VGA mode**, the resolution could be set to the wrong setting, but most likely, there is an issue with the video driver. Another symptom of the resolution being set incorrectly is **oversized images and icons**.

> **Dead pixels** are pixels that do not light up on an LCD screen due to defective transistors. Dead pixels can be (and usually are) present on LCDs—even new ones. Research the LCD manufacturing standard from a particular vendor for dead pixels before purchasing an LCD. LCD panels with dead pixels can still be used and are common. If there are too many dead pixels, it may be necessary to replace the display. Note that LCDs can also have **bright spots** when pixels are permanently stuck in the on position.

> Set the display to the native resolution (that is, the resolution for which the LCD was made).

> If a cursor appears momentarily before the computer boots and then nothing is displayed or a distorted display appears, check for a video driver problem.

> It is possible that a computer may start normally without being able to see the Windows startup screen. Sometimes a **dim image** seems to be evident or no image is displayed, but you can hear the hard drive. In such a case, reset the display to the factory defaults and then try adjusting the brightness and contrast. If these steps do not help, the inverter (the component that converts DC to AC for the backlight) most likely needs to be replaced. This is a commonly replaced component in an LCD. Note that if outputting to a projector that shows a dim image, you might have to adjust the projector brightness/contrast, clean a dirty lens, or the lamp might be failing.

> If a display shows a **flickering image** or appears and then disappears, check the video cable. Horizontal or vertical stripes on the screen are also signs of this problem. Flickering can also be caused by an incorrect refresh rate setting, which can be changed in Windows 7, 8, and 10 in the *Display* Control Panel by selecting *Change Display Settings > Advanced Settings > Adapter* tab. Flickering can also be caused by proximity to other radio signals, video devices, speakers, refrigerators, and fluorescent lighting. In such a situation, move the monitor or offending device.

TECH TIP

What to do if a display goes black, red, dim, or pink
Check cabling. The backlight bulb might be faulty. Try swapping monitors.

> If you change the resolution or number of colors and the output is distorted, change the settings back to the original settings, if possible. If that is not possible, in Windows 7, reboot the computer and use *Advanced Options* and select *Safe Mode* or use the *Last Known Good Configuration* option. In Windows 8 or 10, select *Settings > Change PC Settings > Update and Recovery > Recovery > Restart Now*, and then after restart, select *Troubleshoot > Advanced Options* and try *Automatic Repair* first; if that does not work, return to *Advanced Options >*

Startup Settings > Restart > Safe Mode; if that does not work, use the *Enable Low-Resolution Video* option after the restart.

> If **distorted geometry** occurs (see Figure 4.27) or the screen is not centered correctly, check the video cables or reset the display to the factory default settings.

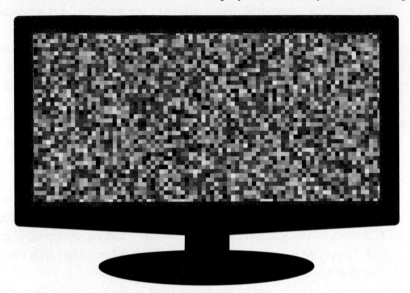

FIGURE 4.27   Geometric distortion

TECH TIP

What to do if a display is dark

Check to see whether the computer is in sleep mode or won't come out of sleep mode. Check the video cable. Hold down the power button and try restarting. Check the power management settings.

> Windows is not supposed to hang during the boot process because of video driver incompatibility. Instead, the operating system loads a default video driver. If video is a problem while working in Windows, use the *Safe Mode, Last Known Good Configuration*, or *Enable Low-Resolution Video* option and then load the correct driver. You can also use the *Driver Rollback* option if a new driver has just been installed.

> Check the monitor settings to verify that the monitor detection is accurate. In Windows 7/8, in the *Display* Control Panel, select *Display Settings > Settings* tab. In Windows 10, use the *Settings > System > Display* link.

> If a blue screen of death (BSOD) appears, log any error message or code that appears (see Figure 4.28) and try rebooting the computer. Do not take a hammer to it. Researching the error is a much more productive way of repairing the computer. You can also boot to safe mode and reload a video driver from there.

TECH TIP

No image on the screen?

Check the following: Is the video card inserted fully into the slot? Are the cables properly attached? Is the adapter supported by the motherboard? Is the auxiliary power attached to the adapter? Is sufficient power coming from the power supply? Is the driver properly installed?

as been shut down to prevent damage

s stop error screen,
ears again, follow

ftware is properly installed.
ardware or software manufacturer

ny newly installed hardware
such as caching or shadowing.
 disable components, restart
d Startup Options, and then

0xFFFFFA80042BCB30,0xFFFFFA80042BCC40,0

FIGURE 4.28   BSOD

> If horizontal or vertical lines appear, check for loose connections and bent or broken pins. Use built-in diagnostics, if available. Reset to factory default settings.

> An LCD or plasma display that has been left on and unchanged for too long may show a **burn-in**, image imprint, or ghost image. In such a case, try turning off the display for a few hours. If that does not work, create an all-white image in a graphics program and use it as the screen saver. Turn the display brightness to low and leave the monitor on for a few hours.

TECH TIP

See or smell smoke or sparks?

Disconnect the display, if possible, from the power source. Use an appropriate fire extinguisher as necessary. Report the incident.

> Any monitor that won't come out of power saver mode might need one of the following done: (1) update the video driver, (2) flash the system BIOS/UEFI, (3) check the BIOS/UEFI power settings to ensure that ACPI is enabled so Windows settings can be used, or (4) determine whether the problem is being caused by the monitor or the port. Connect a different monitor. If the video port is built into the motherboard, disable it through BIOS/UEFI and insert a video card; otherwise, replace the video adapter to see if the port/adapter is causing the problem. Most likely it is a driver or a Windows/BIOS ACPI setting problem.

> If video performance appears to be slow, adjust the monitor to a lower resolution or a lower number of colors (or both). An exercise at the end of this chapter provides step-by-step instructions. Check the video adapter driver to determine whether it matches the installed adapter or whether it is generic. Obtain the specific adapter's latest driver from the Internet.

> If the computer is on for a while, but then the display has issues or you have an **overheat shutdown** situation, check for overheating in the computer or on the video adapter. Check for adequate power output from the power supply.

> An **artifact** is something that appears on your screen that should not appear, such as green dotted or vertical lines, colored lines on one side of the screen, tiny glitters, or an unusual pattern. If the display shows an artifact, check for an overheating GPU, insufficient air flow, or a problematic video driver. An integrated video chip may also be going bad.

> If Windows does not show the *Multiple Displays* option, then Windows does not recognize the second monitor. Check *Device Manager* for possible driver issues. Check cabling. Check the adapter. Note that not all adapters work with one another, so there may be a conflict between the two adapters. If an adapter and a motherboard port are used, the computer may not support this configuration.

> For display problems involving projectors, check the correct input using the projector remote control. For presentation software, the Display Control Panel may need to have the *Duplicate the Display* option so that the output can be seen on the screen. Ensure that the projector light shows (that is, that the bulb is good). If flickering occurs, check cabling.

TECH TIP

Monitor disposal rules

Many states mandate that specific disposal procedures be followed for monitors.

Troubleshooting Configurations

The following are possible indications that a device is not working:

> A new device is installed and the new device or a previously installed device does not work.
> The computer locks up or restarts when performing a specific function, such as when playing or recording audio.
> The computer hangs during startup or shutdown.
> A device does not work properly or fails to work at all.

TECH TIP

Verifying hardware with Device Manager

A small down arrow by a device's icon in Device Manager means the device is disabled, and an exclamation point (!) on a yellow field usually indicates a resource conflict or driver problem. An "i" indicates that the Use Automatic Settings feature is not being used for the device, and resources were manually configured.

In Device Manager, if an exclamation point (!) appears, the hardware device is not working properly, and you should check for cabling issues, resource conflicts, and configuration issues. If a yellow question mark appears, Windows does not recognize the device, and you can try one of the following:

> Perform a Windows update to ensure that you have the latest drivers, security updates, and fixes.
> Manually update the driver by right-clicking the device in *Device Manager* and selecting *Properties* > *Driver* tab > *Update Driver*. You can download this driver from the device manufacturer's website or let Windows try to find the driver.

TECH TIP

Using the General tab for troubleshooting

On the *General* tab of the Properties dialog for any adapter or port, check the *Device Status* section for any error codes, including those for resource conflicts.

With any Device Manager issue, you can right-click the device and select *Properties*. Look at the *General* tab to see if there are error codes.

Configuration problems can also be associated with specific BIOS/UEFI settings. Table 4.7 lists some problems and how you might be able to solve them.

TABLE 4.7 Troubleshooting BIOS/UEFI-related issues

Issue	Things to try
Message appears stating that the date and time are not set, the clock is not set, or all saved BIOS/UEFI settings are lost, or unexpected issues occur in more than one application.	Check the date and time through the operating system. Check the date and time setting in BIOS/UEFI to see if it matches. Replace the motherboard CMOS battery.
Cannot configure a system for virtualization or XP mode.	Enable virtualization in BIOS/UEFI.
Attached device does not work.	If the device connects to a motherboard port, ensure that the port is not disabled in BIOS/UEFI. Ensure that the device connects to the correct port, including a possible port on an adapter instead of the motherboard. If the device connects to a port on an adapter that is the same type of port as one found on the motherboard, the integrated port may need to be disabled in BIOS/UEFI.
System locks up sporadically.	If overclocking, put the system back to its original settings.
System is slow to boot or boots from the wrong device.	Check the BIOS/UEFI boot order setting.

SOFT SKILLS: A GOOD TECHNICIAN PRACTICE: CHANGING ONLY ONE THING AT A TIME

The least effective type of computer technician is a "gun slinger." The term *gun slinger* brings to mind images of Wild West ruffians who had shooting matches with other gangsters in the town's main street. Gun slingers drew their guns frequently and with little provocation. They did not put much thought into their method or consider other possible resolutions. You must strive *not* to be this type of technician.

A gun slinger technician changes multiple things simultaneously. For example, if there is no display on the output, the technician might swap out the monitor, disable the onboard video port, add a new video adapter, power on the computer, and, when output appears, call the problem "solved." If a computer problem is repaired using such a technique, the technician never knows exactly what solved the problem. A gun slinger technician might get frustrated easily because it is easy to forget what has been tried when multiple things have been tried simultaneously—and it is almost impossible to know which one worked (see Figure 4.29).

FIGURE 4.29   A gun slinger technician in action

A good technician, on the other hand, makes a list of symptoms (even if it is simply a mental list) followed by a list of things to try. Then the technician tries the possible solutions, starting with the simplest one (the one that costs the least amount of time to the computer user). The technician documents each step. After each approach that does not fix the problem, the technician puts the system back to the original configuration before attempting the next possible solution. This method keeps the technician focused on what has been tested, and if another technician takes over, the steps do not have to be repeated. Best of all, when one of the possible solutions fixes the problem, the exact solution is known.

Gun slinger technicians do not learn as fast as other technicians because they do not determine the real causes of problems. Each time they are presented with a problem similar to one they have seen in the past, gun slinger technicians use the same haphazard troubleshooting method. These technicians are actually dangerous to an organization because they are not good at documenting what they have done and determining exactly what fixes a particular problem. A good computer technician should methodically troubleshoot a problem by making only one change at a time and reverting the change if the change does not solve the problem. Furthermore, the technician needs to document the issue and its resolution for future problems.

Chapter Summary

> The BIOS/UEFI is used to enable/disable, configure, and troubleshoot motherboard components, expansion slots, and ports, and it sets power-on and BIOS passwords. When the computer is off, a motherboard battery holds saved settings in CMOS.

> An updated type of BIOS is BIOS/UEFI, which allows the use of a mouse and a graphical environment. Security options, support for larger hard drives, antivirus software, remote management, and utilities may also be included.

> Each port and card uses system resources such as interrupts, I/O addresses, and memory addresses.

> System resources can be viewed and changed using Device Manager. Specific Device Manager codes and messages can assist in troubleshooting conflicts.

> A USB or eSATA card or bracket can be added to a computer to provide additional ports.

> If you are not using the onboard video port for dual displays, disable the port in BIOS/UEFI. Note that some adapters will not work when you disable the onboard port and that BIOS/UEFI may automatically disable the port.

> Video memory can be separate from motherboard RAM, can be shared system memory, or can be a combination of both. The amount of available memory affects the maximum resolution and the number and depth of colors that can be seen.

> When a computer shows a blank screen, check the power source, the display cable, the power cable, and the surge protector/UPS. Try rebooting to safe mode or select the Windows 8/10 Enable Low Resolution Video boot option.

> If an artifact appears, check for heat problems.

> If an LCD or plasma display has burn-in, try turning off the display for a few hours. Create an all-white image in a graphics program and use it as the screen saver. Turn the display brightness to low and leave the monitor on for a few hours.

> If geometric distortion occurs or the screen is not centered correctly, check video cables or reset the display to the factory default settings.

> If the computer boots in VGA mode, check the video driver.

> If the display image is dim or blank, try adjusting the brightness controls and contrast. Reset to the factory defaults. Replace the inverter.

> If the display flickers, check the video cable or refresh rate. Check for external radio or other interference sources.

CHAPTER 4

A+ CERTIFICATION EXAM TIPS

✓ A lot of questions from both exams can come from this chapter, especially in the troubleshooting areas. Review the troubleshooting bullets. Research issues on the Internet and read people's postings. Their stories and frustrations (and successes) will stick in your mind and help you with the exam.

✓ Using at least one computer, go through the BIOS/UEFI menus. Review what types of things can be configured through BIOS/UEFI. Important settings include the following: Boot Options, Firmware Updates, Security Settings (Passwords, Drive Encryption, TPM, LoJack, and Secure Boot), and Interface Configurations. Know the purpose of and how to change out the CMOS battery.

✓ Be able to install and configure the following: video card (onboard and add-on card), network interface card (NIC), and USB/eSATA bracket or card.

✓ Know what to do if a system tries to boot to an incorrect device or how you can use the indicator lights when troubleshooting.

✓ Recognize symptoms and what to do when the following video problems occur: system booting into VGA mode; no image on the screen; an overheat shutdown situation; dead pixels; artifacts; incorrect color patterns; a dim, flickering, or distorted image; distorted geometry; burn-in; or oversized images and icons. Note that projector troubleshooting of similar issues like dim display, no image on the screen, flickering artifacts, or distorted geometry are also possible.

✓ Review the Setup options listed in Table 4.1 and what each of these options controls.

Key Terms

add-on video card 140
artifact 148
boot option 120
bright spots 145
Built-in Diagnostics 121
burn-in 147
CMOS 123
CMOS battery 123
dead pixel 145
Device Manager 128
dim image 145
Disable Execute Bit 121
distorted geometry 146
distorted image 144
Drive Encryption 121
eSATA bracket 138
eSATA card 138
ESCD 132
firmware updates 124

flash BIOS 118
flickering image 145
GDDR 141
GPU 140
I/O address 127
incorrect color pattern 144
indicator lights 116
Interface Configuration 121
Intrusion Detection/
Notification 121
IRQ 127
jumper 124
LoJack 121
M.2 slot 121
memory address 127
MSI 128
MSI-X 128
network interface card 139
onboard video card 140

overheat shutdown 148
oversized images and icons 145
Passwords 120
POST 116
registry 132
Secure Boot 121
security settings 120
Setup 116
shared system memory 142
system attempts to boot to an
incorrect device 120
system resources 126
TPM 121
UEFI 116
USB expansion card 134
VGA mode 145
video card 140
Virtualization Support 121

Review Questions

1. When would a technician flash a BIOS/UEFI?

    a. When the date and time start to be incorrect

    b. When a port or motherboard component does not perform at its maximum potential

    c. When the driver for a motherboard port is out of date

    d. When the motherboard has an upgrade, such as a new processor, extra RAM, or an additional adapter installed in an expansion slot

2. What is the effect of setting an administrator password in BIOS/UEFI?

    a. It prevents the computer from having multiple devices that can boot the system.

    b. It prevents the BIOS/UEFI from being infected with a virus.

    c. It prevents a user from accessing the computer operating system.

    d. It prevents a user from changing system Setup settings.

3. Which program is used to determine the driver version being used for a card installed in a computer?

    [BIOS | CMOS | Task Manager | Device Manager | system Setup]

4. Which program is commonly used to verify that a new piece of hardware is recognized by the operating system, functions, and the system resources assigned?

    [BIOS/UEFI | CMOS | manufacturer-provided application | Device Manager]

5. Where would a CR2032 lithium battery most likely be used in a tower PC?

    a. As a laptop battery

    b. Inside the processor

    c. As a component on the motherboard

    d. In the CMOS

6. Which BIOS/UEFI option might need to be modified in order to boot a Windows computer from a flash drive that contains Ubuntu, a Linux-based operating system?

    [LoJack | Secure Boot | Virus Protection | USB Configuration | Hyper-Threading]

7. What is shared system memory?

    a. A method of sharing resources between adapters

    b. A situation in which a video adapter uses its own RAM as well as motherboard RAM

    c. The technique used by a USB hub when multiple devices are attached to it

    d. A way to use RAM from one computer in a second computer

8. A technician is looking at a used computer that was recently purchased by someone and the computer is requesting a password before the operating system loads. What can the technician do to remove the password?

    a. Press the key to enter BIOS

    b. Press the F8 key as the computer boots

    c. Remove the CMOS battery for a minute and then reinstall it

    d. Hold the power button down for 10 seconds as the computer is booting.

9. Which tab of a device's Properties dialog has a *Device Status* section that might contain helpful troubleshooting information or the status of the device?

    [General | Advanced | Driver | Details | Management]

10. A technician receives a complaint about a computer being slow to respond to typed keystrokes. The technician installs more memory and a new keyboard. The customer is happy. What, if anything, could have been done better?

    _____

    _____

    _____

11. What is the maximum wattage that can be provided by a USB 3.1 port?

[100 | 5 | 2.5 | 4.5]

Consider the following BIOS/UEFI configuration menu options for answering Questions 12–15.

Main Menu	Onboard Devices	Boot Device Priority
BIOS Information	PCIe	1st Boot Device
BIOS Version	LAN1 Controller	2nd Boot Device
Build Date	USB 2.0 Controller	3rd Boot Device
EC F/W Version	USB 3.0 Controller	4th Boot Device
CPU Information	Audio	
Memory Information	OnChip SATA Controller	
System Information	SATA	
System Language	HDMI/DVI	
System Date		
System Time		

12. Which menu would you use to determine whether the system should be flashed?

a. Main Menu

b. Onboard Devices

c. Boot Device Priority

13. A computer is mounted inside a cabinet, and you want to know if the USB 3.0 port has been disabled. Which menu would you use?

a. Main menu

b. Onboard Devices

c. Boot Device Priority

14. Which menu would you use to determine whether the particular SATA port you used to connect to an eSATA bracket is enabled?

a. Main menu

b. Onboard Devices

c. Boot Device Priority

15. A technician wants to boot from an eSATA external hard drive. Which submenu item should she use?

[OnChip SATA controller | SATA | PCIe training | 1st Boot Device]

16. A technician keeps having to configure the date and time. What component is suspect?
[CPU | BIOS/UEFI | battery | chipset | CMOS]

17. What are three ways to get more USB ports? (Choose three.)

a. Connect a USB hub to an existing USB port.

b. Connect a network hub to an existing USB port.

c. Install a PCIe adapter that has USB ports.

d. Install an AGP adapter that has USB ports.

e. Install a USB bracket that has USB ports and attaches to motherboard pins.

f. Use a USB port multiplexer.

18. When would a technician use UEFI?

    a. When managing configuration through Device Manager

    b. When the date and/or time continues to be wrong

    c. When an adapter has just been installed

    d. When replacing a motherboard

19. A computer is being used in a medical office. For security reasons, the technician has been asked to reasonably ensure that no one attaches any external media. What would the technician probably do?

    a. Password protect the BIOS/UEFI and disable unused ports.

    b. Swap out the motherboard for one that doesn't have extra ports.

    c. Assign user rights through user passwords on the computer.

    d. Encrypt the hard drive.

    e. Flash the chipset.

20. A technician for a small company set a BIOS/UEFI password on every computer. The technician leaves the company, and the replacement technician needs to access the BIOS/UEFI. What should the new technician do?

    _____

    _____

    _____

Exercises

Exercise 4.1 System Expansion

Objective: To be able to explore different ways to expand a system

Parts: None

Procedure: Use the documentation in Table 4.8 to answer the questions.

TABLE 4.8   Motherboard specifications

Component	Description
CPU	Support for Intel Celeron, Core i3, and Core i5
Chipset	Intel B150 Express
Memory	2 DDR4 DIMM sockets supporting up to 32 GB Dual-channel support Support for DDR4 2133 MHz
Onboard graphics	Integrated Graphics Processor 2 HDMI ports Maximum shared memory of 512 MB
Audio	Realtek ALC887 codec 2/4/5.1/7.1-channel Support for S/PDIF out
LAN	2 Intel GbE LAN chips that support 10/100/1000 Mb/s
Expansion slots	1 PCIe 3.0 x16 slot 1 M.2 Socket 1 connector for wireless module

Component	Description
USB	Chipset: 4 USB 2.0/1.1 ports (2 on back and 2 through the internal USB header) 6 USB 3.0/2.0 ports (4 on back and 2 ports through the internal USB header)
Internal connectors	1 24-pin ATX main power connector 1 4-pin ATX 12 V power connector 6 SATA 6 Gb/s connectors 1 M.2 Socket 3 connector 1 CPU fan header 1 system fan headers 1 front panel header 1 front panel audio header 1 USB 3.0/2.0 header 1 USB 2.0/1.1 header 4 serial port headers 1 S/PDIF Out header 1 speaker header 1 clear CMOS jumper
Back panel connectors	2 USB 2.0/1.1 ports 1 PS/2 keyboard/mouse port 2 WiFi antenna connectors 2 HDMI ports 4 USB 3.0/2.0 ports 2 RJ-45 ports 6 audio jacks

1. The computer that uses this motherboard has one SATA hard drive attached. The person who owns this computer wants to use an eSATA drive.

   Based on the documentation given, can the user attach an eSATA drive to the computer as it is configured now?

   [Yes | No]

2. The technician wants to use an eSATA bracket that has two eSATA ports/cables in addition to one internal SATA device.

   Does the motherboard support this? Explain how you know.

   _____

   _____

3. The user who owns the computer does not like to use USB hubs.

   What is the maximum number of devices the user can connect to the back of the computer without using USB hubs? What advice might you give the user regarding these ports?

   _____

   _____

4. The user wants additional USB ports on the back of the computer. The technician would like to use a USB bracket to provide two additional ports.

   Based on the documentation, can a USB bracket be used with this motherboard? How can you tell? Be specific.

   _____

   _____

Exercise 4.2 BIOS/UEFI Options

Objective: Use information found on the BIOS/UEFI screen to determine which option to use

Parts: None

Procedure: Use Figures 4.30 and 4.31 to answer the questions.

Use Figure 4.30 to answer Questions 1–5.

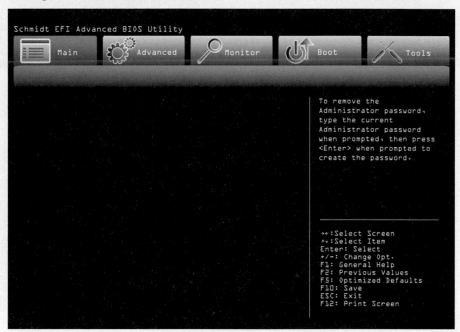

FIGURE 4.30   Sample BIOS/UEFI window 1

1.   The user has modified BIOS/UEFI options to the point where half the ports don't work and the computer is running slowly.

   Which menu option or keystroke should the technician use in order to solve this problem?

   _____

2.   The technician has modified some settings but now wants to research some alternatives and doesn't want to keep the settings he just changed.

   Which menu option or keystroke should the technician use in this situation?

   _____

3.   The computers in the research lab have to have extra security. A technician configuring a new computer for that lab is using the BIOS/UEFI to disable all USB ports on the front and rear panels.

   Which menu option is used to complete this task?

   [Main | Advanced | Monitor | Boot | Tools]

4.   The technician wants to see the last time anyone opened the case.

   Which menu option is used to complete this task?

   [Main | Advanced | Monitor | Boot | Tools]

5.   The user has complained that the system takes too long to boot. One thing a prior technician did was to always have the system try to boot from an external drive used to re-image the computer. If the external drive wasn't found, then it used the internal hard drive to load the operating system.

   Which menu option should the new technician use to change the system to use the internal hard drive to load the operating system as the computer's first choice?

   [Main | Advanced | Monitor | Boot | Tools]

Use Figure 4.31 to answer Questions 6–10.

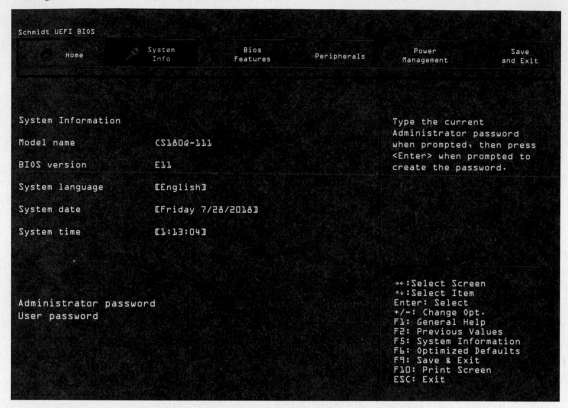

FIGURE 4.31   Sample BIOS/UEFI window 2

6.   The technician wants to stop the user from changing BIOS/UEFI settings.

Which menu option or keystroke should the technician use in order to set a BIOS/UEFI administrator password?

[Home | System Info | Peripherals | Power Management]

7.   A week ago, a user complained about the computer time being wrong. The technician changed the time and date. Now the user has complained again that the date and time are incorrect. If the technician changes the time again and checks the computer the next day and finds it off again, what should the technician do?

a. Flash the BIOS/UEFI.

b. Replace the motherboard.

c. Replace the motherboard battery.

d. Reset the time a third time.

8.   A gamer has been adjusting timing features on this motherboard to make the system go faster.

Which keystroke could the user use in order to take a screenshot of the current settings?

_____

9.   The technician has been modifying BIOS/UEFI settings.

What keystroke should the technician use when exiting the Setup screen?

_____

10. The technician wants to enable two SATA ports so a two-port eSATA bracket can be cabled to the motherboard.

Which menu option should the technician use to ensure that the two SATA ports are enabled?
[Home | System Info | Peripherals | Power Management]

Activities

Internet Discovery

Objective: To obtain specific information on the Internet regarding a computer or its associated parts

Parts: Computer with Internet access

Procedure: Use the Internet to answer the following questions. Assume that the customer owns a Lenovo A740 all-in-one computer when answering Questions 1 and 2.

Questions:

1. A customer owns a Lenovo A740 all-in-one computer. Determine the procedure for accessing the computer's Setup program. Write the key(s) to press and the URL where you find this information.

_____

2. What is the latest BIOS/UEFI version for the Lenovo A740?

_____

3. A Windows 8 HP computer owner just updated the BIOS/UEFI, but after the upgrade, the following message appeared on the screen: `Error: CMOS Checksum bad`. What should the customer do next if the BIOS/UEFI version is 7? Provide the URL where you found this information.

_____

_____

_____

4. A customer owns a Tyan S7025 motherboard. How many and which type of PCIe slots does this motherboard have? Write the answer and the URL where you find the answer.

_____

_____

5. On the same Tyan S7025 motherboard as in Question 4, which motherboard jumper is used to clear CMOS? Write the answer and the URL where you find the information.

_____

6. On the same Tyan S7025 motherboard as in Question 4, which BIOS/UEFI menu option is used to configure the order in which the system looks for devices to boot the computer? Write the answer and the URL where you find the answer.

_____

Soft Skills

Objective: To enhance and fine-tune a future technician's ability to listen, communicate in both written and oral forms and support people who use computers in a professional manner

Activities:

1. In teams, come up with a troubleshooting scenario that involves a computer technician who uses gun-slinging techniques and the same scenario involving a technician who is methodical. Explain what each technician type does and how each one solves the problem. Also, detail how these two technicians treat the customer differently. Determine ways that a gun-slinging technician might be harmful to a computer repair business. Either demonstrate or report on your findings.

2.   After exploring the BIOS/UEFI options, turn to a fellow student, pretend he or she is a customer over the phone, and walk the student through accessing Setup. Explain the purposes of at least five of the options. Reverse roles and cover five other options. Be sure to act like a typical computer user when playing the customer role.

3.   Brainstorm a troubleshooting scenario in which you fix a problem that involves accessing the Setup program and/or an adapter. Document the problem using a word processing application. Create an invoice using either a word processing or spreadsheet application. Share your documents with others in the class.

Critical Thinking Skills

Objective: To analyze and evaluate information as well as apply learned information to new or different situations

Activities:

1.   Why do you think so few computers today have very few PCI adapters or slots?

_____

2.   Compare and contrast a post office with IRQs, I/O addresses, and memory addresses shown in Device Manager. For example, how might something that happens in a post office relate to an IRQ in a PC (or I/O address or memory address)?

_____

_____

_____

_____

_____

_____

_____

_____

_____

3.   Your parents want to buy you a new computer, and they are doing research. They ask you to explain whether they should buy a PCIe 3.1 or 2.1 video adapter. Explain to them (either verbally or in writing) the differences between PCIe 3.1 or 2.1 and your recommendation.

_____

_____

_____

_____

5

Disassembly and Power

In this chapter you will learn:

> How to prevent static electricity, RFI, and EMI from harming or interfering with a computer

> The tools needed to work on computers

> How to take apart a computer and put it back together

> How to perform basic voltage and continuity checks

> How to upgrade or replace a power supply

> Tips for good written communication

CompTIA Exam Objectives:

What CompTIA A+ exam objectives are covered in this chapter?

✓ 1001-2.8   Given a scenario, use appropriate networking tools.

✓ 1001-3.1   Explain basic cable types, features, and their purposes.

✓ 1001-3.2   Identify common connector types.

✓ 1001-3.5   Given a scenario, install and configure motherboards, CPUs, and add-on cards.

✓ 1001-3.7   Summarize power supply types and features.

✓ 1001-5.2   Given a scenario, troubleshoot common problems related to motherboards, RAM, CPUs, and power.

✓ 1002-4.4   Explain common safety procedures.

✓ 1002-4.5   Explain environmental impacts and appropriate controls.

✓ 1002-4.7   Given a scenario, use proper communication techniques and professionalism.

Disassembly Overview

It is seldom necessary to completely disassemble a computer. However, when a technician is first learning about PCs, disassembly can be both informative and fun. A technician might disassemble a computer to perform preventive cleaning or to troubleshoot a problem. It might also be appropriate to disassemble a computer when it has a problem of undetermined cause. Sometimes, the only way to diagnose a problem is to disassemble the computer outside the case or remove components one by one. Disassembling a computer outside the case might help with grounding problems. A **grounding** problem occurs when the motherboard or adapter is not properly installed and a trace (a metal line on the motherboard or adapter) touches the computer frame, causing the adapter and possibly other components to stop working. Don't forget to remove jewelry and use proper lifting techniques, as described in Figure 1.34 (refer to Chapter 1, "Introduction to the World of IT") before disassembling a computer.

Electrostatic Discharge (ESD)

You must take precautions when disassembling a computer. The electronic circuits located on the motherboard and adapters are subject to ESD. Electrostatic discharge (**ESD**) is a difference of potential between two items that cause static electricity. Static electricity can damage electronic equipment without the technician's knowledge. The average person requires a static discharge of 3,000 volts before he or she feels it. An electronic component can be damaged with as little as 30 volts. Some electronic components might not be damaged the first time static electricity occurs. However, the effects of static electricity can be cumulative, weakening or eventually destroying a component. An ESD event is not recoverable: Nothing can be done about the damage it induced. Electronic chips and memory modules are most susceptible to ESD strikes

---

TECH TIP

Atmospheric conditions affect static electricity

When humidity is low, the potential for ESD is greater than at any other time; however, too much humidity is bad for electronics. Keep humidity between 45% and 55% to reduce the threat of ESD.

A technician can prevent ESD by using a variety of methods. The most common tactic is to use an **antistatic wrist strap**, also called an **ESD strap**. One end encircles the technician's wrist. At the other end, an alligator clip attaches to the computer. The clip attaches to a grounding post or a metal part such as the power supply. The electronic symbol for ground is ⏚ .

An antistatic wrist strap allows the technician and the computer to be at the same voltage potential. As long as the technician and the computer or electronic part are at the same potential, static electricity does not occur. Technicians should use an ESD wrist strap whenever possible.

A resistor inside an antistatic wrist strap protects the technician in case something accidentally touches the ground to which the strap attaches while he or she is working inside a computer. This resistor cannot protect the technician against the possible voltages inside a CRT monitor or power supply. See Figure 5.1 for an illustration of an antistatic wrist strap. Figure 5.2 shows a good location for attaching an antistatic wrist strap.

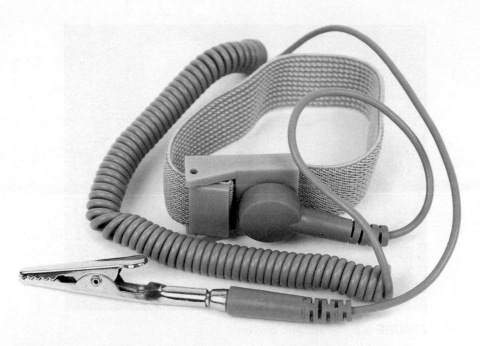

FIGURE 5.1   Antistatic wrist strap

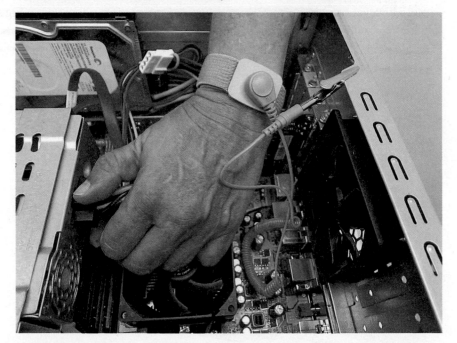

FIGURE 5.2   Where to attach an antistatic wrist strap

TECH TIP

When *not* to wear an antistatic wrist strap

Technicians should not wear an ESD wrist strap when working inside a CRT monitor or power supply because of the high voltages there. Of course, a technician should not be inside these devices unless properly trained in electronics.

Antistatic gloves can be used instead of an antistatic wrist strap. Laptops frequently do not have good places to attach a wrist strap, and in such a case, antistatic gloves work better. Figure 5.3 shows what they look like.

FIGURE 5.3 Antistatic gloves

Antistatic bags are good for storing spare adapters and motherboards when the parts are not in use. However, antistatic bags lose their effectiveness after a few years. Figure 5.4 shows an antistatic bag with an adapter inside it. **ESD mats** are available to place underneath a computer being repaired, and such a mat might have a snap for connecting the antistatic wrist strap. Antistatic heel straps are also available.

FIGURE 5.4 Antistatic bag

If an antistatic wrist strap is not available, you can still reduce the chance of ESD damage. After removing the computer case, stay attached to an unpainted metal computer part. One such part is the power supply. If you are right-handed, place your bare left arm on the power supply. Remove the computer parts one by one, always keeping your left elbow (or some other bare part of your arm) touching the power supply. If you are left-handed, place your right arm on the power supply. By placing your elbow on the power supply, both hands are free to remove computer parts. This **self-grounding** method is an effective way of keeping the technician and the computer at the same voltage potential, thus reducing the chance of ESD damage. However, it is not as safe as using an antistatic wrist strap. Also, removing the power cable from the back of the computer is a good idea. A power supply provides a small amount of power to the motherboard even when the computer is powered off. Always unplug the computer and use an antistatic wrist strap when removing or replacing parts inside a computer!

TECH TIP

Good news about ESD

Because your body and clothing can store up to 2,500 V of static electricity, you will be happy to note that electronics manufacturers are designing components that are less susceptible to ESD. However, you should still ground yourself using any means possible. Each zap weakens a component!

Electromagnetic Interference (EMI)

Electromagnetic interference (**EMI**, sometimes called EMR, for electromagnetic radiation) is noise caused by electrical devices. Many devices can cause EMI, such as a computer, a pencil sharpener, a motor, a vacuum cleaner, an air conditioner, and fluorescent lighting. The electrical devices around the computer case, including a CRT-type monitor and speakers, cause more EMI problems than the computer.

A specific type of electromagnetic interference that negatively affects computers is radio frequency interference (**RFI**). RFI is simply noises that occur in the radio frequency range. If a computer has an intermittent problem, check the surrounding devices for the source of that problem. For example, if a computer goes down only when a pencil sharpener operates or when using the optical drive, EMI could be to blame. EMI problems are very hard to track to the source. Any electronic device, including computers and printers, can be a source of EMI or RFI. EMI/RFI can affect any electronic circuit. EMI can also come through power lines. Move the computer to a different wall outlet or to a totally different circuit to determine whether the power outlet is the problem source. EMI can also affect files on a hard drive.

TECH TIP

Replacing empty slot covers

To help with EMI and RFI problems, replace slot covers for expansion slots that are no longer being used. Slot covers are shown in Figure 4.16 (refer to Chapter 4, "Introduction to Configuration"). Slot covers also keep out dust and improve the airflow within the case.

Tools

No chapter on disassembly and reassembly would be complete without mentioning tools. Tools are used in removing/replacing field replaceable units (FRUs), which are parts of the computer or other electronic devices such as the power supply or motherboard. Tools can be divided into two categories: (1) those you should not leave the office without and (2) those that are nice to have in the office, at home, or in the car.

Many technicians do not go on a repair call with a full tool case. The vast majority of all repairs are completed with the following basic tools:

> Small and medium flat-tipped screwdrivers
> #0, #1, and #2 Phillips screwdrivers
> 1/4- and 3/16-inch hex nut drivers

> Small diagonal cutters
> Needle-nose pliers

Screwdrivers take care of most disassemblies and reassemblies. Sometimes manufacturers place tie wraps on new parts, new cables, or the cables inside the computer case. Diagonal cutters are great for removing these tie wraps without cutting cables or damaging parts. Needle-nose pliers are good for straightening bent pins on cables or connectors, and they are useful for doing a million other things. Small tweaker screwdrivers and needle-nose pliers are indispensable. Figure 5.5 shows the common basic tools.

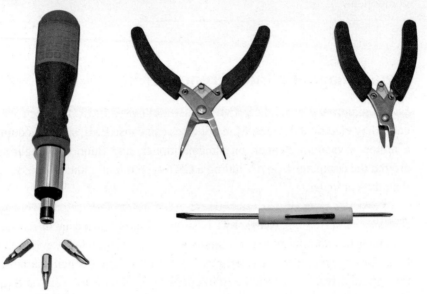

FIGURE 5.5   Basic PC technician tools

TECH TIP

Getting those wayward screws

Magnetic screwdrivers are handy for picking up dropped screws. However, they can affect memory, so avoid using them, if possible. If a screw rolls under the motherboard and cannot be reached, tilt the computer so that the screw rolls out. Sometimes the case must be tilted in different directions until the screw becomes dislodged.

Many technicians start with a basic $15 microcomputer repair kit and build from there. A bargain table 6-in-1 or 4-in-1 combination **screwdriver** that has two sizes of flat-tipped and two sizes of Phillips screwdrivers is a common tool among new technicians. A specialized Swiss army knife with screwdrivers is the favorite of some technicians. Other technicians prefer to carry an all-in-one tool in a pouch that connects to their belt.

There are tools that no one thinks of as tools but that should be taken on a service call every time. They include a pen or pencil with which to take notes and fill out the repair slip and a bootable disc containing the technician's favorite repair utilities. Usually a technician has several bootable discs for different operating systems and utilities. Often a flashlight comes in handy because some rooms and offices are dimly lit. Finally, do not forget to bring a smile and a sense of humor.

A multimeter is a tool used to take voltage readings from power supply connectors and electrical wall outlets. A multimeter can also measure current (amps) and resistance (ohms), as discussed later in the chapter. Figure 5.6 shows a multimeter, a #1 Phillips screwdriver, and a set of nut drivers. Tools that are nice to have but not used daily include a multimeter and the following devices:

> Screw pick-up tool
> Screwdriver extension tool
> Soldering iron, solder, and flux
> Screw-starter tool
> Medium-size diagonal cutters
> Metric nut drivers
> Cable-making tools
> Cable tester
> Loopback plug
> Punch-down tool
> Toner generator and probe
> Wire/cable stripper
> Crimper
> WiFi analyzer
> External enclosure

> AC circuit tester
> Right-angled, flat-tipped, and Phillips screwdrivers
> Hemostats
> Pliers
> Optical laser cleaning kit
> Nonstatic low-airflow vacuum or toner vacuum
> Compressed air
> Disposable gloves
> Safety goggles
> Air filter/mask
> Small plastic scribe
> T8, 10, 15, 20, and 25 Torx (star) screwdriver

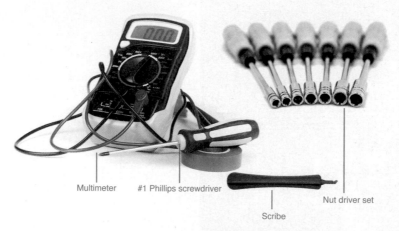

Multimeter   #1 Phillips screwdriver   Scribe   Nut driver set

FIGURE 5.6   Tools: Multimeter, #1 Phillips screwdriver, scribe, and nut driver set

You could get some nice muscle tone from carrying all these nice-to-have, but normally unnecessary, tools. When starting out in computer repair, get the basics. As your career path and skill level grow, so will your toolkit. Getting to a job site and not having the right tool can be a real hassle. However, because there are no standards or limitations on what manufacturers can use in their product lines, it is impossible to always have the right tool on hand.

Disassembly

Before a technician disassembles a computer, the following disassembly steps should be considered:

> Do not remove the motherboard battery; if you do, the configuration information in CMOS will be lost.
> Use proper grounding procedures to prevent ESD damage.
> Keep paper, a pen, a phone, and a digital camera nearby for note taking, diagramming, and photo taking. Even if you have taken apart computers for years, you might find something unique or different inside this one.
> Have ample flat and clean workspace.
> When removing adapters, do not stack the adapters on top of one another.
> If possible, place removed adapters inside a special ESD protective bag.
> Handle each adapter, motherboard, or processor on the side edges. Avoid touching the gold contacts on the bottom of adapters. Sweat, oil, and dirt cause problems.

CHAPTER 5

> Remember that hard drives require careful handling. A very small jolt can cause damage to stored data.
> You can remove a power supply but do not disassemble a CRT-style monitor or power supply without proper training and tools.
> Document screw and cable locations. Label them if possible.

The following section describes the steps in disassembling a computer.

Step 1. Remove Power and External Cables

The first step in disassembling the computer is to remove the power cord. A small amount of power is sent to the motherboard even when the computer is powered off so that the computer can be "woken up" in a corporate environment and updates can be applied. Next is removing external cables. Make notes about which cable attaches to each specific port. Figure 5.7 shows the back of the computer where this is done.

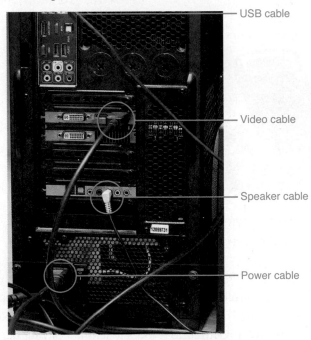

FIGURE 5.7 Removing power and external cables

Step 2. Open the Case

Opening or removing the case is sometimes the hardest part of disassembly. Some manufacturers have tabs or covers over the retaining screws, and others have retention levers or tabs that have to be pressed before the cover slides open or away. For some computers, you must press downward on a tab on top of the computer while simultaneously pressing upward on a tab on the bottom of the computer. Once the tabs are pressed, the cover can be pried open. Sound like a two-person job? Sometimes it is.

Some cases have screws that loosen but do not have to be removed all the way to remove or open the case. For all computer screws, make diagrams and place the screws in an egg carton with each section of the carton labeled with where you got the screws. Remember that to remove or loosen a screw, turn the screwdriver to the left. When possible, refer to the manufacturer's directions when opening a case. Most of the time, you can access inside the computer by simply removing the screws that hold down the side panel, as shown in Figure 5.8.

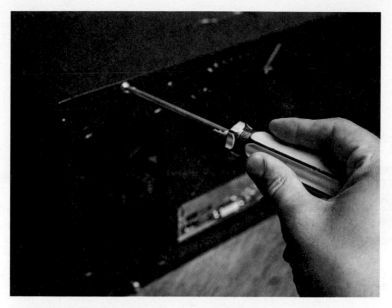

FIGURE 5.8   Removing case screws

Step 3. Remove Internal Cables and Connectors

Internal cables commonly connect from a device to the motherboard, the power supply to a device, the motherboard to the front panel buttons or ports, and/or from a card that occupies an expansion space to a device. Cables can be tricky. Inserting a cable backward into a device or an adapter can damage the device, motherboard, or adapter. Most cables are keyed so the cable inserts only one way into the connector. However, some cables or connectors are *not* keyed.

Removing a cable for the first time requires some muscle. Many cables have a pull tab or plastic piece used to remove the cable from the connector and/or device. Use this if possible and do not yank on the cable. Some cables have connectors with locking tabs. Release the locking tab *before* disconnecting the cable; otherwise, damage can be done to the cable and/or connector.

Be careful with drive cables. Some of the narrow drive cables, such as the one shown in Figure 5.9, are not very sturdy and do not connect as firmly as some of the other computer cables. Also, with this particular cable type, it does not matter which cable end attaches to the device. A 90°-angled cable (see Figure 5.10) might attach to devices in a case that has a limited-space design and might have a release latch.

FIGURE 5.9   Both cable ends are the same

FIGURE 5.10   90°-angled cable with a latch

Pin 1 is the cable edge that is colored

Pin 1 on a ribbon cable is easily identified by the colored stripe that runs down the edge of the cable.

Each cable has a certain number of pins, and every cable has a **pin 1**. Pin 1 on a cable connects to pin 1 on a connector. In the event that the pin 1 is *not* easily identified, both ends of the cable should be labeled with either a 1 or 2 on one side or a higher number on the other end. Pins 1 and 2 are always on the same end of a cable. If you find a higher number, pin 1 is on the opposite end. Also, the cable connector usually has an arrow etched into its molding to show the pin 1 connection. Figure 5.11 shows pin 1 on a ribbon cable.

Arrow
shows pin 1
on the cable

Stripe
shows pin 1
on the cable

Arrow
shows pin 1
on the cable

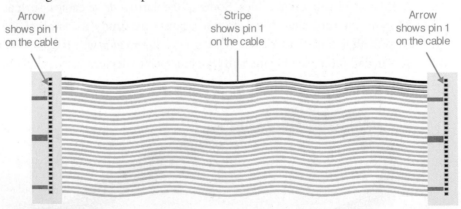

FIGURE 5.11   Pin 1 on a 40-pin IDE PATA ribbon cable

Snug connections

When connecting cables to a motherboard or internal components, ensure that each cable is connected tightly, evenly, and securely.

Motherboard connectors are usually notched so that the cable inserts only one way; however, not all cables are notched. Some motherboards have pin 1 (or the opposite pin) labeled. Always refer to the motherboard documentation for proper orientation of a cable into a motherboard connector. Figure 5.12 shows the Serial Advanced Technology Attachment connectors (**SATA connectors**) used for the cables shown in Figures 5.9 and 5.10. These connectors commonly have hard drives and/or optical drives attached. Figure 5.13 shows two other motherboard connectors: The top connector is an **IDE connector** for older Parallel ATA (PATA) drives, and the bottom one is for motherboard power. Notice that the top connector has a notch (opening). Also notice that the bottom connector has certain connector openings that are different from the square ones to prevent inserting the cable in the wrong direction.

FIGURE 5.12   Motherboard SATA drive connectors

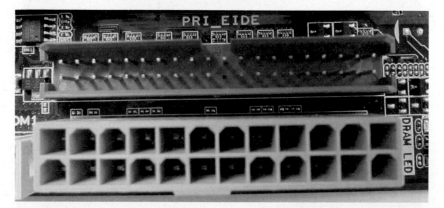

FIGURE 5.13   Two motherboard connectors (older IDE on top and standard 24-pin motherboard power on bottom)

Specific cables connect from the motherboard **front panel connectors** to lights, ports, or buttons on the front panel. These include the power button, a reset button, USB ports, IEEE 1394 (FireWire) ports, a microphone port, a headphone port, speakers, fans, the drive activity light, and the power light, to name a few. Be very careful when removing and reinstalling these cables. Usually, each one of them has a connector that must attach to the appropriate motherboard pins. Be sure to check all ports and buttons after you have reconnected these cables. Refer to the motherboard documentation if your diagramming or notes are inaccurate or if you have no diagrams or notes. Figure 5.14 shows the motherboard pins and the cables. Figure 5.15 shows how the motherboard cables connect to the front panel.

FIGURE 5.14 Motherboard front panel cables

TECH TIP

Carefully connecting front panel cables

Ensure that you connect the front panel cables to the appropriate pins and in the correct direction. Some manufacturers label the cables. As shown in Figure 5.14, once you have one oriented correctly (such as the words appearing toward the outside of the motherboard), the others are commonly oriented in the same direction. Also notice in this figure that all the white cables orient in the same direction.

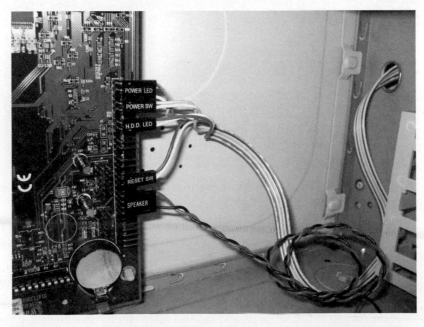

FIGURE 5.15 Front panel connections to a motherboard

The motherboard also contains pins that are used to connect cables such as those that go to the CPU or case fans. Look back at Figure 3.24 (refer to Chapter 3, "On the Motherboard") to see how fans connect to pins on the motherboard. Note that the fan might be a 3- or 4-pin cable, and the motherboard might have a 3- or 4-pin connector. Even if a 3-pin cable has to attach to a 4-pin connector or if a 4-pin cable connects to a 3-pin motherboard connector, the fan still works.

Step 4. Remove Adapters

Adapters commonly have retaining screws or a bar that keeps the adapters firmly in the case. (Refer to Figure 4.16 in Chapter 4 for an illustration of these two methods.) Adapters do have electronic components on them, so observe good ESD avoidance techniques. Use the edges of the adapter to pull it upward out of the expansion slot. Do not touch the gold contacts on the bottom of the adapter. Never pile adapters on top of one another. If an adapter will not be re-installed, insert an expansion slot blank cover in the empty expansion slot so proper airflow will be maintained within the case. Figure 5.16 shows an adapter being removed.

FIGURE 5.16   Adapter removal

Step 5. Remove Storage Devices

Hard drives must be handled with care when disassembling a computer. Inside traditional mechanical hard drives are hard platters with tiny read/write heads located just millimeters above the platters. If dropped, the read/write heads might touch the platter, causing damage to the platter and/or the read/write heads. The platter holds data and applications. Today's mechanical hard drives have self-parking heads that pull the heads away to a safe area when the computer is powered off or in a power-saving mode. Always be careful neither to jolt nor to jar a hard drive when removing it from a computer. Even with self-parking heads, improper handling can cause damage to the hard drive.

A solid-state drive (SSD) does not contain fragile heads. However, these drives are susceptible to ESD. Use proper antistatic handling procedures when removing/installing them. Store a solid-state drive in an antistatic bag when not in use.

A hard drive slides into a drive bay. Some cases require the hard drive to have hard drive rails that attach to the side of the drive, and then the drive slides into a drive bay. Other cases require that the drive be screwed into the hard drive bay. Figure 5.17 shows a hard drive being removed. You can see that this particular case requires screws to secure drives inserted into the drive bays. The screws must be removed before a drive can be removed.

Figure 5.18 shows a hard drive that has a guide rail attached and a different set of guide rails below the drive. When replacing a drive, the drive rails would have to be removed from the old drive and attached to the replacement drive. When installing a new drive, drive rails might have to be purchased.

FIGURE 5.17   Removing a hard drive

FIGURE 5.18   Hard drive rails

Step 6. Remove the Motherboard

Chapter 3 covers motherboard replacement extensively, so here we discuss issues related to building a computer from scratch or disassembling a computer: I/O shield, standoffs, and retaining clips. Some cases include a standard I/O panel shield that might need to be removed to install the I/O shield that comes with some motherboards. The **I/O shield** is a part that allows for optimum airflow and grounding for the motherboard ports. The I/O shield helps ensure that the motherboard is installed correctly and properly aligned with the case. Figure 5.19 shows a motherboard I/O shield.

Some computer cases have plastic or metal (commonly brass) **standoffs** that allow the motherboard to be screwed into the case without the motherboard solder joints touching and grounding to the computer case, causing the motherboard not to work. Some standoffs are plastic, and they slide into slots on the computer case. Do not remove these types of standoffs; just leave them attached and slide the motherboard out of the slots. The most common type of standoff is a metal standoff that screws into the case; this standoff has a threaded side that the motherboard sits on and a screw that attaches the motherboard to the standoff, as shown in Figure 5.20.

FIGURE 5.19   Motherboard I/O shield

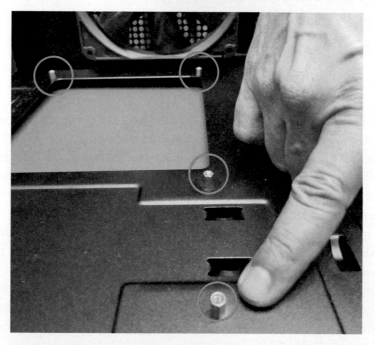

FIGURE 5.20   Motherboard standoff

Some motherboards have not only screws that attach them to the metal standoffs but also one or more retaining clips. A retaining clip might need to be pressed down, lifted up, or bent upward in order to slide the motherboard out of the case. The case might contain one or more notches, and the motherboard might have to be slid in a particular direction (usually in the direction going away from the back I/O ports) before being lifted from the case.

All-in-One Computers

The same disassembly concepts apply to all-in-one computers as to desktop computers regarding cabling, storage device removal, RAM removal, motherboard removal, and power. The difference is the space in which the devices are installed: An all-in-one computer has everything installed on the back of the display, as shown in Figure 5.21.

FIGURE 5.21   All-in-one computer parts

Reassembly

Reassembling a computer is easy if the technician is careful and properly diagrams the disassembly. Simple tasks such as inserting the optical drive in the correct drive bay become confusing after many parts have been removed. Writing reminders or taking photos takes less time than having to troubleshoot the computer because of poor reassembly. A technician should reinsert all components into their proper places, being careful to replace all screws and parts and to install missing slot covers, if possible.

Three major reassembly components are motherboards, cables, and connectors. When reinstalling a motherboard, reverse the procedure used during disassembly. Ensure that the motherboard is securely seated into the case and that all retaining clips and/or screws are replaced. This procedure requires practice, but eventually a technician will be able to tell when a motherboard is seated into the case properly. Visual inspection can also help. Ensure that the ports extend fully from the case through the I/O shield. As a final step, ensure that the drives and cover are aligned properly when the case is reinstalled.

Cables and connectors are the most common sources of reassembly problems once the motherboard is installed. Ensure that cables are fully attached to devices and the same motherboard connector. Ensure that power cables are securely attached. Matching pin 1 on the cable to pin 1 on the motherboard connector is critical for older ribbon cables. Attaching the correct device to the correct cable can be difficult if proper notes were not taken.

Preventive Maintenance

In the course of daily usage, computers get dirty, especially inside. Dust accumulates on top of electronic components, in air vents and fans, around ports and adapters, and between drives, thus creating insulation and increasing the amount of heat generated. Additional heat can cause electronic components to overheat and fail. It can also cause the processor to consistently run at a lower speed. Dust is an enemy of computers. Look at Figure 5.22 to see how dust accumulates inside a computer.

FIGURE 5.22   Dust inside a compartment

Preventive maintenance includes certain procedures performed to prolong the life of a computer. A computer in a normal working environment should be cleaned at least once a year. Typical preventive measures include vacuuming the computer and cleaning the optical drive laser, keyboard keys, printers, and display screen. Be sure to power down the computer and remove the power cord for any computer, remove the battery and AC adapter for a laptop or other mobile device, and allow a laser printer to cool before accessing internal parts. Always ensure that the device has proper ventilation and that vents are clear of any obstructions. Preventive measures for many individual devices are described in their respective chapters. For example, the steps detailing how to clean optical discs are included in Chapter 8, "Multimedia Devices." This section gives an overview of a preventive maintenance program and some general tips about cleaning solvents.

TECH TIP

Carefully cleaning LCD monitors and laptop displays

Use one of the following to clean LCD monitors and laptop displays: (1) wipes specifically designed for LCDs or (2) a soft lint-free cloth dampened with either water or a mixture of isopropyl alcohol and water. Never put liquid directly on the display and ensure that the display is dry before closing the laptop.

When performing preventive maintenance, power on the computer to be certain it operates. Perform an audio and visual inspection of the computer as it boots. Ensure that the room temperature is appropriate for the device. Electronic equipment such as PCs and mobile devices is designed to operate at room temperature (around 73°F [23°C]). Anything above 80°F (27°C) should warrant additional cooling methods for the device.

It is a terrible feeling to perform preventive maintenance on a computer but then power it on and find that it does not work. You will wonder if the cleaning you performed caused the problem or if the computer had a problem before the preventive maintenance. Be sure to document removal of any parts.

Repair companies frequently provide a preventive **maintenance kit** for service calls. The kit normally includes the components listed and described in Table 5.1.

TABLE 5.1   Preventive maintenance items

Item	Description
Portable vacuum	Used to suck dirt from inside the computer. Be sure to use nonmetallic attachments. With a vacuum cleaner that has the ability to blow air, vacuum first and then set the vacuum cleaner to blow to get dust out of hard-to-reach places. Hold fan blades in place.
Toner vacuum	Used to clean computers and laser printers. Special vacuum bags are used to prevent the toner from melting and potentially damaging the vacuum cleaner.
Special vacuum bags	Used for laser printers so that the toner does not melt on the vacuum motor.
Compressed air	Used to remove dust in hard-to-reach places (preferably after vacuuming).
Urethane swabs	Used to clean between keys on a keyboard. If a key is sticking, disconnect the keyboard before spraying or using contact cleaner on it.
Monitor wipes	Used on the front of the display. Wipes with an antistatic solution work best.
Lint-free cloths	Used to clean laptop touchpads and other components. Dampen the cloth to remove residual finger oil.
General-purpose cloths	Used to clean the outside of the case and to clean the desktop areas under and around the computer.
General-purpose cleanser	Used with soft lint-free cloths or lint-free swabs. Never spray or pour liquid on any computer part.
Denatured alcohol	Used on rubber rollers, such as those inside printers.
Antistatic brush	Used to brush dirt from hard-to-reach places.
Optical drive cleaning kit	Can include a lens cleaner that removes dust and debris from an optical lens; a disc cleaner that removes dust, dirt, fingerprints, and oils from the disc; and a scratch repair kit to resurface, clean, and polish CDs, DVDs, and BDs.
Gold contact cleaner	Used to clean adapter contacts as well as contacts on laptop batteries and the contacts where the battery inserts.
Safety goggles	Used in dusty environments or when dealing with chemicals in a poorly ventilated area. Indirect vent goggles prevent a splash from coming into contact with eyes. Nonvented goggles protect from dust, splash, and chemical vapors.
Air filter/mask	Used for protection from airborne fumes, dust, and smoke. There are two types of filters: those for vapors and those for particles. Filtering for vapors helps when using chemical cleaners and solvents. Filtering for particles helps with things that make you sneeze, such as dust, pollen, and mold.

A cleaning solution company may provide a material safety data sheet (**MSDS**) or safety data sheet (**SDS**) that contains information about a product, including its toxicity, storage, disposal, and health/safety concerns. Computer components have the potential to contain toxic substances. Larger companies have very specific rules about how electronic waste is handled, but in both large and small companies, an IT person who deals with hardware needs to be familiar with toxic waste handling. Each state commonly has specific disposal procedures for chemical solvents and toxic waste. Check with the company's safety coordinator for storage and disposal information, use the MSDS/SDS, and research handling and disposal guidelines according to local government regulations.

TECH TIP

Knowing your state aerosol can disposal laws

Some states have special requirements for disposal of aerosol cans, especially those that are clogged and still contain some product. Always comply with government regulations.

To perform the preventive maintenance, power off the computer, remove the power cord, and vacuum the computer with a nonmetallic attachment. Do not start with compressed air or by blowing dust out of the computer because the dirt and dust will simply go into the air and eventually fall back into the computer and surrounding equipment. Figure 5.23 shows vacuuming inside a computer. Remember to hold your finger or a brush on the fan blade so it does not spin out of control and damage the fan. The technician should have removed the watch before performing this maintenance.

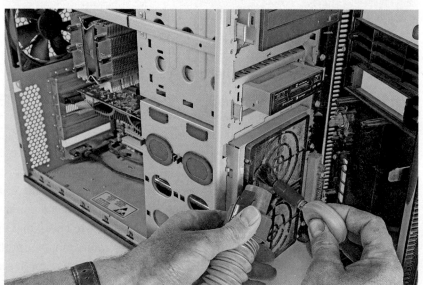

FIGURE 5.23 Preventive maintenance vacuuming

After vacuuming as much as possible, use compressed air to blow the dust out of hard-to-reach places, such as inside the power supply and under the motherboard (see Figure 5.24). If you are performing maintenance on a laptop computer, remove as many modules as possible, such as the optical drive, battery, and hard drive, before vacuuming or using compressed air. Inform people in the immediate area that they might want to leave the area if they have allergies. Use appropriate safety equipment, including safety goggles and an air filter/mask, when performing preventive maintenance.

If you remove an adapter from an expansion slot, replace it into the same slot. If the computer battery is on a riser board, it is best to leave the riser board connected to the motherboard so the system does not lose its configuration information. The same steps covered in the "Disassembly" section, earlier in this chapter, hold true when you are performing preventive maintenance.

TECH TIP

Using a preventive maintenance call as a time for updates

A preventive maintenance call is a good time to check for operating system, BIOS/UEFI, antivirus, and driver updates.

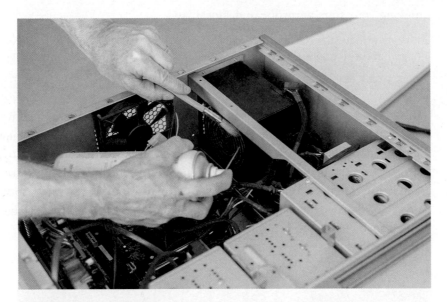

FIGURE 5.24   Preventive maintenance using compressed air

When you perform preventive maintenance, take inventory and document what is installed in the computer, such as the hard drive size, amount of RAM, available hard drive space, and so on. During the maintenance procedure, communicate with the user. Ask whether the computer has been giving anyone trouble lately or if it has been performing adequately. Computer users like to know that you care about their computing needs. Also, users frequently ask questions such as whether sunlight or cold weather harms the computer. Always respond with answers the user can understand. Users appreciate it when you explain things in terms they comprehend and that make sense.

A preventive maintenance call is the perfect opportunity to check that the computer is protected against viruses. Preventive maintenance measures help limit computer problems as well as provide a chance to interact with customers and help with difficulties that might seem minuscule but could worsen. The call is also a good time to take inventory of all hardware and software installed.

Basic Electronics Overview

A technician needs to know a few basic electronic terms and concepts when testing components. The best place to start is with electricity. There are two types of electricity: AC and DC. The electricity provided by a wall outlet is alternating current (**AC**), and the type of electricity used by computer components is direct current (**DC**). Devices such as radios, TVs, and toasters use AC power. Low-voltage DC power is used for a computer's internal components and anything powered by batteries. A computer's power supply converts AC electricity from the wall outlet to DC for the internal components. Electricity involves electrons flowing through a conductor, similar to the way that water runs through a pipe. With AC, electrons flow alternately in both directions. With DC, electrons flow in one direction only.

Electronics: Terminology

Voltage, current, power, and resistance are terms commonly used in the computer industry. **Voltage**, which is a measure of the pressure pushing electrons through a circuit, is measured in **volts**. A power supply's output is measured in volts. Power supplies typically put out +3.3 volts, +5 volts, +12 volts, and –12 volts. You will commonly see these voltages shown in power supply documentation as +5 V or +12 V. Another designation is +5 VSB. This is for the computer's **standby power**, which is always provided, even when the computer is powered off. This supplied voltage is why you have to unplug a computer when working inside it.

TECH TIP

Polarity is important only when measuring DC voltage

When a technician measures the voltage coming out of a power supply, the black meter lead (which is negative) connects to the black wire from the power supply (which is ground). The red meter lead connects to either the +5 or +12 volt wires from the power supply.

The term *volts* is also used to describe voltage from a wall outlet. Wall outlet voltage is normally 120 VAC (120 volts AC). Figure 5.25 shows a multimeter being used to take a DC voltage reading on the power connectors coming from a power supply. When the meter leads are inserted correctly, the voltage level shown is of the correct polarity.

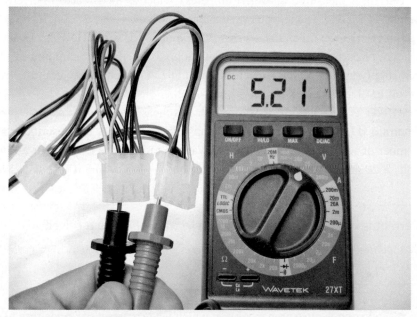

FIGURE 5.25   DC voltage reading

The reading on the meter could be the opposite of what it should be if the meter's leads are reversed. Because electrons flow from one area where there are many of them (negative polarity) to an area where there are few electrons (positive polarity), polarity shows which way an electric current will flow. Polarity is the condition of being positive or negative with respect to some reference point. Polarity is not important when measuring AC. Figure 5.26 shows rules to observe when working with meters.

1. Select AC or DC on the meter (some meters automatically select AC or DC).

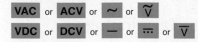

2. Select the appropriate voltage range (0-10V, 0-100V, etc). The meter can be damaged if you measure a high voltage in a low range (but not the reverse). Use the highest range for unknown voltages.

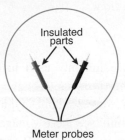

Insulated parts

Meter probes

3. Touch only the insulated parts of the meter probes.

FIGURE 5.26 Meter rules

Monitors and power supplies can have dangerous voltage levels. Monitors can have up to 35,000 volts going to the back of the CRT. Flat panel displays and mobile device displays also contain high voltage levels (but not at the voltage levels of CRTs). 120 volts AC is present inside the power supply of a desktop computer. Power supplies and monitors have capacitors inside them. A capacitor is a component that holds a charge even after the computer is turned off. Capacitors inside a monitor can hold a charge for several hours after the monitor has been powered off.

TECH TIP

Do not work inside a CRT monitor unless you have special training

Monitors require high-voltage meters and special precautions.

Current is measured in **amps** (amperes), which is the number of electrons going through a circuit every second. In the water pipe analogy, voltage is the amount of pressure applied to force the water through the pipe, and current is the amount of water flowing. Every device needs a certain amount of current to operate. A power supply is rated for the amount of total current (in amps) it can supply at each voltage level. For example, a power supply could be rated at 20 amps for the 5-volt level and 8 amps for the 12-volt level.

Power is measured in **watts**, which is a measurement of how much work is being done. It is determined by multiplying volts by amps. Power supplies are described as providing a maximum number of watts or having a specific wattage rating. It is the sum of all outputs (for example, [5 volts × 20 amps] (100 watts)+ [12 V × 8 amps] (96 watts)= 100 watts + 96 watts = 196 watts.

TECH TIP

Current is what kills people when an electrical shock is received

Voltage determines how much current flows through the body. A high-current and low-voltage situation is the most dangerous.

Resistance is measured in **ohms**, which is the amount of opposition to current in an electronic circuit. The resistance range on a meter can be used to check continuity or check whether a fuse is good. A **continuity** check is used to determine whether a wire has a break in it. A conductor (wire) in a cable or a good fuse will have very low resistance to electricity (close to zero ohms). A broken wire or a bad fuse will have a very high resistance (millions of ohms, sometimes shown as infinite ohms, or OL). For example, a cable is normally made up of several wires that go from one connector to another. If you measure the continuity from one end of a wire to the other, it should show no resistance. If the wire has a break in it, the meter shows infinite resistance. Figure 5.27 shows examples of a good wire reading and a broken wire reading.

TECH TIP

Always unplug a computer before working inside it

The power supply provides power to the motherboard, even if the computer is powered off. Leaving the power cord attached can cause damage when replacing components such as the processor or RAM.

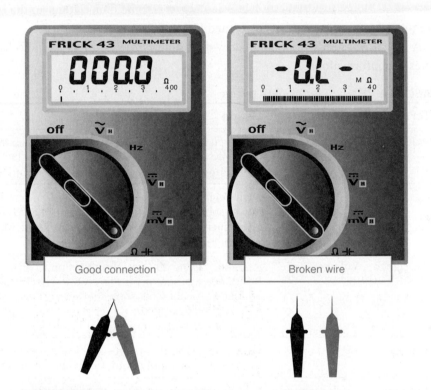

FIGURE 5.27   Sample resistance meter readings

Digital meters have different ways of displaying infinity. Always refer to the meter manual. When checking continuity, the meter is placed on the ohms setting, as shown in Figure 5.27. The ohms setting is usually illustrated by an omega symbol (Ω).

TECH TIP

Dealing with small connections and a meter

With connectors that have small pin connections, use a thin meter probe or insert a thin wire, such as a paper clip, into the hole and touch the meter to the wire to take your reading.

Polarity is not important when performing a continuity check. Either meter lead (red or black) can be placed at either end of the wire. However, you do need a pin-out diagram (wiring list) for the cable before you can check continuity because pin 1 at one end could connect to a different pin number at the other end.

The same concept of continuity applies to fuses. A fuse has a tiny wire inside it that extends from end to end. The fuse is designed so that the wire melts (breaks) if too much current flows through it. The fuse prevents excessive current from damaging electronic circuits or starting a fire. A fuse is rated for a particular amount of current. For example, a 5-amp fuse protects a circuit if the amount of current exceeds 5 amps.

CHAPTER 5

TECH TIP

Using the right fuse

Never replace a fuse with one that has a higher amperage rating. Allowing too much current to be passed by the fuse would defeat the purpose of the fuse and could destroy electronic circuits or cause a fire.

Take a fuse out of the circuit before testing it. A good fuse has a meter reading of (or close to) 0 ohms. A blown fuse shows a meter reading of infinite ohms. Refer to the section "Electronics: Terminology," earlier in this chapter, and Figure 5.27.

A technician needs to be familiar with basic electronics terms and checks. Table 5.2 consolidates this information.

TABLE 5.2   Basic electronics terms

Term	Value	Usage
Voltage	Volts	Voltage is relevant when checking AC voltage from a wall outlet (typically 120 VAC) and when checking the DC output voltage from a power supply (typically ±12, +3.3, and ± 5 VDC).
Current	Amps (amperes)	Each device needs a certain amount of current to operate. A power supply is rated for total current in amps for each voltage level (such as 24 amps for 5-volt power and 50 amps for 12-volt power).
Resistance	Ohms	Resistance is the amount of opposition to electric current. Resistance measurements are used to check continuity on cables and fuses. A cable that shows little or no resistance has no breaks in it. A good fuse shows no resistance. If a cable has a break in it or if a fuse is bad, the resistance is infinite.
Wattage (power)	Watts	Watts is a measure of power and is derived by multiplying amps by volts. Power supply output is measured in watts.
Apparent power	Volt-ampere	Volt-ampere is used with watts to describe how much power an uninterruptible power supply (UPS) can deliver. A UPS, as discussed later in this chapter, is used to provide power when AC power is lost.

Power Supply Overview

A power supply is an essential component within a computer; no internal computer device works without it. A power supply converts AC to DC, distributes lower-voltage DC power to components throughout the computer, and provides cooling through the use of a fan located inside the power supply. The AC voltage a power supply accepts is normally either 100 to 120 volts or 200 to 240 volts. Note that the A+ certification exam objectives list this as **115 V vs. 220 V input voltage**. Some **dual-voltage** power supplies can accept either. This type of power supply might have a selector switch on the back or may be able to automatically detect the input voltage level.

Power supplies can also be auto-switching. An **auto-switching** power supply monitors the incoming voltage from the wall outlet and automatically switches itself accordingly. Auto-switching power supplies accept voltages from 100 to 240 VAC at 50 to 60 Hz. These power supplies are popular in mobile devices and are great for international travel.

TECH TIP

Powering on a power supply without anything attached could damage the power supply

Do not power on a power supply without connecting to the motherboard and possibly a device such as an optical drive or hard drive. An ATX power supply usually requires a motherboard connection at a minimum.

Power Supply Form Factors

Just as motherboards come in different shapes and sizes, so do power supplies. Today's power supply form factors are ATX, ATX12V, and micro-ATX. The ATX power supply form factor was the first type to allow a small amount of voltage to be provided to the motherboard so that both hardware and software could be used to "wake up" the device and/or lower voltage to conserve power. This was known as a soft switch. The ATX12V version 2 standard has a **24-pin motherboard connector** instead of a 20-pin version 1 connector.

The **micro-ATX power supply form factor** is a smaller version than a full-sized ATX power supply to fit in smaller cases. Other form factors include LFX12V (low profile), SFX12V (small form factor), EPS12V (used with server motherboards and has an extra 8-pin connector), CFX12V (compact form factor), SFX12V (small form factor), TFX12V (thin form factor), WTX12V (workstation form factor for high-end workstations and select servers), and FlexATX (smaller systems that have no more than three expansion slots).

Intel, AMD, and video card manufacturers certify specific power supplies that work with their processors and video cards. A computer manufacturer can also have a proprietary power supply form factor that is not compatible with different computer models or other vendors' machines. Laptop power supplies are commonly proprietary.

Power Supply Connectors

Table 5.3 lists the possible ATX power supply connectors, and Figure 5.28 shows them.

TABLE 5.3 ATX power supply connectors

Connector	Notes	Voltage(s)
24-pin main power	Main ATX power connector to the motherboard	+3.3, +5, +12, –12
15-pin SATA power	Internal SATA power connector	+3.3, +5, +12
8-pin 12 V	12 V for CPU used with an ATX12V v1 power supply	+12
8-pin PCIe	PCIe video; connects to a PCIe video adapter (Note that some connectors are 6+2-pin, meaning they accept either the 6- or 8-pin cable.)	+12
6-pin PCIe	PCIe video; connects to PCIe video adapter	+12
6-pin	Sometimes labeled AUX; connects to the motherboard if it has a connector	+3.3, +5
4-pin **Molex**	Connects to peripheral devices such as hard drives and CD/DVD drives	+5, +12
4-pin Berg	Connects to peripheral devices such as a floppy drive	+5, +12
4-pin 12 V	Sometimes labeled AUX or 12 V; connects to the motherboard for the CPU	+12
3-pin	Used to monitor fan speed	N/A

The motherboard, case, and power supply must be size compatible

The motherboard and case form factor and the power supply form factor must fit in the case and must work together. For optimum performance, research what connectors and form factors are supported by both components.

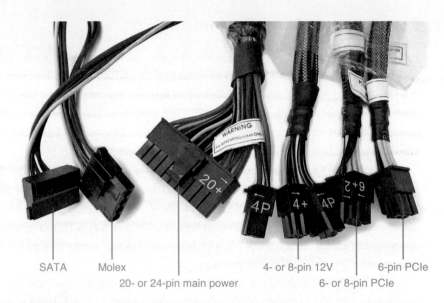

SATA   Molex   4- or 8-pin 12V   6-pin PCIe
         20- or 24-pin main power   6- or 8-pin PCIe

FIGURE 5.28   ATX power supply connectors

Figure 5.29 illustrates the ATX 24-pin motherboard connector standards. Notice in Figure 5.29 that the power cable is only one connector, and the cable inserts into the connector one way only. Also notice that a power good signal (labeled PWR_OK in Figure 5.29) goes to the motherboard. When the computer is turned on, part of POST is to allow the power supply to run a test on each of the voltage levels. The voltage levels must be correct before any other devices are tested and allowed to initialize. If the power is okay, a power good signal is sent to the motherboard. If the power good signal is not sent from the power supply, a timer chip on the motherboard resets the CPU. Once a power good signal is sent, the CPU begins executing software from the BIOS/UEFI. Figure 5.29 also shows the +5 VSB connection to provide standby power for features such as Wake on LAN or Wake on Ring (covered later in this chapter).

A high-quality power supply delays sending the power good signal until all of the power supply's voltages have a chance to stabilize. Some cheap power supplies do not delay the power good signal. Other cheap power supplies do not provide the power good circuitry but instead tie 5 volts to the signal (which sends a power good signal even when it is not there).

The quantity and type of connectors available on a power supply depend on the power supply manufacturer. If a video card needs a PCIe connector and two Molex power connectors are free, a dual Molex-to-PCIe converter can be purchased. If a SATA device needs a power connection and only a Molex cable is free, a Molex-to-SATA converter is available. Figure 5.30 shows a dual Molex-to-PCIe converter on the left and a Molex-to-SATA converter on the right.

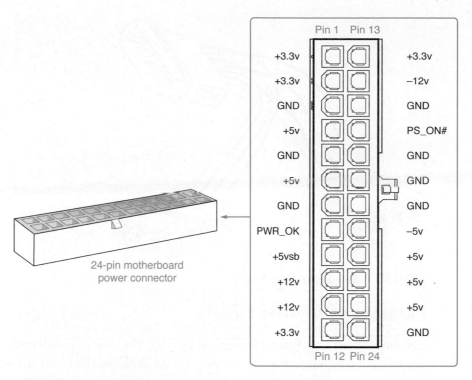

FIGURE 5.29 ATX 24-pin motherboard connectivity

FIGURE 5.30 Dual Molex-to-PCIe and Molex-to-SATA converters

Power supply connectors can connect to any device; there is not a specific connector for the hard drive, the optical drive, and so on. If there are not enough connectors from the power supply for the number of devices installed in a computer, a Y power connector can be purchased at a computer or electronics store. The Y connector adapts a single Molex connector to two Molex connectors for two devices. Verify that the power supply can output enough power to handle the extra device being installed. Figure 5.31 shows a Y power connector.

TECH TIP

Power converters and Y connectors in your toolkit

In case a service call involves adding a new device, having various power converters available as part of your toolkit is smart.

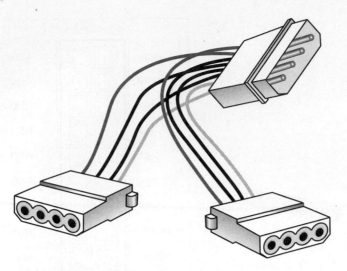

FIGURE 5.31   Molex connector

Purposes of a Power Supply

The power from a wall outlet is high-voltage AC. The type of power computers need is low-voltage DC. All computer parts (the electronic chips on the motherboard and adapters, the electronics on the drives, and the motors in the hard drive and optical drive) need DC power to operate. Power supplies in general come in two types: linear and switching. Computers use switching power supplies. The main functions of a power supply include the following:

> Convert AC to DC
> Provide DC voltage to the motherboard, adapters, and peripheral devices
> Provide cooling and facilitate airflow through the case

One purpose of a power supply is to convert AC to DC so the computer has proper power to run its components. With the ATX power supply, a connection from the front panel switch to the motherboard simply provides a 5-volt signal that allows the motherboard to tell the power supply to turn on. This 5-volt signal allows ATX power supplies to support ACPI, which is covered later in the chapter, and also lets the motherboard and operating system control the power supply. Look back at Figure 5.15 to see front panel connections to the motherboard.

TECH TIP

Setting an ATX power supply on or off to the *on* position

On an ATX power supply that has an on/off switch, ensure that it is set to the *on* position. If an ATX power supply switch is present and in the off position, the motherboard and operating system cannot turn on the power supply. Some ATX power supplies do not have external on/off switches, and the computer can be powered down only via the operating system.

TECH TIP

Checking the input voltage selector

Some power supplies and laptops have input voltage selectors; others have the ability to accept input from 100 to 240 volts for use in various countries (dual-voltage). Ensure that the power supply accepts or is set to the proper input voltage.

Another purpose of a power supply is to distribute proper DC voltage to each component. Several cables with connectors come out of the power supply. With ATX motherboards, there is only a 24-pin connector used to connect power to the motherboard. The power connector inserts only one way into the motherboard connector. Figure 5.32 shows an ATX connector being inserted into a motherboard.

FIGURE 5.32 Installing an ATX power connector on a motherboard

Another purpose of a power supply is to provide cooling for the computer. The power supply's fan circulates air throughout the computer. Most computer cases have air vents on one side, on both sides, or in the rear. The ATX-style power supply blows air inside the case instead of out the back; with this reverse-flow cooling method, the air blows over the processor and memory to keep them cool. This type of power supply keeps the inside of the computer cleaner than older styles.

TECH TIP

Don't block air vents

Whether a computer is a desktop model, a tower model, or a desktop model mounted in a stand on the floor, ensure that nothing blocks the air vents in the computer case.

Because heat sinks generate a lot of heat, it is important to have the proper amount of airflow and in the right direction. Additional fans can be installed to provide additional cooling for a PC. Figure 5.33 shows an extra cooling fan mounted in the rear of a case (as well as over the processor). Notice that this computer needs to have preventive maintenance performed.

CHAPTER 5

FIGURE 5.33   Computer case auxiliary fan

TECH TIP

Airflow and ventilation

Airflow should be through the computer and over the motherboard to provide cooling for the motherboard components.

If you install an additional fan to help with cooling, there are two likely places for fan placement: (1) near the power supply, directly behind the CPU, and (2) on the lower front part of the case. Cases have different numbers of and locations of mounting spots for the case fan(s). Figure 5.34 shows two possible installation sites for an additional fan.

Electronic components generate a great deal of heat but are designed to withstand fairly high temperatures. Auxiliary fans can be purchased to help cool the internal components of a computer. A case may have an extra mount and cutout for an auxiliary fan. Some auxiliary fans mount in adapter slots or drive bays.

TECH TIP

Being careful when installing an auxiliary fan

Place a fan so the outflow of air moves in the same direction as the flow of air generated by the power supply. If an auxiliary fan is installed inside a case in the wrong location, the auxiliary airflow could work against the power supply airflow, reducing the cooling effect.

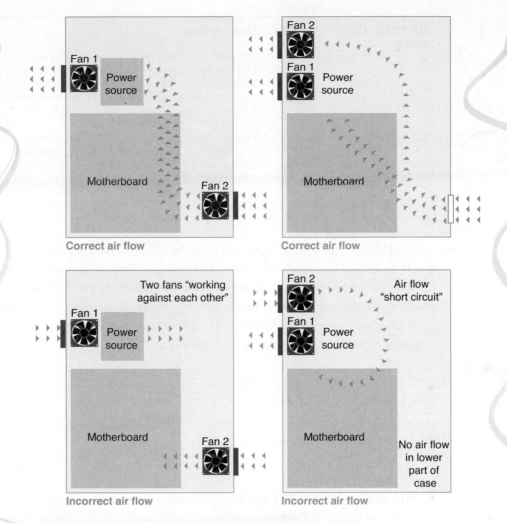

FIGURE 5.34 Placement of auxiliary fans

Advanced Configuration and Power Interface (ACPI)

Advanced Configuration and Power Interface (**ACPI**) gives the BIOS/UEFI and operating system control over various devices' power and modes of operation. ACPI has various operating states, as shown in Table 5.4.

TABLE 5.4 ACPI operating states

Global system state	Sleep state	Description
G0 Working	S0	The computer is fully functional. Software, such as the autosave function used with Microsoft products, can be optimized for performance or to reduce battery usage.
G1 Sleeping		Requires less power than the G0 state and has multiple sleep states: S1, S2, S3, and S4.
	S1	CPU is still powered, and unused devices are powered down. RAM is still being refreshed. Hard drives are not running.
	S2	CPU is not powered. RAM is still being refreshed. System is restored instantly upon user intervention.
	S3	Power supply output is reduced. RAM is still being refreshed. Some information in RAM is restored to the CPU and the cache.

Global system state	Sleep state	Description
	S4	Lowest-power sleep mode, which takes the longest to come up. Information in RAM is saved to nonvolatile memory such as a hard drive or flash media. Some manufacturers call this the hibernate state.
G2 Soft off	S5	Power consumption is almost zero. Requires the operating system to reboot. No information is saved anywhere.
G3 Mechanical off		Also called off. This is the only state in which the computer can be disassembled. You must power on the computer to use it again.

ACPI allows apps to work with the operating system to manage power, such as when an application is set to automatically save a document, but might not do so until the hard drive is being used for something else in order to conserve power in a laptop. In the Windows environment, the **sleep mode** also known as **suspend mode** uses one of the G1 sleeping ACPI states to allow the device to be awakened to continue working. The **hibernate mode** uses the G1 S4 mode and takes the longest to bring a device back to a working state.

TECH TIP

Which power option to select: standby or hibernate?

Most people who want to quickly re-access the device would select the standby option. However, the hibernate mode saves more energy.

Two common BIOS/UEFI and adapter features that take advantage of ACPI are Wake on LAN and Wake on Ring. The **Wake on LAN** feature allows a network administrator to control the power to a workstation remotely and directs the computer to come out of sleep mode. Software applications can also use the Wake on LAN feature to perform updates, upgrades, and maintenance tasks. The feature can also be used to bring up computers immediately before the business day starts. Wake on LAN can be used with web or network cameras to start recording when motion is detected or to bring up a network printer so that it can be used when needed.

Wake on Ring allows a computer to come out of sleep mode when the telephone line has an incoming call. It lets the computer receive phone calls, faxes, and emails when the user is not present. Common BIOS/UEFI settings related to ACPI are listed in Table 5.5.

TECH TIP

Why leave computers on at the office?

In Windows, when a computer is shut down, it is put in soft off, or S5, state. Wake on LAN is not officially supported from this state, and for this reason, corporate environments request that users leave their computers turned on but logged off on specific days or every day.

TABLE 5.5   Common BIOS/UEFI power settings

Setting	Description
Delay Prior to Thermal	Defines the number of minutes the system waits to shut down the system when an overheating situation occurs.
CPU Warning Temperatures	Specifies the CPU temperature at which a warning message is displayed on the screen.
ACPI Function	Enables or disables ACPI. This is the preferred method for disabling ACPI in the event of a problem.
Soft-off	Specifies the length of time a user must press the power button to turn off the computer.
Deep S4/S5	Uses less power and wakes from S4/S5 states only with the power button or an RTC (real-time clock) alarm, such as waking the computer to complete a task.
Power on by Ring, Resume by Ring, or Wakeup	Allows the computer to wake when an adapter or an external device supports Wake on Ring.
Resume by Alarm	Allows a date and time to be set when the system is awakened from Suspend mode. Commonly used to update the system during nonpeak periods.
Wake Up on LAN	Allows the computer to wake when a Wake on LAN signal is received across the network.
CPU THRM Throttling	Allows a reduction in CPU speed when the system reaches a specific temperature.
Power on Function	Specifies which key (or key combination) will activate the system's power.
Hot Key Power On	Defines what keystrokes will reactivate system power.
Doze Mode	When the system is in a reduced activity state, the CPU clock is throttled (slowed down). All other devices operate at full speed.
After Power Failure	Sets power mode after a power loss.

If the computer does not go into the sleep mode, check the following:

> Determine whether ACPI is enabled in the BIOS/UEFI.
> Try disabling the antivirus program to see whether it is causing the problem.
> Set the screen saver to *None* to see if it is causing the problem.
> Determine whether all device drivers are ACPI compliant.
> Determine whether power management is enabled through the operating system (using the Power Options Control Panel).
> Disconnect USB devices to see whether they are causing problems.

Replacing or Upgrading a Power Supply

Power supplies are rated in watts. Today's typical computers have power supplies with a **wattage rating** ranging from 250 to 500 watts, although powerful computers, such as network servers or higher-end gaming systems, can have power supplies rated 600 watts or higher. Each voltage level has a maximum number of amps (amperage). For example, the +5 V part of the power supply might provide a maximum of 20 amps (which is equal to 100 watts of the total power supply wattage). Internal and external devices powered by a particular type of port, such as USB, are affected by the number of amps available from the +5 and +12 V DC power supply output and the total amount of wattage available.

Each device inside a computer uses a certain amount of power, and the power supply must provide enough power to run all the devices. The power each device or adapter requires is usually defined in the documentation for the device or adapter or on the manufacturer's website. The computer uses the wattage needed, not the total capacity of a power supply.

> ## TECH TIP
>
> ### Watching the wattage
>
> Many manufacturers overstate the wattage. The wattage advertised is *not* the wattage available at higher temperatures, such as when mounted inside a computer. Research a model before purchasing.

Some power supplies are listed as being dual or triple (or tri) rail. A **dual-rail power supply** has two +12 V output lines that are monitored for an over-current condition. A triple-rail power supply simply has three +12 V output lines monitored. Keep in mind that most manufacturers do not have two or more independent 12 V sources; they all derive from the same 12 V source but have independent output lines. Figure 5.35 shows how the +12 V rails might be used.

+12V
Look on top of the power supply for the various voltage levels and maximum current output in amps.

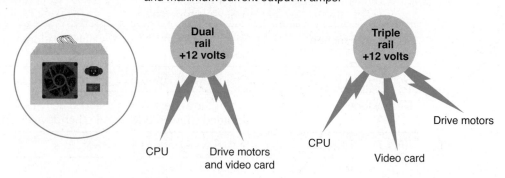

FIGURE 5.35   12 V rails

The second thing to consider is watts. Power supplies are rated in watts. Today's typical computers have a power supply with a wattage rating ranging from 250 to 500 watts, although a powerful computer, such as a network server or higher-end gaming system, can have a power supply rated 600 watts or higher. Each device inside a computer uses a certain amount of power, and the power supply must provide enough power to run all the devices. The power each device or adapter requires is usually defined in the documentation for the device or adapter or on the manufacturer's website. The computer uses the wattage needed, not the total capacity of a power supply. The efficiency is what changes the electricity bill; the less AC is required to convert power to DC, the higher the efficiency.

Some people are interested in exactly how much power their system is consuming. Every device in a computer consumes power, and each device may use one or more different voltage levels (for example, +5 V, –5 V, +12 V, –12 V, and +3.3 V). A power supply has a maximum amperage for each voltage level (for example, 30 amps at +5 volts and 41 amps at +12 V). To determine the maximum power being used, in watts, multiply the amps by the volts. If you add all the maximum power levels, the amount will be greater than the power supply's rating. This means that you cannot use the maximum power at every single voltage level; however, because –5 V and –12 V are not used very often, normally this is not a problem.

Number of Devices/Types of Devices to Be Powered

To determine the power being consumed, you must research every device to determine how much current it uses at a specific voltage level. Internet power calculators are available to help with this task. It is important to have a power supply powerful enough for the number of devices and types of devices installed in the computer. Table 5.6 lists sample computer component power requirements.

TABLE 5.6 Sample computer component power requirements

Component	Power consumption
Motherboard (without processor)	5 to 150 W
Processor	10 to 140 W
PATA IDE hard drive	3 to 30 W
SATA hard drive	2 to 15 W
Optical drive	10 to 30 W
Nonvideo adapter	4 to 25 W
AGP video adapter	20 to 50 W
PCIe video card with one power connector	50 to 150 W
PCIe video card with two power connectors	100 to 300 W
Extra fan	3 W
RAM module	15 W

Choosing a Power Supply

When choosing a power supply, the first things to consider are size and form factor because the power supply has to fit in the case. Different physical sizes of power supplies are available. The second thing to consider is wattage: You should buy a power supply that is equal to or more wattage than the original power supply. Finally, do not forget to ensure that the on/off switch on the new power supply is in a location that fits in the computer case.

TECH TIP

All power supplies are not created equal

A technician needs to replace a power supply with one that provides an equal or greater amount of power. Search the Internet for power supply reviews. A general rule of thumb is that if two power supplies are equal in wattage, the heavier one is better because it uses a bigger transformer, bigger heat sinks, and higher-quality components.

The 80 PLUS is a power supply efficiency rating system that has been incorporated into ENERGY STAR specifications. Efficiency involves converting more AC to DC. The rating system consists of six levels of efficiency. Each level must provide a particular level of efficiency at a specific amount of load (number of components being used simultaneously that require power). Table 5.7 shows the levels and efficiency requirements of each level that relate to PCs.

TABLE 5.7   80 PLUS levels and energy efficiency requirements

Level	Efficiency		
	20% load	**50% load**	**100% load**
80 PLUS	80%	80%	80%
80 PLUS Bronze	82%	85%	82%
80 PLUS Silver	85%	88%	85%
80 PLUS Gold	87%	90%	87%
80 PLUS Platinum	90%	92%	89%
80 PLUS Titanium	92%	94%	90%

Just because a power supply is not certified as 80 PLUS does not mean that it is not an energy-efficient power supply, but these levels do give you an idea of the difference between power supplies. When choosing a power supply, the most important things to consider are as follows:

> Size and form factor
> Wattage
> Number and type of connectors
> Energy efficiency
> Number of 12 V rails monitored for an over current condition

Some people like extra features such as colored lights inside the power supply, power supply fan, and/or ports. Some power supplies come with detachable cables (see Figure 5.36) so that cables that are not used are simply not attached to the power supply to aid in cable management.

FIGURE 5.36   Power supply with detachable cable ports

TECH TIP

Power values for energy-efficient monitors

Always keep the screen saver timeout value shorter than the power saver timeout value, especially with green (energy-efficient) monitors!

Power Protection

Power supplies have built-in protection against adverse power conditions. However, the best protection for a computer is to unplug it during a power outage or thunderstorm. Surge protectors and uninterruptible power supplies (UPSs) are commonly used to protect against adverse power conditions. A line conditioner can also be used. Each device has a specific purpose and guards against certain conditions. A technician must be familiar with each device in order to make recommendations for customers. Figure 5.37 shows a surge protector, and Chapter 19, "Operational Procedures," covers these devices in more detail.

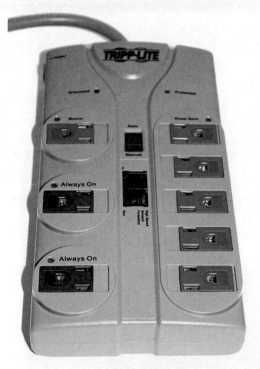

FIGURE 5.37   Tripp Lite surge protector

Symptoms of Power Supply Problems

The power supply is sometimes a source of unusual problems. The effects of the problems can range from those not noticed by the user to those that shut down the system. The following is a list of symptoms of power supply problems:

> The power light is off and/or the device won't turn on (**no power**)
> The power supply fan does not turn when the computer is powered on.
> The computer sounds a continuous beep. (This could also be a bad motherboard or a stuck key on the keyboard.)
> When the computer powers on, it does not beep at all. (This could also be a bad motherboard.)
> When the computer powers on, it sounds repeating short beeps. (This could also be a bad motherboard.)
> During POST, a 02X or parity POST error code appears (where X is any number); one of the POST checks is a power good signal from the power supply, and a 021, 022, … error message indicates that the power supply did not pass the POST test.
> The **computer reboots** or powers down without warning or reboots continuously.
> The power supply fan is noisy (emits a **loud noise**).
> The power supply is too hot to touch.

> The computer emits a **burning smell**, emits **smoke**, or is **overheating**
> The **power supply fan spins, but no power** goes to other devices.
> The monitor has a power light, but nothing appears on the monitor, and no PC power light illuminates.

Checking Power Supply Voltages

Refer to Figure 5.29 and notice how +3.3 V, +5 V, –5 V, +12 V, and –12 V are output and supplied to the motherboard (with **+5 V** and **+12 V** being the most common voltages supplied to devices). The motherboard and adapters use +3.3 V and +5 V, but –5 V is seldom used. Hard drives and optical drives commonly use +5 V and +12 V. The +12 voltage is used to operate the device motors found in drives, the CPU, internal cooling fans, and the graphics card. Drives are now being made that use +5 V motors. Chips use +5 V and +3.3 V, and +3.3 V is also used for memory, AGP/PCI/PCIe adapters, and some laptop fans. The negative voltages are seldom used.

A technician must occasionally check voltages in a system. There are four basic checks for power supply situations: (1) wall outlet AC voltage, (2) DC voltages going to the motherboard, (3) DC voltages going to a device, and (4) ground or lack of voltage with an outlet tester. A **power supply tester** can be used to check DC power levels on the different power supply connectors. Figure 5.38 shows a PC power supply tester. The type of connectors varies from vendor to vendor, so make sure you get a tester that can handle Molex, SATA, and main system power at a minimum.

FIGURE 5.38   PC power supply tester

Solving Power Supply Problems

When you suspect that a power supply is causing a problem, swap the power supply, make the customer happy, and be on your way! Power problems are not usually difficult to detect or troubleshoot.

TECH TIP

Do not disassemble a power supply

Power supplies are not normally disassembled. Manufacturers often rivet them shut. Even when a power supply can be disassembled, you should not take it apart unless you have a background in electronics.

Do not overlook the most obvious power supply symptoms. Start by checking the computer power light. If it is off, check the power supply's fan by placing your palm at the back of the computer. If the fan is turning, it means the wall outlet is providing power to the computer, and you can assume that the wall outlet is functioning. Check the motherboard for LEDs and refer to the manual for their meaning. Test the power outlet with another device. Ensure that the power cord is inserted fully into the wall outlet and the computer. If you suspect that the wall outlet is faulty, use an **AC circuit tester** to verify that the wall outlet is wired properly.

The following troubleshooting questions can help you determine the location of a power problem:

> Did the power supply work before? If not, check the input voltage selector switch on the power supply and verify that it is on the proper setting.

> Is the power supply's fan turning? If yes, check voltages going to the motherboard. If they are good, maybe just the power supply fan is bad. If the power supply's fan is not turning, check the wall outlet for proper AC voltages.

> Is a surge strip used? If so, check to see whether the surge strip is powered on and then try a different outlet in the surge strip or replace the surge strip.

> Is the computer's power cord okay? Verify that the power cord plugs snugly into the outlet and into the back of the computer. Swap the power cord to verify that it is functioning.

> Is the front panel power button stuck?

> Are the voltages going to the motherboard at the proper levels? If they are low, something might be overloading the power supply. Disconnect the power cable to one device and recheck the voltages. Replace the power cable to the device. Remove the power cable from another device and recheck the motherboard voltages. Continue doing this until the power cord for each device has been disconnected and the motherboard voltages have been checked. A single device can short out the power supply and cause the system to malfunction. Replace any device that draws down the power supply's output voltage and draws too much current. If none of the devices is the cause of the problem, replace the power supply. If replacing the power supply does not solve the problem, replace the motherboard.

If a computer does not boot properly but does boot when you press Ctrl+Alt+Del, the power good signal is likely the problem. Some motherboards are more sensitive to the power good signal than others. For example, say that a motherboard has been replaced, and the system does not boot. At first glance, this might appear to be a bad replacement board, but the problem could be caused by a power supply failing to output a consistent power good signal, so try replacing the power supply.

TECH TIP

Checking the power good signal

Check the power supply documentation to see whether the power supply outputs a power good signal, sometimes called a power OK signal, rather than the normal +5 V. Turn on the computer. Check the power good signal on the main motherboard power connector (attached to the power supply). Do this before replacing the motherboard. A power supply with a power good signal below +3 V needs to be replaced.

Sometimes, when a computer comes out of sleep mode, not all devices respond, and the computer's power or reset button has to be pressed to reboot the computer. The following situations can cause this to happen:

> A screen saver conflicts with ACPI.

> All adapters/devices are not ACPI compliant.

> An adapter/device has an outdated driver.
> The system BIOS/UEFI or an installed adapter BIOS needs to be updated.

To see whether the screen saver causes a problem, use the Display Control Panel and set the screen saver option to *None*. Identifying a problem adapter, device, or driver requires Internet research. Check each adapter, device, and driver individually. Use the Power Options Control Panel to change the power scheme. For each device, check for a *Power Management* tab on the *Properties* dialog box and make changes if needed.

SOFT SKILLS: WRITTEN COMMUNICATIONS SKILLS

When technicians are in school, they seldom think that the skills they should be learning involve writing. However, in the workplace, technicians use **written communication** skills when they document problems and use email (see Figure 5.39). Advisory committees across the country say that in addition to having technical knowledge, it is important that technicians be able to communicate effectively both in writing and orally, and they should be comfortable working in a team environment. In addition, technicians should possess critical thinking skills—that is, be able to solve a problem without having been taught about the specific problem.

FIGURE 5.39 Technicians must frequently provide written communication

Regardless of the size of a company, documentation is normally required. The documentation might be only the number of hours spent on a job and a basic description of what was done, but most companies require a bit more. Documentation should be written so others can read and understand it. Keep in mind that if another technician must handle another problem from the same customer, good documentation saves time and money. The following is a list of complaints from managers who hire technicians:

> Avoids doing documentation in a timely manner
> Does not provide adequate or accurate information on what was performed or tried
> Has poor spelling, grammar, capitalization, and punctuation skills
> Writes in short, choppy sentences, using technical jargon
> Does not provide updates on the status of a problem

You can use this list to know where to improve your skills and avoid making the same mistakes.

Email is a common means of communication for technicians. However, most technicians do not take the time to communicate effectively using email. The following is a list of guidelines for effective email communication:

> Do not use email when a meeting or a phone call is more appropriate.
> Include a short description of the email topic in the subject line.
> Do not write or respond to an email when you are angry.
> Send email only to the appropriate people; do not copy others unnecessarily.
> Stick to the point; do not digress.

CHAPTER 5

> Use a spelling and grammar checker; if one is not included in the email client, write the email in a word processing application, check it, and then paste the document into the body of the email.
> Use proper grammar, punctuation, and capitalization; do not write in all uppercase or all lowercase letters.
> Smile when you are typing. Your good attitude will come across in your writing.
> Focus on the task at hand. Read your note out loud if it is a critical one.
> Write each email as if you were putting the message on a billboard (see Figure 5.40); you never know how the content might be used or who might see it.

The number-one complaint about technical support staff is not their lack of technical skills but their lack of communication skills. Spend as much of your education practicing your communication skills as you do your technical skills.

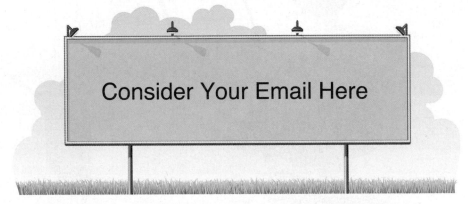

Consider Your Email Here

FIGURE 5.40   Consider what you write in written communications; it could be publicized

Chapter Summary

> Wearing a wrist strap or staying in contact with unpainted metal keeps you and the computing device at the same electrical potential so you won't induce current into any part and weaken/ damage it.
> EMI and RFI cause issues. Move the computer or the offending device and replace all slot covers/openings.
> When removing parts, have the right tools, lighting, and antistatic items, as well as ample workspace. Take notes. Don't use magnetized tools. Avoid jarring hard drives.
> Be careful when installing an I/O shield and be aware of standoffs when dealing with the motherboard.
> Preventive maintenance procedures prolong the life of the computer. Vacuum before spraying compressed air.
> An MSDS/SDS describes disposal and storage procedures and contains information about toxicity and health concerns. Cities/states have specific disposal rules for chemicals, batteries, CRTs, electronics, and so on. Always know the disposal rules in the area where you work.
> AC power goes into the power supply or mobile device power brick. DC power is provided to all internal parts of the computing device. AC and DC voltage checks can be done, and only with DC power does polarity matter. Use the highest meter setting possible with unknown voltage levels. Power is measured in watts.
> Continuity checks are done on cabling, and a good wire shows close to 0 ohms.
> A power supply converts AC to DC, distributes DC throughout a unit, and provides cooling. The power supply must be the correct form factor and able to supply the current amount of

wattage for a particular voltage level, such as +5 V or +12 V. Multiple "rails" are commonly available for +12 V because the CPU commonly needs its own connection. The numbers and types of connectors vary, but converters can be purchased.

> Use ACPI to control power options through the BIOS/UEFI and the operating system. Wake on LAN and Wake on Ring are power features that allow a device to be powered up from a lowered power condition for a specific purpose.
> The Power Options Control Panel is used to configure the power scheme in Windows.
> AC circuit testers, multimeters, and power supply testers are tools used with power problems.
> A UPS provides battery backup.
> In all communications and written documentation, be professional and effective. Use proper capitalization, grammar, punctuation, and spelling.

A+ CERTIFICATION EXAM TIPS

✓ Review the chapter summary. Quite a few exam-related questions are about preventive maintenance procedures. Don't forget that other chapters have preventive maintenance tips, too, including the chapters on storage devices, multimedia devices, and other peripherals.

✓ Always remember to power down a computer, remove the power cord/power brick/battery, and allow a laser printer to cool before performing maintenance.

✓ Be familiar with proper component handling and storage, including the use of self-grounding techniques, antistatic bags, ESD straps, and ESD mats.

✓ Know the purpose of a MSDS.

✓ Know that both with safety issues and when dealing with chemicals and components that could have potential environmental impact, IT personnel must comply with local government regulations.

✓ Know the purpose of an antistatic ESD strap, ESD mats, antistatic bags, and self-grounding techniques. Don't use an antistatic ESD strap when working inside an old CRT monitor or power supply.

✓ Know when to use a toner vacuum and when to use a regular vacuum and compressed air to deal with dust and debris. Wear safety goggles and an air filter/mask for protection from airborne particles. Know when an enclosure is needed.

✓ Know the purpose of and what is contained within a preventive maintenance kit. Be aware of temperature risks, effects of humidity on electronic equipment, and when ventilation is needed.

✓ Be familiar with SATA and IDE motherboard connectors as well as front panel connectors.

✓ Be able to identify and explain basic SATA and IDE hard drive cables.

✓ Identify common connector types, such as a Molex connector.

✓ Know that the power supply outputs 5 V and 12 V and that electronics commonly use the 5 V and motors use 12 V. If the computer is to be used internationally, ensure the computer supports an auto-switching power supply that accepts either 115 V or 220 V as input voltage.

✓ Understand computer component power requirements and that the power supply must be powerful enough to power the number of devices and types of devices installed in the computer.

✓ Be familiar with common power problem symptoms, including the fan spinning but no power being provided to other devices, lack of power, noisy or inoperative fan, and the computer rebooting or powering down without warning.

✓ Be familiar with motherboard connections to the top and front panels (USB, audio, power button, power light, drive activity lights, and reset button).

✓ The following communication and professionalism skills are part of the 220-1002 exam: Use proper language and avoid jargon, acronyms, and slang when applicable; and provide proper documentation on the services provided.

Key Terms

+12 V   198
+5 V   198
115 V vs. 220 V input
voltage   184
24-pin motherboard
connector   185
4-pin 12 V   185
6-pin PCIe   185
8-pin 12 V   185
8-pin PCIe   185
15-pin SATA power   185
24-pin main power   185
AC   180
AC circuit tester   199
ACPI   191
air filter   178
air filter/mask   178
amp   182
antistatic bag   164
antistatic wrist strap   162
auto-switching   184
burning smell   198
compressed air   178
computer reboots   197

continuity   182
DC   180
dual-rail power supply   194
dual-voltage   184
EMI   165
ESD   162
ESD mat   164
ESD strap   162
front panel connector   171
grounding   162
hibernate mode   192
I/O shield   174
IDE connector   171
loud noise   197
maintenance kit   178
mask   178
Molex   185
MSDS   179
no power   197
ohm   182
overheating   198
pin 1   170
power   182

power supply fan spins, but no
power   198
power supply tester   198
preventive maintenance   177
resistance   182
RFI   165
safety goggles   178
SATA connector   171
screwdriver   166
self-grounding   164
SDS   179
sleep mode   192
smoke   198
standby power   181
standoff   174
suspend mode   192
toner vacuum   178
volt   181
voltage   181
Wake on LAN   192
Wake on Ring   192
watt   182
wattage rating   193
written communication   201

Review Questions

1. What would happen if you removed the battery from the motherboard by accident?

    _____

    _____

2. List three tasks commonly performed during preventive maintenance.

    _____

    _____

    _____

3. Computers used in a grocery store warehouse for inventory control have a higher part failure rate than do the other company computers. Which of the following is most likely to help in this situation?

    a. an antistatic wrist strap

    b. a preventive maintenance plan

    c. antistatic pads

    d. high-wattage power supplies

4. Which of the following can prolong the life of a computer and conserve resources? (Select all that apply.)

    a. a preventive maintenance plan

    b. antistatic mats and pads

    c. upgraded power supply

    d. a power plan

    e. Li-ion replacement batteries

    f. extra case fans

5. Which power component has a 24-pin connector?

    a. main motherboard connector

    b. power supply fan

    c. case fan

    d. AUX power for the CPU

6. An optical drive randomly becomes unavailable, and after replacing the drive, the technician now suspects that the drive may not be getting 5 volts consistently. What could help in this situation?

    a. a UPS

    b. a surge protector

    c. antistatic wipes

    d. a preventive maintenance plan

    e. a power supply tester

7. When disassembling a computer, which tool will help you remove the memory module?

    a. magnetic screwdriver

    b. needle-nose pliers

    c. #1 or #2 Phillips screwdriver

    d. antistatic wrist strap

CHAPTER 5

8. A user had a motherboard problem last week, and a technician fixed it. Now the same computer has a different problem. The user reports that the USB ports on the front do not work anymore. What is the first thing you should check?

   a. power supply

   b. power connection to the front panel

   c. motherboard connections to the front panel

   d. voltage output from the power supply to the USB connectors

9. Which of the following items would be specialized for use with a laser printer?

   [surge strip | vacuum | power supply tester | antistatic wrist strap]

10. Which two of the following would most likely cause a loud noise on a desktop computer? (Choose two.)

    [motherboard | USB drive | power supply | case fan | memory | PCIe adapter]

11. A computer will not power on. Which of the following would be used to check the wall outlet?

    [power supply tester | UPS | multimeter | POST]

12. A computer will not power on. After checking the wall outlet and swapping the power cord, what would the technician use next?

    a. resistance

    b. power supply tester

    c. antistatic wrist strap

    d. magnetic screwdriver

    e. nonmagnetic screwdriver

13. Which of the following is affected by the power supply wattage rating?

    a. number of internal storage devices

    b. number of power supply connectors

    c. speed of the processor

    d. type of processor

    e. type of power supply connectors

14. Which of the following would help with computer heat?

    a. increasing the power supply wattage

    b. upgrading to a larger power supply form factor

    c. unplugging unused power connectors

    d. installing case fans

15. [T | F] Power supply disassembly is a common requirement of a PC technician.

16. Consider the following email.

> From: Cheryl a. Schmidt
> To: Network Engineering Technology Faculty
> Subj: [None]
> We have little time to get the PMS done on the PCs and N/W gear. What software do you want?

Reword this email to illustrate good written communication skills.

```



```

17. List three recommendations for good technical written communication.

_____

_____

_____

18. A computer is doing weird things, such as shutting down unexpectedly and hanging. You suspect a power problem. You check the power good (power OK) signal on the power supply's main motherboard connector. The voltage reading shows that you have power (+2.5 volts). What are you going to do next?

    a. Check the voltage coming out of a Molex or SATA connector.

    b. Check the wall outlet voltage.

    c. Replace the power supply.

    d. Check the power supply cable for resistance.

19. What is the purpose of the I/O shield?

    a. It prevents dust and dirt from coming in through the front computer ports.

    b. It provides grounding for motherboard ports.

    c. It prevents dust and dirt from coming into the power supply.

    d. It protects the technician from shocks.

20. Which two items would help a technician maintain personal safety while working on PCs and printers in an extremely dusty warehouse? (Choose two.)

[vacuum | toner vacuum | safety goggles | antistatic wrist strap | air filter/mask]

CHAPTER 5

Exercises

Exercise 5.1 Identifying Power Supply Connectors

Objective: To be able to identify the purposes of common power supply connectors

Procedure: Identify the power supply connectors in Figure 5.41.

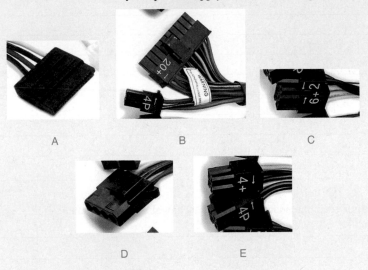

A   B   C

D   E

FIGURE 5.41   Identifying power connectors

_____ 1. Molex for older optical drive

_____ 2. SATA for hard drive

_____ 3. PCIe video

_____ 4. Main motherboard

_____ 5. CPU

Exercise 5.2 Recognizing Computer Replacement Parts

Objective: To be able to recognize parts from a computer

Procedure: Use the following information to answer the questions.

The following parts were ordered by someone building his or her own computer:

a. Intel Core i7 4.4 GHz

b. ASUS Rampage V Extreme X99 (does not include USB 3.1 headers)

c. Triage 8 GB

d. Micro-ATX with two 3.5" internal and two 5.25" external drive bays

e. EVA 450 W

1.   What part is designated by the letter a?
      [memory I hard drive I optical drive I CPU]

2.   What part is designated by the letter b?
      [motherboard I processor I memory I hard drive]

3.   What part is designated by the letter c?
      [motherboard I optical drive I RAM I SATA hard drive I SSD]

4.   What part is designated by the letter d?
      [RAM I case I all storage devices I power supply]

5.   What part is designated by the letter e?
      [case I SSD I optical drive I power supply]

Exercise 5.3 Describing Computer Parts

Objective: To be able to recognize computer parts based on a description

Procedure: Match the description to the computer part affected during disassembly.

_____ 1. 24-pin connector	a. Power supply to motherboard cable
_____ 2. 40-pin ribbon cable	b. Front panel to motherboard cable
_____ 3. Antistatic bag	c. Hard drive to motherboard cable
_____ 4. ESD strap	d. Motherboard to IDE PATA device
_____ 5. Grounding	e. Attaches to wrist and computer
_____ 6. Hard drive	f. Holds an adapter when not in use
_____ 7. HDD LED	g. Helps with EMI
_____ 8. SATA 3	h. Keeping in contact with the computer
_____ 9. Slot cover	i. Attaches motherboard to case
_____ 10. Standoffs	j. Might need guide rails

Activities

Internet Discovery

Objective: To obtain specific information on the Internet regarding a computer or its associated parts

Parts: Computer with Internet access

Procedure: Complete the following procedure and answer the following questions.

1.   Locate an Internet site that provides tips for doing computer preventive maintenance.

Write two of the best tips and the URL where you found the information.

_____

_____

2.   Locate an Internet site where you can buy a computer toolkit that includes an antistatic wrist strap.

List the URL where you found the toolkit and at least three sizes of screwdrivers or bits provided.

_____

3.   Locate a power supply tester that includes a SATA connector.

List the manufacturer and model.

_____

4.   Find a website on good netiquette.

Give three recommendations and the name of the website (not the URL).

_____

_____

_____

5.   You have just started working at a place that uses the HP Elite 800 G2 23-inch nontouch all-in-one computer.

You have been sent to do power checks on the power supply of one of these units. How do you get the cover off? Explain in detail, using complete sentences.

_____

_____

_____

_____

CHAPTER 5

What recommendation does HP give for cleaning the case of stubborn stains that might be found on the computers in the maintenance shop?

_____

According to the documentation, what is different about removing an AMD processor than removing an Intel processor?

_____

_____

Soft Skills

Objective: To enhance and fine-tune a future technician's ability to listen, communicate in both written and oral forms, and support people who use computers in a professional manner

Activities:

1. Prepare a business proposal for a replacement power supply. Present your proposal to the class.

2. Write an informal report on the skills learned while taking apart a computer and reassembling it. Share your best practices with a small group.

3. Work in teams to decide the best way to inform a customer about the differences between a line conditioner and a UPS. Present your description to the class as if you were talking to the customer. Each team member must contribute. Each classmate votes for the best team explanation.

Critical Thinking Skills

Objective: To analyze and evaluate information as well as apply learned information to new or different situations

Activities:

1. Use the Internet to find a description of a particular computer that lists each device that is installed and the type of motherboard, integrated ports, and so on. Then locate a power supply calculator. Find a replacement power supply, based on the calculations performed. Write the details of what you looked for in the replacement power supply, the power supply, vendor, number and type of connectors, and cost.

2. For one of the computers in the classroom, locate the documentation on how to disassemble it. Looking through the documentation, find at least three things that are good tips that you might not have thought of immediately if you were disassembling the computer. Then find at least three safety tips. Place all of this information in an outline. An alternative is to be creative and present the tips graphically on one page or presentation slide.

6
Memory

In this chapter you will learn:

> Different memory technologies

> How to plan for a memory installation or upgrade

> How to install and remove memory modules

> How to optimize memory for Windows platforms

> Best practices for troubleshooting memory problems

> The benefits of teamwork

CompTIA Exam Objectives:

What CompTIA A+ exam objectives are covered in this chapter?

✓ 1001-3.3   Given a scenario, install RAM types.

✓ 1001-5.2   Given a scenario, troubleshoot problems related to motherboards, RAM, CPUs, and power.

✓ 1002-1.5   Given a scenario, use Microsoft operating system features and tools.

✓ 1002-4.7   Given a scenario, use proper communication techniques and professionalism.

Memory Overview

Computer systems need software to operate. The software must reside in computer memory. A technician must understand memory terminology, determine the optimum amount of memory for a system, install the memory, fine-tune it for the best performance, and troubleshoot and solve any memory problems.

The two main types of memory are random-access memory (**RAM**) and read-only memory (ROM), and the difference between them is shown in Figure 6.1.

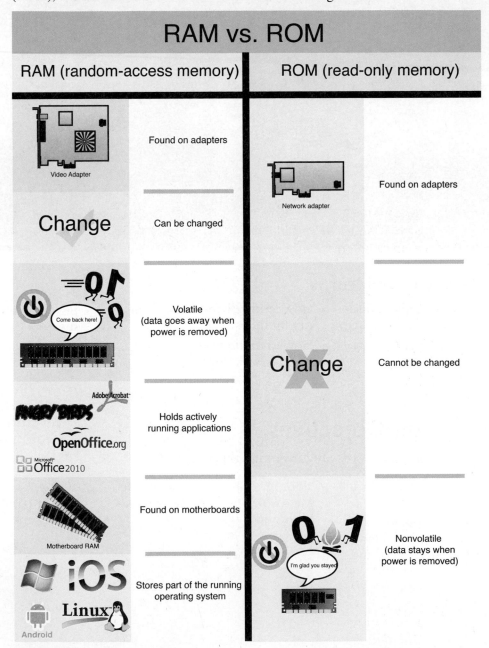

FIGURE 6.1   RAM vs. ROM

RAM is divided into two major types: dynamic RAM (**DRAM**) and static RAM (**SRAM**). DRAM is less expensive but slower than SRAM. With DRAM, the 1s and 0s inside the chip must be refreshed. Over time, the charge, which represents information inside a DRAM chip, leaks out. The information, which is stored in 1s and 0s, is periodically rewritten to the memory chip through the **refresh** process. The refreshing is accomplished inside the DRAM while other processing occurs. Refreshing is one reason DRAM chips are slower than SRAM.

Most memory on a motherboard is DRAM, but a small amount of SRAM can be found inside the processor, just outside the processor inside the processor housing, and sometimes on the motherboard. SRAM is also known as **cache memory**. Cache memory holds the most frequently used data so the CPU does not return to the slower DRAM chips to obtain the data. For example, on a motherboard with a bus speed of 233 MHz, accessing DRAM could take as long as 90 nanoseconds. (A nanosecond, abbreviated ns, is one-billionth of a second.) Accessing the same information in cache could take as little as 23 nanoseconds.

TECH TIP

The CPU should never have to wait to receive an instruction

Using pipelined burst cache speeds up processing for software applications.

The data or instruction that the processor needs is usually found in one of three places: cache, DRAM, or the hard drive. Cache gives the fastest access. If the information is not in cache, the processor looks for it in DRAM. If the information is not in DRAM, it is retrieved from the hard drive and placed into DRAM or the cache. Hard drive access is the slowest of the three. In a computer, it takes roughly a million times longer to access information from the hard drive than it does to access information from DRAM or cache.

TECH TIP

Don't forget hard drive space and video memory

RAM is only one piece of the puzzle. All of a computer's parts—including RAM, hard drive space, and video memory—must work together to provide good (optimal) system performance.

As noted in Chapter 3, "On the Motherboard," to determine a computer's memory requirements, you must consider the operating system, applications, and installed hardware. Memory is one of the most critical things on the motherboard that can easily be upgraded. Let's start with the physical memory module.

Memory Physical Packaging

A dual in-line package (DIP) chip has a row of legs running down each side. The oldest motherboards use DIP chips for the DRAM. Single in-line memory modules (SIMM) came along next. Sometimes you might see SIMMs as memory in laser printers. The memory chip used on motherboards today is a dual in-line memory module (**DIMM**), which has 168, 184, 240, or 288 pins. Memory can also be called a memory stick, or a technician might call one memory module a stick of memory or simply RAM. Laptops and printers use a smaller DIMM called a small outline DIMM (**SODIMM**). Figure 6.2 shows the progression of memory packaging. Figure 6.3 shows a SODIMM.

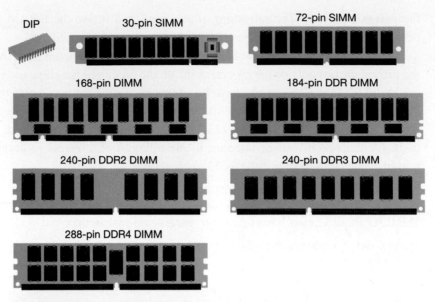

FIGURE 6.2   Memory chips/modules

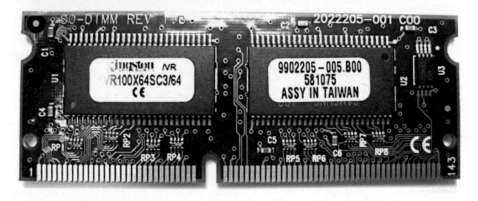

FIGURE 6.3   SODIMM

Planning a Memory Installation

Now that you know a little about memory types, let us look at how to go about planning a memory installation. Some key points follow:

> Refer to the system or motherboard documentation to see what type of memory is supported.
> Determine what features are supported.
> Determine how much memory is needed.
> Determine what memory module(s) you need and how many of them.
> Research prices and purchase the memory module(s) you needed.

Planning the Memory Installation: Memory Module Types

Technology has provided faster DRAM speeds without increasing the cost too greatly. Table 6.1 lists some of the memory technologies available today.

TABLE 6.1 Memory module types

Technology	Explanation
Synchronous DRAM (SDRAM)	Performs very fast burst memory access. New memory addresses are placed on the address but before the prior memory address retrieval and execution is complete. SDRAM synchronizes its operation with the CPU clock signal to speed up memory access. Used with DIMMs.
Double data rate (DDR)	Sometimes called DDR SDRAM or DDR RAM and developed from SDRAM technology. DDR memory can send twice as much data as the older PC133 SDRAM because data is transmitted on both sides of the clock signal (that is, on the rising and falling edges instead of just on the rising edge).
DDR2	Sometimes called DDR2 RAM. DDR2 uses 240-pin DIMMs and is not compatible with DDR.
DDR3	An upgrade from DDR2 (8-bit prefetch buffer compared to 4-bit with DDR2). DDR3 uses 240-pin DIMMs and is not compatible with DDR2 or DDR. The technology better supports multicore processor-based systems and more efficient power utilization.
DDR3L	A DDR3 module that runs at a lower voltage (1.35 V) than the 1.5 V or higher DDR/DDR2/DDR3 modules. Less voltage means less heat and less power consumed.
DDR4	Operates at a lower voltage and faster speeds than DDR3 modules. DDR4 uses 288-pin DIMMs and is not compatible with DDR, DDR2, or DDR3. Allows for storage up to 512 GB on a single module.
DDR4L	Uses a lower voltage (1.05 V) than a standard DDR4 module.

Whether a motherboard supports faster memory chips is determined by the chipset, which performs most functions in conjunction with the processor. A chipset is one to five electronic chips on the motherboard. The chipset contains the circuitry to control the local bus, memory, DMA, interrupts, and cache memory. The motherboard manufacturer determines which chipset to use.

TECH TIP

Using the right type of memory chips

The chipset and motherboard design are very specific about what type, speed, and features the memory chips can have. Refer to the motherboard documentation.

Most people cannot tell the difference among DDR, DDR2, DDR3, and DDR4 memory modules. Even though DDR uses 184 pins, DDR2 and DDR3 use 240 pins, and DDR4 has 288 pins, they are the same physical size. Even though both DDR2 and DDR3 modules have 240 pins, a DDR3 module does not fit in a DDR2 or DDR4 memory slot. Figure 6.4 shows DDR3 DIMMs.

Notice in Figure 6.4 the metal casing, called a **heat spreader**, on the outside of the memory module. Aluminum or copper is commonly used on heat spreaders in order to dissipate heat away from the memory. Table 6.2 lists many of the DIMM models.

FIGURE 6.4 DDR3 DIMMs

TABLE 6.2 DIMMs

Memory type	Alternative name	Clock speed	Data rate
PC2-9200	DDR2-1150	575 MHz	1.15 GT/s
PC2-9600	DDR2-1200	600 MHz	1.2 GT/s
PC3-6400	DDR3-800	400 MHz	800 MT/s
PC3-8500	DDR3-1066	533 MHz	1.06 GT/s
PC3-10600	DDR3-1333	666 MHz	1.33 GT/s
PC3-12800	DDR3-1600	800 MHz	1.6 GT/s
PC3-16000	DDR3-2000	1000 MHz	2 GT/s
PC3-17000	DDR3-2133	1066 MHz	2.13 GT/s
PC4-1866	DDR4-1866	933 MHz	1.86 GT/s
PC4-2400	DDR4-2400	1200 MHz	2.4 GT/s
PC4-2666	DDR4-2666	1333 MHz	2.66 GT/s
PC4-3000	DDR4-3000	1500 MHz	3 GT/s
PC4-25600	DDR4-3200	1600 MHz	3.2 GT/s

Because a DIMM can be shown with either the PCX- or DDRX- designation, which type you buy can be confusing. A brief explanation might help. DDR3-2000 is a type of DDR3 memory that can run on a 1000 MHz front side bus (the number after DDR3 divided in half). Another way of showing the same chip would be to use the designation PC3-16000, which is the theoretical bandwidth of the memory chip in MB/s. The good news about DDR4 is that the module names now match the standard names.

Planning the Memory Installation: Memory Features

In addition to determining what type of memory chips are going to be used, you must determine what features the memory chips might have. The computer system or motherboard documentation delineates what features are supported. Table 6.3 helps characterize memory features.

TABLE 6.3 Memory features

Feature	Explanation
Parity	A method for checking data accuracy. (See the tech tip "How parity works.")
Non-parity	Chips that do not use any error checking.
Error correcting code (**ECC**)	An alternative to parity checking that uses a mathematical algorithm to verify data accuracy. ECC can detect up to 4-bit memory errors and correct 1-bit memory errors. ECC is used in higher-end computers and network servers. **Non-ECC** memory modules are simply modules that do not support ECC.
Unbuffered memory	The opposite of registered memory, used in low- to medium-powered computers. Unbuffered memory is faster than registered or fully buffered memory.
Buffered memory (registered memory)	Memory module that has extra chips (registers) near the bottom of the module that delay all data transfers by one clock tick to ensure accuracy. Buffered memory is used in servers and high-end computers. If you install a registered memory module into a system that allows both registered and unbuffered memory, all memory must be registered modules. These modules are sometimes advertised as fully buffered DIMMs (FBDIMM).
Serial presence detect (**SPD**)	A module that has an extra EEPROM that holds information about the DIMM (capacity, voltage, refresh rates, and so on). The BIOS/UEFI reads and uses this data for best performance. Some modules have **thermal sensors** (sometimes listed as TS in an advertisement) used to monitor and report memory heat conditions.
Single-sided memory	A memory module that has one "bank" of memory, with 64 bits transferred out of the memory module to the CPU. A better term for single-sided memory is single-banked memory. The module might or might not have all of its "chips" on one side.
Double-sided memory	A single memory module developed in such a way that it actually contains two memory modules in one container (two banks). If the motherboard slot has been designed to accept this type of memory module, data is still sent to the CPU 64 bits at a time. This is a way to have more banks of memory on the motherboard without requiring more memory slots. These modules normally have memory chips on both sides, but all modules with chips on both sides are not double-sided memory.
Dual-voltage memory	A module that can operate at a lower voltage level (thus with less heat) if the motherboard supports this feature. Note that all installed modules must also support the lower voltage for the system to operate in this mode.
Extreme memory profile (XMP)	A type of memory module that allows the BIOS to configure voltage and timing settings in order to overclock the memory.

TECH TIP

How parity works

If a system uses even parity and the data bits 10000001 go into memory, the ninth bit, or parity bit, is a 0 because an even number of bits (2) are 1s. The parity changes to a 1 only when the number of bits in the data is an odd number of 1s. If the system uses even parity and the data bits 10000011 go into memory, the parity bit is a 1. There are only three 1s in the data bits. The parity bit adjusts the 1s to an even number. When checking data for accuracy, the parity method detects if 1 bit is incorrect. However, if 2 bits are in error, parity does not catch the error.

Keep in mind that some motherboards might support both non-parity and ECC (error correcting code) or might require a certain feature such as SPD. It is important that you research this *before* you purchase memory.

A memory module might use more than one of the categories listed in the Tables 6.2 and 6.3. For example, a DIMM could be a DDR3 module, could be registered, and could support ECC for error detection and correction. Most registered memory also uses the ECC technology. Memory modules can support either ECC or non-ECC, and they can be registered or unbuffered memory.

Memory technology is moving quite quickly today. Chipsets also change constantly. Technicians are continually challenged to keep up with the features and abilities of the technology so that they can make recommendations to their customers. Trade magazines and the Internet are excellent resources for updates. Don't forget to check the motherboard's documentation when dealing with memory. Information is a technician's best friend.

TECH TIP

If error correction isn't mentioned in the advertisement...

If error correction is not mentioned, the chip is a non-parity chip. Most memory modules today are non-parity because the memory controller circuitry provides error correction.

Planning for Memory: How Much Memory to Install

When you want to improve the performance of a computer, adding memory is one of the easiest upgrades. The amount of memory needed depends on the operating system, applications, number of applications open at the same time, type of computer, and the maximum amount allowed by the motherboard.

The operating system you use determines to a great extent the starting point for the amount of memory to have. Generally, the older or less powerful your operating system, the smaller amount of RAM you need. Table 6.4 provides a starting point for calculating memory requirements. Remember that as you want to run more applications simultaneously and the higher the application function (such as gaming or photo/video/sound manipulation), the more memory you will need. Also note that the memory recommendations shown in Table 6.4 are not the minimum requirements listed by the operating system creators. Notice that Apple computers (macOS) have similar memory recommendations to PCs.

TABLE 6.4   Minimum operating system starting memory recommendations

Operating system	Minimum amount of RAM to start calculations
Windows 7	1 GB
Windows 8/10	1 GB (32-bit)/2 GB (64-bit)
macOS Mavericks/Yosemite/El Capitan/ Sierra/High Sierra/Mojave	2 GB
Linux	Depending on the version, from 64 MB

When upgrading memory, you need to know a couple of key pieces of information:

> How much memory are you starting with?
> How many motherboard RAM slots are currently being used, and are there any slots free?
> What is the maximum amount of memory that your motherboard supports?

TECH TIP

Windows might have memory limitations

Even if the motherboard allows more memory, your operating system has limitations. Upgrade the operating system if this is the case. Table 6.5 shows the Windows memory limits.

TABLE 6.5   Windows 7/8/10 memory limits

Operating system	32-bit version limit	64-bit version limit
Windows 7 Starter edition	2 GB	N/A
Windows 7 Home Basic	4 GB	8 GB
Windows 7 Home Premium	4 GB	16 GB
Windows 7 Business/Professional/ Enterprise/Ultimate	4 GB	192 GB
Windows 8	4 GB	128 GB
Windows 8 Professional/Enterprise	4 GB	512 GB
Windows 10 Home	4 GB	128 GB
Windows 10 Pro/Enterprise	4 GB	2 TB

Use Windows Explorer (in Windows 7) or File Explorer (in Windows 8/10). In Windows 7 to see the amount of installed memory, right-click *Computer > Properties*. In Windows 8/10 right-click (or tap and hold briefly) *This PC > Properties*. Or, in any version of Windows, access the *System Information* window from a command prompt by typing `msinfo32` and pressing Enter. Scroll down to see the memory information. Figure 6.5 shows the System Information window for a computer system that currently has 24 GB of RAM installed (24.0 GB Total Physical Memory).

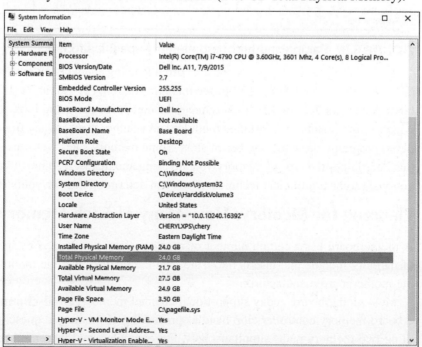

FIGURE 6.5   System Information window

Every motherboard has a maximum

Each motherboard supports a maximum amount of memory. You must check the computer or motherboard documentation to see how much this is. There is not a workaround for this limitation. If you want more memory than the motherboard allows, you must upgrade to a different motherboard.

Figure 6.6 shows a sample advertisement for a micro-ATX motherboard. The *Specifications* tab commonly shows the type of memory supported (and may also show the exact speeds supported), the maximum amount of memory, and the number of memory slots.

Overview	Specifications	Warranty

Specifications

Motherboard Specifications	
Motherboard Type	Desktop
Processor Socket	Intel
Processor Interface	LGA1150
Form Factor	Micro ATX
Processors Supported	Intel® Core™ i3, i5, i7, Pentium, Celeron, Xeon
Chipset	
Northbridge	Intel H81 Express
Memory	
Memory Type	DDR3
Maximum Memory Supported	16GB
Number of Slots	2

FIGURE 6.6　Sample motherboard memory specifications

To determine how many slots you are currently using and whether you have any free, you need to either (1) access the BIOS/UEFI to see this information; (2) use the *Task Manager > Performance* tab in Windows 7, 8, or 10; or (3) remove the computer cover and look at the motherboard to see which memory slots have installed modules and whether there are any free slots. Some BIOS/UEFI Setup programs show the number of slots. Some memory sales websites have a software program that determines the type of memory you are using and makes recommendations. However, because you want to be a proficient technician, you can determine this for yourself.

Planning for Memory: How Many of Each Memory Type?

A motherboard has a certain number of memory slots, determined by its manufacturer. The type of memory module that inserts into a slot and the features that the module has are determined by the motherboard manufacturer.

Most motherboards today support dual-channel memory. **Dual-channel** means that the motherboard memory controller chip handles processing of memory requests more efficiently by handling two memory paths simultaneously. For example, say that a motherboard has four memory slots. Traditionally, the memory controller chip, commonly called the MCH (memory controller hub), had one channel through which all data from the four slots traveled. With dual-channeling, the four slots are divided into two channels, and each channel has two slots. Figure 6.7 shows this concept.

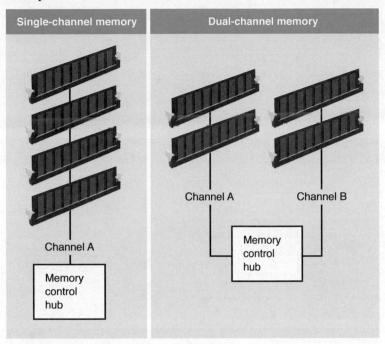

FIGURE 6.7   Dual-channel memory

Dual-channeling increases a system's performance. However, it speeds things up only if the memory modules match exactly—same memory type, same memory features, same speed, and same capacity. Note that on some motherboards, the memory modules on Channel A and Channel B do not have to have the same capacities, but the total capacity of the memory module in Channel A should match the total capacity of the memory modules installed in Channel B. Some motherboards require this. Figure 6.8 illustrates this concept.

TECH TIP

Dual-channel should use exact memory module pairs

Channel A and Channel B (sometimes labeled Channel 0 and Channel 1) should have matching memory modules. Buy a kit (a package of pre-tested memory modules that are guaranteed to work together) to ensure that the two modules are the same.

Notice in Figure 6.8 that in the first example, two identical memory modules are inserted: one memory module in Channel A and the other in Channel B. Motherboard manufacturers frequently require that the memory modules match in all respects—manufacturer, timing, and capacity—in order to support dual-channeling.

The middle section of Figure 6.8 shows three DIMMs being used. Some manufacturers support dual-channeling with three DIMMS, but you should check the motherboard or system documentation to ensure that this is the case. Another example that is not shown in the figure is when an uneven amount of memory is installed in Channel A and Channel B. For example, Channel A might have 2 GB and Channel B a 1 GB memory module. Some motherboards can dual-channel for the first 1 GB. But only if the motherboard supports this can dual-channeling be achieved.

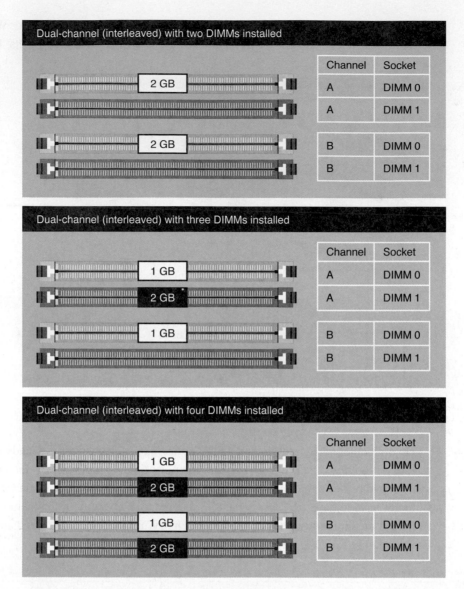

FIGURE 6.8 The total capacity of the memory module installed in Channel A should match the total capacity in Channel B

In the last section shown in Figure 6.8, all four DIMMs are installed. Notice that the Channel A total capacity matches the Channel B total capacity (3 GB in both channels, for a total of 6 GB). When dual-channeling, buy memory modules in pairs from a single source. Memory vendors sell them this way.

TECH TIP

Beware of RAM over 4 GB

Do not install over 4 GB on a computer with a 32-bit operating system such as 32-bit Windows. The operating system will not be able to recognize anything over 4 GB. As a matter of fact, even when a system has 4 GB installed, the 32-bit operating system shows the installed amount as slightly less than 4 GB because some of that memory space is used for devices attached to the PCI/PCIe bus.

To plan for the correct amount of memory, you must refer to the motherboard documentation. An example helps with this concept. Figure 6.9 shows a motherboard layout with four memory slots that has different labeling than shown in Figure 6.8. Remember that motherboard manufacturers can label their motherboards any way they want. This is one of the reasons documentation is so important.

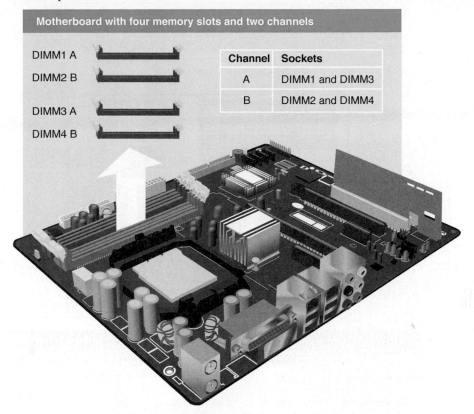

Channel	**Sockets**
A	DIMM1 and DIMM3
B	DIMM2 and DIMM4

FIGURE 6.9   Motherboard with four memory slots and two channels

The motherboard in Figure 6.9 allows 512 MB, 1 GB, and 2 GB unbuffered non-ECC DDR2-533 240-pin DIMMs, for a maximum of 8 GB. Pretend the customer wants 2 GB of RAM. What could you do? How many memory modules would you buy, and what capacities? Table 6.6 shows the possible solutions. The best solution is the second one because it has the largest-capacity chips and takes advantage of dual-channeling, with slots left over for more upgrading.

TABLE 6.6   Possible solutions

Solution	Number and size of memory module(s) needed
1	Four 512 MB DIMMs installed in DIMM1, DIMM2, DIMM3, and DIMM4 slots (dual-channeling)
2*	Two 1 GB DIMMs installed in DIMM1 and DIMM2 slots (dual-channeling)
3	Two 1 GB DIMMs installed in DIMM1 and DIMM3 slots (not dual-channeling)
4	One 2 GB DIMM installed in DIMM1 (not dual-channeling)

*Best solution

Many newer motherboards and server motherboards support **triple-channel** memory, where three memory modules work together, or **quadruple-channel** memory, where four memory modules are accessed simultaneously. Figure 6.10 shows a motherboard that has six memory expansion slots and that supports triple-channeling.

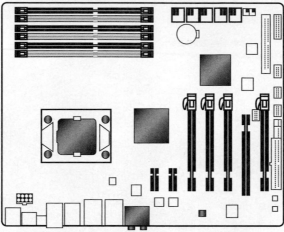

Dual-channel Configuration						
	DIMM 1	DIMM 2	DIMM 3	DIMM 4	DIMM 5	DIMM 6
Two modules	X		X			
Four modules	X	X	X	X		

Triple-channel Configuration						
	DIMM 1	DIMM 2	DIMM 3	DIMM 4	DIMM 5	DIMM 6
Three modules	X		X		X	
Six modules	X	X	X	X	X	X

FIGURE 6.10 Motherboard with six memory slots and three channels

Planning for Memory: Researching and Buying Memory

The researching and buying step in the process of planning for a memory installation/upgrade is the step most likely to make your head spin. Different websites list memory differently. Some give you too much information and some too little. A few, such as Kingston Technology (http://www.kingston.com) and Crucial (http://www.crucial.com), specialize in memory and make it as painless as possible. Nevertheless, as a technician, you should be familiar with all aspects of memory and memory advertisements.

A confusing aspect of buying memory is memory speed. Memory speed can be represented as MHz or the PC rating. The higher the number, the faster the speed of the module.

To further understand memory, it is best to look at some examples. Table 6.7 shows examples of how different amounts of memory might be advertised.

TABLE 6.7 Sample DIMM advertisements

Memory module	How it might be advertised
2 GB	DDR3 PC3-10600 • CL=9 • UNBUFFERED • NON-ECC • DDR3-1333 • 1.35 V • 256 Meg×64
2 GB	DDR3 PC3-12800E • CL=11 • REGISTERED • ECC • DDR3-1600 • 1.35 V • 256 Meg×72
2 GB kit (1 GB×2)	DDR3 PC3-10600 • CL=9 • REGISTERED • ECC • DDR3-1333 • 1.5 V • 128 Meg×72
2 GB	DDR2 PC2-5300FB • CL=5 • FULLY BUFFERED • ECC • DDR2-667 • 1.8 V • 256 Meg×72

Notice in Table 6.7 (as in most memory advertisements) that the memory capacity is shown first. The third row lists a kit for a motherboard that has dual-channeling capabilities. It includes two 1 GB memory modules, for a total of a 2 GB memory gain. Also pay attention to the type of memory module being advertised. Notice in Table 6.7 that the first three memory modules are DDR3 and show the PC3 rating. Later, the advertisement also shows the effective data transfer rate of 1333 MHz or 1600 MHz. Some vendors add an E to the PC3 number to show an ECC module or an F or FB to the PC3 number to show that the module has the fully buffered feature.

Another listing in the memory advertisement shown in Table 6.7 is the **CL rating**. CL (column address strobe [CAS] latency) is the amount of time (based on clock cycles) that passes before the processor moves on to the next memory address. RAM is made up of cells that hold data. A cell is the intersection of a row and a column. (It is much like a cell in a spreadsheet application.) The CAS signal picks which memory column to select, and a signal called RAS (row address strobe) picks which row to select. The intersection of the two is where the data is stored.

TECH TIP

CL ratings and speed

The lower the CL rating, the faster the memory. Think of access time like a track meet: The person with the lowest time wins the race and is considered to be the fastest. Chips with a lower CL rating are faster than those with higher numbers.

Motherboard manufacturers sometimes list a minimum CL or CAS latency value for memory modules. Motherboard documentation, memory magazine advertisements, and online memory retailers list the CL rating as a series of numbers, such as 3-1-1-1. The first number is the CL rating—a CL3, in this example. The 3-1-1-1 is more detailed in that for a 32-bit transfer, it takes three clock cycles to send the first byte (8 bits), but the next 3 bytes are sent using one clock cycle each. In other words, it takes six clock cycles to transfer the 32 bits.

TECH TIP

Buying the fastest type of memory a motherboard allows

Buying memory that is faster than the motherboard allows is like taking a race car on a one-lane unpaved road: The car has the ability to go faster, but it is not feasible with the type of road being used. Sometimes you must buy faster memory because the older memory is no longer sold. This is all right, as long as it is the correct type, such as DDR2, DDR3, or DDR4.

CHAPTER 6

Also notice in Table 6.7 that memory features are listed—fully buffered, unbuffered, and regis-tered. Make sure you know the type of memory you need before buying. The voltage level for the memory module is shown (these are standard values), as is the capacity. With the capacity, if you see the number 64 at the end, the module is a non-parity one. If you see 72, the memory module uses ECC.

TECH TIP

Usually, you can mix CL memory modules

Most systems allow mixing of CL modules; for example, a motherboard could have a memory module rated for CL8 and a different memory module rated for CL9. However, when mixing memory modules, the system will run at the slower memory speed (CL9).

Installing Memory Overview

Memory is an important part of computer performance. Installation involves planning (see Figure 6.11), installing, and possibly removing some older modules. Lack of planning can lead to less-than-optimal performance.

FIGURE 6.11   Plan a memory installation

The following is the best process for determining which memory chips to install in each bank:

Step 1. Determine which chip capacities can be used for the system. Look in the documenta-tion included with the motherboard or computer for this information.

Step 2. Determine how much memory is needed. Ask the users which operating system is installed and which applications they are using (or look yourself). Refer to documen-tation for each application to determine the amount of RAM recommended. Plan for growth.

Step 3. Determine the capacity of the chips that go in each bank by drawing a diagram of the system, planning the memory population on paper, and referring to the system or motherboard documentation.

Depending on the type of motherboard, the number of banks available on the motherboard, whether the computer memory is being upgraded, and whether the memory is a new installation, some memory modules might need to be removed in order to put higher-capacity ones into the bank. Look at what is already installed in the system, refer to the documentation, and remove any existing modules, as necessary, to upgrade the memory.

TECH TIP

Memory safety reminder

Before installing a memory module, power off the computer, disconnect the power cord from the back of the computer, and use proper antistatic procedures. Memory modules are especially susceptible to ESD. If ESD damages a memory module, a problem might not appear immediately and could be intermittent and hard to diagnose.

Removing/Installing Memory

When removing a DIMM and using proper ESD-prevention techniques, push down on the retaining tabs that clasp over the DIMM. Be careful not to overextend the tabs when pushing on them. If a plastic tab breaks, the only solution is to replace the motherboard. The DIMM lifts slightly out of the socket. Always ensure that you are grounded to prevent ESD by using an antistatic wrist strap or maintaining contact with metal and a bare part of your arm (self-grounding). Lift the module out of the socket once it is released. Figure 6.12 shows how to remove a DIMM.

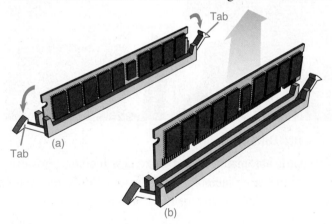

FIGURE 6.12   DIMM removal

A DIMM has one or more notches on the bottom, where the gold or tin contacts are located. The DIMM inserts into the memory socket only one way. Verify that the notches on the bottom of the module align with the notches in the motherboard socket. The DIMM will not insert into the memory socket unless it is oriented properly.

A DIMM is inserted straight down into the socket, not at a tilt, as a laptop module is inserted. Make sure the side tabs are pulled out before you insert the DIMM and close the tabs over the DIMM once it is firmly inserted into the socket. If the DIMM does not go into the slot easily, do not force it and check the notch or notches for correct alignment. However, once the DIMM is aligned correctly into the slot, push the DIMM firmly into the slot, and the tabs should naturally close over the DIMM or on the sides of the DIMM. Figure 6.13 illustrates how to insert a DIMM. Figure 6.14 shows a close-up of how the tab needs to fit securely in the memory module notch.

CHAPTER 6

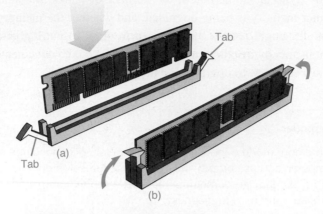

FIGURE 6.13   DIMM installation

FIGURE 6.14   Secure DIMM tab

Today's motherboards automatically recognize new memory; however, some advanced BIOS/ UEFI options exist for tweaking memory performance. With some computers, the Setup program can be used to select parity, non-parity, or ECC options. Always refer to the motherboard or the computer system documentation.

TECH TIP

POST error codes are normal after a memory installation/upgrade

Some computers show a POST error message or automatically go into the Setup program. This is normal. The important thing to notice during POST is that the memory shown in the BIOS/UEFI should equal the amount of memory installed.

Adding More Cache/RAM

Most computers today have cache built into the processor. The motherboard manufacturer determines whether any cache can be installed. Check the documentation included with the motherboard or computer to determine the amount of cache (SRAM).

Adding more RAM can make a noticeable difference in computer performance (up to a point, of course). When a computer user is sitting in front of a computer waiting for a document to appear or waiting to go to a different location within a document, it might be time to install more RAM. If you have several opened applications on the taskbar, click one of them. If you have to wait several seconds before it appears, it might be a good idea to upgrade your RAM.

Windows Disk Caching

Virtual memory is a method of using hard drive space as if it were RAM. Virtual memory allows the operating system to run larger applications and manage multiple applications that are loaded simultaneously. The amount of hard drive space used is dynamic—that is, it increases or decreases as needed. If the system begins to page frequently and is constantly swapping data from RAM to the hard drive, the cache size automatically shrinks.

A **paging file** is a block of hard drive space that applications use like RAM. Other names for the paging file include pagefile, pagefile.sys, page file, and swap file. Look back at Figure 6.5, which shows the System Information screen, and you can see the data related to the paging file next to Total Virtual Memory, Available Virtual Memory, and Page File Space. For optimum performance in any Windows operating system, set aside as much free hard drive space as possible to allow ample room for virtual memory and caching. Keep the hard drive cleaned of temporary files and outdated files/applications.

TECH TIP

Hard drive paging file tips

If multiple hard drives are available, a technician might want to move the paging file to a different drive. Always put the paging file on the fastest hard drive unless that hard drive lacks space. It is best to keep the paging file on a hard drive that does not contain the operating system. You can configure the computer to place the paging file on multiple hard drives. The amount of virtual memory is dynamically created by the operating system and does not normally need to be set manually. If it is manually set, however, the minimum amount should be equal to the amount of RAM installed.

Adjusting the virtual memory size involves the following procedures:

> In Windows 7, access the *System and Security* Control Panel > *System* > *Performance Information and Tools* link > *Advanced tools* > *Adjust the Appearance and Performance of Windows* link > *Continue* if a user account control (UAC) dialog box appears > *Advanced* tab > *Change* button. Change the parameters and click *OK* twice.

> In Windows 8, access the *System and Security* Control Panel > *System* > *Advanced System Settings* link > *Advanced* tab. Locate and select the *Settings* button in the *Performance* section > *Advanced* tab > *Change* button. Change the parameters and click *OK* twice.

> In Windows 10, access the *Start* button > *Settings* > in the *Find a Setting* search textbox, type performance > select the *Adjust the Appearance and Performance of Windows* link > *Advanced* tab > *Change* button. Change the parameters and click *OK* twice.

32-bit Windows uses 32-bit demand-paged virtual memory, and each process gets 4 GB of address space divided into two 2 GB sections. One 2 GB section is shared with the rest of the system, and the other 2 GB section is reserved for one application. All the memory space is divided into 4 KB blocks of memory called **pages**. The operating system allocates as much available RAM as possible to an application. Then the operating system swaps or pages the application to and from the temporary swap file, as needed. The operating system determines the optimum setting for this swap file; however, the swap file size can be changed. Figure 6.15 illustrates how Windows uses virtual memory.

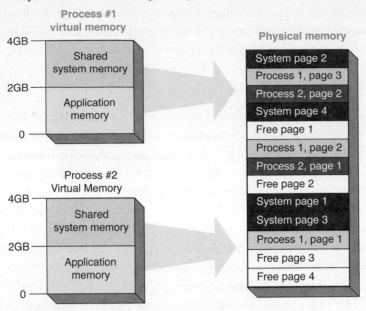

FIGURE 6.15 Windows virtual memory usage

In Figure 6.15, notice that each application has its own memory space. The memory pager maps the virtual memory addresses from address space of each individual process to physical pages in the computer's memory chips. Figure 6.16 shows how all this relates to RAM and hard drive space.

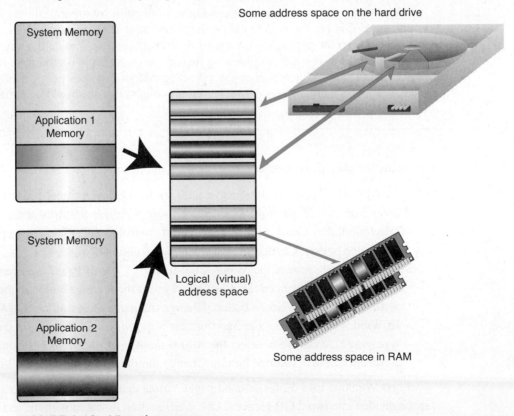

FIGURE 6.16 Virtual memory

32-bit Windows has a natural limitation of 4 GB of physical memory. Physical address extension (**PAE**) is supported only on some motherboards, and it is relevant only when 32-bit Windows operating systems are being used. PAE allows up to 64 GB or 128 GB of physical memory to be used. You can view whether a system supports PAE by viewing the computer's properties through Windows Explorer (in Windows 7) or File Explorer (in Windows 8/10).

Windows 64-bit processes are similar to Windows 32-bit processes except that Microsoft doesn't split virtual memory evenly between shared system memory and an application. Instead, on a desktop computer, the application portion is limited to 8 TB of the 16 EB theoretical maximum.

Monitoring Memory Usage in Windows

Windows has a **Performance utility** in Task Manager for monitoring memory usage. To access Task Manager, press Ctrl+Alt+Del. Select the *Performance* tab, which has graphs that visually demonstrate the CPU and memory usage. Figure 6.17 shows the Task Manager *Performance* tab, and Table 6.8 lists the fields of the Task Manager *Performance* tab.

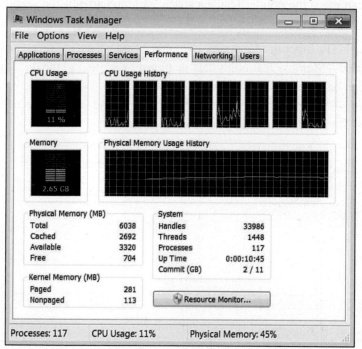

FIGURE 6.17   Windows 7 Task Manager Performance tab

TABLE 6.8   Windows 7 Task Manager Performance tab fields

Field	Description
Total Physical Memory	The amount of RAM installed.
Cached Physical Memory	Memory pages that could be written to disk and be made available.
Available Physical Memory	The amount of memory (physical and paged) for application use.
Free Physical Memory	The amount of available physical RAM.
Paged Kernel Memory	Memory that can be used by applications as needed that can be copied to the paging file (to free up RAM).
Nonpaged Kernel Memory	Memory available only to the operating system that stays in RAM.
Handles	The number of resources the operating system is currently dealing with.
Threads	The number of objects contained within currently running processes that are executing program instructions.

Field	Description
Processes	A running executable program, such as Notepad or a service that is currently running.
Up Time	How long the system has been up.
Commit (GB)	A snapshot of virtual memory requests. Note that if the commit charge exceeds the total physical memory, the system is probably paging to the hard drive too much, and it is time to add more RAM.

Windows 8 and 10 have a redesigned Task Manager, as shown in Figure 6.18 and clarified in Table 6.9. Note that in order to see the memory-related data, you must click the Memory option in the left pane. In the Memory Composition section, there are several sections separated by vertical bars. You can place the pointer inside a space, and the name of the section appears. The sections, from left to right, are as follows:

> *In Use*—The amount of memory currently being used
> *Modified*—Memory that holds data that must be written to the drive before the memory location can be used by something else
> *Standby*—The amount of memory that is cached and currently is not being used
> *Free*—The available memory to be used

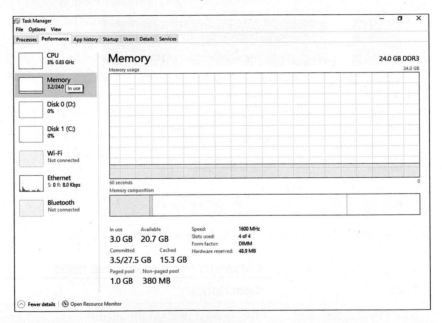

FIGURE 6.18   Windows 8/10 Task Manager Performance tab—Memory

TABLE 6.9   Windows 8/10 Task Manager Performance tab memory-related fields

Field	Description
In Use	The amount of memory currently being used by applications, the operating system, drivers, and processes.
Available	The amount of physical memory for application/operating system use.
Committed	This is shown as two numbers. The first number is how much memory the operating system has identified that needs memory (and that might get removed or paged out of RAM if other, more important, processes need the space). The second number is the amount of physical and virtual memory available.

Field	Description
Cached	The memory space that includes data that needs to be written to disk before being available, as well as cached data that is currently not being used.
Paged Pool	Memory set aside for operating system functions or device drivers that could be written to disk, if necessary.
Non-Paged Pool	Memory set aside for operating system functions or device drivers that must remain in physical memory (that is, cannot be paged out).
Speed	Speed of the RAM chips.
Slots Used	Number of memory slots used for memory modules and total number of slots.
Form Factor	Type of memory module, such as DIMM or SODIMM (used in laptops). Chapter 11, "Computer Design and Troubleshooting Review," covers mobile devices and SODIMMs.
Hardware Reserved	Memory reserved for device drivers or firmware that cannot be used by Windows for any other function.

Older Applications in Windows

Older applications are sometimes challenging in the newer versions of Windows. Some dated applications do not operate in the newer Windows versions because these programs frequently make direct calls to hardware, which Windows 7, 8, and 10 do not allow. These programs might also require that you change the color depth and resolution settings through the Display Control Panel.

For Windows 7 and higher, Microsoft states that some older software might not run properly and offers **Compatibility mode**. Right-click the application icon from the *Start* menu or right-click the program executable file and select *Properties*. Use the *Compatibility* tab to select the Windows version for which the application was written. If you do not know the version, you can select the *Run Compatibility Troubleshooter* button and then select the *Try Recommended Settings* link. Figure 6.19 shows the Compatibility tab.

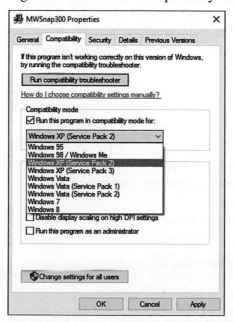

FIGURE 6.19 Windows Compatibility tab

You can also configure virtual machines by using virtualization software such as Microsoft's Virtual PC, Hyper-V, Oracle VM VirtualBox, or VMware Workstation to run older operating systems as well as run older applications. A **virtual machine** (VM) allows you to reduce hardware costs by running multiple operating systems simultaneously on a single computer (without one interfering with the other). Virtualization used to be used only with servers, but many home computers and corporate desktops are virtualized today. Virtualization is covered in more detail in Chapter 12, "Internet Connectivity, Virtualization, and Cloud Technologies."

Troubleshooting Memory Problems

You can get "out of memory" errors, **POST code beeps**, motherboard diagnostic lights or codes, **system lockups**, system slowdowns, and application locking due to memory problems with any operating system. With any of these problems, no matter which operating system is being used, check the amount of available memory and free hard drive space. Sometimes you must close all applications, reboot the computer, and open only the application that was running when the out of memory error occurred because some applications do not release the memory space they hold. The following tips and troubleshooting steps help with memory management:

> Add more RAM. To see the amount of physical memory (RAM) currently installed, access *Windows Explorer* or *File Explorer*, right-click (or tap and hold briefly) *Computer* or *This PC*, and select *Properties*.
> If you just installed new memory and an error appears, this is normal. Enter *Setup* because the system BIOS/UEFI knows something has changed.
> If you just installed new memory and the computer will not boot, check your installation by carefully pushing harder on the memory module (after shutting down and removing power, of course) to ensure that the module is fully seated into the slot. Check for loosened cables near the memory module(s). Ensure that you are installing the right memory type. You might need to upgrade your BIOS/UEFI so that your motherboard recognizes the increased amount of RAM.
> Use the **Windows Memory Diagnostic Tool**, by using one of the following methods:
  > In Windows 7, use the *System and Security* Control Panel > *Administrative Tools* > *Windows Memory Diagnostic* link. In Windows 8 or 10, search using the words `memory diagnostic`. Select the *Diagnose Your Computer's Memory Problems* (Windows 8) or *Windows Memory Diagnostic* (Windows 10) link.
  > Boot into the *Advanced Boot Options* menu (by pressing [F8] upon startup). Press [Esc]. Press [Tab⇆] to move to the *Tools* section. Press [↵Enter] to use the *Windows Memory Diagnostic Tool* to thoroughly test your RAM.
  > Use the original Windows operating system disc to boot the computer. Enter the language requirements and then click the *Repair Your Computer* link. From the *System Recovery Options* window, select *Windows Memory Diagnostics Tool*.
  > Use the command `mdsched`.
    > Delete files/applications that are no longer needed and close applications that are not being used. Empty the Recycle Bin.
    > Adjust the size of the virtual memory.
    > Do not put the paging file on multiple partitions that reside on the same hard drive. Use multiple hard drives, if necessary.
    > Put the paging file on a hard drive partition that does not contain the operating system.
    > Put the paging file on the fastest hard drive.
> Remove the desktop wallpaper scheme or use a plain one.

> Adjust your Temporary Internet Files setting. From Internet Explorer (Windows 7 or 8), select the *Tools > Internet Options > Settings* button. Adjust how much drive space is set aside for caching web pages. For Microsoft Edge in Windows 10, search for Internet Explorer (not Microsoft Edge) and use the same directions for Windows 7/8 to adjust the drive space setting.

> Defragment the hard drive. See Chapter 7, "Storage Devices," for the steps.

TECH TIP

Upgrading memory is an easy solution

Upgrading memory is one of the easiest ways to solve performance issues. Keep in mind that sometimes you simply must buy more RAM, but you should try the previously mentioned tips before resorting to that.

If you receive a message that SPD device data is missing or inconclusive, your motherboard is looking for SPD data that it cannot receive from the memory module. If this is a new module, ensure that it supports SPD. If it is an older module, you need to replace one of your memory modules.

POST usually detects a problem with a memory chip, and most systems show an error code or message. The motherboard might also contain diagnostic lights or a code. In either case, turn off the computer, remove the cover, press down on any memory modules, and reboot. Another option is to clean the memory module slots with compressed air and reinstall the module. The key to good memory chip troubleshooting is to divide and conquer. Narrow the problem to a suspected memory module and then swap banks, if possible. Keep in mind that most memory problems are not in the hardware but in the software applications and operating system.

TECH TIP

When adding more memory doesn't help

Today's operating systems rely almost as much on hard drive space as they do on RAM because of multitasking. Lack of hard drive space is almost as bad as not having enough RAM. If the system still runs slowly after adding RAM, look at used hard drive space and delete files to free up space, upgrade drive storage, or add another drive.

Flash Memory

Flash memory is a type of nonvolatile, solid-state memory that holds data even when the computer power is off. PCs use flash memory as a replacement for the BIOS chip. Network devices, smartphones, and tablets use flash memory to store the operating system and instructions. Some tablets can use external flash media for storage. Solid-state drives (SSDs) also use flash memory (see Chapter 7). Digital cameras use flash memory to store pictures, scanners use flash memory to store images, and printers use flash memory to store fonts. Unlike DRAM, flash memory does not have to be refreshed, and unlike SRAM, it does not need constant power. Figure 6.20 shows various flash memory devices.

USB flash drives (sometimes called thumb drives, memory bars, or memory sticks) allow storage up to 256 GB, and higher capacities are expected in the near future. In Figure 6.20, the blue and lime green items are USB flash drives. Flash drives connect to a USB port and are normally recognized by the Windows operating system. After attaching a flash drive to a USB port, a drive letter is assigned, and Windows Explorer or File Explorer can be used to copy files to the drive.

FIGURE 6.20   Flash memory

If you cannot find the Safely Remove Hardware icon in Windows 10, right-click the taskbar and select *Taskbar Settings*, and in the *Notification Area*, access the *Select Which Icons Appear on the Taskbar* link and ensure that the *Windows Explorer Safely Remove Hardware and Eject Media* option is set to *On*. Note that not all flash drives show in this area, and you might need to right-click a drive in File Explorer and select the *Eject* option.

Various models are available, including drives that fit on neck chains, inside watches, and on key rings. Security features that are available on flash drives include password protection to the drive and data encryption. Flash drives are a very good memory storage solution, and they are inexpensive and easy to use. Figure 6.21 shows the interior of a flash drive. Chapter 11 goes into more detail about the types of flash memory used with such devices.

FIGURE 6.21   Inside a USB flash drive

Memory is one of the most critical components of a computer, and it is important for a technician to be well versed in the different memory technologies. Because memory is one of the most common upgrades, becoming proficient and knowledgeable about populating memory is important.

SOFT SKILLS: TEAMWORK

Technicians tend not to like working in teams as much as they like working on their own. Much of a technician's job is done alone. However, a technician normally has one or more peers, a supervisor, and a network of partners involved with the job, such as suppliers, subcontractors, and part-time help. It is easy to have tunnel vision in a technical support job and lose sight of the mission of the business. Many technical jobs have the main purpose of generating revenue—solving people's computer and network problems for the purpose of making money. Other technicians have more of a back-office support role—planning, installing, configuring, maintaining, and troubleshooting technologies the business uses to make money.

Technicians must focus on solving customers' problems and ensuring that customers feel that their problems have been solved professionally and efficiently. However, you cannot lose sight of the business-first mentality; remember that you play a support role whether you generate revenue or not. You are a figure on someone's balance sheet, and you need to keep your skills and attitudes finely tuned to be valuable to the company. No matter how good you are at your job, you are always better to a company if you are part of a team than if you're on your own. Make sure to **be on time** and **maintain a positive attitude**. Being a person who is late, takes off early, chats too much with customers, blames others, and so on, is not being a good team member. If you are going to be late for work or leave early, inform your supervisor and coworkers so they can take care of any issues that arise while you're gone. If you are going to be late for a customer appointment, contact the customer and let him or her know you are running late.

Technicians need to be good team players and see themselves as a reflection of their company when on the job (see Figure 6.22). Employers see **teamwork** as an important part of a technician's skill set—just as important as technical skills. Think of ways that you can practice teamwork even as a student and refine those skills when you join the workforce.

FIGURE 6.22 Teamwork

Chapter Summary

> Memory on a motherboard is SDRAM, a type of RAM that is cheaper and slower than SRAM, the type of memory inside the CPU and processor housing.

> A DDR module fits in a DDR slot. A DDR2 module requires a DDR2 slot; a DDR3 module requires a DDR3 slot; a DDR4 module requires a DDR4 slot.

> Unbuffered non-parity memory is the memory normally installed in computers.

> ECC is used for error checking and is commonly found in high-end computers and servers. An older method of error checking is called parity.

> The CL rating or the timing sequence's first number shows how quickly the processor can access data in sequential memory locations. The lower the first number, the faster the access.

> SPD is a technology used so the memory module can communicate specifications to the BIOS/UEFI.

> Double-sided memory is one module that acts like two modules (not that it has chips on both sides, even though it most likely does). A motherboard must support using double-sided modules.

> Before installing memory, plan your strategy: Read the manual to determine the type of memory; determine the total amount of memory; determine whether any memory is to be removed; determine the memory to purchase; and be mindful of getting the most out of your memory by implementing dual-, triple-, or even quadruple-channeling.

> When implementing dual-, triple-, or quadruple-channeling, buy matching memory modules.

> Any 32-bit operating system is limited to 4 GB of memory.

> Particular versions of Windows have memory limitations. For example, any 32-bit version of Windows is limited to 4 GB. Windows 7 Starter edition is limited to 2 GB, but any of the other Windows 7 versions can go to 4 GB for the 32-bit versions. 64-bit versions allow much more memory to be installed and accessed. Windows 10 Home 32-bit version is limited to 4 GB, but the 64-bit version can handle up to 128 GB.

> RAM is very susceptible to ESD events. Use proper antistatic-handling procedures, including using an antistatic wrist strap.

> Before removing or installing memory, disconnect the power cord and remove the battery on a mobile device.

> Having as much RAM in a system as possible is an important performance factor, and so is having free hard drive space because hard drive space is used as memory. This is called virtual memory, and the information stored temporarily on a hard drive is stored in an area known as a paging file, page file, or swap file. The paging file should be on the fastest drive that has the most free storage.

> Use Task Manager to monitor memory performance.

> Use POST, motherboard LED/display output codes, BIOS/UEFI diagnostics, and the Windows Memory Diagnostics Tool to diagnose memory problems.

> Flash media is used to provide memory or additional storage space for computing devices and includes USB flash drives.

> A technician is part of a business and should contribute to the team. A technician should professionally represent a company.

A+ CERTIFICATION EXAM TIPS

✓ Know different RAM form factors and types, including DIMMs, SODIMMs, DDR2, DDR3, and DDR4.

✓ Know how to calculate what memory is needed for an upgrade or a new install.

✓ Be able to identify memory slots on a motherboard.

✓ Know how to populate memory when single-, dual-, or triple-channeling is being implemented.

✓ When populating memory, consult the motherboard documentation before you go any further.

✓ Be able to describe the difference between parity, non-parity, and error correcting code (ECC) memory.

✓ Know that memory chips are especially susceptible to ESD and how to prevent ESD damage when installing or removing memory.

✓ Remember that if any application is slow to respond, the computer may need more RAM.

✓ Review the troubleshooting symptoms and tips. Know that adding memory is one of the easiest ways to improve computer performance.

✓ Know when and how to use Compatibility mode and the Windows Memory Diagnostics Tool.

✓ Keep in mind that the following professionalism skills are part of the 220-1002 exam: (1) Maintain a positive attitude and (2) be on time (or, if late, contact the customer). Do not forget to review the professionalism skills.

Key Terms

be on time   237
buffered memory   217
cache memory   213
CL rating   225
Compatibility mode   233
DDR2   215
DDR3   215
DDR4   215
DIMM   213
double-sided memory   217
DRAM   212
dual-channel   220
ECC   217
error correcting   217

flash memory   235
heat spreader   215
maintain a positive attitude   237
non-ECC   217
non-parity   217
PAE   230
page   229
paging file   229
parity   217
Performance utility   231
POST code beep   234
quadruple-channel   223
RAM   212
refresh (process)   213

single-sided memory   217
SODIMM   213
SPD   217
SRAM   212
system lockup   234
teamwork   237
thermal sensor   217
triple-channel   223
unbuffered memory   217
USB flash drive   235
virtual machine   234
virtual memory   229
Windows Memory Diagnostic Tool   234

Review Questions

The following specifications for motherboard RAM are used for Questions 1–5:

> Four 240-pin DDR3 SDRAM DIMM sockets arranged in two channels
> Support for DDR3 1600+ MHz, DDR3 1333 MHz, and DDR3 1066 MHz DIMMs
> Support for non-ECC memory
> Support for up to 16 GB of system memory

1. Of the given features, which one(s) would be applicable to this computer? (Select all that apply.)

   [unbuffered | registered | 204-pin SO-DIMM | 240-pin DDR2 DIMM | 240-pin DDR3 DIMM | ECC]

2. Say that this computer has 4 GB of memory and four memory slots. Write all combinations of memory population in the slots.

   _____

3. [T | F] The memory used in this system does not perform error checking.

4. What does the statement "four 240-pin DDR3 SDRAM DIMM sockets arranged in two channels" mean?

   _____

5. Would there be an issue if this motherboard contained 6 GB of RAM and the computer had 32-bit Windows 10 installed? If so, explain the issue.

   _____

Consider the following memory advertisements for desktop memory used in Questions 6–9:

   a. 2 GB (1 GB×2) 240-pin DIMM PC2-6400 memory module
   b. 2 GB DDR3 1600 DIMM
   c. 2 GB ECC registered DDR2 SDRAM DIMM
   d. 4 GB : 2×2 GB DIMM 240-pin DDR2 800 MHz/PC2-6400 CL6 1.9–2.0 V
   e. 4 GB 1333 MHz DDR3L ECC CL9 DIMM SR x8 1.35 V with TS desktop memory
   f. 4 G FB DDR2 800 memory PC2-5300 5-5-5-18
   g. 8 GB kit (2×4 GB) DDR3 DIMM (240-pin) 1333 MHz PC3-10600/PC3-10666 9-9-9-25 1.5 V
   h. 16 GB kit (2×8 GB) 1600 MHz DDR3 non-ECC CL9 DIMM XMP
   i. 16 GB kit (2×8 GB) 1600 MHz DDR3 CL10 DIMM

6. In these advertisements, which DDR2 option would hold the most data in a single memory module and be best suited for a desktop computer?

   _____

7. In option e, what does the L in DDR3L mean?

   _____

8.   A customer wants to dual-channel 8 GB of RAM on a desktop computer. Which memory module(s) would be best to buy, given the following documentation from the motherboard manual? (Memory module slots are in order from closest to the CPU: 1, 3, 2, and 4.)

> Do not install ECC memory modules.

> If you remove your original memory modules from the computer during an upgrade, keep the old ones separate from any new modules you might have. If possible, do not pair an original module with a new module. Otherwise, the computer might not start properly.

> The memory configurations are as follows:

>> A pair of matched modules in DIMM connectors 1 and 2

>> A pair of matched modules in DIMM connectors 1 and 2 and another pair in connectors 3 and 4

> If you install mixed pairs, the memory modules function at the speed of the slowest memory module installed.

---

9.   When comparing options h and i and imagining that both modules cost the same, which one would be the better purchase? Explain your reasoning.

---

10. What type of memory feature will be needed if data accuracy is paramount for a new computer?

[buffered | ECC | registered | XMP]

11. What is the minimum amount of RAM recommended to install 32-bit Windows 8?

[512 MB | 1 GB | 2 GB | 4 GB]

12. What method is most effective for preventing an ESD event when installing RAM?

   a. placing the computer on an antistatic mat

   b. wearing an antistatic wrist strap

   c. staying in contact with an unpainted metal part of the computer

   d. wearing rubber-soled shoes and using the buddy system by having another technician standing by

13. Which of the following would be the first sign that a computer needs more RAM?

   a. The computer is slow to respond.

   b. The computer makes a ticking noise.

   c. A POST error message appears.

   d. A recommendation to use the *Windows Memory Diagnostics Tool* appears.

14. How would a technician adjust Internet Explorer (Windows 7 and 8) for how much drive space is configured for caching web pages?

   a. *Windows Explorer/File Explorer* > right-click Computer > *Manage*

   b. *Settings > Safety*

   c. F8 on startup > *Windows Memory Diagnostics Tool*

   d. *Tools > Internet Options*

15. List one easy way to tell how much RAM is installed in a computer.

---

16. [T | F] A DDR4 DIMM can fit in a DDR3 memory expansion slot.

17. You have just added two new memory modules to a computer, but now the system will not boot and is beeping multiple times. What will you check first?

---

18. Give an example of how a technician might show teamwork while working on a help desk.

_____

_____

19. A system already has two 1333 MHz memory modules installed, and a technician adds two more modules that operate at 1600 MHz. What will be the result of this action?

    a. The computer won't boot.

    b. The computer might freeze at times.

    c. The memory will operate at the 1333 MHz speed.

    d. All memory will operate at the 1600 MHz speed.

20. A technician has received a complaint that a computer is not performing as well as it used to. Which Windows 10 tool would the technician get the user to open to quickly tell how much RAM is currently being used by the open applications?

    [Performance Monitor | Device Manager | System Information Tool | Task Manager]

Exercises

Exercise 6.1 Configuring Memory on Paper

Objective: To be able to determine the correct amount and type of memory to install on a motherboard

Parts: Internet access or access to magazines or ads that show memory prices

Procedure: Refer to Figure 6.23 and Table 6.10 to answer the questions. This motherboard supports 533/667/800 MHz DDR2 memory modules. The capacities supported are 1 GB and 2 GB, for a total of 8 GB maximum. It is not recommended to use a three-DIMM configuration with this board. Memory channel speed is determined by the slowest DIMM populated in the system.

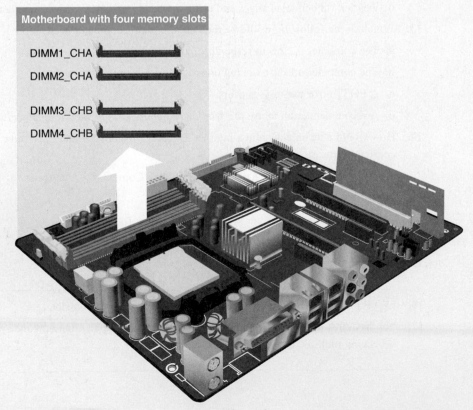

FIGURE 6.23   Motherboard with four memory slots and two channels

TABLE 6.10   Motherboard single-/dual-channel combinations

		Sockets			
Mode	**Scenario**	**DIMM1**	**DIMM2**	**DIMM3**	**DIMM4**
Single	1	Populated			
	2		Populated		
	3			Populated	
	4				Populated
Dual-channel	1	Populated		Populated	
	2		Populated		Populated
	3	Populated	Populated	Populated	Populated

Questions:

1. What memory modules are needed if the customer wants 3 GB of RAM? What capacities and how many modules of each capacity are required?

   _____

   _____

2. Is triple-channeling supported by this motherboard? [Yes | No]

3. Using the Internet, a computer parts magazine, or a list of memory modules, determine the exact part numbers and quantities of memory modules that you would buy. List them as well as the location where you obtained the information.

   _____

4. This motherboard already has 1 GB of RAM installed in the DIMM1 slot. The customer would like to upgrade to 4 GB total memory, use the existing module if possible, and use dual-channeling. What memory modules are needed? What capacities and how many of each capacity are required?

   _____

5. What memory slots will be used to install the memory, based on the information provided?

   _____

6. What does the documentation mean when referencing DDR2 533/667/800 MHz RAM?

   _____

7. How do you know which one of the 533, 667, or 800 types of modules to use?

   _____

   _____

8. Using the Internet, a computer parts magazine, or a provided list of memory modules, determine the exact part numbers and quantities of memory modules that you would buy. List them, along with the location where you obtained the information.

   _____

   _____

Exercise 6.2 Configuring Memory on Paper

Objective: To be able to determine the correct amount and type of memory to install on a motherboard

Parts: Internet access or access to magazines or ads that show memory prices

Procedure: Refer to Figure 6.24 and Table 6.11 to answer the questions. This motherboard supports the following memory configurations:

- Up to 2 GB utilizing 256 MB technology
- Up to 4 GB utilizing 512 MB or 1 GB technology
- Up to 8 GB utilizing 1 GB technology

The desktop board supports either single- or dual-channel memory configurations. The board has four 240-pin DDR2 SDRAM DIMM connectors with gold-plated contacts. It provides support for unbuffered, non-registered single or double-sided DIMMs, non-ECC DDR2 533/667/800 MHz memory, and (SPD) memory only.

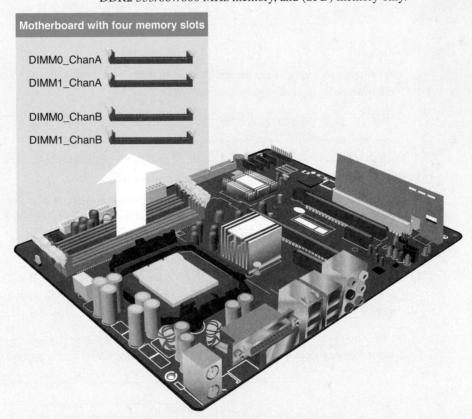

FIGURE 6.24   Motherboard with four memory slots and two channels

TABLE 6.11   Motherboard single-/dual-channel guidelines

Installed memory	Guidelines
2 DIMMs dual-channel	Install a matched pair of DIMMs equal in speed and size in DIMM0 of both Channel A and Channel B.
4 DIMMs dual-channel	Follow the directions for two DIMMs and add another matched pair of DIMMs in DIMM1 of both Channels A and B.
3 DIMMs dual-channel	Install a matched pair of DIMMs equal in speed and size in DIMM0 and DIMM1 of Channel A. Install a DIMM equal in speed and total size of the DIMMs installed in Channel A in either DIMM0 or DIMM1 of Channel B.
Single-channel	All other memory configurations result in single-channel memory operation.

Questions:

1. How can this motherboard support 8 GB of RAM with only four slots?

    _____

2. What memory features, if any, are used? (Select all that apply.)
    [parity | non-parity | ECC | registered | fully buffered | unbuffered | SPD]

3. What memory modules are needed if the customer wants 3 GB of dual-channel RAM? (What capacities and how many of each capacity are required?)

    _____

4. What memory slots will be used to install the memory, based on the information provided?

    _____

    _____

5. Using the Internet, a computer parts magazine, or a list of memory modules, determine the exact part numbers and quantities of memory modules you would buy. List them, along with the location where you obtained the information.

    _____

    _____

6. Will it matter if the motherboard has tin contacts in the memory slots? Why or why not?

    _____

7. Can DDR memory modules be used with this motherboard? How can you tell?

    _____

8. If this motherboard already has 1 GB of RAM installed in the DIMM0_ChanA slot and the customer would like to upgrade to 2 GB of dual-channel RAM, what memory modules are needed? (What capacities and how many of each capacity are required?)

    _____

9. What suggestions, if any, would you make to the customer before researching prices?

    _____

10. What memory slots will be used to install the memory, based on the information provided?

    _____

    _____

11. Using the Internet, a computer parts magazine, or a list of memory modules, determine the exact part numbers and quantities of memory modules that you would buy. List them, along with the location where you obtained the information.

    _____

Exercise 6.3 Configuring Memory on Paper

Objective: To be able to determine the correct amount and type of memory to install on a motherboard

Parts: Internet access or access to magazines or ads that show memory prices

Procedure: Refer to Figure 6.25 to answer the questions. The motherboard supports the following memory configurations:

- 1 GB, 2 GB, 4 GB unbuffered and non-ECC DDR3 DIMMs can be used in the DIMM slots (1, 2, 3, and 4) for a total of 32 GB max using DDR3 1066/1333 MHz modules.

- Recommended memory configurations are modules in DIMMs 1 and 3 or modules in DIMMs 1, 2, 3, and 4.

- Single- and dual-channel modes are supported.

- You may install different sizes in Channel A and B. The dual-channel configuration will be the total size of the lowest-sized channel. Any excess memory will operate in single-channel mode.

- >1.65 V DIMMs are recommended.

- Use the same CAS latency and obtain from the same vendor, if possible.

- The default memory operation frequency is dependent on SPD.

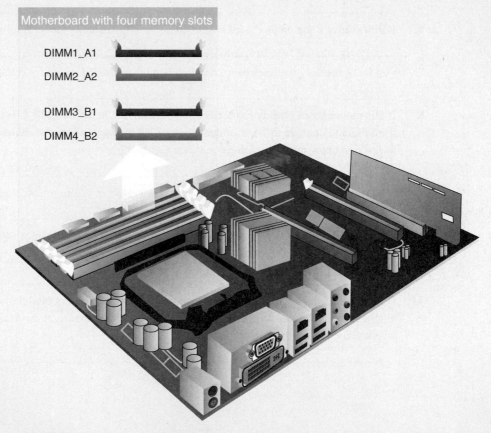

FIGURE 6.25   Second motherboard with four memory slots and two channels

Questions:

1. What memory features, if any, are used? (Select all that apply.)
    [parity | non-parity | ECC | registered | unbuffered | SPD]

2. The customer wants 4 GB of RAM. What memory modules are needed? (What capacities and how many of each capacity are required?)

    _____

3. What memory slots will be used to install the memory suggested in Question 2?

    _____

4. Using the Internet, a computer parts magazine, or a list of memory modules provided by the instructor, determine the exact part numbers and quantities of memory modules that you would buy. List them, along with the location where you obtained this information.

    _____

5. In what type of systems would ECC modules most likely be used?

    [student desktop | smartphones | tablets | servers | laptops]

6. What is the purpose of ECC modules?

    _____

7. What is the purpose of SPD?

    _____

Exercise 6.4 Configuring Memory on Paper

Objective: To be able to determine the correct amount and type of memory to install on a motherboard

Parts: Internet access or access to magazines or ads that show memory prices

Procedure: Refer to Figure 6.26 to answer the questions. The motherboard supports the following memory configurations:

- Max memory supported: 16 GB
- Memory types: DDR4-4600/4400/4266/4200
- Memory channels: 3
- Number of DIMMs: 4
- ECC supported: Yes
- Connectors use gold-plated contacts
- Unbuffered, non-registered single- or double-sided SPD DIMMs with a voltage rating of 1.65 V or less
- Optimal performance can be achieved by installing three matching DIMMs in the ChanA, ChanB, and ChanC memory slots.
- Dual-channel operation can be achieved by installing matching DIMMs in ChanB and ChanC or all four memory slots.

CHAPTER 6

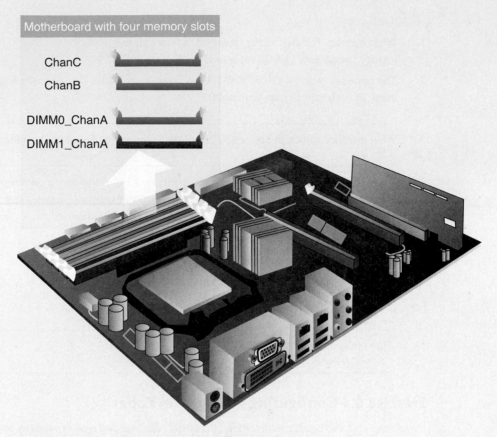

Motherboard with four memory slots

ChanC

ChanB

DIMM0_ChanA

DIMM1_ChanA

FIGURE 6.26   Triple-channel motherboard

Questions:

1.   What memory features, if any, are used? (Select all that apply.)

[parity | non-parity | ECC | registered | unbuffered | SPD]

2.   The customer wants 8 GB of RAM performing triple-channeling. Can this be done? Why or why not?
[Yes | No]

_____

3.   What memory modules are needed to put 8 GB of memory on the motherboard? (What capacities and
how many of each capacity are required?) Justify your choice.

_____

_____

4.   What memory slots will be used to install the memory suggested in Question 3?

_____

5.   Using the Internet, a computer parts magazine, or a list of memory modules provided by the instructor, determine the exact part numbers and quantities of memory modules that you would buy. List
them, along with the location where you obtained this information.

_____

6.   The user has 32-bit Windows 7 installed on this computer. Will there be any issues with the 8 GB of
RAM? If so what might those issues be?

_____

7.   List one method a technician could use to ensure that the 8 GB are recognized by the system.

_____

Activities

Internet Discovery

Objective: To become familiar with researching memory chips using the Internet

Parts: A computer with Internet access

Procedure: Use the Internet to complete the following procedure:

- Power on the computer and start an Internet browser.
- Using any search engine, locate two vendors that sell memory chips.
- Create a table like the one below and fill in your findings for each of the memory sites.

	Site 1	Site 2
Internet URL		
Type of DIMM		
Largest-capacity DIMM		
Pros of website		
Cons of website		

Soft Skills

Objective: To enhance and fine-tune a future technician's ability to listen, communicate in both written form and oral forms, and support people who use computers in a professional manner

Activities:

1. On your own, use the Internet to find a utility that tests soft skills or your personality. Compare your scores with those of others in the class. Make a list of how you might improve in specific weak areas. Present your findings to a group and share your group findings with another group.

2. Note that this activity requires two computers. In groups of two, have one person describe in great detail to the other person how to upgrade the computer's memory by removing memory from one computer and adding it to the other. The person doing the physical installation can do nothing except what the partner describes how to do. Reverse roles for removing the memory and reinstalling back in the original computer. At the end of the exercise, the two participants describe to the teacher what they experienced.

3. In small groups, find a video that describes how to do something on a computer. Critique the video in terms of how the speaker might do a better job communicating to people who are not technicians. Share the video with the class, along with your recommendations for doing it better. As an option, script a short presentation for how to do something. Tape/record it if possible and have the class critique each group's presentation.

Critical Thinking Skills

To analyze and evaluate information as well as apply learned information to new or different situations

Activities:

1. Refer to Figure 6.9 and Table 6.6 in this chapter. Compare and contrast Solution 2 with Solution 3 in terms of dual-channeling. Write a list of your findings and share them with the class.

    _____

    _____

    _____

    _____

    _____

2. List the repercussions of discovering that a motherboard supports both single-sided and double-sided memory modules. For example, what would the memory population look like for 8 GB (the maximum) of RAM in Figure 6.9?

    _____

    _____

    _____

3. Download a motherboard manual from the Internet or use one provided in the classroom. Find the memory section and make a list of any terms or directions that are given that you do not understand. In groups of four or five, share your lists and come up with as many solutions as possible. Share your group list with the class. Write any unsolved questions on the board and bring the answers to those questions back in a week.

7

Storage Devices

In this chapter you will learn:

> Basic storage terms
> About PATA, SATA, SSD, and SSHD technologies
> How to install and configure storage devices, including RAID

> How to fix storage device problems
> How to keep a hard drive healthy
> How to create and troubleshoot a RAID

> How to create and use Windows Storage Spaces
> Effective phone communication

CompTIA Exam Objectives:

What CompTIA A+ exam objectives are covered in this chapter?

✓ 1001-3.1   Explain basic cable types, features, and their purposes.

✓ 1001-3.2   Identify common connector types.

✓ 1001-3.4   Given a scenario, select, install, and configure storage devices.

✓ 1001-5.3   Given a scenario, troubleshoot hard drives and RAID arrays.

✓ 1002-1.3   Summarize general OS installation considerations and upgrade methods.

✓ 1002-1.4   Given a scenario, use appropriate Microsoft command line tools.

✓ 1002-1.5   Given a scenario, use Microsoft operating system features and tools.

✓ 1002-2.9   Given a scenario, implement appropriate data destruction and disposal methods.

✓ 1002-3.1   Given a scenario, troubleshoot Microsoft Windows OS problems.

✓ 1002-4.7   Given a scenario, use proper communication techniques and professionalism.

Storage Devices Overview

Storage devices hold the data we are so fond of generating and keeping—photos, PDFs, movies, word processing documents, spreadsheets, and whatever else we can think to save. Data can be stored on optical media, flash media, and magnetic media such as hard drives, as shown in Figure 7.1.

FIGURE 7.1   Storage devices

Many folks, especially those who travel frequently, use data storage servers at their company. Data can also be stored "in the cloud." This means that there are storage devices available through the Internet to store data. Some storage is provided by an Internet provider or as a service for a mobile device. Companies such as Amazon, Microsoft, Google, SugarSync, and Dropbox provide cloud storage. Some companies charge for cloud storage and others offer limited amounts of cloud storage for free and have an option to pay for more. The services of such a site include backing up the data stored on their drives and having redundant hard drives in their servers. This is known as *cloud storage* or *offsite storage*. Microsoft, Google, Apple, and other companies have made it very easy to store data in the cloud or to synchronize data to the cloud. More information on how to do this is provided in Chapter 11, "Computer Design and Troubleshooting Review," and Chapter 17, "macOS and Linux Operating Systems." Figure 7.2 illustrates this concept, but keep in mind that "in the cloud" is just a ton of hard drives, servers, and other devices in some remote location.

FIGURE 7.2 Cloud storage

Hard Drive Overview

Hard drives are popular devices for storing data. A hard drive can be mounted inside a computer case or attached externally to a USB, IEEE 1394 (FireWire), eSATA, or eSATAp port. Hard drives store more data than flash drives and move data more quickly than tape drives. Today's hard drive capacities extend into the terabytes. Hard drives are frequently upgraded in computers, so it is important for you to understand all the technical issues. These issues include knowing the parts of the hard drive subsystem, how the operating system and the BIOS/UEFI work together with a hard drive, and how to configure and troubleshoot a hard drive.

Hard drives come in different physical sizes (form factors). For desktop and small server models, 5.25-inch (not very popular) and **3.5-inch drives** are available. The **2.5-inch drive** form factor is designed for laptops. A 1.8-inch form factor is available for use and can be found for solid state drives (SSDs), tablets, and in ultraportable devices such as MP3 players. Figure 7.3 shows two hard drive sizes.

FIGURE 7.3 Desktop hard drive form factors

A hard drive can also be placed inside an external enclosure and attached using USB, eSATA, eSATAp (USB/SATA) combo, or IEEE 1394 (FireWire). Figure 7.4 shows a 3.5-inch IDE PATA or SATA to USB or eSATA Sabrent enclosure that includes a cooling fan. Notice that the cooling fan has a filter that protects the fan from dust particles.

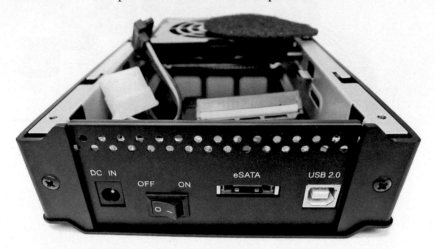

FIGURE 7.4   Sabrent external hard drive enclosure

Magnetic Hard Drive Geometry

Traditional mechanical hard drives are magnetic hard drives. These hard drives have multiple hard metal surfaces called *platters*. Each platter typically holds data on both sides and has two read/ write heads: one for the top and one for the bottom. The read/write heads float on a cushion of air without touching the platter surface. Data is written by using electromagnetism. A charge is applied to the read/write head, creating a magnetic field. Figure 7.5 shows the major components found inside a mechanical hard drive. The metal hard drive platter has magnetic particles that are affected by the read/write head's magnetic field, allowing 1s and 0s to be "placed" or "induced" onto the drive, as shown in Figure 7.6.

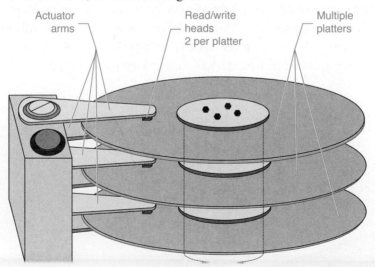

FIGURE 7.5   Hard drive geometry

FIGURE 7.6   Writing to a hard drive

Magnetic hard drives typically have two motors: one to turn the platters and one to move the read/write heads. A hard drive spins at different rotational rates called *revolutions per minute (RPMs)*. Common speeds are **5,400 RPM**, **7,200 RPM**, **10,000 RPM**, and **15,000 RPM**. The faster the drive RPM, the faster the transfer rate and generally the higher the cost. A 7,200 RPM drive typically transfers data 33% faster than a 5,400 RPM drive.

If a read/write head touches the platter, a **head crash** occurs. This is sometimes called HDI (head-to-disk interference), and it can damage the platters or the read/write head, causing data corruption. Another important concept is mean time between failures (**MTBF**)—the average number of hours before a drive is likely to fail. Mechanical hard drives do fail, and that is why it is so important to back up the data stored on them. Figure 7.7 shows the inside of a hard drive. You can see the top read/write head and the platters. Keep in mind that you should not remove the cover from a hard drive because you could allow particles into the sealed drive area.

FIGURE 7.7   Hard drive with cover removed

The magnetic hard drive surface is metallic and has concentric circles, each of which is called a *track*. Tracks are numbered starting with the outermost track, which is called track 0. One corresponding track on all surfaces of a hard drive is a *cylinder*. For example, cylinder 0 consists of all track 0s; all the track 1s comprise cylinder 1, and so on. Whereas a track is a single circle on one platter, a cylinder is the same track on all platters. Figure 7.8 shows the difference between tracks and cylinders. Notice in Figure 7.8 that a concentric circle makes an individual track, and a single track on all the surfaces makes an individual cylinder.

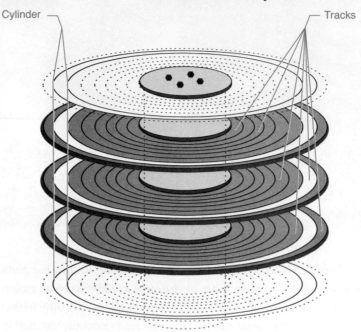

FIGURE 7.8   Cylinders versus tracks

Each track is separated into **sectors**, and the circle is divided into smaller pieces. Normally, each sector stores 512 bytes, as shown in Figure 7.9.

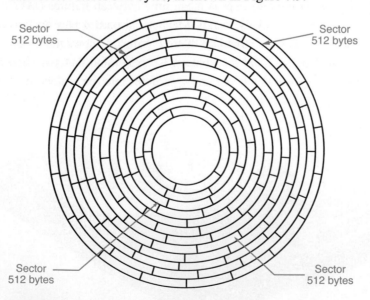

FIGURE 7.9   Hard drive sectors

Solid State Drive (SSD) Overview

SSDs are storage devices that use DRAM (older ones) or nonvolatile flash memory (newer ones) technologies instead of traditional mechanical hard drive technologies. SSDs eliminate the number one cause of hard drive failure: moving parts. SSDs typically use flash memory, and therefore they produce little heat and are reliable, quiet, secure, long-lasting, and fast. SSDs are installed in laptops and desktop models as internal and external units. SSDs are common in tablets and some mobile devices. They are also used in environments such as temperature extremes or where a drive might be jolted. SSDs can be used in conjunction with mechanical hard drive storage. SSDs are used in the following industries:

> *Medical*—CRT/MRI image storage, monitoring equipment, portable devices
> *IT*—Video surveillance, wireless base stations, security appliances
> *Industrial*—Robotic systems, test equipment, manufacturing devices
> *Automotive*—Diagnostics, store safety information, store travel statistics

Another difference between mechanical hard drives and SSDs is how data is actually written. Write amplification and wear leveling are two terms used with SSDs that technicians should understand. To write data, an SSD may have to do an erase operation, move data to another location, and then write the information to memory. Still, overall performance is increased compared to a mechanical hard drive. **Write amplification** is the minimum amount of memory storage space affected by a write request. For example, if there is 4 kB of information to be written and the SSD has a 128 kB erase block, 128 kB must be erased before the 4 kB of information can be written. Some SSDs clean up data blocks when the SSD is not busy. Writing takes longer than reading with SSDs.

Wear leveling is a technique used to erase and write data using all of the memory blocks instead of using the same memory blocks repeatedly. SSD manufacturers use various technologies: (1) software to track usage and direct write operations, (2) a certain amount of reserved memory blocks to use when a memory block fails, and (3) a combination of the two techniques.

SSDs use a NAND structure, where a 1 bit indicates that no data is stored in a particular location, and a 0 bit indicates the presence of data. **NAND flash memory** retains data even when the device is powered off. Two types of technologies used with SSDs are single-level memory cell (SLC) and multi-level memory cell (MLC). **SLCs** store 1 bit in each memory cell and last longer than MLCs, but they are more expensive. **MLCs** store more than 1 bit in each memory cell and are cheaper to manufacture, but they have slower transfer speeds.

The main drawback to SSDs is cost. SSDs are expensive compared to mechanical hard drives. As with flash drives, each memory block of an SSD has a finite number of reads and writes. An SSD that writes data across the entire memory capacity will last longer. Some companies include software with the drive that tracks or estimates end of life. Figure 7.10 shows inside an SSD.

FIGURE 7.10   Solid state drive without a cover

Today, hybrid SSDs are available. A **hybrid SSD**, or solid state hybrid drive (**SSHD**), provides a combination of mechanical and flash technologies. The SSHD has some flash memory integrated with a traditional mechanical drive (see Figure 7.11).

The flash memory in an SSHD typically contains the most frequently used data that would be sent to the host interface. Advanced algorithms are used to predict this data. Only if requested data was not in flash memory would data be pulled from the slower mechanical drive. SSHDs provide the best of both worlds: Costs are lower per byte because you have a little bit of really fast memory storage, thanks to the SSD, and there is a lot of storage space, thanks to the traditional mechanical drive. You also do not require a faster RPM traditional drive with an SSHD.

A similar technology is a flash cache module (**FCM**), which requires software that predicts what data is going to be used and puts data on an SSD that is separate from the mechanical hard drive. At the time this book was going to press, specific Intel chipsets were required in order to use this technology.

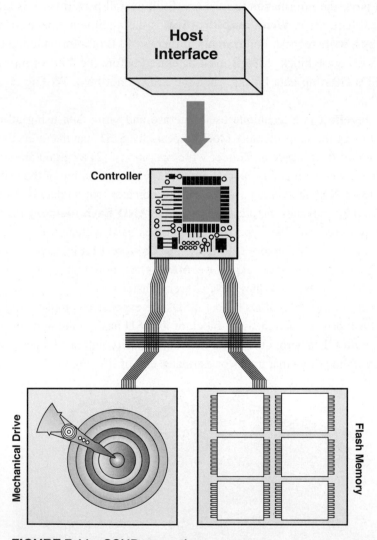

FIGURE 7.11   SSHD operation

Hard Drive Interfaces Overview

A hard drive system must have a set of rules in order to operate. These rules specify the number of heads on the drive, what commands the drive responds to, the cables used with the drive, the number of devices supported, the number of data bits transferred at one time, and so on. These rules make up a standard called an *interface* that governs communication with the hard drive.

There are two major hard drive interfaces: Integrated Drive Electronics (**IDE**)—also known as the AT Attachment (ATA) or Enhanced IDE (**EIDE**) standard—and Small Computer System Interface (SCSI). IDE is the most common in home and office computers. SCSI is more commonly found in storage networks or used with network servers.

Note that other interfaces can also be used to attach external storage devices. Almost everyone has seen a flash drive or an external hard drive attached to a USB port. This chapter focuses more on the internal storage interfaces.

Both IDE and SCSI started out as parallel architectures, in which multiple bits are sent over multiple paths. This architecture requires precise timing as transfer rates increase. With both IDE and SCSI, multiple devices can attach to the same bus. Whereas Parallel IDE, or Parallel ATA (**PATA**), supports only two devices, parallel SCSI supports more. However, the concept is the same. When multiple devices share the same bus, they have to wait their turn to access the bus, and there are configuration issues with which to contend. Figure 7.12 shows the concept of parallel transfer.

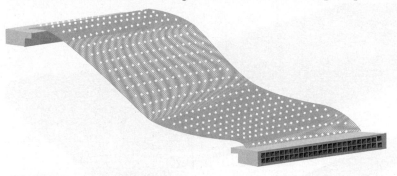

FIGURE 7.12 Parallel transfer

Today serial architectures are used. Both the IDE and SCSI standards have serial architectures available. The ATA serial device is known as a Serial ATA (**SATA**) device, and the SCSI serial device is known as a Serial Attached SCSI (**SAS**) device. SATA drives are used with laptops and PCs. Both SATA and SAS drives are used with network-attached storage (NAS) devices, servers, and storage area networks (SANs). A **NAS drive** is used in a NAS, runs at higher RPMs, and stores data for one or more servers and/or computers; this type of device is relatively expensive because it is designed to run 24/7 with optimized performance. Figure 7.13 shows a technician removing a SAS drive.

FIGURE 7.13   SAS drive being removed

CHAPTER 7

A serial architecture is a point-to-point bus in which each device has a single connection back to the controller. Bits are sent one at a time over a single link. More devices can attach to this type of architecture because it scales easily and is easy to configure. Figure 7.14 illustrates the concept of serial data transfer.

FIGURE 7.14   Serial transfer

Figure 7.15 is a photo of a **SATA cable** and a data PATA **IDE cable**.

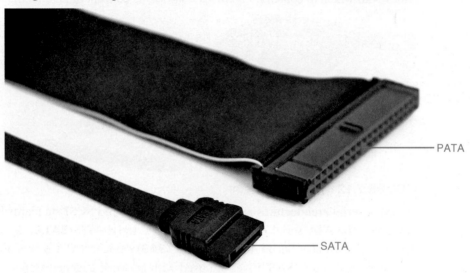

FIGURE 7.15   SATA and PATA data cables

M.2 and NVMe

SATA in laptops is being replaced by an interface known as M.2. An **M.2** connector allows modules of varying sizes to be connected. This serves well for mobile devices and specifically for SSDs. Some desktop motherboards include the M.2 connector. Figure 7.16 shows two M.2 SSDs. (For more information and graphics of the M.2 connector, see Chapter 10, "Mobile Devices.")

SSDs can also use Non-Volatile Memory Express (**NVMe**), which provides faster performance when accessing the NAND flash memory in SSDs. SSDs perform better when attached to the PCIe 4 lane-based NVMe standard. To use NVMe, the SSD could be on a PCIe card or attached through an M.2 connector (see Figure 7.17).

TECH TIP

Windows 7 does not have NVMe boot drive support

To get a Windows 7 computer to boot from an NVMe SSD, the computer must have the BIOS/UEFI compatibility support module setting enabled and must support booting from a UEFI device (and loading the appropriate driver for that device).

FIGURE 7.16   M.2 SSDs

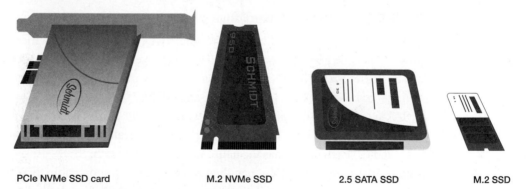

PCIe NVMe SSD card   M.2 NVMe SSD   2.5 SATA SSD   M.2 SSD

FIGURE 7.17   NVMe and non-NVMe SSDs

PATA, SATA, and SAS Connectivity

The original Integrated Drive Electronics (IDE) standard was developed only for hard drives and is officially known as ATA (AT Attachment). Later, other devices were supported by the standard, and the standard evolved to ATA/ATAPI (AT Attachment Packet Interface). ATAPI increased support for devices such as optical and tape drives. There are two types of ATA: Parallel ATA (PATA) and Serial ATA (SATA).

PATA is the older type and uses a 40-pin IDE cable (refer to Figure 7.15) that connects the hard drive to an adapter or the motherboard and transfers 16 bits of data at a time. Each PATA motherboard connector allows two devices to be attached. Some motherboards have both SATA and PATA IDE connectors. Figure 7.18 shows the difference between PATA and SATA motherboard connectors.

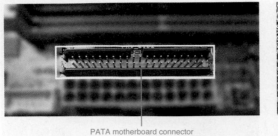
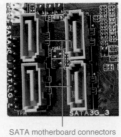

PATA motherboard connector   SATA motherboard connectors

FIGURE 7.18   PATA and SATA motherboard connectors

Figure 7.19 shows PATA IDE hard drive connectors. Notice the 40-pin connector on the far left and the power connector on the far right.

FIGURE 7.19   PATA IDE hard drive connectors

The newer ATA standard is SATA (Serial ATA). The original specification transfers data at 1.5 Gb/s and is called **SATA 1** or SATA I. The 3 Gb/s version is known as **SATA 2** or SATA II, and the latest release, **SATA 3** or SATA III, runs at a maximum of 6 Gb/s. These devices are commonly seen marked as SATA 1.5 Gb/s, 3 Gb/s, and 6 Gb/s.

SATA is a point-to-point interface, which means that (1) each device connects to the host through a dedicated link (unlike with a traditional parallel IDE, where two devices share the host link), and (2) each device has the entire interface bandwidth. SATA uses a smaller, 7-pin cable that is more like a network cable than the traditional IDE ribbon cable. SATA supports both internal and external devices. Figure 7.20 shows an internal SATA drive with the cable attached. The data connector is to the left of the power connector.

There are several connectors for SAS drives, but the one most commonly seen by PC technicians is the **SCSI connector** for a SAS drive. The SAS connector looks similar to the connectors on a SATA drive except that on a SAS drive there is no space between the two sets of gold connectors; instead, it is solid plastic, as shown in Figure 7.21.

An internal SATA device commonly uses a 15-pin SATA power connector rather than the Molex connector used by older hard drives. However, some drives do ship with Molex connectors. A Molex-to-SATA converter can be purchased, but the connector can only provide 5 and 12 volts, not 3.3 volts. The good news is that most SATA drives do not use the 3.3 V line. Figure 7.22 shows an older Molex power connector compared to an internal SATA power connector.

FIGURE 7.20　SATA hard drive and data cable

FIGURE 7.21　SAS drive connector

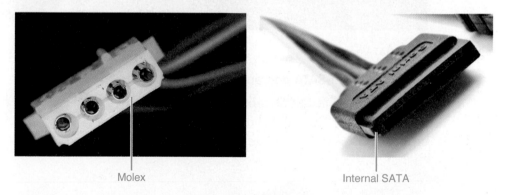

Molex　　　　　　　　　　　　　　　　Internal SATA

FIGURE 7.22　Hard drive power connectors

Internal SATA data cables are limited to a maximum of 3.3 feet (1 meter). The internal SATA data cable is more likely to be inadvertently unplugged or partially unplugged than the PATA cable. Special cables with locking mechanisms are in an L shape for hard-to-reach places, and low-profile form factor cases can also be purchased. Figure 7.23 shows these 7-pin internal SATA device cables.

Standard   Locking   L-shaped

FIGURE 7.23   Internal SATA data cables

External SATA (**eSATA**) provides external device connectivity. It allows shielded cable lengths up to 6.56 feet (2 meters), with faster connections than USB 2.0 or 3.0. However, the standard eSATA connection does not provide power to external devices, but an eSATAp combo USB/eSATA port can provide power. Note that eSATA is currently not faster than USB 3.1 gen 2.

Figure 7.24 shows an eSATA cable and eSATA port. An eSATA cable can be rated for 1.5 Gb/s, 3 Gb/s, or 6 Gb/s. eSATA cables are limited to 3.3 feet (1 meter) for 1.5 Gb/s devices and 6.56 feet (2 meters) for 3 Gb/s or 6 Gb/s transfers.

eSATA port   eSATA cable

FIGURE 7.24   eSATA port and cable

A Serial-Attached **SCSI cable**, or SAS cable, is used to connect hard drives or tape drives to a SAS controller. The cable shown in Figure 7.25 is used to connect a SAS hard drive to a SATA controller that supports SAS drives. One cable provides both power and data connections.

FIGURE 7.25   SAS (Serial-Attached SCSI cable)

Storage Device Configuration Overview

Drive configuration sometimes includes setting jumpers on the drive and sometimes on the associated adapter to ensure proper termination. *Termination* is a method used to prevent signals from reflecting back up the cable. Each drive type has a normal configuration method. However, individual drive manufacturers may develop their own configuration steps. Always refer to the documentation included with the drive, adapter, or motherboard for configuration and installation information. The overall steps for installing a storage device are as follows:

Step 1. Keep the drive in the protective antistatic container until you are ready for the installation. Then use proper antistatic handling procedures when installing the drive and handle the drive by the edges; avoid touching the drive electronics and connectors.

Step 2. Turn off the computer and remove the computer power cord before installing the drive.

Step 3. Physically mount and secure the device in the computer and attach the proper cable.

Step 4. Reconnect the power cord and power on the computer. Configure the BIOS/UEFI, if necessary.

Step 5. If a hard drive is being installed, prepare the drive for data, as described later in the chapter.

PATA Physical Installation

A PATA cable allows two storage devices to connect to a single motherboard connector. Each cable can have a master device and a slave device. To distinguish between the devices, the words **master** or **slave** are used. The two settings are simply used to distinguish between the two devices because only one of the two devices (master or slave) can transmit data at a time. Motherboards used to have at least two PATA connectors, but now some may not have any. The first motherboard connector is known as the primary connector. If a second one is installed, it is called the secondary connector. To distinguish between the devices that connect to each cable, the devices are called the *primary master* and *primary slave*.

TECH TIP

Attach PATA cable correctly to avoid damage

Devices, adapters, controlling circuits, and so on can be damaged if a cable plugs into the connector the wrong way. Some cables are keyed so they insert into the connector only one way.

PATA devices are configured using jumpers. The four options commonly found are single, master, slave, and cable select. The single IDE setting is used when only one device connects to the cable. The master IDE setting is used in conjunction with the slave setting, and both are used when two IDE devices connect to the same cable. One device is set to the master setting, and the other device uses the slave setting. The **cable select** IDE option replaces the master/slave setting. With this setting, the device automatically configures itself to either the master setting or the slave setting, depending on the specific cable connector to which the device attaches. A special 80-conductor, 40-pin cable is needed to use the cable select option. Figure 7.26 shows the connections for an 80-conductor cable.

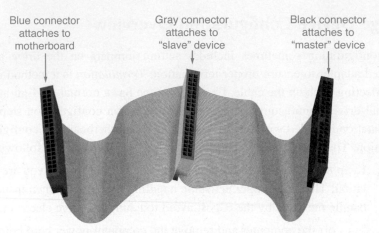

Blue connector attaches to motherboard

Gray connector attaches to "slave" device

Black connector attaches to "master" device

FIGURE 7.26   PATA cable connections

There are two methods of configuring PATA IDE devices: (1) Configure one device as master and the other device as slave or (2) configure both devices to the cable select option. With the cable select option set, the device that connects to the black connector becomes the "master," and the device that connects to the gray connector becomes the "slave." Figure 7.27 illustrates how multiple PATA devices connect to the motherboard.

TECH TIP

Closed means jumpered or enabled

When documentation shows an option as closed, jumpered, or enabled, this means you need to put a jumper over the two pins to configure the option.

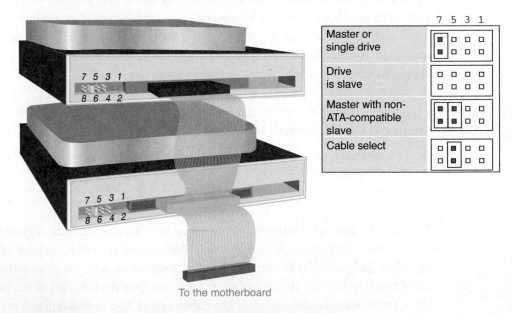

To the motherboard

FIGURE 7.27   Two PATA devices configured with cable select

TECH TIP

Adjusting to poorly written documentation

Technicians must learn to adjust to poorly written and sometimes confusing documentation. Jumpers other than the master/slave jumpers may be present, but you must refer to the documentation for the proper settings.

SATA Physical Installation

SATA drives are easy to install. Most internal drives require a special host adapter that supports one to four drives or an integrated motherboard connection. Each drive is seen as a point-to-point connection with the host controller.

SATA drives do not have any master/slave or cable select jumpers/settings. A serial 7-pin data connector attaches from the SATA controller to the internal SATA drive. A 15-pin cable connects power to the drive. The internal SATA power connector is unique but could possibly be an older Molex connector. A cable converter can be obtained if a Molex connector is the only one available from the power supply. Figure 7.28 shows an internal SATA hard drive with associated cabling. Notice the Molex-to-internal SATA cable converter in the photo.

FIGURE 7.28 **SATA hard drive and cables**

There are also products available that allow a Serial ATA hard drive to connect to a standard IDE controller. Figure 7.29 shows how cables connect to an internal SATA drive. Figure 7.30 shows how two SATA drives attach to a motherboard that has two SATA connectors.

FIGURE 7.29 **SATA data (left) and power (right) cabling**

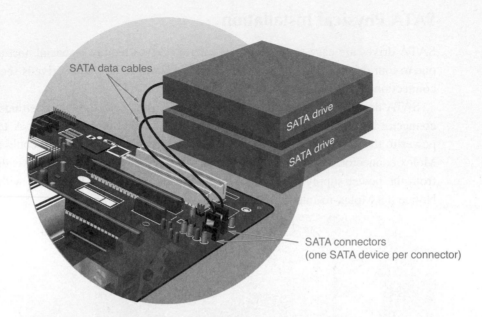

SATA data cables

SATA drive

SATA drive

SATA connectors
(one SATA device per connector)

FIGURE 7.30   SATA connectivity

Figure 7.31 shows a SATA adapter that has two internal ports on the far end and one eSATA port. To install a SATA host adapter, power off the computer and remove the computer power cord. Remove the computer cover and locate an open expansion slot. Some adapters have jumpers for configurable options. For most adapters the default settings will work, but always refer to the adapter's documentation for details.

FIGURE 7.31   eSATA card

TECH TIP

Enabling a SATA port in BIOS/UEFI

Some manufacturers require that you enable the motherboard port through the system BIOS/UEFI before any device connected to the port is recognized.

To install an internal SATA hard drive, power off the computer and remove the computer's power cord. Physically mount the drive into a drive bay. Connect the SATA data cable between the drive and the host controller (usually on the motherboard). Connect the SATA power cable. Figure 7.32 shows an installed internal SATA hard drive.

FIGURE 7.32   Installed SATA hard drive

An external (eSATA) drive normally has no jumpers, terminators, or switches to configure. However, when connecting a faster drive to a slower port—such as when installing a 3.0 Gb/s drive in a 1.5 Gb/s port—a jumper may need to be configured so the drive is compatible with the port. Always refer to the drive manufacturer's documentation when installing a drive. Attach the power cord to the drive, if applicable, and insert the other end of the power cord into a wall outlet. Attach one end of the eSATA cable to the drive. Plug the other end of the cable into an eSATA port on the computer. eSATA ports are sometimes disabled in BIOS/UEFI. Figure 7.33 shows an external hard drive that supports IEEE 1394 (FireWire), eSATA, and USB, as you can see from the ports on the back of the unit.

FIGURE 7.33   External hard drive

Before switching on eSATA drive power, ensure that the drive is positioned where it will stay during operation and that all data and power cords are attached securely. Switch on the drive power. The drive will **mount**. When a drive mounts, a communications channel is opened between the drive and the operating system. Whenever the drive is to be disconnected, it is to be unmounted. Some drive manufacturers provide software for backing up data or configuring the drive in a RAID configuration. Use the Windows *Disk Management* tool to ensure that the drive is recognized. Both RAID and the Disk Management tool are covered later in this chapter.

> **TECH TIP**
>
> **Unmounting an eSATA drive**
>
> To unmount an eSATA drive, click the *Safely Remove Hardware* icon in the notification area and select the appropriate drive letter. Remove the drive when prompted by the operating system. If you cannot find this icon in Windows 10, use *File Explorer* to locate the drive, right-click on it, and select *Eject*.

SSD Physical Installation

For a desktop computer, an SSD can be internally mounted and connected to a SATA/PATA motherboard or an adapter port. Figure 7.34 shows an internal SSD. An SSD can also attach as an external device to an eSATA or USB port. SSDs do not normally require special drivers. Always refer to the SSD mounting directions provided by the manufacturer. The following steps are generic ones:

Step 1. Power off the computer, remove the power cord, and locate an empty drive bay, a power connector of the appropriate type (or buy a converter), and an available SATA/PATA port or free PATA connector on a PATA cable.

Step 2. Attach mounting brackets to the SSD. Mounting brackets may have to be purchased separately, may be provided with the drive, or may be provided with the computer.

Step 3. Slide the SSD into the drive bay and secure it, if necessary.

Step 4. Connect the data cable from the motherboard or adapter to the drive.

Step 5. Attach a power cable to the SSD.

Step 6. Reinstall the computer cover, reattach the power cord, and power on the computer.

FIGURE 7.34   Internal SSD

> **TECH TIP**
>
> **Beware of static electricity**
>
> SSDs are flash memory and are susceptible to static electricity. Use proper ESD handling procedures when installing an SSD.

If installing an external SSD, use the following steps:

Step 1. Attach the appropriate USB or eSATA cable from the drive to the computer.

Step 2. Power on the SSD. The system should recognize the new drive.

> **TECH TIP**
>
> **Using only one technology**
>
> If an external drive supports more than one technology, such as eSATA and USB, attach only one type of cable from the drive to the computer.

System BIOS/UEFI Configuration for Hard Drives

A hard drive is configured through the system BIOS/UEFI Setup program. Setup is accessed through keystrokes during the boot process. In today's computers, the BIOS/UEFI automatically detects the hard drive type. The drive type information is saved in CMOS.

> **TECH TIP**
>
> **Configure BIOS/UEFI according to the drive manufacturer's instructions**
>
> Drive manufacturers normally include documentation describing how to configure the drive in BIOS/UEFI Setup. Also, they provide software for any system that does not recognize the drive.

Hard drives are normally configured using the Auto-Detect feature included with BIOS/UEFI. The Auto-Detect feature automatically determines the drive type for the system. Table 7.1 shows the most commonly used PATA/SATA hard drive settings. SATA drives can be set in different modes of operation: (1) legacy mode, which is used in a system that does not have SATA drivers natively; (2) Advanced Host Controller Interface (**AHCI**) mode, which, when enabled, allows SATA drives to be inserted/removed when power is on and use commands to allow the host circuits to communicate with attached devices in order to implement advanced SATA features; and (3) RAID mode. RAID is discussed later in this chapter. Note that the BIOS/UEFI is also where you select the drive that will boot the system.

TABLE 7.1 Common hard drive BIOS/UEFI settings

Hard drive type	BIOS/UEFI setting
IDE PATA/SATA/SCSI/SAS	AUTO
SATA	SATA mode: IDE mode (no AHCI or RAID)
SATA	SATA mode: SATA or AHCI (AHCI enabled)
SATA	SATA mode: RAID (AHCI and RAID enabled)

CHAPTER 7

Hard Drive Preparation Overview

After a hard drive is installed and configured properly and the hard drive type is recognized and seen within the Setup program, the drive must be prepared to accept data. The two steps of hard drive preparation are as follows:

Step 1. Partition the drive.

Step 2. Perform a high-level format on the hard drive.

TECH TIP

Low-level formatting

Low-level formatting may be done at the hard drive factory. Some manufacturers provide software that enables you to do low-level formatting on the drive, but you should do this only at the direction of the manufacturer.

Partitioning a hard drive allows a drive letter to be assigned to one or more sections of the hard drive. **High-level formatting** prepares the drive for use for a particular file system. This allows the drive to accept data from the operating system. For today's computers, a drive cannot be used until it has been partitioned and had high-level formatting done; thus, technicians must be very familiar with these steps.

Partitioning

The first step in preparing a hard drive for use is partitioning. Partitioning a hard drive means dividing the drive into separate sections so the computer system sees the hard drive as more than one drive. Each drive section gets a drive letter. Figure 7.35 shows a hard drive platter with some colored sections. Each section between the colored lines can be a volume and can receive a different drive letter.

FIGURE 7.35 Visualization of partitioning

Partitioning can be done during the Windows installation process or by using the Windows **Disk Management** program. Similarly, the `diskpart` utility can be used from the command prompt. Disk Management is normally used to partition additional hard drives and to manage all of them. The first hard drive in the system is normally partitioned as part of the Windows installation process. Additional partitions can be created using Disk Management after the operating system is installed.

Partitioning provides advantages such as the following:

> Dividing a hard drive into separate subunits that are then assigned drive letters, such as C: or D:, by the operating system
> Organizing the hard drive to separate multiple operating systems, applications, and data
> Providing data security by placing data in a different partition to allow ease of backup as well as protection
> Using the hard drive to its fullest capacity

TECH TIP

How to determine what file system is being used

Right-click any drive in *Windows Explorer* (Windows 7) or *File Explorer* (Windows 8/10) and select *Properties*. The *General* tab shows the type of file system being used.

The original purpose of partitioning was to make it possible to load multiple operating systems. This is still a good reason today because placing each operating system in its own partition eliminates the crashes and headaches caused by multiple operating systems and multiple applications coexisting in the same partition. The type of partition and how big the partition can be depends on the file system being used. A **file system** defines how data is stored on a drive. The most common Windows file systems are FAT16, FAT32, exFAT, and NTFS. What file system can be used depends on what operating system is installed, whether the device is an internal device or external, and whether files are to be shared. Table 7.2 lists file systems and explains a little about each one.

TABLE 7.2 File systems

File system type	Description
Compact Disk File System (**CDFS**)	A file system for optical media.
FAT	Also called FAT16. Used with all versions of Windows. 2 GB partition limitation with old operating systems. 4 GB partition limitation with XP and higher versions of Windows.
FAT32	Supported with all versions of Windows. Commonly used with removable flash drives. Supports drives up to 2 TB. Can recognize volumes greater than 32 GB but cannot create them that big.
exFAT	Commonly called FAT64. A file system made for removable media (such as flash drives and SD cards) that extends drive size support up to 64 ZB in theory, but 512 TB is the recommended max. Made for copying large files such as disk images and media files. Supported by all versions of Windows.
NTFS	Used with Windows 7, 8, and 10. Supports drives up to 16 EB (16 exabytes, which equals 16 billion gigabytes), but in practice is only 16 TB. Supports file compression and file security (encryption). NTFS allows faster file access and uses hard drive space more efficiently. Supports individual file compression and has the best file security.

CHAPTER 7

File system type	Description
Hierarchical File System (**HFS**)	Used with Apple computers. Was been upgraded to HFS+ and then later upgraded to Apple File System (APFS) in 2017.
Network File System (**NFS**)	An open source file system developed by Sun Microsystems that is used in Linux-based systems. Allows access to remote files over a network.
ext3	Also known as third extended file system. Used in Linux-based operating systems and is a journaling file system (which means it tracks changes in case the operating system crashes, allowing it to be restarted without reloading).
ext4	An update to ext3 that allows for larger volumes and file sizes within Linux-based operating systems.

An even better reason for partitioning than loading multiple operating systems or separating the operating system from data is to partition the hard drive for more efficient use of space. The operating system sets aside at least one cluster for every file. A **cluster** is the smallest amount of space reserved for one file, and it is made up of a specific number of sectors. Figure 7.36 illustrates the concept of a cluster. Keep in mind that the number of hard drive sectors per track varies. The outer tracks hold more information (have more sectors) than the inner tracks.

TECH TIP

How to convert partitions

Use the `convert` program in Windows to convert a FAT16, FAT32, or exFAT partition to NTFS without loss of data. Access a command prompt window. Type the following command: `convert x: /fs:ntfs`, where x is the drive letter of the partition being converted to NTFS.

Press (Enter) and then press (Y) and press (Enter). You can add a /V switch to the end of the command for a more verbose operation mode.

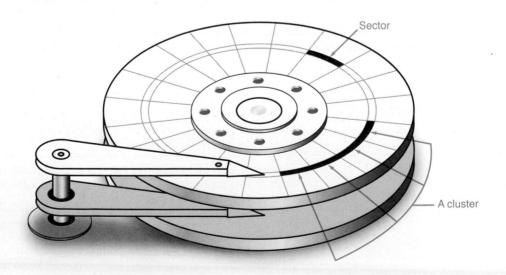

Sector

A cluster

One cluster is the minimum amount of space for a file.

FIGURE 7.36   Cluster

Any type of partition conversion requires free hard drive space. The amount depends on the size of the partition. Table 7.3 shows that partitioning large drives into one FAT partition wastes drive space. An efficiently partitioned hard drive allows more files to be saved because less space on the hard drive is wasted.

TABLE 7.3   FAT16 partitions and cluster sizes

Partition size	Number of sectors	Cluster size
0–32 MB	1	512 bytes
32 MB–64 MB	2	1 kB
64 MB–128 MB	4	2 kB
128 MB–256 MB	8	4 kB
256 MB–512 MB	16	8 kB
512 MB–1 GB	32	16 kB
1 GB–2 GB	64	32 kB
2 GB–4 GB	128	64 kB

Applications should be in a separate partition from data files. The following are some good reasons for partitioning a hard drive and separating data files from application files:

> Multiple partitions on the same hard drive divide the drive into smaller subunits, which makes it easier and faster to back up the data (which should be backed up more often than applications).
> The data is protected from operating system failures, unstable software applications, and any unusual software problems that occur between the application and the operating system.
> The data is in one location, which makes backing up, organizing, and locating the files easier and faster.

FAT32 partitions have been around a long time and are still used. Flash drives are commonly formatted for FAT32 due to the NTFS "lazy write," which prolongs a write and might not release an external drive for some time. The FAT32 file system makes more efficient use of the hard drive than FAT16. NTFS is an efficient file system. Table 7.4 lists the default cluster sizes for all versions of Windows 7 and higher.

TABLE 7.4   NTFS partitions and cluster sizes

Partition size	Number of sectors	Cluster size
0–16 TB	8	4 kB
16 TB–32 TB	16	8 kB
>32 TB–64 TB	32	16 kB
>64 TB–128 TB	64	32 kB
>128 TB–256 TB	128	64 kB

Figure 7.37 shows a screen capture of the Windows 7 Disk Management window. Notice that the external drives and optical drives are also displayed in the Disk Management window. The file system is shown for each drive; for example, you can see the FAT32 file system on an attached flash drive (G:).

Benefits of NTFS

NTFS supports disk quotas, which means that individual users can be limited in the maximum amount of usable hard drive space. NTFS can also automatically repair disk problems. For example, when a hard drive sector is going bad, NTFS moves the entire cluster to another cluster.

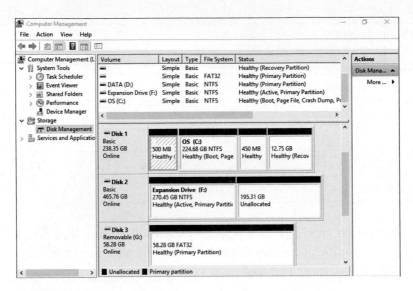

FIGURE 7.37   Windows 7 Disk Management tool

Partitions are defined as primary and extended. If there is only one hard drive installed in a system and the entire hard drive is one partition, it is the **primary partition**. The primary partition on the first detected hard drive is assigned the drive letter C:.

eSATAs are already partitioned

Most eSATA drives are already partitioned and formatted, but these drives can be repartitioned and reformatted as necessary by using the *Disk Management* tool.

If a drive is divided, only part of the drive is the primary partition. In older operating systems, the rest of the cylinders can be designated as the **extended partitions**. An extended partition allows a drive to be further divided into **logical drives**. A logical drive is sometimes called a **volume**. A volume is assigned a drive letter and can include a logical drive and removable media such as a CD, DVD, BD, or flash drive. There can be only one extended partition per drive. In operating systems older than Windows Vista, a single hard drive could be divided into a maximum of four primary partitions. Remember that a partition is a contiguous section of storage space that functions as if it is a separate drive. Figure 7.38 shows an illustration of how one hard drive can be divided into partitions.

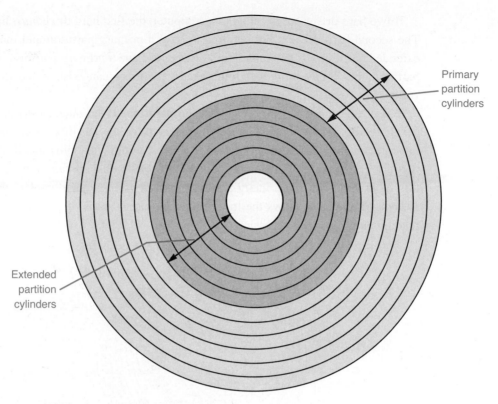

Primary partition cylinders

Extended partition cylinders

FIGURE 7.38   Hard drive partitioning

The first hard drive in a computer system must have a primary partition, but an extended partition is not required. If the drive has an extended partition, it can be further subdivided or split into logical drives that appear as separate hard drives to the computer system. Logical drives created in the extended partition are assigned drive letters such as D: or E:. The only limit for logical drives is the number of drive letters. A second operating system can reside in a logical drive. Figure 7.39 shows an illustration of a hard drive divided into a primary partition and an extended partition that is further subdivided into two logical drives.

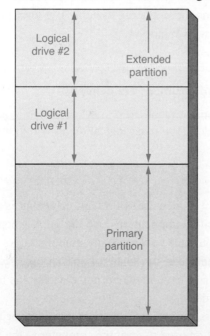

Logical drive #2
Logical drive #1
Extended partition
Primary partition

FIGURE 7.39   Two logical drives

CHAPTER 7

If two hard drives are installed in a computer, the first hard drive *must* have a primary partition. The second hard drive is not required to have a primary partition and may simply have a single extended partition. If the second hard drive does have a primary partition, it can have an extended partition, too. Today, more than four primary partitions can exist, so the sections are simply called *volumes*.

When a hard drive is first installed and partitioned, the outermost track on the platter (cylinder 0, head 0, and physical sector 1) is reserved for the partition table. The partition table holds information about the types of partitions created and in what cylinders these partitions reside. The partition table is part of the master boot record (**MBR**) that contains a program that reads the partition table, looks for the primary partition marked as active, and goes to that partition to boot the system. Figure 7.40 shows the locations of important parts of the hard drive that allow booting, reading partitions, and accessing files.

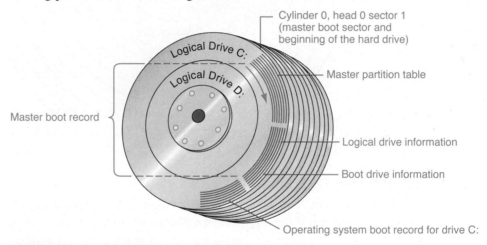

FIGURE 7.40   Hard drive structure

NTFS has two additional terms that you need to be aware of as a technician: system partition and boot partition. A Windows **system partition** is the partition on the hard drive that holds the hardware-specific files needed to load the operating system. A Windows **boot partition** is the partition on the hard drive that contains the operating system. The boot partition and the system partition can be on the same partition with Windows.

TECH TIP

What happens when different types of partitions are deleted?

When a partition is deleted, all information in the partition is lost. When logical drives in an extended partition are deleted, all data is lost. The other logical drives within the extended partition retain their information.

The Host Protected Area (**HPA**) is a hidden area of a hard drive that is used to hold a copy of the operating system; sometimes installed applications use the HPA when the operating system becomes so corrupt that a reinstallation is necessary. Many manufacturers provide a BIOS/UEFI setting or a keystroke that can be used when the system boots in order to access this area. The HPA is commonly found on the hard drive beyond the normal data storage locations; it reduces the amount of storage space available for data.

Look back to Figure 7.37, at the first line of the center section. Under the status, you can see that this computer has a recovery partition used to reset the computer to the way it was when it was purchased. Look down to the graphical section in the center and locate Disk 1. The area to the left of OS (C:) is an extensible firmware interface (EFI) partition. This type of partition is supported by the UEFI specification and supports the running of specific applications, including diagnostics and potentially antivirus software, in a graphical environment before the operating system loads. The Disk Management tool also shows external drives such as the FAT32 external flash drive (G:).

A partition type that is not shown is GPT, which is available with 64-bit Windows operating systems. GUID, or globally unique identifier, partition table (**GPT**) allows up to 128 partitions and volumes up to 9.4 ZB. GPT partitioning is accomplished using the Disk Management tool or using the diskpart command-line utility. GPT makes it possible to have a backup partition table in case the primary partition becomes corrupt. A GPT disk can also have more than the MBR-based disk limit of four primary partitions.

> **TECH TIP**
>
> **You lose data when converting to GPT**
>
> MBR-based partitions can be converted to GPT and vice versa, but data is not preserved. This is seen only with systems that have a UEFI BIOS. Back up data if you convert!

Special products can be used to partition a hard drive and also repartition without any data loss. Examples include Acronis's Disk Director, EaseUS's Partition Master, and Avanquest's Partition Commander.

How Drive Letters Are Assigned

An operating system assigns drive letters to hard drives during the partitioning step. The order in which partitions are assigned drive letters depends on three factors: (1) the number of hard drives, (2) the type of volume on the hard drives (primary or extended), and (3) the operating system.

Note that if a new drive is installed, drive letters for devices, volumes, partitions, or logical drives are added afterward. Drive letters can be changed through the Disk Management tool (by right-clicking on the drive letter) or by using the diskpart command-line utility. Be careful, though, because some applications have pointers to specific files on specific drive letters.

High-Level Formatting

The second step in preparing a hard drive for use is high-level formatting. High-level formatting must be performed on all primary partitions, logical drives located within extended partitions, and GPT partitions before data can be written to the hard drive. The high-level format sets up the file system so it can accept data.

NTFS allows support for multiple data streams as well as support for every character in the world. NTFS also automatically remaps bad clusters to other sections of the hard drive without any additional time or utility. During the installation process, Windows allows for a **quick format** (where you see the word "(quick)" after the option) or a full format (sometimes called a standard format). The **full format** scans for and marks bad sectors. This prevents the operating system from being installed on a sector that may cause operating system issues. The quick format simply prepares the drive for data and takes a lot less time than a full format. Use the full format if you suspect that the drive has issues. Figure 7.41 shows the NTFS partition structure once it has been set up and the high-level formatting is completed.

High-level formatting creates two file allocation tables (FATs): one primary and one secondary. The formatting process also creates the root directory that renumbers the sectors. The **FAT** keeps track of the hard disk's file locations. It is similar to a table of contents in a book as it lists where the files are located in the partition. Table 7.5 shows the differences between the file systems.

FIGURE 7.41 NTFS volume structure

TABLE 7.5 Comparing Windows file systems

Specification	FAT16	FAT32	NTFS	exFAT
Maximum file size	4 GB	4 GB	~16 TB	~16 EB
Maximum volume (partition) size	4 GB (2 GB, if shared with a really old computer)	32 GB (max format)	2 TB (or greater)	64 ZB (512 TB recommended)
Maximum files per volume	~64,000	~4 million	~4 billion	Not defined (but 1,000 per directory)

High-level formatting can be performed using the `format` command or by using the Windows Disk Management tool. The area of the disk that contains information about the system files, the DOS boot record (**DBR**), is located on the hard drive's cylinder 0, head 1, sector 1. The more common term for this today (because DOS is no longer a major operating system) is **boot sector**, or volume boot record.

Additional drive partitions and drives installed after the first hard drive partition is created use the Windows Disk Management tool to apply high-level formatting to the drive. The first hard drive partition normally has high-level formatting done as part of the operating system installation process.

Windows Disk Management

In the Windows environment, storage devices are managed with the Disk Management tool. With Windows, there are two types of storage: basic storage and dynamic storage. The big difference between these two is that you can make partitions and resize changes with a dynamic disk but not with a basic disk. Table 7.6 explains these and other associated terms. Figure 7.42 shows some of these concepts.

> **TECH TIP**
>
> **Hibernation affects disk space**
>
> Whenever you put your computer in hibernate mode, information in RAM is stored temporarily on the hard drive. This requires free hard drive space.

TABLE 7.6 Logical disk management terms

Term	Description
Basic storage	One of the two types of storage. This is what has traditionally been known as a partition. It is the default that is used by all operating systems.
Basic disk	Any drive that has been partitioned and set up for writing files. A basic disk has primary partitions, extended partitions, and logical drives contained within the extended partitions.

Term	Description
Dynamic storage	The second type of storage; contrast with basic storage. Allows you to create primary partitions, logical drives, and dynamic volumes on storage devices. More powerful than basic storage in that it allows creation of simple, spanned, or striped volumes using dynamic disks.
Dynamic disk	A disk made up of volumes. A volume can be the entire hard disk, parts of the hard disk combined into one unit, and other specific types of volumes, such as single, spanned, or striped volumes. Cannot be on a removable drive.
Simple volume	Disk space allocated from one hard drive. The space does not have to be contiguous.
Spanned volume	Disk space created from multiple hard drives. Also known as "just a bunch of disks" (**JBOD**). Windows writes data to a spanned volume in such a way that the first hard drive is used until the space is filled. Then, the second hard drive's space is used for writing. This continues until all hard drives in the spanned volume are utilized.
Striped volume	Disk space in which data is written across 2 to 32 hard drives. It is different from a spanned volume in that the drives are used alternately. Another name for this is striping, or RAID 0 (covered in the next section).
System volume	Disk space that holds the files needed to boot the operating system.
Boot volume	Disk space that holds the remaining operating system files. Can be the same volume as the system volume.
RAW volume	A volume that has never had high-level formatting performed and that does not contain a file system.

A basic disk, simple volume, or spanned volume can be resized, shrunk, or expanded without affecting data. When working within Disk Management, right-click on a drive to see all the available options, such as seeing the properties of the drive, marking a partition as active, changing the drive letter and paths, formatting, extending a volume, shrinking a volume, adding a mirror, or deleting a volume.

TECH TIP

Managing dynamic disks

Use the *Disk Management* tool (found in the *Computer Management* console or by right-clicking the Start button in Windows 10 and selecting *Disk Management*) to work with dynamic disks or to convert a basic disk to a dynamic one. This conversion process cannot be reversed.

TECH TIP

Determining what type of partition you have

To determine what type of partition is on a computer, use the Disk Management tool.

CHAPTER 7

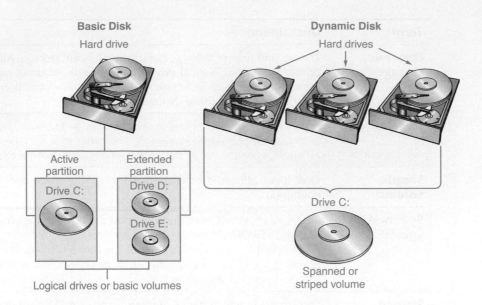

FIGURE 7.42   Disk Management concepts

To **extend** (make larger), **split** (break into two sections), or **shrink** (reduce the size of) a partition, use the following steps:

Step 1. Access the Windows *Disk Management* tool.

Step 2. Right-click on the drive volume.

Step 3. Select either *Shrink Volume* or *Extend Volume*.

Figure 7.43 shows a hard drive partition and settings used to shrink it so that another partition can be created.

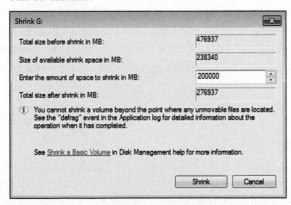

FIGURE 7.43   Resizing a partition

Fault Tolerance

A **drive array** involves using two or more hard drives configured for speed, redundancy, or both (see Figure 7.44). Redundant array of independent (or inexpensive) disks (**RAID**) allows reading from and writing to multiple hard drives for larger storage areas, better performance, and fault tolerance. Fault tolerance is the ability to continue functioning after a hardware or software failure. A RAID array can be implemented with hardware or software. Hardware RAID is configured through the BIOS/UEFI.

FIGURE 7.44 RAID

Generic steps for configuring hardware RAID are as follows:

Step 1. Ensure that the motherboard ports that you want to use are enabled.

Step 2. Ensure that you have RAID drivers for the hard drives used in the RAID.

Step 3. Physically install and cable the hard drives.

Step 4. Enter BIOS/UEFI and enable RAID.

Step 5. Configure RAID in BIOS/UEFI or through a special key sequence to enter the RAID BIOS configuration.

Step 6. Install Windows on a RAID by using the Custom (Advanced) Installation option.

Software RAID is configured through Windows or through software provided by the RAID adapter manufacturer. If you want to be able to control a RAID through Windows and resize the volumes or make adjustments, use software RAID.

RAID can also be implemented with flash cache modules (FCMs) and a traditional mechanical hard drive. Intel has specific processors and chipsets that support RAID configurations. Software on the host device and/or device drivers provides optimization and oversight.

RAID comes in many different levels, but the ones implemented in the Windows environment are 0, 1, and 5. The ones on the A+ certification exam are RAID levels 0, 1, 5, and 10. Some motherboards support "nested" RAID, in which RAID levels are combined. This method also increases the complexity of the hard drive setup. Table 7.7 explains the RAID levels.

TABLE 7.7   RAID

RAID level	Description
0	Also called **disk striping** or disk striping without parity. Data is alternately written on two or more hard drives, which increases system performance. These drives are seen by the system as one logical drive. **RAID 0** does not protect data when a hard drive fails. It is not considered fault tolerant. It has the fastest read and write performance.

CHAPTER 7

RAID level	Description
1	Also called disk mirroring or disk duplexing. **RAID 1** protects against hard drive failure. **Disk mirroring** uses two or more hard drives and one disk controller. The same data is written to two drives so that if one drive fails, the system continues to function. Disk duplexing is similar except that two disk controllers are used. With disk duplexing, performance is slightly degraded when writing data because it has to be written to two drives.
0+1	A striped set and a mirrored set combined. At least four hard drives are required, and they need to have an even number of disks. A second striped set mirrors a primary striped set of disks. Also called RAID 01, this mode can read from the drive quickly, but there is a slight degradation when writing.
1+0	A mirrored set and a striped set combined with at least four hard drives. The difference between 1+0 and 0+1 is that 1+0 has a striped set from a set of mirrored drives. This mode, also called **RAID 10**, can read from the drive quickly but has a slight degradation when writing.
5	Also called disk striping with parity. **RAID 5** writes data to three or more hard drives. Included with the data is parity information. If a drive fails, the data can be rebuilt based on the information from the other two drives. This level can read and write data quickly.

Figure 7.45 shows the different types of RAID. With RAID 0, blocks of data (B1, B2, B3, and so on) are placed on alternating drives. With RAID 1, the same block of data is written to two drives. RAID 5 has one drive that contains parity information (P) for particular blocks of data such as B1 and B2.

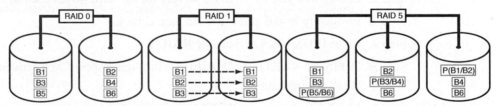

FIGURE 7.45   RAID concepts

Windows 7/8/10 Professional and higher support simple, spanned, striped, and mirrored volumes. Refer to Table 7.6 to reacquaint yourself with these terms. Keep in mind that a spanned volume does not provide redundancy or fault tolerance, as most of the RAID levels do.

RAID drives are often **hot swappable**—that is, they can be removed or installed while power is applied to the computer. USB, SATA, and Serial-Attached SCSI (SAS) all support hot swapping, but RAID is not required to be supported. Always refer to the drive and computer manual before hot swapping any hard drive. RAID rebuilds are time and input/output (I/O) intensive. Be prepared for the system to be out of commission for a while; the amount of time the system will be unavailable depends on the size of the drive and the RAID type.

Hardware RAID for home or business computer used to require a separate RAID adapter and software to perform the RAID. Now many motherboards support RAID, and so do the Windows 7, 8, and 10 operating systems. Many times, you must configure the motherboard BIOS/UEFI for RAID as part of your initial configuration. Table 7.8 shows some common RAID BIOS configuration parameters.

TABLE 7.8   RAID BIOS/UEFI configuration settings

BIOS/UEFI setting	Description
SATA mode: AHCI Mode	A mode that may mean that hot swapping is supported. A set of commands can be used to increase storage performance.
SATA mode: RAID Mode or Discrete SATA Mode	Allows you to select a particular RAID level and the drives associated with the RAID.
SATA drives: Detected RAID Volume	Usually an information screen that shows the type of RAID configured, if any.
SATA drives: eSATA Controller Mode	Allows configuration of RAID through the eSATA port.
SATA drives: eSATA Port x Hot Plug Capability	Allows hot swapping to be enabled or disabled for eSATA ports.

Removable Drive Storage

PATA and SATA interfaces have been used for quite some time to connect hard drives. PATA was used for internal devices. SATA has been used for both internal and external storage devices, such as optical drives and tape drives. **Tape drives** can be attached using SATA or can attach to USB, eSATA, or eSATAp ports if they are external devices. External drives might require two USB ports (see Figure 7.46) when an external power source is not attached. Tape drives are installed using methods similar to those used with other devices that use these ports. The types of tapes most commonly used for backups are DAT (digital audio tape) and Traven. Tape capacities tend to be lower than optical storage capacities (covered in Chapter 8, "Multimedia Devices"), which in turn are usually lower than the capacities of hard drives. Tape capacities can be anywhere from 12 GB to 10 TB but are typically less than this. The most common types of removable storage are optical discs (CD/DVD/BD), USB flash drives, and hard drive storage devices.

FIGURE 7.46   External hard drive with two USB connectors

Windows Storage Spaces

Microsoft Windows 8 and Windows 10 support **Windows Storage Spaces**, which combines drives into a flexible data storage option. An administrator first creates a **storage pool**, which is two or more physical disks that can be different types, such as a SATA drive and a USB drive. A **storage space** is a virtual disk created from available space in a storage pool. There are three types of storage spaces:

> *Simple*—Data is striped across physical disks. No resiliency is provided. This type of storage space provides the highest performance, but there is a loss of data if one disk fails.

> *Parity*—Data is striped across the physical disks and includes parity information. Slows performance.

> *Mirror*—Data is striped across multiple disks, and the same data is copied for the highest level of resiliency.

Unlike with RAID, if you add a drive to a storage space, the data will not be rewritten to include the new drive. Instead, new data will use all of the drives. To create a storage space, follow these steps:

Step 1. Access the *Storage Spaces* Windows Control Panel link. Select *Create a new pool and storage space*.

Step 2. Select the drives to be used and then select *Create Pool* (see Figure 7.47).

Step 3. Name the storage space and select the drive letter, file system, resiliency type, and pool size, (see Figure 7.48) and then select *Create Storage Space*.

When the storage space created, the storage drive letter appears in File Explorer, as shown in Figure 7.49.

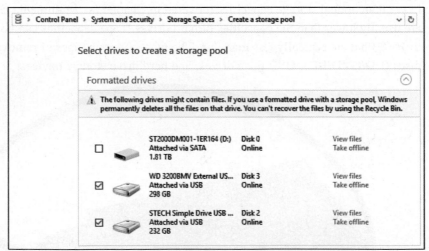

FIGURE 7.47   Windows Storage Spaces—Creating a storage pool

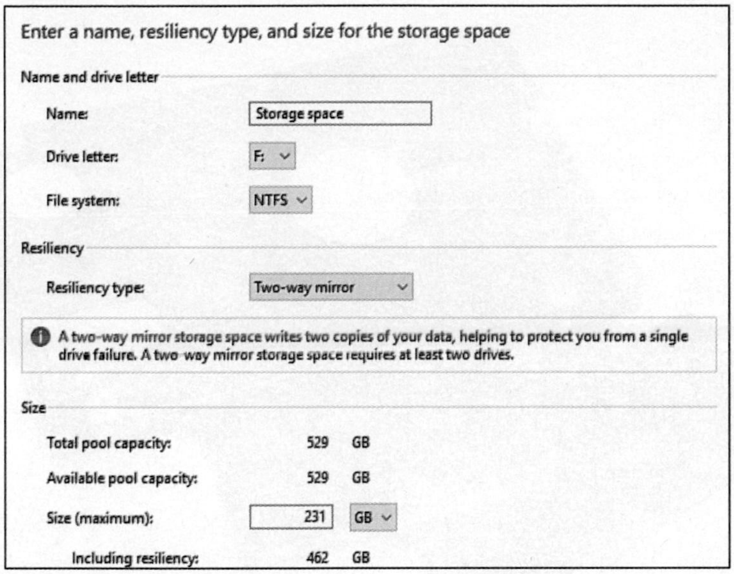

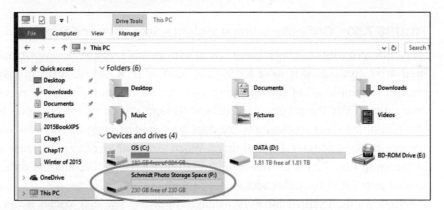

FIGURE 7.48   Windows Storage Spaces—Defining parameters

FIGURE 7.49   Windows Storage Spaces, as shown in File Explorer

Disk Caching/Virtual Memory

Hard drive storage, cache memory built into a hard drive and motherboard RAM (see Figure 7.50) are all used as part of any computer's storage system. An easy way to speed up a hard drive is to create a **disk cache**, which involves putting data into RAM, where it can be retrieved much faster than if the data were still on the hard drive. When data is read from the hard drive, the next requested data is frequently located in the adjacent clusters. Disk caching reads more data from the hard drive than requested. Cache on a hard drive controller, sometimes called a data buffer, allows the read/write heads to read more than just one sector at a time. A hard drive can read up to an entire track of information and hold this data until needed without returning to the hard drive for each sector.

Both PATA and SATA drives can contain 2 MB to 128 MB or more of RAM (cache memory). Because many drives are mechanical devices, they take time to reorder write data to the platters. With cache memory installed, information can be prefetched from the computer's system RAM and stored in the hard drive's cache memory. This frees up the system RAM for other tasks and improves the performance of the system and the hard drive.

FIGURE 7.50   Computer storage system—hard drive and RAM

A different way of using a hard drive is with virtual memory. Using virtual memory means using hard drive space as if it were RAM. The amount of RAM installed in a system is not normally enough to handle all of the operating system and the multiple applications that are opened and being used. Only the program and data of the application that is currently being used is in RAM. The rest of the open applications and data are stored in a paging file (also called a swap file, pagefile.sys, or page file) on the hard drive. When you click over to a different application that is held in the swap file, data is moved from RAM into the swap file, and the data you need to look at is moved into RAM for faster access and data manipulation.

Windows uses virtual memory manager (VMM). The disk cache is dynamic, which means it increases and decreases the cache size as needed. If the system begins to page (that is, constantly swap data between RAM and the hard drive), the cache size automatically shrinks. In Windows, the virtual memory swap file is called pagefile.sys. Here is how to adjust it:

> In Windows 7, in Windows Explorer, right-click *Computer* > *Properties*. In the left pane, se-lect *Advanced System Settings* > *Advanced* tab. In the *Virtual Memory* section, click *Change*. Then, to manually configure the settings, clear the *Automatically Manage Paging File Size for All Drives* checkbox and adjust the settings as needed.

> In Windows 8, access the *System and Security* Control Panel > *System* > *Advanced system settings* link > *Advanced* tab > the Performance section's *Settings* button > *Advanced* tab > *Change* button. Change the parameters and click the *OK* button twice.

> In Windows 10, access the *Start* button > *Settings*. In the *Find a Setting* search textbox, type `performance`. Select the *Adjust the Appearance and Performance of Windows* link > *Advanced* tab > *Change* button (as shown in Figure 7.51). Change the parameters and click the *OK* button twice.

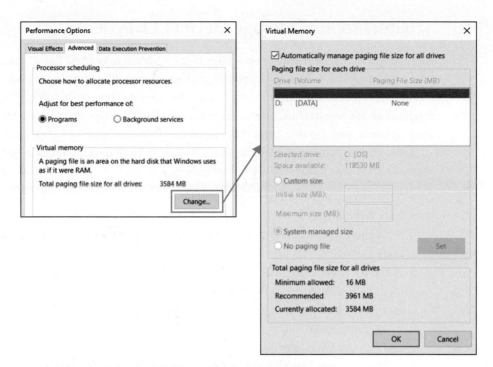

FIGURE 7.51   Windows 10 virtual memory manager

TECH TIP

Where to keep a swap file

If multiple hard drives are available, a technician might want to move the swap file to a different drive. Always put the swap file on the fastest hard drive, unless that hard drive lacks space. The swap file can reside on multiple hard drives. It is best to keep the swap file on a hard drive that does not contain the operating system.

Memory space is divided into 4 KB blocks of memory called *pages*. The operating system allocates as much available RAM as possible to an application. Then the operating system swaps or pages the application to and from the temporary swap file as needed. The operating system determines the optimum setting for this swap file; however, the swap file size can be changed.

The page file can also get corrupted. If it does, boot the Windows 7 system and press F8 while booting. Select the option to repair the computer. In Windows 8 or 10, hold down ⬆Shift while selecting *Restart* from the power icon > *Troubleshoot* > *Advanced Options* > *Startup Repair*. If this does not repair the system, you may have to make manual adjustments from the command prompt, including removing the attributes from the `pagefile.sys` file, and then manually delete it so it can be rebuilt when Windows boots. Search the Windows website for more details on this and more difficult and detailed method.

TECH TIP

Adding more physical RAM helps with caching

One of the most effective ways to speed up a computer is to reduce the amount of data that has to be swapped from the hard drive to RAM. This is done by increasing the amount of motherboard RAM.

Troubleshooting Storage Devices Overview

Storage devices are critical to computer users because they hold users' data. Sadly, users do not back up their data or system frequently. Blackblaze (www.blackblaze.com) did a study of more than 25,000 mechanical drives and found that over a four-year period, 78% of the drives lasted longer than four years, but 22% of them failed during the first four years. Mechanical drives have moving parts, and moving parts fail. Expect it!

Tools that a technician needs to troubleshoot storage devices include both hardware and software. The list that follows is a good starting point:

> Screwdriver to loosen or remove screws.
> External hard drive enclosure to be able to check a drive from another system or be able to determine whether the problem is the drive or the motherboard port (refer to Figure 7.4 to see one).
> Software such as the chkdsk, format, or bootrec commands, and Windows tools such as Error-checking or Disk Management. chkdsk checks a drive for physical and file structure errors and can attempt to fix them. The format command is used to format a disk. The bootrec command is used from the Windows Recovery Environment (WinRE) to repair and recover from hard drive issues.
> Companies can buy **file recovery software** or hire other companies to provide it as a service. Technicians who do not have this software should at least have the name of a company they recommend or use.

The specific hardware or software tool to use depends on the situation, as described in the sections that follow. One thing to remember when troubleshooting a storage device is the user. A technician is often faced with angry users when dealing with their storage devices. Stay calm and do the best you can. Just because a system will not boot from the hard drive does not mean it is bad. There are things you can do, as you will soon see.

Dealing with Slow Performance

Keeping a computer system in a clean and cool operating environment extends the life of the hard drive. Hard drive failures are due to problems with moving parts (heads and motors), power fluctuations, and/or failures. Performing preventive maintenance on the entire computer is good for all components inside the computer, including the hard drive subsystem (see Figure 7.52).

Windows has three great tools to use in hard drive preventive maintenance: Error-checking (*Check Now* or *Check* button), Disk Cleanup, and Disk Defragmenter.

In Windows, you can use Error-checking/Check Now (Windows 7) to locate **lost clusters**, which are clusters that have become disassociated from data files but still occupy disk space. Error-checking/Check Now is also good for dealing with intermittent read/write errors. Locate the drive in Windows Explorer (Windows 7) or File Explorer (8/10), right-click the drive, and then select *Properties > Tool* tab *> Check Now (Windows 7)/Check (8/10)*.

FIGURE 7.52   Disk maintenance

The Windows program **Disk Cleanup** removes temporary files, removes offline Internet files, empties the Recycle Bin, compresses unused files, and removes unused programs—and it prompts you before doing any of this. To access Disk Cleanup, follow these steps:

Step 1. Access *Windows Explorer* (Windows 7)/*File Explorer* (8/10).

Step 2. Right-click on the drive letter (commonly C:) and select *Properties*.

Step 3. On the *General* tab, select the *Disk Cleanup* button.

Step 4. In the Disk Cleanup window, select the checkboxes for the options desired and click *OK* (as shown in Figure 7.53). Table 7.9 lists the types of files that can be removed with this tool.

FIGURE 7.53   Disk Cleanup window

TABLE 7.9   Disk Cleanup file removal

File type	Description
Downloaded program files	Java applets and ActiveX controls that might be downloaded automatically when a particular website is accessed
Temporary Internet files	Frequently accessed web pages stored on the hard drive for quicker access
Offline web pages	Web pages that can be retrieved from the hard drive even when the computer does not have Internet connectivity
Recycle Bin files	Files marked for deletion that are still stored on the hard drive until the Recycle Bin is emptied
Setup log files	Files created by Windows when the configuration has changed
System error memory dump files	Data from memory at the time of a blue screen of death (BSOD) crash
Temporary files	Files generated by programs that are usually deleted when the application is closed
Thumbnails	Copies of pictures, videos, and document thumbnails that display quickly when a folder is opened if thumbnails view is being used
Per user archived/queued Windows error report	Files used for error reporting and when checking for possible solutions
System archived/queued Windows error report	Files used for error reporting and when checking for possible solutions

TECH TIP

Running Disk Cleanup from a command prompt

To run Disk Cleanup from a command prompt, type `cleanmgr` and then press ⏎Enter.

Over time, as files are added to a hard drive, the files become fragmented, which means the clusters that make up a file are not adjacent to one another. Fragmentation slows down the hard drive in two ways: (1) The FAT has to keep track of scattered clusters, and (2) the hard drive read/write head assembly must move to different locations on the drive's surface to access a single file. Figure 7.54 illustrates fragmentation of three files (F1, F2, and F3) and the results after defragmentation has been executed on the hard drive. **Defragmentation** is the process of placing files in contiguous sectors. Notice the results of the defragmentation process in Figure 7.54.

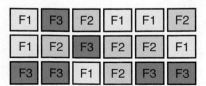
Three fragmented files

Three contiguous files

FIGURE 7.54   Fragmented hard drive/defragmented hard drive

Defragmenting a hard drive makes for faster hard disk access. This process also extends the life of the hard drive by reducing the drive's mechanical movements. The methods used in Windows to defragment are as follows:

> In Windows 7, open *Windows Explorer*, locate a hard drive letter, right-click it, and select *Properties > Tools* tab > *Defragment Now* button.
> In Windows 8/10, open *File Explorer*, locate a hard drive letter, right-click it, and select *Properties > Tools* tab > *Optimize*.
> From a command prompt, use the `defrag` command.

TECH TIP

SSD defragmentation kills

Do not defragment an SSD as you would a magnetic hard drive. Defragmentation causes more reads and writes, which reduces the life span of the SSD.

You should periodically defragment files on a mechanical PATA or SATA hard drive. Users who delete files often and have large files that are constantly revised should especially make use of the defragmentation tool. You can use the Disk Defragmenter tool to check whether a drive partition needs to be defragmented.

TECH TIP

Tool order matters

Use the Error-checking (Check Now or Check) and Disk Cleanup tools before running the Disk Defragmenter tool.

Note that Windows 7 automatically schedules a hard drive to be defragmented every Wednesday at 1 a.m. if the computer is powered on. Otherwise, defragmentation runs automatically the next time the computer is powered on. Windows 8 and 10 perform hard drive optimization as needed. You can manually execute optimization using the Disk Defragmenter tool.

Troubleshooting New Storage Device Installation

Most problems with new drive installation stem from improper configuration of jumpers on PATA drives or problems with cabling. BIOS and the operating system can display a multitude of symptoms, including POST error codes, beeps, and messages, such as the following:

> Hard drive not found
> No boot device available
> Hard drive not present
> Inaccessible boot device
> Invalid boot disk

The following tips assist with checking possible problems when **drive not recognized** errors occur in the system.

> Check the physical settings (such as the power cable, jumper settings, secure data cable, data cable pin 1 orientation, and device placement on data cable).
> Check the drive type setting in BIOS/UEFI Setup and ensure that the ports are enabled (especially SATA ports).
> If after you have configured the drive, installed it, and powered it on, the BIOS/UEFI shows the drive type as "None" or "Not installed," or if it displays all 0s in the drive parameters even though you set it to automatically detect the drive, then the BIOS/UEFI is not able to detect

it. Check the BIOS/UEFI SATA mode and BIOS/UEFI version. Check all jumper settings, check the cable connection(s), and check the power connection. If two PATA drives connect to the same cable, disconnect the slave drive. In Setup, reduce any advanced features to their lowest values or disable them. Increase the amount of time the computer takes to initialize the hard drive by going into Setup and modifying features such as hard drive boot delay or set the boot speed to the lowest value. This gives the hard drive more time to spin up and reach its appropriate RPM before data is read from it. Make sure the motherboard port is enabled.

> Determine whether the drive has been partitioned and one partition has been marked as the active partition. Also determine whether high-level formatting has been applied to the drive.

> Verify that the mounting screw to hold the drive in the case is not too tight. Loosen the screw and power up the computer. Figure 7.55 shows the mounting screws for a hard drive installed in a tower case.

> If the hard drive does not format to full capacity, (1) your BIOS/UEFI may not support the larger drive and/or the BIOS/UEFI must be upgraded, (2) you have selected a file system that does not support larger partitions, or (3) you need an updated driver.

> If during power-on the hard drive does not spin up or the hard drive spins down after a few seconds, check the power connector, the data cable, the drive recognized in BIOS/UEFI, jumper settings, energy management jumpers or settings in Setup, and any software that came with the drive that enables power management. Disable power management in BIOS/UEFI and/or the operating system. Try installing the drive in another system.

> If the system locks or you get a blue screen of death (**BSOD**), write down the message or code, if any, and try a warm boot (Ctrl + Alt + Del). If the drive is recognized after the warm boot, the Setup program may be running too fast for the drive to initialize. Refer to the hard drive documentation to see if the hard drive has a setting to help with this problem.

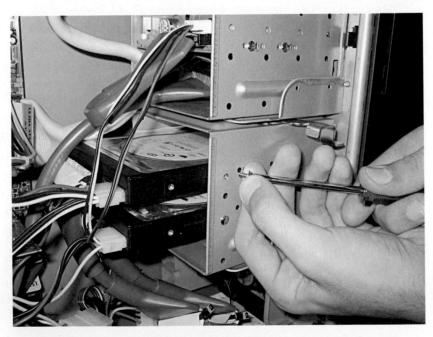

FIGURE 7.55 Hard drive mounting screws

Troubleshooting Previously Installed Storage Devices

Previously installed boot devices can have all of the same symptoms as a newly installed storage device plus the following additional ones:

> **Loud clicking noise**
> Read/write errors
> Slow to respond
> Blue screen of death (BSOD) or pinwheel of death (macOS)

Because many drives are mechanical devices, they make noises. Sometimes these noises are because the hard drive is being used too much as virtual memory due to a lack of physical RAM. Some noises are normal, and others indicate problems, as shown in Figure 7.56.

Normal noises

Whining noise on spin up

Periodic clicking or whirling sounds when the drive is being accessed

Clicking sound made by heads parking during power saving modes or when powering off

Abnormal noises

High-pitched whining sound

Repeated clicking or tapping sounds when computer is idle

High-frequency vibration in mounting hardware

Hard drive clicks and/or a POST error

ERROR\\

FIGURE 7.56 Hard drive noises

When a hard drive starts making that loud clicking, tapping sound, back up the drive immediately and go ahead and purchase a replacement drive. The drive is failing!

The following are generic guidelines for hard drives that have worked but are now having problems or for when a computer **fails to boot**:

> Run a virus-checking program after booting from virus-free boot media. Many viruses are specifically designed to attack hard drives. If you have to wipe the hard drive to ensure that the virus is erased before reinstalling the operating system, applications, and data, ensure that you do a full format and not a quick one as part of the operating system installation process.
> Has there been a recent cleaning of the computer, or has someone recently removed the top from the computer? If so, check all cables and verify that they correctly connect. Check the power connection to the hard drive.

TECH TIP

Does your hard drive stick?

Place a hand on top of the drive as you turn on the computer. Does the drive spin at all? If not, the problem is probably a "sticky" drive or a bad drive. A hard drive must spin at a certain RPM before the heads move over the surface of the hard drive. To check to see whether the drive is sticking, remove the drive and try spinning the spindle motor by hand. If it is not moving, remove the drive, hold the drive in your hand, and give a quick jerk with your wrist. Another trick that may work is to remove the hard drive from the case, place the drive in a plastic bag, and put it in the freezer for a couple of hours. Then remove the drive and allow it to warm up to room temperature and reinstall the drive into the system and try it.

> If the hard drive light flashes quickly on bootup, the controller is trying to read the partition table in the master boot record. If this information is not found, various symptoms are possible, such as the error messages "Invalid boot disk," "Inaccessible boot device," "Invalid partition table," "Error loading operating system," "Missing operating system," or "No operating system found." Use the `diskpart` command from the Windows Recovery Environment (WinRE) to see whether the hard drive partition table is okay. Here are a few commands

to help within this utility: `list disk`, `list volume`, `list partition`, `detail disk`, `detail volume`, and `detail partition`. Try running `bootrec /fixmbr` or use a hard drive utility to repair the partition table.

> A common problem is that the operating system cannot be found, which is indicated with the **OS not found message**. In addition, message or other messages such as "Disk Boot Failure," "Non-System Disk," and "Disk Error" that may indicate a boot record problem. The solution is to boot from a bootable disc or USB flash drive to see if drive C: is available. When doing so, change the BIOS/UEFI boot order settings to boot to your removable media. The operating system may have to be reloaded. Also, verify that the primary partition is marked as active and that there is not nonbootable media such as a disc or USB flash drive inserted into or attached to the system. Check the first boot option setting in BIOS/UEFI and make sure it is set to the appropriate drive.

> If you receive a message such as "Hard drive not found," "No boot device available," "Fixed disk error," or "Disk boot failure," the BIOS/UEFI cannot find the hard drive. Check cabling. Place the drive in an external enclosure and attach to a working computer.

> If a self-monitoring, analysis, and reporting technology (**S.M.A.R.T.**) error appears, back up data and research the error to take immediate action. S.M.A.R.T. is used to monitor both mechanical hard drives and SSDs. A S.M.A.R.T. error may appear immediately before a failure. Table 7.10 lists a few of the S.M.A.R.T. errors, but remember that drive manufacturers may have their own.

TABLE 7.10   S.M.A.R.T. errors

Error	Description
Reallocated sectors count	The number of sectors that were marked as bad, causing the data within those sectors to be moved
Spin retry	The number of times the drive was not up to speed in order to read and write from the drive
SATA downshift error count or runtime bad block count	The number of data blocks that contained uncorrectable errors
Reported uncorrectable errors	The number of uncorrectable errors detected
Reallocation event	How many times data had to be remapped
Soft read error rate or TA counter detected	The number of off-track errors

> When Windows has startup problems, the Windows Recovery Environment (WinRE) and *Advanced Options* menu (press F8 on startup) are used. With Windows 8 or 10 devices, if the system boots too quickly to access this menu, hold down ⬆Shift while restarting the system. Then select *Troubleshoot > Advanced Options >* either *Automatic Repair* (in Windows 8)/ *Startup Repair* (in Windows 10) or *Command Prompt*. Startup problems are often due to a virus. Other utilities that help with MBR, boot sector, and system files are System File Checker (SFC) and the *Advanced Boot Options* menu. Use `bootrec /fixmbr` or `bootrec / fixboot` from the Windows Recovery Environment (WinRE).

TECH TIP

Using System File Checker

You can run the System File Checker program from the command prompt by typing `sfc /scannow`. The System File Checker should also be run after removing some viruses.

> When Windows has startup problems due to incompatible hardware or software or a corrupted installation process, the *Advanced Boot Options* menu can help.

> If an insufficient disk space error appears or if the user is experiencing **slow performance** (the computer takes a long time to respond), delete unnecessary files, including .tmp files, from the hard drive, empty the Recycle Bin, and save files to an optical disc, a flash drive, or an external hard drive and remove the moved files from the hard drive. Use the Disk Cleanup and Defragmenter tool. Another option is to add another hard drive and move some (or all) data files to it.

> For eSATA drives, check the power cabling and data cabling. Ensure that the data cable is the correct type for the port and device being used. Partition and format the drive before data is written to it. Ensure that the port is enabled through BIOS. The BIOS/UEFI may require an update, or a device driver may be required (especially if the drive is listed under "other devices" in Device Manager). Note that some operating systems report SATA drives as SCSI drives.

> If the computer reports that the hard drive may have a defective area or if you start getting **read/write failure** notices, right-click on the hard drive volume > *Properties* > *Tools* tab > *Check Now* (Windows 7)/*Check* (8/10). The drive may need to be replaced soon.

> If drives fail frequently in a particular computer, check for heat problems, power fluctuations, vibrations, improper mounting screws or hardware that might cause vibrations, and environmental issues such as dust, heat, magnetic fields, smoke, and nearby motors. Consider using an SSD if the computer is in a harsh environment.

> If a USB drive is the boot device and the system will not boot, unplug the drive, reattach it, and restart the system.

> If a **proprietary crash screen** appears, note the message and/or code and research it from another computer.

> If a **spinning pinwheel**, ball, hourglass, or other application-specific icon appears, if a message that an application is not responding (sometimes asking you if you want to wait or kill the application) appears, or if a drive takes forever to respond within an application, use the Disk Management tool to view the status of the drive. (Note that the Mac's colored spinning pinwheel is covered in Chapter 17.) Table 7.11 shows some of the normal and problem **drive status** messages seen in the Windows Disk Management tool. These status messages can help with drive management, troubleshooting, and recovery.

TABLE 7.11   Disk Management status states

Status state	Description
Active	The bootable partition, usually on the first hard drive, is ready for use.
Dynamic	An alternative to the basic disk, the dynamic disk has volumes instead of partitions. Types of volumes include simple volumes, volumes that span more than one drive, and RAID volumes.
Failed	The basic disk or dynamic volume cannot be started; the disk or volume could be damaged; the file system could be corrupted; or there may be a problem with the underlying physical disk (turned on, cabled correctly) or with an associated RAID drive. Right-click the disk and select *Reactivate Disk*. Right-click the dynamic volume and select *Reactivate Volume*.
Foreign	A dynamic disk from another computer has just been installed. Right-click the disk and select *Import Foreign Disks*.
Healthy	The drive is ready to be used.

CHAPTER 7

Status state	Description
Not Initialized	A basic disk is not ready to be used. Right-click the disk and select *Initialize Disk*. The **Initialize Disk** option enables a disk so that data can be stored.
Invalid	The operating system cannot access the dynamic disk. Convert the disk to a basic disk (by right-clicking the disk number and selecting *Convert to Basic Disk*).
Offline	Ensure that the physical disk is turned on and cabled correctly. Right-click it and select *Reactivate Disk* or *Activate*.
Online (errors)	Use the hard drive Error-checking tool. In Windows Explorer/File Explorer, right-click the hard drive partition and then select *Properties*, the *Tools* tab, and *Check Now* (Windows 7)/*Check* (8/10) button.
Unallocated	Space on a hard drive has not been partitioned or put into a volume.
Unknown	A new drive has not been initialized properly. Right-click the drive and select *Initialize Disk*. The volume boot sector may be corrupted or infected by a virus.
Unreadable	The drive has not had time to spin up. Restart the computer and rescan the disk (using the *Action* menu item).

RAID Issues

When you add RAID to a computer, you increase the complexity of the disk management. When two hard drives are configured in a RAID, they are seen as one volume and managed as one volume. Because of the different types of RAID and the number of hard drives involved in the RAID, a lot of problems could occur. Symptoms of RAID problems are similar to those that occur with a hard drive failure (read/write failure, slow system performance, loud clicking noise, failure to boot, drive not recognized, operating system not found, or a BSOD). The following issues can help you with RAID configurations:

> If you have done RAID through the BIOS/UEFI, you cannot manage RAID through Windows (it is grayed out and shows as no fault tolerance). If you want to manage RAID through Windows, you have to break the RAID in BIOS/UEFI (remove the RAID) and then re-create the RAID in Windows. Back up your data before doing this.

> Sometimes as part of the RAID configuration, you need driver media for the Windows installation or RAID failure troubleshooting process. Follow the motherboard or RAID adapter's manufacturing directions on how to create this media (usually a USB drive or optical disc, even though the directions on the screen may say floppy disk).

> If Windows doesn't allow you or give you the option to create a RAID, check the BIOS/UEFI settings and ensure that AHCI has been enabled for the drives.

> If disk mirroring is not an option in Windows Disk Management, check your Windows version. You must have Windows Professional or a higher edition to create a RAID.

> If Windows no longer boots, a BSOD appears, and the Windows boot drive is part of a RAID, reinstall Windows if you want to keep the RAID. You may have to get drivers before doing this. If you do not care about RAID and just want Windows to boot again, remove the hardware RAID. You can also use the BSOD code shown to research the error.

> If a RAID partition suddenly goes missing, check for a virus.

> If you receive a message such as **RAID not found**, check the hardware or software configuration (depending on which type of RAID was configured). A power surge can corrupt a

hardware RAID configuration done through BIOS/UEFI Setup. A system upgrade, application upgrade, or new application can affect software RAID.

> If the **RAID stops working**, use the Windows Disk Management tool to check the status of the drives. Then check the RAID configuration if the drives are okay.

SSD Issues

The BIOS should recognize an internally installed SSD. If it does not, go into the system BIOS/UEFI Setup and ensure that the connector to which the SSD attaches is enabled. Be especially careful with SATA ports and port numbering. Configure the system to automatically detect the new drive, save the settings, and reboot the system. Here are some things to try, but remember that other hard drive tips still apply, such as those related to the computer not booting or the operating system not being found:

> Restart the PC.
> Try another SATA port or cable.
> Uninstall/reinstall the driver.
> Turn off the Wake on LAN BIOS option.

CHAPTER 7

SOFT SKILLS: PHONE SKILLS

Technicians must frequently use the phone in the normal course of business to speak with customers, vendors, and technical support staff. Many technicians' full-time jobs involve communication via the telephone.

Phone communication skills are different from the skills needed for in-person communication because on the phone, you have only your words and voice intonation to convey concepts, professionalism, and technical assistance (see Figure 7.57).

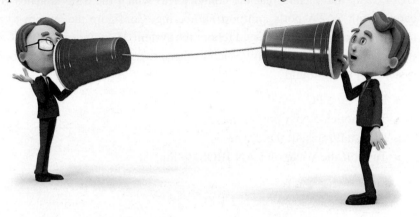

FIGURE 7.57   Telephone communication skills

When dealing with someone in person, you can use some of the following techniques that are not as effective in a phone conversation:

> Gesture to emphasize points.
> Draw a graphic to illustrate a concept.
> Perform steps needed for troubleshooting faster because you can do them rather than step someone through them.
> Show empathy more easily with your body language, actions, and voice.

When dealing with someone on the phone, the following pointers can help. Some of the tips apply to everyday technical support as well:

> Identify yourself clearly and pleasantly.
> Avoid using a condescending tone.
> Be patient and speak slowly when giving directions.
> Use active listening skills (covered in Chapter 2, "Connectivity"); avoid doing other tasks when on a call with someone.
> Avoid using acronyms and technical jargon.
> Avoid being accusatory or threatening.
> If the customer is irate, try to calm the customer down and help him or her; however, if the customer continues to be belligerent, turn the call over to your supervisor.
> Escalate the problem if it is beyond your skill level; do not waste the customer's time.
> Do not leave people on hold for extended periods without checking back with them and updating them.
> Speak clearly and loudly enough to be heard easily.
> Avoid having a headset microphone pulled away so it is hard to hear you; if you are asked to repeat something, speak louder or adjust the microphone or handset.
> Avoid eating, drinking, or chewing gum when on the phone.

Good interpersonal skills are even more important when on the phone than with face-to-face interactions. Before getting on the phone, take a deep breath and check your attitude. Every customer deserves your best game, no matter what type of day you have had or what type of customer you have previously spoken to.

Chapter Summary

> Hard drive form factors include 5.25-, 3.5-, 2.5-, and 1.8-inch drives. Hard drives come in different speeds: 5,400, 7,200, 10,000, and 15,000 RPM. Faster RPM rates mean more expensive drives but also faster data transfers.
> Common drives today are PATA, SATA, and SSD for desktop and mobile computers.
> PATA drives are internal only and connect to a 40-pin ribbon cable that can have two devices per motherboard connector/cable.
> SATA drives can be internal or external and connect using a 7-pin 3.3-foot (1 meter) maximum internal connector, an external eSATA connector (3.3-foot [1-meter] maximum for 1.5 Gb/s devices and 6.56-foot [2-meter] maximum for 3 or 6 Gb/s devices), or an eSATAp combo eSATA/USB port. SATA 1 (I) drives operate at a maximum of 1.5 Gb/s, SATA 2 (II) drives at 3 Gb/s, and SATA 3 (III) drives at 6 Gb/s. SATA internal drives use a unique SATA power connector. A Molex-to-SATA converter can be purchased, but 3.3 V is not supplied to the drive; most drives do not use the 3.3 V line. External drives use an external power source unless plugged into an eSATAp combo port, which can provide power.
> SATA drives require no jumper, and only one device can connect to a SATA motherboard/adapter port.
> SSDs have become more common in desktops, laptops, and tablets. They are often used in harsh environments, dirty environments, heavy movement environments, and harsh temperature environments. They are extremely fast but expensive. They connect using PATA, SATA, USB, or eSATA connections.
> SSDs erase data in blocks instead of by marking available clusters in the FAT with traditional drives. SSDs should not be defragmented. SSDs use various technologies to ensure functionality, such as using all the memory evenly (wear leveling) and using reserved spare memory blocks.
> SSHD is a combination of a mechanical hard drive and flash memory holding the most frequently used data.
> Hard drives must be partitioned and have high-level formatting applied before they can be used to store data.
> Partitioning separates a drive into smaller sections (volumes) that can receive drive letters. The smaller the volume, the smaller the cluster size. A cluster is the smallest space in which a single file can reside. A cluster consists of four or more sectors, and each sector contains 512 bytes.
> Partitioning can be done through the Windows installation process or by using the Disk Management tool.
> A simple volume is the most common type of partition volume created.
> To create a spanned volume (otherwise known as JBOD), space from two or more hard drives is seen as one drive letter. One drive is filled before any other hard drives are used.
> A striped volume writes data to two or more drives but does not provide redundancy.
> The system volume holds files needed to boot the operating system (usually C:).
> The boot volume holds the majority of the operating system files (usually C:).
> Computer manufacturers may use an HPA or protected partition for system recovery.
> Multiple drives can be configured in a hardware or software RAID implementation. Hardware RAID is done using the BIOS/UEFI or a RAID adapter. Software RAID is done using the Windows Disk Management tool.

> RAID 0, or disk striping, does not provide fault tolerance, but it does provide fast, efficient use of two or more drives.
> RAID 1 is disk mirroring, and this method does provide fault tolerance by ensuring an exact copy of a drive in case one drive fails.
> RAID 5 is disk striping with parity, where parity data is kept on one of the three or more drives. This parity data can be used to rebuild one drive if one of the three or more drives fails.
> RAID 10 is a mirrored set and a striped set combined with four hard drives at a minimum. This mode can read from the drive quickly but with slight degradation when writing.
> Windows Storage Spaces can use a variety of drive types to create a single storage space that can have RAID-like qualities.
> File systems in use are FAT16 (FAT), FAT32, exFAT, NTFS, CDFS, HFS, HFS+, APFS, NFS, ext3, and ext4. FAT32 and exFAT are used for external drives, such as flash thumb drives. NTFS, which is used for internal drives, provides features such as better cluster management, security, compression, and encryption. CDFS is used for optical media. NFS, ext3, and ext4 are used in Linux-based systems.
> Two ways of changing from one file system to another are by using the `convert` command and by formatting the drive. The `convert` command preserves existing data. High-level formatting does not preserve any saved data.
> If a drive fails to be recognized as a new installation, check cabling and BIOS/UEFI settings, especially for a disabled SATA port.
> Normal mechanical drive noises include a clicking when going into sleep mode or being powered down due to self-parking heads.
> Abnormal drive noises include a couple of clicks with a POST beep and/or error, repeated clicking noises, high-frequency vibration due to improper or poor mounting hardware, and a high-pitched whining sound.
> If a drive fails after operating for a while, check for a virus. See if the BIOS has a virus checker. Try a warm boot to see whether the drive has not spun up to speed yet. Check cabling, especially on SATA. Review any recent changes. Use the Windows Advanced Boot Options menu, Windows Recovery Environment (WinRE), System File Checker (SFC), and the `bootrec /fixmbr` and `bootrec /fixboot` commands. Boot from an alternate source and check Disk Management for status messages related to the hard drive.
> Hard drive space used as RAM is known as virtual memory. Ensure that enough storage space is available for the operating system.
> When speaking on the phone to anyone, be clear in your statements, don't use technical jargon, keep your tone professional, and do not do other tasks, including eating or drinking.

A+ CERTIFICATION EXAM TIPS

✓ Be able to select, install, and configure SATA, SSD (M.2 and NVMe), and hybrid drives.

✓ Make sure you know about and can recognize SATA, IDE (PATA), and SCSI (SAS) cabling. Be able to recognize SCSI, eSATA, and Molex connectors.

✓ Know the purposes of the Error-checking (Check Now/Check), Disk Cleanup, and Disk Defragmenter tools.

✓ Use a computer to review the disk tools and how to get to them.

✓ Review all the troubleshooting tips right before taking the exam.

✓ Be familiar with the following Disk Management concepts: drive status and what to do if the status is not in a healthy state, mounting, extending partitions, splitting partitions, assigning drive letters, adding drives, and adding arrays.

✓ Know what a normal hard drive sounds like and what sounds a hard drive in trouble makes. Ensure you back up the data before the drive fails.

✓ Know the difference between RAID levels 0, 1, 5, and 10.

✓ Know the various file systems, including exFAT, FAT32, NTFS, CDFS, HFS, NFS, ext3, and ext4.

✓ Know the difference between a quick format and a full format.

✓ Know the differences between basic and dynamic disks and understand primary, extended, and logical partitions and volumes.

✓ Be able to troubleshoot common symptoms such as read/write failures, slow performance, loud noises, failure to boot, drive not recognized, OS not found, RAID not found, and RAID stops working.

✓ Be familiar with BSOD and spinning pinwheel proprietary crash screens.

✓ Know how and when to use Microsoft command-line tools such as `format`, `diskpart`, `SFC`, and `chkdsk`.

✓ Install a couple of practice drives for the exam. Misconfigure the BIOS/UEFI and leave a cable unplugged or the drive power removed so you see the POST errors and symptoms.

✓ Be able to suggest the best type of drive for a particular situation (SSD, hybrid, or mechanical as a type) as well as an appropriate capacity.

✓ Know how and when to configure RAID and the differences between the various RAID levels.

✓ Be able to configure a drive for Storage Spaces, initialize a drive, convert a drive to a dynamic disk, create a simple volume, and select a particular file system.

✓ Know how to speak on the phone professionally.

Key Terms

Review Questions

Consider the following internal hard drive specifications when answering Questions 1–7:

> SATA 6 Gb/s transfer rate
> 1 TB capacity
> Minimizes noise to levels near the threshold of human hearing
> 3.5-inch 7,200 RPM
> 32 MB buffer size

1. Which SATA version is being used?

   [1 | 2 | 3 | Cannot be determined from the information given]

2. Which Windows file system should be placed on this drive if encryption will be used?

   [exFAT | FAT | FAT32 | NTFS]

3. Which drive preparation steps are *required* to be done if this drive is added as a new drive? (Select all that apply.) [defragmentation | low-level format | high-level format | error checking | RAID | virus checking | partitioning | striping | duplexing]

4. This drive is meant to be quiet. List two noises that the drive could make that would indicate issues to you.

   _____

   _____

5. Is this drive internal or external? Explain your reasoning. [Internal | External | cannot be determined]

   _____

6. What is this drive's form factor?

   [6 Gb/s | 1 TB | 3.5-inch | 7,200 RPM | 32 MB]

7. How many other devices could be on the same cable that connects this device to the motherboard?

   [0 | 1 | 2 | 3 | cannot be determined]

8. If only two drives are available, which RAID levels can be used? (Select all that apply.)

   [0 | 1 | 5 | 10]

9. A technician has been called to help with a problem. A S.M.A.R.T. error displays, and the user reports that the system has been running slowly for several months. Which two tools or actions should the technician use immediately? [chkdsk | partition the drive | apply high-level formatting to the drive | convert | diskpart | back up the data | attach external drives and configure Storage Spaces]

10. What is the difference between spanning and striping?

    a. Spanning is done in hardware, and striping is done in software.

    b. Spanning is done within RAID, and striping is done in Windows or through BIOS.

    c. Spanning takes two drives, and striping takes three drives.

    d. Spanning fills one drive before moving to the next drive, whereas striping alternates between the drives.

    e. Spanning is RAID 0, and striping is RAID 1.

CHAPTER 7

11. A tile and carpet warehouse uses several computers for the inventory process. The computers in the warehouse area have a higher hard drive failure rate than those in the office area. Which solution will help this company?

    a. Replace the hard drives with SSDs.

    b. Place antistatic mats under the computers and on the floor where people stand or sit to use the computer.

    c. Install more powerful power supplies.

    d. Install additional CPU fans.

    e. Replace the drives with higher-RPM drives.

12. Which of the following can provide the fastest transfer rate for an internal hard drive?

    [PATA | SSD | SATA | USB 3.0]

13. Which of the following can provide the fastest transfer rate for an external hard drive?

    [PATA | RS-232 | eSATA | USB 2.0]

14. Which Windows 8/10 feature allows space on an external USB and eSATA hard drive to be seen as one drive letter and provide resiliency?

    [Storage Spaces | RAID 10 | RAID 5 | Disk Management]

15. What is a drawback of SSDs?

    [installation time | MTBF | maintenance requirements | cost | speed | reliability]

16. You are installing an older PATA optical drive.

    Which cable connector attaches to the motherboard?

    [gray | black | white | blue]

    Which cable connector attaches to the drive if it is the only device on the cable?

    [gray | black | white | blue]

17. Which tool do most Windows users use to check for lost clusters?

    [Error-checking (Check/Check Now) | diskpart | Disk Defragmenter | Disk Cleanup]

18. By default, during what time and on what day does Windows 7 automatically defragment all attached hard drives if the computer is powered on?

    a. 1 a.m. on Wednesday

    b. 5 a.m. on Friday

    c. Midnight on Sunday

    d. 4 a.m. on Tuesday

19. [T | F] If you have enough RAM installed, the hard drive will not be used as cache memory.

20. You are speaking on the phone to a customer who is upset. The customer curses and starts yelling. What should you do?

    a. Hang up on the caller.

    b. Ask the caller if you can put her on hold while she calms down.

    c. Speak to the customer using a calm, professional tone.

    d. Stay calm but raise your voice level a little to show the importance and professionalism of your technical response.

Exercises

Exercise 7.1 Configuring a PATA IDE Hard Drive on Paper

Objective: To be able to configure a PATA IDE hard drive

Procedure: Refer to the following figures and answer the accompanying questions.

Questions: See Figure 7.58 to answer Question 1.

Jumper	Setting	Comments
J17	Cable Select	Open = disabled* Jumpered = enabled
J18	Master/Slave	Open = slave in a dual-drive system Jumpered = master in a dual-drive system Jumpered = master in a single-drive system*
J19	Write Cache	Open = disabled Jumpered = enabled*
J20	Reserved	For factory use
J21	Spare	

IDE Hard Drive #1
SchmidtMeister 9000
J21 J20 J19 J18 J17

* - Default setting

FIGURE 7.58   Exercise 7.1 documentation

1.   Using Figure 7.58, circle the jumpers to be enabled (set) to configure IDE Hard Drive #1 as if it is the only drive connected to an IDE port.

_____

_____

2.   Now pretend that you have two hard drives that use the same jumpers as in step 1. Draw the drive jumpers. Circle the jumpers to be enabled (set) to configure IDE Hard Drive #1 as the master drive connected to an IDE port. Keep in mind that IDE Hard Drive #2 shares the same cable with Hard Drive #1.

_____

_____

3.   Draw the drive jumpers. Circle the jumpers to be enabled (set) to configure IDE Hard Drive #2 as the slave drive. Keep in mind that IDE Hard Drive #2 shares the same cable with Hard Drive #1.

_____

CHAPTER 7

See Figure 7.59 to answer Questions 4 and 5.

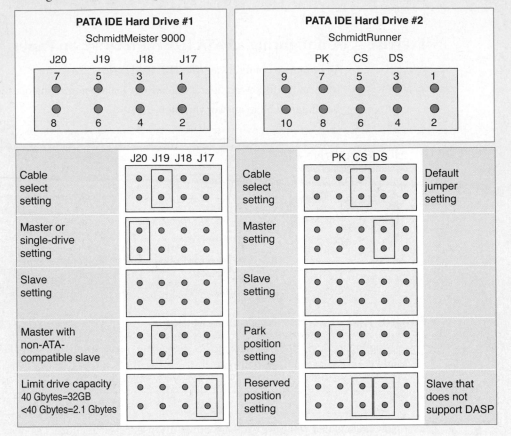

FIGURE 7.59 Exercise 7.1 documentation #2

4. List the jumper(s) that will be enabled (set) to configure IDE Hard Drive #1 as the master drive connected to a PATA IDE port. Keep in mind that IDE Hard Drive #2 shares the same cable with Hard Drive #1.

5. List the jumper(s) (if any) that will be enabled (set) to configure IDE Hard Drive #2 as the slave drive. Keep in mind that IDE Hard Drive #2 shares the same cable with Hard Drive #1.

Exercise 7.2 Configuring a SATA Hard Drive on Paper

Objective: To be able to configure SATA hard drive jumpers

Parts: Internet access is needed for one question

Procedure: Refer to the following figures and answer the accompanying questions

Questions: See Figure 7.60 to answer Questions 1–3.

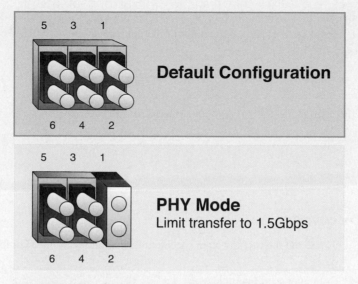

FIGURE 7.60 Exercise 7.2 documentation

1.   Considering the information provided, when would you change the jumpers on this drive?

_____

2.   If the drive has pins 1 and 2 jumpered, what version of SATA is the drive using?

[SATA 1 | SATA 2 | SATA 3]

3.   If this hard drive were to be installed in a desktop model, what form factor would this drive most likely be?

_____

4.   Refer to Figure 7.61. The information provided is for a laptop computer used in a business environment. What do you think would be the effects of installing a jumper on pins 1 and 2 on this drive?

_____

_____

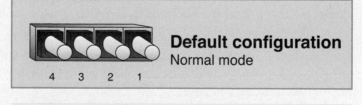

FIGURE 7.61 Exercise 7.2 documentation #2

5. Use the Internet to determine SATA jumper settings for a particular vendor's replacement hard drive. Write the jumper settings and explanation for the jumpers. Write the URL where you found this information.

_____

_____

6. What is the form factor for the hard drive referenced in Question 5?

_____

Activities

Internet Discovery

Objective: To use the Internet to obtain specific information regarding a computer or its associated parts

Parts: Computer with Internet access

Questions: Use the Internet to answer the following questions. Write the answers and the URL of each site where you found information. In answering Questions 1–3, assume you have just purchased a Seagate Barracuda 3 TB 7,200 RPM 6 Gb/s hard drive.

1. What types of cables are needed for this drive? Do they come with the drive? Write the answers and the URL where you found this information.

_____

2. How much cache does this drive have?

_____

3. If the computer does not have an available SATA connector, what one recommendation could you make?

_____

4. A customer has a Western Digital WD3200AAKB Caviar Blue PATA hard drive. What are the possible jumper settings for this drive? Write the answer and the URL where you found this information.
[single | master | slave | cable select | dual (master) | dual (slave) | slave present]

_____

5. Based on the same drive as in Question 4 and information you learned in this chapter, if a customer had a drive already configured to cable select and wanted you to install the Western Digital drive, what setting must be set on the new drive?
[single | master | slave | cable select | dual (master) | dual (slave) | slave present]

6. Find an eSATA and an internal SATA hard drive that are equal or close to equal in capacity. What is the price difference between the two? Write the answer and the URL where you found this information.

_____

Watch the *How to Fully Use Your 3 TB Hard Drive on Windows 7 (MBR to GPT)* YouTube video, at https://www.youtube.com/watch?v=7KwNaR170mg, to answer Questions 7–10. (If this link does not work when you try to use it, find a video that shows how to install a GPT partition.)

7. How many hard disk drives did the presenter have installed, based on what you see in the Disk Management window?

_____

8. Even though the Disk 1 drive was originally unpartitioned, before the presenter did anything to the drive, the drive showed as [1 | 2 | 3] unallocated sections.

9. If a drive has already been partitioned (but doesn't have data on it), what must you do before converting the drive to a GPT disk?

_____

10. List one comment that you found interesting and informative.

_____

Soft Skills

Objective: To enhance and fine-tune a technician's ability to listen, communicate in both written and oral forms, and support people who use computers in a professional manner

Activities:

1. In groups of two, pretend one of you has a hard drive problem. The other student should pretend to help the first student on the phone. Share your phone conversation with two other groups. Select the best group and scenario.

2. With two other classmates, come up with 10 additional tips for good phone support that were not listed in the chapter. Share your ideas with the class.

_____
_____
_____
_____
_____
_____
_____
_____
_____
_____

3. As a team, plan the installation of three storage devices. Two devices are internal SATA drives and an external USB drive. In your plan, detail what drives you are using for the plan, what things you will check for, how you will obtain the documentation, and what obstacles could appear as part of the installation process. The user also would like some type of redundancy. What choices might you present to the user? Share your plan with other teams.

Critical Thinking Skills

Objective: To analyze and evaluate information as well as apply learned information to new or different situations

Activities:

1. List three things that could cause a computer to lock up periodically that relate to the hard drive. What could you do to fix, check, or verify these three things?

_____
_____
_____
_____
_____

CHAPTER 7

2. A customer wants to either upgrade or replace his hard drive. Go through the steps you would take from start to finish to accomplish this task.

_____

_____

_____

_____

_____

3. Your team supports a department of 20 workstations. Some people store very important information on their local hard drives. Use the Internet to research redundancy options as well as options presented in the chapter. Develop a list of possible redundancy plans for the department.

_____

_____

_____

8 Multimedia Devices

In this chapter you will learn:

> To compare optical drive and disc technologies

> To determine optical drive specifications and features from an advertisement or specification sheet

> To determine the best interfaces and ports for connecting optical drives

> How to install, configure, and troubleshoot optical drives, sound, scanners, camcorders, and digital cameras

> How to use Windows to verify optical drives, audio ports, scanners, and digital camera installations

> About KVMs and projectors

> How to install and configure other peripheral devices, including barcode readers, biometric devices, game pads, joysticks, digitizers, motion sensors, smart card readers, and MIDI-enabled devices

> How to provide support with a positive, proactive attitude

CompTIA Exam Objectives:

What CompTIA A+ exam objectives are covered in this chapter?

✓ 1001-3.4   Given a scenario, select, install, and configure storage devices.

✓ 1001-3.5   Given a scenario, install and configure motherboards, CPUs, and add-on cards.

✓ 1001-3.6   Explain the purposes and uses of various peripheral types.

✓ 1002-1.6   Given a scenario, use Microsoft Windows Control Panel utilities.

✓ 1002-4.7   Given a scenario, use proper communication techniques and professionalism.

Multimedia Devices Overview

The term *multimedia* has different meanings because there are many types of multimedia devices. This chapter focuses on the most popular areas—optical drive technologies, sound cards, cameras, and speakers. These devices collectively enable you to create and output sound, music, video, and movies. Video, music, and picture files are known as media files. The chapter is not intended to be a buyer's guide for multimedia devices or an electronics "how it works" chapter; instead, it is a guide for technicians with an emphasis on installation and troubleshooting.

Optical Drive Overview

Compact disc (**CD**), digital versatile disc or digital video disc (**DVD**), and **Blu-ray** drives are collectively called optical disk drives (**ODDs**) because they use optical discs that are read from, written to, or both. Optical discs are used when creating or playing music CDs or movie DVDs and also for backing up data. CDs are the older technology, but they are still in use today in combination with DVD and Blu-ray disc (**BD**) technologies. Blu-ray discs tend to be used for film distribution and for video games. Purchased applications tend to be on CDs or, more commonly, DVDs. Applications can also be downloaded from a remote Internet location or remote site or available on a USB drive. Drives can be obtained that can handle CD, DVD, and BD media. Figure 8.1 shows a BenQ CD drive and its various front panel controls.

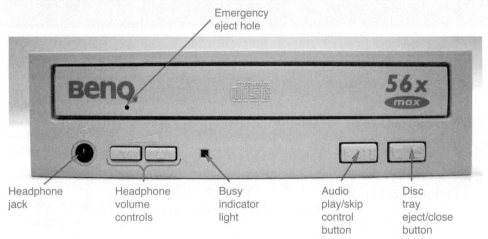

FIGURE 8.1   BenQ CD drive front panel controls

A CD has pits or indentations along the track. Flats, sometimes called lands, separate the pits. Reading information from a CD involves using a laser diode or similar device. The laser beam shines through the protective coating to an aluminum alloy layer, where data is stored. The laser beam reflects back through the optics to a photo diode detector that converts the reflected beam of light into 1s and 0s. The variation of light intensity reflected from the pits and lands is detected as a series of on/off signals that are converted into binary code. CD and DVD drives use red laser technology, whereas Blu-ray drives use blue-violet laser technology. The blue-violet laser technology has a shorter wavelength, which means smaller data pit sizes can be used to create higher disc capacities. This translates to more cost, too. Figure 8.2 shows an inside view of a CD drive. The newer technologies operate in a similar fashion.

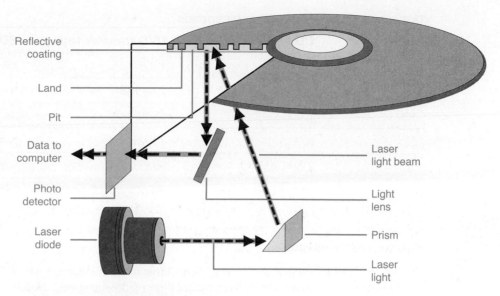

Reflective coating
Land
Pit
Data to computer
Photo detector
Laser diode
Laser light beam
Light lens
Prism
Laser light

FIGURE 8.2 Inside a CD drive

Optical Drive Features

Optical drives that have an "R" designation can read only from a disk. For example, a **CD-ROM** (read-only memory), **BD-R**, or **DVD-ROM** disc cannot be written to. Drives that have an "RW" or "RE" designation—such as a **CD-RW**, **BD-RE**, or **DVD-RW** drive—can perform both reads and writes. Drives with a "DL" designation, such as **DVD-RW DL**, use dual-layer technology, so that two physical layers are available on the same side of the disc, and the laser shines through the first layer to get to the second layer. Table 8.1 lists common media types.

TABLE 8.1 Optical writable media

Media type	Capacity
CD	650 or 700 MB
CD-RW	650 or 700 MB
DVD-5/RW	4.7 GB single-sided single layer
DVD-9/RW (DVD-9DL)	8.5 GB single-sided dual-layer
DVD-10/RW	9.4 GB double-sided single-layer
DVD-18/RW (DVD-18DL)	17.1 GB double-sided dual-layer
BD/BD-RE	25 GB single-layer
BD DL/BD-RE DL	50 GB dual-layer
BD XL	100 or 128 GB multi-layer
Mini BD	7.8 GB single-layer
Mini BD DL	15.6 GB dual-layer

Optical drives come in a variety of types, classified by an x factor: 1x (single-speed), 2x (double-speed), 32x, 48x, 52x, and higher. Optical drives do not operate at just a single speed, though; the speed varies depending on the type of media being read and whether writing is being done. Table 8.2 shows the generic transfer rates for the different x factors and types of optical drives.

TABLE 8.2   Optical drive transfer speeds

x factor	CD transfer rate	DVD transfer rate	BD transfer rate
1x	150 kB/s	1.32 MB/s	4.5 MB/s
2x	300 kB/s	2.64 MB/s	9 MB/s
12x	1,800 kB/s	15.85 MB/s	54 MB/s
22x	N/A	29 MB/s	N/A
52x	7,800 kB/s	N/A	N/A

TECH TIP

How to read the numbers

ODDs are frequently shown with three consecutive factor numbers, such as 52x32x52. The first number is the write speed, the second number the read/write speed, and the third number is the maximum read speed that is used when reading a disc.

A lot of factors can influence how quickly a drive transfers data, including how much RAM the computer has, what other applications are running, how much free hard drive space (virtual memory) is available, and the interface used to connect the optical drive; even how much RAM is on the video card can influence an ODD that has video content. Data is stored as one continuous spiral of data on optical discs. This concept is shown in Figure 8.3. Data is, of course, in 1s and 0s, and spaced a lot closer than shown in the figure, but the idea of one continuous spiral is important for the write-once technologies. Pits on a DVD are half the size of those on a CD, and the tracks are closer together so more data can be stored.

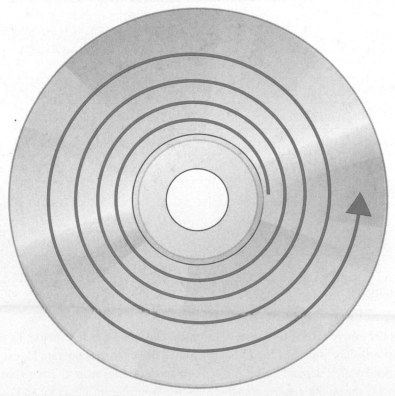

FIGURE 8.3   Optical disc

TECH TIP

Some optical drives cannot read Blu-ray discs

Some optical drives cannot read Blu-ray discs because CD/DVD drives use a red laser, and Blu-ray drives use a blue-violet laser. Drives that have both lasers are available.

The steps for copying files to a disc using Windows/File Explorer in Windows follow:

Step 1. Insert an optical disc into an optical drive. From the window that appears, select *Burn Files to Disc* using Windows Explorer (Windows 7) or File Explorer (8/10).

Step 2. Name the optical disc and select the format type. Click *OK*.

Step 3. Open *Windows/File Explorer* and select any file(s) you want to copy. Drag the file(s) to the optical disc drive in the left panel. Repeat the process with any files located in other folders.

Step 4. After selecting files, click the optical drive letter in the left panel. All files should be listed in the right panel.

Step 5. Right-click the optical drive letter and select *Close Session*.

One way to reduce transfer time when writing data to the drive is by having buffer memory on the drive. When requesting data, the drive looks ahead on the disc for more data than requested and places the data in the buffer memory. **Buffer memory** holds the extra data in the drive and then constantly sends data to the processor so the processor does not have to wait for the drive's slow access time. However, buffer memory is not enough. Having little hard drive space or RAM can still slow down or stop the recording process. Microsoft has a free utility called Virtual CD-ROM Control Panel utility for Windows 7 that can be used with an ISO disk image for a specific application or a backup disk image. The utility allows the ISO file to be mounted or seen as a virtual optical disk (and assigned a drive letter). A benefit of using such software is that you do not have to burn the ISO image to a disc. Windows 8 and 10 have this feature built into the operating system. To use it, right-click on a file with the extension .iso or .img and select *Mount*.

TECH TIP

Keep the data coming

One problem with ODDs occurs when data is written to the disc. If the drive does not receive data in a steady stream, a buffer underrun error occurs, and the disc is ruined if it is a -R or +R disc. To avoid this problem, do not perform other tasks when burning data to disc.

One feature that you might use to compare whether two drives have the same x factor is the random access time. The **random access time** is the amount of time the drive requires to find the appropriate place on the disc and retrieve information. Another important comparison point is mean time between failures (MTBF), which is the average number of hours before a device is likely to fail. A closely related term that you might see instead of MTBF is mean cycles between failure (**MCBF**), which is found by dividing the MTBF by the duration time of a cycle (operations per hour). The MCBF is actually a more accurate figure because drives are not used the same amount of time per hour. Keep in mind that for any of these metrics, the lower the number, the better the performance.

Both DVD and BD drives have **region codes**. The world is divided into six regions for DVD drives and three regions for BD drives. The drive must be set for the correct region code, or the optical disc made for that area will not work. Some drives allow the region code to be changed a specific number of times. When a disc is inserted, the decoder checks which region it is configured for (or, in the case of software decoding, which region the drive is configured for) and then checks for the region code. If the two match, then the movie plays. Table 8.3 shows the region codes for DVD and Blu-ray drives.

TABLE 8.3   DVD/Blu-ray region codes

DVD region code	Geographic area	Blu-ray region code	Geographic area
1	United States and Canada	A	North/Central/South America, Southeast Asia, Taiwan, Hong Kong, Macau, and Korea
2	Europe, Near East, Japan, and South Africa	B	Europe, Africa, Southwest Asia, Australia, and New Zealand
3	Southeast Asia	C	Central/South remaining Asian countries, China, and Russia
4	Australia, Middle America, and South America		
5	Africa, Asia, and Eastern Europe		
6	China		

Many drive features or capabilities can be determined by looking at the symbols on the front of the drive, as shown in Figure 8.4.

FIGURE 8.4   Optical drive symbols

Optical Drive Interfaces and Connections

An optical drive can be internally mounted and attached to a PATA or SATA interface, or the drive can be externally attached to a USB, IEEE 1394 (FireWire), eSATA, or eSATAp (combo SATA/USB) port. In both desktop and portable computers, the SATA interface is the most common for internal devices, and USB is most common for external devices. An all-in-one computer, laptop, or ultrabook is likely to have a slot-loaded drive (like a car optical disc player) instead of the tray-loaded drives that are common in desktop models. Figure 8.5 shows a laptop with a slot-loaded drive.

FIGURE 8.5   Slot-loaded optical drive

The following will help you decide which optical drive interface to recommend:

> Is the drive going to be internal or external? If it will be internal, open the case to see if a drive bay is available. Check for a PATA or SATA interface on the motherboard. If PATA is being used, remember that in desktop models, two devices can connect to a single motherboard connector; however, SATA requires one port for each device. Remember that internal devices tend to be cheaper than external ones.

> If the drive is internal, check that a power connection is available. A Y connector or Molex-to-SATA power converter may have to be purchased.

> If the drive is external, check what eSATA, eSATAp, USB, or IEEE 1394 ports are available. Some USB hard drives take two ports. Ensure that the drive comes with the needed cable or purchase one separately.

> Check with the customer about features such as buffer memory and writing disc labels.

> If the customer wants to upgrade the drive, find out why. Slow access is often due to other components in the computer, not the drive.

Optical Drive Installation

One thing to be concerned about with an optical drive is whether the drive is to be installed horizontally or vertically. Not all drives can be installed vertically.

The steps for installing an internal optical drive are almost identical to the steps for installing a hard drive:

Step 1. Download the latest drivers before installation.

Step 2. Install any necessary mounting brackets.

Step 3. Ensure that a proper port/interface is available. Ensure that a power connector is available. Set the appropriate configuration jumpers, if necessary. Refer to the drive documentation.

Step 4. Turn off the power. Remove power cords. Remove the laptop battery.

Step 5. Install the drive.

Step 6. Attach the power and data cables.

Step 7. Enter BIOS/UEFI to check the drive status. Ensure that the port is enabled. Ensure that the drive is recognized. Note that you may need to reboot the machine once to see this. If the drive is not recognized in BIOS/UEFI (or if the fact that there is a drive attached is not recognized), recheck settings and cabling.

Step 8. If necessary, install drivers and/or software as part of the installation process. See Figure 8.6. Get the drive functional by using the driver that came with the drive, if possible. Then upgrade the driver after the drive is recognized by the system.

FIGURE 8.6   Installing software

TECH TIP

PATA IDE connectivity considerations

When connecting an optical drive to a PATA connector that already has a drive attached to one of the PATA cable connectors, you have to know the jumper settings on the already installed drive to correctly install the optical drive. The installed drive settings may have to be adjusted when a second device is added to the cable. The optical drive should be the slave device.

For an external drive, download the latest drivers, ensure that you have the correct port, attach external power to the device as necessary before attaching to the port, attach the cable to the device, and attach the other end of the cable to the computer. Again, you may need a driver upgrade and/or may need to install some software as part of this process. Remember to check Device Manager to ensure that the device is recognized by the operating system.

TECH TIP

Always test the installation

Test the installation by using the device to play something or write to a disc that you bring along. Ensure that the customer tries the disc and is comfortable with the changes caused by the installation.

Troubleshooting Optical Drive Issues

Windows has troubleshooting tools in the Help and Support Center. Here's how you use them:

Step 1. In Windows 7, click *Start* and select *Help and Support*. In Windows 8 and 10, access the *Search* textbox.

Step 2. In Windows 7, 8, or 10, type **troubleshoot** in the Search textbox.

Step 3. In Windows 7, open the *Hardware and Devices Troubleshooter* link and progress through the wizard, as appropriate for the problem.

In Windows 8, select the first *Troubleshooting* option to go to the Troubleshoot Computer Problems Control Panel > *Hardware and Sound*.

In Windows 10, you are in the *Troubleshoot* window.

Step 4. Access the link that relates to the problem that is occurring.

TECH TIP

Checking the easy stuff first

Verify that the correct type of optical disc is in the drive, is inserted correctly (label side up), and is not dirty or damaged. Test the disc in another drive. Verify that the ODD has a drive letter. Check Device Manager for errors.

The following is a list of problems, along with possible solutions and recommendations:

> If a drive tray cannot be opened, make sure there is power. Use Windows/File Explorer to locate the drive, right-click the drive, and select *Eject*. Some drives have an emergency eject button or a hole you can insert a paperclip into to eject the disc. Refer to Figure 8.1 to see an example of the eject hole.

> If a drive is not recognized by the operating system, check cables, the power cord, and the configuration (master/slave, cable select, SATA speed, and the port enabled in BIOS/UEFI).

> If a drive busy indicator flashes more slowly than normal, the disc or laser lens might be dirty. Refer to the manufacturer's recommendations for cleaning. See the next section, on preventive maintenance, for details on how to clean a disc.

> If the drive cannot read a disc, ensure that the drive supports the disc being used. Ensure that the disc label is facing up. Ensure that the disc is clean and without scratches. Try the disc in another machine or try a different disc to see if the problem is with the drive or the disc.

> If a drive is not recognized as a recordable device (from Windows Explorer [Windows 7]/File Explorer [Windows 8/10], right-click or tap and hold briefly on the drive letter, select *Properties,* look to see if the Recording tab is missing), an updated driver or registry edit is probably needed.

> If a DVD sound track works, but video is missing or distorted, check the cabling. Verify the video drivers. Try changing the display resolution and the number of colors.

> If a message appears about an illegal DVD or BD region error or region code error, change the region, if possible. You can't use the disc without using a drive that matches.

Seeing video, but no audio

If you can see video but can't hear audio or vice versa, verify that the computer has the hardware and software requirements for DVD playback. Update the optical drive drivers.

> If a drive reads only CDs and not DVDs or Blu-ray discs, update the driver.
> Some optical drive problems are resolved by using DirectX. **DirectX** allows people who write software to not have to write code to access specific hardware directly. DirectX translates generic hardware commands into special commands for the hardware, which speeds up development time for hardware manufacturers and software developers. DirectX may need to be reinstalled or upgraded. Access the DirectX Diagnostic Tool in Windows by entering `dxdiag` in the Start/Run or Search dialog box. Notice that the System tab shows the DirectX version. The Sound tab is also useful.
> Check to see whether there is a more recent driver for the drive.
> If a drive keeps opening the tray, check for a stuck eject button. Check for a virus. Remove the data cable (but leave the power cable attached) to see whether the problem is the drive or a signal being sent to the drive to open. If you can hear sound from a DVD, but not a CD, get an updated optical drive driver.
> If you continue to see errors when writing to a disc, clean the laser lens or record at a lower speed. Avoid multitasking when writing.
> If you get a message stating that the DVD decoder is not installed, download a decoder from the DVD drive manufacturer or the computer manufacturer if the drive came with the computer. A **decoder** makes it possible for the disc images to be played/viewed through software on your computer.
> Do not worry if you get a message from an application that requires a disc in a specific drive letter, as happens when you have added more drives. You can change the drive letter by using the Windows Disk Management tool. Right-click the drive in the left panel and select *Change Drive Letter and Paths*.
> Blu-ray requirements are much more stringent than requirements for other optical formats, so ensure that your video drivers, DVD drivers, the display, and the video cable are appropriate for playing Blu-ray discs.

Preventive Maintenance for ODDs and Discs

CDs and DVDs have a protective coating over the aluminum alloy-based data layer that helps protect the disc. Blu-ray has a requirement that BD media be scratch resistant, so BDs are less likely to need preventive maintenance than other optical formats. However, fingerprints, dust, and dirt can still negatively affect CD and DVD performance.

Handling discs with care

Always handle a disc by the edges and keep the disc in a sleeve or case to aid in good performance. Never touch a disc's surface. Store discs in a cool location.

When reading information, the optical drive laser beam ignores the protective coating and shines through to the data layer. Even if the disc has dirt on the protective coating, the laser beam can still operate because the beam is directed at the data layer rather than the disc surface. However, if dust or dirt completely blocks the laser beam, the laser beam could be reflected or distorted, causing distortion or data corruption. Special cleaning discs, cloths, and kits are available for cleaning optical discs. A soft lint-free cloth and water or glass cleaner works, too. Figure 8.7 shows proper handling during the cleaning process.

FIGURE 8.7 Disc cleaning

Mild abrasives or special disc repair kits can be used to repair scratched discs. Examples of mild abrasives include plastic, furniture, or brass polish. When applying the abrasive, do not rub in circles. Instead, use the same technique as for cleaning: Start from the innermost portion and rub outward. The abrasive can remove a scratch that is not too deep. A wax such as furniture or car wax can be used to fill a scratch that is not removed by the abrasive.

TECH TIP

Cleaning discs

When using a cleaning cloth, wipe the disc from the inside (near the center hole) to the outside of the disc (not in a circular motion) on the side of the disc that holds data.

A special component of the optical drive, the **laser lens** (also known as the objective lens), is responsible for reading information from discs. If the laser lens gets dust, dirt, or moisture on it, the drive may report data or read errors. Some drives have the lens encased in an airtight enclosure, and others have a self-cleaning laser lens. If a drive does not have this feature, look for a laser lens cleaning kit. Also, the laser lens can be cleaned with an air blower like ones used on a camera lens. Cleaning the laser lens should be part of a preventive maintenance routine. Some drive manufacturers include a special plate to keep dust away from the internal components. In any case, keep the disc compartment closed to prevent dust and dirt from accumulating on the laser lens and other drive parts.

CHAPTER 8

Introduction to Audio

Video and sound technologies are important today. No multimedia chapter would be complete without mentioning sound (and other devices, such as digital cameras, covered later in the chapter). Sound is important to the end user, but sound is also important to a technician in many instances, such as when a computer does not boot. A motherboard has a small integrated speaker or a speaker that attaches to motherboard pins that allows POST sounds to be heard even if the more advanced sound system is not working. Figure 8.8 shows a motherboard speaker.

FIGURE 8.8   Motherboard speaker

On a motherboard, ports for speakers and headphones are typically 1/8-inch (3.5 mm) connectors that accept TRS (tip ring sleeve) connectors. Figure 8.9 shows common motherboard sound ports.

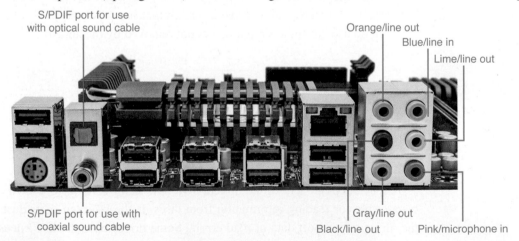

FIGURE 8.9   Motherboard audio ports

Notice in Figure 8.9 the connection for Sony/Philips Digital Interface Format (S/PDIF). S/PDIF is a newer type of sound port that can be used to carry digital audio signals between audio devices and stereo components or the output of a DVD or BD player in a PC to a home theater or some other external output device. S/PDIF ports can attach using an RCA jack attached to coaxial cable or a TOSLINK connector attached to a fiber-optic cable.

One connection that is not shown in Figure 8.9 is an older 15-pin female MIDI port. Musical instrument digital interface (**MIDI**) is used to create synthesized music. Traditionally, a MIDI device such as a digital piano keyboard would connect using the MIDI interface and the traditional microphone or line out ports. MIDI instruments today typically have a USB connection. If not, a cable converter can be purchased. A MIDI device is considered to be both an input device and output device.

Optical drives have the capability to produce sound, usually through a front headphone jack and through a connection to sound through the motherboard or an installed sound adapter. Audio discs can be played on these drives, but the audio does not sound as good through the drive's headphone jack as it does through a stereo system or speakers. Figure 8.10 shows how an audio device connects to a sound card. Figure 8.11 shows typical sound card ports and the types of devices that might connect to these ports. Table 8.4 shows the colors that are normally found on sound ports.

FIGURE 8.10   Audio ports on an adapter and an audio cable

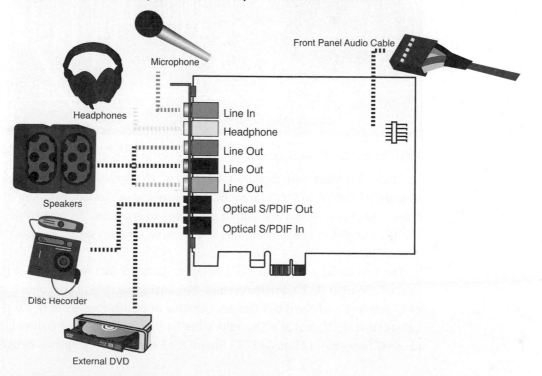

FIGURE 8.11   Sound card port connectivity

TABLE 8.4   Sound port colors

Color	Purpose
Orange/gold	Center speaker or subwoofer
Black	Rear speaker
Light blue	Line in
Lime green	Line out/front channel speakers
Pink	Microphone
Gray	Side speaker

Theory of Sound Card Operation

Sound cards can include a variety of options, such as an input from a microphone, an output to a speaker, a MIDI interface, and the ability to generate music (for example, bringing sound into the computer through a microphone connected to a sound card). Sound waves are shown as an analog waveform, as shown in Figure 8.12.

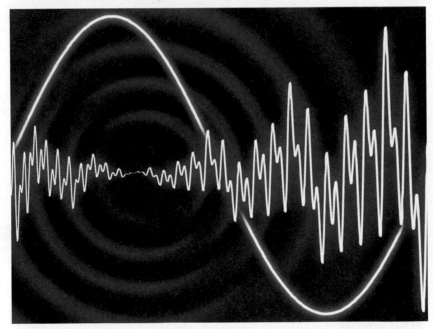

FIGURE 8.12   Sound waves

Computers work with digital signals (1s and 0s), so a sound card must convert an analog signal to a digital format to send the sound into a computer. Sound cards can also take the digital data from optical disc media and output the sound to speakers. To convert an analog waveform to 1s and 0s, samples of the data are taken. The more samples taken, the truer the reproduction of the original signal.

The first sound cards made for computers sampled data using 8 bits. Eight 1s and 0s can give a total of 256 (that is, 2^8) different values. The analog waveform goes above and below a center value of 0. Because 1 of the 8 bits denotes negative or positive value, only 7 bits can represent sampled values (that is, 2^7, or 128). The values can be 0 through +127 or 0 through −127. (The total value range is between −127 and +127.) Figure 8.13 shows an example of sampling.

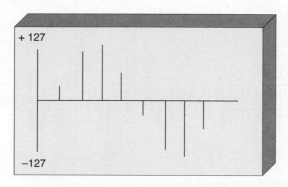

FIGURE 8.13 8-bit sampling

The more samples taken by a sound card, the closer the reproduction is to the original sound signal. The sound card **frequency response** is dependent on the sample rate. This is also known as the sample rate or sample frequency. For a good reproduction of sound, the sound wave is sampled at twice the range desired. For example, a person's hearing is in the 20 Hz to 20 kHz range. Twice that range is approximately 40,000 samples per second. The frequency response for a music CD is 44,100 samples per second—a good-quality sound reproduction for human ears. The first sound cards for computers used 8 bits to sample the sound wave and had a frequency response of approximately 22,000 samples per second (22 kHz). The sound produced from the original sound cards was better than the beeps and chirps previously heard from the computer. The sound was still grainy, though; it was better than the sound from an AM radio station but not as good as the sound from an FM radio station or a music CD.

Next, 16-bit sound cards arrived for computers. The number of possible levels sampled with 16 bits is 65,536 (that is, 2^{16}). When positive and negative levels are sampled, the range is –32,767 to +32,767. The frequency response with 16-bit sound cards is 44 kHz—the same resolution as stereo audio CDs. 24-bit sampling results in a 96 kHz sample rate that is sometimes called the audio resolution. The increase in the number of sampling levels and the frequency response allow sound cards to produce quality sound equal to that of audio discs. See Figure 8.14 for an example of 16-bit sampling. Keep in mind that when more samples are taken, the sound card provides a better frequency response (see Figure 8.15). DVDs require a 48 kHz sampling rate for audio output. Therefore, sound card sampling rates should be a minimum of 48 kHz for DVDs and 44.1 kHz for CDs.

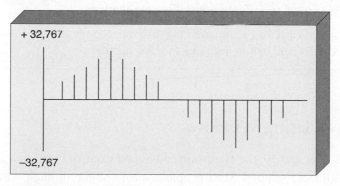

FIGURE 8.14 16-bit sampling

FIGURE 8.15 Digitized sound

Installing Sound Cards

The steps involved in installing a sound card are similar to the steps involved in installing any other adapter. Refer to the manufacturer's instructions when installing devices and adapters. The basic steps are as follows:

Step 1. Power off the computer, remove the computer case and power cord, and locate an empty expansion slot (making sure it is the appropriate type of slot).

Step 2. Attach the appropriate cables, such as the audio cable, from the optical drive to the adapter.

Step 3. Attach external devices, such as speakers. Attach power to the external devices as necessary.

Step 4. Power on the computer. Windows should detect that new hardware has been installed (if it does not, use the *Hardware and Sound* Control Panel > *Add a Device* link.

Step 5. Load the appropriate device drivers for the sound card.

After a sound card is installed, there are normally other programs and utilities from the sound card manufacturer that you can install as you would any other application.

> **TECH TIP**
>
> **Disabling motherboard sound when installing an adapter**
>
> If you install a sound card into a computer that has sound built into the motherboard, you must disable the onboard sound before installing the new adapter.

Sound Cards Using Windows

With Windows 7, 8, and 10, the Hardware and Sound Control Panel link is used to change sound and adjust multimedia settings. Most people control volume through a notification area volume control icon located in the lower-right portion of the screen. This icon can be used to mute or adjust sound.

Audio drivers have been vastly improved in Windows to accommodate multiple streams of real-time audio and allow a kernel-mode process to handle audio management. This means the operating system can control all aspects and improve audio performance. Digital audio can be redirected to any available output, including USB.

TECH TIP

Check for muting

If sound is not coming from the computer, look for the *Mute* checkbox or icon located in the volume control in the notification area and ensure that the volume is not muted.

Windows includes a set of application programming interfaces (APIs), which are commands that developers use to communicate with sound cards. DirectX has specific APIs that provide commands related to audio. In DirectX, Microsoft adds such things as DirectSound3D, which has more 3D audio effect commands, supports hardware acceleration, and allows simulation of audio sounds in certain environments, such as a tunnel or underwater. It allows software and game developers to create realistic audio environments such as muffling effects and audio directional effects (that is, the direction a sound comes from).

You can tell whether a device has integrated sound or a sound adapter installed by inspecting the *Sound, Video and Game Controllers* category in Device Manager. Figure 8.16 shows a screen capture of Device Manager from a computer that has integrated sound on the motherboard. Note that integrated sound may be located in the *System Devices* category or the *Other Devices* category.

FIGURE 8.16   Integrated sound in Device Manager

Microphones are commonly used in conference calls and voice over IP (VoIP) calls. VoIP is a technology in which phone calls are digitized and transmitted using a data network rather than using a traditional corporate digital voice network or the public switched telephone network (PSTN)—in other words, the traditional phone network. Microphones can be attached to a headset or a separate device, integrated into the computer display, or integrated into the device (as with mobile devices). To see microphone settings on a Windows device, open the *Hardware and Sound* Control Panel, and in the Sound section, locate and select *Manage Audio Devices* and click the *Recording* tab. Figure 8.17 shows an integrated microphone built into a laptop. After you select the microphone, you can use the *Properties* button to adjust the microphone settings.

FIGURE 8.17 Integrated display microphone

Speakers

Most people connect speakers to a sound card or integrated sound ports. Others use a **headset**, as shown in Figure 8.18. The quality of sound is personal; sounds that are acceptable to one person are not always acceptable to others. Table 8.5 shows some features to look for in speakers.

FIGURE 8.18 Sound quality is personal

TABLE 8.5   Speaker features

Feature	Description
Amplification	Increases the strength of the sound. Sound cards usually have built-in amplification to drive speakers. Amplification output is measured in watts, and most sound cards provide up to 4 watts of amplification (which is not enough for full-bodied sound). Many speakers have built-in amplifiers to boost the audio signal for a much fuller sound.
Power rating	Indicates how loud the volume can go without distorting the sound. This is expressed in watts per channel. Look for the root-mean-square (RMS) power rating; 10 to 15 watts per channel is an adequate rating for most computer users.
Frequency response range	Indicates the range of frequency (sounds) that a speaker can reproduce. Humans can hear from 20 Hz to 20 kHz, and the range varies for each person. Therefore, whether a computer speaker is appropriate depends on the person listening to the speaker. Speaker quality is subjective. Room acoustics and speaker placement also affect sound quality.
Shielding	Cancels out magnetic interference and keeps magnetic interference away from other devices. Speakers usually have a magnet inside them that can cause distortion to a device such as a monitor. These magnets can also cause damage to disks and other storage media. The best optical drive and sound card combination can be downgraded by using inexpensive, poorly shielded speakers.

Most computers come with internal or external speakers. Sometimes the external speakers produce poor-quality sound. Also, some external speakers are battery or AC powered, which might not be desired. One speaker commonly connects to the sound card port, and the other speaker is usually daisy-chained to the first speaker. Some speakers have an external volume control. Be mindful of this as it is another thing to check for when sound does not occur. Figure 8.19 shows computer speakers that are USB powered.

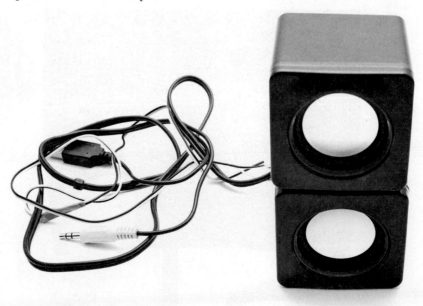

FIGURE 8.19   USB speakers

How to choose speakers

Listen to them without headphones, using an audio (non-software) disc.

USB and wireless solutions can also be used to provide connectivity for speakers. Digital audio is sent over the bus, and an external speaker converts the signal into sound. When audio is converted inside the computer, interference from internal electronic components and external sources (especially if an expansion slot does not have an adapter installed and the case has an opening) can cause audio interference. The drawback to USB is that it puts more work on the CPU. However, in today's multicore processor environment, this may not be an issue. The following are some extras to look for in speakers:

> An external volume control
> Headphone jacks
> Headphone and microphone pass-through connectors (so you do not have to dislodge the computer to reach the jacks)
> AC adapter
> Connectors for the speakers to connect to the sound card
> 7.1 and 5.1 surround sound
> Four- or six-speaker system

Two speakers are normally joined by a cable that may or may not be removable. Figure 8.20 shows a single power cable, a thin cable just right of center that goes to the computer, and the cable on the right that plugs into the second speaker.

When speakers power on, they sometimes emit a popping sound. This is normal, but if the popping sound continues, the speaker is probably picking up interference from the computer or another device. Try moving the speakers farther away from the computer.

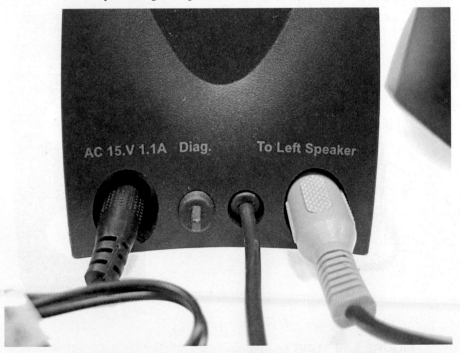

FIGURE 8.20   Speaker connections

Troubleshooting Sound Problems ◼◌

The best place to start troubleshooting sound problems is to check the easy potential problems first. Here are some basic steps to get started:

> Are the speakers plugged into the correct port on the sound card?
> Is the volume control muted? If it is, take it off mute.
> Is the volume control on the speakers turned up?
> From within Windows, check whether the device appears to be playing without sound being heard. In this case, the problem is definitely in the sound system.
> Do the speakers have power?

The following is a list of common sound problems and solutions:

> If a speaker is emitting unwanted sounds, make sure there are no empty adapter slots in the computer. Next, check the speaker wires for cuts, move the sound card to another expansion slot, and move the speakers farther away from the computer. Finally, move the computer away from the offending device or the offending device away from the computer. If the speakers produce a humming noise and are AC powered, move the speaker power cord to a different wall outlet. Plugging the speakers into the same circuit as the computer is best.
> If sound is a problem or if any solution directs you to update your sound driver, access *Device Manager* and expand the *Sound, Video, and Game Controllers, System Devices*, or *Other Devices* option. Locate and right-click the integrated sound or the sound card and select *Properties*. Select the *Driver* tab and click the *Update Driver* button.
> If the sound card is not working, check Device Manager to see whether the sound card is listed twice. If there are two entries for the same sound card, remove both of them by clicking each entry and clicking the *Remove* button. Restart Windows, and the operating system should detect the adapter and either install a device driver or prompt for one. For best results, use the latest device driver from the sound card manufacturer or computer manufacturer (in the case of an integrated port). Note that frequently this is provided through an operating system update.
> In Windows 7, if you do not see a sound icon in the bottom-right corner of the screen, access the *Appearance and Personalization* Control Panel > in the *Taskbar and Start Menu* section, select *Customize Icons on the Taskbar Link* > locate the *Volume* icon. Use the drop-down menu to select the *Show Icon and Notifications* option.

  In Windows 8, if you do not see a sound icon on the screen, access the *Appearance and Personalization* Control Panel. In the *Taskbar and Navigation* section, select *Customize Icons on the Taskbar*. Select the *Notification Area* tab and locate the *Volume* icon. Use the drop-down menu to select the *Show Icon and Notifications* option.

  In Windows 10, if you do not see a sound icon on the screen, access *Settings > System > Notifications & Actions > Select Which Icons Appear on the Taskbar* link > locate the *Volume* icon > select the *On* side.
> If the computer emits no sound, use the Windows audio troubleshooter. Search the Windows Control Panel by typing the word `Troubleshooting`. In the *Hardware and Sound* section, select the *Troubleshoot Audio Playback* link.
> If the audio volume is low no matter what sound is played (see Figure 8.21), the speakers may not be amplified speakers, or they may not be connected to the correct sound card port. Also, do not forget to check the computer sound settings through the icon in the notification area. Check Device Manager to see if a yellow question mark is beside the sound card. If so, right-click the sound card, select *Properties*, and then check the *Device Status* section for the issue. Many issues require driver updates.

FIGURE 8.21 Low or no sound

> If one disc does not output sound, but other discs work fine, the disc may use a later version of DirectX than the one installed. Check the recommended DirectX version for the disc. Also, the disc may have a problem.

> If building a computer, install the sound card after installing the video card, hard drive, and optical drive but before anything else. Some sound cards are inflexible about system resource changes.

> For headphone issues, ensure that the cable attaches to the correct line out port. Determine whether you want the speakers disabled. Normally, if you plug into the headphones' line out port, the speakers cut off.

> If sound does not come out of the optical drive after the drivers and software load, try the following troubleshooting tips:

> > Be sure an audio disc is inserted into the drive.

> > If sound no longer comes out of the speakers, check the speaker cables.

> > Check to make sure the audio cable is properly installed.

> > Ensure that the speakers or headphones connect to the drive or to the sound card or integrated sound port.

> > If using speakers, ensure that the cable jack is inserted into the proper port on the sound card. Verify that the speakers have batteries installed or an AC adapter connected.

> > If using headphones, verify that the headphones work on another device before using them to test the drive.

> > Get updated drivers from the sound card manufacturer's website.

> > If the monitor's image quality decreases after installing a sound card with speakers, move the speakers farther away from the monitor.

Scanners

A **scanner** is an input device that allows documents including text and pictures to be brought into the computer and displayed, printed, emailed, written to an optical disc, and so on. A scanner is commonly built into a multifunction device (MFD) such as a printer, scanner, copier, and/or fax machine. These are also called all-in-one (AIO) devices. The most common types of scanners are listed in Table 8.6. Figure 8.22 shows a flatbed scanner. Figure 8.23 shows a barcode reader, which is another type of scanner. Portable and handheld scanners are being made obsolete due to cameras in mobile devices.

TABLE 8.6   Types of scanners

Scanner type	Comments
Flatbed (sometimes called desktop scanner)	Can scan books, paper, photographs, and so on; can take up desk space
ADF (automatic document feeder) or sheetfeeder	Enables a document to be fed through an automatic document feeder similar to a fax machine; good for scanning multiple-page documents
Handheld	Slowly moves across the document; user must have patience and a steady hand; portable unit
Film	Scans picture film instead of picture prints
Barcode scanner	Handheld device that reads barcodes in checkout lanes and in retail establishments; uploads performed wirelessly or by connecting to a PC
QR scanner	A scanner on a smartphone or handheld scanner that can read a Quick Response (QR) code that links to more information, such as further information about the item the QR code is attached to, contact information, or a web link

FIGURE 8.22   Flatbed scanner

FIGURE 8.23 Barcode reader

Figure 8.24 outlines how a flatbed scanner works.

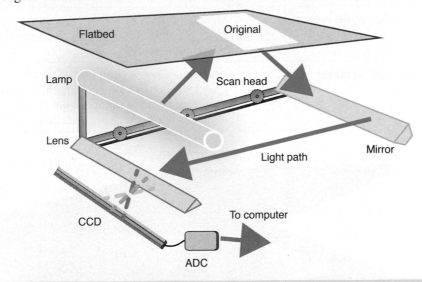

1. A document is placed on the scanner's glass plate. There is a lamp under the glass.

2. The lamp (fluorescent, CCFL [cold cathode fluorescent lamp], or Xenon) turns on. Light reflects from the document.

3. The scan head is used to capture the reflected light. It moves slowly down the document by way of a belt. The light reflects through a series of mirrors to the CCD (charge-coupled device) array.

4. The CCD array holds light-sensitive diodes. The diodes convert light into varying voltage levels. The voltage levels are sent to an ADC (analog to digital converter).

5. The ADC converts the voltage levels to pixels. A pixel is a dot and is the smallest unit in a picture or document.

6. The pixels are sent through the scanner interface to the computer where the image is displayed.

FIGURE 8.24 How a flatbed scanner works

A scanner normally attaches to a computer using one of the following options:

> USB

> RJ-45 Ethernet

> Wireless

USB is the most common connectivity option. USB devices are easy to install, and USB hubs allow system-integrated USB ports to be turned into multiple USB ports. To install a USB scanner, always follow the manufacturer's directions. The following steps are generic:

Step 1. Install software and drivers.

Step 2. Unpackage and unlock or remove special packaging.

Step 3. Connect the data or network cable as well as the power cable.

Step 4. Power on the scanner. Some scanners have a calibration process that needs to be performed. There may be a special switch or push button that locks/unlocks the scan head.

Step 5. Configure options and default settings.

Step 6. Scan a document to test it.

Step 7. Ensure that the customer is trained and has all scanner documentation.

A scanned image can be saved in several formats. When scanning a document or graphic for web pages, select PNG, PDF, JPEG, or GIF format. The most common graphic file formats are listed in Table 8.7. There are many terms associated with scanning, and Table 8.8 lists the most common of them.

TABLE 8.7   Scanner file formats

File format	Comments
Joint Photographic Experts Group (JPEG)	Small file size; good for web pictures but not good for master copies. Always compresses the file; the file extension is .jpg.
Graphic Interchange Format (GIF)	Limited to 256 colors, small in size, and good for web pictures; the file extension is .gif.
Tag Image File Format (TIFF)	Good for master copies and large size; the file extension is .tiff or .tif.
Portable Network Graphics (PNG)	Not supported by all applications or older applications; supports 24- and 48-bit color. The file extension is .png.
Portable Document Format (PDF)	Used for web-based forms and scanned words; the file extension is .pdf.

TABLE 8.8   Scanner terms

Scanner term	Comments
Resolution	Measured in DPI (dots per inch); determined by the number of sensors in the CCD array and by the precision of the stepper motor; common resolutions include 300, 600, 1,200, 2,400, 3,200, 4,800, 6,400, and 9,600.
Bit depth	The number of bits used for color; the more bits, the more colors and color depth. Common configurations are 24, 30, 36, and 48 bits.
Interpolation	Software used by the scanner to achieve a greater resolution by filling in the pixels around the scanned pixels.
OCR (optical character recognition)	Software that processes printed or written text characters; not all scanners ship with OCR software.
TWAIN	An API and communications protocol that is used so that applications can access and acquire images directly from the scanner.

Resolution is an important concept when scanning a document or photo. When scanning something, always think about whether the output is intended for a printer or for a monitor. Setting the scanner's resolution to the maximum settings for every scan is not a good idea. Table 8.9 shows some sample resolutions for scanning.

TABLE 8.9   Sample scanner resolutions

Type of document and use	Scanner color setting	Recommended resolution (DPI)
Any document for display on a monitor	Color, grayscale, or black and white	150
Text for copying or emailing	Color, grayscale, or black and white	150
Black-and-white photo for saving, using on a website, or using in email	Grayscale	75–300
Color photo for copying, printing, or creating a document such as a photo or postcard	Color	300
Color photo for use in a website or email	Color	75–150
Color photo for saving	Color	75–300

A scanner's plate glass needs to be cleaned periodically (see Figure 8.25). To test whether cleaning has been successful, scan a full page without a document loaded onto the scanner. See if the results yield any smudges or streaks. Consider these best practices:

> The best cleaning method is to put optical surface cleaning fluid on an antistatic cleaning cloth and then wipe the glass.
> Never spray cleaner directly on the glass.
> Do not use rough paper towels.
> A commercial glass cleaner or water can be used.
> Always remove all cleaner residue from the glass.
> Do not press down on the glass.
> Do not use an abrasive or corrosive solvent.
> Keep the glass dust free.

TECH TIP

Protecting scanner glass

Be careful with sharp objects such as staples around a scanner. A scratched or damaged glass surface results in marks on all scanned images.

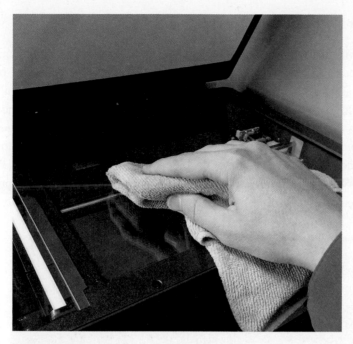

FIGURE 8.25   Scanner glass cleaning

KVMs

Some network administrators, technicians, or businesses want the ability to use the same monitor (and sometimes mouse and keyboard) for two or more different computers. This is best done through a keyboard, video, mouse (**KVM**) switch, which allows at least one mouse, one keyboard, and one video output to be used by two or more computers. Figure 8.26 shows a KVM switch.

FIGURE 8.26   KVM switch

KVM switches usually require no software. They are sometimes used with projectors to allow multiple inputs. Connect the cables to the port and use the dial or push buttons on the front of the KVM switch in order to select which device to use for input or output.

Many people would rather use software than a KVM switch to remotely access the desktop of another computer. Windows calls this built-in software feature Remote Desktop. Remote Desktop is covered in Chapter 16, "Advanced Windows."

CHAPTER 8

Projectors

Monitors, cameras, TVs, and webcams are not the only peripherals that connect to computer video ports. Projectors have become common devices, and technicians must be familiar with them. A projector allows information displayed on a computer, laptop, camera, or other device to be projected onto a larger screen. A projector has connections similar to those described for video cards. Cables that convert between the different formats are available. Figure 8.27 shows some of the connectors available on a projector. A projector sometimes connects to other audio and video devices besides computers, such as a document camera, speakers, optical disc players, and smart boards. The VGA in and out ports are two ports commonly seen on a projector for connecting video. S-video is also quite common. Newer projectors have DVI, DisplayPort, HDMI, and USB ports.

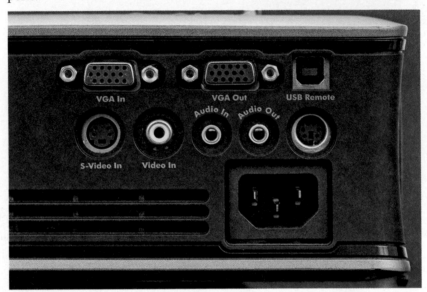

FIGURE 8.27   Projector ports close up

To connect a projector to a PC and a monitor, you need a video distribution (sharing) device, a KVM switch, or two video ports from a PC. A laptop frequently has a video port available for connecting an external monitor or a projector.

Figure 8.28 shows a projector that has a lot of ports. As with video cards, you expect to see VGA, DVI, or HDMI ports, but ports that are often seen on TVs, gaming consoles, optical disc players, or stereos are also available on projectors. Composite video is normally a yellow port (like the one labeled VIDEO in Figure 8.28). The audio RCA ports are normally red and white. **Component/RGB video** analog ports are normally colored red, green, and blue and have the symbols Y, Pr, and Pb above them. (Y is for the luminescence, or brightness, and Pr and Pb are for the color difference signals.) An RJ-45 connector connects a projector to an Ethernet network. Many projectors also have wireless network capabilities.

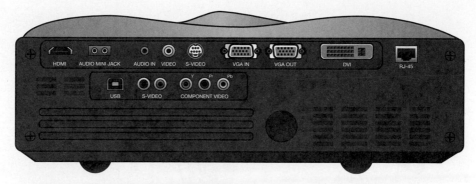

FIGURE 8.28 Projector ports

Table 8.10 lists key features to look for in a professional projector.

TABLE 8.10 Projector features

Projector feature	Comments
Brightness or luminance	How much light a monitor or projector can produce. Two factors affect brightness: how much light the projector outputs and the reflective properties of the screen being used. Some projectors have optimization, so you can't base comparisons just on lumen ratings.
Lumens	A measure of light output or brightness—how much visible light is coming out of equipment, such as lamps, lighting equipment, or projectors. This measure is important when comparing products for a room that has lots of exposure to sunlight, for example.
Resolution	The number of pixels used to create an image. The more pixels, the higher the resolution. Shown using two numbers, where the first number indicates the number of horizontal pixels used and the second number indicates the number of vertical pixels.
Wired Ethernet capability	The ability for a projector to be connected through an RJ-45 port to a wired Ethernet network.
Wireless	The ability for a projector to be connected and monitored through an 802.11 wireless network.
Remote control or desk controller	The ability to control a projector through either a remote control or a control panel mounted near a computer in the room.

DLP

Digital Light Processing (**DLP**) is a Texas Instrument technology used in projectors and rear projection TVs. DLP has an array of mounted miniature mirrors, one of which is smaller than the width of a human hair and represents one or more pixels. The mirrors are used to create a light or dark pixel on a projection surface by being repositioned to different angles to reflect light. A color wheel or LEDs are used for the primary colors red, green, and blue. Figure 8.29 shows this concept.

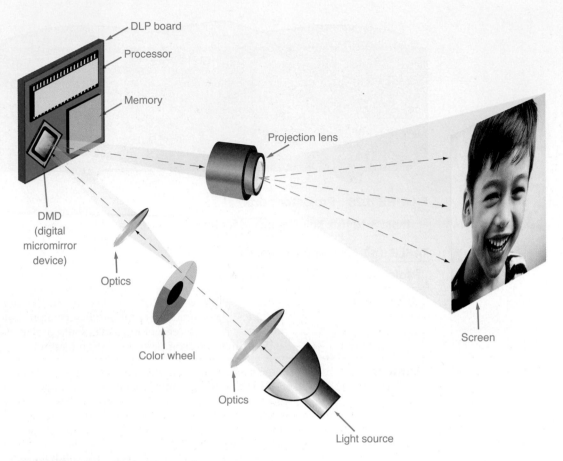

FIGURE 8.29   Projector ports

Projector Maintenance

Treat your projector well. Do not immediately unplug the power to a projector after a presentation; instead, allow the projector to cool down first. You can turn off the projector, but the fan still runs on some models to quickly cool the projector. Keep the filter clean to extend the life of the projector bulb.

Video Recording

Video recording capabilities can be built into a computer or a mobile device, an attachment to a computer, or a standalone digital camera or camcorder used for the purpose of taking photographs or recording movies. A digital camera has a sensor that converts light into electrical charges or digital 1s and 0s. A digital camera's resolution—the number of horizontal and vertical pixels the camera can use to display an image—is measured in pixels. Today, digital camera resolution technology has evolved into megapixels (MP). A camera's photosensors determine how many pixels can be used. Common resolutions for integrated tablet cameras and smartphones are now comparable to those of digital cameras.

TECH TIP

Caring for a digital camera

Remove disposable (alkaline) batteries from a digital camera when it's not being used for an extended period so they do not leak battery fluid into the camera.

Some cameras store photographs or movies on flash media (miniSD, microSD, xD, CompactFlash, and so on) or hard drives, usually in the JPEG file format, but some cameras can save in RAW or TIFF formats. Table 8.11 shows camera storage media. Figure 8.30 shows a digital camera with flash storage to the side. Table 8.12 lists common file formats.

TABLE 8.11   Digital camera data storage

Storage type	Comments
CompactFlash (CF)	Introduced by SanDisk; uses flash memory; does not require a battery to store photos after power is removed; includes CF-I and CF-II
SmartMedia	Developed by Toshiba; smaller and lighter than CF; adapter cards with PC Card/ExpressBus ATA are available for data transfers
Memory Stick	Created by Sony; small in size; can read/write with a Memory Stick reader; includes Memory Stick (MS), Memory Stick Duo (MSD), Memory Stick Micro (M2)
Secure Digital	Size of a postage stamp; does not require power to retain data; uses flash memory technology; supports cryptographic security; different types include SD, miniSD, microSD, and SDHC
ExpressBus drive	Consumes more power than memory technology
MMC (multimedia card)	A type of flash memory used in many portable devices, including cameras; works in many devices that support SD cards and is less expensive; types include MMC, embedded MMC (eMMC), reduced size MMC (RS-MMC), MMCmicro, dual voltage (DV-MMC), MMCplus (faster MMC), MMCmobile, and MiCard (has two detachable parts—one side for USB and the other side for use with a card reader)

FIGURE 8.30   Digital camera with flash memory

TABLE 8.12   Digital camera file formats

File type	Description
RAW	Outputs raw, unprocessed data; image is not directly usable without further processing
JPEG	Most common type; saves more photos due to compression

File type	Description
TIFF	Larger file size (fewer photos) due to retaining image quality
WAV	Used for voice memos
MOV	Used for movie files

Camcorders are similar to digital cameras in that they store still images and videos, but they are better than digital cameras for creating and storing videos. Camcorders commonly connect to computers or directly to hard drives so that the videos can be transferred and stored. Digital cameras and camcorders can connect to computers via USB and mini-USB. Attach the cable from the camera to the computer. Power on the camera or camcorder and follow the directions given on the screen. Frequently on a computer, a dialog box appears, asking if you want to transfer images/videos. Some camera/camcorder manufacturers provide software that allows you to modify the images or movies.

An alternative is to remove the media storage card and install it into a memory card reader. A memory card reader or multi-card reader is a popular device that many people attach externally or have integrated into a computer or mobile device. A reader has multiple slots that allow different memory media to be read. These devices have many names, such as 15-in-1 reader, 8-in-1 reader, or 5-in-1 reader (depending on how many different slots or types of memory modules the device accepts). A memory card reader instantly recognizes inserted memory cards, whose contents can be copied to the computer and manipulated. The media card slots are assigned drive letters that are accessible through Windows/File Explorer. Figure 8.31 shows one of these readers.

TECH TIP

No drive letter

If the media does not appear in Windows/File Explorer, the reader may have been temporarily un-installed. Use the Safely Remove Hardware and Eject Media tool in the Notification area, unplug the cable from the port, and re-insert the cable to ensure that the operating system recognizes the reader. If the card reader or ports are still not available or if they are integrated into the computer, restart the computer.

FIGURE 8.31 Memory card reader

Another popular type of digital camera is a **webcam**, which is short for web camera—a digital camera that attaches to a PC for use in transmitting live video or recording video. Web cameras can also attach to VoIP phones and activate when a phone session occurs for instant web conferencing. A webcam may have a small visor that can be flipped over the lens to prevent video when desired. Figure 8.32 shows a wired webcam, but keep in mind that webcams can connect wirelessly or can be integrated into displays or mobile devices.

FIGURE 8.32 Webcam

To access an integrated camera in a flat panel display, you normally use the Control Panel or software that comes with the camera, such as the Logitech Webcam Software shown in Figure 8.33. If you ever get a "Bandwidth exceeded" message when a camera is being used, try reducing the camera's resolution in whatever software is being used.

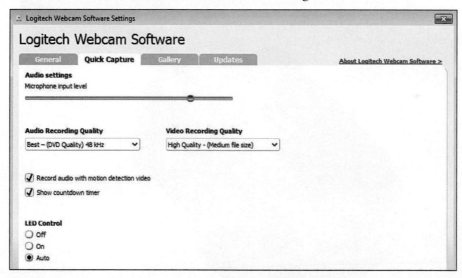

FIGURE 8.33 Logitech Webcam control software

Regardless of whether multimedia devices are integrated into a computer or connect to a computer, all devices attach and install similarly. When installing a new device for a customer, don't forget to allow the customer to test the device while you are still there. Also, remember to leave all documentation related to the installation with the customer. The customer paid for the device and is entitled to the documentation.

Installing and Configuring Other Peripheral Devices

Some peripheral devices commonly connect to the computer via a USB port. Each device may be configured with software and possibly drivers provided by the manufacturer. Many USB devices have drivers provided with the Windows operating system. Let's examine a few that you might see.

Barcode Scanners

Barcode scanners, which have already been mentioned in this chapter, commonly connect via USB cable or wirelessly. You might have to reset a barcode scanner by turning it off and back on or reattaching it to the computer. Some scanners respond to a specific bar code that, when scanned, resets the barcode scanner to defaults, adds the time and date after a barcode scan, omits the first digit, adds four zeros to the beginning of the barcode, and other modifications.

Biometric Devices

A **biometric device** is commonly used to authenticate someone or prove identity. Examples of biometric devices include retina scanners and **fingerprint readers** (see Figure 8.34). These are discussed further in Chapter 18, "Computer and Network Security." To install a fingerprint reader, always follow the manufacturer's instructions. Following are the common steps involved:

Step 1. Install the software provided by the manufacturer.

Step 2. Attach the fingerprint reader to the computer and ensure the device is recognized by the system. Use Device Manager to verify this, if necessary.

Step 3. Use the fingerprint software to register users who are allowed to access the system.

Step 4. Verify the configuration by powering off the computer and having each user practice accessing the system.

FIGURE 8.34   Fingerprint reader

Use Windows Device Manager for biometric devices to verify that Windows recognizes such a device. Sometimes a biometric device is integrated into a computer or a mobile device and must be enabled through BIOS/UEFI. It is important to use a BIOS/UEFI password so that it is not possible for someone to bypass the biometric device by simply disabling it in BIOS/UEFI.

Apple provides Touch ID with its devices. Touch ID allows a fingerprint to be used to unlock the device as well as make online purchases. Touch ID is built into the home button of an Apple mobile device so that the fingerprint can be detected without actually pressing the button.

Microsoft Windows 8.1 provides a fingerprint management application as part of the operating system, which means a fingerprint reader manufacturer does not have to provide software. To access the option, access *Settings > Accounts > Sign-in Options*. If a fingerprint reader is attached or integrated into the device, the option will be available.

Similarly, Microsoft Windows 10 includes Windows Hello, a biometric device application that supports facial recognition and fingerprint detection. The facial recognition uses iris-scanning technology. To configure Windows Hello, access *Settings > Accounts > Sign-in Options*.

Most biometric software requires configuration with the persons who will be allowed access. If a technician does not train the computer user how to do this, multiple service calls might have to be made. Sometimes biometric devices require that the software be reinstalled. Biometric devices also commonly require preventive maintenance, such as wiping the surface of the fingerprint scanner or cleaning the lens of an iris scanner.

Game Controllers, Joysticks, and Motion Sensors

Game controllers (see Figure 8.35), **joysticks** (see Figure 8.36), and motion sensors are used to interact with games. These devices commonly come with software that, if misplaced, can usually be downloaded from the manufacturer's website and used to customize the control buttons. Game pads, joysticks, and motion sensors have hardware and software minimum requirements. Game pads and joysticks attach to USB ports and are verified through Device Manager.

FIGURE 8.35 Game controller

FIGURE 8.36 Joystick

Motion sensors are used to detect movement. A motion sensor may be a device that connects to the game console, it might be integrated into the game console, or it might be in a hand controller. Usually such a device has an accelerometer that detects and transmits details related to movement, direction, and degree of acceleration. A camera may be part of the system.

Some motion sensors require external power bricks. External motion sensors are normally placed on a stable surface. Those that connect to computers usually do so through a USB port or connect wirelessly. Software is used to calibrate such a device.

Digitizers

A **digitizer** (see Figure 8.37) provides input into documents such as architectural drawings, technical plans, and photos. It can also be used to draw electronic pictures.

A digitizer comes with a pen that may or may not need a battery. Some pens have replaceable ends. Digitizers either connect through a wired USB connection or can be wireless. A digitizer tablet comes with software that commonly allows the pen and digitizer tablet buttons to be customized in terms of what a button does and the speed at which a button reacts. Some digitizers come with diagnostics as part of the software.

FIGURE 8.37   Digitizer

Smart Card Readers

A **smart card reader** can attach to a PC or mobile device, connect to a point of sale (POS) system, be integrated into a keyboard, or be an expansion card that can be inserted into a laptop. Smart card readers are used with credit cards that have a special embedded chip that holds data. The chip is read by the smart card reader. Smart cards can require contact or they can be contactless. Smart card readers are also used with a common access card (CAC) issued to active duty military personnel, government employees, and civilian contractors. Figure 8.38 shows a smart card reader.

FIGURE 8.38   Smart card reader

External smart card readers commonly attach to a USB port, but they can sometimes attach through a wireless connection. Download the latest driver from the manufacturer's website and install it. The device can be verified in Device Manager. Device Manager has a smart card reader section, but the device may show up as an unknown device if a device driver has not been installed properly. You may have to install a security certificate provided by the employer.

A technology called near field communication (NFC) is related to smart card readers. NFC-enabled devices can be used in close proximity to an NFC reader in order to perform financial and ticketing types of transactions. NFC is covered in more detail in Chapter 10, "Mobile Devices."

SOFT SKILLS: ATTITUDE

A technician's **attitude** (see Figure 8.39) is one of his or her greatest assets. Some consider having a good attitude as simply being positive at work, but that is not the entire picture.

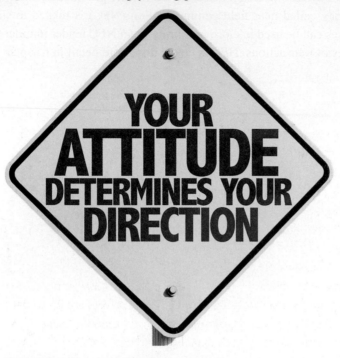

FIGURE 8.39   Your attitude is important

A technician with a good attitude has the following traits:

> *Is proactive, not reactive*—A good technician actively looks for a solution rather than waiting for someone to instruct him or her.

> *Projects confidence*—A technician who lacks confidence is easily spotted by end users. A confident technician isn't arrogant but instead is secure in the knowledge that a problem can be solved.

> *Seeks solutions instead of providing excuses*—A positive person does not continually apologize or talk in a subservient tone. For example, a positive technician explains issues such as late deliveries in a professional, positive manner.

> *Accepts responsibility for actions taken*—If you forget something or take a misstep, you should apologize and explain to the customer what happened. Truth goes a long way with customers. A positive technician does not constantly shift blame to other departments or technicians. Even if the other department or technician is responsible, a person with a positive attitude handles the customer and then talks to the other department or technician about the problem.

> *Deals with priority changes professionally*—In the IT field, computer and network problems may require tasks to be reprioritized weekly, daily, and even hourly. These are normal occurrences, and a person with a positive attitude understands this.

> *Cooperates and works well with others*—A positive attitude is contagious, and others like being around it.

> *Maintains professionalism even when working with a coworker who is unethical, unprofessional, or uncooperative*—A technician with a good attitude does not let someone else's poor attitude be a negative influence.

> *Embraces problems as challenges to learn and develop skills*—Sometimes, after joining the IT field, a technician becomes complacent and does not seek new skills. The IT field requires that you constantly improve and refine your skills. See a tough problem as a challenge, not a burden. With such an attitude, problems will not frustrate you but will serve as catalysts for advancement and make you a better technician.

You should exhibit all these traits consistently to establish a positive mental attitude and make it part of your daily habits.

Chapter Summary

> Install ODDs using the same rules of configuration as for SATA and PATA hard drives.
> Use the appropriate media for the type of drive installed.
> Don't multitask when writing data to an optical disc.
> Optical drives and discs have region codes that must match.
> When purchasing an optical drive, features to look for include ample buffer memory and reduced random access times, MTBF, and MCBF.
> For stuck optical discs, use the *Eject* option from Windows/File Explorer or the emergency eject hole.
> Keep the laser lens clean.
> Wipe dirty discs in an inward-to-outward (not circular) motion.
> It's important to ensure that device and video drivers are up-to-date.
> DirectX (`dxdiag`) is used to troubleshoot multimedia issues.
> A motherboard normally has a small speaker used for POST codes when sound does not work properly.
> If a sound card is installed, disable the motherboard sound ports.
> The higher the sampling rate, the better the audio quality.
> For sound issues, check muting, volume controls, cables, and device conflicts.
> Microphones are used for VoIP and are tested/managed through the *Recording* tab of the Sound window.
> Scan documents at a resolution suited for the final output (print, web, display).
> Do not spray cleaner directly on scanner glass but do keep the glass clean.
> KVM switches allow multiple computers to share monitors, a mouse, and/or a keyboard.
> Projectors come with a variety of ports, including VGA, DVI, HDMI, composite, and component/RGB.
> Digital cameras commonly have storage media that can be removed and attached directly to a PC or mobile computer, using a memory card reader.
> Webcams can be integrated into a display or mobile device or an external unit that is used for conference calls or for recording video.
> When installing and configuring common peripheral devices, always follow manufacturers' directions. Software is commonly provided to configure device options.
> A technician should have a positive attitude and project confidence, be proactive, and maintain professionalism when working with others.

A+ CERTIFICATION EXAM TIPS

✓ Ensure that you know how to install and configure an optical drive, a sound card, and a scanner.

✓ Know features and capacities for the following types of optical drives and media: CD-ROM, CD-RW, DVD-ROM, DVD-RW/DVD-RW DL, Blu-ray, BD-R, and BD-RE.

✓ Be able to explain when you would use an ADF/flatbed scanner, barcode or QR scanner, optical drive, DVD drive, game controller, camera/webcam, microphone, speakers, headset, projector, KVM, and smart card reader.

✓ Know what lumens and brightness are in regard to a projector.

✓ Know that a digital camera transforms light into 1s and 0s.

✓ Know the various types of flash-based storage media and technologies, including CompactFlash, SD, miniSD, microSD, and xD.

✓ Know the purpose of a KVM switch.

✓ Maintaining a positive attitude and projecting confidence are the professionalism and communication skills that are part of the 220-1002 exam.

Key Terms

ADF scanner   335
amplification   331
attitude   350
barcode scanner   335
BD   314
BD-R   315
BD-RE   315
biometric device   346
Blu-ray   314
brightness   341
buffer memory   317
CD   314
CD-ROM   315
CD-RW   315
component/RGB video   340
decoder   322

digitizer   348
DirectX   322
DLP   341
DVD   314
DVD-ROM   315
DVD-RW   315
DVD-RW DL   315
dxdiag   322
fingerprint reader   346
flatbed scanner   335
frequency response   327
frequency response range   331
game controller   347
headset   330
joystick   347
KVM   339

laser lens   323
lumens   341
MCBF   317
MIDI   324
motion sensor   348
ODD   314
power rating   331
QR scanner   335
random access time   317
region code   317
scanner   335
shielding   331
smart card reader   348
webcam   344

Review Questions

Consider the following optical drive specifications as you answer Questions 1–7:

> SATA interface half-height internal BD-ROM
> Maximum 4x BD-ROM/BD-RE SL and 4x BD-ROM/BD-R/BD-RE DL CAV reading
> Maximum 8x DVD-ROM/+R/+RW/+RDL/-R/-RW/-RW DL CAV reading
> Maximum 32x CD-ROM/R/RW CAV reading
> Random access times: BD, 250 ms; DVD, 160 ms; CD, 150 ms
> Buffer size 2 MB
> System requirements for HD Blu-ray playback: 3.0 GHz, 1 GB of RAM, Windows 7 or higher, HDCP capable display, or TV for digital output.

1. Which SATA version is being used?

   [1 | 2 | 3 | Cannot be determined from the information given]

2. Can Blu-ray discs be created on this unit? How can you tell?

   _____

3. Pretend you are adding this device to a computer. What is the maximum number of devices (if any) that can be on the same cable that connects this drive to the motherboard?

   [None | 1 | 2 | Cannot be determined from the information given]

4. What does the term *random access time* mean?

   _____

5. What is the purpose of buffer memory?

   _____

6. Can a DVD±RW disc be read in this drive? How can you tell?

   _____

7. What does BD-RE DL mean?

   _____

8. What Apple biometric technology supports fingerprint recognition?
   [Hello world | Touch ID | IT ID | Watch me]

9. Select the non-sound port.
   [RJ-45 | S/PDIF | TOSLINK | RCA | 1/8-inch TRS]

10. Which optical media has the highest capacity? [DVD | CD | BD]

11. Which drive would have two lasers?

    a. a drive that can handle an 8.5 GB single-sided dual-layer disc

    b. a drive that can handle a double-sided single-layer disc

    c. a drive that can handle a 25 GB dual-layer disc

    d. a drive that can handle a DVD or a Blu-ray disc

12. A PCIe sound card is being installed. Which two steps are most likely going to be done by the technician? (Choose two.)

    a. Upgrade the power supply.

    b. Install a driver.

    c. Flash the BIOS/UEFI.

    d. Disable the integrated ports in BIOS/UEFI.

    e. Configure jumpers on the adapter.

    f. Delete the integrated port drivers.

13. Which utility is best used to troubleshoot sound issues?

    [Disk Management | DirectX | BIOS/UEFI diagnostics | Device Manager]

14. Why should a battery be removed from a camera that is not used very often?

    a. in case the battery leaks

    b. in order to preserve the saved files on the memory card

    c. to keep the battery charged

    d. to keep the battery cool

15. A user has attempted a scanner installation to the computer's front USB ports because all the back ports were taken. However, the scanner will not function. What should the technician try next?

    a. Replace the scanner.

    b. Replace the USB port.

    c. Reattach the USB cable that leads from the front panel to the motherboard.

    d. Add a version 2.0 or higher USB hub to the back USB port.

16. [T | F] A technician can clean a scanner using paper towels.

17. [T | F] Part of the installation process for a tablet is to calibrate the camera.

18. Which multimedia device requires calibration as part of the installation process?

    [camera | sound card | scanner | optical disc drive]

19. Which item would more likely be used with a digital camera than with a scanner?

    [flash media | 1.8-inch hard drive | laser lens | optical cleaning cloth]

20. Which scenario is one that most shows a positive attitude?

    a. A technician returns a borrowed disc to a team member after having the disc more than six months.

    b. A technician leaves documentation for a newly installed optical drive with the customer, even though the customer treated the technician poorly during the installation.

    c. A technician eagerly helps reorganize a wiring closet for the company.

    d. A technician smiles when an angry customer is taking out her computer problems on the technician.

Exercises

Exercise 8.1 Multimedia Device Research

Objective: To be able to use the Internet to locate device drivers and technical specifications

Parts: A computer that has Internet access

Procedure: Using the Internet, find the cost, latest device driver, and most important technical specification for the devices listed in Table 8.13.

TABLE 8.13   Multimedia device information

Device type	Cost	Device driver version	Most important technical specification
Flatbed scanner			
Barcode reader			
Fingerprint scanner			
Game pad			
Joystick			
Digitizer			
Motion sensor			
Smart card reader			
Digital camera			
Webcam			
Camcorder			
MIDI device			
Sound card			
Speakers			

Exercise 8.2 Which one will you buy?

Objective: To be able to use the Internet to locate multimedia devices for a specific purpose

Parts: A computer that has Internet access

Procedure: Using the Internet, find a device to meet the user specification

1.   A 10-person conference room has an oval table. A computer is in the corner. The company would like to add to the room a projector and a projection screen. Do the following:

   • List three criteria you looked for in the projector.

   • List at least one projector you recommend.

   _____

   _____

   _____

   _____

2.   A 25-person computer training room needs a scanner. The people who use the room scan forms completed by trainees. Each person completes a three-page form. Because of the nature of the information, the form cannot be put onto a web page.

   • List three criteria you looked for in the scanner.

   • List at least one scanner you recommend to the company.

   _____

   _____

   _____

   _____

3.   A person owns a home business creating movies for events such as weddings, receptions, showers, and so on and providing a digital copy of each edited video. Previously, the owner provided the digital copy on an external drive, but now the owner wants to offer optical media as well. Even though folders are backed up to a remote site, what type of optical drive and media supported by the drive would you recommend for this home business owner?

   • List the type of optical drive you recommend and give at least two reasons for why you chose this type.

   • Would you recommend an internal or external drive? Describe why you chose this type.

   • List at least one drive you would recommend for this desktop computer. Include the part number and website where you found the drive.

   _____

   _____

   _____

   _____

Activities

Internet Discovery

To obtain specific information on the Internet regarding a computer or its associated parts

Computer with access to the Internet

Use the Internet to answer the following questions.

1.   Find a website that sells external optical drives. List the cost of one drive and the website URL.

2.   What is the cost of a disc that works in a DVD±RW drive? List the cost and website URL.

3.   Find the driver version for a Sound BlasterX AE-5 PCIe adapter that is going in a 64-bit Windows 10 computer. Document the driver download filename and URL where you find this information.

4.   An HP G4050 Scanjet scanner attaches to a Windows 8.1 computer. When the scanning software is accessed, the error "Scanner initialization failed" appears. List the four recommended steps.

5.   The president of a company purchased a Canon EOS Rebel T4i digital camera. Which type of memory media does this camera accept? Write the answer and URL where you find the answer.

6.   A customer has a Plextor PX-891SAF CD-RW, DVD+/-RW drive. How much buffer memory does the drive contain, and which interface(s) does it support? Write the answers and website URL where you find the information.

Soft Skills

To enhance and fine-tune a technician's ability to listen, communicate in both written and oral forms, and support people who use computers in a professional manner

1.   List some tips for determining whether a computer has an optical drive installed, as if you were stepping through it over the phone with a customer who is not a technician. Using your instructions, practice with a classmate.

2.   With the class divided into groups of five, each group makes a list of three categories that relate to multimedia devices. The five groups share their lists and determine which group works on which category. In 30 minutes, each team comes up with five answers with corresponding questions for their category. The answers are rated from 100 to 500, with 100 being the easiest. The teams play *Jeopardy!*, with the rule that the teams cannot choose their own category.

Critical Thinking Skills

Objective: To analyze and evaluate information and apply information to new or different situations

Activities:

1. For this activity, you need an advertisement for a sound card, including the technical specifications. Make a list of all terms used in this ad that you do not know. Using books, the Internet, or other resources, research these terms and define them.

2. Form teams of two and obtain several multimedia devices. The devices are numbered. Each team selects a number and installs, configures, and tests the associated device. Each team documents its installation and shares its experience (including lessons learned) with the rest of the class.

9

Printers

In this chapter you will learn:

> How each type of printer operates

> The steps required to install a printer

> Preventive printer maintenance

> How to control printers from Windows and make printer adjustments

> How to solve common printer problems

> Techniques for ethical and professional behavior

CompTIA Exam Objectives:

What CompTIA A+ exam objectives are covered in this chapter?

✓ 1001-2.5   Summarize the properties and purposes of services provided by networked hosts.

✓ 1001-3.6   Explain the purposes and uses of various peripheral types.

✓ 1001-3.10 Given a scenario, configure SOHO multifunction devices/printers and settings.

✓ 1001-3.11   Given a scenario, install and maintain various print technologies.

✓ 1001-5.6   Given a scenario, troubleshoot printers.

✓ 1002-1.5   Given a scenario, use Microsoft operating system features and tools.

✓ 1002-1.6   Given a scenario, use Microsoft Windows Control Panel utilities.

✓ 1002-1.8   Given a scenario, configure Microsoft Windows networking on a client/desktop.

✓ 1002-4.7   Given a scenario, use proper communication techniques and professionalism.

Printers Overview

Printers are commonly used output devices. They can be a difficult subject to cover because many different models exist. Of course, that can be said about any peripheral, but the basic principles are the same for all printers. The best way to begin is to look at what printers have in common. Every printer has three subsystems: (1) the paper transport subsystem, (2) the marking subsystem, and (3) the print engine subsystem. Table 9.1 describes these subsystems.

TABLE 9.1   Printer subsystems

Subsystem	Description
Paper transport	Subsystem that pulls, pushes, or rolls paper through the printer. This can be done using a belt, tractor feed, or rollers. Some printers can have a duplexer or **duplexing assembly**, which is an attachment option that allows printing on both sides of the paper.
Marking	Parts responsible for placing the image on the paper (also called the marking engine). This includes ribbons, ink (print) cartridges, toner cartridges, any moving part that is inside one of these, and anything else needed to print the image.
Print engine	The brains of the operation. The print engine accepts data and commands from the computer and translates them into motion. It also redirects feedback to the computer.

Keep the three printer subsystems in mind when setting up a printer and troubleshooting it. Knowing how a specific type of printer places an image on the paper also helps when troubleshooting the printer.

TECH TIP

Dealing with sensitive printed material

If any printouts are on a printer, ask the user to remove them and put them away. Demonstrate professionalism any time you are exposed to corporate or personal information that might be found on printers, desks, or within documents.

Printer Ports

Printers can connect to Ethernet or USB ports, and they can also connect wirelessly. Most wired printers attach to a PC by using the USB port and are near the computer. Printers can also be shared using a variety of techniques covered later in this chapter.

With USB printers, the USB host controller (which may be built into the motherboard or on an adapter) powers up and queries all USB devices about the types of data transfer they want to perform. Printers use bulk transfer on USB, which means data is sent in 64-byte sections. Even though a USB port can provide power to smaller devices, a USB printer normally has its own power source.

USB is a good solution for printers because it is fast, and there are usually several USB ports available—or a USB hub can be added to provide more ports. USB uses only one interrupt for the devices connected to the bus.

Categories of Printers

Printers can be categorized according to how they put an image on paper. There are five main categories of printers: impact (also known as dot matrix), inkjet, laser, thermal, and 3D. There are other types, but these five account for the majority of printers used in businesses and homes. Computer users normally choose a printer based on the type of printing they need to do. Table 9.2 describes the five major printer categories.

Each of the five basic printer types is discussed in greater detail in the following sections. The theory of operation for each printer type mainly concerns the marking subsystem.

TABLE 9.2   Printer categories

Type of printer	Description
Impact printer	Also known as a dot matrix printer, good for printing multiple copies of text and can produce limited graphics. Uses ribbons, which keeps costs down. It is the only printer that can do multiple-part forms using impact printer paper/forms and supports the 132-column paper needed in some industries.
Inkjet printer	Much quieter, weighs less, and produces higher-quality graphics than an impact printer. Uses a print cartridge, sometimes called an ink cartridge, that holds the ink used to produce the text and graphics; an ink cartridge costs $10 to $60 and can print 100 to 200 pages, depending on the manufacturer, the size of the cartridge, what is printed, and the print quality settings. Color can be done by impact printers, but inkjet printers are best for color printing.
Laser printer	Produces the highest-quality output at the fastest rate. Toner cartridges can cost $20 to $350. They are common in the corporate network environment, where users share peripherals and require fast printing, often in bulk. Used for graphic design and computer-generated art where high-quality printing is a necessity. Some can produce color output but at a much higher cost than for black and white. Some even have stapling capabilities.
Thermal printer	Uses special thermal paper that is sensitive to heat. An image is created where the heat is applied. Commonly used as ticket printers or receipt printers in retail outlets and gas stations.
3D printer	Used to create 3D objects using various types of materials, including plastics, thermoplastics, clay, alloys, rubber, stainless steel, and metal alloys.

Impact Printers

Impact printers (see Figure 9.1) are also called dot matrix printers because of the way they create an image on paper. Such a printer has an **impact print head** that holds tiny wires called **print wires**. Figure 9.2 shows an Oki Data Americas, Inc., print head. The print wires are shown on the front of the print head. The print wires can get out of alignment and produce malformed characters.

The wires individually strike a **print ribbon** hard enough to create a dot on the paper. The dots collectively form letters or images. The speed at which the print head can place characters on a page is its characters per second (**cps**) rating. The number of print wires in the print head determines the quality of printing: The more print wires, the better the print quality. The most common numbers of print wires are 9, 18, and 24. The 24-pin impact printers can print near letter quality (NLQ) output.

Each print wire connects to a solenoid coil. When current flows to the print wire, a magnetic field causes the wire to move away from the print head and out a tiny hole. The print wire impacts a ribbon, creating a dot on the paper. Figure 9.3 shows an impact printer print head. To show the individual print wires, the casing that covers the print wires has been removed from the illustration.

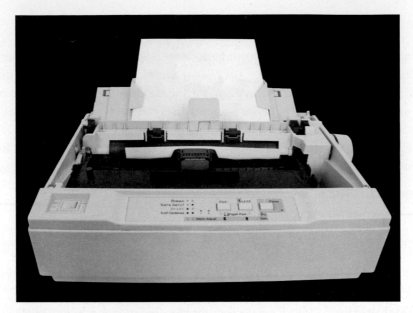

FIGURE 9.1 Impact printer

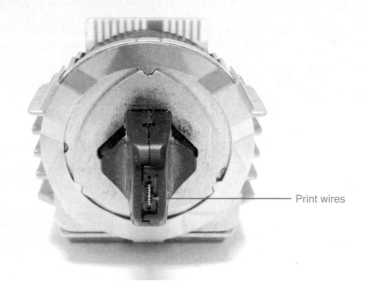

FIGURE 9.2 Impact printer head

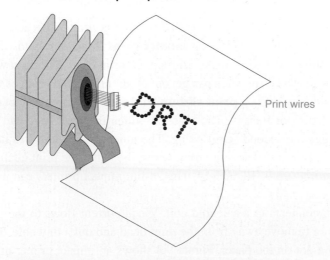

FIGURE 9.3 Impact print head operation

Each wire connects to a spring that pulls the print wire back inside the print head. The images created are a series of dots on the page. Dot matrix printers are also called impact printers because the print wire springs out of the print head. The act of the print wire coming out of the print head is called pin firing. The impact of the printer physically striking the ribbon, which in turn touches the paper, causes impact printers to be noisy.

TECH TIP

Printing in one direction is not a problem

Most impact printers print bidirectionally. When the print head gets too hot, the printer prints only in the left-to-right direction. This is normal.

Because the print wire impacts the ribbon, one of the most common points of failure with impact printers is the print head. It can be expensive to replace print heads frequently in a high-usage situation; however, refurbished print heads work fine and are available at a reduced price. The companies that refurbish them usually replace the faulty wires and test each print head thoroughly.

Impact printers are the workhorses of printers. One advantage of an impact printer is that it can print multiple-part forms such as invoices, purchase orders, shipping documents, and wide forms. Multiple-part forms print easily on an impact printer because the printer impacts the paper so hard. Special **impact paper** can be purchased so duplicates are made each time a print job is sent. The maximum number of multiple copies each printer handles depends on the printer model. Laser and inkjet printers cannot produce multiple-part forms. They can only make multiple copies of the same document.

TECH TIP

Don't stack

Don't stack things on top of a printer, especially an impact printer. Keep a printer in a cool environment to avoid overheating.

Inkjet Printers

Inkjet printers, which are much quieter than impact printers, are used to print black-and-white, grayscale, and color output. Like an impact printer, an inkjet printer also has a print head, but the inkjet's print head does not have metal pins that fire out from the print head. Instead, the inkjet's print head has many tiny nozzles that squirt ink onto the paper. Each nozzle is smaller than a strand of human hair. Figure 9.4 shows a photo of an **ink cartridge**. Notice the three rows of nozzles on the cartridge on the left.

One great thing is that an **inkjet print head** includes the nozzles and the reservoir for ink. When the ink runs out, you replace the entire print head. The inkjet printer print head is known as the print, or ink, cartridge. An ink cartridge has up to 6,000 nozzles instead of the 9-, 18-, or 24-pin configuration of the impact printer. This is one reason inkjet quality is better than the quality of an impact printer. Replacing the print head, one of the most frequently used parts, keeps repair costs low, but consumable costs are high. Two alternatives are for the manufacturers to use (1) a combination of a disposable print head that is replaced as needed and a disposable ink tank or (2) a replaceable print head similar to that of an impact printer.

FIGURE 9.4   Inkjet print cartridge

Inkjet printers, also called bubble jet printers, use thermal (heat) technology to place the ink on the paper. Each print nozzle attaches to a small ink chamber that attaches to a larger ink reservoir. A small amount of ink inside the chamber heats to a boiling temperature. Once the ink boils, a vapor bubble forms. As the bubble gets hotter, it expands and goes out through the print cartridge's nozzle onto the paper. The size of the ink droplet is approximately two ten-thousandths (.0002) of an inch, which is smaller than the width of a human hair. As the small ink chamber cools down, suction occurs. The suction pulls more ink into the ink chamber for the production of the next ink droplet.

An alternative for producing the ink dots is to use piezo-electric technology, which uses pressure, rather than heat, to eject the ink onto the paper. Some companies use this technology to obtain high resolutions. **DPI** is the number of dots per inch a printer outputs. The higher the DPI, the better the quality of inkjet or laser printer output. Figure 9.5 shows the basic principle of how an inkjet printer works. Figure 9.6 shows how paper feeds through the printer and the parts associated with that process. Table 9.3 lists the major parts found inside an inkjet printer.

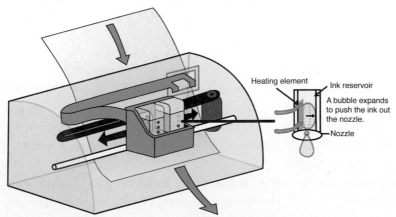

FIGURE 9.5   How an inkjet printer works

TABLE 9.3   Inkjet parts

Part	Description
Print head	Contains nozzles used to dispense ink
Print head assembly	Holds the print head and possibly ink cartridge(s)

Part	Description
Ink cartridge	Also known as a print cartridge or simply as a cartridge; may be one color or may have sections for separate colors and may include the print head
Stepper motor	Used to move the print head/ink cartridge from one side of the printer and back as well as move the print head assembly (see Figure 9.6)
Belt	A belt connects to the stepper motor and print head assembly to move the print head and ink cartridge from one side of the printer to the other side (see Figure 9.6)
Stabilizer bar	Acts as a guide for the print head assembly for smooth motion
Power supply	Converts wall outlet AC to DC for inside the printer
Carriage	The part that moves from one side of the printer and back; includes the belt, stabilizer bar, and print head assembly (and the print head that may be included with the ink cartridge(s) (see Figure 9.6))
Paper tray and/or paper **feeder**	Holds paper (see Figure 9.6)
Roller	Moves paper through the printer (see Figure 9.6)
Duplexing assembly	Supports two-sided printing

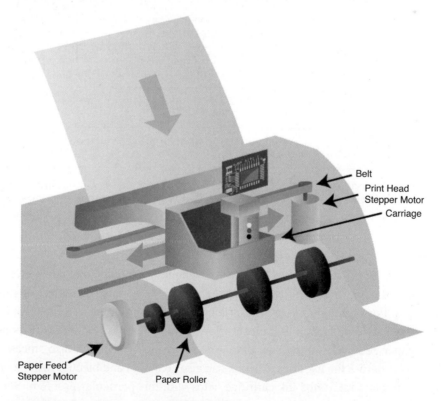

FIGURE 9.6   Major inkjet printer parts

Most inkjet printers have different modes of printing. The draft mode uses the least amount of ink, and the NLQ mode uses the most ink. The quality produced by an inkjet printer is equal to or sometimes higher than that of a laser printer, and inkjet printers print in color, whereas many laser printers print only in monochrome (black and white).

Be aware of optimized DPI

Many inkjet printers now show their DPI as *optimized* DPI. Optimized DPI does not describe how many drops of liquid are in an inch but in a specific grid.

Color inkjet printers usually have a black cartridge for text printing and a separate color cartridge or separate cartridges for colored ink. Buying an inkjet printer that uses a single cartridge for all colors means a lower-priced initial printer purchase but is more expensive in the long run. The black ink usually runs out much more quickly than the colored ink. Users should buy an inkjet model with separate cartridges for black ink and for colored ink.

There are some alternatives to inkjet technology. Table 9.4 outlines four of them.

TABLE 9.4   Other printer technologies

Type of printer	Description
Solid ink printer	Sometimes called a phase change or hot melt printer; uses colored wax sticks to create vivid color output. A wax stick is melted and sprayed through tiny nozzles onto the paper. The wax is smoothed and pressed as the paper is sent through rollers. The sticks can be installed one at a time, as needed. The wax does not melt or bleed onto hands, clothing, or internal printer parts. This type of printer can print more colors, is faster, has fewer mechanical parts, and is cheaper than color laser printers but is more expensive than normal inkjet printers.
Dye sublimation printer	Also known as a dye diffusion thermal transfer printer; uses four film ribbons that contain color dyes. The ribbons are heated and applied to the paper. The quality is high, but the printers are expensive.
Thermal wax transfer printer	Uses wax-based inks like a solid ink printer but prints at lower resolutions.
Large-format inkjet printer	A wide printer to print large-scale media such as CAD drawings, posters, and artwork.

An inkjet printer can also be integrated with a scanner and operate like a copier as an all-in-one unit. With these units, there are frequently two or even three paper feeds: from the rear paper tray, from a paper tray accessed from the bottom front of the unit, and from the top, which is commonly used for the copying or scanning.

Inkjet printers are perfect for small businesses, home computer users, and individual computer office work. Some inkjet printer models include faxing, scanning, copying, and printing capabilities. For higher output, a laser printer is more appropriate. A drawback to using ink is that sometimes the ink smears. Ink manufacturers vary greatly in how they respond to this problem. If the paper gets wet, some inkjet output becomes messy. The ink also smears if you touch the printed page before the ink dries. The ink can also soak into and bleed down the paper. Using good-quality paper and ink in the ink cartridge helps with this particular problem. Some manufacturers have a printer operation mode that slows down the printing to give the ink time to dry or a heating process to prevent smudges. See this chapter's section on printer supplies for more information on choosing the correct paper for different printers.

Laser Printers

The term *laser* stands for light amplification by stimulated emission of radiation. A laser printer uses a process similar to a copy machine's electrophotographic process. Before describing how a laser printer works, identifying the major parts inside the printer helps to understand how it works. Figure 9.7 shows a side view of a laser printer with a toner cartridge installed.

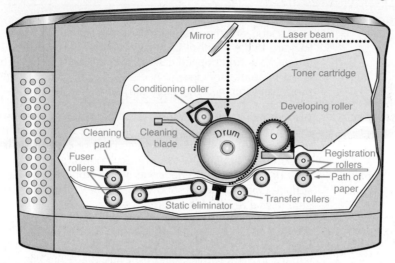

FIGURE 9.7   Inside a laser printer

The computer sends 1s and 0s out the port and down the cable to the printer. Because data gets written to a laser drum by placing "dots" close together—similarly to how an inkjet printer squirts dots close together—the data must be prepared before the seven steps of getting the data onto the paper begin. The processing is the preparatory step, in which the data is rasterized or converted into dots. Data transmits either through an array of LEDs or through a laser beam. The light beam strikes the photosensitive imaging drum located inside the toner cartridge (see Figure 9.8). Laser toner particles are attracted to the drum. The paper feeds through, and the toner transfers to the paper. The toner is then fused or melted onto the paper. Table 9.5 summarizes the seven-step laser printer imaging process.

FIGURE 9.8   Laser imaging drum

TABLE 9.5   Laser printer imaging process steps

Step	Description
Processing	Also known as raster image processing. Gets the data ready to print. The laser printer converts the data from the printer language, such as HPPCL (Hewlett-Packard Printer Control Language), Adobe PostScript, or Microsoft OpenXPS (Open XML Paper Specification), into a bitmap image. The laser printed page is made up of very closely spaced dots. Each row of dots is a scan line. The processing step gets the data ready to "write" a scan line.
Charging	Also known as conditioning. Gets the drum ready for use. Before any information goes onto the drum, the entire drum must have the same voltage level. The primary corona (main corona) or **conditioning roller** has up to –6,000 VDC applied to it. A primary control grid located behind the corona wire or conditioning roller controls the amount of voltage applied to the drum's surface (approximately –600 V to –1,000 V). The drum gets a uniform electrical charge as a result of this step.
Exposing	Also known as the writing phase. Puts 1s and 0s on the drum surface. Whether the printer uses a laser beam or an LED array, the light reflects to the drum surface in the form of 1s and 0s. Every place the beam touches, the drum's surface voltage is reduced to approximately 100 volts (from the very high negative voltage level). The image on the drum is nothing more than dots of electrical charges and is invisible at this point.
Developing	Gets toner on the drum (develops the image). A **developing cylinder** (or developing roller) is inside the toner cartridge (right next to the drum) and contains a magnet that runs the length of the cylinder. When the cylinder rotates, toner is attracted to the cylinder because the toner has iron particles in it. The toner receives a negative electrostatic charge. The magnetic charge is a voltage level between –200 V and –500 V. The magnetized toner particles are attracted to the places on the drum where the light beam strikes. A **density control blade** controls the amount of toner allowed through to the drum. The image is no longer transparent on the drum: The image is black on the drum surface.
Transferring	Transfers an image to paper. A **transfer belt** (or an equivalent part, such as a **transfer roller**, **transfer corona**, or **transfer pad**) is located at the bottom of the printer. It places a positive charge on the back of the paper. The positive charge is strong enough to attract the negatively charged toner particles from the drum. The particles leave the drum and go onto the paper. At this point, the image is on the paper, but the particles are held only by their magnetic charge.
Fusing	The **fuser assembly** melts the toner onto the paper. Heat and pressure make the image on the paper permanent. The paper, with the toner particles clinging to it, immediately passes through fusing rollers or a belt that applies pressure to the toner. The top roller applies intense heat (350°F) to the toner and paper that literally squeezes and melts the toner into the paper fibers. Figure 9.9 shows an example of a fuser assembly and the motor used with it.
Cleaning	Wipes off any toner left on the drum. Some books list this as the first step, but the order does not matter because the process is a continuous cycle. During the cleaning stage, a wiper blade or brush clears the photosensitive drum of any excess toner. Then an **erase lamp** neutralizes any charges left on the drum so the next printed page begins with a clean drum.

Power supply

Fuser assembly

Fuser motor

Registration
assembly

FIGURE 9.9   Laser printer parts

A mnemonic (where the first letter of a saying helps you remember another word) for the laser printer imaging process is as follows: `People Can't Expect Dummies To Fix Computers.`

TECH TIP

Laser printers *do* make weird noises

A laser printer frequently makes an unusual noise that is a result of the fusing rollers turning when the printer is not in use. If the rollers didn't turn like this, they would have an indentation on one side. Users not familiar with laser printers sometimes complain about this noise, but it is a normal function of a laser printer.

Every laser printer that uses the seven-phase imaging process is known as a **write-black laser printer**. Such laser printers produce a black dot everyplace the beam touches the drum. Most laser printers use write-black technology. Write-white laser printers reverse the process, and the toner attracts everywhere the light beam does *not* touch the drum surface. Write-black printers print finer details, but write-white laser printers can produce darker shades of black areas.

To help with this flood of data about laser printers, Table 9.6 lists the major parts of a laser printer and briefly describes the purpose of each part.

TABLE 9.6   Laser printer parts

Part	Purpose
AC power supply	Acts as the main power supply for the printer
Cleaning blade	Wipes away excess toner from the drum before printing the next page
Cleaning pad	Applies oil to the fusing roller to prevent sticking; also removes excess toner during the fusing stage
Conditioning roller	Used instead of a primary corona wire to apply a uniform negative charge to the drum's surface

Part	Purpose
Control panel assembly	Acts as the user interface on the printer
Density control blade	Controls the amount of toner allowed on the drum (usually user adjustable)
Developing cylinder	Rotates to magnetize the toner particles before they go on the drum (also called the developing roller)
Drum (photo-sensitive)	Also known as **imaging drum**; accepts light beams (data) from LEDs or a laser; can be permanently damaged if exposed to light; humidity can adversely affect it
Duplexing assembly	Supports two-sided printing
ECP (electronic control package)	The main board for a printer that usually holds most of the electronic circuitry, the CPU, and RAM
Erase lamp	Neutralizes any residual charges on the drum before printing the next page
Fuser (fusing) assembly	Holds the fusing roller, conditioning pad, pressure roller, and heating unit
Fusing rollers	Applies pressure and heat to fuse the toner into the paper
High-voltage power supply	Provides a charge to the primary corona or conditioning roller, which puts a charge on the drum
Main motor	Provides the power to drive several smaller motors that drive the gears, rollers, and drum
Pickup rollers (feed rollers)	Rollers used along the paper path to feed paper through the laser printer
Primary corona (main corona)	Applies a uniform negative charge to the drum's surface
Registration assembly	Holds the majority of the rollers and gears to move paper through the unit
Separate pad (separation pad)	A bar or pad in a laser printer that can have a rubber or cork surface that rubs against the paper as it is picked up
Scanner unit	Includes a laser or an LED array that is used to write the 1s and 0s onto the drum surface
Toner	Powder made of plastic resin particles and organic compounds bonded to iron oxide
Toner cartridge (EP cartridge)	Holds the conditioning roller, cleaning blade, drum, developing cylinder, and toner; always remove the toner cartridge before shipping a laser printer
Transfer corona wire (transfer belt or roller)	Applies a positive charge on the back of the paper to pull the toner from the drum onto the paper

Figure 9.10 shows a photograph of a toner cartridge.

FIGURE 9.10 Inside a laser printer cartridge

A word about spilled toner

Toner melts when warmed; small toner spills outside a printer can be wiped using a cold, damp cloth. Toner spills inside a printer require a special type of vacuum with special bags. Toner on clothing can normally be removed by washing in cold water. Do not put the clothing in a dryer if the toner has not yet been removed, or the toner will melt into the clothing and become impossible to remove.

Thermal Printers

Thermal printers are used in a lot of retail establishments and at kiosks, gas pumps, trade shows, and basically anywhere someone needs a little printer to print a small document, such as a receipt. IT staff commonly have to service thermal printers. Thermal printers are also known as point of sale (POS) or cash register printer.

A thermal printer uses **special thermal paper** that is sensitive to heat. A print head has closely spaced heating elements that appear as closely spaced dots on the heat-sensitive paper. A **feed assembly** is used to move the thermal paper through the printer. Figure 9.11 shows examples of thermal printers. Figure 9.12 shows how a thermal printer works.

FIGURE 9.11 Thermal printers

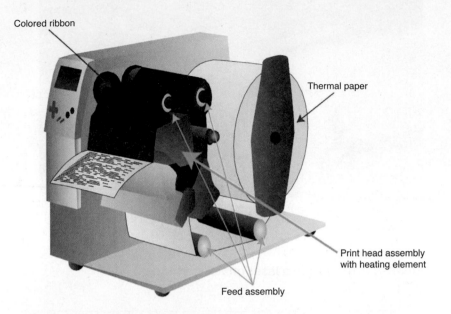

Colored ribbon

Thermal paper

Print head assembly
with heating element

Feed assembly

FIGURE 9.12   Inside a thermal printer

The thermal print head is one of the most important parts of a thermal printer. The print head can be damaged in several ways:

> Residue or material buildup causing uneven printing or missing dots
> Opening the print mechanism while printing
> Poor-quality thermal paper
> Dirty environment
> Other objects (stuck labels, staples, paper clip, and debris)
> ESD (Very little voltage can damage the print head. Use self-grounding or an antistatic wrist strap when handling the print head.)
> Excessive moisture, such as in high-humidity environments

3D Printers

3D printers are used to "print" 3D solid objects out of various types of materials, including plastic, ceramics, metals, metal alloys, and clay. A 3D image is scanned into the computer, drawn, or downloaded from the Internet. Software slices the image into thousands of layers. The printer "prints" each layer until the object is formed. The end result is that a solid object is created. Think of the possibilities—from being able to print a toy, a cat dish, or that hard-to-get-plastic piece that always breaks on the pool vacuum. Figure 9.13 shows a 3D printer.

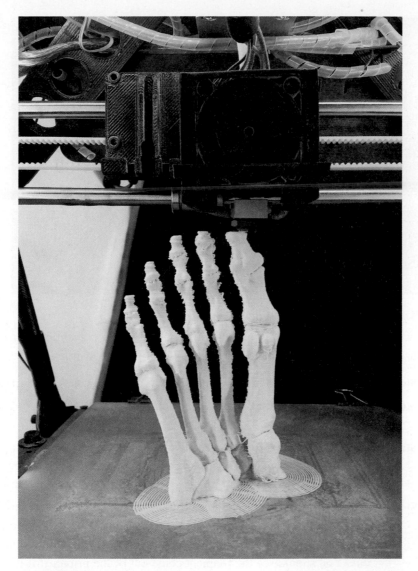

FIGURE 9.13 3D printing

Installing Plastic Filament

3D printers commonly use plastic known as **plastic filament**, or printer filament, that comes in different types and colors. The type you need depends on the 3D printer model and the type of object being created. Two common types of plastic filament are acrylonitrile butadiene styrene (ABS) and polylactic acid (PLA). Figure 9.14 shows what plastic filament looks like on the reel that attaches to a 3D printer.

FIGURE 9.14   3D printing filament

Always follow the manufacturer's instructions and safety precautions for replacing/installing the plastic filament in a 3D printer. The following are generic instructions:

Step 1. Use side cutters to trim the end of the filament to create a sharp taper.

Step 2. Mount the reel onto the printer, ensuring that the filament spool unwinds in the correct direction.

Step 3. Use a printer menu to select the load filament option. Some models use options such as *Material > Change*. On printers that allow multiple reels, you might need to choose which reel is being loaded, such as right or left, as shown in the Figure 9.15 menus.

Step 4. After the printer preheats the extruder (the part that ejects material to create the 3D object), insert the end of the filament into the hole on the 3D printer, as shown in Figure 9.16. Note that you might have to insert the filament through a sleeve before doing this. You should see the filament come out of the printer if it is feeding properly.

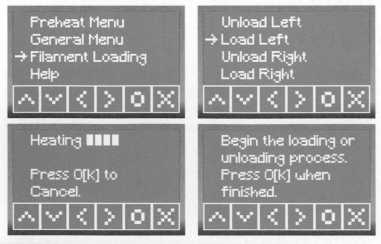

FIGURE 9.15   Sample 3D printer menu options

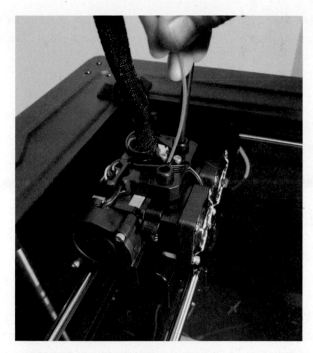

FIGURE 9.16   Inserting plastic filament into a 3D printer

Paper

The type of paper used in a printer can affect its performance and cause problems. Impact printers are the most forgiving because a mechanism physically impacts the paper. On the other hand, because inkjet printers spray ink onto the paper, the quality of paper determines how well the ink adheres. If the paper absorbs too much of the ink, the printout appears faded. For a laser printer, how well the paper heats and absorbs the toner affects the printed output. Paper is a big factor in the quality of the printouts produced and how long the ink lasts.

Erasable-bond paper does not work well in laser printers because the paper does not allow the toner to fuse properly. Many types of paper are available for inkjet and laser printers: transparency paper for overhead projectors, high-gloss paper, water-resistant inkjet paper, fabric paper, greeting cards, labels, recycled paper, and so on. Recycled paper may cause printer jams and can produce lower print quality.

TECH TIP

Paper and pounds

Paper is rated in pounds (abbreviated lb) and shown as 20 lb or 20#. A higher number indicates heavier, thicker paper.

The highest-quality paper available does not work well if the surrounding area is too humid. Humidity causes paper to stick together and reduces the paper's strength, which causes feed problems. Paper affected by humidity may be noticeably lumpy. If you detect that paper is damaged, recycle it or make it into scrap paper. For best printing results, store paper in a non-humid storage area and fan the paper before you insert it into the printer's bin.

Some impact printers allow you to remove the normal paper feeder and attach a tractor-feed option that allows continuous-feed paper to be fed through the printer. Figure 9.17 shows how the paper with holes on both sides feeds through an impact printer. Both impact and inkjet printers have special feeders or a slide bar to feed envelopes or unusual-sized paper through. Laser printers sometimes ship with additional trays and must be configured for this option.

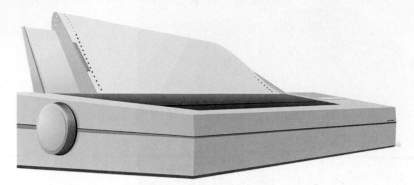

FIGURE 9.17 Tractor-fed paper

Another paper option is a duplexing assembly that enables two-sided printing. You may have seen and heard a duplexing assembly in action on a copier. A duplexing assembly is more commonly purchased for a laser printer than any other printer types, but certain inkjet printers also have this optional part. The duplexer is commonly attached to the bottom of a laser printer and the rear of the printer and selected through the *Print* menu of any application. Figure 9.18 shows a duplexing assembly.

FIGURE 9.18 Duplexing assembly

TECH TIP

How to control printer trays and manual feed options

In Windows, the *General* tab on the printer *Properties* window is commonly used to view the current paper settings. Click the *Preferences* button to configure where you want the printer to look for paper to be used. See Figure 9.19.

Most printers allow you to set a default order in which the printer looks for paper. You can typically configure this through either manufacturer-provided software or the printer *Properties* window. Many printers have both *Properties* and a *Printer Properties* options (see Figure 9.20). Figure 9.21 shows the difference between the windows these options bring up. You will most likely want the *Printer Properties* option shown on the right.

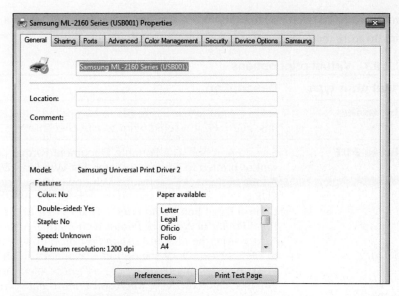

FIGURE 9.19   Paper options for a printer

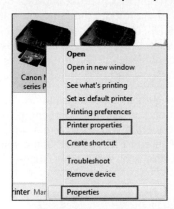

FIGURE 9.20   Right-click menu options for a printer

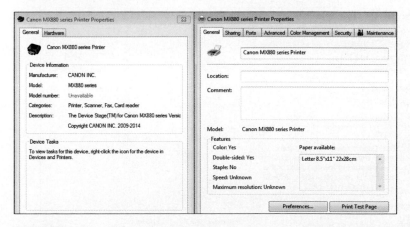

FIGURE 9.21   Properties window (left) and Printer Properties window (right)

Virtual Printing

Printing of any type takes information formatted in a specific application (web browser, word processor, spreadsheet, photo viewer, and so on) and puts it into a format the printer understands. One way to save paper is to use virtual printing. **Virtual printing** means printing to somewhere other than the directly connected printer and commonly to a specific file type so the file can be viewed, saved, or even emailed instead of printed or eventually sent to a printer. Four common virtual printing techniques are outlined in Table 9.7.

TABLE 9.7   Virtual print options

Virtual print type	Description
Print to file	Saves a print job as a .prn file to be printed later. Not all printers support this. *File > Print >* select *Print to File* checkbox (see Figure 9.22) > *OK.*
Print to PDF	Saves a print job as a Portable Document Format (.pdf) file that can be sent or printed to any printer later. For Windows 7/8, download free Adobe Systems, Inc. software. Windows 10 includes a native print-to-PDF option. If it is not shown, search for the *Advanced Printer Setup* Control Panel link > *The Printer That I Want Isn't Listed* link > *Add a Local Printer or Network Printer with Manual Settings* radio button > *Next >* from the *Use an Existing Port* drop-down menu, select *File: (Print to File) > Next.* Once the option is available, in all Windows versions, from any application, select *File > Print >* select *Adobe PDF* (Windows 7/8) (see Figure 9.23) or *Microsoft Print to PDF* (Windows 10)> *OK.*
Print to XPS	Saves a file as a Microsoft XPS file that allows a document to be printed on any printer but not modified. From any application, *File > Print >* select *Microsoft XPS Document Writer > Properties > XPS Documents* tab > ensure the *Automatically Open XPS Documents Using the XPS Viewer* checkbox is enabled. To view the document in the XPS Viewer, browse to the file location and double-click on the file name.
Print to image	Saves a file to an image file. When documents cannot print to PDF due to a poor download or damaged content, print to image is a great option. It is also good when you are giving a sample of something but do not want to give an entire document. Some software allows you to save in a JPEG, TIFF, PNG, or some other image file type.

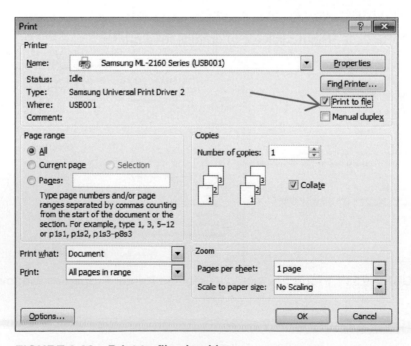

FIGURE 9.22   Print to file checkbox

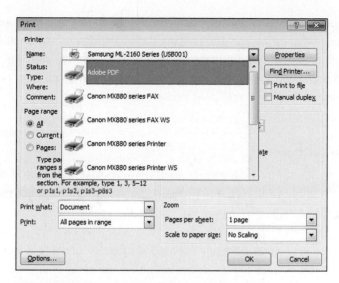

FIGURE 9.23   Print to Adobe PDF option

Refilling Cartridges, Re-inking Ribbons, and Recycling Cartridges

Controversy exists about re-inking impact printer ribbons, refilling inkjet cartridges, and buying remanufactured laser cartridges. Many people who are concerned about the environment recycle cartridges. Even if a company or an individual user decides not to purchase remanufactured products, some send empty cartridges to companies that do the remanufacturing or take them to a local office supply company for credit. Refilling ink cartridges significantly lowers printing costs.

If you refill ink cartridges, you should add new ink before an old cartridge runs completely dry. Also, be sure the refill ink emulates the manufacturer's ink. Some ink refill companies use inferior ink that, over time, has a corrosive effect on the cartridge housing. A leaky cartridge or one that bursts, causing ink to get into the printer, is trouble.

Some ink refill companies have exchange systems. The old ink cartridges are placed into a sealed plastic bag and returned to the company, where they are remanufactured. In return, the company ships a remanufactured cartridge filled with ink. If the empty ink cartridge sent to the company does not meet the company's standards criteria, the cartridge is thrown away.

Some manufacturers offer a **continuous ink system** (CIS) that does not require changing out ink cartridges so often. Other companies sell a product that modifies a printer to use a CIS. Figure 9.24 shows a CIS. Notice how the CIS connects to the printer via tubes. The tubes have to connect to the print head assembly so that ink can be supplied to the print head.

FIGURE 9.24   Refilling a CIS

When it comes to laser cartridge remanufacturing, the most important components are the drum and the wiper blade that cleans the drum. Many laser cartridge remanufacturers use the same parts over and over again. A quality refill company will disassemble the cartridge and inspect each part. When the drum and wiper blade are worn, they are replaced with new parts. Some states have disposal requirements for inkjet and laser printer cartridges.

TECH TIP

Beware of toner cartridges

Toner powder is harmful if inhaled. Wear a mask when refilling. Also, wear disposable gloves when replacing or refilling a toner cartridge to prevent toner from entering your skin pores.

Re-inking an impact printer ribbon is not a good idea. It can cause a mess, and the ink is sometimes an inferior quality that causes deterioration of the print head over time. Because impact printer ribbons are so inexpensive, you should just replace them.

Upgrading Printers

Printers can be upgraded in many ways, and the options available are vendor and printer dependent. The most common upgrades include memory and tray/paper feed options. The most commonly upgraded printers are inkjet and laser printers.

The most common upgrade for laser printers is memory. Many laser printer manufacturers use DIMMs and SO-DIMMs now, but some printers have proprietary memory modules. The amount of memory storage available for printers (especially those shared by multiple users) is important because printing errors can occur with too little memory. It is also important to have some means of storage so that the documents can be sent and stored away from the computer that requested the print job. This frees up the computer's memory and hard drive space to do other tasks.

TECH TIP

Printer memory upgrades

Many memory technologies are available for printers, but the common ones are RAM modules, flash memory, and proprietary memory modules. These technologies are installed in the same manner as on a computer. Hard drives can also be attached to some printers for additional storage.

Paper storage trays and feeders are another common upgrade. Laser printers frequently come with various paper storage tray options. When multiple people share a printer, a small-capacity paper tray can be a nuisance. Inkjet printers often have different paper feed options for photograph printing. Paper designed for printing photographs is available in various sizes. Special paper feed options can be purchased that are mounted onto a printer for rolls or different sizes of paper. With the increased popularity of digital photography, these printer options are quite popular.

Printer Maintenance

Maintenance is important for all types of electronics, but printers have maintenance and preventive maintenance requirements that are a bit different than those of other devices. For some printers, preventive maintenance kits are available for purchase. Quality printer replacement parts and preventive maintenance kits are important to a technician. Let's examine the maintenance procedures associated with each printer type.

Impact Printer Maintenance

Maintenance done on an impact printer commonly involves the following:

> Replacing the ribbon (see Figure 9.25)
> Replacing the print head
> Replacing paper
> Clearing and cleaning the paper path

FIGURE 9.25   Impact printer ribbon

You know it is time to replace the ribbon when the print output is consistently light. The time to replace the print head is when the output shows one or more white horizontal lines. When replacing the printer print head, always follow the manufacturer's instructions. Generic steps to install an impact printer print head are as follows:

Step 1. Power off the printer and allow the print head to cool.

Step 2. Press the release lever or button that allows the print head to be removed.

Step 3. Insert the replacement print head.

Step 4. Power on the printer and send a sample print job to ensure that the print head is firing all pins.

To replace paper, simply insert the paper inside the paper tray. If continuous paper or forms are installed, you may be required to clear and clean the paper path. Ensure that the paper aligns properly and evenly to the pins in the continuous (tractor-fed) paper. A sample form may have to be printed to ensure that data is placed in the appropriate form fields.

Impact printers usually require cleaning more often than any other type of printer because they are frequently used for continuously fed paper or multiform paper and are often installed in industrial environments. Paper chafe, dust, and dirt cause an insulating layer of heat to form on the printer components, which causes them to fail faster. It is important to vacuum impact printers more often than other printers as a preventive maintenance task.

Inkjet Printer Maintenance

Maintenance done on an inkjet printer commonly involves the following:

> Replacing the cartridge (see Figure 9.26)
> Performing calibration/print head alignment
> Clearing paper jams
> Cleaning the print head

FIGURE 9.26   Inkjet ink cartridge assembly

You know it is time to replace an ink cartridge when the print output is consistently light, a particular color does not print, or a message appears. The generic steps to install an ink cartridge are as follows:

Step 1. Ensure that the printer is powered on.

Step 2. Open the printer cover or door to gain access to the print cartridge assembly. Most printers automatically move the assembly to a place where access is easiest. Give the printer time to complete this process.

Step 3. Release the old print cartridge. There might be a release lever to access the cartridge. Some cartridges require pressing down to eject or simply pulling out, pulling out and then up, or lifting up. Always refer to the manufacturer's directions.

Step 4. Remove the protective tape from the new cartridge. Be careful not to touch any ink nozzles and/or the copper contacts on the cartridge.

Step 5. Insert the new cartridge, reversing the removal procedure.

Step 6. Replace the printer cover or access door.

Step 7. Print a test page.

On most inkjet printers you have to **calibrate**, or perform a print head alignment process, on the print head to ensure quality output. Many inkjet printers come with their own optional software that can be installed to perform this process. Each inkjet printer has a different calibration process, but the generic steps are as follows:

Step 1. Locate the printer in the appropriate Windows Control Panel.

Step 2. Right-click the printer and select *Properties* or *Printer Properties*.

Step 3. Locate the calibration function, which is commonly found on a *Tools*, *Maintenance*, or *Advanced* tab.

Step 4. Perform the calibration, which normally involves printing a page and then selecting specific values through another menu. See Figure 9.27 for an example of the calibration or print head alignment page that is printed as part of the calibration process.

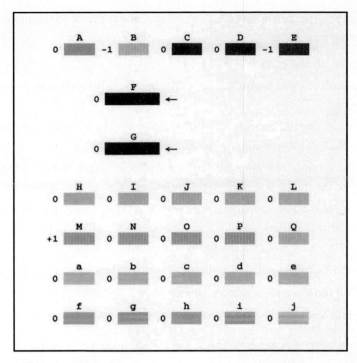

FIGURE 9.27   Sample inkjet print head/calibration output page

A **paper jam** involves paper getting stuck somewhere along the paper path. The key to clearing or fixing paper jams on any printer is patience. Power off the printer and unplug it. Open the main cover and inspect to determine where the jam occurred. Remove all loose paper from the paper path and paper tray. Sometimes fixing a jam is simply a matter of pulling gently backward on the paper from the paper tray (although it is always best to try to take the paper through the natural direction of the paper path), fanning through the paper in the paper tray to loosen one piece of paper from the others, or pulling the paper the rest of the way through the paper path. Do not tug; do not tear paper, if possible, as doing so will make fixing the jam more difficult for you.

It may be easier to move the cartridge assembly to the side of the printer. Not all printers allow this. You might also gain access to an area by removing the ink cartridges. Needle-nose pliers and tweezers are great tools for stuck paper. Again, try to pull in the direction the paper would naturally roll through the printer.

Inkjet printers require little preventive maintenance. Keep the interior and exterior clean of dust and particles. Use a soft brush or nonmetallic vacuum nozzle to remove dust. Do not use any type of lubricants on the print cartridge bar. Use the printer's software or maintenance procedure for aligning the print cartridge each time it is replaced.

Some printers have a "clean" maintenance procedure that can be done through the software that ships with the printer. Some of these processes do not clean the print head well enough, and the print heads tend to clog during usage. In such a case, remove the print head and clean it with a lint-free cloth or with a dampened cotton swab. Allow the cartridge to dry thoroughly before reinstalling it.

Laser Printer Maintenance

Maintenance done on a laser printer commonly involves the following:

> Replacing a toner cartridge
> Applying a maintenance kit
> Performing calibration
> Clearing paper jams
> Cleaning the printer

To replace the toner cartridge on a laser printer, always refer to the manufacturer's instructions. These are the generic steps:

Step 1. Power off the printer.

Step 2. Access the toner cartridge. This may involve lifting the top cover or opening an access door.

Step 3. Remove the old cartridge by lifting up or sliding forward and then lifting up (see Figure 9.28). If this model has a release tab, press it.

Step 4. If the original covering and bag are available, attach the covering and insert the cartridge inside the bag. Recycle if possible.

Step 5. Remove the new cartridge from the box. Avoid doing this in sunlight. Avoid touching the cartridge drum. Many cartridges have a plastic strip that must be pulled out and thrown away. Remove the protective drum covering.

Step 6. Install the new cartridge and ensure that it snaps securely in place.

Step 7. Close the top cover or access door.

Step 8. Print a test page to ensure that the printer works well.

FIGURE 9.28 Replacing a laser printer cartridge

A **laser printer maintenance kit** is available for some models. The contents of the kit are vendor specific and might include any of the following: separation pad, pickup roller, transfer roller, charge roller, and fuser assembly. Always follow the manufacturer's directions for installing a maintenance kit. The separation pad and pickup rollers commonly require removal of an e-clip that holds rollers tightly on a bar. An e-clip looks like the letter C or letter E, as shown in Figure 9.29.

FIGURE 9.29 E-clip

There is a specific tool for removing e-clips, but needle-nose pliers and a small flat-tip screwdriver can work, too. Hold the closed side of the e-clip tightly with the pliers and use the tip of the screwdriver to gently pry the e-clip off the bar.

A common process done at the end of applying the maintenance kit is to reset the **maintenance counter**. This counter is used to count the number of pages until the next time the message to apply the maintenance kit appears again. Usually this counter is reset through the laser printer menu, but some printers require you to press a special button sequence.

TECH TIP

Allow laser printer to cool

Before working on a laser printer, allow the printer to cool down. Look for warnings where hot components are located.

A laser printer may have software options for cleaning and calibration. The cleaning mode cleans the paper path so that no corner or random specks appear on the output. Calibration can help with environmental issues (see the bulleted point on ozone that follows) or print cartridge quality issues. Cleaning mode and calibration are commonly accessed through the printer menu or from manufacturer-specific software on a PC. Some laser printers have automatic calibration and also allow it to be done manually.

Laser printers do require some periodic maintenance. The list that follows can help:

> Be careful about using compressed air to clean a laser printer that has loose toner in it. The compressed air could push the toner into hard-to-reach places or into parts that heat up, causing the parts to fail. Be sure to vacuum up laser printer toner before using compressed air inside a laser printer.

> If a transfer corona is used, clean it when replacing the toner cartridge. Some printers include a small cleaning brush for this purpose. Some toner cartridges include a cotton swab. The transfer corona wire is normally in the bottom of the printer, protected by monofilament wires. Be extremely careful not to break the wires or the transfer corona.

TECH TIP

Laser printer preventive maintenance is important

If any toner appears inside a laser printer, do *not* use a normal vacuum cleaner to get it out. Toner particles can seep through the vacuum cleaner bag and into the vacuum's motor, where the particles melt. Also, the toner can become electrically charged and ignite a fire. Special high-efficiency particulate air (HEPA) vacuum bags are available for some computer and/or laser printer vacuum cleaners.

> Laser printers that use a corona wire can produce ozone gas. Some printers have an ozone filter that removes the ozone gas as well as any toner and paper dust particles. The ozone filter needs to be replaced after a specific number of usage hours. Check the printer documentation for the filter replacement schedule. If you forget to replace the ozone filter, people in the immediate vicinity may develop headaches, sore eyes, dry throat, nausea, irritability, and depression. Most home and small office laser printers do not have ozone filters. When using these printers, the surrounding area must be well ventilated.

> The fuser cleaning pad (sometimes known as the fuser wand) sits above the top fusing roller and is normally replaced at the same time as the toner cartridge. However, the cleaning pad

sometimes becomes dirty before it is time to replace the cartridge. If the cleaning pad needs to be cleaned, remove it and hold it over a trash can. Use the shaft of a small flat-tipped screwdriver to rub along the felt pad. Replace the cleaning pad and wipe the screwdriver with a cloth.

> The fusing roller sometimes has particles cling to it. When the assembly cools, *gently* scrape the particles from the roller. A small amount of isopropyl alcohol on a soft, lint-free cloth or an alcohol pad can help with stubborn spots.

> If the laser printer uses a laser beam to write data to the photosensitive drum, the laser beam does not directly touch the drum. Instead, at least one mirror is used to redirect the laser beam onto the drum's surface. The mirror needs to be cleaned periodically with a lint-free cloth.

Thermal Printer Maintenance

Maintenance done on a thermal printer commonly involves the following:

> Replacing special thermal paper
> Cleaning the print head/heating elements
> Removing debris
> Checking the feed assembly

Thermal printer preventive maintenance involves cleaning the print head/heating elements and removing debris from the printer and paper path. Isopropyl alcohol or premoistened thermal cleaning swabs can be used to clean the thermal print head and rollers. Compressed air can be used, too. It is recommended that with some thermal printers, you use a cleaning card, cleaning file, cleaning pen, or cleaning swabs. Remember to always use proper ESD procedures and to allow the thermal printer to cool before performing preventive maintenance.

Printer Maintenance Conclusion

Printers are critical to some users. Keeping a printer well maintained and recommending a maintenance routine is part of the routine for many technicians. If any type of printer must be sent out for repair, for warranty work, or for some other reason, make sure to remove the toner cartridge, platen knobs, and power cords before packing the printer in a box (or remind the user to do so). Check with the receiving company to see if you should send the toner cartridge separately.

TECH TIP

What if you just performed maintenance on a printer, and now the printing looks bad?

After performing preventive maintenance on a printer, the pages may appear smudged or slightly dirty. Run a few print jobs through the printer to allow the dust to settle (so to speak). Never perform any maintenance on any computer part or peripheral without testing the results.

USB Printer Installation

A printer is one of the easiest devices to install. Refer to the printer documentation for exact installation and configuration specifics (see Figure 9.30).

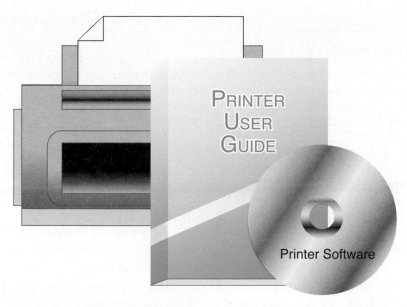

FIGURE 9.30 Printer installation, using software and a manual

The following steps explain how to install a printer that attaches to a USB port:

Step 1. Take the printer out of its box and remove the shipping materials. The number-one reason new printers do not work properly is failure to properly remove all the shipping safeguards.

Step 2. Connect the power cord from the printer to the wall outlet, surge protector, or UPS outlet. Note that most UPS units are not rated high enough for a laser printer to be connected to them.

Step 3. Load paper and the ribbon, ink, and cartridge into the printer, according to the manufacturer's instructions.

Step 4. Turn on the printer and verify that the power light is on.

Step 5. Install the print driver by following the manufacturer's instructions for the particular operating system being used.

Step 6. Attach the USB cable to the printer and to the computer. Note that this cable might not be provided with the printer.

Step 7. Configure options and default settings.

Step 8. Verify that the operating system recognizes the printer. Perform a test print to verify communication between the computer and printer. Perform the calibration/print head alignment procedure.

Step 9. Train the user on printer operation and leave all printer documentation with the customer.

TECH TIP

Educating the user on printer functionality and print cartridges

As part of the installation process, ask the user to print something and show him or her any unique features. Inform the user that the cartridge that comes with the printer does not last long and to order a new one as soon as possible.

CHAPTER 9

TECH TIP

For a successful printer installation

The keys to a successful printer installation are to read the printer documentation, use a good cable, load the latest printer drivers (from the manufacturer), and test the printer's operation. Many hours of frustration for the computer user and the technician can be avoided by doing research before the installation rather than after a problem occurs.

Installing a Local Printer

A local printer is a printer that connects to a computer. The steps for installing a local printer depend on how the printer connects to the computer, but the generic steps are discussed in this section. Refer to the manufacturer's directions for specifics.

Local printers commonly connect through a USB port, a wired or wireless network, or a Bluetooth network. You may sometimes see old 9- or 25-pin serial or 25-pin parallel printers still in use. As mentioned earlier in this chapter, you may have to install software before attaching the printer cable. Table 9.8 describes some tips for the various installation types.

TABLE 9.8   Printer installation notes per connection type

Connection type	Notes
USB	If software was installed before attaching the cable, Windows should detect it and automatically start the installation process.
Wired network	To set up a computer on a wired network, use the *Add Printer* wizard. A prompt asks whether the printer is local or networked. A local printer is directly attached to the computer, and a networked printer is attached to another workstation, a print server, or directly to the network.
Wireless network	Setting up a printer on a wireless network is similar to setting up a printer on a wired network except that you have to know a few details about the wireless network, such as the wireless network name (SSID) and security password.
Bluetooth	Bluetooth may have to be enabled first through a switch on the computer or through the Control Panel. Bluetooth must be enabled on the printer to make it discoverable. Note that some Bluetooth devices are always in discovery mode.

If a printer is not discovered, you can use the *Add a Printer* Control Panel link. If the printer does not appear, you can select the link *The Printer That I Want Isn't Listed* > *Add a Local Printer or Network Printer with Manual Settings* link > *Next* > *Use an Existing Port* > select the appropriate port > select the manufacturer and printer model from the list or click the *Have Disk* button to browse to the downloaded file.

Printers in the Windows Environment

The operating system plays a big part in controlling a printer. When working in a Windows environment, there are three essential areas for a technician to know (besides knowing how to print): (1) configuration utilities, (2) managing the print driver, and (3) printer settings. Sometimes these areas overlap.

To print in Windows, use one of the following methods:

> Open the file in the appropriate application. Click the *File* menu item and click the *Print* option.
> Drag the file to print to the printer's icon in the *Printers* folder.

> Create a shortcut icon on the desktop for a specific printer and drag the file to that icon.
> Right-click the filename and select the *Print* option.
> Open the file in the appropriate application and press Ctrl+P to bring up the *Print* window.
> Open the file in the appropriate application and click the printer icon located under the menu bar.

TECH TIP

Using the printer icon in the notification area

When a print job occurs, Windows normally shows an icon of a printer in the notification area (the right side of the taskbar). When the print job is still accessible, you can double-click the printer icon, click the document, and pause or cancel the print job by using the *Documents* menu option.

You can use the *Devices and Printers* Control Panel to add a printer, remove a printer, temporarily halt a print job (that is, pause the printer), and define or change printer settings, such as resolution, paper type, and paper orientation. The Windows *Add a Printer* wizard steps you through the installation process. This utility starts automatically when Windows detects a newly connected printer. After the wizard starts, you must select whether the printer is a local printer (used by only one computer) or a network printer. If the local printer option is selected, you have to install a print driver. (Device sharing and networking printers are covered later in this chapter.) For best performance, always use the latest driver from the printer manufacturer for the operating system installed.

A **default printer** is a printer that applications use without any configuration changes. Even if you reply *No* to this prompt, you can change a printer to the default printer at a later date. Right-clicking a specific printer icon also gives you access to the *Printer Properties* window. In this window, several tabs are available, depending on the printer model. Common tabs include *General*, *Sharing*, *Ports*, and *Advanced*. Figure 9.31 shows the *Printer Properties* window. Notice that the *General* tab has a *Print Test Page* button that can be used to test connectivity between the computer and the printer, and the test can be used to ensure that the print driver is working.

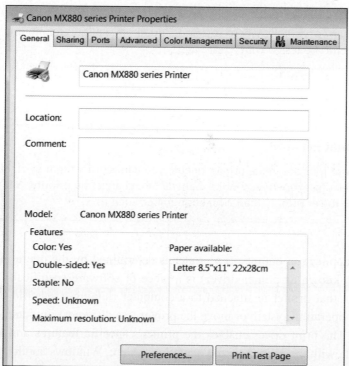

FIGURE 9.31   Printer Properties window

TECH TIP

Setting a printer as the default printer

Locate the printer using the *Devices and Printers* Control Panel. Right-click the appropriate printer > *Set as Default Printer*. The default printer has a check mark next to the printer icon.

A printer's *Properties* window contains useful tools and settings. Table 9.9 lists the common printer *Properties* window tabs and their general purposes.

TABLE 9.9 Printer Properties window tabs

Tab	Description
General	Displays the printer name and has a button for printing a test page
Sharing	Shares the printer over a network
Ports	Sets the LPT port number or displays the current port
Advanced	Allows setting of resolution, graphics intensity (darkness), graphics mode, spooling (transmission delay), and defaults
Maintenance	Printer type dependent; contains links to various maintenance functions, including cleaning, calibration, print head alignment, nozzle check, roller cleaning, and quiet mode
Fonts	Displays and installs printer fonts
Device Options	Adjusts print density and quality, displays the amount of RAM installed in the printer, and adjusts printer memory tracking

TECH TIP

Print Test Page button on the printer Properties General tab

The *General* tab is normally where you find a button that allows communication between the PC and the printer to be tested with a test page.

TECH TIP

I want my print job now!

If multiple print jobs are in the printer queue, you can reorder them by right-clicking on a document and selecting *Properties*. On the *General* tab, change the priority. A lower number, such as 1, indicates a lower priority than a higher number, such as 3.

How an application outputs to a printer is determined by the operating system used. A **print driver** (also known as printer driver) is a piece of software specifically written for a particular printer when that printer is attached to a computer running a specific operating system. If you upgrade the operating system or move the printer to a different computer, a different printer driver is required. The print driver enables the printer's specific features and allows an application to communicate with the printer via the operating system. Windows applications use one print driver per printer. If you have two printers attached, two print drivers have to be installed.

Using the latest print driver

For best results and performance, use the manufacturer-provided driver that is designed for the operating system being used.

The print driver and software from the printer manufacturer provide customizable configuration settings for a particular operating system. These settings can be accessed by right-clicking on the printer within the *Devices and Printers* Control Panel and selecting *Printing Preferences*. Commonly used configuration settings include the following:

> **Orientation** (see Figure 9.32)—The vertical or horizontal presentation of the document. Portrait orientation is taller than it is wide, and landscape is wider than it is tall.

> **Duplex** (see Figure 9.32)—Also known as double-sided printing. Note that the printer featured in Figure 9.32 does not have a duplexer assembly, so printing on two sides would require turning the paper over and sending it back through the printer.

> **Collate** (see Figure 9.33)—The collation setting affects the order in which the pages are printed when multiple copies of a multipage document are being made. For example, if you want to make three copies of a 10-page document, with collation enabled, you would get the first copy of the 10-page document, then the second copy, and finally the third copy. Without collation enabled, you would get three copies of the first page, three copies of the second page, and so on.

> **Quality** (see Figure 9.34)—This setting controls the resolution (DPI for example) and amount of ink/toner used.

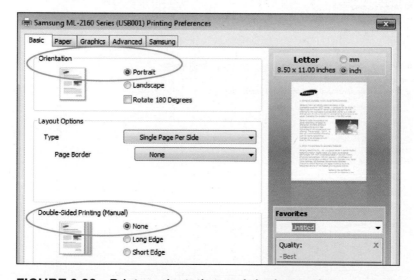

FIGURE 9.32   Printer orientation and duplex settings

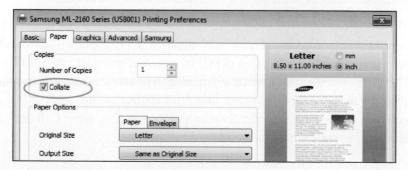

FIGURE 9.33   Printer collate option

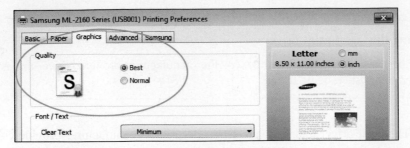

FIGURE 9.34   Printer print quality option

Printers accept as much data as possible from a computer, process that data, output it, communicate to the computer the need for more data, accept more data, and repeat the process. With Windows, a print spooler is used. A **print spooler**, or print manager, is a software program that intercepts an application's request to print. Instead of going directly to the printer, the data goes on the hard drive. The print spooler service that is built into the Windows operating system controls the data that is going from the hard drive to the printer. A print spooler allows multiple print jobs to be queued on the hard drive so that other work can be performed while the printer prints. The data is sent from the hard drive when the printer is ready to accept more data. A printer may come with its own print manager that replaces the Windows print spooler.

If you right-click a printer and select *Properties* (or sometimes the window is under *Printer Properties*), you can control the print spooler from the *Advanced* tab, as shown in Figure 9.35.

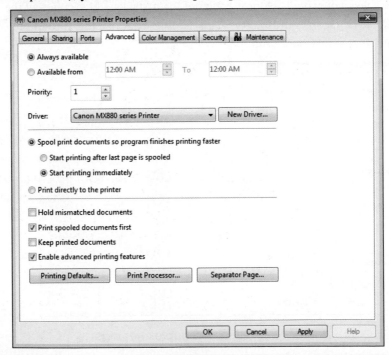

FIGURE 9.35   Spooling settings

A print spooler runs as a service in Windows. The print spooler service relies on another service, called the Remote Procedure Call (RPC) service, and optionally the HTTP service in order to operate. To verify whether the services are running, type services.msc at a command prompt, in the *Run* textbox, or in the *Search Programs and Files* textbox on the *Start* button menu. In the resulting screen, you can see that the Print Spooler and Remote Procedure Call (RPC) services have a status of *Running*, as shown in Figure 9.36.

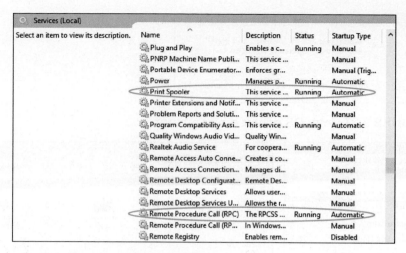

FIGURE 9.36   Print Spooler service

When not to use spooling

If you have less than 300 MB of hard drive space, turn off spooling because the system needs the free drive space to operate. Remove files from the hard drive and clean up if possible or add more storage so spooling can be re-enabled. Note that if a printer is shared, spooling must be enabled.

Printers in the macOS Environment

There are three ways to connect a printer to a Mac computer: (1) Use a USB cable and attach it directly, (2) print through an Apple AirPort router or AirPort Extreme Base Station, or (3) use an Apple Time Capsule. An AirPort router can be used to create a wireless network. The Apple Time Capsule acts as a wireless router and has USB ports for sharing a printer on the network.

macOS includes many print drivers, so no printer driver needs to be installed on an Apple computer. Once a printer is installed, you can power on the printer and select Software Update from the Apple menu. The computer will check for driver updates for the printer connected to the Mac. If there is a printer update, click the Update button shown on the screen.

The following are the generic steps for installing a printer in the macOS environment:

Step 1. Unpack the printer and install ink, toner, paper, and so on and then power on the printer.

Step 2. Connect the printer through a cable or to the wireless network.

Step 3. Normally, the driver loads if it is part of the operating system (OS). Otherwise, the OS prompts you to download it, as shown in Figure 9.37.

Step 4. Use the Apple menu to select *System Preferences > Print & Scan/Printers and Scanners* (see Figure 9.38). If the printer is not listed, click the add (plus sign) button at the bottom of the list and select the printer.

Note that once the printer is selected, the printer options are configured the same way in macOS as in the Windows environment.

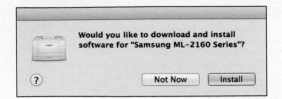

FIGURE 9.37 macOS printer driver prompt

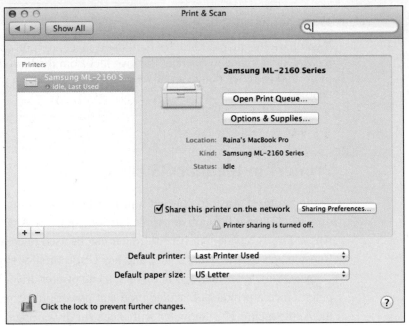

FIGURE 9.38 macOS Print & Scan

In order to see print jobs on a Mac, you can view the print history as follows:

Step 1. Open the *Terminal* application. A window that allows commands to be entered appears.

Step 2. Type `cupsctl WebInterface=yes` and then press ⏎Enter.

Step 3. Open a web browser and type `http://localhost:631` in the address bar. Then press ⏎Enter.

Step 4. Select the *Jobs* tab and click the *Show Completed Jobs* button to see print jobs.

Printing Device Sharing

Many home users and almost all businesses use printing device sharing (that is, printers that can be used by more than one computer). Printers can be shared using the following methods:

> Connect a printer to a port (USB or the older serial/parallel) on a computer that is connected to the network and share the printer.

> Connect a printer with a wired or wireless NIC directly on the network. Some printers can be upgraded to have a wired or wireless network port added to them. Figure 9.39 shows a wired Ethernet port that can be inserted into a printer expansion slot.

> Set up a computer or device that is designated as a print server. Connect the printer to the print server. Connect the print server to the network.

> Use public/shared devices.

A networked printer can reduce costs. Laser printers can be expensive—especially ones that produce high-speed, high-volume, high-quality color output. Buying one printer and allowing users to access it from their individual desktops, laptops, and mobile devices can be cost-effective. It also reduces the amount of office or home space needed. Network printing is a viable alternative to using a computer's USB port. Wired printers can connect to a computer and then be shared or can connect to a wired network so that everyone on the network can use the printer.

FIGURE 9.39   Wired network port printer

Sharing Through Windows

To share a workstation-connected printer across the network, follow these steps:

Step 1. Enable *File and Print Sharing* by selecting the *Network and Sharing Center* Control Panel > *Change Advanced Sharing Settings* > expand the current network profile > *Turn On File and Printer Sharing* > *Save Changes*. See Figure 9.40.

Step 2. To share a directly connected printer so others can access it, right-click the printer to be shared > *Properties* (or possibly *Printer Properties*) > *Sharing* tab > enable (select) the *Share This Printer* option so it is checked > in the *Share Name* textbox, type a name for the printer > *OK*. See Figure 9.41.

Notice in Figure 9.41 that you can install additional drivers for other Windows operating systems so that when other computers access this shared printer, they do not have to download and install the driver for this printer.

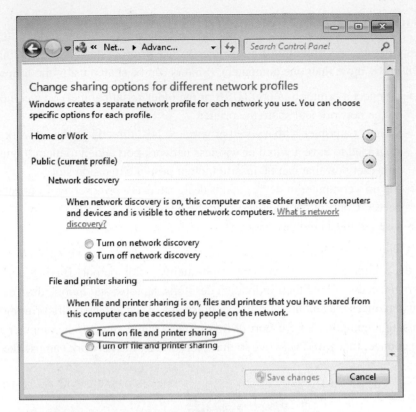

FIGURE 9.40   Enable print sharing

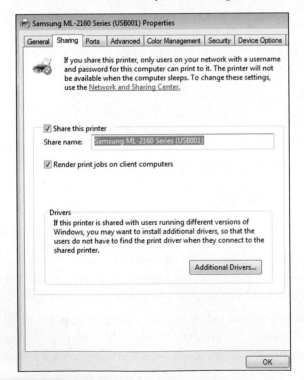

FIGURE 9.41   Printer Sharing tab

Wireless Printers

A PC can use different methods to connect wirelessly to a printer:

> The printer can have an 802.11 wireless NIC installed, or the NIC can attach to a USB port.
> The printer can have integrated Bluetooth capabilities or a Bluetooth adapter attached via a USB port.
> The wireless printer can communicate directly with another wireless device.
> The print server to which the printer connects can have wireless capabilities, and wireless PCs and devices can connect to the printer through the print server (as discussed in the next section).

Printers with wireless capabilities are common, but a wireless adapter may have to be purchased separately. Refer to Chapters 13, "Networking," and 14, "Introduction to Operating Systems," for more information on wireless networking theory and issues related to installing wireless devices.

The first method is the most common. An 802.11 wireless network has an 802.11 access point or combination access point and router that coordinates communication between all devices on the wireless network.

TECH TIP

Doing your wireless homework

When installing an 802.11 wireless network printer, obtain the SSID and security information before starting the installation.

There are different types of 802.11 networks (a, b, g, n, and ac). Each type has its own frequency and rules of operation. The wireless NICs in all the devices on the wireless network must be of compatible types. See Chapter 13 for more information.

The steps for installing a wireless printer are similar to the steps for installing a wired network printer once the printer is attached to the wireless network . Before installing a wireless printer, you need to ensure that a functional wireless network is in the area. You need to know the SSID and any security settings configured on the wireless network. Normally, you can configure wireless printers using one of the following methods:

> Install software that comes with the printer *before* connecting the printer. Then use the software to enter the wireless network SSID and optional security parameters.
> Use the controls on the front panel of the printer to configure the wireless settings.
> Use a USB connection to the printer until the wireless network configuration options are entered.

Some Bluetooth printers are configured by first connecting them via USB and then configuring the Bluetooth option. To install a Bluetooth printer, always follow the manufacturer's directions, but the following generic steps are provided:

Step 1. Install the print driver for the operating system version being used.

Step 2. Ensure that Bluetooth is enabled on the computer or mobile device.

Step 3. Ensure that Bluetooth is enabled on the printer (usually through a front panel control). Note that you may have to set the visibility option to *Visible to All*.

Step 4. If in Windows, use the Windows *Devices and Printers* Control Panel to access the *Add a Printer > Add a Network, Wireless or Bluetooth Printer* link. Some manufacturers simply recommend using the Bluetooth icon in the notification area to select *Add a*

CHAPTER 9

Bluetooth Device. On a device, something may have to be tapped or pushed in order to start pairing with the Bluetooth printer.

Step 5. Ensure that the two devices pair properly and that the print function works.

Some wireless printers support **ad hoc wireless printing**, which allows two 802.11 wireless devices to communicate directly, without the use of a wireless access point or a wireless router. When a wireless access point or wireless router is used, the alternative mode is known as **infrastructure mode**. To install and configure an ad hoc wireless printer, use the recommended procedures from the printer manufacturer. These are the generic steps:

Step 1. Place the printer in ad hoc mode by using the front panel controls or software from the printer manufacturer.

Step 2. Place the computer, tablet, or mobile device in ad hoc mode. In Windows, access the *Network and Sharing Center* Control Panel > *Set up a new connection or network* link > configure the wireless network name and security options.

Note that you might have to manually configure the wireless NIC IP address and subnet mask. See Chapter 13 for more information on how to do that.

Print Servers

A **print server** connects to a network and allows any computer that is also connected to a network to print to it if the networks are the same or connected to one another. Some print servers can handle both wired and wireless connections. In such a case, the print server attaches to a network switch, and a network wireless router or wireless access point attaches to the same switch. Any PCs (wired or wireless) can print to the printer that attaches to the print server. Figure 9.42 illustrates this concept.

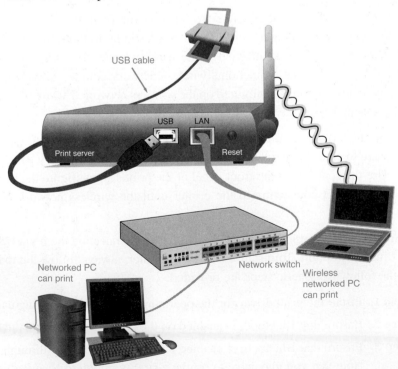

FIGURE 9.42 **Wireless and wired print server connectivity**

Accessing a Network, Wireless, or Bluetooth Printer

To access a networked printer, use the Windows *Devices and Printers* Control Panel > *Add a Printer* > *Add a Network, Wireless or Bluetooth Printer* link. If the printer does not display in the list, select *The Printer That I Wanted Is Not Listed*. Three options are available (see Figure 9.43):

> Browse for a network printer
> Type the path to the printer
> Enter the IP address or printer hostname

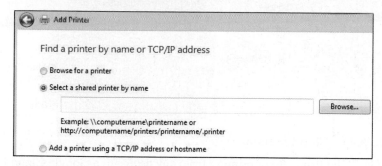

FIGURE 9.43   Finding a shared printer

See Chapter 13 for more information on configuring network devices.

An older PC can be used as a software print server so that it does nothing except handle print jobs sent to the printer attached to the PC. Software such as Apple's AirPrint or Bonjour can also be used to create a print server.

Apple's **AirPrint**, which is included with devices running macOS, can be used to print to any AirPrint printer without the need to download device drivers. The printer and the device must be on the same wireless network. Older printers can also support AirPrint by using a third-party print server. To print from an Apple device by using AirPrint, access *Tools > Print > Share and Print*. If using Mail, select the *Reply* button > *Print*. From the Safari web browser, access the shortcut button left of the address bar > *Print*.

Apple's **Bonjour** printer server is available on Apple devices and can be downloaded for free for Windows devices (or installed automatically when the Apple Safari web browser or iTunes is installed). The Bonjour print server allows Apple and Windows devices to share printers without any configuration.

Cloud Printing

What if you want to print something in a remote location or you are on a wired computer and want to print to a wireless printer? **Cloud printing** can let you do that or print using any device, whether it is connected to the network where the printer is located or not. Cloud printing can be done through a service provided by the printer manufacturer or through a provider such as Google. People already access email, files, music, and other devices by using the cloud, so it makes sense that an app can allow a print job to do the same. Figure 9.44 shows how a document or a photo can be printed from a cell phone if cloud printing is enabled.

FIGURE 9.44 Cloud printing

Google Cloud Print allows printing from any device to a Google Cloud Print–connected printer. This means you can print a picture or a document from your phone or mobile device. To determine whether the printer is Google Cloud ready, open a Chrome web browser window. In the address bar, type `chrome://devices`. You then see a list of any Google Cloud devices. To add a printer, click *Add Printers* (see Figure 9.45). Select whatever printers you would like to add to Google Cloud Print and click the *Add Printer(s)* button (see Figure 9.46). From the resulting screen, click *Manage My Printers* to see the options within Google Cloud Print (see Figure 9.47).

FIGURE 9.45 Viewing Google Cloud–ready devices

Once you have printers registered to the cloud, you can download an app on your phone or mobile device. Some apps only allow printing from a particular browser. Other apps have you upload a document or photo to the app and then print from there. Finally, you may have to share a photo or document with the app and then print from the app. Many printer manufacturers have their own cloud-based print solutions and apps.

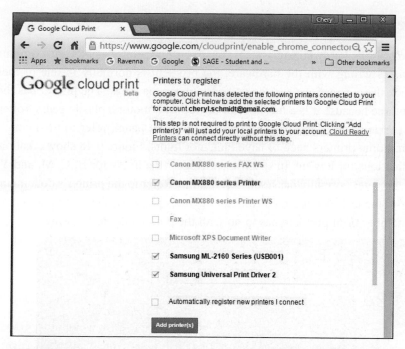

FIGURE 9.46   Viewing Google Cloud printers to register

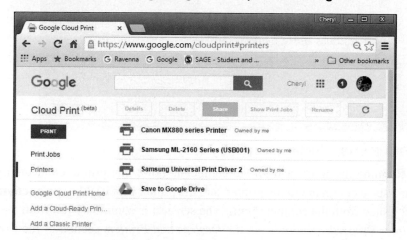

FIGURE 9.47   Google Cloud Print

Printing Data Privacy

Technicians need to be aware of the drawbacks to printing to a shared, public, or cloud-based printer:

> Printers shared through a PC require that the PC be powered on at all times.

> Sharing a printer through a PC means that print jobs are spooled to the PC hard drive (**hard drive caching**). If someone sends an inappropriate print job or prints something that is sensitive corporate information, a technician must realize that the spooled data can be recovered even after the print job completes.

> Privacy can be an issue. For printers shared wirelessly, it may be necessary to give the wireless network password to anyone who wants to print. Printers involved in cloud-based printing require a user to authenticate and register with the app vendor. There can be no expectation of **data privacy** or security.

General Printer Troubleshooting

The printing hardware subsystem consists of the printer, cable, and communications port. If something is wrong with the hardware, the problem is normally in one of these three areas. Always check the connections and the power between the areas. The printer has the highest failure rate of the three because it is a mechanical device with motors, plastic gears, rollers, and moving parts. If an **error code** or message appears on the front panel, refer to the manual or online documentation. Some printers beep or have indicator lights. Figure 9.48 shows that one particular printer has indications for low ink in specific cartridges (the lights for B, C, M, and Y).

A printer normally has a self-test routine. Refer to the printer's documentation to determine how to run the test. If a printer's self-test operates properly, the printer is operational. In this case, any remaining print problem has to do with the port, cable, or software.

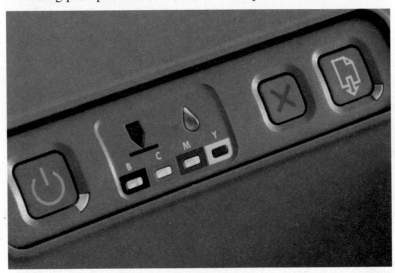

FIGURE 9.48 Printer indicator lights

Running the self-test from the computer shows that printer connectivity works (the computer can issue a command to the printer, and the printer gets it). **No connectivity** is evident if the self-test issued from the computer fails. The self-test is commonly run from the printer's *Properties or Printer Properties* option from the *Devices and Printers* section of the Control Panel. Access the *General* tab > *Print Test Page* button. Refer to Figure 9.31.

TECH TIP

When paper is not feeding

If a printer is having trouble with the **paper not feeding**, you should look to see how far the paper went along the paper path before it jammed or could not go any farther. Many paper-feeding problems are due to poor paper quality or inefficiency of the rubber rollers that move the paper along the paper path. Rubber rollers are normally found in the paper transport system on all printer types, and over time, the rollers become slick from use and stop working properly.

If the **printer will not print**, perform the following generic steps:

Step 1. If the printer attaches to a computer, see if any message appears on the computer.

Step 2. See if any message appears on the printer's control panel.

Step 3. Determine whether the correct printer was chosen.

Step 4. Ensure that the printer has ink or toner and paper.

TECH TIP

The paper could be the culprit

If a printer has trouble feeding paper, ensure that you're using the correct type of paper. One vendor says that 80% of all paper jams are due to inferior paper quality, poor paper condition (such as damage due to humidity), or operator-related problems such as the wrong paper size selected in the software program.

If you are **unable to install the printer** using the manufacturer's instructions, try the following steps:

Step 1. Check the cabling and power.

Step 2. Reread the manufacturer's directions and ensure that they have been followed.

Step 3. Delete the print driver and try the installation again, following the manufacturer's instructions.

Step 4. Download a different print driver and try the installation again.

Step 5. Research the error on the printer manufacturer's website. In some cases, it may be necessary to back up the registry, modify the registry, and restart the print spooler in order to repair this issue.

If there is **no image on the printer display**, check that the printer is powered on. Also check the wall outlet by plugging a known working device into the same socket; if applicable, check the power surge strip. The printer power brick may be faulty.

TECH TIP

Mixed-up output

If you see **garbled characters** on the output, check the cable and then the print driver.

If a printer gives a "paper out" message (see Figure 9.49), but the paper is installed in the printer, check the paper sensor. Sometimes this sensor is an optical sensor, and sometimes it is a plastic piece that flips out. Take out the paper and reinsert it. Ensure that there is no blockage and that the sensor is not sticking (that is, not flipping out properly). Dust and debris can cause both blockage and sensor sticking.

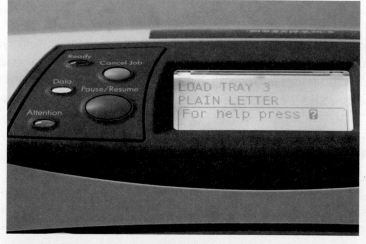

FIGURE 9.49 Printer front panel message

TECH TIP

Faded or totally missing print

When the print output is **faded print**, check the ribbon (in impact and thermal printers), ink levels (in inkjet printers), or toner (in laser printers). Check the quality setting. In a thermal printer, reduce the print head energy or print head pressure setting; ensure that the ribbon and media are compatible. Do the same checks if the printer is **printing blank pages** and also ensure the print driver is working properly. You may have to roll back the driver in Device Manager if a Windows Update has just occurred.

If the printer outputs **creased paper**, check the following:

> Ensure that the paper guides in the paper tray are set to the correct size and do not push too tightly against the paper.
> Fan the paper before printing.
> Ensure that the paper being used meets the printer manufacturer's specifications.
> Check the paper path for obstructions, such as a label, staple, or paper clip.

Some printers have upgradable firmware. Just as a computer's flash BIOS can be upgraded, printers may need a firmware upgrade to correct specific problems. Printer firmware updates can normally be obtained from the printer manufacturer's website.

Another problem could be that the printer is not configured for the correct port. Check that the printer is configured for the proper port. Refer to the printer's documentation for specifics on how to configure the printer for a specific port. To verify which port is currently configured, access the printer manufacturer's software or use Windows *Printer Properties* from the Control Panel (by right-clicking the printer) > *Ports* tab. You can also connect a working printer to the port, install the proper print driver, and verify that the port works.

TECH TIP

What to do with slick printer rollers

Special cleaners such as Rubber Rejuvenator are available for rubber printer rollers that have a hard time picking up paper and sending it through the printer. Some printers have a special cleaning page for cleaning rollers. Refer to the printer's manual for exact procedures. If a cleaner is unavailable, scrub the rollers with a wire brush or sandpaper to roughen them up a bit, which will enable them to pick up the paper better. If you do not have a wire brush or sandpaper, use the sharp edge of a paper clip to roughen up the rubber part of the roller so it can grip the paper. Vacuum all debris before using the printer.

Another common problem is that a printer may not have enough memory. One symptom of this is that when printing, the printer blinks as if it is accepting data. Then the printer quits blinking, and nothing appears or the printer prints only half the page. This could also be caused by insufficient hard drive space when spooling is enabled. Some printers display a **low memory error** message or error code.

TECH TIP

What if a printer needs more memory?

Alternatives to adding memory are to send fewer pages of the print job at a time, reduce the printer resolution, reduce the size of the graphics, or standardize the fonts (by not using as many font types, styles, or font sizes). Also ensure that there is ample free hard drive space on the computer being used to send the print job.

USB-Attached Printer Troubleshooting

If a printer that uses a USB port is displaying problems, consult the following list of troubleshooting options:

> If the computer stops responding and the USB device is suspect, power off the computer and then turn it back on again.

> The BIOS/UEFI settings may have to be enabled for USB devices. Different BIOS/UEFI manufacturers list the USB settings differently. The USB settings may be located under the heading *Enabling Onboard USB* or within the PCI section. If you install a USB host adapter and the motherboard also supports USB ports, you may have to disable the motherboard ports through BIOS/UEFI.

> Use *Device Manager* to check whether USB is listed. Look at the *Universal Serial Bus Controllers* section. If USB is not listed, check the BIOS/UEFI settings or update the BIOS. If the USB device is listed, ensure that there are no resource conflicts.

> If there is a USB hub connected to the USB port, disconnect the hub and connect the USB printer directly to the USB port to see if the hub is the problem.

> With the computer's power on, disconnect the USB printer and reconnect it. Go into *Device Manager* and ensure that there is only one listing for the USB printer.

> Disconnect the USB printer while the computer is powered on. Power down the computer. Then power on the computer. Insert the USB printer cable into the USB port. The system should automatically detect and install the printer.

> Verify that the USB device works by plugging it into another USB port or another computer's USB port.

> Check that the proper USB cable is being used.

A USB cable can be rated as SuperSpeed+, SuperSpeed, Hi-Speed, or Low-Speed. The SuperSpeed and Hi-Speed cables have more shielding and can support higher speeds. If a SuperSpeed or Hi-Speed USB device is attached to a Low-Speed cable, the device operates at the lower speed. Make sure you have the proper USB cable for a printer that attaches to a USB port.

On the software side, troubleshooting involves narrowing down the problem to the print driver. Because Windows uses one print driver for all applications, check the printing from within several software packages. Use a simple text program such as Notepad to see if simple text will print. Printers need memory to print multiple pages of complex graphics. If a printer prints a couple pages and then stops, or if it prints half a page, ejects the paper, and then prints the other half of the page and ejects the paper, the printer's memory needs to be upgraded. If printing does not occur in all the software packages tested, the problem is most likely the software driver. See the next section for specific Windows printer troubleshooting tips.

Windows Printer Troubleshooting

The most common printing test is a test page from an application or from a specific printer's *Properties* or *Printer Properties* window, using the *General* tab. Remember that Windows uses a single print driver for all applications. Windows has a troubleshooting tool that you access differently, depending on the Windows version being used:

> Windows 7: *Start* button > *Control Panel* > type `troubleshooting` in the Search Control Panel textbox > *Search Windows Help and Support for "Troubleshooting"* link > *Troubleshooting* > locate the *Open the Printer Troubleshooter* link > *Click to Open the Printer Troubleshooter* link > follow the directions on the screen.

> Windows 8: In the *Search* textbox, type `troubleshooting` > *Hardware and Sound* link > in the *Printing* section, select *Printer* link > follow the directions on the screen.

> Windows 10: In the *Search the Web and Windows* textbox, type `troubleshooting` > *Troubleshooting* section of the Control Panel > *Hardware and Sound* link > in the *Printing* section, select *Printer* link > follow the directions on the screen.

If the Windows troubleshooting tool does not help, run a self-test on your printer by following the manufacturer's directions. If the self-test works, the printer is likely fine, and the problem lies in the cable, port, software driver, or printer settings.

TECH TIP

Print from Notepad

If a printer self-test works, try printing from Notepad. If the file prints, your problem may be a print problem that affects only one application, or the printer may not have enough memory for complex output, such as high-end graphics.

Free hard drive space is important for print spooling. Insufficient free space can cause problems with print jobs. Even if there appears to be enough hard drive space to spool a print job, the printer may still need more RAM installed to print a large or complex document.

A print spooler and/or associated services, such as RPC and HTTP, can cause problems and can be stopped or paused. Locate the Print Spooler, RPC, or HTTP service used by the printer (by typing `services.msc`). Right-click on the service and select *Properties*. In the window that appears, you can start, stop, pause, or resume a service. Figure 9.50 shows the Print Spooler Properties window. Because the service is started automatically, the only button currently available is Stop.

If the printer works, then you know the printer, port, and printer cable are all operational, and the problem is in the operating system. To see if the printer driver is the problem, use the *Add Printer Wizard* to install the Generic/Text Only printer driver.

FIGURE 9.50   Managing the Print Spooler service

If you reload a printer driver, the old version of the printer driver must be removed first. Some manufacturers have specific instructions for removing their drivers. Always follow their directions. Most of them say to do something similar to the following: Right-click the specific printer icon and click the *Delete* option. Click the *Yes* button when prompted if all the associated printer files are to be deleted. To reinstall the printer, use the *Add Printer Wizard*.

The print queue sometimes causes problems. A single document may be in the queue but not print for some reason, causing other print jobs added later to fail to print. Always check the print queue to see if there are **multiple failed print jobs**. Multiple failed print jobs indicate a problem with the printer such as a paper jam or lack of paper, being out of ink/toner, and so on. Check the printer's front panel to see if it indicates any errors.

After a problem is rectified, the print queue might need to be cleared. Depending on what rights the user has, sometimes a technician must clear the print queue. The following methods can be used:

> Open the *Devices and Printers* (Windows 7)/*Printers* (Windows 8)/*Printers & Scanners* (Windows 10) Control Panel. Right-click the printer icon > *Open*. Right-click the first document (the one that is causing the problem) > *Cancel*. To cancel all print jobs, select *Cancel All Documents* from the *Printer* menu option.

> If the print job has already gone to the printer and is no longer stored on the hard drive, you may not be able to use the first method. In this case, use the *Printer* menu or *Cancel* function on the printer to cancel the print job.

> Turn the printer off and back on again.

Note that if you get an access denied message, it means you must be logged on as an administrator to control the print queue. If a user gets the **access denied** message, then the user account must be added to the printer. Access the printer within the *Devices and Printers* Control Panel > right-click the printer > *Printer Properties* > *Security* tab > add the user account.

You can use the Windows Event Viewer to both set up and check the **print log**. Access the *Administrative Tools* Control Panel > *Event Viewer* > expand *Applications and Services* > expand *Microsoft* > expand *Windows* > expand *Print Service* > right-click on *Operational* > *Enable Log*. Return to this same area to view information related to printing problems.

If you are having trouble sharing a printer, ensure that Windows Firewall is not blocking printer sharing. Take these steps if Windows Firewall is being used (and for another vendor's firewall, follow directions from the vendor):

Step 1. Open the *Windows Firewall* Control Panel.

Step 2. In Windows 7, select the *Allow a Program or Feature Through Windows Firewall* link. On Windows 8/10, select the *Allow an App or a Feature Through Windows Firewall* link.

Step 3. Locate and check (enable) the *File and Printer Sharing* option. Click *OK*.

TECH TIP

Network printers

If a printer can be seen on the network but cannot be printed to, verify that the printer is on and shows no error conditions on the front panel or LEDs. Print a test page using the front panel menu, if possible. Verify that the network printer has a static IP address and is not configured for DHCP. These concepts are covered in Chapter 13.

Impact Printer Troubleshooting

When technicians state that a print head is not firing, this means that one or more of the print wires are not coming out of the print head to impact the ribbon. A print head that is not firing is evidenced by one or more white lines appearing where the printed dots should be. On a printed page, the white line appears horizontally in the middle of a single printed line. The most likely problem is the print head. However, the problem could be a bad driver transistor on the main circuit board or a loose print head cable. However, because the print head is a mechanical part, it is the most suspect.

If the print is light and then dark, the printer ribbon may not be advancing properly. One of the shafts that insert into each end of the ribbon may not be turning, or the set of gears under the shaft may not mesh properly. Also, there is a motor that handles ribbon movement, and it may need to be replaced. A faulty ribbon can also cause the carriage to seize up. Remove the ribbon and power up the printer. If the carriage moves when the ribbon is removed, but it will not move when the ribbon is installed, replace the ribbon. Some printers have belts that move the print head across the page. A worn, loose, or slipping belt can cause erratic printing.

> **TECH TIP**
>
> **How to fix light printing**
>
> Light printing can be caused by several issues. Adjust the print head gap to place the print head closer to the ribbon or replace the ribbon. Also, the platen could be misaligned with the bottom paper-feed rollers.

If the printer prints continuously on the same line, be sure the setting for tractor-fed paper or friction-fed paper is correct. Or, the motor that controls paper movement may need to be replaced. If the printer moves the paper up a small bit after printing, the model may have the Auto Tear Off feature enabled. The Auto Tear Off feature is used with the perforated forms that are needed in many businesses. See the printer's documentation to disable this feature.

Inkjet Printer Troubleshooting

Most inkjet printer troubleshooting involves the print head. Inkjet printers frequently have a built-in print head cleaning routine. Access the routine through the printer's buttons or through software. Most manufacturers recommend cleaning the inkjet cartridge only when there is a problem, such as lines or dots missing from the printed output. Otherwise, cleaning the inkjet cartridge with this method wastes ink and shortens the life span of the print cartridge.

Usually, inkjet manufacturers include an alignment program to align the dots more precisely. Use the alignment program when vertical lines or characters do not align properly. If the colors do not appear correctly (for example, the page **prints in the wrong color**), check ink levels and run the printer manufacturer–provided color calibration routine. Refer to the printer's documentation for troubleshooting programs, such as the print head cleaning, calibration, and alignment routines.

> **TECH TIP**
>
> **Troubleshooting color**
>
> If a page does not print in color, check the printer properties to see if the grayscale option is selected.

Laser Printer Troubleshooting

Laser printers have more mechanical and electronic circuitry than the other printer types, which means more things can go wrong. The following list contains some common symptoms and possible solutions:

> If black **streaks** appear on the paper, the problem may be the drum, toner cartridge, fusing assembly, or paper. If the drum cannot hold a charge in a particular place, it can't attract toner to that area, and the drum might have to be replaced. The drum can be part of the toner cartridge or might be a separate unit. The toner cartridge is the easiest thing to replace to see if the streaks stop. Some cartridges have a sliding plastic strip that can be used to remove excess toner from the opening. A dirty or damaged fusing assembly can also cause black streaks. Allow the printer to cool and check the fuser cleaning pad for toner particles and then use a small screwdriver to scrape off excess particles. Finally, the paper might have a static charge, especially on low-humidity days, so fan the paper before re-inserting it.

> If output appears darker in some spots than others, remove the toner cartridge. Gently rock the toner cartridge back and forth to redistribute the toner. If this does not fix the problem, turn down the toner density by using the *Devices and Printers* Control Panel or software provided by the printer manufacturer. Also, the paper could be too smooth.

> If printing appears light, adjust the darkness setting on the printer or through the printer's operating system settings. The toner cartridge could be low. Damp paper could also cause this symptom. Use fresh paper of the proper weight and finish. If the print appears consistently dark, adjust the darkness setting.

> If a horizontal line appears periodically throughout the printout, the problem is one of the rollers. Check all the rollers to see if one is dirty or gouged and needs to be replaced. The rollers in a laser printer are not all the same size; the distance between the lines is the circumference of the roller. This allows you to easily tell which rollers are definitely not the problem and which ones are likely candidates.

> When white **vertical lines** appear, the corona wires may have paper bits or something else stuck on them. Or something might be caught in the developer unit (located in the cartridge). Replace the cartridge to see if this is the problem.

> If the back side of the printed page is smudged, the fuser could be faulty, needs adjusting, the wrong type of paper could be being used, or the toner might be leaking. Some printers allow temperature adjustments. Increase the temperature if the image smears; decrease the temperature if the paper curls or burn marks appear.

Many laser printer problems involve the toner cartridge, which is a good thing because the cartridge is a part that people normally have on hand. Various symptoms can occur because of the toner cartridge, including **ghost images**, smearing, **horizontal streaking**, **vertical streaking**, faded printing, one vertical black line, one horizontal black line, a white streak on one side, and a wavy image. One of the easiest things to do is to remove the toner cartridge, hold the cartridge in front of you with both hands, and rock the cartridge away from you and then back toward you. Reinsert the cartridge into the printer and test it.

Sometimes, the primary corona wire or the conditioning roller inside the toner cartridge needs to be cleaned. Clean the corona wires with the provided brush or with a cotton swab. Dampen the cotton swab with alcohol, if necessary. Clean the conditioning roller with a lint-free cloth and dampen the cloth with alcohol, if necessary.

When **toner is not fused** to the paper, you need to determine whether a problem is in the fuser assembly or elsewhere in the printer. Send any output to the printer. When the printer is through with the writing stage and before the toner fuses to the paper, open the laser printer cover and remove the paper. If the paper is error free, the problem is most likely in the transfer corona/roller or fusing assembly.

Experience is the best teacher when it comes to printers. If you work on a couple impact models, a couple inkjet printers, and a couple laser printer models, you will see the majority of problems. Printers have very few circuit boards to replace. Normally, the problems are in the moving parts or are software related.

SOFT SKILLS: WORK ETHICS

Ethics is a set of morals by which you live or work. Employers want employees to possess high ethical standards. This means they want people who are honest, trustworthy, and dependable. IT technicians are exposed to many personal things—passwords, private data, and visited Internet sites, just to name a few. Employers do not want to worry about technicians taking things that belong to others, looking at data that does not relate to the computer problem at hand (such as the information that might be on the desk shown in Figure 9.51 or printed material in the printer tray), or taking/giving away things from the office.

FIGURE 9.51   Work ethics: Do not look at or take information when working in an office

The best guideline in terms of ethics is to always be professional. For example, if you are in a situation where someone asks you to share another person's password, ask yourself whether divulging the information is professional. When opening a customer's documents and reading them, ask yourself whether you are being professional. If the answer is no, stop reading. If you are in a customer's office and accidentally see the person's password taped to a keyboard, let the person know that you have seen it, suggest that passwords should not be kept in a conspicuous place, and recommend that the password be changed right away. One of the biggest assets an IT professional can have is his or her reputation. Being ethical at work goes a long way in establishing a good reputation.

Finally, every IT person can probably remember at least one instance in which he or she was asked to do something unethical—charge for more time than was actually spent on a job, provide access to a room or an area where access is normally restricted, or grant privileges that others at the same level do not have. When put in such a situation, there are a few options: (1) Politely refuse, (2) adamantly refuse, or (3) report the person to a supervisor. Recommending what to do is difficult, but for most offenses, politely refusing is the best course of action and is the most professional. If a request is against corporate policy or could hurt others in the company, you need to report it to a company manager or security. Your own boss may be the best person to inform.

Chapter Summary

> Five types of printers commonly seen in businesses are impact, inkjet, laser, thermal, and 3D printers. Laser and inkjet printers do high-quality printing. A laser printer's supplies cost more than other printers' supplies, but laser printers last longer, and the cost per page is lower than for other types of printers.

> Printers can be shared using the operating system and a computer connected to a network. A printer can also have its own wired or wireless networking connectivity. With wired networking, the printer has a direct connection to the network. Wireless networking includes 802.11 and Bluetooth technologies. A hardware print server can be attached to a printer to allow sharing, too.

> Impact printers use print wires to impact a ribbon. Inkjet printers use pressure or heat to squirt ink dots onto paper.

> A laser printer works like a copying machine to produce output.

> The steps in printing from a laser printer include processing the data, charging, exposing, developing, transferring, fusing, and cleaning.

> Impact printers can use normal-sized paper and fan-folded paper with pin holes that are fed by a tractor. Laser printers can have extra drawers for paper. A duplexing assembly option can be attached to allow a printer to print on both sides of the paper without human intervention. Impact printers use special heat-sensitive paper.

> Print drivers must match the operating system version.

> A printer uses a print spooler or hard drive space that keeps data flowing to the printer in large print jobs. The print spooler can be stopped and started using the Services window (services.msc).

> If a printer doesn't work, check the printer display, check the computer for any messages, and ensure that the correct printer was chosen.

> A laser printer maintenance kit includes parts from a manufacturer that need to be changed after the printer has been used for a given number of hours. The contents of such a kit are vendor specific. The maintenance counter must be reset after a maintenance kit has been applied.

> Printers can be networked with wired or wireless networking or they can connect to a print server, be registered in the cloud, or be shared through the printer to which they attach.

> Virtual printing can be accomplished through the print to file, print to PDF, print to XPS, and print to image options.

> Common printer problems include streaks, light print, ghost images, toner not fusing to the paper, paper path issues, problems with connectivity to the printer, print driver problems, security settings, and error codes that appear on the printer display.

> A computer technician needs to behave ethically around customers and peers.

A+ CERTIFICATION EXAM TIPS

✓ Know how impact, inkjet, laser, thermal, and 3D printers work.

✓ Know the parts of a laser printer: imaging drum, fuser assembly, transfer belt, transfer roller, pickup rollers, separate pads, and duplexing assembly. Some printers allow adjustments to the fuser assembly. The temperature should be hotter if the image smears and turned down if the paper curls or has burn marks.

✓ Know the laser imaging process: processing, charging, exposing, developing, transferring, fusing, and cleaning.

✓ Know the parts of an inkjet printer: ink cartridge, print head, roller, feeder, duplexing assembly, carriage, and belt.

✓ Know the parts of a thermal printer: feed assembly, heating element, and special thermal paper.

✓ Know the parts of an impact printer: print head, ribbon, tractor feeder, and impact paper.

✓ Know the virtual printing types: print to file, print to PDF, print to XPS, and print to image.

✓ Know the appropriate laser printer maintenance techniques, including replacing toner, applying a maintenance kit, calibrating, and cleaning.

✓ Know the appropriate thermal printer maintenance techniques, including replacing paper, cleaning the heating element, and removing debris.

✓ Know the appropriate impact printer maintenance techniques, including replacing the ribbon, replacing the print head, and replacing paper.

✓ Know the appropriate inkjet printer maintenance techniques, including cleaning the heads, replacing cartridges, calibration, and clearing jams.

✓ Be able to describe the steps needed to install/replace the plastic filament in a 3D printer.

✓ Be able to configure printer options, including duplex, collate, orientation, and quality settings.

✓ Know how to review and control the print driver and print spooler.

✓ Know how to network a printer by using a print server, printer sharing, cloud printing, Bonjour, and AirPrint

✓ Be aware of data privacy issues, including user authentication that may be required, hard drive caching, and access to corporate/private information that may be onscreen or printed.

✓ Review all the troubleshooting sections (especially the key term items) before taking the exam.

Key Terms

Review Questions

1. What method does a technician *normally* use to print a test page to prove that connectivity exists between a computer and a printer and to prove that the driver is working properly?

   a. Use a self-test button on the printer.

   b. Use Notepad and print.

   c. Use at least two applications and print.

   d. Use the *Print Test Page* button from the *General* tab of the printer Properties window.

2. Which type of printer would a glass blower who sells art at trade shows most likely use to print receipts? [impact | inkjet | thermal | laser]

3. Which program is used to restart the print spooler in Windows?

   [Device Manager | Services | System Information | DirectX]

4. A Samsung laser printer is showing an error message on the screen that says that the paper is out, but the user shows you that there is plenty of paper in the bin. What should you do?

   a. Turn the printer off and back on again.

   b. Check the paper sensor for debris or dust.

   c. Use the reset sensor to reset the printer paper counter.

   d. Use the Print Test Page button in Windows to verify connectivity.

5. Which type of printer contains a fuser assembly?

   [impact | inkjet | laser | thermal]

6. [T | F] Use compressed air with a plastic nozzle to remove toner from a laser printer.

7. For what do you use a printer-duplexing assembly?

   a. two-sided printing

   b. multiple paper trays

   c. wired and wireless network connectivity

   d. rasterization

8. Which component causes ghost images on laser printer output?

   [drum | fusing assembly | LED array/laser | pickup rollers | paper sensor]

9. A college president's administrative assistant calls to report that some pages of a 500-page board of trustees document are printing only half a page. What is the problem and what can the technician recommend to do to get the document printed?

   a. The print cartridge is defective. Replace the cartridge and reprint.

   b. The print cartridge has toner that is not evenly distributed. Remove the cartridge, gently shake it back and forth, reinstall the cartridge, and reprint.

   c. The printer does not have enough memory. Ask the user to print a smaller number of pages at a time.

   d. The printer mainboard has issues. Use compressed air to remove dust and debris. Then try to reprint the pages. Order a replacement mainboard and use another printer if the printing fails again.

10. One of the technicians in your shop frequently swaps parts that do not fix the problem. The parts taken out of customer machines are taken to build private customer computers. This is an example of poor _____. [communication skills | work ethics | relations | troubleshooting skills]

11. Which type of printer maintenance commonly requires resetting a maintenance counter?
    [impact | thermal | laser | inkjet]

12. Which printer option allows multiple copies of a document to be printed in page 1, 2, 3 order instead of all the page 1s to be printed, then all the page 2s, and then all the page 3s?
    [fusing | collating | duplexing | conditioning]

13. A networked printer is visible through the network, but no one can print to it. What is the first thing the technician should check?

    a. print spooler setting

    b. printer IP address

    c. errors or indicators on the printer

    d. cabling

14. A laser printer outputs streaks on the paper. What is the issue?
    [drum | roller | ink cartridge | laser]

15. An inkjet printer's output appears to have missing elements. What is the first thing a technician should try if the ink cartridge appears to be full?

    _____

16. A printer menu displays the following message, "Filament Loading." Which type of printer is being used?

    [3D | impact | inkjet | laser]

17. What is the purpose of the belt in an inkjet printer?

    a. It limits the amount of paper fed through the printer to one page.

    b. It controls the amount of ink allowed onto the paper.

    c. It moves the paper through the paper path.

    d. It moves the carriage from one side to the other.

18. What happens if a heating element fails on a thermal printer?

    a. missing printed output

    b. paper doesn't feed through

    c. incorrect colors output

    d. garbled output

19. How is laser printer calibration commonly performed?

    a. with a multimeter

    b. with a special tool that is part of the maintenance kit

    c. through the printer menu

    d. with calipers

20. Which option is relevant to virtual printing?
    [duplexing | PDF | collating | cloud]

Exercises

Exercise 9.1 Research a Local Printer

Objective: To use the Internet or a magazine to research information about a printer

Parts: A computer with Internet access

Notes: A printer is not required to be attached to the computer for this exercise to be executed.

Procedure: Complete the following procedure and answer the accompanying questions.

A business user is interested in purchasing two printers. Details for each printer are as follows:

Printer A: A printer to be shared by all employees through the wired Ethernet network. Output should be high-quality black-and-white, grayscale, or color. The printer will not be used for huge print jobs but to print a proposal for a client or a few handouts for a small number of participants in a presentation. Speed is not an issue.

Printer B: A printer model that will be standard for those who need a printer attached to their workstations. The printer should be able to support wired connectivity to the Ethernet LAN or IEEE 802.11 wireless connectivity. The printer might be shared with computers that do not have a local printer attached. The printer should support quality black-and-white, grayscale, or color. The printer will not be used for a large number of copies. Speed is not an issue. A scanner needs to be part of the printer, too. The cost of supplies is a concern.

1. Using the Internet, provide the business user with three suggestions for Printer **A.** List the model number and at least five facts related to the criteri**a.** Find three price quotes for each suggested model and the name of the company for each one.

_____

_____

_____

_____

_____

_____

_____

2. Using the Internet, provide the business user with three suggestions for Printer B. List the model number and at least five facts related to the criteria. Find three price quotes for each suggested model and the name of the company for each one.

_____

_____

_____

_____

_____

_____

_____

Exercise 9.2 Printer Driver Research

Objective:	To use the Internet to research information about three printer drivers
Parts:	A computer with Internet access
Notes:	A printer is not required to be attached to the computer for this exercise to be executed.
Procedure:	Complete the following procedure and answer the accompanying questions.

Locate the latest driver for each of the following printers and operating systems. Write the driver version in the third column.

Printer model	Operating system	Latest print driver version
HP OfficeJet 3830 All-in-One	Windows 10 (64-bit)	
Lexmark MC2535adwe color laser	Windows 7 (64-bit)	
Okidata ML1190 dot matrix	Windows 8.1 (64-bit)	

Activities

Internet Discovery

Objective:	To obtain specific information on the Internet regarding a computer or its associated parts
Parts:	Computer with access to the Internet
Questions:	Use the Internet to answer the following questions.

1. A customer has a broken USB inkjet printer that would cost more to repair than to replace. The customer is considering an Epson Expression XP-440 all-in-one printer as a replacement. The customer would also like to have wireless connectivity, individual color cartridges, and the ability to print from a camera memory card. Will this printer meet the customer's needs? Explain your answer and write the URL where the information was found.

    _____

    _____

2. What is the latest print driver version for a Canon PIXMA MG3120 printer if the customer has 64-bit Windows 10 installed? Note that you just want to reload the printer driver. Write the version number and the URL where you found the information.

    _____

3. A customer has a Lexmark E460 laser printer connected to a computer that runs 32-bit Windows 7. Does Lexmark provide a Windows 7–capable printer driver for this printer? Write the answer and the URL where you found the solution.

    _____

4. How do you reset the HP LaserJet P2035 to factory default settings? Write the answer and list the URL where you found the answer.

    _____

    _____

5. You had to replace the drum on a Brother HL-L8250CDN color laser printer. What process is used to reset the drum unit counter?

    _____

    _____

Soft Skills

Objective: To enhance and fine-tune a technician's ability to listen, communicate in both written and oral forms, and support people who use computers in a professional manner

Activities:

1.   The class is divided into seven groups. Each group is assigned a laser printing process. The group has 20 minutes to research the process. At the end of 20 minutes, each team explains its process to the rest of the class.

2.   Pretend you have a job as a computer technician. You just solved a printer problem. Using good written communication skills, document the problem as well as the solution in a professional format. Exchange your problem/solution with a classmate and critique each other's writings. Based on suggestions and your own background, refine your documentation. Share your documentation with the rest of the class.

Critical Thinking Skills

Objective: To analyze and evaluate information as well as apply learned information to new or different situations

Activities:

1.   Two networked PCs and a printer are needed for this activity. Connect a printer to a **PC.** Install the printer, configure the default settings to something different from the current settings, share the printer, and then print from another PC that connects to the same network.

2.   Interview a technician regarding a printing problem. List the steps the technician took and make notes about how he or she might have done the steps differently, based on what you have learned. Share the experience with the class.

10 Mobile Devices

In this chapter you will learn:

> About the operating systems mobile devices use

> How to configure mobile devices

> How to back up and secure mobile devices

> How to troubleshoot mobile devices

> The importance of appearance in the IT field

CompTIA Exam Objectives:

What CompTIA A+ exam objectives are covered in this chapter?

✓ 1001-1.1 Given a scenario, install and configure laptop hardware and components.

✓ 1001-1.2 Given a scenario, install components within the display of a laptop.

✓ 1001-1.3 Given a scenario, use appropriate laptop features.

✓ 1001-1.4 Compare and contrast characteristics of various types of other mobile devices.

✓ 1001-1.5 Given a scenario, connect and configure accessories and ports of other mobile devices.

✓ 1001-1.6 Given a scenario, configure basic mobile device network connectivity and application support.

✓ 1001-1.7 Given a scenario, use methods to perform mobile device synchronization.

✓ 1001-2.4 Compare and contrast wireless networking protocols.

✓ 1001-2.7 Compare and contrast Internet connection types, network types, and their features.

✓ 1001-2.8 Given a scenario, use appropriate networking tools.

✓ 1001-3.1 Explain basic cable types, features, and their purposes.

✓ 1001-3.2 Identify common connector types.

✓ 1001-3.3 Given a scenario, install RAM types.

✓ 1001-3.4 Given a scenario, select, install and configure storage devices.

✓ 1001-3.6 Explain the purposes and uses of various peripheral types.

✓ 1001-3.9 Given a scenario, install and configure common devices.

✓ 1001-5.5 Given a scenario, troubleshoot common mobile device issues while adhering to the appropriate procedures.

✓ 1001-5.7 Given a scenario, troubleshoot common wired and wireless network problems.

✓ 1002-1.1 Compare and contrast operating system types and their purposes.

✓ 1002-2.8 Given a scenario, implement methods for securing mobile devices.

✓ 1002-3.4 Given a scenario, troubleshoot mobile OS and application issues.

✓ 1002-3.5 Given a scenario, troubleshoot mobile OS and application security issues.

Mobile Device Overview

Mobile devices are an integrated part of today's society. **Wearable devices** such as smart watches, fitness monitors, glasses, and headsets allow us to take our technology wherever we go. New laptops, Android phones, Apple iPhones and iPads, and other electronics are continuously being introduced. Many mobile devices are all-in-one units. Because some mobile devices have no keyboard, much of the device is devoted to being a touchpad. Mobile devices are designed to be quick, light, durable, and portable (see Figure 10.1) and for some, are often a user's second computer: People commonly use the smaller mobile devices while on the go and leave their desktops and laptops at home. Table 10.1 lists characteristics of various mobile devices.

FIGURE 10.1   Mobile devices

TABLE 10.1   Mobile devices

Device	Description
Tablet	A tablet is a mobile device that has a touchscreen, camera(s), microphone, and possibly one or more ports, such as sound, USB, miniDisplayPort, or miniThunderbolt. Tablets connect to the Internet; take, send, receive, and store pictures and video; and are often a good choice for people who travel, people with small hands, and young adults. See Figure 10.2.
GPS	The Global Positioning System (GPS) is a series of satellites that provide location, movement, and time information to other devices. A device that supports GPS can be a standalone unit, software that communicates with satellites, or an app on a mobile device. Figure 10.3 shows a self-driving car that is using GPS.
Smartphone	A smartphone has the capability to make calls and run apps, play music, track movement using GPS, connect to wireless networks, connect wirelessly to other devices, connect to the Internet through the phone network or wireless network (see Figure 10.4), and take high-resolution pictures and videos. Two popular smartphone operating systems are Android and Apple iOS. Microsoft also has the Windows Mobile operating system; Windows 10 Mobile will not get bug or security fixes after December 2019.

Device	Description
Phablet	A phablet, which is a cross between a smartphone and a tablet, tends to have a larger screen than a smartphone. Phablets are designed for taking notes and viewing documents more easily. May include a stylus, as shown in Figure 10.5.
E-reader	Also known as an e-book reader, an e-reader has an LCD screen designed for reading and storing digital books (see Figure 10.6), magazines, and other online materials. Battery life is extended; some e-readers can adapt to the ambient light to enable users to more easily read the text and use e-ink technology to provide contrast and easy viewing angles.
Smart camera	A smart camera has one or more extra capabilities beyond what a digital camera has and is used for such things as facial recognition, measuring, inspection for quality assurance, surveillance, and robot guidance. A smart camera may include a mobile operating system, have Internet access, and have support for wired and wireless networking. To operate an integrated camera on an Apple iOS or Android device, use the Camera option from the home page. Use the Photos application (iOS) or Gallery application (Android) to see saved images. Figure 10.7 shows a smart camera attached to a drone.

FIGURE 10.2 Tablet

FIGURE 10.3 GPS

FIGURE 10.4   Smartphone

FIGURE 10.5   Phablet

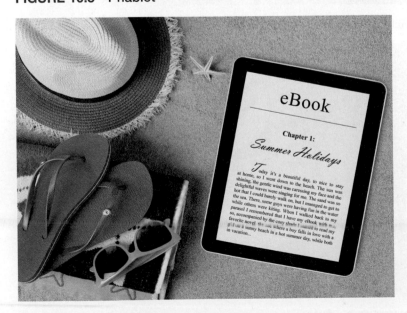

FIGURE 10.6   E-reader

FIGURE 10.7 Smart camera

Mobile Operating System Basics and Features

A mobile device, like any other computer, needs an operating system (OS). The mobile operating system can be proprietary to a particular vendor, but four common mobile operating systems are Android, iOS, Windows, and Chrome. **Android** is an open source OS that is based on the Linux kernel and used mainly on phones and tablets but is also available on laptops and PCs. **Open source** operating systems allow vendors to use the core source code and enable them to customize the operating system. Google, Inc. purchased Android in 2005, and it continues to be one of the most popular mobile operating systems in the world.

Apple's **iOS** is used only on Apple devices. This is an example of a **closed source operating system** or **vendor-specific operating system**. This type of operating system is not allowed to be modified or distributed by anyone other than those designated by the developer (in the case of iOS, Apple Inc.).

Microsoft has several closed source Windows Mobile operating systems that are used on mobile devices. Note that some mobile devices support the normal Windows desktop operating system versions. The following operating systems are specifically related to mobile devices and are not the full version of Windows:

> *Windows Phone*—An older family of operating systems designed for smartphones.
> *Windows 10 Mobile*—Successor to Windows Phone, which integrates some features common to Windows desktop and mobile devices into smartphones and small tablets.
> *Windows RT*—An operating system based on the reduced instruction set computing (RISC) architecture, which allows for thinner, lighter, cooler mobile devices and can run longer on a battery charge. Only executes software digitally signed by Microsoft and Microsoft Store apps.

Many are familiar with Chrome as a browser option, but **Chrome** is also an operating system that was developed by Google as an open source project (called the Chromium OS project). Developers can use or modify the code developed from this group, but the Chrome OS is supported by Google and Google partners. Laptops that use Chrome OS, known as Chromebooks, are very popular in schools and commonly use cloud-based apps.

Mobile Storage

Mobile devices need a place to store data, and mobile storage uses the same technology as some PC storage, but of course, the storage media is smaller. Mobile devices do have RAM. Sometimes this RAM is not upgradable in mobile devices such as tablets and smartphones. However, mobile devices commonly use flash memory. **Flash memory** is a type of nonvolatile, solid-state memory that holds data even when the computer power is off. Smartphones, tablets, and other mobile devices use flash memory to store the operating system, apps, and data/video. Flash memory for mobile devices includes various types of Secure Digital (**SD**) cards: SD, **miniSD**, **microSD**, SDHC, miniSDHC, microSDHC, SDXC, microSDXC, Extreme Digital (**xD**), and probably more since this book has been published. On some phones, the micro memory chip is found by removing the back cover and the battery.

Another flash technology used with mobile devices is CompactFlash. **CompactFlash** (CF) has two main standards: CompactFlash and CF+. CompactFlash is a small, 50-pin removable storage device that allows speeds up to 133 MB/s. CF cards can store 512 GB or more. The CF+ standard allows increased functionality with cards available for Ethernet, fax/modem/wireless, and barcode scanners.

CF cards can be inserted directly into many devices, such as cameras, smartphones, network devices, and tablet PCs. A CF card uses flash memory, which does not require a battery to keep the data saved to it. A CF card can also be installed into a computer with a CF card reader. The CF technology is also used in solid-state drives. Figure 10.8 shows a photo of three flash memory cards (with the CF card on the left and two types of SD cards on the right).

FIGURE 10.8 Flash storage

Flash memory cards, or **storage cards**, are found in mobile devices and laptops, as well as in desktop computers. A device may have an SD card slot built in, as in the case of the laptop shown in Figure 10.9. If a device has an SD tray that pulls out, insert the flash card into the tray (with the contacts facing down), and then push the tray into the device. Sometimes in order to insert a microSD card into a laptop or tablet, an adapter may have to be purchased so that the microSD card can be used. Figure 10.10 shows how the microSD card inserts into an adapter. That adapter must match the slot size (normally SD) of the mobile device.

Flash media is commonly installed in Apple and Android products. When you install flash media into an Android tablet or phone, you can use the *Settings > Storage* option to view the internal memory capacity and any additional memory storage. For an iOS-based device, go to *Settings > General* to see the amount of memory installed.

Some people like to use a **smart card reader** (also known as a multi-card reader, media card reader, or flash/flash memory card reader) to quickly and easily transfer pictures, data, movies, and so on to a PC. Some card readers accept 75 different types of media storage. A card reader attaches to a USB port or is integrated into a laptop. Insert the flash media into an appropriate slot. Look at Figure 10.11 to see some of the media slots. Once inserted, the OS will assign a drive letter.

FIGURE 10.9   Laptop SD card slot

FIGURE 10.10   Flash media adapter

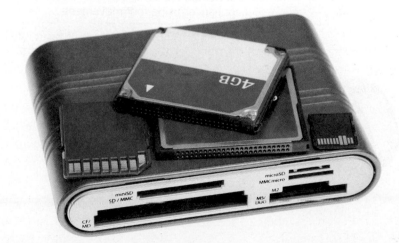

FIGURE 10.11   Smart card reader

Don't format CF cards with Windows

If Windows is used to format a CF card, it will place a different file system on the card. Windows can be used to read files from the card or place files on the card, but best practice is to use the formatting option on the device instead of using Windows to format a CF card.

Mobile Technology Devices

Mobile technology includes some cool wearable items, such as watches, shoes, and even earrings. Table 10.2 lists some wearable technologies.

TABLE 10.2   Wearable technologies

Device	Description
Smart watch	Functions as a tiny computer strapped to your wrist (see Figure 10.12). Smart watches are expensive, and they are not capable of doing all that a tablet can do. Most smart watches will sync up with a smartphone and support app downloading. Usually a smart watch must be paired with a phone to make phone calls (and some require a nearby microphone). Some are or can be GPS-enabled so they can be used for tasks such as tracking fitness goals.
Fitness monitor	Detects movement (step counting), calculates distances (some have a GPS feature), counts calories, measures heart rate and pulse, and measures sleep. Some can automatically sync up with a smartphone to keep track of daily/weekly workout activities. Usually water and dust-resistant, with a common battery life of a week. Figure 10.13 shows how a smart watch, fitness monitor, and smartphone might all be able to share information.
Glasses	A wearable technology that has a tiny computer display visible to one eye; can take photos, make videos, and make calls; commonly has a processor, RAM, and storage. May be able to support 3D. See Figure 10.14.
Smart shoes	Allows control of wireless devices such as smartphones and appliances using foot movements.
Earring	Wearable technology that tracks heart rate and calories burned.

FIGURE 10.12   Smart watches

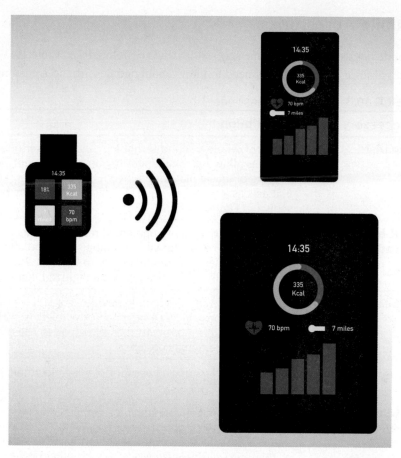

FIGURE 10.13   Fitness monitor

FIGURE 10.14   Wearable technology glasses

Mobile Accessories

Mobile devices also have some accessories that are unlike PCs. Table 10.3 outlines various mobile accessories a technician may need to know about and describe to a customer.

TABLE 10.3   Mobile accessories

Accessory	Description
Headset	Wired or wireless sound technology that fits over one or both ears. Some headsets allow for song control by head movement, voice control, and pausing of music play for an incoming call. A headset may support an app that acts as a trainer or track fitness. A headset may be for only one ear, as shown in Figure 10.15.
VR headset/AR headset	A virtual reality (VR) or augmented reality (AR) headset can be used in gaming and in educational or training settings to allow users to interact with a simulated environment (refer to Figure 1.25). VR replaces what you would normally see or hear. AR puts digitized items into reality.
Speaker	Speakers are built in to mobile devices; some devices have an audio port for external speakers. Can be wired or wireless (see Figure 10.16 for a wireless speaker). Apps exist that allow you to use other mobile devices in the area as additional speakers.
Game pad	Wired or wireless device used for playing electronic games, as shown in Figure 10.17.
Mobile docking station	Provides a stable environment for mobile computers while traveling, such as for a laptop in a police car or for military operations. Docking stations are also available to charge one or more mobile devices. Some docking stations also synchronize a device with other devices or applications while charging. Figure 10.18 shows a mobile docking station.
Extra **battery pack** or **battery charger**	All mobile devices operate on battery power and need to be charged. Portable battery chargers are available that are charged and then can be carried around to charge a mobile device without having to attach the mobile device to a wall outlet or PC. Figure 10.19 shows a portable charger.
Protective cover	Because mobile devices are easily dropped, they frequently have either a protective cover for the entire device or a protective cover for just the screen. Figure 10.20 shows the two concepts.
Waterproofing	Waterproofing protects mobile devices from liquids, but there are different levels of protection. A cover may be waterproof, a device itself might come in a waterproof model, or a waterproof option may be available for the entire device. Waterproof bags are available for mobile devices. There are also treatments that can protect electronics for accidental immersion.
Credit card reader	Can be wired or wireless. If wired, a credit card reader can be attached to a USB port on the laptop, and a driver can be installed, if necessary. For wireless credit card readers, see the "Mobile Device Wireless Connectivity" section, later in the chapter. Some readers allow printed receipts; others allow an email address to be input instead. Figure 10.21 shows a credit card reader.
Magnetic card reader	A device that reads encrypted data on small ID-sized cards. Used in government IDs, driver's licenses, some credit cards, and employee badges. Figure 10.22 shows a magnetic card reader.

FIGURE 10.15   Wireless headset

FIGURE 10.16   Wireless speaker

FIGURE 10.17   Game pad

FIGURE 10.18   Mobile docking station

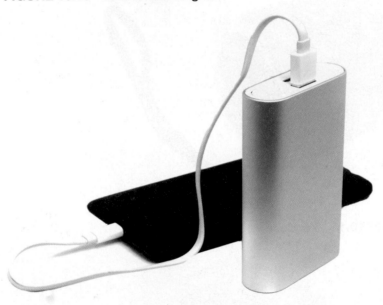

FIGURE 10.19   Portable charger

FIGURE 10.20   Mobile device screen protection

FIGURE 10.21   Mobile credit card reader

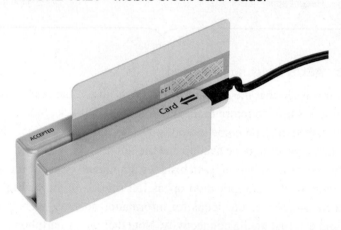

FIGURE 10.22   Magnetic card reader

Using Mobile Devices

A mobile operating system is different from other operating systems in that, instead of primarily using a mouse or keyboard to interact with the operating system, a finger, a stylus, spoken word, or multiple fingers are used. Figure 10.23 shows the home page of an ASUS tablet that uses Android as the operating system.

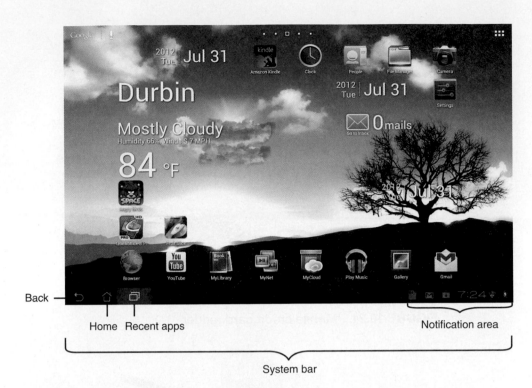

Back

Home   Recent apps

Notification area

System bar

FIGURE 10.23   ASUS tablet home screen

Notice in Figure 10.23 that the **system bar** extends across the bottom of the screen. The back button on the far left is used to return to the previous page. If the keyboard screen is open, the back button closes the keyboard. The home button is used to return to the main home page, but keep in mind that other home pages may be available to the left or right. The third icon from the left on the system bar is the recent apps button, which shows thumbnail views of recently used applications. If you touch a thumbnail, the application opens full screen. In the far-right corner is the mobile **notification area**, which contains icons for information such as the battery life, wireless signal strength, time, and external media connectivity. Note that on a smartphone (refer to Figure 10.24), the notification area is commonly available with a swipe from the top of the display.

Figure 10.25 shows an Apple iOS home screen. An Apple iPad or iPhone has a physical home button (not an icon to tap) beside or below the screen. Note that on an iPhone X, you swipe up from the bottom of the screen. On an iPad, pushing the home button removes the keyboard.

FIGURE 10.24 Android smartphone home screen

FIGURE 10.25   iOS home screen

Interacting with a Mobile Operating System

Configuration is commonly performed through a mobile device's *Settings* option, but before this chapter discusses configuration, you need to understand touch displays. Touching a display instructs the operating system to do something. Swiping is used to go to the next (or previous) page of an application or go to the next (or previous) photo. Multitouch technology makes a device capable of accepting multiple touches, such as when two fingers or a finger and a knuckle are used. 3D touch involves lightly tapping the touchscreen to open an application, tapping and holding for a second to perform a different function, or pressing down firmly on the same area to perform a third function. This technology is continually evolving.

Table 10.4 lists the terms commonly used for different means of interacting with a mobile OS. As you can see from this list of terms, some interaction requires multitouch, and not all screens support this feature. Figure 10.26 shows some multitouch techniques.

TABLE 10.4 Mobile operating system interaction terms

Term	Description	Function
Touch or tap	Press an icon or area.	Opens an application.
Double-tap	Press an icon or area twice in quick succession.	Enlarges an area of a screen or an item such as a picture.
Long touch or touch and hold	Press and hold on an icon or area.	Moves an icon from one home screen to a different home screen or to unlock a tablet.
Swipe or flick	Press and move to the left or right or up and down.	Moves from one home screen to another or opens the notification area on a smartphone.
Scroll	Press and move up or down.	Quickly goes through a list of files or pictures.
Pinch or pinch close	Using two fingers spread apart, bring the fingers closer together.	Zooms out from an object or area.
Spread or pinch open	Using two fingers close together, move the fingers apart.	Zooms in on an object or area, such as when you want to be able to see a closer view of a map or to enlarge words.

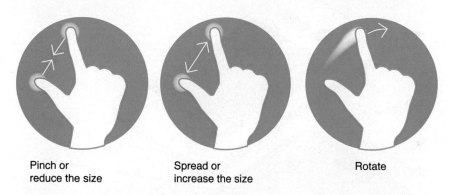

Pinch or reduce the size   Spread or increase the size   Rotate

FIGURE 10.26 Multitouch techniques

TECH TIP

What if a device goes to sleep?

Press the power button and optionally enter the appropriate pattern, PIN, or passcode. On an Android device, press and drag the lock icon to the unlock icon in the center of the display. Pressing the home button, swiping up from the bottom edge, or tapping the screen quickly also awakens an iPhone or iPad. Slide the *Slide to Unlock* bar to the right and enter the passcode if one is set.

Cell Phones

Most people are familiar with what a cell phone is, but technicians need to know a little more than the normal user about phones. Also, some companies issue phones to employees and have technicians support them. Learning about how phones are identified and when they should be updated is important.

IMEI and IMSI

International Mobile Equipment Identity (**IMEI**) is a unique number—much like a serial number—given to a particular cell phone or satellite phone. IMEI numbers are stored in a database or the

Equipment Identity Register (EIR). When phones are reported stolen, the database can be updated to mark the number as invalid. When buying a used phone, you might want to check the IMEI number against a mobile blacklist to ensure that the phone has not been lost or stolen.

A company may ask the IT department to track cell phones paid for by the company. The IMEI number is commonly found using one of the following methods:

> Look on the back of the phone.
> Look under the battery. Figure 10.27 shows two smartphones that have the back removed and the battery exposed.
> Use the phone's *Settings* > *General* or *Settings* > *About Phone* option.
> Dial ***#06#**.
> Look in the SIM card tray or under the SIM card for an engraved number.
> For an iPhone, plug the phone into a PC and then open *iTunes*. Select the phone from the *Device* menu > *Summary* tab.
> For an Android phone, use Google Dashboard (www.google.com/settings/dashboard) > expand *Android* > locate and then select the phone.
> Look on the original box the device came in.
> Use the network provider's website.

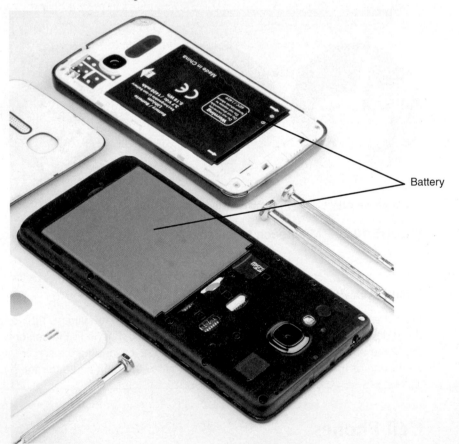

FIGURE 10.27   Cell phones with backs removed

The international mobile subscriber identity (**IMSI**) is a unique number that is stored in your smartphone's subscriber identification module (SIM) card. **SIM** cards are used in mobile phones, satellite phones, mobile devices, and laptops. A SIM card contains electronics that store information such as personal contacts, numbers, phone services on a Global System for Mobile communications (GSM) network, security authentication, and a security personal identification number (PIN). Figure 10.28 shows a SIM card.

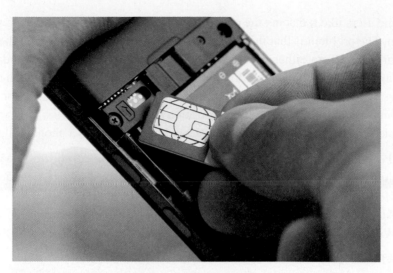

FIGURE 10.28 SIM card

The IMSI has three parts: the country code, the network code (which identifies the provider network), and a unique number. The IMSI is used when your phone's network connects to any other network or type of network, such as when you call someone who uses another phone network or call someone's home using your cell phone. This is important because roaming charges may be assessed on calls that go through or to another network.

PRI and PRL Updates

Each phone contains a specific product release instruction (**PRI**) configuration file. This file contains what frequency bands can be used and the default preferred roaming list (**PRL**) to use. The PRL is created by the cell network provider. The information is stored in your phone and used when connecting to a cell tower. The PRL includes service provider IDs and prioritized systems the device may access, such as companies with which a particular company has agreements so that the user may "roam" and still maintain the ability to make/receive calls. **PRI updates** and **PRL updates** are automatically pushed out to phones. Most companies have a specific code that can be dialed and used to update the PRL to the latest information.

> **TECH TIP**
>
> **Why update the PRL?**
>
> If a phone is frequently used outside the "home network" area, it is a good idea to manually update the PRL.

The PRL is what allows a phone to provide a roaming indicator, such as when the phone is in its home network (not roaming), when it is off the home network (roaming), or when roaming is disabled. Phone and data roaming can usually be enabled/disabled through a phone's *Settings* option.

Baseband Updates and Radio Firmware

Baseband is a type of signal used in telecommunications networks. A baseband signal is used to send updates to mobile devices such as mobile phones. Actually, the **baseband update** is applied to the phone's **radio firmware**, which is low-level software that manages items related to a phone's radio. The radio is what allows a phone to connect to a cellular network, send and receive data, and send and receive phone calls. Firmware is specific to a device and sometimes to a phone network provider.

Some users like replacing the operating system that comes with a phone with another operating system. The problem is that the phone vendor will send updates for both the operating system and the firmware. When either the operating system or the firmware gets updated without the other (such as when someone loads a different operating system), problems such as dropped calls, over-heating, reduced battery life, reduced time on a single battery charge, poor or no performance on a particular port, and high resource utilization can occur.

To determine the software version and baseband version on a phone, follow these generic steps:

> iPhone: *Settings > General > About > Check iPhone Firmware Version* in the *Version* section for the main operating system version and then *Check iPhone Baseband Version* in the *Modem Firmware* section for the radio firmware version.
> Android: *Settings > About/About Device > Software Information*.
> Windows: From *Start*, swipe left to access the *App List > Settings > About > More Info*.

See Figure 10.29 for a screenshot from an Android phone.

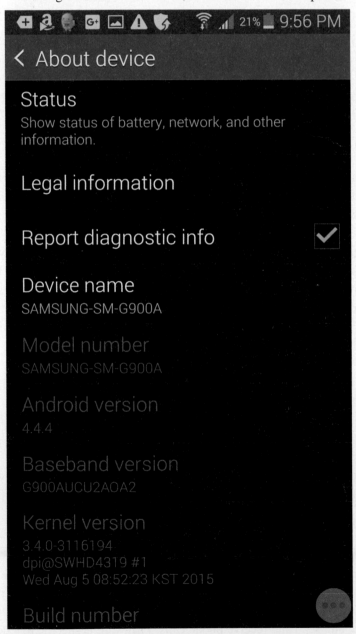

FIGURE 10.29 Cell phone operating system/radio firmware versions

Mobile Apps

Applications, commonly called *apps*, for mobile devices come with a device, can be downloaded free of charge, or can be purchased through the App Store (Apple iOS devices), Google Play (Android devices), or Store (Windows devices). New apps are being developed constantly, and applications that might not be of much use with a desktop computer are very handy on mobile devices. Table 10.5 lists common mobile apps.

TABLE 10.5   Common mobile apps

Android app	iOS app	Windows app
Gmail	Mail	Mail
Google Maps	Maps	Maps
Gallery/Photos	Photos	Photos
MyLibrary	iBooks	Reader
Chrome	Safari	Edge
Play Music	iTunes	Music
Clock	Calendar	Calendar
Play Store	App Store	Microsoft Store

Common Apps and Features

Apps on mobile devices have individual settings that users might need help with. For example, some people hate the clicking noise a camera makes when taking a picture. This can be disabled within the app. Another common one is disabling sound on the app (not the phone) for online games. Always check the settings of the particular app for changes possible within just that app. Personal information on the phone can also be shared to the app developer, including stored phone numbers, email addresses, text messages, and phone call logs. In both Android and iOS apps, use the *Settings* menu and selecting either *Permissions* or *Privacy* to remove unnecessary permissions.

One commonly used feature is GPS. With GPS, satellites send location information to a receiver on a mobile device. Most mobile devices have GPS capability. Mobile apps provide directions to get to a store or where another person is located, and they show how far you have walked.

Some people disable the GPS capability until they want to use it because of geotracking. **Geotracking** involves tracking the location and movement of a mobile device. Social media and other applications, known as **locator apps**, rely on such data to "publish" your current location or the locations of friends you have selected. Vendors have pay plans that include the ability to track family members. Companies use geotracking to locate lost and stolen mobile devices. Note that some devices also use a geotagging feature; for example, a camera app may use geotagging to include with a photo information such as where the photo was taken. It is possible to disable the geotagging feature, and may users do so for privacy reasons (see Figure 10.30).

Gaming on smartphones and tablets has been enhanced through the use of accelerometers and gyroscopes. An **accelerometer** detects the orientation of the device and adapts what is shown on the screen based on that orientation. This is how you can hold a tablet in portrait mode and then move it to a horizontal position to see a better view in landscape mode. It is also used by some manufacturers to detect that a laptop is falling so that the hard drive heads can be parked to prevent data loss and hard drive damage. A **gyroscope** measures and maintains orientation.

Because a mobile device screen is used to interact with the operating system, screen calibration may need to be performed. Android users use the *Settings* app. Windows users use *Settings > Calibrate the Screen for Pen and Touch Input > Calibrate*. You can also download an app to perform screen calibration tasks, such as the following:

> Color calibration
> Sensitivity
> One-hand configuration
> Motion/gestures configuration

FIGURE 10.30 Geotracking

Table 10.6 explains some mobile operating system features.

TABLE 10.6   Mobile operating system features

Feature	Description
Internet calling	Use an app such as Skype, Google Hangouts, or WhatsApp to call another person.
WiFi calling	Make a call using a WiFi connection rather than the cell phone network; beneficial when the phone network has a weak signal or to avoid using cell phone network minutes or roaming. Some vendors offer this as a built-in service and allow you to use your existing phone contacts.
Virtual assistant	Use voice commands to obtain information such as directions or current sports scores and to dictate emails or texts; examples include Apple's Siri, Microsoft's Cortana, Google Now, and SVoice.
Emergency notification	Obtain wireless emergency alerts (WEA); a U.S. method for propagating emergency alerts such as announcements from the National Weather Service, presidential messages, and emergency operation centers messages to mobile devices.
Mobile payment service	Pay for services or goods by using a mobile device instead of with money or a credit card. This is popular in developing countries where banking is not as prevalent as it is in developed nations. Transactions can be conducted using technologies such as near field communication (NFC), Wireless Application Protocol (WAP), direct mobile billing, and Short Message Service (SMS). See Figure 10.31.
Launcher	Perform administrative tasks such as creating and managing multiple applications using a tool found in the Windows and Apple versions of the software development kit (SDK). On Android, it is the part of the user interface that allows management of apps that are not on the home screen. A launcher allows manipulation of the graphical user interface (**GUI**) so that multiple apps and/or commands are easily deployed. Some mobile operating systems allow the creation of app groups.

FIGURE 10.31   Mobile wallet

Obtaining, Installing, and Removing Apps

Mobile device apps are obtained from a source such as **Google Play**, Apple's **App Store** (or iTunes), **Microsoft Store** or **Marketplace**, Amazon's Appstore for Android, and a host of other content sources. There are other ways to get an app: manually installing it (called *side loading*), using a USB cable (which commonly requires a file management app), using your storage media and a media reader, using an app such as Bump to transfer an application (or photos), or using a quick response (QR) code between two devices. For an example of a QR code, look at the bottom of the cell phone screen in Figure 10.31. Note that whatever method you use to install an app, you must ensure that the app is from a trusted source or a trusted app developer. Be sure to see what permissions are given when an app is installing. Table 10.7 lists tasks that are commonly done with apps.

TABLE 10.7   Mobile device tasks*

Task	Android	iOS	Windows
Delete an app	Press and hold the app's icon and drag it to the trash can.	Press and hold the app's icon until it jiggles and press the X that appears beside the icon. Press the menu key to stop the jiggling.	Press and hold the app's icon > tap *Uninstall* > *Yes*.
Close an app/force it to stop	*Settings* > *Applications* > *Manage Applications* > tap the specific application name > tap *Force Stop*.	Press the Home button quickly two times or swipe up on iPhone X > swipe left to locate the app if using the Home button > swipe upward on the app preview.	Swipe down from the top of the screen and drag the app to beyond the bottom of the screen.
Install an app	Access Google *Play Store* > locate and select the app to download > tap *Install*.	Access *App Store* > locate and select the app to install > tap *Install*.	Access *Microsoft Store/Marketplace* > locate and select the app to install > tap *Install*.
Move an app icon	Press and hold the app icon until it jiggles and drag the icon to another location. If the location is another home screen, hold the icon on the edge of the screen until the new location appears.	Press and hold the app icon until it jiggles and drag the icon to another location. If the location is another home screen, hold the icon on the edge of the screen until the new location appears.	Press and hold the tile until the app bar appears. Then drag the tile to the new location.
Create a folder to hold apps	Press an empty part of the home screen and select *Folder*. To move an item to the folder, press and drag the icon into the folder.	Press and hold the app icon until it jiggles. Drag the icon onto another app icon. A folder is created that contains both icons. Other icons can now be added by dragging and dropping into the folder.	From the *Start* screen, tap and drag one tile on top of another.

*Because Android is open source, the exact steps may vary. Also, Apple devices are constantly being updated/upgraded.

Two important terms related to apps are APK and SDK. Android application package (**APK**) is the file format used to distribute and install Android apps. So if you download an app, it is an APK file. A software development kit (**SDK**) is a set of tools (application programming interfaces [APIs], documentation, programming tools, analytic tools, sample code, and so on) used to develop an app for a specific mobile OS or platform.

Mobile Device Wired Connectivity

Mobile devices have many of the same ports as computers but in smaller versions. **Proprietary vendor-specific ports** are primarily for power connections or provide communication option(s). Let's explore these ports in a little more detail, starting with the ports you are most familiar with—USB.

Mobile USB and Lightning Ports

Mobile devices frequently have either a **micro-USB**, **mini-USB**, or **USB-C** port. There is even a mini-/micro-AB port that accepts either a mini-/micro A or a mini-/micro-B cable end. Figure 10.32 shows the standard Type-A USB port found on a PC and the mini-B, micro-B, and USB-C ports found on mobile devices. The USB-C port is now a standard interface for smartphones.

Standard Type A   Mini-   Micro-   Type-C
USB   USB   USB   USB

FIGURE 10.32   USB Type-A, mini, micro, and USB-C ports

Apple designed a proprietary 30-pin connector for docking Apple mobile devices. Later, Apple released the 8-pin replacement **Lightning port** for its devices. Now Apple is moving to the USB Type-C port. Both the Lightning port and USB-C cables can be inserted either face up or face down, because they are non-directional. Figure 10.33 shows a Lightning connector and port. You can also refer to Figure 2.31 to see a photo of the cable and connector. Figure 10.34 shows Apple's two connectors on the left followed by the micro-USB, mini-USB, and traditional USB connectors.

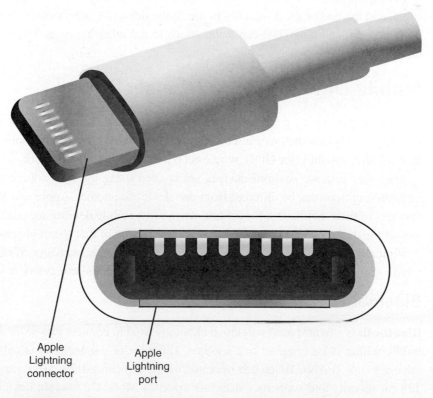

Apple
Lightning
connector

Apple
Lightning
port

FIGURE 10.33   Apple Lightning port and connector

Apple 30-pin dock connector   Apple Lightning connector   Micro-USB   Mini-USB   Traditional USB

FIGURE 10.34 Mobile connectors

With devices that don't have a wired RJ-45 network connection but do have a USB port, a **USB-to-RJ-45 dongle** can be used. Wired network connections are faster than wireless connections and commonly found on laptops, but other mobile devices lack RJ-45 jacks. Refer to Figure 2.27 for a photograph of a USB-to-RJ-45 (Ethernet) dongle.

When an HDMI, miniHDMI, or microHDMI connector is on an Android-based device, you connect the correct cable between the Android device and a video output device, such as a monitor or TV. Then, you launch an application such as your photo gallery. Tap the *HDMI Play* control icon. Some applications require no interaction for the HDMI output to work. Note that you might have to use the *Settings > HDMI* option to adjust the resolution. In addition, note that some applications do not support HDMI output from a smartphone.

For Apple iOS devices, you can purchase an Apple Digital AV adapter. This cable is like a Y cable, and the end of the Y attaches to the Apple device. A power connector can connect to one of the Y prongs, and an HDMI cable can attach to the other Y prong. This cable supports TV standards up to 1080p.

Mobile Device Wireless Connectivity

The whole purpose of having a mobile device is being able to move around with it. However, mobility is only half the picture. The other half involves connecting to some type of network, such as a cellular, satellite (for GPS), wireless (WiFi), or Bluetooth network.

Note that because Android devices are created using an open source operating system, configuration options can be different from one device to another. Apple and Windows have different versions of their mobile OS. By default, when most mobile devices are configured for wireless networks, the device will connect. If you walk out of range of that wireless network and another one is configured, the device will switch over to the second wireless network. If no wireless networks are within range, the mobile device will switch over to the cellular network if you are connected to it.

Bluetooth

Bluetooth is a radio-based wireless technology used to connect two or more devices that are commonly within close range of one another. This type of connectivity is called a wireless personal area network (PAN). Bluetooth operates in the unlicensed 2.4 GHz range. Bluetooth includes 128-bit security and supports a data rate up to 24 Mb/s. Up to eight devices can be connected in a master/slave relationship (with only one device being the master). Bluetooth has three classes of devices:

> *Class 1*—Range up to 328 feet (100 meters)
> *Class 2*—Range up to 33 feet (10 meters)
> *Class 3*—Range up to 3 feet (1 meter)

Note that the Bluetooth 5 standard supports a longer range of up to 800 feet (242 meters). The Bluetooth standards do not define the maximum range. Rather, the range depends on the type of Bluetooth radio installed. Most mobile devices use a Class 2 radio but seldom can have connectivity 33 feet away.

Many mobile devices support Bluetooth. Refer to Figure 10.15 to see a Bluetooth headset used with a cell phone. Figure 10.35 shows controls in a car to enable Bluetooth connectivity. The Bluetooth symbol is shown in Figure 10.36.

FIGURE 10.35   Enabling Bluetooth connectivity

FIGURE 10.36   Bluetooth symbol

The basic concept behind configuring Bluetooth is that each device must have Bluetooth enabled and must "pair," or connect, with another Bluetooth-enabled device. Once enabled, Bluetooth broadcasts a wireless signal that other Bluetooth-enabled devices can detect. The basic steps for configuration are as follows:

Step 1. Enable Bluetooth.

Step 2. Ensure that pairing is enabled.

Step 3. Pair with another Bluetooth-enabled device.

Step 4. Enter the security pin code.

Step 5. Test connectivity.

To enable Bluetooth on an Android phone, you can swipe from the top and tap the *Bluetooth* icon. On an iPhone, swipe up from the bottom edge of the screen to display the *Control Center*. Then tap the *Bluetooth* button to enable/disable it.

Laptops frequently use a function or Fn key along with a key that has the Bluetooth symbol (F1–F12) to activate Bluetooth. In Windows, search for **bluetooth** > *Change Bluetooth Settings* option > *Options* tab > ensure that the *Allow Bluetooth Devices to Find This Computer* checkbox is enabled.

Table 10.8 shows basic Bluetooth configurations for the various operating systems after a device is powered on and ready for pairing.

TABLE 10.8   Bluetooth installation steps

Windows	Apple iOS	Android
Ensure that Bluetooth is enabled. Use the *Add a Bluetooth Device* link > select the device > *Next*. If the device is a Bluetooth printer, use the *Add a Printer* link. You may have to enter a passkey or PIN. Verify connectivity.	Access *Settings* > *General* > *Bluetooth* > *ON*. In the *Devices* field, you should see the name of the device. Select the device > *Pair*. You may have to enter a passkey or PIN. Verify connectivity.	Access *Settings* > *Wireless and Network* > *Bluetooth Settings*. Ensure that Bluetooth is enabled > *Scan Devices*. Select the device once it appears > *Accept*. You may have to enter a passkey or PIN. Verify connectivity.

Laptops commonly have Bluetooth installed. To determine whether Bluetooth is installed in Windows 7/8/10, open the *Network and Sharing Center* Control Panel > *Change Adapter Settings* link. If installed, a Bluetooth adapter displays. Right-click on the adapter to enable or disable the adapter and to pair it with other devices.

If a device does not have Bluetooth capability or if the Bluetooth circuitry fails and the device has a USB port, a **USB-to-Bluetooth dongle** can be obtained and used. Plug the dongle into a USB port on your laptop. In the Windows environment, the device will register and the Control Panel should pop up. In Windows 7 and 8, look under *Hardware and Sound* > *Add a Device* link. In Windows 10, use the *Settings* > *Devices* > *Bluetooth* option. Your Bluetooth device model number displays > select *Next* > follow any additional instructions such as entering a PIN. Always remember to follow the manufacturer's directions. Figure 10.37 shows a USB Bluetooth dongle.

FIGURE 10.37   USB Bluetooth dongle

IEEE 802.11 Wireless

The 802.11 wireless standard is used to connect the mobile device to a wireless network that operates in the 2.4 GHz and/or 5 GHz range. A wireless access point is used to coordinate and connect multiple wireless devices in the immediate area. Data rates depend on the distance from the access point and what type of walls and materials are between the mobile device and the access point. 802.11 wireless networks are commonly referred to as WiFi. Table 10.9 shows the 802.11 standards related to wireless and the frequency range/speed used with each type.

TABLE 10.9   IEEE 802.11 wireless standards

Standard	Frequency range and speed
802.11a	5 GHz up to 54 Mb/s
802.11b	2.4 GHz up to 11 Mb/s
802.11g	2.4 GHz up to 54 Mb/s
802.11n	2.4 GHz and 5 GHz up to 600 Mb/s
802.11ac	5 GHz up to 1+ Gb/s

The reason it is important to know the frequency is so you can determine whether your mobile device can attach to the wireless network. If an 802.11n access point is used, it has the capability to be programmed in both the 2.4 and 5 GHz ranges, but someone could just configure it to operate in one of these ranges, such as 2.4 GHz. That would mean your mobile device would have to support the 802.11b, 802.11g, or 802.11n standard. The access point could also be configured to support only 802.11n devices (but this is not common except perhaps within a company). The more devices that connect and transmit/receive data on a wireless network, the worse its performance. Some access points allow a limited number of wired connections in addition to all the wireless devices connected to it, as shown in Figure 10.38.

FIGURE 10.38   IEEE 802.11 wireless network

To configure a wireless mobile device for IEEE 802.11 wireless networking, ensure that the WiFi option is enabled. Use the same process as outlined for accessing Bluetooth but select WiFi instead. The basic configuration steps for accessing 802.11 wireless networks are as follows:

Step 1. Enable WiFi through the device's *Settings* option.

Step 2. Select the WiFi wireless network to join.

Step 3. Enter the security password, if required.

For wireless networks that do not broadcast the SSID (see Chapter 13, "Networking," for more information on that), the network can be manually configured on a mobile device. To manually add a wireless network on an Android device, use *Settings > Add Network* and manually enter the SSID, security type, and password. Similarly, on an iOS device, use *Settings > Wi-Fi* and follow the same process.

If the 802.11 WiFi circuitry fails or is unavailable on a mobile device, and the device has a USB port, a **USB-to-WiFi dongle** can be obtained and installed. Figure 10.39 shows one of these.

FIGURE 10.39   USB wireless NIC

Airplane Mode

Airplane Mode allows you to disable all wireless communication—WiFi, mobile broadband, Bluetooth, GPS or GNSS (Global Navigation Satellite System), and NFC. In this mode, you could still view a movie or play a game, as long as doing so does not require Internet, cellular, or wireless connectivity. To turn on Airplane Mode, use the *Settings > Airplane Mode* option. Airplane Mode saves on power, secures your mobile device because no wireless communication can occur, and is used when flying (thus the name) and in other communication-sensitive situations.

Table 10.10 lists the basic network connectivity configuration options for Android and Apple iOS devices.

TABLE 10.10   Mobile device network configuration options

Connectivity method	Android	iOS
802.11 wireless	*Settings > Wireless and Networks > Wi-Fi*	*Settings > Wi-Fi*
Bluetooth	*Settings > Wireless and Networks > Bluetooth*	*Settings > Bluetooth*
Cellular	*Settings > Wireless and Networks > More Networks > Mobile Networks*	*Settings > General > Cellular Data*
GPS	*Settings > Location Services > Location*	*Settings > Location*
Airplane Mode	*Settings > Wireless and Networks > Flight Mode > Airplane Mode*	*Settings > Privacy > Location Services*

Hotspot/Tethering

A WiFi **hotspot** is a wireless network that has free Internet access. Hotspots can be found in cities, parks, stores, restaurants, hotels, libraries, government buildings, airports, and schools. Security is a concern with hotspots because no encryption or authentication is commonly required.

Another way of gaining access to the Internet is through tethering. Say you are at a gas station and need to look up something on the Internet on your PC. Your phone has Internet connectivity, but there is no free WiFi. You could have Internet access on the PC through the phone by using tethering. **Tethering** allows sharing of an Internet connection with other mobile devices in the nearby area. Tethering might also be considered to be a hotspot. Common methods of using tethering are through Bluetooth, WiFi, or a wired USB connection. Some phone vendors charge for the tethering option. Configure tethering on an Android device using the *Settings > Wireless & Networks* option. Then select whether you are using USB, WiFi, or Bluetooth to tether. On an iPhone, access *Settings > enable Personal Hotspot >* the directions for connecting through WiFi, Bluetooth, and USB appear. Figure 10.40 shows wired tethering through USB and the concept of wireless tethering. Note that companies might implement bandwidth throttling to limit the amount of data sent over the corporate wireless network.

FIGURE 10.40   Wireless tethering

Radio Frequency Identification (RFID)

Radio frequency identification (**RFID**) uses wireless radio waves to locate something. RFID is used to track and locate shipped good or items in a warehouse, clothing in a store, pets, and people. RFID tags are also used in devices that mount in cars and are used for toll collection as the cars pass through toll booths.

RFID tags can be active or passive. An active tag has a battery and periodically sends out a signal. A passive tag does not have a battery and gets its power from the RFID reader. Figure 10.41 shows an RFID tag like one you might have seen in your textbook when you bought it.

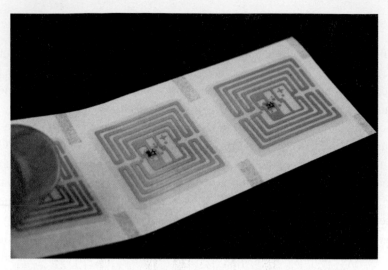

FIGURE 10.41   RFID tag

Near Field Communication (NFC)

Near field communication (**NFC**) is a radio-based wireless technology similar to RFID that allows two devices to exchange information. There are three modes of NFC operation:

> *NFC card emulation*—Enables a mobile device to act like a smart card and perform business transactions such as wireless payment-related or ticket purchasing, displaying, inspection, or invalidation transactions
> *NFC reader/writer*—Allows an NFC device to read information from a tag
> *NFC peer-to-peer*—Allows two NFC-enabled devices to exchange information

The devices must be within close proximity of one another (4 inches or less). Smart phones are commonly used as **NFC/tap pay devices**. If your phone has NFC capability and your printer supports NFC, then you can stand next to the printer, tap the *Print* option, and send something to the printer. Figure 10.42 shows someone making a payment for purchases by using an NFC-enabled smartphone. Note that NFC transactions are secure and commonly include a haptic (vibration) and/or audio feedback that a transaction has occurred.

FIGURE 10.42   NFC transaction

NFC can also be used to establish other types of connections, such as Bluetooth, WiFi, and data exchange transfers. NFC is also used to allow keyless entry into cars, connect speakers, and provide wireless charging.

To configure an Android device for NFC, go to *Settings > NFC* and ensure that it is turned on. To be able to pay using your phone, you need to have an app such as Google Wallet or Samsung Pay installed.

To configure an iOS device for NFC and Apple Pay, go to *Settings > Wallet & Apple Pay >* add a credit or debit card and follow the directions for the type of card chosen.

Infrared

Infrared (**IR**) is a radio-based wireless technology that operates in the 300 GHz to 430 THz range, but many devices use either 2.4 GHz or 27 MHz. IR is used for very short distances and is cheaper than other wireless technologies. IR requires line of sight; anything from a human to a chair can get in the way and cause lack of connectivity. For that reason, IR is commonly used for short distances to connect wireless devices such as motion detectors, intrusion detectors, TV remotes, hand scanners, a mouse, or a keyboard.

Cellular Networks

A cellular network is a collection of devices that allow mobile phones/smartphones to communicate. A cellular network is divided into cells, and each cell provides coverage within a specific geographic area. Table 10.11 lists the cellular network technologies a technician needs to be familiar with.

TABLE 10.11   Cellular network technologies

Technology	Description
3G	Third generation of wireless cellular technology that allowed mobile devices to have faster Internet connectivity (at least 200 kb/s up to 2 Mb/s).
4G	Fourth generation of cellular network that supports IP telephony, gaming services, mobile TV, and video conferencing at speeds up to 1 Gb/s.
LTE (Long Term Evolution)	Long Term Evolution (LTE), a version of 4G that optimized the network for video streaming and online games.
5G	Fifth generation of cellular networks that docs not have formal standards yet; includes faster speeds at some new lower frequencies; frequency range is 600 MHz to 6 GHz to support speeds up to 10 Gb/s.

Cellular Data

Two methods for sending data over a cellular network are Short Message Service (SMS) and Multimedia Message Service (MMS). SMS is used for text messages. MMS is used for visual data such as photos or video. Many phone providers charge for these services, so some users disable them. On an iOS device, use *Settings > General > Cellular Data*. On an Android device, access *Wireless and Networks Settings > Mobile Networks > Data*.

VPN

A virtual private network (**VPN**) is used to connect one device to another device through a public network such as the Internet. Figure 10.43 shows an example of the concept. A salesperson might have a tablet in order to demonstrate a product as well as input customer information. To upload the customer information, the salesperson might need to establish a VPN, and a technician might be required to configure this on a phone or another mobile device. Specific network information is required from the network support staff in order to create this type of connection.

FIGURE 10.43   Concept of a VPN

The general steps to start the VPN configuration are as follows:

> iOS: *Settings > General > VPN*
> Android: *Settings > > More from the Wireless & Networks section> VPN > +* (plus sign)

In order to use the VPN, the user has to connect using his or her own username and password:

> iOS: *Settings >* set *VPN* to on (as seen in Figure 10.44)
> Android: *Settings > General > VPN*

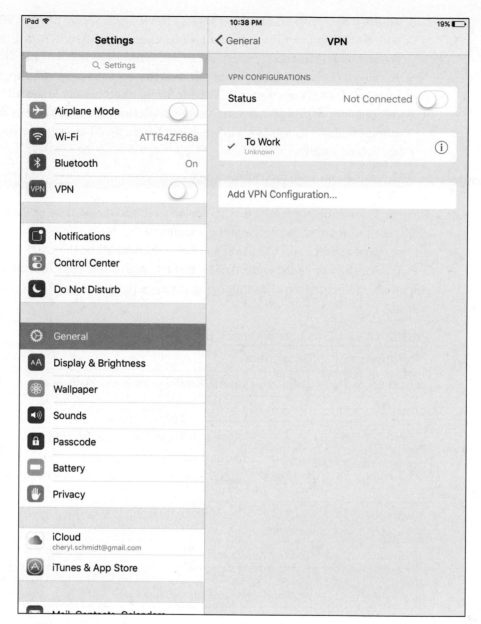

FIGURE 10.44 Accessing VPN configuration on an iOS device

Mobile Device Email Configuration

Many people want to check their email on a mobile device. Email can be accessed and delivered using a variety of protocols, including the following:

> *Post Office Protocol version 3 (**POP3**)*—Used to retrieve email using TCP port 110; saves email to the local device.

> *Internet Message Access Protocol (**IMAP**)*—Used to retrieve email using TCP port 143; good when two or more people check the same account or a user wants email access from multiple devices.

> *Secure Sockets Layer (**SSL**)*—Used to encrypt data between an email client and the email server.

> *Simple Mail Transfer Protocol (SMTP)*—An older protocol used to send emails using TCP port 25.

> *Multipurpose Internet Mail Extensions (MIME) and Secure MIME (**S/MIME**)*—Used along with SMTP so that pictures and attachments are supported; S/MIME allows encryption and signing of MIME data.
> *Exchange Online*—Microsoft's application that uses the messaging application programming interface (MAPI) to connect to Microsoft Exchange servers for email, calendar, and contact information. Microsoft supports storing copies of messages or calendar events in personal storage table (.pst) files, such as when items from the Microsoft Exchange server are archived and stored locally.

The email server used determines which email client may be used on the mobile device. Several key pieces of information are commonly needed to configure that client; see Table 10.12. (See Chapter 13 to learn more about how protocols work and the purpose of them.) Some organizations configure the email server to support autoconfiguration (sometimes called autodiscovery) so that all you have to enter is a username and password and all of the other configuration parameters are automatically provided to the device. Not all email client apps support autoconfiguration. You might have to get the email configuration parameters from the IT support staff, an FAQ page, or website.

TABLE 10.12   Email configuration parameters

Parameter	Description
Email address	The address used to send you an email, such as cheryl.schmidt@gmail.com.
Email protocol	Protocol(s) used to send and receive email.
Server name or host name	The name of the incoming or outgoing mail server (which you can get from network staff).
Username	The name assigned to you by the company that hosts the email server. This may be your email address.
Password	The password used in conjunction with a username to access an email account.
Domain	The network domain name.
SSL	Secure Sockets Layer (SSL) when enabled is used to encrypt data between the mobile device and the email server.

Most mobile devices include email configuration as part of the mobile OS. Examples include the following:

> **Google/Inbox**
> **Yahoo**
> **Exchange Online**
> **iCloud**

When you first configure an Android device, you are prompted to either enter your Google account information or create a Google account. The email app that comes with the phone simply opens Gmail. You can add an account by selecting *Settings > Email* option. Use the *Personal (IMAP/POP)* option for configuring Yahoo, Outlook, AOL Mail, and other IMAP/POP type email accounts. Use the *Exchange* option for configuring Microsoft Exchange. Similarly, on Apple iOS devices, use *Settings >Passwords & Accounts* (or *Mail, Contacts, Calendars* on older versions as seen in Figure 10.45) to select *Add Account >* select the particular type of account desired (Exchange, Google, Yahoo, and so on).

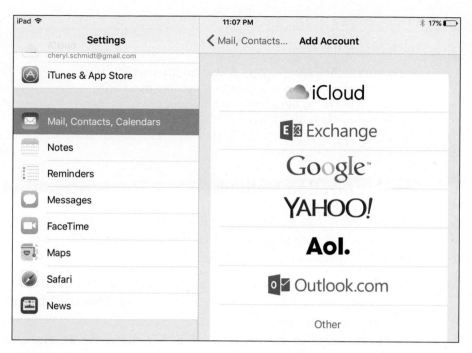

FIGURE 10.45   Email configuration on iOS device

Mobile Device Synchronization and Backup

Synchronization means making the same data available on multiple devices and/or multiple locations. This is sometimes known as a **remote backup**, cloud backup, or cloud storage. The types of data synchronized include personal contacts, applications, email, pictures, music, videos, calendar appointments, browser bookmarks, documents, folders, location data, social media data, e-books, and passwords. Make sure you know what type of data can be synchronized if you are going for the A+ certification.

Synchronization makes life easier because you do not have to log in to a work computer or bring up a web browser in order to see what is scheduled tomorrow. You can also synchronize your fitness results and maintain them on both your cell phone and mobile fitness device or smart watch (see Figure 10.46).

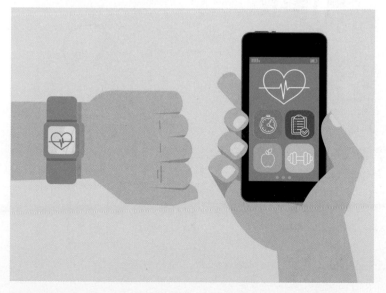

FIGURE 10.46   Fitness app synchronization

Think before you sync

Be careful synchronizing cached passwords (passwords you have directed the browser, operating system, or app to save) across the cloud because of security reasons. There are also issues synching music files due to file formats and multiple platforms (Apple, PC, car, mobile device, for example). Be sure to research your synchronization method.

Synchronization Methods

Synchronization can be done through a particular operating system, browser, email provider, applications, and/or third-party vendors. People commonly use one or more of the following synchronization methods for mobile devices:

> **Synchronize to the cloud**—It is possible to store data in a remote location where it can be viewed, retrieved, saved, shared, and/or forwarded based on the cloud vendor used and user preferences. See Figure 10.47.

> **Synchronize to the desktop**—A mobile device can be synchronized with one or more desktop computers using an app, software, the operating system, or a combination of these.

> **Synchronize to the automobile**—It is possible to connect and synchronize a Bluetooth headset, smartphone, or other mobile device to a car. A Ford vehicle, for example, can sync to a cell phone, and the address book is transferred to the car and kept in an internal database. Many vehicles support text-to-speech and can read text messages.

Note that whichever type is used, it is important that the software requirements needed to install the app and actually synchronize the data are met on each of the devices that have data to be synchronized.

FIGURE 10.47 Synchronization to the cloud

TECH TIP

Use vCards for synching contacts

A vCard (also known as a virtual contact file (VCF)) is used for electronic contact information like an e-business card. A vcard file extension can be .vcf or .vcard. If a vCard is imbedded in an email, right-click on it and you normally have the option to add to your contacts.

Synchronization Connection Types

In order for devices to synchronize data, they have to establish connectivity with each other. Synchronization commonly occurs using one of three types of connections:

> *Wired USB connection*—The two devices may attach to one another using a USB port on each device. An example is an iOS device connected via USB to a computer and using iTunes to synchronize music.
> *Wireless connection*—Devices can attach to one another using any wireless method, including an 802.11 WiFi connection and cellular network.
> *Wired network connection*—Devices can attach to a wired network and access the Internet and a cloud-based solution through a web browser.

Figure 10.48 shows synchronization between a mobile phone and a desktop computer.

FIGURE 10.48   Synchronization between a mobile phone and a PC

Synchronization on Android Devices

Google software is commonly used to synchronize data between an Android device and other devices. Google Drive can be used to store and share documents for free. The Google Chrome browser allows synchronization of bookmarks. Google Photos allows storage and sharing of photos. When you use Google software to synchronize, an Android user authenticates once in order to access multiple services. This is known as **mutual authentication for multiple services** or single sign-on (**SSO**), and it is available through the other mobile operating systems as well. When you use a third-party product to synchronize data, you may be required to install an app on one or more mobile devices and PCs.

An Android device is configured with a Google ID and password using the *Settings > Accounts* option and then the three vertical dots in the top-right corner can be tapped to select what to synchronize. Figure 10.49 shows the synchronization settings for email (which is turned on).

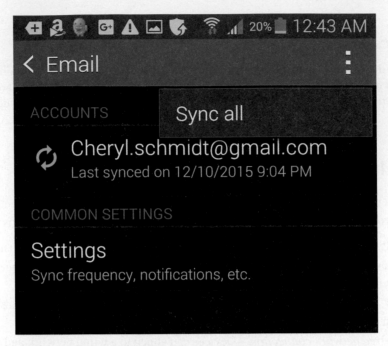

FIGURE 10.49   Android email synchronization

Synchronization on iOS Devices

iOS devices can use Google Gmail and other apps to synchronize Google contacts and calendar. An individual app may also support synchronization with Google. You can view and add apps by using *Settings* > *Personal* (which is not used on some Android devices) > *Accounts and Sync* or whatever method is used by the particular application.

However, iOS users tend to use Apple solutions, such as iCloud and iTunes, for synchronization. iCloud is used to store, share, and manage data from any device, including contacts, calendar, ringtones, photos/videos, and data. Apple provides iCloud Photo Library for photos and video and iCloud Drive for document storage. Apple provides free storage (5 GB at press time) with the option to pay for more. A Windows device requires a download and installation of iCloud for Windows in order to access data stored there. Figure 10.50 shows the configuration for iCloud on an iOS device, and Figure 10.51 shows iCloud Drive configuration.

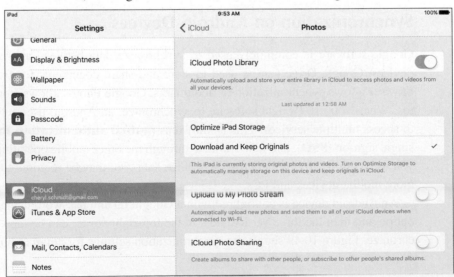

FIGURE 10.50   iCloud configuration screen

FIGURE 10.51   iCloud Drive configuration screen

iTunes can be used to synchronize Apple devices and to play and manage music, video, books, and lectures. iTunes used to require a USB connection between a mobile device and a PC or Mac but now supports WiFi connectivity. Through iTunes, you can back up personal data (settings, messages, voicemails, and so on) and the Apple device operating system.

iTunes has a 64-bit version for 64-bit Windows 7 and higher operating systems. There is no such application for Android devices. However, you can connect an Apple mobile device to an Android device and use the Android *File Transfer* app to transfer files such as music files (found on the Apple device in the following folder *Music > iTunes > iTunes Media*).

To use iTunes, open it from an Apple device that has Mac OS X 10.8.5 or higher or connect the Apple device to a computer or PC. Select the device by choosing the correct device icon in the upper-left corner of the iTunes window. In the left panel of the *Settings* area are various sections based on what types of items are in the iTunes library (such as Music, Movies, TV Shows, Info, Podcasts, iTunes U, Books, AudioBooks, Tones, and Photos). Each section can be accessed to sync that particular type of content. The Info section is used to sync contacts and calendars. iTunes cannot sync browser email accounts, bookmarks, and other such information.

Backup and Restore Overview

Synchronization of apps is one way of backing up information, but it doesn't provide an operating system backup. A mobile device should have the system backed up in case of an operating system update failure, a virus infection, or inability to remove malware. Apps are available that allow you to remotely back up a mobile device. Backup and restore techniques are just as important in the mobile environment as they are in the desktop arena.

Android-Based Backup and Restore

Android devices have different backup options based on what type of data you want to back up and/or restore. Table 10.13 lists the major ones.

TABLE 10.13   Android backup options

Type of data to back up	Method
Photos/videos	Use Auto Backup. Open *Google Photos* app > top left, access the menu icon (three horizontal bars) > *Settings* > *Back Up & Sync* > enable or disable. **Important note:** Turning off the backup settings affects all apps that use Back Up & Sync, such as Google Drive.
Files, folders, images, videos	Use Google Drive. Open a web browser and go to http://drive.google.com. Use the menu to create new folders or upload files or drag and drop files/folders into the window.
Data	Use Android Backup Service: *Settings* > *Backup & Reset* > enable *Back Up My Data*. Figure 10.52 shows this screen.

The Android Backup Service backs up the following data and settings: Google Calendar, WiFi networks and passwords, home screen wallpaper, Gmail settings, apps installed through Google Play and backed up using the Play Store app, display settings, language settings, input settings, date and time, and some third-party app settings and data.

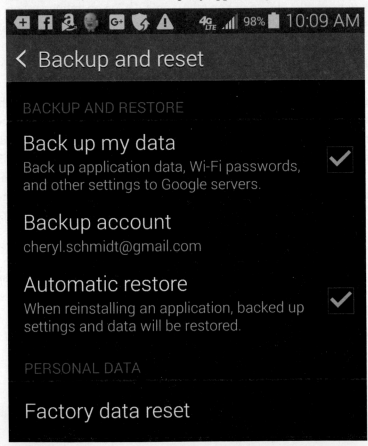

FIGURE 10.52   Android Backup and Reset screen

Notice in Figure 10.52 that you can also use this screen to perform a factory reset. A **factory reset** is used when a device cannot be repaired using any other method. As the name of the option implies, it resets the mobile device to the original settings. Android phones keep the OS separate from the apps and data. The OS is read-only. A factory reset resets only the apps and data. That is why you need to back them up. Generic steps to back up an Android-based mobile device are as follows:

Step 1. Boot the device into *Recovery Mode*, which is typically accessed by holding down two or more specific buttons (such as the power, volume, and/or home buttons) while the device boots. See the mobile device manufacturer's website for specific instructions.

Step 2. From the boot menu, select *Backup & Restore > Backup*.

Step 3. When the backup is complete, restart the device and boot normally.

The generic steps for the restore process are as follows:

Step 1. Boot the device into *Recovery Mode*.

Step 2. From the boot menu, select *Backup & Restore > Restore*.

Step 3. When the restore is complete, reboot the device to ensure that it boots normally.

Note that there are other apps that can be used to back up the operating system and the installed apps.

iOS-Based Backup and Restore Overview

With iOS you can back up your operating system using iCloud or iTunes. If you use iCloud, the backup is stored in the cloud (up to 5 GB free at press time), it is encrypted, and it can be accomplished wirelessly. With iTunes, the backup is stored on a Mac or PC, the storage limit is based on storage available on that Mac or PC, and encryption is optional.

iCloud Backup and Restore Overview

iCloud backups do not include data that is already in the cloud, data from other cloud services, Apple Pay information, Touch ID, or content that you got from other vendors (even if available in iTunes or iBooks). In order to make a backup using iCloud, ensure that the device connects to a WiFi network > *Settings > iCloud Backup/Storage & Backup* > enable (turn on) iCloud Backup > *Back Up Now*.

You can verify that the backup is stored by using the following steps: *Settings > iCloud > Storage > Manage Storage* > select the device. The details shown include the date, time, and backup file size. Backups are automatically made on a daily basis if the device meets the following criteria:

> The device connects to a power source.
> The device connects to a WiFi network.
> The device has a locked screen
> iCloud storage space is available.

To reset and restore an iOS device using iCloud, follow these generic steps:

Step 1. Boot the device and look for a hello screen. Note that if the device is still functional, you cannot restore from an iCloud backup if the device is configured. Use the *Settings > Erase All Content and Settings option* to wipe the device.

Step 2. Follow the directions on how to set up the device, including the requirement of joining a WiFi network.

Step 3. Select *Restore from an iCloud Backup* and sign in to iCloud.

Step 4. Select a backup. Do not disconnect from the WiFi network. Note that this may take a period of time.

iTunes Backup and Restore Overview

Use the following steps to make a backup of an iOS device using iTunes:

Step 1. Open the iTunes application on a Mac or PC.

Step 2. Connect the iOS device to the Mac or PC, using a USB cable. The device icon should display in the top-left corner, as shown in Figure 10.53.

Step 3. Make a backup of content downloaded from the iTunes Store or Apple App Store by using *File > Devices > Transfer Purchases*. Note that when the file transfer is complete, you might need to press Ctrl+B.

Step 4. Select whether the backup is to be kept in the cloud (by selecting the *iCloud* radio button) or on the PC or Mac (by selecting the *This Computer* radio button). See Figure 10.53.

Step 5. On a Mac, select *Back Up Now* (as shown in Figure 10.53). On a Windows PC, use *File > Devices > Back Up*.

Step 6. When the process is finished, use the iTunes *Summary* option to see the date and time of the backup. In Windows, use *Preferences > Devices*. If the file is encrypted, there is a lock icon beside the device name.

FIGURE 10.53 iTunes backup options

A reinstallation of the operating system is known as a **clean install**. To restore a device using iTunes, connect the device to the Mac or PC that contains the backup. Cable the device to the Mac or PC. Open iTunes. Select *File > Devices > Restore from Backup*. Select the latest backup and click *Restore*. Note that the file transfer can take some time.

OneDrive

Microsoft has a product called **OneDrive** that can be used for synchronization and/or backup and restore operations. At the time this book went to press, new users could use up to 5 GB of free storage and share files and folders with others, and Office 365 subscribers could use 1 TB of free storage. Users may place deleted files in a recycle bin and recover them up to three months later without that storage capacity counting. People who use Microsoft Outlook through an Exchange server from any mobile operating system can save files and photos to OneDrive and then access them through a web browser or mobile device app. Some mobile Outlook users save their email attachments to OneDrive. Microsoft reserves the rights to monitor any content saved in OneDrive and can remove any files that do not adhere to its strict policy. Figure 10.54 shows a screenshot of OneDrive.

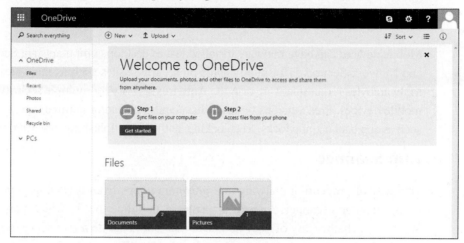

FIGURE 10.54 Microsoft OneDrive

Other Mobile Software Tools

Mobile devices sometimes require other tools for troubleshooting and management. You might also have to download apps to perform specific tasks or to help with troubleshooting. You might consider installing some of the apps described in the following sections as a standard in a business environment.

Mobile Device Management

Mobile device management **(MDM)** is the ability to view and manage multiple mobile devices (see Figure 10.55). In the corporate environment, mobile devices are challenging for IT staff. Some companies purchase software in order to push updates, track, and remotely wipe data and configurations. Mobile application management (MAM) is used to control apps on mobile devices in the corporate environment instead of trying to control the entire device.

FIGURE 10.55 Mobile device management

The **Apple Configurator** free app is an example of an MDM product. It allows business support staff to configure settings on iOS-based devices before issuing them to users. Using configuration profiles, IT personnel can install specific iOS versions and ensure that security policies are applied. Apple Configurator can also be used to wipe the device and provide basic management of deployed devices. Similar products can be purchased to allow more corporate management capabilities.

Mobile Antimalware

Mobile devices can have malware installed just as desktop computers can. See Chapter 18, "Computer and Network Security," for more details on security issues such as malware. Some products, such as Malwarebytes for antimalware or AVG Antivirus security for multiple security threats, are available for mobile devices. Free versions typically have antivirus and/or antimalware. Paid versions add features such as app backup, app locks, SIM locking, antitheft, antiphishing, tracking, and secure web browsing.

App Scanner

One way of preventing malware and preventing apps from revealing your personal information is to install an app scanner. An **app scanner** is an online tool in which you can type the name of an app to see whether any of your data is at risk and generate a risk score to get an idea of how risky the app is. One example is a web-based tool called Zscaler Application Profiler (ZAP). Other app scanners may be part of security apps, such as Sophos Mobile Security. There are also app scanners that manage particular apps and ensure compliance, cloud-based management for specific mobile devices, and enterprise-based mobile device management.

WiFi Analyzer

A **WiFi analyzer** app (sometimes known as a **wireless locator**) is used to identify what wireless networks are in the area and what frequencies (channels) are being used and to find less crowded channels for any wireless installations, hotspot, or tethering that may be needed in a particular area. Some WiFi analyzers give you additional feedback such as a quality rating based on the channel you might select. One optional feature is a signal meter to see the wireless range of a particular wireless network. WiFi analyzers are particularly useful to technicians in allowing them to identify potential sources of other wireless interference. See Chapter 13 for more detail on wireless networks and wireless configuration. Figure 10.56 shows a WiFi analyzer (called WiFi Analyzer) designed for Windows 10 devices and available in the Microsoft Store.

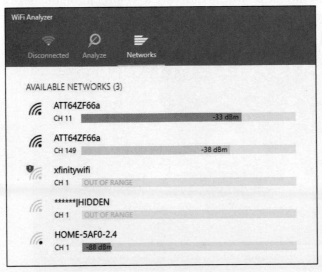

FIGURE 10.56   WiFi Analyzer app screen

Cell Tower Analyzer

A **cell tower analyzer** app (also known as a cell signal analyzer) details information about the cell phone network and possibly wireless networks. The information can include signal strength, data state, data activity, mobile network code (MNC), mobile country code (MCC), IP address, roaming state, phone type, and so on. You can use other apps to see all the cell towers in the area in order to get an idea of cell phone coverage in the areas most used. Figure 10.57 shows a screenshot from a cell tower analyzer app (called Network Signal Info).

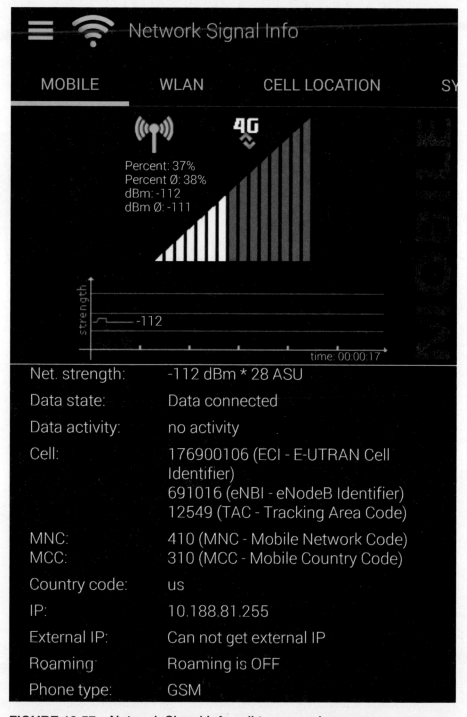

FIGURE 10.57   Network Signal Info cell tower analyzer app

Laptops Overview

Mobile devices are fun to explore, but let's move on to laptops now. Laptops were the first mobile device that technicians had to support. They are an integral part of the IT scene. Anyone in an IT position is expected to know some technical laptop basics. Technical support staff are expected to know more. Always remember that every laptop is different. Always consult the particular computer manufacturer's website for instructions on replacing anything on your laptop.

Laptop Hardware

A laptop has similar parts and ports to a desktop computer, but some of these components are, naturally, smaller. Figure 10.58 shows common laptop parts. Notice in the figure how many of the components are built into the laptop motherboard.

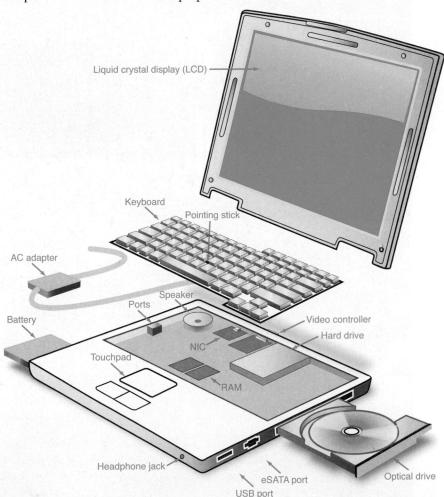

FIGURE 10.58   Laptop parts

Whenever taking anything out of a laptop, one of the major issues is tiny screws. Use a magnetic screwdriver to remove the screws or place the screws on a magnetized tray. Many manufacturers label the type of screws or location for ease of explaining disassembly (see Figure 10.59). Always keep like screws together (in containers or an egg carton) and take notes and photos. All the parts are manufacturer dependent, but the following explanation and graphics/photos should help.

FIGURE 10.59   Laptop screws and covers

External Laptop Devices

Laptops might also have external devices attached. The USB port is the most common port used for external connectivity. For laptops that do not have a USB port, you can use an eSATA port for an external device or add an Express-to-USB card if the laptop has an ExpressCard slot. Note that these USB ports on an ExpressCard (covered in the next section) might not be able to provide the power that a normal integrated USB port could provide. Types of external connectivity include the following:

> *External monitor*—An external monitor attaches to a video port. Common video ports on laptops include VGA, HDMI, Thunderbolt, and DisplayPort. HDMI can carry audio and video signals. Thunderbolt can carry not only video but data and power as well. That is why Thunderbolt can be used for other connections besides video connections. Thunderbolt is also used to connect to docking stations (covered next). Some devices have miniature versions of these ports. Figure 10.60 shows the difference between a DisplayPort and a mini DisplayPort.

> *External hard drive*—An external hard drive commonly connects to a USB, Thunderbolt, or eSATA port.

> *External optical drive* (see Figure 10.61)—An external optical drive commonly connects to a USB port; such drives are useful for tablets, too.

DisplayPort

Mini
DisplayPort

FIGURE 10.60   DisplayPort and mini DisplayPort

FIGURE 10.61   USB optical drive

Some people like having more expandability when in the office than when traveling with a laptop. For these folks, two devices can help: a docking station and a port replicator. A **laptop docking station** allows a laptop computer to be more like a desktop system. A docking station can have ports for charging devices and connections for a full-size monitor, keyboard, mouse, and printer. In addition, a docking station can have expansion slots or cards and storage bays.

Docking stations tend to be vendor proprietary, which means that if you have a particular brand of laptop, you must use the same brand of docking station. Typically, to install a laptop into a docking station, you close the laptop and slide the laptop into the docking station. Optionally (depending on the model), you can secure the laptop with locking tabs. Figure 10.62 shows the concept of a laptop docking station and the ports that can be found on the back. Figure 10.63 shows the back of an older laptop docking station. Notice the male 9-pin serial port on the bottom row.

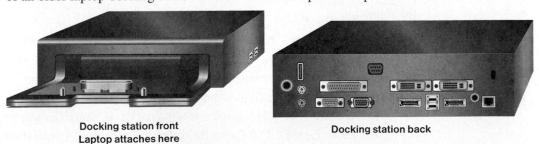

Docking station front
Laptop attaches here

Docking station back

FIGURE 10.62   Laptop docking station

A **port replicator** is similar to a docking station but does not normally include expansion slots or drive storage bays. A port replicator attaches to a laptop and allows more devices to be connected, such as an external monitor, keyboard, mouse, joystick, and printer, or port replicator. Port replicators can be proprietary or may support multiple laptop vendors.

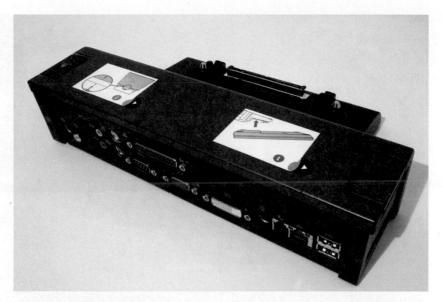

FIGURE 10.63 Laptop docking station with VGA, DVI, USB, and RJ-45 ports

Other Laptop Expansion Options

Laptops can also be expanded by adding expansion cards. The miniPCI 32-bit 33 MHz standard was developed to allow PCI upgrades and interface cards to be added to laptops, docking stations, and printers. MiniPCI cards have three form factors: Type I, Type II, and Type III.

The **miniPCIe** is a popular 52-pin card that fits in the bottom of a laptop or on the motherboard/ system board, not a tablet. Three common uses are to install a modem card, a wireless card, or a cellular card. A **modem card** is used to allow a PC to connect to a remote modem using an analog phone line. A **wireless card** is used to connect a laptop to an IEEE 802.11 or Bluetooth wireless network. A **cellular card** is used to connect a laptop to the cell phone network. Note that some adapters have both wireless and cellular abilities built into the same card. Also, these adapters could be attached via a USB port instead of a miniPCIe adapter.

To install a miniPCI/PCIe adapter, you may have to disassemble the laptop or remove a screw from the bottom, as shown in Figure 10.64, or you may have to lift a lid to access the slot. An expansion slot is shown in Figure 10.65.

FIGURE 10.64 Laptop underside

FIGURE 10.65   Laptop adapter

M.2 and NVMe

A type of expansion slot found in both laptops and desktop computers is M.2. The **M.2** expansion slot is quite flexible in that the specification allows different module sizes, including widths of 12, 16, 22, and 30 mm and lengths of 16, 26, 30, 38, 42, 60, 80, and 110 mm. Usually a longer slot allows the short cards to be installed.

M.2 expansion cards in laptops and desktop computers are used for WiFi, Bluetooth, and cellular network cards as well as solid-state drives (SSDs). The support of various card lengths and advanced technology makes M.2 an attractive expansion capability option for solid-state drives and cards in all computer systems and mobile devices. Figure 10.66 shows an M.2 WiFi expansion card and an SSD.

SSD storage comes in the form of 2.5-inch cases, mounted on a PCIe card for desktops, on an M.2 card, and on a Non-volatile Memory Express (**NVMe**) card. For a laptop, an SSD on an NVMe is the fastest option. M.2 and the 2.5-inch case connect to a μSATA (microSATA) connection. The NVMe card uses the PCIe bus and provides a faster connection but is more expensive. Look back to Figure 7.17 in Chapter 7, "Storage Devices," to see an NVMe card.

FIGURE 10.66   M.2 wireless card and SSD

Laptop Power

A laptop normally uses a battery as its power source, but a laptop can also be powered through an AC wall outlet connection that recharges the laptop battery. Figure 10.67 shows the woman in the white shirt working on a laptop that is being charged. A power adapter (sometimes called a wall adapter) converts the AC power from the wall outlet to DC and connects to the rear of the laptop (near where the battery is located). When a laptop has an AC adapter attached, the battery is being recharged on most models. The port sometimes has a DC voltage symbol below or beside it. This symbol is a solid line with a dashed line below it (═╍╍). Figure 10.68 shows an example of a power adapter that would be connected between the laptop and the AC outlet and the power connection on a laptop.

When purchasing a new power supply for a laptop or battery for a mobile device, ensure that it has the same specifications as the one from the manufacturer. Less expensive models might not provide the same quality as approved models. Ensure that the replacement has a power jack that does not wiggle when it is inserted into the device. Ensure that a laptop power brick has the appropriate DC voltage required by the laptop. Current (amperage) should be equal to or greater than in the original power brick.

FIGURE 10.67   Laptop powered by AC power

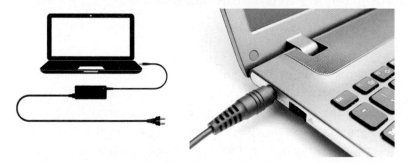

FIGURE 10.68   Laptop power adapter and power connector

> **TECH TIP**
>
> **Do not power on after a temperature change**
>
> Computers are designed to work within a range of temperatures, and sudden change is not good for them. If a mobile device is in a car all night and the temperature drops, allow the device to return to room temperature before powering it on. Avoid direct sunlight. It is usually 40°F hotter inside the computer case than outside it.

Laptop Battery Removal

Laptop batteries fail and have to be replaced. Ensure that you disconnect the AC adapter and power the laptop off before removing the battery. You may have to turn the laptop over to access the battery compartment. Laptop batteries are normally modules that have one or two release latches that are used to remove the module (see Figure 10.69).

FIGURE 10.69   Release latch for laptop battery removal

Battery technologies have improved in the past few years, probably driven by the development of more devices that need battery power, such as tablets, digital cameras, and portable optical drive players. Laptops use lithium-ion (**Li-ion**) **batteries**, which are very light and can hold a charge longer than any other type. They are also more expensive than other battery types. Mobile phones, tablets, portable media players, and digital cameras also use Li-ion batteries. These batteries lose their charge over time, even if they are not being used. Use your laptop with battery-provided power. Some vendors recommend to not leave a laptop with a Li-ion battery plugged into an AC outlet all the time.

TECH TIP

Keep Li-ion batteries cool

Li-ion batteries last longer if they are kept cool (not frozen). When you store a Li-ion battery, the battery should be only 40% charged and placed in a refrigerator to prolong its life.

Li-ion polymer batteries are similar to other Li-ion batteries except that they are packed in pouched cells. This design allows for smaller batteries and a more efficient use of space, which is important in the portable computer and mobile device industries. For environmentalists, the zinc-air battery is the one to watch. AER Energy Resources, Inc., has several patents on a battery that uses oxygen to generate electricity. Air is allowed to flow during battery discharge and is blocked when the battery is not in use. This battery holds a charge for extended periods of time. Another upcoming technology is fuel cells. Fuel cells used for a laptop can provide power for 5 to 10 hours.

Getting the Most from Your Laptop Battery

Mobile devices rely on their batteries to provide mobility. The following tips can help you get more time out of your batteries:

> Most people do not need a spare Li-ion battery. If you are not using a Li-ion battery constantly, it is best not to buy a spare. The longer the spare sits unused, the shorter the life span it will have.
> Buy the battery recommended by the laptop manufacturer.
> For a mobile device or smartphone, use an AC outlet rather than a USB port for faster charging.
> If using a USB port for charging a mobile device or smartphone, unplug all unused USB devices. Note that not all USB ports can provide a charge if the host device is in sleep mode.
> Avoid using an optical player when running on battery power.

> Turn off the wireless adapter if a wireless network is not being used.
> In the power options, configure the mobile device for hibernate rather than standby.
> Save work only when necessary and turn off the autosave feature.
> Reduce the screen brightness.
> Avoid using external USB devices such as flash drives or external hard drives.
> Install more RAM to reduce swapping of information from the hard drive to RAM to CPU or to just be more efficient.
> In mobile devices, keep battery contacts clean with a dab of rubbing alcohol on a lint-free swab once a month.
> Avoid running multiple programs.
> If possible, disable automatic updates.
> Avoid temperature extremes.
> Turn off location services.
> The laptop manufacturer might also support a wireless charging mat that allows a laptop battery to be charged without an AC adapter.

Windows *Power Options* Control Panel settings for a laptop include the following links: Require a Password on Wakeup, Choose What the Power Button Does (as shown in Figure 10.70), Choose What Closing the Lid Does, Create a Power Plan, Choose When to Turn Off the Display, and Change When the Computer Sleeps. Laptop power settings affect battery life. Users and technicians should adjust these settings to best fit how the laptop or mobile device is used.

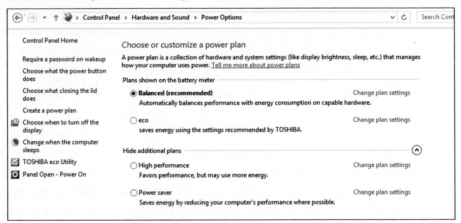

FIGURE 10.70   Laptop power settings

Another way to control the power settings on a Windows laptop is through the battery meter in the bottom-right corner of the screen on the taskbar. When you hover a pointer over the battery meter, the percentage of battery power remaining is shown. By clicking on the meter you can change the power option or adjust the screen brightness. Figure 10.71 shows the screen that displays when the battery meter icon is clicked.

FIGURE 10.71   Laptop battery meter

Laptop Repairs Overview

It is a bit more difficult to get replacement or upgrade parts in a laptop than in a desktop PC because the parts are smaller and a bit different due to manufacturers keeping the laptops light, portable, and maintaining speeds equal to those of desktop computers. Most laptop parts are manufacturer-dependent (except for storage devices and memory). Laptop repairs require more attention to detail than do desktop models because there are so many screws, the screws are much smaller, and there is little space in which to work. Be patient. The following is a good list of items to remember when disassembling and reconnecting everything in a laptop:

> Use proper antistatic procedures. There are not always good places to attach an antistatic wrist strap. Consider using antistatic gloves (refer to Figure 5.3). Maintain skin contact when touching parts if no other antistatic tools are used; this is known as self-grounding.

> Organize your parts. Use an egg carton and label individual sections with screws of like length and type, as well as where the screws came from. Otherwise, use tape sticky side up to place like screws on and make notes to go with them.

> Take photos.

> Take notes.

> Use appropriate tools. Scribes are very handy when removing plastic pieces. Very thin needle-nose pliers are great with laptop connectors. It is important to have #1 and #0 Phillips screwdrivers.

> Always refer to the manufacturer's directions when removing and installing parts. Having a tablet or phone where you can pull this document up while you work is fine. Use your resources. No person can know all models of all machines they work on.

Some laptop and mobile device compartments require levering the compartment cover away from the case or removing plastic parts such as the cover or frame that fits over a mobile computer keyboard. A plastic **scribe** is the best tool to use for this levering. Figure 10.72 shows a plastic scribe being used to lift the plastic part that is between the keyboard and the laptop screen. Go back to Figure 5.6 to see another photo of a scribe.

FIGURE 10.72   Plastic scribe

Laptop System Board/Processor Replacement

Laptop motherboards (**system boards**) are similar to desktop motherboards. A mobile device motherboard holds the majority of the electronics, contains a processor, has memory, and supports having ports attached. The processor on a mobile device is typically not as powerful as that on a desktop model, it might have less memory that may not be upgradeable, and it has fewer ports. However, some powerful laptops have more power, upgradability, and ports than some low-end desktop models.

In order to get to the system board, at a minimum, screws from the underside of the laptop have to be removed. Sometimes a hard drive, a drive that inserts on the side, the keyboard, and memory must be removed before you can remove the motherboard. Figure 10.73 shows a laptop system board.

FIGURE 10.73 Laptop system board

Before replacing a motherboard, it is important to do all the following:

> Disconnect the AC power connector.
> Remove the battery.
> Disconnect external devices, such as the mouse, keyboard, and monitor.
> Remove adapters.
> Remove memory from expansion slots.

> Disconnect cables, taking care to use any release tabs and not to pull on the cables but on the connector. Needle-nose pliers may be needed.
> Remove the optical drive and hard drive.
> Remove the processor and cooling assembly. Note that this may be done after removing the motherboard. Store the processor in an antistatic bag. It will have to be reinstalled and possibly some new thermal paste will need to be applied when the new system board is installed.
> Remember that replacement system boards do not come with RAM, a processor, or adapters.
> Make a note or take a photo of the CPU orientation before removing it from the bad/older system board.

Laptop processors are not normally upgraded, but they do sometimes have to be replaced. Always refer to the laptop documentation for motherboard removal procedures. Always power off the laptop and remove the laptop battery before working inside the laptop. Use proper grounding procedures. A laptop processor may have a heat sink and/or fan assembly attached (look back to Figure 10.73). Furthermore, some processor sockets must be loosened or a screw loosened/removed before you lift the processor from the socket, as shown in Figure 10.74. Figure 10.75 shows a processor being removed.

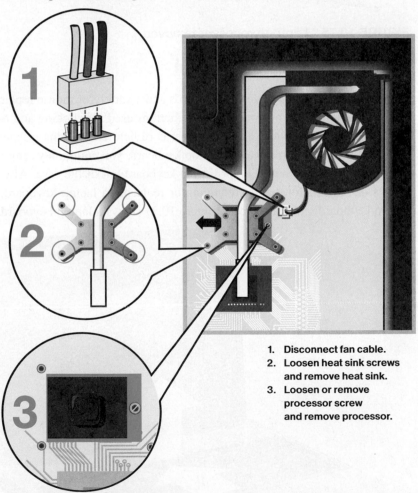

1. Disconnect fan cable.
2. Loosen heat sink screws and remove heat sink.
3. Loosen or remove processor screw and remove processor.

FIGURE 10.74   Laptop processor removal steps

FIGURE 10.75   Laptop processor removed

Laptop Keyboards/Touchpad

Laptops usually have integrated keyboards and a variety of mouse replacement devices, such as a touch stick, touchpad, and/or one or two buttons used for clicking and right-clicking. You should always remove the battery and AC power cord before removing a laptop keyboard or any other internal laptop part. To remove a laptop keyboard, you commonly remove screws from the top or bottom of the laptop and slide or lift the keyboard out of the case. Always refer to the manufacturer's documentation before removing or replacing a laptop keyboard. Figure 10.76 shows the laptop keyboard removal process. Figure 10.77 shows a laptop keyboard that has been removed.

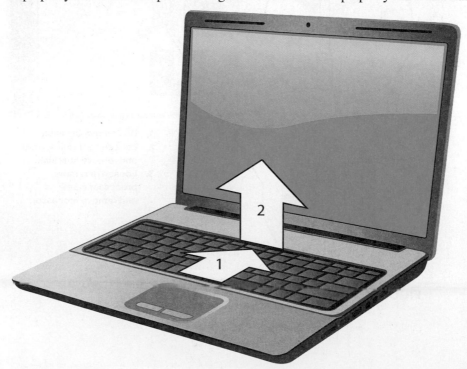

FIGURE 10.76   Laptop keyboard removal process

These concepts relate to Apple computers, too

Even though this book focuses on PCs, concepts related to CPUs, motherboards, expansion slots, caches, and chipsets also apply to Apple computers. Apple computers and PCs have similar CPU and memory requirements.

FIGURE 10.77 Removed laptop keyboard

Replacing the touchpad or mouse-like devices on laptops requires a little more work and disassembly than a keyboard. Sometimes an internal drive, memory, the keyboard, the wireless network card, and/or the system board must be removed before you can access the screws, connector, and/or cable that hold the touchpad in place. Sometimes the keyboard must be turned upside down to get to the touch stick. Look back at Figure 10.77, and you can see the blue touch stick attached to the keyboard.

Touchpads are also sensitive and may need to be adjusted through the operating system during regular use or after replacement. For a Mac, use the Apple icon in the upper-left corner to select *System Preferences > Trackpad*. The touchpad settings in Windows 7, 8, and 10 are accessed through the *Hardware and Sound* Control Panel > *Mouse*, as shown in Figure 10.78. Notice that this vendor has its own tab. Some vendors have their own touchpad Control Panel.

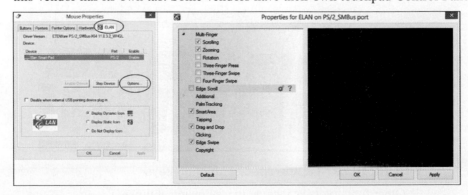

FIGURE 10.78 Touchpad area of the Control Panel

What to do if the laptop keyboard or touchpad goes bad

You can replace mobile keyboards/pointing devices or use external wired or wireless ones.

Laptops have **special function keys**. These keys are in the uppermost part of the keyboard. They are labeled (F1), (F2), and so on through (F10) or (F12). They allow you to quickly control screen brightness and hibernation, turn WiFi on/off, mute sound, and perform other functions. For example, on some laptops when you press the (Fn) key (lower-left side of keyboard) while simultaneously pressing the (F5) key, your screen brightness increases. Refer to your particular device's user manual or look at the symbols on the keyboard for a clue about what they can do when combined with the (Fn) key. Table 10.14 lists one vendor's function keys. Figure 10.79 shows a close-up of some of the laptop function keys. See if you can guess what features they perform.

TABLE 10.14   Sample laptop function keys

(Fn) + ____	Description
(F1)	Mute the speaker
(F2)	Decrease sound
(F3)	Increase sound
(F4)	Turn the system off
(F5)	Refresh the browser window
(F6)	Enable/disable the touchpad
(F7)	Decrease display brightness
(F8)	Increase display brightness
(F9)	Switch display output to an external device
(F10)	Switch power modes
(F11)	Enable/disable Bluetooth
(F12)	Enable/disable WiFi

FIGURE 10.79   Laptop special function keys

Other function keys include the following abilities:

> Enable/disable cellular
> Enable/disable the touchpad
> Change the screen orientation

> Enable/disable GPS
> Enable/disable Bluetooth
> Enable/disable Airplane Mode
> Enable/disable keyboard backlighting
> Media options such as fast forward and rewind for videos or audio playback
> Video controls such as dual displays, external display, laptop display and external display, and blanking the display (See Figure 10.80 for a couple examples of video controls that require the use of a function key.)

FIGURE 10.80   Laptop video output special function keys

Laptop Memory

The memory chips used with laptops are different from the ones used in desktop or tower computers. Laptops use a special form factor called a small-outline DIMM (**SODIMM**). Other types exist (microDIMMs and small-outline RIMMs [SORIMMs]), but SODIMMs are the most popular, and they come in a 72-pin version for 32-bit transfers and 144-, 200-, 204-, or 260-pin versions for 64-bit transfers. Figure 10.81 shows the difference between DDR2, DDR3, and DDR4 SODIMMs. Each type of SODIMM is notched differently and cannot fit in another type of slot (that is, a DDR4 SODIMM requires a DDR4 SODIMM memory slot).

200-pin SODIMM DDR 2

204-pin SODIMM DDR 3

260-pin SODIMM DDR 4

FIGURE 10.81   SODIMM form factors

Some laptops cannot be upgraded. Many laptops have only one memory slot, so when you upgrade, you must replace the module that is installed. Some smartphones, tablets, and laptops can be upgraded with flash memory cards. Refer to Figures 10.8, 10.9, 10.10, and 10.11 to see some examples of flash media.

Planning the Laptop Memory Upgrade

In addition to determining what type of memory chips are going to be used, you must determine what features the memory chip might have. The computer system or motherboard documentation delineates what features are supported. Refer to Table 6.3 for a refresher on memory technologies. Laptop memory advertisements are similar to desktop memory advertisements, as shown in Table 10.15.

TABLE 10.15 Sample SODIMM advertisements

Memory	Advertisement
2 GB	204-pin SODIMM DDR3 1333 Unbuffered 1.35V CAS Latency 9
4 GB	204-pin SODIMM DDR3 1333 Unbuffered 1.5V CAS Latency 10
8 GB kit (2×4 GB)	204-pin SODIMM DDR3 1600 Unbuffered 1.5V CAS Latency 9
16 GB kit (2×8 GB)	260-pin SODIMM DDR4 2,400 MHz (PC4-19200) CL16 (16-16-16-39 Non-ECC Unbuffered 1.2V

Notice in Table 10.15 that the 2 GB memory module runs at 1.35 V, and the others run at 1.5 V or 1.2 V. Some motherboards support **dual-voltage memory**, which   means the motherboard supports the memory module that runs at the lower 1.35 V or 1.2 V level. 1.35 V memory modules use less power and generate less heat. Note that all memory modules must be 1.35 V modules to operate at 1.35 V.

Say that you want to upgrade memory for a laptop. First, you would open a web browser and search for the specific model and look for the memory specifications (that is, how many slots and what type of memory the laptop allows). Say that the laptop came with 4 GB of RAM, but it has the capacity to hold 8 GB; it has two memory slots, and it currently has two 2 GB SODIMMs installed. In order to upgrade, you will have to purchase two memory modules of 4 GB each and replace the modules that are currently in the laptop.

Laptop Memory Removal/Installation

Many laptops have only one memory slot, so when you upgrade, you must remove the module that is installed. Always refer to the manufacturer's documentation when doing this. Before installing or removing laptop memory, always turn off the laptop, disconnect the AC power cord (if installed), and remove the battery.

When installing memory into a mobile device, refer to the documentation to see whether a retaining screw on the bottom of the unit must be removed or if the keyboard must be removed in order to access the memory slots. Be sure the laptop memory notch fits into the key in the memory slot. Laptop memory is normally installed at a 45-degree angle into the slot. Press down on the module until it locks into the side clips. The trick to installing memory is to push firmly into the slot and then into the side clamps. Figure 10.82 shows how to access the memory module in a laptop and the installation process. Notice that the laptop battery has been removed.

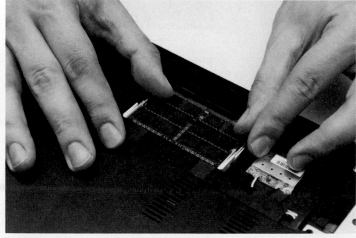

FIGURE 10.82 Accessing and installing a laptop memory module

Laptop Storage

Laptop hard drives come in two major form factors—1.8-inch and 2.5-inch. The **2.5-inch** form factor is designed for laptops. A **1.8-inch** form factor is found in laptops, ultrabooks, and ultra-portable devices such as MP3 players, and it is also used for SSDs. Figure 10.83 shows a 2.5-inch hard drive installed in a laptop.

FIGURE 10.83 Installed 2.5-inch laptop hard drive

TECH TIP

What to do if you want more storage space for a laptop

A laptop typically does not allow a second hard drive. However, you can add an additional hard drive to the USB, eSATA, or combo eSATAp port.

Hard drives in laptops tend to be one of three types, as described in Table 10.16.

TABLE 10.16 Laptop hard drive types

Type	Description
Mechanical drive	This is a traditional drive that requires a motor to spin and has read/write heads that float over the hard drive platters.
SSD	An SSD uses flash memory technology to store data. It has no moving parts and produces less heat than a mechanical drive. It is very fast but more expensive than a mechanical drive.
Hybrid drive	This type of drive is sometimes known as a solid-state hybrid drive (SSHD). Part of the drive is an SSD to store the operating system, and the other part is a traditional mechanical drive to hold user data.

Internal Laptop Drives

Laptops traditionally had a PATA or SATA hard drive installed, but today they have an SSD instead of or in addition to these hard drive types. Other mobile devices, such as ultrabooks and tablets, use SSDs as well. A miniPCIe adapter, $_\mu$SATA (microSATA) connector, or an M.2 connector can be used to connect the drive to the system, or the drive can be directly attached to the motherboard using traditional SATA data and power connectors. Additional storage can be provided by devices that connect to USB, eSATA, or eSATAp ports.

External Drives

An external drive may need to be attached to external power. Some USB devices use external power, some are powered and connect to one USB port, and still others require two USB ports. Some manufacturers may require you to install software before attaching the drive. Once a drive is installed, use *Device Manager* to ensure that the drive is recognized by the operating system.

Replacing a Hard Drive

Two methods are used with hard drives installed in portable computers: proprietary or removable. With a proprietary installation, the hard drive is installed in a location where it cannot be changed, configured, or moved very easily. Proprietary cables and connectors are used. With removable hard drives, the laptop has a hard drive bay that allows installation/removal through a single connector that provides power as well as data signaling. Otherwise, the drive could have separate data and power connectors.

To remove a laptop hard drive, always follow the manufacturer's instructions. Also ensure that you are replacing the drive with the correct size and interface before starting the process. The following are generic steps for removing/replacing a laptop hard drive:

Step 1. Power down the laptop and remove the battery.

Step 2. Turn the computer upside down to locate the panel used to access the hard drive. Take appropriate antistatic precautions. Note that some laptop models have hard drives that release to the side of the computer.

Step 3. Remove any screws to gain access to the drive. A sliding lock release may also allow access to the drive area. Do not lose these screws as screws may not come with the replacement drive.

Step 4. Slide the drive out of the connector and remove it from the unit. Do not force it. Some units have release levers, are mounted on a frame, and/or are mounted on rubber feet. You may need to gently rock the drive back and forth while pulling gently to ease the drive out of the laptop. Remember that this drive has probably never been removed since it was initially installed.

Reverse the process to install a new drive that has the same form factor. Figure 10.84 shows a SATA hard drive being mounted inside a frame before being installed in a laptop.

FIGURE 10.84   Installing a laptop hard drive

Upgrading a Hard Drive to an SSD

When replacing a laptop hard drive with an SSD, because there is only one drive bay, an external drive enclosure that holds the SSD is needed for the installation process. The enclosure might later be used for the current hard drive to make it an external drive. Also, third-party software that clones your computer and allows you to move selected applications over to the SSD without reinstallation of the software is useful.

Figure 10.85 shows an SSD drive being installed in a laptop. Remember to have AC power attached during this process. The following are generic steps used to replace a hard drive with an SSD:

Step 1. Delete any unneeded files and folders. Uninstall any unneeded, unwanted, or unused applications.

Step 2. Defragment the hard drive or run Disk Cleanup.

Step 3. Create a system image.

Step 4. Put the SSD in an external enclosure, if necessary, and connect it to the laptop or install the M.2 SSD into the M.2 slot.

Step 5. Use the *Disk Management* tool to verify that Windows recognizes the drive. If the drive is listed as "Not initialized," right-click on the drive and select *Initialize Disk*. Also ensure that the used space on the current hard drive is less than that the space available on the SSD. Depending on the software you use, you may have to shrink your current hard drive partition that has the operating system installed to less than that of the SSD. If you do, reboot the computer after all operations to ensure that the hard drive is still working properly.

Step 6. Use third-party software to clone the current hard drive to the SSD.

Step 7. If you used an external enclosure, power off the laptop. Remove the old hard drive and install the SSD.

Step 8. Power on the laptop and ensure that the SSD boots and all applications work.

FIGURE 10.85   Installing a laptop SSD

Optical Drive Replacement

Mobile devices that have optical disc drives can be slot-loaded drives (where you insert the disc into a slot on the side or front of the mobile device) or mounted drives. For mounted drives, you typically need to turn over the laptop to access the drive. You might even have to remove the keyboard in order to gain access to the drive. Look for the little symbol of the optical disc. Not all manufacturers use this symbol, so be sure to research the particular mobile device model. Remove the appropriate screw(s) and then pull out the drive. Before replacing an optical drive, blow compressed air on the drive to clear out any collected residue. Reinstall and retest the drive. Figure 10.86 shows an internal laptop optical drive.

FIGURE 10.86   Internal laptop optical drive

Smart Card Reader Replacement

A laptop may have an integrated smart card reader that can be used to easily copy files from various flash media. You should always refer to the laptop manufacturer's documentation on how to replace the reader, but generic steps are provided:

Step 1. Disconnect the power brick and remove the battery.

Step 2. Use appropriate antistatic measures and remove any other parts, such as the keyboard, in order to gain access to the smart card cable.

Step 3. Disconnect the smart card cable.

Step 4. Remove any retaining screws from the smart card reader. Remember not to press hard downward to remove the screw for the first time. Do not strip the screw.

Step 5. Slide the smart card reader out of the laptop.

Reverse the steps to install the replacement reader.

Laptop Wireless/Bluetooth Card Replacement

The laptop wireless card is commonly located under the keyboard or accessible from the underside of the laptop. Figure 10.87 shows an 802.11ac WiFi and Bluetooth card.

FIGURE 10.87   802.11ac WiFi and Bluetooth laptop card

Refer to the manufacturer's website for the exact procedures. The generic removal steps are as follows:

Step 1. Disconnect the AC power and remove the battery. Take appropriate antistatic precautions.

Step 2. Locate the wireless card. In Figure 10.83, a WLAN card is shown to the immediate left of the hard drive and is labeled WLAN (upside down in the photo).

Step 3. Disconnect the one or two wireless antenna cables from the card (see Figure 10.88). Notice that the wires attach to two posts on the wireless NIC. These wires connect the antenna to the wireless NIC. A small flat-tipped screwdriver, small needle-nose pliers, or tweezers might be used for this task. Be very careful with this step. Cables are not typically included with a replacement wireless card. Take a picture or make a note about which cable attaches to which connector if multiple cables are used.

Step 4. Ease the wireless card out of the laptop. Note that a lever or tab may be used, depending on the vendor. Make a note or take a photo of how the wireless card inserts into the slot.

Simply reverse these steps to install the replacement card.

TECH TIP

Where is the wireless antenna on a laptop?

For laptops that have integrated wireless NICs, the wireless antenna is usually built into the laptop display for best connectivity. This is because the display is the tallest point of the laptop and is therefore closest to the wireless receiving antenna. The quality of integrated antennas varies.

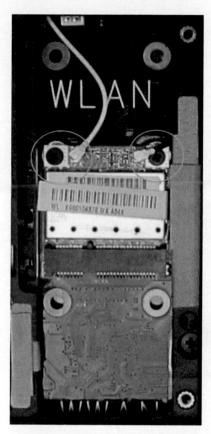

FIGURE 10.88   Laptop wireless NIC

Laptop DC Jack Replacement

Because of the numerous times the AC-to-DC power brick is attached to a laptop, it makes sense that laptop power jacks need to be replaced sometimes. The **DC jack** is where you attach power to the laptop. You know the jack is problematic when a new power brick doesn't work, when you can see a broken pin or loose pin in the DC jack, or when you use a multimeter to test the DC voltage level coming out of the power brick, and it is fine.

The power jack is a DC connector because the power brick takes the AC power from the wall and converts it to DC for input into the laptop. The DC jack comes with an internal power cable that usually winds through the laptop and attaches to the motherboard. It may actually be mounted on a small circuit card. Always refer to the manufacturer's replacement steps.

Figure 10.89 shows how a DC connector might connect. Always disconnect the power brick and remove the battery before starting any repair. Note that the cable attached to the DC jack may have retaining clips or might be threaded through a very narrow space. Do not damage adjacent parts. Document any parts that you have to remove in order to remove the defective DC jack.

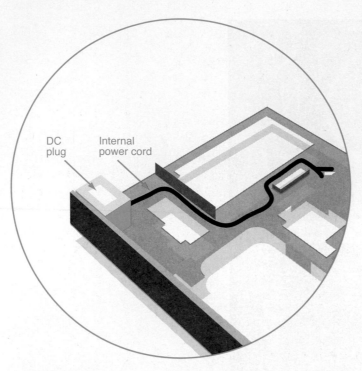

DC plug

Internal power cord

FIGURE 10.89   Laptop DC jack (plug) and power cable

Mobile Device Sound

Laptop speakers are not always of the highest quality. Compared to desktop computers, mobile devices are limited in their sound options. A mobile device normally has an integrated microphone, a line out connector for headphones, and sound integrated into the system board.

Laptop devices normally allow the user to control sound with buttons above the keypad or by selecting a combination of Fn and another key.

For Android mobile devices, use the *Setting > Sound* option to mute and modify the ringtone. Optionally, you can also select sounds to be played, such as when the screen unlocks or when switching between screens.

For Apple iOS devices, use the *General > Settings > Sounds* option. The speaker volume and sounds heard for email, phone calls, reminders, keyboard clicks, and so on are set on this screen. Both Android and Apple iOS-based mobile devices have volume controls on the sides.

Consider using wireless or USB speakers if a laptop speaker fails. Keep in mind that if a sound device is powered by the USB port, this shortens battery life. Laptop speakers are commonly located in the sides or back corners of the laptop. Figure 10.90 shows two different models of mobile device speakers.

When replacing laptop speakers, be careful when tracing and removing the speaker wires. Always refer to the manufacturer's directions. Speaker wires must sometimes be wiggled gently in order to detach them. They commonly screw into the motherboard. Inspect the speaker wire path before removing the wire. Other parts may have to be removed in order to remove the faulty speakers.

Microphones in tablets normally do not have controls, as laptops and PCs. Instead, the microphone is controlled through an application that supports a microphone, such as a notepad that allows you to add audio notes or record a lecture or an online conference application. Inside the application, there is normally a little icon of a microphone that you tap in order to start recording. External microphones can be added using wireless Bluetooth connectivity or an external microphone (if the tablet has a jack). Smartphones, of course, have integrated microphones.

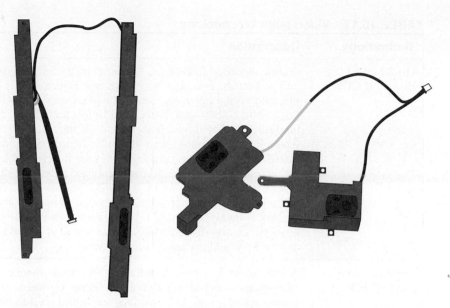

FIGURE 10.90   Internal laptop speakers

Laptop Video Card Replacement

A laptop is likely to have a GPU built into the motherboard or soldered onto the motherboard. Video cards are not a common replacement item because replaceable video cards make the laptop heavier and thicker. You can achieve extra graphics output to additional external displays by using a USB-to-HDMI (see Figure 10.91) or USB-to-DVI external adapter.

FIGURE 10.91   USB-to-HDMI adapter

Laptop Display

The laptop display is one of the most complex parts of a laptop. Three of the most popular display technologies are listed in Table 10.17.

TABLE 10.17 Video output technology

Technology	Description
Liquid crystal display (**LCD**)	Technology used in laptops, flat panel monitors, TVs, tablets, smartphones, and projectors. Two glass substrates (see Figure 10.92) have a thin layer of liquid crystal between them. One glass substrate is the color filter, with three main colors—red, green, and blue—that allow millions of colors to be displayed. The other glass substrate is the thin film transistor (TFT) array, which has the technology to direct the liquid crystal to block the light. A **backlight** (which can be a cold cathode fluorescent lamp (**CCFL**) or LED technology) extends behind the combined glass assembly, and the light is always on. This is why an LCD monitor appears to sometimes glow even when it's off and why crystals are needed to block some of the light to create the intensities of light. Liquid crystals are sensitive to temperature changes. Laptop displays may appear distorted in cold or hot temperatures due to the liquid crystals.
Light-emitting diode (**LED**)	A low-power, low-heat, long-lasting electronic device used in many technologies, including calculators, home, business, and auto lighting, fiber optics, and displays. LED displays use liquid crystals as well as an LED backlight instead of a CCFL. LED displays have better color accuracy than LCDs, are thinner than the LCDs that use CCFLs, and are commonly used for large displays.
Organic LED (**OLED**)	Does not require a backlight, like LCDs, but has a film of organic compounds placed in rows and columns that can emit light. Is lightweight, has a fast response time, low power usage, and a wide viewing angle; found in TVs, mobile phones, and handheld game consoles.

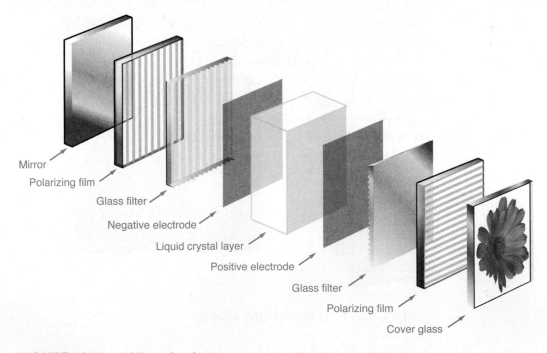

Mirror
Polarizing film
Glass filter
Negative electrode
Liquid crystal layer
Positive electrode
Glass filter
Polarizing film
Cover glass

FIGURE 10.92 LCD technology

TECH TIP

Liquid crystals are poisonous

Be careful with cracked LCDs. If liquid crystals (which are not actually liquid) get on you, wash with soap and water and seek medical attention.

A laptop may have a **rotating/removable screen**. If the display is removable, it normally can be used as a tablet. A laptop with a rotating display is useful in offices where information is to be shared or shown to a person sitting in front of a desk. The display can be rotated in the opposite direction or just turned a bit, as shown in Figure 10.93.

FIGURE 10.93   Laptop with rotating screen

To rotate the screen, always follow the manufacturer's instructions. Many models have a display release latch located near the area where the display connects to the part of the laptop case where the keyboard is located. Press the release latch and turn the display.

If a laptop doesn't have a display that physically rotates but you want to change the orientation of the information on the screen, you can adjust the rotation through Windows. In Windows 7, 8, or 10, locate the *Display* Control Panel, and if multiple monitors are present, select the one to be changed, locate the *Orientation* drop-down box and select the orientation you would like, and click *Apply*. Note that if you have a special graphics card, you may use an application like the Intel Graphics Media Accelerator to configure the graphics properties.

Besides the laptop screen, the display assembly contains other parts, and some of them have nothing to do with the screen. Table 10.18 outlines some common components found in a laptop display.

TABLE 10.18   Laptop display components

Component	Description
WiFi antenna	Attaches to the WLAN card (which is commonly under the computer and/or attached to the system board) in order to receive/transmit wireless signals.
Webcam	A camera used for video conferencing (and as a camera/video recorder in other mobile devices). Some laptops have the ability to use the integrated camera for facial recognition as a security measure. However, because the biometric software cannot distinguish between a living face and a digitized image, it is possible to fool the software by using a photograph.
Microphone	A device used to digitize voice into 1s and 0s so that sound may be heard on a conference call or in a recording. Microphones are used for voice over IP (VoIP) and are tested through the *Recording* tab of the Sound Control Panel.
Inverter	Converts DC to AC for the CCFL backlight.
Digitizer	Found in a touchscreen display; a thin layer of plastic that translates pressure, swipes, or other touch actions into digital signals. Replacement is sometimes difficult and usually cheaper than replacing the display.

Laptops use LCDs and have a video cable that connects the LCD to the motherboard. Either a CCFL or LED backlight bulb is used on many models so images on the screen can be seen. The CCFL type connects to an inverter (see Figure 10.94). The inverter converts low DC voltage to high AC voltage for the backlight bulb. Screens larger than 15.4 inches may need two CCFL backlight bulbs. An LCD with an LED backlight does not need an inverter. An OLED display doesn't need an inverter or a backlight.

TECH TIP

Is it worth fixing a laptop display?

Laptop displays might be too expensive to repair, but if the inverter or backlight is the faulty part, the repair cost is negligible.

The lid close detector (displayed in Figure 10.94) can be a physical switch or a magnetic switch located close to the back edge of the keyboard portion of a laptop. The laptop can be configured through power management configuration to go into hibernation, sleep, or standby mode when the laptop is closed.

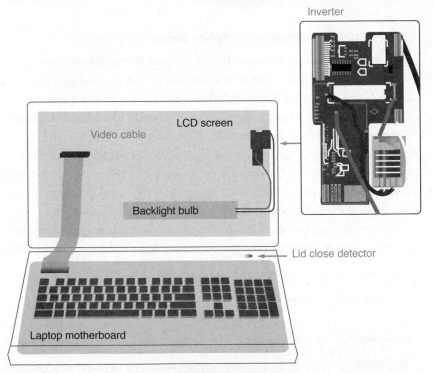

FIGURE 10.94   **Laptop video connectivity**

The laptop display may need to be replaced as part of a repair. When removing a laptop display, always refer to the directions from the computer manufacturer. The following steps are generic:

Step 1. Use proper antistatic precautions and remove the screws that hold the screen bezel in place.

Step 2. If you have a display that is inside the plastic cover (and does not go right to the edge of the laptop), you must gently pry the plastic bezel that protects the screen edge from the case. Note that there may be little covers over screws. Remove the covers and then the screws, if necessary. There is a light adhesive, and you might want to use a hair dryer on low heat to warm up the adhesive so it is easier to pry off. The screen might also be held in place by hinge covers. Turn the laptop upside down and use a tool to separate the hinge cover at the seam.

Step 3. Remove the screen's retaining screws.

Step 4. Gently lift the screen from the case. Be very careful with the connectors. Flip the screen so the back of the screen is visible.

Step 5. Notice the ribbon cable that runs up the back of the display. Gently disconnect the cable at the top of the display and the cable that connects to the motherboard. Some cables you must squeeze to release; others have pull tabs or need to be gently pulled from the socket. Figure 10.95 shows the back side of an LCD that uses a CCFL backlight.

TECH TIP

What is the best resolution for a laptop display?

Set a laptop to the native resolution (the resolution for which the LCD was made).

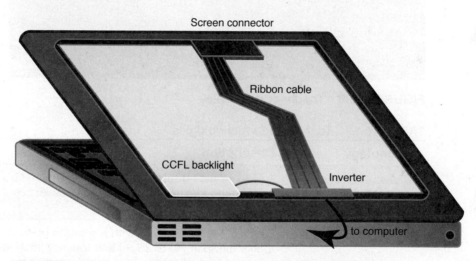

FIGURE 10.95 Removing an LCD with an LED backlight

Touchscreens

Touchscreen displays are used with PCs, tablets, and smartphones. They respond to contact on the screen rather than keyboard or mouse input. A touchscreen is both an input device and an output device. Touchscreens are commonly used in situations where information is to be controlled and in public areas, such as for kiosks at airports, malls, and entrance areas of schools or businesses. A touchscreen monitor normally attaches to a USB, VGA, DVI, or HDMI port, a combination of these ports, or wirelessly (on a desktop model). Special drivers and software are used to control the monitor.

Several technologies are used to manufacture a touchscreen display. The two most common ones are resistive and capacitive. A resistive touchscreen has a flexible membrane stretched over the face of the display. The membrane contains a special metal oxide coating and has spacers that are used to locate the touched spot on the screen. Resistive touchscreens are good in manufacturing or in the medical industry where personnel wear gloves. A stylus can also be used with both types of displays.

Capacitive touchscreens are more durable than resistive screens. They respond to a touch or multiple touches on the display and easily detect contact. Most touchscreens are the capacitive type. Some mobile devices allow you to calibrate the screen or lock the screen orientation by using the *Settings* option. Figure 10.96 shows a touchscreen. Table 10.19 lists some of the technologies used with touchscreen displays.

FIGURE 10.96   Touchscreen display

TABLE 10.19   Touchscreen technologies

Technology	Description
Four-wire resistive	1.7- to 24-inch displays with high resolution. Has a short life span (1 to 2 million touches) and low brightness. Accepts input from fingers, a gloved hand, or a stylus.
Five-wire resistive	10.4- to 24-inch displays with resolution up to 1,024×1,024. Has a longer life span (30 to 35 million touches) than four-wire resistive and low brightness. Accepts input from fingers, a gloved hand, or a stylus.
Capacitive	12- to 27-inch displays with resolution up to 2,560×1,440. Has a longer life span than any of the resistive types (100 million touches) and high brightness. Accepts finger input.
Surface wave	10.4- to 30-inch displays with high resolutions. Lasts a long time (50 million touches) and has high brightness. Accepts input from fingers, a gloved hand, or a soft stylus. Tends to have the longest warranties.
Infrared	10.4- to 42-inch displays with high resolutions, long-term reliability (more than 100 million touches), and high brightness. Accepts input from fingers, a gloved hand, and a stylus.

Touchscreen Replacement

The touchscreen may be part of the LCD, and if it is, you just replace the LCD as described earlier. Alternatively, a touchscreen may be a separate assembly, in which case you remove the retaining screws and lean the screen backward so that the screen doesn't fall forward when all screws are removed. The screen may have to be pried from the outside casing, using a metal or plastic prying tool that has a small flat edge. Gently lean the screen forward and notice the cable/connector that connects to the screen. There may be a retaining bar and/or tape or a tab on the connector.

Figure 10.97 shows a touchscreen that has just been removed. Only one cable is the video cable that goes to the motherboard. The other cables connect to the WiFi/Bluetooth and cellular cards.

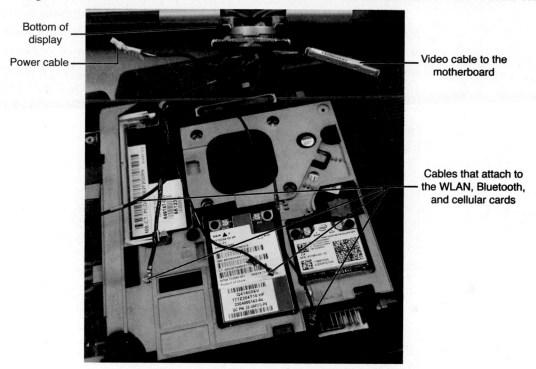

FIGURE 10.97 Removing a touchscreen from the motherboard

After a touchscreen is replaced, use Device Manager to verify that it is recognized by the operating system. Expand the *Human Interface Devices* (HID) section to ensure the device and driver are shown. Most manufacturers provide their updates through Windows updates, but you might want to check the manufacturer's website to see if there is a newer driver.

The technologies that enable touchscreens allow users to interact with mobile devices and displays of all types with ease. A touchscreen has multiple configurations that can be controlled, including how swiping is controlled, as shown in Figure 10.98.

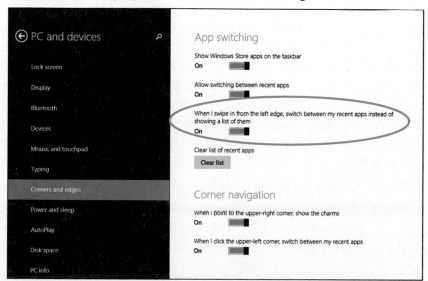

FIGURE 10.98 Sample swipe configuration

After replacing a touchscreen, you might need to calibrate it. In Windows 7, use the *Start* button > *Control Panel* > *Hardware and Sound* > under the *Tablet PC Settings*, select *Calibrate Your Pen or Touch Input* > *Display* tab > locate *Display Options* > *Calibrate*. Follow the instructions on the screen.

In Windows 8, use the *Settings* > *PC and Devices* > *Calibrate the Screen for Pen or Touch Input*, as shown in Figure 10.99. To access this area of the Control Panel in Windows 8, simply search for the word **calibrate** and select the *Calibrate the Screen for Pen or Touch Input* link in the resulting list. Use the *Setup* button to calibrate the screen for either a pen or for touch. In Windows 10, search on the word **calibrate** and select *Calibrate Display Color*. To calibrate a Mac display, access the Apple menu > *System Preferences* > *Displays* > *Color* > click *Calibrate*.

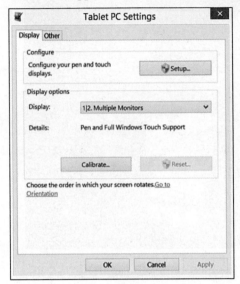

FIGURE 10.99   Windows touchscreen calibration

If the new touchscreen does not function, make sure the replacement screen is really a touchscreen and that the digitizer cable(s) are attached.

Webcam/Integrated Microphone Replacement

If a webcam and microphone are built into the display, they are commonly on the same circuit board. Before replacing a webcam or microphone, make sure that the part is actually faulty. Start by checking to see if Device Manager recognizes it. If you just upgraded the operating system, such as to Windows 10, you might need an updated driver rather than a new webcam. Try another application with it, use a different browser with the application, use the testwebcam.com website, or try a video chat session with a friend. You might also consider adding an external device by using USB or Bluetooth instead of repairing the built-in device.

If the webcam or integrated microphone really is faulty, always use the documentation provided by the manufacturer. The generic directions for dealing with a webcam that is built into the display are as follows:

Step 1. Remove the screen bezel, as described earlier in this chapter, to expose the webcam.

Step 2. If the webcam is held by a screw or a horizontal connector that has light adhesive holding it to the back of the display case, use a flat-tipped screwdriver or plastic scribe to pry the webcam from the case.

Replace the device by reversing the process.

Inverter Replacement

If the inverter needs to be replaced, always follow the recommended installation directions provided by the manufacturer. Generic instructions for replacement are as follows:

Step 1. Remove the screen bezel, as described earlier in this chapter, to expose the inverter at the bottom of the display.

Step 2. If the inverter has a connector on either side of it, remove those cables from the inverter.

Step 3. Remove the retaining screw, if necessary.

Step 4. Remove the bad inverter.

Reverse the process to install the replacement part.

Mobile Device Security

Laptops have special physical security needs, and locking and tracking devices are available for them. Use a nondescript bag to carry a laptop to reduce the chance of theft. Have an engraved permanent asset tag attached. A **physical laptop lock** or laptop locking station can be purchased and installed on a desk. A user can place a laptop into the locking station without worrying about someone coming by and taking it.

Another option is to use the universal security slot (USS), which allows a **cable lock** or laptop alarm to be attached. Special software packages enable a laptop to automatically contact a tracking center in case of theft. Figure 10.100 shows a USS on a notebook computer.

FIGURE 10.100   Laptop cable lock

Many of the issues for wireless connectivity for laptops also apply to smartphones and tablets. But smartphones and tablets also have issues of their own. Many people think that because the devices do not have hard drives, they do not need antivirus or antimalware software. This is a misconception. It is important to install—and run—antivirus/antimalware software on mobile devices. Depending on the device, the software may not be able to automatically scan for viruses or even have a set scheduled scan time. Here are some more security suggestions:

> Mobile devices can run each app in a sandbox—a space separated from other apps. Using a sandbox provides a natural security mechanism for applications.

> Mobile device OS upgrades and updates are just as important as updates on a full-sized computer.

> Many mobile devices have GPS tracking capability that can be used to locate a lost or stolen device. This may be a paid service.

> A paid service or an app on the phone can provide the capability to perform a remote lock or a remote wipe. The remote lock disables the phone so it cannot be accessed. The remote wipe deletes all data from the device. A **remote wipe** uses software to send a command to a mobile device to do one or any of the following: delete data, factory reset, remove everything from the device so it cannot be used, or overwrite data storage to prevent forensic data recovery.

> Doing a factory reset can help when some of the app issues and resolutions discussed below do not work.

> Verifying that the phone firmware is the latest version as an update may fix a security issue.

> A mobile device may have a lost mode option that enables you to display messages on the screen for anyone who might find the device.

Most mobile devices have the ability to do some of the following types of locks or **screen locks**: have a **swipe lock**, PIN, **passcode lock**, security pattern, **facial recognition lock** or unlock, **fingerprint lock**, or password enabled that activates when the device is inactive. **Authenticator apps** can also be downloaded. To configure basic mobile security, perform the following:

> Android: *Settings > Location & Security > Set Up Screen Lock*.
> iOS: *Settings > General > Passcode Lock On* option. Use *Settings > Passcode* for more passcode options (see Figure 10.101). You can also configure the *Auto-Lock* time. On an iPad, you can use the *iPad Cover Lock/Unlock On* option.

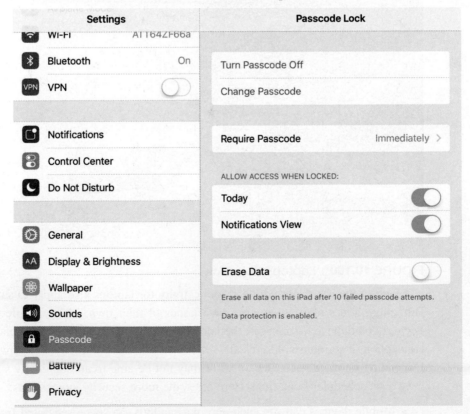

FIGURE 10.101   iOS Passcode settings

Failed Login Attempts or Unauthorized Account Access

Some mobile devices have configuration settings for when the security method fails, such as an incorrectly entered password or **system lockout**. Some devices allow a default number of attempts. For extra security, some devices can be configured to take an action after a set number of failed attempts, such as disabling the device or even erasing the data. Most mobile device users who have this capability enabled have the data backed up to the cloud or onto a machine.

On an Android device, perform a factory reset from the Android system recovery menu. In iOS, you can use the *Passcode Lock* setting (refer to Figure 10.101) to set how long the system waits for the passcode (*Require Passcode* setting). After 6 failed attempts, the iOS mobile device will be disabled for 1 minute; after 7 failed attempts, it will be disabled for 5 minutes; after 9 failed attempts, it will be disabled for an hour. If you enable the *Erase Data* option, the device will be wiped after 11 failed attempts.

So what happens if someone gets your account? Change your password immediately. Change the credit card used on the account. Notify the vendor (Apple, Microsoft, Google, and so on). If possible, enable two-step verification to prevent future issues. Some email products allow viewing account activity. Many vendors have an option to send you an email when an unusual device was used to access your account.

Unauthorized Location Tracking

Although not all mobile devices have GPS, they can obtain information from other networks and browsers to provide location services. Apps that use location services also use battery life. To turn on location services, use the following:

> On Android: *Settings > Location*.
> On iOS: *Settings > Privacy > Location Services*. (Note that you can use the *System Services* option to select which services are allowed to track your location.) You can also use *Settings > Privacy > Advertising >* enable *Limit Ad Tracking* and *Reset Advertising Identifier* in order to be prompted for which apps can track. Another option is to change your Safari or other browser settings. For Safari, *Settings > Safari >* enable *Do Not Track*.

Android and iOS have apps for dealing with mobile devices that have been lost or stolen:

> Android: *Settings > Security > Device Administration*
> iOS: *Settings > Find My iPhone*

In addition, other free and paid apps are available for dealing with mobile devices that have been lost or stolen.

Leaked Personal Files or Data

The way to protect personal files and/or data on a mobile device is to protect the device itself, secure the device, and encrypt the files (see Figure 10.102). Don't enable Bluetooth or GPS except when you need it. If you think data has already been compromised, change all passwords on all accounts and devices. Watch accounts and notify credit companies, if applicable. You can also do a factory reset on the device.

FIGURE 10.102 Leaked data on a mobile device

Unauthorized Camera/Microphone Activation

As discussed earlier in this chapter, some apps intentionally gather information about you by using your location and possibly the integrated camera and microphone. One app has the capability of figuring out where you are, who is in the room, and the sounds being heard and then correlating the data with others in the same vicinity to create a social network environment. Other apps are used for spying on people. Research each app that you or the customer installs.

Every Android app is supposed to state what access permissions are required by the app. With Android, you can ensure that *Android Device Manager* is enabled (*Settings > Security > Device Administration*). It is enabled by default. See Figure 10.103.

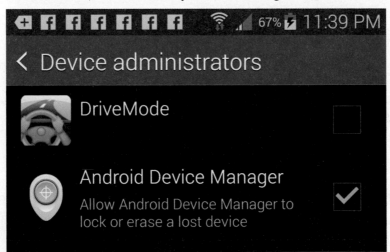

FIGURE 10.103 Android Device Manager

With iOS devices, use *Settings > Privacy > Camera/Microphone* to show what apps have requested access to either the camera or the microphone.

Not all reported activity occurs through an app. So how can you tell if someone has accessed your phone and potentially your camera and microphone as well? Here are some signs:

> Look for strange Short Message Service (SMS) text messages.
> Look for increased phone bills.
> Take notice of any weird activity on your phone, such as apps locking or opening mysteriously or slow performance.
> Take note of battery life to see if it is losing its charge faster than normal.

Data Transmission over Limit

Many mobile devices that connect to the cellular network have a specific amount of text, photo, and video allowed in the user's specific rate plan. To view how much data has been used in a specific period or to turn off cellular data, use these steps:

> Android: *Settings > Data Usage* (optionally, you can set the mobile data limit)
> iOS: *Settings > Cellular > Cellular Data*

Unauthorized Root Access

A user who has unauthorized root access has access to the mobile device's file system (see Figure 10.104). Through the file system, malicious programs can be installed, files can be downloaded and copied, and private information can be gleaned. **Jailbreaking** (iOS) and **rooting** (Android) are two terms that mean that the operating system has been compromised in such a way that the user has an increased level of privilege on the phone. On Android, this is known as having root access. For iOS devices, users bypass some of the restrictions placed on the device. People do this for several reasons, including the following: to be able to remove apps that are preinstalled and typically unremovable; to gain free access to features such as tethering that typically might require an additional charge; to enable the device to operate faster; to ensure that the device is not tied to or monitored by the operating system vendor or the phone vendor; and/or to modify the operating environment.

FIGURE 10.104   Root access to a mobile phone

Android is an open source operating system, and vendors are allowed to make modifications and customize it. For both iOS and Android devices, security and operating system releases are not received by phones that have been rooted or jailbroken. Rooting or jailbreaking a device may void a manufacturer's warranty; makes a device more susceptible to viruses, malware, and security issues; and increases the possibility of access to the root directory (the starting place for all files). If an iOS device has been jailbroken, the original iOS can be restored by using iTunes.

Mobile Device Travel and Storage

When traveling with a laptop, remove all cards that insert into slots and store them in containers so that their contacts do not become dirty and cause intermittent problems. Remove all media discs such as CDs, DVDs, or BDs. Check that drive doors and devices are securely latched. Ensure that the mobile device is powered off or in hibernate mode (not in sleep/suspend or standby power mode).

Carry the device in a padded case. If you have to place the device on an airport security conveyor belt, ensure that the device is not placed upside down, which can cause damage to the display. Never place objects on top of a mobile device or pick up a laptop by the edges of the display when the laptop is opened. When shipping a mobile device, place it in a properly padded box. The original shipping box is a safe container.

The United States has regulations about lithium batteries on airplanes. If the battery contacts come in contact with metal or other batteries, the battery could short-circuit and cause a fire. For this reason, any lithium batteries are to be kept in original packaging. If original packaging is not available, place electrical tape over the battery terminals or place each battery in an individual bag. Spare lithium batteries are not allowed in checked baggage but can be taken in carry-on bags.

Mobile Device Troubleshooting Overview

Troubleshooting mobile devices is similar to troubleshooting desktop devices. Whether Android, iOS, or Windows is being used as an operating system, you use *Settings* or various control panels in order to make changes to or adjust configuration settings on the device. The software and hardware of mobile devices are similar to those of desktop devices. Things that go wrong in a mobile device touchscreen are similar to those that occur on a laptop touchscreen.

Hard and Soft Resets

Sometimes a simple soft reset is all it takes to fix a problem. A **soft reset** is simply a restart of a mobile device. Some phones have a restart option. In some instances, a phone might not restart, and you might need to remove the battery in order to power off the device. Reasons to do a soft reset include the following abnormal behaviors:

> Unresponsive touchscreen
> Slow system response
> Cannot receive, make, send, and/or receive text messages or calls
> Audio issues
> Error codes appear (in which case you should record the codes before restarting; see Figure 10.105)

In contrast, a **hard reset** is a factory reset. (Hard resets for Android devices are covered earlier in this chapter.) You may need to do a hard reset if no other solution helps with the problem, if you have forgotten your password, if the screen is unresponsive and a soft reset does not help, or if you installed a software app that you cannot uninstall or it caused erratic behavior that cannot be solved in any other way.

FIGURE 10.105 Cell phone error

In Android, boot the device into *Recovery Mode* (typically accessed by holding down two or more specific buttons, such as the power, volume, and/or home buttons) while the device boots > *Wipe Data/Factory Reset* (press *Power* button to select) > *Yes – Erase All User Data.*

In iOS, you perform a hard reset with *Settings > General > Reset > Erase All Content and Settings > Erase iPhone/iPad.*

In Windows, check the manufacturer. Commonly holding down the power button (or the power button and the increase volume button) for several seconds prompts a hard reset. Sometimes, you might have to disconnect the AC power cord and remove the battery.

Some devices can be fixed by removing the power brick (wall adapter) and the battery and leaving the battery out for about 30 seconds. On some Apple devices, you must hold the power button down for 5 seconds afterward. This is known as a System Management Controller (SMC) reset. Apple devices also keep configuration settings such as volume, date, and time in parameter RAM (PRAM). A small separate battery keeps these settings current. To reset these settings on an Apple laptop, hold the following keys down at the same time while the system is booting: Cmd +Option+P+R.

The following sections discuss troubleshooting of mobile devices by area of concern. Remember that the Internet has a wealth of technical information available at your fingertips. Research is an important troubleshooting step in order to see how others have solved similar problems.

Mobile Device App Concerns

Many apps that are free (and even the ones that we pay for) do not play well with one another or with specific operating system versions. In order to troubleshoot apps, sometimes you need to stop the app (that is, perform a forced stop) or stop other apps because the mobile device is slow to respond due to **high resource utilization** (that is, apps taking all of the memory and processor power). Here are the generic steps for stopping an application, but remember that Android is open source so vendors can implement things differently, and iOS and Windows have different versions so the exact steps may be different than those shown:

> Android: *Settings* > *Apps/Application Manager* > locate and select a particular application > *Force Stop*
> On iOS 8 and lower, press the *Home* button two times quickly; on an iPhone X, swipe up from the bottom > swipe to find the app to close > swipe up on the app's preview to close it

You might also be required to uninstall and reinstall an app if the app fails to respond or is not working. There are free app managers that allow you to do this easily, but the mobile operating systems allow you to delete apps, too (though some apps that come with a mobile device cannot be installed but may be disabled). Deleting an app deletes the data and settings. These are the generic steps for deleting an app:

> Android: *Settings* > *Apps/Application Manager* > locate and select a particular app > *Uninstall/Disable*
> iOS: Press and hold on top of the app icon until all the icons shake (see Figure 10.106) > tap the *x* in the corner of the icon > *Delete*

FIGURE 10.106   iOS app deletion

Depending on the type of mobile device you are on, you might be able to use the operating system to check for **app log errors**. In Windows, use *Event Viewer*. On a Mac, access the *Utilities* folder from within the *Applications* folder. Ensure that the sidebar is shown (by clicking the leftmost button in the toolbar if it is not shown). Select *All Messages* from the tab bar. There are also log files located in the *Library* > *Logs* > *DiagnosticReports* folder.

Apps Not Installing

When an app does not install, ensure that your hardware/operating system is compatible with the app and has available storage space. Some apps do not run well from an SD card and might need to be installed onto the phone's internal storage. Ensure that an antivirus program isn't blocking app installation. If an app hangs during the installation process, ensure that you have a connection to a WiFi or cellular network, restart the device, and start the process again. Try downloading the app from a different WiFi network. Follow these generic steps when apps are not installing:

> Android: *Settings* > *Apps/Application Manager* > *All* > locate and tap on *Market* > *Clear Data* > *Clear Cache*.
> iOS: Try resetting the network settings: *Settings* > *General* > *Reset* and try again. You could reset all settings or take the device to an Apple Store.

Apps Not Loading

When you are faced with **apps not loading**, see if the mobile device believes it to be running already. Windows has *Task Manager* and Android has *Settings > Apps/Application Manager*. With iOS, some apps refresh their content automatically. You can see these settings with *Settings > General > Background App Refresh*. You can also try closing the app and opening it again. Try restarting the mobile device. Try powering down the device and restarting it. Check for operating system updates as well as app updates. If all else fails, delete the app and reinstall it.

TECH TIP

Email not current on your smartphone?

Check connectivity. If you have Internet/cellular access, restart the phone.

Unable to Decrypt Email

On a mobile device, a user may not be able to open an email because the device is **unable to decrypt email**. With iOS devices, you can use S/MIME to send and possibly receive encrypted email messages. Use the *Passwords & Accounts* (or *Mail, Contacts, Calendars* on older versions) option > select the appropriate email account > *Account* > depending on the email account type, you can set the S/MIME setting there or go into *Advanced*. Some vendors allow encrypting all messages by default.

Within Android, support for S/MIME is built into email clients and can be accessed through the email app > *Settings* option. Also, web browser add-ons can be used. Some email apps might require that a security certificate (file) be obtained and copied to the *root directory* (see Chapter 17 for more information on this) or the *Download* folder. Then access your email account > *Settings > Security Options > Email Certificate* > tap + (plus sign) > select the certificate.

Mobile Device Keyboard/Trackpad Issues

Sometimes when symptoms appear, the solution is not simply to replace the part. The key to such issues is to research what others have done when the particular problem has occurred. For example, software updates sometimes fix hardware issues.

Keyboard Issues

Not all devices have keyboards. Mobile devices can have wireless keyboards, optional keyboards, and wired keyboards. Three common keyboard issues are [Num Lock] indicator light, sticking keys, and ghost cursor/pointer drift.

The [Num Lock] key is used to allow keys on the numeric pad to be used as something besides numbers (arrow keys, a Home key, Page Up and Page Down keys, Delete key, Insert key, and End key), as shown in Figure 10.107. Pressing the [Num Lock] key so the **Num Lock indicator light** illuminates on the keyboard causes numbers to be used. Again pressing the [Num Lock] key so the indicator turns off causes the keys to be used for arrow keys and the like. Configure the system BIOS/UEFI for the default action (enabled or not enabled) per the customer's preference.

FIGURE 10.107   Num Lock and numeric key pad

Mobile devices that have keyboards can get dirtier than desktop systems. For **sticking keys**, follow the same process you would use for a desktop keyboard. Shake out the dirt and spray with compressed air, as shown back in Figure 1.22. Keys might have to be removed in order to get to the dirt or debris, to clean, or to spray compressed air. Figure 10.108 shows a close-up of a laptop key that has been removed. The key may have to be pushed toward the top of the keyboard and then lifted up in order to remove it. Peek under the key to see how it attaches before prying off the key.

FIGURE 10.108   Removed laptop key

A polyurethane cover that is clear, thin, and soft allows the user full function of the keyboard while protecting the keyboard from liquids and debris; it is easy to pop off and wash with dish detergent and water. Laptop backpacks are available that offer good protection against dropping, banging, temperature changes, and liquids. Rugged tablets and laptops offer military-type construction, glove-capable touch instead of bare fingertip, and an outdoor adaptable/readable display. Flexible rubber keyboards are also available.

Trackpad Issues

An annoying keyboard problem is the illustrious **ghost cursor** or **pointer drift**, in which the pointer moves across the screen even if no one is touching it. This is commonly caused by improper touchpad sensitivity settings. You might also need to update the touchpad driver that is installed. Malware or a virus can cause this symptom. In Windows, you can search for **troubleshoot touchpad** for guidance. Some users disable the touchpad and use a wired mouse.

Mobile Device Display Issues

Displays are critical to mobile devices. They get viewed, touched, and swiped more than any other part. Displays can go out, dim, stop responding, flicker, and otherwise cause user dissatisfaction. Let's tackle some of the common issues.

Dim Display, No Display, or Flickering Display

A **dim display** is commonly caused by a lack of interaction, display setting, or low battery. Move the pointer or tap the screen, adjust display settings, and attach AC power to see if the problem is a battery-related issue. On a laptop, the problem could also be caused by an improperly adjusted backlight or sticky lid actuator switch (the switch that detects when the laptop is closed or opened).

If the device has **no display**, attach an external display if possible and use the appropriate Fn key combination to send the output to the external display. If you **cannot display to external monitor** or if showing a presentation, you might have to use the Windows *Change Display Settings* link to adjust the output to duplicate what is showing on the screen. Check video cabling. Also use the appropriate Fn key combination, even if an external display is not available in case the settings have been changed by mistake.

Check the laptop close switch that is located in the main part of the laptop, near the back, where the display attaches to the laptop. The lid close detector can be a physical switch or a magnetic switch located near the back edge of the keyboard portion of a laptop. A laptop and some mobile devices can be configured to go into hibernation, sleep, or standby mode when the laptop is closed. Check the power management settings. Also check the video cable from the laptop system board to the display.

TECH TIP

What to do if a laptop display goes black, red, dim, or pink

If a laptop display goes black, red, dim, or pink, most likely this is because the backlight bulb is faulty. Otherwise, the problem is the DC-to-AC inverter. Connect an external monitor to the laptop external video port. If the external monitor works, most likely the backlight bulb is the culprit.

For a mobile device, try turning it off and back on. On a laptop or tablet, see if the device appears to boot normally. If the device has recently been exposed to liquid, power off the device, remove the battery, and allow the device to thoroughly dry before trying to power it back on again. A bad LCD backlight or inverter can cause a dim or blank display, too.

A **flickering display** can sometimes be fixed by simply adjusting the resolution (to the native resolution) or refresh rate or tightening the display cable. If you have recently changed the display, check the driver. Move the display to see if the flicker is related to display movement. An inverter and backlight can also cause this problem or show horizontal/vertical lines. Figure 10.109 shows a disassembled phone so you can see how the display attaches.

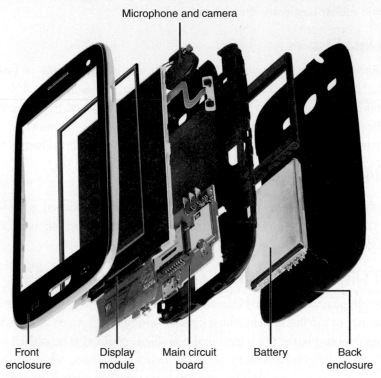

Microphone and camera

Front enclosure   Display module   Main circuit board   Battery   Back enclosure

FIGURE 10.109   Disassembled smartphone

Touchscreen Does Not Respond or Is Inaccurate

The touchscreen is a critical part of a mobile device. Users get frustrated by **touchscreen non-responsive** issues. The following list suggests things to try if the touchscreen is non-responsive or doesn't respond the way you expect it to:

> Close some apps to free up memory.
> See if the problem is app-specific, if possible.
> Restart the device. Force a shutdown even if doing so requires disconnecting the AC power cord and/or removing the battery.
> If the display has had any liquid on it, turn off the device and remove the battery. Allow the device to dry thoroughly before powering it on.
> If a screen protector is in place, remove it.
> Shut down the device and remove any memory cards, the SIM card, and the battery for about 60 seconds. Reinstall these items and power up.
> A device may have a calibration utility, or you may be able to download one to calibrate for touch input. On an Android device, try *Settings > Display*. In Windows 7/8/10, search for and use *Calibrate the Screen for Pen and Touch Input > Calibrate*. For iOS devices, try resetting the phone.
> Perform a factory restart.

If the touchscreen is broken, you should be able to still see what is on the device. When the LCD is damaged and cracks appear or the screen has dark spots, the touchscreen might still work in places. Screens can be ordered and replaced. Some repair shops specialize in mobile device displays.

Slow Performance

Slow performance means a system is not responding as fast as it normally does. The problem can be a lot of things, but some folks first notice the responsiveness of a touchscreen or slowness for data to download. If you suspect that the touchscreen is the problem, troubleshoot that. But if you have ruled out the touchscreen, consider the following tips:

> Check the battery power level.
> Close apps that aren't being used.
> Close services (WiFi, GPS, location services, Bluetooth, and so on) that are not being used. Put the device in Airplane Mode.
> Attach to a WiFi network.
> Move closer to the wireless access point if attached to WiFi.
> Newer Android devices have an option to reduce the amount of data needed by the Chrome browser: *Settings > (Advanced) Data Saver.*

Mobile Device Power Issues

A mobile device quickly becomes useless if it has power issues. Power is required for a device to be mobile. Power issues can include extremely short battery life, no power, swollen battery, and the battery not charging.

Battery Issues

A battery is critical for operations in a mobile device. A battery that has an **extremely short battery life** (that is, it won't hold a charge for long or has a power drain) commonly needs to be replaced. However, the problem could be the many apps, wireless, location services, GPS, and Bluetooth settings that are turned on. Check the display settings. Set the brightness/contrast setting to a lower setting instead of Auto. You should inspect the battery to see if it is swollen. A **swollen battery** is a battery that bulges and might even leak (see Figure 10.110). Most batteries that won't hold a charge need to be replaced (and replaced immediately if swollen). Also, verify that the phone shows the battery actually being charged. Don't just assume that it is charged, based on the amount of time it has been plugged in. The physical connection to the charger could be a tenuous one. The charger could be faulty, too.

FIGURE 10.110   Swollen battery in a cell phone

Battery Not Charging

The problem of a **battery not charging** properly could be happening because of the battery, the charger, or the connection on the phone. Inspect the connection on the phone first. Do you see any debris or dirt, or do you see pins that look like they do not align with the other pins? If so, power off the device, remove the battery, and clean it with compressed air; gently try to align pins that are misaligned. Do the same inspection on the charge connector. Take a voltage reading on the charger, if possible. See if it is outputting power. See if the same cable and/or charger can charge other devices that require the same voltage and connector type. Try to charge with a different connector, such as a car adapter.

No Power or Frozen System

An electronic device that has **no power** or is a **frozen system** is useless. Try the following when troubleshooting a mobile device that will not power up:

> Check for the power light.
> Ensure that the device has not gone into sleep mode. Try waking up the device or power it down and then power it on again.
> Check for a misbehaving app.
> Attach the device to an AC adapter and power it up.
> Disconnect the AC power brick, remove the battery, and hold down the power button for a few seconds. Replace the battery and reconnect to AC. Try to power on the laptop again.
> Inspect the power button and think about whether it has felt strange lately.
> When you attach the power brick to the mobile device, does the connector attach easily, or does it wiggle? Consider replacing the DC power jack if on a laptop.
> Check brightness displays.
> If on a laptop, check the lid close sensor.
> If on a laptop or a tablet with a keyboard, try closing the display and opening it back up fully (see Figure 10.111).
> Check for malware or viruses.

FIGURE 10.111   Close and reopen the laptop display

Overheating: Warm/Hot to the Touch

Heat is one of the worst enemies of electronic devices. Symptoms of **overheating** include the device is warm to the touch, loses battery strength faster than normal, and shuts down unexpectedly. Leaving mobile devices in hot vehicles and in the sun is bad. If a device is overheating, power down the device and let it cool. Do not just move it to a cooler spot.

See if you can determine a specific spot that is getting hotter than other places on the device. Determine whether that spot is where the battery or power is located or whether it is another spot on the mobile device. If near the battery, troubleshoot power problems after the device has cooled completely.

Check the battery health icon on the device. Inspect the battery. Replace the battery if you think that is the cause. Close unneeded apps and services. Remove the device from a case, if applicable. Ensure that you are not covering the device's air vents, such as by placing it on a lap or pillow. Place a laptop on something that elevates it from the desk, such as drink coasters. In addition, pads, trays, and mats can be purchased with fans that are AC powered or USB powered. Research the device vendor to determine if others are having similar issues.

Mobile Device Sound Issues

Mobile devices, like desktop computers, can have sound issues. If the problem is **no sound from speakers**, verify that the speakers are plugged into the correct port. Determine whether the volume is muted or low. Is the correct output selected? Do the speakers require external power, and is that power being provided?

For headphone issues, ensure that the cable attaches to the correct line out port. Determine whether you want the speakers disabled. Normally, if you plug into the headphones line out port, the speakers cut off. For Android or iOS devices, check the volume control and whether the device is muted. On tablets or smartphones, check whether other applications are using the microphone.

Another common complaint is that, when headphones are attached, sound still comes through the speakers. Ensure that the headphones connect to the device securely. Power off the device, remove the battery, and clean the headphone jack. Also try these steps:

> Android: Press and hold the power/lock button to change the sound setting to mute everything except the media sound. Close unused apps.
> iOS: Try muting sound and then re-enabling it.

Mobile Device Network Issues

Chapter 13 goes into more details on networking, but this chapter presents some basic troubleshooting techniques you can perform on mobile devices without providing more involved details about how these technologies work. The issues can be broken down into three areas: WiFi, GPS, and Bluetooth.

WiFi Issues

Use the following list to help when troubleshooting WiFi issues such as **intermittent wireless** or **no wireless connectivity** on a mobile device:

> Ensure that the mobile device is not in Airplane Mode.
> Ensure that WiFi is enabled.
> Ensure that the correct WiFi network is chosen. If prompted, provide the appropriate security/ login credentials.
> Turn off WiFi and then re-enable it.
> If a laptop always has low signal strength, ensure that the wire(s) are attached to the wireless NIC. If the display has been replaced recently, ensure that all connectors have been reattached properly and have not been damaged.
> For any device that has low signal strength, move around and try to see if you get more signal bars by moving. The more bars you see, the better the signal strength and speed of transmission. See Figure 10.112.
> With some laptops, you must turn the laptop to a different angle to attach to an access point or find a stronger signal strength (which means faster transfers). Antenna placement is important in a wireless network. Antennas on mobile devices tend to be in the edges or built into the displays.

> If a mobile device connects to a WiFi network unintentionally, turn off WiFi. Some mobile devices have the ability to automatically switch between WiFi and mobile networks in order to keep a solid Internet connection. To disable this in iOS, use *Settings > Wi-Fi >* disable *Auto-Join*. On Android devices that have Wi-Fi enabled, use *Settings > Wi-Fi >* select and hold on the wireless network that is not wanted *> Forget Network*.

> Whenever a question mark appears at the top of a mobile device, it means there are WiFi networks in the area and you need to select the one that you want to attach to. A lock on the wireless network name means you need a password to access the wireless network.

> Slow or intermittent transmissions can be related to distance to the access point, other WiFi networks and devices, and the number of devices attached to the same wireless access point.

FIGURE 10.112   Wireless signal strength

GPS Issues

GPS is not provided in all mobile devices. The geographical environment affects GPS reception and can cause intermittent connectivity. If GPS is installed, but the problem is **GPS not functioning** properly, try turning off *Location Services* and then turning it back on. If that fails, restart the device. Some Android devices have assisted GPS, which uses GPS satellites, cell towers, and WiFi networks to provide location services. The device might be in an area where connectivity is limited or missing. Ensure that *Use Wireless Networks* and *Use GPS Satellites* are enabled on an older phone. Some phones have a *High Accuracy* setting instead. Another problem is that the user might have denied a particular app the right to have access to location services, and an app like Google Maps might not be as beneficial as it could be without it. Access the app settings to verify. You can try uninstalling and reinstalling the app. Turn off any apps that might be using the GPS, but are not needed.

Bluetooth Issues

If you have **no Bluetooth connectivity**, the suggestions are the same as for all other network connectivity issues: Turn the device off and back on again, move the device closer to the other Bluetooth device(s), and put the device in Airplane Mode and then turn off Airplane Mode to toggle off all radios and then re-enable them. Other troubleshooting hints are as follows:

> Check for interference from other devices, including wireless devices on the same frequency. Also look for Windows, Apple iOS, or Android configuration issues.

> If a Bluetooth device is not working in Windows, try the following: Select the Bluetooth icon ( ) in the notification area on the taskbar and select *Show Bluetooth Devices*. If the device is not listed there, select *Add a Device* and try to add it.

> Ensure that the Bluetooth device is charged, powered on, and in the appropriate mode to pair with another Bluetooth device, such as a computing device or car with Bluetooth capability.

> Ensure that other wireless devices, such as wireless networks, automatic lighting and remote controls, cell phones and other portable phones, and microwave ovens, are not interfering with the device.

> Remove unused USB devices.

> If passkeys (PINs) are used, ensure that the keys match.

> If a Bluetooth transceiver is used, move the transceiver to another USB port.

> Remove all other Bluetooth devices to aid in troubleshooting the problematic device.
> In Windows, ensure that Bluetooth services are enabled. See Chapter 16, "Advanced Windows," for more information on Windows services.
> In Windows, ensure that Device Manager shows no issues with the Bluetooth transceiver driver (under the *Bluetooth Radios* section) or the Bluetooth device (sometimes shown under the *Other Devices* category). The Bluetooth driver for the host computer may need to be updated for a newer device.
> You can use similar tricks with Apple iOS and Android devices: (1) Ensure that the device is powered, (2) ensure that Bluetooth is enabled, and (3) ensure that no other wireless networks/ devices are nearby (by moving to another location to see if they appear).
> A common method used with Bluetooth devices is to restart the pairing mode on the Bluetooth device or rescan for a device from the iOS/Android computing device.
> If a mobile device unintentionally pairs with another Bluetooth device, turn off Bluetooth— and keep it off except when you are using it. Move the mobile device closer to the Bluetooth device.
> USB-to-RJ-45, USB-to-Bluetooth, and USB-to-WiFi adapters/dongles can be used when a network ports fails.

SOFT SKILLS: A WORD ABOUT APPEARANCE

John T. Mallow's 1975 book *Dress for Success* heightened awareness of concepts like the power tie, color coordination, and proper wardrobe with the aim of getting ahead in one's professional and personal life. Some of you are simply too young to have read this. Although some of the book's advice may seem a bit quaint today, the fact is, you are nonetheless judged on your personal appearance. This is one soft skill area you cannot afford to ignore; if you do, you risk hindering your chances for advancement, client relationships, or reputation.

Why does appearance matter so much? Research shows that we form opinions about each other within mere seconds of meeting. And some people decide whether you are trustworthy in less than a second! Look at Figure 10.113 and imagine that each of these people is a technician coming in to fix your computer. What would be your impression of each person, based only on his or her attire?

FIGURE 10.113   Professional attire options

To make good impressions on your boss and your customers, strive to project a competent and professional appearance and demeanor. A good rule of thumb is to dress to the level of the client. For example, you would probably dress more professionally for a job in a law office or doctor's office than you would for a job at Joe the plumber's business. If you knew you were going to be working on laser printers, you probably wouldn't want to wear your best clothes, or you might take a lab coat to protect your clothes.

Be aware of generational bias. In the United States today, four generations have different values. The Traditionalists, or silent generation, born 1925–1945, value suits, coats and ties for men and dresses for women. Most of these people are now age 70+, so there are few of them left in workplaces. The Baby Boomers, 1946–1964, are a little more relaxed about dress codes but still believe in good appearance (think business casual). Now aged in their 50s to 60s, they are likely to be the bosses and senior managers. Next come the GenXers, generally born 1965–1980, who value flexibility and freedom and are even more relaxed—even casual. Finally comes the GenYers, or Millennials, born between 1981 and the present. Millennials value change, diversity, and individual freedom. These are the ones most likely to express themselves with tattoos, piercings, extreme grooming, and so on. To Millennials, dress codes are much less important than they are to members of the other generations.

The following are some common-sense guidelines:

> Above all, avoid tattered jeans, sneakers, and t-shirts, as you could run the risk of looking too scruffy to be taken seriously.

> If your job involves dirty work, such as pulling fiber optic cables through the overhead space or working on laser printers, jeans and button-down shirts are acceptable. Or consider wearing a lab coat. It doesn't hurt to let the client know upon checking in that you are dressed for a dirty job.

> Watch your haircuts and (for men) beards. Don't forget to groom your hands and nails, which will be noticed (either consciously or unconsciously) by your boss and customers.

> Women are more likely to be better liked and trusted if they use a moderate makeup and little to no perfume.

Table 10.20 lists recommendations for attire according to the environment.

TABLE 10.20   Attire in specific environments

Environment	Recommended attire
Business dress	Men: Coat and tie. Women: Dress, skirt, pant suit.
Business casual	Men: Dress shirt (tie optional). Women: Dress, skirt/blouse, pants/shirt
Casual	Men: Collared shirt, polo shirt, nice pants, slacks. Women: Pants, polo shirt

TECH TIP

The colors you wear send subliminal messages

Colors can profoundly affect how other people view you. Here are some of the main ones to bear in mind:

> Black or dark gray—Represents authority and confidence

> Blue—Suggests trust and traditional values

> Green—Portrays empathy and tranquility

> Red—Conveys that you are passionate and likely to be an extrovert

> Brown—Says that you are loyal and reliable

It is usually the subconscious mind that notices how others look. So even if you don't consider appearances to be very important, keep in mind that, without your realizing it, appearances have helped you form an opinion of just about everyone you have ever met. Don't underestimate the importance of dressing appropriately on the job but don't let your wardrobe impede your ability to do the job.

Chapter Summary

> Mobile devices are used for different purposes and therefore come in a variety of types—laptops, tablets, smartphones, wearable technology, e-readers, cameras, and GPS.

> Mobile devices have the following common hardware parts: display, flash memory, battery, DC jack, speaker, microphone, speaker, wireless antenna, system board, processor, and expansion options. Other parts that may be more for laptops or tablets include ExpressCards, SODIMMs, mechanical, SSD, and hybrid storage, ports and adapters, keyboards, miniPCI/PCIe cards, touchpad, and touchscreen.

> Mobile devices have various methods of expansion and connectivity, including the following: NFC, proprietary, USB, miniUSB, microUSB, Lightning, infrared, tethering, Bluetooth, GPS, cellular, satellite, WiFi, miniPCI/PCIe, docking stations, and port replicators.

> Mobile devices commonly have accessories that need to be installed and/or attached, including headsets, speakers, game pads, battery packs/chargers, protective covers, waterproofing, credit card readers, and memory.

> Mobile device operating systems include the open source Android, closed source Apple iOS, and various Microsoft Windows-based mobile operating systems.

> Laptops use Fn to control specific functions, such as WiFi, Bluetooth, speakers, display output, and keyboard backlight.

> Mobile devices need their operating system and data backed up. Two common methods to do this are to back them up to another device or use storage in the cloud.

> Mobile devices need security. Laptops can have locks. All mobile devices need operating system security, personal files and identity security, antimalware, and antivirus. Remote data wiping can be configured if a device is compromised or stolen.

> A plastic scribe helps with prying off plastics and covers. Laptop speakers and DC power plugs frequently have cables that run along the back or sides of the device. Keep screws separated and take notes and photos for any parts that are removed.

> Conserve mobile device power by adding more RAM, turning off wireless/Bluetooth, turning off unnecessary apps, configuring power options, reducing screen brightness, and avoiding temperature extremes.

> Li-ion batteries are used with mobile devices. If a device must be attached to AC power or a USB port in order to work, replace the battery with the correct DC power jack, appropriate DC voltage level, and current (amperage) equal to or higher than the original power brick.

> Before removing or installing memory, disconnect the power cord and remove the battery on a mobile device.

> Laptops can sometimes be upgraded with SODIMMs. Tablets and smartphones can sometimes be upgraded and gain additional storage through flash memory cards.

> AC power goes into the power supply or mobile device power brick. DC power is provided to all internal parts of a computing device.

> Microphones are used for VoIP and are tested/managed in Windows through the *Recording* tab of the *Sound* window.

> Secure a mobile device with a PIN, facial recognition, a password, or a passcode/pattern.

> When replacing a laptop processor, you may have to loosen a screw before you can remove the old processor.

> When replacing a laptop motherboard, additional components may have to be removed.

> Troubleshooting mobile devices commonly includes a soft reset or a restart or a hard reset, which is another name for a factory reset. Android and iOS devices use *Settings* to manage most configurations. Windows uses either various Control Panels or *Settings*.

> Troubleshooting commonly involves disabling apps, connectivity, and features.

> Troubleshooting sometimes involves removing AC power and the battery.

> Mobile device repairs commonly require different tools, including scribes, antistatic gloves, and smaller tools.

A+ CERTIFICATION EXAM TIPS

✓ Be able to explain the difference between Windows, Android, iOS, and Chrome mobile devices.

✓ Be able to identify, describe the purpose of, and replace/install and configure the following hardware components: wireless card, smart card reader, Bluetooth module, video card, display, flash memory, battery, DC jack, speaker, microphone, wireless antenna, system board, processor, and expansion options. Other parts that may be more for laptops or tablets include SODIMMs, mechanical drives, SSDs, hybrid storage, ports and adapters, keyboards, miniPCIe cards, touchpads, and touchscreens.

✓ Know that each app has configurable settings that might need to be adjusted.

✓ Know the difference between a docking station and a port replicator.

✓ Watch a few videos on laptop disassembly.

✓ Be able to describe how to connect an external monitor to a laptop and make adjustments for various combinations of laptop only, external monitor only, and laptop along with the external monitor. Also know how power options might need to be adjusted.

✓ Be able to install components within the laptop display: LCD, OLED, inverter, digitizer/touchscreen, WiFi antenna placement, webcam, and microphone.

✓ Study how to configure and connect NFC, tethering, Bluetooth, GPS, cellular, and WiFi. Know that airplane mode disables Bluetooth, cellular, and WiFi communications as well as saves on battery life. Right before the exams, use an Android simulator or practice on Android, iOS, and Windows device configurations. Know that bandwidth throttling might be implemented on wireless networks that affects those that might be streaming video, creating a hotspot, or using tethering.

✓ A cell phone requires an NFC chip in order to use the mobile pay feature.

✓ Realize that quick battery drain could be more than just a battery that needs to be replaced. Check for running apps, brightness levels, and open communications (Bluetooth, cellular, WiFi, GPS, and so on).

✓ Review the types of things you might control with function keys. Know that you might use these keys to solve problems such as erratic mouse actions (touchpad) and display output.

✓ If you can't easily reattach a cell phone back, check for a swollen battery.

✓ Know that Android devices synchronize to the cloud by default. Know that iTunes can be used to back up/restore an iOS device. Know that OneDrive is used to access saved attachments from Microsoft Outlook. Configuring a mobile device to an email account synchronizes associated data, such as calendars and contacts.

✓ Be able to configure security settings on Android, iOS, and Windows devices.

✓ If you cannot connect to a wireless network, see if there are multiple networks in the area and select one. Note that a wireless network might need to be "forgotten" so that you can reattach with an updated password or to just reassociate if Internet connectivity is unavailable.

✓ Know that geotracking is what allows social media apps and tracking apps to locate a phone/person. The location feature might need to be enabled.

✓ Read and reread all the troubleshooting scenarios in the chapter. Troubleshooting mobile devices is a part of both the CompTIA A+ 220-1001 and 220-1002 exams.

Key Terms

1.8 inch 483	802.11ac 447	Android 423
2.5 inch 483	802.11b 447	APK 442
3G 451	802.11g 447	app log errors 506
4G 451	802.11n 447	app scanner 464
5G 451	accelerometer 439	App Store 442
802.11a 447	Airplane Mode 448	Apple Configurator 464

Review Questions

1. How can you control sending display output to an external monitor on a laptop?

   _____

2. Which mobile device feature allows for tracking how far someone has walked this week?
   [virtual assistant l accelerometer l gyroscope l geothermal sensor]

3. In which of the following situations would Bluetooth most likely be used?

   a. to connect to a corporate wireless network

   b. to attach a keyboard to a PC

   c. to connect a PC to a phone line

   d. to connect a flash drive to a camera

4. Which type of operating systems allow vendors to use the core source code and customize the OS?

   a. closed source

   b. proprietary

   c. open source

   d. vendor-specific

5. List three recommendations for saving power on a laptop.

   _____

Consider the following memory advertisements for laptop memory used in Question 6.

   a. 16 GB (2×8GB) 204-pin DDR3 SODIMM DDR3L 1600 (PC3L 12800) 1.35 V unbuffered

   b. 4 GB (2×2GB) 1,333 MHz DDR3 unbuffered DIMM

   c. 8 GB 260-pin DDR4 SODIMM 2400 (PC4 19200)

   d. 8 GB DDR3 204-pin SODIMM PC3-12800 memory

6. In these advertisements, which memory module(s) would work as an upgrade for a laptop, given the following specifications:

   Maximum of 16 GB. Configured with 4 GB DDR3 1 main memory slot (which is occupied).

   _____

7. List one way that a tablet computer's memory might be upgraded.

   _____

   _____

8. Which two options are used to back up an iOS device? (Choose two.)
   [iBooks l iTunes l Tips l iCloud l iBackup l Backup]

9. Which type of laptop hard drive would provide the best performance?
   [mechanical l SSD l hybrid l stock]

10. What is a drawback of SSDs?

    [installation time l MTBF l maintenance requirements l cost l speed l reliability]

11. A technician has been troubleshooting a laptop power issue, and now the speakers don't work. What should the technician do first?

    a. Replace the speakers.

    b. Reinstall the original power supply.

    c. Check the speaker cabling.

    d. Replace the power supply with another one.

12. Which icon would be used on a laptop to turn down the volume?

   a.

   b.

   c.

   d.

13. A laptop display is not showing anything, but the technician can hear the hard drive working. The technician connects an external monitor, and the monitor works. What should the technician try next?

   a. Replace the laptop display.

   b. Try connecting another external monitor.

   c. Replace the laptop display connector.

   d. Use the appropriate key to retest the output to the display.

14. What is the purpose of a laptop inverter?

   a. to convert DC to AC for the CCFL backlight

   b. to attach the keypad to the keyboard

   c. to allow specific keys to be used as a numeric keypad, when enabled

   d. to allow the display to be flipped backward

15. List three recommendations for laptop security.

   _____

   _____

16. A hybrid drive is:

   a. a mechanical hard drive.

   b. an SSD.

   c. a combination of an SSD part and a mechanical drive in the same case.

   d. an upgraded flash drive.

17. Which of the following should be tried first if a mobile device is frozen?

   a. factory reset

   b. soft reset

   c. hard reset

   d. recovery

18. A user complains that he has slow data speeds on his mobile device. List three things you will check.

   _____

   _____

19. A mobile device continuously attaches to a nearby Bluetooth-enabled computer that is not the computer the user wants to attach to. What should be done?

   a. Disconnect the Bluetooth adapter from the nearby computer.

   b. Move the Bluetooth device closer to the desired computer.

   c. Power off the nearby computer.

   d. Put the mobile device in Airplane Mode.

20. [T | F] An accelerometer detects the screen orientation and adapts what is shown on the screen based on that orientation.

Exercises

Exercise 10.1   Identifying Laptop Parts

Objective: To identify various laptop parts correctly

Procedure: Identify each part in Figure 10.114 by matching the component name to the identified part in the photo.

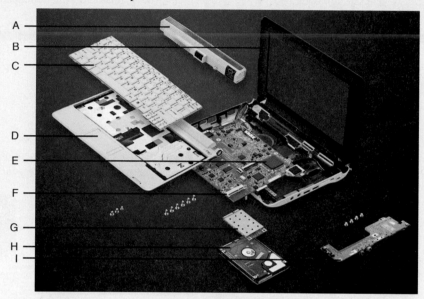

FIGURE 10.114   Laptop part identification photo

Components

LCD	Keyboard
Ports assembly	System board
Mounting bracket for touchpad	Processor
Hard drive	Palm rest assembly
Battery	

A. _____   F. _____

B. _____   G. _____

C. _____   H. _____

D. _____   I. _____

E. _____

Exercise 10.2 Common Laptop Keys

Objective: To identify various keys used on a laptop

Procedure: Match each laptop function key in Figure 10.115 to the description in Table 10.21.

FIGURE 10.115   Laptop function key identification photo

TABLE 10.21   Keyboard functions

a.	Increase volume	**g.**	Mute
b.	Decrease display brightness	**h.**	Increase display brightness
c.	Decrease keyboard backlight brightness	**i.**	Pair with Bluetooth Device 2
d.	Pair with Bluetooth Device 1	**j.**	Increase keyboard backlight brightness
e.	Play/pause	**k.**	Pair with Bluetooth Device 3
f.	Cycle through open apps	**l.**	Enable/disable touchpad

F1 _____	F4 _____	F7 _____	F10 _____
F2 _____	F5 _____	F8 _____	F11 _____
F3 _____	F6 _____	F9 _____	F12 _____

Exercise 10.3   Cell Phone Parts

Objective: To identify various cell phone parts correctly

Procedure: Identify each part in Figure 10.116 by matching the component name to the identified part in the photo. Note that not all identified parts are used. Write your answers in Table 10.22.

FIGURE 10.116   Cell phone parts identification

TABLE 10.22   Cell phone parts

Part	Corresponding letter
Front enclosure	
Display	
Microphone and camera	
Back enclosure	
Main printed circuit board	
Battery	

Activities

Internet Discovery

Objective: To obtain specific information from the Internet regarding a computer or its associated parts

Parts: Computer with Internet access

Procedure: Complete the following procedure and answer the accompanying questions.

Questions:

1. Watch the laptop hard drive replacement video at the following URL to answer Questions 1–5 (if this link does not work, find a video that shows a laptop hard drive replacement) https://www.youtube.com/watch?v=wSa3Owia-2k:

    List one piece of software mentioned in the video that might be obtained or purchased in order to clone the operating system.

    _____

2. Use the Internet to find an alternative cloning software that could be used. Detail why you think this software would be appropriate and why you chose it.

    _____

3. What were the two locations for the hard drives in the two laptops, and how were they removed?

    _____

    _____

4. What power safety procedures were recommended?

    _____

5. What power procedure was recommended in the chapter that was not done in this video?

    _____

    A customer owns a Toshiba Satellite R845-ST6N02 laptop. Use the Toshiba troubleshooting assistant program to help with a battery problem. Use this information to answer Questions 6–9.

6. What output values should be on the AC adapter?

    _____

7. Assume that the values on the AC power brick match those required on the computer. How long should the power button be held down after the external power and battery have been removed from the computer?

    _____

8. Which two colors can be used for the power indicator light (if it is working, of course)?

    _____

9. Assume that you have power, and you shut down the computer and remove the AC adapter. What might you do before assuming that the battery is dead?

    _____

10. A student has an HP ENVY notebook model 15-ae041nr. The screen seems blurry when displaying a browser or even some Windows configuration screens, but other screens appear fine. Use the Internet to find what some people have done. List one or two solutions.

    _____

    _____

Soft Skills

Objective: To enhance and fine-tune a future technician's ability to listen, communicate in both written and oral forms, and support people who use computers and mobile devices in a professional manner

Activities:

1. In groups of three, each person finds a video that shows a particular model of laptop being taken apart. Share your findings with the others. Each team selects the best video to share with the class or submits the web link to the teacher.

2. Record yourself describing a mobile device problem and what you did to fix it, in three minutes or less. If you have never had a mobile device problem, use the Internet to find someone else's problem that you describe in your own words. No reading aloud. Tell the story.

3. In groups of six, three people must each find a cartoon or story that describes a funny mobile device situation. The other three people should find a cartoon or story that illustrates the need to dress professionally in the IT field. Each person must share findings with the group. Have a category for mobile and a category for appearance. Each person rates each cartoon or story. Summarize your findings in electronic format or verbally.

4. Each group is assigned one of the following laptop parts: (1) processor and heat solution, (2) mechanical, SSD, or hybrid storage device, (3) display, (4) system board, (5) inverter, (6) backlight. Work in teams to outline in words and illustrations how to replace the part and issues related to the replacement. Present the work to the class.

Critical Thinking Skills

Objective: To analyze and evaluate information as well as apply learned information to new or different situations

Procedure:

1. Locate two laptop manuals from two different manufacturers. They cannot just be two models from the same manufacturer. Compare and contrast how the CPU is replaced in each one.

2. Select a laptop that has a mechanical hard drive and pretend it is yours and has been yours for at least a year. Now pretend that you are upgrading to an SSD or a hybrid drive. Select what hardware and software you might need and price it all out. Develop a step-by-step plan of action of how you are going to do this.

3. On a separate piece of paper, describe why WiFi networks are so important to cell phone users. Are there any drawbacks to using them?

4. Find a technical job at monster.com, dice.com, or indeed.com. Then look online for at least three graphics or photos showing clothes you think a male or a female would wear to the interview for this job. Find another three graphics or photos that depict what a male or female would wear on a daily basis for the job.

11 Computer Design and Troubleshooting Review

In this chapter you will learn:

> To select computer components based on the customer's needs

> The components best suited for a particular computing environment

> How to design for specific computer subsystems, such as the video or storage subsystem

> How to perform basic troubleshooting procedures

> How BIOS/UEFI controls the boot sequence and how that helps when troubleshooting

> The purpose of POST error codes

> A list of troubleshooting symptoms that could be on the CompTIA A+ 220-1001 exam

> How to deal with difficult customers or situations

CompTIA Exam Objectives:

What CompTIA A+ exam objectives are covered in this chapter?

✓ 1001-2.8   Given a scenario, use appropriate networking tools.

✓ 1001-3.8   Given a scenario, select and configure appropriate components for a custom PC configuration to meet customer specifications or needs.

✓ 1001-5.1   Given a scenario, use the best practice methodology to resolve problems.

✓ 1001-5.2   Given a scenario, troubleshoot problems related to motherboards, RAM, CPUs, and power.

✓ 1001-5.3   Given a scenario, troubleshoot hard drives and RAID arrays.

✓ 1002-4.7   Given a scenario, use proper communication techniques and professionalism.

Design Overview

Why would employers want technicians to be able to design computers? If you needed a car repaired, wouldn't it be nice to have a person who could design cars to advise you? A designer would know the best engines, the most fuel-efficient body design, what parts might not work well with other parts, and so on. A designer would know a lot about all parts of the car. The same is true about those who can design computers: They know a lot about computer parts and how those parts interact with one another.

When you first learn about computers, you learn the language, or lingo. You learn terms such as RAM and processor. Later, when you hear such words, you form images in your mind. You do more than just recognize the words; you actually know what different parts look like. You can explain to someone else what a part does. You continue to grow in a particular area. Designing something is right up there with troubleshooting something well: It requires knowing what you are talking about.

Benjamin Bloom chaired a committee that created a classification of learning objectives that was named Bloom's Taxonomy. Look at Figure 11.1 to see how people normally progress through the learning process from the bottom to the top. Notice that creating is at the top. Of course, employers want people who can design: They are the folks who know all the things it takes to be able to design.

FIGURE 11.1   Bloom's Taxonomy

This chapter helps you learn how to select components within subsystems, such as video or audio, and the components needed for complete computer builds, based on the type of customer and the customer's needs. Even if you are designing just a subset of a computer, such as the video subsystem or an optical drive subsystem, you must know how that subset interacts with other components that might need to be upgraded as well. Be sure to check out the exercises at the end of the chapter, which help put all this together. Practice is one of the best teachers.

Computer System Design

Computer users need different types of computer systems. What the user does with a computer dictates the components and peripherals needed. Looking at computer systems by purpose is a good place to start with design.

Note: In the following sections, the bullets with asterisks (*) are components emphasized on the CompTIA A+ 220-1001 exam.

Graphic/CAD/CAM Design Workstations

Engineers and design engineers use computer-aided design (CAD) and computer-aided manufacturing (CAM) systems in manufacturing plants to create things. Graphic design personnel also use a similar type of system (see Figure 11.2). A **graphic/CAD/CAM design workstation** would need the following key components:

> Powerful multicore processor(s)
> *Maximum system RAM
> *An SSD
> *High-end video card(s) with maximum video RAM and graphics processing unit (GPU)
> Large display or dual displays
> Large-capacity hard drive(s)
> Optional peripherals such as digital tablets, scanners, plotters, and 3D printers
> Good-quality mouse or input device

FIGURE 11.2 CAD/CAM design workstation

Gaming PCs

Gaming computers are a unique type of PC. Gamers frequently build their own systems, but some computer manufacturers make gaming PCs. A **gaming PC** (see Figure 11.3) tends to have the following key components:

> Powerful multicore processor(s)
> *High-end video cards (with maximum video RAM and specialized GPU)
> *High-definition sound card and speakers
> *High-end system cooling
> *An SSD
> Large amount of RAM
> Large display or dual displays
> Quality mouse
> Optional gaming console
> Headphone with microphone
> Optional 3D glasses (if supported by the video card and monitor)

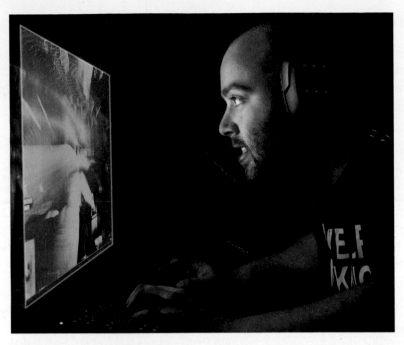

FIGURE 11.3 Gaming PC

Audio/Video Editing Workstations

An **audio/video editing workstation** (see Figure 11.4) is used to manipulate sounds (shorten, add, overlay, and so on) or video. This type of system requires a lot of hard drive space and RAM. These are the most common configuration elements for such a computer:

> *Specialized video card with maximum video RAM and GPU
> *Specialized audio (sound) card and speakers
> *Very fast and large-capacity hard drive
> *Dual monitors
> Powerful multicore processor(s)
> Large amount of system RAM
> Quality mouse
> Possible digital tablet or scanner

FIGURE 11.4 Audio/video editing workstation

Network-Attached Storage (NAS) Devices

A **network-attached storage** (NAS) **device** can be a single box that contains multiple hard drives used for storing photos, movies, and files from multiple computers in a home or small office environment (see Figure 11.5). It is commonly used for media streaming of videos and music and file sharing in the home environment. A diskless NAS is a storage container that comes without disks so you can add your own mechanical drives or SSDs.

FIGURE 11.5   Home or small business NAS

In the corporate environment, a NAS can also be rows of hard drives in a larger company environment (see Figure 11.6). These drives provide storage for multiple servers and users and are commonly configured in a RAID array for data recovery in case one drive fails.

FIGURE 11.6   Corporate NAS

A NAS device would have the following components and capabilities:

> *Media streaming
> *File sharing
> *Gigabit NIC (possibly multiple NICs)
> *RAID array
> *Multiple hard drives
> Multiple SSDs

Virtualization Workstations

Virtualization workstation can mean two things: (1) a workstation that has at least one operating system, in its own virtual machine that is separate from the host operating system (see Figure 11.7) or (2) a workstation that uses hardware and software virtualization techniques to provide an end user with a controlled workstation environment. Each of these situations requires different hardware and software. In terms of the CompTIA A+ certification, a virtualization workstation is considered to be the first example (a computer that has more than one operating system in a virtual environment). The second example, also known as a thin client, is covered in the next section.

A virtualization workstation would have the following components:

> *Maximum CPU cores
> *Maximum RAM
> Multiple, fast, large-capacity hard drives
> Possible SSDs
> Possible network-attached storage for increased storage space that can be shared with other devices

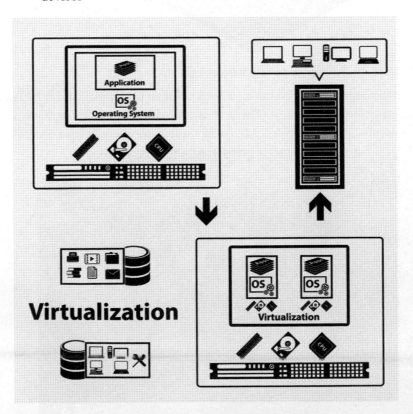

FIGURE 11.7 Virtualization workstation concepts

Thin Client Workstations

A **thin client** workstation is a desktop or laptop that has a display, mouse, keyboard, and network connectivity and runs applications from a server. There is very little software added to the computer. Thin client computers provide better security to critical data and applications and are commonly used in airports, hotels, and corporate areas where the information accessed or software used is centralized.

Thin client computers are less expensive than normal workstations; however, the network infrastructure (for example, servers, software, storage area network [SAN]) to support thin clients costs money. Storage tends to be cloud based or on remote storage media. Both the hardware and software environments can be virtualized (commonly referred to as desktop virtualization) in order to provide a controlled environment. Corporations, medical offices, and call centers commonly use thin clients (see Figure 11.8).

FIGURE 11.8 Thin client workstations

Characteristics to look for in a thin client computer include the following:

> *Meets minimum requirements for selected operating system
> *Network connectivity (1 Gb/s preferred)
> *Only used for basic applications, such as word processing, spreadsheet manipulation, and web-based apps
> Optional display privacy screen

Standard Thick Client Workstations

In contrast to a thin client workstation, a **thick client** computer is the most common type of desktop or laptop in the work environment. Applications are installed, and documents are commonly stored on the local hard drive. An all-in-one computer could be a thick client computer. Computers in small businesses tend to be thick client workstations. A **standard thick client** computer has the following characteristics:

> *Meets minimum hardware requirements for the selected operating system
> *Desktop applications (each one should meet recommended hardware and software requirements)
> Optional display privacy screen
> Optional dual displays

Home Servers

A **home server** computer is used to store data; function as a web server, print server, or file server; control media streaming; be accessible from outside the home; control devices; and manage backups of other computers. Notice in Figure 11.9 that the home server in the top-right corner can be used to backup files from other home devices such as a laptop. Servers and networks are discussed in Chapter 13, "Networking." Typical components found in a home server include the following:

> Multiple hard drives in a RAID array configuration
> 1 Gb/s (1000 Mb/s) NIC
> Medium to large case
> Multiple processors or multiple cores in the processor
> 8 GB or more RAM
> Server applications, including media streaming, file sharing, and print sharing applications
> Optional NAS
> Optional KVM switch

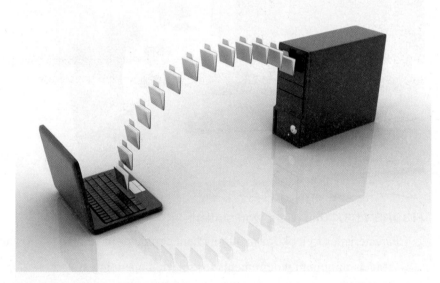

FIGURE 11.9   Home server

Industrial Computers

An industrial computer is a computer used for a specific trade. For example, in a car repair shop, the standard computers used both inside the showroom and in the service and repair center might be in an enclosure (see Figure 11.10) or have keyboard coverings. A kiosk in a mall or school might contain or be controlled by a computer. Kiosks are commonly used to show maps, provide directions, locate personnel, or provide information. The following are some characteristics and components to consider for an industrial computer:

> Meets recommended hardware requirements based on applications installed
> Optional enclosure for wet, dry, or outdoor environments
> Optional enclosure for a laptop's external keyboard and mouse for non-secure or outdoor environments
> Optional LCD enclosure for harsh, outdoor, public, high-traffic, or industrial environments
> Optional privacy display screen
> Case with air filters that may be removable for cleaning

FIGURE 11.10   Industrial computer in a car repair shop

Mobile Computers

A mobile computer for someone who travels as part of his or her job requires special design considerations. Considerations for a mobile computer include the following:

> Laptop or tablet
> Sufficient RAM
> Optional mobile broadband connectivity
> Optional SSD (if jarring or dropping due to handling is a concern or if high speed is needed)
> Optional projector
> Optional thermal or portable printer
> Optional portable speakers and headphones with noise cancellation

Go Green

Keep in mind that there are many ways to go green and conserve energy in computer design. The company requesting a design may require green specifications. Cases, motherboards, processors, power supplies, printers, displays, and other computing devices can be designed with energy conservation in mind. The Electronic Product Environmental Assessment Tool (EPEAT) can help with that.

The **EPEAT rating system** was designed to work with the EPA in identifying products that have a green (and clean) design. **ENERGY STAR** is another program that requires strict energy efficiency. Products that earn the ENERGY STAR rating today have low total energy requirements, low-power modes, and efficient power supplies.

Another aspect of being green is recycling old components. Always check with the local disposal requirements and find places to take electronics that have been redesigned and replaced for recycling (see Figure 11.11).

You can also be conscientious of energy requirements when designing a subsystem. Upgrade requests might be for a computer subsystem. In such a case, the best practice is to look at the subsystem as a unit. The following sections examine the various computer subsystems.

RECYCLE HERE

FIGURE 11.11   Computer parts recycling

Motherboard and Associated Component Design

The motherboard, chipset, and CPU are all directly related to one another and should be designed in conjunction with one another. If you buy an Intel motherboard, then you have to get an Intel processor; alternatively, you can use an AMD motherboard and processor. Using a motherboard that has the Intel B360 chipset, for example, gives you up to 12 USB ports, including support for version 3.1 ports and support for up to three displays. You might consider the AMD X370 chipset to get support for both the CrossFire and Scalable Link Interface (SLI) technologies. Some technicians choose a motherboard based on a specific chipset, depending on what the user needs. Newer technologies may influence your choices.

TECH TIP

Don't forget the cooling

If you select a high-end CPU, you must have appropriate cooling for it.

When comparing processors, you may want to consider the nanotechnology used. Processor technology length is measured in **nanometers**. A nanometer is 0.000000001 in length (1×10^{-9}). Processors and chipsets created using 14 nm or 22 nm technology can have more transistors in the same amount of space compared to processors and chipsets created using 32 nm or 45 nm technology.

Traditionally, the smaller the technology, the less heat produced. With lower heat, some components can be made to run faster, but that is not always the case.

Memory ties into processor technology because the type of motherboard/chipset dictates the type of memory supported, the maximum amount of memory the motherboard manufacturer might consider putting on the motherboard, and the maximum memory speed that can be used. Whenever a technician is upgrading or replacing a motherboard, compatibility with existing components is a requirement.

The most important design consideration for memory is to take advantage of dual, triple, and quad channeling, when possible. Ensure that the memory modules are purchased together and installed according to the recommendations set forth in the motherboard/computer manual. Encourage the end user to buy as much RAM as he or she can initially afford. This area is one of the most influential considerations on the user computing experience. Beef up this subsystem component as much as possible.

When dealing with the motherboard, consider the following:

> Motherboard form factor
> Chipset
> Whether the CPU is included or needs to be purchased separately
> CPU size
> Motherboard socket size
> Nanotechnology used with the processor and/or chipset (14 nm, 22 nm, 32 nm, 45 nm, and so on)
> CPU cooling
> RAM
> Number and type of ports

Power Supply and Case Design

When selecting a power supply, the main concerns are size (form factor), total wattage for specific voltage levels, number of connectors, and power efficiency. One issue you must consider is how many connectors connect to the same cable. When you have several high-powered devices, you want to be able to connect them with separate power cables, if possible, instead of using two connectors along the same cable. Also, be careful with cables that do not have at least four wires. These are peripheral cables to power 12-volt fans and are normally labeled as fan connectors. Some power supplies have detachable cables that connect between a power supply connector and a device connector. You attach the number and type of cables you need. Buy additional cables of a specific type, as needed. Figure 11.12 shows detachable cables.

When replacing, upgrading, or purchasing a power supply, consider the following:

> Enough power cables for video cards
> Number and type of power cables (SATA, Molex, PCIe, and fan)
> Form factor
> Wattage for the 12-volt line
> Total wattage, determined using an online power-use calculator
> Quietness
> Mean time between failures (MTBF)
> Overvoltage, overcurrent, undervoltage, and short-circuit protection
> Warranty

FIGURE 11.12 Detachable cables for some power supplies

Keep in mind that the power supply and the case (and the motherboard, too) have to be the same form factor. Some cases accept multiple motherboard form factors. A case may or may not include a fan that goes with the case. Most cases have at least two locations for fans—one at the front of the case and one at the rear. Fans tend to come in 40, 60, 80, 90, 92, 120, or 140 mm sizes. Look for the following key features in a new case:

> Size (ATX, micro-ATX, BTX, ITX, mini-ITX, and so on), type (desktop, tower, or all-in-one), and physical dimensions
> Number and type of front panel ports
> Number and placement of fans
> Cable management
> Number of case expansion slots (matching or coming close to matching the number of slots on the motherboard)
> Number and type of accessible drive bays, including internal or external
> Outside texture and design (metal, aluminum, plastic, acrylic, see-through)
> Ease of cover removal
> Method of securing expansion cards (screw, plastic tab, or single plastic bar)
> Ability to lock case panels to deter entry

Table 11.1 lists recommendations for cases and power supplies for different types of users.

TABLE 11.1   Power supply and case design

Use	Design considerations
Graphic/CAD/CAM, gaming PC, home server PC, audio/video editing computer, or virtualization computer	500 W or higher power supply ATX mid- or full-sized tower Two or more case cooling fans
Thin client	300 W or higher power supply Mini-ATX or micro-ATX tower
Standard thick client or normal user	300 W or higher power supply ATX, mini-ATX, micro-ATX, or mid-sized ATX tower

Air filters can be cheaply purchased for intake openings (not exhaust) to filter dirt and dust. It is important that you know the direction air is flowing through a system before installing a filter. Some cases come with removable air filters that can be cleaned thoroughly. Some power supplies have air filters installed. Air filters, external storage device enclosures, and special computer and laptop enclosures can help protect against airborne particles that can harm a computer or other device.

Figure 11.13 shows a computer case that has removable drives for internal hard drives. Note that even though SATA drives are hot swappable (you can remove them while power is applied), your SATA controller (motherboard) must support this feature, the drive must support it, a SATA power connector must be used, and the drive cannot be in use or used to boot the operating system. For best results, power down the computer before removing an internal SATA drive just to be safe.

FIGURE 11.13   Case with removable internal hard drive trays

Storage Subsystem Design

The storage subsystem consists of magnetic or flash technologies for internal or external hard drives, flash storage (including SSDs), or optical drives.

When adding, replacing, or building a storage subsystem, you must take into account the customer needs, how long the customer plans on storing the data, and how long the customer thinks the storage subsystem will be in use before being upgraded or replaced. Table 11.2 helps with the storage device options.

TABLE 11.2   Storage subsystem design considerations

Feature	Design considerations
Internal connectivity	SATA or M.2
Internal power	Molex or SATA power connector
Internal physical size	1.8, 2.5, 3.5, or 5.25 inches, with an available expansion slot in the case
External connectivity	USB, IEEE 1394 (FireWire), eSATA, or eSATAp port NIC, if required, for cloud (Internet) storage Media reader for flash media, if needed
External power	Either external power cord or power provided by the USB, IEEE 1394, or eSATAp port

Feature	Design considerations
Storage technology	Magnetic (hard drive or optical drive); SATA 1.5, 3, or 6 Gb/s (SATA1, SATA2, or SATA3), M.2, flash memory (SSD, flash drives, and flash media), or hybrid (magnetic and SSD)
Special storage considerations	Multiple drives, if RAID is used NAS to share storage with other computers
Storage device speed	5400, 5900, 7200, 10000, or 15000 RPM for magnetic drives Transfer rate for SSDs Input/output operations per second (**IOPS**) for both magnetic drives and SSDs, which is a measurement that takes into account sequential reads/writes as well as random reads/writes
Optical drive capability	Read-only or read/write
Optical drive technology	Red-violet and/or blue laser(s)
Drive buffers	Both hard drives and optical drives can have buffers that increase data transfer rates
External considerations	What other devices may share the port External cages/enclosures, if needed, to turn an internal device into an external device

Audio Subsystem Design

The audio design consists of the audio ports and speakers. When upgrading or building an audio subsystem, let the customer listen to the speakers, if possible. Table 11.3 lists audio design considerations.

TABLE 11.3 Audio subsystem design considerations

Feature	Design considerations
Number of speakers	Two for a casual user or gamer; three to seven for a music, video, or gaming enthusiast 5.1 surround-sound system: center channel speaker, two front channel speakers for left/right audio, two rear channel speakers for left/right audio, and a subwoofer for low-frequency (bass) sound effects 7.1 surround-sound system: the same speakers as 5.1, with two additional center channel speakers for left/right audio
Microphone	Integrated into the display, headset, or external, with a headset being best for conference calls
2.0 or 2.1	2.0 audio subsystem: two channels (left and right), with an amplifier within one of the two speakers 2.1 audio subsystem: two speakers and a subwoofer for lower-frequency sounds
Port connectivity	3.5 mm mini-plug, S/PDIF TOSLINK, S/PDIF fiber, or wireless
Sound card	PCI, PCIe, or integrated into the motherboard Number and type of sound ports matching the speaker connectivity
Logistics	Elimination of trip hazards Shelving, wall plates, wall inserts, wall hangers Speaker location planning

Display Subsystem Design

Displays are important to the computing experience. With respect to replacing, upgrading, and installing displays, design specifications are important. Many consider multiple displays in the work environment the norm. Some jobs require many displays, as shown in Figure 11.14.

FIGURE 11.14   Multiple displays

Table 11.4 lists some design considerations for displays.

TABLE 11.4   Display subsystem design considerations

Feature	Design considerations
Size/aspect ratio	Common determining factors include physical location, space available, and cost Common aspect ratios: 4:3, 16:9, 16:10, and 1.9:1
Number of displays	Two displays or a single widescreen display
Type of display	Plasma, LCD with CCFL backlight, LCD with LED backlight (LED), or OLED Touchscreen
Display conferencing features	Integrated microphone or webcam
Contrast ratio	A higher number appropriate (Keep in mind that not all vendors give true numbers.)
Video adapter	Slot type Number and type of ports Number of cards and support for sharing of resources (for example, SLI, CrossFire) RAM GPU Power and cooling requirements Power connectivity requirements

   If you can design computer subsystems or an entire computer, you know a lot about the pieces that go into a computer and how they interact. Practicing with different scenarios can help, and there are exercises at the end of the chapter to help you build this skill. Looking at component specifications can help you learn a lot. Investigate component specifications when you shop to increase your knowledge.

Troubleshooting Overview

When a computer does not work properly, technicians must exhibit one essential trait: the will to succeed. The main objective is to return the computer or peripheral to service as quickly and economically as possible. When a computer is down, a business loses revenue and productivity. Therefore, a technician must have a good attitude and a large amount of perseverance and drive to resolve the problem at hand quickly, efficiently, and in a professional, helpful manner.

TECH TIP

Back up data

Before any changes are made to a system, ensure that its data is backed up, if possible.

Technicians must use all available resources, including documentation for a particular peripheral, motherboard, or computer; the Internet; their five senses; other technicians; corporate documentation; textbooks; experience with similar problems; training materials; previous service history on a particular customer/computer; information from users or those around them (see Figure 11.15); or an online database provided by a company or partner. Technicians can be stubborn, but they must always remember that time is money, and solving a problem quickly and with the least amount of downtime to the customer is a critical component of a computer support job.

FIGURE 11.15   Technician gathering information from a computer user

---

TECH TIP

Before making changes...

You must always consider corporate policies, procedures, and impacts before implementing changes.

Evaluating and solving a technology problem is a high-level objective in Bloom's Taxonomy, as shown earlier in the chapter (Figure 11.1). Teaching someone to troubleshoot is challenging. Not every problem can be described in a step-by-step fashion. Troubleshooting is easier if a technician uses reasoning and takes logical steps. Logical troubleshooting can be broken down into six simple steps:

Step 1. Identify the problem.

Step 2. Establish a theory of probable cause (question the obvious).

Step 3. Test the theory to determine the cause.

Step 4. Establish a plan of action to resolve the problem and implement a solution.

Step 5. Verify full system functionality and, if applicable, implement preventive measures.

Step 6. Document findings, actions, and outcomes.

Step 1. Identify the Problem

Computer problems come in all shapes and sizes. Many problems relate to the people who operate computers—the users. Users may fail to choose the correct printer, push the wrong key for a specific function, or issue an incorrect command.

Have the user demonstrate or re-create the problem. Because the user is often the problem, you can save a great deal of time by taking this step. Do not assume anything! A user may complain that "my hard drive does not work" when, in fact, there is no power to the computer. Often users repeat computer terms they have heard or read, but they do not use them correctly or in the right context. By asking a user to re-create a problem, a technician creates a chance to see the problem as the client sees it. This should be done even during a phone consultation. Whether diagnosing a problem on the phone or in person, be sure to follow these guidelines:

> Do not assume anything; ask the user to re-create the problem step-by-step.

> Question the user. Ask the user if anything has been changed. Do not be threatening; otherwise, the user will not be forthright and honest. Ask open-ended questions to get an idea of what is wrong. Use closed-ended questions (those that require a yes or no answer) to narrow the problem. Refer to Figure 1.2 in Chapter 1, "Introduction to the World of IT," to see examples of these techniques.

> Inquire about any environmental or infrastructure changes in the work environment. Has anything been added to the computer or network recently? Has any maintenance work been done in the area?

> Verify obvious conditions, such as power to the monitor or speakers muted through the Control Panel.

> Do not assume that there is not a problem if the user cannot re-create it. Some problems occur intermittently.

> Use all your senses. Listen for noises such as from the power supply, case/CPU fans, speaker feedback, hard drive, or optical drive. Power off if you detect a burning smell.

> **Review system and application logs**. Operating systems contain logs that document what occurs during normal and abnormal conditions. Applications also log issues. For hardware issues such as those related to motherboards, RAM, CPU, or power, make sure you examine **log entries and error messages** displayed. Use the Windows Advanced Boot Options window to select *Enable Boot Logging* > reboot > and examine the logging file `ntbtlog.txt`. See Chapter 16, "Advanced Windows," for more information on Windows Advanced Boot Options.

> Back up data, if possible, before making changes (see Figure 11.16).

FIGURE 11.16   Back up user data before making changes

Step 2. Establish a Theory of Probable Cause (Question the Obvious)

In order to establish a theory of probable cause, you have to have heard or seen the problem as explained by the user. A lot of times, you establish a theory based on analyzing the problem and determining whether the problem is hardware or software related (or both) by using your senses: Sight, hearing, and smell can reveal a great deal. Smell for burning components. Watch the computer boot, look for lights, listen for beeps, and take notes. Use internal resources such as coworkers or your boss; use external resources including the Internet to research symptoms. Do not forget to question the obvious.

The Boot Process

One thing that might help you establish a theory of probable cause is to examine the boot process. Frequently, a hardware problem is detected during the power-on self-test (POST) executed by the BIOS/UEFI when the computer is first powered on. Remember that the traditional BIOS is looking for the boot loader (a small bit of code on a drive). The computer is configured with a specific device boot order. Knowing the steps taken during the boot process can help you troubleshoot an older machine that has a traditional BIOS:

Step 1. The power supply sends a power good signal.

Step 2. The CPU looks in BIOS for software.

Step 3. The CPU executes POST from BIOS. Note that any errors are usually audio or motherboard LEDs or codes at this point.

Step 4. System resources (I/O address, memory addresses, and interrupts) are retrieved from nonvolatile RAM (NVRAM), (which is RAM that can be changed, but data is not lost when power is removed) and assigned to ports, devices, and adapters.

Step 5. Video is initialized, and a cursor appears.

Step 6. POST continues to check hardware and error messages and/or codes can now appear on the display.

Step 7. Based on the boot order configuration in System Setup, the system checks for an operating system from the specified devices.

Step 8. The computer loads an operating system found from the first device that contains an operating system or displays an error.

On a newer computer that has a UEFI BIOS, things can be a bit different. A UEFI BIOS can optionally have a BIOS compatibility mode in which the computer behaves as previously described. However, if the system is natively booting using UEFI, the UEFI standards require a common format for executable code. This allows much more flexibility in the boot process, as UEFI has to be able to interpret (not just recognize) globally unique identifiers (GUID) partition table (GPT) partitions and the traditional master boot record (MBR). UEFI supports larger drives and partitions.

UEFI has a boot manager. This boot manager can load UEFI drivers and applications and is customizable. These are not operating system drivers. This means that if the operating system has issues, through the UEFI, you can still use your mouse and other devices that have UEFI drivers within the UEFI environment and with UEFI applications that could help with troubleshooting. Refer to Chapter 4, "Introduction to Configuration," for a refresher on the UEFI BIOS. Figure 11.17 shows the boot sequence for a UEFI-based device.

FIGURE 11.17 UEFI boot order

POST Codes and Error Messages

During the firmware phase—whether UEFI or BIOS is used—POST checks out the hardware in a sequential order, and if it finds an error, the BIOS/UEFI issues a beep, displays a numeric error code, or displays an **error message**. Make note of any error codes, beeps, or messages. The number or duration of beeps, the meaning of numeric error codes, and the type of error messages that appear are different for different computers.

TECH TIP

Audio POST code: Checking video and RAM first

Have you ever been working on a computer which gives a POST code that you didn't want to take the time to look up? Audio codes are frequently related to video and memory. Check connections and reset the card or module.

The secret is knowing the BIOS/UEFI chip manufacturer. The computer or motherboard documentation sometimes contains a list of codes or beeps used for troubleshooting. A single beep is a common tone heard on a successful completion of POST because hardware errors were not detected. Listening is an important part of troubleshooting.

Table 11.5 lists the audio beeps heard on Dell computers. Look at the first line. The 1-1-2 means the computer beeps once, pauses, beeps again, pauses, and then beeps two times. Table 11.6 lists audio beeps for computers that have an AMI BIOS/UEFI chip installed. Table 11.7 lists the audio beeps heard on a computer with a Phoenix BIOS/UEFI chip installed.

TABLE 11.5 Dell computer POST audio beeps

Beeps	Description of problem
1-1-2	Processor register failure
1-1-3	NVRAM
1-1-4	BIOS checksum failure
1-3-1 through 2-4-4	Memory modules not identified or used
3-2-4	Keyboard controller test failure
3-3-1	NVRAM power loss
3-3-2	NVRAM configuration
3-3-4	Video memory test failure
3-4-1	Screen initialization failure
4-3-4	Time-of-day clock stopped

TECH TIP

Troubleshoot the first POST code heard or seen

If multiple POST errors occur, start by troubleshooting the first one heard or seen.

TABLE 11.6 AMI BIOS/UEFI audio beeps

Beeps	Description of problem
1, 2, or 3	Memory error
4, 5, 6, or 7	Motherboard component
8	Video issue
1 long 3 short	Memory test failure
1 long 8 short	Display test failure
2 short	POST failure

TABLE 11.7   Phoenix audio beep codes

Beeps	Description
1-2-2-3	BIOS ROM (flash the BIOS/motherboard)
1-3-1-1	Memory refresh (RAM contacts/RAM)
1-3-1-3	8742 keyboard controller (keyboard/motherboard)
1-3-4-1	Memory address line error (RAM contacts/RAM/power supply/motherboard)
1-3-4-3	Memory error (RAM contacts/RAM/motherboard)
1-4-1-3	CPU bus clock frequency
2-2-3-1	Unexpected interrupt (adapter/motherboard)
2-4-2-3	Keyboard error
3-1-1-1	Onboard I/O port issue

Don't get frustrated at error messages that appear on the screen. Error messages are good things in that they assist you in troubleshooting. Table 11.8 lists the POST error messages sometimes seen on other computers.

TABLE 11.8   BIOS/UEFI POST error messages

Message	Description
BIOS ROM checksum error—System halted	The BIOS/UEFI has a problem and needs to be replaced.
CMOS battery failed/error	Replace the motherboard battery.
CMOS checksum error—Defaults loaded	CMOS has detected a problem. Check the motherboard battery.
CMOS timer error	The system date/time has not been set. Check/replace the motherboard battery if this is not the first time this computer has been powered on.
Hard disk install failure	The BIOS/UEFI could not find or initialize the hard drive. Check the hard drive connectivity and power.
Intruder detection error	The computer chassis has been opened.
Keyboard error or no keyboard present	The keyboard could not be found. Check the cabling.
Keyboard is locked out—Unlock the key	Ensure that nothing rests on the keys during the POST.
Memory test fail	A RAM error occurred. Swap the memory modules.
Memory size decrease error	The amount of system RAM has decreased. Check to see whether RAM has been stolen, needs to be reseated, or needs to be replaced.
Memory optimal error	The amount of memory in channel A is not equal to channel B. For optimal memory performance, the channels should have equal memory. See Chapter 6, "Memory," for more details.
Override enabled—Defaults loaded	The current settings in CMOS could not be loaded, and the BIOS/UEFI defaults are used. Check the battery and CMOS settings.

Message	Description
Primary master hard disk fail	The PATA hard drive attached to the primary IDE connector and configured as master could not be detected. If it is a new installation, check the cabling, power, and master/slave/cable select settings. See Chapter 7, "Storage Devices," for more details.
Primary slave hard disk fail	The PATA hard drive attached to the primary IDE connector and configured as slave could not be detected. If it is a new installation, check the cabling, power, and master/slave/cable select settings. See Chapter 7 for more details.

A BIOS/UEFI can be sold to various computer manufacturers that are then allowed to create their own error codes and messages. Always look in the motherboard/computer manual or on the manufacturer's website for a list of exact error messages.

In addition to generating audio tones or numeric error codes or written messages, the motherboard might provide additional troubleshooting information, such as the following:

> You might see a **proprietary crash screen** or a screen showing something that is unique to a specific manufacturer.
> In Windows, you might see a blue screen of death (**BSOD**) with a XE "monitors:BSOD" numeric code and/or a message. You might also see the system display a message saying a particular application is not responding. Use *Task Manager* to stop the application or give the application more time to complete the task. Close other open applications. See Chapter 16 for more Windows troubleshooting.
> On macOS or Linux operating systems, you might see a colored **pin wheel** that appears to turn forever. Use *Activity Monitor* to check for processor and RAM performance and free disk space and/or to stop the problematic application. See Chapter 17, "macOS and Linux Operating Systems," for more troubleshooting tips on Mac and Linux systems.

When a numeric code appears or when certain lights illuminate, you have to use the Internet or motherboard/computer manual to determine the issue. Some motherboards have a numeric display or colored indicators that display as part of the POST. The meaning of the visual clues can be found in the motherboard or computer manual.

Other Diagnostics

Some technicians carry a POST card as part of their toolkit. A **POST card** is a PCI/PCIe adapter or USB-attached card that performs hardware diagnostics and displays the results as a series of codes on an LED display or LED light(s). These are not as popular today as they once were because many UEFI-based motherboards include powerful diagnostics (see Table 11.9) that can be executed from or downloaded from the computer manufacturer's website. However, a POST card is useful if a system does not boot and no other symptoms appear.

TABLE 11.9   UEFI diagnostic types

Diagnostic	Description
Express, start, or system test	Similar to POST, checks the main hardware components needed to load the operating system.
Component test	Allows selection of individual parts to test.
Hard drive test	Checks the drive for bad areas and has the capability to mark an area and not use it in the future.

Diagnostic	Description
Memory test	Performs multiple reads/writes to memory locations.
Battery test	Checks the battery's power level.

Some motherboard LEDs are used in conjunction with switches that can be pressed to test components. Figure 11.18 shows a motherboard LED, and Figure 11.19 shows some common uses of motherboard LEDs.

FIGURE 11.18   Motherboard LED

Examples of Motherboard Switches and LEDs

Switch	LED	Explanation
MemOK!	MemOK	Depress the MemOK switch to determine if the RAM modules are compatible. The MemOK LED illuminates if so.
EPU	EPU	Enable the EPU switch or enable through BIOS to allow the motherboard to moderate power consumption. When enabled, the EPU LED is lit.
	RAM	The RAM LED illuminates for a memory error.
	Power	The power LED commonly illuminates when power is applied, or if the computer is in either the sleep or soft off power mode.

FIGURE 11.19   Motherboard switches and LED usage

Hardware Errors

Hardware errors sometimes occur. For example, a display might suddenly go black, an optical drive's access light might not go on when it attempts to access the optical disc, or a printer might repeatedly flash an error code. If you suspect a physical port problem, you can use a loopback plug to test the port. A **loopback plug** sends a signal out one or more electrical pins and allows the signal to come back in on one or more different pins. Loopback plugs are commonly used with older ports, such as parallel and serial ports. Today, one of the most common uses for a loopback plug is to test a communication circuit port or an RJ-45 loopback plug to test network port functionality.

TECH TIP

What to do if you smell smoke coming from a computer

Unplug the device if you can. Pull the fire alarm. Call 911. If you see smoke, get a fire extinguisher and PASS (pull the pin, aim at the base of the fire, squeeze the trigger, and sweep slowly side to side).

Hardware errors are usually obvious because of POST error codes or errors that occur when accessing a particular device. Also, some peripherals, such as hard drives and printers, include diagnostics as part of the software that is loaded when the device is installed. These diagnostics are frequently accessed through the device's *Properties* window.

Intermittent Device Failure

Sometimes, none of the hardware troubleshooting actions described so far work. In such a case, a grounding problem might be the issue. Symptoms of a grounding problem include intermittent or unexplained shutdowns.

To troubleshoot an intermittent device failure, build the computer outside the computer case on an antistatic mat, if possible. Start with only the power supply, motherboard, and speaker connected. Even though it will normally produce a POST audio error, verify that the power supply fan turns. Most power supplies issue a click before the audio POST beeps. Next, verify the voltages from the power supply. If the fan turns and the voltages are correct, power down the machine and add a video adapter and monitor to the system. If the machine does not work, put the video adapter in a different expansion slot and try again. If placing the video adapter in a different expansion slot does not work, swap out the video adapter.

If the video adapter works, continue adding devices one by one and checking the voltages. Just as any one device can prevent the system from operating properly, so can any adapter. If one particular adapter causes the system to malfunction, try a different expansion slot before trying a different adapter. If the expansion slot proves to be a problem, check the slot for foreign objects. If none are found, but the problem still occurs, place a note on the expansion slot so that no one will use it.

An **intermittent device failure** is one of the hardest things to troubleshoot. Devices commonly associated with intermittent device failure are the motherboard, RAM, processor, and power supply; however, a failing hard drive can also present itself as an intermittent device failure if the drive is starting to have problems.

When considering the motherboard, RAM, processor, and power supply, RAM is the easiest to troubleshoot of these four components if there are multiple memory modules installed. Before trying anything else, remove power to the system and push firmly on the memory modules. They can creep up a bit even with the side locking levers in place. Power on and see if the problem reappears.

If it doesn't, swap the modules to see whether symptoms change or remove one of the modules. If the system stays stable, reinsert the module and see whether the intermittent failure returns.

For intermittent power issues, first check the power output with a power supply tester. Also check the power supply wattage and ensure that it is adequate for the number of installed devices. Inspect power connectors to ensure that they have not gotten caught or crimped in the cover.

Determining whether a problem is a motherboard or a processor is tough. The easiest thing to do is check the processor on a different (compatible) motherboard. You might see whether you can use a particular UEFI diagnostic to do an extended test on the motherboard and processor.

Software Errors

Software errors occur when a computer user accesses a particular application or file or when the system boots. Applications sometimes present error messages like POST does, but they are application specific. Sometimes an application restarts itself or needs to be manually stopped through Task Manager. Then open the application again.

Some software errors relate to hardware, such as a USB-to-serial adapter. If the application being used with the adapter locks, unplugging the USB cable and reinserting may cause the hardware and software to start working again.

Sometimes a software problem can be resolved with a **warm boot**. Warm booting causes any changes that have been made to take effect without putting as much strain on the computer as a cold boot does. Here are the warm boot (restart) procedures for the different Windows versions:

> Windows 7: Select the *Start* button > click on the right arrow adjacent to the lock button or Shutdown and select *Restart*.

> Windows 8: Move the mouse to the upper-right corner or swipe from the right edge to access the *Charms* menu > *Settings* > *Power* > *Restart*.

> Windows 10: Select the *Start* button > *Power* > *Restart*.

> In all Windows versions, a warm boot can be performed through Task Manager by pressing `Ctrl`+`Alt`+`Del` > *Task Manager* > *Shut Down* option > select *Restart* from the drop-down menu > *OK*.

TECH TIP

Check motherboard manual or website for the latest error codes

Manufacturers constantly produce BIOS/UEFI upgrades, and you can use the Internet to verify POST errors that occur and the recommended actions to take.

Files that affect the booting process, such as files in the Startup folder, are dependent on the operating system. If in doubt as to whether a problem is hardware or software related, use Windows *Device Manager* to test the hardware to eliminate that possibility. Every software program has problems (bugs). Software manufacturers typically offer software **patches** or **service releases** to fix known problems. Patches or service releases are usually available on the Internet from the software manufacturer. It is important to keep applications and the operating system patched. A **service pack** (in Windows 7) usually contains multiple patches and installs them at the same time rather than in multiple downloads.

Step 3. Test the Theory to Determine the Cause

Once you have a theory or suspect a general area and your theory is confirmed, you need to determine the next steps needed to resolve the problem. If you go through the process for what you suspect and the problem is still unresolved, you might have to step back and reevaluate the problem. From there, you can establish a new theory or, if needed, escalate the problem to a more senior technician.

Divide the problem into logical areas and continue subdividing the problem until you have isolated it. For example, if an error appears each time the computer user tries to write data to a CD, the logical place to look is the optical drive system. The optical drive system includes the user's disc, the optical drive, electronics that tell the drive what to do, a cable that connects the drive to the controlling electronics, and the software program currently being used. Any of these may be the cause of the problem.

Ernie Friend, a technician of many years, advises students to divide a problem in half, and then divide it in half again, and then continue to divide it until the problem is manageable. This way of thinking carries a technician a long way. Also, always keep in mind that you will beat the problem at hand! You are smarter than any problem!

TECH TIP

Reinstall the original part if it does not fix the problem

Always reinstall the original part if the symptoms do not change. Then continue troubleshooting.

Here's how you could use Ernie's philosophy with an optical drive problem: Divide the problem in half and determine whether the problem is hardware or software related. To determine whether the software application is causing the problem, try accessing the disc from another application. If the second application works, then the problem is in the first application. If both applications have problems, the problem is most likely in the disc or in the drive hardware system. The next easiest thing to eliminate as a suspect is the CD. Try a different disc. If a different disc works, then the first disc was the problem. If neither disc accepts data, the problem is the optical drive, cable, or electronics. Swap parts one at a time until you locate the problem.

If a hardware problem is evident after a POST error or peripheral access/usage error occurs, consider the problem a subunit of the entire computer. For example, if a POST error occurs for the optical drive, the subunit is the optical drive subsystem, which consists of the drive, the cable, and the controlling circuits that may be on an adapter or the motherboard.

If a problem is software related, narrow it to a specific area. For example, determine whether the problem is related to printing, saving, or retrieving a file. This may give you a clue about what section of the application is having a problem or may even lead you back to considering other hardware components as the cause of the problem.

TECH TIP

Change or check the easy stuff first

When isolating a problem to a specific area, be practical; change or check the easy stuff first (see Figure 11.20). Time is money—to the company or person whose computer is down and to the company that employs the technician.

When multiple things could cause a problem, make a list of possibilities and eliminate the potential problems one by one. If a display is faulty, swap the display with another one before opening the computer and replacing the video adapter.

"It could be that it's not plugged in, but that would be too easy."

FIGURE 11.20   Check the easy stuff first

Also, check with the computer user to see whether anything about the computer has changed recently. For example, ask if anyone installed or removed something from the computer or if new software was loaded before or has been loaded since the problem started. If the problem is hardware related, you can use the Device Manager and Windows troubleshooting wizards to narrow it down to a subunit.

If you do not hear any unusual audio beeps or see any POST error codes and you suspect a software error, reboot the computer. Before Windows starts, press the F8 key to bring up the *Advanced Boot Options* menu. Select a menu option, such as *Repair Your Computer*, *Safe Mode*, or *Last Known Good Configuration*. In newer computers, it is not always easy to press the F8 key during startup. Here's how to do this for Windows 8 and 10:

> In Windows 8: Access *Settings* > *Advanced Startup Options* > locate the *Advanced Startup* section > click the *Restart Now* button.

> In Windows 10: Access *Settings* > *Update & Security* > *Recovery* > locate the *Advanced Startup* section > click the *Restart Now* button.

Swapping a part, checking hardware settings, and referring to documentation are necessary steps in troubleshooting. Noting error or beep codes is just one element in the diagnostic routine. Determining what the problem is usually takes longer than fixing it. Software problems frequently involve reloading software applications and software drivers or getting software updates and patches from the appropriate vendor. The Internet is an excellent resource for these files and vendor recommendations. Hardware problem resolution simply involves swapping the damaged part. Sometimes, it is necessary to remove or disable unnecessary components and peripherals, especially in notebook computers.

If swapping a part or reloading the software does not solve the problem, go back to logical troubleshooting. Step 2 reminds you to divide the problem into hardware- and software-related issues. Go back to that step, if necessary.

Step 4. Establish a Plan of Action to Resolve the Problem and Implement the Solution

Every repair should involve a plan of action. Having a plan helps you through the problem-resolution process. The plan of action should take you through resolving the problem and implementing the solution. Some repairs take multiple steps. You might have to apply a BIOS/UEFI update before installing a new adapter. You might have to update the operating system or remove a virus before reinstalling or upgrading an application. Having a plan instead of just doing things in a random order saves time—and time is money!

Step 5. Verify Full System Functionality and, if Applicable, Implement Preventive Measures

Never assume that a hardware component or replaced software repairs a computer. The computer can have multiple problems, or one repair may not offer a complete solution. Verify full system functionality and have the user test the computer in normal conditions to ensure that the problem is indeed solved. You may need to implement preventive measures, such as cleaning the computer or device or installing a legal copy of antivirus/anti-malware software and making sure that software is updated. Preventive measures also include using disk maintenance utilities to clean up the hard drive, cleaning the optical drive laser lens, scheduling disk maintenance, and creating a recovery image.

Step 6. Document Findings, Actions, and Outcomes

Many technicians feel that their work is done once a problem is solved, but it is not. It is important to document the steps taken to resolve a problem in a clear, concise manner. A lot of times, this documentation is put in a customer's record, or an invoice is generated as a result of the repair. Having easy-to-read and easy-to-understand documentation is important for nontechnical users who see this documentation as well as any follow-up repairs that you or another technician must do. The old adage that a job is not done until the paperwork is done is still true, even though the paperwork is usually electronic documentation. Documentation remains an important last step.

The best computer technicians can repair problems, build trust with users, and explain problems in a way customers can understand. A repair is never finished until the user is informed. Technical training on new equipment or a procedure/process may be necessary. Realize that computer users are intelligent, even if they are not proficient in technical terminology.

A good recommendation is to follow up with a customer a week after a repair to make sure the customer is satisfied and verify that the problem is solved. If the customer is unhappy, jump at the chance to redo the repair. The best advertising is good referrals from satisfied customers. Keep in mind that the general rule of thumb is that if a customer is satisfied, he or she will tell 1 or 2 other people about the service, but if a customer is dissatisfied, he or she will tell 10 other people about the problem.

Each computer repair is a different scenario because of the plethora of vendors, products, and standards in the marketplace. But this is one thing that makes the job so interesting and challenging. Break down each problem into manageable tasks, isolate the specific issue, and use all available resources, including other technicians, documentation, and the Internet, to solve the problem. Keep a "can do" attitude with intermittent problems, which are the most difficult-to-solve types of problems. Never forget to give feedback to the user.

Sample Troubleshooting Flowcharts

Technical documentation commonly includes troubleshooting flowcharts. Learning how to read and use them is helpful. Figure 11.21 shows a flowchart that does not have any words in it. The symbols in the sample flowchart are as follows:

> The powder blue and dark orange rectangles with rounded edges are terminal blocks that show where to start or where to end. Not all flowcharts have these blocks.
> The lime green parallelogram shows input or output, which could be generating a report or receiving some type of diagnostic data
> The yellow rectangle is the most common shape you will see in a flowchart. It shows an action to take, a task to do, or an operation to perform.
> The purple diamond is a decision box. Which direction you take out of the decision box depends on what happens. Notice in Figure 11.21 that there are three results that could occur from the decision box. If they were Yes, No, and Not applicable, and whatever you did resulted in the question posed in the purple box having an answer of yes, the left output from the purple decision box could lead to another action box, labeled Yes. If the answer were not applicable and the bottom of the purple decision box were labeled N/A, then you would terminate and be done (drop to the orange terminal block). If the answer out of the purple decision box was no and the right side of the decision box was labeled No, you would do the action listed in the blue action box on the right

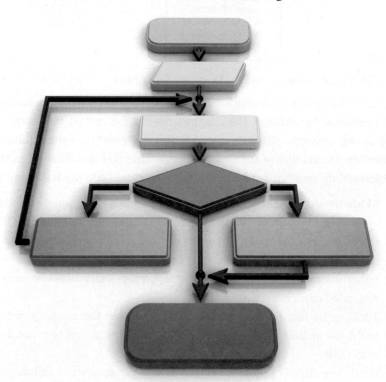

FIGURE 11.21   Sample flowchart

Figure 11.22 shows a simple troubleshooting flowchart, and Figure 11.23 shows a USB troubleshooting flowchart.

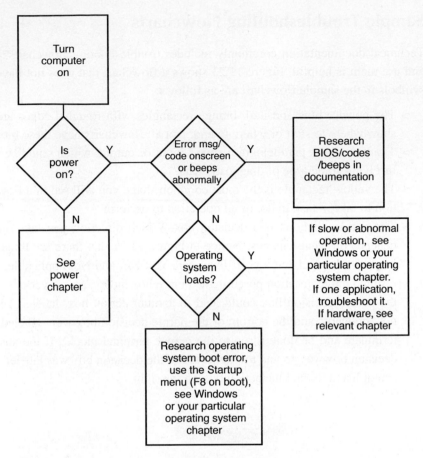

FIGURE 11.22 Basic troubleshooting flowchart

Keep in mind that each chapter of this book has one or more troubleshooting sections to help with problems. In addition, the chapters toward the end of this book address problems related to operating systems. Also, the list that follows provides information that is important for the troubleshooting section of the CompTIA A+ 220-1001 certification exam. Review each chapter's troubleshooting sections before taking the exam and keep the following information in mind:

> Motherboard, RAM, CPU, and power problem symptoms include unexpected shutdowns, system lockups, POST code beeps, blank screen on bootup, BIOS/UEFI time and settings resets, attempts to boot to incorrect devices, continuous reboots, no power, overheating, loud noise, intermittent device failure, fans spin but no power goes to other devices, indicator lights illuminate, smoke, burning smell, proprietary crash screens (BSOD/pin wheel), and distended capacitors.

> Tools to be familiar with when troubleshooting the motherboard, RAM, CPU, and power problems include the following: multimeter, power supply tester, loopback plugs, and POST card/USB.

> Hard drive/RAID problem symptoms include read/write failure, slow performance, a loud clicking noise, failure to boot, drive not recognized, OS not found, RAID not found, RAID stops working, proprietary crash screens (BSOD/pin wheel), and S.M.A.R.T. errors.

> Tools to be familiar with when troubleshooting hard drive and RAID problems include the following: screwdriver, external enclosures, `chkdsk`, `format`, file recovery software, `bootrec`, `diskpart`, and the defragmentation tool.

> Video, projector, and display problem symptoms include VGA mode, no image on the screen, overheat shutdown, dead pixels, artifacts, incorrect color patterns, dim images, flickering images, distorted images, distorted geometry, burn-in, and oversized images and icons.

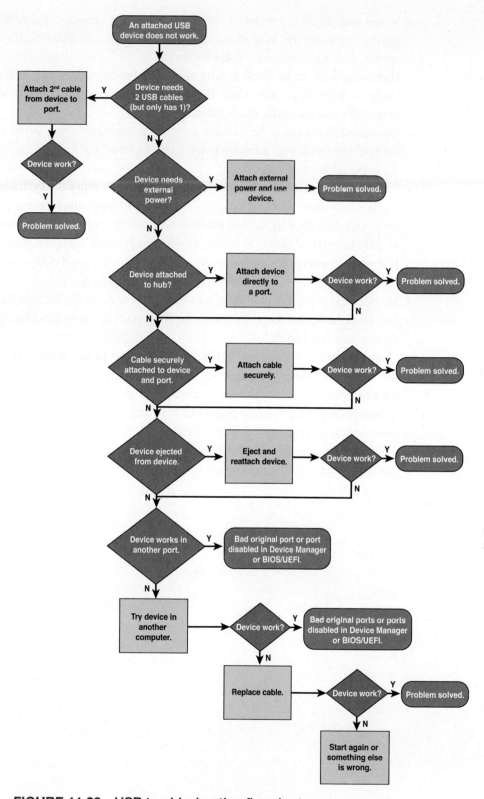

FIGURE 11.23   USB troubleshooting flowchart

> Wired and wireless problem symptoms include no connectivity, APIPA/link local address, limited connectivity, local connectivity, intermittent connectivity, IP conflict, slow transfer speeds, low RF signal, and SSID not found.

> Hardware tools to be familiar with when troubleshooting wired and wireless problems include the following: cable tester, loopback plug, punch down tools, tone generator and probe, wire strippers, crimpers, and wireless locator.

> Command-line tools to be familiar with when troubleshooting wired and wireless problems include the following: `ping`, `ipconfig/ifconfig`, `tracert`, `netstat`, `nbtstat`, `net`, `netdom`, and `nslookup`.

> Mobile device problem symptoms include no display, dim display, flickering display, sticking keys, intermittent wireless, battery that doesn't charge, ghost cursor/pointer drift, no power, num lock indicator lights, no wireless connectivity, no Bluetooth connectivity, inability to display to external monitor, nonresponsive touchscreen, apps not loading, slow performance, inability to decrypt email, extremely short battery life, overheating, frozen system, no sound from speakers, GPS not functioning, and swollen battery.

> Mobile device disassembly processes for proper reassembly include the following: document and label cable and screw locations, organize parts, refer to manufacturer resources, and use appropriate hand tools.

> Printer problem symptoms include streaks, faded print, ghost images, toner not fused to the paper, creased paper, paper not feeding, paper jams, no connectivity, garbled characters on paper, vertical lines on page, backed-up print queue, low memory errors, denied access, printer failing to print, color prints in the wrong print color, inability to install a printer, error codes, printing blank pages, and no image on the printer display.

> Tools to use with printer problems include the following: maintenance kit, toner vacuum, compressed air, and printer spooler.

SOFT SKILLS: DEALING WITH IRATE CUSTOMERS

One of the most difficult tasks a technician faces is dealing with people who are angry, upset, or frustrated. This is a common issue for those who come to help or try to troubleshoot a problem over the phone. Dealing with irate customers is a skill that you can fine-tune. Listening to peer technicians tell how they have successfully (or unsuccessfully) dealt with a difficult customer can also help. Realize that not only do customers want their computer problems fixed, they sometimes just need to vent and be heard. Because a technician is the person with the knowledge for at least the start of the resolution and the technician is in front of or on the phone with the person who is not able to do something on the computer, the technician may be a scapegoat and must try to listen to the irritated customer. Some key tips for dealing with customers are shown in Figure 11.24.

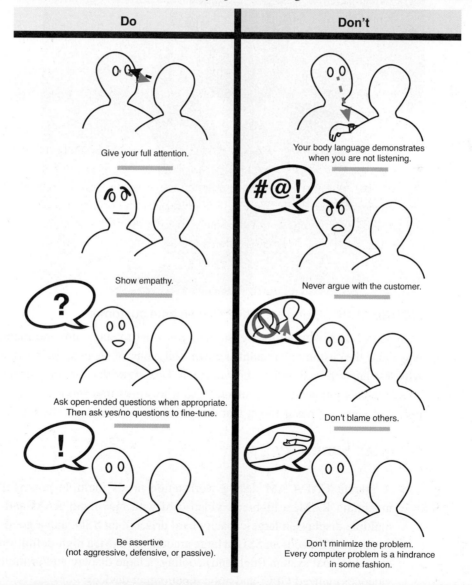

FIGURE 11.24   Dealing with irate customers

The last suggestion in Figure 11.24 about being assertive is one that many people do not understand. Aggression involves dominating a conversation or situation by threatening, bullying, being sarcastic, or showing belittling behavior and/or actions. Some technicians consistently demonstrate aggressive behavior. This reflects poorly on the technician and the company that the technician represents. Passive behavior involves letting others dominate you and expressing yourself apologetically. Technicians who are passive frequently apologize while the customer is trying to explain the problem. Assertive behavior involves being respectful of another person but not allowing him or her to take advantage or dominate the situation. This is the middle ground you want to strive for when dealing with customers. It would be appropriate to raise a hand to indicate that you want an irate customer to stop what he or she is doing (see Figure 11.25). This would be an assertive way to show that the current behavior is inappropriate.

FIGURE 11.25   Being assertive with an irate customer

When dealing with an irate customer, you want to stay calm and maintain your professionalism. Once the customer has calmed down a bit, you can glean more information about the problem with less anger mixed into the conversation. Dealing with angry customers is an important part of a technician's job, as it is for anyone else who works in a service industry. Consider customers' points of view and never forget that they are the ones who must use the devices that you repair.

Chapter Summary

> A graphic/CAD/CAM design workstation needs multiple powerful multicore processors, maximum RAM, a high-end video card with maximum RAM and GPU, a large display/multiple displays, a large-capacity hard drive(s), an SSD, and a good input device(s).

> A gaming PC needs an SSD, a large amount of RAM, a high-definition sound card and speakers, additional system (high-end) cooling, a large display and/or multiple displays, high-end video/specialized GPU, and good input/output devices.

> An audio- or video-editing workstation needs powerful multicore processors, maximum RAM, a good video card with maximum RAM and GPU, a specialized sound card, a fast and large-capacity hard drive, dual monitors, and good input device(s).

> A virtualization workstation needs maximum multicore processors, maximum RAM, multiple fast hard drives, an SSD, and at least 1 Gb/s NIC.

> A standard thick client computer supports desktop applications and meets recommended requirements for the selected OS.

> A thin client computer supports basic applications and meets minimum requirements for the selected OS. A thin client must also have network connectivity.

> A network-attached storage device can be used for media streaming and file sharing. It should include a gigabit NIC, RAID array, and large hard drive.

> A mobile computer is commonly a laptop with lots of RAM and an SSD, a mobile tablet, or a smartphone, and it may require devices such as a projector, thermal printer, portable speakers, or headphones with noise cancellation.

> A home server PC has a medium to large case, multiple powerful multicore processors, lots of RAM, RAID, a 1 Gb/s NIC, and server applications such as media streaming, file sharing, and print sharing.

> Processors and chipsets are created using a specific nanotechnology. Common technologies used are 14, 22, 32, and 45 nm. The smaller the number, the less space for the same number of transistors.

> When designing a motherboard, the CPU size and motherboard CPU socket must match.

> The power supply, motherboard, and case form factors must match.

> Power supplies must have the correct amount of wattage, the correct wattage for a specific power level, and an appropriate number/type of power cables.

> Air filters and enclosures can help in environments where airborne particles are a concern.

> When designing for internal devices, use SATA or M.2 and have the correct power connector. Ensure that an internal connector is available.

> When designing for external connectivity, ensure that a USB, eSATA, or eSATAp port is available; ensure that enough power is provided to power the device through the port or use an external power supply; and ensure that the port is not being shared by too many devices, which can affect performance.

> For audio, ensure that the correct number and type of input/output ports are available.

> For common usage, the 2.0 two-channel audio subsystem is used. A 2.1 audio subsystem adds a subwoofer as a third output device for lower frequencies.

> Display design should include considerations about physical space, type of display, features that might be integrated into the display (such as a microphone or camera), video port, and memory, GPU, and additional power requirements.

> Mobile designs include all the same major components as a desktop system plus 802.11 and Bluetooth wireless capabilities, as well as integrated input devices such as a keyboard and touchpad.

> The six steps of troubleshooting are as follows: (1) identify the problem, (2) establish a theory, (3) test the theory, (4) establish a plan of action, (5) verify full system functionality and, if applicable, implement preventive measures, and (6) document findings, actions, and outcomes as well as provide feedback.

> BIOS/UEFI controls the boot process. Knowing the following traditional BIOS steps can help with the troubleshooting process. The basic steps that the computer goes through to start up are as follows:

Step 1. The power supply sends a power good signal.

Step 2. The CPU looks in BIOS for software.

Step 3. The CPU executes POST from BIOS (only audio errors available at this point).

Step 4. The computer assigns system resources to ports, devices, and adapters.

Step 5. Video is initialized, and a cursor appears.

Step 6. POST continues to check hardware.

Step 7. The computer looks for an operating system from the BIOS-specified boot order devices.

Step 8. The computer loads the operating system or halts with an error.

> Like a traditional BIOS, UEFI checks the hardware. The UEFI boot manager can load drivers that allow devices such as the mouse and NIC to be used with UEFI applications. In a Windows environment, the UEFI boot manager turns over control to a Windows boot manager; then the Windows operating system loader controls the loading of the operating system kernel.

> POST error codes are determined by the BIOS/UEFI vendor and the company that makes the motherboard.

> POST codes can be audible beeps, numeric codes, or words.

> The BIOS/UEFI can contain advanced diagnostics.

> The motherboard can contain diagnostic LEDs or a display.

> A POST card can be used to perform diagnostics.

> A loopback plug can be used in conjunction with diagnostics to check older ports and communication ports or to test network interface ports.

> Reinstall parts that do not solve the problem.

> Always document a problem as part of the troubleshooting process. Give users the appropriate documentation. Be professional in your oral and written communication. Provide feedback to the user.

A+ CERTIFICATION EXAM TIPS

✓ The specific types of custom configurations on the exam include the following computer types: (1) graphic/CAD/CAM design, (2) audio/video editing, (3) virtualization, (4) gaming, (5) network-attached storage device, (6) standard thick client, and (7) thin client. Be able to select the appropriate components and configure them for each type. Focus on the starred components in each computer type within the chapter, because these are the ones on the certification.

✓ Know what type of problem would need a loopback plug.

✓ For troubleshooting motherboards, RAM, CPUs, and power, a new symptom has been added to the A+ 1001 exam objectives: log entries and error messages. When something happens within a computer, the operating system logs it, and a technician should know to look in the logs and pay attention to error messages.

✓ Remember that proprietary crash screens, the BSOD, and the spinning pin wheel can occur when troubleshooting hard drives and RAID arrays.

✓ If you know any technicians, ask them to tell you about the problems they have solved this week. Another idea is to get them to tell you a problem and you see if you can guess the top things that could cause that problem.

✓ Review the section "Soft Skills: Dealing with Irate Customers" for communication skills best practices. The communication questions can sometimes have answers that are very similar. Use the review questions at the end of the chapter to help practice with those types of questions.

✓ The 220-1002 exam has very specific criteria for proper communication and professionalism, including difficult customers and situations. Remember to avoid arguing with a customer and/or being defensive. Do not minimize the customer's problem. Avoid being judgmental. Clarify customer statements by asking open-ended questions (which allow the customer to freely explain the situation) to narrow the scope of the problem and by restating the issue or question to verify your understanding. Never disclose work-related experiences via social media outlets.

✓ Be able to choose between components (power supplies, storage options, video options, RAM, and so on) for two different types of computers, such as between a thick client and a thin client, a gaming machine versus a regular home computer (thick client), a video editing computer and a computer used for virtualization, and so on.

✓ Know the six steps in resolving problems and ensure that you consider company policies, procedures, and impacts before implementing any changes. Even though these steps are logical, when the steps are placed into written questions, they can become tricky. On the 220-1001 exam, the six troubleshooting steps could be applied to specific troubleshooting scenarios Try to think of the computer problems and relate them to the six troubleshooting steps:

Step 1. Identify the problem. Question the user and determine if there have been any environmental, infrastructure, or computer changes. Review system and application logs. Do a backup before making changes.

Step 2. Establish a theory of probable cause (question the obvious).

Step 3. Test the theory to determine the cause. If you cannot confirm a theory, find a new theory or escalate the problem.

Step 4. Establish a plan of action to resolve the problem and implement the solution.

Step 5. Verify full system functionality and, if necessary, implement preventive measures.

Step 6. Document findings, actions, and outcomes.

Key Terms

air filter   538
audio/video editing workstation   530
BSOD   548
ENERGY STAR   535
EPEAT rating system   535
error message   545
gaming PC   529
graphic/CAD/CAM design workstation   529
home server   534

intermittent device failure   550
IOPS   540
log entries and error messages   543
loopback plug   550
nanometer   536
network-attached storage device   531
patch   551
pin wheel   548
POST card   548

proprietary crash screen   548
review system and application logs   543
service pack   551
service release   551
standard thick client   533
thick client   533
thin client   533
virtualization workstation   532
warm boot   551

Review Questions

1. _____ executes POST. [BIOS/UEFI I CMOS I NAS I RAM]

2. Which technology is most likely to require dual monitors as part of the configuration?
    [virtual computer I home server I audio/video editing workstation I NAS]

3. A person comes into a computer store wanting a custom built computer. The customer will be using the computer to stream video; video chat with remote family; standard computer usage such as word processing, spreadsheet, and Internet browsing; and a child will use the computer to play games. Which computer component will the technician focus on to satisfy this customer?

    [500 GB hard drive I RAID array I multicore processor I 10G NIC]

4. To troubleshoot a variety of possible system startup problems, press the Windows 7 _____ key during the system startup process to bring up the Advanced Boot Options menu. [F1 I F2 I F8 I F12]

5. Which of the following would most likely be a design consideration for a gaming PC rather than a computer used for virtualization?

    a. high amount of RAM

    b. NAS

    c. multiple fast, large-capacity hard drives

    d. additional system cooling

6. If a computer beeps once during POST, what does this commonly mean to a technician?

    a. There is not a problem.

    b. A CPU register test is occurring.

    c. A DRAM refresh is occurring.

    d. A video initialization error has occurred.

7. An adapter or a USB device that performs diagnostics and displays a code or illuminates LEDs is known as a _____.
    [DIGI card I probe I torx I POST card]

8–10. Group the following computer components into three design subsystems. In other words, group the components that need to be considered together when designing a subsystem of a computer. Each group must include at least two components. All components are used.

power supply	CPU	chipset
video card	case	CPU cooling
motherboard	display	RAM

Group 1 components: _____

Group 2 components: _____

Group 3 components: _____

11. A motherboard advertisement lists UEFI as one of the motherboard features. What is UEFI?

    a. a port

    b. a BIOS replacement

    c. an internal interface

    d. a type of storage device

12. Which three design environments would have the largest display needs? (Choose three.)

    [CAD I industrial I gaming I audio/video editing I virtualization I thick client I home server]

13. Which type of computer design would be implemented if a workstation ran its applications from a remote server?

    [CAD | industrial | home theater | virtualization | thin client | thick client]

14. When designing, with what computer component would you consider the nanometer measurement?

    [hard drive | motherboard | display | CPU | power supply | air filter]

15. Which two components could have an ITX form factor? (Choose two.)

    [hard drive | motherboard | display | CPU | power supply | air filter]

16. Place the six steps of troubleshooting in the order in which they occur.

    _____ Step 1   **a.** Test the theory to determine cause.

    _____ Step 2   **b.** Establish a theory of probable cause.

    _____ Step 3   **c.** Document and provide feedback.

    _____ Step 4   **d.** Identify the problem.

    _____ Step 5   **e.** Verify system functionality and, if applicable, implement preventive measures.

    _____ Step 6   **f.** Establish a plan of action to resolve the problem and implement the solution.

17. [T | F] During the *troubleshooting* phase in which you test the theory, you might be required to escalate the problem to a more experienced technician.

18. A _____ is used to test a communications circuit or RJ-45 port.

    [multimeter | probe | torx | loopback plug]

19. Which computer design environment would have the most need for a laptop enclosure?

    [industrial | gaming | virtualization | mobile | home server]

20. [T | F] When dealing with an irate customer, it is best to listen to the customer vent.

Exercises

Exercise 11.1 Computer System Design

Objective: To be able to recommend a complete system based on the customer's needs or placement of the system

Parts: Internet access

Procedure: Use the Internet to research specific computers, based on the given scenario.

1. A homebound elderly person has just had her hard drive fail. The drive was installed in a really old computer, and the person has decided to replace the computer rather than fix the broken one. The elderly person uses the computer to shop for family members, check email, play basic computer card games with others online, and view pictures on CDs or DVDs sent by family members. Internet access is through a DSL modem that connects to the USB port and still works. Find a suitable computer on the Internet. The customer would like to keep the cost around $700, including installation, if possible. Write the computer model, basic description, cost, and cost of installation.

    _____

    _____

    _____

    _____

2. A graphic artist would like a second computer as a mobile solution and would like your assistance finding a suitable laptop. The graphic artist does mostly video graphics creation but would like to be able to work while traveling. Find three possible solutions. Provide the computer model, basic description, and costs of the three laptops.

    _____
    _____
    _____
    _____

3. A sports complex wants to have a kiosk with a touchscreen and that holds a computer that runs specialized software. The software allows people to search for events and get detailed walking directions to the events and/or a specific sports field. No network connectivity is required. Locate a computer with an HDMI output for connectivity with the touchscreen for this outdoor kiosk located in a year-round sports complex. List the model number, basic description, and your fee for installing this system.

    _____
    _____
    _____
    _____

4. A 10-person purchasing department is going to a thin client environment. Select one desktop thin client computer model and one mobile thin client model from different manufacturers that can be used in the department. The models need to support dual displays. Detail any model numbers, basic parts descriptions, and costs.

    _____
    _____
    _____
    _____

5. A small company is expanding and is hiring an administrative assistant for the sales manager. Select a computer, monitor, keyboard, and an inkjet all-in-one printer for this assistant, who will be using Microsoft Office–type applications. The boss has put a $1,200 limit (not counting shipping) on the entire purchase. Provide a detailed list, description, and costs of parts chosen.

    _____
    _____
    _____
    _____
    _____
    _____
    _____

6. Select a CAD/CAM manufacturing design computer that uses 64-bit AutoCAD Mechanical 2019 software. Research the AutoCAD Mechanical application's video requirements. Provide a detailed list, description, and cost of parts chosen, including the video card and display. Assume that there is no price limit. (Note that AutoCAD Mechanical requires a 1920×1080 display with true color.)

    _____
    _____
    _____
    _____
    _____

7. You have an unlimited budget to build the best gaming rig possible. Choose two PC manufacturer sites at which you can select components, monitors, applications, and accessories for your new system.

    _____

    _____

    _____

    _____

8. You have an unlimited budget and need to build two systems from scratch. You will need cases, power supplies, motherboards, CPUs, RAM, hard drives, video cards, and more. List two websites at which you can compare and buy all the components you need to build the two systems.

    _____

    _____

Exercise 11.2 Design Components

Objective: To be able to recognize the unique components for a specific computer design scenario

Procedure: Using the list of components, identify which components would be used in the scenarios given. Note that any one component can be used multiple times.

Components

a. Multiple powerful processor cores
b. Maximum RAM
c. Lots of RAM
d. Multiple large-capacity hard drives
e. Large-capacity hard drive
f. RAID
g. Sound card and speakers
h. Powerful video card and RAM on the card

i. Multiple displays
j. Large display
k. DVR
l. TV tuner or cable card
m. 1 Gb/s NIC
n. Computer enclosure
o. KVM switch
p. SSD

Scenario 1

Identify the unique components from the provided list for a computer used for audio and video editing.

_____

Scenario 2

You need to build a computer to test the Chrome operating system, along with your current Windows operating system. You have decided to do this in a virtual environment. Identify the unique components that would be in the computer.

_____

Scenario 3

A customer wants to try out thin client workstations in one department. Identify one or more unique components that would be in one computer of this type.

_____

Scenario 4

A tire shop would like to have a computer in the lobby where information about the latest and upcoming sales are displayed. The owner is concerned about theft. What unique component would be needed for this situation?

_____

Scenario 5

A computer programmer works from home but likes to work from several types of computers—a mobile tablet, laptop, and desktop—and to be able to work on any mobile device when traveling. The programmer has decided to create a server to store and access everything from anyplace. The programmer does not want to have to buy another keyboard, mouse, or display for the server but wants to share these components connected to the desktop computer with the server. What unique components would be part of this system?

Exercise 11.3 Subsystem Design Components

Objective: To be able to design a subsystem of a computer, based on design requirements

Parts: Internet access

Procedure: Use the Internet to research specific computers, based on the given scenario.

Scenario 1

You have just ascertained that a customer's older ATX Pentium 4 motherboard in a home computer is bad. The customer wants a motherboard upgrade or replacement. The existing motherboard has a PCI sound card and VGA port that the user would like to continue using. The RAM on the existing motherboard has 512 MB of DDR2 memory. The hard drive and optical drive use PATA for connectivity, and the customer would like to continue using these devices and the current operating system. The customer does light computer work but likes listening to broadcasts and music on the computer. Locate suitable replacement upgraded components. The budget is $250, including labor. Detail each item, item description, and cost.

Scenario 2

A customer has been given a micro-ATX motherboard, an Intel Core i5 quad-core processor, and RAM. The customer has two 3.5-inch SATA drives and one 5.25-inch optical drive from other computers. The customer would like assistance getting a case and a power supply to handle all these devices. The customer does not have a lot of room but wants a tower case that provides good airflow through the computer. The customer has a budget of $200 for this. Locate a power supply and case for the customer. Detail the items, item descriptions, and costs.

Scenario 3

A retired naval officer has just gotten into classical music and now wants surround-sound in his office. Select an appropriate sound subsystem. The budget is $200. The office system has both PCI and PCIe expansion slots available. List the components, a description of each component, and the cost.

Scenario 4

A college graduate has started her own website design business. She wants a video card that supports two 18- to 20-inch displays. Recommend a video subsystem for her. The budget is $500 maximum. List the components, a description of each component, and the costs.

_____

_____

_____

Scenario 5

Locate a motherboard, power supply, RAM, CPU, and midsized case that are compatible with one another for an administrative assistant. The budget is $600. List the components, a description of the components (ensure that you list the type of RAM the motherboard supports), and the costs.

_____

_____

_____

_____

_____

_____

Exercise 11.4 Determine the Troubleshooting Theory Step

Objective: To be able to determine which step of the troubleshooting process is occurring

Procedure: Match one of the six troubleshooting steps to the situation. Note that a particular step may be the answer for more than one situation.

Troubleshooting steps

a. Identify the problem.

b. Establish a theory of probable cause.

c. Test the theory.

d. Establish a plan of action.

e. Verify full functionality.

f. Document findings.

_____ A USB flash drive is not being recognized in a computer. You move the drive to a different USB slot.

_____ You provide the user with the registration/authentication code for the antivirus software that was installed into the computer after a virus was removed.

_____ You ask open-ended questions.

_____ The user explains what has happened in the past few days that was unusual.

_____ You phone the user to ask if the system appears to be running faster since the new memory module was installed.

_____ You order a new motherboard.

_____ You re-enable automatic Windows updates so they get applied in the future and prevent future issues.

_____ You believe that the problem is either the motherboard or processor.

Activities

Internet Discovery

Objective: To become familiar with researching computer items used in designing systems or subsystems

Parts: Internet access

Procedure: Use the Internet to answer the following questions. Write the answers and the URL of the site where you found the information.

1. Locate the Bloom's Taxonomy chart that has been modified by Andrew Churches to include verbs for the digital age. Write at least five verbs that Andrew Churches recommends as being relative to the top level of the taxonomy—the creating level—and the URL where you found the chart.

   _____

2. Locate minimum requirements for either a student computer or a staff computer at a particular school. Write the requirements, school name, and the URL where you found this information.

   _____

   _____

   _____

3. What are the recommended video standards for use when playing Kerbal Space Program on a PC? Write the answer and the URL where you found this information. Then find a video card that meets those specifications. Document the video card and the price.

   _____

4. What are the minimum processor, RAM, and display resolution requirements for a client who wants to run AutoCAD 2019 software? Write the answer and the URL where you found the information.

   _____

5. Find a monitor that supports the minimum AutoCAD 2019 display resolution found for Question 4. List the monitor manufacturer, model number, and URL where you found the information.

   _____

6. Locate a website that has a troubleshooting flowchart. Write three things the flowchart provides that you find helpful or confusing. Write the URL where the chart was found.

   _____

   _____

   _____

7. Locate one website that lists at least two BIOS/UEFI error codes. Write the URL where this information was found.

   _____

8. Find a website that shows at least three recommendations for dealing with irate customers. Write three recommendations and the URL where you found this information.

   _____

   _____

   _____

Soft Skills

Objective: To become familiar with researching computer items used in designing systems or subsystems and to learn how to deal with difficult customers or situations

Activities:

1. Interview or email someone who works in your school to determine the school's minimum hardware requirements for its new computers. Document your findings.

    _____

    _____

    _____

2. In teams of two, find a video that shows how to deal with an irate customer. Document at least three observations from the video and the URL.

    _____

    _____

    _____

3. In teams of two, three, or four, design a computer for a specific purpose. State the purpose and provide all the models, descriptions, and costs. Compete with other teams for the best design.

Critical Thinking Skills

Objective: To become familiar with researching computer items used in designing systems or subsystems

Activities:

1. Refer to Tables 11.1 through 11.4, which provide recommendations for hardware components. Find at least one type of computer configuration for which you disagree with the special hardware components; if you agree with them all, then think of one that should be added. List the component and the reason for your disagreement or addition.

    _____

    _____

2. Locate an image that shows a map of Bloom's Taxonomy, as modified by Andrew Churches. Explain why designing (in the creating stage) requires higher-level skills than working in the evaluating stage, which includes experimenting, judging, monitoring, and testing.

    _____

    _____

    _____

    _____

    _____

3. Do you think most technicians are good at designing computers for specific purposes? Explain your opinion.

    _____

    _____

    _____

12 Internet Connectivity, Virtualization, and Cloud Technologies

In this chapter you will learn:

> To describe dial-up networking

> Other Internet connectivity options, such as satellite, cable, DSL, fiber, WiMAX and line-of-sight wireless Internet service, as well as cellular

> To configure a browser and other basic issues related to a browser

> How cloud computing is used for personal and corporate purposes

> Terms associated with cloud computing

> The basics of virtualization, including terms and features associated with it

> The benefits of mentoring in the IT field

CompTIA Exam Objectives:

What CompTIA A+ exam objectives are covered in this chapter?

✓ 1001-2.2 Compare and contrast common networking hardware devices.

✓ 1001-2.7 Compare and contrast Internet connection types, network types, and their features.

✓ 1001-4.1 Compare and contrast cloud computing concepts.

✓ 1001-4.2 Given a scenario, set up and configure client-side virtualization.

✓ 1002-1.5 Given a scenario, use Microsoft operating system features and tools.

✓ 1002-1.6 Given a scenario, use Microsoft Windows Control Panel utilities.

✓ 1002-1.8 Given a scenario, configure Microsoft Windows networking on a client/desktop.

✓ 1002-2.4 Given a scenario, detect, remove, and prevent malware using appropriate tools and methods.

✓ 1002-3.2 Given a scenario, troubleshoot and resolve PC security issues.

Internet Connectivity Overview

Connecting to the Internet can be done in a variety of ways: via analog modem, ISDN, cable modem, DSL modem, satellite modem, fiber, wirelessly, power line, or cellular network. These technologies have unique installation and configuration methods, but they all have in common the capability to connect a computer to an outside network. Each technology is a viable option for connectivity in a specific situation. By examining and understanding the technologies, you can offer customers connectivity options. More information about troubleshooting network connectivity is provided in Chapter 13, "Networking." Let's start with the oldest method: analog modems.

Dial-up Overview

One of the first devices still in operation that was used to connect to the Internet is the modem. A modem (which stands for *modulator/demodulator*) connects a computer with the outside world through a phone line. This type of technology is frequently called a **dial-up network** or just **dial-up** because the modem uses the traditional phone line to "dial up," or call, another modem. Modems can be internal or external peripheral devices. An internal modem is an adapter installed in an expansion slot. An external modem attaches to a USB port. A modem converts a signal transmitted over the phone line to digital 1s and 0s to be read by the computer. It also converts the digital 1s and 0s from the computer and modulates them onto the carrier signal and sends the data over the phone line. Modems normally connect to a remote modem through the phone line. Figure 12.1 shows two modems connecting two computers.

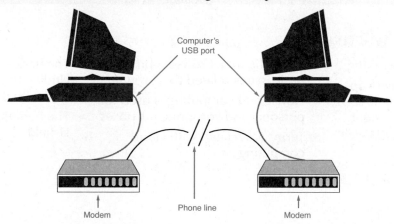

FIGURE 12.1   Sample modem connection

TECH TIP

When connecting a modem to a phone line, be careful with the cabling

Some modems have two jacks on the back. The labeling varies, but one jack is usually labeled PHONE and the other LINE. The LINE jack is for the cable that goes from the modem to the phone wall jack. The modem's PHONE jack is an optional jack that connects a telephone to the modem. Figure 12.2 shows the ports on an internal modem.

FIGURE 12.2   Internal modem ports

Serial Communication Overview

A serial device such as a modem transmits or receives information 1 bit at a time and is tradition-ally connected to a serial port. With modern computers, a USB-to-serial converter (see Figure 12.3) is used to attach an external serial device such as a modem. An internal modem may be on an adapter. Serial ports are also known as asynchronous ports, COM ports, or RS232 ports. **Asynchronous** transmissions add extra bits to the data to track when each byte starts and ends. Synchronous transmissions rely on an external clock to time the data reception or transmission. Basic terminology associated with asynchronous transmissions is found in Table 12.1.

TECH TIP

Configuring transmission speeds

When configuring a serial port or using an application, the configured speed is the rate at which the serial port transmits. This is not the speed for an external serial device that connects to the port (such as a modem).

FIGURE 12.3   USB-to-DB-9 serial converter

TABLE 12.1   Serial asynchronous transmission terminology

Term	Description
Baud	Number of times an analog signal changes in 1 second. Some use this term to speak of the modem speed. With today's modulation techniques, modems can send several bits in one cycle, so it is more accurate to specify modem speed in bits per second (bps or b/s).
Bits per second (**bps**)	Measurement used to describe the transmission speed of serial devices and ports. Settings include 110, 300, 1200, 2400, 4800, 9600, 19200, 38400, 57600, and 115200. The application software must match the serial device or serial port's bits per second rate.
RS232C	Standard approved by the Electronic Industries Alliance (EIA) for the serial port used in a computer. Because serial devices use the 9- or 25-pin connector defined by this standard, they are commonly called RS232 serial devices.
Start bit	Bit used in asynchronous transmissions to signal the start of the data.
Stop bit	Bit used in asynchronous transmissions to signal the end of the data.
Universal Asynchronous Receiver/ Transmitter (UART)	A chip on the motherboard for an integrated serial port or on the adapter of an internal modem. It converts a data byte into a serial data stream of single 1s and 0s for transmission. It also receives the bit stream and stores data in its own buffers until the processor can accept the data.

Configuring Traditional Serial Devices

Serial ports and devices such as internal modems have three important configuration parameters (as well as some others, as discussed later): interrupt, input/output (I/O) address, and COM port number. An internal modem has all these parameters; an external modem uses these same parameters, but they are assigned to the serial port to which the external modem connects. Use Device Manager to identify these system resources.

TECH TIP

Application settings and hardware settings must match

For applications that communicate or control serial devices, the application settings must match the hardware settings; otherwise, communication will not occur.

An understanding of how serial devices operate is essential to a technician's knowledge base if analog modems are in the geographic area. Before installing a serial device and configuring its associated software, a technician must be familiar with the terminology associated with serial device installation. Table 12.2 lists the various serial port settings.

TABLE 12.2   Serial port settings

Setting	Description
Data bits	Determines how many bits make up a data word. It is usually 8 bits per data word, but it can be 7 or lower.
Parity	Checks for basic data accuracy. When parity is used, both computers must be set to the same setting. The choices for parity include none, odd, even, space, and mark. With a space parity setting, both computers always set the parity bit to 0. With the mark parity setting, both computers always set the parity bit to 1. The most common setting is none for modems.
Stop bits	Controls the number of bits sent to indicate the end of the data word. The number of stop bits can be 1, 1.5, or 2. One stop bit is the common choice.
FIFO setting	Enables or disables the UART chip's FIFO buffer. This setting gives the processor time to handle other tasks without the serial device losing data. If data is lost, it will have to be retransmitted later, when the microprocessor turns its attention back to the serial device.
Handshaking	Determines the order in which things happen to allow two serial devices to communicate. Knowing this order helps with troubleshooting.
Flow control	Determines how two serial devices communicate. Can be set using software or physical pins on the serial port (hardware). Also called handshaking, which allows a serial device to tell the sending serial device, "Wait, I need a second before you send any more data." Two methods used for flow control are XON/XOFF and RTS/CTS.

TECH TIP

How does parity work?

Parity can be either even or odd. Consider, for example, a computer that uses even parity. If the data sent is 10101010, a total of four 1s is sent, plus a 0 for the parity bit. Four is an even number; therefore, the parity bit is set to 0 because the total number of 1s must be an even number when even parity is used. If the data sent is 10101011, a total of five 1s is sent, plus an extra 1 for the parity bit. Because five is an odd number and the system uses even parity, the extra parity bit is set to 1 to make the total number of 1s an even number.

56 kbps Modems

An analog modem is one of the slowest types of Internet connectivity. Modems transmit and receive at different speeds. A faster modem means less time on the phone line and less time for processor interaction. However, because modems connect to other modems, the slowest modem determines the fastest connection speed. A slow modem can operate only at the speed for which it was designed. Connecting to a faster modem will not make the slower modem operate any faster. Fortunately, speedy modems can transmit at lower speeds. As a general rule, a modem's speed setting should be set to its maximum throughput.

The phone line limit was once thought to be 28.8 kbps, and then it was raised to 33.6 kbps, and finally to 56 kbps. The 56 kbps data transfer rate is possible only if the transmitted (analog) signal converts to digital one time during the data transmission. Digital phone lines are quieter than their analog counterparts, have less noise on the line, and allow faster data transmissions. For example, consider the scenario of a person dialing into an office network from home that is shown in Figure 12.4.

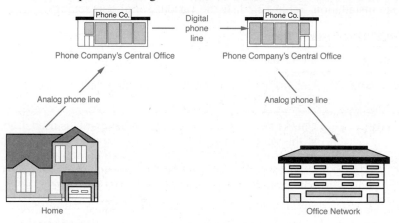

FIGURE 12.4   Normal modem usage

Notice in Figure 12.4 that the signal is converted twice. The first time is when the analog signal enters the phone company's central office. Between central offices, the signal stays digital. Then, when the signal leaves the central office to travel to the office building, the signal is converted from a digital signal to an analog signal.

56 kbps transmission speeds do not support two conversions. If, however, the workplace has a digital line from the phone company or if a person dials into an Internet provider that has a digital phone connection, 56 kbps throughput on a 56 kbps modem is achievable. Figure 12.5 shows the difference.

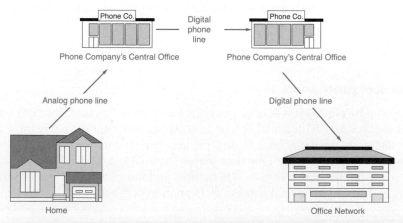

FIGURE 12.5   56 kbps modem connection

In Figure 12.5, only one analog-to-digital conversion exists—the one between the home and the first central office. 56 kbps speeds, in theory, can exist when only one conversion takes place. However, if the modem cannot run at 56 kbps, the modem supports lower speeds, such as 33.6 kbps and 28.8 kbps.

To configure a dial-up connection using a 56 *kbps* modem, install the internal modem or connect the external modem to the computer. Ensure that the modem connects to a working phone outlet. In Windows, use the following generic procedure, but always check the manufacturer's instructions because some modems have their own installation software:

> Windows 7: Use the *Network and Sharing Center* section of the Control Panel > *Set Up a New Connection or Network* link > *Set Up a Dialup Connection* > *Dial-up* > enter the remote modem phone number, username and password, and name the connection > *Connect.*

> Windows 8: Access the *Network and Internet* section of the *Control Panel* > *Dial-up* > enter the remote modem phone number, username and password, and name the connection > *Connect.*

> Windows 10: *Access Settings* > *Network & Internet* > *Network and Sharing Center* link > *Set Up a New Connection or Network* link > *Connect to the Internet* > *Next* button > *Dial-up* > enter the remote modem phone number, username and password, and name the connection > *Connect* button.

Digital Modems and ISDN

A digital modem connects a computer directly to a digital phone line rather than to a traditional analog phone line. One type of digital phone line available from the phone company is an ISDN line. An Integrated Services Digital Network (**ISDN**) line has three separate channels: two B channels and a D channel. The B channels handle data at 64 kbps transmission speeds. The D channel is for network routing information and transmits at a lower 16 kbps. The two B channels can combine into a single channel for video conferencing, thus allowing speeds up to 128 kbps. They are available in large metropolitan areas for reasonable rates, making it an affordable option for home office use. However, due to recent technologies, such as cable modems and xDSL modems (covered later in this chapter), ISDN is not a popular option today.

VoIP

Traditionally a company had separate networks for voice and data (the network where computers and printers connect). Voice over IP (**VoIP**) uses a corporate data network and/or the Internet for phone traffic rather than using the traditional public switched telephone network (**PSTN**). Free and purchased VoIP software can be used to enable a user to call someone for free using the Internet. Figure 12.6 shows a VoIP phone that cables to a PC and into the corporate data network.

FIGURE 12.6 Corporate VoIP phone

Companies also used a separate network structure for the video network, but that has also now been moved onto the data network. **Convergence** is a term used to describe how these data, voice, and video technologies now use one network structure instead of multiple networks. Figure 12.7 shows a video conference in the corporate environment where people join using tablets, laptops, corporate conference rooms, and desktop computers.

FIGURE 12.7   Corporate video conference call

Some free software applications and email accounts also support video conferencing using the Internet. You might have experienced this by using programs such as Skype, Google Hangout, or FaceTime. Through these applications, the quality may not be as good as with the traditional PSTN. This is because a guaranteed quality of service (**QoS**) is not provided. QoS prioritizes traffic so important traffic—such as business transaction traffic and VoIP traffic—is sure to get through. Figure 12.8 shows this concept.

Bandwidth Use with No QoS

Bandwidth Use with QoS Implemented

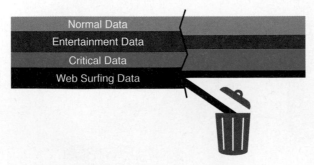

FIGURE 12.8   QoS

Technicians must be aware of VoIP for two reasons: (1) A digital phone installed in a corporate office must be connected to the network in a similar fashion to a PC and (2) a digital phone may be a software application (a soft phone) that has to be installed and configured on a computer.

VoIP has also affected fax capabilities. A VoIP adapter can be installed in a fax machine to connect it to a VoIP gateway. The VoIP gateway connects to a phone line that has a destination fax machine attached. Keep in mind that once something on a network-connected device is converted into 1s and 0s, then it is just data to the network and can be transmitted.

One last thing to remember about VoIP in the corporate environment is that no corporate network can do away with the PSTN connection to the traditional phone network. A corporate environment will always need to be able to communicate with the outside world and especially be able to contact emergency services such as police, fire, and emergency responders.

Cable Modems

One of the most popular items in the modem industry is the **cable modem**, which connects a computer to a cable TV network. Cable modems can be internal or external devices but commonly are external. If a cable modem is external, two methods commonly exist for connectivity to a PC: (1) A NIC built into the motherboard is used or an adapter is installed, and a cable attaches between the NIC and the cable modem or (2) the cable modem connects to a USB port on the computer. Figures 12.9 and 12.10 show these two types of connections. Figure 12.11 shows a cable modem that has the coaxial cable on the top for connection to the wall coax connector, both USB and RJ-45 network connectors for connectivity to a PC, and two additional RJ-45 jacks for a printer or additional network devices.

> **TECH TIP**
>
> **Cable TV and cable modems**
>
> Some cable Internet providers will not provide Internet access through their network unless you have their cable TV service as well.

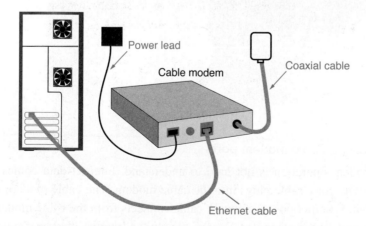

FIGURE 12.9 Cable modem and NIC connectivity

FIGURE 12.10   Cable modem and USB connectivity

FIGURE 12.11   Cable modem ports

Cable modem operation is not hard to understand. Internet data comes in through cable TV coax cable. The coax cable plugs into the cable modem. The cable modem sends the information out its built-in Ethernet port. A network cable connects from the cable modem's Ethernet port into an Ethernet port on the computer. To send data to the Internet, the reverse happens: The computer sends the data out its Ethernet port into the cable modem. The cable modem sends the data out the coax cable onto the cable TV company's network. Notice in Figure 12.11 how there are additional Ethernet ports below the yellow cable. If the cable modem needs to connect to a company or home router, one end of an Ethernet cable is attached to one of the cable modem Ethernet ports and the other end to the router.

Fiber Networks

A high-speed **fiber network** connection is commonly used to bring bundled technologies to subscribers. Such bundles may include phone, Internet, and cable TV connectivity. A fiber network has many fiber-optic cables used to connect between buildings, multiple companies, and home users. A single fiber carries voice, data, and video using three different optical wavelengths. This same type of connectivity is offered at higher speeds to small businesses. Light flows through a fiber-optic cable (instead of electrical pulses flowing through copper cables). Instead of an electrical pulse being a 1, the light being on is a 1. A 0 is the light being turned off. Figure 12.12 shows the basic construction of fiber-optic cable.

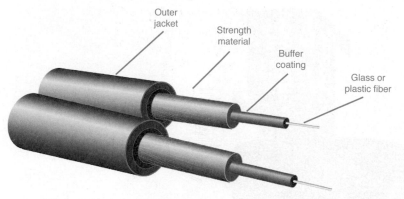

FIGURE 12.12 Fiber-optic cable

Fiber-optic cable has many advantages, including security, long-distance transmission, and bandwidth. Many government agencies use fiber-optic cable because of the high security it offers. Unlike signals from other cable media, light signals that travel down fiber are impossible to detect remotely. Also, because light is used instead of electrical signals, fiber-optic cable is not susceptible to electromagnetic interference (EMI) or radio-frequency interference (RFI). Fiber-optic cable is the most expensive cable type, but it also handles the most data with the least amount of data loss. Figure 12.13 shows how fiber-optic cable is installed under a city street, along with electrical conduits.

FIGURE 12.13 Laying fiber-optic cable

Cable Mode Transmissions

Two terms that are often associated with cable modems are upstream and downstream. **Upstream** refers to data sent from your home to the Internet. **Downstream** refers to the data pulled from the Internet into your computer, as when you download a file or view a web page (see Figure 12.14). With cable modems, downstream (download) transfer rates are faster than upstream (upload) transfers. Downstream speeds can be as high as 1 Gbps for consumers and even higher for businesses. Upstream speeds vary; with an external cable modem, they tend to be between 384 kbps and 35 Mbps. Even though upstream speeds are slower, cable modems greatly improve speed over analog (dial-up) modems.

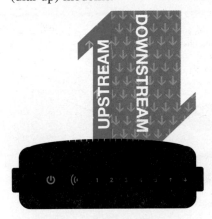

Cable or ADSL Modem

FIGURE 12.14   Upstream and downstream

The speed of a cable modem connection depends on two things: (1) the cable company and (2) how many people in the area share the same cable TV provider. Each cable channel uses 6 MHz of the cable's bandwidth. **Bandwidth** is the capacity of the communications channel. Bandwidth is also known as *throughput* or *line speed*. The cable company designates one of the 6 MHz channels as Internet access. Several homes can use the same channel, which reduces the amount of bandwidth each house has available. If you have three neighbors who all use the same cable vendor and they are Internet warriors, you will have slower access than if you were the only person in the neighborhood connected.

The minimum amount of hardware needed to have a cable modem depends on the cable company's specifications. Whether you need an internal modem, Ethernet card, or other equipment or software depends on the company from which you receive the cable modem. Some companies include them as part of their rate. Some cable companies install the cable modem and associated software and hardware as part of their package. If you need to install a cable modem, always follow the manufacturer's installation instructions. Chapter 13 includes tips on configuring network adapters.

xDSL Modems

xDSL is another modem technology. The *x* in the term xDSL refers to the various types of digital subscriber line (**DSL**) that are on the market. The most common one is Asymmetric DSL (**ADSL**), but there are many others. ADSL uses faster downstream speeds than upstream. This performance is fine for most home Internet users. DSL uses the traditional phone line to send and transmit not only voice but also Internet data. Table 12.3 shows the most common DSL types.

TABLE 12.3   DSL technologies

DSL type	Comments
ADSL	Asymmetric DSL is the most common, with faster downloads than uploads. It has upstream speeds from 0.5 to 3.5 Mbps and downstream speeds from 5 to 150 Mbps. It uses a different frequency level for upstream and downstream communications.
G.SHDSL	Symmetric High-speed DSL is an upgrade to SDSL that supports symmetric data rates up to 4.6 Mbps.
HDSL	High bit rate DSL is a symmetrical transmission (equal speed for downloads/uploads); it has speeds up to 1.5 Mbps.
PDSL	Power line DSL modulates data speeds from 256 kbps to 2.7 Mbps onto electrical lines and is sometimes called Broadband over Powerline (BPL).
RADSL	Rate-adaptive DSL, which was developed by Westell, enables a modem to adapt to phone line conditions. It has speeds up to 2.2 Mbps.
SDSL	Symmetric DSL has the same speed, up to 1.5 Mbps, in both directions.
UDSL	Also known as Uni-DSL or Ultra-high-speed DSL, UDSL has speeds up to 200 Mbps and is backward compatible with ADSL, ADSL2+, VDSL, and VDSL2.
VDSL2	VDSL2 is an upgrade of VDSL that supports voice, video, data, and HDTV, with speeds from 1 to 150 Mbps downstream.

With DSL modems, bandwidth is not shared between people in the same geographic area. The bandwidth paid for is exclusive to the user. DSL is not available in all areas. The DSLReports website (http://www.dslreports.com) lists major DSL vendors, other Internet technology vendors, and geographic areas, and it provides ratings on the services.

An internal or external DSL modem can be connected to a regular phone line. The phone line can be used for calls, faxes, and so on at the same time the modem is being used. An external modem can connect to a USB port or an Ethernet network card. Figure 12.15 shows DSL modem ports, including the DSL connector, which connects to the wall outlet and is labeled ADSL, and the multiple Ethernet LAN connections, which could be used to connect to one or more computers, printers, external network storage, or other wired network devices.

FIGURE 12.15   DSL modem ports

TECH TIP

Corporate DSL, cable, or fiber

Corporate Internet connectivity can use DSL, cable, or fiber connections. Chapter 2, "Connectivity," provides more information on fiber cabling.

A drawback to DSL is that the DSL signal needs to be separated from the normal phone traffic. DSL providers normally ship **phone filters** that must connect to each phone outlet, and a phone, fax machine, or voice recorder attaches to the filter. The connection from the DSL modem to the phone outlet does not have a filter on it.

This chapter does not go into detail about firewalls and network security; they are discussed in later chapters. It is important when installing cable modems and DSL modems to also be familiar with proxy servers, firewalls, port forwarding, file sharing, and so on. When such technologies are improperly implemented or configured, a computer is more prone to attacks, viruses, theft of computer files, and computer takeover. Figure 12.16 shows three different ways to connect a cable or DSL modem. The example on the left is the least secure. File sharing should not be enabled on computers connected in this manner.

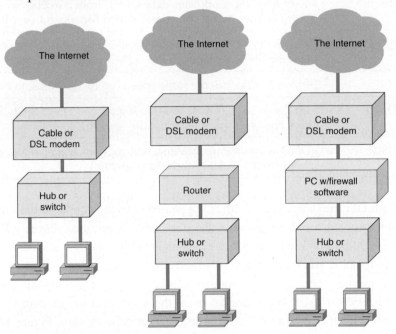

FIGURE 12.16   Cable/DSL modem connectivity

Satellite Modems

An option available to areas that do not have cable or DSL service is satellite connectivity. The satellite relays communication back to receivers on Earth. Satellite connectivity requires a satellite dish and a **satellite modem** at a minimum. It may also require an analog modem and other equipment, depending on the satellite provider. With a satellite connection, the data goes from the computer to the satellite dish mounted outside the home or business (see Figure 12.17) to another satellite dish (and maybe more), up to the satellite orbiting Earth, down to the Internet service provider (**ISP**), and from the ISP to the website requested; the web page returns via the same path it took. Satellite connectivity is not as fast as cable or DSL connectivity, but it can be five to seven times faster than dial-up. The downstream speeds can be from 9 kbps to 24 Mbps, but they are typically around 500 kbps. Some providers offer the same upstream speeds.

FIGURE 12.17   Satellite modem and dish

With a satellite modem, TV programs accessed via the satellite can be watched at the same time that web pages are downloaded from the Internet. However, drawbacks to satellite modems are important to mention:

> The initial cost of installing a satellite modem can be high.
> If other people in the area subscribe to the same satellite service, speed is decreased during peak periods.
> Initial connections have a lag time associated with them, so playing multiplayer games is not very practical.
> Virtual private networks (VPNs) are not always supported.
> Weather elements, such as high winds, rain, and snow, affect performance and connectivity.

Modem Preventive Maintenance

The old adage "an ounce of prevention is worth a pound of cure" is especially true in the case of modems. A power surge can come across a phone line just as it can travel over an electrical power line. Most people think and worry about the computer problems that could result from power surges, but they do not think about surges through the phone line. To provide protection for a modem and a computer, purchase a special protection device called a phone line isolator or a modem isolator at a computer or phone store. A power surge through a phone line or cable can take out many components inside a computer, including the motherboard.

Some surge protectors also include modem protection. A cable from the computer plugs into the surge protector. A separate cable connects to another jack on the surge protector, and the other end plugs into the phone or cable company wall jack. The surge protector must, of course, be plugged into a grounded outlet.

Mobile Connectivity Overview

Today's working environment is a mobile one with laptops, cell phones, and tablets. Connecting to the Internet through an 802.11 wireless network is common, as introduced in Chapter 10, "Mobile Devices" (and even more information is provided in Chapter 13). Smartphones, computers, and tablets can become **mobile hotspots**. Using a connection such as a USB port, Bluetooth wireless connectivity, or the cellular network, can provide wireless Internet connectivity to others in the immediate vicinity. Some cell service providers offer this option as part of a cellular plan. The term *mobile hotspot* is also used to refer to an area of wireless connectivity (normally free), such as in a park, coffee shop, or museum. Another way of getting onto the Internet is through the use of tethering. **Tethering** allows the sharing of an Internet connection with other mobile devices in the nearby area wirelessly through Bluetooth or WiFi, or wired through a USB connection.

Cellular Connectivity

Mobile devices use the cellular network to connect to the Internet. Table 12.4 recaps the different cellular network types.

TABLE 12.4   Cellular Network Types

Cellular Network Type	Features
3G	Speeds of 200 kbps up to 2 Mbps
4G	Speeds up to 1 Gbps to support gaming, mobile TV, and video conferencing
LTE (Long Term Evolution)	An optimized version of 4G for video streaming and gaming
5G	Slated to support speeds up to 10 Gbps (though it had not been formalized at press time)

Wireless Broadband

An increasingly popular feature with laptops and tablets is **wireless broadband**, with download speeds up to 45 Mbps. This technology is sometimes referred to as wireless WAN, mobile broadband, or cellular WAN. Cell phone companies and Internet providers offer USB modems, mobile data cards, or integrated laptop connectivity to enable users to receive, create, and communicate Internet information within a coverage area. For people who travel a lot, this option allows for connectivity in places where data connectivity has not previously been feasible.

WiMAX

Another wireless technology that can be used to connect to the Internet is Worldwide Interoperability for Microwave Access (**WiMAX**). WiMAX is similar to a home or corporate wireless network but on a much larger scale for a larger coverage area. WiMAX, which is defined in the IEEE 802.16 standard, can provide Internet access at speeds up to 1 Gbps. WiMAX can also be used for connectivity as part of a cellular network, and many WiMAX installations are being replaced with cellular LTE.

WiMAX has two major types of connections: non-line-of-sight and line-of-sight. As an example of the non-line-of-sight connection type, a home or portable device can have a WiMAX receiver similar to a wireless broadband receiver, that communicates with a tower that has a WiMAX antenna attached.

With **line-of-sight wireless Internet service**, a WiMAX antenna mounted on a tower connects wirelessly to another WiMAX antenna mounted on a tower (which might connect to a third WiMAX tower). These connections are also known as line-of-sight backhauls. Eventually, the last WiMAX tower connects via cable to the ISP. A newer alternative to this is similar but involves a wireless bridge. Figure 12.18 shows WiMAX connectivity options.

A similar concept to WiMAX is mobile wireless broadband (**WiBro**), or mobile WiMAX, which allows wireless connectivity for moving devices such as from a vehicle or train. Figure 12.19 summarizes WiMAX concepts.

TECH TIP

Laptop wireless WAN connectivity

A laptop that ships with integrated wireless WAN capabilities does not need an additional adapter or antenna. However, the BIOS/UEFI must have the option enabled. Some laptops might have a key combination or a switch to enable the connection. The wireless application software is available through the Start button.

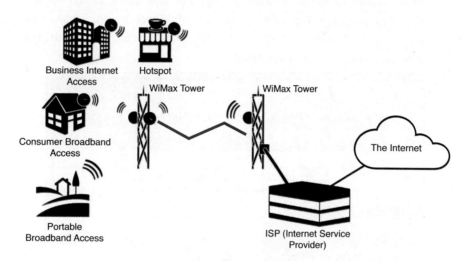

FIGURE 12.18   WiMAX connectivity

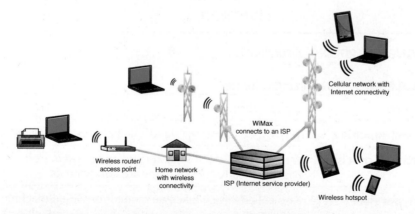

FIGURE 12.19   Wireless Internet connectivity

Virtualization Basics

An optional technology you might want to implement in any operating system is virtualization. Have you ever seen a TV service that allows you to watch multiple sports channels at once in smaller windows, or a service that allows you to watch a smaller screen of a different channel in the corner of a larger window? That is like virtualization in the computer world. **Virtualization** allows multiple operating systems to be installed on the same computer without affecting each other (or even knowing about each other); share hardware such as CPU, RAM, USB ports, a NIC, and hard drive space; and provide a test environment for a different operating system or an operational environment for software that might not be compatible on a specific platform.

Virtualization of a PC involves a computer that has a virtual application such as a VMware Workstation, Oracle VirtualBox, or Microsoft Hyper-V, which has instances of one or more operating systems. Figure 12.20 shows the concept of virtualization, and Table 12.5 defines some terms commonly used with virtualization.

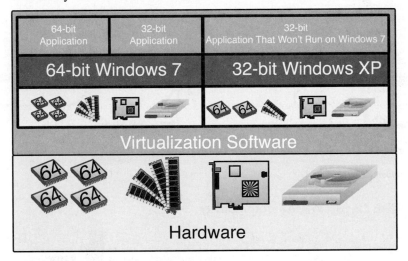

FIGURE 12.20   PC virtualization

TABLE 12.5   Virtualization terms

Term	Description
Host machine	The real computer that holds multiple operating systems
Virtual machine	Also called a VM, a separate operating system from the host computer that has specifically chosen hardware components
Hypervisor	Also called virtual machine monitor or virtual machine manager, the software that can create a virtual machine and allocate resources to the virtual machine
Snapshot/ checkpoint	A copy or backup of the VM at a particular point in time, which can revert the VM to that point in time (which is a similar concept to a Windows restore point)

The hypervisor is like an orchestra conductor for virtualization. The hypervisor is responsible for managing and overseeing the operation of the virtual machines (VMs). The hypervisor oversees RAM, hard drive space, and any processor(s) shared between the VMs.

There are two types of hypervisors: Type 1 and Type 2. A **Type 1 hypervisor** is also known as a native hypervisor because the operating system runs on top of the hypervisor. Examples of

Type 1 hypervisors include VMware's ESXI and Microsoft's Hyper-V. A **Type 2 hypervisor**, also known as a hosted hypervisor, runs on top of a host operating system such as Windows 10. VMware Player, Oracle VirtualBox, and Windows Virtual PC are examples of Type 2 hypervisors.

In Figure 12.20, there are fewer CPUs and there is less RAM in the VM (virtual machine) on the right than CPUs virtually "installed" in the VM on the left. Within one virtual environment, you should not (and, in some instances, cannot) "install" more hardware than is on the host machine (the real machine), even though some virtual software allows you to do so. For example, say that the VM on the left in Figure 12.20 is assigned the full amount of RAM that is on the host machine, 4 GB, and the VM on the right is assigned 2 GB. The total is 6 GB, but the host machine has only 4 GB. This is allowed and common in the virtual environment. Some virtualization software (but not all) enables you to select 6 GB for the VM on the left, but doing so causes degradation in the virtual environment.

Working with VMs makes restoring an operating system (or a VM that holds an operating system) much easier than using the traditional operating system-based restoration methods. Technicians today are expected to know the basics of working in a virtual environment.

> **TECH TIP**
>
> **You have to buy the OS license**
>
> A common misconception about virtualization is that you don't have to buy both operating systems when two operating systems are installed. This is not always true and depends on the virtual software used. If you want to install Windows 7 in one virtual machine, Windows 10 in another virtual machine, and Windows Server 2016 in a third virtual machine, you have to purchase all three operating systems.

Each virtual machine can connect to a network using one of two basic options. Note that in Hyper-V, this is configured through a virtual switch:

> *Internal network*—The internal network option allows a particular VM access to other virtual machines that connect to the same network (though they may be on a different computer or another VM on the same computer).
>
> *External network*—The external network option allows a particular VM access to a different (external) network from within the VM. In a college environment, for example, if a student computer can access the Internet and that same computer is configured for virtualization, a VM on that student computer can be configured for the external network and have access to the Internet.

Virtualization Resource and Emulator Requirements

Most Windows versions today have some type of emulation or virtualization included with them. Windows XP Mode is a program that you can download from Microsoft.com designed for Windows 7 in order to run Windows XP applications in a protected environment. Windows Virtual PC allows other Windows operating systems to run inside Virtual PC as well as one-click access to Windows XP Mode, which is integrated into Virtual PC. Table 12.6 lists the requirements for Virtual PC, which is Microsoft's emulator. An **emulator** is hardware or software that makes one operating system behave like an older or different one.

TABLE 12.6 Microsoft Virtual PC requirements

Component	Requirement
Processor	1 GHz
RAM	2 GB
Available hard disk space	15 GB per virtual machine

Microsoft provides the Hardware-Assisted Virtualization Detection Tool to quickly determine if your computer can support Windows XP Mode or Virtual PC:

> If the message "There is no hardware-assisted virtualization support in the system" appears, then virtualization is not supported.
> If the message "Hardware-assisted virtualization is disabled" appears, then virtualization has not been enabled in the BIOS/UEFI.

Windows 8 and 10 Pro and higher versions have replaced Virtual PC with Hyper-V, a virtualization product. See Table 12.7 for the minimum hardware requirements for the Hyper-V client.

TABLE 12.7 Microsoft client Hyper-V requirements

Component	Requirement
Processor	At least 1 x64 CPU
RAM	4 GB
Operating system version	Windows 8/10 Enterprise, Pro, or Education

To enable Windows Hyper-V, access the *Programs and Features* Control Panel > select *Turn Windows Features On or Off* > enable the *Hyper-V* checkbox (see Figure 12.21) > *OK*. Virtualization has been popular with network servers but now applies to desktop operating systems as well. Technicians are expected to be familiar with virtualization because it is used in both home and corporate environments.

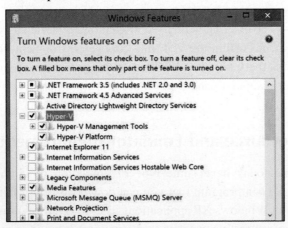

FIGURE 12.21 Enable Hyper-V in Windows

Virtualization Security

When using virtualization, each virtual machine needs the same protection as an individual computer. All security concepts apply not just to the host machine but to each virtual machine as well.

TECH TIP

You can still get a virus

A common misconception about virtualization is that you don't have to worry about security because you are in a "protected" environment. This is not true. The protection is that one operating system is protected from the other operating system, but all virtual machines are susceptible to viruses and security attacks. Install the appropriate protection and see Chapter 18, "Computer and Network Security," for more information on security.

Cloud Computing

Cloud computing was briefly introduced in Chapter 9, "Printers," with printing to the cloud. You should learn a bit more about it because cloud technologies are prevalent in small, medium, and large businesses alike. So what does it mean to say that something is "in the cloud"? It simply means the network device, application, storage, connectivity, server, and more are not located within the company's physical location. Cloud technologies have been around for years. They might be used, for example, for a small business that doesn't have the resources or staffing to create and maintain a web server. That web server can be hosted elsewhere, in which case it is considered "in the cloud," or out on the Internet somewhere (see Figure 12.22).

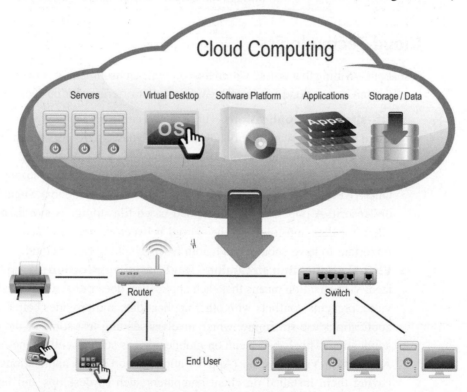

FIGURE 12.22 The concept of "in the cloud"

Cloud Services and Models

Different types of services are provided by cloud vendors, as outlined in Table 12.8.

TABLE 12.8   Cloud service types

Cloud service type	Description
Software as a Service (**SaaS**)	Applications such as learning management, enterprise resource planning (ERP), human resources management (HRM), payroll, antivirus, and inventory management systems that are hosted by another company. Cloud-based applications that you might be more familiar with such as Microsoft Office 365, Git Hub, a personal calendar, or diet tracker are also considered SaaS.
Desktop as a Service (DaaS)	Users access a **virtual desktop** that is managed by another company or for which the equipment is located elsewhere. This would simply be the computer in a virtual environment so that the company that uses this service does not have to worry about software licenses, technicians to maintain operating system updates, and backups. A virtual desktop also includes a virtual network interface card (NIC), or **virtual NIC**, as covered in more detail in Chapter 13.
Platform as a Service (**PaaS**)	Servers, databases, operating system, storage, and development tools provided in an outside environment to relieve the support burden on companies that need an environment to perform high-level programming and develop applications.
Infrastructure as a Service (**IaaS**)	Routers, switches, servers, virtual machines, load balancers, access points, storage, and any other infrastructure device that is provided through the online environment.

Cloud Technologies

Just about anything that is used within the corporate environment or personal computing environment can be offered as a cloud service. The most popular offerings for business include the following:

> **Off-site email applications**—Instead of a company having to house its own email servers, email services are commonly housed in the cloud environment, either on the company's own servers located in a remote location or provided by a cloud-hosted email provider.

> **Cloud file storage services**—Many people use external storage, such as Microsoft's OneDrive, Google's Google Drive, Apple's iCloud, Dropbox, SugarSync, Box, SpiderOak, or Tresorit. A popular feature of cloud-based file storage is **synchronization apps**, which allow for data and folders to be synced between devices and accessed from anywhere. It is important to have enough bandwidth when synching to the cloud.

> **Virtual application streaming/cloud-based applications**—Applications can be virtualized; virtualization means that each application doesn't have to be installed on individual devices, prevents conflicts with other applications, and provides better security controls. Some applications use streaming, which involves sending just some of the code needed to run the application. This is beneficial on mobile devices such as cell phones and tablets. Microsoft's Application Virtualization (App-V) allows cloud-based applications to be used instead of having them installed on client computers such as desktops and laptops. You might have heard of Microsoft's Office 365 or Wine, which is software that allows Windows applications to run on Linux machines.

> **Cloud-based network controller**—Vendors commonly have network controllers that control network devices such as switches and access points. Switches and access points, which are discussed further in Chapter 13, are used in wired networks to connect devices to the network. As shown in Figure 12.23, a cloud-based network controller might be used to monitor and control switches located at the company and branch offices. Figure 12.24 shows a cloud-based network controller that is used to control and monitor access points.

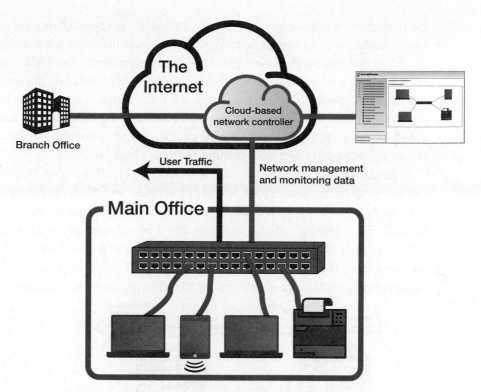

FIGURE 12.23 Cloud-based network controller for switch control

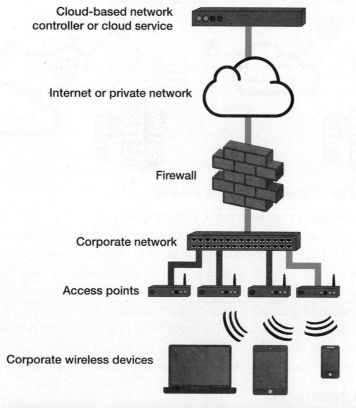

FIGURE 12.24 Cloud-based network controller for access point control

Cloud Service Deployment Methods

Cloud services can be deployed in a combination of ways: private, public, hybrid, and community (see Figure 12.25). A **private cloud** is part of a company's network infrastructure located outside the business in a remote location, but the company has responsibility for managing the software and/or hardware. For example, a college may purchase licenses for a learning management system (LMS) so that students can view grades and see assignments. The LMS could run on servers that are located in a remote vendor's location, but the college network administrators install, update, and maintain responsibility for supporting the LMS. Large businesses tend to be the biggest users of private clouds. With a private cloud deployment, the business doesn't have to worry about providing power, cooling, and space for the equipment and optionally can pay for redundant Internet access and equipment and other features from the cloud provider.

A **public cloud** is an environment operated by a cloud provider. The cloud provider provides services to all business sizes for a cost. Again consider an LMS as an example; the servers and software for the LMS could be provided by the LMS vendor who has the servers in a service provider's building. In a public cloud, the vendor or cloud provider has the responsibility for managing the software and/or hardware. In a public cloud deployment model, several companies would pay for the services of the public cloud vendor. For an LMS, many colleges would purchase the public cloud option and allow another company to configure, monitor, and maintain the LMS.

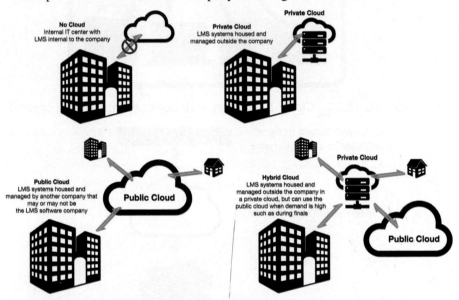

FIGURE 12.25 Cloud deployment models

A **hybrid cloud** is a combination of a private cloud and a public cloud. The company using cloud services is responsible for the licensing and maintenance of the LMS in the private cloud but might need additional storage or servers during peak times. A hybrid cloud solution could be implemented as a failover solution as well. In such a case, the private cloud is used, but if a disaster occurs or during planned maintenance periods, the company uses the application in the public cloud instead.

With a **community cloud**, a number of organizations have access to IT resources that are in the community cloud. An example of this might be an IT system created by a consortium of colleges in one state that are co-developing the system. The system could be housed in the cloud and tested on systems in the cloud. The cost for the community cloud would be shared by all the colleges.

Cloud Advantages

Cloud computing has many benefits to businesses including reduced costs, increased flexibility, increased efficiency, and consistently applied software patches and upgrades. Costs related to network operations centers have increased due to the use of and reliance on technology throughout a business. Common network center costs and overhead include power, hardware, hardware redundancy, storage, fire protection system, licensing, cabling/interconnectivity, and backups.

Other advantages of using cloud technology include the following:

> Corporate focus—Cloud computing enables a company to focus on core IT services or the true function of the company while an outside vendor focuses on its particular strengths (technical expertise on a particular product, staffing levels, quality of service, customer service, and so on).

> 24/7 access—Cloud computing supports continuous access from anywhere and possibly any device. Access is **on-demand**, meaning that it is available when the customer needs it.

> **Rapid elasticity**—Cloud computing facilitates quick expansion of services, software, and/or hardware. For example, if another server or more storage or more of anything else is needed, the outside vendor can access resources that allow expansion on demand. For some companies, such expansions might take several months for an internal system because of the time needed to requisition and obtain the resources.

> **Resource pooling**—A big part of cloud computing is taking advantage of **shared resources**. Shared resources can include servers, applications, hardware components like RAM and CPUs, data storage, Internet connections, or network infrastructure equipment. Think back to virtualization, which is a big part of the cloud environment. Within one computer, the virtualized environment provides resource pooling, such as sharing RAM or CPUs between the multiple operating systems loaded. The resources could be resources owned by the company but housed elsewhere (**internal shared resources**) or shared with other companies (**external shared resources**) when hosted by an external vendor. By using an outside vendor's services, a company can pool resources with other companies that have the same need. A vendor might have access to hundreds of servers. Say that Company A needs just a few servers right now, but Company B has a high usage rate. The outside vendor can allocate servers to Company B to handle the load right now but later reallocate the additional servers to Company A, when its usage increases.

> Measured service—An outside vendor can allocate resources easily by providing a **measured service**: the capability to track (and charge for) cloud consumer usage and apply resources when needed.

> Metered service—With **metered service**, a company pays an amount based on how much of the service is used on an hourly or monthly basis. A company can select how much memory or how many CPUs to use on a particular server or how much time on Oracle's Java Cloud Service in order to develop Java apps. In contrast, **non-metered service** involves a fixed charge and usually has fixed resources or configurations.

Web Browsers

Whether working from a web server in the cloud or surfing the Internet, a web browser is often used. A web browser is a graphical interface between a user and the Internet. Common web browsers include Microsoft's Internet Explorer (commonly called IE), Microsoft's Edge (which is the Windows 10 IE replacement), Mozilla's Firefox, and Google's Chrome. Because Internet Explorer ships with Windows, most textbooks use this browser to explain concepts.

Most browsers are customizable, and many of the settings relate to security, so they are covered in Chapter 18. To get to those settings, click on *Tools* or the icon that looks like a gear in the top-right corner of Internet Explorer (see Figure 12.26). The *Tools* menu option or the gear icon in new versions has configuration items that can be used for web browsing issues. For example, the Compatibility View settings menu option is used when a particular website doesn't display properly. Internet Explorer 11 has seven main Internet Options tabs (see Figure 12.27) for configuring the browser experience. Note that these options can also be reached by using the Internet Options Control Panel in all versions of Windows and some of these options affects other browsers. Table 12.9 explains the primary purposes of the main tabs.

FIGURE 12.26   How to get to Internet Options

FIGURE 12.27   Internet Options window

TABLE 12.9   Purposes of the Internet Options tabs

Tab	Purpose
General	Enables configuration of the home page (the page that opens every time Internet Explorer opens or the home icon is clicked), deletes or configures how long the browsing history (the websites visited) is kept, configures how tabs are organized and behave, and enables customization of the font, language, and color scheme.
Security	Enables customization of security options for sites that you trust and ones that you want blocked (see Chapter 18).
Privacy	Allows you to configure how your private information is handled, including cookies and pop-ups (see Chapter 18).
Content	Provides options for controlling security certificates, AutoComplete for ease of completing online forms, and Feeds and Web Slices for providing updated content directly into the browser.
Connections	Provides options for configuring an Internet connection, dial-up (phone line) connection, proxy server, or VPN (virtual private network) information. (Proxy servers and VPNs are also covered in Chapters 13 and 18.)

Tab	Purpose
Programs	Provides options for configuring email access, add-ons such as toolbars and extensions, and HTML-editing program options.
Advanced	Shows a list of options that might be set throughout the other tabs, also presented here in one easily configured list of checkboxes.

Internet Options General Tab

The General tab is one of the most commonly used Internet Options tabs. Table 12.10 explains the purpose of its main sections.

TABLE 12.10 Internet Options General tab sections

Section	Purpose
Home page	Allows you to configure the page that opens every time Internet Explorer opens or the home icon is clicked.
Startup	Enables you to set whether to start Internet Explorer with tabs previously opened or with the home page website.
Tabs	Allows configuration of the browsing tabs (not the configuration tabs) and other features, such as warnings and pop-ups (see Figure 12.28).
Browsing history	Enables you to delete or configure how long the browsing history (the websites visited) is kept. If you click on the Settings tab, three tabs are available. The *Temporary Internet Files* tab, shown in Figure 12.29, allows you to specify the maximum amount of space to use (and where that data is stored). The *History* tab lets you set the number of days to keep a history of your browsing (see Figure 12.30). Use the *Caches and Databases* tab to set the amount of cache storage space that can be used before a message is displayed (see Figure 12.30).
Appearance	Enables you to customize the browser environment, including the colors (see Figure 12.31), language (see Figure 12.31), fonts (see Figure 12.32), and accessibility options (see Figure 12.32).

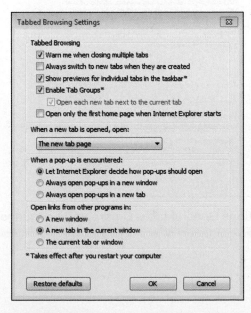

FIGURE 12.28 Internet Options General tab > Tabs button

CHAPTER 12

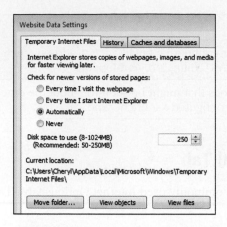

FIGURE 12.29   Internet Options General tab > Temporary Internet Files tab

FIGURE 12.30   Internet Options General tab > History and Caches and databases windows

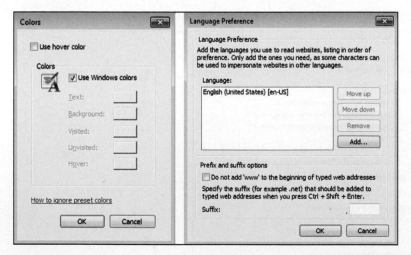

FIGURE 12.31   Internet Options General tab > Colors and Languages windows

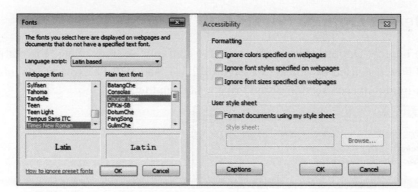

FIGURE 12.32   Internet Options General tab > Fonts and Accessibility windows

Internet Options Security Tab

The Internet Options Security tab is used to configure security settings related to dangerous or risky online content. Figure 12.33 shows the Security tab window. Table 12.11 explains the differences between the four zones.

FIGURE 12.33   Internet Options Security tab

TABLE 12.11   Internet Explorer Security tab zones

Zone	Purpose
Internet	Allows you to set the security level related to websites (excluding sites from the other three zones).
Local intranet	Allows you to set the security level related to a private network such as the one found inside a company (as opposed to the Internet, which is the rest of the world).
Trusted sites	Allows you to set the security level related to websites you believe do not have content that will infect the computer.
Restricted sites	Allows you to set the security level for websites you definitely do not trust.

Internet Options Privacy Tab

The Internet Options Privacy tab is used to configure settings related to your personal information and how it is used by others (see Figure 12.34). Table 12.12 explains the information that can be configured in each section of the Privacy tab window.

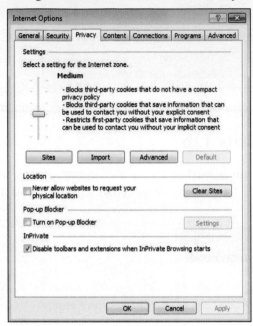

FIGURE 12.34   Internet Options Privacy tab

TABLE 12.12   Internet Explorer/Edge Privacy tab window

Section	Purpose
Settings	Allows you to set the security level for how cookies are handled. (See Chapter 18 for more information on cookies.) The Sites button enables you to select whether a site is always allowed to use cookies or never allowed (blocked) to use cookies (see Figure 12.35). The Advanced button enables you to choose how cookies are automatically handled (see Figure 12.35).
Location	Allows you to configure whether websites can request to know where you are located using location services. Even if you allow this, you are prompted whether or not to allow once or always allow the site to know your physical location.
Pop-up Blocker	Allows you to controls pop-ups from websites. If you select Turn on Pop-up Blocker, the Settings button is enabled. You can click it and then select which websites are allowed to produce pop-ups, as shown in Figure 12.36.
InPrivate	Enables you to prevent the browser from storing history information and passwords.

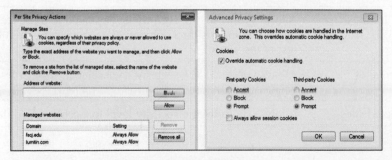

FIGURE 12.35   Internet Options Privacy tab > Sites window and Advanced Privacy Settings window

FIGURE 12.36   Internet Options Privacy tab > Pop-up Blocker Settings windows

Private browsing might be important in a corporate environment, when using a browser on someone else's computer, when going to a website you have never used before, or when using a public computer. Here is how to do it in some common browsers:

> Microsoft Internet Explorer: On a desktop, right-click the *Internet Explorer/Edge* icon > *Start InPrivate Browsing*. For a mobile device, open *Internet Explorer > Tools > Safety > InPrivate Browsing*.
> Microsoft Edge: *More Actions* (three dots option in top-right corner) > *New InPrivate Window*.
> Mozilla Firefox: *Tools > Start Private Browsing*.
> Google Chrome: *Wrench* icon > *New Incognito Window*.

Internet Options Content Tab

The Content tab change settings related to what can be seen in the browser window. Figure 12.37 shows the overall screen, and Table 12.13 details what each section is for.

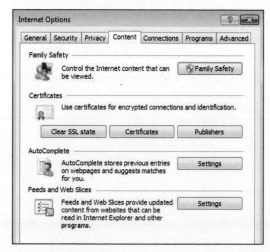

FIGURE 12.37   Internet Options Content tab

TABLE 12.13   Internet Explorer Content tab window

Section	Purpose
Family Safety	Within Windows 7/8 the Family Safety option links to users and the controls applied, if any. Figure 12.38 shows the Parental Controls window and the security warnings that can occur there. For a Windows 10 computer, you create a child account in order to set up parental controls. Chapter 18 goes into further detail about securing accounts.
Certificates	This section is used to verify the authenticity of a person, file, or device when making online purchases or sending an encrypted file.
AutoComplete	Click the Settings button to specify settings related to filling in information on a web page such as your name, address, and email address (see the left side of Figure 12.39).
Feeds and Web Slices	This area provides settings related to Rich Site Summary (RSS) feeds to receive data, audio, and video information from news sources and the like (see the right side of Figure 12.39)

FIGURE 12.38   Internet Options Content tab > Parental controls window

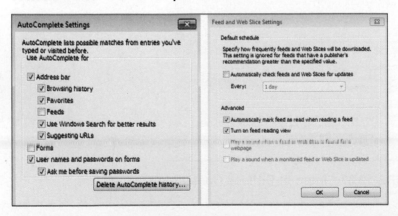

FIGURE 12.39   Internet Options Content tab > AutoComplete Settings window and Feeds and Web Slices Settings window

Internet Options Connections Tab

The Connections tab (see Figure 12.40) is where you go to configure your Internet connection (see Figure 12.41), configure a computer to use a proxy server, and set up a new VPN so that someone can securely access company resources while working from home or away from the office (see Figure 12.42), and configure connections related to LAN settings (see Figure 12.43). Chapters 13 and 18 detail more information about VPNs and proxy servers. For now, concentrate on knowing where you go in Internet Explorer/Edge to configure browser settings.

FIGURE 12.40   Internet Options Connections tab

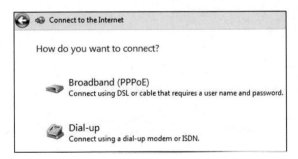

FIGURE 12.41   Internet Options Connections tab > Setup button window

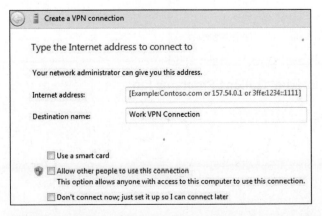

FIGURE 12.42   Internet Options Connections tab > Add VPN button window

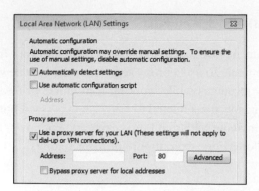

FIGURE 12.43   Internet Options Connections tab > LAN Settings window

Internet Options Programs Tab

How many times do you think someone downloads a software update of some type and gets the default browser changed to something else? The Programs tab (see Figure 12.44) can help with this and with managing add-ons. An **add-on** is an extension or plug-in that provides the browser an additional feature, such as a toolbar or the capability to dim everything on the screen except for a running video. Add-ons can present security risks. Figure 12.45 shows the Manage Add-ons window.

The HTML Editing section of the Programs tab has a drop-down menu to select the application used to edit HTML files. Examples include Microsoft Windows, Excel, and Notepad. The last section of the tab is used to access the Set Default Programs section of the Control Panel, where you can select which application opens a music file, for example. It is similar to choosing your default browser but for other applications.

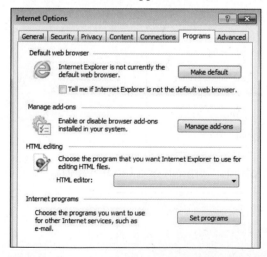

FIGURE 12.44   Internet Options Programs tab

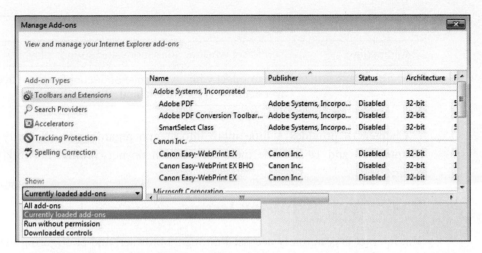

FIGURE 12.45   Internet Options Programs tab > Manage Add-ons window

Internet Options Advanced Tab

The last tab in Internet Options is the Advanced tab (see Figure 12.46). This tab is used for all types of options not covered on the other tabs. Table 12.14 outlines just a few examples of the sections.

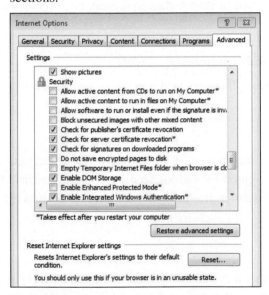

FIGURE 12.46   Internet Options Advanced tab

TABLE 12.14   Internet Explorer Advanced tab window

Section	Purpose
Accelerated graphics	Used to enable software rendering instead of GPU rendering
Accessibility	Used to play system sounds, provide alt text for images, and reset text sizes
Browsing	Used to set browsing options (such as notification of script errors or when a download completes), automatic crash recovery, and loading content in the background to improve performance
HTTP settings	Used to set the HTTP version
International	Used to set settings such as Unicode UTF-8 format, which is a standard way to display characters found in different languages

Section	Purpose
Multimedia	Used to set whether animations and sounds play
Security	Used to select which version(s) of Secure Sockets Layer (SSL) and Transport Layer Security (TLS) are enabled

Chapter 18 provides a little more information regarding the Security Internet Options tab. Chapters 13 and 18 provide more information on networking, network security, and Internet security.

Basic Web Browser Issues

The Internet is commonly accessed through a browser, and configuring the browser is one of the first steps in configuring security. Browsers are commonly upgraded to provide improved security options. Before upgrading an Internet browser, you must determine the current web browser version. With many Windows-based applications, the version is determined by starting the application, clicking *Help > About x* (where *x* is the name of the application), or selecting the question mark menu item. With Internet Explorer (IE), the first two numbers listed are the software version numbers. There is another value called cipher strength that is a bit value for encryption; **encryption** is a protection method used to change data so it cannot be recognized.

TECH TIP

Why keep your Windows and web browser current?

Internet hackers frequently target browsers, and constant updates are provided to counter these attacks.

When people connect to the Internet, they normally do so through a web browser. A web browser can usually be configured for various security options. Because the Microsoft operating systems ship with Internet Explorer, it is covered here. Similar options are available in most other browsers.

Hijacked Browser

One issue with browsers is that they can be hijacked (see Figure 12.47). A hijacked browser either replaces the home page with another one or directs whatever web page is being used to a different one. This is called a **browser redirect**. Besides sending you to another web page, a browser redirect can also be used to install a rootkit or install more malware ("bad software"), such as keystroke loggers (to record your keystrokes, including your typed usernames and passwords), perform a DNS hijack, or install a rogue HOSTS file. A **rootkit** can be used to act as a backdoor to your operating system and may be used to do things that require administrator access. Rootkits can also be downloaded and installed to a flash drive. The HOSTS file is a text file used to manually map a hostname to a particular IP address.

FIGURE 12.47   Web browser redirect

The following recommendations can help with hijacked browser issues:

> Change the home page URL to your normal home page and not the hijacked page. In any browser, go to the web page you want to be the home page and copy that web address. In Internet Explorer, access *Tools* (gear) icon > use the *Home Page* section on the General tab to type the home page address to use > *Apply* > *OK*. In Microsoft Edge, access the *More* (three dots) option > *Settings* > in the *Open With* section, select the *A Specific Page or Pages* radio button > use the down arrow to select *Custom* > type a web address in the *Enter a Web Address* textbox.

> Clear the browser history/cache. In Internet Explorer, access *Tools* (gear) icon > *Internet options* > use the *Delete* button in the *Browsing history* section on the *General* tab > ensure *Temporary Internet files, Cookies*, and *History* are checked > *OK*. In Microsoft Edge, access the *More* (three dots) option > *Settings* > in the *Clear browsing data* section, select *Choose what to clear* > ensure *Cached data and files, Cookies and stored website data*, and *Browsing history* are checked > *Clear*.

> If clearing the browser history/cache did not work, reset the browser settings. In Internet Explorer, access *Tools* (gear) icon > *Internet options* > *Advanced tab* > under the *Reset Internet Explorer settings*, select *Reset* > *Reset*. If that doesn't work, you could try selecting the *Delete personal settings* option. In Microsoft Edge, access the *More* (three dots) option > *Settings* > in the *Clear browsing data* section, select *Choose what to clear* > enable all options > *Clear*.

> Try a different browser to see if the symptom remains. You could also uninstall the browser and reinstall it.

> If **pop-ups** (unwanted messages, screens, or windows) appear continuously, use Task Manager to stop the `iexplore.exe` process. Reopen Internet Explorer and ensure that the pop-up blocker is turned on: *Internet Options* > *Privacy* tab > enable *Turn on Pop-up Blocker*. Otherwise, use a different browser, such as Google Chrome or Mozilla Firefox. Install anti-malware software. You can always uninstall and reinstall a browser, too.

> If necessary, start the computer in *Safe Mode with Networking*. If the web browser works properly in this mode, but not when normal booting straight to Windows, a DLL file might have been added to the computer. Run a scan with your antimalware application.

> Start the browser with no add-ons to see if one of them is causing the problem. How you do this depends on the browser. In Internet Explorer, perform the following:

> > Windows 7: *Start > All Programs > Accessories > System Tools > Internet Explorer (No Add-ons)*.

> > Windows 8/10: Start *Internet Explorer > Tools > Manage Add-ons >* in the *Show* drop-down menu, select *All Add-ons >* select the add-on you want to turn off *> Disable > Close*.

> If the browser starts working, turn on the add-ons one by one to determine which one caused the problem.

> Determine whether the HOSTS file has been modified and includes some rogue entries. The HOSTS file can be found in the C:\Windows\system32\drivers\etc folder.

Slow Browser

If your browser seems like it is getting slower and slower, but the rest of the machine is running fine, there are a few things you can do:

> Disable unnecessary add-ons.
> Disable all add-ons and re-enable them one at a time.
> Disable extensions (which, in Chrome, are different from plug-ins).
> Uninstall and reinstall the web browser.
> Clear browser cache/history (steps are in Hijacked Browser section).
> Reset browser settings (steps are in Hijacked Browser section).
> Use a different web browser.

SOFT SKILLS: MENTORING

Every great technician can tell you that he or she has had at least one mentor along the way. When you hear the word *mentor*, it probably conjures up other words and phrases in your head—coach, guidance, teacher, adviser, positive influence, leadership, setting an example, and so on. No technician can attain his or her ultimate level without being mentored. Also, no technician can learn everything from a book or from experience. Others helping us along the way enable us to learn faster and more efficiently.

When you enter your first (second, third, or fourth) job in the IT field, you should take a few days to look around the company. Find someone who appears to be very professional and knowledgeable—someone you want to emulate. Talk to that person and explain your goals. Ask if he or she will mentor you—whether to get help with problems you cannot solve or advice about office politics (see Figure 12.48).

FIGURE 12.48   Mentoring

Mentoring is an important part of life. Not only should you consider being mentored, you should consider mentoring others. Many technicians hoard information from other technicians and computer users. Knowledge is power, and by sharing information with others and helping them along the way, you cement and expand your own knowledge.

Chapter Summary

> Serial devices use either XON/XOFF (software method) or RTS/CTS (hardware method) for flow control.
> Serial devices must be configured for the number of bits, parity, stop bits, FIFO setting, flow control, and handshaking.
> The two sides of a connection must match.
> The speed at which a 56 kbps modem can transmit is limited by the number of analog-to-digital conversions.
> Internet connectivity can be provided by an analog modem, satellite modem, ISDN, cable modem, fiber, DSL modem, or wirelessly through the cell phone network, a wireless bridge, a mobile hotspot, WiMAX, or a wireless network.

> Cable modem bandwidth is shared by the subscribers in an area. If the number of subscribers is too many and the cable bandwidth is unacceptable, a direct fiber connection might be an option.
> A DSL modem uses a phone line. ADSL has a faster downstream speed than upstream speed.
> WiMAX networks and wireless bridges are used with line-of-sight networks.
> VoIP uses a corporate network and/or the Internet for voice connectivity. Internet-based VoIP does not offer QoS.
> Cloud technology services are classified as SaaS, IaaS, and PaaS. Cloud deployment models include private, public, hybrid, and community.
> Shared resources can be internal or external.
> The cost of metered service is based on how much the service is used on an hourly or monthly basis. In contrast, measured service involves payment based on usage.
> A computer that uses virtualization must have more hardware to run more than a single operating system environment.
> A virtual desktop is an operating system that is in a virtual machine and used within a corporate environment to more easily manage multiple computers.
> Technicians frequently have to configure Internet browsers. In Internet Explorer, you use the *Internet Options* tabs for configuration. In Edge, use *More > Settings*.
> Keep a web browser current for security reasons.
> Private browsing prevents a web browser from storing browsing history information and passwords.
> A hijacked browser redirects a browser to a different web page.
> Pop-ups can be managed by using a pop-up blocker (in Internet Explorer, on the *Privacy* tab).
> Disable add-ons to prevent pop-ups and help with a hijacked browser.
> Mentoring is important when you get started as a technician and as you gain experience.

A+ CERTIFICATION EXAM TIPS

✓ The Internet connection types that are on the 220-1001 exam are as follows: cable, DSL, dial-up, fiber, satellite, ISDN, cellular (mobile hotspot/tethering), and line-of-sight wireless Internet service. Be able to compare and contrast these technologies.

✓ Know pros and cons of each Internet connection type. Do and/or review Exercise 12.1 at the end of the chapter.

✓ Know when each Internet connection type would be used.

✓ The 220-1002 exam includes the *Internet Options* Control Panel, which includes the tabs that can also be accessed from within Internet Explorer. Be familiar with each tab and why a technician would use it. Before the exam, re-examine those options using Internet Explorer.

✓ Know the difference between SaaS, PaaS, and IaaS and the four types of cloud deployment (public, private, hybrid, and community).

✓ Be able to set up and configure client-side virtualization and know what resources, emulator, security, and network requirements are needed.

✓ Know the purpose of setting up a virtual machine and what hypervisor is being used.

✓ Know the meanings of the following terms: shared resources (internal and external), rapid elasticity, on-demand, resource pooling, as it relates to cloud technologies and virtualization, measured service, metered, offsite email applications, cloud file storage services including synchronization apps, virtual application streaming and cloud-based applications for both mobile devices and computers, as well as virtual desktop/virtual NIC.

Key Terms

3G 588

4G 588

5G 588

add-on 606

ADSL 584

asynchronous 575

bandwidth 584

baud 576

bps 576

browser redirect 608

cable modem 581

checkpoint 590

cloud-based application 594

cloud-based network control-ler 594

cloud file storage service 594

community cloud 596

convergence 580

data bits 577

dial-up 574

dial-up network 574

downstream 584

DSL 584

emulator 591

encryption 608

external shared resources 597

fiber network 583

FIFO setting 577

flow control 577

handshaking 577

host machine 590

hybrid cloud 596

hypervisor 590

IaaS 594

internal shared resources 597

ISDN 579

ISP 586

line-of-sight wireless Internet service 588

LTE 588

measured service 597

metered service 597

mobile hotspot 587

non-metered service 597

off-site email application 594

on-demand 597

PaaS 594

parity 577

phone filter 586

pop-up 609

private cloud 595

PSTN 579

public cloud 596

QoS 580

rapid elasticity 597

resource pooling 597

rootkit 608

RS232C 576

SaaS 594

satellite modem 586

shared resources 597

snapshot 590

start bit 576

stop bit 576

synchronization app 594

tethering 588

Type 1 hypervisor 590

Type 2 hypervisor 591

upstream 584

virtual application streaming 594

virtual desktop 594

virtual machine 590

virtual NIC 594

virtualization 589

VoIP 579

WiBro 589

WiMAX 588

wireless broadband 588

xDSL 584

CHAPTER 12

Review Questions

1. A company outsources corporate payroll to a company that provides a cloud-based solution. What type of cloud service is being provided?
   [DaaS | SaaS | PaaS | IaaS]

2. A company has its email server in the cloud. The company has a network administrator assigned to maintain and manage the email server. Which cloud deployment model is used?
   [community | private | public | hybrid]

3. Which port is used to connect a cable modem to a business or home router?
   [RJ-11 | eSATA | USB | Ethernet]

4. What is the biggest limitation of using a 56 kbps modem transmitting at 56 kbps as a dial-up connection to the Internet?

   _____

5. What is VoIP?

   a. A cable modem technology

   b. A method used to wirelessly connect to the Internet

   c. A method of using a network to carry voice traffic

   d. Network communication that is faster on downloads than on uploads

6. To connect to the Internet and transmit data and voice using DSL, which component would you need to add to phone jacks that have a phone or answering machine attached to them?
   [modem surge protector | phone filter | ISP | RJ-11 connector]

7. A customer has an older 16-bit game as well as some newer 32-bit games. The customer is considering upgrading to 64-bit Windows 10. Will there be any issues with this? If so, what are they, and how might they be resolved?

   _____

   _____

8. Which type of hypervisor is used with Windows 10's Virtual PC and is also known as a hosted hypervisor?
   [Super | UEFI | Type 2 | Internal]

9. List one drawback to a cable modem.

   _____

10. What does asymmetrical mean in relation to an ADSL modem?

    _____

11. Which virtualization component manages VMs?
    [hypervisor | filter | virtual NIC | virtual BIOS/UEFI]

12. What is the first thing you should check if your Internet connectivity is down and you have a DSL modem installed?

    _____

13. What is wireless broadband?

    _____

14. What is most important when synching data to the cloud? [CPU speed | amount of free hard disk space | amount of RAM | speed of RAM | Internet connection bandwidth]

15. A new laptop has an integrated wireless LAN. The customer thinks there is a missing wireless antenna. What should you advise the customer?

    _____

16. [T | F] A hotspot provides wired network connectivity.

17. What would be the purpose of an Ethernet connection on a cable modem or a DSL modem?

   a. To connect a PC to the phone jack on the wall

   b. To connect a PC to the jack provided by the Internet provider

   c. To connect a PC to the modem

   d. To connect the modem to the jack provided by the Internet provider

18. A customer has a new laptop with wireless WAN capabilities; however, the software does not connect to the Internet. What would you suggest to the customer?

   _____

   _____

19. Which Internet Connection window tab would be used to configure a proxy server?
   [Security | Content | Privacy | Connections]

20. List two ways mentoring can help in the IT field.

   _____

   _____

Exercises

Exercise 12.1 Exploring Internet Connectivity Options

Objective: To explore different methods of Internet connectivity

Note: This exercise can be done with information found in the chapter or as an Internet research exercise (which would require a device with Internet access).

Procedure: Research and document two advantages and two disadvantages of each of the types of Internet connectivity listed in Table 12.15.

TABLE 12.15   Research of Internet connectivity types*

Type	Two disadvantages	Two advantages
56 kbps modem		
ISDN		
Cable modem		
DSL modem		

Type	Two disadvantages	Two advantages
Satellite modem		
Wireless broadband		
WiMAX		

* Answers may vary; possible answers are given.

Exercise 12.2 Exploring the Internet Options Window

Objective: To explore the different tabs in the Internet Options window

Note: This exercise can be done with information found within the chapter, as an Internet research exercise (which would require a device with Internet access), or on a Windows computer.

Procedure: Indicate in Table 12.16 the Internet Options tab (General, Security, Privacy, Content, Connections, Programs, or Advanced) that would be used to perform the task.

TABLE 12.16   Internet Options tabs to use for specific tasks

Task	Internet Options tab
Enable pop-up blocker	
Specify the maximum amount of disk space for temporary Internet files	
Configure security certificates	
Disable an add-on	
Designate which program opens sound files found in web pages	
Configure a proxy server	
Configure the version of HTTP supported	
Configure a VPN	
Designate the URL to be used as the home page	
Configure settings related to inside the corporate network (as opposed to the Internet)	
Set the default font used for a web page	

Activities

Internet Discovery

Objective: To obtain specific information regarding a computer or its associated parts on the Internet

Parts: Computer with Internet access

Questions: Use the Internet to answer the following questions.

1. Locate a cable modem website that explains how to increase speed on a cable modem. Write the URL where you found the answer as well as the recommendation.

   _____

   _____

2. Determine whether cable or DSL modems are supported in your area. If so, determine as many vendors as you can for these products.

   _____

3. Find one vendor of VDSL in the United States and write down the name of the vendor and the URL where you found the answer.

   _____

   _____

4. Find a website that describes how modem chat scripts are done and that provides an example of one. Write the URL and your own explanation of chat scripts.

   _____

   _____

5. Determine how much a vendor charges to enable the mobile hotspot option or determine a phone/device that supports the mobile hotspot option. Document the price or phone model number and the URL where you found this information.

   _____

6. Find a vendor in your state that sells wireless broadband for a laptop. What type of technology does it use (USB, integrated, and so on)? Write the URL, the vendor name, the model number, and the cost.

   _____

Soft Skills

Objective: To enhance and fine-tune a future technician's ability to listen, communicate in both written and oral forms, and support people who use computers in a professional manner

Activities:

1. Divide the class into three groups—two groups that will be debating against one another and a third group of judges. The judges have 45 minutes to determine the rules and consequences of how the debate is to be conducted. During the same 45 minutes, the two debating groups will research material and plan a strategy for either cable modems or DSL modems. At the end of 45 minutes, the debate will start, and the judges will mediate with the rules they establish and present to the two teams before the debate begins. The judges, along with the instructor, determine which group proved its point the best.

   Using whatever resources are available, research one of the following that has been assigned to you. Share the results with the class.

What is the largest number of IRQs supported by an analog modem that you could find?

_____

What is the fastest DSL, cable, or analog connection within a 60-mile radius of your school?

_____

What is the most common type of Internet connectivity for home users in your area?

_____

What is the most common type of Internet connectivity among businesses in your area?

_____

What are the type and speed of the Internet connectivity at your school?

_____

What are the type and speed of the Internet connectivity at a college in your state?

_____

Which types of DSL services are available in your state?

_____

Which types of cable modem services are available in your state?

_____

Critical Thinking Skills

Objective: To analyze and evaluate information as well as apply learned information to new or different situations

Activities:

1.   In groups of three, research one of the following issues, as designated by the instructor. Share your findings with the other groups.

 > What are the pros and cons of changing the settings on a smartphone so that it can be a hotspot? Be prepared to share the group findings.

 > What wireless broadband options are available from one of the most popular mobile phone providers in the area? Detail one option and its rate plan and cost. Be prepared to share your findings.

 > Determine the best Internet connectivity rates for a small business in the area where your school is located. Share at least two competitors' rates, if possible. Detail the connectivity speeds and costs per vendor and be prepared to share your findings.

 > Find at least three VoIP solutions for home users. Prepare a chart that shows vendors, options, pros and cons of each option, costs, and customer ratings (and comments, if possible). Be prepared to share your findings.

2.   In groups of two, write two analog/cable/DSL modem problems on two separate index cards. Give one problem to another class group and the other problem to a different class group. Your group will receive two index cards from two different groups as well. Solve the problems given to you, using any resource available. Share your group findings with the class.

13 Networking

In this chapter you will learn:

> To identify common network cables
> About Ethernet networks
> About the OSI and TCP/IP models, different networking protocols, and important TCP or UDP port numbers

> To identify MAC, IPv4, and IPv6 addresses
> To set up wired and wireless networks
> Common network troubleshooting tools

> To configure and access a network printer
> Important network servers
> To share data using a network
> How to be a proactive technician

CompTIA Exam Objectives:

What CompTIA A+ exam objectives are covered in this chapter?

✓ 1001-2.1 Compare and contrast TCP and UDP ports, protocols, and their purposes.

✓ 1001-2.2 Compare and contrast networking hardware devices.

✓ 1001-2.3 Given a scenario, install and configure a basic wired/wireless SOHO network.

✓ 1001-2.4 Compare and contrast wireless networking protocols.

✓ 1001-2.5 Summarize the properties and purposes of services provided by networked hosts.

✓ 1001-2.6 Explain common network configuration concepts.

✓ 1001-2.7 Compare and contrast Internet connection types, network types, and their features.

✓ 1001-2.8 Given a scenario, use appropriate networking tools.

✓ 1001-3.1 Explain basic cable types, features, and their purposes.

✓ 1001-3.2 Identify common connector types.

✓ 1001-3.9 Given a scenario, install and configure common devices.

✓ 1001-3.10 Given a scenario, configure SOHO multifunction devices/printers and settings.

✓ 1001-4.1 Compare and contrast cloud computing concepts.

✓ 1001-4.2 Given a scenario, set up and configure client-side virtualization.

✓ 1001-5.6 Given a scenario, troubleshoot common wired and wireless network problems.

✓ 1002-1.4 Given a scenario, use appropriate Microsoft command line tools.

✓ 1002-1.6 Given a scenario, use Microsoft Windows Control Panel utilities.

✓ 1002-1.8 Given a scenario, configure Microsoft Windows networking on a client/desktop.

✓ 1002-2.6 Compare and contrast the differences of basic Microsoft Windows OS security settings.

✓ 1002-2.10 Given a scenario, configure security on SOHO wireless and wired networks.

✓ 1002-4.4 Explain common safety procedures.

Networking Overview

Networks are all around us. A few examples include the following:

> A network of roads and interstate highways
> A telephone network
> The electrical network that provides electricity to our homes
> The cellular network that allows cell phones/smartphones to connect to one another as well as connectivity between cell phones/smartphones and the wired telephone network and the Internet
> The air traffic control network
> Your network of friends and family

A network as it relates to computers is two or more devices that have the capability to communicate with one another and share resources. A network allows computer users to share files; communicate via email; browse the Internet; share a printer, modem, or scanner; and access applications and files. Networks can be divided into major categories based on the size and type of network. Table 13.1 describes these different networks.

TABLE 13.1   Types of networks

Network type	Description
Personal area network (**PAN**)	Personal devices such as keyboard, mouse, TV, cell phone, laptop, desktop, mobile device, and pocket video games that can communicate in close proximity through a wired or wireless network. Using a Bluetooth keyboard with a PC is an example of a PAN.
Local area network (**LAN**)	A group of devices that can share resources in a single area, such as a room, home, or building. The most common type of LAN is Ethernet. A LAN can be wired or wireless. The computers in a networked classroom are an example of a LAN.
Metropolitan area network (**MAN**)	Connectivity between sites within the same city. A MAN connects multiple LANs. MANs can be wireless or can use fiber-optic cable. Multiple college campuses connected in a city are an example of a MAN.
Wide area network (**WAN**)	Connectivity between LANs on a large geographic scale. Two remote locations that have connectivity between them as part of the company network are a WAN.
Wireless LAN (**WLAN**)	A wireless network that consists of an access point and some wireless devices including laptops, tablets, and smartphones. A wireless network can be short range, such as when Bluetooth is used, or have wider coverage, as in a wireless network for a home or business. Wireless bridges might be used to connect devices between two buildings.
Wireless WAN (**WWAN**)	Wireless connectivity for a larger geographic area, using a mix of technologies, such as cellular or WiMAX.
Wireless mesh network (**WMN**)	Wireless connectivity that is especially good in emergency situations because WMNs do not require traditional access points, pass data between peer radio devices, and can be used over large distances.

Today, networks are vital to businesses. They can also be found in many homes. A technician must have a basic understanding of the devices that make up networks and learn how to connect them to existing networks.

Attaching to Different Types of Networks

Computers can attach to different types of networks. A technician must be familiar with attaching computers to three basic types:

> A server-based network
> A workgroup
> A Microsoft HomeGroup

With a **server-based network**, computer users log in to a main computer called a *server*, where they are authenticated (authorized to use the network). The server is a more powerful computer than a normal workstation. The server contains information about who is allowed to connect to the network and to what network resources (files, printers, and applications) the network user is allowed access. Windows computers in a server-based network are commonly called a **domain**, or a Microsoft Active Directory domain. One or more dedicated servers log and track users and resources. Domains are commonly found in the business environment. Don't worry that you don't know all the components in this picture yet. Those terms are coming.

When working in a corporate environment, technicians commonly have to install new computers, replace computers, or repair computers on the domain. This requires special rights to be assigned to the technician; end users are not normally allowed to add computers to a domain. If a computer ever displays a message that the trust relationship is broken, the computer must be reconnected to the domain.

A Microsoft HomeGroup or a workgroup network does not have a centralized server and has a smaller number of devices. Each computer is its own server, and resources are shared between the workstation computers. This is sometimes known as a client/server relationship. One computer acts as the server and allows information to be obtained by the client or another device. Another name for any network that allows sharing of resources on a small network is *peer-to-peer network*.

Windows computers in a peer-to-peer network are known as a **workgroup**; Microsoft uses the term **HomeGroup** in Windows 7, 8, and 10 (although it has been removed from Windows 10 version 1803 and higher). Two or more computers configured with the same workgroup name can share devices such as printers as well as files and folders. No central server or domain controller is used. Many homes and small businesses use a workgroup environment.

In the workgroup environment, the computer user sets up passwords to allow others access to the resources through the network. A person uses the network to access remote files, printers, applications, and so forth from his workstation.

A special type of workgroup network is Microsoft's HomeGroup. A HomeGroup network is assigned a single password, and other devices within that HomeGroup simply need that password to access resources such as files and photos. A HomeGroup is easier to manage than a workgroup because it does not require setting up individual accounts and passwords as a workgroup does. Figure 13.1 shows a workgroup/HomeGroup network. Again, don't worry about knowing the parts shown at this point of the chapter.

Server-based networks are more common in businesses, whereas workgroup and HomeGroup networks are more common in homes and small businesses. A server-based network can consist of 20 or more computers; in contrast, a workgroup network usually has fewer (2 to 20) computers. End-user devices on the different types of networks tend to be the same, and configuration of those devices is similar.

A server-based network is more secure than a peer-to-peer network. This is because the server is normally in a locked network room or wiring closet. A server has a special operating system loaded on it, called a network operating system (NOS), such as Microsoft Windows Server, Red Hat Enterprise Linux, or Oracle Solaris. A network operating system has utilities that allow computer user management (who is allowed onto the network), resource management (what network applications, files, printers, and so on a user can use), and security management (what a user is allowed to do with a resource, such as read, write, or read and write). One user ID and password is all a remote user needs to access many network resources located throughout the business organization.

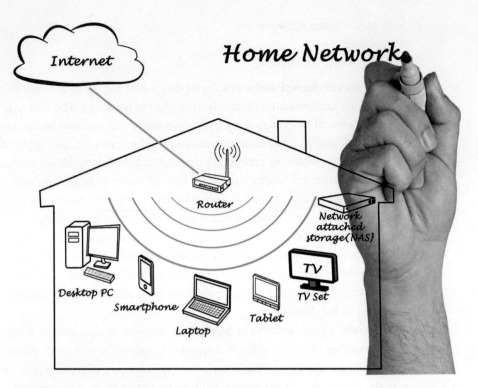

FIGURE 13.1   Workgroup network design

Figure 13.2 shows how a server-based network can be configured. The network has one server in the center, four workstations, and two laser printers. The server has a database of users—CSchmidt, RDevoid, and MElkins—and their associated passwords. The server also has three applications loaded—Microsoft Excel, Microsoft Project, and Microsoft Word. These applications and associated documents are stored on the server. Whether the users can access these applications and documents and what they can do within each document is also stored on the server. In the Permission column of the table in Figure 13.2 is either R for Read or R/W for Read/Write, which indicates what the user can do in a particular application. For example, user CSchmidt has read and write access to Excel, Project, and Word. This means that she can open, look at, and modify documents in any of these three applications. MElkins can read Excel and Word documents, and she can read and write Microsoft Project documents. CSchmidt can print to either of the laser printers, but RDevoid prints only to the LP1 laser printer.

A workgroup network is not as expensive or as secure as a server-based network. A server is more expensive than a regular workstation, and it requires a network operating system. Because workgroup networks do not use a dedicated server, costs are reduced. Instead of a network operating system, each workstation uses an operating system such as Windows 7, 8, and/or 10. A workgroup network is not as secure as a server-based network because each computer must be configured with individual user IDs and passwords. Figure 13.3 shows how a workgroup network is configured.

Figure 13.3 shows three workstations, labeled Workstation 1, Workstation 2, and Workstation 3. Workstation 2 has a shared printer for everyone to use. There are three people in this company: Raina Devoid, Cheryl Schmidt, and Melodie Elkins. RDevoid normally works at Workstation 1, and she has shared a folder on the hard drive called *WORDDOCS* that has the password Stealth2. CSchmidt and MElkins can access the documents located in *WORDDOCS* from their own workstations as long as they know the password is Stealth2. If RDevoid wants to access MElkins's *WAN* folder, RDevoid must know and remember that the password is Tech2001. If MElkins changes the password on the *WAN* folder, MElkins must remember to tell the new password to anyone who needs access. The password is used only when accessing the WAN folder documents.

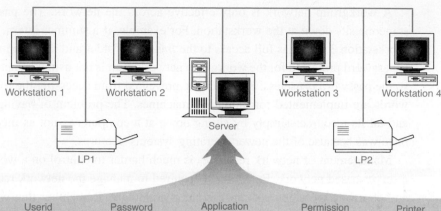

Userid	Password	Application	Permission	Printer
CSchmidt	hellØ	Excel	R/W	LP1
		Project	R/W	LP2
		Word	R/W	
RDevoid	Teeny18	Excel	R/W	LP1
		Word	R	
MElkins	bØdy89	Excel	R	LP2
		Project	R/W	
		Word	R	

FIGURE 13.2   Server-based network

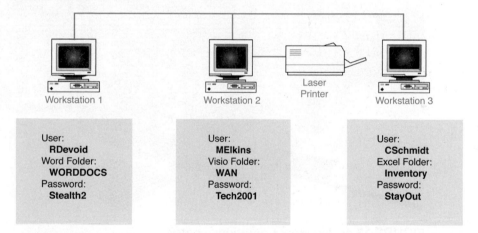

FIGURE 13.3   Workgroup network

Now if someone made this workgroup network into a HomeGroup, the HomeGroup would be assigned a single password, such as Schm1dt$hare. Any devices accessing the shared resources within the HomeGroup would need that password. The single password makes it easier to manage the network environment because most things shared at home would not need specialized usernames, passwords, and specified rights.

TECH TIP

Workgroup networks are for small networks

You can see that the more resources that are shared on a workgroup network, the more passwords and the more cumbersome password management will be unless you use a Windows Home-Group. That is the reason workgroup networks are used in small network environments.

A workgroup network is only effective across the network. The password is not effective if someone sits down at the workstation. For example, if a summer intern, Ken Tinker, sits down at Workstation 3, Ken has full access to the *Inventory* folder and documents. Even though the folder is password protected for the workgroup network, Ken is not using the network to access the folder, so the password is useless. Ken could be prevented from accessing the folder if user IDs and passwords are implemented for individual machines. The problem of having access to a workstation and all its resources simply by sitting down at a computer is not as much of a threat today as it once was because of the newer operating systems' features.

Management of network resources is much harder to control on a workgroup network than on a server-based network. Each user is required to manage the network resources on one computer, and password management can become a nightmare. Remember that with workgroup networks, anyone who knows the password can access the resource such as a folder across the network. Server-based networks are normally more secure than workgroup networks because (1) passwords are managed centrally at the server and (2) the server is normally locked in a wiring closet, server room/network operations center (see Figure 13.4), or at least a locked cabinet.

FIGURE 13.4   Network operations center

When configuring Windows for a network, you are presented with three or four choices: home network, work network, public network, or domain. The option chosen defines, to some extent, the type of network you could configure, as shown in Figure 13.5. Table 13.2 describes each option.

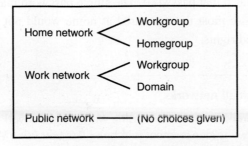

FIGURE 13.5   Types of Windows network options

TABLE 13.2   Windows network options

Network option	Description
Home	Used to configure a device participating in a workgroup or a HomeGroup. Network discovery is enabled. Network discovery allows detection by other network devices.
Work	Used to configure a device participating in a workgroup or domain. Network discovery is enabled.
Public	Used to configure a device on a network where the other devices are unknown. Network discovery is disabled.
Domain	Used to configure a device in the enterprise corporate environment where policies are enforced and deployed.

To have a network, the following are required: network adapters (also called NICs), network media (cable or air), and an operating system with network options enabled. The following sections explore these concepts.

Network Topologies

The physical network topology is how a network is wired. Figure 13.6 shows the physical topologies used in networking. Keep in mind that a large business may have combinations of these topologies.

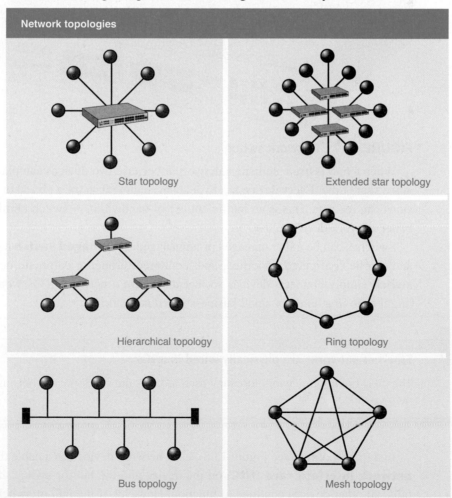

FIGURE 13.6   Network topologies

Ethernet Star Topology

Ethernet is the most common type of LAN. Each network device connects to a central device, normally a hub or a switch. Both the hub and the switch contain two or more RJ-45 network jacks. The hub is not as intelligent as a switch. The switch takes a look at each data frame as it comes through the switch. The hub cannot do this. Figure 13.7 illustrates a switch (although it could be a hub). You sometimes have to look at the model number to tell the difference between a hub and a switch because they are similar in appearance.

Why a switch is better than a hub

When a workstation sends data to a hub, the **hub** broadcasts the data out all ports except for the port that received the original data (the port the data came in on). A better solution is a switch. A **switch** keeps a table of addresses. When a switch receives data, the switch looks up the destination MAC address (an address burned into a NIC) in the switch table and forwards the data out the port for which it is destined.

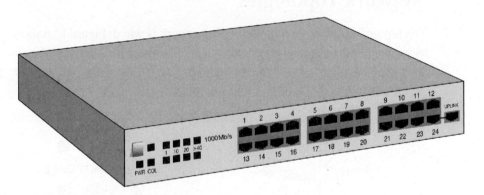

FIGURE 13.7   Network switch

When a hub is used, collisions may occur because two devices can place data onto the network at the same time. Every device has to delay in sending data for a period of time, and then transmissions can reoccur. This is an inefficient use of bandwidth. A switch eliminates collisions and is a better network device to use.

Switches can be either managed or unmanaged. A **managed switch** has an IP address assigned and can be configured, modified, and monitored through a corporate network. An **unmanaged switch** simply connects devices so that they form a network. This would be like a switch you might have in a home or small business wired network.

Ethernet networks are physically wired in a star

The most common network topology used today is the star topology because it is used with Ethernet networks.

In a star topology (see Figure 13.8), each network device has a cable that connects between the **network interface card** (**NIC**) on the device and the hub or switch. If one computer or cable fails, all other devices continue to function. However, if the hub or switch fails, the network goes down.

Star topologies are easy to troubleshoot. If one network device goes down, the problem is in the device, cable, or port on the hub/switch. If a group of network devices goes down, the problem is most likely in the device that connects them together (the hub or switch).

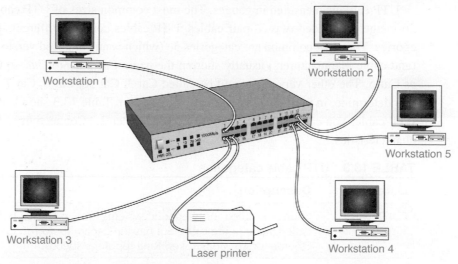

FIGURE 13.8 Star network topology

Network Media Overview

A network requires some type of medium to transmit data. This medium is normally some type of cable or air (wireless using radio, microwave, and electromagnetic signals). The most common types of cable are twisted pair copper and fiber-optic cable, although some older networks used coax cable. Video networks also use coax. Air is used in wireless networking when data is sent over radio frequencies.

Copper Media

Copper media is the most common cabling used to connect devices to a network. It is also used to connect network devices. Copper media comes in two major types: twisted pair and coaxial.

Twisted Pair Cable Overview

Twisted pair cable comes in two types: shielded and unshielded. The acronyms used with this type of cable are STP (shielded twisted pair) and UTP (unshielded twisted pair). The most common type of copper media used with computer networking and phone cabling is **UTP** cable. Most people are familiar with twisted pair cable because UTP is used in homes for telephone wiring. **Twisted pair cable** has four pairs of conductors entwined around each other—hence its name. Figure 13.9 shows the physical properties of an unshielded twisted pair cable.

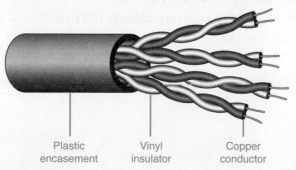

Plastic encasement   Vinyl insulator   Copper conductor

FIGURE 13.9 UTP cable

STP cable has extra foil that provides more shielding. Shielded twisted pair cable is used in industrial settings, such as factories, where extra shielding is needed to prevent outside interference from adversely affecting the data on the cable.

UTP cable is measured in gauges. The most common sizes of UTP cable are 22-, 23-, 24-, and 26-gauge unshielded twisted pair cables. UTP cables come in different specifications called categories. The most common are categories 5e (which is an enhanced version of 5), 6, and 7. People (and cable manufacturers) usually shorten the name *Category* to *Cat*, so Category 5 is spoken of as Cat 5. The other versions would be called Cat 3, Cat 5e, Cat 6, Cat 7, and so on. The categories determine, in part, how fast the network can run. Table 13.3 shows some of the categories of UTP cable. You can also refer to Table 2.6 in Chapter 2, "Connectivity," for a recap of the major characteristics.

TABLE 13.3   UTP cable categories

Category	Description
Cat 3	Mainly installed for telephone systems in many office buildings. Commonly called voice-grade cable but has the capability to run up to the older 10 Mbps Ethernet or 16 Mbps Token Ring topology speeds.
Cat 5	No longer a recognized standard; replaced by Cat 5e.
Cat 5e	Known as Cat 5 enhanced. Can be used with 10BaseT, 100BaseT, and 1000BaseT (Gigabit) Ethernet networks. Cables are rated to a max of 328 feet (100 meters). However, Ethernet cabling from the end device to the network device normally consists of three runs: (1) the cable from a patch panel to the wall at a maximum of 295 feet (90 meters), (2) the 16-foot (5 meter) maximum patch cable from the wall to a network device, and (3) a 16-foot (5 meter) patch cable from a patch panel to a switch. The total length of cable from device to patch panel is 328 feet (100 meters). Supports frequencies up to 100 MHz per pair (speeds up to 1 Gbps).
Cat 6	Supports Gigabit Ethernet better than Cat 5e but uses larger-gauge (thicker) cable. Supports frequencies up to 250 MHz per pair (speeds up to 1 Gbps). More stringent specifications to prevent crosstalk (signals from one wire going over into another wire). Commonly used in industry.
Cat 6a	Supports 10GBaseT Ethernet and frequencies up to 500 MHz (speeds up to 10 Gbps).
Cat 7	Backward compatible with Cat 5e and 6. Supports 10GBaseT Ethernet and frequencies up to 600 MHz (speeds up to 10 Gbps).

A special type of UTP or STP cable is plenum cable. A plenum is a building's air circulation space for heating and air conditioning systems. **Plenum cable** is treated with Teflon or alternative fire-retardant materials to make it is less of a fire risk. Plenum cable is less smoke producing and less toxic when burning than regular networking cable.

The alternative to plenum cable is polyvinyl chloride (**PVC**) cable that has a plastic cable insulation or jacket. PVC is cheaper than plenum cable, and it can have flame retardant added to make the cable flame retardant if necessary for compliance with building codes. PVC is usually easier to install than plenum cable.

Terminating Twisted Pair Cable

Twisted pair cable has an RJ-45 connector that has a tang (a little plastic clip) to securely insert the connector into an RJ-45 jack. Tangs frequently get broken, and many times a technician must simply make an Ethernet cable as part of the job. If a tang breaks off, the RJ-45 connector is cut off and a new RJ-45 connector attached. This is known as *terminating* a cable. To create a new cable, you purchase a spool of twisted pair cable, cut off a suitable length, and add an RJ-45 connector to each end.

Twisted pair cable uses either an **RJ-45** (8 conductor) or **RJ-11** (4 conductor) connector. RJ-45 connectors are used with network cabling. Twisted pair cable used with networking has eight copper wires. The wires are grouped in colored pairs (see Figure 13.10). Each pair is twisted together to prevent crosstalk, which occurs when a signal on one wire interferes with the signal on an adjacent wire.

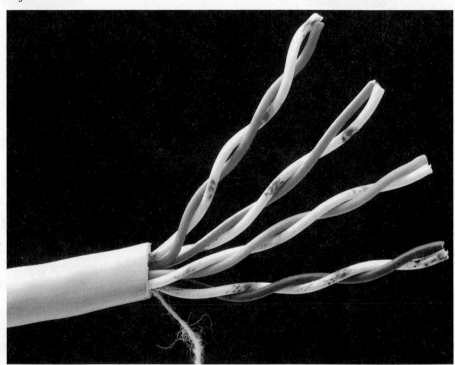

FIGURE 13.10 UTP color pairs

To connect a computer to a switch or network wall outlet, a **straight-through cable** (also known as a patch cable) is used. Both ends of the cable would be wired to the **T568A** standard, or both ends of the cable would be wired to the **T568B** standard (more popular method). When connecting two computers (or two switches) together, a **crossover cable** is used. A crossover cable has one RJ-45 connector created to the T568A standard and the other end to the T568B standard. Figure 13.11 shows the color codes associated with the T568A and T568B standards. Figure 13.12 shows the location of pin 1 on an RJ-45 port and on a connector. Notice in both figures how the tang is pointing down toward the floor.

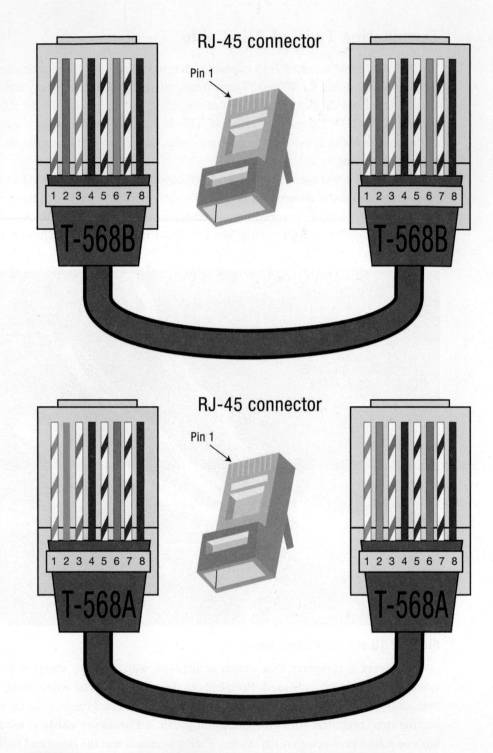

FIGURE 13.11   UTP cabling by color and wiring standards

FIGURE 13.12   Pin 1 on an RJ-45 port and connector

TECH TIP

Network two PCs without a switch or hub

If you have two PCs with Ethernet NICs installed, you can connect them with a crossover cable attached to the RJ-45 jack on each NIC.

To start creating your own cable, the plastic encasement (refer to Figure 13.9) must be stripped away with a **cable stripper** (also known as a **wire stripper**) to expose approximately 1 inch (2 centimeters) of the vinyl insulator that covers the copper conductors. Figure 13.13 shows a cable stripper. A **crimper** that is used to secure the cable to the RJ-45 connector sometimes includes a blade and/or a cable stripper. In the first photo in Figure 13.14, the cable is being stripped of the plastic encasement. It's important not to cut into the vinyl insulator. The second photo in Figure 13.14 shows the vinyl insulator stripped away.

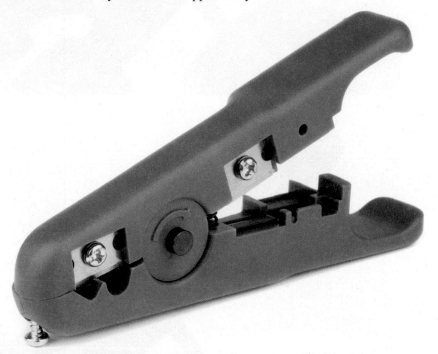

FIGURE 13.13   Cable stripper

After the plastic encasement is removed, untwist the cable pairs and place them in the proper color order. Wiggle each cable back and forth to make it more pliable. Cut the cables straight across, leaving 1/2 inch (1 centimeter) of cable. Insert the cables into the RJ-45 connector in the correct color order. Ensure that the tang points toward the floor.

A common mistake when making a cable is not pushing the wires to the end of the RJ-45 connector. Before crimping, look at the end of the RJ-45 connector. You should see each wire jammed against the end of the RJ-45 connector. You should see what looks like a set of eight gold eyes staring at you when you turn the connector end toward you to verify that the conductors are pushed far enough into the connector before crimping.

FIGURE 13.14   Crimper used as a wire stripper

Another check to do before crimping is ensure the plastic encasement is inside the RJ-45 connector. You do not want the vinyl insulator outside the connector, or data errors can occur. Notice in Figure 13.15 how the blue plastic encasement is in the wider part of the RJ-45 connector. No unprotected wires are outside the RJ-45 connector.

TECH TIP

Push the cable firmly into the jack

It is important to fully insert the UTP cable into the RJ-45 jack and in the standardized order. A common mistake new technicians make is putting on the RJ-45 connector upside down.

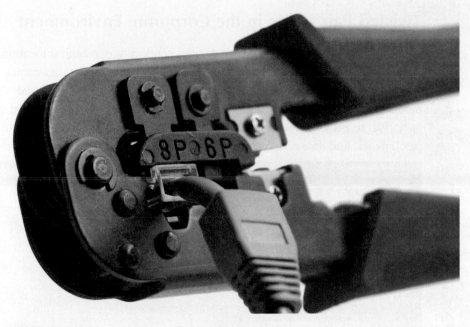

FIGURE 13.15   Crimping an RJ-45 connector

When you have verified the color order, ensured that the eight gold connectors are pushed to the end, and verified the plastic encasement inside the RJ-45 connector, you are ready to crimp. Crimping involves carefully inserting the RJ-45 connector into the crimper (while maintaining the wires pushed firmly into the connector) and pressing the crimper handles together firmly until the cable clicks and releases. Figure 13.15 shows a store-bought Ethernet cable that probably had a broken tang. A store-bought Ethernet cable has a protective sleeve that goes over the RJ-45 connector. The sleeve must be moved back before cutting off the damaged RJ-45 connector and replacing it. The sleeve is slid back over the RJ-45 connector when crimping is complete.

After crimping, you must use a **cable tester** to ensure that the cable is ready for use. Figure 13.16 shows a cable tester. Plug one end of the cable into the RJ-45 jack on the main tester piece (yellow case) and the other end into the RJ-45 cap. Each cable tester is different, so review the instructions, if necessary.

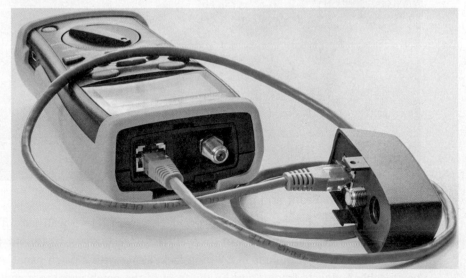

FIGURE 13.16   Cable tester

Twisted Pair Cable in the Corporate Environment

With twisted pair cable, all network devices connect to one central location, such as a patch panel, hub, or switch. Refer to Figure 13.8 to see how straight-through cables connect each network device to a switch. In a corporate environment, a patch panel is used. A **patch panel**, which mounts in a network wiring rack, has network ports on the front of it and wiring connected to the back of it to provide network connectivity. In Figure 13.17, the first photo shows the front of the patch panel, and the second photo shows the back.

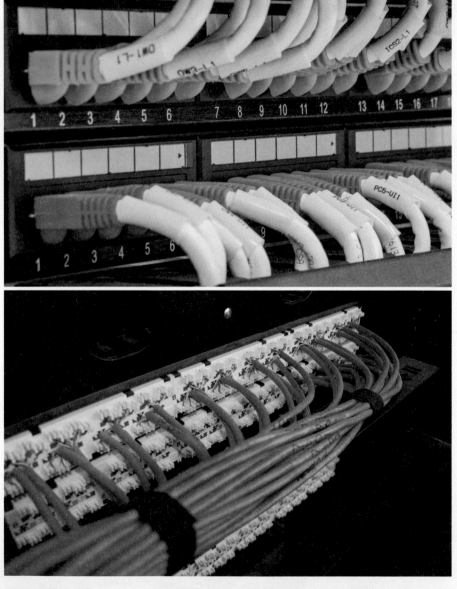

FIGURE 13.17 Front and back of a patch panel

A UTP cable connects from a network device to an RJ-45 wall jack. That wall jack has UTP cabling that goes from the back of the wall jack (see Figures 13.18 and 13.19) to the back of a patch panel. A switch mounts in a wiring rack, along with a patch panel. A straight-through UTP patch cable connects from a port on the front of the patch panel to a switch located in the same network rack. Figure 13.19 shows the cabling from PCs to a switch in a corporate environment.

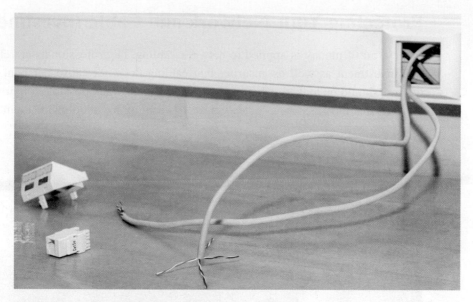

FIGURE 13.18 Network wall jack

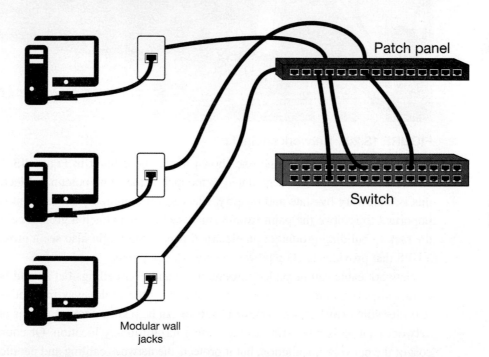

FIGURE 13.19 Corporate network connectivity from PCs to a switch

TECH TIP

Label both cable ends

When installing any type of network cable, you should label both ends with a unique identifier that normally includes the building and/or room number.

Protecting Your Network and Cable Investment

Quite a bit of money is applied to network cabling. IT professionals are charged with protecting this investment as well as ensuring that cabling does not cause personal safety risks. Network devices should be locked in a secure room or cabinet when possible. Figure 13.20 shows network cabinets that have network devices as well as cabling installed inside them.

FIGURE 13.20   Network cabinets

Network racks, such as the one shown inside the cabinet in Figure 13.20, require grounding so that all of the equipment mounted to the rack is the same potential. Electrical codes as to how this is done vary by state and country. Electricians commonly do this, but on painted racks, it is important to remove the paint from a small section and attach a ground cable that connects from the rack to building ground or an electrical panel. You might also see a ground wire connected to a UPS that provides backup power to network equipment.

Network cable can be pulled through walls and over ceilings but should be installed in conduit or raceways (mesh racks or ladder racks that keep the cable away from other things), if possible. A professional **cable management system** can help keep network cables organized. Ensure that network cabling is not a trip or other safety hazard in any location. Of course, this increases the cost of the network installation, but it protects the network cabling and people. Figure 13.21 shows a network closet that is typical of the closets in many companies. Figure 13.22 shows a network wiring rack with a cable management system.

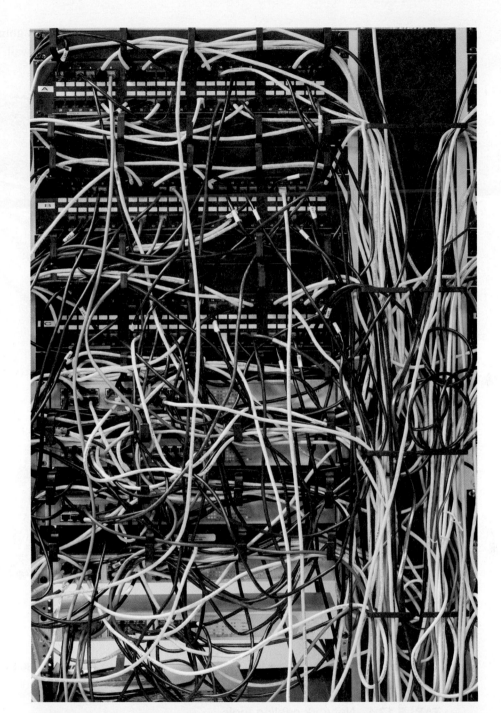

FIGURE 13.21 Messy (and dangerous) network wiring rack

FIGURE 13.22 Cable management system

A ladder rack is a network cable accessory that holds multiple cables going across a room or from one side of the room to a network rack that is located away from the wall. Figure 13.23 shows a network cable ladder rack with bundles of cables.

FIGURE 13.23   Network cable ladder racks

Network Cabling and Troubleshooting Tools

Table 13.4 and Figure 13.24 show and describe network-related tools used in making cable and troubleshooting cable issues.

TABLE 13.4   Network cabling tools

Tool	Description
Cable stripper	Creates straight-through UTP patch cables or crossover cables. (Refer to Figures 13.13 and 13.14.) Also called a wire stripper.
Cable tester	Checks coaxial and UTP cable (depending on the model). (Refer to Figures 13.16 and 13.24.)
Crimper	Permanently attaches an RJ-45 or RJ-11 connector to cable. (Refer to Figure 13.15 to see an RJ-45 connector being crimped.)
Loopback plug	Attaches to a specific port and tests a port or communications circuitry to see if a signal can be sent out and received. If the test succeeds, the port and communication circuits are good.

Tool	Description
Multimeter	Takes voltage, resistance, and current readings. Can be used to check if data racks are grounded. (Refer to Figure 5.6.)
Punch-down tool	Connects network cables to a patch panel (see Figure 13.24) or phone cables to a punch-down block.
Tone generator and probe	A **tone generator** connects to a cable or is inserted into a network jack. The tone generator injects a tone down the cable. The toner **probe** (see Figure 13.25) is touched to the other end of a cable to identify it. The tone generator/toner probe combination can be used to identify cables when they are not labeled or are labeled incorrectly.

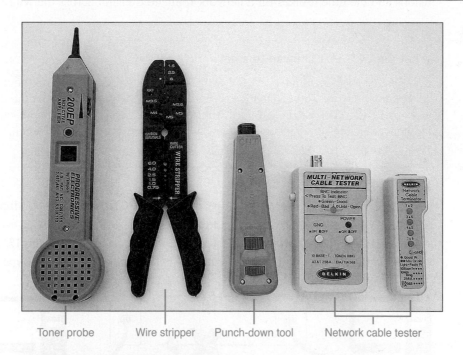

Toner probe   Wire stripper   Punch-down tool   Network cable tester

FIGURE 13.24   Network tools

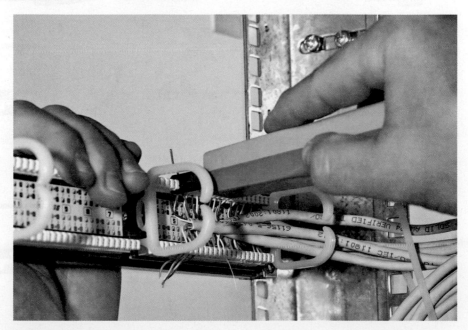

FIGURE 13.25   Punch-down tool

Ethernet Concepts

An Ethernet LAN is the most common type of LAN, and more time must be spent on understanding it because technicians constantly add and remove devices from Ethernet networks. Some issues related to Ethernet include full-duplex and half-duplex transmissions, network slowdowns, and increasing bandwidth.

Ethernet networks were originally designed for **half-duplex** (both directions, but only one direction at a time) transmission on a 10 Mbps bus topology. The more workstations on the same network, the more collisions occur and the more the network slows down. In addition, with half-duplex Ethernet, less than 50% of the 10 Mbps available bandwidth could be used because of collisions and the time it takes for a network frame to transmit across the wire.

> **TECH TIP**
>
> **What does CSMA/CD mean to a network?**
>
> CSMA/CD is the access method used with Ethernet networks: It specifies the rules for how data gets on the network. The CS stands for "Carrier Sense," which means that the PC checks the network cable for other traffic. MA, for "Multiple Access," means that multiple computers can access the network cable simultaneously. CD, which stands for "Collision Detection," provides rules for what happens when computers access the network at the same time.

Today's Ethernet networks support speeds of 10 Mbps, 100 Mbps, 1,000 Mbps (1 Gbps), and 10,000 Mbps (10 Gbps). Most Ethernet NICs are 10/100/1,000, which means they can run at either 10, 100, or 1,000 Mbps using **full duplex** (transmit/receive simultaneously). Figure 13.26 illustrates the difference between half- and full-duplex operations. Table 13.5 lists the different types of Ethernet networks.

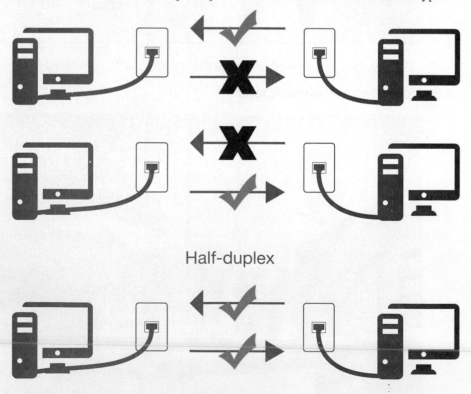

Half-duplex

Full-duplex

FIGURE 13.26   Half-duplex and full-duplex communication

TABLE 13.5 Ethernet standards

Ethernet type	Description
10BaseT	10 Mbps over Cat 3 or Cat 5 UTP cable
100BaseT	100 Mbps over Cat 5 or higher UTP cable
1000BaseT	Also known as Gigabit Ethernet; 1,000 Mbps or 1 Gbps over Cat 5 or higher UTP cable
1000BaseSX	1 Gbps using multi-mode **fiber** (a type of cable made of plastic or glass that carries data using light)
1000BaseLX	1 Gbps using single-mode fiber
10GBaseSR	10 Gbps over multi-mode fiber
10GBaseLX4	10 Gbps over multi-mode and single-mode fiber
10GBaseLR	10 Gbps up to 6.2 miles (10 km) using single-mode fiber
10GBaseER	10 Gbps up to 24.85 miles (40 km) using single-mode fiber
10GBaseT	10 Gbps over UTP (Cat 6 or higher) or STP cable

In the term 100BaseT, the 100 means that the network runs at 100 Mbps. The T at the end of 100BaseT means that the computer uses twisted pair cable. The *1000* in 1000BaseT means that 1,000 Mbps is supported. Base means that the network uses baseband technology. Baseband describes data that is sent over a single channel on a single wire. In contrast, broadband is used in cable TV systems, and it allows multiple channels using different frequencies to be covered over a single wire.

TECH TIP

Switches support full duplex and microsegmentation

With full duplex, collisions are not a problem because full duplex takes advantage of the two cable pairs (one for receiving and one for transmitting). Full-duplex Ethernet creates a direct connection between the transmitting station at one end and the receiving circuits at the other end (thus segmenting the network) and allows 100% of the available bandwidth to be used in each direction.

Full duplex more than doubles the amount of throughput on a network because of the lack of collisions and because it transmits in both directions simultaneously. Full duplex is used when a switch is used to connect network devices together. Full-duplex connectivity uses four wires (two pairs). Two of the wires are used for sending data, and the other two wires are used for receiving data. This creates a collision-free environment. Using a switch instead of a hub as a central connectivity device speeds up Ethernet transactions because a switch has more intelligence than a hub and creates a collision-free, full-duplex environment. Switches are common devices in today's business network environment.

Ethernet over Power

One way to create an Ethernet network without switches, hubs, or a crossover cable between two PCs is to use electrical outlets. **Ethernet over Power** (EoP) (also known as powerline communication) sends network data to EoP modules plugged in to power outlets to extend Ethernet networks. Some EoP modules support wireless connectivity as well. To use EoP, you need a minimum of two EoP modules. One module plugs in to a power outlet near the Internet modem. An Ethernet cable attaches from the Internet modem to the EOP module. A second EoP module connects somewhere else in the home or business, near a device that has trouble connecting to the Internet due to the absence of Ethernet wiring or weak wireless RF signal. Attach an Ethernet cable between the stranded device and the EoP module, and the device will have Internet access. Figure 13.27 shows this concept.

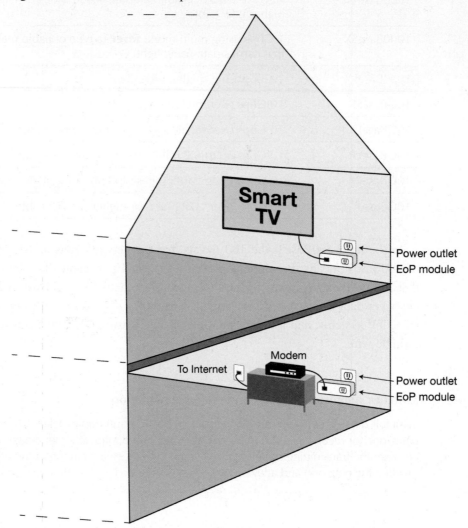

FIGURE 13.27   Ethernet over Power connectivity

The OSI Model

The International Organization for Standardization (ISO) developed a model for network communications known as the OSI (Open Systems Interconnect) model. The **OSI model** is a standard for information transfer across the network. The model sets several guidelines, including (1) how the different transmission media are arranged and interconnected, (2) how network devices that use different languages communicate with one another, (3) how a network device contacts another network device, (4) how and when data gets transmitted across the network, (5) how data is sent to the correct device, and (6) how it is known if the network data was received properly. All these tasks must be handled by a set of rules, and the OSI model provides a structure into which these rules fit.

Can you imagine a generic model for building a car? This model would state that you need some means of steering, a type of fuel to power the car, a place for the driver to sit, safety standards, and so forth. The model would not say what type of steering wheel to put in the car or what type of fuel the car must use but would just be a blueprint for making the car. The OSI model is a similar model in networking.

The OSI model divides networking into different layers so that it is easier to understand (and teach). Dividing the network into distinct layers also helps manufacturers. If a particular manufacturer wants to make a network device that works on Layer 3, the manufacturer has to be concerned only with Layer 3. This division helps networking technologies emerge much faster. Having a layered model also helps in teach network concepts at each layer can be taught as a separate network function.

The layers of the OSI model (starting from the top and working down) are application, presentation, session, transport, network, data link, and physical. Figure 13.28 shows this concept.

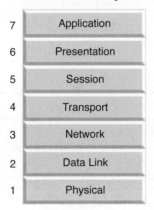

FIGURE 13.28   OSI model layers

Each layer of the OSI model uses the layer below it (except for the physical layer, which is at the bottom). Each layer provides some function to the layer above it. For example, the data link layer cannot be accessed without first going through the physical layer. If communication needs to be performed at Layer 3 (the network layer), the physical and data link layers must be used first.

TECH TIP

OSI mnemonic

A mnemonic to help remember the OSI layers is Active People Seldom Take Naps During Parties. For example, A in Active reminds you of the application layer, P in People reminds you of the presentation layer, and so on.

Each layer of the OSI model from the top down (except for the physical layer) adds information to the data being sent across the network. Sometimes, this information is called a *header*. Figure 13.29 shows how a header is added as the packet travels down the OSI model. When the receiving computer receives the data, each layer removes the header information. Information at the physical layer is normally called *bits*. When referring to information at the data link layer, use the term *frame*. When referring to information at the network layer, use the term *packet*.

Each of the seven OSI model layers performs a unique function and interacts with the layers surrounding it. The bottom three layers handle the physical delivery of data across the network. The top four layers handle the ins and outs of providing accurate data delivery between computers and their individual processes, especially in a multitasking operating system environment.

The OSI model can be confusing when you first learn about networking, but it is important. Understanding the model helps when troubleshooting a network. Knowing where a problem occurred narrows the field of possible solutions. Table 13.6 summarizes the OSI model.

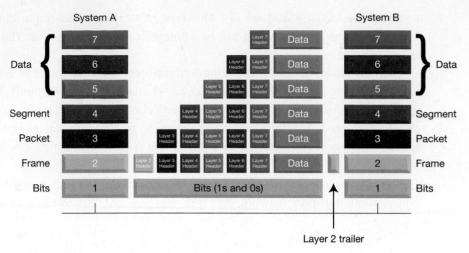

FIGURE 13.29 OSI peer communication

TABLE 13.6 OSI model

OSI model layer	Description
Application	Provides network services (file, print, and messaging) to any software application running on the network. **Firewalls** (devices or software that inspect data for security purposes and filter traffic based on networking protocols and rules established by a network administrator) operate at this layer.
Presentation	Translates data from one character set to another.
Session	Manages the communication and synchronization between network devices.
Transport	Provides the mechanisms for how data is sent, such as reliability and error correction.
Network	Provides path selection between two networks. **Routers** reside at the network layer and send data toward the destination network. Encapsulated data at this layer is called a *packet*. Multilayer switches can operate at this layer.
Data link	Encapsulates bits into frames. Can provide error control. A MAC address is at this layer. Layer 2 switches operate at this layer.
Physical	Defines how bits are transferred and received. Defines the network media, connectors, and voltage levels. Data at this level is called bits. Hubs, cables, and NICs operate at this level.

The TCP/IP Model

A **network protocol** is a data communication language. A protocol suite is a group of protocols that are designed to work together. Transmission Control Protocol/Internet Protocol (**TCP/IP**) is the protocol suite used in networks today. It is the most common network protocol and is required when accessing the Internet. Most companies and homes use TCP/IP as their standard protocol. The TCP/IP protocol suite consists of many protocols, including Transmission Control Protocol (TCP), Internet Protocol (IP), Dynamic Host Configuration Protocol (DHCP), File Transfer Protocol (FTP), and Hypertext Transfer Protocol (HTTP), to name a few. The TCP/IP model describes how information flows through the computer when TCP/IP-based protocols are used. The TCP/IP model has only four layers, in contrast to the seven layers in the theoretical OSI model. Because there are fewer layers and because the TCP/IP model consists of protocols that are in production, it is easier to study and understand networking from a TCP/IP model perspective. Figure 13.30 shows the TCP/IP model and message formatting, and Table 13.7 describes the layers.

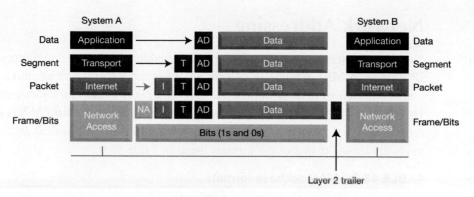

FIGURE 13.30   TCP/IP model and message formatting

TABLE 13.7   TCP/IP model layers

TCP/IP model layer	Description
Application	TCP/IP-based application layer protocols format data specific for the purpose; equivalent to the application, presentation, and session layers of the OSI model. Protocols include HTTP, Telnet, DNS, HTTPS, FTP, TFTP, TLS, SSL, POP, SNMP, IMAP, NNTP, and SMTP.
Transport	Transport layer protocols add port numbers in the header, so the computer can identify which application sends the data. When data returns, this port number allows the computer to determine into which window on the screen to place the data. Protocols include TCP and UDP.
Internet	Sometimes called the internetwork layer, IP is the most common Internet layer protocol. IP adds a source and destination **IP address** to uniquely identify the source and destination network devices. An IP address is a unique 32- or 128-bit number assigned to a NIC.
Network access	Called link layer in the original RFC (Request for Comments). Defines how to format the data for the type of network used. For example, if Ethernet is used, an Ethernet header, including unique source and destination MAC addresses, will be added here. A **MAC address** is a unique 48-bit hexadecimal number burned into a chip on the NIC. The network access layer would define the type of connector used and put the data onto the network, whether it be voltage levels for 1s and 0s on the copper cable or pulses of light for fiber.

Table 13.8 shows what devices operate at the OSI and TCP/IP model layers. Wireless devices are covered later in the chapter.

TABLE 13.8   Devices and the OSI and TCP/IP models

Network devices	OSI layer	TCP/IP layer	Description
Router, wireless router	Network	Internet (internetwork)	Connects two or more networks
Switch, wireless access point, wireless bridge	Data link	Network access	A switch connects devices to a LAN and learns MAC addresses. An access point connects wireless devices to form a WLAN. A wireless bridge connects two networks.
Hub, wireless antenna, cable, connectors	Physical	Network access	A hub connects devices to a LAN. An antenna receives wireless signals. A cable connects a device to a wired network. A connector attaches to a cable.

Network Addressing

Network adapters normally have two types of addresses assigned to them: a MAC address and an IP address. A MAC address is a 48-bit unique number that is burned into a chip located on a NIC and is represented in hexadecimal. A MAC address is unique for every computer on the network. However, the MAC address has no scheme to it except that the first 24 bits represent the manufacturer. The MAC address is known as a Layer 2 address or a physical address. A MAC address is normally shown in one of the formats listed in Table 13.9.

TABLE 13.9   MAC address formats

Address format	Description
00-11-11-71-41-10	Groups of two hexadecimal digits are separated by hyphens.
01:11:11:71:41:10	Groups of two hexadecimal digits are separated by colons.
0111.1171.4110	Groups of four hexadecimal digits are separated by periods.

The IP address is a much more organized way of addressing a computer and is sometimes known as a Layer 3 address, in reference to the OSI network layer. There are two types of IP addresses: IPv4 (IP version 4) and IPv6 (IP version 6). **IPv4** is the most common IP addressing used on LANs. An IPv4 address is a 32-bit number that is entered into a NIC's configuration parameters. This address is used when multiple networks are connected and when accessing the Internet. The IPv4 address is shown using dotted decimal notation, such as 192.168.10.4.

TECH TIP

What is in an IPv4 address?

An IPv4 address is separated into four sections called octets. The octets are separated by periods, and each one represents 8 bits. The numbers that can be represented by 8 bits are 0 to 255.

IPv6 addresses are 128 bits in length and shown in hexadecimal format. IPv6 addresses are used by corporate devices and by some Internet service providers, and more conversions of IPv4 to IPv6 are coming soon. Computers today have both an IPv4 address and IPv6 address assigned. An example of an IPv6 address is fe80::13e:4586:5807:95f7. Each set of four digits represents 16 bits. Anywhere there are just three digits, such as 13e, there is a "silent" zero in front that has been left omitted (013e). Anywhere there are double colons (::), a string of zeros has been omitted. Only one set of double colons is allowed in an IPv6 address. Many network cards are assigned IPv6 addresses, even if IPv6 is not used.

One IPv6 address assigned to a NIC is a link-local address. An IPv6 **link-local address** is used to communicate on a particular network. This address cannot be used to communicate with devices on a different network. A link-local address can be manually assigned or, more commonly, may be automatically assigned. Figure 13.31 shows a home computer that has an IPv6 link-local address that has been automatically assigned. You can also see the IPv4 address.

```
Ethernet adapter Local Area Connection:

   Connection-specific DNS Suffix  . : gateway.2wire.net
   Link-local IPv6 Address . . . . . : fe80::13e:4586:5807:95f7%10
   IPv4 Address. . . . . . . . . . . : 192.168.1.64
   Subnet Mask . . . . . . . . . . . : 255.255.255.0
   Default Gateway . . . . . . . . . : 192.168.1.254
```

FIGURE 13.31   IPv6 link-local address and IPv4 address

IPv4 addresses are grouped into five classes: A, B, C, D, and E. Class A, B, and C addresses are used by network devices. Class D addresses are used for multicasting (sending traffic to a group of devices such as in a distributed video or a web conference session), and Class E addresses are used for experimentation. It is easy to tell which type of IP address is used by a device: All you have to look at is the first number shown in the dotted decimal notation. Table 13.10 shows the common classes of addresses.

TABLE 13.10 Classes of IPv4 addresses

Class	First octet (number) of the IP address
Class A	0 to 127
Class B	128 to 191
Class C	192 to 223

If a computer has the IP address 12.150.172.39, the IP address is a Class A address because the first number is 12. If a computer has the IP address 176.10.100.2, it is a Class B IP address because the first number is 176. A computer with an IP address of 200.1.1.1 has a Class C address. Addresses are also classified as public addresses and private addresses. A **private IP address** is used inside a home or business. This address is not allowed to be transmitted across the Internet. The service provider or company translates the address to a **public IP address** that is seen on the Internet. Table 13.11 shows the private IP address ranges for each of the IPv4 classes.

TABLE 13.11 IPv4 private IP addresses

Class	First octet (number) of an IP address
Class A	10.x.x.x (where the x represents any number from 0 to 255), or 10.0.0.0 through 10.255.255.255
Class B	172.16.x.x through 172.31.x.x, or 172.16.0.0 through 172.31.255.255
Class C	192.168.x.x, or 192.168.0.0 through 192.168.255.255

More IPv4 Addressing

An IP address is broken into two major parts: the network number and the host number. The **network number** is the portion of an IP address that represents which network the computer is on. All computers on the same network have the same network number. The **host address** (or host portion of the address) represents the specific computer on the network. All computers on the same network have unique host numbers; if they didn't, they could not communicate.

The number of bits that represent the network number and the host number depends on which class of IP address is used. With Class A IP addresses, the first 8 bits (the first number) represent the network portion, and the remaining 24 bits (the last three numbers) represent the host number. With Class B IP addresses, the first 16 bits (the first two numbers) represent the network portion, and the remaining 16 bits (the last two numbers) represent the host number. With Class C IP addresses, the first 24 bits (the first three numbers) represent the network portion, and the remaining 8 bits (the last number) represent the host number. Figure 13.32 illustrates this point.

To see how IP addressing works, it is best to use an example. Say that a business has two networks connected with a router. On each network, there are computers and printers. Each of the two networks must have a unique network number. For this example, one network has the network number 193.14.150.0, and the other network has the network number 193.14.151.0. Notice that each network number represents a Class C IP address because the first number is 193.

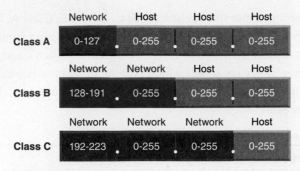

FIGURE 13.32   IP addressing (network and host portions)

With a Class C IP address, the first three numbers represent the network number. The first network uses the numbers 193.14.150 to represent the network part of the IP address. The second network uses the numbers 193.14.151 in the network part of the address. Remember that each network must have a different network part of the IP address from any other network in the organization. The last part of the IP address (the host portion) will be used to assign a number to each network device. On the first network, each device will have a number that starts with 193.14.150 because that is the network part of the number, and it stays the same for all devices on that network. Each device will then have a different number in the last portion of the IP address—for example, 193.14.150.3, 193.14.150.4, and 193.14.150.5.

On the second network, each device will have a number that starts with 193.14.151 because that is the network part of the IP address. The last number in the IP address changes for each network device—for example, 193.14.151.3, 193.14.151.4, 193.14.151.5, and so on. In this example, no device can have a host number that has 0 in the last octet because that number represents the network, and no device can have an IP address where the last octet number of 255 in the host portion of the address because that represents something called the broadcast address. A **broadcast address** is the IP address used to communicate with all devices on a particular network.

In this example, no network device can be assigned the IP addresses 193.14.150.0 or 193.14.151.0 because these numbers represent the two networks. Furthermore, no network device can be assigned the IP addresses 193.14.150.255 or 193.14.151.255 because these numbers represent the broadcast address used with each network. An example of a Class B broadcast is 150.10.255.255. An example of a Class A broadcast is 11.255.255.255. Figure 13.33 shows this configuration.

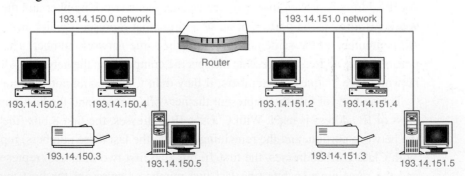

FIGURE 13.33   IP addressing (two networks example)

Notice in Figure 13.33 that each device to the left of the router has an IP address that starts with 193.14.150 (the network number), and each device has a unique last number. The same is true for the devices to the right of the router, except that they are on the 193.14.151.0 network.

VLANs

Another way of creating networks is by using VLANs. A virtual local area network (**VLAN**) is a method used to create multiple networks within a switch. For example, IP phones, PCs, and printers typically connect to a switch, and companies that have switches that support VLANs tend to create separate networks for different types of devices or devices in a particular location. For example, if you had two IP phones, three PCs, and a printer connected to the same switch, you might configure the switch ports that connect to the IP phones as VLAN 17, the switch ports that connect to the PCs as VLAN 18, and the port that connects to the printer as VLAN 19. The IP addressing schemes used within a company commonly include the VLAN number as part of the IP addressing. Notice in Figure 13.34 that the phones have IP addresses 192.168.17.x (where x is a unique number) and that the PCs have IP addresses 192.168.18.x. The printer has the IP address 192.168.19.3.

Switch configured with VLANS*

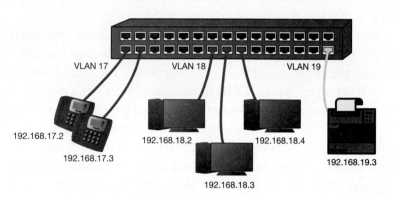

*A switch that supports VLANS has all ports in VLAN 1
unless they are configured otherwise.

FIGURE 13.34 VLANs

Not all switches can be configured with VLANs, but on a switch that does support VLANs, all ports are assigned to VLAN 1 as a default. If a switch does not support VLANs, then all ports need to be considered to be in the same network, and all devices connected to the switch will be in the same network.

Benefits of VLANs include the following:

> Separation of networks at Layer 2
> Reduced broadcast messages
> Easier to apply security
> Easier to apply quality of service (QoS)

Subnet Masks

In addition to assigning a computer an IP address, you must also assign a subnet mask. The **subnet mask** (sometimes shortened to *mask*) is a number that a computer uses to determine which part of the IP address represents the network and which portion represents the host. The default subnet mask for a Class A IP address is 255.0.0.0, the default subnet mask for a Class B IP address is 255.255.0.0, and the default subnet mask for a Class C IP address is 255.255.255.0. Table 13.12 recaps this important information.

TABLE 13.12   IP address information

Class	First number	Network/host number	Subnet mask
A	0–127	N.H.H.H*	255.0.0.0
B	128–191	N.N.H.H*	255.255.0.0
C	192–223	N.N.N.H*	255.255.255.0

*N = network number; H = host number

Sometimes subnet masks are shown with a slash (/) followed by a number. The number represents how many consecutive 1s are in the subnet mask. For example, /8 indicates that there are eight consecutive 1s in the subnet mask, or 11111111.00000000.00000000.000000000. Notice that the subnet mask is all 0s after the eight 1s are shown. This is known as showing the subnet mask in a prefix notation format. A technician might have to refer to network documentation, and the subnet mask to use will be shown in prefix notation format. The prefix notation format for a Class A address is /8, Class B is /16, and Class C is /24.

A subnet mask does not always have to follow classful boundaries. Sometimes, a technician might see a subnet mask that looks like the following examples: 255.255.254.0 or /23, 255.255.255.192 or /26, and 255.255.255.240 or /28. These are known as classless inter-domain routing (CIDR) subnet masks. **CIDR** (pronounced "cider") is a method of allocating IP addresses based on the number of host addresses needed for a particular network. Because the subnet mask dictates where the network portion ends and where the host portion begins, CIDR subnet masks are numbers different from the standard 255.0.0.0, 255.255.0.0, and 255.255.255.0 subnet masks.

So you understand the concept, let's look at how a /23 subnet mask becomes 255.255.254.0. The /23 means there are 23 1s in a row in the subnet mask, with the rest being 0s; keep in mind that there are just eight 1s in each of the subnet mask sections where you enter the number. Write down the 23 1s with only eight digits in each section. Place 0s after the 1s for the remaining digits, keeping in mind that the subnet mask, like an IP address, has 32 bits. Then you perform simple binary-to-decimal conversion to get the subnet mask in dotted decimal notation, as it must be when you enter it on a network device:

11111111.11111111.11111110.00000000
  255 . 255 . 254 . 0

Appendix A, "Subnetting Basics," goes into CIDR in a lot more detail.

Wireless Networks Overview

Even though wireless devices are covered elsewhere in the book (when discussing mice, keyboards, and mobile devices), no networking chapter would be complete without a thorough knowledge of wireless networking. Wireless networks are networks that transmit data over air using either infrared (1 THz to 400 THz range) or radio frequencies (**2.4 GHz** or **5 GHz** range). Most wireless networks in homes and businesses use radio frequencies. Wireless networks operate at Layers 1 and 2 of the OSI model.

Wireless networks are popular in home and business computer environments and are great in places that are not conducive to having cabling, such as outdoor centers, convention centers, bookstores, coffee shops, and hotels, as well as between buildings and in between nonwired rooms in homes or businesses. Wireless networks can be installed indoors or outdoors.

TECH TIP

What if I want wireless connectivity for my desktop computer?

Desktop workstations usually have integrated RJ-45 Ethernet connections, but for wireless networking, a wireless NIC is required.

Laptops and portable devices are frequently used to connect to wireless networks and have wireless capabilities integrated into them. Laptops also normally have wired network connections. A technician must be familiar with installation, configuration, and troubleshooting of both wired and wireless technologies.

Wireless Network Standards

The IEEE 802.11 committees define standards for wireless networks, and they can be quite confusing. Table 13.13 shows the current and proposed wireless network standards.

TABLE 13.13 IEEE 802.11 standards

Standard	Purpose
802.11a	Came after the 802.11b standard. Has speeds up to 54 Mbps but is incompatible with 802.11b. Operates in the 5 GHz range.
802.11b	Operates in the 2.4000 and 2.4835 GHz radio frequency ranges, with speeds up to 11 Mbps.
802.11e	Provides standards related to quality of service.
802.11g	Operates in the 2.4 GHz range, with speeds up to 54 Mbps, and is backward compatible with 802.11b.
802.11i	Relates to wireless network security and includes AES (Advanced Encryption Standard) for protecting data.
802.11n	Operates in the 2.4 and 5 GHz ranges and is backward compatible with the older 802.11a, b, and g equipment. Speeds up to 600 Mbps using MIMO antennas. Maximum of four simultaneous data streams.
802.11ac	Operates only in the 5 GHz range, which makes it backward compatible with 802.11n and 802.11a. Speeds up to 6.93 Gbps. Maximum of eight simultaneous data streams using MU-MIMO antennas.
802.11ad	Also known as WiGig and works in the 60 GHz range. Speeds up to 6.76 Gbps.

Bluetooth

Bluetooth is a wireless technology for PANs. Bluetooth devices include audio/visual products, automotive accessories, keyboards, mice, phones, printer adapters, cameras, wireless cell phone headsets, sunglasses with radios and wireless speakers, and other small wireless devices. Bluetooth works in the 2.4 GHz range, similarly to business wireless networks. Traditional Bluetooth has three classes of devices (1, 2, and 3) that have a range of less than 30 feet (less than 10 meters), 33 feet (10 meters), and 328 feet (100 meters), respectively, and a maximum transfer rate of 24 Mbps. Bluetooth version 5 is a newer standard that supports longer distances. Vendors tout ranges of up to 800 feet (243 meters) for version 5, although such distances are not defined in the standard.

Bluetooth supports both data and voice transmissions. Up to eight Bluetooth devices can be connected in a piconet or PAN (a small network). Bluetooth has always had security features integrated into it, including 128-bit encryption (scrambling of data, as discussed later in this chapter) that uses a modified form of SAFER+ (Secure and Fast Encryption Routine). Bluetooth is a viable network solution for short-range wireless solutions. Figure 13.35 shows a Bluetooth cell phone headset.

FIGURE 13.35   Bluetooth cell phone headset

A Bluetooth network provides computer-to-computer connectivity between Bluetooth devices. Each computer must support a PAN to join the network. In Windows 7/8, use *Devices and Printers* > *Add a Device* (or *Add a Printer*). In Windows 10, use *Settings* > *Devices* > *Bluetooth*. Review Chapter 10, "Mobile Devices," for complete installation steps. Chapters 2 and 10 provide more information on how to configure and troubleshoot Bluetooth connectivity.

> **TECH TIP**
>
> **Missing Bluetooth section of the Control Panel**
>
> If the Bluetooth Devices Windows Control Panel does not display or if the Bluetooth icon is not in the notification area on the taskbar, type `bthprops.cpl` at a command prompt.

Wireless Network Components

The most common components of a wireless network are wireless NICs, access points, wireless bridges, and wireless routers. Table 13.14 describes the purposes of these parts.

TABLE 13.14   Common wireless devices

Wireless device	Description
Access point (AP)	The central connecting point for a wireless network. Coordinates wireless access for wireless devices. Commonly connects to a wired network.
Wireless **bridge**	A physical device or software that connects two or more networks. Could connect a wireless network to a wired network. An example of a wireless bridge is a building where all devices connect wirelessly to the bridge. The bridge connects to the wired network, which eventually connects to the Internet. Many access points or wireless routers can be placed in bridged mode.
Wireless NIC	Integrated into a wireless device, such as a laptop, smartphone, or tablet.
Wireless router	An AP/router device that normally has both wireless capability and a few wired Ethernet ports.

Major types of wireless NICs include integrated ports, USB, and PCIe. Figure 13.36 shows a wireless USB NIC with a detachable antenna.

FIGURE 13.36   Wireless USB NIC

To determine whether you have a wireless NIC installed on a Windows-based device, perform the following steps:

> Windows 7/8: Access the *Network and Sharing Center* Control Panel > *Change Adapter Settings* link on the left > *Wi-Fi* appears in the window, if installed.

> Windows 10: Access *Settings* > *Network & Internet* > *Wi-Fi* appears in the window, if installed.

Figure 13.37 shows the Network Connections windows of a Windows computer with a wireless NIC installed.

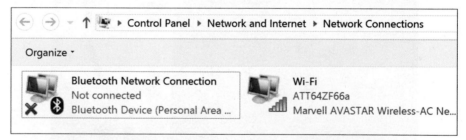

FIGURE 13.37   Wireless NIC in Network Connections window

A wireless access point (AP) is a device that receives and transmits data from multiple computers that have wireless NICs installed. The AP can be a standalone unit or can be integrated into an ADSL router, as shown in Figure 13.38. It is the wireless AP part of the router that needs the three antennas shown.

FIGURE 13.38   Access point integrated with an ADSL router

Wireless routers commonly have switch ports built into them. This is referred to as having **router/switch functionality**. You might hear these referred to as being a router/switch, or they might just be called a wireless router, but regardless of the name, such a device has switch ports integrated as shown in Figure 13.39. A wireless router is used as any router to connect devices between networks such as a home network and the Internet. The switch part of the device is used to create a wired LAN, and each wired device would have an Ethernet cable that runs between the device and the switch port on the wireless router.

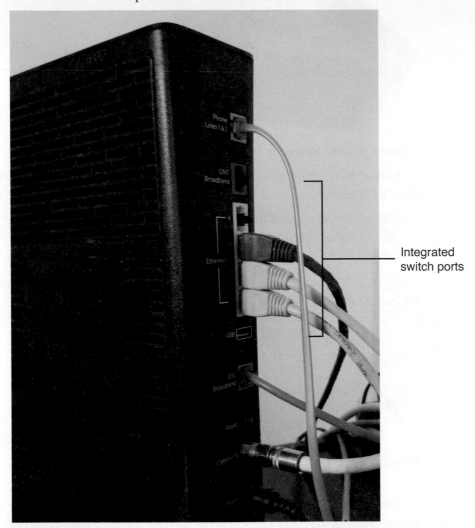

FIGURE 13.39   Wireless router with integrated switch ports

Wireless Network Design

The easiest way to describe an access point is to think of it as a network hub, but instead of connecting wired devices and sharing bandwidth, the AP connects wireless devices that share bandwidth. When a wireless network or device is in **infrastructure mode**, an AP is part of the wireless network. The alternative to infrastructure mode is **ad hoc mode**, in which two wireless devices communicate directly with one another (without an AP). This was discussed in Chapter 9, "Printers," in relationship to wireless printers. Figure 13.40 shows a wireless network with an access point and multiple wireless devices.

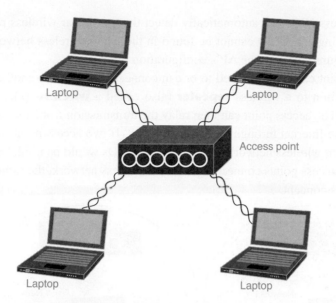

FIGURE 13.40   Wireless network

It is common for a home network to use an integrated services router that allows wireless and wired connectivity. Figure 13.41 shows how a wireless access point connects in this type of environment. Notice how the access point connects to a wired network and gives the wireless devices access to the Internet.

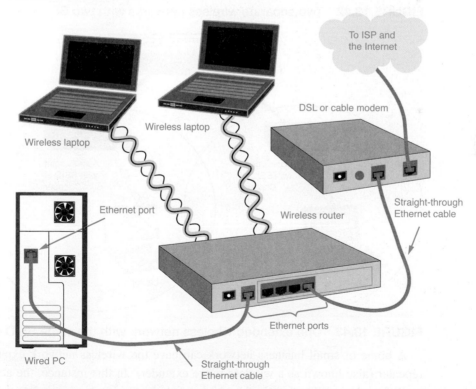

FIGURE 13.41   Wireless and wired network connectivity

Each access point can handle 30 to 250 wireless devices, depending on the vendor, wireless network environment, amount of usage, and type of data sent. Each AP is assigned a service set identifier (**SSID**). It is common for an AP to have a default SSID that can be changed. An SSID is a set of 32 alphanumeric characters used to differentiate between different wireless networks. An AP broadcasts the SSID by default, but this setting can be changed. When the AP is broadcasting the SSID, wireless NICs can automatically detect that particular wireless network. When the AP is not broadcasting (the SSID cannot be found in the list of wireless networks), the SSID can be manually configured through the AP's configuration window.

An access point can also be wired to or can connect wirelessly to another AP, have a wired or wireless connection to a wireless **repeater** (also called a **wireless extender**), or connect to a wired network. The access point can then relay the transmission from a wireless device to another network or to the Internet through the wired network. If two access points are used and they connect two different wireless networks, two different SSIDs would be used. Figure 13.42 shows this concept. If two access points connect to the same wireless network, the same SSID is used. Figure 13.43 shows this concept.

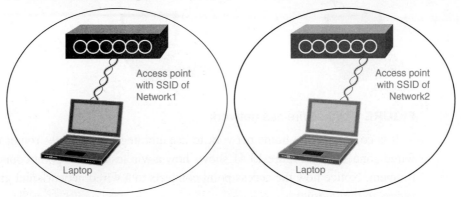

FIGURE 13.42   Two separate wireless networks with two SSIDs

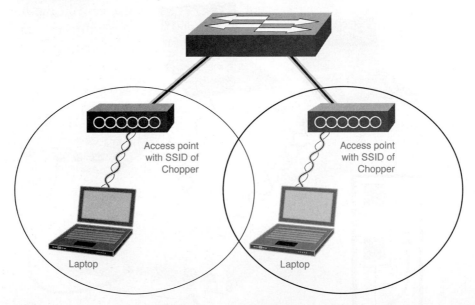

FIGURE 13.43   One extended wireless network with the same SSID on both APs

A home or small business network can have the wireless network expanded using a wireless repeater (also known as a wireless range extender). In this instance, the access point cannot normally be connected to the wired LAN. Instead, the repeater access point attaches to a "root" access point. The repeater access point allows wireless devices to communicate with it and relays the data to the other access point. Both access points will have the same SSID. Figure 13.44 shows this concept.

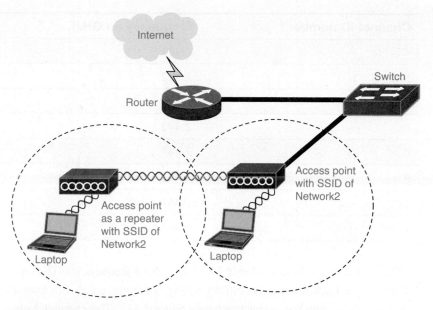

FIGURE 13.44 Access point as a repeater

Power over Ethernet (PoE)

Corporate APs are commonly powered through the attached Ethernet cable that goes from the mounted AP to a switch. The switch provides the power through the Ethernet cable, using a standard called Power over Ethernet (**PoE**). A switch that has PoE capability is sometimes called a **PoE switch**. If the switch does not support PoE, a **PoE injector** (sometimes called power injector) is needed to inject DC voltage power. Figure 13.45 demonstrates these concepts.

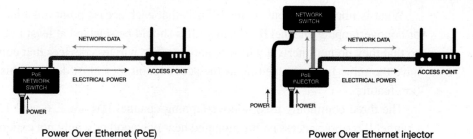

Power Over Ethernet (PoE)   Power Over Ethernet injector

FIGURE 13.45 AP with PoE and PoE injector

Wireless Channel ID

In addition to having an SSID, an access point can be configured with a number known as a channel ID. The **channel ID** (sometimes called a **channel**) defines at what frequency the access point operates. With APs that have a 2.4 GHz antenna, up to 14 channels are available, depending on where in the world the wireless network is deployed. In the United States, only 11 channels are used; they are listed in Table 13.15.

TABLE 13.15 Wireless frequency channels

Channel ID number	Frequency (in GHz)
1	2.412
2	2.417
3	2.422

Channel ID number	Frequency (in GHz)
4	2.427
5	2.432
6	2.437
7	2.442
8	2.447
9	2.452
10	2.457
11	2.462

The frequencies shown in Table 13.15 are center frequencies. The center frequencies are spaced 5 MHz apart. Each channel is actually a range of frequencies. For example, the channel 1 range is 2.401 to 2.423, with the center frequency being 2.412. The channel 2 range is 2.406 to 2.428, with the center frequency being 2.417.

TECH TIP

Channel ID must match

The channel ID (frequency) must be the same between an access point and a wireless NIC for communication to occur between any wireless devices on the same network.

What is important about channel IDs is that each access point must have a different frequency or nonoverlapping channel ID. Channel IDs should be selected at least five channel numbers apart so that they do not interfere with one another. The wireless devices that connect to an access point have the same frequency setting as the access point. For most devices, this is an automatic detection feature.

The three commonly used nonoverlapping channel IDs are 1, 6, and 11. By using these three channel IDs, three access points mounted near one another would not experience interference from the other two. This is because each center frequency does not overlap with the adjacent frequency channels. Figure 13.46 shows this concept.

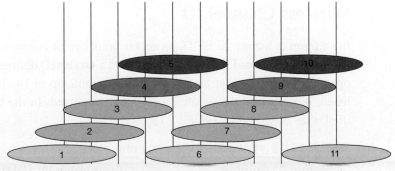

802.11b, g, and n Center Frequencies (in GHz)   2.412 2.417 2.422 2.427 2.432 2.437 2.442 2.447 2.452 2.457 2.462

FIGURE 13.46   802.11b/g/n 2.4 GHz nonoverlapping channels

Notice in Figure 13.46 that each center frequency is 5 MHz from the next center frequency. Also notice that each channel is actually a range of frequencies, shown by the shaded ovals. Channels 1, 6, and 11 clearly do not overlap and do not interfere with each other. Other nonoverlapping channel combinations could be Channels 2 and 7, Channels 3 and 8, Channels 4 and 9, and Channels 5 and 10. The combination of Channels 1, 6, and 11 is preferred because it gives you three channels with which to work. Figure 13.47 shows a different way of looking at how Channels 1, 6, and 11 do not overlap.

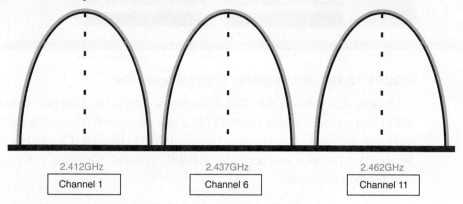

2.412GHz	2.437GHz	2.462GHz
Channel 1	Channel 6	Channel 11

FIGURE 13.47   2.4 GHz channel IDs 1, 6, and 11

Figure 13.48 shows how the three nonoverlapping channels can be used to attain extended coverage even with multiple access points.

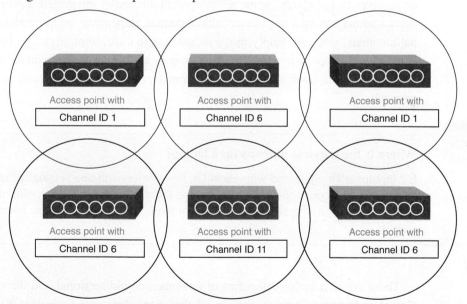

FIGURE 13.48   802.11b/g/n nonoverlapping channel IDs

With 802.11a, 12 20 MHz channels are available in the 5 GHz range. 802.11n supports 20 and 40 MHz channels. 802.11ac supports 20, 40, 80, and 160 MHz channels. The 5 GHz range has three subranges called Unlicensed National Information Infrastructure (UNII): UNII-1, UNII-2, and UNII-3. Before 2014, UNII-1 was for indoor use only, UNII-2 for both indoor and outdoor use, and UNII-3 for outdoor use only. Now all bands can be used for indoor and outdoor usage. Figure 13.49 shows the 5 GHz channels.

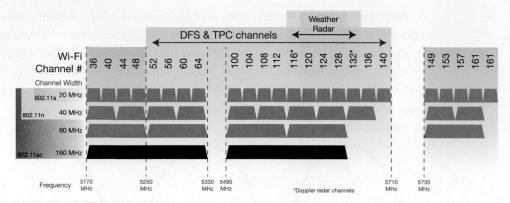

FIGURE 13.49   802.11 a/n/ac 5 GHz channel IDs

Devices that work in the UNII-2 frequency ranges must support dynamic frequency selection (**DFS**) and transmit power control (TPC) to avoid interference with military applications. These two terms are most often shortened to simply DFS channels. Channels 120, 124, and 128 are used for terminal Doppler weather radar (TDWR) systems. Channels 116 and 132 may optionally be used for Doppler radar.

Antenna Basics

Wireless cards and access points can have either external or built-in antennas. An antenna radiates or receives radio waves. Some access points also have integrated antennas. Wireless NICs and access points can also have detachable antennas, depending on the make and model. With external antennas, you can simply move an antenna to a different angle to obtain a better connection. With some laptops, you must turn the laptop to a different angle to attach to an access point or get a stronger signal (and, therefore, faster transfers). Antenna placement is important in a wireless network.

TECH TIP

Where is the wireless antenna on a laptop?

For laptops with integrated wireless NICs, the wireless antenna is usually built in to the laptop display for best connectivity. This is because the display is the tallest point of the laptop and therefore closest to the wireless receiving antenna. The quality of these integrated antennas is diverse.

There are two major categories of antennas: omnidirectional and directional. An **omnidirectional antenna** radiates energy in all directions. Integrated wireless NICs use omnidirectional antennas. Refer to Figure 10.88 to see how the antenna wires attach to two posts on the wireless NIC. These wires connect the antenna to the wireless NIC. If a laptop always has low signal strength, ensure that these two wires are attached.

A **directional antenna** radiates energy in a specific direction. Directional antennas are frequently used to connect two buildings together or to limit wireless connectivity outside a building. Each antenna has a specific radiation pattern (sometimes called a propagation pattern), which is the direction(s) the radio frequency is sent or received. It is the coverage area for the antenna that is normally shown in a graphical representation in the antenna manufacturer's specifications. Figure 13.50 shows the difference in radiation patterns between omnidirectional and directional antennas.

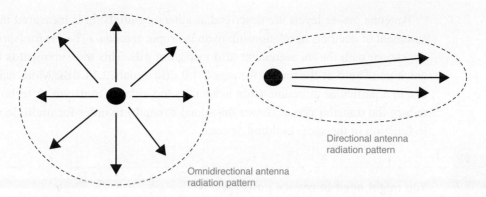

Directional antenna
radiation pattern

Omnidirectional antenna
radiation pattern

FIGURE 13.50   **Basic antenna radiation patterns**

A wireless network installer must be familiar with an antenna's radiation pattern so that the appropriate type of antenna can be chosen for the installation. As a signal is radiated from an antenna, some of the signal is lost. Attenuation is the amount of signal loss of a radio wave as it travels (is propagated) through air. Attenuation, which is sometimes called *path loss*, is measured in decibels (dB). The decibel is a value that represents a measure of the ratio between two signal levels.

Factors that affect an antenna's path loss are the distance between the transmitting antenna and the receiving antenna, any obstructions between the two antennas, and how high the antenna is mounted. Another factor that affects wireless transmission is interference, including radio frequencies being transmitted using the same frequency range and external noises. Other wireless devices, wireless networks, cordless phones, and microwave ovens are common sources of interference.

TECH TIP

What is the maximum distance of a wireless network?

The maximum distance of a wireless network depends on the wireless network standard used, the antenna attached to the AP, and the attenuation experienced.

An important concept related to antennas is gain, and to understand gain, an isotropic antenna must be discussed. An isotropic antenna is not real; it is an imaginary antenna that is perfect in that it theoretically transmits an equal amount of power in all directions. The omnidirectional radiation pattern previously shown in Figure 13.50 would be the pattern of an isotropic antenna. A lot of ceiling-mounted APs have omnidirectional antennas. Figure 13.51 shows an AP that could be mounted on the ceiling and have integrated omnidirectional antennas.

FIGURE 13.51   Ceiling-mounted AP

Antenna power levels are described as antenna gain. Gain is measured in dBi, which is a measurement of decibels in relationship to an isotropic antenna. (The *i* is for *isotropic*.) Some antennas are shown with the measurement dBd instead of dBi. This measurement is referenced to a dipole antenna. (The *d* at the end is for *dipole*.) 0 dBd equals 2.14 dBi. More gain means more coverage in a particular direction. Gain is actually logarithmic in nature. A technician must sometimes reduce the transmit power (lower the signal strength) in order for multiple wireless access points to function in the same building or area.

TECH TIP

You might need to reduce power levels

If an open wireless network is being used by adjacent businesses, reduce the power level of the antenna to reduce the wireless network coverage area.

Imagine that a round balloon is blown up. The balloon represents an isotropic radiation pattern: It extends in all directions. Push down on the top of the balloon, and the balloon extends out more horizontally than it does vertically. Push on the side of the balloon, and the balloon extends more in one horizontal directional than the side being pushed. Now think of the balloon's shape as an antenna's radiation pattern. Antenna designers can change the radiation pattern of an antenna by changing the antenna's length and shape, similarly to how the look of a balloon can be changed by pushing on it in different directions. In this way, different antennas can be created to serve different purposes.

TECH TIP

Understanding gain

A 3 dB gain is twice the antenna output power. 10 dB is 10 times the power, 13 dB is approximately 20 times the power, and 20 dB is 100 times the power. Gain that is shown with a negative value means there is a power loss. For example, a –3 dB gain means the power is halved.

A **site survey** is an examination of an area to determine the best wireless hardware placement. To conduct such a survey, temporarily mount an access point (or use a telescoping pole to place it at different heights). With a laptop that has a wireless NIC and site survey software (or a WiFi analyzer/WiFi locator, as mentioned in Chapter 10 and described later in this section), walk around the wireless network area to see the coverage range. Some vendors provide site survey software with their wireless NICs.

A site survey can also be conducted by double-clicking the network icon on the taskbar. The signal strength is shown in the window that appears. Move the access point as necessary to avoid attenuation and obtain the largest coverage area. Radio waves are affected by obstructions such as walls, trees, rain, snow, fog, and buildings, so for a larger project, a site survey may need to be done over a period of time. You can see the wireless antenna signal strength in the notification area part of the taskbar. You can also see it from within the wireless NIC properties window. Figure 13.52 shows a laptop wireless antenna signal strength display on a laptop.

FIGURE 13.52 Signal strength

The higher the decibel rating, the better the signal

The type of radio antenna and antenna gain also affect the signal strength. However, no matter how good the antenna, as a wireless device is moved farther away from an access point or another wireless device, the more attenuation occurs. Walls, trees, obstacles, and other radio waves can cause attenuation.

A **WiFi analyzer** or wireless locator can determine whether there are wireless networks or hotspots in the area. Wireless devices can also be attached to pets, people, keys, remotes, and so on. A WiFi analyzer or wireless locator device can locate these devices. A phone or mobile device app can also locate a powered mobile device or locate a person who has a mobile device with this enabled.

Many different types of antennas exist, but four common ones are parabolic, Yagi, patch, and dipole. Parabolic antennas can come in either grid or dish type models and are usually used in outdoor environments. Parabolic dishes provide the greatest distances in a wireless network. Parabolic dish antennas may not come with mounting hardware, so you should research whether additional hardware is needed before purchasing one.

Other antennas include Yagi, patch, MIMO, and dipole. A Yagi antenna can be used indoors or outdoors, depending on the manufacturer. It is used for long-distance communication and normally is not large or difficult to mount. A patch antenna can also be used indoors or outdoors. Patch antennas can be mounted to a variety of surfaces, including room columns or walls.

Multiple input/multiple output (**MIMO**) uses multiple 2.4 GHz and 5 GHz antennas. Figure 13.53 shows an example of MIMO transmissions. Note that although each client that attaches to an AP using MIMO can have multiple data streams, the AP handles one client at a time.

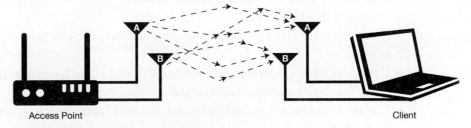

Access Point   Client

FIGURE 13.53 MIMO transmissions

MIMO antennas may be external or built in to a wireless device. Greater wireless speeds can be achieved by using multiple antennas. 802.11n and 802.11ac radios are defined by how many antennas can transmit and receive as well as the number of data streams supported. The documentation is commonly in a number formatted such as 2x2:1 or 4x4:4 (the maximum for an 802.11n device). The first number is the maximum number of antennas that can transmit. The second number is the number of antennas that can receive data. The last number is the number of data streams supported. 802.11ac uses multi-user MIMO (**MU-MIMO**) and allows up to eight simultaneous streams. MU-MIMO serves multiple devices simultaneously, whereas with pre-802.11ac implementations, an AP serves only one user at a time.

Wireless Data Transfer Speeds

The data transfer speed between a wireless NIC and an access point or another wireless device is automatically negotiated for the fastest transfer possible. The farther away from an access point a wireless device is located, the lower the speed. A low radio frequency signal (or **low RF signal**) could simply mean the device is too far from the access point. Move closer or change the angle of the device to get a better signal. Figure 13.54 shows this concept.

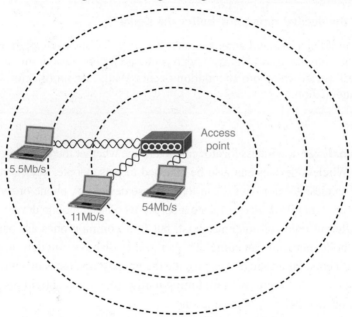

FIGURE 13.54 AP speed ranges

End-User Device Configuration Overview

When you are connecting a device to a wired or wireless network, many things might have to be done, such as the following:

> Give the computer a unique name and optionally join a workgroup or domain.
> Configure IP addressing.
> If the computer connects to a workgroup network, file and print sharing might need to be enabled.
> If the device is on a corporate network, the device might have to be put on the domain.
> Name the device a unique name on the network.
> If a wireless device is being configured, the SSID and possibly security parameters need to be entered.

TECH TIP

How to name a computer

In Windows, name a computer using the *System* section of the Control Panel. Each device on the same network must be given a unique name.

Adding a Computer to a Windows Domain

In a corporate environment, computers are in a network domain. This means that all the network devices are registered with (joined to) one or more network servers, called *domain controllers*, as shown in Figure 13.55.

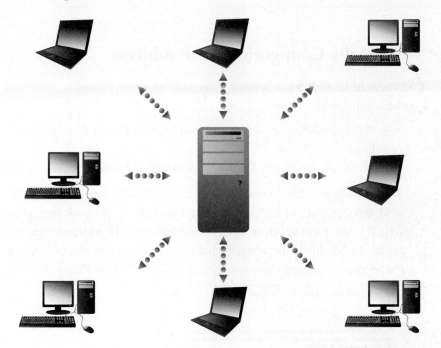

FIGURE 13.55   Network domain

A technician who has a domain user account that has the appropriate permission can add devices to the domain. On a Windows computer, use the *System* Control Panel to access the *Change Settings* link in the Computer Name, Domain, and Workgroup Settings section > from the Computer Name tab, select *Network ID* button > *This Computer Is Part of a Business Network* radio button > *Next* > *My Company Uses a Network with a Domain* > *Next* > *Next* > enter a domain user account name that has permission to add a computer to the domain and password > enter a computer name and the domain name > *Next*. Restart the computer.

With macOS, use the *System Preferences* option by clicking the Apple in the top-left corner > *Accounts* > select *Lock* > *Join* button > *Open Directory Utility* button > select *Lock* > highlight *Active Directory* and select the pencil icon > enter the domain name and a unique computer ID > *Bind* button > enter the domain user account name/password that has permission to add a computer to the domain.

Configuring an End-User Device: Addressing

No matter what device connects to a wired or wireless network, the **end-user device configuration** includes an IP address so that it is uniquely identified and can communicate on the network. Every device on a wired and wireless network needs an IP address and a subnet mask configured. The IP address is what makes the network device unique and allows it to be reached by other network devices. There are two ways to get IP addressing information: (1) statically define the IP address and subnet mask or (2) dynamically obtain the address by using DHCP. The device also needs a default gateway IP address in order to communicate with other networks.

My computer's IP address changes

The IP address can change each time a computer boots because with DHCP you can configure the DHCP server to issue an IP address for a specific amount of time.

Statically Configuring an IP Address

When an IP address is statically defined, someone manually enters an IP address and mask into the computer as follows:

> Windows 7/8: Access *Network and Sharing Center* Control Panel > *Change Adapter Settings* link.
> Windows 10: access *Settings* > *Network & Internet* > *Change Adapter Options* link.

Most support staff do not statically define IP addresses except for devices that are important network devices, such as web servers, database servers, network servers, routers, or switches. Instead, DHCP is used. However, in home-wired networks, IP addresses are sometimes statically assigned. Figure 13.56 shows the window that appears when you right-click a particular adapter and select *Properties > Internet Protocol Version 4 (TCP/IPv4) > Properties* button.

FIGURE 13.56   IP address configuration

What happens if you assign the same IP address to two devices?

Entering an IP address that is a duplicate of another network device renders the new network device inoperable on the network and could affect the other device's traffic as well.

Using DHCP

Dynamic host configuration protocol (**DHCP**) is a protocol used to assign IP addresses to network devices. A **DHCP server** (software configured on a network server, router, or multifunction router/AP) contains a pool of IP addresses. When a network device has been configured for DHCP and it boots, the device sends out a DHCP request for an IP address. A DHCP server responds to this request and issues an IP address to the network device. DHCP makes IP addressing easy and keeps network devices from being assigned duplicate IP addresses.

An important configuration on a DHCP server is a **DHCP reservation**, which is an IP address reserved for a particular device such as a server or printer. Instead of statically assigning an IP address to a device, a technician enters the physical address (the MAC address) of the device, such as a network printer, into the DHCP server and the IP address to be assigned to the device. No other device will get that IP address, and the device will always get the reserved IP address. On the DHCP server, each network is configured with a DHCP pool. A technician can also create a range of reserved IP addresses that will not be issued to network devices by the DHCP server but can be statically configured on the device as an alternative to making an individual reservation on the DHCP server for each device. Figure 13.57 shows this concept.

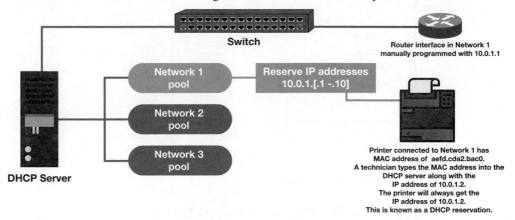

FIGURE 13.57   DHCP reservations

To configure **client-side DHCP** in Windows, access the *Network and Sharing Center* Control Panel > access the *Change Adapter Settings* link > right-click or tap and briefly hold on the wired and wireless NIC and select *Properties* > double-click or double-tap on the *Internet Protocol Version 4 (TCP/IPv4)* option > ensure the *Obtain an IP Address Automatically* radio button is enabled. Refer to Figure 13.56 to see this option.

> **TECH TIP**
>
> **Watch out for duplicate IP address messages**
>
> If a device displays a message relating to a duplicate IP address, check the device to see if a static IP address has been assigned (and the DHCP server issued the same address to a different device or vice versa). If a computer cannot communicate on a network, verify that the computer received an IP address using the `ipconfig` command. If a computer cannot communicate on a remote network, use the `ipconfig` command to verify the computer received a default gateway.

APIPA

Windows computers support automatic private IP addressing (**APIPA**), which assigns an IP address and mask to the computer when a DHCP server is not available but continues trying to contact the server in 5 minute intervals. The IP addresses assigned are 169.254.0.1 to 169.254.255.254. No two computers get the same IP address. If you can connect to other computers on your local network but cannot reach the Internet or other networks, it is likely that the DHCP server is down and Windows has automatically assigned an APIPA address. To determine if APIPA is configured, open a command prompt window and type `ipconfig /all`. If you see the words *Autoconfiguration Enabled Yes,* APIPA is turned on. If the last word is *No*, APIPA is disabled.

Alternative IP Address

An **alternative configuration** is used when a DHCP server cannot assign an IP address, such as when there are network problems or the DHCP server is down. An **alternative IP address** could also be used on a laptop when DHCP is used at work, but addresses are statically assigned at home, for example. Figure 13.58 shows the *Alternate Configuration* tab settings. Note that this tab appears only if you have the *Obtain an IP Address Automatically* radio button enabled on the *General* tab of the *Internet Protocol Version 4 (TCP/IPv4) Properties* window.

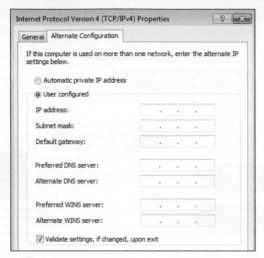

FIGURE 13.58   Alternate Configuration tab

Default Gateway

Another important concept that relates to IP addressing is a default gateway (sometimes called *gateway of last resort* or simply **gateway**). A **default gateway** is an IP address assigned to a network device that tells the device where to send a packet that is going to a remote network. Default gateway addresses are important for network devices to communicate with network devices on other networks. The default gateway address is the IP address of the router that is directly connected to that immediate network. Keep in mind that the primary job of a router is to find the best path to another network. Routers send traffic from one network to another throughout the Internet. Your router at home might be used to get traffic from your wireless network and your wired network out to the Internet. Consider Figure 13.59, which shows a router moving traffic from the network on the left to the network on the right (or vice versa).

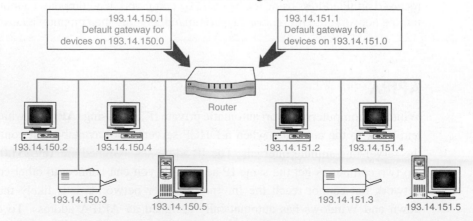

FIGURE 13.59   Default gateway

In the network shown in Figure 13.59, network devices on the 193.14.150.0 network use the router IP address 193.14.150.1 as a default gateway address. When a network device on the 193.14.150.0 network wants to send a packet to the other network, the device sends the packet to the default gateway, the router. The router, in turn, looks up the destination address in its routing table and sends the packet out of the other router interface (193.14.151.1) to the device on the 193.14.151.0 network.

The default gateway address for all network devices on the 193.14.151.0 network is 193.14.151.1, the router's IP address on the same network. Any network device on 193.14.151.0 sending information to another network sends the packet to the default gateway address.

TECH TIP

How do I assign a default gateway?

If you are statically assigning an IP address, the default gateway address is configured using the *Network and Sharing Center* Control Panel. Your computer can automatically receive a default gateway through DHCP just as it receives an IP address and mask.

DNS

Other elements of TCP/IP information that may need to be configured or provided through DHCP include DNS server IP addresses. Domain Name Service (**DNS**) is an application that runs on a network server (sometimes called a domain name server, or **DNS server**) that provides translation of Internet names into IP addresses. DNS is used on the Internet, so you do not have to remember the IP address of each site to which you connect. For example, DNS would be used to connect to Pearson Education, Inc. by translating the uniform resource locator (URL) http://www.pearsoned.com into the IP address 159.182.16.65. **Client-side DNS** involves configuring a computer to use one or more DNS servers. A computer can be programmed for one or more DNS server IP addresses by using DHCP. The DHCP server must be configured for this. Otherwise, a technician can manually configure the system for one or more DNS server IP addresses through the *Network and Sharing Center* Control Panel.

TECH TIP

DNS servers provide name resolution

If a Windows computer is on an Active Directory domain, Active Directory automatically uses DNS to locate other hosts and services using assigned domain names.

If a DNS server does not know a domain name (that is, if it does not have the name in its database), the DNS server can contact another DNS server to get the translation information. Common codes used with DNS (three letters used at the end of a domain name) are .com (commercial sites), .edu (educational sites), .gov (government sites), .net (network-related sites), and .org (miscellaneous sites). Wired and wireless adapters require IP addresses, default gateways, and DNS configuration, but before any wired or wireless adapters are installed or configured, the basic configuration parameters should be determined.

Wireless NIC–Specific Settings

Not all computers in a wireless network need the same type of wireless NIC, but each NIC does require configuration to join a wireless network. After the wireless adapter is installed, SSID and security options can be entered. Specific security options are covered in Chapter 18, "Computer and Network Security." Wireless parameters can be configured through a utility provided by the wireless NIC manufacturer or through Windows by selecting the wireless network icon in the notification area, selecting the wireless network shown, and entering the required security information.

If the SSID is not being broadcast (**SSID not found** in the list of available wireless networks), a wireless network can be manually entered using the following procedures for Windows 7, 8, and 10: *Network and Sharing Center* Control Panel > *Set Up a New Connection or Network* link > *Manually Connect to a Wireless Network* option (see Figure 13.60).

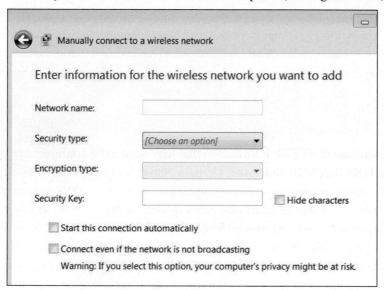

FIGURE 13.60   Windows 7 wireless network configuration window

TECH TIP

Ensure laptop wireless NIC is enabled

If a laptop cannot connect to a wireless network, make sure the wireless NIC is enabled. It can be enabled/disabled through the use of a [Fn] key.

Another common setting for wireless NICs is the type of encryption used. Encryption is covered in Chapter 18, along with other wireless security measures. The following types of encryption can be chosen and must match what is configured on the wireless AP/router (see Figure 13.61):

> *Wireless Encryption Protocol (**WEP**)*—64- and 128-bit versions
> *Temporal Key Integrity Protocol (**TKIP**)*—May be seen in combination with WiFi Protected Access (WPA) and/or WPA2
> **WPA**—Might be seen with Preshared Keys (PSK), meaning a passphrase and/or TKIP
> **WPA2**—Uses the Counter Mode Block Chaining Message Authentication Code Protocol (CCMP) for added security (might be seen as PSK and/or TKIP)

> *WPA2 with Advanced Encryption Standard (**AES**)*—Uses a block cipher and has key lengths of 28, 192, or 256 bits with the longer key lengths being the stronger.

FIGURE 13.61 Wireless security options

Wireless NICs are easy to install. Always follow the manufacturer's instructions. All the screens and configuration utilities have the same type of information. Understanding what the configuration parameters mean is important. The hardest part about configuring wireless NICs is obtaining the correct parameters before installation begins. Incorrectly inputting any one of the parameters causes the wireless NIC to not join the wireless network. Planning is critical for configuring wireless NICs.

Advanced NIC Properties

Both wired and wireless NICs have some optional parameters that can be manually configured. These options are shown in Figure 13.62 and discussed in Table 13.16. Access these parameters by right-clicking the NIC from within the *Networking and Sharing Center* section of the Control Panel > *Properties* > *Configure* button > *Advanced* tab.

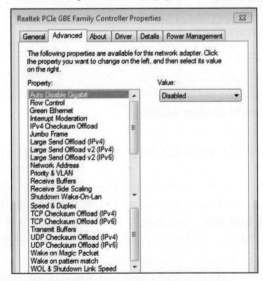

FIGURE 13.62 NIC advanced properties

TABLE 13.16 Network card properties

Configuration property	Description
Duplex	Options include half duplex/full duplex/auto. The default is auto or auto negotiation, to automatically configure full-duplex or half-duplex mode. Duplex might be combined with the Speed configuration option. Speed/Duplex should be manually configured on an important device such as a server. Figure 13.63 shows common speed and duplex options.
On-board NIC (BIOS/UEFI)	If a wired or wireless NIC is integrated into the motherboard or mobile device, you might have to access BIOS/UEFI to configure some of the settings related to the NIC.

Configuration property	Description
Quality of service (QoS)	Some NICs have the capability to have QoS features enabled. This allows tagging certain packets for priority transmission. Other similar options might be Priority and VLAN or Tagging.
Speed (NIC property)	Normally automatically configured but manual options include 10 Gbps, 1 Gbps, 100 Mbps, and 10 Mbps.
Wake-on-LAN	Wake-on-LAN allows the computer to be brought out of a low power mode to have configuration changes or updates made. Usually enabled through the BIOS but also through the NIC properties *Advanced* tab. Other options might include Wake on magic packet or WOL.

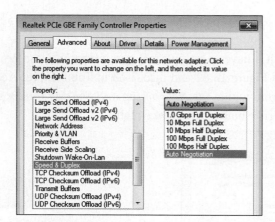

FIGURE 13.63   NIC Speed and Duplex options

NIC Configuration When Using Virtualization

Virtualization allows a single computer to host multiple operating systems that share hardware resources. When you configure a computer for virtualization, part of that virtualization is a virtual network interface card, or **virtual NIC**. One virtual NIC is standard in a virtual machine. More virtual NICs can be assigned. The physical device has at least one NIC, but if the device is a server, it has more than one NIC.

Each virtual NIC has its own MAC address and can have an IP address assigned. If more than one virtual machine is installed, each can communicate with the other machine based on the NIC settings configured. Furthermore, the virtual NIC can go through the physical NIC and have Internet access in the virtual environment. If the virtual machine doesn't have network connectivity, but the host workstation does, verify the virtual NIC settings. Figure 13.64 shows the concept of three virtual machines (one Linux, one Windows 10, and one Microsoft Server 2016, for example) in one physical machine connecting to the one physical NIC even though each virtual machine has its own virtual NIC.

Rather than go into all of the different virtualization vendors' products, let's examine VMware Workstation's NIC settings. Other vendors have similar configurations. In VMware Workstation, a NIC can be configured for bridged, network address translation (NAT), host-only, or custom mode. Table 13.17 describes these modes.

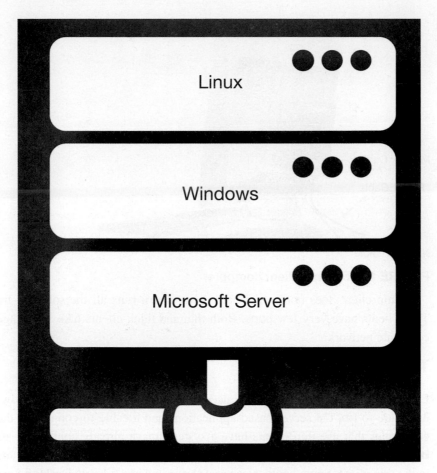

FIGURE 13.64   Virtualized machines connecting to a network

TABLE 13.17   Virtualized NIC modes of operation

Mode	Description
Bridged	The NIC is normally manually configured and has access to the host machine's NIC (which normally is connected to the Internet and provides Internet access to the virtual machine).
Custom	Select the VM network that the NIC is assigned to.
Host-only	Other virtual machines configured with an IP address on the same network can see and communicate with one another. DHCP is supported.
NAT (network address translation)	Cannot be seen by other virtual machines but can use the host machine's NIC for Internet access. DHCP is also supported.

Thin or Thick Client Installation Overview

Thin client and *thick client* are terms used in the corporate environment. A business computer that is a tower under someone's desk is likely to be a thick client and thick clients are the most common. A thick client has software applications loaded on the local hard drive. In contrast, a thin client is an all-in-one unit or a small computer that usually mounts to the back of a monitor, as shown in Figure 13.65.

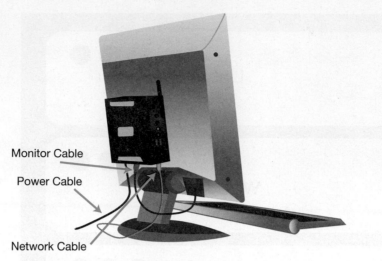

Monitor Cable

Power Cable

Network Cable

FIGURE 13.65   Thin client computer

A thin client does not have a hard drive, and it runs all the software from a network server. Thin clients have very few ports. Both thin and thick clients take advantage of and attach to the corporate network.

Thin Client Installation

Before installing a thin client, you need to ensure that the thin client hardware has the minimum hardware to run the server-based applications and a cable to connect to the network. Normally, companies that use thin clients have a system image already configured and stored somewhere. **Image management software** is used for creating, storing, modifying, and deploying an image to the thin client. Some companies use a server and use Remote Desktop Services (which was previously called **Terminal Services**). **Remote Desktop Services** is software on a server that can be accessed by multiple client sessions running simultaneously. This is important when thin clients are used because you can deploy and manage Windows-based applications. Remote Desktop Services can also be used to access and control (manage) remote Windows-based computers and servers.

Settings that relate to thin client installation through the image management software or Remote Desktop Services include the following:

> MAC and/or IP address of the thin client
> Schedule settings, including what days and within which time periods the thin client can be used
> Monitor settings, such as resolution, color depth, and refresh rate
> Domain/username, such as the Windows network domain name and the username of the person(s) using the thin client computer
> Hardware drivers

To install a thin client computer, always follow corporate guidelines, but here are the generic steps involved:

Step 1. The thin client may be an all-in-one unit which requires no assembly or a computer and a monitor (which might include a stand to attach both components). If using a computer, monitor, and stand, place the pieces into the stand and secure with screws as needed.

Step 2. Attach power to the thin client.

Step 3. Attach the Ethernet network cable from the wall outlet or cubicle outlet to the Ethernet port on the thin client.

Step 4. Attach the mouse and keyboard to the proper ports.

Step 5. If using a computer and monitor, attach the appropriate video cable from the computer video port to the monitor port.

Step 6. If using an external monitor, attach power to the monitor.

Step 7. Power on the computer and monitor and ensure that the device has network connectivity.

Step 8. If needed, set **account settings** such as language, time zone, display resolution, and network type.

Step 9. If required, use image management software or Remote Desktop Services to image the computer.

Step 10. Put the computer on the network domain.

Step 11. Ensure that the common applications work.

Step 12. Apply company-required settings or profile.

Thick Client Installation

Before installing a thick client, you need to ensure that the minimum hardware is available to run the applications that will be loaded. As with thin clients, medium to large companies tend to have a system image already configured, stored and available somewhere on the network, and the same tools are used to get the image onto the computer as for a thin client. Smaller companies might have a technician load each application individually and then configure the account settings manually.

You can also use Remote Desktop Services or Terminal Services, just as with a thin client, and push an image to the computer. In small companies, the applications are commonly installed by the technician one by one, or a standard image with the most common applications might be used. Then the technician would have to possibly configure the following settings:

> Network printer

> Local printer

> Application account settings

> Computer settings, such as wireless, display, and desktop icons

Wireless AP/Router Basic Configuration

A wireless AP frequently has the capability to route. This type of device is made for a small office/home office (SOHO) environment. The graphical environment used to configure a SOHO AP varies per vendor, but the process is common. The generic steps follow:

Step 1. Connect an Ethernet cable between the wireless AP and another device that has a web browser.

Step 2. Open a web browser and in the address textbox, enter the default IP address of the AP, such as http://192.168.1.1.

Step 3. Enter the default username (if needed) and default password.

TECH TIP

Change the default username/password

When an access point or wireless router is purchased, sometimes a default username and/or password is assigned. Because default passwords are available on the Internet, the password needs to be changed immediately so that unauthorized access is not permitted. Manufacturers recognized this weakness, and as a result many newer devices enable you to create a password during the initial setup.

Typical AP configuration menu options are shown in Table 13.18.

TABLE 13.18   Common AP configuration options

Area	Description
Wireless	Used to configure basic wireless settings, such as the SSID. Also includes a link to security options such as MAC filtering, authentication, and encryption (covered in Chapter 18).
Security	Used to enable/disable a firewall and configure firewall features such as VPN or allow particular network ports to be opened to allow certain types of traffic through.
Storage	Allows monitoring and control of an attached storage device or even supports a File Transfer Protocol (FTP) server.
Maintenance	Allows viewing the current status of the various components as well as access to any logging that is enabled.
Administration	Allows configuration of the device, such as password, IP address assignment, and event logging. Could also include configuration of features such as VoIP or QoS. QoS allows one type of traffic such as voice, which cannot tolerate delay to take priority over another type of traffic.

Wireless SOHO access points/routers frequently include network functions such as demilitarized zone (DMZ), QoS, DHCP server (sometimes seen as the DHCP on/off setting), router, integrated switch ports, and sometimes a port to add a hard drive and support network-accessible storage. Chapter 18 provides explanations and configuration details related to wireless security, and Table 13.19 introduces some common configuration features.

TABLE 13.19   Common wireless network device configuration settings

Option	Description
Basic QoS	Used to enable QoS so that traffic such as gaming traffic or Voice over IP (VoIP) traffic is prioritized over other data types.
Blacklist/whitelist	Lists that control which users, websites, protocols, and apps can be used on a device. A blacklist denies, whereas a whitelist specifically permits or allows network traffic.
Channel ID	Used to specify a particular 2.4 or 5 GHz channel.
Demilitarized zone (**DMZ**)	Might be seen as DMZ host. An advanced option that allows a PC or server to be accessed from a remote location.
DHCP	Used to enable or disable DHCP as well as the specific network number, mask, and range of addresses to use.
Firmware	Used to update the embedded code within a device. Frequently contains security, performance, and software updates.

Option	Description
Network address translation (**NAT**)/ destination NAT (**DNAT**)	NAT, which is used to translate from private IP addresses to a public address, is enabled by default. DNAT maps a public IP address to a specific private IP address and is used in a home or small business network.
Port forwarding/port triggering	An alternative to using a DMZ in which specific port numbers, ranges of port numbers, and applications are allowed to be used instead of opening all ports. One example of this is when a small company has a web server inside the company, and the server needs to be accessed by external users. Port triggering allows data through on a limited basis when a specific/configured situation occurs.
SSID	Used to name the wireless network. Cannot contain spaces. Commonly has the SSID broadcast option to enable or disable.
Universal Plug and Play (**UPnP**)	An alternative to configure port forwarding that allows peer-to-peer (P2P) gaming applications to function without further configuration. Could be a security risk for other devices on the network.

WWAN Cellular Configuration

Another type of wireless device that you might configure is a wireless broadband device or a WWAN (cellular) connection. A wireless broadband (WWAN cellular) device is normally a USB device, but this technology is integrated into some mobile devices. Software is normally installed either by using a disc or from the device. The device commonly has a phone number/account number associated with the broadband card. Figure 13.66 shows the type of information provided for a wireless broadband USB device.

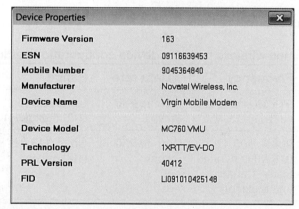

FIGURE 13.66   WWAN cellular properties

IoT and Smart Devices

The Internet of Things (**IoT**) is a term that describes the interconnectivity of sensors and devices that in the past have not been connected. IoT has affected all industries, but home devices are particularly common. Smart homes (see Figure 13.67) are becoming popular even in older existing homes. Smart homes include devices that can monitor water consumption, air and heat, and electricity, as well as control locks, lights, thermostats, garage doors, computers, sound systems, TVs, refrigerators, and the list just keeps growing. The devices are controlled through an app on a phone, tablet, laptop, or computer. The smart devices can connect to a wired Ethernet network, an

802.11-based wireless network, or using two other standards that are used in smart homes: Zigbee and Z-Wave. Table 13.20 shows how they compare.

FIGURE 13.67 Smart home controls

TABLE 13.20 Common wireless network device configuration settings

Standard	Frequency	Data rate	Range	Security
Zigbee	915 MHz and 2.4 GHz	Up to 250 kbps	Up to 328 feet (100 meters)	128-bit AES encryption
Z-Wave	908.4, 908.42, and 916 MHz (United States, Canada, and Mexico)	Up to 250 kbps	Up to 328 feet (100 meters)	Proprietary and improved with Security2 (S2)

Both Zigbee and Z-Wave involve a mesh network, in which wireless signals go from device to device, and a central hub/coordinator that commonly connects to the Internet. Each device can connect to multiple other devices.

Zigbee Configuration

Zigbee is a standard managed by the Zigbee Alliance. Zigbee devices do not have a maximum number of hops (that is, a maximum number of devices the signal can go through to reach the destination). However, before Zigbee version 3.0, there were different Zigbee standards and different protocols for these standards. A Zigbee network includes a Zigbee coordinator and Zigbee devices. The network might include a Zigbee router, also called a Zigbee gateway, which extends the range of the wireless network. Figure 13.68 shows two sample topologies used with Zigbee: one without a Zigbee router and one with one.

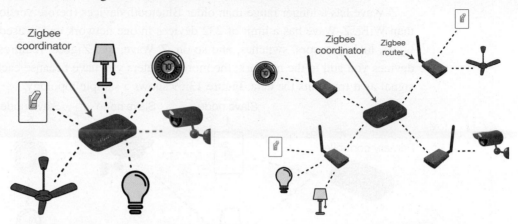

A Zigbee coordinator registers and receives data from the Zigbee end devices.

A Zigbee router extends the Zigbee network.

FIGURE 13.68   Zigbee topologies

Generic Zigbee configuration parameters are listed here, but always remember to refer to the manufacturer's instructions. For the central hub that is the coordinator, you have to configure the following:

> *PAN ID*—This must be the same for all devices on the same network. An example is 100.
> *Channel ID*—This must be the same for all devices on the same network. An example is 1000.
> *Sleep Mode*—This must be the same for all devices on the same network. The three sleep modes are (1) Normal—does not sleep, relays sleep sync messages to other devices, but does not generate sleep sync messages; (2) Cyclic—sleeps as directed by the sleep coordinator; and (3) Sleep support mode—does not sleep but can generate and relay sleep sync messages to other devices.
> *API or Transparent Mode*— API mode is required to see data from the other devices' I/O pins, but is more complicated than Transparent mode; with Transparent mode, all data is transmitted.
> *Save Configuration*—This saves the settings to non-volatile memory.

For an individual Zigbee device, the following configuration settings must be entered:

> Matching PAN ID
> Matching Channel ID
> Matching sleep mode
> The coordinator's unique address (found on the coordinator device)
> For each device, a permanent unique 64-bit serial address
> Destination Address Low, which is usually 0
> Destination Address High setting (If you want all devices to be able to hear the messages, you can configure a PAN broadcast address such as 0xFFFF. If only the coordinator is to be used, you can set the coordinator's address.)

Z-Wave Configuration

Z-Wave is a wireless standard from Silicon Labs. Z-Wave supports only four hops between one particular device and the controller. If DeviceX has to go through Device1, Device2, and Device3 to get to the controller, all is good, but if DeviceX had to go through an additional device to get to the controller, DeviceX cannot be controlled. Devices are known as *slave nodes*.

Z-Wave has a longer range than older Bluetooth devices (before version 5) and has less power than WiFi. Z-Wave has a limit of 232 devices in one network and is used to support thermostats, lights, locks, sensors, switches, and so on. Z-Wave, like Zigbee, requires a controller. The more devices you add to the network, the more repeaters you have because each device then boosts the signal as it transmits the data. Figure 13.69 shows a sample topology.

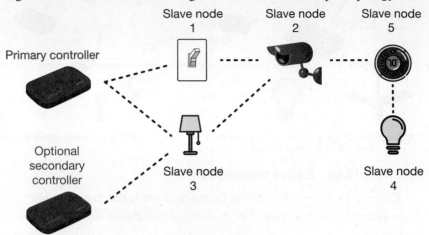

FIGURE 13.69   Z-Wave sample topology

A Z-Wave system is an event-driven network, which means the devices send data only when an event occurs, such as a gesture triggering a motion detector. Otherwise, they sit silently on the network. When an event is reported by a network device (node), the controller might be programmed with what to do in that case (for example, if motion is detected, turn on a particular light).

For the central hub that is the coordinator, you have to do the following as an example (but you should always use the instructions provided with a specific controller):

> Plug the controller into a wired network or use the wireless network.
> Open a web browser and enter the IP address that was assigned to the controller.
> For some controllers, use a setup dialog to set options such as the name of the controller, which modes you want to enable and configure, such as when you are home, what hours are considered to be night hours, when you have any planned vacations, authorized users, and so on.
> Navigate to the controller management area to select an option such as Add Node or Include a Node in order to add a device to the network.

Thermostat

A smart **thermostat** is programmable and adjustable like a normal thermostat. What makes it smart is that you can remotely control it, it can show you data such as your energy consumption, and it can make adjustments based on other installed sensors, such as humidity and temperature sensors. When a change is made, a smart thermostat can give you information about the changes you just requested and might even discourage one or more of them or suggest an alternative setting.

Installing a smart thermostat involves some wiring. Make sure you follow the manufacturer's installation instructions. Here are some generic instructions to give you an idea of the process:

Step 1. Turn off power at the circuit breaker.

Step 2. Remove the cover from the existing thermostat and take a photo of the wiring.

Step 3. Loosen the screws to remove each of the wires. It is a best practice to label which connector each wire went to.

Step 4. Connect the wires to the new IoT thermostat. These connections are like connections for speaker wires, where you press down on a tab, insert the wire, and release the tab.

Step 5. Attach the IoT thermostat cover, reapply power, and set up the device (usually through an app). You might have to add your thermostat to your network. On some thermostats, you might have to push or turn it to get a key that is entered into the app in order to add the thermostat so it can be controlled and monitored through the app.

IoT Light Switch Installation

An IoT or smart **light switch** can be programmed and set on a timer, motion-activated, and/or controlled by voice or by using an app on a phone or tablet, as shown in Figure 13.70.

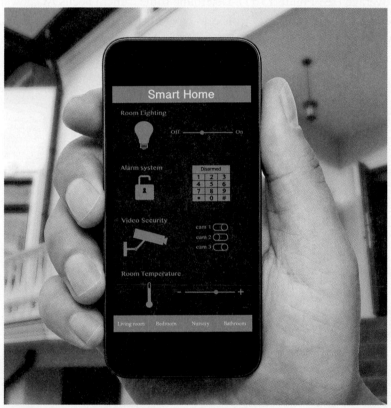

FIGURE 13.70   App to control an IoT light

With light switches, you really have to be careful and follow the manufacturer's instructions or hire an electrician. Here are some generic steps for installation:

Step 1. Ensure that there is a neutral line installed.

Step 2. Turn off power to the outlet at the breaker box.

Step 3. Remove the outlet faceplate and identify the ground, live/load, and neutral wires.

Step 4. Disconnect the wires from the face plate.

Step 5. Connect the smart switch wires to the electrical wires.

Step 6. Mount the smart switch into the wall outlet.

Step 7. Turn on the power at the breaker box.

Security Camera Installation

Security cameras can connect through a wired or wireless network. People have different reasons for wanting to install a **security camera** other than the obvious reason of security; for example, parents might want to monitor babies and young children, remote monitoring may be used for day care centers so parents can check in or for home pet monitoring.

Before buying a smart security camera, you need to first identify where you want the camera to be, including whether it is to be installed indoors, outdoors, or both. When considering where to install the camera, you must also consider the lighting around that area. A motion detector that turns on a light might be needed for the recording.

Some cameras come with motion detectors. Make sure you do not put the camera in an enclosure that might cause overheating due to poor airflow. Outdoor cameras should be placed in a sheltered area, and they should be at least 10 feet high to avoid vandalism and provide a wide angle of coverage (see Figure 13.71). Determine if the camera needs AC power or will run on batteries. Determine which of the protocols is to be used (wired TCP/IP, 802.11 WiFi, Bluetooth, Zigbee, or Z-Wave). If you are recording, you can save the data to an SD card, cloud-based account, home server, or hard drive.

FIGURE 13.71   Security camera installation

To install a security camera, always follow the manufacturer's instructions. Generic installation steps are as follows:

Step 1. Install any power or cabling that is required.

Step 2. Install the camera mounts.

Step 3. Attach the camera to the mount and position it for best coverage.

Step 4. Connect the camera to the network (which is probably wired Ethernet, wireless, Zigbee, or Z-Wave).

Step 5. Ensure that enough storage space is available. Some cameras come with a digital video recorder (DVR) that can connect to the home wired network.

IoT Door Lock Installation

A smart **door lock** allows keyless entry. Depending on the model, you might get to keep the traditional key as well. When looking at features, if you want to keep your key system, then make sure you buy the correct adapter. Also make sure the smart door lock attaches to the network the way you want (using WiFi, Bluetooth, Z-Wave, or Zigbee).

Always follow the manufacturer's recommended installation process. The following is a generic process for installing a smart door lock when you are keeping the deadbolt:

Step 1. Insert the batteries into the door lock.

Step 2. Make sure the lock is in the unlock position and tape over the keyhole on the outside part of the door to hold it in place.

Step 3. From the inside, remove the thumb latch assembly, which is usually held by two screws. If there is a mounting plate for the thumb latch assembly, remove it, too.

Step 4. Align and connect the lock-specific adapter to the part of the deadbolt that is protruding through.

Step 5. Align and insert another adapter into the smart door lock.

Step 6. Attach the smart door lock onto the mounting plate and secure.

Step 7. Use the appropriate app to configure the door lock and attach to the network.

If you are replacing the entire deadbolt, remove it and insert the smart deadbolt (ensuring that any wires are fed through the opening) and secure it in place. Thread any wires through the back plate and secure the back plate. Connect the wires and then attach and secure the smart lock. Use the app or controller program to attach the device to the network.

Voice-Enabled Smart Speakers or Digital Assistants

Many people use Google Assistant or Siri on a cell phone to get answers to questions or perform actions such as scheduling an event or playing a particular type of music. A **voice-enabled smart speaker** is a wireless device that is designed to respond to voice commands for music control, but some of these devices include voice-activated **digital assistants** and can do much more, including control smart IoT devices. It is also possible to control smart home devices by using a smartphone app and the phone's speaker, as shown in Figure 13.72.

To enable a digital assistant, you need to check the phone app, mobile app, or device settings. Always follow the manufacturer's instructions. The following are some generic installation instructions:

Step 1. Power on the device.

Step 2. Download the app that can control the device, open the app, and select the device.

Step 3. Configure the device with the appropriate settings for the type of wireless network being used.

FIGURE 13.72   Smart speaker controlled by an app

Network Troubleshooting

One step in troubleshooting a network is to determine how many devices are affected. For example, if only one computer cannot communicate across a network, it will be handled differently than if several (or all) computers on a network cannot communicate. If a network port is suspect, you can try another cable or use a loopback plug to test the port. The easiest way to determine how many devices are having trouble is by using a simple test. Because most computers use TCP/IP, one tool that can be used for testing is the `ping` command.

The `ping` Command

The `ping` command can be used to check connectivity around the network (if you suspect **no connectivity** or **intermittent connectivity**). Figure 13.73 shows a sample network that is used to explain how `ping` is used to check various network points.

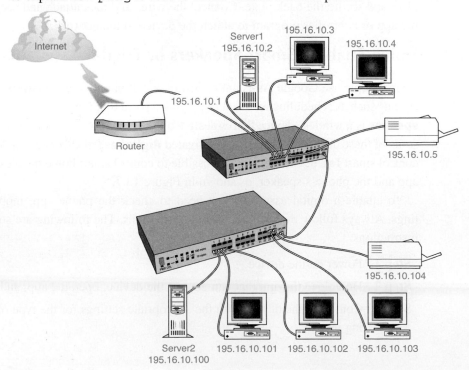

FIGURE 13.73   Sample network troubleshooting scenario

TECH TIP

What does `ping` **do?**

The `ping` command can be used to determine whether the network path is available, whether there are delays along the path, and whether the remote network device is reachable. `ping` sends a packet to an IP destination (that you determine), and a reply is sent back from the destination device if everything works fine.

The network shown in Figure 13.73 consists of various network devices, including two servers and two laser printers. The devices connect to one of two switches that are connected using the uplink port. This port allows two similar devices to be connected with a standard Ethernet cable or fiber cable. A router connects to the top switch, and the router connects to the Internet.

If the 195.16.10.3 workstation cannot access a file on Server2 (195.16.10.100), the first step in troubleshooting is to ping Server2 from the workstation. If this is successful, you know the problem is with Server2 or the file located on the server.

If the ping is unsuccessful, there is a problem somewhere between the workstation and the server or on the server. To test this, ping another device that connects to the same switch; for example, from workstation 195.16.10.3, ping Server1 (195.16.10.2). A successful ping tells you the connection between the 195.16.10.3 workstation and the switch is good, the switch is working, the cable connecting to Server1 is fine, and Server1 is functioning.

What Resources Are Unavailable?

One of the first signs of network issues is a user complaining about **unavailable resources**. This might mean the user can't reach the Internet or can't reach **local resources** within the company, such as network shares, printers, or email. Troubleshooting each of these problems helps you narrow down where you should ping and verify exactly what network resource(s) cannot be reached.

Pinging devices on the same network is a good check of local connectivity. The term **local connectivity** describes devices on the same network, including the default gateway. If a network device can ping other devices on the same network as well as the default gateway, the network device (and all its components and basic settings) is configured correctly.

TECH TIP

Use `ping -t`

Use `ping x.x.x.x -t` (where you replace `x.x.x.x` with an IP address or a URL) to issue a continuous ping to a remote location. The ping does not stop until you press Ctrl+C.

Now ping workstation 195.16.10.101 (a device other than the server on the remote switch) by typing `ping 195.16.10.101`. If the ping is successful, (1) the uplink cable is operational; (2) the second switch is operational; (3) the cable that connects workstation 195.16.10.101 to the switch is good; and (4) the 195.16.10.101 workstation has been successfully configured for TCP/IP. If the ping is unsuccessful, one of these five items is faulty. The problems could be the (1) Server2 cable, (2) switch port to which the server connects, (3) server NIC, (4) server configuration, or (5) file on Server2.

TECH TIP

How can I check the TCP/IP protocol stack on my own NIC?

The `ping` command can be used to test a NIC as well as the TCP/IP protocol running on the NIC, with the command `ping 127.0.0.1` (IPv4), `ping ::1` (IPv6), or `ping localhost`, where *localhost* is a hostname that is translated to an IP address known as a private IP address, or loopback address, which means it cannot be used by the outside world.

Use the `ping` command followed by the name of the device (or website) being tested (for example, `ping www.pearsoned.com`). A DNS server translates the name (pearsoned.com) to an IP address (52.4.47.53). If you can reach the site by pinging the IP address, but not the name, there is a problem with the DNS server.

TECH TIP

What the `ping localhost` results mean

If a ping is successful (that is, you get a message that a reply was received from 127.0.0.1 or ::1), you know the TCP/IP protocol stack works correctly on the NIC. If the ping response is nothing (appears to hang) or a 100% packet loss error, TCP/IP is not properly installed or is not functioning correctly on that one workstation.

The `ipconfig` Command

To see the current IP configuration on a Windows computer, use the **`ipconfig`** command from a Windows command prompt or the **`ifconfig`** command with Linux or macOS. The `ipconfig` /all command can be used to see both wired and wireless NICs if both are installed, as shown in Figure 13.74. The `ipconfig /all` command also allows you to view MAC addresses.

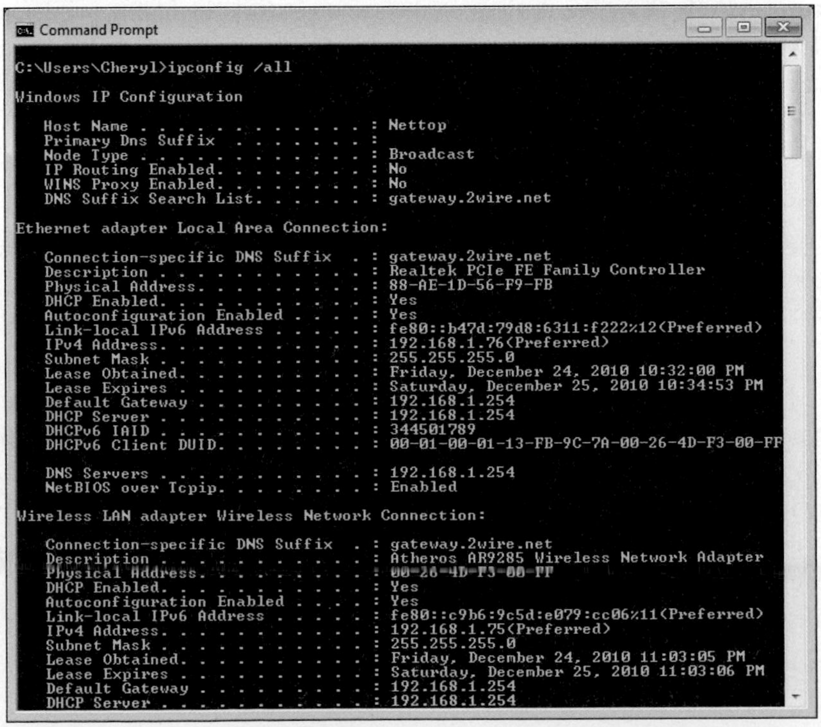

```
Command Prompt

C:\Users\Cheryl>ipconfig /all

Windows IP Configuration

    Host Name . . . . . . . . . . . . : Nettop
    Primary Dns Suffix  . . . . . . . :
    Node Type . . . . . . . . . . . . : Broadcast
    IP Routing Enabled. . . . . . . . : No
    WINS Proxy Enabled. . . . . . . . : No
    DNS Suffix Search List. . . . . . : gateway.2wire.net

Ethernet adapter Local Area Connection:

    Connection-specific DNS Suffix  . : gateway.2wire.net
    Description . . . . . . . . . . . : Realtek PCIe FE Family Controller
    Physical Address. . . . . . . . . : 88-AE-1D-56-F9-FB
    DHCP Enabled. . . . . . . . . . . : Yes
    Autoconfiguration Enabled . . . . : Yes
    Link-local IPv6 Address . . . . . : fe80::b47d:79d8:6311:f222%12(Preferred)
    IPv4 Address. . . . . . . . . . . : 192.168.1.76(Preferred)
    Subnet Mask . . . . . . . . . . . : 255.255.255.0
    Lease Obtained. . . . . . . . . . : Friday, December 24, 2010 10:32:00 PM
    Lease Expires . . . . . . . . . . : Saturday, December 25, 2010 10:34:53 PM
    Default Gateway . . . . . . . . . : 192.168.1.254
    DHCP Server . . . . . . . . . . . : 192.168.1.254
    DHCPv6 IAID . . . . . . . . . . . : 344501789
    DHCPv6 Client DUID. . . . . . . . : 00-01-00-01-13-FB-9C-7A-00-26-4D-F3-00-FF

    DNS Servers . . . . . . . . . . . : 192.168.1.254
    NetBIOS over Tcpip. . . . . . . . : Enabled

Wireless LAN adapter Wireless Network Connection:

    Connection-specific DNS Suffix  . : gateway.2wire.net
    Description . . . . . . . . . . . : Atheros AR9285 Wireless Network Adapter
    Physical Address. . . . . . . . . : 00-26-4D-F3-00-FF
    DHCP Enabled. . . . . . . . . . . : Yes
    Autoconfiguration Enabled . . . . : Yes
    Link-local IPv6 Address . . . . . : fe80::c9b6:9c5d:e079:cc06%11(Preferred)
    IPv4 Address. . . . . . . . . . . : 192.168.1.75(Preferred)
    Subnet Mask . . . . . . . . . . . : 255.255.255.0
    Lease Obtained. . . . . . . . . . : Friday, December 24, 2010 11:03:05 PM
    Lease Expires . . . . . . . . . . : Saturday, December 25, 2010 11:03:06 PM
    Default Gateway . . . . . . . . . : 192.168.1.254
    DHCP Server . . . . . . . . . . . : 192.168.1.254
```

FIGURE 13.74 `ipconfig /all` **command output**

If a network device does not get an IP address properly from the DHCP server, use the `ipconfig /release` command. Then issue the `ipconfig /renew` command. A symptom of this is a device getting an APIPA (IPv4) or link local (IPv6) address because a DHCP server is unavailable. Also ensure that the device is actually configured for DHCP. A message appears on Windows-based devices when two devices have been manually assigned the same IP address. Note that not all operating systems and/or devices do this. Check any device that has a manually configured IP address for any duplicate IP addresses that are causing an **IP address conflict**.

The `tracert` Command

The `tracert` command is a commonly used tool in Microsoft, macOS, and Linux environments. The `tracert` command is used to display the path a packet takes through the network. The benefit of using the `tracert` command is that you can see where a fault is occurring in a larger network. It also allows you to see the network latency. Network latency is the delay measured from source to destination and results in **slow transfer speeds**. The `tracert` command is also useful when you have intermittent connectivity. An example of output from the command is as follows:

```
C:\Users\Cheryl>tracert comptia.org
Tracing route to comptia.org [198.134.5.6] over a maximum of 30 hops:
 1 <1 ms <1 ms <1 ms vankman1 [192.168.1.1]
 2 8 ms 7 ms 8 ms 10.126.208.1
 3 10 ms 8 ms 7 ms 72-31-92-20.net.bhntampa.com [72.31.92.20]
 4 11 ms 14 ms 12 ms ten0-6-0-11.tamp27-car1.bhn.net [71.44.3.186]
 5 17 ms 16 ms 19 ms hun0-4-0-3.tamp20-car1.bhn.net [72.31.117.170]
 6 22 ms 19 ms 18 ms ten0-8-0-0.orld71-CAR1.bhn.net [71.44.1.211]
 7 17 ms 16 ms 19 ms 72-31-217-88.net.bhntampa.com [72.31.217.88]
 8 23 ms 19 ms 14 ms 10.bu-ether15.orldfljo00w-bcr00.tbone.rr.com
[66.109.6.98]
 9 36 ms 31 ms 31 ms bu-ether18.atlngamq47w-bcr01.tbone.rr.com [66.109.1.72]
10 23 ms 23 ms 24 ms 0.ae2.pr1.atl20.tbone.rr.com [107.14.17.188]
11 26 ms 29 ms 23 ms 67.106.215.89.ptr.us.xo.net [67.106.215.89]
12 50 ms 51 ms 50 ms 207.88.13.54.ptr.us.xo.net [207.88.13.54]
13 52 ms 56 ms 49 ms 207.88.12.174.ptr.us.xo.net [207.88.12.174]
14 50 ms 51 ms 51 ms 207.88.12.31.ptr.us.xo.net [207.88.12.31]
15 49 ms 57 ms 55 ms ae0d0.mcr1.chicago-il.us.xo.net [216.156.0.162]
16 54 ms 52 ms 53 ms 216.55.11.62
17 52 ms 60 ms 52 ms 198.134.5.6
Trace complete.
```

The `nslookup` Command

The `nslookup` command is a program tool that helps with DNS server troubleshooting. `nslookup` enables you to see domain names and their associated IP addresses. When an Internet site (server) cannot be contacted by its name but can be contacted using its IP address, there is a DNS problem. The `nslookup` command can make troubleshooting these types of problems easier. To see this tool in action, bring up a command prompt, type `nslookup http://www.pearsonhighered.com`, and press ⏎Enter. The IP address of the Pearson web server appears. Type `quit` to return to the command prompt. Note that if the nslookup command shows a domain name such as a computer, for example, but the domain name cannot be used to contact the device, then the `ipconfig /flushdns` command can be used to clear the DNS cache.

The `net` Command

The `net` command is used to manage just about everything on a network from a command prompt. The `net` command is followed by other options, and each option has different parameters. Here is the command syntax:

```
net [ accounts | computer | config | continue | file | group | help |
helpmsg | localgroup | name | pause | print | send | session | share | start
| statistics | stop | time | use |user | view ]
```

Table 13.21 lists some of the most commonly used `net` command options.

TABLE 13.21   net command options and descriptions

Command	Description
net help	Used to get help for the `net` commands. You can also use `net help` followed by the command (`net help computer`) or `net computer / help` or `net computer /?`.
net computer	Used to add or remove a computer from a Microsoft domain.
net config	Used to display information about the server or workstation service.
net share	Used to create, remove, or view network share resources
net start	Used to start a network service.
net stop	Used to stop a network service.
net use	Used to map a drive letter to a network resource.
net user	Used to manage user accounts.
net view	Used to view network devices.

The `netdom` command

The `netdom` command, which is similar to `net`, is used to manage workstations in a domain environment. Use the `netdom /?` command to see all the options. Table 13.22 shows some of the most popular `netdom` command options.

TABLE 13.22   netdom command options and descriptions

Command	Description
netdom add	Used to add a workstation account to the domain
netdom join	Used to join a workstation to a domain
netdom remove	Used to remove a workstation from the domain
netdom renamecomputer	Used to rename a computer and its domain account
netdom reset	Used to reset the connection between a workstation and a network domain controller
netdom resetpwd	Used to reset the computer account password
netdom verify	Used to verify the connection between a workstation and a Microsoft domain controller

NIC Troubleshooting

The following methods can help with NIC troubleshooting:

> From a command prompt window, use `ping localhost` to test the NIC.
> Ping another device on the same network. If successful, you know the NIC, device, cable, switch or hub, and the same on the other device are all working.
> Ping the default gateway. If successful, connectivity and configuration of the device for communication on the local network works and has the potential to communicate with other networks.
> Ping a device on a remote network. If successful, the Layer 3 device serving as the default gateway is working.
> Use the `tracert` command to see if the location of the fault (such as whether the problem is inside or outside the company).
> Check the status light(s) on the NIC (see Figure 13.75) to see if the physical connection is good. Different NICs have different colored lights, but the two most common colors used with status lights to indicate a good connection are green and orange. Some status lights indicate the speed at which the NIC is operating (10 Mbps, 100 Mbps, or 1 Gbps).
> Check the status light on the hub or switch (see Figure 13.76) that is used to connect the workstation NIC to the network. Green is a common color for a good connection on these devices.

Status lights

FIGURE 13.75   NIC status lights

> Check cabling. Even if the status lights indicate that the connection is good, the cabling may still be faulty.
> Update the device driver by obtaining a newer one from the NIC manufacturer's website.
> Check the IP addressing used. Use the `ipconfig` command from a prompt to ensure that the NIC has an IP address assigned. If you get a duplicate IP address error message, change the IP addressing to DHCP or another statically assigned (not used already) address.
> On a mobile device, ensure that wireless is enabled and that the wireless NIC is enabled. Look for a button or a keystroke combination that re enables the wireless antenna and ensure that the NIC is not disabled in the *Network and Sharing Center* Control Panel.
> If your network connection on the desktop or from within the *Network and Sharing* section of the Control Panel shows **limited connectivity** (see Figure 13.77) or you cannot reach the Internet at all, try rebooting the PC (because of a 169.254.*x.x* address) or the router (if in a home or small business network). With a wireless connection, check security settings, the

wireless button that controls the wireless antenna, or a wireless key that toggles the wireless NIC. If on a wired network, the cable could be an issue.

Status lights

FIGURE 13.76   Switch or hub status lights

> If the network connection is intermittent or slow on a wireless connection, move closer to the AP, change the position of the wireless device, or add another AP in the area to extend the wireless network. On a wired connection, check cabling and duplex settings. Replace a hub with a switch.

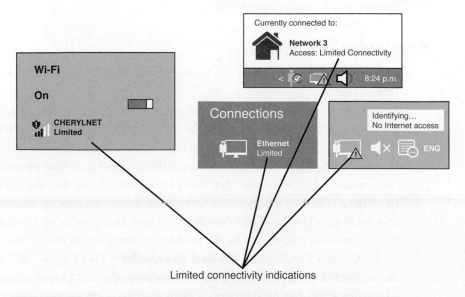

Limited connectivity indications

FIGURE 13.77   Windows limited connectivity network indications

Troubleshooting Cable and DSL Modems

Because most cable and DSL modems are external, the best tools for troubleshooting connectivity problems are the lights on the front of the modem (see Figure 13.78). The lights vary from vendor to vendor, but common ones are listed in Table 13.23.

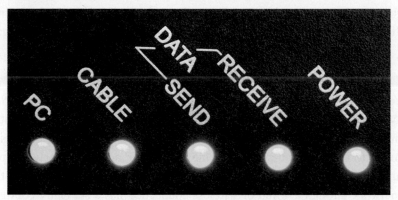

FIGURE 13.78   Cable/DSL modem lights for troubleshooting

TABLE 13.23   Cable/DSL modem lights and troubleshooting*

Light	Explanation
Cable, Data, or D/S	Usually blinks to indicate connectivity with Internet provider
ENET, E, or Ethernet	Usually indicates connectivity between the PC and the modem; if unlit, ensure that you are using Ethernet (if using USB, this will be unlit), check cabling, and check PC network card settings
Internet, Ready, or Rdy	Stays lit when the modem has established an Internet connection
Link Status	Usually flashes when acquiring a connection with a provider and is steadily on when a link is established
PC	Used instead of Ethernet or USB lights to show the status of the connection between the modem and the PC
Power	Indicates power to the modem
USB or U	Usually indicates connectivity between the PC and the modem; if unlit, ensure that you are using USB (if using a NIC, this light will be unlit), check cabling, and check *Device Manager* to see if the modem is recognized

* Refer to the modem documentation for the exact status of the lights.

After you have checked lights and possibly checked cables, if you still have a problem, power off the modem, wait for 2 minutes, power it back on, and reboot the computer. Give the modem a couple minutes to initialize. Most modems have a reset button that can also be used, but powering off and powering back on works without having to wipe all the configuration information. If a modem is still not working after you take these steps, contact the service provider.

Network Printers

Chapter 9 outlines how to share a printer across a network as well as how to access a wired or wireless network printer. Now that you know a bit more about networking, it might be easier to understand if you go back and review those processes. **Printer sharing** is commonly done in a home or small business environment. In a corporate environment, a print server is used, and printers are published or visible to network users. A printer may or may not be controlled by a printer server, but it will definitely have an IP address assigned. Users can perform **network printer mapping**, which enables network users to add a printer to their computer by using the domain printer name or IP address. A print server or printer is assigned an IP address so that other devices on the network can use the printer. This is sometimes called **TCP printing**, or TCP/IP printing. To find printers by name in a corporate network domain, do the following:

> Windows 7: Use *Windows Explorer* to explore the network for printers.
> Windows 8/10: Use *File Explorer* to explore the network for printers.

You can also use the *Add Printer* Control Panel link > enable the *Select a Shared Printer by Name* radio button and enter the domain name (an example might be the domain name Schmidtworks, in this format: \\Schmidtworks\) and select from the printers that are listed. Another option is to add the printer by using the printer's IP address. A network printer commonly has a front panel that is used to access network configuration settings. A printer that connects directly to the network through a wired or wireless connection has a statically configured IP address, mask, and default gateway. Many times technical support staff attach a label to the printer that shows the IP address. You could access the network settings from the *Devices and Printers > Printers* section of the Control Panel to view the assigned IP address. Refer to Chapter 9 for how to connect using a printer's IP address.

Network Printer Troubleshooting

To begin troubleshooting a network printer, do all the things that are normally done when troubleshooting a local printer, checking the obvious things first. Does the printer have power? Is the printer online? Does the printer have paper? Are the printer's connectors secured tightly? Is the correct printer driver loaded? If all these normal troubleshooting steps check out correctly, try the following steps:

> Print a test page and see if the printer's IP address outputs or see if the printer is labeled with its IP address. If so, ping the printer's IP address to see if there is network connectivity between the computer and the printer. Use the `tracert` command to see if there is a complete network path to the printer.
> Check the printer's *Properties* page to see if the printer has been paused.
> Cancel any print jobs in the print queue and resubmit the print job.
> Reset the printer by powering it off and back on. If it connects to a print server device, reset that, too.
> Be sure the print job has been sent to the correct printer. Companies commonly have several network printers to use.
> If a network printer fails and a user has a USB-attached printer, the USB printer can be shared. Chapter 9, "Printers," shows how to share a printer across a network.
> If the printer has never worked, try a different version of the print driver.

Network Servers

Servers are an important part of networking and provide different functionality. One server could provide more than one function. For example, a corporate server might act as a web server as well as a DHCP server. Figure 13.79 shows several network servers mounted in a rack. Each physical box could contain several virtualized servers.

FIGURE 13.79   Network servers

Table 13.24 summarizes the most common servers on a network.

TABLE 13.24   Server types and descriptions

Server type	Description
Authentication server	Used to verify credentials (usually username and password), such as when someone logs in to a domain workstation.
DHCP server	Used to issue IP-related information, including IP address, subnet mask, default gateway, DNS server, and domain name. Commonly has a block of addresses that are in a pool to be assigned to common devices such as PCs and IP phones. A few addresses are reserved for statically assigned devices such as routers, switches, APs, and printers.
DNS server	Used to translate domain names to IP addresses.
End-point management server	A centralized solution used for discovering devices, distributing software, provisioning, updating, configuring, managing security, managing profile, imaging/re-imaging computers, and managing inventory.
File server	Used to store files that can be accessed and managed from a remote location.
Mail server	Also known as an email server. Used to maintain a database of email accounts, store messages (email) sent and received, communicate with other mail servers, and use the DNS protocol to locate other servers.
Print server	Used to manage one or more network printers. See Chapter 9 for more information.
Proxy server	Used as a go-between between an application such as a web browser and a physical server. Details on how to configure a network device for a proxy server are found in Chapter 18.
Syslog server	Also called a logging server, used to receive information from multiple network devices and used as a historical record of events such as devices losing power, a particular interface going down, and logins or logouts on a particular device.
Web server	Used to provide web-based content that is accessed through a web browser that commonly requests the information through TCP port 80.

Embedded and Legacy Systems

An **embedded system** is a computer that has a specific function within a larger system. Embedded systems have many of the same components as desktop or mobile computers: processor, RAM, flash memory, and ports. Embedded systems can be found in many places, including airports, manufacturing plants, medical equipment, electrical systems, mechanical systems, and telecommunication systems. Embedded systems tend to be self-contained, but they commonly attach to a wired or wireless network and may be part of an IT person's responsibility.

A **legacy system** is an outdated computer system or piece of network equipment that in an ideal world would be replaced or updated with something new but is commonly kept because it might cost too much to replace it, it is used with a particular system that can't be replaced, or it provides a functionality that will not be needed too much longer. A legacy system might contain ports that require converters to be attached to the newer equipment, outdated methods used for access, or proprietary cables that might not be easy to obtain or find. Legacy systems are challenging for technicians because of the lack of support and documentation, but they may still be part of the job requirements.

Network Terminology

In the networking field, you must be familiar with a great many acronyms and terms. Table 13.25 shows a few of the most common terms.

TABLE 13.25   Common network terms

Term	Description
Address Resolution Protocol (**ARP**)	A protocol used to discover MAC addresses. To send a message using the TCP/IP protocol stack, a computer needs four key addresses: source IP, source MAC, destination IP, and destination MAC. The computer sending the message knows its own source IP and MAC addresses. When the computer does not know the destination MAC address (but knows the destination IP address), ARP is used to discover that destination MAC address.
Backbone	The part of the network that connects multiple buildings, floors, networks, and so on together.
Bandwidth	The width of a communications channel, which defines its capacity for data. Examples include up to 56 kbps for analog modems, 64 to 128 kbps for ISDN, and up to 100 Gbps for an Ethernet network.
Baseband	A system in which the entire cable bandwidth is used to transmit a digital signal. Because LANs use baseband, there must be an access method used to determine when a network device is allowed to transmit such as CSMA/CD.
Broadband	Cable bandwidth that is divided into multiple channels, on which simultaneous voice, video, and data can be sent.
Code Division Multiple Access (CDMA)	A protocol used in cellular networks as an alternative to GSM. Devices that attach to a CDMA-based network use a mobile equipment ID (MEID) and do not require a subscriber identity module (SIM) card.
Common Internet File System (**CIFS**)	A version of Server Message Block (SMB) used for providing shared network access to files and printers.

Term	Description
Fast Ethernet	An extension of the original Ethernet standard that permits data transmission of 100 Mbps. Fast Ethernet uses CSMA/CD, just like the original Ethernet standard.
Fiber Distributed Data Interface (FDDI)	A high-speed fiber network that uses the ring topology and the token passing method of access.
Global System for Mobile Communication (GSM)	The most widely used digital technology for cellular networks. Devices that attach to a GSM network require a subscriber identity module (SIM) card.
Hypertext Markup Language (HTML)	The programming language used on the Internet for creating web pages.
Internet Control Message Protocol (ICMP)	A Layer 3 protocol used when troubleshooting or evaluating networks. The `ping`, `pathping`, and `tracert` commands use ICMP.
Network Address Translation/Port Address Translation (NAT/PAT)	A method of conserving IP addresses. NAT uses private IP addresses that are translated to public IP addresses. PAT does the same thing, except it uses fewer public IP addresses by "overloading" one or more public IP addresses by tracking port numbers.
Point of Presence (POP)	An Internet access point. Also, Post Office Protocol, which is covered in the next section.
Secure Sockets Layer (SSL)	A protocol used to transmit Internet messages securely. This protocol is used with HTTPS and online shopping websites to secure credit card information.
Transmission Control Protocol (**TCP**)	A connection-oriented protocol that ensures reliable communication between two devices. TCP and UDP are the two most common transport layer protocols. TCP is used when a connection needs to be made, and if the data is not received, the data is re-sent. Website connections and some file transfer protocols use TCP.
User Datagram Protocol (**UDP**)	A Layer 4 connectionless protocol that applications use to communicate with a remote device. TCP and UDP are the two most common transport layer protocols. UDP is used when a connection is not very important, low overhead is needed (the UDP header is a lot smaller than a TCP header), or speed is of the essence. VoIP and DHCP use UDP.
Voice over IP (VoIP)	A method of sending a phone conversation over a data network instead of using traditional telephone circuits and wiring. It can include connectivity through the Internet. VoIP can be implemented by installing software on your computer and using speakers or headphones and an integrated or external microphone. Another method is to use special network-enabled phones that connect to an RJ-45 jack on your DSL or cable modem the same way your computer connects. In businesses, VoIP phones connect to an RJ-45 data jack that is wired to a PoE network switch. Most VoIP phones have a second RJ-45 port so that a PC can connect directly to the phone instead of having to have a second RJ-45 wall data jack wired to a switch. Corporate VoIP phones commonly use PoE.

The TCP/IP Model in Action

To see the TCP/IP model in action, imagine opening a web browser with two separate windows: `http://www.pearsoned.com` and `http://www.google.com`. Two separate packages of data would be formed. For example, because HTTP data is sent, HTTP specifies how the data is to be formatted at the application layer. So, web page 1 gets HTTP data at the application layer and moves down to the transport layer (inside the computer). At the transport layer, TCP is used for HTTP traffic, and TCP adds a source port number 51116 and a destination port number 80 as part of building the transport layer header. All this HTTP and TCP information moves down to the Internet layer, where IP adds source and destination IP addresses. Because Pearson Education's web server has the IP address 74.125.47.99, that is the destination IP address. The packet continues moving down the model to the network access layer, and because the LAN is an Ethernet LAN, a source MAC address and destination MAC address are added. The data and all the headers are placed onto the Ethernet cable and sent on their way. The same thing happens with the second web page, except that at the transport layer, TCP adds port number 51117 and destination port number 80.

TECH TIP

Use `netstat` to view current connections

To see current connections and associated port numbers, bring up a command prompt and type `netstat`.

When the Pearson Education web server delivers the web page to the computer, the data is, of course, from the web server, but the TCP port numbers are reversed. The web server places port number 80 as the source port number and port number 51116 as the destination port number. The source and destination IP addresses and MAC addresses are reversed as well. When the original computer gets the message, it knows which browser window generated port number 51116, and it places the Pearson Education information from the web server into the correct browser window. The same is true when the Google request comes back from the Google web server. TCP/IP-based protocols are required to send and receive data through the Internet. Table 13.26 shows some of the most popular protocols, a description, and the TCP/IP port number commonly used. Table 13.27 lists some of the common protocols or network standards and the TCP/IP model layers at which they operate.

TABLE 13.26   TCP/IP protocols and port numbers

Protocol	Common port number	Description
Apple Filing Protocol (**AFP**)	548	Provides file services for macOS.
Dynamic Host Configuration Protocol (DHCP)	67/68	Issues IP addressing information, such as IP address, subnet mask, default gateway, and DNS server address to network devices.
Domain Name System (DNS)	53	Translates Internet names and URLs into IP addresses.
File Transfer Protocol (**FTP**)	21	Sends/receives files from one computer to another network device; actually requires two port numbers: one to issue commands and the other one for data. Port 20 is sometimes but not always used for data.
Hypertext Transfer Protocol (**HTTP**)	80	Provides browser-based Internet communication.

Protocol	Common port number	Description
HTTP over SSL (Secure Sockets Layer) Protocol (**HTTPS**)	443	Provides encrypted HTTP communication through an SSL session.
Internet Message Access Protocol (**IMAP**)	143	Supports email retrieval . Allows synchronization from multiple devices.
Lightweight Directory Access Protocol (**LDAP**)	389	Provides records related to directory services (any type of network resource such as users, printers, phone numbers, files, access points, and so on)
NetBIOS over TCP/IP (**NetBT**)	137-139	Supports outdated applications that rely on the NetBIOS API to use a TCP/IP-based network. Also known as NBT.
Network Time Protocol (NTP)	123	Synchronizes time between network devices.
Post Office Protocol version 3 (**POP3**)	110	Supports email retrieval and stores email on a single network device (contrast with IMAP).
Remote Desktop Protocol (**RDP**)	3389	Connects one Windows computer to a remote Windows computer.
Secure File Transfer Protocol (SFTP)	22	Supports file transfer using the SSH protocol suite.
Secure Shell (**SSH**)	22	Supports secure connectivity to a remote device and allows secure file transfer.
Server Message Block (**SMB**)/CIFS (Common Internet File System)	445	Provides access to shared network devices, files, and printers, especially in a mixed environment, such as a combination of MAC and Windows computers. CIFS is a version of SMB. SMB/CIFS can use TCP port 445, but when used with the NetBIOS API, UDP ports 137 and 138 as well as TCP ports 137 and 139 are used (see NBT).
Service Location Protocol (**SLP**)	427	Announces and discovers services in a LAN.
Simple Mail Transfer Protocol (**SMTP**)	25	Transmits email and commonly used with MIME (Multipurpose Internet Mail Extensions) to include non-ASCII character sets and other rich media content within the email.
Simple Network Management Protocol (**SNMP**)	161/162	Used to monitor, communicate with, and manage network devices.
Telnet	23	Supports connecting to a remote network device; is not secure.

TABLE 13.27   TCP/IP layers and associated protocols/standards

Layer	Protocols
Application	HTTP, HTTPS, Telnet, SSH, FTP, SFTP, DNS
Transport	TCP, UDP
Internet (Internetwork)	IP, DHCP, ICMP
Network access	ARP, 802.3 (Ethernet), 802.11a, b, g, n, and ac (wireless)

Using the Network and Sharing Center Section of the Control Panel

Even though you can control many things from the notification area or from some of the Settings options on Windows 8 and 10, the bulk of network configuration settings are available through the *Network and Sharing Center* Control Panel. The *Network and Sharing Center* Control Panel has been used both in this chapter and Chapter 12, "Internet Connectivity, Virtualization, and Cloud Technologies," but knowing the details and purpose of the options is important to IT personnel. Figure 13.80 shows the *Network and Sharing Center* window. Note that the options are the same in Windows 7, 8, and 10.

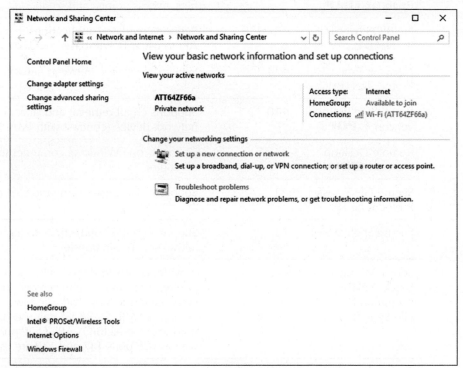

FIGURE 13.80   Windows 10 Network and Sharing Center window

Notice in the main portion of the screen that you can see what network is currently being used. You can see whether the connection is wired or wireless and the name of the network. You can also tell in home or small business networks if the computer can share files with others using the HomeGroup option (which is covered in the next section). This main screen is where you set up a dial-up, VPN, or broadband connection using the *Set Up a New Connection or Network* link. You can also use the *Troubleshoot Problems* link to get help if issues arise.

There are two important links in the left pane: *Change Adapter Settings* and *Change Advanced Sharing Settings*. The *Change Adapter Settings* link enables you to access the network adapters installed, as shown in Figure 13.81. If a network adapter that is installed in the computer is not listed, use *Device Manager* to troubleshoot and ensure that the device is enabled through UEFI/system BIOS.

FIGURE 13.81 Windows 10 Network Connections window

The *Network Connections* window is important when configuring an adapter. In it you can perform some of the following tasks:

> Double-click or tap the adapter icon to view device information. A wireless NIC shows wireless connectivity (see Figure 13.82), a wired NIC shows the wired network information (see Figure 13.83), and a Bluetooth adapter shows any Bluetooth pairs. At the bottom of each of the wired and wireless NIC windows, you can see the number of sent and received bytes (refer to Figures 13.82 and 13.83).

> Click the *Details* button in the wireless or wired NIC windows (*Wi-Fi Status or Local Area Connection Status*) to see information similar to that provided with the `ipconfig /all` command (see Figure 13.84).

FIGURE 13.82 Wireless NIC window

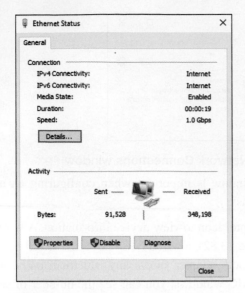

FIGURE 13.83   Wired NIC window

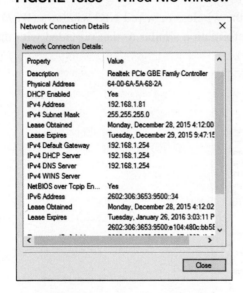

FIGURE 13.84   Wired or Wireless NIC details

> Click the *Wireless Properties* button in the wireless NIC window (*Wi-Fi Status* window) to view information about the specific type of wireless network. Use the *Security* tab to view the type of security applied.

> In both the wireless and wired NIC windows, click the *Properties* button to manually configure the NIC properties or modify a connection, such as the TCP/IPv4 or TCP/IPv6 parameters (see Figure 13.85).

> Double-click or tap the *Internet Protocol Version 4 (TCP/IPv4)* (or *TCP/IPv6*) link to configure the adapter for DHCP, statically assign an IP address (refer to Figure 13.56), or complete an alternative configuration (refer to Figure 13.58).

> Click or tap the *Configure* button to set wired or wireless NIC-related settings, such as speed and duplex (refer to Figure 13.63).

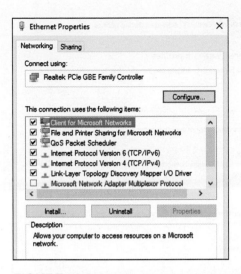

FIGURE 13.85   Wired or wireless networking properties window

> Manually configure the wireless NIC for a specific nonbroadcasting wireless network (refer to Figure 13.60).

> Set up a new Bluetooth connection. In Windows 7/8/10, access the *View Devices and Printers* Control Panel > *Add a Device* link. Ensure that the Bluetooth device is turned on and visible in the *Add a Device* window (see Figure 13.86). Select the device and click *Next*. Sometimes, a PIN or passcode must be verified in Windows and on the device.

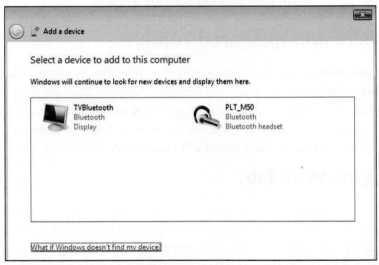

FIGURE 13.86   View Bluetooth devices in the Add a device window

> Finally, from the *Network and Sharing Center* Control Panel, select *Change Advanced Sharing Settings*. These settings relate to what the next section covers: sharing information across the networks you are now familiar with. Figure 13.87 shows the *Advanced Sharing Settings* window. Notice in Figure 13.87 there are three distinct and expandable sections: Private, Guest or Public, and All Networks. The Private section has been expanded so you can see the available options.

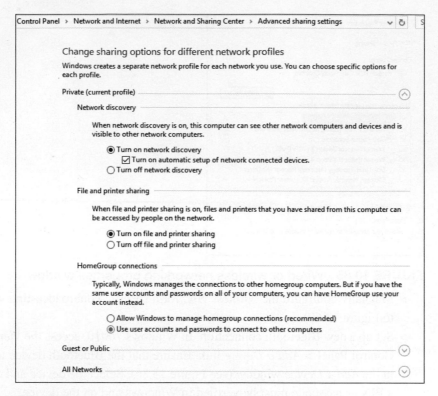

FIGURE 13.87   Advanced Sharing Settings window

Introduction to Shared Folders

When you double-click the *Network* option in Windows Explorer (Windows 7) or File Explorer (Windows 8/10), you can view other network devices by their assigned names. You can also view network device names by typing nbtstat -n at a command prompt. Knowing a network device name is important when accessing a network share across the network. A **network share** is a folder or device that has been shared and is accessible from a remote network device.

Using the *Share* Tab

The command prompt can be used to access network shares by typing the computer name and the share name, using the Universal Naming Convention (UNC). For example, say that a computer called *CSchmidt* has a network share called *TESTS*. By typing \\CSchmidt\TESTS at the command prompt, you can access the network share. Or you can type the IP address of the computer instead of the computer UNC. For example, if the CSchmidt computer had IP address 192.168.10.5, you could use \\192.168.10.5\TESTS from the command prompt instead. The problem with this method is that computer IP addresses are commonly provided by DHCP and could change. Next week, the CSchmidt computer could have the IP address 192.168.10.77, and the command would have to be adjusted. Figure 13.88 shows the *Sharing* tab.

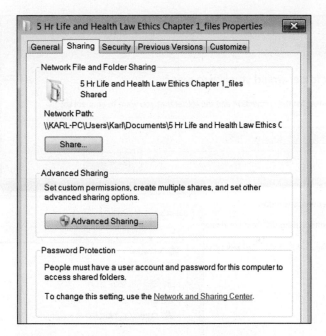

FIGURE 13.88 Windows 7 Sharing tab

CHAPTER 13

TECH TIP

How to share a folder

To share a folder, use *Windows Explorer/File Explorer*. Locate the folder to be shared and right-click it > *Properties* > *Sharing* tab > *Advanced Sharing* button. In the *Advanced Sharing* > *Share Name* textbox, type a name for the network share. On a remote computer, this name appears in Windows Explorer/File Explorer—in the *Network* section.

Mapping to a Share

In a network, it is common to map a drive letter to a frequently used network share. To map a drive letter to a network share in Windows 7, click the *Start* button > *Computer* > *Map Network Drive* > select a drive letter in the *Drive* box > in the *Folder* textbox type the UNC for the network share or click the *Browse* button to select the network share. The *Reconnect at Logon* checkbox allows you to connect to the mapped drive every time you log on.

In Windows 8 or 10, use File Explorer to locate and right-click or tap and briefly hold *This PC* > *Map Network Drive* > select a drive letter in the *Drive* box > in the *Folder* textbox type the UNC for the network share or click the *Browse* button to select the network share. The *Reconnect at Logon* checkbox allows you to connect to the mapped drive every time you log on. Figure 13.89 shows the windows to map drive letter Z: to the shared folder on the computer called CHERYL-PC. Expand the CHERYL-PC option to see the shared folders on this computer.

TECH TIP

Mapping from a prompt

A drive can be mapped from a command prompt. Use the net /? command for more help. For example, say that a computer with the name *TECH01* has a share called *Cheryl*. The following command can be used to attach to it using the drive letter M:

```
net use m: /persistent:yes \\TECH01\Cheryl
```

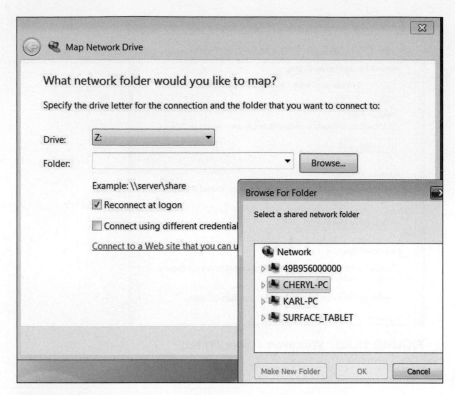

FIGURE 13.89   Windows 7 Map Network Drive window

Computer users commonly have network shares mapped to a drive letter for frequently used network shares. It is faster to access a network share by the drive letter than by searching around for the share through *Network*.

Creating a HomeGroup

Windows 7 and higher make it easier to create a network at home with the *HomeGroup* option. Here are some pointers to be aware of with Windows HomeGroup:

> Windows 7, 8, and 10 versions can create a HomeGroup. (However, note that Windows 10 versions 1803+ no longer include HomeGroup.)
> Windows Starter and Home Basic versions can join a HomeGroup but cannot create one.
> If Windows XP or Vista computers need to access information from a Windows 7, 8, or 10 computer that is on a HomeGroup network, access the *User Account* section of the Control Panel link on the Windows 7, 8, or 10 computer to create a new *Standard User* account username and password. Then, from the XP or Vista computer, use Windows Explorer to access the *Network/My Network Places* option in the left panel. Double-click the Windows computer that has the shared documents. Enter the username and password that was created on the Windows 7, 8, or 10 computer. Double-click the *Users* share that appears in the window, and all files and folders shared on the Windows computer are accessible.
> If a firewall other than the Windows firewall is active, the following ports need to be opened to find other PCs, find network devices, and use a HomeGroup: UDP ports 137, 138, 1900, 3540, 3702, and 5355; TCP ports 139, 445, 2869, 3587, 5357, and 5358.
> Each computer in the HomeGroup needs to have a unique name, and they all need to belong to the same workgroup. Make these changes in the *System* Control Panel.
> In the *Network and Sharing Center* window, ensure that the network type is set to a home or work network.

To access the HomeGroup Wizard to create or join a network, access the *HomeGroup* Control Panel. Part of the process is to create a password that is used to add other computers to the HomeGroup. Another part of the configuration process is to determine what to share, such as pictures, music, videos, documents, and printers. These particular libraries are then made available to other computers on the same network. On another computer, use the *HomeGroup* Control Panel and enter the password to join. Figure 13.90 shows the process for a computer to join a HomeGroup. Click the *Join Now* button > select what folders to share > *Next* > enter the password that is on the computer that created the HomeGroup.

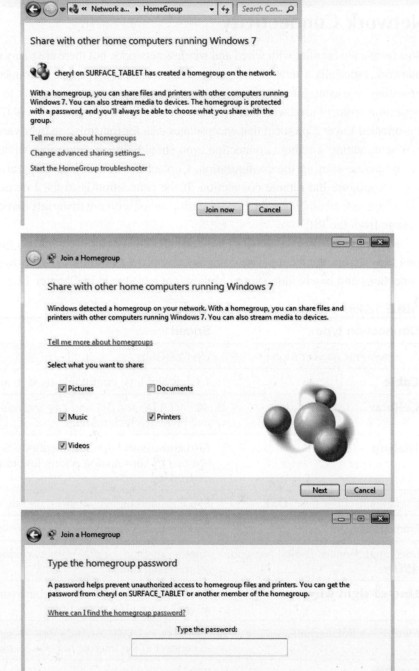

FIGURE 13.90 Windows 7 HomeGroup configuration window

For corporate users, you commonly must use a domain username (a username that has been configured on a centralized server) and a domain password. The rights you have been given determine the network resources you are allowed to access. Common parameters that must be entered when logging in to a domain to access corporate resources are a username and password. Commonly, the domain name must also be specified. If a company domain called GoBig had a user with the username JTech (who had the password 5tay-ouT), Joe Tech might be prompted for a username and password and would have to type GoBig\JTech for the username because the *Domain_name\ Username* format specifies the name of the domain and then the appropriate user ID, followed by the appropriate password in the password textbox.

Network Connectivity

Most people are familiar with wired and wireless networks, but there are many methods used to create a network, especially a network that gets you into a building. The type of connection, the protocol, and the settings you configure on the remote computer depend on the company to which you connect. A connection protocol used with dial-up networking is Point-to-Point Protocol (PPP). PPP is a connection-oriented Layer 2 protocol that encapsulates data for transmission over various connection types.

When creating a remote connection, you should always determine what parameters are to be entered *before* starting the configuration. Contact the network administrator for exact details on how to configure the remote connection. If the connection is to the Internet via an ISP, detailed instructions are available on the ISP's website and/or with the materials that come with the Internet package from the ISP.

There are many types of network connections. Businesses use various types of network connections leased from the local phone company or a provider. Table 13.28 shows the types of network connections and bandwidth. (Some of these are introduced in Chapter 12.)

TABLE 13.28   Network connection types

Connection type	Speed
Asynchronous Transfer Mode (ATM)	Up to 2 Gbps
Cable	1 Gbps and less; commonly used to also bring video
Cellular	3G, 4G, LTE, and 5G and can use non-line-of-sight and fixed wireless technologies
Dial-up	Also known as Plain Old Telephone Service (POTS); 2,400 bps to 115 kbps analog phone line to perform dial-up networking
Digital Subscriber Line (**DSL**)	256 kbps and higher; shares data line with voice line
Frame Relay	56 kbps to 1.544 Mbps
Integrated Services Digital Network (**ISDN**)	Another method for dial-up networking—64 kbps to 1.544 Mbps digital line
Line-of-sight wireless	Used with WiMAX to connect between WiMAX antennas as well as for LTE connections
MetroE (MetroEthernet)	Speeds of 1, 10, 40, or 100 Gbps, using Ethernet technology to connect to the Internet or connect multiple sites/buildings
Satellite	750 kbps and higher
T1	1.544 Mbps guaranteed bandwidth between two points
T3	44 Mbps guaranteed bandwidth between two points

SOFT SKILLS: BEING PROACTIVE

A good technician is **proactive**, which means the technician thinks of ways to improve a situation, anticipates problems, and fixes problems before being told to. A proactive technician follows up after a service call to ensure that a repair fixed the problem rather than waiting for another help desk ticket that states that the problem is unresolved. When something happens or a problem with a customer occurs, a proactive technician provides a list of recommended solutions or procedural changes to the supervisor rather than waiting for the supervisor to delineate what changes must occur.

For example, consider a technician at a college. The technician is responsible for any problems logged by computer users through the help desk. The technician is also responsible for maintaining the computer classrooms used by various departments. Each term, the technician reloads the computers with software updates and changes requested by the teachers. A proactive technician checks each machine and ensures that the computers boot properly and that the load is successful.

Another example involves checking new software. When the computers are reloaded each term, a faculty member is asked to check the load. A proactive technician has a list of "standard" software loaded on the computer, such as the operating system, service pack level, and any applications that are standard throughout the college. A separate list would include the changes that have been applied to the computer. Then the faculty member can simply look at the list and verify the load. Being proactive actually saves both the technician and the faculty member time.

The opposite of proactive is reactive. A reactive technician responds to situations only when there is a problem reported. A reactive technician does not look for ways to avoid problems. For example, a proactive technician ensures that a computer is configured with automatic updates of virus scanning software. A reactive technician waits until a help desk ticket is created for a computer that exhibits unusual behavior (for example, it has a virus) even though the technician notices the unusual behavior when installing a second monitor.

As a student, practice being proactive. Start an assignment a day before you would normally start it. Talk to your teacher about your grade in advance (before the day preceding the final). Bring something to write with and paper to school. Finally, take this practice into your IT career: Be proactive as an IT professional and increase the level of service and professionalism to the field.

Chapter Summary

> Networks are created to share data and devices and connect to the Internet. Types of networks include PANs, LANs, MANs, WANs, and WMNs.
> Networks can be wired or wireless.
> A workgroup/HomeGroup network is composed of a small number of computers, whereas the client/server type of network is used in companies in a domain environment. A domain environment has a server that provides authentication to resources with a centralized user ID and password. A workgroup network manages the usernames on a computer-by-computer basis, which grows less secure and more difficult to manage as the network grows. A Microsoft HomeGroup network has a single password.
> An Ethernet LAN, which is the most common type of LAN, is wired in a star or extended star topology. A switch is used to connect the devices. Each network connects to a router for communication with other networks. The router's IP address is the default gateway for all network devices on a particular LAN.

> Computers must have IP addresses to participate in a TCP/IP-based network (and gain access to the Internet). IPv4 is the most common addressing used on computers today, but IPv6 addresses are slowly being assigned and used by corporate devices and Internet providers.

> IP addresses are grouped by classes, with a particular subnet mask for each class. Each default mask can be changed to further subdivide a network for more efficient and manageable addressing. DHCP can provide addresses to network devices, or a static address can be assigned. Public addresses are routable on the Internet. Private addresses are used within homes and companies. These addresses can be translated to public addresses by using NAT/PAT.

> TCP/IP is a suite that includes the following important protocols: FTP, Telnet, SMTP, DNS, DHCP, HTTP, HTTPS, POP3, IMAP, RDP, LDAP, SNMP, SSH, SFTP, TCP, UDP, IP, AFP, and ICMP.

> The OSI model is a networking model that has seven layers: application, presentation, session, transport, network, data link, and physical. The TCP/IP model is a working model that contains four layers: application, transport, Internet (internetwork), and network access. The devices and applications that work at Layer 3 (network or Internet layers) include routers, IP, and ICMP. The devices and applications that work at Layer 2 (data link or network access) include switches, access points, and ARP. Keep in mind that Ethernet has Layer 2 specifications. This is why a MAC address is a Layer 2 address. The devices that work at Layer 1 (physical layer or network access layer) are cables, connectors, hubs, and wireless antennas.

> 802.11 and Bluetooth are types of wireless networks. Bluetooth is used in PANs, and 802.11 is used in wireless LANs. 802.11 wireless NICs include 802.11a, b, g, n, and ac. 802.11a, n, and ac work in the 5 GHz range; 802.11b, g, and n work in the 2.4 GHz range. 802.11 antennas are either directional or omnidirectional.

> The key tools for troubleshooting a networked computer are the `ipconfig`, `ping`, `nslookup`, and `tracert` commands, and a cable tester.

> Network sharing can be done by sharing folders or by using a HomeGroup.

> A technician should be proactive as opposed to reactive and should prevent problems and situations whenever possible.

A+ CERTIFICATION EXAM TIPS

✓ This chapter provides information related to both the 220-1001 and 220-1002 exams. The information related to the 1002 exam includes how to create a HomeGroup, the *Network and Sharing Center* Control Panel, and network installation items (alternative address, dial-up, wireless, wired WWAN [cellular], network-related commands—`ipconfig`, `ifconfig`, `tracert`, `netstat`, `net use`, `net user`, `ipconfig /flushdns`, and `ping`—NIC properties, network shares, and drive mapping).

✓ Know the difference between a LAN, WAN, PAN, MAN, and WMN.

✓ Know the purpose of the network devices: hub, router, access point, bridge, modem, firewall, patch panel, cloud-based network controller (see Chapter 12), cable/DSL modem (see Chapter 12), repeater, PoE (injectors and switch), Ethernet over Power, and switch (both managed and unmanaged).

✓ Know the purposes of key networking protocols, port numbers used by the protocols, and the difference between TCP and UDP.

✓ Know when to use a particular type of networking tool, whether it is a physical tool or a command. Be able to determine if a network rack is grounded by looking for a ground strap.

✓ Describe how a hub and switch operate and the differences between the two.

✓ Know what to do when one or more computers cannot connect to the Internet or when they have an IP address conflict. Be able to tell whether the problem is an Internet connection problem or what specific network resources the device can't reach, such as network shares, printers, or email.

✓ Know how to manually configure an IP address on a network device such as a computer, an AP, or a printer.

✓ Know how to configure an alternative configuration on a computer.

✓ Know the different types of wireless networks and their compatibility with each other.

✓ Be able to configure a wireless network and 2.4 GHz and 5 GHz channels so multiple wireless APs can coexist as well as other parameters, such as an administrator password and DHCP.

✓ Know the purpose of an IP address, a default gateway, and a subnet mask.

✓ Know the difference between an IPv4 address and an IPv6 address.

✓ Recognize when an address is a private IP address and understand the difference between a public IP address and a private IP address.

✓ Know the different types of network cabling and connectors.

✓ Recognize when a computer gets assigned an IP address from APIPA.

✓ Know the port numbers and purposes of the following protocols as well as the difference between TCP and UDP: 21 (FTP), 22 (SSH), 23 (Telnet), 25 (SMTP), 53 (DNS), 67/68 (DHCP), 80 (HTTP), 110 (POP3), 143 (IMAP), 443 (HTTPS), 3389 (RDP), 137–139 (NetBIOS/NetBT), 161–162 (SNMP), 389 (LDAP), 445 (SMB/CIFS), 427 (SLP), and 548 (AFP).

✓ Know the purposes of different servers: web, file, print, DHCP, DNS, proxy, mail, authentication, end-point management, and syslog.

✓ Review the section on troubleshooting network printer problems.

✓ If a wireless laptop cannot get on a wireless network, you might have to forget the network, reconnect, and provide credentials. You can also check if wireless has been disabled.

✓ Be able to recognize and troubleshoot problems with IP addressing information that comes from a DHCP server (IP address, default gateway, subnet mask, and DNS server address).

✓ Be able to troubleshoot wireless problems. Move the device to a different location. Make sure that the wireless NIC is turned on.

✓ Know the difference between a PAN, LAN, MAN, WAN, WLAN, WWAN, and WMN.

✓ Be able to use the `ipconfig` command and review the options available (`ipconfig /?` to see).

✓ Know the difference between how a hub operates and a switch operates.

✓ Be able to configure the following IoT devices: thermostat, light switch, security camera, door lock, and voice-enabled smart speaker/digital assistant. Also know that these devices may connect via Bluetooth, 802.11 wireless, Zigbee, or Z-Wave. You should know the differences between these wireless standards.

Key Terms

2.4 GHz 650	alternative IP address 668	cable 706
5 GHz 650	APIPA 667	cable management system 636
access point 652	ARP 694	cable stripper 631
account settings 675	authentication server 693	cable tester 633
ad hoc mode 654	Basic QoS 676	Cat 5 528
AES 671	blacklist 676	Cat 5e 528
AFP 696	bridge 652	Cat 6 528
alternative configuration 668	broadcast address 648	cellular 706

Review Questions

1. Match the network type on the left with the scenario on the right.

    _____ MAN   **a.** Home network of four PCs

    _____ LAN   **b.** City of Schmidtville networks

    _____ PAN   **c.** Hewlett-Packard corporate networks

    _____ WAN   **d.** Bluetooth network of two devices

2. Match the following. Note that even though an answer may be valid for more than one answer, only one answer will allow all answers to be used. No term is used twice.

    a. Cat 3 UTP   _____ Common type of LAN cable

    b. Cat 6 UTP   _____ 1 Gbps over UTP

    c. 1000BaseT   _____ Voice-grade phone network cable

    d. 1000BaseSX _____ 1 Gbps over fiber

3. Which network device would be best to use to connect wired devices and can send data directly to the destination device without sending the data as a broadcast to every connected device?

    [access point | hub | router | switch]

4. Match the TCP/IP model layer to the description. Note that a layer can be used more than once.

    a. Application   _____ HTTP   _____ a straight-through cable   _____ a NIC

    b. Transport   _____ a router   _____ UDP   _____ DNS

    c. Internet   _____ a switch   _____ IP   _____ TCP

    d. Network access _____ ICMP   _____ MAC address   _____ a wireless antenna

5. Some computers (both wired and wireless) in a specific area of the building are having problems connecting to printers, servers and the Internet. What should the technician do?

    a. Use a tone generator

    b. Check the access point

    c. Check the DHCP server

    d. Check problem computers for a DNS server address

6. What does the *1000* mean in the term 1000BaseT?

    a. The speed of transmission, which is 1000 Mbps

    b. The maximum distance for a cable in meters

    c. The maximum distance for a cable in feet

    d. The speed of transmission, which is 1000 bps

7. Which network device works at Layer 1 and sends received data out all its ports (except the port that received the data)?

    [switch | antenna | router | hub]

8. What is the most common network protocol suite and the protocol suite required to communicate on the Internet?

    [LTE | TCP/IP | Bluetooth | ISO]

9. Which type of address is 48 bits long? [IP | TCP | MAC | NAT]

10. Which type of address is called a Layer 3 address? [IP | TCP | MAC | NAT]

11. Which type of IP address uses 128 bits? [IPv4 | IPv32 | IPv6 | IPv64]

12. Draw a vertical line between the network number and the host number for each of the following IP addresses (assuming the default subnet mask):

    130.5.15.177   130.5.| 15.177

    192.168.13.15   192.168.13.| 15

    10.12.17.18   10.| 12.17.18

13. What protocol could be used to issue an IP address and the IP address of the DNS server to network devices?
    [DNS | DHCP | ICMP | ARP]

14. What protocol is used to convert URLs to IP addresses?
    [HTTP | SSH | SSL | UDP | DNS]

15. Two access points connect and extend *the same* wireless network. List the SSIDs for each access point in the following chart.

Access point	SSID
Access Point 1	
Access Point 2	

16. Two access points (AP1 and AP2) operating in the 2.4 GHz range have overlapping coverage areas. List the two channel IDs to assign to each access point by filling in the following chart.

Access point	Channel ID
AP1	
AP2	

17. Two 802.11n access points (AP1 and AP2) operating in the 5 GHz range have overlapping coverage areas. List the two channel IDs to assign to each access point by filling in the following chart.

Access point	Channel ID
AP1	
AP2	

18. [T | F] When communicating with an access point, a wireless NIC and an access point must be configured to the same frequency.

19. Match the following definitions. Note that not all options on the right are used.

____ 802.11a   **a.** Operates in the 2.4 GHz range, with speeds up to 54 Mbps

____ 802.11b   **b.** Operates in the 2.4 GHz range, with speeds up to 2 Mbps

____ 802.11g   **c.** Operates in the 2.4 GHz range, with speeds up to 11 Mbps

____ 802.11i   **d.** Security specification

____ 802.11n   **e.** Operates in the 5 GHz range, with speeds up to 54 Mbps

____ 802.11ac   **f.** Specifies interoperability between access points

g. Standard for quality of service

h. Standard for wireless interference

i. Backward compatible with 802.11a, b, and g

j. Allows eight simultaneous data streams

20. In Figure 13.91, what IP address is the default gateway for host 203.145.15.2?

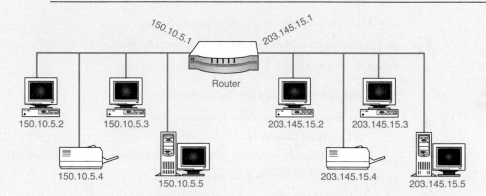

FIGURE 13.91   Review question network scenario

21. Which command determines whether another network device is reachable?

`[ ping | ipconfig | ipconfig /all | arp -a ]`

22. On which network device would VLANs be configured?

`[ hub | switch | router | firewall ]`

23. Which two port numbers could be used to remotely access a network server? (Choose two.)

`[ 21 | 22 | 23 | 53 | 69 | 80 | 443 ]`

24. What command can be used to see a computer's MAC address?

`[ netdom | net | netstat | ipconfig /all ]`

25. A technician is setting up a new printer and notices that the computer is running unusually slowly. The technician decides to do only the job that was logged (install the new printer). Is the technician being reactive or proactive?

`[ proactive | reactive ]`

Exercises

Exercise 13.1 Understanding Wireless AP Paper Configuration

Objective: To determine what menu item would be used for specific functions

Procedure: Use the given menu options to determine which one would be used to perform a common configuration task on a wireless AP.

Note: Many times an IT professional must deal with a device or a particular model that is unfamiliar. Many wireless AP menus are similar so practicing which menu option might be the one chosen is a good activity.

Wireless AP sample menu and submenu options:

a. Setup—Language, Date/Time

b. Wireless—Basic Wireless Settings, Wireless Security, Wireless MAC Filter, Advanced Wireless Settings

c. WAN/LAN—Internet Setup and Network Setup

d. Administration—Management, Access, Security, Factory Defaults, Firmware Upgrade

e. Status—Access Point, Wireless Network, About

Select which menu option would be used to do the following:

_____ 1. Change the password used to access the AP menu.

_____ 2. Configure for UPnP.

_____ 3. Configure to only allow 802.11n 2.4 GHz devices to attach (not 802.11b or g).

_____ 4. Check connectivity with another device.

_____ 5. Change the SSID.

_____ 6. Disable SSID broadcasting.

_____ 7. Configure the device as a DHCP server for wireless clients.

_____ 8. Set the year.

_____ 9. Reset the device.

_____ 10. Determine how many wireless hosts are currently attached to the AP.

Exercise 13.2 Understanding T568B Color Sequence

Objective: To articulate the proper colored order of a T568B straight-through cable

Procedure: Use the given graphic to denote which color of cable goes into the connector from left to right.

Use Figure 13.92 to designate which color of vinyl insulator should go into making a T568B connector.

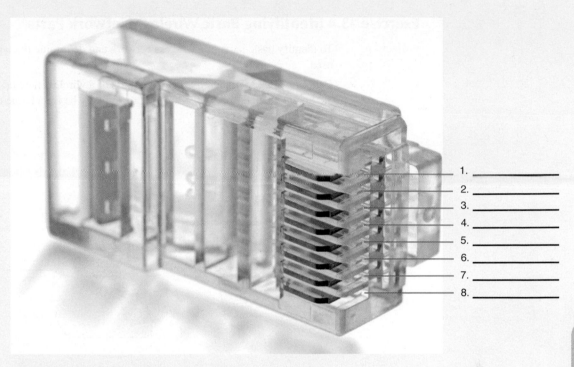

FIGURE 13.92   RJ-45 connector/cabling exercise

Exercise 13.3 Recognizing Network Devices

Objective: To recognize a network device on sight

Procedure: Use Figure 13.93 to identify each network device.

Note: Possible answers could include the following. Note that not all devices are used. No device is shown twice.

Possible devices:

Internet router	Termination plate	Switch
Hub	Patch panel	Repeater
Bridge	Wireless router	Firewall

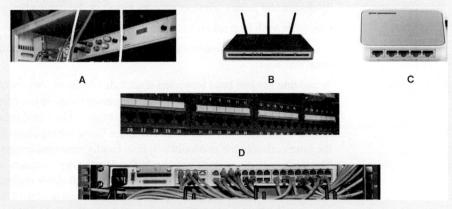

FIGURE 13.93   Network device identification

A _____

B _____

C _____

D _____

E _____

Exercise 13.4 Identifying Basic Wireless Network Parts

Objective: To identify basic parts of a wireless network and determine the type of wireless network used

Procedure: Using Figure 13.94, identify the major parts of a wireless network. For the number 5 blank, document whether this network would most likely be for a home or a corporate network and explain why.

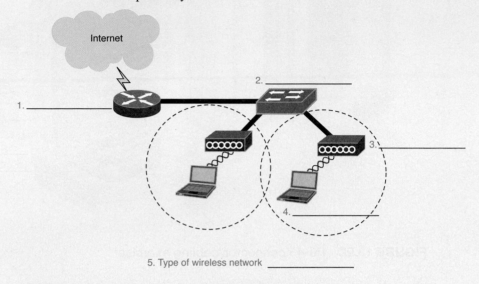

5. Type of wireless network _____

FIGURE 13.94   Wireless network components

1. _____
2. _____
3. _____
4. _____
5. _____

Exercise 13.5 Wireless Network Case Study

Objective: To design and price a wireless network based on the parameters given

Parts: Computer with Internet access

Note: The instructor or lab assistant can speak on behalf of the faculty members if any design questions arise.

Scenario: A building has just been renovated to include faculty offices and two new classrooms, as shown in Figure 13.95. The only wired networks are in the computer classroom (not shown) and the administrator's office (not shown). The wired network allows access to the Internet. The wired network connections are in the wiring closet shown in the diagram at the intersection of the two hallways. Five faculty members are issued laptop computers. The laptops do not include wireless NICs. The faculty members want to use their laptops in their classrooms and offices. There are also comfortable chairs in the hallways, and faculty would like to use their laptops in the hallways as well. The faculty would like (1) access to the Internet and (2) access to a printer. Currently, there are no printers in the classrooms or the faculty area that they can use.

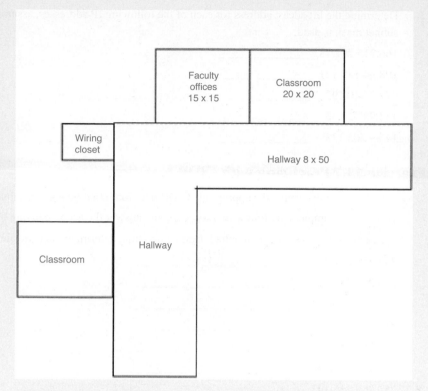

FIGURE 13.95   Building floor plan for wireless design

Tasks:

> Design a wireless network to allow faculty to use their laptops to gain access to the Internet. Provide this drawing in an electronic form to the instructor. This can be done in Word, Visio, PowerPoint, or some other drawing program.

> Provide a detailed list of wireless network parts, part numbers, prices, and a web link where the prices were obtained. This will include the antenna type, a printout of the wireless antenna radiation pattern, and antenna coverage range.

> Provide the instructor with a typewritten list of policies and configuration settings for the wireless network. You are the designer and implementer and what you decide goes.

Exercise 13.6 Practicing with Network Numbers and Broadcast Addresses

Objective: To determine the subnet numbers, broadcast addresses, and IP addresses that can be assigned to network devices

Procedure: Complete the following procedure and answer the accompanying questions.

1.   Determine the network address for each of the following IP addresses, assuming that the default subnet mask is used.

210.141.254.122 _____

206.240.195.38 _____

14.130.188.213 _____

129.89.5.224 _____

110.113.71.66 _____

2. Determine the broadcast address for each of the following IP addresses, assuming that the default subnet mask is used.

166.215.207.182 _____

198.94.140.121 _____

97.57.210.192 _____

133.98.227.36 _____

14.89.203.133 _____

Exercise 13.7 Practicing with CIDR Notation

Objective: To determine the appropriate CIDR notation based on a given subnet mask

Procedure: Complete the following procedure and answer the accompanying questions.

For each subnet mask given in dotted decimal notation, determine the equivalent CIDR notation.

255.255.255.0   _____

255.255.255.224   _____

255.255.255.252   _____

255.255.254.0   _____

255.255.0.0   _____

255.255.255.128   _____

255.255.255.192   _____

255.0.0.0   _____

255.255.240.0   _____

255.255.255.240   _____

Exercise 13.8 Determining the Default Gateway

Objective: To determine the appropriate default gateway for a PC based on a given situation.

Procedure: Complete the following procedure and answer the accompanying questions.

1. Determine the appropriate IP address, subnet mask (in dotted decimal notation, x.x.x.x), and default gateway for PC1 shown in Figure 13.96.

IP address: _____

Subnet mask: _____

Default gateway: _____

2. Determine the appropriate IP address, subnet mask (in dotted decimal notation, x.x.x.x), and default gateway for PC2 shown in Figure 13.96.

IP address: _____

Subnet mask: _____

Default gateway: _____

3. Determine the appropriate IP address, subnet mask (in dotted decimal notation, x.x.x.x), and default gateway for PC3 shown in Figure 13.96.

    IP address: _____

    Subnet mask: _____

    Default gateway: _____

4. Determine the appropriate IP address, subnet mask (in dotted decimal notation, x.x.x.x), and default gateway for PC4 shown in Figure 13.96.

    IP address: _____

    Subnet mask: _____

    Default gateway: _____

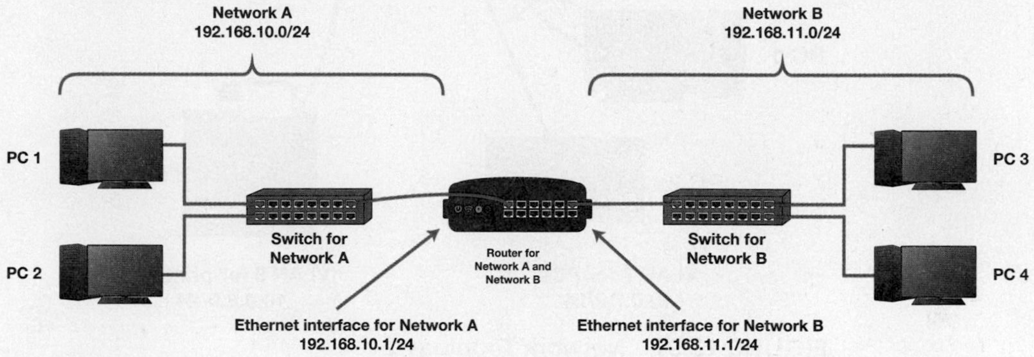

FIGURE 13.96   Network Topology 1

5. Determine the appropriate IP address, subnet mask (in dotted decimal notation, x.x.x.x), and default gateway for PC1 shown in Figure 13.97.

    IP address: _____

    Subnet mask: _____

    Default gateway: _____

6. Determine the appropriate IP address, subnet mask (in dotted decimal notation, x.x.x.x), and default gateway for PC2 shown in Figure 13.97.

    IP address: _____

    Subnet mask: _____

    Default gateway: _____

7. Determine the appropriate IP address, subnet mask (in dotted decimal notation, x.x.x.x), and default gateway for the printer shown in Figure 13.97.

    IP address: _____

    Subnet mask: _____

    Default gateway: _____

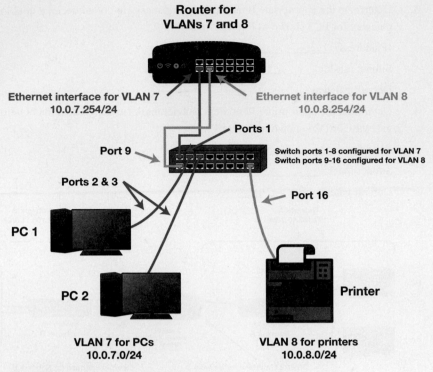

FIGURE 13.97   Network Topology 2

Activities

Internet Discovery

Objective: To obtain specific information regarding a computer or its associated parts on the Internet

Parts: Computer with Internet access

Procedure: Complete the following procedure and answer the accompanying questions.

1. On an HP Pavilion dm3z laptop, you cannot get the wireless NIC to attach to the wireless network. What are some steps you can take, as recommended by HP, to help in this situation?

   Write at least three solutions as well as the URL where you found the solution.

   _____

   _____

   _____

2. What does the term Wake on Wireless mean, and at what URL did you locate the answer?

   _____

   _____

3. Locate a website that describes how to reserve an IP address on a Netgear router. Write the one router model the answer applies to, the menu option used to configure, and the URL where you found this information.

   _____

   _____

   _____

4. Find an Internet forum that discusses Bluetooth and Windows 7 on Lenovo laptops. Write one key piece of information you found about configuring Bluetooth. Write the URL where you found the information.

    _____

    _____

5. Find an Internet site that explains the differences between Cat 5e and Cat 6 UTP cable. Write which standard you would recommend to the CIO and why. List the URL where you found this information.

    _____

    _____

Soft Skills

Objective: To enhance and fine-tune a technician's ability to listen, communicate in both written and oral form, and support people who use computers in a professional manner

Activities:

1. Using the Internet, find and access a utility that tests your soft skills. Compare your scores with those of others in the class and determine how you might improve in specific weak areas.

2. In groups of two, one person puts a network problem in a computer, while the other person is out of the room. When the other person comes back, they troubleshoot the problem by asking questions of the user (as if they were on the phone helping them). The person performing the troubleshooting cannot touch the computer. Discuss strategies for doing this better before swapping roles.

3. In groups of two or three, brainstorm three examples of a technician being reactive rather than proactive. List ways the technician could have been more proactive for each example. Share your findings with other teams.

Critical Thinking Skills

Objective: To analyze and evaluate information as well as apply learned information to new or different situations

Activities:

1. A home user connects to the Internet. The ISP provides hard drive space for the user's web page. Is this a network? Why or why not? Write your answer in a well-written paragraph using good grammar, capitalization, and punctuation.

    _____

    _____

    _____

    _____

    _____

    _____

2. Use the Internet, magazines, newspapers, or books to find a network installation case study. Make a table of terms they use that were introduced in this chapter. On the left side, list the term, and on the right side, define or describe how the term relates to the network installation. Analyze the installation and discuss with a team. Make a checklist of approved processes and of recommended changes to implemented processes. Share your team findings with the class.

3. In a team environment, design a wired and wireless network for a small business with 10 computers. Name the business, provide a design and implementation plan, and provide a list of items for which you should do more research. Share your plan with the class.

14 Introduction to Operating Systems

In this chapter you will learn:

> To identify the basic features and functions of an operating system

> To identify various types of operating systems: desktop, workstation, and mobile device operating systems

> To identify end-of-life, compatibility, and updating operating system concerns

> To identify specific corporate needs

> To identify and use common desktop icons in Windows 7/8/10

> To manage files and folders in Windows

> To work with the Windows registry

> To create backups and to create a system image

> Techniques to stay current in the field

CompTIA Exam Objectives:

What CompTIA A+ exam objectives are covered in this chapter?

✓ 1002-1.1 Compare and contrast common operating system types and their purposes.

✓ 1002-1.2 Compare and contrast features of Microsoft Windows versions.

✓ 1002-1.5 Given a scenario, use Microsoft operating system features and tools.

✓ 1002-1.6 Given a scenario, use Microsoft Control Panel utilities.

Operating Systems Overview

The operating system (OS) is the most important piece of software on a computer because without it, no application can run and the hardware cannot work. While today's operating systems provide many services, the basic service of an **operating system** is to be the interface between the user and the hardware as well as software applications installed on or executed by the computer.

You might be asking yourself what kind of things the operating system can do. The operating system does many tasks, but some that really affect you as a student are recognizing what you type on the keyboard (or do using a mouse or a touchpad) and bringing that information into the computer as input. The operating system controls output to the display, keeping track of files and folders, managing and keeping track of open applications, and controlling peripherals such as printers.

The **boot process** is the steps a device goes through when a computer is first turned on. The central processing unit (CPU) initializes itself. It looks to the system's basic input/output system (BIOS or UEFI BIOS) for its first instruction. It runs the power-on self-test (POST), which makes sure the hardware is functioning properly. When this is complete, the BIOS looks for an operating system to load.

At this point, the operating system takes control of the boot process. The operating system loads the necessary device drivers to control devices such as a printer, CD/DVD drive, mouse, and keyboard. Once drivers are loaded, the user can access the system's applications and begin to work.

Virtually everything today's users do with their computers is done through an application, and every application must run through the operating system. The list of applications is endless, and new applications are being developed daily. The operating system allows a computer to do almost anything—from the baby monitor installed by new parents, to the tablet a hospital nurse uses to enter patient information, to the digital music player a teenager uses to listen to his favorite tunes, to the computer a microbiologist is using to analyze data.

Each application must be written to communicate with a specific operating system because each operating system has its own specific code and syntax. Therefore, the choice of operating system largely determines the applications a computer can run. Many applications today are developed for multiple operating systems, and this requires that multiple versions of the application be created.

TECH TIP

Buy an application for a particular operating system

You must be careful, when buying or installing an application, to get the version created for your operating system.

User Interaction with Operating Systems

When you click on something or type something in a search box, you are interacting with the operating system. The operating system therefore has to be programmed with what to do based on what you do. At the most basic level, an operating system responds to a set of commands. The commands are accepted and processed by the operating system's command processor. Today's operating systems allow most commands to be entered by clicking on something through the graphical user interface (**GUI**) or by entering a command through the command line interface. The **command line interface** is not graphical and is only used to enter or view commands. For example, you can use the command line interface to rename a file as shown at the top of Figure 14.1, or you can use the GUI interface as shown below the command. Through the GUI, simply right-click on the file in Windows Explorer or File Explorer and select the *Rename* option.

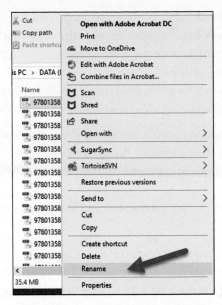

FIGURE 14.1 Command line interface (top image) and GUI (bottom image)

The operating system is also responsible for handling file and disk management. That is why the Windows Explorer (renamed File Explorer in Windows 8 and 10) tools are part of the standard Windows operating system. Figure 14.2 shows Windows Explorer from a Windows 7 computer.

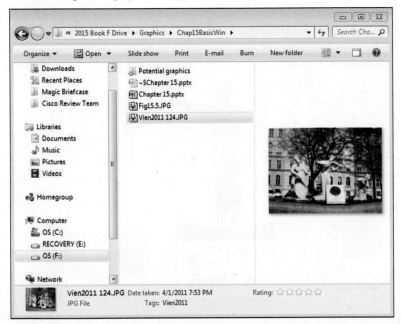

FIGURE 14.2 Windows Explorer

A **file** is an electronic container that holds computer code or data. Another way of looking at a file is to think of it as either a box of bits or an electronic piece of paper with information on it. A **folder** holds files and can also contain other folders. In Figure 14.2, *Potential Graphics* is a folder. With Windows Explorer/File Explorer, you can create, copy, or move files or folders.

An alternative environment used by technicians when there is a problem is the command prompt environment, also called the command line interface. From a command prompt, you can enter commands that are specific to the operating system. For example, say that you type the word

hop at the command prompt. The word "hop" is not a command that the computer has been programmed to understand, so an error message appears because the computer does not know what to do. However, if you type **dir** at a command prompt, the computer recognizes the command and displays a *directory*, which is a listing of files.

To access the command prompt from within Windows, use the following steps, but always remember that there are several ways of accomplishing almost anything within the Windows environment:

> Windows 7: Access the *Start* button menu > select *All Programs* > locate and click the *Accessories* option > double-click the *Command Prompt* option.
> Windows 8/8.1: Access the *Command Prompt* tile located as an option under *Windows System*.
> Windows 10: Type **command** in the *Search the Web and Windows* textbox > select *Command Prompt* from the search result.

Chapter 15, "Introduction to Scripting," covers using the command prompt in greater depth.

Technicians must be familiar with the GUI environment and must also be able to function from a command prompt because sometimes the only way to execute a fix is by typing a command at a command prompt. Not only must technicians be familiar with the tools and environments, they must know multiple operating systems. This makes for a challenging and ever-changing environment. Figure 14.3 shows that the operating system is the coordinator of all hardware and software. The operating system is the software that any computer device needs to function.

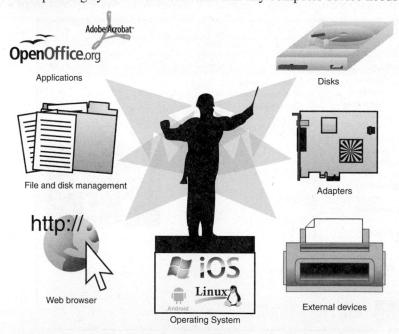

FIGURE 14.3   The operating system coordinates everything

Overview of Popular Operating Systems

Six of the most common operating systems today are Microsoft's Windows, Apple's macOS, Linux, Chrome OS, Android, and Apple's iOS. The last two are specifically used for mobile devices, such as cell phones and tablets, and Windows also has a version of its operating system for mobile devices.

In 2018 it was estimated that more than 90% of all personal computers use some version of Windows, and the remainder use Linux or macOS. It's important to remember that these numbers reflect worldwide usage.

The **Microsoft Windows** operating system dominates the personal computer world and remains the most popular operating system for home and office computers. Microsoft Windows was announced by Bill Gates in November 1983. Since then, there have been numerous versions and updates.

DOS 3.1 was used as the first operating system for Apple computers in 1978. The **Apple Macintosh OS** that might be more familiar to you was not introduced until 1997, as Mac OS 8. Mac OS 9 was introduced in 1999, the same year as Mac OS X Server was introduced. At the time of press, the latest version is macOS X. Apple has used the Roman numeral X as the major version number 10 throughout the version X development history. The **macOS** runs only on Apple laptops and desktops, so it is a **proprietary system**.

In 1991 a Finnish student, Linus Torvalds, began work on a personal project: to build a new free operating system kernel known as Linux. The **kernel** is the core of a computer's operating system. People from all over the world continue to collaborate on the Linux **open source** code to submit tweaks to the central kernel.

The Windows operating system can be used on a wide variety of computers manufactured by many different companies. Apple computers, on the other hand, are the only computers that can use macOS. **Linux** has maintained its original goal of being a free and open source operating system. When you purchase an operating system license, there are several types available: (1) an open and free license such as when you download and install Linux, (2) a personal license such as when you buy the rights to use the operating system on one computer such as a home computer or for each small business computer, (3) a corporate license where you get a discount for a specific number of installs for Microsoft Windows, for example, and (4) an enterprise license, which might include more security, cloud, and virtualization options.

32-bit vs. 64-bit Operating Systems

Operating systems can use either a **32-bit architecture** or **64-bit architecture**. The number of bits is determined by the processor. Some versions of Windows and macOS are available in both 32-bit and 64-bit options.

The main difference between the two is the type of processors that can be supported. A 64-bit operating system supports 64-bit processors. A 64-bit processor features multiple cores, and the more cores, the more processing power a CPU has. This makes a 64-bit operating system better suited to handling tasks such as video editing and image rendering.

It is also significant to note that a 32-bit operating system can run only programs and use only drivers that are written specifically for a 32-bit operating system's instruction set. However, a 64-bit system supports software written for 64-bit architecture and also allows the computer to run 32-bit applications. Table 14.1 lists the differences between 32-bit and 64-bit Windows.

TABLE 14.1   32-bit and 64-bit Windows

32-bit Windows	64-bit Windows
32-bit or 64-bit processor	64-bit processor
4 GB **RAM limitation** (that is, the operating system can view no more even if more RAM is installed)	Up to 2,048 GB RAM supported, depending on the version of Windows used
32 bits processed at a time	64 bits processed at a time
32-bit drivers required	64-bit device drivers required, and they must be digitally signed

32-bit Windows	64-bit Windows
32-bit applications and some support for older 16-bit applications	32- or 64-bit application support; 16-bit application support using the Program Compatibility Wizard or downloading and using Windows XP Mode in Windows 7; use the Program Compatibility Troubleshooter to help with running older applications
Use of DEP (Data Execution Prevention), which prevents a specific type of security attack by using both hardware and software technology	"Always-on" DEP support for 64-bit processes
N/A	Protection for the operating system kernel (the core of the operating system) Better support for multiple processors

Windows 7/8/8.1/10 Versions

Windows 7 was similar in looks and operation to Windows XP, so people loved going to it. Windows 8 was a different look and feel, which was modified in Windows 8.1 to have either a Windows 7 look or the tiled look of Windows 8. Windows 10 is a mixture of both, but was an operating system designed from the beginning to be across all platforms—desktop, laptops, and mobile devices. Windows 10 updates device drivers automatically through Windows update. Table 14.2 shows the various versions of Windows that can be purchased and briefly describes each one. Each version can be 32- or 64-bit, except where noted.

TABLE 14.2   Windows 7, 8, 8.1, and 10 editions

Windows edition	Description
Starter: Windows 7	A 32-bit-only version used with low-cost computers and with tablets.
Home: Windows 10	Designed for home use for PCs and tablets; it is the new equivalent to Windows 7 and Windows Vista Home editions.
Home Basic: Windows 7	Used to surf the Internet and do basic computing. Comes with Internet Explorer, Windows Media Player, Windows Movie Maker, and Windows Mail. CDs can be created, but not DVDs. It does not allow connecting to a network domain (but can join a HomeGroup home network created from a Windows 7 or higher computer); it does not support EFS encryption or provide the full Aero user experience. Windows 7 Home Basic is sold only in certain areas.
Home Premium: Windows 7	More robust than Home Basic, includes the Aero GUI interface, DVD creation, ability to create/join a HomeGroup (Windows 7 and higher, but removed starting with Windows 10 version 1803) home network, and other tools for media creation and editing.
Windows 8	Sometimes known as Windows 8 (Core).
Basic Edition: Windows 8.1	The equivalent of Windows Home versions in prior versions.
Professional: Windows 7, 8, and 8.1	The continuation of the Business edition found previously in Vista. Designed for computers in the workplace and the domain environment. Aero, encryption, Shadow Copy, and Remote Desktop are supported, but not all the multimedia capabilities are supported.
Pro: Windows 10	The equivalent of Windows Professional in prior versions.

Windows edition	Description
Enterprise: Windows 7, 8, 8.1, and 10	Designed for corporate environments where multimedia editing and creation are used; supports BitLocker drive encryption and provides multilingual support. Not sold through retail centers but to corporate and educational institutions using bulk licensing.
Ultimate: Windows 7	Contains all the Enterprise features, including support for multiple processors, but includes some extras that are downloadable from Microsoft. These include fun utilities and work-related tools, such as the Windows BitLocker Drive Preparation Tool, AppLocker to prevent unwanted corporate applications, and DirectAccess for connecting to the corporate network without a VPN (virtual private network).
Education: Windows 10	Provides everything offered in the Enterprise version of Windows 10 but is designed for use by schools and universities.
Mobile: Windows 10	Supports mobile device encryption, mobile device management, and side-loading of apps. This mobile operating system grew from the Windows Phone operating system and works on smartphones, phablets, and tablets.
Mobile Enterprise: Windows 10	Has all the features of Windows Mobile and additionally supports Windows Update for Business and Current Branch for Business features.

Workstation Operating Systems

A workstation is a computer used by one or more users. It normally includes one or more high-resolution displays and a fast processor, designed to handle complex manipulation of data such as data analysis, video editing, animations, or mathematical plots. Sometimes, however, the term is applied to any individual computer location that is hooked up to a mainframe.

Microsoft has a Windows 10 Pro for Workstations operating system, which is a higher-end version of Windows 10 Professional. It includes features that were already available on Windows Server but were brought over to a desktop version of Windows. macOS and Linux are also operating systems used on workstations.

Operating Systems for Mobile Devices

A mobile operating system is an operating system for phones, tablets, smartwatches, and other mobile devices. Mobile operating systems tend to take less memory and combine features of a personal computer operating system with features needed on mobile devices, such as a touchscreen, Bluetooth, GPS navigation, speech recognition, and more. Some specialized mobile devices need specialized operating systems. For example, drones use Robot Operating System (ROS).

The **Android OS**, developed by Google, Inc., is based on the Linux kernel. Worldwide, Android dominates the field; in the first quarter of 2018, nearly 86% of the 383 million smartphones sold use the Android OS. Android's early releases (before 2.0) were used exclusively on mobile phones. Android version 4.0 is used by both smartphones and tablets.

Chrome OS is an operating system designed by Google that is also based on the Linux kernel. It was conceived as an operating system with a design goal that allows both applications and user data to reside in the cloud. Therefore, it uses the Chrome browser as its principal user interface. It is available only on hardware from Google manufacturing partners. Even though primarily used on laptops and tablets, the Chrome OS can be used on desktops.

The **iOS** mobile operating system was created and developed by Apple, Inc. to run only on Apple devices such as the iPhone, iPad, and iPod Touch. It is the second-most-popular mobile operating system worldwide but still is a distant second after Android, with only about 14% of the market (at the time of press).

The **Windows Mobile** operating system developed by Microsoft is still found on devices, but has been discontinued. Windows Mobile was succeeded by Windows Phone, but in 2015 Windows 10 Mobile replaced Windows Phone. However, in late 2017, work on Windows 10 Mobile was discontinued. For more information on mobile devices, refer to Chapter 10, "Mobile Devices."

End-of-Life Concerns

Most IT departments replace their workstations, servers, and phones regularly in a replacement cycle. In other cases, users may be forced to move on because of liabilities caused when companies stop issuing OS updates or a warranty ends. There can be serious consequences associated with using software that has reached its **end-of-life**, which can mean the end of support from the vendor or the end of the software's usefulness. Some of these consequences are listed here:

> **Security threats**—The operating system becomes far more vulnerable to security threats.
> **Software incompatibility**—Software vendors often cannot guarantee that new applications will be compatible with older operating systems.
> *Compliance issues*—Regulated industries, such as health care and e-commerce, deal with sensitive data. It is dangerous to entrust critical information to an outdated and possibly insecure system.
> *Operating costs*—It costs a lot to maintain and fix bugs in unsupported software. The expense of, for example, paying a company to patch an operating system that has reached its end-of-life can exceed the price of updating to a new system.
> *Performance and reliability*—Software, as it ages, can grow slow or fail to always perform as expected. Also, normally, old software is installed on old hardware, which is prone to breaking down.

Update Concerns

While there are many excellent reasons to update an operating system that has reached its end-of-life, the process of updating may cause problems. Those who have been through the process before face the task of updating with anxiety and concern. Some potential problems are listed here with possible solutions or ways to avoid the problems.

> *Insufficient hardware*—Normally, a new operating system requires better hardware than the previous version. Hardware requirements should be checked before doing an upgrade. Insufficient hardware may cause a new operating system to run slowly. Often a fast processor and more memory are required, but other components may also need to be upgraded.
> *Setup errors and freezes*—Such problems could be caused by insufficient disk space, RAM, or drivers.
> *Drivers*—Drivers often cause trouble related to operating system upgrades. Unfortunately, sometimes vendors don't update their drivers to work with the newest systems, and this may mean you need to buy a new card or other component.
> *Application incompatibilities*—There are some workarounds that can be tried to get an older application to work with a new operating system, but sometimes the best course of action is to upgrade the application to a compatible version.
> *Data loss*—Data loss can be tragic, but it is the most preventable of all possible problems. User data should be stored on a different partition or physical hard disk, a different server, or in the cloud and backed up regularly.

Compatibility Concerns

Computers are considered compatible if software that runs on one of the models can run on all other models of that family, even if that software differs in performance, reliability, or some other feature. Hardware compatibility means that some components, such as a RAM chip, can be used on various models.

One consideration is related to 32-bit vs. 64-bit systems. Most new systems today include processors based on a 64-bit architecture. These systems are compatible with 32-bit operating systems and 32-bit applications, but the converse is not true: 32-bit hardware cannot support 64-bit operating systems and applications. While there are many benefits to a 64-bit system and not many cons, it is important to understand that there are differences and to be aware of which system you are dealing with.

Software **compatibility** can refer to whether a particular application must be used with a specific CPU architecture, such as Intel. It can also refer to the ability of software to run on one or more operating systems or version of operating systems.

When purchasing software, it is important to consider compatibility. Sometimes even upgrading software you are already running can cause incompatibility issues. Software released for a newer version of an operating system may not work or may not work as expected on an older version of the same operating system.

Forward compatibility, also known as **upward compatibility**, is designed by the software manufacturer. It means that a system should be able to accept input intended for a later version and is meant to allow older devices to recognize when data has been generated for new devices. An application that has been designed with forward compatibility usually also has **backward compatibility**, which means the new system can still process data from the older software.

Software with both forward and backward compatibility is not the same as software that is extensible. A forward-compatible system only means that the software is able to process some of the data from a new version of itself, but an extensible system, or **extensible software**, can be upgraded easily.

Because of the nature of operating systems, software is never completely compatible between different operating systems. While there are rarely file type incompatibility issues between macOS and Windows, applications are not compatible across these operating systems. A **file type** is commonly defined by the application that created it or the type of application that can open the file. For example, a text file (a file that ends with .txt) is a file that doesn't have any special formatting and can be opened with Microsoft Word, WordPerfect, Notepad, WordPad, and a variety of other applications. The bottom line is that software must be chosen for a specific operating system.

Computers can have more than one OS installed. By dividing the hard drive into multiple sections, it is possible to use a dual-boot system. For example, when a Mac hard drive is partitioned, Windows runs on one partition and Mac on the other. With this type of setup, you would have to buy Windows-compatible software for the Windows partition and Apple-compatible software for the Apple partition.

One thing that must be considered when using a dual-boot system is what happens with the data. Luckily, most file types are compatible with both macOS and Windows. However, sharing folders may result in some issues since macOS and Windows deal with folders differently.

Corporate Operating System Needs

In a business environment, users have different needs than they would have at home, and corporate computers may have different operating systems than do computers used at home. The operating system in the corporate environment needs to be one that supports being on a corporate network, has rules imposed on it, and is controlled in a different way than a home computer. Let's take a look at some of these differences.

Business computers tend to be organized in either a domain or a workgroup. In Windows, the concept of a domain is different from that of a workgroup:

> *Domain*—Domains are used to create networks in medium to large companies. **Active Directory (AD)**, which is part of the Microsoft Windows Server operating system, provides authentication and authorization for the network devices and people using the domain. Within AD, an organizational structure can be created to separate devices and people by location, department, or function. AD enables IT staff to implement security policies and provide support and changes easily and efficiently.

> *Workgroup*—In Windows, a workgroup is an alternative to a domain. Each computer has a user account, and if a user wants to use another computer, a separate user account must be created on the second computer. Software is usually installed on each computer that is part of a workgroup.

Windows workgroups are difficult to manage when there are more than a dozen clients, so they are more suitable for small businesses or home office networks. Active Directory, on the other hand, offers single sign-on, disaster recover functionality, and many security features that are lacking with workgroups. This makes Active Directory a better choice for larger businesses and organizations.

Domain Access

Computers in a business environment that has more than 10 computers commonly are registered with one or more domain controllers. A *domain controller* is a network server that has a network operating system installed. When a user logs into a company computer, the domain controller verifies the username and password to ensure that the user is allowed on the company network.

A medium to large company is organized into one or more domains created on the domain controller. The domain controller has a centralized database that contains all the registered users and network devices. An authorized user who successfully logs into the domain is granted **domain access**.

BitLocker

BitLocker Drive Encryption is a Windows data protection feature that scrambles the data on drives. This is of particular interest to companies because laptops are often lost, computers stolen, and drives removed/upgraded. BitLocker helps reduce the threat of unauthorized access by enhancing file and system protections. When computers are decommissioned or recycled, BitLocker protection helps render data inaccessible.

There are two additional tools that can be used to manage BitLocker: BitLocker Recovery Password Viewer and BitLocker Drive Encryption. A best practice is for technicians to back up BitLocker recovery passwords. The BitLocker Recovery Password Viewer allows a technician to see those passwords. BitLocker Drive Encryption, which is used from the command line, is used when scripts involving drive deployment or refreshes are created and deployed. Chapter 15 covers PowerShell cmdlets and scripting in more detail.

Media Center

Windows **Media Center** can be used to turn a computer into a home entertainment hub. It's included in some editions of Windows 7. For Windows 8, it is available for purchase as an add-on through the Add Features option. However, Microsoft removed Media Center from Windows 10 and is no longer supporting it.

BranchCache

Wide area network (WAN) links are slower than local area network (LAN) connections. This is because WANs connect buildings, locations in different cities, or locations in different countries. Microsoft has introduced a technology called **BranchCache** that helps users more quickly retrieve data from remote locations. BranchCache is available on Windows 7, 8, and 10 and some Windows Server versions.

The beauty of BranchCache is that whenever a user accesses content from a remote server or cloud server, that information is stored locally. The next time the user needs to access that content, the information is retrieved faster and without using WAN resources. If another user needs that same information, that user retrieves it from the local storage and doesn't use WAN resources either. Only authorized users can access the information, so even though it is stored locally, it is secure.

Encrypting File System (EFS)

Some corporate environments require that specific files and folders be encrypted, especially on a laptop that might be stolen or on a computer that contains sensitive data. Corporate versions of Windows include a feature called Encrypting File System (**EFS**) that allows you to encrypt a file or folder as easily as making a file or folder read-only. Whereas BitLocker encrypts an entire drive, EFS allows you to control the encryption on a file or folder basis.

To enable EFS, right-click on any file or folder and select *Properties* > click the *Advanced* button > enable the *Encrypt Contents to Secure Data* checkbox > click *OK*. If you are encrypting a folder, you may be asked if you want the encryption for just this folder or all subfolders and files as well. Click *OK* again if necessary. When are prompted to back up the file encryption certificate and key for security purposes, save the certificate to a separate drive. This file is very important for decrypting files and folders.

When you have a file or folder encrypted, you see what looks like a little lock over the file icon. To store and retrieve a file or folder, the user must request a key from a program that is built into Windows.

Basic Windows Usage Overview

If you have been using a Windows-based computer your entire life, you might find this first look at the Windows environment a little dry. It's the basics. However, little technical tricks and tips are among these basics, and even veteran technicians are likely to at some points say, "I didn't know that." So, look for those.

Windows Desktop/Start Screen

On a Windows computer, the user is initially presented with a logon screen. A user ID and password or PIN is entered as part of the operating system installation process or created as part of adding a new user, and is then used thereafter.

When in the Windows environment, the desktop appears. The **desktop** is the area on the screen of a GUI environment in which all work is performed. It is the interface between the computer user and files, applications, operating system, and installed hardware. The desktop contains **icons**, which are pictures that provide access to various devices, files, applications/apps, or other resources, such as a printer. The desktop can be customized so that the most commonly accessed applications or files are easily accessible. Figure 14.4 shows a Windows 7 desktop.

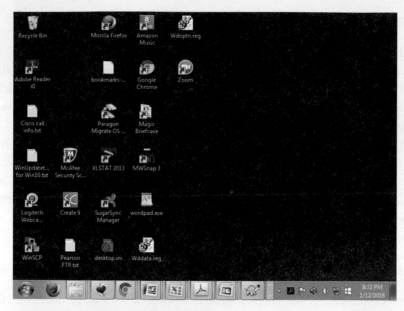

FIGURE 14.4 Windows 7 desktop

Windows 8 has a **Start screen**. Windows 8.1 can have a Start screen or a traditional desktop. The Start screen contains tiles instead of icons. These **tiles** provide the same access to files and apps as the traditional icons. Figure 14.5 shows a Windows 8/8.1 Start screen. Notice that tiles are used instead of the traditional Windows icons. A scrollbar at the bottom enables you to see more desktop tiles. The specific tile labeled *Desktop* is used to access a more traditional desktop. You can also configure Windows 8.1 to use the traditional desktop all the time.

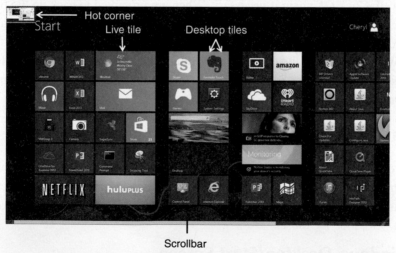

FIGURE 14.5 Windows 8/8.1 Start screen

One particular tile of interest is a live tile. A **live tile** represents an app with content that periodically changes. Apps for weather, news, and photos commonly have live tiles. You can right-click a live tile to disable the "live" feature.

Windows 8/8.1 has hot corners on the Start screen. By moving the pointer to one of the four corners of the screen, you can bring up different options. From the Start screen, the top-left corner shows other windows that are open (refer to Figure 14.5).

Click a window area for quick access to that particular application. For example, point to the right corner and see the charms appear (see Figure 14.6). A **charm** is a menu you can use to quickly access commonly used Windows features, as outlined in Table 14.3.

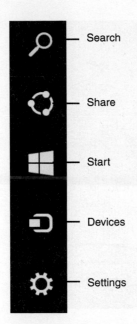

FIGURE 14.6   Windows 8 charms

TABLE 14.3   Purposes of Windows 8/8.1 charms

Charm	Purpose
Search	Used to find apps, settings, and files. Some apps allow the Search charm to find content within the app. The shortcut is ⊞+Ⓕ to search for files, ⊞+Ⓠ to search for apps, and ⊞+Ⓦ to search settings.
Share	Used to share content with other people, using specific apps that support this feature.
Start	Used to open the Start screen.
Devices	Used to send data from the current app to another device, such as a printer or an external display.
Settings	Used to change settings and access the traditional Control Panel utilities.

TECH TIP

Using the Windows key

The ⊞ brings up the Start menu/screen.

Windows 10 enables you to choose the desktop style that you want. Figure 14.7 shows a Windows 10 desktop, but you can also choose to show the tiles (tablet mode) in Windows 10, much as in Windows 8. The *Search the Web and Windows* textbox enables you to search for anything from the desktop. The *Task View* icon enables you to create multiple desktops and switch between them.

TECH TIP

Keeping the desktop organized

Sometimes, the desktop is cluttered with icons the user puts on it. To organize the desktop nicely, right-click an empty desktop space, point to *View* > select *Auto Arrange Icons*.

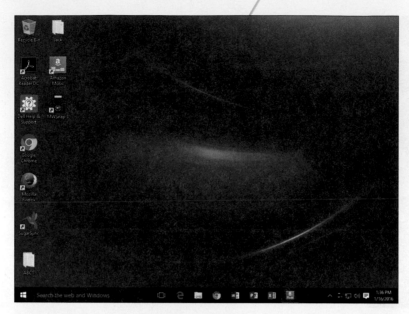

FIGURE 14.7   Windows 10 desktop

One way to modify the desktop is to change the wallpaper scheme. A wallpaper scheme is a background picture, pattern, or color. Other changes to the desktop include altering the color scheme in folders and enabling a screen saver, which is the picture, color, or pattern that displays when the computer is inactive.

Shortcuts and Tiles

Each of the tiles in the Windows 8/8.1 or 10 tablet mode is a shortcut. A **shortcut** represents a **path** (a location on a drive) to a file, folder, or program. It is a link (pointer) to where the file or application resides on a disk. On the traditional desktop, a shortcut has a small arrow in the left corner. When a shortcut icon is double-clicked, Windows knows where to find the specific file the icon represents by the associated path. Users and technicians frequently place shortcuts or tiles on the desktop, so it is important to know how to create, remove, modify, and troubleshoot them.

By default, the Windows 7 desktop displays the Recycle Bin icon only. However, some people like to have Windows icons displayed. Common desktop icons or tiles are listed in Table 14.4.

TABLE 14.4   Common Windows desktop icons or tiles

Icon	Purpose
Documents	Maps to a folder located on the hard drive that is the default storage location for files
Computer/This PC	Accesses hardware, software, and files
Network	Accesses network resources, such as computers, printers, scanners, fax machines, and files
Recycle Bin	Holds files and folders that have been deleted
Internet Explorer/Edge	Starts the Microsoft browser used to access the Internet

To discover the path to the original file used to create a shortcut, right-click the shortcut icon and select *Properties*. Click the *Shortcut* tab and look in the *Target* textbox for the path to the original file. In Windows 7 the *Open File Location* button can be used to locate the original file. If tiles are shown in Windows 8 or 10, right-click a tile and select *Open File Location*. Note that you may have to point to the *More* option to access *Open File Location*.

Recycle Bin

An important Windows desktop icon is the Recycle Bin, which holds files and folders that the user deletes. When a file or folder is deleted, it is not actually gone. Instead, it goes into the Recycle Bin, which is just a folder on the hard drive. The deleted file or folder can be removed from the Recycle Bin just as a piece of trash can be removed from a real trash can. Deleted files and folders in the Recycle Bin use hard drive space.

TECH TIP

Need hard drive space? Empty the Recycle Bin

A technician must remember that some users do not empty the Recycle Bin. Emptying the Recycle Bin frees up space on the hard drive.

The contents of the Recycle Bin take up hard drive space. To change how much space is reserved for the Recycle Bin or the drive on which the deleted files in the Recycle Bin are stored, right-click the *Recycle Bin* and select *Properties*.

TECH TIP

How to delete a file permanently

If you hold down the (⬆Shift) key when deleting a file, the file is permanently deleted and does not go into the Recycle Bin.

TECH TIP

Removable media files are permanently deleted

When deleting a file or folder from an optical disc, a memory card, an MP3 player, a digital camera, a remote computer, or a flash drive, the file or folder is permanently deleted. It does not go into the Recycle Bin, as is the case when a file is deleted from a hard drive.

Windows 7 Desktop Components

The traditional Windows desktop has specific desktop components. Figure 14.8 shows a Windows 7 desktop, with the primary components labeled.

The **taskbar** is the bar that commonly runs across the bottom of the traditional desktop. The taskbar holds icons that represent applications or files currently loaded into computer memory. The taskbar also holds icons that allow access to system utilities such as a clock for the date and time and a speaker symbol for access to volume control. Refer to Figure 14.8 to ensure that you know the location of the taskbar. The taskbar consists of the four areas shown at the bottom of Figure 14.8: the Start button, the Quick Launch Bar, the Notification area, and the Show Desktop button.

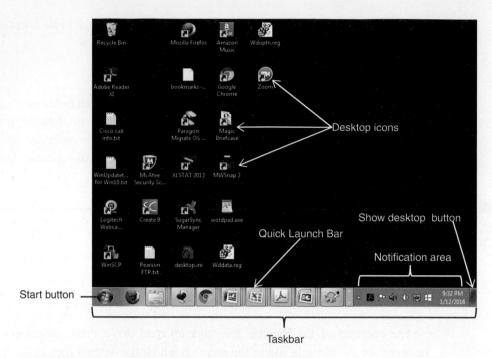

FIGURE 14.8   Windows 7 desktop components

The **Start button** by default is located in the desktop's lower-left corner on the taskbar and is used to launch applications and utilities, search for files and other computers, obtain help, and add/ remove hardware and software. Windows 8.1 has the Start button, but Windows 8 does not. Figure 14.9 shows the Windows 7 Start button menu.

FIGURE 14.9   Windows 7 Start button menu

Notice in Figure 14.9 that applications are listed on the far left. There is a line between the top five applications and the rest of the applications. The top five applications (Hearts, Google Chrome, Calculator, Snipping Tool, and Printkey in Figure 14.9) are "pinned" to the Start button menu. The bottom part of the applications list contains the most commonly used applications.

Start button missing?

If the Start button is missing, press the ▦ key or the Ctrl+⬆Shift key combination.

On the far right of the Start button are commonly used options and the power off option. Click *Shut Down* to power off the computer properly. Click the arrow to the right of the *Shut Down* option, and you can see other shutdown options (Switch User, Log Off, Lock, Restart, and Sleep), as shown in Figure 14.10. *Standby*, *Hibernate*, and *Sleep* options are available on computers that support power-saving features and are commonly used with laptops and Ultrabooks. If a Windows shield appears to the left of *Shut Down*, Windows updates are ready and will be installed before the computer is shut down.

FIGURE 14.10   Windows 7 Shut Down options

The Windows 7 taskbar has four main areas (refer to Figure 14.8): (1) the Start button on the far left, (2) icons for commonly used applications or open applications (Quick Launch Bar), (3) the notification area on the right, and (4) the Show Desktop button on the farthest right. The two closest icons to the right of the Start button (Mozilla Firefox and Windows Explorer) are "pinned" to the taskbar; that is, they are always on the taskbar. The other icons (Hearts, Google Chrome, Microsoft Word, Microsoft Excel, Adobe Acrobat, Microsoft PowerPoint, and Tortoise SVN in Figure 14.8) are open applications.

How to modify the buttons shown on the taskbar

To pin an application to the taskbar, launch the application, locate the application icon on the taskbar, and right-click and select *Pin This Program to Taskbar*.

On the far right of the taskbar is the **notification area**, where you can find information about an application or a tool. In Figure 14.8, for example, the icons from left to right are an Adobe Acrobat notification of an impending update, the Windows Action Center section of the Control Panel, the Realtek HD Audio Manager, the Windows speaker control (to quickly mute or adjust sound volume), a network icon (which a technician could use to quickly ascertain if Internet access is available), a Windows Update icon, and the date and time. Other icons are available by clicking the up arrow to the left of the Adobe Acrobat update icon. Notice the space to the far right, immediately after the date/time. Click this area to instantly show the desktop area. Click the area again, and whatever window you were working in reappears. The *Show Desktop* option is also available by simply right-clicking an empty space on the taskbar.

Windows Desktop/Start Screen Components

The Windows Start screen (the desktop replacement that uses tiles instead of icons) can be used on Windows 8, 8.1, and 10 desktop computers as well as mobile devices. Figure 14.11 shows a Windows 8.1 desktop with the primary components, and Table 14.5 lists the purpose of each one.

FIGURE 14.11   Windows 8/8.1 Start screen components

TABLE 14.5   Windows Start screen components

Component	Purpose
Account settings	Shows the person/account currently logged on. Can be used to change users, change the account picture, lock the screen, or sign out.
Power options	Used to shut down the device, put the device in sleep mode, or restart it (see Figure 14.12).
Search	The same as the Search charm; used to share content with other people using specific apps that support this feature. In Figure 14.13, notice that you can click the down arrow by the word *Everywhere* to select where the search is performed.
Apps arrow	Used to access all the app tiles. Click the up arrow at the bottom of the screen to return to the Start screen.

FIGURE 14.12   Windows 8/8.1 Power options menu

FIGURE 14.13   Windows 8/8.1 Search options

Notice in Figure 14.14 that the apps are in alphabetical order. Scroll all the way to the right to see Windows accessories and programs commonly seen from a traditional Start button.

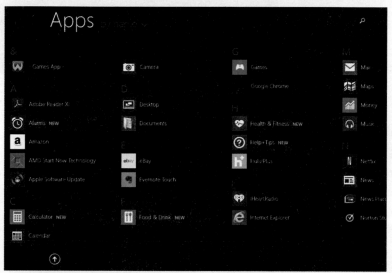

FIGURE 14.14   Windows 8.1 all apps screen

TECH TIP

Adding or removing an app tile on the Start screen

Right-click any tile that does not currently appear on the Start screen, and you can select the *Pin to Start* option to put it there. Select any tile on the Start screen that the user does not want there and select *Unpin from Start*.

Windows 8.1 also supports the traditional desktop. Press the ▦ key after the Start screen, and the traditional desktop appears. Press the same key again, and the Start screen reappears. You can also access the traditional desktop by using the *Desktop* tile.

Windows 10 Desktop Components

The Windows 10 desktop can look similar to the Windows 7 desktop but can also use the Windows 8/8.1 Start screen look or a combination of the two. Figure 14.15 shows a Windows 10 computer with the traditional desktop. The search function is built into the taskbar and can appear as a search icon, the Cortana search textbox, or the *Search the Web and Windows* search textbox. With the Cortana feature, you can type or speak a question or statement, such as "What's on TV tonight?" or "Show me the latest news."

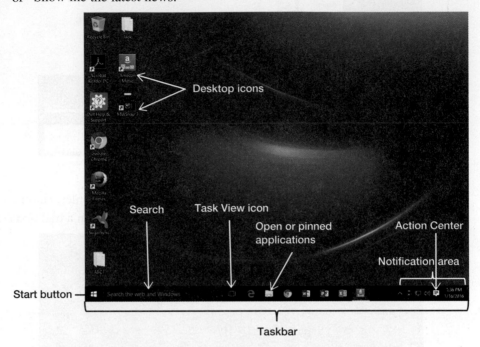

FIGURE 14.15   Windows 10 desktop components

The Windows 10 Start button can be configured to show some tiles (see Figure 14.16) or the Start screen (all tiles), as shown in Figure 14.17. Use the icons on the top and bottom left to re-access the Start button, access the power options, or view the apps in alphabetical order. Scroll down to see the rest of the tiles.

FIGURE 14.16   Windows 10 Start button with some tiles

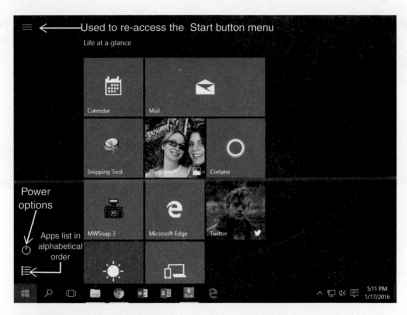

FIGURE 14.17   Windows 10 Start screen view

Windows 10 Task View

The Task View icon (refer to Figure 14.15) is new to Windows 10. The **Task View** button enables you to view thumbnails of open apps and easily select which one to access, as shown in Figure 14.18. You may be familiar with using the Alt + Tab key combination to select an open window; Task View does the same thing but more efficiently. Task View also enables you to create more than one desktop. Select the *New Desktop* option in the bottom-right corner to create one. Figure 14.18 shows two desktops created. The windows open in Desktop 1 (selected at the bottom) are shown as thumbnails in the top window.

FIGURE 14.18   Windows 10 Task View window

Interactions Within a Window

Whenever anything is double-clicked in Windows, a window appears. A **window** is a normal part of the Windows environment, a square section on the screen, and common options can appear within a window. Technicians frequently interact with the Windows operating system through a dialog box. A dialog box is used within the operating system and with Windows applications to allow configuration and operating system preferences. The most common features found in a dialog box are checkboxes, textboxes, tabs, drop-down menus, a Close button, an OK button, a Cancel button, and an Apply button. Figure 14.19 shows a sample dialog box.

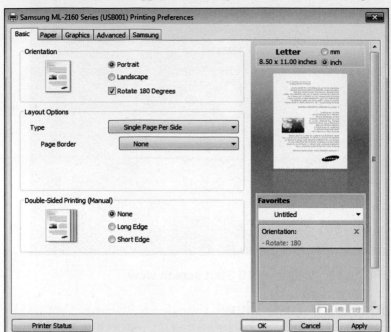

FIGURE 14.19 Samsung Printing Preferences dialog box

A textbox is an area in which you can type a specific parameter. When the inside of a textbox is clicked, a vertical line or an entire default word appears. Any typed text is placed to the right of the insertion point, or you can just type to replace the highlighted word. Textboxes sometimes have up and down arrows that can be used to select an option or enable a user to type in a new parameter.

Tabs frequently appear across the top of a dialog box. Each tab holds a group of related options. Click a tab once to bring that particular major section to the window's forefront. The tabs in Figure 14.19 are Basic, Paper, Graphics, Advanced, and Samsung.

The Close button, which is an X in the upper-right corner of the dialog box, closes the dialog box. When you click the Close button, changes made inside the dialog box are not applied. When you click the OK button, all options selected or changed within the dialog box are applied. When you click the Cancel button, anything changed within the dialog box is not applied; the options are left in their original state. The **Apply button** makes changes immediately (before clicking the OK button).

TECH TIP

Select *OK* or *Apply* to make it work

To apply a change, inexperienced technicians often make the mistake of clicking the *Close* button (the red X button in the top right) instead of the *OK* or *Apply* button. When the *Close* button is used, changes in the dialog box are neither saved nor applied.

When checked, a checkbox option is enabled or turned on. Clicking inside a checkbox option places a check mark inside the checkbox, such as the one for *Rotate 180 Degrees* in Figure 14.19. If you click again inside the checkbox, the check is removed, and the option is not enabled.

A similar dialog box option is a radio button. A radio button is a circle that, when enabled, has a solid dot inside it. If a radio button that already has a dot in it is clicked, the dot disappears, and the option is disabled. For example, in Figure 14.19, the *Portrait* radio button is enabled, and the *Landscape* radio button is disabled.

A drop-down menu is presented when you click a down arrow to see the options. Refer to Figure 14.19 to see two drop-down menus: *Type* and *Page Border*. After a drop-down menu is selected, the options appear in the drop-down menu.

Within a dialog box, help is commonly provided through context-sensitive help. Simply hold the pointer over a particular item, and one or more words appear.

Another popular type of interaction is with a **context menu**, which appears when you right-click an item. The context menu that appears is different in every application but usually includes options that are available from the main menu or from a Windows Settings or Control Panel option. Context menus frequently save time and are commonly used by technicians.

Managing Windows Files and Folders

Technicians often create, delete, and move files and folders. You need to do these tasks quickly and without error. It is important to think about what file and folder you want to work with, where the files and folders are located now, and where you want the files or folders to be eventually.

Each drive in a computer is represented by a drive letter followed by a colon. For example, the first hard drive partition is represented by C:. The optical drive, flash drive, and any external drives are each represented by a drive letter followed by a colon. Windows Explorer (Windows 7) or File Explorer (Windows 8/8.1/10) is used to manage files and folders. Figure 14.20 shows drive letters within File Explorer on a Windows 10 computer.

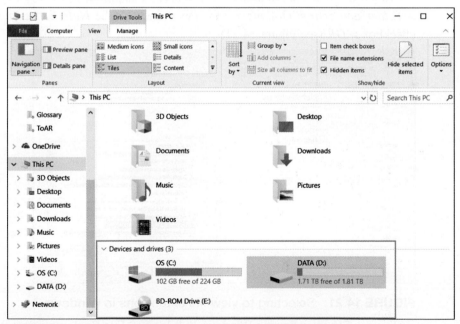

FIGURE 14.20   Windows 10 File Explorer drive letters

Discs or drives hold files. A file is kept on some type of media, such as a flash drive, a hard drive, a tape, or an optical disc. Each file is given a name that includes two parts: the **filename** and the extension, separated by a dot. For example, in the filename WIN8CHAP.DOCX, the name of the file is WIN8CHAP, and the extension is DOCX. Regardless of whether you use lowercase or uppercase letters, Windows remembers the case; however, it does not require you to remember. Case does not matter when searching for a file or typing the name of a file to open.

Characters you cannot use in filenames and folder names

Folder names and filenames can include all keyboard characters, numbers, letters, and spaces *except* the following: / (forward slash), " (quotation mark), \ (backslash), | (vertical bar), ? (question mark), : (colon), and * (asterisk).

Filenames and Extensions

Files are usually organized in folders. In older operating systems, a folder was called a *directory*, and you still see this term today, especially when using the command line interface. A folder within a folder is called a **subfolder** or **subdirectory**. Windows 7 and higher have automatic groupings, each one called a **library**, for saving files. The Windows 7 libraries, for example, include the following: Documents, Music, Pictures, and Videos. By default, applications save files in these libraries. You can also create additional libraries, as needed.

Every file is given a filename and an extension. An **extension** is added to the filename, separated by a dot, and can be two or more characters. An example of a filename with an extension is myShow.PPTX, where myShow is the name of the file, and PPTX is the extension.

Normally with Windows, the application used to create a file automatically adds an extension to the end of the filename. In most views, Windows does not automatically show the extensions. To view the extensions in Windows 7 Windows Explorer, select the *Organize* drop-down menu > *Folder and Search Options* > *View* tab > uncheck the *Hide Extensions for Known File Types* checkbox > *OK* (see Figure 14.21).

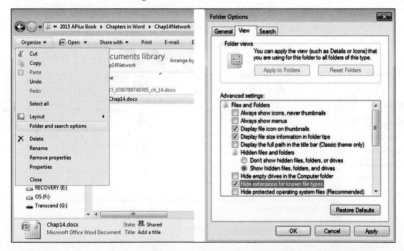

FIGURE 14.21 Selecting to view file extensions in Windows 7

To view file extensions in Windows 8, 8.1, or 10 File Explorer, select the *View* tab, as shown in Figure 14.22 > enable (select) the *File Name Extensions* checkbox. As shown in Figure 14.22, the context-sensitive help appears when the pointer is hovered over the *File Name Extensions* option. The checkbox has a check inside it if the option is enabled.

When Windows recognizes an extension, the operating system associates the extension with a particular application. Filename extensions can tell you a lot about a file, such as what application created the file or what its purpose is. Table 14.6 lists some common file extensions and their purpose or the application that creates the extension.

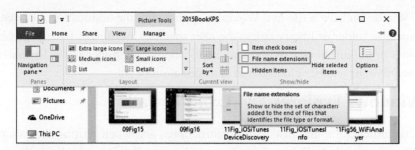

FIGURE 14.22   Selecting to view file extensions in Windows 10

TABLE 14.6   Common file extensions

Extension	Purpose or application	Extension	Purpose or application
AAX	Audible enhanced audio file	JPG or JPEG	Joint Photographic Experts Group graphics file
AI	Adobe Illustrator or Corel Trace file	MPG or MPEG	Movie clip file
BAT	Batch file, for executing commands from one file	ONE	Microsoft OneNote file
BMP	Bitmap file	PCX	Microsoft Paintbrush file
CAB	Cabinet file, a compressed file that holds operating system or application files	PDF	Adobe Acrobat portable document format file
COM	Command file, an executable file that opens an application or a tool	PNG	Microsoft Paint or Snipping Tool graphics file
DLL	Dynamic Link Library file, contains executable code that can be used by more than one application and is called upon from other code already running	PPT or PPTX	Microsoft PowerPoint file
DOC or DOCX	Microsoft Word file	RTF	Rich text format file
DRV	Device driver, a piece of software that enables an operating system to recognize a hardware device	TIF or TIFF	Tag image file
EPS	Encapsulated PostScript file	TXT	Text file
EXE	Executable file, a file that opens an application	VXD	Virtual device driver
GIF	Graphics interchange file	WPS	Microsoft Works text file
HLP	Windows-based help file	WRI	Microsoft WordPad file
INF	Information or setup file	XLS or XLSX	Microsoft Excel file
INI	Initialization file, used in older Windows environments	ZIP	Compressed file

CHAPTER 14

When you save a file in a Windows application, the application automatically saves the file to a specific folder or library unless the user specifies a different folder. This is known as the default folder or default library. With many applications, this folder is the *Documents* folder, Microsoft's OneDrive, or another cloud-based storage solution.

Windows Explorer/File Explorer Path

In documentation and installation instructions, and when writing the exact location of a file, the full path is used. A file's path is like a road map to the file. It includes the drive letter plus all folders and subfolders that must be followed to get to that file's filename and extension. For example, if the `Chap1.docx` file is in the `Documents` folder on the first Windows hard drive partition and the author, Cheryl, is logged on, the full path is as follows:

`C:\Users\Cheryl\Documents\Chap1.docx`

The first part is the drive letter where the document is stored: `C:` represents the first hard drive partition. Each user of a specific computer has a unique folder in the `Users` folder. The name of the document is always at the end of the path. In the example given, `Chap1.docx` is the name of the file. Everything in between the drive letter and the filename is the name of one or more folders to get to where the `Chap1.docx` file is located. The folder in this example is `Users`. In the `Users` folder is the `Cheryl` subfolder. In the `Cheryl` subfolder is another subfolder called `Documents`. Finally, within that `Documents` folder is the `Chap1.docx` document. Figure 14.23 shows this concept.

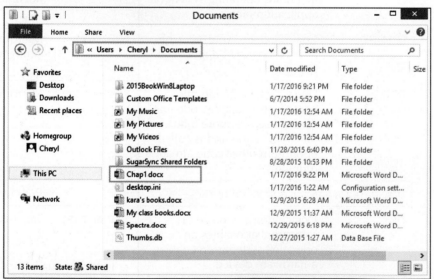

FIGURE 14.23 Windows File Explorer path

Notice that the path appears at the top of the File Explorer Window, and the filename appears within the Documents folder. Note that this was done intentionally to show you the full path. Normally, when you open File Explorer, expand *This PC* on the left and select *Documents*, the `Users` or `Cheryl` folder is not shown. The path would simply show as `This PC > Documents`,

When writing a complete path to a folder, a backslash (the keyboard key above the ⏎Enter key) is always used to separate the folder names from each other as well as the drive letter from the first folder name. In Windows 8, 8.1, or 10 File Explorer, the greater than sign (>) is used to separate folders.

In Windows 7, the full path does not appear automatically. From Windows Explorer, click anywhere to the right of the words in the address bar, and the full path appears and is highlighted, as shown in Figure 14.24.

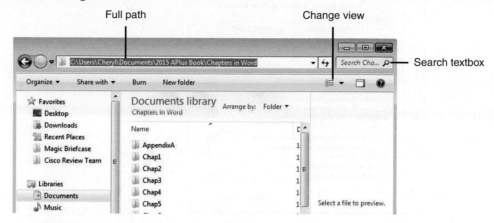

FIGURE 14.24 Windows 7 full path in Windows Explorer address bar

Windows Explore/File Explorer View Options

You can change what information displays or how the information displays in Windows Explorer by using the *Change View > More Options* down arrow in Windows 7 (see the upper-right corner of Figure 14.24). Table 14.7 explains these options.

TABLE 14.7 Windows Explorer display options

Windows 7 option	Explanation
List	File/folder name shown
Details	File/folder shown with size, extension, and modification date
Small Icons	Small graphics with the file or folder name shown under the icon
Content	Reduced size icons with file/folder contents shown
Tiles	Multiple columns of file/folder icons with name, application, and size shown
Medium Icons, Large Icons, Extra Large Icons	Varying size file/folder icons

It is important for a technician to be able to control how files and folders display in Windows Explorer/File Explorer. To display the full path in File Explorer (Windows 8/8.1/10), open *File Explorer* > select the *View* menu option > access the *Options* down arrow on the far right > select *Change Folder and Search Options* > select the *View* tab (see Figure 14.25) > enable the *Display the Full Path in the Title Bar* option.

To change the options of how files, folders, images, and so on display in Windows 8 or 10 in File Explorer, refer to Figure 14.22 to see how the *View* option can be used and is easier to find than in Windows 7.

Figure 14.26 shows the options that are available in the *General* tab of the *File Explorer Options* window. The *General* tab has three main sections: Browse Folders, Click Items as Follows, and Privacy. Each section has either radio buttons or checkboxes to enable various items.

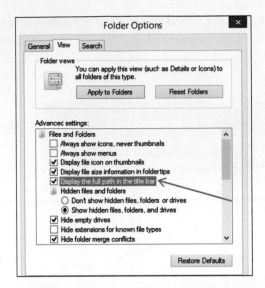

FIGURE 14.25   Windows 10 *Display the Full Path* option

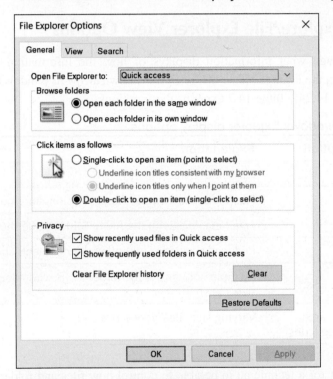

FIGURE 14.26   Windows 10 *File Explorer* Options > *General* tab

The *File Explorer Options* window can also be accessed using the File Explorer Options Control Panel. Control Panels are covered later in the chapter. A technician should be able to set the following important options through this window:

> View hidden files using the *Hidden Files and Folders* section of the *View* tab
> Hide file extensions using the *Hide Extensions for Known File Types* checkbox on the *View* tab
> Use other options on the *View* tab, including how to reset the settings or to apply to subfolders and display the full path
> Use any of the three major options found on the *General* tab

Searches and Indexing

You can use the *Folder Options* Windows Explorer/File Explorer window to help with file searches. You can perform a search from within Windows Explorer/File Explorer by typing a filename or phrase within the search textbox. In Windows 7 you can also start searches from the *Search Programs and Files* textbox in the *Start* button menu. In Windows 8/8.1, an alternative to File Explorer is to use the *Search* charm. In Windows 10 you can search using the textbox on the taskbar or the Cortana search feature.

The *Folder Options* window also has a *Search* tab that has some technical significance. Figure 14.27 shows the contents of this tab in both Windows 7 (left) and Windows 8/8.1/10 (right).

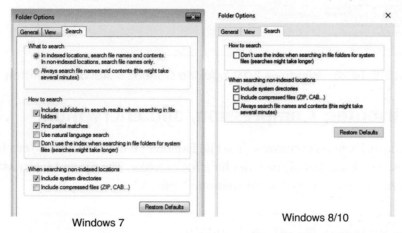

Windows 7   Windows 8/10

FIGURE 14.27   Windows 7 and 8 (8.1)/10 Folder Options > *Search* tab

The first section in Windows 7 is what to search for. Windows 8, 8.1, and 10 always include filenames and data within the files, as well as web searches. The search feature in the operating system deals with searches and is affected by the Windows index feature. **Indexing** is the process used in Windows to quickly search common locations for files and folders, including all libraries, the Start button menu, and Internet Explorer/Edge browsing history. How to modify what is included in the index is covered in the next section.

The *How to Search* section in Windows 7 offers several more options than the same section in Windows 8, 8.1, or 10. In Windows 7, unchecking the first box in this section means that all the files and folders in the drive, folder, or subfolder will be searched. In Windows 8, 8.1, and 10, you can see that the index is used by default, but you may enable this option. Files and folders outside the non-indexed locations can be specified in the last section (in the *When Searching Non-indexed Locations* section).

Modifying Index Locations

To modify what locations get indexed, use a search function and type **indexing** > select *Indexing Options* from the resulting list. Use the *Modify* or *Advanced* buttons to change the settings. Figure 14.28 shows the Indexing Options window as well as the window that appears if you click the *Advanced* button.

If you don't want a file to be indexed and easily found, you can right click the filename, select *Properties* > *Advanced* button > disable (uncheck) the *Allow This File to Have Contents Indexed in Addition to File Properties* option.

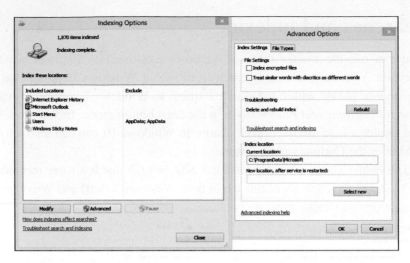

FIGURE 14.28   Windows 8/10 *Indexing Options > Advanced* button

Attributes, Compression, and Encryption

Windows Explorer (Windows 7) or File Explorer (Windows 8/8.1/10) can be used for setting attributes, which are specific qualities for a file or folder. The file and folder **attributes** are read-only, hidden, archive, and system, as shown in Figure 14.29.

TECH TIP

How to change a file or folder's attributes

To change a file or folder's attributes, right-click the filename or folder name > *Properties* > click attribute checkboxes to enable them. If the file is not a system file, the system attribute is unavailable. Click A*pply*.

All Windows-based applications can read from and write to compressed files. The operating system decompresses the file, the file is available to the application, and the operating system recompresses the file when that file is saved. For the archive attribute, Windows files and folders have the archive attribute set by default. This is sometimes referred to as having the archive bit set.

If a hard drive is partitioned for the NTFS file system, files and folders can be compressed or encrypted. Figure 14.30 provides more information on these concepts.

TECH TIP

Compression causes your computer to slow down

When **compression** is enabled, the computer's performance can degrade because when a compressed file is opened, the file must be uncompressed, and then it must be recompressed to be saved or closed. Degradation can also occur if a compressed file is transferred across a network because the file must be uncompressed before it is transferred.

TECH TIP

What happens when a compressed file is moved or copied?

Moving or copying a compressed file or folder can alter the compression. When moving a compressed file or folder, the file or folder remains compressed. When copying a compressed file or folder, it is compressed only if the destination folder (where you are moving it to) is already compressed. When adding a file to an encrypted folder, the file is automatically encrypted.

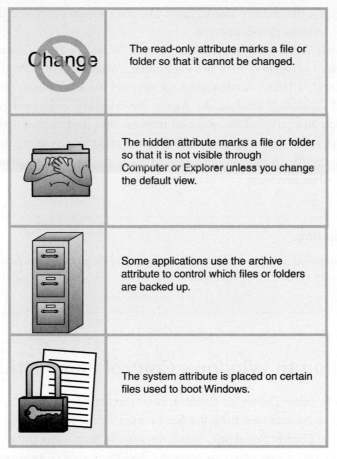

Change	The read-only attribute marks a file or folder so that it cannot be changed.
	The hidden attribute marks a file or folder so that it is not visible through Computer or Explorer unless you change the default view.
	Some applications use the archive attribute to control which files or folders are backed up.
	The system attribute is placed on certain files used to boot Windows.

FIGURE 14.29   Windows file/folder attributes

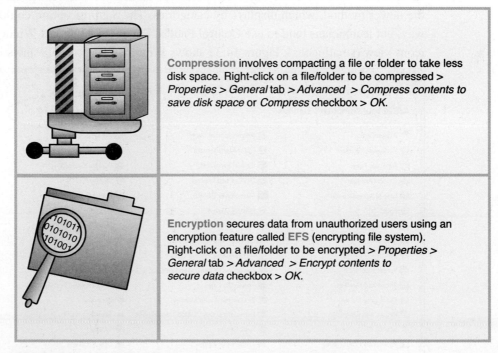

	Compression involves compacting a file or folder to take less disk space. Right-click on a file/folder to be compressed > *Properties > General* tab > *Advanced > Compress contents to save disk space* or *Compress* checkbox > *OK*.
	Encryption secures data from unauthorized users using an encryption feature called **EFS** (encrypting file system). Right-click on a file/folder to be encrypted > *Properties > General* tab > *Advanced > Encrypt contents to secure data* checkbox > *OK*.

FIGURE 14.30   Windows compression and encryption

Compressed files, system files, and read-only files cannot be encrypted. Windows 7 Starter, Home Basic, and Home Premium versions do not fully support encryption, but the other Windows 7 versions do. In the Home Windows versions, the `cipher` command can be used at the command prompt to decrypt a file, modify an encrypted file, and copy an encrypted file to the computer. The older Windows versions cannot encrypt.

Similarly, with Windows 8, the basic edition of Windows 8/8.1 (sometimes called Windows 8/8.1 Core) does not support EFS file encryption. Windows 8/8.1 Professional and Enterprise do. The Windows 10 Home version does not support file encryption, but the Windows 10 Pro, Enterprise, and Education versions do. Again, the `cipher` command can be used to decrypt, modify, and copy an encrypted file obtained from another computer or server that does support it.

When a file or folder is encrypted with EFS (Encrypting File System), only authorized users can view or change the file. Administrators designated as recovery agents have the ability to recover encrypted files when necessary.

TECH TIP

Copying and moving

When you are copying a file or folder, use the *Copy* and *Paste* functions from the Windows Explorer/File Explorer *Edit* menu option. When you move a file or folder, use the *Cut* and *Paste* functions.

Introduction to Windows Control Panel Utilities

Control Panels (also known as Control Panel applets or utilities) configure all aspects of Windows and can be accessed from the Start button menu or, in Windows 8/8.1, from *Settings* charm > select the *Control Panel* link. You have actually been using some of the Windows Control Panels already in this chapter (see the section "Modifying Index Locations"). Control Panels can be viewed in two different ways: the older view, where all Control Panels are shown as icons, or the newer method, which displays by categories. The *Settings* option could be considered a third way, but technicians tend to use Control Panels. Figure 14.31 shows Windows 7 Control Panel in icons view (small icons). Figure 14.32 shows Windows 10 Control Panels in category view.

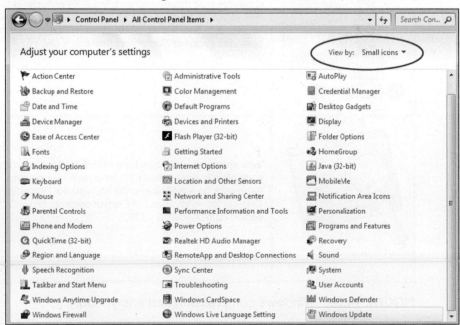

FIGURE 14.31 Windows 7 Control Panel utilities—icon view

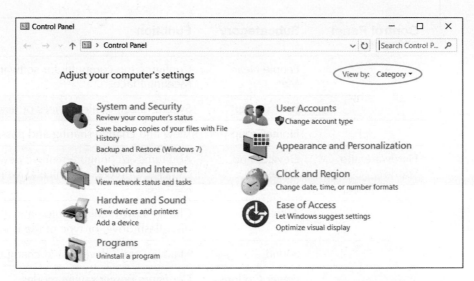

FIGURE 14.32   Windows 8 Control Panel utilities—category view

Table 14.8 shows all the Windows 7 Control Panel categories and subcategories. Control Panel utilities are similar across Windows versions, and Windows 8, 8.1, and 10 configure some things through Settings. Keep in mind that a particular Control Panel utility might be accessible through two or more Control Panel categories.

TABLE 14.8   Common Windows 7 Control Panel categories*

Control Panel category	Subcategory	Function
System and Security	Backup and Restore	Save or restore files and folders to or from a different location.
	System	View basic computer properties, such as RAM, processor type, and computer name.
	Windows Update	Customize how updates are received and installed.
	Power Options	Configure power saving modes.
	Administrative Tools	Free up hard disk space, manage hard drive partitions, schedule tasks, and view event logs.
	Action Center	View personal information, view a history of computer problems, view performance information, configure backup, troubleshoot problems, and restore the computer to a previous point.
	Windows Firewall	Enable and customize security features.
	Windows Update	Customize how updates are received and installed.
	Windows Defender*	Scan the computer for unwanted software.
	BitLocker Drive Encryption	Change or use encryption options.
Network and Internet	Network and Sharing Center	Check the status and modify network-related settings as well as share files, folders, and devices on the network.
	Internet Options	Customize Internet Explorer.

Control Panel category	Subcategory	Function
	People Near Me*	Configure the computer for software such as Windows Meeting Place.
	Sync Center*	Synchronize mobile devices or network shares.
	HomeGroup	View and change sharing and password options.
Hardware and Sound	Devices and Printers	Add/remove/configure/remove devices, scanners, cameras, printers, and mice as well as access Device Manager.
	AutoPlay	Change how media is automatically handled when a disc, flash drive, or type of file is added or inserted.
	Sound	Manage audio devices and change sound schemes.
	Power Options	Configure power saving modes.
	Keyboard*	Customize keyboard settings.
	Phone and Modem Options*	Install a modem and control modem and phone dialing properties.
	Game Controllers*	Add, remove, and customize USB joysticks, gamepads, and other gaming devices.
	Pen and Input Devices	Configure pen options for a tablet PC.
	Color Management*	View/change advanced color settings on disc plays, scanners, and printers.
	Tablet PC Settings	Configure tablet and screen settings on a tablet PC.
	Display	Adjust resolution, configure an external display, or make text larger/smaller.
	Bluetooth Devices	Install, configure, and adjust Bluetooth wireless devices.
Programs	Programs and Features	Uninstall and change programs as well as enable/disable Windows features such as games, Telnet server, Telnet client, TFTP client, and print services.
	Windows Defender*	Scan the computer for unwanted software.
	Default Programs	Remove a startup program, associate a file extension with a particular application, or select the program used with a particular type of file.
	Desktop Gadgets	Add/remove/restore desktop interactive objects.
Mobile PC	Windows Mobility Center	Adjust laptop screen brightness, audio volume, wireless enabling and strength status, presentation settings, and external display control.
	Power Options	Used on laptops to configure power saving modes.
	Personalization	Assign visuals and sounds such as the Windows theme used.

Control Panel category	Subcategory	Function
	Tablet PC Settings	Used on mobile devices to calibrate the screen, set tablet buttons, and control screen rotation.
	Pen and Input Devices/Touch	Used on laptops to change pen settings, enable flicks, change touch input, and change handwriting settings.
	Sync Center	Configure synchronization options, view sync settings, conflicts, and results, and manage offline files.
User Accounts and Family Safety	User Accounts	Add, remove, or modify accounts on the computer.
	Parental Controls	Create a user that has security control settings available for children.
	Windows CardSpace	Manage relationships and information such as a user ID and password for websites and online services. The personal card information is kept encrypted on the local hard drive.
	Credential Manager	Store username/password in a vault for easy logon to sites and/or computers.
Appearance and Personalization	Personalization	Assign visuals and sounds such as the Windows theme.
	Taskbar and Start menu	Customize the Start menu and taskbar by adding or removing icons.
	Fonts	Customize available fonts.
	Folder Options	Configure how folders are viewed and acted upon, including what files are seen.
Clock, Language, and Region	Date and Time	Configure time, date, time zone, and clocks for different time zones.
	Region and Language Options	Configure the format for date, time, currency, and so on that are region-specific options. Also used to customize keyboard settings.
Additional Options		Holds special Control Panel utilities that are system specific, such as an NVIDIA video display or Java Control Panel.

* Note that particular options can be found by typing in the subcategory in the Search Control Panel textbox.

Determining the Windows Version

One Control Panel that is important for technicians is the *System* Control Panel. With this utility you can determine the amount of RAM installed, processor installed, and Windows version. The version of an operating system is important when troubleshooting because it is one more piece of information that can be placed within a search parameter. You can access the *System* Control Panel by using *Windows Explorer* (7)/*File Explorer* (8/10) > right-click or tap and briefly hold *Computer* (7)/*This PC* (8/10) > *Properties*. Figure 14.33 shows the *System* Control Panel in Windows 10.

FIGURE 14.33   Windows 10 System Control Panel

With Windows 7, 8, and 8.1, upgrades or patches to the operating system are provided as service packs. A **service pack** has multiple fixes to the operating system. Technicians must determine what operating system version is on the computer so that they can research whether a service pack is needed or research a particular problem. Windows 10 provides updates automatically.

Windows Registry

Every software and hardware configuration is stored in a database called the **registry**. The registry contains such things as folder and file property settings, port configuration, application preferences, and user profiles. A **user profile** contains specific configuration settings such as which applications the user can access, desktop settings, and each user's network configuration. The profile is different for each person who has an account on the computer. The registry loads into RAM (memory) during the boot process. When in memory, the registry is updated continuously by changes made to software, hardware, and user preferences.

The registry is divided into five subtrees. Subtrees are also sometimes called branches or hives. The five standard subtrees are Hkey_Local_Machine, Hkey_Users, Hkey_Current_User, Hkey_Current_Config, and Hkey_Classes_Root.

Each of these subtrees has keys and subkeys that contain values related to hardware and software settings. Table 14.9 lists the five subtrees and their functions. The registry can contain other subtrees that are user defined or system defined, depending on what hardware or software is installed on the computer.

TABLE 14.9   Windows registry subtrees

Registry subtree	Subtree function
Hkey_Local_Machine	Holds global hardware configuration. Included in the branch is a list of hardware components installed in the computer, the software drivers that handle each component, and the settings for each device. This information is not user specific.
Hkey_Users	Keeps track of individual users and their preferences.

Registry subtree	Subtree function
Hkey_Current_User	Holds a specific user's configuration, such as software settings, how the desktop appears, and what folders the user has created.
Hkey_Current_Config	Holds information about the hardware profile that is used when the computer first boots.
Hkey_Classes_Root	Holds file associations and file links. The information held here is what allows the correct application to start when you double-click a filename in Windows Explorer/File Explorer or My Computer/Computer (provided that the file extension is registered).

Editing the Windows Registry

Most changes to Windows are done through the various Control Panel utilities, but sometimes the only way to make a change is to edit the registry directly. Depending on the Windows operating system used, one or two registry editors are available from a command prompt: **regedit** and **regedt32**. Figure 14.34 shows the Windows 7 regedit utility.

Notice in Figure 14.34 that subtrees such as Hkey_Classes_Root and Hkey_Current_User appear in the left window. If you click the arrow beside a subtree, more subkeys appear. After several layers, when you click a folder in the left window, values appear in the right window. These values are the ones you must sometimes change to fix a problem.

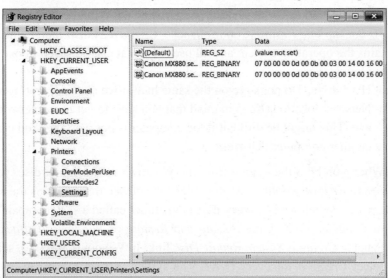

FIGURE 14.34 REGEDIT in Windows 7

TECH TIP

Make a backup of the registry before you change it

Before making changes to the registry, you should always make a backup of it. This way, if the changes do not work properly, they can be easily reversed.

For 64-bit versions of Windows, the registry is divided into 32- and 64-bit keys. The 32-bit keys are kept in a subfolder called *Wow6432Node*, located within the Hkey_Local_Machine key (*Software* folder). On some machines, the vendor may have a subfolder under *Software*; it is this vendor subfolder that contains the *Wow6432Node* folder. Just do a search for *Wow6432Node* to find it. 64-bit software keys are kept in `Hkey_Local_Machine\Software` subfolders.

Backing Up Data

Having a data **backup**, or a copy of that data, is important. Many people store their data in a remote location, using cloud storage. Those who have accounts with Google (Gmail or another Google product) have access to Google Drive; Microsoft users have OneDrive; Apple users have iCloud; and there are other vendors such as Dropbox or SugarSync. Windows 7 and 10 allow backing up the entire system and files/folders by using the Windows 7 *Backup and Restore* or the *Windows 10 Backup and Restore* Control Panel. Windows 8, 8.1, and 10 use *File History*, which saves files that are contained in the libraries (and you can create new libraries), contacts, desktop files, and favorites to external media or a network storage location.

Recovering the Windows OS

When a computer starts performing poorly and the operating system tools do not seem to help, you may need to repair, replace (**reload OS**), or uninstall/reinstall the operating system. A virus could also cause extensive damage, resulting in the need for an operating system recovery. How you do this depends on what measures have been taken (or have not been taken, in some cases) and the type of environment in which the computer is located (home or work). The following list describes some of the common methods used to recover an operating system:

> Create a Windows 7/10 **system image** using the Windows 7 *Backup and Restore* or *Windows 10 Backup and Restore* Control Panel > *Create a System Image* link. The system image contains the operating system and all user files that can be saved to one of three locations:
> > Optical discs
> > Hard drive (Do not store on the same hard drive as the operating system.)
> > Network location (Keep in mind that you have to get to the network location to get the image. This might be difficult if the computer is not working. You could burn the image from another computer that works.)

> When you boot the system from the Windows 7/10 original disc, you can select the *System Image Recovery* option and then select the device that contains the system image.

> Create a Windows **recovery disc** (sometimes called a system repair disc or a recovery drive) in Windows 7 using the *Backup and Restore* or *Windows 10 Backup and Restore* Control Panel > *Create a System Repair Disc* link. In Windows 8/8.1/10, search for **recovery** and select *Create a Recovery Drive*. The system recovery disc can boot the system when you don't have an original Windows disc and then restore the computer from a previously saved system image.

> Use a recovery disc provided by the computer manufacturer to restore the computer to the original "as sold" condition. *Caution:* With this option, none of the user's data will be restored.

> A recovery partition or section of the hard drive (sometimes called the HPA, or host protected area) is created by the computer manufacturer and commonly accessed through *Advanced Boot Options* (press F8 while booting) in Windows 7. To do the same in Windows 8/10 with an SSD installed or on a mobile device, perform the following:
> > Windows 8/8.1: Access *Settings* > *Advanced Startup Options* > locate the *Advanced Startup* section, and click the *Restart Now* button.

> Windows 10: Access *Settings* > *Update & Security* > *Recovery* > locate the *Advanced Startup* section, and click the *Restart Now* button.

> You can use imaging software. Companies frequently have a standard image stored on a server that can replace a failing operating system or can be used on a new computer.

> Backup/restore software may be provided by an external hard drive manufacturer.

> You can use the original operating system disc or image. This method is a risky one because the original disc or image does not contain the latest service packs. Download service packs and copy them to an optical disc *before* reinstalling the operating system. Research the service pack requirements before installing. Ensure that the computer is disconnected from any network before reinstalling the operating system and service packs! Do not connect to the network until the service packs have been installed, or virus infection may result.

> You can select *Safe Mode* from *Advanced Boot Options* (while booting) and use the *System Restore* tool to restore the operating system to a time when it worked.

WinRE

Windows Recovery Environment (**WinRE**) is used when Windows 7/8/10 does not boot and other tools and startup options do not solve a problem. WinRE has a list of recovery options, including a command prompt–only environment. The WinRE environment provides access to tools to troubleshoot the operating system when the tools within the operating system cannot be accessed or don't work properly. The tools are available through a special recovery partition accessed through Advanced Boot Options (which you access by pressing F8 while booting) or from the original Windows installation disc. Select *Repair Your Computer* and use the *System Recovery Options*. Note that if you are in Windows 8 or 10 and an SSD is installed, you can still get to the Advanced Boot Options by using the following process:

> Windows 8/8.1: Access *Settings* > *Advanced Startup Options* > locate the *Advanced Startup* section, and click the *Restart Now* button.

> Windows 10: Access *Settings* > *Update & Security* > *Recovery* > locate the *Advanced Startup* section, and click the *Restart Now* button.

SOFT SKILLS: STAYING CURRENT

Technicians must stay current in the rapidly changing field of computers. Benefits of staying current include understanding and troubleshooting the latest technologies, recommending upgrades or solutions to customers, saving time (and therefore money) troubleshooting, and being someone considered for a promotion. Technicians use a variety of methods to stay current, including the following:

> Subscribe to a magazine or an online magazine.
> Subscribe to a news list that gives you an update in your email.
> Join or attend association meetings.
> Register for and attend a seminar.
> Attend an online webinar.
> Take a class.
> Read books.
> Talk to your department peers and supervisor.

Staying current on technology in the past few years has been challenging for all, but the rapidly changing environment is what draws many to the field.

Chapter Summary

> An operating system performs all the basic tasks to communicate between hardware and software, to communicate between hardware and users, and to facilitate communication between software and users.
> The user communicates with the operating system through commands or a GUI interface.
> The most popular desktop/laptop operating systems are Microsoft's Windows, Apple's macOS, Chrome OS, and Linux. The most popular mobile operating systems are Android and iOS.
> Operating systems use either 32-bit or 64-bit architecture. A 64-bit system has more processing power than a 32-bit system.
> When replacing or upgrading an operating system, end-of-life concerns must be addressed. Concerns include security threats, software incompatibility, compliance issues, performance, reliability, and cost.
> Computers are considered compatible if software that runs on one model can run on all other models in that family, even if this results in performance issues. Forward and backward compatibility as well as extensibility are considerations.
> While specifics may differ, all Windows versions (7/8/10) offer the user a desktop or Start screen that consists of icons, the taskbar, shortcuts, and the Recycle Bin.
> Right-click a shortcut or tile and select *Properties* to see the path to the original file.
> Windows Explorer (Windows 7)/File Explorer (Windows 8/8.1/10) is commonly used to manipulate files and folders. Windows libraries (Documents, Music, Pictures, and Videos) are commonly part of the path to stored documents and subfolders.
> Deleted files are stored on the hard drive in a folder called Recycle Bin. The Recycle Bin must be emptied to release hard drive space. This is relevant only to files stored on hard drives.
> Windows supports encryption and compression. Encrypted files that are moved or copied on NTFS volumes remain encrypted. Compressed files, system files, and read-only files cannot be encrypted. When a file or folder is encrypted with EFS, only authorized users can view or change the file.
> Technicians commonly use the Control Panel to modify how the hardware, software, and operating system environment functions and appears. The *System* section of the Control Panel

can be used to determine the Windows version and to modify the registry. Other uses for the important Control Panel utilities are covered in Chapter 16, "Advanced Windows."

> The Windows registry is a database of everything within the Windows environment. Configuring Control Panel settings modifies the registry. Use `regedit` or `regedt32` to manually modify the registry.

> You can recover the operating system in various ways: using a Windows or manufacturer-provided recovery disc, a recovery partition, a previously created image, a reload of the operating system and service packs, and the System Restore tool.

> Technicians must stay current in the IT field to move up or maintain their current job status. Methods used to stay current include joining associations, reading relevant magazines, taking classes, reading current books, and interacting with peers.

A+ CERTIFICATION EXAM TIPS

✓ Know the differences between 32-bit and 64-bit architecture.

✓ Know the types and uses of operating systems, including Microsoft Windows, Apple's macOS, and Linux. Know the different types of licenses for OSes: open, personal, corporate, and enterprise.

✓ Know the types and uses of cell phone/tablet operating systems, including Microsoft Windows, Android, iOS, and Chrome OS.

✓ Describe the differences and similarities between Windows 7, Windows 8/8.1, and Windows 10, paying special attention to desktop styles and the user interface.

✓ Describe how the following are addressed in a corporate environment and on a personal computer: domain access, BitLocker, Media Center, BranchCache, and EFS.

✓ Be able to set various folder options, including hiding file extensions, viewing hidden files, view options, and the options available through the *Folder Options* Control Panel > *View* tab.

CHAPTER 14

Key Terms

32-bit architecture 727	end-of-life 730	RAM limitation 727
64-bit architecture 727	extensible software 731	recovery disk 760
Active Directory (AD) 732	extension 746	Recycle Bin 736
Android OS 729	file 725	regedit 759
Apple Macintosh OS 727	file type 731	regedit32 759
Apply button 744	filename 745	registry 758
attribute 752	folder 725	reload OS 760
backup 760	forward compatibility 731	security threat 730
backward compatibility 731	GUI 724	service pack 758
BitLocker 732	icon 733	shortcut 736
boot process 724	indexing 751	software incompatibility 730
BranchCache 733	Internet Explorer 736	Start button 738
charm 734	iOS 729	Start screen 734
Chrome OS 729	library 746	subdirectory 746
command line interface 724	Linux 727	subfolder 746
compatibility 731	live tile 734	system image 760
computer 736	macOS 727	Task View 743
compression 752	Media Center 732	taskbar 727
context menu 745	Microsoft Windows 727	This PC 736
Control Panel 754	network 736	tile 734
desktop 733	notification area 740	upward compatibility 731
documents 736	open source 727	user profile 758
domain access 732	operating system 724	window 743
Edge 736	path 736	Windows Mobile 730
EFS 733	proprietary system 727	WinRE 761

Review Questions

1. The key piece of software that provides an interface between the user and installed hardware is a(n) _____.

   [application | time machine | operating system | registry]

2. What is the core of a computer's operating system?

   [CPU | kernel | RAM | commands]

3. [T | F] Programs and drivers written for 64-bit systems can always run on 32-bit systems.

4. Two methods of interacting with the operating system are through a(n) ____ or a(n) _____. (Choose two.)

   [tunnel | GUI | OS cache | command line | core | workstation]

5. Name two features specifically needed on a mobile device's operating system.

   _____

6. Name three possible consequences associated with using software that has reached its end-of-life.

   _____

   _____

7. Name two potential problems associated with updating an operating system.

   _____

8. [T | F] Backward compatibility means that a new application can still process data from older software.

9. [T | F] A folder and a directory are the same thing.

10. A file's name consists of a filename and a(n) _____.

    [path | size | folder | extension]

11. Describe how to show a file's extension if it is not displayed in Windows Explorer/File Explorer. Choose one version of Windows (7, 8, 8.1, or 10).

    _____

12. In the following path, which is(are) the subfolder(s)?

    `C:\Users\Cheryl\NewFiles\review.docx`

    _____

13. [T | F] Deleted files stored on a hard drive can be recovered from the Recycle Bin.

14. What Windows option can access various icons or links that can configure the computer?

    [Control Panel | Time Machine | registry | Quick Launch]

15. What is the maximum memory that can be recognized by a Windows 32-bit operating system?

    [1 GB | 2 GB | 4 GB | 16 GB | 64 GB]

16. In the filename `Opsys_Quiz 4.docx`, what is the extension?

    [`Opsys_Quiz 4.docx` | `Opsys` | `4` | `docx`]

17. A user is working in Microsoft Word. She saves the document called `Ltr1.docx` to a folder called *Homedocs*. The *Homedocs* folder is a subfolder of the *Work* folder located on the D: hard drive volume. Write the complete path for the `Ltr1.docx` file.

    _____

18. [T | F] File and folder compression can degrade computer performance.

19. List three methods that can be used to recover an operating system.

_____

_____

20. What is the name of a registry editor?

[registry | regedit | edit | nano]

21. Describe two common methods used to recover an operating system.

_____

_____

22. List two methods that you think you will use to stay current in the IT field.

_____

_____

Exercises

Exercise 14.1

Objective: To recognize common Windows Control Panel categories

Procedure: Match the task to the appropriate Windows Control Panel category. Note that a category can be used more than once.

a. System and Security	**e.** User Accounts/User Accounts and Family Safety
b Network and Internet	**f.** Appearance and Personalization
c. Hardware and Sound	**g.** Clock, Language, and Region
d. Programs	**h.** Ease of Access

Task:

_____ Configure a HomeGroup.

_____ Require a password to be entered when the computer comes out of sleep mode.

_____ Enable screen reading for any text shown on the screen.

_____ Determine whether a computer is on a domain or workgroup.

_____ Access Device Manager.

_____ Customize the Start button menu.

_____ Configure whether hidden files display.

_____ Configure power saving options.

_____ Disable the showing of Microsoft-provided games.

_____ Back up the system.

_____ Configure the home page for the default Microsoft browser.

_____ Set the proper time zone.

_____ Change the Windows password for a home computer.

_____ Verify that a camera shows as attached.

_____ Configure the Ethernet NIC for DHCP.

Exercise 14.2

Objective: To differentiate between operating systems used today

Procedure: Match the OS to the description. Note that an operating system can be used more than once.

a. Windows

b. Linux

c. macOS

d. iOS

e. Chrome

Task:

_____   1.   Microsoft's operating system

_____   2.   The operating system most commonly used for office computers

_____   3.   Has version numbers that include the Roman numeral X

_____   4.   An open source operating system

_____   5.   A mobile operating system

_____   6.   Apple's operating system

_____   7.   A proprietary operating system

_____   8.   An operating system designed for cloud-based apps

_____   9.   Torvalds worked on the kernel

_____   10.   Runs on Apple desktop computers

_____   11.   Has the Control Panel

_____   12.   Has worldwide development efforts

_____   13.   Operating system developed by Google

Exercise 14.3

Objective: To differentiate between when a command line environment is used and when a graphical user interface is used

Procedure: Determine whether the action is using a (a) GUI environment or (b) command line interface. Note that an option can be used more than once. You may have to do some research on your own to determine the answers.

Task:

_____   1.   Working with File Explorer

_____   2.   Typing `dir` to see a list of files

_____   3.   Making a batch file

_____   4.   Working with Windows Explorer

_____   5.   Setting a configuration using the System Control Panel utility

_____   6.   Using `regedit`

_____   7.   Creating a script

_____   8.   Trying to fix a system on which the Windows operating system does not load

Activities

Internet Discovery

Objective: Access the Internet to obtain specific information regarding a computer or its associated parts

Parts: Access to the Internet

Procedure: Complete the following procedure and answer the accompanying questions.

1. Locate an Internet site that has a tutorial for Windows 8 troubleshooting or usage. Document the site and one thing you learned from the tutorial.

_____

_____

2. Find a web-based article on the differences between Windows 8 and Windows 8 Pro editions. Write the name of the article, three important differences, and the URL.

_____

_____

_____

_____

3. Locate a website that demonstrates how to edit the Windows registry for any version of the Windows 8 operating system. Describe the registry hack using at least one complete sentence. State whether you would deploy such a hack and explain why or why not.

_____

_____

4. Locate a website that describes three things to do if Windows 7 (any version) will not boot. Briefly describe the three things and document the URL.

_____

_____

_____

_____

_____

_____

_____

Soft Skills

Objective: To enhance and fine-tune a technician's ability to listen, communicate in both written and oral form, and support people who use computers in a professional manner

Activities:

1. Access a monitor *Setup* menu. Make a list of some of the settings that would be helpful to a computer user. Include in your list a description of each function. Document this in such a way that it could be given to users as a how-to guide.

2. On an index card, write a paragraph describing a problem and how a technician might look at the problem from a different perspective than that of a user. Exchange cards with one classmate and discuss both paragraphs. Comment on anything you find unclear in the classmate's paragraph, listen to suggestions from your classmate, and rewrite your paragraph, if necessary.

Critical Thinking Skills

Objective: To enhance and fine-tune a technician's ability to listen, communicate in both written and oral form, and support people who use computers in a professional manner

Activities:

1. On a piece of paper or an index card, list two topics you would like to hear about if you were to attend a local association such as a PC users' group meeting. Share this information with your group. Consolidate ideas and present five of the best ideas to the class.

2. In a team environment, select one of the five ideas presented in Activity 1 to research. Every team member should present something about a new technology to the rest of the class. The class will vote on the best presented topic and the most interesting topic.

3. On an index card, document a question that several students have asked the teacher about how to do a particular task. Exchange cards with a classmate. Correct each other's grammar, punctuation, and capitalization. When you have your original card back, exchange cards with a different classmate and perform the same task. Rewrite your index card based on the recommendations of your classmates. Keep in mind that all their suggestions are just that—suggestions. You do not have to accept any of them. A complaint in the industry is that technicians do not write well. Practice helps with this issue.

15 Introduction to Scripting

In this chapter you will learn:

> How to work from a command prompt

> How to use specific commands

> How to define environment variables and distinguish between system and user environment variables

> How to view and modify environment variables

> The basics of shell scripting and scripting in Python, JavaScript, VBScript, batch files, and PowerShell

> The building blocks of scripting: variables and data types

> The three programming constructs used to build all scripts: sequence, selection, and repetition

> How to use relational and logical operators in a script

> The pros and cons of each of six scripting languages

> About changing your perspective when troubleshooting

CompTIA Exam Objectives

What CompTIA A+ exam objectives are covered in this chapter?

✓ **1002-1.4** Given a scenario, use appropriate Microsoft command line tools.

✓ **1002-1.5** Given a scenario, use Microsoft operating system features and tools.

✓ **1002-4.8** Identify the basics of scripting.

Scripting Overview

While the Windows operating system offers technicians many dialog boxes that provide assistance in fixing problems and accessing various settings, sometimes technicians need to do things that cannot be done through a dialog box. In such cases, the command prompt environment can be used. From a command prompt, a technician can type commands that are specific to the operating system and to the required task. However, to do this, you must know the commands that a computer understands as well as the appropriate syntax to get the command to work. *Syntax* refers to the rules that specify the correct sequence of symbols or words. For example, in English, the phrase "table on this is book the" is meaningless, but the same words in a different order make perfect sense: "this book is on the table." In English, the correct syntax must be followed for the words to be understandable. Similarly, typing `/p dir w/` at a command prompt will give you an error, but typing `dir /p /w` will display the list of files and folders in a directory one page at a time in wide format. The same characters and symbols must be used in correct order—with correct syntax—for a command at the command prompt to work.

Access the command prompt from within Windows as follows:

> Windows 7: Access the *Start* button menu > select *All Programs* > locate and click the *Accessories* option, double-click the *Command Prompt* option.
> Windows 8: Access the *Command Prompt* tile located as an option under *Windows System*.
> Windows 10: Type `command` in the *Search the Web and Windows* textbox > select *Command Prompt* from the search result.

Remember, of course, that there are always several ways to accomplish almost anything in the Windows environment.

Some actions performed from the command prompt can only be done as an administrator of the machine. To open the command prompt window with administrator rights, right-click the *Command Prompt* option and select *Run as Administrator*. Figure 15.1 shows a command prompt environment.

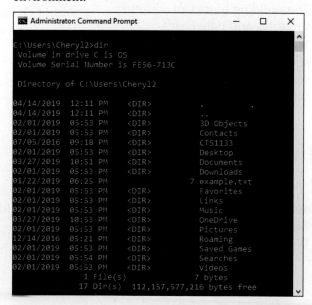

FIGURE 15.1   Windows command prompt

Network technicians can use scripts to automate tasks, to save time when completing complex procedures, to ensure consistency in tasks that must be executed over multiple servers in different locations, and to reduce human error. A script is a program that is designed to do a specific task. You can often find scripts written by others that you can use, and you can also create your own. Scripts are created in a text editor and are run from the command line prompt. In this chapter you will learn the basics of scripting in some of the many scripting languages, including PowerShell, VBScript, Python, JavaScript, as well as shell scripts for Unix and batch files for Windows.

Command Prompt Overview

Even with the advent of newer and more powerful operating systems, a technician still must enter basic commands into computers while troubleshooting, when deploying computers, and when updating computers in a corporate environment. Functioning from a command prompt is a skill that a technician still must use sometimes.

Following are several ways to access a command prompt when a computer is functional:

> Access the *Search* function > type **cmd** and press ⏎Enter.
> Access the *Search* function > type **command** and press ⏎Enter. (*Note:* When this option is used, the keyboard arrow keys do not bring up previously used commands, as they do when you use cmd.)
> Access *Accessories* > *Command Prompt* (7, and 10).
> Access the *Command Prompt* tile (Windows 8/8.1/10).

TECH TIP

Use the command prompt with administrative privileges

When issuing commands from a prompt, you might need to log in or provide credentials that allow you to execute a particular command with administrative privileges. Right-click or tap and briefly hold the *Command Prompt* option > select *Run as Administrator*.

You can close the command prompt window in several ways:

> Use the Close button in the upper-right corner.
> Click or tap the little black box in the upper-left corner > select *Close*.
> Type the **exit** command.

Command Prompt Basics

Drive letters are assigned to hardware devices when a computer boots. For example, the first hard drive partition gets the drive letter C:. The colon is part of the device drive letter. The devices detected by the operating system can use and be assigned drive letters A: through Z:.

All communication using typed commands begins at the **command prompt**, also called simply a *prompt*. A command prompt might look like F:\> or C:\> or C:\Windows>. Commands can be typed using a keyboard or entered through a touchscreen. Capitalization does not matter when using a command prompt, but commands *must* be typed in a specific format and in a specific order. Practicing using commands from a command prompt is the best way to become proficient at using them.

Files can be organized like chapters in a book; however, on a computer, a file grouping is called a folder (in a GUI environment) or a **directory** (in a command prompt environment). The starting point for all directories is the **root directory**. From the root directory, other directories can be created or accessed. The root directory can hold only a limited number of files, and the quantity depends on the file system used. The root directory is shown with a backslash after the letter: C:\ or E:\. In the command prompt environment, when you are at the root directory, a greater than sign (>) follows the letter and the backslash: C:\> and E:\>.

Any number of files can exist under each directory. Each filename within a directory must be unique, but multiple directories can contain the same file. For example, assume that the *Cheryl.txt* file exists in the *Documents* directory. A different *Cheryl.txt* file can exist in the *Lotus* or *Utility* directory (or all three directories for that matter). The file called *Cheryl.txt* that contains the same information could also exist in all three folders. However, a second *Cheryl.txt* file cannot exist in the same folder (directory).

Files are kept in directories (folders) or in the root directory. A **subdirectory** can be created beneath another directory. For example, if a directory (folder) has the name *Book*, below the directory can be subdirectories titled *Chap1*, *Chap2*, *Chap3*, and so on. Since the word *root* identifies the start of the directory structure, many people describe the directory structure as a tree. Figure 15.2 illustrates this concept.

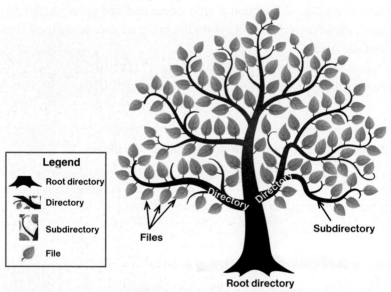

FIGURE 15.2   Tree structure concepts

Sometimes it's easier to see the file structure concepts from File Explorer than from the command prompt. Figure 15.3 shows the *Documents* directory of the C: drive for the user *Cheryl*. Notice that the path is listed at the top of the File Explorer window because that option has been enabled through the *Folder Options* window. Also notice the address bar, which shows part of the path (<<Users > Cheryl > Documents). The File Explorer window also it shows folders (for example, *2015BookWin8Laptop*, *Custom Office Templates*, *Outlook Files*, and *SugarSync Shared Folders*). It also shows shortcuts to the *My Music*, *My Pictures*, and *My Videos* folders. Finally, it shows one hidden file (*desktop.ini*) and four other files (*Chap1.docx*, *kara's books.docx*, *My class books.docx*, and *Spectre.docx*). Settings in the *Folder Options* section of the Control Panel allow you to determine whether the filenames and hidden files are seen.

Now let's view this same structure from the command prompt by using the tree command. Figure 15.4 shows this perspective from the command prompt.

In Figure 15.4 notice that two commands have actually been given. The first one, tree, asks the computer to display a "tree," or the structure starting from C:\Users\Cheryl\Documents. The second command uses a /f at the end causing files to be shown.

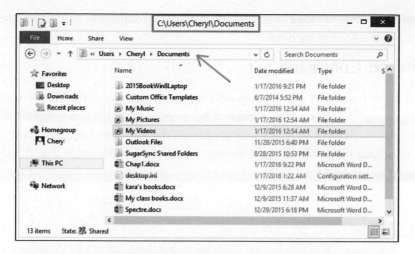

FIGURE 15.3   Sample file structure in File Explorer

FIGURE 15.4   Tree structure from a command prompt

Every folder along the path is shown, starting with the root directory, `C:` (`C:\`). The path tells you exactly how to reach the file. When something goes wrong in a particular application and Microsoft or another vendor posts a solution online, the solution commonly shows the complete path. It is the only way to clearly tell you where to find, put, delete, or replace a file.

Moving Around from a Command Prompt

One of the most important skills when working in the command line environment is to be able to move around within that environment. The `cd`, `md`, `rd`, and `dir` commands are the four most popular commands used within the Windows environment to move around the directory structure. Let's take a look at each one.

The cd Command

The most frequently used command for moving around in the cumbersome tree structure is cd (for *change directory*). The cd command enables you to "change" to a different directory so that the prompt changes to where you are within the directory (tree) structure. For example, say you have a flash drive with a *Test1* directory that has subdirectories called *Sub1*, *Sub2*, and *Sub3*, as shown in Figure 15.5.

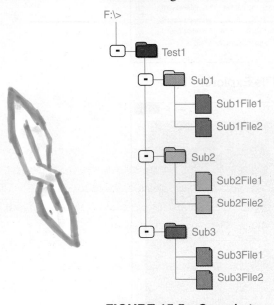

FIGURE 15.5   Sample tree structure

Assume that the prompt is at F:\>. (To get to this prompt, you simply type the drive letter of your flash drive and press ⏎Enter.) To move to the *Sub2* subdirectory (subfolder), type the command **cd Test1\Sub2**. The prompt changes to F:\Test1\Sub2>. Another command that does the same thing is **cd F:\Test1\Sub2**. The difference is that with the second command, the full path was given. The F:\ is not required because the prompt was already at the root directory of F: (F:\>).

To move to a subdirectory that is on the same level as the *Sub2* directory (such as *Sub1* or *Sub3*), several commands are possible. For example, you can type **cd..** to move back one level and then type **cd Sub1**. Notice that there is no a backslash (\) between cd and Sub1. You omit the backslash only when moving one level down the tree structure, as shown in Figure 15.5.

From the F:\Test1> prompt, you can type **cd Sub1**, **cd\Test1\Sub1**, or **cd F:\ Test1\Sub1** to get to the *Sub1* subfolder. However, if the prompt shows that you are at the root directory (F:\>), you must use either **F:\Test1\Sub1** or **cd Test1\Sub1**. The other commands given do not operate properly because of the current location within the tree structure (as shown by the prompt such as F:\>). Practice is the best way to master moving around from a prompt.

The dir Command

The dir command lists all the files and directories from wherever you are at the prompt. Figure 15.6 shows the dir command from the root directory of a flash drive (G:\>).

Notice in Figure 15.6 that directories are shown with <DIR>. There is nothing listed in that column to identify a file. Directories in the root directory of G: are *Chip, Dale, cotlong, Photos*, and *classes*. Files in the root directory of the same flash drive are *Dinfo.txt* and *Ninfo.txt*.

FIGURE 15.6 `dir` command from a prompt

When you use the `dir` command on a hard drive, you might notice a directory for `.` and `..` (see Figure 15.7). The `.` and `..` are used with commands like `cd` to move around the directory structure. A single period (`.`) represents the current directory but can also be used to move to the root directory. Two periods (`..`) represents the parent directory. That is why the command `cd..` moves you back one directory structure and the `cd\.` command takes you back to the root directory. In Figure 15.7, if someone were to type the command `cd..` from the `C:\Users\Cheryl2>` prompt, the prompt would change to `C:\Users`. If the `cd\.` command were issued from the `C:\Users\Cheryl2>` prompt, the prompt would change to `C:\`.

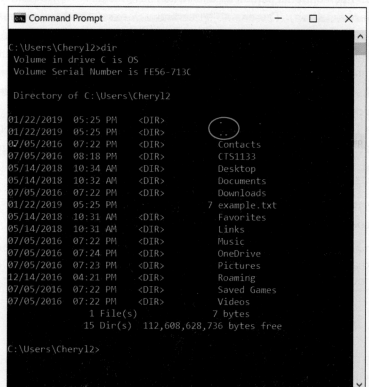

FIGURE 15.7 `dir` command showing the `.` and `..` directories

Each command commonly has one or more optional **command switches** that change how the command operates. To determine what switches are available with any command, type the following:

`command_name /?`

where *command_name* is any one command. For example, the command `dir /?` shows all the possible options that can be used with the `dir` command (see Figure 15.8). Notice how the `dir` is the *command_name* and the `/?` is how to get help for the `dir` command. In the third and fourth lines from the top of Figure 15.8 you can see that there is an order to the listing of the switches. Normally, they are shown in alphabetical order.

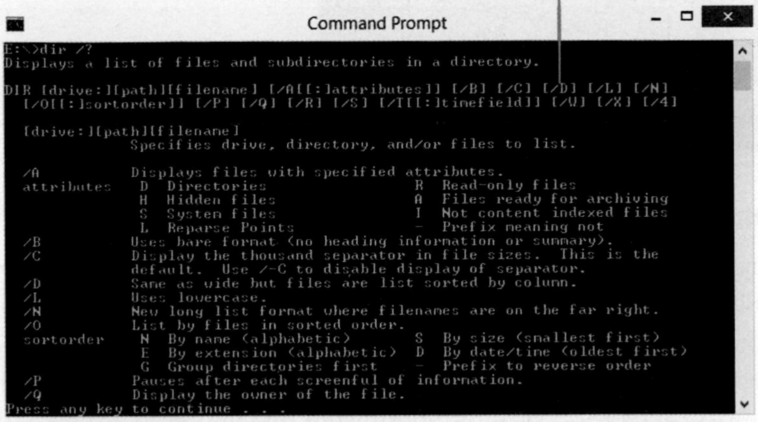

FIGURE 15.8 `dir` command switches

Notice in the output shown in Figure 15.8 that there are optional parameters such as `drive:` and `path`. Each optional parameter and switch has brackets ([ ]) around it. Switches are preceded by a / (forward slash). There is no space between the / and the optional switch. For example, with the `dir` command, you could simply type `dir` and press ↵Enter. You could also type `dir /p` to display things one page at a time or `dir /w` to display the output in a wide format. You can use multiple switches together, such as `dir /p /w`. While it is not necessary to put a space after each switch, you must put a space between the command and a switch. The command `dir /p/w` works exactly the same way as `dir /p /w`.

Figure 15.8 shows that each command switch is described below the options. Also notice in this figure that when some commands list more than one page of output, you get a `Press any key to continue...` message at the bottom of the screen.

TECH TIP

Make a command output one page at a time

If a command outputs more than one page at a time, you can use the | more option after the command and make it show only one page at a time. Note that the | (pipe) symbol is created by holding down the ⬆Shift key and pressing the Ⓘ key located directly above the ↵Enter key.

TECH TIP

Limited commands in WinRE

Not all command parameters or switches shown may be available when using the Windows Recovery Environment (WinRE), which is discussed in Chapter 14, "Introduction to Operating Systems" and Chapter 16, "Advanced Windows." The WinRE has a limited number of commands. Type the `help` command to see a list of available commands.

The `md` and `rd` Commands

Sometimes as an IT staff person, you might be required to create or remove a directory from a command prompt to install software or as part of a repair. The md and rd commands are used to perform these tasks.

The `md` Command

The **md** (for *make directory*) command makes a directory from wherever you are in the directory structure (as shown from the prompt on the screen). Consider the following command: `F:\>md CTS1133` (the Classes folder on the F: drive). The *CTS1133* directory would be made in the root directory of the F: drive. Now consider the following set of commands:

```
F:\>
F:\>cd classes
F:\Classes>md CTS1133
F:\Classes>
```

What is different about this set of commands is that before the md CTS1133 command was issued, the cd classes command was issued. The cd classes command changed the prompt to F:\Classes> (the Classes folder on the F: drive). Then the md CTS1133 command was issued, thus creating a subdirectory called *CTS1133* under the *Classes* folder.

An alternative way of doing the same thing is to issue the full path with the command, as shown here:

```
F:\>md \classes\CTS1133
```

Or:

```
F:\>md F:\classes\CTS1133
```

Note that the second command would work from any prompt, including the C:\> prompt, because it includes the full path as part of the command.

TECH TIP

The full path works from everywhere

If you begin learning the command prompt by typing the full path no matter where you are in the directory structure, you will be better prepared for working in this environment.

The `rd` Command

The **rd** command removes a directory or subdirectory. Note that if the directory has files in it, this message will appear: `The directory is not empty.` You can only use the rd command on an empty directory. The examples here show how to remove a directory from the different prompts:

```
F:\>rd F:\classes\cts1133
F:\>rd \classes\cts1133
F:\Classes>rd cts1133
```

Note that the first example here works from any prompt, even if it is another drive letter.

Two Useful Commands: `del` and `type`

When problems occur and a technician is working at a command prompt, two tasks that might need to be accomplished are to delete a particular file or to read the contents of a file such as a log file. The `del` and `type` commands can be used to do this so let's look at them next.

The `del` Command

Sometimes a file has to be deleted as part of the repair process. The **del** (for *delete*) command removes a file. It cannot be used to remove a directory. That is an important point to remember. To issue the command, simply type the `del` command followed by the name of the file you want to delete. You must be in the correct directory (as shown by the prompt) to use this method, and you must include the file extension as part of the filename. In the commands shown below, the user is in the root directory of the `F:` drive and wants to delete a file named `homework1.docx` that is in the `cts1133` subdirectory of the `classes` directory. Before issuing the `del` command, the user must change directories to be in the `cts1133` subdirectory:

```
F:\>
F:\>cd F:\classes\cts1133
F:\Classes\CTS1133>del homework1.docx
F:\Classes\CTS1133>
```

An alternative method can work from any prompt. This method requires that you type the full path of the file to be deleted, as shown here:

```
F:\>del F:\classes\cts1133\homework1.docx
```

The `type` Command

Another useful command is the **type** command, which displays text (`.txt`) or batch (`.bat`) files on the screen. Many times *Readme.txt* files are included with software applications and utilities. The `type` command allows you to view these files from the command line interface; however, most of the time, these files occupy more than one screen. So, using the `| more` parameter after the `type` command permits viewing the file one screen at a time. After viewing each screen, press the Spacebar key to see the next screenful of content. For example, `type readme.txt | more` allows you to view the text file called *readme.txt* one page at a time.

Copying Files

Commands that can copy files are `copy`, `xcopy`, and `robocopy`. The **copy** command is used to make a duplicate of a file. The **xcopy** command is used to copy and back up files and directories. The **robocopy** command enables you to copy a directory, its contents, all its subdirectories (and their subdirectories), and each attribute.

We focus on the `copy` command because it is the command you can use in any environment. The `copy` command is an internal command, meaning it cannot be found as an executable file on the hard drive or Windows disc. The operating system can always find an internal command no matter where in the directory structure the command is located. The command enables you to copy a file to a different disk, copy a file from one directory to another, copy a group of files using wildcards, or rename a file as it is being copied. A **wildcard** replaces one or more characters. `?` and `*` are examples of wildcards; `?` represents a single character, and `*` represents any number of characters.

The copy command has three parts, separated by spaces:

> The command itself (copy or xcopy)
> The source (the file being copied)
> The destination (where the file is being copied to)

In technical documentation, this would be shown using the syntax copy *source destination.* *destination* is optional if the file is being copied into the current directory. For example, if you are working from the E:\> command prompt and copying a file called *Document.txt* from the hard drive's root directory, the command could be copy C:\Document.txt. The destination is omitted because the file automatically copies to the current drive and directory (which is E:\). The same function can be accomplished by typing copy C:\Document.txt E:\, which has all three parts: the copy command, the *source* (a file called *Document.txt* located on the hard drive or C:\Document.txt), and the *destination* (the root directory of E: or E:\).

The command requires all three parts if the destination is *not* the current drive and directory. For example, consider the situation of being at the C:\> command prompt. To copy the *format. com* file from the hard drive (the *System32* subfolder of the *Windows* folder) to a disk shown as E:, type the following command:

```
C:\> copy C:\Windows\System32\format.com E:\
```

Note that the copy command is first. Then you use the source, location, and name of the file being copied—C:\Windows\System32\format.com. Finally, you include the destination, E:\, or the root directory of the flash drive where the file is to be placed. If the current directory is the C:\Windows\System32 hard drive directory, then the source path does not have to be typed. Instead, the command would look like the following:

```
C:\Windows\System32>copy format.com E:\
```

The backslash (\) after the E: is not necessary if the flash drive does not have directories (folders). The copy command does not need the entire path in front of the command because copy is an internal command.

TECH TIP

Getting the command straight in your head

Before using any command, consider the following questions:

> What command do you want to issue?
> Where in the directory structure are you currently working? Look at the prompt to determine where you are.
> If you are copying a file or moving a file, what is the name of the file, and what is the full path to it? This is the source file.
> If you are copying a file or moving a file, in what directory does the file need to be placed? This is the destination file.

The attrib Command

The **attrib** command sets, removes, or shows the attribute(s) of a file or a directory. Attributes change how a file or directory is displayed on the screen or what can be done with the file or directory. Possible attributes are read-only, archive, system, and hidden:

> The read-only attribute protects files so that they cannot be accidentally changed or deleted.
> The archive attribute marks files that have changed since they were last backed up by a backup program.

> The system attribute designates a file as a system file; files with this attribute do not appear in directory listings.
> The hidden attribute allows you to hide files and even directories.

Set each attribute using the +*x* switch, where *x* is r for read-only, a for archive, h for hidden, or s for system. Remove each attribute by using the -r, -s, -h, or -a switch with the attrib command. Similarly, you can add an attribute by using the +r, +s, +h, or +a switch with the attrib command. One command can set more than one attribute on a file or directory. For example, to make the *Cheryl.txt* file hidden and read-only, type **attrib +r +h Cheryl.txt**.

Why Learn Commands?

With many Windows problems, some solutions involve working from a command prompt until a Windows update fixes the problem. Other problems simply involve using a command from a prompt. Commands can also be used in a script. A *script* is a group of commands in a file that together automate a particular task. For example, say that you want to write a script to stop a computer print spooler and delete all spooled files that are in the queue to be printed. The following commands could be written in Notepad and saved to a file called *DeletePrint.cmd*:

```
net stop spooler
del %systemroot%\system32\spool\printers\*.shd
del %systemroot%\system32\spool\printers\*.spl
net start spooler
```

After the file is saved, you could copy this file to a hard drive, type DeletePrint, and press ↵Enter, and the four commands would execute.

> **TECH TIP**
>
> **Start your favorite tools using a command**
>
> For example from a command prompt or from the *Search* textbox, type **mmc devmgmt.msc** to start Device Manager. Note that you can access the Microsoft Management Console and still get to Device Manager by simply typing **mmc**.

PowerShell

In today's computing environment, a technician frequently has to do things to hundreds, or even thousands, of computers. Scripts and Windows PowerShell can help. Windows PowerShell is a tool that helps technicians and network administrators automate support functions through the use of scripts and snippets. Windows 7, 8, 8.1, and 10 ship with PowerShell as an accessory. Every command that you can type from a command window (and a lot more) can be executed from within PowerShell.

> **TECH TIP**
>
> **How do you open PowerShell?**
>
> Access Windows PowerShell by typing **powershell** in the search window, right-clicking on the resulting Windows PowerShell app, and selecting *Run as Administrator*. It can also be found through the *Start* button (Windows 8.1 or 10), *Start* screen > *Apps View* > *Windows System* section > *Windows PowerShell* (Windows 8 or 8.1), or *All Programs* > *Accessories* > *Windows PowerShell* (Windows 7).

Other Commands You Should Look Over

Some commonly used commands are discussed in other chapters of this book or are beyond the basics of learning how to function from a command prompt. When you understand how to work from a prompt, you can execute any command fairly easily. In the "Command Format" section that follows, commands shown as key terms (bolded and colored) are objectives for the certification exam.

The following are the most common and, perhaps, most important commands that you as a technician should be familiar with:

> [command name] /?	> format	> notepad
> ..	> gpresult	> nslookup
> bootrec	> gpupdate	> ping
> cd	> help	> rd
> chkdsk	> ipconfig	> regedit
> command	> md	> regsvr32
> copy	> mmc	> robocopy
> defrag	> msconfig	> services.msc
> del	> msinfo32	> sfc
> dir	> mstsc	> shutdown
> diskpart	> nbtstat	> taskkill
> dism	> net	> tasklist
> dxdiag	> net use	> tracert
> exit	> net user	> xcopy
> expand	> netdom	
> explorer	> netstat	

Command Format

When Windows does not boot, a technician must work from a command prompt. Some of the most frequently used commands are outlined in detail on the following pages. Items enclosed by brackets ([ ]) are optional. Items in italics are command-specific values that you must enter. When the items are separated by a | (called a pipe, or bar), one of the items must be typed.

The following pages provide a command reference. Some of these commands are used elsewhere in this chapter or in others. This list is by no means comprehensive. You can expect to see the bold and colored terms on the CompTIA A+ Core 1 (220-1001) and CompTIA A+ Core 2 (220-1002) certification exams. Visit the microsoft.com website for a complete listing; the TechNet area is a good asset.

CHAPTER 15

> **TECH TIP**

How to get help when working from a prompt

To get help while working from a prompt, type **help** *command_name* or type *command_name* **/?**. For example, to get help for the attrib command, type **help attrib** or **attrib /?**.

[command name] /?

The **[command name]** /? command displays help information about a specific command.

Syntax: [command_name] /?

Explanation: [command_name] is the name of the command for which you want help.

Example: dir /?

Notes: If you do not specify the *command_name* parameter when using this command, no commands are listed and an error appears that /? is not recognized as an internal or external command, operable program, or batch file.

attrib

The attrib command controls the attribute for a file or folder.

Syntax: attrib [+|-h] [+|-r] [+|-a]

[+|-s] [*drive:*] [*path*] *filename* [/S] [/D]

Explanation: + adds an attribute.

- takes away an attribute.

h is the hidden attribute.

r is the read-only attribute.

a is the archive file attribute.

s is the system attribute.

[*drive:*] is the drive where the file is located.

[*path*] is the directory/subdirectory where the file is located.

filename is the name of the file.

[/S] includes subfolders.

[/D] includes folders

Example: attrib +h c:\cheryl.bat

This command sets the hidden attribute for a file called *Cheryl.bat* located on the hard drive.

Notes: The dir command (typed without any switches) is used to see what attributes are currently set. You may set more than one attribute at a time.

bcdedit

The bcdedit command is used at the command prompt or in the System Recovery environment to modify and control settings contained in the BCD (boot configuration data) store, which controls how the operating system boots.

Syntax: bcdedit [/createstore] [/copy] [/create] [/delete] [/deletevalue] [/set] [/enum] [/bootsequence] [/default] [/displayorder] [/timeout]

Explanation: [/createstore] creates a new empty BCD store that is not a system store.

[/copy] makes a copy of a specific boot entry contained in the BCD store.

[/create] creates a new entry in the BCD store.

[/delete] deletes an element from a specific entry in the BCD store.

[/deletevalue] deletes a specific element from a boot entry.

[/set] sets a specific entry's option value.

[/enum] lists entries in a store.

[/bootsequence] specifies a display order that is used one time only. The next time the computer boots, the original display order is shown.

[/default] selects the entry used by the boot manager when the timeout expires.

[/displayorder] specifies a display order that is used each time the computer boots.

[/timeout] specifies, in seconds, the amount of time before the boot manager boots using the default entry.

Example:　bcdedit / set Default debug on

This command troubleshoots a new operating system installation for the operating system. It is the default option that appears in the Boot Manager menu.

Notes:　Use the bcdedit /? types command to see a list of data types. Use the bcd /? formats command to see a list of valid data formats. To get detailed information on any of the options, type bcdedit /? followed by the option. For example, to see information on how to export the BCD, type bcd /? export.

bootrec

The bootrec command is used in the System Recovery environment to repair and recover from hard drive problems.

Syntax:　bootrec [/FixMbr] [/FixBoot] [/ScanOs] [/RebuildBcd]

Explanation:　[/FixMbr] repairs the hard drive MBR (master boot record) by copying a new MBR to the system partition. The existing partition table is not altered.

[/FixBoot] repairs the hard drive boot sector if it has been corrupted and replaces it with a higher boot sector or, if an earlier version of Windows has been installed after Windows 7, 8/8.1, or 10.

[/ScanOs] looks for compatible operating system installations that do not currently appear on the Boot Manager list.

[/RebuildBcd] scans all disks for operating systems compatible with Windows Vista or higher and optionally rebuilds the BCD (boot configuration data) store. The BCD store provides structured storage for boot settings that is especially helpful in multiple operating system environments. Discovered operating systems can be added to the BCD store.

Example:　bootrec /fixmbr

This command could be used if a virus has destroyed the master boot record.

Notes:　If you receive an Element not Found error when using the bootrec command, the hard drive partition might not be active. Use the Windows Recovery Environment command prompt and the diskpart command to select the drive disk number (if you only have one and it has one partition, it will be the command select disk 0, as an example), and then type the command active. Exit the `diskpart` utility and reboot the computer. Re-access the System Recovery environment and rerun the `bootrec` command.

If the system needs a new BCD and rebuilding it did not help, you can export the existing BCD and then delete the current BCD. To export the BCD, type `bcdedit /export x:\folder` (where `x:\folder` is the location where you want the BCD store exported). Then type `c:`, `cd boot`, `attrib bcd -s -h -r`, `ren c:\boot\bcd bcd.old`, `bootrec /RebuildBcd` to create a backup copy of the BCD store, make it so it is not hidden and can be deleted, and then rebuild it.

cd

The **cd** command is used to navigate through the directory structure.

Syntax: `cd [drive:] [path] [..]`

Explanation: `[drive:]` specifies the drive (if it is different from the current drive) to which you want to change.

`[path]` is the directory/subdirectory to reach the folder.

`[..]` changes to the parent directory (moves you back one directory in the tree structure).

Examples: `C:\Windows>cd..`

`C:\>`

This command moves you from the *Windows* directory (folder) to the parent directory, which is the root directory (`C:\`).

`C:\>cd \Windows`

This command moves you from the root directory to the *Windows* directory on the `C:` drive.

chkdsk

The **chkdsk** command checks a disk for physical problems, lost clusters, cross-linked files, and directory errors. If necessary, the `chkdsk` command repairs the disk, marks bad sectors, recovers information, and displays the status of the disk.

Syntax: `chkdsk [drive:] [/r] [/f] [/i] [/b]`

Explanation: `[drive:]` specifies the drive to check.

`[/r]` locates bad sectors and attempts recovery of the sector's information.

`[/f]` fixes drive errors.

`[/i]` checks only index entries on NTFS volumes.

`[/b]` re-evaluates bad clusters.

Example: `chkdsk d:`

This command checks the disk structure on the `D:` drive.

Notes: This command can be used without switches. For the `chkdsk` command to work, the file *Autochk.exe* must be loaded in the *System32* folder or used with the correct path and run from the Windows disc. If one or more files are open on the drive being checked, `chkdsk` prompts you to schedule the disk to be checked the next time the computer is restarted.

chkntfs

The chkntfs command can display whether a particular disk volume is scheduled for automatic disk checking the next time the computer is started, or it can be used to modify automatic disk checking.

Syntax: chkntfs *volume*: [/D] [/X] [/C]

Explanation: *volume*: specifies the drive volume to display or modify.

[/D] places the computer back to default behavior. (All drives are checked at boot time, and chkdsk is run on those that are dirty.)

[/X] excludes a particular volume from the default boot-time check.

[/C] schedules a drive to be checked at boot time. The chkdsk command will be run if the drive is dirty.

Example: chkntfs c:

This command displays whether the drive is dirty or scheduled to be checked on the next computer reboot.

cipher

The cipher command displays or alters file or folder encryption.

Syntax: cipher [/e] [/d] [/f] [/q] [/k] [/u] [/n] [*path*]

Explanation: [/e] encrypts the specified folder, including files that are added in the future.

[/d] decrypts the specified folder.

[/f] forces encryption or decryption because, by default, files that have already been encrypted or decrypted are skipped.

[/q] reports essential information about the encryption or decryption.

[/k] creates a new file encryption key.

[/u] updates the encryption key to the current one for all encrypted files if the keys have been changed. /u works only with the /n option.

[/n] finds all encrypted files. It prevents keys from being updated. It is used only with /u.

[*path*] is a pattern, file, or folder.

Examples: cipher /e Book\Chap1

This command encrypts a subfolder called *Chap1* that is located in a folder called *Book*.

cipher /e /s:Book

This command encrypts all subfolders in the folder called *Book*.

cipher Book

This command displays whether the *Book* folder is encrypted.

cipher Book\Chap 1*

This command displays whether any files in the *Chap1* subfolder of the *Book* folder are encrypted.

Notes: Multiple parameters are separated with spaces. Read-only files and folders cannot be encrypted.

CHAPTER 15

cls

The cls command clears the screen of any previously typed commands.

Example: C:\Windows>cls

command

The command command is executed from the *Search* textbox by simply typing command and pressing Enter. A command prompt window appears. Type exit to close the window.

Syntax: command

Explanation: When command is entered, a command prompt window opens.

copy

The **copy** command is used to copy one or more files to the specified destination.

Syntax: copy [/a] [/y] [/-y] source [destination]

Explanation: [/a] indicates an ASCII text file.

[/y] suppresses the prompt to overwrite an existing file.

[/-y] prompts to overwrite an existing file.

source is the file that you want to copy, and it includes the drive letter and the path if it is different from your current location.

[destination] is the location in which you want to put the file and includes the drive letter and path if it is different from your current location.

Example: copy c:\cheryl.bat f:\

This command takes a file called *cheryl.bat* that is located in the root directory of the hard drive and copies it to a flash drive.

Notes: You do not have to include a target if the file is going to the current location specified by the command prompt. If a file already exists, you will be prompted whether to overwrite the file. Compressed files that are copied from the Windows media are automatically uncompressed to the hard drive as they are copied.

defrag

The defrag command is used to locate and reorder files so that they are contiguous (not fragmented) to improve system performance.

Syntax: defrag [drive:] [/a] [/c] [/x]

Explanation: [drive:] is the drive letter where the files are located.

[/a] analyzes the drive volume specified.

[/c] includes all volumes.

[/x] consolidates free space on the specified volume.

Example: defrag c: d: /a

This command defragments the C: and D: drives and analyzes them.

Notes: Multiple switches can be used, as long as spaces appear between them.
Multiple drive letters (volumes) can be used with a single command.

del

The del command is used to delete a file.

Syntax: `del name [/p] [/f] [/s]`

Explanation: `name` is the file or directory (folder) that you want to delete, and it includes the drive letter and the path if it is different from your current location.

[/p] prompts for confirmation before deleting.

[/f] forces read-only files to be deleted.

[/s] deletes files from all subdirectories.

Example: `C:\Windows>del c:\cheryl.bat`

This command deletes a file called *cheryl.bat* that is located in the *Windows* directory on the hard drive.

dir

The **dir** command list files and folders and their attributes.

Syntax: `dir [drive:] [path] [filename] [/a:attribute] [/o]`
`[/p] [/s] [/w]`

Explanation: `[drive:]` is the letter of the drive where the files are located.

`[path]` is the directory/subdirectory to reach the folder.

`[filename]` is the name of a specific file.

`[/a:attribute]` displays files that have specific attributes, where the attributes are D, R, H, A, and S. D is for directories; R is for read-only, H is for hidden, A is for archive, and S is for system files.

`[/o]` displays the listing in sorted order. Options you can use after the o are E, D, G, N, and S. E is by alphabetic file extension; D is by date and time, with the oldest listing shown first; G shows the directories listed first; N displays by alphabetic name; and S displays by size, from smallest to largest.

`[/p]` displays the information one page at a time.

`[/s]` includes subdirectories in the listing.

`[/w]` shows the listing in wide format.

Example: `dir c:\windows`

This command shows all the files and folders (and their associated attributes) for the *windows* folder that is located on the C: drive.

disable

The disable command disables a system service or hardware driver.

Syntax: `disable name`

Explanation: `name` is the name of the service or driver that you want to disable.

Notes: You can use the `listsvc` command to show all services and drivers that are available for you to disable. Make sure that you write down the previous *START_TYPE* before you disable the service in case you need to restart the service.

diskpart

The **diskpart** command is used to manage and manipulate the hard drive partitions.

Syntax: `diskpart [/add|/delete] [devicename] [drivename | partitionname] [size]`

Explanation: `[/add |/delete]` creates a new partition or deletes an existing partition.

`[devicename]` is the name given to the device when creating a new partition, such as `\Device\HardDisk0`.

`[drivename]` is the drive letter used when deleting an existing partition, such as `E:`.

`[partitionname]` is the name used when deleting an existing partition and can be used instead of the *drivename* option. An example of a *partitionname* is `Device\HardDisk0\Partition2`.

`[size]` is used when creating a new partition and is the size of the partition, in megabytes.

Notes: You can just type the `diskpart` command without any options, and a user interface appears that helps when managing hard drive partitions.

dism

The **dism** command is a Windows utility, Deployment Image Servicing and Management, which can be used to repair and prepare Windows images.

Syntax: `dism /Online /Cleanup-Image /[/CheckHealth] [/ScanHealth] [/RestoreHealth]`

Explanation: `[/CheckHealth]` checks whether the image has been flagged as corrupted and whether the corruption can be repaired.

`[/ScanHealth]` scans the image for component store corruption and records that corruption to the log file.

`[/RestoreHealth]` scans the image for component store corruption, performs repair operations automatically, and records that corruption to the log file.

dxdiag

The **dxdiag** command is used to perform DirectX diagnostics.

Syntax: `dxdiag [/dontskip] [whql:on|/whql:off] [/64bit target] [/x filename] [/t filename]`

Explanation: `[/dontskip]` causes all diagnostics to be performed, even if a previous crash in `dxdiag` has occurred.

`[/whql:on]` checks for WHQL digital signatures.

`[/whql:off]` prevents checking for WHQL digital signatures.

`[/64bit target]` uses 64-bit DirectX diagnostics.

`[/x filename]` saves XML information to the specified filename and quits.

`[/t filename]` saves TXT information to the specified filename and quits.

Notes: When DirectX diagnostics checks for WHQL digital signatures, the Internet may be used.

enable

The enable command is used to enable a system service or hardware driver.

Syntax:	enable `name` [`start-type`]
Explanation:	`name` is the name of the service or driver that you want to disable.

[`start-type`] is used when you want the service or driver scheduled to begin. Valid options are as follows:

SERVICE_BOOT_START

SERVICE_SYSTEM_START

SERVICE_AUTO_START

SERVICE_DEMAND_START

Example:	enable DHCP client service_auto_start
Notes:	You can use the listsvc command to show all services and drivers that are available for you to enable. Make sure that you write down the previous value before you enable the service in case you need to restart the old service or driver.

exit

The exit command closes the command prompt environment window.

Example:	C:\Windows>exit

expand

The expand command uncompresses a file from a CAB (short for *cabinet*) file. A CAB file holds multiple files or drivers that are compressed into a single file. Technicians sometimes copy the CAB files onto the local hard drive so that when hardware and/or software is installed, removed, or reinstalled, the application disc does not have to be inserted.

Syntax:	expand [-i] `source` [`destination`]
Explanation:	[-i] renames files but ignores the directory structure.

`source` is the name of the file, including the path that you want to uncompress.

[`destination`] is the path where you want to place the uncompressed file.

Example:	expand d:\i386\access.cp_ c:\windows\system32\access.cpl

This command expands (uncompresses) the compressed file *Access.cp_* and puts it into the *C:\Windows\System32* folder with the name *Access.cpl*.

Notes:	You may not use wildcard characters with the `source` parameter.

explorer

The **explorer** command is used to start Windows Explorer or File Explorer from a command prompt.

Syntax:	explorer

format

The **format** command is used to format a disk or drive and can format it for a particular file system.

Syntax:	`format [driveletter:] [/q] [/fs:filesystem] [/v:label][/x]`
Explanation:	`[driveletter:]` is the drive letter for the disk or hard drive volume that you want to format.
	`[/q]` is the parameter used if you want to perform a quick format.
	`[/fs:filesystem]` is the parameter used if you want to specify a file system. Valid values are FAT, FAT32, exFAT, and NTFS.
	`[/v:label]` The `/v:` must be part of the command, followed by the name of the volume assigned.
	`[/x]` dismounts the volume first, if necessary.
Example:	`format c: /fs:ntfs`
Notes:	If no `/fs:filesystem` parameter is specified, the NTFS file system is used. FAT is FAT16. FAT16 hard drive volumes cannot be more than 4 GB in size.

gpresult

The **gpresult** command is used to display Group Policy settings. A Group Policy determines how a computer is configured for both system and user (or a group of users) settings.

Syntax:	`gpresult [/s computer] [/u domain\user] [/p password] [/user target_user] [ /r] [/v] [/z]`
Explanation:	`[/s computer]` is an optional parameter that specifies a remote computer using the computer name or IP address; otherwise, the local computer is selected by default.
	`[/u domain\user]` specifies authentication for the remote computer.
	`[/p password]` specifies a password for the remote computer user ID.
	`[/user target_user]` specifies to display a user's Group Policy settings.
	`[/v]` outputs data in verbose mode.
	`[/z]` displays all available data about the Group Policy.
Examples:	`gpresult /r`
	`gpresult /s 10.3.207.15 /u pearson\cschmidt /p G#t0Ut0fH3R3`

gpupdate

The **gpupdate** command refreshes local- and Active Directory–based Group Policy settings.

Syntax:	`gpupdate [/target:{computer	user}] [/force] [/wait:value] [/logoff] [/boot]`
Explanation:	`[/target:{computer	user}]` is an optional parameter used to specify whether either the *Computer* settings or the current *User* settings are used. When neither is specified, both computer and user settings are processed.
	`[/force]` reapplies all settings.

[/wait:*value*] specifies the number of seconds policy processing waits to finish. The default is 600 seconds. A 0 wait value processes immediately. A -1 value places the wait time at indefinitely.

[/logoff] forces a logoff after the refresh completes.

[/boot] forces the computer to restart after the refresh completes.

Example: gpupdate /force /boot

help

The help command displays information about specific commands.

Syntax: help [*command*]

Explanation: [*command*] is the name of the command for which you want help.

Example: help expand

Notes: If you do not specify the *command* parameter when using the help command, all commands are listed.

ipconfig

The **ipconfig** command is used to view and control information related to a network adapter.

Syntax: ipconfig [/allcompartments] [/all|/renew [*adapter*]
                   | /release [*adapter*]|/renew6 [*adapter*]|/release6
                   [*adapter*]| /flushdns|displaydns|/registerdns|/
                   showclassid [*adapter*]| /setclassid *adapter*
                   [*classid*]|/showclassid6 [*adapter*]| /setclassid6
                   adapter [*classid*]]

Explanation: [/allcompartments] displays information regarding all compartments and, when used with the /all option, shows detailed information about all compartments.

[/all] displays all configuration information, including IP and MAC addresses.

[/renew] renews the IPv4 address for a specific adapter.

[/release] releases the IPv4 address for a specific adapter.

[/renew6] renews the IPv6 address for a specific adapter.

[/release6] releases the IPv6 address for a specific adapter.

[/flushdns] removes all entries from the DNS resolver cache.

[/displaydns] shows the contents of the DNS resolver cache.

[/registerdns] refreshes DHCP leases and re-registers recently used DNS names.

[/show classid] displays all configured IPv4 DHCP class IDs allowed for a specific adapter.

[/setclassid *adapter*] configures an adapter for a specific IPv4 DHCP class ID. A class ID is used to have two or more user classes that are configured as different DHCP scopes on a server. One class could be for laptops, whereas a different class could be for desktop computers in an organization.

[/showclassid6 *adapter*] displays all configured IPv6 DHCP class IDs allowed for a specific adapter.

[/setclassid6 *adapter*] configures an adapter for a specific IPv6 DHCP class ID.

Examples: ipconfig /all

This command verifies whether an IP address has been configured or received from a DHCP server.

ipconfig /release

This command releases a DHCP-sent IP address.

ipconfig /renew

This command starts the DHCP request process.

md

The md command is used to create a directory (folder).

Syntax: md [driveletter:] [*dirname*]

Explanation: [*driveletter:*] is the drive letter for the disk or volume on which you want to create a directory (folder). It can also include the path.

[*dirname*] is the parameter used to name the directory (folder).

Example: md c:\test

Notes: You may not use wildcard characters with this command.

mmc

The **mmc** command is used to open the Microsoft Management Console in Windows 2000 and its successors.

Syntax: mmc [*path**filename*.msc] [/a] [/64] [/32]

Explanation: [*path**filename*.msc] is an option to specify where to locate a saved console.

[/a] opens the console in author mode.

[/64] opens the 64-bit console.

[/32] opens the 32-bit console.

Notes: Use the /32 parameter if you are in a 64-bit operating system and want to run 32-bit snap-ins.

more

The more command is used to display a text file.

Syntax: more *filename*

Explanation: *filename* is the path and name of the text file you want to display on the screen.

Example: more c:\boot.ini

Notes: The [Spacebar] enables you to view the next page of a text file. The [↵Enter] key enables you to scroll through the text file one line at a time. The [Esc] key enables you to quit viewing the text file.

msconfig

The msconfig command starts the System Configuration utility from a command prompt instead of a Control Panel. The System Configuration utility is commonly used to troubleshoot boot issues specifically related to software and services. The Startup tab lists software that is loaded when the computer boots, and a checkbox enables you to disable and enable the particular application. The same concept is used with the Services tab, which contains checkboxes next to services that are started when the computer boots.

> *Syntax:*   msconfig

msinfo32

The **msinfo32** command brings up the System Information window from a command prompt. The System Information window contains details about hardware and hardware configurations as well as software and software drivers.

> *Syntax:*   msinfo32 [/computer *computer_name*]

> *Explanation:* [/computer *computer_name*] starts the System Information utility for a remote computer.

> *Examples:*   msinfo
>
>   msinfo /computer Cheryl_Dell

mstsc

The **mstsc** command starts the Remote Desktop Connection utility.

> *Syntax:*   mstsc [/v:*computer*[:*port*]]

> *Explanation:* [/v:*computer*[:*port*] specifies the specific remote computer—by name or IP address and port number—to which you want to connect.

> *Example:*   mstsc /v:Cheryl-PC

> *Notes:*   The default port number for Remote Desktop is 3389, but if a different port has been specified, then you can specify a port by using this command.

nbtstat

The nbtstat command is used to display statistics relevant to current TCP/IP connections on the local computer or a remote computer using NBT (NetBIOS over TCP/IP).

> *Syntax:*   nbtstat [-a *remotename*] [-A *IPaddress*] [-c] [-S]

> *Explanation:* [-a *remotename*] shows the NetBIOS name table for a remote computer designated by *remotename*.
>
>   [-A *IPaddress*] shows the NetBIOS name table for a remote computer designated by *IPaddress*.
>
>   [-c] shows the NetBIOS name cache, names, and resolved IP addresses.
>
>   [-S] shows NetBIOS client and server sessions.

> *Examples:*   nbtstat -S
>
>   nbtstat -A 10.5.8.133

CHAPTER 15

net

The net command has many options, and each of those options has specific parameters. A few options are shown. Use the net /? command to see all options.

Syntax: net [computer] [group] [localgroup] [print] [session] [share] [use] [user] [view]

Explanation: [computer] adds or removes a computer from the network domain.

[group] adds, views, or modifies domain groups.

[localgroup] adds, views, or modifies local groups.

[print] displays or controls a specific network printer queue.

[share] manages share resources.

[session] manages sessions with remote devices.

[use] attaches to a remote network device.

[user] adds, modifies, or views a network user account.

[view] lists resources or computers shared by the computer this is used on.

net use

The **net use** command attaches to a remote network device.

Syntax: net use [drive_letter] [\\server_name\share_name / user:domain_name\user_name [password]]

Explanation: drive_letter is the letter (followed by a colon) that net use assigns to the network device connection.

\\server_name is the name of the network device to which to connect.

share_name is the name of the share.

domain_name is the domain used to validate the user.

user_name is the user to be validated.

[password] is an optional entry, so the system does not prompt for a password. If this option is not entered, a password prompt appears, and the system automatically assigns a drive letter once a connection is made.

Example: net use \\ATC227-01\cisco /user:cisco\student

net user

The **net user** command is used to add, delete, and make changes to someone on a Windows domain.

Syntax: net user [username [password | *] [options]] [/ domain]

Explanation: username is the domain username assigned to the person in the company.

password is used to change a password or assign one to a particular user.

* is used instead of the password option to force the password to be entered after the net user command is entered.

options include things like /add, /delete, /times, and /active.

/domain executes the command on the Microsoft domain controller instead of the local computer.

Examples: `net user cschmidt`

This command allows you to see account information related to the cschmidt account.

`net user cschmidt /active:no`

This command allows you to disable the cschmidt account.

`net user cschmidt /delete`

This command allows you to delete the cschmidt account; note that common practice is to disable, not delete.

netdom

The `netdom` command manages Active Directory domains and trust relationships. This command has many operations, as shown in the syntax and explanation section.

Syntax: `netdom {add | computername | join | move | query | remove | renamecomputer | reset | resetpwd | verify} [<Computer>] [{/d: | /domain:} <Domain>] [<Options>]`

Explanation: add adds a workstation to the domain.

[computername] manages the primary and alternative names for a domain controller.

[join] joins a computer to the domain.

[move] moves a computer to a new domain.

[query] presents information about the domain membership, trust, and so on.

[remove] deletes a computer form the domain.

[renamecomputer] renames a domain workstation.

[reset] resets the connection between a domain workstation and the domain controller.

[resetpwd] resets a computer account password for a domain controller.

[verify] verifies the connection between a domain workstation and the domain controller.

netstat

The **netstat** command attaches to a remote network device.

Syntax: `netstat [-a] [-e] [-n] [-o] [-p protocol] [-r] [-s]`

Explanation: [-a] shows all connections and listening port numbers.

[-e] shows Ethernet statistics and can be used with the -s option.

[-n] shows addresses and port numbers.

[-o] shows active TCP connections.

[-p protocol] shows specific connections that use a specific protocol. The protocol parameter can be one of the following: IP, IPv6, ICMP, ICMPv6, TCP, TCPv6, UDP, or UDPv6.

[-r] shows the routing table.

[-s] shows statistics for a particular protocol.

Examples: `netstat`

                       `netstat -a`

                       `netstat -p TCP`

Note: The parameters used with this command must be preceded by a dash rather than the / (slash) used by most commands.

notepad

The **notepad** command starts the Windows Notepad accessory.

Syntax: `notepad`

nslookup

The **nslookup** command is used to troubleshoot DNS issues.

Syntax: `nslookup [-option] [hostname] [server]`

Explanation: `[-option]` has a variety of options that can be used, such as `exit`, `finger`, `help`, `ls`, `lserver`, `root`, `server`, and `set`. See Microsoft TechNet for a complete listing.

                `[hostname]` is a name of a host, such as the computer name for a specific computer in the organization.

                `[server]` is the URL of a specific server, such as www.pearsoned.com.

Examples: `nslookup www.pearsoned.com`

                `nslookup -querytype=hinfo -timeout=10`

                The second example changes the default query type to a host and the timeout to 10 seconds.

Notes: You must have at least one DNS server IP address configured on a network adapter (which you can view with the `ipconfig /all` command) to use the `nslookup` command. There are two modes of operation: non-interactive and interactive. The non-interactive has more commands than those shown in the examples given. The interactive mode is started by simply typing `nslookup` and pressing ↵Enter.

ping

The **ping** command tests connectivity to a remote network device.

Syntax: `ping [-t] [-a] [-n count] [-l size] [-i ttl] [-S source_addr] [-4] [-6] target`

Explanation: `[-t]` pings the destination until stopped with Ctrl+C keystrokes. To see the statistics and continue, use the Ctrl+Break keys.

                `[-a]` resolves IP addresses to hostnames.

                `[-n count]` defines how many pings (echo requests) are sent to the destination.

                `[-l size]` defines the buffer size (length of packet).

                `[-i ttl]` defines a Time to Live value from 0 through 255.

                `[-S source_addr]` defines the source IP address to use.

[-4] forces the use of IPv4.

[-6] forces the use of IPv6.

target is the destination IP address.

Examples: ping -t www.pearsoned.com

This example pings the Pearson Technology Education website indefinitely until the Ctrl+C key combination is used.

ping -n 2 -l 1450 165.193.130.107

This example sends two echo requests (pings) that are 1450 bytes to the Pearson Technology Education website.

rd

The rd command is used to remove a directory (folder).

Syntax: rd [*driveletter*:] [*path*] *name*

Explanation: [*driveletter*:] is the drive letter for the disk or hard drive volume from which you want to remove a directory (folder).

[*path*] is the optional path and name of the directory (folder) you want to remove.

name is the name of the folder/directory to remove.

Example: rd c:\Test\Junkdata

This command removes a directory (folder) called *Junkdata* that is a subdirectory under a directory (folder) called *Test*. This directory is located on the hard drive (C:).

Notes: You do not have to use the *driveletter:* parameter if the default drive letter is the same as the one that contains the directory to be deleted.

regedit

The **regedit** command accesses the Windows registry editor.

Syntax: regedit

Explanation: All the Windows configuration information is stored in a hierarchical database. The registry editor can modify specific registry keys, back up the registry, or set specific values to the defaults.

Notes: The regedt32 command brings up the same registry editor window as regedit.

regsvr32

The regsvr32 command registers .dll files in the Windows registry.

Syntax: regsvr32 [/u] *name*

Explanation: *name* is the name of the .dll file that will be registered.

[/u] is an optional switch used to unregister a .dll file.

Example: regsvr32 wuapi.dll

This command registers a Windows update DLL file.

Notes: There is a 64-bit version of this file in the *SysWow64* folder.

CHAPTER 15

ren

The ren command renames a file or directory (folder).

Syntax: ren [driveletter:] [path] name1 name2

Explanation: [driveletter:] is the drive letter for the disk or hard drive volume where you want to rename a file or a directory (folder).

[path] is the optional path telling the operating system where to find the file or directory (folder) you want to rename.

name1 is the old name of the file or directory (folder) that you want to rename.

name2 is the new name of the file or directory (folder).

Example: ren c:\cheryl.bat c:\newcheryl.bat

Notes: The renamed file cannot be placed in a new location with this command. Move or copy the file after you rename it if that is what you want to do. The * and ? wildcard characters are not supported.

robocopy

The **robocopy** command is used to copy files but has a lot more parameters than copy or xcopy.

Syntax: robocopy [source] [destination] [file [file]...] [options]

Explanation: [source] specifies the source directory in the drive: | path format or the \\server\share path format.

[destination] specifies the destination directory in the drive:| path format or the \\server\share path format.

[file] is the files to copy, including wildcards. The default is *.*.

[options] includes various options, such as /s to copy subdirectories (but not empty ones), /e to copy subdirectories (including empty ones), /mov to move files and delete the source, /move to move files and directories and delete the source, /a to copy files with the archive attribute set, and /m to copy files with the archive attribute set and to reset the archive bit.

Examples: robocopy c:\users\cschmidt\My Documents\Book d:\ /e

This command copies the contents of the *Book* subfolder to the D: drive and includes any empty directories.

robocopy \\CSchmidt\Book \\RLD\SchmidtBook

This command copies all files from the *CSchmidt* computer share called *Book* to the *RLD* computer network share called SchmidtBook.

services.mmc

The **services.msc** command is used to open the Microsoft Management Console and display the Services window.

Syntax: services.msc

Notes: The Services window shows the applications that run as background applications. Some services are manually started by the user or a technician, some start automatically, and some start automatically but delay starting to allow faster booting. This window is commonly used to start a service or to verify that a service such as the print service is still started.

set

The set command is used to display and view different variables.

Syntax:	`set [variable = value]`
Explanation:	`variable` is one of the following:

`AllowWildCards` is the variable used to enable wildcard support for the commands that normally do not support wildcards.

`AllowAllPaths` is the variable that allows access to all the computer's files and folders.

`AllowRemovableMedia` is the variable that allows files to be copied to removable media.

`NoCopyPrompt` is the variable that disables prompting when overwriting a file.

`value` is the setting associated with the specific variable.

Examples:	`set allowallpaths = true`

This command allows access to all files and folders on all drives.

`set allowremovablemedia = true`

This command allows you to use a flash drive.

`set allowwildcards = true`

This command allows you to use wildcards at the command prompt.

Notes: To see all of the current settings, type set without a variable and the current settings display. The set command can be used only if it is enabled using the Group Policy snap-in.

sfc

The **sfc** command starts the System File Checker utility from a command prompt. The System File Checker verifies operating system files.

Syntax:	`sfc [/scannow] [/verifyonly] [/scanfile=file_` `name] [/verifyfile=file_name] [/offwindir=windows_` `directory] [/offbootdir=boot_directory]`
Explanation:	`[/scannow]` scans all protected system files and repairs those that are damaged, if possible.

`[/verifyonly]` scans all protected system files but does not repair any detected problems.

`[/scanfile=file_name]` scans the specified file and repairs it if necessary. `file_name` should contain the full path.

`[/verifyfile=file_name]` verifies the specified file but does not repair it. `file_name` should contain the full path.

`[/offwindir=windows_directory]` is used for offline repairs for the specified Windows directory.

`[/offbootdir=boot_directory]` is used for offline repairs for the specified boot directory.

Examples:	`sfc /scannow`
	`sfc /scannow /offwindir=c:\Windows`

shutdown

The **shutdown** command is used to restart or shut down a local or remote computer.

Syntax: shutdown [-l] [-s] [-r] [-a] [-f] [-m [*computer_ name*]] [-t *xx*] [-c "*message*"]

Notes: If this command is used without any parameters, the command logs off the current user.

You can use the -a parameter only during the timeout period.

Explanation: [/l] logs off the current user.

[-s] shuts down the computer.

[-r] reboots the computer.

[-a] aborts the shutdown process.

[-f] forces active applications to close.

[-m [*computer_name*] specifies a particular computer to shut down.

[/t *xx*] specifies the number of seconds to wait before shutting down the computer.

[-c "*message*"] specifies a 127-maximum-character message to show in the System Shutdown window.

Examples: shutdown -f -m \\Raina-PC -t 30 -c "Going down in 30 seconds, daughter"

systeminfo

The systeminfo command displays detailed configuration information about a specific computer.

Syntax: systeminfo [/s *computer*] [/u *domain**user*] [/p *password*] [/fo [table | list | csv]]

Explanation: [/s *computer*] is an optional parameter that designates a specific remote computer using the computer name or IP address; otherwise, the local computer is selected by default.

[/u *domain**user*] specifies authentication for the remote computer.

[/p *password*] specifies a password for the remote computer user ID.

[/fo [table | list | csv]] defines whether the output displays in table format, list format, or CSV (comma-separated-values) format. The default is to display in table format.

Examples: systeminfo

systeminfo /s CSchmidt /u pearson\cschmidt /p G#T0UT0FH3R#

taskkill

The **taskkill** command is used to halt a process or task.

Syntax: taskkill [/s *computer*] [/u *domain**user*] [/p *password*] [/pid *process_id*] [/im *name*] [/f] [/t]

Explanation: `[/s computer]` is an optional parameter that designates a specific remote computer using the computer name or IP address; otherwise, the local computer is selected by default.

`[/u domain\user]` specifies authentication for the remote computer.

`[/p password]` specifies a password for the remote computer user ID.

`[/pid process_id]` specifies a specific process ID to halt.

`[/im name]` specifies a specific image or application name to halt.

`[/f]` forcefully terminates the process.

`[/t]` is a "tree kill" that kills all child processes associated with the process ID.

Examples: `taskkill /pid 1230 /pid 1231 /pid 1242`

`taskkill /im iexplore.exe`

tasklist

The `tasklist` command is used to list process IDs for active applications and services.

Syntax: `tasklist [/s computer] [/u domain\user] [/p password] [/fo {table|list|csv}] [/v]`

Explanation: `[/s computer]` is an optional parameter that designates a specific remote computer using the computer name or IP address; if no computer is specified, the local computer is selected by default.

`[/u domain\user]` specifies authentication for the remote computer.

`[/p password]` specifies a password for the remote computer user ID.

`[/fo {table|list|csv]` specifies the output format (table, which is the default, list, or CSV).

`[/v]` displays output in a verbose format.

Example: `tasklist /fo csv`

Notes: This command should be used before the `taskkill` command.

telnet

The `telnet` command is used to access a remote network device.

Syntax: `telnet [destination]`

Explanation: `[destination]` is the name or IP address of the remote network device.

Notes: The Telnet client must be enabled through the *Programs and Features* section of the Control Panel > *Turn Windows Features On or Off*. SSH is a better tool to use.

tracert

The **tracert** command verifies the path taken by a packet from a source device to a destination.

Syntax: `tracert [-d] [destination]`

Explanation: `[-d]` speeds up the `tracert` process by not attempting to resolve intermediate router IP addresses to names.

`[destination]` is the targeted end device, listed by IP address or name.

Example: `tracert -d www.pearsoned.com`

type

The `type` command displays the contents of a text file.

Syntax:	`type filename`
Explanation:	`filename` is the path and name of the text file you want to display on the screen.
Example:	`type c:\byteme.txt`
Notes:	The (Spacebar) enables you to view the next page of a text file. The (↵Enter) key enables you to scroll through the text file one line at a time. The (Esc) key enables you to quit viewing the text file.

wbadmin

The `wbadmin` command is used to perform backups and restores.

Syntax:	`wbadmin [start backup] [stop job] [get versions] [get items]`
Notes:	Each parameter listed for `wbadmin` has options (settings) that follow. Use the `/?` after each parameter to see these options, for example, `wbadmin start backup /?`.
Explanation:	`[start backup]` begins the backup process.
	`[stop job]` halts the currently running backup.
	`[get versions]` provides a list of available backups from the local computer or from a remote computer.
	`[get items]` provides a list of items included in a particular backup.
Example:	`wbadmin start backup`
	If no parameters are specified after `wbadmin start backup`, the settings within the daily backup schedule are used.
Notes:	You cannot recover backups that were made with `ntbackup` using the `wbadmin` command, but you can download the `ntbackup` command/application from Microsoft.

wscript

`wscript` is the command that brings up a Windows-based script property sheet. This property sheet sets script properties. The command-line version is `cscript.exe`.

xcopy

The **xcopy** command copies and backs up files and directories.

Syntax:	`xcopy source [destination] [/e] [/h]`
Explanation:	`source` is the full path from where the files are copied.
	`[destination]` is the optional destination path. If the destination is not given, the current directory is used.
	`[/e]` copies all directories and subdirectories, including empty ones.
	`[/h]` copies hidden and system files.

Example: `xcopy c:\users\cheryl\Documents\Chap1\Chap1.docx e:\`
`Book\Chap1`

This command copies a file called *Chap1.docx* (which is located in a folder called *Chap1* that is a subfolder of the *Documents* folder, which is a subfolder of the *cheryl* folder, which is a subfolder of the *users* folder) to the E: drive and places it in the *Chap1* subfolder that is contained in the *Book* folder.

Notes: The xcopy command normally resets read-only attributes when copying.

TECH TIP

Operation requires elevation

Some commands can be executed from a command prompt with **standard privileges** (user privileges). However, if a message appears from within the command prompt window that the requested operation requires elevation, this requires **administrative privileges**. In such a case, close the command prompt window. Right-click the *Command Prompt* Windows accessory. Select *Run As Administrator* and re-execute the command from the prompt.

Introduction to Scripting

A **script** is a little program that is designed to do a specific task. There are many scripts available for networking professionals to use, and you can also create your own. While you don't need to become a code monkey to write useful scripts, you'll find that being able to create short scripts yourself will not only help your career but make many of your tasks easier. This section will help you understand the basics of scripting and introduce you to various script languages, including Python, JavaScript, shell scripts for Unix-based systems, and PowerShell, VBScript, and batch files for Windows-based systems.

What Is Scripting?

A script is a small program that carries out a task or a series of tasks based on specific conditions. Whereas programs written in programming languages you may have heard of, such as C++ or Java, are compiled, scripts are interpreted. The difference is in how the code is executed. A **compiled program** is turned into machine language before it can be run. An **interpreted program** is carried out one line at a time as the computer encounters each line of code. This makes it ideal for use by IT professionals.

A script is a **text file**. This means it can be created in any text editor, like Notepad in Windows. However, each scripting language has its own specific syntax and commands that you need to learn before you can create your own scripts. Running a script is easy. From a command prompt or command line, simply type the name of the script and press (↵Enter).

Scripting allows you to automate some network administration tasks. For example, every time a user logs into a network, that user must be assigned various network drives based on certain conditions. A script can automate this process. This type of script would run each time a user logs on. In other cases a script may only need to run once, but it might be able to be written to be applied in different situations. For example, a script can modify the registry under one specific condition. If many servers on a network need to do this task, the script can be distributed and can run that one task on all the servers.

CHAPTER 15

There are many advantages to being able to create and use scripts as a network administrator. The following are some of them:

> Scripts save time. They can be written to carry out complex tasks that would take you a lot of time if done by hand. While a script runs, you are free to concentrate on other things.

> Scripts ensure consistent operation. Once a script is written, each time it is run, you can be sure it will be completed exactly as before. Scripts make completing a task much less likely to cause errors than if the task were done manually at various times.

> Scripts can be flexible. Since scripts use the basic logical constructs of all programming languages, they can be created to respond in different ways to different conditions.

Script File Types

There are many scripting languages that you can choose from, although some must be used with specific operating systems, and some are more suited to certain tasks than others. Table 15.1 shows the most common and easily learned scripting languages.

TABLE 15.1   Common scripting languages

Language	File extension	Description
Shell script	.sh	A shell script is a set of commands within a text file for a Unix or Linux-based system. Shell scripts may not run correctly on a Windows system.
Batch file	.bat	Batch files are script files that are strictly Windows based. They contain a series of commands to execute one after another. The instructions in a batch file can only be interpreted by the Windows operating system.
Python	.py	Python is a good language for writing scripts because it is relatively easy to learn, and Python scripts can run on most operating systems.
VBScript	.vbs	VBScript is a Microsoft scripting language that has some commands that are part of the Visual Basic programming language. It was designed specifically for use with Microsoft's Internet Explorer. Unless you are certain you will only use a script on a Windows machine, it is probably better to use a more versatile language.
JavaScript	.js	JavaScript is a programming language that has many uses. In some ways, it is valuable for creating script files because it can be run on any operating system. However, it may be more difficult to learn than Python, which also has the benefit of being platform independent. Creating and running command-line JavaScript requires that Node.js be installed.
PowerShell	.ps1	PowerShell is a Windows environment that was created to help in IT task automation and configuration management. It is an interface that allows you to use small programs called cmdlets that run consecutively from a single file that you can use repeatedly and share with others. PowerShell files with the .ps1 extension can be opened, edited, and run in the PowerShell Script pane.

TECH TIP

Scripts are just text files

Scripts contain only text with no special formatting. Each byte of a text file represents one character of ASCII code. Text files must be created in a text editor such as Notepad. Files that have been created with Microsoft Word or OpenOffice's Writer are stored as binary files, which do not have a one-to-one mapping between bytes and characters. If you attempt to copy and paste code from any source that is not a text file, you may get in trouble, even if you see no visible difference between what you copied from and your file because formatting commands are automatically included in the copy process.

Environment Variables

An **environment variable** is a variable that describes the environment in which a program runs. For example, a .docx file runs in the Word environment. Environment variables tell the computer where to find a specific program and can be used to answer questions such as, "Where are saved files stored?" or "Where are the temporary files stored for this particular application?"

In Windows, an environment variable has a name and a value. For example, the variable that represents the Windows program is windir (short for *Windows directory*), and the value associated with that variable is, normally, C:\Windows. This means that the Windows program is located in the C:\ drive in a folder called *Windows*. The value of an environment variable is the path to the program identified by the variable name.

Another important variable is PATH. The PATH variable tells a program where to find the files it may need. Programs that need specific files to run will look for the PATH variable automatically. The value of the PATH variable is set by a program when it is installed.

Two types of environment variables are system and user. System environment variables are global and cannot be changed by any user. They refer to critical system resources, such as the location of Windows or where program files are stored on a computer. They are set by specific programs and drivers. System environment variable values are the same for all user accounts.

User environment variables, however, have values that differ from user to user. They store the location of such things as a user's profile, where that user stores temporary files, and so on. These variables can be set by the user, by Windows, or by various programs that work with user-specific locations.

To access environment variables in Windows 10, you can type **environment** into the search box and then click or select *Edit the System Environment Variables*. The System Properties window will open, and you can click on *Environment Variables* to open the Environment Variables window. There are some minor visual differences between various versions of Windows, but the options and buttons are the same, regardless of which version of Windows you are using.

You can also access the Environment Variables window by accessing the *System and Security* Control Panel > *System* > *Advanced System Settings*. This will take you to the *System Properties* window, where you will see the *Environment Variables* button (see Figure 15.9). Clicking this button opens the *Environment Variables* window (see Figure 15.10).

To edit the path to an environment variable, to add a new environment variable, or to reorder the current environment variables, you can click the *Edit* button in the *Environment Variables* window.

Access the *Run* dialog box by pressing ⊞+ℝ and enter the command **systemproperties-advanced.exe** will also bring you to the *System Properties* window as shown in Figure 15.11.

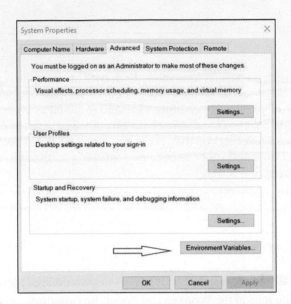

FIGURE 15.9   Accessing Windows environment variables

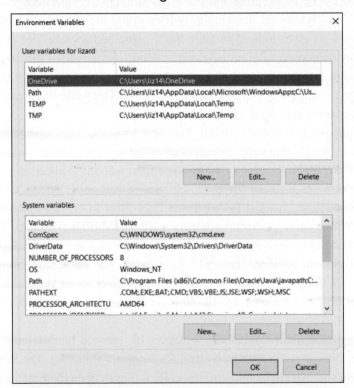

FIGURE 15.10   Environment Variables window

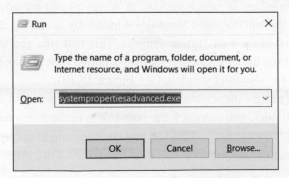

FIGURE 15.11   Accessing the System Properties window through the Run dialog box

From the command prompt, simply typing `set` will show you all the environment variables, as shown in Figure 15.12.

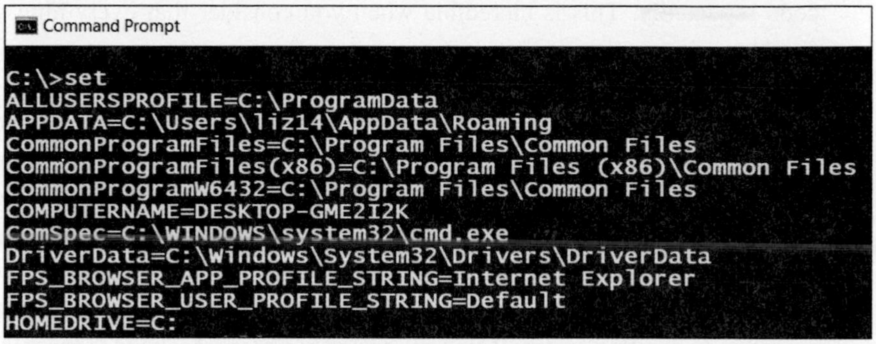

```
Command Prompt
C:\>set
ALLUSERSPROFILE=C:\ProgramData
APPDATA=C:\Users\liz14\AppData\Roaming
CommonProgramFiles=C:\Program Files\Common Files
CommonProgramFiles(x86)=C:\Program Files (x86)\Common Files
CommonProgramW6432=C:\Program Files\Common Files
COMPUTERNAME=DESKTOP-GME2I2K
ComSpec=C:\WINDOWS\system32\cmd.exe
DriverData=C:\Windows\System32\Drivers\DriverData
FPS_BROWSER_APP_PROFILE_STRING=Internet Explorer
FPS_BROWSER_USER_PROFILE_STRING=Default
HOMEDRIVE=C:
```

FIGURE 15.12   Viewing environment variables by using the set command

There may be times when you need to create an environment variable to tell the computer how to find the program needed to run a script. PowerShell (`.ps1` files) and VBScript (`.vbs` files) both run on the .NET framework, which is installed with Windows. Batch (`.bat`) files are run from the command line. Running Python, however, requires a little more work. The Python engine is not preinstalled on Windows even though Windows installers have been included with every release. Still, you may need to create an environment variable to run Python. The same is true for JavaScript, for which you need to install Node.js. Node.js is a free open source environment where you can run JavaScript code without a browser. Node.js is also very flexible in that it can run on most operating systems, including Windows, Linux, and macOS.

Script Syntax

Every programming language has its own syntax. The **syntax** of a language is the set of symbols and rules used to create instructions. Understanding and using correct syntax is the only way you can get a script to work since a computer cannot understand the context of an instruction. If the instruction is not composed in the exact syntax of that language, it will not be executed and, worse, may cause the whole script to crash.

Syntax refers to more than using the correct words in a command. It includes the correct symbols and punctuation. If one language requires an instruction to terminate with a semicolon, leaving off the semicolon invalidates the entire instruction and usually will cause serious errors. Each scripting language has its own specific syntax, which you must learn in order to write a script in that language. However, it isn't as hard as it sounds. Most languages have similar syntax. And all scripting and programming languages use the same logical constructs to write instructions. Once you understand the logic behind programming instructions and commands, learning a language's specific syntax is pretty easy.

For example, the syntax to display a sentence such as `Hello, my friend!` on the console uses the following syntax in these four scripting languages:

> Python: `print("Hello, my friend!")`
> JavaScript: `console.log("Hello, my friend!");`
> Batch file: `ECHO Hello, my friend!`
> Shell script: `echo "Hello, my friend!"`

Introduction to Script Programming

In the 1960s scientists proved that all programming code can be done using three constructs: sequence, selection, and repetition. **Sequence** is how the computer executes code one line at a time from top to bottom. **Selection** is how specific lines of code are run if a specific condition is met. **Repetition** (sometimes called iteration) is how the computer can execute specific lines of code repeatedly. This is incredible when you consider that everything you see and do with any computer or any device that uses a computer runs on programming code, and all of that code is based on the same simple logic described here.

A program is a list of instructions written by a programmer to perform a task or tasks. The instructions are executed one line at a time, in the order in which they are written. A script is simply a type of program. The difference between a scripting language and other types of programming languages lies in how the code executes, not in how the code is written.

Programming languages such as C++ or Java are compiled languages. A compiled language uses a compiler to translate the source code to machine code. Machine code is code specific to a given processor and operating system. Once a program has been translated to machine code, the computer runs the machine code on its own. Before a compiled program can be run, it must be completely error free.

In an interpreted implementation of a language, the computer does not execute the source code directly, but uses an interpreter to execute each line of code. If an error is found, the program will stop and send feedback to the programmer. This allows the programmer to see the error immediately and make necessary changes. Interpreted languages are often called *scripting languages*. They are used by networking professionals because they are relatively easy to learn and use, they are easy to debug, and they are portable across various hardware and network platforms.

All programs rely on input, processing, and output. A program performs a task based on some type of input. The **input** may come from a user typing information at the program's request, from values sent by other parts of the program, or from the computer itself. Then the program processes the information and returns some output (the **processing**). The **output** can be results seen on the screen or console or may be changes sent to other parts of the program or to the computer itself.

Together, the input–processing–output sequence and the three programming constructs form the basis for all programs. Before learning about those constructs, it is important to understand two basic concepts: variables and data types.

Variables

A program **variable** is a named memory location which stores data of a specific type (integer, floating point number, or text). The *value* of that variable is the data contents at that memory location. It is called a variable because its value can change (vary) as the program runs. You can think of a location in the computer's memory as a mailbox. The variable is the name printed on that mailbox, and the value of the variable is the contents of that box. For example, if you have a variable named myNumber and you set its value to 23 using an instruction in the syntax of the language you are using, the memory location named myNumber stores the number 23.

However, as soon as you write another instruction to change the value of myNumber to, for example, 584, the value 23 is lost forever, and the new value takes its place. From now on, every time myNumber is referenced in a program, it means 584—at least until that value is changed by a different instruction.

Previously you saw how to display some text on the screen using the syntax of several different scripting languages. The text that was displayed was hard-coded, which means the programmer wrote the exact words to be displayed. But if the programmer had, instead, used a variable to store that text, the text could be changed every time the program runs, depending on different conditions.

For example, the program could display Good morning if the current time is between 5:00 a.m. and 11:59 a.m., Good afternoon if the current time is between noon and 5:00 p.m., Good evening if the current time is between 5:01 p.m. and 9:00 p.m., and so on. The instructions in this code would include a check of the system for the current time and would assign the correct greeting to the variable, depending on the result of the time check. Then the display would greet the user with a message that is appropriate for the time of day.

For example, if a variable is named myGreeting, the command to display the correct greeting would then be:

> Python: print(myGreeting)
> JavaScript: console.log(myGreeting);
> Batch file: ECHO myGreeting
> Shell script: echo $myGreeting

You can see that, while the specific command to have output displayed on the screen differs for each language, the logic for this instruction is the same for all languages: Use the correct command for outputting something on the screen, followed by the variable name that represents the value to be displayed.

A programmer must follow certain rules in selecting variable names. While not every language has exactly the same rules for naming variables, there are some universal rules:

> A variable name cannot begin with a number but may contain numbers. For example, 1stNumber is not acceptable, but Number1 is fine.
> A variable name may not include any spaces and, except for the underscore and sometimes the hyphen (_ and -), should not include any punctuation. For example, my Greeting is not acceptable, nor is my&Greeting, but my_Greeting is fine.
> Variables are case sensitive. For example, Username is not the same variable as username or userName.
> A variable name cannot begin with a language's keyword. A **keyword** is a set of characters that is an instruction in that language. In the Python language, for example, try is a keyword. Therefore, tryIt is not an acceptable variable name in Python; however, attemptIt is fine.
> Variable names can be long, but each language has a restriction on how many characters are allowed.
> A variable name should indicate what the content is about without being too long. Since you will probably have to type a variable name many times in a script, you want to keep your variable names as short as possible while still indicating what the variable represents. For example, gt is an acceptable variable name but would be confusing to someone who had to work with your code at a later date. Also, the_greeting_to_be_displayed_to_ the_user is an acceptable variable name, but do you really want to type it 20 times in a script? A better option would be greeting.

In order to create a variable, a programmer must declare the variable. This means the programmer writes a line of code to tell the computer that there will be a variable with a specific name and type. (The concept of data types is explained more fully later in this chapter.) Each language has its own way to declare variables, but the concept of a variable **declaration** is the same: The computer must be told that a variable with a given name will exist, and the computer then assigns a memory location to hold the value of that variable.

When a variable is declared, if it is set to a beginning value, this is known as **initialization**. If no value is given when the variable is declared, the computer may leave the memory location empty or may place a default value in that location. The syntax for declaring a variable named myVarName and setting its initial value to 0 is, in four scripting languages, as follows:

> Python: myVarName = 0
> JavaScript: var myVarName = 0;
> Batch file: set myVarName=0
> Shell script: myVarName=0

Notice that JavaScript and .bat files require a keyword before the variable name (var in JavaScript and set in a batch file), but Python and shell scripts don't. However, in Python and JavaScript, the spaces before and after the = symbol are optional, while in a .bat file or a .sh file, putting spaces before and after this symbol will not work. JavaScript requires a semicolon at the end of the variable declaration, while the other languages shown here do not. This is why learning the syntax of each language is important.

Data Types

The value of a variable is stored in computer memory as a specific type of data. Some languages have a long list of possible data types, while others have only a few. However, all languages distinguish between numbers, types of numbers, and characters or strings of characters (which could be numbers that are dealt with as text), sometimes simply called **strings**.

The data type of a variable determines how much space is allotted in memory to store that value and also determines what operations can be performed with that data. For example, numeric data can be multiplied, but you cannot multiply two alphanumeric characters. **Alphanumeric characters** include all the letters of the alphabet, both upper and lowercase, as well as the digits 0 through 9 plus the punctuation marks and symbols available on a normal keyboard (for example, @, #). If you try to perform an operation on data stored as one data type that the data type does not support, your program will either not work or will work incorrectly.

There are two basic types of numbers that a computer program normally deals with: integers and floating-point numbers. **Integers** are whole numbers, including zero and negative numbers. **Floating-point numbers** are numbers that can be written in the form x÷y. A floating-point number can be thought of as a number that includes a decimal value, even if that value is 0. For example, the number 6 is an integer, but the number 6.0 is a floating-point number. Floating-point numbers are handled very differently from integers but, because they are rarely used in scripts, for the purposes of this book, we do not need to concern ourselves with them. When referring to numeric data, we will only consider integers.

In the previous examples, all the variables named myVarName would be stored as numeric data because they were initially given integer values (in this case, 0). In some languages you must specify what data type a variable will be. In others, such as Python and JavaScript, the data type of a variable is set by the computer based on the variable's initial value. Once set, a variable's data type cannot be changed while in use.

Examples of Using Variables

The following examples demonstrate how variables can be used in several of the scripting languages. In each of the first set of examples, two numeric variables, named num1 and num2, are declared and initialized to integer values and then added together. The result is stored in a third variable, named numResult, and then output to the console. The output in all cases would be 7.

> Python:

```
num1 = 3
num2 = 4
numResult = num1 + num2
print(numResult)
```

> JavaScript:

```
var num1 = 3;
var num2 = 4;
var numResult = num1 + num2;
console.log(numResult);
```

> Batch files:

```
set num1=3
set num2=4
set numResult=%num1%+%num2%
Echo %numResult%
```

> Shell scripts:

```
set num1=3
set num2=4
set /anumResult=%num1%+%num2%
echo $numResult
```

The following script snippets demonstrate how to join two string variables (variables that hold alphanumeric data) to output a result. In each case, one string variable named `userName` is joined with the value of a second string variable named `message`, and the resulting string is output to the console. In these examples, it may be assumed that the name of this computer's user, to be stored in `username`, is Joey Jones. The output in all cases would be `Welcome Joey Jones`.

> Python:

```
username = "Joey Jones"
message = "Welcome "
result = message + username
print(result)
```

> JavaScript:

```
var username = "Joey Jones";
var message = "Welcome ";
var result = message + username;
console.log(result);
```

> Batch files:

```
set username=Joey Jones
set message=Welcome
set result=message+" "+username
Echo %result%
```

> Shell scripts:

```
set username="Joey Jones"
set message="Welcome "
set result=$message$username
echo $result
```

You have now seen how to join variables of the same data type (integer and integer, string and string). But it is also possible to join a string variable with an integer variable; however, each language handles this situation differently.

Comments

When a script runs, the computer processes each instruction and does what that instruction says to do. In the examples shown in the previous section, you can see that the computer does the following:

> The first line declares a variable and initializes it with a value.
> The second line declares a second variable and initializes it with a value.
> The third line declares a third variable on the left-hand side of the instruction. Then it joins the values of the first and second variables on the right-hand side of the instruction. Finally, it puts that value into the third variable.
> The last line outputs the value of the third variable to the screen or console.

The purpose of each of these short snippets is clear and easy to see. But you can also see that some of the syntax may be confusing as, for example, when variable names are enclosed in symbols like % (batch files) or require a symbol like $ before the variable name (shell scripts). As your scripts become longer, the purpose of some parts of them may not be immediately clear. You will also see, as you continue to write scripts, that there may be more than one way to write code to do a specific task. And you may be asked to use or edit a script written by someone else who may no longer even be working with you.

For these reasons, it is always a good idea to include **comments** when you write your scripts. Comments are put into scripts to explain what a script or part of a script is supposed to do. They are meant to be read by the person who is using the script, and they are ignored by the computer when the script runs. Each language has its own syntax for writing comments:

> Python: Comments can be on one line or multi-line. Comments that are on one line start with the hash character (#). They may be placed on a new line or following a space at the end of a coded instruction. Multi-line comments begin and end with three double quotes (" " "):
```
# This is a single line comment in Python.
Print(result)   # Here's another comment.
""" This begins a multi-line comment. Everything
until the end of the comment is ignored by the
processor. The comment will end here. """
```

> JavaScript: Comments start with two slashes (//) and go to the end of the line. Comments may be placed on separate lines or following a line of code. If you want to include several lines in a single comment, open the comment with /* and end the comment with */:
```
// This is a single line comment in JavaScript.
Console.log(result)    // Here is another comment.
/* This begins a multi-line comment. Everything
until the end of the comment is ignored by the
processor. The comment will end here. */
```

> Batch files: A comment in a batch file begins with the keyword REM. Comments can also begin with two colons (::). There is a slight danger in using the REM command. If ECHO (the command to output to the screen) is on, then the comment itself will be displayed:
```
REM This is a comment in a batch file.
:: This is also a comment in a batch file.
```

> Shell scripts: The hash symbol (#) is used to identify a comment in a .sh file. It can be placed on a separate line or after the first space following a line of code:
```
# This is a comment in a shell script file.
echo $result  # This is another comment.
```

Basic Script Constructs

All scripts—in fact, all computer programs—are built around three basic **constructs**: sequence, decision (or selection), and repetition (or iteration). Instructions in a script file are executed by the computer in the order in which they are written. Executing instructions in the order in which they appear in the code is known as the *sequence structure*. However, the code may instruct the computer to follow one sequence of instructions under certain conditions and a different sequence of instructions under different conditions. Without this ability to make decisions, a script could only do a very limited number of tasks.

Take, for example, a script that displays a greeting to the user based on the time of day. The computer must be told to check the time and, depending on the result of that check, do only one thing and skip the remaining options. This is known as a selection structure, or a **decision structure**.

A script may also require that a task or part of a task be repeated 2 or 3 or even 1,000 times. Rewriting an instruction many times is tedious and unnecessary. For example, if you want to check a directory to see if it includes a specific file, you need to compare the filename you're searching for with each file in that directory. Instead of writing separate instructions to check the first file, the second file, the third file, and so on, you can write a single structure that says to check a file in that directory and, if it is not the filename you seek, do the same thing again with the next file, and the next, and so on until the list of files in that directory ends or until you have found the file you want. This is known as a repetition structure, or a **loop structure**.

Decisions: The Selection Structure

A *selection structure* is also referred to as a *decision structure*. It consists of a test condition together with one or more groups (or blocks) of statements. The result of the test condition determines which block of statements will be executed. This means that, for any selection structure, some statements will never be executed. For example, if you wrote a script to display a greeting based on the time of day, and it is 10:00 a.m., you only want the block of statements that display Good morning! to be executed. The blocks that display Good afternoon! or Good evening! should be—and are—skipped.

Three main types of selection/decision structures are used in programming: single alternative, dual alternative, and multiple alternative. Before we discuss these three types of selection structures, we need to define the operators used in these structures.

Relational Operators

Operators that compare two expressions are known as **relational operators**. In most programming languages, the symbol >= means "greater than or equal to," the symbol <= means "less than or equal to," and the symbol != means "is not equal to." The > and < symbols mean "greater than" and "less than," but in batch files the > symbol is a redirection operator and cannot be used to compare values. Batch files and shell scripts use other commands to compare two expressions. Table 15.2 shows the various relational operators and their meanings in most languages.

TABLE 15.2   Relational operators

Meaning	Most common	Batch file commands	Shell operator
Equal to	==	EQU	-eq
Not equal to	!=	NEQ	-ne
Less than	<	LSS	-lt
Less than or equal to	<=	LEQ	-le
Greater than	>	GTR	-gt
Greater than or equal to	>=	GEQ	-ge

Three Types of Selection Structures

Remember we started with stating that there are three types of programming structures: sequence, decision (or selection), and repetition (or iteration). There are three different types of the decision/selection structures: single alternative, dual alternative, and multiple alternative. It is also possible to nest a selection structure inside another selection structure. Let's take a look at each one of these.

Single Alternative

With the single-alternative structure, a test is performed. If the outcome of the test is true, a block of statements is executed, and then program control moves to the next instruction after the selection structure. If the outcome of the test is not true, nothing is executed, and the program control proceeds to the next instruction. For example, imagine a script that is written to check whether the current user is named Jonas. If it is, the program displays user found and if it is not, it does nothing. The current user's name is stored in a variable named name. The single-alternative logic for this script in Python would be:

```
if name == "Jonas":
    print("user found!")
continue...
```

If name is anything other than "Jonas", the program continues, and nothing happens. This is known as an if structure.

Note: Notice the double equals sign (==) in the if statement shown in the preceding example. It is called the **comparison operator** or, sometimes, the **equals operator** or the **equality operator**. In most programming languages, a single equals sign (=) sets the value on the right side of the expression to the variable name on the left side. But a double equals sign *compares* the two values. This statement says, basically, "Is the value stored in the variable named name *the same as* "Jonas"?" This distinction is very important; using a single equals sign when trying to compare values is an error that often causes a lot of trouble.

Dual Alternative

With the dual-alternative structure, a test is also performed, but one of two possible blocks of statements will always execute. If the outcome of the test is true, one block of statements is executed, and then program control moves to the next instruction after the selection structure. If the outcome of the test is not true, a different block of statements is performed, and the program control proceeds to the next instruction. In a dual-alternative structure, the example shown above might look like this in Python:

```
if name == "Jonas":
    print("user found!")
else:
    print("user not found!")
continue...
```

In this case, one of the two statements (user found! or user not found!) would always be displayed, and the other would be skipped. This type of structure is called an if-else structure.

Multiple Alternative

Sometimes you need more than two options in a selection structure. For example, a script might assign a student's letter grade based on the numeric result of an exam score. Every language has the ability to create a multiple-alternative structure, but each has its own syntax for doing so. In Python, such a structure is known as an if-elif-else structure. The code to assign a letter grade in Python is as follows:

```
1.  if score >= 90:
2.      print("Congratulations! You have a grade of A.")
3.  elif score >= 80:
4.      print("You have a grade of B.")
5.  elif score >= 70:
6.      print("You have a grade of C.")
7.  elif score >= 60:
8.      print("You have a grade of D.")
9.  else:
10.     print("You have a grade of F.")
11. continue...
```

It is assumed that a variable named score already holds a student's numeric score on the exam. In this code, the value of score is checked against a test condition. If it matches, the block of statements that follows that test condition is executed, and all the other code up to the end of the if-elif-else structure is skipped. If the first condition is not true, the second condition is tested. If that one is also not true, the third condition is tested, and so on. As soon as one condition is found to be true, that block of statements is executed, and any remaining conditions are skipped. In a multiple-alternative structure, only one block of statements is executed and all the others are skipped.

Note: The line numbers described in the information that follows are for clarity only. In a real program, there would be no line numbers.

Note: In Python the indentation of various statements is important. Proper indentation tells the computer which statements are part of the various blocks of code. Other languages use other syntax to define blocks of statements in control structures.

You might wonder how this program works for a score of 96 or 78 or why it is not necessary to specify that a score of 84 must be less than 90 as well as greater than 80. Consider the logic of the program. Line 1 checks to see if score is greater than or equal to 90. This includes everything from 90 and above, including 96. If, however, score is less than 90, line 2 is skipped, and the value of score is tested on line 3. The only way the program can execute line 3 is if the test on line 1 fails. And that means score is less than 90, so there is no need to specify it in the code.

CHAPTER 15

All that is needed is to check whether score is greater than 79. If score is 62, the only way line 8 can be executed is if the tests on lines 1, 3, and 5 have failed, which means score is already known to be less than 70. If score is anything greater than or equal to 60, line 8 is executed. If it is not greater than or equal to 60, then score must be less than 60, and there is no need to specify that in the code. No matter what value score holds, only one block of statements will be executed and, regardless of what that block is, the program will continue on line 11.

Selection Structure Examples

Following are examples of how a multiple-alternative selection structure would be coded in several scripting languages. In each case, it is assumed that one variable (num1) holds the value of a number, and a second variable (num2) holds the value of another number. If the first number is greater than the second number, one message is displayed. If the second number is greater than the first, a different message is displayed. If the two numbers are the same, a third message is displayed:

> Python:
```
if (num1 > num2):
    print(num1," is greater than ",num2)
elif (num1 < num2):
    print(num1," is less than ",num2)
else:
    print(num1," and ", num2 ," are the same")
```

> JavaScript:
```
if (num1 > num2)          {
        console.log(num1 + " is greater than " + num2);
    }
    else if (num1 < num2)      {
        console.log(num1 + " is less than " + num2);
    }
        else
        console.log(num1 + " and " + num2 + " are equal");
```

> Batch files:
```
IF  %num1% GTR %num2% (
    ECHO %num1% is greater than %num2%
        ) ELSE IF %num1% LSS %num2% (
        ECHO %num1% is less than %num2%
        ) ELSE (
            ECHO %num1% and %num2% are the same
        )
```

> Shell scripts:
```
if [ $num1 -gt $num2 ]
    then
        set str=$num1 is greater than $num2"
        echo $str
    elif [ $num1 -lt $num2 ]
    then
        set str="$num1 is less than $num2"
        echo $str
    else
        set str="$num1 and $num2 are the same"
            echo $str
```

Note: In a Shell script comparison, all conditional expressions must be placed inside square brackets with spaces around the expression.

Compound Conditions and Logical Operators

In all the examples of selection structures shown so far, a single condition has been tested. However, it would be restrictive if you could test only one condition at a time. For example, you might want to test whether a computer is registered to a specific user *and* whether this user has a specific version of the operating system. This requires that both conditions must be true in order for any statements that follow to be executed. You could test first to see if the user is the one you are looking for and then nest a second selection structure to test for the operating system version. Or you could use one of the **logical operators** to test both conditions in one statement. When you join two test conditions in a single statement, this is known as a **compound condition**.

The three logical operators that are most commonly used are AND, OR, and NOT. When comparing two expressions, the result of the comparison is, as with relational operators, always either true or false:

> The AND **operator** returns true if and only if both expressions (conditions) are true.
> The OR **operator** returns false if and only if both expressions (conditions) are false. If either expression (condition) is true, then the OR operator returns true.
> The NOT **operator** simply flips the result of an expression. If an expression (condition) is true, it returns false, and if the expression (condition) is false, it returns true.

The following are some examples of compound conditions using the three logical operators:

> Examples of the AND operator: Given that x = 15, y = 8, z = 2,
  (x > y) AND (x > z) returns true; both conditions are true
  (x > y) AND (z > x) returns false; one condition is false
  (x < y) AND (y > z) returns false; one condition is false
  (x < y) AND (z > x) returns false; both conditions are false

> Examples of the OR operator: Given that x = 15, y = 8, z = 2,
  (x > y) OR (x > z) returns true; both conditions are true
  (x > y) OR (z > x) returns true; at least one condition is true
  (x < y) OR (y > z) returns true; at least one condition is true
  (x < y) OR (z > x) returns false; both conditions are false

> Examples of the NOT operator: Given that x = 15, y = 8, z = 2,
  NOT(x > y) returns false since the condition is true
  NOT(z > x) returns true since the condition is false

Combining expressions that use relational operators with logical operators allows you to test many conditions in a single statement.

Loops: The Repetition Structure

The last control structure is called a **repetition structure**, or a **loop**. A loop contains a block of statements that are executed repeatedly. In most programming languages, there are various types of loops, but not all of them are available in every scripting languages. A common type of loop is the **while loop**, discussed first. The **for loop**, a shorthand method of writing while loops, is also discussed in detail. Each time a loop executes its block of statements, it is called an **iteration**.

The while Loop

A while loop begins with the keyword while and a test condition. If the condition is true, the loop will begin, and the block of statements in the loop will repeat until the condition is no longer true. This means that somewhere in that block of statements, something must change the condition, or the loop will repeat forever (an infinite loop). The general syntax for a while loop is as follows:

```
while (test condition) do:
    Block of statements to execute
        Update/change of the test condition
end while
```

Examples of while Loops

The following are examples of the syntax of while loops in several scripting languages. Each program counts by fives and displays the following results:

5   10   15   20   25   30   35   40   45   50

> Python:

```
x = 5
count = 1
while (count < 11, end = "   "):
    print(count * x)
    count++
```

> Shell scripts:

```
x=5
count=1
while [ $count -lt 11 ]
do
    echo "expr $x\*$count   "
    count="expr $count + 1"
done
```

> JavaScript:

```
var x = 5;
var count = 1;
while (count < 11)      {
    console.log(count * x + "   ");
    count += 1;
}
```

> Batch files:

```
SET /A "x=5"
SET /A "count=1"
SET /A "limit=11"
:while
    if %count% LSS %limit% (
        ECHO %x%*%count% " "
        SET /A "count=count + 1"
        Goto :while
        )
```

Note: Batch files do not have a `while` loop, but you can use other batch commands to write a script that closely mimics the logic of a `while` loop, as shown.

Note: `/A` is a switch that is used if a value needs to be numeric.

The `for` Loop

Most often a loop is used to repeat a block of instructions a given number of times. You may or may not know exactly how many times you need a loop to repeat. In the `while` loop shown earlier in this chapter, you know you want the loop to repeat 10 times. However, you may not know how many times the loop should repeat. For example, imagine that you want to check each file in various directories to see how many files are over a certain size. The number of files in each directory to be checked would probably not be known. Most scripting languages have a type of loop known as a `for` loop to handle such situations.

A traditional `for` loop is, in effect, a shorthand way to write a `while` loop. The general syntax is as follows:

```
for variable=value; test condition; variable increment/decrement
{
        Several statements in a block to execute
}
```

In this type of loop, you initialize a variable first—a statement that is generally done before entering the `while` loop. Then you set up a test condition, as you would in a `while` loop. Finally, you increment or decrement the value of the variable; in a `while` loop, this is done within the block of statements. The JavaScript `for` loop version of the `while` loop shown above is as follows:

```
var x = 5;
    for (count = 1; count < 11; count++)      {
        console.log(count * x + "   ");
    }
```

A `for` loop is sometimes referred to as a *collection-controlled loop*. In such a loop, you identify the item to be tested, the collection of items, and, at the same time, the initial value, the ending value, and how much to increment or decrement the item. The general syntax for this type of `for` loop is as follows:

```
for variable in range(start, step, end) list do:
        Block of statements to execute
end loop
```

In most languages, one or more of the `start`, `step`, and `end` values are optional. If they are not specified, the computer will normally default to a value of `0` or `1` (depending on the type of collection) for `start`, a value of `+1` for `step`, and will end at the end of the collection of items.

There are some variations on the `for` loop in most scripting languages that allow for more flexibility. The batch file example shown in the following section demonstrates how the `forfiles` loop, specific to batch files, makes solving the problem of checking all files in a directory easier than using a traditional `for` loop.

Examples of `for` Loops

The following are examples of a loop that searches through a list of filenames in a directory and returns the date each file was last modified. Each of the scripting languages has specific functions that deal with the properties of files and directories, and some of them have other ways to automate this process.

> Python:

```
for file in directory:
    print("modified: %s " %
        time.ctime(os.path.getmtime(str(file)))
```

> Batch files:

```
forfiles /C "cmd /c echo @file @fdate @ftime"
```

Note: Batch files also have a `for` command, but for this particular problem, the `forfiles` command works better.

> Shell scripts:

```
for entry in "$directory"/*
do
modDate=$(stat-c%y "$entry")
modDate=${modDate%%*}
echo $entry:$modDate
```

> JavaScript:

```
for(var i = 0; i < files.length; i++)
{
    console.log(files[i] + "<br>");
}
```

Note: This program is a little trickier in JavaScript. The example here is intended to show how a `for` loop is coded in JavaScript and will only display the names of the files without all the files' properties, including the date modified. As with many other scripting tasks, JavaScript is not the best language to use.

A Brief Look at VBScript and PowerShell

All of the examples in the preceding sections demonstrate how scripts are written in Python, JavaScript, batch files, and shell scripting. Two other scripting tools are VBScript and PowerShell. While VBScript is used exclusively with the Windows operating system, PowerShell can be used with Windows, Linux, Unix, and macOS.

VBScript

VBScript is a Microsoft scripting language that has some commands that are part of the Visual Basic programming language. It allows Windows system administrators to manage error handling, subroutines, and other processes managed by scripting languages. VBScript files have the extension .vbs.

However, VBScript is mainly used to allow functionality and interaction on web pages, and it is not supported by any modern browser. For use on web pages, JavaScript has usurped VBScript. For use in managing system administration tasks, any of the other cross-platform languages or batch files are preferable.

PowerShell

PowerShell was originally created in 2006 by Microsoft as a task automation and configuration management framework for the Windows operating system. A decade later, in 2016, Microsoft released an open source cross-platform version of PowerShell. Windows PowerShell runs on the full .NET Framework, and the cross-platform version runs on the **.NET Core**. PowerShell files are identified by the .ps1 file extension.

In PowerShell, administrative tasks are generally performed by specialized .NET classes called **cmdlets**. There are more than 200 basic cmdlets. Each cmdlet implements a particular operation and has help that includes an example of how to use the cmdlet.

Some of the core cmdlets are Get-Location to get the current directory, Move-item to move a file to a different location, and New-item to create a new file. You can also create PowerShell scripts to do tasks not covered by a cmdlet. A PowerShell script includes a combination of cmdlets and associated logic.

To get help with PowerShell, the man command is used. Figure 15.13 shows the man Get-Location command output and syntax for the Get-Location cmdlet.

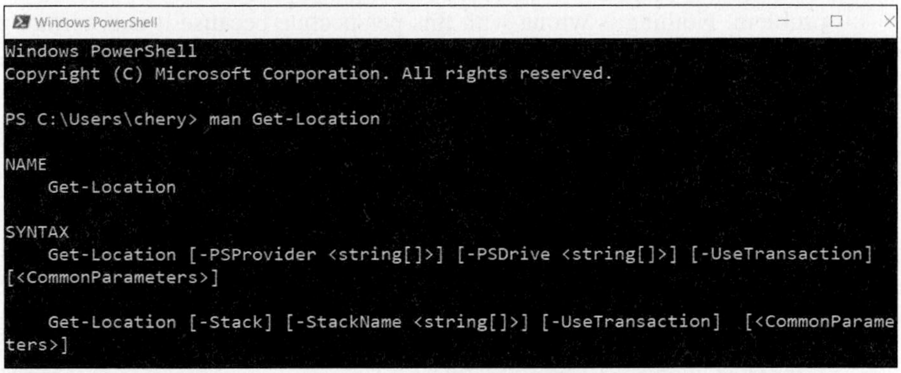

```
Windows PowerShell
Copyright (C) Microsoft Corporation. All rights reserved.

PS C:\Users\chery> man Get-Location

NAME
    Get-Location

SYNTAX
    Get-Location [-PSProvider <string[]>] [-PSDrive <string[]>] [-UseTransaction]
[<CommonParameters>]

    Get-Location [-Stack] [-StackName <string[]>] [-UseTransaction]  [<CommonParame
ters>]
```

FIGURE 15.13   Get-Location **cmdlet syntax**

SOFT SKILLS: CHANGING PERSPECTIVE WHEN TROUBLESHOOTING

Troubleshooting is a hard topic to teach. Experience is the best way to learn how to tackle device problems, including problems with displays. In the classroom, teachers often rely on things going wrong during installation to teach troubleshooting. Also, broken machines can be used to encourage students to jump in and attempt repair. One troubleshooting technique that is seldom practiced in the classroom but that is great to do is to change your perspective.

When troubleshooting a problem, your perspective is that of a trained technician: You look at what is going wrong and determine what you know about that particular area that can cause the problem. Nothing is wrong with this perspective because it is a normal progression for a technician. But what happens when you are stuck or when you are faced with something you have never seen before?

One of the ways you can change your perspective is to put yourself in the mindset of the user. Through talking with a user just a bit, you can get an idea of how the person thinks and works. Then you can try imagining the problem from that person's perspective. First, this may give you troubleshooting ideas that you haven't thought of before. Second, it will make you more empathetic and a better technician. See Figure 15.14.

FIGURE 15.14   See things from a new perspective

Another way to look at things from a different perspective is to imagine a great technician you know. Put yourself in that person's shoes. What would that technician try that you haven't thought of yet? What tricks have you seen tried in the past?

Perspective shapes how we approach problems. By changing our perspective, we change how we troubleshoot problems and how we approach the troubleshooting task. As technicians, we must constantly update and refine our skills because most of our day is spent troubleshooting. See Figure 15.15.

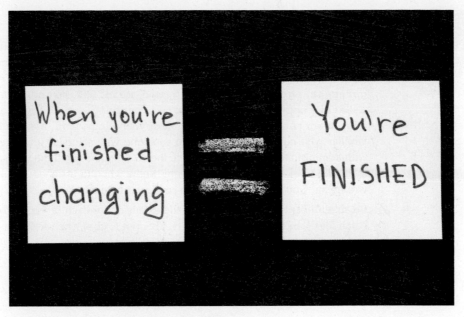

FIGURE 15.15　Changing perspectives

Chapter Summary

> Commands are used in two environments: (1) in a command prompt environment when the GUI tools do not or cannot correct a problem and (2) when using a scripting environment to deploy the operating system and/or updates to multiple computers.

> Command switches alter the way a command performs or outputs information. Use *command* /? or help to receive help on any particular command.

> Important commands to know are dir, cd, .., ipconfig, ping, tracert, netstat, nslookup, shutdown, dism, sfc, chkdsk, diskpart, taskkill, gpupdate, gpresult, format, copy, xcopy, robocopy, net use, net user, [command name] /?, msconfig, regedit, command, services.msc, mmc, mstsc, msinfo32, and dxdiag.

> Environment variables describe the environment in which a program runs. In Windows, each environment variable has a name and a value. The value is the path to the program that is identified by the variable name.

> A script, as referred to in this text, is a small computer program designed to do a specific task. System administrators use scripts for task automation and configuration management. The ability to create and use scripts is valuable because scripts save time, ensure consistency in the execution of tasks, and allow for flexibility in responding to various conditions.

> Scripts can be written in many scripting languages. Some are designed for use on a single operating system, and others are cross-platform. While all scripting languages use the same logic to write a script for a given task, each language has its own unique and specific syntax. Scripting languages discussed in this chapter include batch files, shell scripts, VBScript, PowerShell, Python, and JavaScript.

> The building blocks of scripting include variables and data types. All scripts are written using three basic programming constructs: sequence, selection, and repetition.

> Technicians must stay current in the IT field to move up or maintain their current job status. Methods used to stay current include associations, magazines, classes, books, and peers.

CHAPTER 15

A+ CERTIFICATION EXAM TIPS

✓ Be familiar with the commands and how to work in the command prompt environment. The following commands are on the certification exam: navigation commands (`dir`, `cd`, and `..`), as well as other commands: `chkdsk`, `copy`, `diskpart`, `dism`, `explorer`, `format`, `gpresult`, `gpupdate`, `ipconfig`, `mmc`, `msinfo32`, `mstsc`, `net use`, `net user`, `netstat`, `notepad`, `nslookup`, `ping`, `regedit`, `robocopy`, `services.msc`, `sfc`, `shutdown`, `taskkill`, `tracert`, `xcopy`, and `[command name] /?`. You should also be familiar with commands available to someone with standard privileges vs. those available with administrative privileges. Practice these commands (and the various switches used with them) the week before taking the exam. Know when to use them. Consider what would be wrong that would force you to use a particular command.

✓ Be able to identify the program and file extension for each of the following script file types: batch files (`.bat`), PowerShell (`.ps1`), VBScript (`.vbs`), shell scripting (`.sh`), Python (`.py`), and JavaScript (`.js`).

✓ Understand and identify environment variables.

✓ Identify a comment within a particular script file.

✓ Understand and identify script variables.

✓ Identify basic data types within a script, such as integers and strings.

✓ Describe basic script constructs, including basic selection and repetition structures (decisions and loops).

Key Terms

Review Questions

1. What command is used to create a directory? [CD | MD | DIR | MAD]

2. What command is used to list the contents of a directory?

    _____

3. Consider the following directory structure from the F: drive root directory.

    2019_Term (directory)

    CompRepair (subdirectory)

    Opsys (subdirectory)

    Cisco8 (subdirectory)

    VoIP (subdirectory)

    If the prompt is C:\2019_Term>, and you want to move into the *VoIP* subdirectory, what command do you type?

    a. CD VoIP

    b. CD..

    c. CD C:\

    d. CD C:\VoIP

4. The _____ and _____ file extensions are used with Windows executable files that are used to start applications. [.app | .com | .exe | .js | .ps1]

5. What command would be used on a computer where a specific application has stopped?
    [quit | net stop | taskkill | stop]

6. List one example of where you think a technician might see or use a batch file or a script file.

    _____

    _____

7. A script is created as a _____ file. [Word | csv | text | HTML]

8. A(n) _____ _____ tells the computer where to find a specific program.
    [batch file | environment variable | value variable | scripting language]

9. The two types of environment variables are _____ and _____.
    [experimental | external | internal | system | test | user]

10. The set of symbols and rules used to create instructions in a scripting language is its _____.
    [variable name | keywords | value | syntax]

11. What command would a technician use to apply a change to the security policy?
    [gpupdate | mstsc | regedit | bootrec]

12. The value of a variable is stored in the computer's memory as a specific _____.
    [integer | string | data type | ASCII code]

13. _____ are included in a script to explain what the script or a portion of the script does but are ignored by the computer when the script runs.
    [Comments | Variables | Commands | Syntax lines]

14. Which type of file would have the following command as part of it.

    ```
    format d: /fs:ntfs /v:Corp /p:2
    ```

    [.py | .vbs | .js | .bat]

15. To compare two expressions in a selection structure, you use _____ operators.
    [>= | logic | equals | relational]

16. The _____ operator will return `false` only if both sides of the expression are false.
    [AND | OR | NOT | equals]

17. A _____ structure contains a block of statements that is executed repeatedly.
    [decision | selection | repetition | sequence]

18. Two types of loops are _____ and _____ loops.

    [continuous | decision | else | for | one time | while]

19. The scripting languages that were developed by Microsoft are _____ and _____.
    [Basic | C | Java | PowerShell | VBScript]

20. A script that has the `.sh` extension is a _____ script and works on _____-based systems.

21. The `.py` extension indicates that a script is written in the _____ language.
    [PowerShell | JavaScript | batch | Python]

Exercises

Exercise 15.1

Objective: To recognize which command to use for a specific task

Procedure: Match the command to the task by writing the letter of the command beside the task that would use this command. Note that not all commands will be used.

Commands:

a. dir	**f.** robocopy	**k.** attrib
b. rd	**g.** md	**l.** sfc
c. del	**h.** gpresult	**m.** regedit
d. cd	**i.** type	**n.** tasklist
e. gpupdate	**j.** copy	

Task:

____ Copy a directory, its contents, all subdirectories, and attributes.

____ Create a folder.

____ Remove a file.

____ Copy a file from one place to another.

____ List all files in a particular directory.

____ Delete a directory.

____ Display the contents of a test or batch file.

____ Verify and optionally repair operating system files.

____ Move to a different directory.

Exercise 15.2

Objective: To recognize terms related to scripting.

Procedure: Match the item to its description.

a. .sh   e. shell scripts

b. .py   f. PowerShell

c. .bat   g. strings

d. loop   h. environment variable

Item: Description:

____   A variable that describes the environment in which a program runs

____   A control structure used by a scripting language to write scripts

____   The extension used by the Python language

____   A data type consisting of alphanumeric characters

____   The extension that identifies a batch file

____   Scripts written for a Unix-based system

____   The extension that identifies a shell script

____   A Windows shell that was created to help in task automation and configuration management

Activities

Internet Discovery

Objective: Access the Internet to obtain specific information regarding a computer or its associated parts

Parts: Access to the Internet

Procedure: Complete the following procedure and answer the accompanying questions.

1.   Locate an Internet site that has a specific usage for the chkdsk command.

_____

_____

2.   List three things that you think would be useful from Microsoft's Customizing the Out-of-Box Experience for IT Pros website and explain why you think they would help the technician.

_____

_____

_____

3.   Locate a website that provides a VBScript sample that could be used by a computer technician. Provide a basic description of what the script does and the URL where you found the answer.

_____

_____

4.   You have been asked to add some user accounts to the domain, and the supervisor wants you to get some practice from the command line. Find a website that provides the command and specific instructions on how to use that command. Provide the command, one recommendation found on the website, and the URL of the website.

_____

_____

_____

_____

5. Six scripting languages are described in the chapter. Locate a website that compares and contrasts the use of at least two of these languages. Document the URL. Briefly describe which language you would choose and explain why you made this choice.

_____

_____

_____

Soft Skills

Objective: To enhance and fine-tune a technician's ability to listen, communicate in both written and oral form, and support people who use computers in a professional manner

Activities:

1. On a piece of paper or an index card, list two commands you would like to hear how to use in specific situations. Use the Internet to find reports from other technicians who have used these commands. Write what you have learned, paying special attention to any issues that were brought up. Share this information with your group. Consolidate ideas and present five of the best ideas to the class.

2. In a team environment, select two of the five ideas presented in Activity 1 to research further. Every team member should present a problem and its solution. Present these to the rest of the class. The class votes on the presentation that includes the most interesting and useful topic.

3. In a team environment, assign one scripting language to each member of the team. Each member should research the pros and cons of that language and present the findings to the group. Make a list of when each language should be used and its restrictions to present to the class.

Critical Thinking Skills

Objective: To analyze and evaluate information and to apply learned information to new or different situations

Activities:

1. Write a four-line batch file that does the following tasks:

   > Removes the path (`C:\Whatever`) shown on the screen.

   > Clears the screen

   > Puts a message on the screen about what the batch file is doing.

   > Starts a particular application or opens a specific web browser.

_____

_____

_____

_____

_____

2. Describe what you would do if you were hired for an IT position and asked to create a script.

_____

_____

_____

_____

_____

3. Describe what you would do if you were hired for an IT position and asked to display and modify the environment variable on a given system for a user-installed program.

_____

_____

_____

_____

_____

16 Advanced Windows

In this chapter you will learn:

> To distinguish between the Windows 7, 8, 8.1, and 10 operating systems

> To install, configure, and troubleshoot Windows 7, 8, 8.1, and 10

> To install hardware and software in the Windows environment

> To use various tools and features, such as System Restore, driver rollback, and WinRE

> To use the Control Panel utilities

> To implement the Windows boot process and troubleshoot boot problems

> To use the Computer Management console, Task Manager, and Event Viewer

> How to avoid burnout in the IT field

CompTIA Exam Objectives:

What CompTIA exam objectives are covered in this chapter?

✓ 1002-1.2 Compare and contrast features of Microsoft Windows versions.

✓ 1002-1.3 Summarize general OS installation considerations and upgrade methods.

✓ 1002-1.5 Given a scenario, use Microsoft operating system features and tools.

✓ 1002-1.6 Given a scenario, use Microsoft Windows Control Panel utilities.

✓ 1002-1.7 Summarize application installation and configuration concepts.

✓ 1002-1.8 Given a scenario, configure Microsoft Windows networking on a client/desktop.

✓ 1002-2.6 Compare and contrast the differences of basic Microsoft Windows OS security settings.

✓ 1002-3.1 Given a scenario, troubleshoot Microsoft Windows OS problems.

✓ 1002-3.2 Given a scenario, troubleshoot and resolve PC security issues.

Advanced Windows Overview

Before going into the more technical issues related to Windows, let's go over some of the features you might not have heard of in Windows. Windows 7, 8, 8.1, and 10 come in 32- and 64-bit versions, each having different tiers available: Starter, Home Basic, Home Premium, Business, Professional (Pro), Enterprise, Ultimate, and Education. Depending on the version, enhanced features include the following:

> *Aero*—A Windows 7 graphical environment that introduces rich colors, features such as Aero Peek, and enables you to see all open documents by holding a pointer over application icons.

> *Side-by-side apps or windows*—Achieved in Windows 7, 8, 8.1, or 10 by dragging the top of a window to one side of the screen (until an outline of the window appears). An alternative is to be in an active window and use ⊞+← or ⊞+→, depending on whether you want the active window pinned to the left or right side. Open another window and do the same for the opposite side, and the windows or apps are automatically equally sized.

> *Metro UI*—The tiled look in Windows 8, 8.1, and 10.

> *OneDrive*—Microsoft's cloud storage, which allows files to be synced from multiple devices and accessible from a browser.

> *UAC (User Account Control)*—A method used to notify you of potential security issues before anything is added to or removed from the system.

> *Windows Store*—A store from which apps are optionally purchased and downloaded.

> *Multi-monitor taskbar*—A Windows 8/8.1/10 feature that can be modified with a right-click (or by tapping and briefly holding on an empty spot) on the taskbar > select *Properties* > locate the *Multiple Displays* section > select whether the taskbar shows on all displays and which display buttons should be displayed on.

> *Charms*—A Windows 8/8.1 hidden sidebar that, when displayed, provides quick access to searching, sharing content, the Start screen, devices, and settings.

> *WinRE (Windows Recovery Environment)*—The place to go when things go wrong with Windows, such as when a system will not boot or operate properly.

> *Hyper-V*—A hypervisor for running virtual machines.

> *Cortana*—A Windows 10 virtual assistant.

Preinstallation of Windows

Windows can be installed from either a central location using a network or locally using an optical disc or external drive. The preinstallation of any operating system is more important than the installation. Technicians who grab a disc or just download and load a new operating system without going through a preparation process are asking for trouble. The operating system is a complex piece of software that is critical to the operation of all hardware and other software.

It is important to follow these steps before installing Windows:

Step 1. Decide whether the installation will be an upgrade or a clean install and which version of the operating system is to be loaded. Take into account software application compatibility.

Step 2. Decide whether the computer will have more than one operating system installed.

Step 3. Plan the partition/volume size and select the file system.

Step 4. Determine whether or not the hardware is compatible.

Step 5. Obtain any drivers, upgrades, or hardware replacements.

Step 6. Back up any data files.

Step 7. Scan for viruses and then disable the virus protection during the installation process.

Step 8. Temporarily disable any power management or disk management tools.

Types of Installations

Windows can be installed for a variety of reasons, such as to have the latest features, to have a different operating system, to repair a system that doesn't boot, or to speed up a slow performing operating system. Table 16.1 summarizes the various types of installations.

TABLE 16.1   Windows installation types

Installation type	Description
Unattended installation	A method of installing Windows in which a script or answer file (usually a custom-prepared one for the company) is used; sometimes called zero-touch installation (ZTI).
In-place upgrade	An upgrade of an existing operating system where the user keeps settings and files, such as moving from Windows 8 to Windows 8.1 or 10.
Clean install	An installation of an operating system when no other operating system is present.
Repair installation	Replacement of the Windows operating system when files have been corrupt or the system won't boot properly.
Multiboot	Two or more operating systems on the same system; make sure you load the oldest operating system first.
Remote network installation	A server or network share containing a created image is accessed, and the image is deployed to a computer on a remote network. Network bandwidth is affected, and this may interfere with normal business operations. For this reason, remote installations are commonly done during light network usage time or during off hours.
Image deployment	A file that contains an image that can be deployed with little interaction. Windows operating system, software, drivers, and updates are added to a network share, and configuration files are created. Burn the boot images to optical media or an external drive. Boot the destination computer with the boot image, and the installation occurs without further intervention.
Recovery partition	Sometimes called a **factory recovery partition**; contains the operating system and applications that came with the system when it was purchased.
Refresh/restore	The refresh option reinstalls Windows while keeping any saved files, apps, and settings that you have installed. The restore option brings Windows back to a previous state, such as to a time before a recent update was applied.

CHAPTER 16

In-place Upgrade or Clean Install

The first decision to make when planning to install an operating system is whether to upgrade from another operating system or to perform a clean install. An upgrade or in-place upgrade occurs when a computer already has an older operating system on it, and a newer operating system is being installed. A clean install puts an operating system on a system that does not have one or removes the existing operating system in order to install a new one. There are three reasons to perform a clean install:

> The computer does not already have an operating system installed.

> The current operating system is not upgradable to the desired Windows version.

> The current operating system is upgradable to a specific Windows version, but the existing files and applications are going to be reloaded.

Microsoft describes an in-place upgrade as an installation that requires no movement of files. Although an in-place installation can usually be accomplished to upgrade from one version of Windows to another, this isn't always an option. For example, if someone has an older XP computer, the recommended Microsoft upgrade is to Vista. If the user wanted Windows 10, you can't just go from Windows XP to Windows 7, 8, or 10 and keep all of the settings. To make sure an upgrade is possible, consult the documentation for the version of Windows you want to upgrade to and know which version of Windows you currently have installed. Alternatively, you can use the Windows Upgrade Advisor tool. Figure 16.1 shows how to use the Windows System Control Panel utility to see what version is currently installed. Table 16.2 shows the upgrade paths for Windows 7, 8, and 8.1.

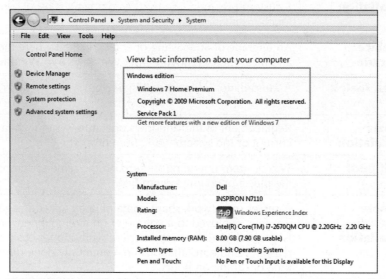

FIGURE 16.1   Windows System section of the Control Panel: current version

TABLE 16.2   Windows upgrade paths

Original operating system	Upgrade to possibilities
Windows 7 Home Basic, Home Premium Windows 8/8.1 Core	Windows 10 Home, Pro, and Education
Windows 7 Professional, Ultimate Windows 8/8.1 Pro	Windows 10 Pro, Education, and Enterprise
Windows 7 Enterprise Windows 8/8.1 Enterprise	Windows 10 Education and Enterprise

When you decide to upgrade, you must take into account which operating system is installed, what hardware is installed, what applications are being used, and whether or not those applications are compatible with the new operating system (see Figure 16.2). When Windows is installed as an upgrade, the user's applications and data are preserved if the operating system is installed in the same folder as the original operating system. If Windows is installed in a different folder, then all applications must be reloaded.

FIGURE 16.2 Applications are affected by an OS upgrade

Windows Upgrade Advisor

The **Windows Upgrade Advisor** application should always be used before upgrading. Upgrade Advisor, sometimes also referred to as Upgrade Assistant in more recent versions of Windows, can be downloaded, installed, and executed to see whether a Windows 7, 8, 8.1, or 10 computer can function well with a higher version of Windows. Upgrade Advisor checks hardware, connected devices, and existing applications, and it makes recommendations before an upgrade. You will want to make sure you have all hardware peripherals that are commonly used with the system are connected when you run the advisor tool.

In order to take advantage of Windows reliability, enhancements, and security features, sometimes a clean installation is the best choice. Because a clean installation involves formatting the hard drive, the user's data must be backed up, and all applications should be reinstalled when the Windows installation is complete. Also, all user-defined settings are lost.

> **TECH TIP**
>
> **OEM OS cannot go to another computer**
>
> An original equipment manufacturer (OEM) version of Windows that is sold as part of a computer sale is not transferable to another computer.

Even when Microsoft states that an in-place upgrade *can* be done, there is no guarantee that all applications and settings will work after the upgrade. In a corporate environment, if custom software is involved, contact the software developer for any known issues or test the software in a test environment before deploying corporate-wide. The information may be posted on the software developer's website. Also, Microsoft has a list of compatible software for many of the popular applications and games on its website.

Easy Transfer and USMT

The **Easy Transfer** program or the User State Migration Tool (**USMT**) can be used to migrate data when updating Windows when an in-place upgrade is not supported. See Figure 16.3 for an example of data migration. Windows Easy Transfer (`migwiz.exe`), which is free from Microsoft, is used to copy files and operating system settings to another drive, to removable media, over a network, or to another storage location. Once the operating system is installed, the files and settings are reapplied to the upgraded computer. This tool can also be used when a computer is being replaced and a data migration is required. The Easy Transfer program works only through Windows 8, but USMT can be used from Windows XP all the way to Windows 10.

CHAPTER 16

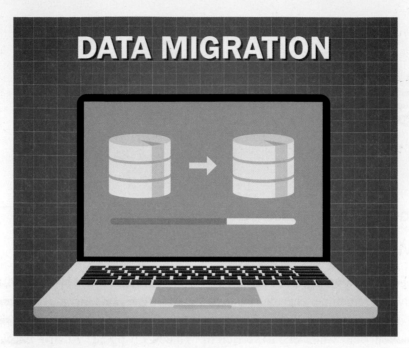

FIGURE 16.3   Local data migration

IT staff use the USMT to perform large deployments of Windows. This tool is used from a command line for more control and customized settings, including registry changes. The `scanstate.exe` and `loadstate.exe` commands are used to transfer file and user settings.

Compatibility Mode

Keep in mind while upgrading that not all 16- or 32-bit applications can be used in the 64-bit Windows environment. If a program is proving to be incompatible, try the **compatibility mode** available using the **Program Compatibility Wizard**: Locate the *Programs* section of the Control Panel > use the *Run Programs Made for Previous Versions of Windows* link.

Another way to manually assign a particular application that was made to be compatible with an older (selectable) Windows version is to locate the application in the Start button menu or find the executable file on disk. Right-click the application and select *Properties > Compatibility* tab > enable (check) the *Run This Program in Compatibility Mode For* checkbox > use the drop-down menu to select the specific operating system > use the specific video and administrator options available in the *Settings* and *Privilege Level* sections > click *Apply* > click *OK*.

Virtual XP Mode

If the Program Compatibility Wizard does not work, the Virtual XP Mode is an option in Windows 7, but it was discontinued for newer versions of Windows. **Virtual XP Mode** (also known as Windows XP Mode) is an optional program that can be downloaded and used in Windows 7 Professional, Ultimate, and Enterprise editions. Once it is downloaded and installed, access the software by clicking on the *Start* button > *All Programs > Windows Virtual PC > Virtual Windows XP*.

TECH TIP

Running a troublesome app in Windows 8 and 10

Windows 8 and 10 include Hyper-V to use for virtualization where you could install and run an older application.

Planning Drive Space

The third step when planning to install Windows is to determine how large to make the **drive partition** (also called volumes) and select the file system to be used. One option is to place the operating system in one partition and data in a separate partition to make it easier to back up the data. Figure 16.4 shows this concept. By default, an entire drive is used; however, drives can be partitioned during the Windows installation process.

FIGURE 16.4 Partitioning (dividing) drive space during OS installation concept

The file system should be NTFS for the following reasons:

> Provides security (individual files can be protected using encryption)
> Makes more efficient use of cluster space
> Supports file compression
> Supports larger hard drive partition sizes
> Includes journaling, which helps in rebuilding the file system after a crash or power failure

An issue that is relevant only when upgrading is whether to convert an old FAT16 or FAT32 hard drive partition to NTFS. Once a partition is converted to NTFS, the partition cannot be changed. If you are unsure whether to convert a partition, leave it unchanged and later use the `convert` command to upgrade (without losing any data).

TECH TIP

Using the `convert` command

The **`convert`** command can be used to change a FAT16 or FAT32 partition to NTFS and keep the data from the old partition. Use `convert x: /fs:ntfs` (where `x:` is the drive to be converted to NTFS). Remember, once you go to a higher file system, you cannot go back.

Types of Partitions

Before a drive can be used by the operating system, it has to be partitioned and formatted. Partitioning allows you to divide a drive into multiple sections or select the entire drive to be used. As part of partitioning, you assign a drive letter to each drive section. You are already familiar with the `C:` drive, where the operating system normally resides. Once a drive is partitioned, that section must be formatted for a particular type of file system, such as NTFS, exFAT, or FAT32. Table 16.3 reviews the types of partitions found in the Windows environment. When Windows is being installed, you have the option of a quick format or a full format. A **full format** identifies and marks bad sectors so they will not be used for data storage. A **quick format** skips this analysis.

TECH TIP

Use the Disk Management tool

Drives are created and managed using the Disk Management tool, accessed through the *System and Security > Administrative Tools > Computer Management > Disk Management* section of the Control Panel. You can also type `diskmgmt.msc` from a prompt or search window to access the tool. The Disk Management tool is covered in more detail later in the chapter.

TABLE 16.3   Windows partition types

Partition type	Description
Basic disk	The most common type of partition that can contain primary partitions, extended partitions, and logical drives. Each primary partition and logical drive must be formatted for a specific file system.
Primary partition	A partition that can hold an operating system. If the operating system is used to boot the system, it must be a primary partition that is configured as an active partition. A primary partition is assigned a drive letter and formatted for a specific file system.
Extended partition	A type of partition that allows hard drive subdivisions called **logical partitions**. Each logical partition (also called logical drive) is assigned a drive letter and formatted for a specific file system. Can only be used with basic disks.
MBR (master boot record partition table)	The traditional type of partition that uses primary and extended partitions.
Dynamic disk	A more advanced type of disk volume that supports simple, spanned, striped, and RAID drive configuration.
GPT (GUID partition table)	A more advanced type of partition that requires a UEFI BIOS and allows partition sizes larger than 2 TB, improved protection of the partition table, and more partitions.
Swap partition	The Linux equivalent of a Windows paging file. Paging uses hard drive space as RAM so that programs that exceed the size of available physical memory can operate.

File System Types

The most common Windows file systems are FAT16, FAT32, exFAT, and NTFS. The file system that can be used depends on what operating system is installed, whether the device is an internal device or external, and whether files are to be shared. Table 16.4 lists file systems used with Windows and other operating systems.

TABLE 16.4   File system types

File system type	Description
Compact Disk File System (**CDFS**)	A file system for optical media.
FAT	Also called FAT16. Used with all versions of Windows. 2 GB partition limitation with old operating systems. 4 GB partition limitation with XP and higher versions of Windows.

File system type	Description
FAT32	Supported with all versions of Windows. Commonly used with removable flash drives. Supports drives up to 2 TB. Can recognize volumes greater than 32 GB.
exFAT	Commonly called FAT64. A file system made for removable media (such as flash drives and SD cards) that extends drive size support up to 64 ZB in theory, although 512 TB is the recommended max. Made for copying large files such as disk images and media files. Supported by all versions of Windows.
NTFS	Used with Windows 7, 8, and 10. Supports drives up to 16 EB (16 exabytes, which equals 16 billion gigabytes) but in practice is only 16 TB. Supports file compression and file security (encryption). NTFS allows faster file access and uses hard drive space more efficiently. Supports individual file compression and has the best Windows file security.
Hierarchical File System (**HFS**)	Used with Apple computers that have been upgraded to HFS+ and then later upgraded to Apple File System (APFS) in 2017.
Network File System (**NFS**)	An open source file system developed by Sun Microsystems that is found in Linux-based systems. Allows access to remote files over a network.
ext3	Also known as third extended file system. Used in Linux-based operating systems, it is a journaling file system, which means it tracks changes in case the operating system crashes, allowing it to be restarted without reloading.
ext4	An update to ext3 to allow for larger volumes and file sizes in Linux-based operating systems.

Hardware

The fourth step when planning to install Windows is to determine what computer hardware is installed. Table 16.5 lists the requirements for most Windows 7/8/8.1/10 installations. One thing that might influence your choice of Windows version is the amount of memory supported by the different flavors.

TABLE 16.5 Windows 7/8/8.1/10 hardware requirements

Component	Minimum
Processor	1 GHz
RAM	1 GB (32-bit)/2 GB (64-bit)
Graphics	Support for DirectX9 or higher with 1.0 WDDM driver
Hard drive space	16 GB (32-bit)/20 GB (64-bit)

Drivers

Once hardware has been verified, you have to obtain hardware device drivers specific to the operating system from the hardware manufacturer's website so that you can **load alternate third-party drivers**, when necessary. The hardware device may have to be upgraded or replaced. Sometimes, older operating system drivers do work, but many times older drivers do not work or do not work properly. This is the cost of going to a more powerful operating system. The customer may also decide at this point not to upgrade but rather to buy a computer with the desired version of Windows already installed instead.

The Microsoft Upgrade Advisor tool may recommend getting updated third-party drivers for specific pieces of hardware. Drivers related to hard drives—for example, drivers for hardware RAID, motherboard AHCI mode, SATA hard drives, and hard drives over 2 TB—are especially critical to the installation process. Obtain any of these hard drive–related drivers *before* the installation, or you will not be able to install the operating system to that hard drive.

If upgrading, ensure that Windows updates are current

If upgrading to a new version of Windows, ensure that the current version has the latest Windows updates.

Backing Up Before an OS Installation

The sixth step in planning to install Windows is one of the most important: In any upgrade, hardware change, or software change, you *must* back up the user data. Whether you do a clean install or an upgrade, if the user has data on the computer, it must be backed up before starting the installation process. Also, before backing up the data, remove any unwanted files and/or applications in order to free up hard drive space. Right-click on the drive letter from Windows Explorer/File Explorer. From the General tab, use the *Disk Cleanup* button to check and defragment the hard drive. Once the data is backed up from a Windows system, create a system image backup and system repair disc.

Security Scan

The seventh step in planning for a Windows installation is to scan the system for viruses and malware (see Figure 16.5).

FIGURE 16.5   Do a security scan before an OS upgrade

Antivirus software causes issues

Whether doing a clean install or an upgrade, disable the antivirus protection until after the installation. If possible, disconnect the computer from the network before disabling the software.

Disabling Interfering Software

The last step in the preinstallation checklist is to disable any power- or disk-management tools that are loaded. They can interfere with the new tools provided with Windows and can prevent an operating system from installing. Some security applications, including anti-malware and firewalls, can interfere with an operating system upgrade as well. Disable these utilities and applications before attempting an operating system installation or upgrade.

Installation/Upgrade of Windows

After completing all the preinstallation steps, you are ready to install Windows. The installation process is easy if you performed the preinstallation steps. The number-one piece of advice to heed is to do your installation/upgrade research first. Doing so will greatly reduce the number of possible problems.

Basically, an installation involves three phases.

> In the first phase of an installation (sometimes called the Windows Preinstallation Environment, or Windows PE), a selection must be made about whether to upgrade or perform a clean installation, the product key must be entered, the **time/date/region/language settings** must be set, and a basic hardware check including available disk space must be accomplished. The computer then restarts.

> After the restart, the second phase begins. During this process, a partition to install Windows can be chosen, and setup files are copied to the partition.

> During the third phase, devices are installed, the administrator password is entered, questions about Windows Update and such are answered, and the operating system is created. The system restarts a final time, and the logon screen is presented.

Part of the installation process is to select the type of network: home, work, or public. Computers on a home network can be a part of a HomeGroup or workgroup. By default, computers on a company network can see and share information with other work computers but cannot create or join a HomeGroup. With a public network, a computer attaches to an unsecured network, as in a restaurant or bookstore. Your computer is not visible to other computers by default when the public network option is chosen. (Table 16.6 shows these types.) Note that you can bypass the network configuration at this point and configure it later.

TABLE 16.6   Network types

Network type	Description
Workgroup	You can configure Windows 7 for this type, but file and print sharing are not automatically enabled as they are with a Windows HomeGroup. Note that Windows HomeGroup is removed starting with Windows 10 version 1803, but you can still share files and folders across a small network.
HomeGroup	Normally created in a Windows 7, 8, 8.1, or 10 home or small business environment that automatically turns on file and print sharing. Note that computers with Windows 7 Starter or Home Basic can join a HomeGroup but not start one. All Windows 7 and higher operating systems can join the HomeGroup. Starting with version 1803, Windows 10 no longer supports HomeGroup as a network choice, but you can still share files and folders across a small network.
Domain	A corporate environment in which users authenticate with a centralized user ID and password. Whatever machine the user goes to, the user ID and password would be the same if the computer has been configured to be on the domain.

You will probably have to set aside some time to allow the computer to receive and install updates issued since the operating system image/version you just installed was created. You may also have to install additional software apps that may not be part of the backup or image that was installed.

Corporate Windows Deployment

Corporate computer installations are much more involved than any other type of deployment. Computers are installed in bulk instead of one at a time, as in a home or small business. The computers are frequently the same model and have the same software installed.

Disk imaging is common in the corporate environment. Disk imaging software makes an exact copy (a binary copy) of the files loaded on the hard drive. The copy is then pressed to an optical disc or an external drive, or it is put on a network drive to be copied and deployed onto other computers. When a computer has an issue, it is faster to just **reimage** the computer than to troubleshoot the Windows problem.

Companies need automated installation tools to help with the corporate Windows deployment process. Tools that can help with this are the Windows Assessment and Deployment Kit (Windows ADK), Windows System Preparation (Sysprep) tool, imaging software such as Symantec Corporation's Ghost program, Microsoft's Setup Manager, and Windows System Image Manager (SIM). An image can be created and deployed to multiple computers. Table 16.7 describes some of these tools.

TABLE 16.7   Corporate computer deployment tools

Tool	Description
Sysprep	When a prototype computer has Windows, Windows updates, all drivers, and applications installed, Sysprep can remove the security identifier (SID)—a unique number assigned to a computer by a network domain controller as well as other unique information, such as the computer name or network domain. The computer is then imaged, and the image is deployed to other computers. A third-party utility such as Symantec Ghost Walker or Microsoft's newsid.exe can be used to reassign the SIDs after the drive image has been deployed.
SIM (System Image Manager)	Used to create and configure answer files, install applications, apply service packs and updates to an image, and add device drivers. After the Windows unattend.xml answer file is created, you can use this file to answer the installation questions as the files are downloaded from a share or server on the network. SIM is part of the Windows ADK download.
WDS (Windows Deployment Services)	Uses the corporate network(s) to deploy Windows-based operating systems, drivers, updates, and applications using a network-based installation.
MDT (Microsoft Deployment Toolkit)	A GUI shell to make Windows deployment easier. Tools such as USMT, Application Compatibility Toolkit (ACT), Microsoft Assessment and Planning Toolkit (MAP), and the volume licensing application are inside the MDT shell.

When making a Windows image, you have to remove the unique identifiers from the computer—that is, computer name, security identifier (SID), a network domain, and so on—before deploying the image to other computers. You must also reset or re-arm the Windows **activation clock** if a single activation key is used. If you do not do this, you are prompted for the Windows product key as soon as the computer boots. By re-arming the activation clock, you have a 30-day (Windows 7)/90-day (Windows 8/10) grace period before having to re-enter the product key.

CHAPTER 16

TECH TIP

Three re-arms with Windows

There is no limit to the number of times a computer can be reimaged, but there is a limit to how many times a computer can be re-armed or have the Windows activation clock reset. You can use the Sysprep tool or the `slmgr -rearm` command to reset the re-arm count. To see how many times the computer has been re-armed, use the `slmgr /dlv` command.

When deploying Windows in the enterprise, licensing is handled a bit differently. Larger businesses buy a volume license key (VLK). Two other choices are MAK and KMS. With Multiple Activation Key (MAK), the Internet or a phone call must be used to register one or more computers. This method has a limited number of activations, but more licenses can be purchased. The Key Management Service (**KMS**) method is used in companies with 25 or more computers to deploy.

TECH TIP

Be responsible

A technician is responsible for ensuring that any computer deployed has an antivirus application installed and that the application is configured to receive virus signature updates. Educate users about viruses and what to do if a computer gets one.

Verifying the Installation

In any upgrade or installation, verification that the upgrade is successful is critical in both home and business environments. After an upgrade has been done, verify that all applications still function. After a new installation has been completed, ensure that all installed hardware is detected by Device Manager (covered in the "Adding Devices" section, later in this chapter).

TECH TIP

Reinitialize antivirus software

If antivirus software was disabled through BIOS/UEFI and through an application, re-enable it after the operating system installation is complete. Verify that all settings are in accordance with the user requirements and departmental/organizational standards.

When you are satisfied that the installation is successful, don't forget to **apply updates** to the operating system, applications, and anti-malware software. You might also want to update device drivers to ensure the most up-to-date security and features for the installed hardware.

Troubleshooting a Windows Installation

Installation problems can be caused by a number of factors. The following are the most common causes of problems and their solutions:

> *No boot device available*—Access BIOS and **update the boot order** so that the device that contains the operating system is listed first.

> *Incompatible hardware drivers*—Obtain drivers for the appropriate Windows version from the hardware manufacturer, if not Microsoft.

> *Incompatible applications*—Obtain upgrades from the software manufacturer, the Program Compatibility Wizard, a multiboot environment, or virtualization.
> *Minimum hardware requirements have not been met*—Upgrade the hardware. The most likely things to check are the CPU and RAM.
> *A virus is present*—Run an antivirus program and remove the virus.
> *Antivirus software is installed and active and is halting the installation/upgrade*—Disable the antivirus software through BIOS/UEFI and through the application. Restart the Windows installation and re-enable the antivirus software when the operating system installation is complete.
> *Preinstallation steps have not been completed*—Go back through the list.
> *The installation disc or download is corrupt (not as likely as the other causes)*—Try the disc in another machine and see if you can see the contents. Check to see if a scratch or dirt is on the disc surface and clean the disc as necessary. Redownload the operating system.
> *Incorrect registration key*—Type in the correct key to complete the installation. The key is located on the disc or disc case or in an email.
> *The Windows installation process cannot find a hard drive*—This is most likely due to a SATA drive being used and a driver not being available for the controller. Download the driver, put it on a flash drive, or use a software program such as NTLite to create a custom installation disc that includes the downloaded driver.
> *A STOP message occurs when installing a multiboot system*—Boot from the Windows installation disc rather than the other operating system.
> *The computer locks up during setup and shows a "blue screen of death" (BSOD)*—Check the BIOS/UEFI and hardware compatibility. Also, if an error message appears, research the error on the Internet.
> *Incompatible BIOS*—Obtain compatible BIOS/UEFI, replace the motherboard with one that has a compatible BIOS, or do not upgrade or install the higher Windows version.
> *BIOS needs to be upgraded*—Upgrade the BIOS/UEFI.
> *You get an "NTLDR is Missing" error*—If you get an **NTLDR is Missing** error on a Windows 7, 8, or 10 computer during the installation process, try the clean install process over again.

TECH TIP

Installation halts

If installation stops, try removing any nonessential hardware, such as network cards, modems, and USB devices and start the installation again. Reinstall the hardware after Windows is properly installed.

> *A message appears during setup that a device driver was unable to load*—Obtain the latest device drivers that are compatible and restart the setup program.
> *After upgrading Windows, the computer freezes*—Boot to Safe Mode and check Device Manager (covered in the "Adding Devices" section, later in this chapter) for errors. **Safe Mode** is a boot option that starts the computer with a minimum set of drivers. If no errors are present within Device Manager, disable the following devices, if present: video adapter, sound card, network card, USB devices and controller (unless using a USB keyboard/mouse), optical drive, modem, and unused ports. Enable each disabled device one at a time until the blue screen appears. When the problem device is known, obtain the appropriate replacement driver.

During the Windows installation there are log files created that can be helpful for resolving installation issues. Table 16.8 outlines important log files for each version of Windows and briefly describes what they contain.

TABLE 16.8 Windows setup log files

Log file location	Description
`X:\Windows\setupapi.log`	Device and driver changes, service pack, and hotfix installations
`X:\$Windows.~BT\Sources\ Panther\ setupact.log`	Setup actions performed during the install
`X:\$Windows.~BT\Sources\Panther\ setuperr.log`	Setup installation errors
`X:\$Windows.~BT\Sources\ Panther\ PreGatherPnPList.log`	Initial capture of devices information
`X:\$Windows.~BT\Sources\Panther\ miglog.xml`	User directory structure and SID information
`X:\Windows\Inf\setupapi*.log`	Plug-and-play devices and driver information
`X:\Windows\Inf\setupapi.app.log`	Application installation information
`X:\Windows\Panther\ PostGatherPnPList.log`	Device information after the online configuration

Reloading Windows

Chapter 14, "Introduction to Operating Systems," has a section called "Recovering the Windows OS" that helps when in the situation of **no OS found**. This section provides a few more technical suggestions for such situations.

Sometimes it's necessary to do a *repair installation* (sometimes called an *in-place upgrade* or a *reinstallation*) of Windows, such as when Windows does not start normally or in Safe Mode, or when it has a registry corruption that cannot be solved with System Restore (covered later in the chapter). Hopefully the user has backed up existing data. The installation process should not disturb the data, but there is always a chance that it could.

Windows Resource Protection (**WRP**) protects operating system files, folders, and important registry keys, using access control lists (**ACL**s), or code that permits or denies changes to the operating system. Changes made to a monitored file or folder cannot be changed even by an administrator unless the administrator takes ownership and adds the appropriate access control entities (ACEs) within an ACL. Any file that cannot be repaired by **System File Checker (sfc)** can be identified with the following command using administrative privileges:

```
findstr /C:"[SR] Cannot repair member file" %windir%\logs\cbs\cbs.
log>sfcdetails.txt
```

Use Notepad or the edit command to open the file (normally located in the `C:\Windows\System32` folder). **Notepad**, as you learned in Chapter 15, "Introduction to Scripting," is a text editor that is handy for creating scripts and opening .txt or log files. From an elevated command prompt, the following commands grant administrators access to the protected files so they can be replaced:

> `takeown  /f  filename_including_path` (where *filename_including_ path* is the full path and filename of the problem file).

> icacls *filename_including_path*/grant administrators:r
> Then use the COPY command to replace the file with a known good one copy *source_filename destination_filename* (where the *source* and *destination* are the full path and file).

TECH TIP

Use sfc to solve system file problems

Use the sfc /scannow command as an administrator to replace any protected system files that have problems.

Newer Windows versions do not normally have to be reloaded as often as older Windows versions did. Modern Windows computers are more likely to allow booting from a flash drive. The operating system image can be copied or downloaded and placed on the flash drive. Change the BIOS/UEFI settings to boot from the flash drive, and the installation process starts. Windows has great tools that help with startup problems, such as a corrupt registry and missing or corrupt boot configuration files. These tools are covered later in this chapter.

TECH TIP

All existing system restore points are removed when Windows is reinstalled

When Windows has been installed, no preexisting restore points are kept. You should ensure that the System Restore utility is enabled and back up your data after Windows is installed. You should also apply any service packs and patches after the reinstallation is complete.

Windows Updates

Almost daily, new vulnerabilities are found in every operating system. Windows has a method called **Windows Update** or **Automatic Updates** for upgrading the operating system. To configure Windows 7 and 8 for automatic updates, locate the *System* section of the Control Panel > *Automatic Updates* tab. Windows 10 does automatic updates by default, but Microsoft has announced it is rethinking this policy. The **System Control Panel** is used to view the Windows version being used, the Windows product key, the processor type and speed, the amount of RAM, the computer name, and the workgroup or domain name.

TECH TIP

What is the difference between a patch, a service pack, and a hotfix?

A **patch** is an update to an operating system. Microsoft releases patches when they are needed for emergency fixes to vulnerabilities and routinely about once a month. A **service pack** is a group of patches that is it easier to install than a large number of separate patches. A **hotfix** has one or more files that fix a particular software problem. Use the systeminfo command to see what hotfixes have been applied.

One way to access Windows Update settings for Windows 7 is from the *Start* button > *All Programs* > *Windows Update* > *Change Settings*. To access this setting in Windows 8, access the *System and Security* section of the Control Panel > *Windows Update* > *Change Settings*. In

Windows 10 the update settings have been moved out of the Control Panel to the new *Settings* menu. To access the update settings in Windows 10, access *Settings >* select *Update and Security.*

For fine-tuning, technicians should always use the *Windows Update* section of the Control Panel in Windows 7, which offers more options. Figure 16.6 shows the options available.

TECH TIP

Roll back Windows updates

When a Windows update causes the computer to not work properly, **roll back Windows updates** to at least one previous version. Note that you might have to do this from Safe Mode. In Windows 7, 8, and 8.1, use the *Programs and Features > View Installed Updates* link > select a particular update > *Uninstall.* In Windows 10, access the *Update and Security* setting > *Windows Update > View Update History* link > *Uninstall Updates* (Windows 10) to perform this task. You can also use the System Restore tool.

FIGURE 16.6 Windows Update options in Windows 7

The Windows 7 and 8 Control Panel settings pane has four options:

> Install updates automatically (recommended)
> Download updates but let me choose whether to install them
> Check for updates but let me choose whether to download and install them
> Never check for updates (not recommended)

Windows 10 has removed the options to disable checking and installing updates. In the Settings menu you are presented with only the option to allow automatic updates or to be notified when to schedule a restart to install updates. By default, a Windows 10 device does not restart when the user is using the computer.

TECH TIP

Updates must be installed

Depending on which option is chosen from the System section of the Control Panel in Windows 7 and 8, updates may be downloaded, but you may have to manually install them. Review the history and try to install the failed updates one update at a time. A system is not protected unless the updates are installed. This is also true for installed applications.

Other options are available, such as how to handle recommended options, whether all users on the computer can install updates, and whether to receive updates for other Microsoft products, such as the Microsoft browser, at the same time as receiving operating system updates (see Figure 16.7). If a newly installed service pack causes problems and must be removed, use the `spuninst.exe` command.

You must be an administrator to change Automatic Updates settings

You must be logged in as the administrator or a user that is a member of the Administrators group to modify Automatic Updates settings.

To customize how the notifications appear in Windows 7, right-click the *Start* button > *Properties* > *Taskbar* tab > locate the *Notification Area* section > *Customize* button > locate *Windows Update* option under *Icons* column > select the appropriate behavior. In Windows 8 and 10, the system tray notification option for Windows updates has been removed.

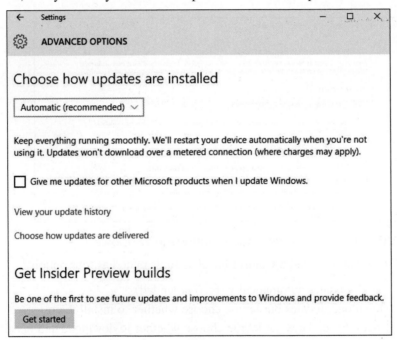

FIGURE 16.7   Windows Update options in Windows 10

Backing Up the Windows Registry and Data

The **registry** is a database that contains information about the Windows environment, including installed hardware, installed software, and users. The registry should be backed up whenever the computer is fully functional and when any software or hardware changes are made.

Back up the registry

The registry should be backed up and restored on a working computer *before* disaster hits. The time to learn how to restore the registry is not when the computer is down.

The registry can be backed up and restored several different ways:

> Using the `regedit` program
> Using the Backup utility (Windows 7)
> Using the System Restore tool (covered later in this chapter)

The **regedit** program enables you to export the registry to a file that has the extension `.reg`. The file can be imported back into the computer if the computer fails. The `regedit` program and the Backup utility both back up the entire registry.

In Windows 7 the Backup utility (introduced in Chapter 14) is launched by accessing the *System and Security* section of the Control Panel > *Backup and Restore*. Using the Backup utility is the preferred method for backing up the Windows registry, but in Windows 7 the full version of the Backup tool (the part that can back up the registry) is available only in the Business, Professional, Enterprise, and Ultimate versions. The Backup and Restore section of the Control Panel can be used to schedule a backup at a specific time and how often it should be performed.

Windows 8 has tried to move away from the Backup and Restore utility in favor of the new **File History** backup feature, for quicker and smaller, spaced backups. File History enables you to back up only a specific user's libraries instead of the entire system. *File History* also allows you to schedule these backups. Windows 10 also uses File History backups (see Figure 16.8), but it still includes the Backup and Restore feature. A user who has a Windows 8 or 10 system would best be served by backing up the entire system to an external drive or backing up the data and using one of the methods described in Chapter 14 to reinstall the operating system.

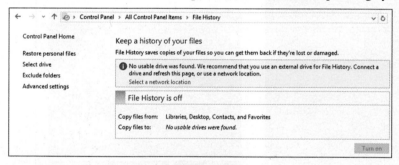

FIGURE 16.8   File History in Windows 10

TECH TIP

Who can use the Backup program?

To use the Backup program, you must be an administrator or have group rights to perform the backup.

To correct a problem with the system files, registry, or boot failure, you may also restore from a **restore point**. Restore points are created by the **System Restore** utility any time a change happens to the system, such as a program or driver being installed or a Windows update occurring. It is possible to revert to a restore point by opening the System Restore application when a change causes Windows to not operate properly or fail to boot.

The Windows 7 Backup and Restore link can also be used to back up the system state. This link can also be used to back up files and an entire disk image. To access this link, click the *Start* button > *Control Panel* > *System and Security* (7) > *Backup and Restore* > *Create a System Repair Disc*.

Windows 8 will do a File History backup, and if you had to recover the system, you would reinstall it and restore the File History. Windows 10, however, brought back the Backup and Restore feature from past versions of Windows, and it can be accessed by using the universal search bar on the Start menu and searching for `Backup and Restore (Windows 7)` or by right-clicking the *Start* button > *Control Panel* > *System and Security* > *Backup and Restore (Windows 7)*.

Configuring Windows Overview

One of the windows technicians use most commonly is the *Control Panel* window. A Control Panel allows you to configure various components. Each Control Panel icon represents a Windows utility that customizes a particular part of the Windows environment. The number of Control Panels displayed depends on the type of computer and the components contained within the computer. Control Panels have been discussed throughout the book, but this chapter explores more in-depth tasks with them. Windows has various Control Panel views, depending on the operating system: classic and category in Windows 7 and category, large icons, and small icons in Windows 8, 8.1, and 10.

With Windows 8, Microsoft tried moving away from Control Panels by offering the *Settings* option. Once *Settings* has been clicked, the options available from the PC settings window are ones that users would want. This frustrated technicians and users because Control Panels utilities were not easy to find. Microsoft changed this in Windows 8.1 and provided a link within the PC settings window to access the Control Panel (see Figure 16.9).

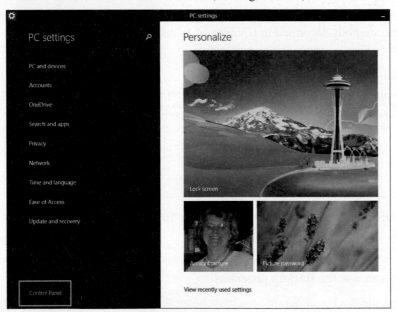

FIGURE 16.9   PC Settings in Windows 8

Windows 10 further improved on the *Settings* option but totally redesigned the categories, as shown in Figure 16.10. The options within each category contain much of what is in Control Panel utilities, but it will take a while before technicians move to using these, especially because not all tools are within these categories.

Technicians must know which Control Panel category to use for changing a computer's configuration. Windows has some configuration options that are unique to particular versions of the operating system. A technician should be familiar with these differences. Table 16.9 shows the unique Control Panel utilities by Windows version.

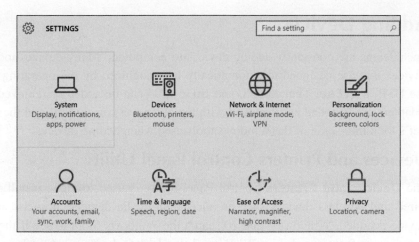

FIGURE 16.10   Settings in Windows 10

TABLE 16.9   Windows unique Control Panel utilities

Windows 7	Windows 8	Windows 10
HomeGroup	Add Features to Windows 8	Security and Maintenance
Action Center	Family Safety	
RemoteApp and Desktop Connections*		
Troubleshooting		
Devices and Printers		
Sync Center		

* RemoteApp and Desktop Connections can be used to access a computer such as a workplace computer from a remote place. The configuration requires a URL from the network administrator to make this connection.

Configuring Windows

Technicians must frequently interact with the operating system when adding new hardware and software. Windows has specific tools for these functions. Using the correct procedure is essential for success. The following sections highlight tasks a technician commonly performs:

> Adding devices
> Removing hardware components
> Adding a printer
> Installing/removing software

Hardware devices are physical components that connect to the computer. A **device driver** is a piece of software that enables hardware to work with a specific operating system. Device drivers are operating system dependent. For example, a printer driver that works with Windows 7 may not work with Windows 10. Not all manufacturers provide updates for the newer operating systems. Some device drivers are automatically included with Windows and are updated continuously through Windows updates. A technician must be aware of what hardware is installed on a system so that the latest compatible drivers can be downloaded and installed.

CHAPTER 16

Adding Devices

Technicians are constantly adding devices to computers. Many devices today are plug-and-play devices that are designed to automatically be recognized by the operating system. Devices that use USB, eSATAp, Thunderbolt, and IEEE 1394 can be added or removed with power applied. Adapters are installed and removed with the computer powered off and the power cord removed. Let's look into some of the Windows tools used when adding devices.

Devices and Printers Control Panel Utility

The **Devices and Printers** Control Panel utility is used to view, install, remove, and manage wired and wireless devices such as mice, multimedia devices, printers, and speakers. When a device is added, Windows 8 and 10 search the Windows Store to see if there is an app from the device manufacturer, whereas Windows 7 simply defaults to searching for a driver. If an installed device isn't detected, use the *Add a Device* or *Add a Printer* link to initiate the process.

Device Manager

Devices that are recognized or at least sensed by the OS are shown in a **Device Manager** utility (see Figure 16.11). Device Manager is a technician's best friend when it comes to adding and troubleshooting devices on a Windows computer. Once you expand a particular category, such as Network adapters (see Figure 16.11), you can look for symbols that indicate trouble. A down arrow beside an icon means the device is disabled. An exclamation point indicates a problem that is usually a resource conflict or driver issue. An "I" beside a device means that the resources for the device were manually configured.

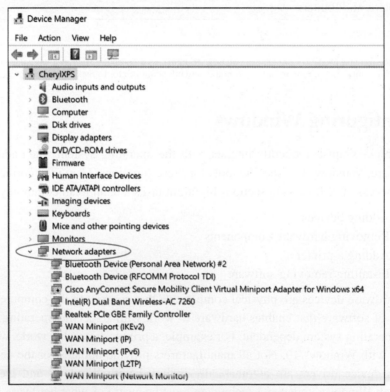

FIGURE 16.11   Device Manager in Windows 10

The keys to a successful device installation follow:

> Possessing the most up-to-date device driver for the specific installed operating system
> Following the directions provided by the device manufacturer

Windows autodetects when a new device is installed or connected and attempts to find the appropriate driver. Windows searches driver packages that are stored in an indexed database. The drivers are stored in the `Windows\System32\DriverStore\FileRepository` folder. All driver files that are not part of the operating system must be imported into this folder before the driver package can be installed. Drivers created for earlier Windows versions may need to be updated.

TECH TIP

Installing a device driver requires Administrator rights

Remember that if the operating system cannot configure a device and prompts for a device driver, you must have Administrator rights to install the driver.

Some Windows device drivers use **digital signatures**, which is sometimes called driver signing or a requiring a signed driver. The digital signature confirms that the device driver for a particular piece of hardware has met certain criteria for WHQL (Windows Hardware Quality Labs) tests and is compatible with Windows. Digital signatures are required for 64-bit kernel mode drivers in Windows. Figure 16.12 shows this concept, and Figure 16.13 shows a signed driver in Device Manager. Notice the little certificate icon to the left of the driver.

Use `verifier.exe` from a prompt to verify installed drivers especially if you have unexplained computer problems.

Use `sigverif.exe` to see signed drivers.

Microsoft

Device Driver

A signed device driver has not been altered and cannot be overwritten by another program's installation process.

FIGURE 16.12   Signed drivers

From the Windows Advanced Boot Options menu (press F8 on startup), select the *Disable Driver Signature Enforcement* option if you suspect that Windows is not booting because of an unsigned driver. The computer boots normally and not in Safe Mode.

CHAPTER 16

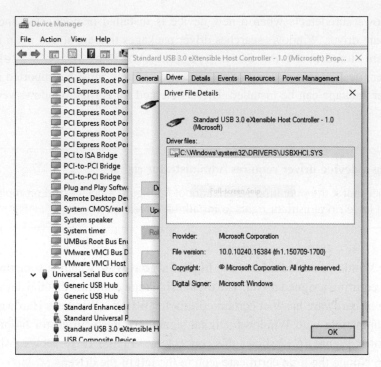

FIGURE 16.13   Signed driver in Device Manager

For Windows 7, 8, and 10, use the *System and Security* section of the Control Panel > *System* > *Advanced System Settings* link > *Hardware* tab > *Device Installation Settings* button. The options available follow:

> Yes, do this automatically (recommended)
> No, let me choose what to do
> Always install the best driver software from Windows Update
> Install driver software from Windows Update if it is not found on my computer
> Never install driver software from Windows Update

In Windows, most hardware is automatically detected. In Windows 7 there is an *Add a Device* link in the Hardware and Sound Control Panel group. This *Add a Device* link was moved to the Devices and Printers group in Windows 8 and 10.

Audio Devices

Device Manager can also help when troubleshooting sound. Locate and expand the *Sound, Video and Game Controllers* category. Verify that a sound card or integrated sound processor is shown. Right-click or tap and briefly hold on the sound card > select *Properties*. Verify the device status on the *General* tab.

The Sound section of the Control Panel is used to adjust volume output and manage sound-related devices, including speakers, headsets, microphones, and integrated audio devices. From the *Sound* section of the Control Panel, select the *Playback* tab to configure and manage headsets and speakers. Use the *Recording* tab to view the properties of and manage microphones and headset microphones. The *Sounds* tab can be used to select a sound scheme and test particular sounds. The *Communications* tab can be used to filter unwanted sounds. Refer to Chapter 8, "Multimedia Devices," for sound troubleshooting tips.

Display/Display Settings

Video settings frequently have to be adjusted because so much time is spent looking at computer output. The *Display* section of the Control Panel is used to adjust the size of text on the screen (without changing resolution), to control and configure multiple monitors, to adjust the resolution if someone has set it to a suboptimum setting, and to configure the refresh rate. Let's look at the most common settings:

> *Adjust Resolution*—**Resolution** is the number of pixels shown as a *horizontal × vertical* number, such as 1920×1080. A display's native resolution is the best resolution that it could be set to. Ensure that the correct display is chosen if multiple displays are used. Use the *Orientation* drop-down menu to select whether the display is shown as landscape or portrait. There are also landscape/portrait (flipped) options that are for displays that can be turned upside down for others to view, such as in a counselor's or salesperson's office. If a user's screen is upside down, this is where you go to change it. Adjust resolution slightly differently in the different versions of Windows:

> > Windows 7/8: Use the *Appearance and Personalization* section of the Control Panel > *Adjust Resolution* link. Use the *Resolution* drop-down menu to see the recommended resolution and resolutions that can be used.

> > Windows 10: Use *Settings* > *System* > *Resolution* drop-down menu to select a resolution and see the recommended resolution.

> *Advanced Display Settings*—Used to view the properties, memory, **refresh rate** (a value shown in hertz [Hz] that describes how long it takes a screen to be drawn in one second; note that the higher the refresh rate, the smaller the pixel/icon appears on the screen), and color settings such as the number of bits, or **color depth** (the number of bits that control color that determine the maximum number of colors that can be displayed). Sometimes this includes a *Troubleshoot* button or tab.

> *Calibrate Color*—Used to configure a display for the best color when set to its best (native) resolution.

> *Change Display Settings*—Same options as *Adjust Resolution*. This screen is also where multiple monitors can be seen and rearranged.

> *Adjust ClearType Text*—Provides a series of questions designed to make your text easier to read.

> *Custom DPI*—Used to adjust the size of text.

Troubleshooting a Device That Does Not Work or Is Not Detected

Use Device Manager to view installed hardware devices, to enable or disable devices, to troubleshoot a device, to view and/or change system resources such as IRQs and I/O addresses, to update drivers, and to access the Roll Back Driver option. The Roll Back Driver option is available in all versions of Windows. When you roll back a device driver, the older driver is reinstalled if the new driver causes the device to not start, not be detected, or not work properly.

TECH TIP

Driver rollback requires Administrator rights

You must have Administrator rights to access or use the Roll Back Driver option in Device Manager.

To access the **roll back device driver** feature, access *Device Manager* > expand the appropriate category > right-click on the hardware device > *Properties* > *Driver* tab > *Roll Back Driver* button > *OK*.

If the device driver has not been updated, driver rollback is not possible. A message screen displays this fact, and the Roll Back Driver button in Device Manager is disabled. The troubleshooting tool should be used instead to troubleshoot the device.

Sometimes, Windows installs the wrong driver for an older device or adapter. To uninstall or disable such a driver in Device Manager, right-click or tap and briefly hold the device icon and select *Disable*. Sometimes the computer must reboot, and Windows reinstalls the wrong driver. The solution to this is to disable the device and then manually install it.

Follow these steps to manually install a device:

Step 1. Open the *Device Manager* utility.

Step 2. Expand categories as needed to locate the device for which the driver is to be installed. To display hidden devices in Device Manager, select *Show Hidden Devices* from the *View* menu option.

Step 3. Right-click the device name and select *Update Driver Software*.

Step 4. Select *Browse My Computer for Driver Software*, select *Let Me Pick from a List of Device Drivers on My Computer*, and select *Have Disk*. Click the *Browse* button to locate the extracted files. Click the .inf file designed to work with the device.

Step 5. Follow the dialogs that continue to update the driver. If you are prompted with a warning about driver compatibility, you can click *No* and continue installing the driver. You can always remove it or roll back the driver if it does not install correctly or if it does not work.

If an .inf file cannot be found in a folder from your driver download, look in subfolders or other folders for the file. You could always download the driver again and pay attention to the folder name in which the driver is stored. If there are multiple .inf files in the folder, you may have to try them one at a time until you find the one that works with your hardware. Always reboot Windows after a driver installation, even if the system does not prompt for a reboot.

If you cannot install a device driver by using its installation program, you can try running the installation program in compatibility mode, using Administrator credentials, or by manually installing it using Device Manager.

To run the driver installation program in compatibility mode, locate and right-click or tap and briefly hold the executable file for the driver installation program. The same can be done for an application. Select *Properties* > *Compatibility* tab > enable the *Run This Program in Compatibility Mode For* checkbox > select a version of Windows that it is known to work on (see Figure 16.14) > click *OK*. Double-click or double-tap the executable file icon to start the installation process.

To use Administrator credentials, locate the executable file used to start the driver installation process. Right-click its filename and select *Properties* > *Compatibility* tab > enable the *Run as Administrator* checkbox, and select the particular operating system that you would want to use, as shown in the side panel of Figure 16.14. Provide the Administrator password, if required. Click *Continue*. Follow the installation instructions as normal.

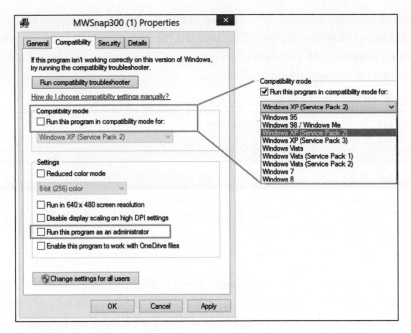

FIGURE 16.14   Installing a driver/application in compatibility mode

Too many tray icons

If any icons in the notification area are not used, remove them. In Windows 7, right-click *Start* button > *Properties* > *Notification Area* tab > *Customize* button. In Windows 8, select the up arrow in the notification area > *Customize*. In Windows 8 or 10, right-click or tap and briefly hold on an empty space in the taskbar > *Properties* > *Taskbar* tab > *Notification Area: Customize* button.

More Troubleshooting: Using Wizards and Troubleshooting Links

Whenever a yellow warning icon appears next to a device in the Devices and Printers section of the Control Panel, select *Troubleshoot* to open the Windows Troubleshooting Wizard. Windows 7 and 8 have the Windows *Action Center* section of the Control Panel that can be used to view Windows Update information, maintenance and backup issues, to access the *Troubleshooting* link to find and repair issues, and to access *Recovery* (which is System Recovery). Windows 10 no longer has the Action Center section of the Control Panel. Use the *Security and Maintenance* Control Panel to locate and use the same tools.

   You can also use the troubleshooting tool to help check for solutions to other problems. Instead of hunting through the Control Panels or Settings, use the search feature. Type `troubleshooting` in the *Search* textbox. The troubleshooting tool appears first in the output list. These Control Panel links can also be accessed through the System Configuration utility (`msconfig`) *Tools* tab.

Installing/Removing Software

Software makes a computer useful. One thing you should know about the newer Windows versions is that they may not support some of the older 16-bit software. Use the Program Compatibility Wizard or download and use the Windows XP Mode virtual environment for older applications loaded in Windows 7. Use the Hyper-V virtual environment in Windows 8 or 10 to run older applications.

Most software today is 32- or 64-bit, comes on an optical disc or is downloaded, and includes an AutoRun/AutoPlay feature. If the disc has the AutoRun feature, an installation wizard steps you through installing the software when the disc is inserted into the drive. Table 16.10 shows common locations for 32- and 64-bit applications.

TABLE 16.10   Default locations for 32- and 64-bit files

Folder	Description
System32	Used for 64-bit Windows system files
Program Files	Used for 64-bit application files
SysWOW64	Used for 32-bit Windows system files (Note that the WOW in the folder name stands for Windows 32-bit on Windows 64-bit.)
Program Files (x86)	Used for 32-bit application files

The Programs section of the Control Panel is used to add and remove applications. This Control Panel utility is also used to configure which programs are the default programs such as for email or a web browser. Desktop gadgets in the Windows 7 Aero environment can be customized from here as well.

TECH TIP

Launch an application

After an application is installed, launch the application by clicking the *Start* button > *All Programs* (*All Apps* in Windows 10) or select the icon for the application (Windows 8) > locate the application name and click it.

Before installing an application, you need to make sure the application meets all **system requirements** (the minimum hardware and software). You should look out for the following, keeping in mind that these concepts relate to all operating systems, including Windows, Linux, and macOS:

> *Drive space*—Does the storage device that will be used to hold the application and files generated by the application have enough room? Do you need to remove some applications first, back up old files and delete them, or delete unwanted files?

> *RAM*—Does the computer have enough RAM for the application, knowing that the minimum might not provide the performance the customer wants?

> *OS requirements*—Is the application 32-bit or 64-bit? If 64-bit, is the computer the application is being installed to 64-bit? If not, the application will not run.

> *Compatibility*—Is the application compatible with the type of computer being installed on? Does it require a Windows, Mac, or Linux machine?

An application can be installed to a computer using a local method of installing, such as by using a CD/DVD/Blu-Ray disc or an application downloaded from the Internet and then installed. Otherwise, a network-based method can be used, with the application installed from a network server or from a shared folder on the network. When installing an application, other considerations also have to be taken into account:

> What local security permissions need to be assigned? Chapter 18, "Computer and Network Security," covers how to make these assignments.

> Which files or folders are needed to install the application? Do the users need access to do it themselves, or does just the technician who will install it need access?
> What are other security considerations are important? What impact does the application have on the computer or network?
> What other devices might be needed as a result of having access to this application? Is a printer, plotter, digitizer, second monitor, or some other device needed?

Synchronization

Synchronization is the process of keeping things together or the same. Windows 7 has a **Sync Center** Control Panel utility that can be used to synchronize files, for example. If a file on one computer has been changed and the same file is on another computer, then the latest version of the file is put on whichever computer needs it. Even if a computer is not connected to the network, you can work on a file and then, when the computer connects, the file is updated (as long as it is not open). If the file is open on one machine and another computer is modifying the file, a conflict might occur. There is a *Resolve* option to help with this situation. Now, file synchronization is done with a cloud solution such as Microsoft's OneDrive.

Windows 8 and 10 have a synchronization feature configured through *Settings > Accounts > Sync Your Settings*. This synchronization is about the look and feel of your Windows working environment and having it the same on all devices you use. You can sync things like the computer theme, language preferences, and Ease of Access settings.

Programs and Features

The *Programs and Features* Control Panel utility is the most commonly used subcategory under Programs because it is used to uninstall an application, view the version of a particular application, and access the *Program Compatibility* option to execute programs written for older Windows versions. The *Turn Features On or Off* link is used to enable or disable Windows features such as Hyper-V, PowerShell, Microsoft Print to PDF, Games, Telnet, TFTP server, or TFTP client. Use the *Installed Updates* link to see when any application or Windows updates were installed and to see the specific update number.

Figure 16.15 shows the *Uninstall or Change a Program* link and displays all the currently installed applications on a Windows 10 computer. This link can do more than be used to uninstall an application. Select an application, and up to three options appear at the top of the column as actions that can be taken: Uninstall, Change, or Repair. From Windows 10, you can also use the *Programs and Features* section of the Control Panel or the *Apps & Features* setting, with which you click on an app and select *Modify* or *Uninstall*.

Figure 16.16 shows the Windows 10 *Turn Windows Features On or Off* window. A check in a feature's checkbox means that feature is enabled. A cleared checkbox means that option is not turned on.

TECH TIP

Application misbehavior

To **repair an application** that is not working or not working properly, select the application in the *Programs and Features* section of the Control Panel > select *Repair*.

CHAPTER 16

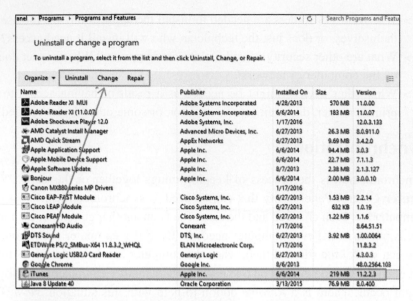

FIGURE 16.15 *Programs and Features* section of the Control Panel > *Uninstall a Program* window

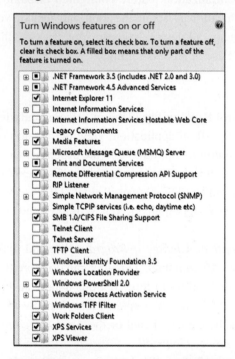

FIGURE 16.16 *Programs and Features* section of the Control Panel > *Turn Windows Features On or Off* window

The *View Installed Updates* window allows you to see updates for specific applications. For example, Figure 16.17 shows the Adobe Reader and Microsoft Windows updates. Select a particular update, and the *Uninstall* option appears at the top, as shown in the figure. Select *Uninstall* to uninstall a particular update that may be causing issues.

Refer to Figure 16.14 to see the compatibility options. If an application or executable used to install a device driver displays a message that the software is incompatible with the current operating system, use this tab to make it work.

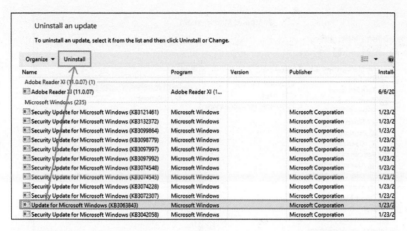

FIGURE 16.17 *Programs and Features* section of the Control Panel > *View Installed Updates* window

Another software-related issue involves dynamic link libraries (DLLs). DLL files contain reusable code that can be used by multiple applications. A DLL must be registered with the Windows registry to function. Sometimes, DLL registry links are broken, and the DLLs must be reregistered using the **regsvr32.exe** command. You might also have to remove and then reinstall a particular application to fix a particular DLL. Microsoft has a database of DLLs to help with DLL version conflicts.

Computer Management Console

The **Microsoft Management Console** holds snap-ins, which are tools that are used to maintain a computer. Open this tool by using the **mmc** command or searching for **mmc** in the search textbox. Microsoft makes use of the Microsoft Management Console with the **Computer Management** console, the mother lode of technical tools for an IT technician. You can start the Microsoft Management Console and open a saved console by using the mmc   path\filename.msc command.

The three major tool categories are System Tools, Storage, and Services and Applications. Expand the System Tools section to see some of the most technical utilities available to a technician. Expand the Storage section to find the Disk Management utility. The expanded Services and Applications section shows access to Services and WMI Control. Access the Computer Management console by using one of the following methods.

> *System and Security* section of the Control Panel > *Administrative Tools* > *Computer Management*.
> Use the search textbox to search for **computer management** or **compmgmt**.
> Make selections as follows, depending on the version of Windows:
>> Windows 7: In Windows Explorer, right-click on *Computer* > *Manage*.
>> Windows 8/8.1: Move the pointer to the bottom-right corner to access the charm bar > *Settings* > *Tiles* > set *Show Administrative Tools* to *Yes*.
>> Windows 8.1/10: *Start* button > *Windows Administrative Tools* > *Computer Management*

Figure 16.18 shows the Computer Management console. The Computer Management console allows a technician to manage shared folders and drives, start and stop services, look at performance logs and system alerts, and access Device Manager to troubleshoot hardware problems.

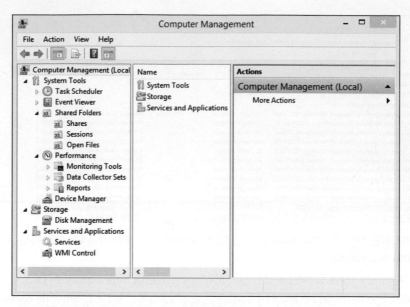

FIGURE 16.18   Computer Management console

Using Component Services?

You can use a particular snap-in called **Component Services** to view, configure, and administer the Component Object Model (COM) components, COM+ applications, and Distribution Transaction Coordinator (DTC). COM applications are a group of components within applications that were designed to work together. When deployed, Component Services can be used to track services and assess performance measures.

System Tools

The System Tools section includes Task Scheduler, Event Viewer, Shared Folders, Local Users and Groups, Performance, and Device Manager. Each of these tools is important when supporting Windows computers. Let's dive into each one.

Task Scheduler

Task Scheduler (taskschd.msc) enables you to plan and execute apps, scripts, and utilities on a regular basis. Use the Actions pane to create a new task, show what tasks are running, and import a task from another machine (see Figure 16.19). If a company has an executable it wants to run at 2 a.m. every week on Wednesday or when a user logs on every time, Task Scheduler is the tool to use.

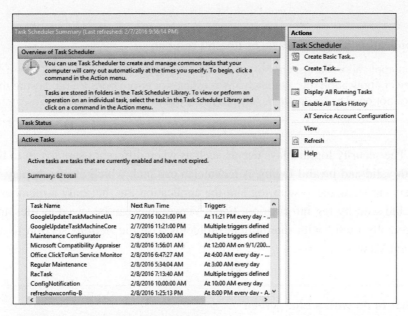

FIGURE 16.19   Task Scheduler

Event Viewer

Logs are created every time something happens in a Windows system, and Event Viewer is what you use to see them (see Figure 16.20). **Event Viewer** is a Windows tool used to monitor various events on your computer such as when a driver or service does not start properly. The Windows Event Log service starts automatically every time a computer boots to Windows. This service allows the events to be logged, and then Event Viewer is used to see the log.

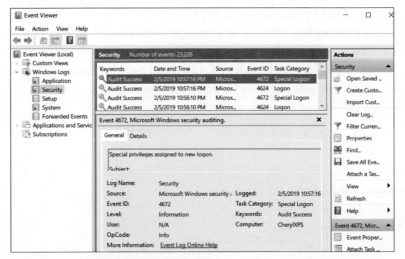

FIGURE 16.20   Event Viewer

Access Event Viewer by selecting the *System and Security* Control Panel > *Administrative Tools* > *Event Viewer*. The application log displays events associated with a specific program. The programmers who design software decide which events to display in Event Viewer's application log.

Application hangs, crashes, or doesn't respond

If an application hangs, crashes, or shows a "not responding" message, take a look at the Event Viewer application log. Research any messages or error codes found. Ensure that the application does not need to be updated. Any proprietary crash screens should be researched in Event Viewer.

The security log displays events such as when different users log in to the computer, including both valid and invalid logins. A technician can pick which events display in the security log. All users can view the system log and the application log, but only a member of Administrators can enable security log information. Event Viewer logs can be saved as files and viewed later. This is especially useful with intermittent problems. Use the *Actions* section to save and retrieve saved Event Viewer log files.

What to do with a blue screen

Sometimes when Windows crashes, a **blue screen** with an error code and numbers appears on the screen. Check the Event Viewer for a system event. Try to reboot with the power button; this may require you to remove the computer's power cord, reinsert the power cord, and once again power on the computer. When the computer has been restarted, you can research the error message and problem on the Internet.

The most commonly used log is the system log. The system log displays events that deal with various system components such as drivers or services that load during startup. The type of system log events cannot be changed or deleted.

Access **system log** errors whenever you want detailed information about Windows-controlled events; look at the **application log** errors when troubleshooting a particular program. Figure 16.21 shows the filters applied to see all system events. Figure 16.22 shows the results. Notice in Figure 16.22 that you can select a particular event. The *General* tab shows the gist of the error. Select the *Details* tab for even more details.

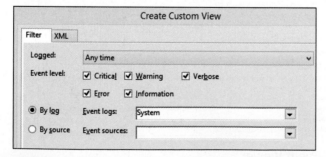

FIGURE 16.21   Event Viewer filter

Windows Event Viewer has two types of logs: (1) Windows logs and (2) applications and services logs. In the Windows Logs section, there are the traditional application, security, and system logs, along with two new ones: setup and forwarded events. Also, there is a new Applications and Services Logs section. Table 16.11 summarizes the types of things you might see in these logs. Event Viewer can display five different types of events. The events and related symbols are shown in Table 16.12.

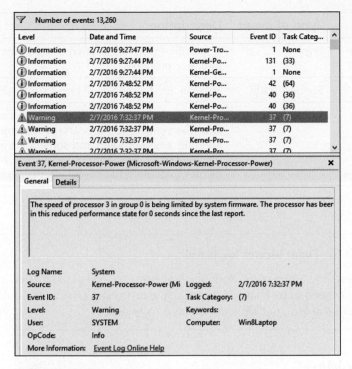

FIGURE 16.22 Event Viewer filter results

TABLE 16.11 Windows Event Viewer logs

Major log category	Log	Description
Windows logs	Application	Contains events logged by software applications. The company that writes the software applications decides what to log.
	Security	Contains events specified by administrators, such as valid and invalid logon attempts and network share usage.
	Setup	Contains setup events logged by software applications.
	System	Contains Windows system events such as when a driver or service fails to load or start.
	Forwarded events	Contains events from remote computers.
Applications and services logs	Vendor specific	Contains logs from a specific application or Windows component. The logs can be one of four types: admin, operational, analytic, and debug. The admin log is for normal users and technical support staff. The operational log is used by technical staff to analyze a problem. The analytic and debug logs would likely be used by the application developer; both of these logs create a large number of entries and should be used for a short period of time only.

TABLE 16.12 Event Viewer symbols

Symbol	Type of event	Description
Lowercase "i"	Information	Normal system operations, such as the system being initialized or shut down.
Exclamation point	Warning	An event that is not critical but that you might want to take a look at. The system can still function, but some features may not be available.

Symbol	Type of event	Description
X	Error	A specific event failed, such as a service or device failing to initialize properly.
Yellow key	Success audit	You can audit a specific event. If successful, this symbol appears.
Yellow lock	Failure audit	When you specify a specific event to audit and the event fails, the yellow lock appears. An example is when you are auditing a system login and someone tries to log in without having a valid username or password; in this case, the system creates a failure audit event.

TECH TIP

What to do if the Event Viewer log is full

Start *Event Viewer* > *Action* menu option > *Properties* > *General* tab > *Clear Log* button. The *Log Size* option may need to be changed to one of the following: *Overwrite Events Older Than 0 Days, Maximum Log Size,* or *Overwrite Events as Needed.*

Shared Folders

The **Shared Folders** tool is used to view shares, sessions, and open files. **Shares** can be folders that have been shared on the computer, printers, or a network resource such as a scanner. *Sessions* list network users who are currently connected to the computer as well as the network users' computer names, the network connection type (Windows or Apple Macs, for example), how many resources have been opened by the network user, how long the user has been connected, and whether this user is connected using the Guest user account. *Open Files* are files that are currently open by network users.

In the left Computer Management window pane, expand the *Shared Folders* option and click the *Shares* option. The network shares appear in the right pane. Double-click any of the shares to view the Properties window. From this window, using the *Share Permissions* or *Security* tabs, permissions can be set for shared resources. Permissions are covered later in this chapter.

User Account Management

User account management in Windows is an important function for a technician and involves creating accounts, managing accounts, and putting people into groups that are used in different situations. Windows 7, 8, 8.1, and 10 store information credentials for Windows and web accounts. You can make configuration changes by using the *User Accounts* Control Panel.

Credential Manager

Have you ever gone to a website or accessed a remote computer and been asked if you want your username and password saved? If you agree to this request while using a Windows computer, your information is saved using Credential Manager. **Credential Manager** is where Windows stores login credentials. You can back up Windows credentials in case the computer crashes and also view or remove forgotten or old credentials. Information stored in Credential Manager can be used by Windows and other applications and can be of several varieties:

> *Windows credentials* Windows services use Windows credentials when you access a spe cific computer or server with a username and password.

> *Certificate-based credentials*—Certificate-based credentials are mainly used in complex business network environments with smart cards.

> *Generic credentials*—Apps such as Microsoft Office, Microsoft Live products, OneDrive, and Xbox Live use generic credentials. Websites that require usernames and password also use generic credentials.

> *Web credentials*—Web credentials include username and password information stored by Windows 8 or 10 for specific websites. Your machine might store your web credentials for logging in to the main portal where you work, a gaming website, email, and shopping sites. Web credentials are also used for password reset links.

TECH TIP

Stored credentials pose a security risk

Storing usernames and passwords saves all of us time. If someone gains access to your computer, however, he or she can quickly use *Back Up Vault* (Windows 7) or *Back Up Credentials* (Windows 8 or 10) to save all your credentials to the cloud or removable media and then use that information from another computer to access accounts.

To open Credential Manager in Windows 7, use the *User Accounts and Family Safety* Control Panel > *Credential Manager*. In Windows 8, 8.1, or 10, use the *User Accounts* Control Panel and select *Credential Manager*, as shown in Figure 16.23. You can also locate Credential Manager by using *Search*. Windows 7 does not have web credentials but does have Credential Manager (see Figure 16.24).

FIGURE 16.23 Credential Manager in Windows 10

Navigating Stored Windows Credentials

In Windows 8, 8.1, and 10 the Credential Manager Control Panel utility shows credentials a little differently than Windows 7. Notice in Figure 16.25 that there are two sections: Web Credentials and Windows Credentials.

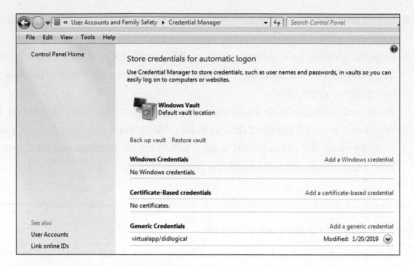

FIGURE 16.24   Credential Manager in Windows 7

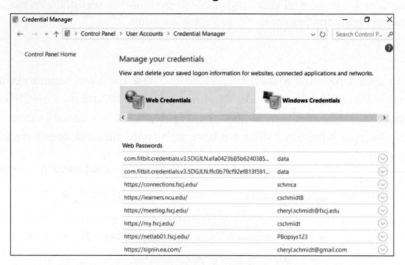

FIGURE 16.25   Credential Manager in Windows 8 and 10

How to Add Credentials to Windows

As a technician, you might find that you need to manually add a credential so Windows can use it. To do this, locate the area that contains the specific type of credential and click *Add a Windows Credential*, *Add a Certificate-Based Credential*, or *Add a Generic Credential*. For example, Figure 16.26 shows the link to use if you want to add a Windows credential.

Before adding the information to Windows Credential Manager, you should access the server, network device, network share, or website and verify the username and password. Then you can enter that information into the appropriate textboxes, as shown in Figure 16.27.

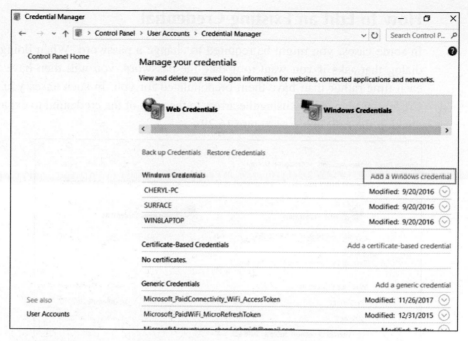

FIGURE 16.26 Adding a Windows credential, step 1

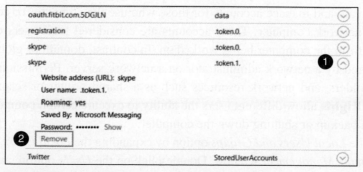

FIGURE 16.27 Adding a Windows credential, step 2

How to Remove a Credential from Windows

If you want to remove a specific credential, such as when you see one that you do not recognize or that you no longer use, click the arrow associated with that credential to expand the section. Then click the *Remove from Vault* (Windows 7) or *Remove* (Windows 8, 8.1, or 10) link, as shown in Figure 16.28.

FIGURE 16.28 Deleting a credential

How to Edit an Existing Credential

In some cases, you might be required to change a password. When doing so, if you decline the dialog that asks if you want to update the password, you will then have to type the credentials each time rather than have them prepopulated for you. In such cases you can edit credentials in Credential Manager by using the arrow to the right of the credential to expand the section and then clicking the *Edit* link (see Figure 16.29).

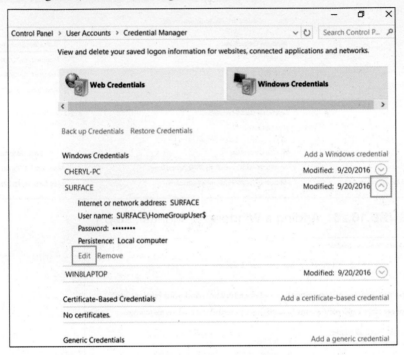

FIGURE 16.29   Editing a credential, step 1

TECH TIP

Use the specific application to change the credentials

Not all applications respond well to editing credentials within Credential Manager. Be especially cautious when editing credentials used to access virtual machines.

Local Users and Groups

The **Local Users and Groups** tool is available only in Windows Professional/Pro versions. It is used to create and manage accounts for those who use the computer or computer resources from a remote network computer. These accounts are considered local users or local groups and are managed from the computer being worked on. In contrast, domain or global users and groups are administered by a network administrator on a network server. Permissions are granted or denied to files, folders, and network resources such as a shared printer or scanner. Rights can also be assigned. **Rights** allow different users the ability to execute certain computer actions such as performing a backup or shutting down the computer.

Open the *Local Users and Groups* option by expanding the *Local Users and Groups* selection in the *Computer Management* window. Double-click on the *Users* option, and a list of current users displays in the right pane. Figure 16.30 shows an example of local users that have been created for a Windows 8 computer.

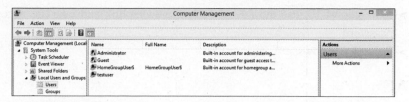

FIGURE 16.30 Local users and groups

Notice in Figure 16.30 that the Guest account has a small down arrow in the lower-right corner of its icon. This means the account has been disabled. Double-click the *Guest* icon. Look at the *Account Is Disabled* checkbox to see if the account is disabled. The box is checked by default, meaning that the Guest account is not available for use. To create a new user, click the *Action* menu option and select *New User*.

TECH TIP

Where are the local user settings?

Windows local user settings are found in the following folder: `%userprofile%\AppData\Local` (for example, `C:\Users\Cheryl\AppData\Local`). You might have to enable *Show Hidden Files* in Windows Explorer/File Explorer to see the *AppData* folder.

Windows has two basic types of user accounts available in the different Windows editions: Standard user and Administrator. The **Administrator** account has full control over the system, as it always has in Windows. By default, a **Standard user** account cannot install most applications or change system settings. Every user on the computer should have a Standard user account that is used for everyday use. Any account designated as an Administrator account should be used only to log on to the system to make system changes and install new software.

In the Windows Professional/Pro and higher versions, there are other types of user accounts that can be used for various security levels. These user groups are covered elsewhere, but one user group that should be mentioned here is Power Users. In older Windows versions (Windows XP and earlier), users who were in the Power Users group had elevated permissions to perform common configuration tasks such as changing user-related Control Panel settings and changing the time zone. Today, the Standard user group has most of these permissions.

Account Recovery Options: Local Account

Windows 8 and 10 support using a Microsoft account as a login or a local account. Windows **account recovery options** are limited for security reasons. You should always have a backup account that is an Administrator account on a local (workgroup) computer. Here are some other ways that you can recover a Windows user account:

> Use the Windows 7 password reset disk that was previously created.
> Have someone who has an Administrator account log into Windows and reset your password for you.
> If you use your Microsoft account, go online and use Microsoft tools to reset that password.
> Boot from a Windows installation disk, boot to a command prompt, and use the `net user` command to create an Administrator account. You will have to do research on this one.
> If there are accidentally no users with Administrator rights, boot the computer into Safe Mode and change one of the accounts to an Administrator account type.

> In Windows 10, use the *I Forgot My Password* link and take the necessary steps to reset the password.
> Reload Windows.

UAC

The Administrator and Standard user accounts are affected by a feature in Windows called User Account Control (**UAC**). UAC works with Internet Explorer/Edge, Windows Defender, and Parental Controls to provide heightened awareness of security issues. A UAC message appears any time something occurs that normally would require an administrator-level decision to make changes to the system. An application that has a security shield icon overlay is going to display a UAC prompt when executed. If a Standard user is logged in, a message appears, stating that the task is prohibited, access is denied, or Administrator credentials must be provided in order to proceed (see Figure 16.31). UAC is meant to protect users from themselves as well as from software that tries to change the system. Even if a person is logged in with an Administrator account, the UAC prompt appears to confirm the action that is about to be performed.

FIGURE 16.31 Administrator credentials required

The following configurations help with UAC:

> To configure a specific application to run in an elevated mode—meaning it has the Administrator access token given to it or permission given to it to run—right-click the application and select *Properties* > *Compatibility* tab > under Privilege Level select *Run This Program as Administrator* > *OK*.
> If a user demands that UAC be disabled, use the System Configuration window (`msconfig`) *Tools* tab. Select *Change UAC Settings*. Also, an individual account can be changed through the *Change User Account Control Settings* link from within the *User Accounts* Control Panel. Figure 16.32 shows this in Windows 10.

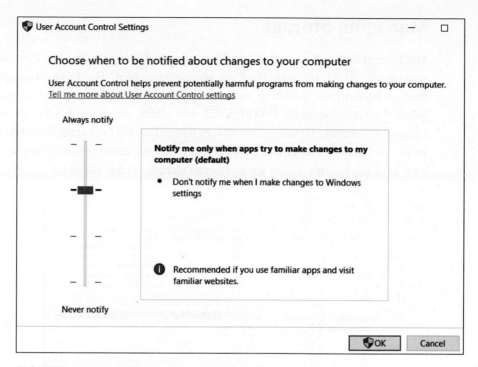

FIGURE 16.32   UAC configuration in Windows 10

Device Manager

Device Manager is introduced in the "Adding Devices" section, earlier in this chapter. Device Manager is used after installing a new hardware device to verify that Windows recognizes the device. Device Manager is also used to change or view hardware configuration settings, view and install device drivers, return (roll back) to a previous device driver version, disable/enable/uninstall devices, and print a summary of all hardware installed.

To verify that a device is working properly, expand a Device Manager section. Double-click or double-tap, and a device's *Properties* window appears. The *General* tab displays a message saying whether the device is working, according to Windows. The number of tabs a device has depends on the device. Figure 16.33 shows the Device Manager window > *General* tab as well as the *Driver* tab for a USB mouse. The *Driver* tab is used to roll back the driver if an updated driver is installed and does not function properly. It also shows the current driver version. The *Driver* tab can be used to disable the device and uninstall the device driver.

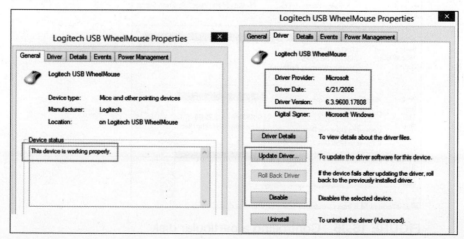

FIGURE 16.33   *Device Manager* > *General* and *Driver* tabs

Managing Storage

Mechanical hard drives and SSDs can be managed using the Storage Computer Management console option, which includes the Disk Management tool. The **Disk Management** tool is used to manage hard drives, including volumes or partitions. With it you can initialize drives; create volumes; format volumes for FAT, FAT32, and NTFS; configure RAID; and manage remote drives. Chapter 7, "Storage Devices," introduces this utility, but let's review the basics again. Figure 16.34 shows the Disk Management utility. Notice that the drive volumes display in the top window as well as at the bottom. Disks are numbered starting with 0 (Disk 0).

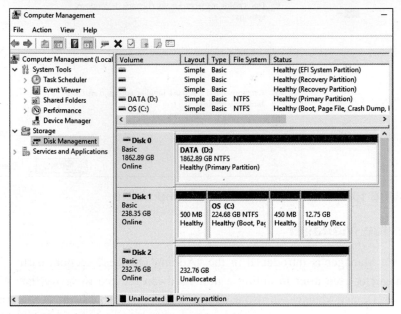

FIGURE 16.34   Disk Management utility

Figure 16.35 shows that you can right-click or tap and briefly hold on a particular drive on the far left to control the drive from there. The menu shown is for a drive that is already in use and online. If a drive shows a **drive status** other than online, actions can be taken from the context menu.

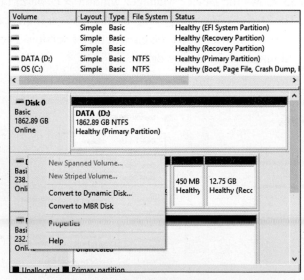

FIGURE 16.35   Controlling a particular disk

Figure 16.36 shows the context menu if you right-click or tap and briefly hold within a disk arrow, such as within the slanted lines of the D: drive (Drive 0). Notice that you can delete, extend, or shrink a volume. You can also change the drive letter. Table 16.13 shows common tasks done within the Disk Management tool.

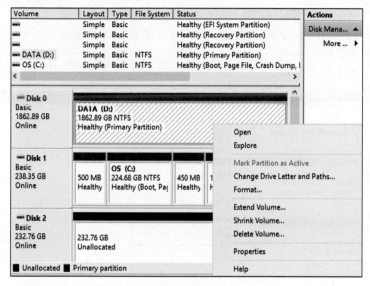

FIGURE 16.36   Managing an existing disk

TABLE 16.13   Disk Management tasks

Task	Description
Mounting	Map an empty folder on an NTFS volume by right-clicking on a partition or volume > *Change Drive Letter and Paths* > *Add* > *Mount in the Following Empty NTFS Folder* and either type the path or browse to an empty folder > *OK* > *OK*.
Initializing	Make a drive available to be used by right-clicking on a drive > *Initialize Disk*.
Extending partition	Increase the size of a partition by right-clicking on the drive letter > *Extend Volume*.
Splitting partition	To divide space on a hard drive or make one partition smaller, right-click the drive > *Shrink Volume*. Then create a new partition with the relinquished drive space.
Shrink partition	Decrease the size of the partition by right-clicking on the drive letter > *Shrink Volume*.
Assigning/changing drive letter	Right-click on a drive volume > *Change Drive Letter and Paths*.
Adding drive	Ensure that the drive is recognized by the BIOS and then create a partition and format for a particular file system.
Adding array	Right-click inside unallocated space of a drive > *New Spanned Volume* or *New Striped Volume*, select another drive to be added, select a drive letter and file system.

Figure 16.37 shows the commands available if you right-click or tap and briefly hold inside the unallocated space in Disk 2. Because the disk is currently a basic disk, only a simple volume can

be created. When you create a volume, you are prompted to select a file system as well as assign a drive letter. See Chapter 7 for more information on volumes and partitions.

All Windows disk management tools require Administrator rights

You must be a member of the Administrators group to perform any disk management tasks.

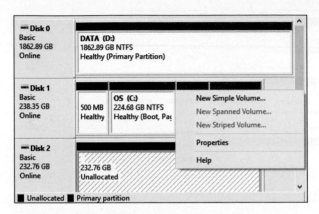

FIGURE 16.37 Managing drive space on a new drive

Storage Spaces

Another Control Panel utility that is used with disk management is Storage Spaces. The **Storage Spaces** Control Panel is used for data storage using two or more drives that the operating system sees as one drive. The unusual thing about Windows Storage Spaces is that the drives can be different types of drives; for example, an eSATA drive and a USB flash drive can be used to create a virtual disk that is seen as one drive. A logical drive created through Storage Spaces is formatted for either the NTFS or ReFS file system. Note that if you use drives in a logical drive created through Storage Spaces, each of those drives cannot be given an individual drive letter.

Step 1. From the *Storage Spaces* Control Panel, select the *Create a New Pool and Storage Space* link.

Step 2. Ensure that at least two drives that you want to use for the virtual drive created using Storage Spaces are attached. Select the drives by clicking in the checkbox beside the drives to be used. Note that any existing files on that drive will be erased and cannot be recovered.

Step 3. Click the *Create Pool* button.

Step 4. Name the storage space and select the drive letter, file system, resiliency type, and pool size > select *Create Storage Space*.

Use the *Change Settings* button within the *Storage Spaces* Control Panel to manage or modify a logical drive.

Disk Maintenance

Mechanical hard drives get sluggish over time. The good news is that disk management and maintenance are now done for you automatically in Windows 7, 8, 8.1, and 10. Let's look at the tools that are available to keep mechanical drives running smoothly.

Right-click or tap and briefly hold a drive letter in Windows Explorer/File Explorer > select *Properties*. On the *General* tab, you can access the **Disk Cleanup** tool (`cleanmgr /d drive`, for example), which scans the drive volume to see what files could potentially be deleted.

The *Tools* tab provides access to two additional tools: Error Checking and Optimize and Defragment Drive. The **Error Checking** tool is extremely important to Windows 7. The tool checks the drive for file system errors, bad hard drive sectors, and lost clusters. Error Checking is the equivalent of running the `chkdsk` command.

Windows 8 and 10 do not need to have the drive checked as often because certain disk errors are fixed immediately and do not need a utility executed to make that happen. In Windows 8, 8.1, and 10, Microsoft integrated some of the new features of the Resilient File System (ReFS). **ReFS** is expected to eventually replace NTFS as the file system used on Microsoft Windows systems, but at the time of press, ReFS volumes cannot be used to boot the system.

With a mechanical drive, **defragment the hard drive** to get better drive performance after you have used the Error Checking tool or used the `chkdsk` command. The **Optimize and Defragment** *drives* tool (Defragment button or `defrag` command), is used to place files in contiguous clusters on the hard drive. Files and folders become fragmented due to file creation and deletion over a period of time. A defragmented volume provides better performance than a volume with files and folders located throughout the drive. Microsoft automatically runs a defragment operation once a week, but you can always defragment the drive volume manually. You can also use the *Action Center* section of the Control Panel (Windows 7) to view the drive status quickly. If a drive status shows as anything but healthy, run a scan or repair the drive status.

> **TECH TIP**
>
> **Defragmentation requires Administrator rights**
>
> Note that only a member of the Administrators group can defragment a hard drive.

In Windows 7, you might want to schedule disk cleanup by using Task Scheduler. Access Task Scheduler, and from the *Action* menu, select *Create Basic Task* > name the task, select *Next* > select how often you want disk cleanup to run (the trigger). A good choice is weekly, especially if the drive has been used for a while. Depending on the frequency, you have to select other options, such as what day of the week you want the task to execute. On the *Action* menu, select the *Start a Program* radio button. In the *Program/Script* textbox, type **`cleanmgr.exe`** or browse to `C:\Windows\System32\cleanmgr.exe`. Click the *Finish* button.

In Windows 8 and 10, search for *Defragment* and select the *Defragment and Optimize Your Drives* option. Select *Change Settings*. Select the option that fits the computer user best:

> *Run on a Schedule*—Select how often the drive optimization executes.
> *Frequency*—Choose daily, weekly, or monthly. (The default is weekly and runs during automatic maintenance.)
> *Notify Me if Three Consecutive Scheduled Runs Are Missed*—Clear this checkbox if the user does not want the notification.
> *Drives*—Click the *Choose* button to select drives. Note that SSDs are not supposed to be defragmented using the drive optimization routine and should be deselected by default.

Managing Services and Applications

The *Services and Applications* section can contain a multitude of options, depending on the computer and what is loaded. Common options include Telephony, WMI Control, Services, and

Indexing Service. A frequently used option is *Services*. A **service** is an application that can be started using this window or configured so that it starts when the computer boots. By clicking the **Services** option, a list of services installed on the computer displays in the right window. Double-click or double-tap any service, and the service *Properties* window appears. From this window on the *General* tab, a service can be started, stopped, paused, resumed, or disabled on the local computer and on remote computers, but you must be logged on as a member of the Administrators group to change a service. Figure 16.38 shows the Computer Management console Services window and some examples of installed services.

If you double-click a service, you can use the *Recovery* tab to determine what happened when a service fails a first time, a second time, and even a third time. For example, if the print service fails the first time, a restart occurs. After the print service fails a second time, the print server can be restarted automatically. The third time the print service fails, a file that pages a technician can be executed.

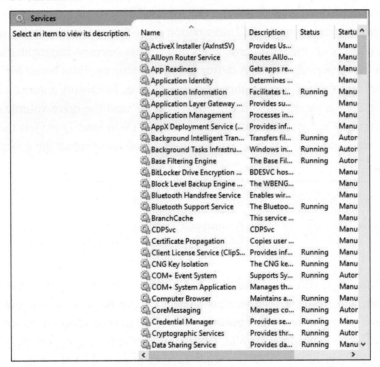

FIGURE 16.38   Computer Management console: Services window

Data Sources (ODBC)

Open database connectivity (ODBC) is a programming interface that enables applications to access data from a database. Use the **Data Sources** (ODBC) administrative tool to select which particular application drive is associated with a particular type of file. Access the *Data Sources (ODBC)* section of the Control Panel by searching for the *Administrative Tools* section of the Control Panel > double-click on *Data Sources (ODBC)*. Figure 16.39 shows the user data source name (DSN). Figure 16.40 shows the *Tracing* tab, which can be used to create logs that help when applications misbehave.

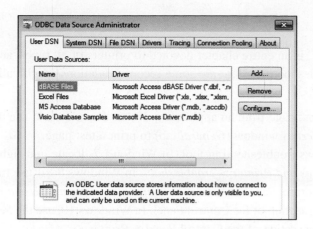

FIGURE 16.39   Data Sources (ODBC) section of the Control Panel

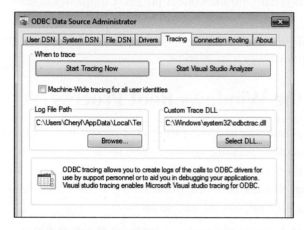

FIGURE 16.40   Data Sources (ODBC) Tracing tab

Print Management Console

The **Print Management** console is used to manage printers on Windows 7, 8, 8.1, and 10 Pro and higher versions. To access the console, use one of the following methods:

> Access the *System and Security* section of the Control Panel > select *Administrative Tools* > double-click or double-tap *Printer Management*.

> Use the `printmanagement.msc` command.

Figure 16.41 shows the Print Management console window. On the left, expand *Custom Filters* to see all the printers, all drivers, the printers that show a not ready status, and printers that currently have print jobs. On the center screen is a list of printers in a home or small business environment. In the corporate environment, there would be more; plus you could use the *Print Servers* option in the left pane.

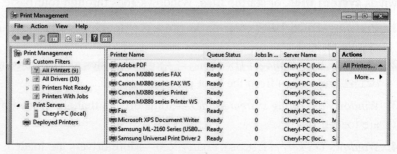

FIGURE 16.41   Print Management console

Printing Issues

Chapter 9, "Printers," is an entire chapter devoted to printers of all types, and each type has a section on printer troubleshooting. Here are some recommendations specifically related to Windows **printing issues**:

> Try printing a test page from an application. If that doesn't work, use the printer's *Properties* or *Printer Properties* window (*General* tab) to print a test page.

> Use the Windows troubleshooting tool. In Windows 7, locate and right-click on the specific printer in *Devices and Printer* > *Troubleshoot*. In Windows 8/8.1 use the *System and Security* section of the Control Panel and select *Find and Fix Problems* > *Use a Printer* from the *Hardware and Sound* section of the Control Panel. In Windows 10, use the *Search* text box to locate the *Troubleshoot* section of the Control Panel > *Printer*.

> Ensure the user is printing to the correct printer. Companies commonly have more than one network printer.

> Clear the print spooler (queue) files and restart the print spooler service from the printer's *Properties* or *Printer Properties* window.

Overview of the Windows Boot Process

When a computer boots and after executing the power-on self-test, the computer looks for an operating system. The Windows operating system can be loaded using several boot methods, and you might have to use an alternative boot method to solve a problem. Here are the most common boot methods, but remember that the boot order in a setting within BIOS/UEFI affects which one the operating system looks for first, second, and so on:

> An **internal hard drive partition** on an **internal fixed disk** that could be a hard disk drive (HDD), solid state drive (SSD), or M.2 SSD. Note that the partition must be a bootable partition.

> **Optical disc** such as a CD, DVD, or Blu-ray disc. Note that this will work only if the BIOS/UEFI boot option is configured correctly and listed before a hard drive.

> **External hard drive** such as a USB or eSATA drive. Check BIOS/UEFI boot options.

> **Network boot**, sometimes called pre-boot execution environment (**PXE**) boot, where the system boots from an image shared on the network from a server. Configure BIOS/UEFI for the appropriate setting, which might be listed as PXE, PXE Boot, Boot to Network, or LAN Boot ROM Enabled, as well as the network boot option, which might be placed before any of the other options.

The **system volume** is the active drive partition that has the files needed to load the operating system. The **boot volume** is the partition or logical drive where the operating system files are located. One thing that people sometimes forget is that the system volume and the boot volume can be on the same partition. These partitions are where certain boot files are located.

Every operating system needs specific files that allow the computer to boot. These files are known as **system files**, or startup files. Windows goes through four basic phases to get started:

1. *Preboot*—BIOS/UEFI controls the process of looking for, finding, and allowing an operating system to load.

2. *Windows boot manager* (bootmgr.exe)—Locates and executes the Windows loader (winload.exe) from the boot partition/volume.

3. *Windows operating system loader*—Some drivers that are needed by the Windows kernel are loaded.

4. *Windows OS kernel* (ntoskrnl.exe)—More drivers are loaded, services start, group and local policies are applied, and the logon screen is shown.

Table 16.14 shows the system files and their specific locations on the hard drive.

TABLE 16.14   Windows system files

Startup filename	File location
bootmgr.exe	Root directory of system partition
hal.dll	%systemroot%\System32*
ntoskrnl.exe	%systemroot%\System32*
winload.exe	%systemroot%\System32*
winresume.exe	Root directory of system partition
bcd (boot configuration data)	%systemroot%\Boot
system (registry file)	%systemroot%\System32\Config\System
winlogon.exe	%systemroot%\System32

* %systemroot% is the boot partition and the name of the folder under the folder where Windows is installed (normally C:\ Winnt or C:\Windows).

Reading about Windows files can be confusing because the file locations frequently have the entries %systemroot% and %systemdrive%. This is because computers can be partitioned differently. If you install Windows onto a drive letter (a partition or logical drive) other than the active partition (normally C:), the startup files can be on two different drive letters. Also, you do not have to take the default folder name of *Windows* to install Windows. To account for these different scenarios, Microsoft uses %systemroot% to represent the **boot partition**, the partition and folder that contains the majority of the Windows files. %systemdrive% represents the root directory. On a computer with a single operating system, this would be C:\.

TECH TIP

Installing Windows with older operating systems

Be careful about installing Windows with an older operating system. Windows overwrites the MBR, boot sector, and boot files. That is why few Windows versions are upgradable to Windows 7.

Speeding Up the Windows Boot Process

Windows can seem to take forever to boot (especially if you do not have an SSD), but there are things a technical person can do to help speed up the OS boot process (see Figure 16.42).

FIGURE 16.42   Fine-tuning the startup process

The following tips can help reduce the time Windows takes to become operational:

> Configure BIOS/UEFI boot options so that the drive used to boot Windows is listed as the first option.

> Configure BIOS/UEFI for the fast boot option or disable hardware checks.

> If multiple operating systems are installed, use the `msconfig` utility *Boot* tab to reduce the boot menu timeout value.

> Remove unnecessary startup applications using the `msconfig` utility. This links to Task Manager in Windows 8 and 10.

> Have available hard disk space and keep the drive defragmented. Note that Windows is automatically configured to defragment the hard drive at 1:00 a.m. on Wednesday. If the computer is powered off, defragmentation occurs when the computer next boots.

> Disable unused or unnecessary hardware by using Device Manager.

> Use Windows **ReadyBoost** to cache some startup files to a 256 MB+ flash drive, SD card, or CF card. Right-click the device to access the *Properties* option and select the *ReadyBoost* tab. Note that ReadyBoost does not increase performance on a system that boots from an SSD, so Windows disables ReadyBoost as an option when an SSD is in use.

> Use the *Administrative Tools* Control Panel > access *Services*. Change services that are not needed the moment Windows boots to use the *Automatic (Delayed Start)* option instead of *Automatic*.

Troubleshooting the Windows Boot Process

Troubleshooting the boot process where Windows will not load (**failure to boot**) is sometimes easier than troubleshooting other types of problems that can occur within the operating system. You can try several tools but always remember that you may need to reload the operating system. If the computer locks, has a BSOD, or will not start, try the following:

> Check the BIOS/UEFI setting to ensure that the boot order is correct.

> Remove the power cord and leave the computer powered down for one to two minutes. Then reinsert the power cord and power on the computer again. Make note of any beeps or error codes. Use these symptoms to start your troubleshooting process.

> Disconnect any unnecessary peripherals from the computer, leaving just the power and monitor connected. If the computer starts, connect peripherals one by one while restarting to see which item is causing a boot to fail.

> Let Windows attempt to repair the computer.

> Determine the last thing that was done before the computer refused to boot. If possible, boot the computer to Safe Mode. Use the System Restore utility to bring the computer back to a date before the issue occurred. The following are some questions to ask the user:
  > Did a Windows Update just occur?
  > Was an application recently installed?
  > Was any hardware added recently?
  > Did any type of application update just occur?

> If on Windows 8/8.1, use the **Refresh Your PC** tool, which installs a new copy of Windows 8 but keeps the user's data, settings, and Windows 8 apps if there is enough hard drive space to back them up.

> Windows 8, 8.1, and 10 have a **Reset This PC** option that reinstalls Windows and gives you the choice of whether you keep the files, remove everything, or, on some computers, restore to factory settings (including Windows and the apps that came with the computer when you bought it).

> Boot to Safe Mode and run the System File Checker (sfc) to replace missing or corrupt operating system files or load an appropriate graphics driver.
> Use the Last Known Good Configuration option from the Advanced Boot Options menu.

For information on recovering the Windows operating system and WinRE, see Chapter 14 and the following text. For information on troubleshooting storage devices, see Chapter 7.

Quite a few things can cause Windows to fail to boot into the graphical interface properly. For example, a nonbootable disk listed as the first boot device or media inserted into an optical drive (and it being listed as a boot device) can cause Windows not to boot. If none of the hard drives contain an active partition or if the hard drive's boot sector information is missing or corrupt, any of the following messages or events could appear:

> *Invalid Partition Table*
> *Error Loading Operating System*
> *Missing Operating System*
> BOOTMGR *Is Missing*
> *Windows Has Blocked Some Startup Programs*
> *The Windows Boot Configuration Data File Is Missing Required Information*
> *No OS found*
> *Windows Could Not Start Because the Following File Is Missing or Corrupt*

Also, if you receive a message that you have an invalid boot disk, a disk read error, or an inaccessible boot device, troubleshoot your hard drive and/or BIOS/UEFI settings.

TECH TIP

How to stop programs that automatically load at startup from running

To disable startup programs, hold down the (⬆Shift) key during the logon process and keep it held down until the desktop icons appear.

Windows has a plethora of tools and start modes that you can use to troubleshoot the system. If Windows boots but still has a problem, try to solve the problem without booting into one of these special modes. For example, if one piece of hardware is not working properly and the system boots properly, use Device Manager and the troubleshooting wizards to troubleshoot the problem. Another problem can be caused by an application that loads during startup.

If a startup problem occurs before the Starting Windows logo appears (**graphical interface fails to load**), the cause is typically missing startup files, corrupt files, or hardware problems. You can use the Windows command bootsect /nt60 all (or a drive letter instead of all if multiple operating systems are installed) to manually repair the boot sector. The bootsect.exe file is available from the *Boot* folder of the Windows DVD and can be executed from within the Windows Recovery Environment (WinRE), covered later in this chapter, or from within Windows. If the Windows logo appears but there is a problem before the logon prompt appears, the problem is usually with misconfigured drivers and/or services. If problems occur after the logon window appears, then (1) look to startup applications (hold down the (⬆Shift) key during startup) or (2) see if the userinit.exe file has issues. Use the *Advanced Boot Options* startup menu (by pressing (F8) during startup), and from a command prompt, use the sfc /scannow command to fix the userinit file.

Black Screen/Video Issues

Windows is not supposed to hang during the boot process because of video driver incompatibility. Instead, the operating system loads a default video driver. If video is a problem while working in Windows (that is, if you get a **black screen** or a blank screen), check your video power and cabling and try booting to *Safe Mode* or use the *Last Known Good Configuration* boot option and then load the correct driver. You could also use the driver rollback option if a new driver has just been installed.

To save time booting into Safe Mode, you could use the *System Configuration* (`msconfig`) tool > *Boot* tab > enable the *Base Video* checkbox > *OK* (see Figure 16.43).

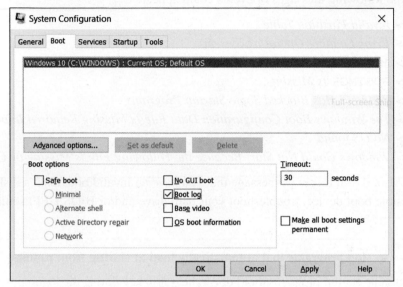

FIGURE 16.43   *System Configuration > Boot* tab

If multiple monitors are installed, another option is to verify that each monitor has power and the data cable attaches securely. Check the monitor settings to verify that the monitor detection is accurate. In Windows 7/8/8.1, use the *Display* Control Panel > *Display Settings* > *Settings* tab. In Windows 10, use the *Settings* > *System* > *Display* link.

> **TECH TIP**
>
> **Display is dark**
>
> If the display is dark, check to see whether the computer is in sleep mode or won't come out of sleep mode. Check the video cable. Hold down the power button and try restarting. Check the power management settings.

Recovery Console

The Windows Recovery Console is accessible by pressing F8 as the computer is booting or by accessing it from the Windows installation or recovery disc. You can also access it through the Advanced Boot Options menu. In Windows 7 and higher, the **Windows Recovery Environment (WinRE)** is accessed by booting from a Windows installation DVD > selecting the language parameters > *Repair Your Computer* > selecting an operating system > *Next*. Some computers have a recovery partition that is available through the Advanced Boot Options menu. See the computer documentation for details. The Windows 10 Advanced Options tools are shown in Figure 16.44 and explained in Table 16.15.

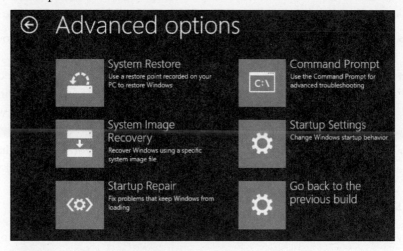

FIGURE 16.44   Windows 10 Advanced Options tools

TABLE 16.15   WinRE tools

Tool	Description
System Restore	Returns the system to an earlier time, such as before a service pack or update was installed and the system stopped booting.
System Image Recovery	Available in all versions of Windows 7 and higher to restore the contents of the hard drive from some type of backup media, such as another hard drive or DVDs.
Startup Repair	Analyzes a computer and tries to fix any missing or damaged system files or Boot Configuration Data (BCD) files. This tool can be run multiple times. After a single repair and system reboot, try the tool again (and again). The system could have multiple problems.
Command Prompt	The *Command Prompt* option allows execution of any command-line program.
Startup Settings	This option takes you to the *Startup Settings* window, which contains many of the same options available through the *Advanced Boot Options* menu that appears when you press F8 during the boot process.
Go Back to the Previous Build	This option, which is available in Windows 10, allows you to downgrade back to the original operating system that was upgraded to Windows 10. Note that this option is available only for 31 days after the Windows 10 upgrade.
Windows Memory Diagnostics	Accessed several ways: (1) from the System Recovery window from the Windows installation DVD, (2) by pressing F8 during the boot process and selecting *Repair Your Computer* > selecting from the System Recovery window, and (3) the *Command Prompt* option and using the mdsched command or through the *Administrative Tools* section of the Control Panel > *Diagnose Your Computer's* Memory Problems link. Used to heavily test RAM modules to see if they are causing the system to fail to boot. Microsoft states that it is unlikely that repeating the test will result in a newly detected error. An extended test is available from the Windows Memory Diagnostics menu.

If the computer shows *Invalid Boot Disk*, ensure that the BIOS/UEFI boot order settings are correct, no virus is installed, and that the first boot device has a valid operating system installed or on disc. Depending on the installed version, you can also use `bootrec /fixmbr` or `bootrec /fixboot`. Use other `bootrec` command options if multiple operating systems are installed. Following is a breakdown of the commands you should try after using the Startup Repair option:

> `bootrec /fixmbr`: Used to resolve MBR issues; writes a Windows-compatible MBR to the system partition.

> `bootrec /fixboot`: Used if the boot sector has been replaced with a non-Windows boot sector, if the boot sector has become corrupt, or if an earlier Windows version has been installed *after* Windows was installed and the computer was started with the `ntldr` instead of `bootmgr.exe`.

> `bootrec /scanos`: Used when any Windows operating system has been installed and is not listed on the Boot Manager menu; scans all disks for any and all versions of Windows.

System Restore

Any hardware or software installation can cause a system not to boot or to operate correctly. You can use the System Restore utility to return the system to an operable state so that you can try the installation again or determine a better method. The System Restore program makes a snapshot image of the registry and backs up certain dynamic system files. The program does not affect your email or personal data files. This program is similar to the Last Known Good Configuration Advanced Boot Options menu item but more powerful. Each snapshot is called a *restore point*, and multiple restore points are created on the computer; you can select which one to use.

In Windows 7 and 8, restore points are created weekly and whenever a system update occurs. You can manually create a restore point at any time, especially before performing an important upgrade or installation. A fixed amount of disk space is used for restore points. When a new restore point is created, the oldest one is removed automatically. System Restore is your number-one tool for solving problems within the operating system and registry. In Windows 10, System Restore is disabled by default. The *System* Control Panel > **System Protection** tab is used to set up and configure System Restore, manage restore points, and manage the amount of disk space used for System Restore. To verify whether it is on or not, use the following steps:

Step 1. Access the *System* section of the Control Panel > *System Protection* link.

Step 2. Access the *System Protection* tab > look in the *Protection Settings* window to see if the system drive (C:) shows *On* in the *Protection* column.

If System Restore is turned off, you can use the following steps to turn it on:

Step 1. Access the *System* section of the Control Panel > *System Protection* link.

Step 2. Access the *System Protection* tab > in the *Protection Settings* window locate and select the system drive (`C:`).

Step 3. Click *Configure* > enable the *Turn On System Protection* radio button > set the amount of disk space to be used > *OK*.

TECH TIP

BSOD after a Windows update

Always research the error code associated with a failed update. Windows updates include device driver updates. If the computer fails to boot after a Windows update, reboot the computer to WinRE Safe Mode and use the System Restore tool to restore the registry to an earlier time so that the problem can be researched. If multiple updates were installed, try loading the updates one at a time.

Use System Restore if you suspect that the registry is corrupt. For example, if an application worked fine yesterday but today displays a message that the application cannot be found, you may have a virus, a corrupt application executable file, or a corrupt registry. Run an antivirus check first with updated virus definitions. If free of viruses, use the System Restore utility to roll back the system to yesterday or the day before this problem occurred. Sometimes System Restore works best if executed from Safe Mode. If System Restore does not fix the problem, reinstall the application.

System Restore requires the NTFS file system. Windows uses **Shadow Copy** technology, which employs a block-level image instead of monitoring certain files for file changes. Backup media can be optical discs, flash devices, other hard drives, and server storage but not tape.

Access the window to configure System Restore by searching for the *System* section of the Control Panel > *System Protection* link > *System Protection* tab. Figure 16.45 shows how you can select a specific date during the System Restore process. You can also select the *Show More Restore Points* checkbox at the bottom of the window to see more of them.

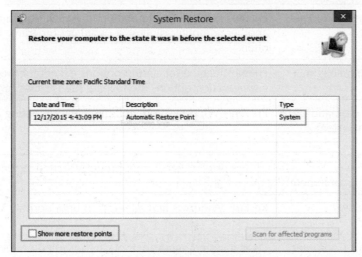

FIGURE 16.45   Windows System Restore

TECH TIP

You can run System Restore from a command prompt

If Windows does not load properly, you can execute System Restore from a command prompt with the command `%systemroot%\system32\rstrui.exe`.

Advanced Boot Options/Startup Settings Menu

When Windows does not boot properly, you can use the Windows **Advanced Boot Options** menu. Tools that troubleshoot Windows boot problems include Last Known Good Configuration, Safe Mode, Windows Recovery Environment, and Startup Repair. Table 16.16 briefly describes these options. Note that the options available vary depending on the version of Windows used.

TECH TIP

Press F8 during startup

When Windows is booting, press F8 to access the Windows Advanced Boot Options menu.

CHAPTER 16

TABLE 16.16   Windows Advanced Boot Options window

Boot option	Description
Safe Mode	Uses a minimum set of drivers and services to start Windows; a commonly used option.
Safe Mode with Networking	Same as Safe Mode but includes a NIC driver.
Safe Mode with Command Prompt	Same as Safe Mode except Windows Explorer (GUI mode) is not used; instead, a command prompt appears. This option is not used often.
Enable Low-Resolution Video (640×480)	Used when Safe Mode does not work and you suspect that the default video driver is not working.
Last Known Good Configuration	A popular option used when a change that was just implemented caused the system to not boot properly.
Debugging Mode	Enables debugging information to be sent through the serial port to another computer running a debugger program. This option is not used often.
Enable Boot Logging	Enables logging for startup options except for the *Last Known Good Configuration* option. The logging file is `ntbtlog.txt`.
Disable Automatic Restart on System Failure	Prevents Windows from automatically rebooting after a system crash.
Disable Driver Signature Enforcement	Allows drivers that are not properly signed to load during startup.
Start Windows Normally	Restarts Windows and attempts to boot normally.
Repair Your Computer	Used if system recovery tools are installed on the hard disk. Otherwise, these tools are available when booting from the Windows installation DVD.
Reboot	Restarts Windows. A reboot can also occur using the *Restart* Start button option.
Disable Early Launch Anti-malware Protection (Windows 8 and higher)	Disables anti-malware protection for booting. Sometimes driver files might be flagged as malware, causing the system not to boot; disable this feature to boot the system to fix it.

Safe Mode enables you to access configuration files and make necessary changes, troubleshoot installed software and hardware, disable software and services, and adjust hardware and software settings that may be causing problems. In other words, Safe Mode puts the computer in a "bare-bones" mode so that you can troubleshoot problems.

TECH TIP

When to use the *Last Known Good Configuration* boot option

Whenever the *Last Known Good Configuration* option is used, all configuration changes made since the last successful boot are lost. However, because the changes are the most likely cause of Windows not booting correctly, Last Known Good Configuration is a useful tool when installing new devices and drivers that do not work properly.

If Last Known Good Configuration does not work properly, boot the computer into Safe Mode. If Windows works, but a hardware device does not work and a new driver has been recently loaded, use the *Roll Back Driver* option for the device.

Accessing *Advanced Boot Options* with an SSD installed

Some devices boot so quickly that pressing F8 is an almost impossible task. For such cases, Windows 8 and 10 have help. Access *Settings > Change PC Settings > Update and Recovery > Recovery >* under *Advanced Startup,* select *Restart Now >* after the restart, select *Troubleshoot* from the *Choose an Option* window > select *Startup Settings.* If you do not have a *Startup Settings* option, select *Advanced Options* to access it. Select an option such as *Disable Driver Signature Enforcement.*

System Configuration Utility

The **System Configuration utility** (**msconfig** command) is used to troubleshoot Windows startup problems by disabling startup programs and services one at a time or several at once. This graphical utility reduces the chances of making typing errors, deleting files, and other misfortunes that occur when technicians work from a command prompt. Only an administrator or a member of the Administrators group can use the System Configuration utility.

To start the System Configuration utility in Windows 7, click *Start > Run* (or press ⊞+R) > type **msconfig** > Enter. In Windows 8 and 10, type **msconfig** in the search textbox.

The first System Configuration utility tab is *General* (see Figure 16.46). The *General* tab has three radio buttons: Normal Startup, Diagnostic Startup, and Selective Startup. *Normal Startup* is the default option, and all device drivers and services load normally when this radio button is selected. Select the *Diagnostic Startup* radio button when you want to create a clean environment for troubleshooting. When *Diagnostic Startup* is chosen and Windows is restarted, the system boots to Safe Mode, and only the most basic device drivers and services are active.

FIGURE 16.46 Windows 8 System Configuration utility: *General* tab

The *Selective Startup* radio button is the most common troubleshooting option on the General tab. When you choose *Selective Startup*, you can pick which startup options load. Use the divide-and-conquer method of troubleshooting to find the startup file that is causing the boot problems. Start with the first checkbox, *Load System Services*, and deselect it > *OK* and restart the computer. When you determine which file is causing the problem (that is, when the problem reappears), select the System Configuration tab that corresponds to the problem file and deselect files until the exact problem file is located.

File fails to open

If a file does not open, check the *System Configuration* utility to verify if *Selective Startup* is used and a file has been left unchecked. Otherwise, ensure that the application is still installed and other files from this application open properly. Finally, change folder options so that extensions can be seen and verify that the file's extension has not been altered.

The *Boot* tab (see Figure 16.47) enables you to control and modify the Windows boot environment. The *Boot* tab functions include selecting the default operating system and the time allotted to wait for the default operating system to load if no other operating system is chosen from the boot menu in a multiple–operating system situation. Notice that **Safe Boot** and other options are available at the bottom of the window. Table 16.17 describes these options.

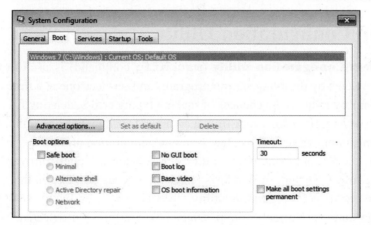

FIGURE 16.47   Windows 7 System Configuration utility: *Boot* tab

TABLE 16.17   *System Configuration Boot tab > Safe Boot options*

Safe boot option	Description
Minimal	Boots in Safe Mode with only critical system services operational (no networking)
Alternate Shell	Boots into a command prompt without GUI or networking
Active Directory Repair	Boots into Safe Mode, running critical system services and Active Directory
Network	Boots in Safe Mode GUI with networking enabled
No GUI	Does not display the Windows welcome screen
Boot Log	Stores information about the startup process in the `ntbtlog.txt` file
Base Video	Starts in VGA mode
OS Boot Information	Displays driver names during the boot process
Timeout	Controls how long the boot menu shows before the default boot entry executes

TECH TIP

Computer boots into Safe Mode for no obvious reason

Check the *System Configuration* utility *Boot* tab to see if some form of *Safe Boot* is enabled.

Click the *Advanced Options* button on the *Boot* tab to define the number of processors and maximum memory used to boot the system if you want fewer than the maximum (see Figure 16.48). When the *PCI Lock* option is enabled, it prevents Windows from changing I/O and IRQ assignments from those set by the system BIOS/UEFI.

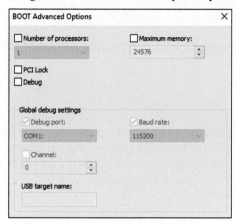

FIGURE 16.48   Windows 10 System Configuration utility: *Boot Advanced Options*

The *Services* and *Startup* tabs in the System Configuration window are also quite useful when troubleshooting boot problems. Certain applications, such as an antivirus program or a printer, run as services. Many of these services are started during the boot process. Use the *Services* tab (see Figure 16.49) to disable and enable these boot services. Enable the *Hide All Microsoft Services* option to view and manipulate third-party (non-Microsoft) services.

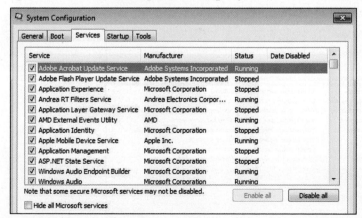

FIGURE 16.49   Windows 7 System Configuration utility: *Services* tab

On the *Startup* tab you can enable and **disable Windows applications** that start automatically when Windows boots. Figure 16.50 shows a sample Startup tab screen.

CHAPTER 16

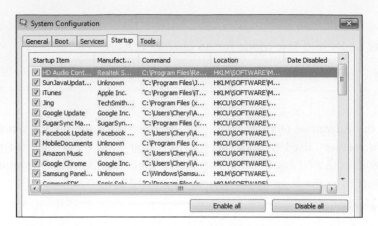

FIGURE 16.50   Windows 7 System Configuration utility: *Startup* tab

The *Tools* tab is useful

The System Configuration *Tools* tab allows you to launch options—such as Task Manager, Performance Monitor, and Internet Options from Internet Explorer—that might need to be changed as a result of a startup issue. In Windows 7, startup options are controlled in the *Startup* tab. However, in Windows 8, 8.1, and 10, this tab links you to Task Manager, which is covered in the next section.

In Windows 7, startup applications are controlled from the *Startup* tab. However, in Windows 8, 8.1, and 10, this tab links you to Task Manager, where you can use the new *Startup* tab to enable and disable an application.

The System Configuration *Tools* tab allows you to launch the majority of the Windows utilities, such as Task Manager, About Windows, Computer Management, System Information, Event Viewer, Programs, Performance Monitor, Registry Editor, System Restore, Command Prompt, and so on, as shown in Figure 16.51.

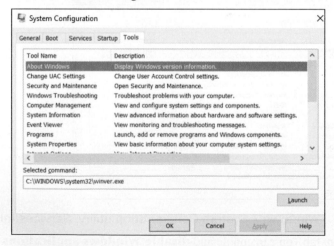

FIGURE 16.51   Windows 10 System Configuration utility: *Tools* tab

Task Manager

Task Manager is a Windows-based utility that displays applications that are currently loaded into memory, processes that are currently running, processor usage, and memory details. To activate Task Manager, right-click or tap and briefly hold an empty spot on the taskbar and select *Task*

Manager. Task Manager is commonly used when an **application crashes**. Access Task Manager to **kill task** (stop) one or more programs that have stopped responding. Using Task Manager is also a great way to get a graphical overview of how the system performs or which programs use a lot of memory. Note that Windows 7 has the following tabs: Applications, Processes, Services, Performance, Networking, and Users. Windows 8, 8.1, and 10 have a few additional tabs: Processes, Performance, App History, Startup, Users Details, and Services.

Figure 16.52 shows the Task Manager *Processes* tab (called *Applications* in Windows 7), which lists the applications currently running on a computer. Notice in the figure that there is a green leaf by two of the apps. If you went over to the *Details* tab, you would see that the applications that have the green leaf beside them would show the status *suspended*. Suspended apps are apps that are running as background apps, such as when you have an application like a calculator minimized and haven't used the app in a while. An app that has a green leaf or is in a suspended state isn't using a lot of system resources.

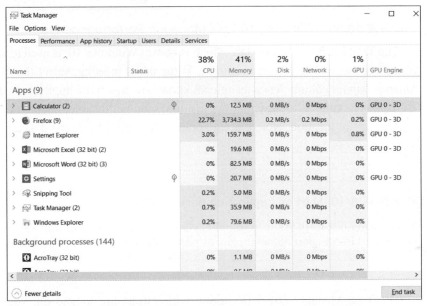

FIGURE 16.52   Windows 10 Task Manager: *Processes* tab

Notice in Figure 16.52 that the Calculator app has a green leaf. You can highlight an app and then click the *End Task* button to stop the application.

TECH TIP

Task Manager tabs are missing

If Task Manager is missing the menu bar and tabs, it is in Tiny Footprint mode. Double-click an empty space in the top border to make the menu and tabs reappear.

The Task Manager *Performance* tab (see Figure 16.53) shows performance indicators for key computer components including the CPU, disk, Ethernet and Wi-Fi for network connectivity, Bluetooth, and GPU. When a user complains about a computer being slow, this is one of the first places for a technician to look.

The Task Manager *App History* tab shows resource usage for individual applications, including CPU time, network utilization, metered network utilization, and the amount of network utilization for any live tile updates. This is helpful with mobile devices to identify which applications are using resources so that you can disable them to conserve battery power.

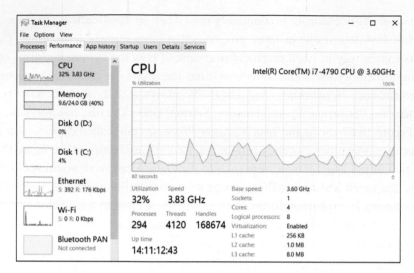

FIGURE 16.53   Windows 10 Task Manager: *Performance* tab

The Task Manager *Startup* tab, which is new in Windows 10, is used to see any app that executes as part of the Windows startup routine. If the tab is missing, select the *More Details* option. The *Startup Impact* column lets a technician know how much the application impacts the startup time. By right-clicking on a particular application, you can disable, enable, view properties, and open the .exe file location. Note that an application cannot be delayed as a service can as part of the startup process.

TECH TIP

Windows 8/10: Start an application during startup

In Windows 8/8.1/10, you can use the *Settings > Apps > Startup* option to turn on any app that you would like to start automatically as part of the Windows boot process.

The Task Manager *Users* tab shows which users are logged on. You can also use the tab to disconnect another user that is logged on, such as when a work cubicle is shared by two people and the other person forgot to log out. The *Users* tab shows what resources that particular user is using in a table format.

The Task Manager *Details* tab (Windows 8/8.1/10) shows more information on the processes that are running. Note that the processes that appear here may not be shown in the *Processes* tab or *Performance* tab. The process ID (PID) is also shown here.

The Task Manager *Services* tab is a handy place to see what services are currently running or stopped. Note that not all services are shown here. There is a link at the bottom to *Open Services*, which provides access to *Services*, where you can see services that were started but that have a delayed start startup type, as well as a list of all services available on the computer.

TECH TIP

What to do if a system appears to lock up or is slow

If a system appears to lock up or is slow, allow the system time to try to respond. If you get no response, access Task Manager by pressing Ctrl+Alt+Del. Keep in mind that it might take a bit of time for Task Manager to open. Access the *Applications* (Windows 7)/*Processes* (Windows 8/10) tab > locate and select the troublesome application > *End Task* button. Normally, if an application is causing a problem, the status shows the application as "not responding." If Task Manager never appears, power down the computer and reboot.

Troubleshooting a Service That Does Not Start

Some Windows services start automatically each time the computer boots. If one of these services has a problem or a particular **service fails to start**, normally an error message appears during the boot sequence. You can use the System Configuration utility (`msconfig`) discussed previously to enable and disable services or **restart services**. You can also use Event Viewer to see if the service loaded properly. Another program that you can use is the Services snap-in used from the Computer Management tool. Or, from a command prompt, type `services.msc` and press ⏎Enter. The *Services* tool enables you to view what services have started and stopped and, if desired, enables you to **disable a service**. In the *Services* snap-in (see Figure 16.54), note the services list in alphabetical order.

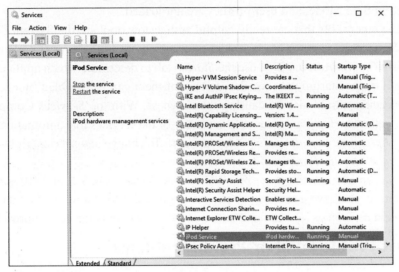

FIGURE 16.54   Windows 10 services

Note that a similar window shows as a tab within *Task Manager*: the *Service* window. On the General tab are the *Stop* and *Start* buttons that control the service. Double-click or double-tap any particular service. Figure 16.55 shows the iPod service. Through this window you can control whether the service starts automatically, starts manually, or is disabled. Notice back in Figure 16.54 that, because the iPod service is already running, the only action that can be performed is to stop the service.

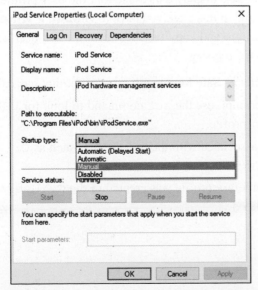

FIGURE 16.55   Windows 10 controlling a service

Slow Boot

Whenever the problem of a **slow boot** is reported to you, several issues could be the culprit. The operating system could be running slowly, the hard drive could be lacking free hard drive space, there might be too many startup applications or services running, or there might be too many startup login scripts. If you recently installed an app, restore the system from a system restore point. If you just received a Windows or application update, remove that update.

If you suspect that the operating system is the problem, use Safe Mode when the computer stalls, slows down, or does not work correctly or when there are problems caused by improper video, intermittent errors, or new hardware/software installation. Safe Mode can start Windows with minimal device drivers and services. Software that automatically loads during startup is disabled in Safe Mode, and user profiles are not loaded.

The other tools that are really helpful with a slow boot are the System Configuration utility and the Services Computer Management tool, which are both covered earlier in this chapter. In the *System Configuration* utility, use the *Startup* tab to determine which applications are having to load as part of the startup process. See if some of them can be disabled (unchecked). One application in particular might also be causing the slowness. With the *Services* Computer Management tool, look in the *Startup Type* column to see if any of the services that automatically start can be changed from *Automatic* to *Automatic (Delayed Start)*. To change any service, right-click on it > *Properties* > use the *Startup Type* drop-down menu.

You can also use the *Reset Your PC* option (Windows 8, 8.1, and 10) and reinstall the operating system. If you have a recovery drive, you could use it to restore or reset the PC. Taking care of the problem as soon as you can and not letting it get worse is the best approach.

Slow Profile Load or Profile Problems

Companies make use of login scripts that run every time a user logs onto a computer. Such a script can reference a local profile, a domain profile, or both. (Profiles are covered in detail in Chapter 18.) A problem that might be reported to you as a slow boot problem may actually relate to a **slow profile load**. A large profile or having too many profiles (a personal one, one that is part of a group, and/or a local one) can cause the user to have to wait a long time for the computer to execute.

The operating system might also display a message that the user profile cannot be loaded. The user profile could be corrupt, and in this case, you have to **rebuild a Windows profile**. One way to fix it is to create a new account and copy the files from the old user account. Otherwise, you will have to make changes to the registry:

Step 1. Log into the computer in Safe Mode with an account that has Administrator rights.

Step 2. From a command prompt, use the `set` command to look for USERPROFILE= to see the problematic user profile.

Step 3. Rename the folder associated with the user profile, such as `C:\Users\CSchmidt`, to something like `Cschmidt.old folder`.

Step 4. Look to see if a temporary profile was created in the `C:\Users\TEMP` folder. Delete the profile if there is one.

Step 5. Access the registry and delete or rename the registry key that matches the SID. Here is the location of that key: `Hkey_Local_Machine\Software\Microsoft\WindowsNT|CurrentVersion\ProfileList`. If you do not know which one matches the SID, click on each folder and look in `ProfileImagePath` to find the SID that matches the user that has the profile issue.

Step 6. Restart the computer and log in with the user profile that had the problem. You will have to copy the user's data from the `.old profile` folder.

Troubleshooting Windows Network Settings

Remember that most corporate devices connect to the wired or wireless network. (Troubleshooting network settings is covered in detail in Chapter 13, "Networking.") If a user cannot access the network, don't forget to check the Windows network settings and keep in mind that you might have to **update network settings** to fix the problem. Check the following:

> Use the *Network and Sharing Center* to see if the network is connected to the Internet.
> If the device is a wireless one, see if the device is connected to the appropriate wireless network.
> See if the device has the appropriate IP address, subnet mask, and default gateway. Remember that without a default gateway, the device cannot access any resource outside its own network (where most servers and connectivity are needed today). Use the `ipconfig` command to verify the IP address and default gateway.
> If the device has an IP address that starts with 169, use the `ipconfig /release` and `ipconfig /renew` commands to get a proper IP address. You can also right-click on the wired or wireless NIC in the *Network Connections* section of the Control Panel > *Properties* > select *Internet Protocol Version 4 (TCP/IPv4)* > *Properties* > *Use the Following IP Address* radio button and input any IP address and mask > *OK* > *OK*. Then re-access the same TCP/IPv4 settings and enable the *Obtain an IP Address Automatically* radio button to receive IP address settings from a DHCP server > *OK* > *OK*. See Figure 16.56. Use the `ipconfig` command to verify that the appropriate adapter received, at a minimum, an IP address, subnet mask, and default gateway, as shown in Figure 16.57.

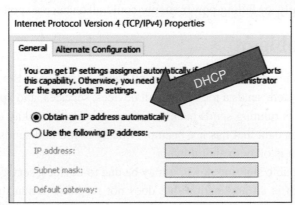

FIGURE 16.56 Configuring a Windows PC for DHCP services

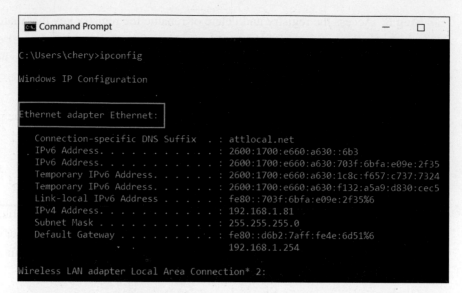

FIGURE 16.57 Verifying IP addressing information using `ipconfig`

Windows Reboots

Some of the hardest problems to solve are intermittent problems, and when Windows reboots spontaneously or shuts down spontaneously, a lot of different things could be the cause. Spontaneous reboots could be caused by a newly installed Windows update, newly installed application, or newly updated driver. A corrupt device driver could also be the culprit, but that is hard to find. An Internet search on your specific hardware device might speed up the troubleshooting process.

A spontaneous reboot can also be caused by a virus or malware. See Chapter 18 for more on those security issues. Other hardware issues could be the RAM, processor, video card, and hard drive. You can quickly see why the cause of spontaneous reboots is one of the hardest problems to narrow down.

However, spontaneous reboots are different from spontaneous shutdowns. Spontaneous shutdowns tend to be heat-related problems. Check the CPU and case fans. Some BIOS/UEFI menus have options that display internal temperatures. Start noting temperature readings. A failing CPU, overloaded power supply, or failing power supply could also cause a spontaneous shutdown.

Shutdown Problems

Windows should be shut down properly when all work is finished. Before Windows can shut down, the operating system sends a message to all devices, services, and applications. Each device or system service that is running sends back a message, saying it is okay to shut down now. Any active application saves data that has not been previously saved and sends a message back to the operating system that it is okay to shut down.

If the system has trouble shutting down, it may be due to devices, services, or applications. The most common problem is an application that does not respond. When this happens, open Task Manager. Manually stop any applications that show a status of not responding. You may also click any other applications and stop them to see if they are causing the problem. Sometimes, a program does not show a status of not responding until you try to manually stop the application from within Task Manager. If a single application continually prevents Windows from shutting down, contact the software manufacturer to see if there is a fix or check online.

TECH TIP

Try the restart option instead of the shutdown option

If you cannot stop a problematic application or determine whether the problem is a service or hardware issue, try restarting the computer instead of shutting down. After the computer restarts, try shutting down again. As a last resort, use the computer power button to power off the computer. If even this does not work in a laptop, remove the battery.

For problems that deal with Windows services, boot the computer into Safe Mode and then shut down the computer. Notice whether the computer had any problems shutting down. If the process works, use the System Configuration window *General* tab *Selective Startup* radio button with the *Services* tab to selectively disable services. Because there are so many services loaded, you might try the divide-and-conquer method: Disable one-half of the services to narrow the list.

Devices do not frequently cause shutdown problems, so eliminate services and applications first. Then, while working on the computer, notice what devices you are using. Common devices are video, hard drive, optical drive, keyboard, and mouse. Boot to the Advanced Boot Options menu by pressing F8 during booting or use *Advanced Options > Startup Settings* in Windows 8 or 10 > select *Enable Boot Logging*. When the system boots, locate the ntbtlog.txt file in the Windows folder. You may have to set folder options in Windows Explorer/File Explorer to list the file and access it. Verify that all your devices have the most up-to-date drivers loaded and that the drivers are compatible with the installed version of Windows.

Sometimes USB or IEEE 1394 FireWire ports can stop a computer from shutting down or powering off. Check the event logs to see if any device did not enter a suspend state. A feature called *USB Selective Suspend* allows the Windows hub driver to suspend a particular USB port and not affect the other USB ports. This is particularly important with laptops, netbooks, and Ultrabooks because of power consumption. Suspending USB devices when a device is not in use conserves power. If USB device suspension is causing the problem, this default behavior can be modified using the *Power Options* section of the Control Panel link and accessing the *Advanced Power Settings*.

Power Options

Windows 7, 8, and 10 have three power plans available, and these plans can be customized. Use the *Change Plan Settings* link followed by the *Change Advanced Power Settings* link to expand a section, such as the *Multimedia Settings* option. The three main power plans are described here, but additional plans might be available from the computer manufacturer:

> *Balanced*—This is the most common plan because it provides full power when you need it and saves power when the computer is not being used.

> *Power Saver*—This plan saves power by running the CPU more slowly and reducing screen brightness.

> *High Performance*—To see this option, select the *Show Additional Plans* link. This plan provides the maximum performance possible.

TECH TIP

Windows power management

Use the *Power Options* section of the Control Panel to configure power in the Windows environment, as shown in Figure 16.58.

CHAPTER 16

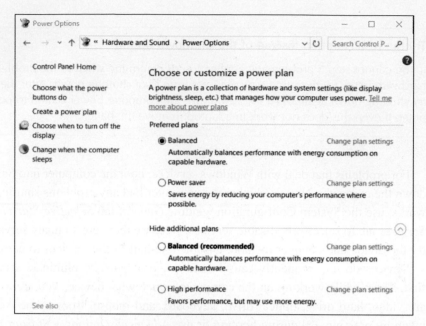

FIGURE 16.58 *Power Options* section of the Control Panel in Windows 10

Monitoring System Performance

It is important for a technician to understand how a computer is performing and to analyze why a computer might have **slow performance** (see Figure 16.59). To do that, a technician must know what applications are run on the computer and their effects on the computer resources. A technician must also monitor the computer's resource usage when problems occur, change the configuration as needed, and observe the results of configuration changes.

FIGURE 16.59   Slow performance

Utilities commonly used to monitor system performance include Task Manager, Performance Logs and Alerts, Reliability Monitor, and Performance Monitor. Sometimes, a computer seems sluggish. The most common cause of a slowdown is that the computer's resources are insufficient or an application is monopolizing a particular resource, such as memory. Other causes of slow-downs include a resource such as a hard drive not functioning properly or being outdated; a resource not being configured for maximum performance and needing to be adjusted; or resources such as hard drive space and memory not sharing workloads properly and needing adjustment.

Viewing system performance when a problem occurs is good, but it is easier to figure out what is happening if the normal performance is known. A baseline can help with this. A **base-line** is a snapshot of computer performance during normal operations (before it has problems). Task Manager can give you an idea of what normal performance is. The Windows Performance Monitor and Reliability Monitor tools are better suited to capturing and analyzing specific computer resource data.

TECH TIP

When do I need to do a baseline of a computer?

A baseline report is needed before a computer slowdown occurs.

Using Task Manager to Measure Performance

Although Task Manager is discussed earlier in this chapter, how to use it to monitor computer performance has not yet been discussed. Using Task Manager is the easiest and quickest way for anyone to quickly and visually see how a computer is performing. Access *Task Manager* and select the *Performance* tab. Task Manager immediately starts gathering CPU and memory usage statistics and displays them in graph form in the window. You can see graphs for CPU performance (refer to Figure 16.53), memory, disk drives, Ethernet, and Wi-Fi performance.

TECH TIP

What to do if you think memory is the problem

To address a memory problem, you can add RAM, create multiple paging files when multiple hard drives are installed in the system, manually set the paging file size, run one application at a time, close unnecessary windows, upgrade or add another hard drive, delete unused files, and defragment the hard drive.

CPU Usage shows the processor usage percentage—that is, what percentage of time the processor is working. Actually, it is more accurate to say that CPU Usage shows the percentage of time the processor is running a thread. A *thread* is a type of Windows object that runs application instructions. The window on the right in the Task Manager is a graph of how busy the processor is over a period of time.

In Windows 7 there is a snapshot of statistics regarding memory at the bottom. In Windows 8/8.1 and 10, you must use the *Memory* option on the left to see these statistics. Note that this might be referred to in articles, documentation, or the CompTIA certification as system **performance (virtual memory)** because any computer's virtual memory affects performance. If you think the page file for virtual memory is too small, you can adjust it with the following steps:

Step 1. Search for and access the *System* section of the Control Panel > *System Protection* > *Advanced* tab > *Performance* section *Settings* button.

Step 2. Select the *Advanced* tab.

Step 3. In the *Virtual Memory* section, look at the total size of the paging file. Click the *Change* button, deselect the *Automatically Manage Paging File Size for All Drives* checkbox, and you can make adjustments, as shown in Figure 16.60.

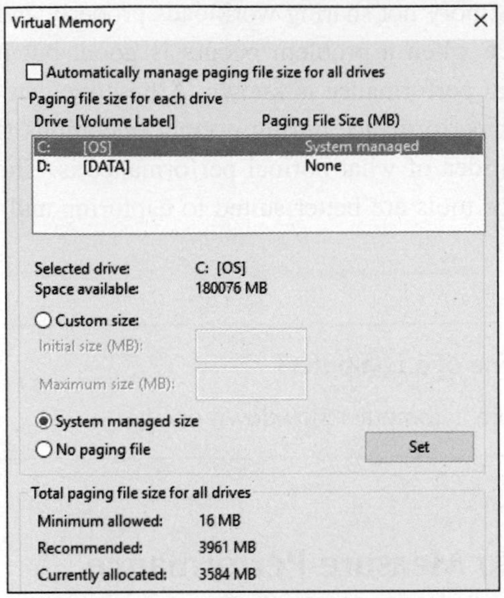

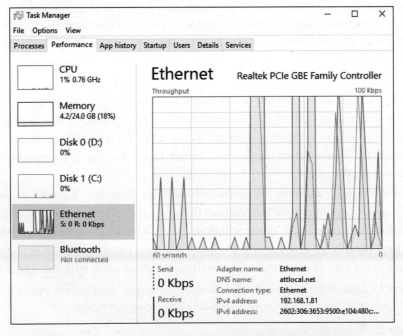

FIGURE 16.60 Manually configuring page file (virtual memory) size in Windows 10

To see how much memory an individual process is using, use the *Processes* tab and locate the program executable file. The CPU and memory usage display in separate columns on the *Processes* tab. Windows 8 and 10 offers disk and network columns as well.

Memory is frequently a bottleneck for computer performance issues. You can also use Task Manager to see the total amount of RAM installed and how much RAM is available. Look in the *Physical Memory* information section of the Task Manager *Performance* tab to see this information.

Click on a particular network card to see a graph of network performance for a particular network interface, including Bluetooth. Figure 16.61 shows the Task Manager *Performance* option for an Ethernet card.

FIGURE 16.61 Task Manager: *Performance* tab, *Ethernet*

The Task Manager *Users* tab shows users that are logged on to the computer and the specific performance statistics for CPU memory, disk, and network for each particular user. This is probably one of the least used Task Manager tabs in either the corporate environment or at home. However, if multiple people are logged on, one of them might have a particular application or service running that is causing the machine to slow down.

Performance Monitor

Performance Monitor is a visual graph in real time or from a saved log file that provides data on specific computer components. Use the *System and Security* section of the Control Panel > *Administrative Tools* > double-click *Performance Monitor*. Inside Performance Monitor, counters are used. A counter is a specific measurement for an object. Common objects include cache, memory, paging file, physical disk, processor, network interface, system, and thread. Use the + (plus sign) in Performance Monitor to select various counters. At the bottom of the window is a legend for interpreting the graph, including what color is used for each of the performance measures and what counter is used. Table 16.18 shows common counters used in Performance Monitor, and Figure 16.62 shows an example of Performance Monitor.

TABLE 16.18   Performance Monitor counters

Computer component	Object name	Counters
Memory	Memory	Available Bytes and Cache Bytes
Hard disk	Physical disk	Disk Reads/sec and Disk Writes/sec
Hard disk	Logical disk	% Free Space
Processor	Processor	% Processor Time (All Instances)

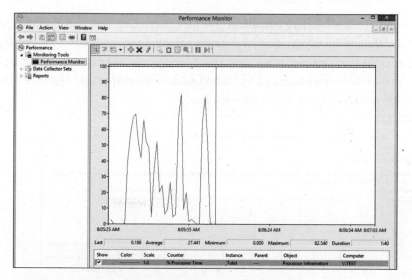

FIGURE 16.62   Windows Performance Monitor

Resource Monitor

The Windows **Resource Monitor** is a nice graphical tool that requires little work and shows the main components of a system. Access the tool by selecting the *Open Resource Monitor* link from within the Performance Monitor window or access the *System and Security* section of the Control Panel > *System* > *Performance Information and Tools* link at the bottom of the left panel > *Advanced Tools* > *Open Resource Monitor*. Figure 16.63 shows Resource Monitor.

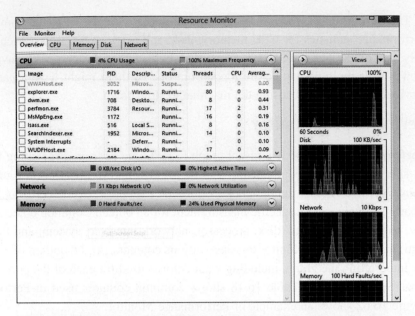

FIGURE 16.63   Windows 8 Resource Monitor

Running any performance monitoring tool affects a computer's performance, especially when using the Graph view and sampling large amounts of data. The following recommendations help when running any performance monitoring tool:

> Turn off any screen saver.
> Use Report view instead of Graph view to save on resources.
> Minimize the number of counters monitored.
> Sample at longer intervals, such as 10 to 15 minutes, rather than at short intervals such as a few seconds or minutes.

Windows **Reliability Monitor** provides a visual graph and detailed report of system stability and details on events that might have affected the computer's reliability. The details can help technicians troubleshoot what has caused the system to become unreliable. Reliability Monitor is found by typing `reliability monitor` in the respective *Search Programs and Files* feature of each release. Figure 16.64 shows this tool.

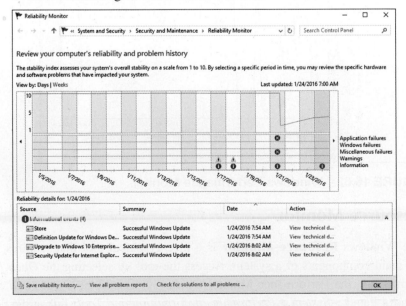

FIGURE 16.64   Windows 10 Reliability Monitor

Supporting Windows Computers Remotely

Windows provides two products for accessing a PC remotely: Remote Desktop and Remote Assistance. Both products allow a computer to be accessed remotely. The difference is that **Remote Assistance** displays a prompt at the remote computer, asking permission to allow the computer to be viewed remotely, and **Remote Desktop Connection** does not display this prompt.

Using Remote Desktop (the `mstsc` command) requires the following elements:

> The remote computer must have some type of network connectivity.
> The computer used to access the remote computer must run Windows 7 Professional or higher, Windows 8/10 Pro or higher, or Windows Server or must have some type of terminal services running.
> Any firewalls between the two computers must allow ports 3389 and 80 to be open.
> The remote PC must have the Remote Desktop application installed.
> You need to know the computer name of the remote PC.
> You need to have a user account with a password on the remote PC.

When you are on a computer that is remotely accessing another computer, there is a bar across the top of the screen that contains the remote computer name. This is how you know that you are on another computer. The user on the remote computer is logged off.

Both Remote Desktop and Remote Assistance are useful for those working at a help desk and for technicians who must support computers in other locations. With Remote Assistance, one computer user (the Expert) views another computer user's (the Novice's) desktop using a secure connection. Remote Assistance (`msra` command) can be initiated using any of the following methods:

> Using Windows Messenger service
> Sending an email an invitation
> Sending an invitation as an email attachment
> Using Easy Connect

Remote Desktop is disabled by default in Windows, and the **Remote Settings** link is used to enable/configure it. Open *Windows Explorer/File Explorer* and right-click *Computer* (*This PC* in Windows 8 and 10) > *Properties* > *Remote Settings* link from left panel. In the Windows environment, Remote Assistance now supports computers that use network address translation (NAT). However, you may have to go into the Windows Firewall application and, in the left panel, select *Allow a Program Through Windows Firewall*. Select the *Exceptions* tab and locate *Remote Assistance*. You must also set up a password for the guest user and manually send the password to the person invited to take over the computer. To use Windows Remote Assistance, type `remote assistance` in the *Search Files and Folders* textbox. Click the *Windows Remote Assistance* option. Figure 16.65 shows the available options.

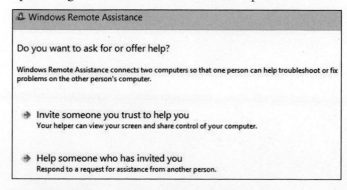

FIGURE 16.65   Windows Remote Assistance

Preventive Maintenance for Your Operating System

Your operating system is a key component of a working system. Preventive maintenance can help avoid issues and reduce downtime when properly applied. No application or hardware can work without an operating system. It is important that you keep your operating system healthy. The following suggestions can help:

> Always have an antivirus software program that has current virus definitions.
> Make frequent data backups.
> Have a backup of your operating system. Many external hard drives include backup software.
> Ensure that the System Restore utility is enabled.
> Update the operating system with service packs and patches.
> Use the Task Scheduler tool to automate some of the preventive maintenance tasks. You can use the **at** command (type **at /?** at a command prompt to see the options) to create a script file or have an application run at a specific time.

SOFT SKILLS: AVOIDING BURNOUT

Burnout—commonly caused by too much work and stress—is a mental state that can also affect emotional and physical capabilities. Many technicians tire of the fast pace of technology (see Figure 16.66). As a person matures, it seems to take more effort to stay current in the skills required for business. One attraction of technology for many students is that technology is always changing; however, it is this speed of change that also provides a challenge, even to seasoned veterans. After being in the same job for multiple years, a technician may show signs of burnout. Technicians should monitor their own attitude and mental state constantly and watch for warning signs associated with burnout:

> Overreaction to common situations
> Constant tiredness
> Reduced productivity
> Poor attitude
> Lack of patience with customers or peers
> Feeling of a loss of control
> Use of food, drink, or drugs as coping mechanisms

FIGURE 16.66 Burnout affects your performance

Burnout can be prevented and dealt with if you recognize the symptoms. Working too much, having too many responsibilities, and expecting too much of yourself can lead to burnout. The following list can help you recognize and cope with burnout:

> Take vacations during which you do not stay in contact with work.
> Set reachable goals, even on a daily basis.
> Take a couple breaks during the day to do something nontechnical.
> Learn something new that is not related to technology.
> Have good eating, sleeping, and exercising routines.
> Subscribe to a positive saying or joke of the day.

Chapter Summary

> Windows operating systems come in different editions that have various features and tools and can be 32-bit or 64-bit. The 32-bit versions are limited to a maximum of 4 GB of RAM; 32-bit operating systems or applications are sometimes referred to as x86 instead of 32-bit.
> Before installing Windows, you should complete the eight preinstallation steps to ensure a smooth, error-free installation.
> The installation of Windows includes three phases: determining whether to upgrade or perform a clean installation, choosing a partition system, and completing the installation.
> Corporate computer installations are more complex than other types of installation. Automated tools and disk imaging software can help with this process.
> Many installation problems are addressed in the chapter, along with possible causes and solutions.
> Updates to Windows may be configured manually, but Windows 10 does automatic updates by default.
> The registry should be backed up whenever the computer is fully functional and when any software or hardware changes are made.
> The System Configuration Utility (`msconfig`) is used to troubleshoot startup issues, set boot conditions, and access services and quick links to Windows tools.
> Tasks that a technician commonly performs to configure Windows includes adding devices, removing hardware components, adding a printer, and installing or removing software.
> The Computer Management console can access three categories: System Tools (Task Scheduler, Event Viewer, Shared Folders, Local Users and Groups, Performance, and Device Manager), Storage, and Services and Applications.
> Managing accounts for those who use computers or computer resources from remote network computers is an important function of a technician or administrator.
> The Storage Computer Management category includes just the Disk Management tool, which is used to manage hard drives, including volumes or partitions.
> A service is an application that can be started using the Services option or configured to start when the computer boots.
> The Data Sources administrative tool can select which application is associated with a particular type of file.
> The Print Management console is used to manage printers.
> There are various methods to speed up and troubleshoot the boot process. The Windows Recovery Environment (WinRE) is accessed by booting from a Windows installation DVD or from within Windows. It includes many diagnostic and other helpful tools.
> Task Manager can perform preventive maintenance on a regular basis. Preventive maintenance can reduce downtime and includes keeping the operating system and applications

patched, keeping the antivirus definitions current, and keeping the hard drive defragmented and with ample space.

> Technicians should understand how a computer is performing by using Task Manager and comparing current performance to a baseline that was taken at a time when the computer was running optimally. Other tools, such as Performance Monitor or Resource Monitor, are also very helpful.

> Technicians may be required to access computers remotely, and this can be done using the Remote Desktop or Remote Assistance products.

> Technicians can do positive things to avoid burnout, including getting good rest, avoiding drugs and alcohol, doing nontechnical things, and having good time-management skills.

A+ CERTIFICATION EXAM TIPS

✓ Know the minimum hardware requirements for installing 32- and 64-bit Windows 7, 8, and 10.

✓ Use all Windows tools before taking the certification exam. Ensure that you pay attention to the purpose of each tool and consider why (or in what situation) you would use each Windows tool.

✓ Review all symptoms and resolutions for a system running slowly and slow boot.

✓ Know the various boot methods.

✓ Review the various types of installations, such as an unattended installation, in-place upgrade, clean install, repair installation, remote network install, image deployment, recovery partition, and refresh/restore Review Table 16.1.

✓ Know the various types of partitions and what they are best used for.

✓ Be familiar with different user/group accounts and Credential Manager.

✓ Be familiar with common symptoms/troubleshooting of software problems. Common symptoms include slow performance, failure to boot, and application crashes.

✓ Be familiar with the following features: Computer Management, Print Management, Device Manager (can be used to disable a device), Local users and groups, Performance Monitor, Services, System Configuration, Task Scheduler, Component Services, Data Sources, Windows Memory Diagnostic Tool, Task Manager, Disk Management (including knowing how to install a drive, create both an MBR, dynamic disk, convert an MBR to a dynamic disk, partition, select files system, and format) Upgrade Advisor, System Restore, and Windows Update.

✓ Interact with and use for troubleshooting the following Windows Control Panel utilities: Display/Display Settings, User Accounts, System, Power Options, Programs and Features, Devices and Printers, Sound, and Troubleshooting.

Key Terms

CHAPTER 16

Review Questions

1. What is the maximum amount of RAM that can be recognized by any version of 32-bit Windows?

    _____

2. A customer has an older 16-bit game as well as some 32- and 64-bit games. The customer is considering upgrading to 64-bit Windows 10. Will there be any issues with this? If so, what are they, and how might they be resolved?

    _____

    _____

3. List three steps to be taken *before* installing Windows.

    _____

    _____

    _____

    _____

    _____

    _____

4. Which tool can limit and control the number of applications used to boot the computer?
    [`taskmgr` | `regedit` | `msconfig` | `diskpart`]

5. Which Windows setting would be used to enable Windows PowerShell, Hyper-V, or Microsoft's Print to PDF option?
    [Turn Windows Features On or Off | Task Manager | System Configuration | Performance Monitor]

6. Which performance tool would a technician use first to see if a computer has enough hardware resources when a particular application executes?
    [Performance Monitor | Task Manager | Reliability Monitor | Device Manager]

7. How could you have both Windows 7 and Windows 10 operating systems installed on one computer?

    _____

8. [T | F] Existing restore points are deleted if Windows is reinstalled.

9. [T | F] Device drivers are specific to a particular Windows operating system version.

10. Which System Configuration tab is used to configure a computer to boot in diagnostic startup mode?
    [Boot | Services | Startup | General | Tools]

11. What user group is allowed to perform driver rollback. (Select all that apply.)
    [Standard User | Guest | Administrator | Backup Operators]

12. What is the purpose of the System Restore utility?

    _____

    _____

13. When Windows boots, nothing appears on the screen. If the display is powered on and attached, which Windows tool would be best to try first?
    [System Restore | Safe Mode | Command Prompt | Reset Your PC]

14. When would a technician use Event Viewer?

    _____

    _____

    _____

CHAPTER 16

15. Detail specifically how Task Manager can monitor computer performance?

_____

_____

_____

16. Which disk management option would be used to create a flexible data storage option from a USB drive and an eSATA drive that is seen as one drive letter?
     [RAID 0 | RAID 1 | RAID 5 | Storage Spaces]

17. Where does Windows store passwords and login details for a particular user?
     [Storage Spaces | Credential Manager | BIOS/UEFI | C:\Windows\System32\Configuration]

18. Which type of Windows installation setup is used for a corporate environment?
     [workgroup | homegroup | domain | peer-to-peer]

19. Which type of Windows boot process is used in conjunction with the PXE BIOS/UEFI option?
     [in-place upgrade | multiboot | network | recovery]

20. List three things a student can do to avoid burnout in school.

_____

_____

Exercises

Exercise 16.1 Windows Tools

Objective: To determine which Windows tool to use, based on the task

Procedure: Match each scenario to the best Windows tool to use for the given situation. Note that one tool is used twice.

Tools:

a. Event Viewer	**k.** Services
b. System Restore	**l.** Performance Monitor
c. System Repair	**m.** Task Manager
d. msconfig	**n.** Computer Management console
e. Device Manager	**o.** Windows Memory Diagnostics Tool
f. Folder Options	**p.** Safe Mode
g. System Properties	**q.** regsvr32
h. Devices and Printers	**r.** safe boot
i. Disk Management	**s.** Print Management
j. Task Scheduler	

Scenarios:

_____ 1. Configure two drives in a RAID configuration.

_____ 2. Determine when a user logged into a computer yesterday.

_____ 3. Restart the program that allows the print spooler to function.

_____ 4. You suspect one of the DDR4 modules has an issue.

_____ 5. Quickest way to see the default printer.

_____ 6. Disable a computer vendor app that keeps running every time the computer boots, trying to get the user to buy storage space.

_____ 7. Configure a specific number of processors the computer uses to boot.

_____ 8. Run a test of hard drive reads per second and writes per second to see if the drive is causing slowdown issues.

_____ 9. Bring the system back to before a particular Windows update was installed.

_____ 10. Instruct the system to perform disk maintenance twice a week instead of just once.

_____ 11. Have the ability to access Device Manager and the Disk Management tool from one window.

_____ 12. View system files through Windows Explorer/File Explorer.

_____ 13. Testing mode with limited drivers loaded.

_____ 14. Unregister a DLL.

_____ 15. Disable a piece of hardware.

_____ 16. Adjust virtual memory.

_____ 17. View all print servers.

_____ 18. Halt a misbehaving app.

_____ 19. Control the Safe Mode boot type the next time the computer restarts.

_____ 20. Let the OS try to figure out why Windows won't boot.

Exercise 16.2 Task Manager Tabs

Objective: To determine which Task Manager tab to use, based on the task

Procedure: Match each scenario to the best Task Manager tab to use in Windows 10. You might want to review figures throughout the chapter. Each tab is used only once.

Tabs:

a. Processes

b. Performance

c. App history

d. Startup

e. Users

f. Details

g. Services

Scenarios:

_____ 1. See a graph of how quickly the SSD used to boot the system is responding to requests for information.

_____ 2. Determine what applications a person has used today and how much memory each of them has used.

_____ 3. Document how much bandwidth a particular application used on a metered network.

_____ 4. Stop and restart Wlansvc.

_____ 5. Learn which apps are considered to be actively used on the computer right now.

_____ 6. Look up the specific process ID (PID) for the firefox.exe application.

_____ 7. Research which applications launched automatically when the computer booted.

Exercise 16.3 System Configuration Tabs

Objective: To determine which System Configuration tab to use, based on the task

Procedure: Match each scenario to the best System Configuration tab to use for the given situation. You might want to review figures throughout the chapter. Each tab is used only once.

Tabs:

a. General

b. Boot

c. Services

d. Startup

e. Tools

Scenarios:

_____ 1. Determine what applications began as part of the Windows boot process.

_____ 2. Allow a technician to choose either a normal, diagnostic, or selective startup.

_____ 3. Quickly access Event Viewer.

_____ 4. Create a log file of the boot process for a computer that doesn't boot properly.

_____ 5. Select only three Windows apps that enable specific Windows features that start as part of the boot process.

Activities

Internet Discovery

Objective: To access the Internet to obtain specific information regarding a computer or its associated parts

Parts: Access to the Internet

Procedure: Use the Internet to answer the following questions.

1. Find a website that offers Windows freeware tools. Write the name of the website and the URL where this information was found.

_____

2. What is the latest update available from Microsoft for Windows 8.1? Write the answer and the URL where you found the answer.

_____

3. Find a website that details what to do if a Windows 10 upgrade results in a black screen. Detail what the website recommends and the URL where you found it.

_____

_____

4. Microsoft always has a planned lifecycle for any of its operating systems. Find a website that tells you what the planned mainstream support end date is for Windows 10 Enterprise version 1709. Write the mainstream support end date as well as the URL.

_____

5. You get the error code 0x80072EE7 on a Windows 10 computer. Find a website that describes this error. Write at least one thing that could cause this error, one solution, and URL where the answer can be found.

_____

_____

6. Find a technical certification related to a Microsoft operating system. List the certification and the average salary associated with the certification. List all URLs used to find this information.

_____

_____

_____

Soft Skills

Flip the CLASSROOM

Objective: To enhance and fine-tune a future technician's ability to listen, communicate in both written and oral forms, and professionally support people who use computers

Activities:

1. In groups of two or three students, one student inserts a problem related to Windows on the computer. The other student or students use the Remote Desktop Connection utility to find the problem and then repair it. Document each problem, along with the solution provided. Exchange roles so that each student practices the repair and documentation.

2. Divide into five groups. Five questions about operating systems follow:

    (1) What should you do *before* installing an operating system?

    (2) What are alternatives to Windows 7, 8, or 10 as an operating system, and what are pros and cons of these alternatives?

    (3) What is the difference between an active partition, a system partition, and a boot partition in regard to Windows?

    (4) What operating systems can be upgraded to Windows 7, 8, or 10? What is the difference between a clean install and an upgrade, and what determines which one you do?

    (5) What differences can be seen for a Windows hard drive that has a FAT32 partition and one that has an NTFS partition?

    Each group is assigned one of these five areas or another set of five questions related to Windows. Each group is allowed 20 minutes (and some whiteboard space or poster-sized paper) to write their ideas. All group members help to present their findings to the class.

3. Find a magazine article related to a Windows solution or feature. Share your findings with the class.

_____

_____

4. Using any research method and resource, determine the pros and cons of upgrading to Windows 10 from Windows 8. Make a list of things to check before upgrading.

_____

_____

_____

_____

_____

_____

CHAPTER 16

17 macOS and Linux Operating Systems

In this chapter you will learn:

> What operating systems are available besides Windows

> How to navigate the user interfaces of macOS and Ubuntu Linux

> How to manipulate files and folders in the graphical and command-line interfaces

> How to create system backups

> How to find UNIX/Linux software

> How to work from a Linux-based command line

> Reasons to be humble in the IT field

CompTIA Exam Objectives:

What CompTIA A+ exam objectives are covered in this chapter?

✓ 1002-1.1 Compare and contrast common operating system types and their purposes.

✓ 1002-1.3 Summarize general OS installation considerations and upgrade methods.

✓ 1002-1.9 Given a scenario, use features and tools of the Mac OS and Linux client/desktop operating systems.

✓ 1002-3.2 Given a scenario, troubleshoot and resolve PC security issues.

✓ 1002-3.3 Given a scenario, use best practice procedures for malware removal.

Introduction to macOS

OS X (pronounced "OS ten") is a UNIX-based operating system that was developed by Apple, Inc., for its Macintosh line of computers, called Mac for short. Today, the operating system is known as **macOS**. This Apple operating system is the second most commonly used desktop operating system, after Windows, and it is the most commonly used type of UNIX/Linux-based desktop operating system.

Like most other UNIX/Linux operating systems, macOS utilizes many open source projects to make up the core and functionality of the operating system, along with a touch of Apple's own customization. **Open source** software is software that is made freely available and that is open to outside contributions. Although many parts of macOS are open source, the operating system is not. macOS is unique to Apple-released hardware (see Figure 17.1) because it comes preinstalled only on Macintosh systems and is not sold or distributed to run on other hardware, as Windows and most other UNIX/Linux distributions are.

FIGURE 17.1   Apple computer running OS X

OS X reached the 11th major desktop release when macOS came out, and it is now up to version 10.14. There was a line of dedicated macOS-based server operating systems, but that has now been discontinued in favor of a separately purchased add-on from the Apple App Store to provide the same functionality. The desktop OS X releases were called by feline names, and the macOS versions are now named after California landmarks. Table 17.1 lists Mac operating system distributions by release number and name.

TABLE 17.1   macOS releases since 2011 by name and number

Release number	Name	Release date
10.7	Lion	July 2011
10.8	Mountain Lion	July 2012
10.9	Mavericks	October 2013
10.10	Yosemite	October 2014
10.11	El Capitan	September 2015
10.12	Sierra	June 2016
10.13	High Sierra	June 2017
10.14	Mojave	June 2018

macOS is a portable operating system interface (**POSIX**)–compliant operating system, which means it meets the specifications for a standardized operating system outlined by the IEEE Computer Society and contains a Bourne shell and other standard programs and services that are found in all POSIX-compliant operating systems. A **shell** is a user interface that is used to interact with an operating system. POSIX standardization makes it easier for end users, IT professionals, and developers to use different operating systems that are POSIX compliant and have familiar tools available. Because of this standardization, many skills that you learn with macOS can be applied to other operating systems.

Navigating the User Interface

macOS is renowned for its intuitive and easy-to-learn graphical user interface (GUI); there are multiple ways to interact with this GUI, including using the standard mouse and keyboard to using the more modern trackpad multitouch gestures. The macOS GUI is called Aqua. Steve Jobs, co-founder of Apple Inc., famously said, "One of the design goals was when you saw it you wanted to lick it." referring to the original water-like theme with heavy use of translucent and reflective design elements within the GUI. Now the GUI is a flatter, toned-down interface that more resembles Apple's mobile operating system iOS than earlier versions of the operating system.

There are four basic elements to the macOS GUI (see Figure 17.2). The one that sticks out first when looking at the desktop is known simply as the Dock. The **Dock** is the shortcut organizational bar used for launching, switching, and managing applications. You can easily customize the Dock by dragging and dropping applications and folder shortcuts to it. By default, the Dock is at the bottom of the screen, but its position can be changed so it is located on the side of the screen.

FIGURE 17.2   OS X desktop

The **Finder**, which is the file manager included in macOS, is used for navigating and managing files or folders in the file system. The Finder is similar to Microsoft's Windows Explorer/File Explorer. You can open the Finder by clicking the iconic Finder icon, known for its smiling face, which is always located on the Dock.

The **menu bar**, which is anchored to the top of the screen, is a dynamically changing bar that presents contextual drop-down menu options on the left side, depending on what window is active. On the right side, the menu bar provides shortcuts for actions such as connecting to a WiFi network or changing volume. The menu bar is also informative, displaying information such as battery life on MacBooks and the time of day.

Another important element of the macOS GUI is the desktop, which can display any mounted drives or disks as well as hold anything the end user wants to save to it, such as documents or pictures, for quick access.

Notice in Figure 17.2 the three colored dots on the upper-left corner of the Finder window. The red dot on the far left is used to close the window. The middle yellow dot is used to minimize the open window down to the Dock. The green dot (the rightmost one) is used to expand the window to full screen mode. These three dots are universal across all windows in the macOS.

TECH TIP

What to do if the Dock is missing

If the Dock is not present, try hovering the pointer toward the bottom or sides of the screen. Many macOS users hide the Dock to gain more screen space, so that it pops up only when the pointer is nearby.

On top of the core GUI elements are a few built-in utilities that make using the GUI easier. macOS supports multiple desktops, much as Microsoft Windows 10 does with Task View. **Mission Control** is a feature that gives an overview for managing all application windows and virtual desktops. It can be invoked by pressing the F3 key (or the F9 on older Mac keyboards), by clicking the Mission Control icon, or by swiping up on a trackpad with three or four fingers at once (depending on the trackpad settings). Mission Control displays all the running applications (see Figure 17.3), their respective windows grouped together, and any extra virtual desktops. From this view, you can create, delete, or rearrange virtual desktops; switch which application windows reside on each virtual desktop; and easily explore all the open application windows.

Although Mission Control is great for managing applications, it cannot launch them. **Launchpad** is an application launcher shortcut. It can be invoked by pressing the F4 key, clicking the Launchpad icon, or using a thumb + three-finger pinch gesture on a trackpad. This view is a grid-like display of all installed applications that you can click to launch (see Figure 17.4). This grid interface can be searched with the available search bar at the top of the Launchpad interface. Applications can also be sorted into folders and multiple pages in this view for easy organization.

Finder is used for navigating the file system, but it can be cumbersome, and it can take a long time to find something, especially if you are not sure where that something is located. For searching the system, you can use Spotlight. **Spotlight** is a universal search tool that can search every file and directory, as well as contacts, email, music, and even the web (see Figure 17.5). It is invoked by holding down Cmd and pressing the Spacebar or by clicking the magnifying glass icon on the right side of the menu bar. A large search bar appears in the middle of the screen, allowing you to type in your search. The results are then presented to you underneath the search bar.

FIGURE 17.3 OS X Mission Control

FIGURE 17.4 OS X Launchpad

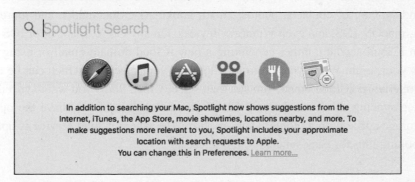

FIGURE 17.5 OS X Spotlight

You may have noticed that many of these shortcuts have their own dedicated gestures that can be triggered using a trackpad. Apple introduced the idea of finger-based **gestures**, a use of fingers to make motions that provide input, in its mobile operating system, iOS. These gestures and functionality were later brought to MacBook laptops. To easily use these gestures, a user could purchase a Magic Mouse, which is a multitouch mouse sold by Apple, or a Bluetooth trackpad known as a Magic Trackpad. Table 17.2 lists the most commonly used trackpad gestures and the actions they trigger. Keep in mind that other gestures can be enabled, and many of them can be changed to have different effects, depending on the user's preference.

TABLE 17.2   Commonly used macOS gestures

Gesture	Action
Swipe left or right with two fingers	Swipe between pages
Swipe left or right with four fingers	Swipe between full screen applications
Swipe up with three or four fingers	Open Mission Control
Pinch in with the thumb and three fingers	Open Launchpad
Spread apart the thumb and three fingers	Show the desktop
Pinch in or out with two fingers	Zoom in or out
Tap with two fingers at the same time	Right-click
Tap and hold down with three fingers	Take control of a window allowing you to drag it around the screen

Basic System Usage, Updates, and Backups

When macOS starts, you may be presented with a login screen if the user accounts have passwords enabled. You can log in with a previously created user account or, if it is enabled, you can use the guest login selection. If you log in as a guest, any changes you make or items you save will be deleted from the system when you log out. Every time you are logged in as a guest user, you are presented with a fresh desktop experience, as if it has never been used before.

The macOS comes bundled with a wide range of software (see Figure 17.6) for general use as well as system upkeep. It includes an office productivity suite, commonly known as **iWork**, which includes a word processor called Pages, a presentation application called Keynote, and a spreadsheet application called Numbers. These productivity applications are Apple's answer to the popular Microsoft Office suite. Other useful bundled applications include Mail, Safari (the default web browser), Calendar, Contacts, and Photos.

macOS also comes with **iCloud**, a cloud-based service offering storage, application support, and syncing of contacts, photos, email, bookmarks, documents, and more between multiple OS X, macOS, iOS, and even Windows devices. On any OS X, macOS, or iOS device, you can create an iCloud account, either generating a new iCloud domain email or using another email address as your login. When you log in to iCloud on your machine, which can be done inside the *System Preferences* iCloud menu, you can then select which items you want synced between devices. The free syncing service includes 5 GB of cloud storage, and you have the option to purchase more storage space with a monthly subscription. The whole iCloud service is optional to use but worth looking into for easy syncing to all devices.

FIGURE 17.6 Apple bundled software

One unique feature of iCloud that sets it apart from other cloud services is that it has built-in remote connectivity. If you log in to iCloud, have Internet access, and enable the **Back to My Mac** feature in the *System Preferences* iCloud menu, you can browse that Mac from another macOS device. The remote Mac appears as a shared device in Finder, enabling you to browse the file system. You can click a Share Screen button to start a remote desktop session.

TECH TIP

iCloud screen sharing requirements

An iCloud screen-sharing session needs at least 300 Kbps of full-duplex bandwidth. You might need to edit firewall settings to allow the connection to go through.

App Store

macOS comes with a wide range of bundled software, and there is also a software marketplace. The **App Store** is a centralized marketplace where developers can list and sell software (see Figure 17.7). You can find a wide range of software, from simple utilities to advanced 3D games. The App Store allows for easy management of purchases, as they are tied to a user's Apple ID, and a user can install the software on multiple systems or re-download past purchases by logging in with his or her account. The App Store also allows for easy application updates because developers can push out updates through this centralized repository to end users. This also provides a layer of security: Users know the applications found in the App Store have been vetted by Apple and most likely include no harmful or malicious code.

TECH TIP

Apple ID

To use the App Store and other Apple cloud services, you need an Apple ID. This login is used for tracking software purchases through all of Apple's stores. You can create one in the App Store, through iTunes (an Apple media player, radio app, and media library), or by going to https://appleid.apple.com/account.

FIGURE 17.7   App Store

Share a Mac Screen

If you have **screen sharing** turned on, another Mac user who is on the same network can view and even control the display of your Apple computer. To view another computer's display remotely, open *Finder* > hover the pointer over the word *Shared* > *Show* > select a particular computer > *Share Screen*. Screen sharing is especially helpful to technicians supporting remote users.

System Updates

Apple uses the App Store to release patches and updates for macOS. It is important to check the Updates tab in the App Store from time to time to get the latest operating system and application updates. You can also have the number of updates available dynamically display on the App Store icon as a reminder that you have updates to perform.

Time Machine

It is easy to recover your previously purchased applications through the App Store, but the App Store is not a backup system. For that you need to set up Time Machine. **Time Machine** is a bundled application in macOS that enables you to do full and incremental system backups to an external hard drive. It gets its clever naming from the capability to navigate your past backups as if you were traveling through time. Notice in Figure 17.8 that the current Finder is on top. The stacked windows behind it are previous snapshots shown in time order from present to the past.

To use Time Machine, you need to connect an external hard drive to the system, typically through a USB or Thunderbolt connection. You can also do the backups to a disk over your network by using Time Capsule, a remote backup system sold by Apple. When an external drive is connected, you simply go into the Time Machine settings, which are located in the *System Preferences* menu, select the disk you want to use, and turn it on. From there, Time Machine performs a full system backup and then continues to do a new incremental backup every hour. It retains the past 24 hours of backups, a daily backup for each day in the past month, and a weekly backup for all prior months. It keeps as many of these backups following those rules as it can until you run out of disk space on the drive used. All these backups are done in the background, without user intervention, after Time Machine is set up.

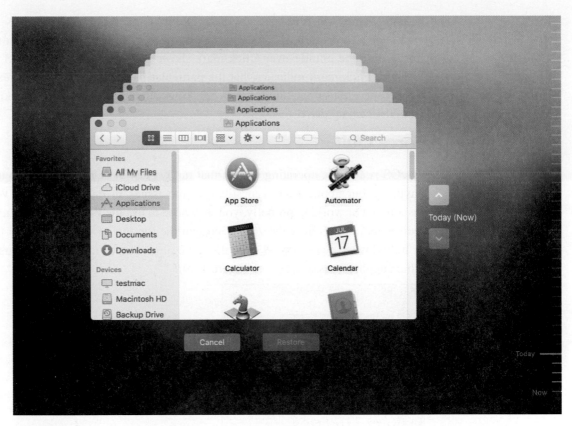

FIGURE 17.8   Time Machine

TECH TIP

Requirements for using a disk for backups

When selecting a drive to use for backups, remember you need to use a drive with a partition that is macOS Extended formatted. By default, macOS cannot write to an NTFS partitioned drive and defaults to using HFS+ partitioning for system partitions. The number of backups possible depends on how big the external drive is. At a minimum, you want the drive to have at least as much disk space as your internal Mac hard drive so that you can always fit at least one full backup set on it. The larger the drive, the better. But remember, creating a single backup is not a reliable way to back up important data. Always have multiple backup options for data that you cannot risk losing (for example, a local backup such as Time Machine as well as a remote or cloud backup).

With the Time Machine interface, you can recover deleted files or even restore older versions of a file, as well as applications that were deleted. If a system failure occurs, you can even restore the entire backup from your Time Machine external drive onto a different Mac. You do this by booting the Mac you want to restore to into recovery mode by holding down the ⌘ key and the ⓡ key while the system is starting up. When recovery mode boots, you see the option to select *Restore from a Time Machine Backup*. Make sure the external Time Machine drive is connected, select this option, and follow the prompts to restore the backup. If using a networked disk for Time Machine, you have the option to connect to the remote disk for the restore process.

To restore an individual file or find an older version of it, simply select the file or navigate to the location where it was saved in Finder. Then open the Time Machine application, and it brings up a timeline view of that particular selected file or the files that have been in the selected location. You can navigate the backups available by scrolling through the timeline presented on the right side. When you find the file or version you want to restore, select it and click the *Restore* button.

If the Time Machine external drive is not connected, local snapshots are automatically created once a day. Figure 17.8 shows tick marks on the right bottom. Each tick mark is a backup. Positioning the pointer over a tick mark shows a particular color. For OS X Yosemite or later, a bright red tick mark indicates that the particular backup can be used to restore the system (from a local snapshot or backup drive). A less bright tick mark indicates a backup that can be restored from the backup drive.

Force Quit

macOS is a stable operating system that rarely crashes or requires you to use backups to recover anything, but applications can still run into issues in day-to-day use. When a program stops responding or working properly, you may need to use the **Force Quit** feature. To access the Force Quit menu, either click the Apple icon on the top left of the screen and then select *Force Quit* or hold down Cmd+Option+Esc at the same time. The window that appears allows you to choose which applications to quit (see Figure 17.9).

FIGURE 17.9   Force Quit window

Another way of stopping an application is through the Terminal application, described later in this chapter. The Terminal program allows access to a command prompt environment. Type **top** to see currently running processes. Locate the process ID associated with the problem application and type `kill -9 process_id` (replacing `process_id` with the process ID number associated with the problem application).

Remote Disc

You may notice that most Macs do not have an optical CD/DVD drive. In fact, no currently released Mac contains an optical drive, as Apple is trying to push software distribution through the App Store. However, Apple realizes that users from time to time may need to access a disc. You always have the option to plug in an external USB optical drive, but that isn't always possible. For such situations, macOS has **Remote Disc**, which enables you to remotely use the optical drive of another Mac or even that of a Windows-based PC.

To set up Remote Disc on another Mac, go to *System Preferences > Sharing >* select the *DVD or CD Sharing* checkbox to activate it (see Figure 17.10). You have the option to enable approval to be granted on that Mac when another system tries to connect to the optical drive. On the Windows side, install the *DVD or CD Sharing Update for Windows*. After you do this, the computer includes a Control Panel entry that allows you to enable remote access to the optical drive. It is also possible to require approval before anyone can access the drive.

To access Remote Disc, open *Finder >* select *Remote Disk* link on the left sidebar > choose the remote machine that you want to use. Be aware that both machines must be on the same local network.

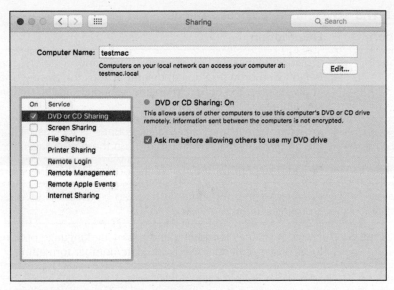

FIGURE 17.10   Remote Disc

Management and Troubleshooting Tools

macOS comes with a robust set of tools to keep the system running smoothly. But as with many other things in technology, they eventually break. As an IT professional, you need to understand what tools are at your disposal for fixing a system.

The most basic tool is the System Preferences menu (see Figure 17.11). **System Preferences** is equivalent to the Control Panels in Windows. System Preferences contains most of the system settings, from desktop backgrounds and screen savers to more advanced settings such as user accounts and file sharing. Third-party applications can also insert their own preferences menu into the System Preferences menu. The System Preferences shortcut by default is located on the Dock, listed in Launchpad. It can also be opened from within Finder. Select the *Applications* menu on the left sidebar and then select the *System Preferences* icon. Table 17.3 lists all the default options in System Preferences and provides a brief description of each option.

FIGURE 17.11   System Preferences window

TABLE 17.3   System Preferences settings

Option	Description
General	Provides settings for button, menu, and window colors; scrollbar behavior; default web browser choice; default actions for closing/opening documents and windows; the option to enable handoff; and the option to enable LCD font smoothing.
Desktop & Screen Saver	Provides settings for desktop backgrounds as well as for screen savers, such as the image to use, and when to turn on the screen saver.
Dock	Provides settings for the size of the dock and how the shortcuts behave.
Mission Control	Provides settings for shortcuts that can be used inside Mission Control as well as grouping settings.
Language & Region	Provides settings for adding and removing language options as well as setting the local region, calendar used, and date/number formatting.
Security & Privacy	Provides settings for general security, such as password requirements to unlock the screen from sleep, disk encryption using FireVault, general firewall settings, and privacy settings (such as using location-based services).
Spotlight	Provides settings for what is and isn't allowed to be searched.
Notifications	Provides settings for what apps can display notifications and how they are displayed.
CDs & DVDs	Allows access to optical discs and control actions for inserted discs.
Displays	Provides settings for managing resolution, brightness, and multiple display settings.
Energy Saver	Provides settings for when to turn the screen off or put the hard disk to sleep.
Keyboard	Provides settings for functions, shortcuts, and auto-correct.
Mouse	Provides settings for mouse speed, scroll direction, and primary mouse button side.
Trackpad	Provides settings for multitouch gestures.
Printers & Scanners	Provides settings for adding and removing printers and scanning devices.
Sound	Provides settings for which audio output/input to use, volume, balancing the sound between speakers, and system sounds for alerts.
Ink	Provides settings for controlling handwriting recognition.
iCloud	Provides settings for the sign-in menu for iCloud and enabling of iCloud services.
Internet Accounts	Provides settings for management of email, contacts, calendars, and messages accounts.
Extensions	Provides settings for managing third-party extensions used for customizing macOS.
Network	Contains all network settings.
Bluetooth	Provides settings for toggling Bluetooth on and off and pairing devices such as Bluetooth headsets.
Sharing	Provides settings for external access, such as enabling remote login and remote file sharing. Also provides settings for sharing of devices such as printers and setting the computer name.

Option	Description
Users & Groups	Provides settings for creating and deleting user accounts, as well as what groups they belong in. Also provides settings for what items open automatically when a user logs in.
Parental Controls	Provides settings for managing restrictions for kids' accounts, such as restricted websites, time limits for computer usage, and application usage.
App Store	Provides settings for when updates are checked for the operating system and any applications purchased in the App Store, as well as how to update them.
Dictation & Speech	Provides settings for dictation for typing as well as text-to-speech to hear written text.
Date & Time	Provides settings for adjusting the time zone and the date and setting the clock.
Startup Disk	Provides settings for selecting a different bootup disk, such as an external drive or Boot Camp partition (and allows Windows to be loaded as well).
Time Machine	Provides settings for toggling Time Machine backups on or off, selecting which external disk to use, and setting how to handle backups.
Accessibility	Provides settings for accessibility options such as colors, zoom, voiceover, captions, and more.

Safe Mode

Safe mode (sometimes called safe boot) allows a Mac computer to be booted with a slimmed-down version of the operating system. The software that is normally loaded automatically is not loaded; user-installed fonts are not installed; and font caches, kernel cache, and other system cache files are deleted. One really important function of safe mode is that the startup disk is checked and repaired, if possible, when issues are detected. Safe mode can also be used when removing malware.

TECH TIP

How to start a Mac in safe mode

Hold down the ⇧Shift key while booting the computer.

Utilities

For more advanced system management, maintenance, and troubleshooting, use the tools located under the *Utilities* directory (see Figure 17.12). This is found by opening *Finder*, selecting the *Applications* section on the left side of the bar, and going into the *Utilities* folder.

CHAPTER 17

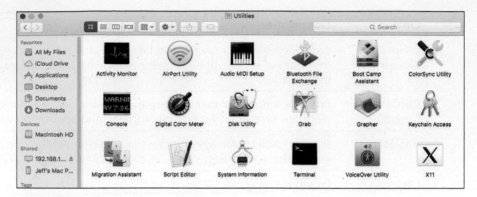

FIGURE 17.12   Utilities window

Activity Monitor

You need to be familiar with a few key utilities to properly troubleshoot a macOS system. **Activity Monitor** is a tool used to see what processes and services are running, as well as what system resources are used. It is extremely useful in discovering why a system is running slowly (such as when an application appears to be frozen or when the system presents a constantly spinning **pin wheel**). You can look at the *CPU* tab, shown in Figure 17.13, to see what is consuming most of the CPU processing power. The *Memory* tab shows how much RAM each process is using, and the *Disk* tab provides a breakdown of how much disk read/write I/O is occurring. The macOS automatically reserves some hard drive space to use as RAM. This is known as swap space. A good rule of thumb is to keep about 15% of the hard drive unused at all times (and more, if possible). All these statistics are great tools for pinpointing poor system performance due to errant processes or lack of resources available for what the system is trying to do.

Process Name	% CPU	CPU Time	Threads	Idle Wake Ups	PID	User
mdworker	9.7	0.51	5	8	677	testuser
Activity Monitor	7.1	0.57	10	3	678	testuser
iconservicesagent	0.6	0.38	6	0	277	testuser
lsd	0.2	0.14	6	0	241	testuser
vmware-tools-daemon	0.2	5.77	4	9	291	testuser
SpotlightNetHelper	0.2	1.67	10	1	320	testuser
Spotlight	0.1	1.03	17	1	308	testuser
Dock	0.1	1.70	6	8	243	testuser
cfprefsd	0.1	0.91	5	0	240	testuser
CoreServicesUIAgent	0.1	0.07	6	0	399	testuser
Finder	0.1	8.57	8	1	641	testuser
fontd	0.0	0.51	3	0	252	testuser
Notification Center	0.0	0.91	5	0	273	testuser
SystemUIServer	0.0	0.38	5	0	244	testuser
swcd	0.0	0.03	4	0	397	testuser
mdworker	0.0	0.05	3	0	350	testuser
distnoted	0.0	0.51	6	0	238	testuser
sharedfilelistd	0.0	0.17	5	0	251	testuser
mdworker	0.0	0.08	4	0	343	testuser
mdworker	0.0	0.05	4	0	344	testuser
Keychain Circle Notification	0.0	0.09	3	0	271	testuser
Photos Agent	0.0	0.42	4	0	302	testuser
storeuid	0.0	0.11	3	0	394	testuser

System:	2.95%	CPU LOAD	Threads	822
User:	6.27%		Processes:	184
Idle:	90.79%			

FIGURE 17.13   *Activity Monitor > CPU* tab

Console

The **Console** is a centralized place to find system and application logs and messages. macOS and the applications running on it constantly send activity logs to the Console, which lets you parse these logs manually or by searching for something specific. This is particularly helpful if you have an application or system service that is not behaving properly but that is not presenting an error message in the user interface. Most likely, if something has a problem, you can find a log explaining why in the Console. Figure 17.14 shows sample output in the Console.

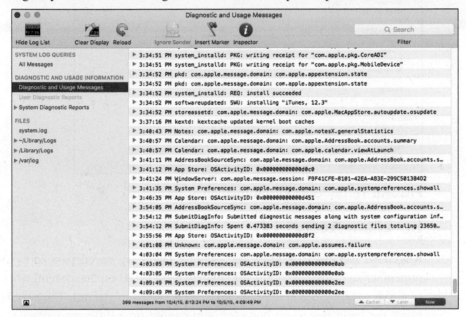

FIGURE 17.14   Console messages

Kernel Panic

The Console is good for troubleshooting **kernel panic**, which is a critical system error that the operating system cannot recover from. When this happens in macOS, the Mac reboots to return to a stable state. Trying to find the cause of kernel panic can be difficult because a wide array of issues can cause it, such as a hardware failure, operating system failure, or a faulty application. If kernel panic happens only once, it is typically fine to ignore it. But if problems continue to occur, the logs in the Console can be helpful for determining the cause. The kernel panic logs are saved in the /Library/Logs/DiagnosticReports directory, which can be viewed from inside the Console.

System Information

System Information is a utility that provides an overview of the Mac, including basic diagnostic information such as installed hardware, software, and network settings. If you need to find information about what is installed, such as the name of a graphic card, or the firmware version used for the network card, this is the place to look. It can be accessed from the *Utilities* directory or by clicking the Apple icon in the upper-left corner on the menu bar, selecting *About This Mac* from the drop-down menu, and then selecting *System Report* from the System Information menu that appears. Figure 17.15 shows sample output for hardware found from the System Information utility.

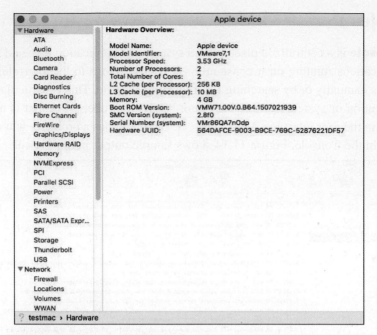

FIGURE 17.15   System Information > *Hardware*

Keychain Access

Keychain Access is a utility for securely managing saved passwords so users do not have to remember so many passwords for any password saved on the system, whether for a WiFi network or a web page login. These passwords are encrypted by default. The keychain file can be unlocked using the login password; however, you can set up a different password for the Keychain, thus providing additional security.

A common problem occurs when a user updates his or her password when logging on, and then Keychain asks for the Keychain password. This happens if someone uses a network-based account and updates his or her account password not by using the standard password change feature, or if he or she uses the reset password feature in macOS recovery mode. Not all users are aware of what Keychain Access is or that they even have a Keychain password because this happens automatically. To remedy this, open the *Keychain Access* utility, from the menu bar select *Edit* > choose *Change Password for Keychain* > enter the previous password > select *OK*. A window opens, allowing you to update the password to the new login password.

A useful feature of the Keychain Access utility is the ability to see saved passwords. It is easy to forget passwords. If you were in a situation in which you were already connected to a WiFi network but did not know the password, you could open the *Keychain Access* utility > select *Local Items* > double-click or double-tap the entry for the WiFi network > enable the *Show Password* option. You are then prompted to authenticate with your Keychain password. You then see the saved password, unencrypted, as shown in Figure 17.16.

TECH TIP

What to do if users cannot remember their Keychain password

A user who cannot remember his or her old Keychain password needs to start a new Keychain. This is done by selecting the Keychain Access *Preferences* drop-down menu > *Reset My Default Keychain*. The user can either delete the old Keychain or opt to keep it in case he or she later remembers the password.

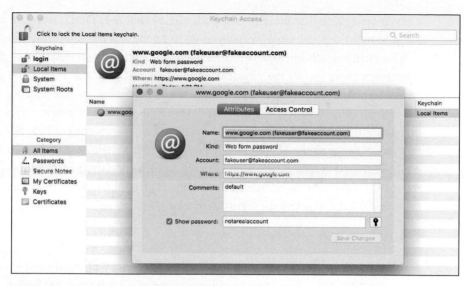

FIGURE 17.16 Keychain Access

Disk Utility

Disk Utility is an application that handles the management of disks and images in macOS (see Figure 17.17). This utility can be used to rename, reformat, erase, repair, and restore disks. It is a powerful tool and should be used with caution because it is easy to delete all data on a system or on an external disk attached to the system.

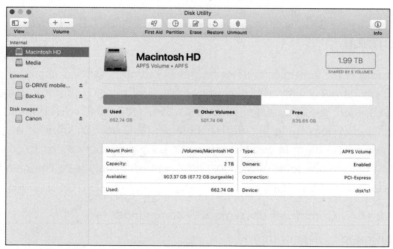

FIGURE 17.17 macOS Disk Utility

When a drive is connected to a Mac, it is mounted and shows up on the left side of the Disk Utility window. Selecting the drive gives you a handful of options: First aid, Erase, Partition, Mount, and Info. The Repair disk option is similar to `fsck` or `chkdsk`. It checks the file system integrity on a system and repairs issues it finds. It is highly advisable not to run repair disk unless you have a system backup and have a reason to run it, such as when a system boots only into safe mode or into recovery mode.

The *Erase* option allows you to wipe a disk, choose the format for the disk, and name the partition. You may also perform a secure erase by going into the security options on the menu. Secure erase has a few options, all of which write 0s or random data over the previous data on the disk to make it unrecoverable. You can choose no passes of zeros to quickly wipe out the disk, one pass of zeros, three passes of various types of data that is Department of Energy (DOE) compliant, or a seven-pass erase that meets the Department of Defense (DOD) standard for safely deleting data. Keep in mind that the more passes you do, the longer it takes to erase the disk.

The *Partition* tab enables you to manage the addition and deletion of partitions on a disk. An interactive chart shows the physical partition layout. You can adjust the chart with your mouse cursor to resize partitions, free up space to add new ones, or free up space to expand a partition. As with all other disk modification, you need to make sure you have any data backed up on a disk that you are repartitioning. Even if this is done properly, there is a risk of corruption and data loss.

macOS supports the Hierarchical File System Plus (HFS+), also known as macOS Extended, as well as the new Apple File System (APFS), which supports SSDs and allows drive volumes to be reduced or increased as needed. To view the type of file system being used on a drive, select the drive in Disk Utility, and the file system type displays.

Boot Camp

Boot Camp is a boot-loading utility designed to assist with partitioning, installation, and support in running Windows on a Mac. Installation requires a USB flash drive with at least 16 GB of space, a Windows installation ISO file or DVD installer, and a minimum of 30 GB of free space on the hard drive. The Boot Camp application guides you through the process of repartitioning your hard drive to make a partition labeled *BOOTCAMP*. It also copies the Windows ISO or DVD installer to the USB flash drive and copies the appropriate Mac drivers to it. After Boot Camp sets up the partition and copies everything you need to the flash drive, it reboots the system into the Windows installer, allowing you to complete the installation. As always, make sure you back up a system before doing anything involving partitioning. Boot Camp can also be used to remove a Windows partition.

Terminal

Terminal is the terminal emulator for macOS. It allows the command-line interface (CLI) access to the operating system. Although the majority of things you do in macOS can be performed in the GUI, there are times when using the CLI is required. The Terminal application can be found in the *Applications* folder > *Utilities* subfolder. You need to know at least a few basic commands and how to use them in case you run into a situation that can be fixed only by using Terminal. Table 17.4 outlines some of the most basic and commonly used commands. (More commands are provided later in the chapter.)

TABLE 17.4   Commonly used macOS commands

Command	Description
c	Lists the contents of the current working directory
pwd	Shows the current working directory path
cd	Moves between directories
touch	Creates a file
mkdir	Creates a directory
cp	Copies a file
mv	Moves a file
rm	Deletes a file or directory
ls	Shows the contents of a directory

Command	Description
chown	Changes ownership
chmod	Changes file permissions
sudo	Temporarily gains root privileges
kill	Stops a process ID associated with a particular application
nano	An easy-to-use text editor
vi	A text editor used by more experienced Linux users
less	Shows the contents of a file
grep	Searches output for a specified search term
man	When followed by another command, brings up a manual for using that command

The basic commands in Table 17.4 are enough to navigate the file system, create and remove files and directories, and do some basic troubleshooting. Keep in mind that for all these commands, you can use a variety of flags. It is best to reference the man page to discover what a command can do if you are unfamiliar with it. For example, the ls command run by itself shows the contents of the current working directory, but you can also specify a directory that is not the one you are working so you can see its contents, as shown here.

```
testmac:~ testuser$ ls
Applications Desktop Documents Downloads Dropbox Library Movies Music
Pictures Public
testmac:~ testuser$ ls Public
Drop Box
```

As you can see here that by using ls and specifying another directory (in this case *Public*), the contents of the *Public* folder can be seen instead of the user's home folder. The following paragraphs provide brief examples of using the commands listed in Table 17.4.

ls lists the contents of a directory, including any directories located inside the current path in the file system. Here is an example:

```
testmac:~ testuser$ ls
Applications Desktop Documents Downloads Dropbox Library Movies Music
Pictures Public
```

pwd identifies the current working path, as shown in this example:

```
testmac:~ testuser$ pwd
/Users/testuser
```

cd, which is short for *change directory*, does exactly what its name indicates. Typing cd followed by a directory takes you to that directory. Notice that the working path is updated on the command line to keep track of the current location:

```
testmac:~ testuser$ cd Applications
testmac:Applications testuser$
```

touch creates a blank file with the specified name. This command is not limited to text files. For example, you could make a file with the extension html if you wanted to work on creating a web page. Notice in the following example that -1 is added to the ls command when showing the file created with the touch command:

```
testmac:~ testuser$ touch test.txt
testmac:~ testuser$ ls -1 test.txt
-rw-r--r-- 1 testuser Editors 0 Sep 29 13:56 test.txt
```

The -1 modifier is a flag for what is called *long listing*, which includes the normal output of the ls command plus add-ins. From left to right, the add-ins are as follows: file permission, number of file links, owner name, owner group, file size, time of last modification, and filename. Also specified is the file that the ls command was used on. Instead of seeing all contents of the directory, you see only the file specifics.

cp is short for *copy*. The syntax of this command is cp followed by the source file and then the destination of the copy. You can also rename the file while copying it. Consider this example:

```
testmac:~ testuser$ cp test.txt testcopy.txt
testmac:~ testuser$ ls
Applications Documents Dropbox Movies Public
test.txt Desktop Downloads Library Music Pictures testcopy.txt
```

mv is short for *move*. It works similarly to cp, except it does not keep the original file in place. It actually modifies the file by moving it in the file system. During this process, you have the option to rename the file. In the following example, the testcopy.txt file was moved to testmove.txt:

```
testmac:~ testuser$ mv testcopy.txt testmove.txt
testmac:~ testuser$ ls
Applications Documents Dropbox Movies Public
test.txt Desktop Downloads Library Music Pictures testmove.txt
```

If the files were listed, testcopy.txt would not exist because it is now named testmove.txt.

rm is short for *remove*. By using the rm command, you can designate which file or files to remove, as in this example:

```
testmac:~ testuser$ rm test.txt testmove.txt
testmac:~ testuser$ ls
Applications Desktop Documents Downloads Dropbox Library Movies Music Public
```

sudo is a command used to gain superuser (also known as root) privileges. In UNIX/Linux, the administrator account is known as **root**. The root user has absolute power on a system, including within macOS. However, by default, this user account is disabled. It is advised that you not log in directly using root because if you were to accidentally run something malicious, the system could be degraded or compromised. However, administrative access is occasionally needed to perform certain tasks, such as running a script or installing an application. When you need such access at the command-line level, use the sudo command, which invokes a temporary root session to complete the command you are running.

In the following example, the file importantdocument.txt is created:

When you run ls -1 for the file, you can see that you are the owner of it. Then you want to make root the owner of the file, so you attempt to use the command chown, which changes file ownership. When chown is run, the message "Operation not permitted" displays, meaning you do not have permission to do this. To fix this, you add sudo to the start of the command. When prompted, you enter your account password for verification. The command runs as the root user. When you use ls -1 again, you can see that the file owner changes from testuser to root.

```
testmac:~ testuser$ touch importantdocument.txt
testmac:~ testuser$ ls -1 importantdocument.txt
```

```
-rw-r--r-- 1 testuser Editors 0 Sep 30 10:39 importantdocument.txt
testmac:~ testuser$ chown root importantdocument.txt
chown: importantdocument.txt: Operation not permitted
testmac:~ testuser$ sudo chown root importantdocument.txt
Password:
testmac:~ testuser$ ls -l importantdocument.txt
-rw-r--r-- 1 root Editors 0 Sep 30 10:39 importantdocument.txt
```

To understand how to use the chmod command, you have to understand UNIX/Linux file permissions. There are three types of permissions a user or group can have for a file: read, write, and execute. Permissions are indicated using the -rwxrwxrwx notation, with r being read, w being write, and x being execute. Notice the three sets of rwx entries. The first set, starting from the left, represents the owner's permissions. The second set represents the group's permissions. The last set represents everyone else (otherwise known as others). In the following example, look at the leftmost entries:

```
testmac:~ testuser$ ls -l importantdocument.txt
-rw-rw-r-- 1 root Editors 0 Sep 30 10:39 importantdocument.txt
```

The root owner of the file can read and write to the file as designated by the first set of letters rw. The users belonging to the Editors group can also read and write to the file as shown by the second set of letters rw. Everyone else can only read the file and is not allowed to modify it in any way as designated by the last r.

To use chmod to change these permissions, there are various syntax options. The easiest to visualize uses letters. For instance, to add a write permissions group to the importantdocument.txt file for those known as others, use o+w, shown in the following example:

```
testmac:~ testuser$ sudo chmod o+w importantdocument.txt
Password:
testmac:~ testuser$ ls -l importantdocument.txt
-rw-rw-rw- 1 root Editors 0 Sep 30 10:39 importantdocument.txt
```

This syntax can be used with the letters u (user), g (group), o (other), and a (all). The letters r, w, and x are then used to signify what permissions to either add or subtract for the subject specified. Then you specify the file for which permissions are to be changed.

There is another way of specifying permissions; it involves using numbers to represent the permissions. The syntax for this is a three-digit number string, with the first number starting from the left representing the owner, the second number representing the group, and the final number representing others. The numbers range from 0 to 7, and they are translated into binary numbers to represent the permissions value, but the easy thing to do is remember that read permission equals 4, write permission equals 2, and execute permission equals 1. All the permissions you want to assign are added together. For example, if you want to give the root user read (4), write (2), and execute (1) permissions, the group read (4) permissions, and others no (0) permissions, you end up with 740. You can then use the command chmod followed by this number and then the file that is changed. The following example shows what this looks like:

```
testmac:~ testuser$ ls -l importantdocument.txt
-rw-rw-rw- 1 root Editors 0 Sep 30 10:39 importantdocument.txt
testmac:~ testuser$ sudo chmod 740 importantdocument.txt
Password:
testmac:~ testuser$ ls -l importantdocument.txt
-rwxr----- 1 root Editors 0 Sep 30 10:39 importantdocument.txt
```

nano is a text editor. When using the command line, it is common to need to use a text editor to fix files. Instead of going through the slow process of using a graphical text editor and navigating to the file to open it, you can quickly edit a file at the command line.

There are a few command-line text editors available to use in macOS and Linux, including vi, emacs, and nano. nano is an easy-to-use command-line text editor. You launch it by typing nano followed by the filename you want to edit. If the file does not exist, nano creates it. Entering the command q cancels the editing session. What makes nano so convenient to use is that it is a powerful editor with many options, such as search and replace, line numbers, and quick navigation with page up/page down. It also has a set of quick controls displayed in its interface, which is helpful for occasional users who have not memorized all the shortcuts.

less is a tool you can use to quickly view the contents of a file. It presents a window of the contents that you can scroll through by using the B key to scroll up and Spacebar to scroll down; you can also page to the bottom by holding down ⬆Shift and pressing the G key. less becomes a powerful tool when combined with a search utility known as grep and using the | (pipe) function. The | key is used for passing output from one command to another. You can use less to see the content of a file and then pipe it to grep to search for something inside it. For example, you can add the following text to the importantdocument.txt file with which you have been working:

```
OS X 10.8 Mountain Lion
OS X 10.9 Mavericks
OS X 10.10 Yosemite
OS X 10.11 El Capitan
```

If you want to find this information somewhere within a few hundred pages, it would be difficult to find it by just reading the document. Using nano to search could also take a long time because you would have to run the search over and over to find all the multiple entries. A better command to use in this case is less to get the output of the file and send it to grep to search for the wanted file:

```
testmac:~ testuser$ less importantdocument.txt | grep Yosemite
OS X 10.10    Yosemite
```

You can see that grep works by taking the input it receives and providing it as a search term. It then outputs every line of the input (importantdocument.txt) that contains the search term.

TECH TIP

Use the manual!

You need to know your commands and their options, but it is easy to forget the ones that you do not use often. When you cannot remember how to use a command, use the command man, which is short for manual and brings up directions on how to use any command for which there is a manual page entry. The syntax is simply the command man followed by the command you want to know more about.

Introduction to Linux

Linux, released in 1991 by developer Linus Torvalds, is a widely used operating system platform that is similar to trademarked UNIX, a group of operating systems that grew from the AT&T-developed UNIX. It is meant to be a free, open source operating system that everyone can use, contribute to, and modify as needed. Because of this, it is widely used in many different areas of technology, such as servers, desktops, embedded systems, and smartphones. It is also mostly POSIX compliant, so some of the concepts you have already learned in this chapter about macOS also apply to most Linux systems.

The terminology of Linux can be confusing for someone who is new to it. The name *Linux* refers to an operating system kernel. A **kernel** is the heart of an operating system. It acts as the controller and interpreter for nearly everything in a system, so hardware and software can interface and work together. It controls things such as memory management, peripherals, and allocation of other system resources to processes.

The Linux kernel is repackaged into different operating system distributions (distros for short). There are hundreds of different distros. Table 17.5 lists the most popular ones and where to find more information about them. Although these distros are all different from one another in some ways, they are all Linux operating systems because they use the Linux kernel.

TABLE 17.5   Linux distros

Distro name	Website
Ubuntu	http://www.ubuntu.com
Debian	http://www.debian.org
Mint	http://linuxmint.com
SUSE	https://www.suse.com
Red Hat	http://www.redhat.com
Fedora	https://getfedora.org
CentOS	https://www.centos.org
Gentoo	https://www.gentoo.org
Arch	https://www.archlinux.org
Kali	https://www.kali.org

Anyone going into IT should explore the different types of Linux distros to see the differences and similarities between them. Ubuntu is the most widely used home desktop distribution, and it also has a server version. Although you probably will not find Ubuntu in an enterprise environment, you are likely to encounter it with end users, developers, and simple servers. And a lot of the skills you learn for Ubuntu are useful with other distros.

You do not have to install Ubuntu onto a computer to experiment with it. Unlike with Windows or macOS, you can use a live CD or DVD, which is simply a disc you can boot to or run from a flash drive. By booting from a CD, DVD, or flash drive, you can run the operating system as if it were installed on the computer. This makes it much easier to try different distributions without having to dedicate a computer solely to running Linux. If you do launch Linux from a CD, DVD, or flash drive, however, you need to be careful because you can still modify the local file system on the computer and cause harm to the installed operating system.

TECH TIP

Downloading Ubuntu

Download Ubuntu's latest release from http://www.ubuntu.com/download/desktop. It will be needed at the end of the chapter to complete the question section.

Navigating the User Interface

There are many types of graphical user interfaces for Linux, such as GNOME, KDE, Xfce, and Cinnamon. Each has unique interface operation and tools. **Unity** is the name of the graphical user interface in Ubuntu. It has some similarities to the user interface of macOS, but it is drastically different from Windows.

Launcher is the shortcut bar on the left side of the screen. It is reminiscent of the macOS Dock, but it doesn't work completely the same. It has the functionality of being an application launcher shortcut as well as having a universal search feature built in to it. When you click the Ubuntu icon at the top of Launcher, a menu allows a local search on the system, as well as the ability to get results from the Internet.

The **Panel** is a menu bar at the top of the screen that contains contextual information on the left side and static information on the right side; it is a lot like the menu bar in macOS. **Nautilus** is the file manager for Ubuntu (see Figure 17.18). You can quickly access it by clicking the *Files* icon on the Launcher. Like all other GUI operating systems, Linux has a standard desktop. Nautilus is the default file manager, but because Linux is so modular and customizable, it can be replaced with an alternative file manager.

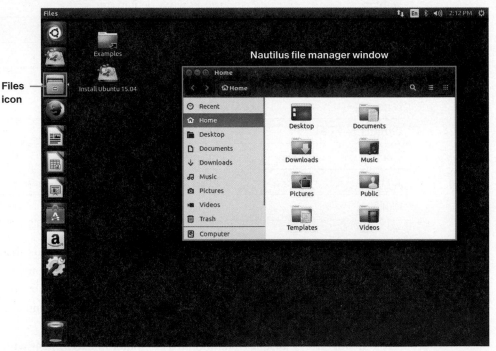

FIGURE 17.18   Nautilus file manager window

Dash is the universal search tool that is built into the Launcher. It searches local content as well as Internet sources, all of which can be enabled or disabled simply by opening up Dash. There are also subcategories at the bottom of the Dash interface, called lenses. By default, there are lenses for universal searching, applications, files and folders, videos, music, and photos, as shown in Figure 17.19.

The Ubuntu user interface is straightforward. A Linux system in an enterprise environment is not accessed through the GUI. Most of the Linux systems in the corporate environment do not even have a GUI installed. However, a few tools should be mentioned, and they are covered in the following sections.

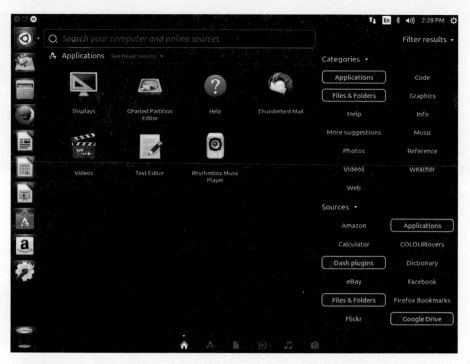

FIGURE 17.19   Dash search tool

Basic System Usage, Updates, and Backups

Numerous useful tools come bundled with Ubuntu for managing the system. Some of these are best used through the GUI. Although everything can be done through the command-line interface, some tools are much easier to use on the desktop.

The best example of this is **GParted**, a disk management tool that allows for the creation, deletion, and resizing of partitions on a physical disk (see Figure 17.20). GParted has an easy-to-use drag-and-drop interface for partition management that is far easier to visualize and understand than the command line. If you experiment with GParted, be mindful that you can wipe out your system if you are unsure of the correct procedures.

Whereas Windows uses NTFS, and macOS uses the HFS+ or APFS, there are many more file system options to choose from on Linux. When installing Linux or partitioning with GParted, you need to be aware of these options. Table 17.6 lists and describes the most common file systems. Most distros, including Ubuntu, default to using a file system known as ext4 (fourth extended file system), an improvement on ext3 (third extended file system), which was the most widely used file system for many years.

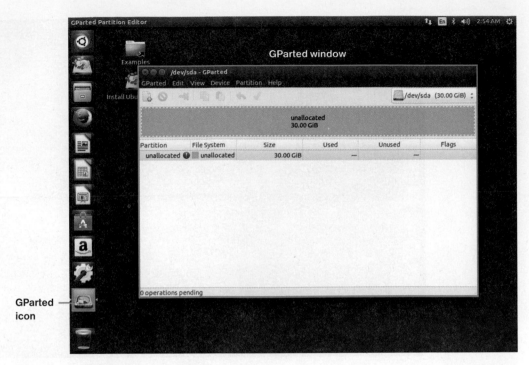

GParted
icon

FIGURE 17.20   GParted window

TABLE 17.6   Linux file systems

File system name	Description
ext3	Third generation of the extended file system, which introduced journaling (that is, the capability for a file system to track changes so that the file system can recover from power failures or crashes).
ext4	Fourth generation of the extended file system, which contains features such as journaling, volume support up to 1 exbibyte (EiB), and file sizes up to 16 tebibytes (TiB). It is a common file system choice.
ZFS	File system that focuses on data integrity and can do integrity checks on mounted disks (unlike ext4). You would not use ZFS on a machine that is using RAID. It is recommended for use on a single drive or just a bunch of disks (JBOD).
Btrfs	Pronounced "butter F S," a contender to be the successor to ext4, adding features such as snapshots, volume spanning, live resizing of file systems, and live addition/removal of disks to live file systems. It can support volumes and file sizes up to 16 EiB.

Ubuntu comes with a fair amount of software installed, but one of the great things about using Linux is the amount of free, open source software available. It isn't always easy to find software, especially if you are new to Linux and are unfamiliar with the tools that are available. The **Ubuntu Software Center** is a software manager that lets you access software from Ubuntu's repositories. With Ubuntu Software Center, shown in Figure 17.21, you can uninstall existing applications and install new ones, many of which are available for free. Although Ubuntu Software Center is useful for finding new software, you need to use the **Software Updater** tool to update your operating system and applications.

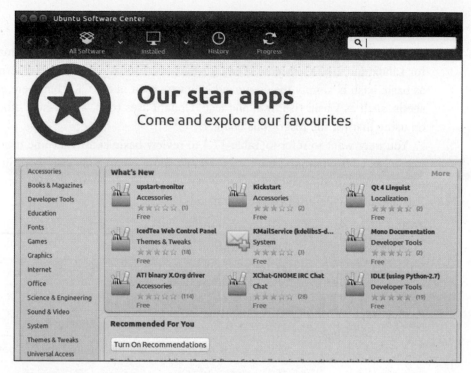

FIGURE 17.21   Ubuntu Software Center

Ubuntu comes bundled with a built-in backup application (see Figure 17.22) that supports local and remote backups, encryption, incremental and full backups, and scheduling; in addition, it can run seamlessly in the background. The backup application can be found by searching for backups in Dash. However, a wide array of other backup software is available for Linux. Many companies have their own backup procedure that involves using custom scripts and various utilities, such as `rsync`, to save on resources compared to doing a full system backup, as experienced in most Windows environments.

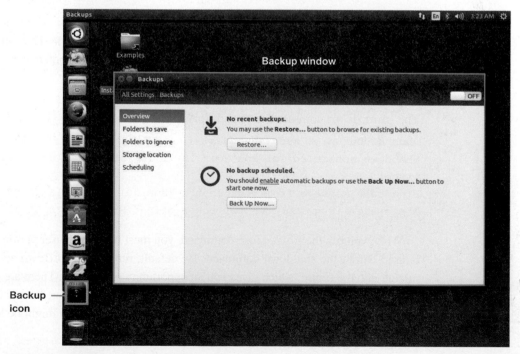

FIGURE 17.22   Ubuntu backup application

Command-Line Interface

The **command-line interface**, abbreviated CLI, is where most system management takes place for Linux and UNIX systems. The CLI for most Linux systems uses a terminal language known as bash. bash is simply the command language used in the CLI, but there are a few other notable shells, such as Dash, fish, zsh, and tcsh. Ubuntu uses bash, as do most other distros, so we focus on using that for the rest of this chapter.

You may want to refer to Table 17.4 to review basic command-line usage in macOS. Because macOS is UNIX (which Linux is based on), those commands also work in Linux. There are also more advanced commands that everyone who supports Linux systems should know. Table 17.7 lists and briefly describes these commands.

TABLE 17.7   Advanced CLI commands

Command	Description
shutdown	Shuts down or restarts the system, depending on the options used
passwd	Sets the password for a user
su	Switches from one user account to another
ifconfig	Shows network interface information for Ethernet ports
iwconfig	Shows network interface information for wireless adapters
ps	Shows a list of all current processes
apt-get	Allows management of packages
dd	Copies and converts files
locate	Searches the system for a file
updatedb	Updates the file database of the system for the locate command

To use the CLI on Ubuntu, click the *Dash* icon and search for *Terminal*. A few options appear, but you might want to use the one specifically labeled *Terminal*. This interface is similar to the macOS in that the command line shows the username and computer name.

Shutting Down the System

The shutdown command is straightforward; it shuts down the system. Here is an example:

```
ubuntu@ubuntu:~$ sudo shutdown
Shutdown scheduled for Sun 2019-10-25 16:13:07 UTC, use 'shutdown -c' to
cancel.
Broadcast message from root@ubuntu (Sun 2019-10-25 16:12:07 UTC):
The system is going down for power-off at Sun 2019-10-25 16:13:07 UTC!
```

When you run the shutdown command, you must have superuser permissions; this is why sudo is used before the shutdown command. By default, running shutdown schedules a shutdown one minute into the future, which gives you an opportunity to cancel it. There are also options to schedule the shutdown for a different time, to happen immediately, or to restart instead of powering off. You can also have a shutdown message broadcast to warn anyone else who might be logged in to the system.

passwd **Versus** pwd

The passwd command, not to be confused with pwd, is used to change a user's password. Remember that the pwd command is used to show you the current working directory. To change the logged-in user, just run the `passwd` command by itself. A prompt appears, where you can enter the current password and then enter the new password twice, as shown here.

```
ubuntu@ubuntu:~$ passwd
Change password for ubuntu.
(current) UNIX password:
Enter new UNIX password:
Retype new UNIX password:
passwd: password updated successfully
```

If you want to change the password of a different user, enter the command followed by the username, as shown here:

```
ubuntu@ubuntu:~$ sudo passwd test
Enter new UNIX password:
Retype new UNIX password:
passwd: password updated successfully
```

Note that you must have superuser permissions to change another user's password. To modify an account, you either need to be logged in to that account or have administrative (root) privileges.

Performing Network Configuration

The command `ifconfig` is an essential Linux command that all Linux administrators and users need to be familiar with. The basic output shows the current network settings, such as IP address, subnet mask, interfaces used, MAC address, and interface statistics, as shown in the following example:

```
ubuntu@ubuntu:~$ ifconfig
eth0 Link encap:Ethernet HWaddr b8:27:eb:43:c3:ad
 inet addr:10.0.0.250 Bcast:10.0.0.255 Mask:255.255.255.0
 UP BROADCAST RUNNING MULTICAST MTU:1500 Metric:1
 RX packets:5633010 errors:0 dropped:6300 overruns:0 frame:0
 TX packets:9370432 errors:0 dropped:0 overruns:0 carrier:0
 collisions:0 txqueuelen:1000
 RX bytes:429577586 (409.6 MiB) TX bytes:3680672251 (3.4 GiB)
lo Link encap:Local Loopback
 inet addr:127.0.0.1 Mask:255.0.0.0
 UP LOOPBACK RUNNING MTU:65536 Metric:1
 RX packets:0 errors:0 dropped:0 overruns:0 frame:0
 TX packets:0 errors:0 dropped:0 overruns:0 carrier:0
 collisions:0 txqueuelen:0
 RX bytes:0 (0.0 B) TX bytes:0 (0.0 B)

wlan0 Link encap:Ethernet HWaddr 80:1f:02:bb:ee:fa
 UP BROADCAST MULTICAST MTU:1500 Metric:1
 RX packets:0 errors:0 dropped:0 overruns:0 frame:0
 TX packets:0 errors:0 dropped:0 overruns:0 carrier:0
 collisions:0 txqueuelen:1000
 RX bytes:0 (0.0 B) TX bytes:0 (0.0 B)
```

As you can see in this output, you are presented with three different interfaces. `eth0` is an abbreviation for ethernet 0, the wired Ethernet connection. `lo` is an abbreviation for localhost, a loopback interface that is used for testing and routing information inside the operating system. Finally, `wlan0` represents wireless LAN interface 0. At the moment, only `eth0` and `lo` have IP addresses assigned, and `wlan0` is yet to be configured.

More advanced use of ifconfig allows you to change interface settings. If you want to set an address for wlan0, you can use ifconfig followed by the interface name wlan0, and then the appropriate settings, as shown in the following example:

```
ubuntu@ubuntu:~$ sudo ifconfig wlan0 10.0.0.200 netmask 255.255.255.0
broadcast 10.0.0.255
ubuntu@ubuntu:~$ ifconfig
eth0 Link encap:Ethernet HWaddr b8:27:eb:43:c3:ad
 inet addr:10.0.0.250 Bcast:10.0.0.255 Mask:255.255.255.0
 UP BROADCAST RUNNING MULTICAST MTU:1500 Metric:1
 RX packets:5668535 errors:0 dropped:6327 overruns:0 frame:0
 TX packets:9430245 errors:0 dropped:0 overruns:0 carrier:0
 collisions:0 txqueuelen:1000
 RX bytes:432348412 (412.3 MiB) TX bytes:3758820467 (3.5 GiB)

lo Link encap:Local Loopback
 inet addr:127.0.0.1 Mask:255.0.0.0
 UP LOOPBACK RUNNING MTU:65536 Metric:1
 RX packets:0 errors:0 dropped:0 overruns:0 frame:0
 TX packets:0 errors:0 dropped:0 overruns:0 carrier:0
 collisions:0 txqueuelen:0
 RX bytes:0 (0.0 B) TX bytes:0 (0.0 B)

wlan0 Link encap:Ethernet HWaddr 80:1f:02:bb:ee:fa
 inet addr:10.0.0.200 Bcast:10.0.0.255 Mask:255.255.255.0
 UP BROADCAST MULTICAST MTU:1500 Metric:1
 RX packets:0 errors:0 dropped:0 overruns:0 frame:0
 TX packets:0 errors:0 dropped:0 overruns:0 carrier:0
 collisions:0 txqueuelen:1000
 RX bytes:0 (0.0 B) TX bytes:0 (0.0 B)
```

In this example, even though an appropriate address has been assigned to wlan0 for the wireless network, wlan0 is not a working wireless interface. Other wireless settings, such as the wireless network SSID, as well as any authentication settings must be configured. That is where the command iwconfig comes into play. Although ifconfig can edit IP settings, it cannot do the wireless-specific settings that iwconfig provides.

Say that you have a Linux computer connected to a wireless network named Test that uses the WEP encryption key 1234567890. You would enter the following command:

```
ubuntu@ubuntu:~$ sudo iwconfig wlan0 essid Test key restricted 1234567890
```

> **TECH TIP**
>
> **iwconfig supports only WEP authentication**
>
> It is important to realize that iwconfig supports only WEP authentication. For more advanced authentication, such as WPA or WPA2, you need to use wpa_supplicant. It is recommended not to use WEP if you can use higher-level encryption because WEP is an older standard that is easily cracked.

Viewing Processes

ps is another command to have in your toolbox for administering a Linux system. ps shows all active processes running on a system. This important information tells you what is running, how long things have been running, and how many resources are being used. Here is an example:

```
ubuntu@ubuntu:~$ ps
 PID TTY TIME CMD
 4093 pts/0 00:00:01 bash
14766 pts/0 00:00:00 ps
```

By default, ps shows only processes being run by the current user and from the current login session. Generally, you use ps along with other modifiers to get useful information. The most common version of ps is ps aux. The a modifier lists all processes from other users; u shows the user who is running the process; and x shows processes from all sessions. The ps command effectively shows everything that is running on the system. Here is an example:

```
ubuntu@ubuntu:~$ ps aux
USER PID %CPU %MEM VSZ RSS TTY STAT START TIME COMMAND
root 1 0.0 0.1 2148 1348 ? Ss Oct23 0:10 init [2]
root 2 0.0 0.0 0 0 ? S Oct23 0:00 [kthreadd]
root 3 0.0 0.0 0 0 ? S Oct23 0:16 [ksoftirqd/0]
root 5 0.0 0.0 0 0 ? S< Oct23 0:00 [kworker/0:0H]
root 7 0.0 0.0 0 0 ? S Oct23 1:53 [rcu_preempt]
root 8 0.0 0.0 0 0 ? S Oct23 0:00 [rcu_sched]
root 9 0.0 0.0 0 0 ? S Oct23 0:00 [rcu_bh]
```

A lesser-known option is to add the f modifier, so the command is ps faux. This shows everything from ps aux and also organizes the processes in a tree format so you can see what processes are the parent and the child. In the following example, a screen session is running for a script being run by the program supervisor. Some of the command output has been omitted here to make it easier to read:

```
root 2316 0.0 0.3 4816 2372 ? Ss Oct23 1:02 SCREEN
root 2317 0.0 0.5 5680 4088 pts/1 Ss Oct23 0:00 \_ /bin/bash
root 2325 0.0 0.3 4592 2660 pts/1 S+ Oct23 0:00 \_ sudo supervise
/etc/init.d/
```

Obtaining Software via the CLI

Earlier in this chapter you read about using the Ubuntu Software Center to obtain software. apt-get is the command-line interface tool that is the equivalent of Ubuntu Software Center. There is another common command-line package manager, named rpm, short for Red Hat Package Manager. Despite its name, it is used on more distros than just Red Hat. There is another lesser-used manager called yum, short for Yellowdog Updater Modified, that builds on rpm.

To use apt-get, start by refreshing the list of available software. Systems that use apt-get have a file located at /etc/apt/sources.list, which lists the software repositories that should be checked for available software. It is common to edit this list to add different sources to get different applications. To update the list of available software from your sources list, you use the command apt-get followed by the modifier update. Only the first few lines of the following example are shown because the complete output can take up a lot of screen space, depending on the number of sources:

```
ubuntu@ubuntu:~$ sudo apt-get update
Get:1 http://archive.ubuntu.com vivid InRelease [218 kB]
Get:2 http://security.ubuntu.com vivid-security InRelease [64.4 kB]
```

After updating the sources, use the `apt-get` command followed by `install` and then the name of the package to install the software. Say that you want to obtain software called `install screen`, which is a tool that enables you to use multiple screens. At the CLI, execute the following command: `apt-get install screen`

It is recommended that you always simulate a software installation first by using the `-s` modifier to make sure the installation will not affect something important on the system. Here is an example:

```
ubuntu@ubuntu:~$ sudo apt-get install screen -s
Reading package lists... Done
Building dependency tree
Reading state information... Done
Suggested packages:
 select screen byobu
The following NEW packages will be installed:
 screen
0 upgraded, 1 newly installed, 0 to remove and 282 not upgraded.
Inst screen (4.2.1.-3 Ubuntu:15.04/vivid [amd64])
Conf screen (4.2.1.-3 Ubuntu:15.04/vivid [amd64])
```

This simulation shows what would happen if it actually installed the screen. Once you determine that the installation would be correct, you can rerun the command without the `-s` modifier to install the software.

> **TECH TIP**
>
> **Always predownload packages**
>
> When working with systems that need high uptime, it is always advisable to predownload the packages you plan to install ahead of time to avoid downtime while waiting for a download to occur. This can be done by running the `apt-get install` command with the `-d` flag.

Copying Data

The command `dd` is a versatile command you can use to copy and convert data. Some common uses include copying the contents of a CD/DVD to an ISO file, cloning a partition to another one, creating a backup, erasing a disk, converting a file or its content, and benchmarking. The general syntax is the command `dd`, followed by the input file and then the output file. You can also use many other modifiers, such as `conv` for conversions, `bs` for block counts, and `count` for the number of blocks used.

Figure 17.23 shows the capabilities of `dd` in an environment with two partitions using the application `gparted`. The partitions are equal in size, are virtually empty, and are named `/dev/sda1` and `/dev/sda2`.

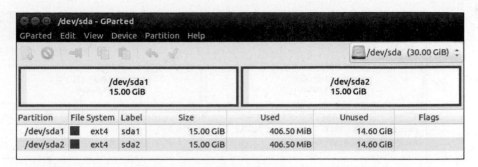

FIGURE 17.23   Disk partitions in GParted

To copy the contents of a DVD onto /dev/sda1, the syntax is dd followed by the input file (the DVD), and the output file, which is /dev/sda1. Here is an example:

```
ubuntu@ubuntu:~$ sudo dd if=/dev/sr0 of=/sda1/test.iso
2247744+0 records in
2247744+0 records out
1150844928 bytes (1.2 GB) copied, 23.0764 s, 49.9 MB/s
```

The output in this example shows 1.2 GB of data copied, the size of the data on the DVD. It took 23 seconds, and it copied at almost 50 MB/s. Look at the partitions with GParted in Figure 17.24. The sda1 file now has more space used, as represented by the yellow highlighted space.

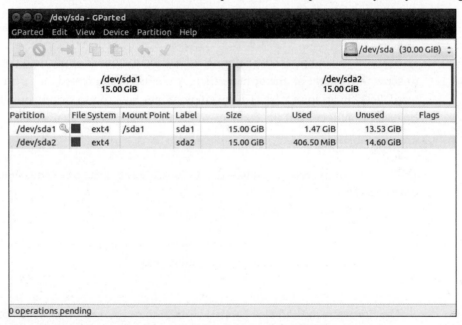

FIGURE 17.24   DVD copied onto the sda1 partition

Now use dd to clone sda1 to sda2. The syntax is virtually the same as before; the only difference is that when you copy one partition to another partition, you use the full device name of the partition rather than the folder to which it is mounted. The following example shows this command and its output, and Figure 17.25 shows the results in GParted:

```
ubuntu@ubuntu:~$ sudo dd if=/dev/sda1 of=/dev/sda2
31455232+0 records in
31455232+0 records out
16105078784 bytes (16 GB) copied, 386.654 s, 41.7 MB/s
```

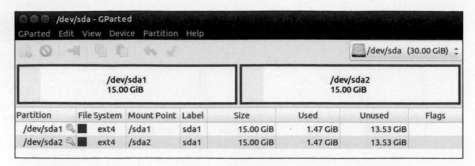

FIGURE 17.25   Cloned partition in GParted

Figure 17.25 shows that you can verify in GParted that the dd command cloned sda1 to sda2. They are exact clones. Comparing Figure 17.25 to Figure 17.24, notice that even the device label copied over to sda2. And now both partitions use the same amount of disk space. Comparing the mounted partitions, both contain the same file: the ISO previously created.

```
ubuntu@ubuntu:~$ ls -l /sda1
total 1123892
drwx------ 2 root root          16384 Oct 26 02:38 lost+found
-rw-rw-r-- 2 root root     1150844928 Oct 26 02:37 test.iso
ubuntu@ubuntu:~$ ls -l /sda2
total 1123892
drwx------ 2 root root          16384 Oct 26 02:38 lost+found
-rw-rw-r-- 2 root root     1150844928 Oct 26 02:37 test.iso
```

In the next example, the dd command is used to convert a file, and the cat command is used to show the content of one or more files. A file has been created on /sda1 that contains only the word "test" in all lowercase. This example shows how to use dd to copy the file to sda2 and the conv option to convert the contents of the file to uppercase characters.

```
ubuntu@ubuntu:/sda1$ cat test.txt
test
ubuntu@ubuntu:/sda1$ sudo dd if=/sda1/test.txt of=/sda2/test.txt
conv=ucase
0+1 records in
0+1 records out
5 bytes (5 B) copied, 0.000263474 s, 19.0 kB/s
ubuntu@ubuntu:/sda1$ cat /sda2/test.txt
TEST
```

The dd command can also be used to erase the sda2 partition. One option is to write all zeros to the partition. You do this by using /dev/zero *device*, where *device* is a software device that is used specifically for outputting just zeros. It is used as the input file, into the output of sda2, using block sizes of 4 kB. This process, shown in the following example, is called zeroing out a drive:

```
ubuntu@ubuntu:~$ sudo dd if=/dev/zero of=/dev/sda2 bs=4k
dd: error writing '/dev/sda2': No space left on device
3932161+0 records in
3932160+0 records out
16106127360 bytes (16 GB) copied, 25.5437 s, 631 MB/s
```

Zeroing out a device is a secure method of erasing data, as the whole drive is filled with zeros, until it runs out of space. This makes typical data recovery methods impossible to use and renders the partition useless until it is repartitioned.

In Figure 17.26 you can see that sda2 now has an error. This is because Ubuntu cannot find a file system for the device; it has been rendered unusable until it is repartitioned.

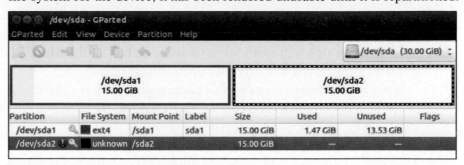

FIGURE 17.26   Unusable partition in GParted

Finding Files

Sometimes, when managing a system (especially an unfamiliar system) at the command line, it is difficult to find the locations of files. This is where two commands called updatedb and locate come into use. updatedb is a command you can run to update a local database on the system that contains the full pathname of each file. You can then use the command locate to search for a file in this database of paths.

This is a much quicker way to search for a file than searching the system itself, but there are limitations to this search method. The database of paths has to be updated regularly to be accurate. Usually, this is done by a scheduled task through the cron service. If you are searching for a file that was recently added, you may need to run the updatedb command and press ⏎Enter to manually refresh the database. Because this command looks at the entire file system, you need to run it with superuser permissions to ensure that it can read all file paths. Here is an example:

```
ubuntu@ubuntu:~$ sudo updatedb
ubuntu@ubuntu:~$
```

You can now search the system. Say that someone left an important file called *testdocument. txt* that you need to retrieve, but the person didn't tell you where the file is located; you could use locate to find the path to the file, as in this example:

```
ubuntu@ubuntu:~$ locate testdocument.txt
/home/test/testdocument.txt
```

You can see from this example that testdocument.txt was left in the test user's home directory.

CHAPTER 17

Missing GRUB/LILO

The bootloader contains all the information about how the disk is organized, such as the size and layout of partitions. Linux distros typically install one of two bootloaders: Grand Unified Boot

Loader (GRUB) or Linux Loader (LILO). LILO used to be the more predominant bootloader, but GRUB is now the default because it supports more modern features; the current version is GRUB2. LILO, which has been marked as discontinued, is an older and more basic bootloader; it is missing some features, such as network boot and a command-line interface, that GRUB supports. The majority of the time you should keep whatever default bootloader your distro comes with unless you need a key feature that only another bootloader offers.

If you have problems booting into a Linux system, there is a chance that the bootloader has been overwritten or corrupted. This problem might happen, for example, if a PC technician decides to install a Windows operating system on the same disk that has Linux installed. When the technician does the installation, the Windows installation could overwrite the bootloader with its own MBR. After that, Linux cannot be loaded because the boot information created by GRUB or LILO no longer exists. To fix this issue, it is necessary to re-create the bootloader for the system. To fix the broken bootloader in this situation, you would boot to an Ubuntu live CD and run a few commands to fix it.

To use LILO to replace the MBR, you would open a command prompt and first install LILO with `sudo apt-get install lilo`. You would then run the command `sudo lilo -M /dev/XXX /mbr` (replacing *XXX* with the device name, such as `sda`), which references the name of the disk device where you installed Linux (or, in a more advanced partition setup, where the boot partition is, which is usually the device containing a /boot partition).

To fix this problem with GRUB, you would install GRUB2 with `sudo apt-get install grub2` and then run the command `sudo grub-install /dev/XXX` (replacing *XXX* with the device, name such as `sda`).

A missing bootloader scenario could require a slightly different fix, depending on the partition layout and the operating systems installed. It is important to read the documentation for either bootloader that you intend to use to make sure you are using a solution that fits the problem.

macOS and Linux Best Practices

Apple macOS and any flavor of Linux, like other operating systems, should be maintained using best practices. Key best practices are as follows:

> *Perform scheduled backups*—Back up the operating system and important data on a regular basis. As an IT staff member, you should gently remind users to do this, too.
> *Schedule disk maintenance*—Drives become fragmented over time. For best system performance, perform disk maintenance on a regular basis.
> *Perform system updates*—Be sure to install the latest operating system updates to prevent security and performance problems.
> *Perform driver/firmware updates*—Ensure that the latest hardware drivers and firmware updates are installed.
> *Perform patch management*—A patch is code changes that fix a particular problem in an operating system or application. Patch management is the process of downloading, testing, installing, retesting, and documenting these changes. Patch management helps with security issues, too. See Chapter 18, "Computer and Network Security," for more information.
> *Install and update antivirus/anti-malware*—Many people believe that Apple computers and Linux-based computers do not need antivirus or anti-malware software. This is not true. Not only should this software be installed, but it needs to be updated regularly.

SOFT SKILLS: BE HUMBLE

As an IT staff member, you have to be confident that you can repair most anything and figure things out. However, that confidence sometimes comes across to others as arrogance. Anyone who has worked in IT knows that you cannot know everything. You might know a little bit about a lot of things. You may know a lot about a specific side of IT. But no one can be an expert in it all. Show a little humility and be humble with your knowledge. Do not lord your knowledge and expertise over those you support. Showing empathy for the people you support and interact with goes a long way. See Figure 17.27.

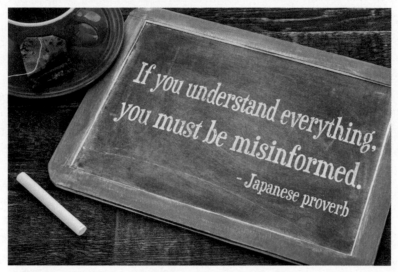

FIGURE 17.27   No technician knows everything

Chapter Summary

- > macOS is a UNIX-based operating system developed by Apple.
- > Open source software is made freely available and is open for modification.
- > macOS can only run on Apple hardware, even in virtual machines.
- > The macOS user interface, known as Aqua, contains the Dock, Finder, and menu bar.
- > Spotlight can be used to quickly search a macOS system to find files, emails, applications, and even web search results.
- > iCloud is Apple's online service that provides online storage and syncing.
- > To get the most out of using macOS, end users should have an Apple ID to use with iCloud and the Mac App Store.
- > Time Machine is the tool used for automated macOS backups.
- > Most system settings can be found and managed in the System Preferences menu, which is equivalent to the Control Panel in Windows.
- > Boot Camp, an application that comes bundled with macOS, guides you through the installation of Windows on a separate partition on a Mac.
- > Basic macOS troubleshooting can be done using the Console and Activity Monitor. The Console allows you to see detailed logs of macOS, applications, and services. Activity Monitor allows you to see what is running on the system and what resources processes are using.
- > Keychain Access is a utility for storing passwords, and users tend not to understand it. Be prepared to show users how to update their Keychain password when they update their passwords.
- > Advanced system administrators use the Terminal application to access the command-line interface of macOS.

> Linux is an open operating system platform built on the principles of UNIX.
> Most Linux administration happens at the command-line level, not in the graphical user interface.
> You must learn the basics of using the command line to properly administer Linux/UNIX systems. Be familiar with the commands in Tables 17.4 and 17.7.
> Be prepared to spend many hours researching how to use Linux/UNIX systems; it can take years to master understanding how they work and how to properly administer them. If you aren't sure about something, use online resources or ask a colleague to get a better understanding.

A+ CERTIFICATION EXAM TIPS

✓ This chapter and the objectives contained within account for only a small percentage of the exam.

✓ Be familiar with the following features: multiple desktops/Mission Control, Keychain, Spotlight, iCloud, gestures, Finder, Remote Disc, the Dock, and Boot Camp.

✓ Know the purpose of the shell/Terminal application and review commands such as su/sudo, ls, cd, shutdown, mv, cp, rm, grep, pwd, passwd, chmod, chown, iwconfig, ifconfig, ps, vi, dd, kill, and apt-get. Know that you would use the sudo command to be able to modify settings within the operating system.

✓ Know macOS and Linux client best practices, including those related to scheduled backups, scheduled disk maintenance, system updates, App Store for macOS, patch management, driver and firmware updates, and antivirus/anti-malware updates.

✓ Be able to use the following tools in a macOS or Linux client: Time Machine backups (and know why you would use), snapshot restores, image recovery, disk maintenance utilities, the Terminal application/shell, screen sharing, and Force Quit.

✓ Know that the Time Machine tool and iCloud can be used to back up/restore Mac images.

✓ Be familiar with the file systems associated with macOS and Linux: ext3, ext4, and HFS.

Key Terms

Activity Monitor   930
App Store   923
apt-get   944
Back to My Mac   923
Boot Camp   934
c   934
cd   934
chmod   935
chown   935
command-line interface   944
Console   931
cp   934
Dash   940
dd   944
Disk Utility   933
Dock   919
ext3   942
ext4   942
Finder   919
Force Quit   926
gestures   922
GParted   941
grep   935
iCloud   922
ifconfig   944

iwconfig   944
iWork   922
kernel   939
kernel panic   931
Keychain Access   932
kill   935
launcher   940
Launchpad   920
less   935
Linux   938
locate   944
ls   934
macOS   918
man   935
menu bar   920
Mission Control   920
mkdir   934
mv   934
nano   935
Nautilus   940
open source   918
OS X   918
Panel   940
passwd   944
pin wheel   930

POSIX   919
ps   944
pwd   934
Remote Disc   926
rm   934
root   936
safe mode (Mac)   929
screen sharing   924
shell   919
shutdown   944
Software Updater   942
Spotlight   920
su   944
sudo   935
System Information   931
System Preferences   927
Terminal   934
Time Machine   924
touch   934
Ubuntu Software Center   942
Unity   940
updatedb   944
vi   935

Review Questions

1. What are the four main parts of the macOS graphical user interface? (Choose four.)
   [Desktop | Finder | Time Machine | Console | Spotlight | Dock | Menu bar]

2. [T | F] Ubuntu 15.04 uses the GNOME user interface.

3. What wireless encryption does `iwconfig` support, and what is an alternative to using `iwconfig`? (Choose one answer from each set of distractors.)
   Choose one of these: [WEP | WPA | WPA2 | AES]
   Choose one of these: [ipconfig | ipconfig /all | WPA supplicant | TSA]

4. In what ways could you quickly launch an application in macOS?

   _____

5. What type of account do you need to create to purchase software through the Apple App Store?

   _____

6. Write out the steps you would take to create a file with the Terminal application in macOS or Linux.

   _____

7. What `dd` command would you use to copy the contents of a partition named /dev/drive1 to another partition, called /dev/backup?

   _____

8. What command is used to look for the word *mouse* in a filename?
   [sudo | apt-get | grep | rd]

9. The _____ command lists the contents of the current directory.
   [apt-get | grep | ls | sudo]

10. Which macOS tool is used to display and modify the main system settings?
    [Launchpad | Activity Monitor | Safari | System Preferences]

11. How would you create a file from the command-line interface?

    _____

12. What steps would you take in Ubuntu, from the command line, to install a new package named lynx?

    _____

    _____

    _____

    _____

13. If an application is not starting properly on macOS, what steps could you take to resolve this?

    _____

14. If a Mac is running slowly, what utility could you use to identify the cause of the slowdown?
    [Activity Monitor | Dash | Launchpad | Mission Control]

15. What is the difference between `passwd` and `pwd`?

    _____

16. How large should a Time Machine backup drive be?

    _____

17. If you wanted to use `chmod` to give a file owner read, write, and execute permissions, what command would you use?

    _____

CHAPTER 17

18. Which command grants temporary superuser permissions? [ls | less | root | sudo | app-get]

19. [T | F] The locate command searches the Linux file system.

20. How would you find out more information about a Linux command?

_____

Exercises

Exercise 17.1

Objective: To become familiar with macOS tools

Procedure: Match each tool to the correct description.

_____ **a.** Time Machine   Stop a non-responsive application

_____ **b.** Screen sharing   Configure file sharing

_____ **c.** App Store   Get system updates

_____ **d.** Force Quit   Use an optical disc on another computer

_____ **e.** Remote Disc   Troubleshoot kernel panic

_____ **f.** System Preferences   View processes and used system resources

_____ **g.** Activity Monitor   View a remote Mac

_____ **h.** Console   Create a system backup

Exercise 17.2

Objective: To become familiar with Mac/Linux commands

Procedure: Match each command to the correct description.

_____ **a.** cd   Delete a file

_____ **b.** rm   Gain root privilege

_____ **c.** touch   Move a file

_____ **d.** chown   Move to a different directory

_____ **e.** mv   Change the owner of a directory

_____ **f.** grep   Get help for a particular command

_____ **g.** man   Create a file

_____ **h.** sudo   Search output for a specific value

Activities

Internet Discovery

Objective: Access the Internet to obtain specific information regarding a computer or its associated parts

Parts: Internet access

Procedure: Complete the following procedure and answer the accompanying questions.

1. Search online to find a Linux distro besides Ubuntu. Document the website and give a brief description of the distro.

_____

_____

2. What are some of the common business uses of the distro you found?

_____

_____

3. Research why Linux servers usually do not have a graphical user interface installed. Write down the URL of the website you used to help come to your conclusion and explain your reasoning for not installing a GUI.

_____

_____

4. Linux is a stable platform but still has issues and can crash. Research to determine what log files are useful in Linux for troubleshooting.

_____

_____

5. Find a website that describes how to troubleshoot a Linux system that will not boot. Write the URL you used and one thing you learned from the site.

_____

_____

Soft Skills

Objective: To enhance and fine-tune a future technician's ability to listen, communicate in oral form, work together in a group on technical problems, and support people who use computers in a professional manner.

Activities: Complete the following questions in a group of three and share your opinions.

1. Write down two things you find confusing about using macOS or Linux and share them with your group. See which areas are the most common problems for everyone.

_____

_____

2. With your group, do more research on your group's list of the most common confusing items from step 1; as a group, try to come to a better understanding of each issue. For any topics that you cannot get a better grasp on, create a plan to better understand them and describe your plan.

3. Working with UNIX or Linux requires the ability to do independent research to discover and understand new technologies in the field. You need to know how to properly search on the Internet to effectively find information, especially when troubleshooting an issue you are unfamiliar with. Have everyone in the group search to find what is the most popular web server application used to run on Linux. Compare answers to see if everyone got the same results. Also compare what terms each person used to search for the answer. Some searches will be more precise at finding the answer than others. It is important to take a look at how you search to get results as quickly as possible. List the most common answer for the most popular web server to run on Linux, as well as what was the most concise search phrase or term used.

_____

_____

Critical Thinking Skills

Objective: To analyze and evaluate information as well as apply learned information to new or different situations

Activities:

1. You have a Ubuntu user who cannot read a file. What is the first thing you should look at to resolve this? Why?

   _____

   _____

2. Write a paragraph explaining why you think businesses prefer to use Linux rather than Windows for server environments.

   _____

   _____

   _____

   _____

   _____

   _____

3. What would be the drawbacks of using Linux rather than Windows for a server?

   _____

   _____

18 Computer and Network Security

In this chapter you will learn:

> What a company might put in a security policy

> How to perform operating system and data protection

> How to share and protect data

> How to optimize security for Windows

> Methods to use for data destruction and disposal

> How to configure wireless security options

> How to build customer trust

CompTIA Exam Objectives

What CompTIA exam objectives are covered in this chapter?

✓ 1001-2.3 Given a scenario, install and configure a basic wired/wireless SOHO network.

✓ 1001-2.5 Summarize the properties and purposes of services provided by networked hosts.

✓ 1001-2.6 Explain common network configuration concepts.

✓ 1001-3.5 Given a scenario, install and configure motherboards, CPUs, and add-on cards.

✓ 1002-1.6 Given a scenario, use Microsoft Windows Control Panel utilities.

✓ 1002-1.8 Given a scenario, configure Microsoft Windows networking on a client/desktop.

✓ 1002-2.1 Summarize the importance of physical security measures.

✓ 1002-2.2 Explain logical security concepts.

✓ 1002-2.3 Compare and contrast wireless security protocols and authentication methods.

✓ 1002-2.4 Given a scenario, detect, remove, and prevent malware using appropriate tools and methods.

✓ 1002-2.5 Compare and contrast social engineering, threats, and vulnerabilities.

✓ 1002-2.6 Compare and contrast the differences of basic Microsoft Windows OS security settings.

✓ 1002-2.7 Given a scenario, implement security best practices to secure a workstation.

✓ 1002-2.8 Given a scenario, implement methods for securing mobile devices.

✓ 1002-2.9 Given a scenario, implement appropriate data destruction and disposal methods.

✓ 1002-2.10 Given a scenario, configure security on SOHO wireless and wired networks.

✓ 1002-3.2 Given a scenario, troubleshoot and resolve PC security issues.

✓ 1002-3.3 Given a scenario, use best practice procedures for malware removal.

✓ 1002-4.1 Compare and contrast best practices associated with types of documentation.

✓ 1002-4.3 Given a scenario, implement basic disaster prevention and recovery methods.

✓ 1002-4.6 Explain the processes for addressing prohibited content/activity, and privacy, licensing, and policy concepts.

✓ 1002.-4.9 Given a scenario, use remote access technologies.

Security Overview

Computer and network security relates to the hardware, software, and data protection of PCs and mobile devices. Large books are devoted to this topic. This chapter focuses on issues related to a PC technician's job and the processes and terminology with which a technician should be familiar. Security should be of concern to everyone in a business or a home—including, of course, the people who repair and support PCs: the technicians. A technician must be able to implement and explain security concepts. Every technician has the responsibility to promote security consciousness and to train users to be good stewards of equipment and data.

Security Policy

Companies struggle with information technology (IT) security as much today as when computers were first used in the corporate environment. Actually, the corporate landscape has become complicated today because people bring their own electronic devices to work. This is commonly referred to as *bring your own device*, or **BYOD**. Management must define and make clear what devices may be put on corporate wired or wireless networks and also what devices are unacceptable, along with the consequences for doing so.

A **security policy** is one or more documents that provide rules and guidelines related to computer and network security. Every company, no matter its size or number of employees, should have a security policy. Small businesses tend to have general operating procedures that are passed verbally from one employee to another, but it is best to have these processes documented in detail. **Non-compliant systems**, or systems that do not meet security policy guidelines, are some of the biggest threats to companies today. Some sectors, such as education, health care, and government, require IT security policies.

Common elements of a security policy are listed in Table 18.1.

TABLE 18.1   Security policy elements

Security policy component	Description
Physical access	Describes who is allowed into a building, to what part of the building they have access, and badge/key control. Defines who has keys to the wiring closets and server rooms as well as who is allowed in such places. Delineates what type of security log is kept when a person is allowed access to a space.
Antivirus	States whether antivirus software is required on every system, possibly what product is used, how updates are obtained, and steps taken when a machine is not compliant or if a person refuses to be compliant.
Acceptable use policy (AUP)	Defines who has access to, and what level of usage is appropriate for, company-provided information resources such as email and Internet usage. Sometimes, an AUP defines what data can be taken from the company or data storage limitations (for example, "no personal data is to be stored on a server or workstation PC"). This section normally includes statements about gaming and web surfing during work hours as well as consequences for violations. The details might include defining what web browser and hardware platforms are supported. It might include the process for assigning folder and file rights and what to do if an account has been disabled.
Password policy	Spells out guidelines for protecting passwords, such as not writing them down, a timeline for changing passwords, the number and types of characters required, and processes for forgotten passwords, such as whether the new password can be given by phone or by email only.

Security policy component	Description
Email usage	Defines who owns email that resides on a company server, how long email is stored, proper usage of email, and when it is backed up. Lawsuits related to this area continue to find for the company regarding email rights because the data is stored on company-owned and company-provided servers.
Remote access	Contains statements related to who is allowed remote access, the type(s) of remote access permitted, company resources that can be accessed remotely, the process to obtain desired rights and access, and the security level required.
Emergency procedures	Details what to do when something is missing and the steps to take if a natural disaster such as a hurricane occurs. Stipulates who overrides a security policy and authorizes access to someone.

Many corporate security policies are implemented based on user profiles. Within each profile, mandatory requirements such as password length and frequency of password changes are dictated and enforced. The profile also can enforce what network resources a particular user has access to. Even though not every company has a formal security policy, specific points related to a security policy are referenced throughout this chapter. Whether written or just commonly accepted guidelines, many implementations are based on a particular company's rules for computer and network security.

To ease into the topic of security, the easiest place to start is security prevention methods. Security prevention methods deal with security measures that might prevent a security breach from occurring in the first place. Four methods of security prevention are physical security, logical security, end-user education, and the principle of least privilege.

Physical Security

Typical physical security includes door locks, cipher locks, keys, guards, and fences, but physical security regarding computers can mean much more. Companies commonly use electronic key cards, instead of keys, for physical access to rooms. Electronic key cards (see Figure 18.1) are part of an access control system, which includes the key cards, door readers, and software to control and monitor the system.

Electronic key cards have many benefits, including the following:

> They are easy to program and issue/revoke compared to issuing a key and getting it back from an employee who quits or is dismissed.
> Data is stored in a database instead of on a checkout form.
> Access to information, such as who entered a room and at what time, can be logged and monitored more easily than with a checkout sheet.
> More layers of control can be exercised with key cards. With metal keys, the usual process is to give a key for each room, issue a submaster key for an entire wing, or issue a master key for the entire building.
> When keys are issued and one is lost, the lock must be rekeyed and new keys issued. When an electronic key card is lost, the old card is deactivated, and a new one is issued.

Other electronic devices and technologies also provide access to computers and rooms—in other words, authenticate the user. **Authentication** is the process of determining whether a network device or person has permission to access a network. Table 18.2 lists and describes security devices that help with the physical security of computers.

FIGURE 18.1   Electronic key cards

TABLE 18.2   Physical security devices

Device/technology	Description
Smart card	A small ID-sized card that can store data, which can be encrypted, and that requires authorization for changing. A smart card can be swiped through a card reader or may interact wirelessly with a card reader. Smart cards are used in government IDs (with such information as medical/dental records), mobile phones as subscriber ID modules, driver's licenses, and employee badges (see Figure 18.2).
Key fob	Used for keyless entry to cars and buildings and interior doors, such as a fitness room in an apartment complex.
Radio frequency ID (**RFID**)	A technology that allows automatic identification of people, objects, or animals. Uses an RFID tag that is read wirelessly by an RFID reader. Used in libraries and inventory systems and used for computers, hospital equipment, and locating lost pets or people. An **RFID badge** can be used to access and track access to a locked area.
Badge reader	A device that can be contactless or that may require a swipe or insertion of an identification card to allow entry into a space.
Security guard	A human who provides security by controlling access into a controlled space such as a network closet or server room.
Security token	Also called an authentication token, USB token, hardware token, or software token. As a physical security option, this is a device that authorizes access to something. A **hardware token** (see Figure 18.3), for example, is a physical device used to gain access to a resource such as a file or company. Examples of hardware tokens are smart cards, one-time passwords, and Bluetooth tokens.
Door lock	A physical security device that should be used for key equipment such as servers, firewalls, switches, and data storage devices. Even with a locked room, it is important to **disable unused ports** on devices in case the room is compromised.

Device/technology	Description
Entry control roster	Also known as an access control roster, lists employees who are authorized access to a particular area.
Biometric lock	A lock that is operated using a physical trait such as a fingerprint, retina scan, hand scan, or facial recognition to allow access into a controlled space such as a research lab or network closet. See the "Biometrics" section, later in this chapter.
Trusted Platform Module (**TPM**)	A microcontroller chip on a motherboard used for hardware/software authentication. Stores information such as security certificates, passwords, and encryption keys. **Encryption** is the process of converting data into an unreadable format. The TPM can also authenticate hardware devices. Applications can use TPM for file and folder encryption, local passwords, email, VPN/PKI authentication, and wireless authentication.
Cable lock	Used with devices in common areas such as libraries or lobby areas. Also used to secure laptops. Refer to Figure 10.100.
Server lock	A physical or electronic lock on a server cabinet that can provide monitoring and security for individual server cabinet doors.
USB lock	A lock that can prevent USB storage devices from being used in USB ports in order to prevent moving, transferring, and copying of files.
Mantrap	A method of separating a nonsecure area from a secured area (see Figure 18.4). This could be two doors with a guard, keypad, or some other security means on the second door. Useful in preventing unauthorized access and tailgating (in which an unauthorized person enters directly behind an authorized person).
Privacy screen	Also called a privacy filter; prevents **shoulder surfing**, in which someone looks over your shoulder to gain information from looking at your screen; allows viewing the screen clearly only if you are sitting directly in front of the monitor (see Figure 18.5).
Tracking module	Used to track assets and provide recovery options if a device is lost or stolen. Might include a remote data wiping service.

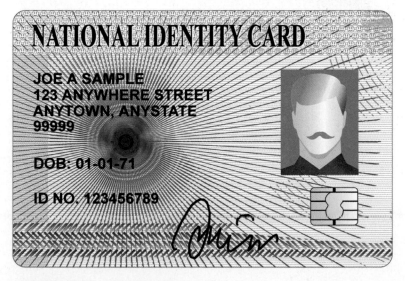

FIGURE 18.2 Smart card

FIGURE 18.3   Hardware token

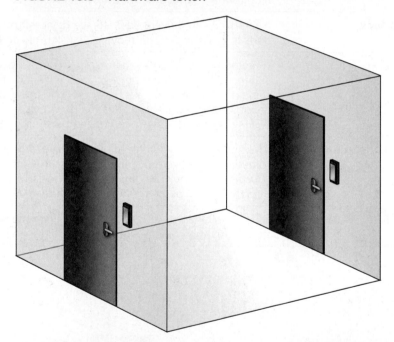

FIGURE 18.4   Mantrap

FIGURE 18.5   Shoulder surfing

Document Security

Some computer data must be printed as part of normal business operations. Some of this printed material must be kept in a locked environment (such as a safe, cabinet, or file cabinet). When others who do not have a "need to know" are in the room, turn the printed material over or, better yet, put it inside a folder. When the material is no longer needed, it can be shredded by a shredding service or using a shredder in the office. Outside companies should provide a **certificate of destruction** or proof of **incineration** (destruction by fire).

Shredders are available for reasonable prices, but they are not the best option in a corporate environment because shredded paper from most models can still be reconstructed (see Figure 18.6). For day-to-day business and personal documents, shredding is still a good practice to keep other people from taking documents out of trash bins (**dumpster diving**) and using the information for some malicious intent.

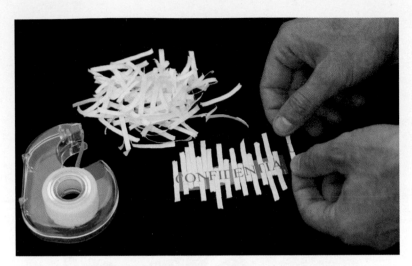

FIGURE 18.6 Reconstructing shredded documents

Authentication

Authentication involves proving who a particular person or device is by using something someone has, something a person knows, something a person is, or somewhere a person is located. Smart cards or security tokens are often described as two-factor authentication, or **multifactor authentication**. With this type of authentication, which is familiar to most people, you need something you possess, such as your ATM card, your current location, or a security token device, and something you know, such as a PIN, in order to gain access to something (such as a room, bank account, shared folder, or data stored in the cloud). This is more secure than **single-factor authentication**, which uses only one means of authentication, such as a username/password.

Software tokens and authenticator apps can be used as part of multifactor authentication. A **software token**, sometimes called a *soft token*, is a code generated through software. It could be a code provided through a text message, email, phone call, and so on. An **authenticator app** provides a one-time password that comes from a previously configured website and is used in addition to the commonly required user ID and password.

Two other technologies used with authentication are RADIUS and TACACS. The Remote Authentication Dial-in User Service (**RADIUS**) protocol is used to centralize authentication, authorization, and accounting (AAA). A RADIUS server can provide a way to authenticate wired and wireless users as well as devices before they are allowed to communicate on the network. Terminal Access Controller Access Control System (**TACACS**) also supports AAA, and it also makes it possible to separate the pieces of AAA so you don't have to do all three on the same server. You could do authentication on a different server but still support authorization and accounting on a TACACS server, for example.

Multifactor authentication is used to gain access to a computer, network room, or other shared media. With computers, one of the two security measures could be something the users know, such as a password or PIN, and the second security measure could be an answer to a question, a token, a smart card, a USB security key device, or a biometric feature such as a fingerprint, voiceprint, or facial features identified with software and a webcam. Mobile devices sometimes enable additional multifactor authentication measures, such as a touch pattern. Biometrics, which adds one more security layer to authentication, is covered in the next section.

Biometrics

An expanding field related to authentication and used in multifactor authentication is **biometrics**, which is authentication based on one or more physical traits, such as a fingerprint, an eyeball (retina), or a hand. Behavioral traits, such as voice, common web surfing, or purchase habits, can also be used. Voice can actually be both physical and behavioral. A less complex system might just compare voice with a stored voice print. A more complex system might compare tone and inflection, too, which is more in the behavioral realm.

Biometrics provide extra security because a biometric system is more difficult to bypass than a user ID and password. The trait is less likely to be lost than a password. Also, biometrics require that the person being authenticated be present in order to gain access. Implementing biometrics is more expensive than implementing a user ID/password scheme.

Table 18.3 lists examples of biometric devices used to allow someone to gain access to a room, locker, or device.

TABLE 18.3 Biometric devices

Device	Description
Fingerprint reader/lock	Requires a finger to be placed on a reader and compared against a stored image. Used in laptops, with some vendors having these devices already installed. Currently one of the best security measures for touch mobile devices. Can be easily attached to an existing computer via an ExpressCard or USB (see Figure 18.7).
Facial recognition	Commonly used with integrated laptop webcams. Another system takes a photo and compares it with an image database (though this process is resource intensive) (see Figure 18.8).
Hand scanner	Requires a palm of the hand to be placed against a reader and is more secure than a fingerprint reader. Higher-end systems can analyze veins in the palm.
Retinal scanner	Sometimes called an eye scanner and closely related to an iris scanner. According to LG Electronics, the iris is the most distinguishable human characteristic.
Voice recognition	Involves a person speaking into a microphone in order to gain access to a computer or physical space. Also called speech recognition but not the same as the software used to input data that replaces typing.

FIGURE 18.7 Fingerprint scanner

Applications for biometric devices are not limited to computer/network security. Disney World uses biometrics to ensure that the same person uses a multiday pass. Airports use biometrics for access to employee-only areas. Police departments use biometrics to gain access to evidence and gun lockers. These devices need to be installed and maintained by computer and network support staff.

You might be required to use the system/UEFI BIOS Setup program to activate an integrated biometric device. To use a biometric device, optionally download a driver, install it, and use a specific application that is available for download, that comes with the device or computer, or that is preinstalled on the computer.

FIGURE 18.8   Facial recognition

Logical Security

Logical security involves protection through the use of software. All types of devices and techniques can help in this area. The types of logical security prevention methods on the CompTIA A+ certification exam are briefly outlined here, and some of them are explained in more detail later in the chapter:

> **Antivirus/anti-malware**—This type of software is used to protect the operating system and applications from small programs that wreak havoc on the system, even causing it not to work at all. It is best to just have one application installed as these programs do not work well together and cause the system to run slowly. An application that can perform heuristic analysis can detect previously unknown viruses that are variants of known viruses.

> **Firewall**—A **software firewall** is a tool provided with a device or an application that can be configured on a PC, a router, an access point, and so on. A firewall can also be a hardware device that protects an organization. A company may have more than one firewall, depending on the network design (see Figure 18.9).

> **User authentication/strong passwords**—User authentication and strong passwords help ensure that the person accessing a device or network is a person who is allowed to do so.

> *Multifactor authentication*—With this type of authentication, more than one digital method is used to verify and identify the person using the device or network resources.

FIGURE 18.9   Corporate firewall design

> **Directory permissions**—When data is shared across a network or stored in one or more folders on a server, permissions can be assigned to differentiate between people who just need to see the data and those who need to change or even delete the data.

> *Virtual private network (VPN)*—A **VPN** enables secure connectivity across an unsecure network such as the Internet to a remote location; an example of someone who would need to use a VPN is a mobile user who must connect to the corporate network to upload data weekly or to access corporate data stored in folders on a server. See the section "VPN Configuration," later in this chapter, for more information on how to configure a VPN.

> **Data loss prevention (DLP)**—DLP software is used to protect corporate data from being sent outside the corporate network.

> *Disabling ports*—In highly sensitive areas, ports such as USB, IEEE 1394 FireWire, eSATA, Thunderbolt, and more are disabled so that an external device cannot be attached to gain access to corporate or government-sensitive data.

> **Access control lists (ACLs)**—ACLs are security rules that permit or deny the types of traffic flowing into a device, out of a device, or toward a particular network, or that specify the type of traffic, such as HTTP or HTTPS packets.

> *Port security*—When people bring their own devices to work, they sometimes attach those devices to the physical network. **Port security** is used on a corporate switch to allow only a device with a particular MAC address to attach. Whenever someone unplugs the specified device and attaches a different one, port security settings shut down the switch port because a device with a different MAC address has been attached.

> **Email filtering**—Security rules can be used to process incoming email messages before putting them into specific users' email inboxes. These rules search for and remove suspicious and harmful emails, and they may potentially scan outgoing emails to ensure security or legal compliance (see Figure 18.10). Security settings might also have to be adjusted for the email application, such as when graphics or images do not appear. The spam folder in a user's email

inbox provides evidence of such filtering. Technical staff must sometimes remind users to check the spam folder for email that was sent from an external source.

> **Trusted sources** *vs.* **untrusted sources**—Windows and mobile device users commonly have security software that tells them whether a website or a downloaded file is a trusted or untrusted software source. Linux users have repositories of open source software that has been approved or tested on specific Linux platforms. Linux users should be cautious about downloading software from unknown developers who do not make their source code public. All users, no matter the operating system, should be aware of untrusted software sources when downloading files.

Let's dive a little more deeply into some of these security items, starting with the one we all are familiar with: the password. Actually, different types of passwords authenticate users (and devices, for that matter). BIOS/UEFI passwords are a great place to start.

FIGURE 18.10 Email filtering

BIOS/UEFI

Most computers have BIOS/UEFI options that prevent others from altering the settings. A BIOS/UEFI password can also be assigned to require a password before the operating system loads. Table 18.4 shows some BIOS/UEFI options related to security.

TABLE 18.4   BIOS/UEFI security options

Option	Description
Supervisor	Unrestricted access to all BIOS options.
User	Enables a limited number of configuration changes, such as time and boot sequence.

Option	Description
Trusted Platform Module (TPM)	Allows initialization and viewing of a password for the TPM motherboard chip that generates and stores cryptographic keys.
LoJack	Locates a mobile device and displays a message on the lost device.
Secure boot	Prevents an unauthorized operating system from loading.
Boot or power-on password	Required before BIOS/UEFI looks for an operating system. This is not the Windows user password.

In a corporate environment, the supervisor password is commonly configured. Other options that may affect the corporate environment include the following:

> Enabling/disabling device options
> Enabling/disabling ports
> Encrypting a drive
> Enabling TPM
> Enabling LoJack (which allows a mobile device to be located, remotely locked, and to display an "if found" message)
> Viewing/changing security levels/passwords
> Restoring security settings to the default values

Laptops, netbooks, Chromebooks, and ultrabooks sometimes have an additional password for their internal storage drive. That way, if the device is stolen, the hard drive cannot be inserted into another device and used without the hard drive password. This password is in addition to the power-on password or Windows password. If this option is available, it is configured through the BIOS/UEFI.

Password Security

Passwords are used to authenticate people and should always be required. A great analogy for authentication is the clubhouse that many of us made as children. A secret tap at the door or a special password was the only way to gain access to the private domain.

Most people are familiar with the user ID and password method of authentication. Other means can also be used, including the previously discussed biometric methods, to provide additional layers of security beyond the user ID and password method. Windows and other operating systems and applications use the Kerberos protocol. Kerberos uses a key distribution center (KDC) to authenticate users, applications, and services in the corporate environment. Table 18.5 lists some password guidelines.

TABLE 18.5   Computer/network password guidelines

Guideline	Description
Reminders	Do not write down your password. Many computer users write down their password and keep it close to the computer. Do not put your password in a document stored on the same computer. Passwords can be kept digitally through an app or an encrypted file.
Number of characters/complexity	Use eight or more characters, including uppercase and lowercase letters, interspersed with numerals and special characters.

Guideline	Description
Format	Do not use consecutive letters or numbers on the keyboard, such as *asd* or *123* because doing so makes it easy for someone who is watching to guess the password. Do not use passwords that are words such as *children* or *happiness* because password-cracking programs use **dictionary** attacks to hack passwords. These dictionaries even include foreign words and names.
Expiration	On servers, this is known as the minimum password age and the maximum password age. The minimum password age is how long a user must keep a password before changing it. Microsoft recommends 3 to 7 days. The maximum is how long before the user is required to change it. Common values are 30, 60, and 90 days.
Reuse	Authentication servers often have a setting that dictates the number of times you have to change to new passwords before an old password can be used again. It is best practice to not allow users to reuse passwords and to prevent them from changing a password immediately and repeatedly to go right back to an old password.
Screen saver/lock computer	Use a screen saver or lock the computer with the ⊞+Ⓛ option. Configure the screen saver using the *Personalization* Control Panel link to configure the screen saver and require login credentials to re-access the computer. This is especially important for a private PC in a public or visible area.
Failed attempts	A common setting for the number of times a person is allowed to try a password that is wrong before being locked out is three failed attempts.
Social	People's eyes tend to stray toward movement. If someone is standing near enough to you that he or she could be shoulder surfing when you log in, ensure that the person's eyes are averted or wait until the person moves away to type your password into the system. Obtain a privacy filter.

Windows allows several user ID and password options, including the following:

> Local user ID and password created and maintained on the local PC
> An ID and password for a computer that is part of the workgroup where the user ID and password are created, stored, and maintained on the local computer (similar to the local PC)
> A HomeGroup password that is used on all Windows HomeGroup computers
> An ID and password for a computer that is part of a domain and the user ID and password are created, stored, and maintained on a centralized network server
> PINs
> Microsoft account password

Different password requirements, user IDs, and passwords cause stress for many people. Research is ongoing into the effectiveness of requiring frequent password changes since many write the password down, use a weaker password, or use a password easily modified. One solution people are turning to is a password manager, an application that is on a computer or a USB drive, mobile app, or web browser plug-in that locally or remotely stores passwords used to access accounts. When stored remotely, the passwords and associated data (site, device, and so on) should be encrypted. Research shows that password policies frequently

End-User Education

End-user education is a great way to prevent security events and issues. Technical staff frequently forget this step because they would rather deal with the machines and the technology than the people who operate and access the devices. Training should start when someone is first hired. New hires should be presented with the acceptable use policy (AUP), described earlier in this chapter. Some companies present this policy every time a user logs in to the network. Users should be reminded that every employee is required to follow corporate end-user policies and apply security best practices with every device used to perform business tasks.

Remind users that everyone is inconvenienced by good security practices that are time-consuming, bothersome, and may sometimes even seem meaningless (until a security event occurs!). People tend to take shortcuts, and humans are the weakest security link. Users should be reminded that if their computer is remotely accessed by a technician, they should close windows that contain corporate or personal information prior to agreeing to the remote connection. Any time a technician removes a virus or malware from a user device, training should be part of solving the problem. Violations of security best practices are a common security threat and make a company more vulnerable to other security problems. Let's explore some of the common areas that apply to users.

Licensing

An ethical problem technicians often face is being asked to install software or other content that is not legitimate. Digital rights management (**DRM**) is the technology used to implement controls placed on digital media (software, hardware, songs, videos, and more). Users often request that technicians share with them methods to break copyright laws or work around copy protection controls. Technicians must maintain their professionalism and ethics to ensure that corporate interests are protected.

Instances like these provide a great opportunity to talk to users about different software sources:

> *Open source*—Software for which the original software code is provided.
> *Freeware*—Software that doesn't cost anything but could include some harmful software.
> *Shareware*—Software that might be free at first but may require later payment; may include only part of a particular software package with the option to buy the rest.
> **Commercial license**—Purchased software for a specific number of users and/or machines. Even when commercial licensing is obtained, there is an end-user licensing agreement (**EULA**) that specifies what can be done with that particular license.
> **Personal license**—Purchased software for a specific number of users and/or machines. Commonly used for home or small business environments and also covered by a EULA.

A 2015 Business Software Alliance (BSA) global software piracy survey found that 37% of PC software did not have a legitimate license. **Piracy** (see Figure 18.11) is defined by the BSA as follows:
> Copying or distribution of copyrighted software that is not authorized
> Purchasing a copy of a particular application or software and putting it on more than one computer
> Installing, sharing, selling, copying, downloading, or uploading stolen software to another site
> Installing company software on or permitting access to unauthorized devices

Software companies have different pricing structures for individual or personal licenses and corporate or enterprise licenses. An enterprise license gives a company permission to load the software on unlimited or a maximum number of devices. A personal license is more limiting (usually to one device).

People use software piracy websites to obtain illegal software. These sites are riddled with security threats that are downloaded along with the desired software. The current penalty in the United States for software piracy is $150,000 per program copied. If prosecuted for copyright infringement, fines can be up to $250,000 and/or up to five years in jail. Don't be persuaded to risk your personal life and professional future for software piracy.

FIGURE 18.11 Software pirate

Regulated Data

As ever-increasing computing power has made the mining, collection, and storage of private data more efficient and invasive, so too have the world's standards for privacy protection increased. Inadvertently disclosing regulated data embarrasses you and your employer, and it could subject you both to civil and/or criminal penalties.

Regulated data is defined by federal law or regulation according to its purpose, such as in the areas of education, health care, financial institutions, arms trafficking, exports administration, and online children's privacy. There are numerous categories, but in this chapter we focus on four specific types to give you an overall framework for privacy protections:

> *PII*—personally identifiable information
> *PCI*—payment card information
> *GDPR*—European General Data Protection Regulation
> *PHI*—protected health information

Personally identifiable information (**PII**) is information that uniquely identifies someone, such as a Social Security number, an employee ID, a patient number, a passport number, or a user ID. It is important to stress to users that they should not have such information lying around, taped somewhere, or available in the work environment except where needed. There are two broad types of PII: nonsensitive and sensitive. Nonsensitive PII is information that can be found publicly, such as a person's name, telephone number, and email address. Nonsensitive information can be transmitted unencrypted (unscrambled and with no security) without causing harm to an individual. In contrast, transmitting sensitive PII non-encrypted may cause harm and breach someone's privacy. Sensitive PII should be encrypted (scrambled with security algorithms) if sent or if the data is data stored. In other words, sensitive PII should always be in encrypted form.

All members of the payment card (for example, credit card, debit card) industry (financial institutions, credit card companies, and merchant services) must comply with standards related to payment card industry (**PCI**) information. The Payment Card Industry Data Security Standard (PCI DSS) was developed to encourage and enhance the security of personally identifiable information and payment data. Compliance is enforced by the Discover, MasterCard, American Express, Visa, and JCB International credit card brands. As a technician, you may have exposure to PII and PCI data. You are obligated to protect the privacy of this data.

The General Data Protection Regulation (**GDPR**) was adopted in 2016 by the European Union (EU). The GDPR unifies protection for the personal data of European Union residents, including U.S. expatriates, and sets forth restrictions on processing and transferring personal data outside the EU. Any entity (such as a business) that offers goods or services to, or monitors the behavior of, residents in the EU must comply with the GDPR. For example, an American business selling products to an EU resident would be subject to the GDPR. Violations of GDPR provisions subject organizations to financial penalties of up to 4% of the organization's global annual turnover.

EU residents have the right to access, correct, or erase their data. They also have the right to restrict further processing and the right to receive copies of their data. In some cases, according to the GDPR, a client's consent is necessary to process his or her information or transfer it to the United States. If special categories of information (for example, data related to race, religion, or political beliefs) are processed, then the client's explicit consent must be obtained. Organizations are required to report a data breach "without undue delay" (typically within 72 hours) to their country's data protection authority in the EU and, where applicable, to affected individuals.

The Health Insurance Portability and Accountability Act (HIPAA) of 1996 required the U.S. Department of Health & Human Services (HHS) to develop privacy and security regulations for certain health information. HHS developed the HIPAA Privacy Rule, which defines protected health information (**PHI**) as "individually identifiable health information," including demographic data, that relates to an individual's past, present or future physical or mental health or condition; the provision of health care to the individual; the past, present or future payment for providing health care; and the individual's identity. Common identifiers are name, Social Security number, birth date, and address.

Security Threats and Vulnerabilities

Several types of security threats and vulnerabilities exist. Many of them fall into multiple categories because there might be multiple threats. They all do bad and weird things to devices. Malware is a good place to start.

Malware

Malware is software code that is designed to damage a computer system (causing lockups, slowness, applications crashing or failing to run or running incorrectly, operating system update failures, and so on). In most cases, allowing more users to bring their own devices to work increases the risk of introducing malware into the network. Table 18.6 lists common types of malware.

TABLE 18.6   Types of malware

Type	Description
Spyware	Collects personal information without consent through logging keystrokes, accessing saved documents, and recording Internet browsing. Results in unsolicited pop-ups and identity theft.
Virus	Does something harmful to a computer (for example, displays a message, prevents the computer from booting, makes it run slowly, changes file or application permissions, or logs keystrokes). A virus commonly attaches itself to an installed program.

Type	Description
Worm	Spreads to other devices and may or may not do anything that causes suspicion.
Trojan	Disguises itself as a legitimate program to gain unauthorized access to a device. Also known as a trojan horse (see Figure 18.12).
Rootkit	Gains administrator access (known as root access in Linux) to the operating system. Check for unknown processes running to see if a rootkit is installed.
Ransomware	Restricts access to a device until a user pays money to regain access (see Figure 18.13).
Keylogger	Records every keystroke entered in an attempt to collect users' ID and passwords.
Botnet	Software that spreads from hacked device to hacked device and that is under control of someone else (called zombie computers or zombies; see Figure 18.14).

"Sure, bring her in. I've always wanted to work on one of these babies."

FIGURE 18.12 Trojan (disguising itself)

FIGURE 18.13 Ransomware

FIGURE 18.14 Zombies and botnets

The following are common symptoms of a virus:

> Computer does not boot.
> Computer hard drive space is reduced.
> Applications do not load.
> An application takes longer to load or function than it used to.
> Hard drive activity increases (especially when no work is being done by the user and the antivirus software is not currently scanning).
> An antivirus software message appears.

> The number of hard drive sectors marked as bad steadily increases.
> Unusual graphics or messages appear on the screen.
> Files are missing (deleted).
> A message indicates that the hard drive cannot be detected or recognized.
> Strange sounds come from the computer.

Antivirus applications can be configured to run in manual mode (on demand) or as scheduled scans. When you have an infected computer, you should quarantine it. This means you should disconnect the computer from the network until the computer is virus free. Some antivirus programs can quarantine a computer automatically if the computer has a virus. Many antivirus software programs have the capability to quarantine files—files that appear to the antivirus program as possible virus-infected or suspicious files that might be dangerous. A message normally appears with a list of files that have been quarantined, and each one must be identified as a valid file or to be left in the quarantine (unusable) until a new version of the antivirus signature files has been updated and can identify the file.

Social Engineering

All technicians (and employees) should be aware of social engineering. **Social engineering** involves tricking people into divulging information, including their own personal information or corporate knowledge. Social engineering does not just relate to computers but can be done over the phone, through online surveys, or through mail surveys. A common social engineering technique is **impersonation**, in which someone pretends to be from a trusted bank or company, such as Microsoft.

Shoulder surfing and looking at someone's computer screen while standing behind them is a type of social engineering. Another one is dumpster diving, where someone looks in a trash bin inside or outside the office to gather information. No auditing or network security applications and devices can help with such deviousness. Good security awareness helps prevent unintentional disclosures.

TECH TIP

Watch out for tailgating

Tailgating (also known as piggybacking) is a type of social engineering in which an unauthorized person enters a building or an area of a building behind an authorized person. Prevention of tailgating requires training and diligence by all employees.

Phishing

Closely related to social engineering is the concept is phishing. **Phishing** (pronounced "fishing") is a type of social engineering that involves attempting to get personal information by using email messages from a company that appears to be legitimate. Phishing emails target ATM/debit or credit card numbers and PINs, Social Security numbers, bank account numbers, Internet banking login IDs and passwords, email addresses, security information such as a mother's maiden name, full name, home address, or phone number. Most browsers include a phishing filter, which proactively warns computer users when they go to a site that is a known phishing site or when a site contains characteristics common to phishing sites.

A variant of phishing is **spear phishing**, which is a targeted method of phishing in which the attacker knows some information about you. The subject line or first part of the message may include your name. The body of the message may reference someone you know or may appear to be from a legitimate company with which you do business (see Figure 18.15).

FIGURE 18.15   Spear phishing

Security Attacks

Security attacks can come from outside or from within a corporate network. Table 18.7 lists various types of network attacks.

TABLE 18.7   Types of network attacks

Type of attack	Description
Access	A type of attack that frequently uses multiple dictionaries, including foreign ones, to gain access to accounts, databases, servers, and/or network devices. Types of access attacks include man-in-the-middle, port redirection, buffer overflow, and password.
Backdoor	Also known as a trapdoor, a planted program that executes to bypass security and/or authentication.
Botnet	Software that spreads from hacked device to hacked device (called zombie computers or zombies) and that is under control of someone else (refer to Figure 18.14).
Brute force	Repeated attempts to check all possible key combinations to gain access to a network device or stored material.
Dictionary	A brute-force attack to try to determine a password or decryption key by trying different words found in a dictionary.
DoS (denial of service)	A string of data/messages sent to overload a particular firewall, router, switch, server, access point, or computer in an attempt to deny service to other network devices.
DDoS (distributed denial of service)	A group of infected computers attacking a single network device by flooding the network with traffic.
Man-in-the-middle (MITM)	A technique in which a hacker inserts a device between a sender and a receiver so the device can receive the intended traffic. Access points, DHCP servers, and default gateways are commonly simulated in this type of attack.
Rainbow table	A method of obtaining a password in a short amount of time by using a table that contains previously discovered hash values that are used to encrypt a password.

Type of attack	Description
Reconnaissance	A technique that involves attempting to gather information about a network before launching another type of attack. Tools used include port scanners, pings, and packet-sniffing programs.
Replay	A technique in which a valid network message or certificate is re-sent, usually in an attempt to obtain logon information.
Smurf	A technique that involves using Internet Control Message Protocol (ICMP) to ping a large amount of network traffic at a specific device to deny that device network access, ping a nonexistent device to generate network traffic, or ping all network devices to generate traffic in ICMP replies.
Spoofing	A technique that involves sending an Ethernet frame with a fake source MAC address to trick other devices into sending traffic to a rogue device. Can be used in conjunction with a man-in-the-middle attack.
TCP/IP hijacking	A technique in which a stolen IP address is used to gain access and/or authorization information from a network.
Vulnerability scanner	A software program used to assess network devices to identify weaknesses such as unpatched operating systems, open ports, or missing/outdated virus-scanning software.
Zero day	A type of attack that takes advantage of a vulnerability in a particular software application that is found by hackers before it is known/fixed by the software developer.
Zombie	A device that has been hacked and is controlled by someone else or that carries out malicious tasks. Refer to Figure 18.14.

Workgroups and Domains

A workgroup or HomeGroup is a LAN in which each computer maintains its own networked resources, such as a file or printer that is shared with others. Workgroup networks are most common in small office/home office (SOHO) environments. A **domain** environment is more common in the business world, in which network servers authenticate logins, provide file storage, and provide services such as email and web access. Another name for a domain environment is a server-based network. Figure 18.16 illustrates a workgroup environment; Figure 18.17 shows how a domain environment is different.

Some companies use single sign-on (SSO) for user authentication. **Single sign-on** enables a user to authenticate with a minimum of a user ID and password. With that authentication, the user is allowed access to multiple systems/servers, devices such as printers and copiers, and networked-based applications. With so many mobile devices and cloud-based applications today, single sign-on is even more important to users. The alternative is that users are prompted to authenticate or log in each time they access network connections such as a work computer, an email server, or a shared file server.

FIGURE 18.16   Windows workgroup model

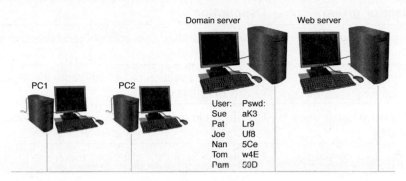

FIGURE 18.17 Windows domain model

Protecting Access to Local and Network Resources

Several techniques exist to protect computer access, and some of them have already been considered in this chapter as part of physical access. Authentication is used to determine what network resources can be used. **Authorization** involves the operating system or network granting access to specific resources, such as files, folders, printers, video conferencing equipment, scanners, and so on, on a computer system or network.

TECH TIP

Prevent a computer from being seen through the network

Search and access the *Administrative Tools* section of the Control Panel > *Services* > double-click or double-tap *Computer Browser* > from the *Startup Type* drop-down menu, select *Disabled* > *Apply* > *OK* > restart the computer.

User Management

Users can be added and placed into groups for ease of management. Table 18.8 shows the default local users/groups for Windows 7, 8, and 10. Note that in Windows Home versions, local groups are not supported.

TABLE 18.8 Windows default users/groups

User or group	Description
Administrator (user)	Has total control of the computer; best practice is to rename the account and password protect it; create another user account that belongs to the administrator group and has a complex password.
Administrators (group)	A user account that has been created and placed in this group that has total control of the computer.
Guest (user)	A member of the Guest group; disabled by default; no default user rights.
Guests (group)	Used by those who do not have an account on the computer; normally does not require a password; best practice is to disable.
Standard user (user)	Default type of account created when you create a common corporate staff worker; the user is required to request an administrator to make changes to software, hardware, or security settings.
Backup operators (group)	Can back up and restore files and folders, regardless of permissions assigned; cannot change security settings; can access the computer from a remote location.

User or group	Description
Power users (group)	Same as a Standard user account (and can change things like time zone or date/time).
Users (group)	Can perform common tasks and create local groups but cannot share folders or printers.
Remote desktop users (group)	Can log on to the computer from a remote location.
Offer Remote Assistance Helper (group)	Can use the Remote Assistance program to help a computer user.
Network Configuration Operators (group)	Can make TCP/IP changes and release/renew IP addresses.
Performance Log Users (group)	Can manage local or remote performance logs and alerts.

TECH TIP

Always change the default admin password

Whether it is a Windows computer, a router, or any other electronic device, always **change the default admin user account password** or create an account that has administrator access and disable the default account.

A security best practice in Windows 7 is to create an account that has administrator access and to disable the Administrator account. Another option in Windows 7 is to just change the username to something other than Administrator. The Guest account should always be disabled unless you have the situation of a computer in an open area that does not require a login and is used to find an office location, for example. (The Guest account is disabled by default.)

Windows 8 and 10 do not allow you to disable the Administrator account, but you can add a user that has administrator access. In Windows 8, access the *User Accounts* Control Panel. Select the *Manage Another Account* link > select the *Add an Account* link. If you don't want to use an email address, you can select the *Sign In Without a Microsoft Account (Not Recommended)* link > *Local Account* button > enter the information and select *Next* > *Finish*. Select the account just created > *Edit* > change the account type to *Administrator* > *OK*.

In Windows 10, access the *User Accounts* Control Panel. Select the *Manage Another Account* link > select the *Add a New User in PC Settings* link > in the *Other Users* section, select the *Add Someone Else to the PC* option > if you don't want to use a Microsoft, Skype, Xbox, or other type of email or phone number and account information, select the *I Don't Have This Person's Sign-in Information* link > select the *Add a User Without a Microsoft Account* link. Select the newly created user and select the *Change Account Type* button > change the account type to *Administrator* > *OK*.

The following list describes some best practices for securing a workstation in a corporate environment.

> Apply **logon time restrictions**. If someone works during the daytime Monday through Friday, then restrict Saturday and Sunday or evenings.
> **Disable the Guest account**. Use the Computer Management Console > expand *System Tools* > expand *Local Users and Groups* > double-click on the *Guest* account > select the *Account Is Disabled* checkbox.

> Enable the **failed attempts lockout** feature to lock out users after a specific number of failed login attempts.
> Configure a **timeout/screen lock** for when users are away from their workstation to automatically lock the screen after a period of nonuse.
> Implement user permissions and apply the principle of least privilege (which is covered later in this chapter).

TECH TIP

Use the Lock Computer option

When away from your desk, use the *Lock Computer* option by pressing Ctrl+Alt+Del and selecting *Lock* or *Lock This Computer*.

Basic Active Directory Functions

Technicians sometimes have to use a Windows server and specifically the **Active Directory** (AD) service on the server to manage users and devices on the network as part of security best practices in the corporate environment. You can use Active Directory to define domains. Remember that a domain is a way of organizing all user accounts and devices such as computers and printers.

Tasks that a technician should be familiar with include creating and deleting an account, resetting a domain password for a user, unlocking a user account, and disabling an account. Let's take a look at these.

Within Active Directory, users can be placed in either organizational units or groups so that administration is easier (for example, assigning security rights). Figure 18.18 shows a corporate structure in which one group of users is the Information Technology Services group. By expanding the group, you can see the users listed there.

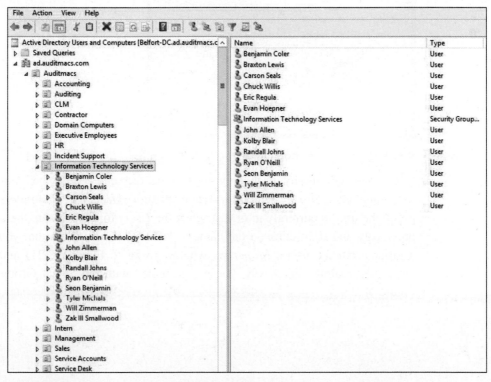

FIGURE 18.18 Active Directory Groups

CHAPTER 18

To do **account creation** in AD (that is, add a user to a particular group), open the User Manager by going to the *Start* button > *Programs* > *Administrative Tools* > *Active Directory Users and Computers*. Expand the domain (the section that starts with "ad.xxx") until you see the group you want; click on that group. From the menu bar, select *Action* > *New* > *User*. In the dialog box shown in Figure 18.19, enter the user information and click *Next*. Enter the password and select any appropriate security settings, such as *User Must Change Password at Next Logon*, as shown in Figure 18.20. Figure 18.21 shows the user account properties screen, where you click *OK*.

FIGURE 18.19 Active Directory > creating a new user

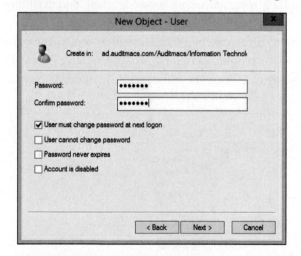

FIGURE 18.20 Active Directory > setting a new user password

Users are commonly placed in groups so that they can be managed more easily. To place a user in a group, click *Start* or search for *Active Directory Users and Computers* > expand the particular group the user is currently in or just select the *Users* folder > locate the user that has been added previously and right-click on the name > *Add to a Group*. Note that you can also add a user to a group from the user's *Properties* window (refer to Figure 18.21) and select the *Member Of* tab > *Add* button. Either way, you are presented with the Select Groups window, as shown in Figure 18.22.

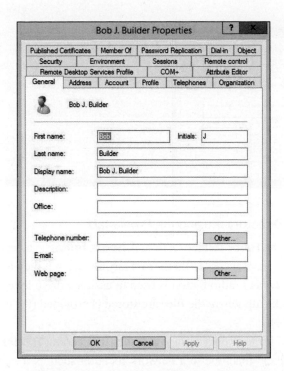

FIGURE 18.21   Active Directory > viewing properties of a new user

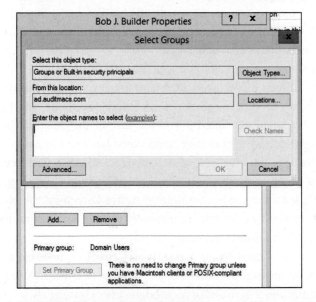

FIGURE 18.22   Active Directory > adding a user to a group

At the bottom of the textbox, type the name of the group you want the user to be in. Look at the groups within the domain shown to the left of this window (refer to Figure 18.18), such as HR or Information Technology Services. You can also click on the *Advanced* button and the *Find Now* button to see a list of all the groups and then simply click on one of them. A user can be a member of multiple groups, and those groups are shown on the *Members Of* tab.

Other functions within the user account properties that might need to be set by a technician are the logon script, home folder, and folder redirection. A logon script (sometimes referred to as a **login script**) is a set of tasks configured in one file that run when a user logs in, such as running a specific application, performing an operating system function on the local computer, or setting system environment variables. The logon script can be defined as part of a group policy (covered in the next section) or through the *Properties* window > *Profile* tab, as shown in Figure 18.23.

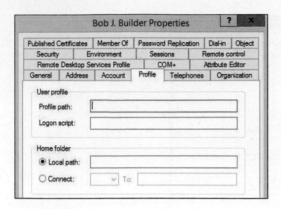

FIGURE 18.23   Active Directory > using the *Profile* tab

Notice in Figure 18.23 the Home Folder section. A **home folder** is a network folder that allows users to store their files and have access to them from any device that they log onto within the same domain. Commonly the *Connect* radio button is used to assign a drive letter in the first drop-down menu, and then the network path where the files are stored is provided (for example, \\ServerName\ FolderName\%username%).

Another technique used for user data storage is folder redirection. **Folder redirection** involves mapping a folder on the local machine to a network location such as a server. The user then has access to the files within that folder from any device on the network domain. Folder redirection is commonly implemented in conjunction with offline files and roaming user profiles. (Profiles are covered in the next section.) This way, data is available to the user through any device on the network, even if the network or server is down.

A few more things you might need to do as a technician are delete or disable an account, reset a user password, and unlock a user account. There are several ways to do **account deletion** in AD. One way commonly used is to right-click on someone's name (see Figure 18.24) and select the *Delete* option > *Yes* when prompted if you are sure of the deletion. Some companies have a policy of not deleting user accounts in case users come back or in case you might for some other reason need to access accounts. Instead, some managers **disable the account** and put that disabled account into a group with all the other disabled accounts. Starting with Microsoft Server 2012, Microsoft included a recycle bin for deleted Active Directory objects such as user accounts, but this feature is not enabled by default. To manually disable an account, locate and right-click on the user account and select *Disable Account*.

A technician might also need to do a **password reset** or **unlock an account**. To reset a password, right-click on the user account and select *Reset Password*. A security best practice is to select the *User Must Change Password at Next Logon* checkbox, as shown in Figure 18.25, so that the user will be forced to select a password that is not known to the technician. Also notice that if the user account is locked for any reason, you can use this window to unlock a user account by selecting the *Unlock the User's Account* checkbox.

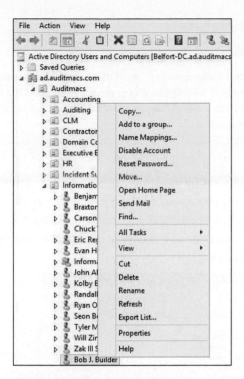

FIGURE 18.24   Active Directory > right-clicking on user account

FIGURE 18.25   Active Directory > resetting a password or unlocking an account

Local and Group Policies

Another method of controlling login passwords is through a local- or domain-based group account policy. Policies do more than just define password requirements. They can define the desktop, what applications are available to users, what options are available through the *Start* menu, whether users are allowed to save files to external media, and so on. A domain policy, or **group policy**, can be created, updated, and applied to every computer on the domain. This practice is common in Microsoft Active Directory (AD) domain networks.

A **local security policy** is created on a computer, and it could be used to disable auto-playing of optical discs, prevent users from shutting down or restarting a computer, turn off personalized menus, or prevent someone from changing the Internet Explorer or Microsoft Edge home page. A local security policy might be implemented in a workgroup setting. A group policy is more common in a corporate environment, and a group policy can overwrite a local policy. If any computer settings on a networked computer in a corporate environment are grayed out, the settings are probably locked out due to the policy deployed throughout the domain.

Accessing the local security policy and group policy

Access the local security policy by typing `gpedit.msc` at a command prompt or in the *Search* textbox. Use the `gpresult` command to display group policy settings. Use the `gpupdate` command to update all domain users with a newly deployed group policy. Use the `secedit` command to configure or analyze a security policy.

Through the defined policy, criteria for auditing can also be set. **Auditing**, sometimes called *event logging* or just *logging*, is the process of tracking events that occur on the network, such as someone logging in to the network. In a business environment, a server with special auditing software is sometimes devoted to this task because it is very important to security. Figure 18.26 shows the Local Group Policy Editor window.

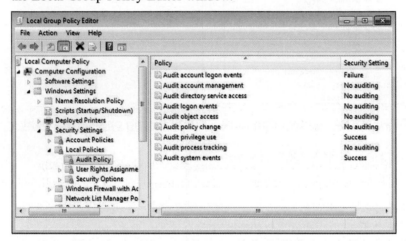

FIGURE 18.26   Local Group Policy Editor window

Requiring password protection

You can enable or disable password protection through the Network and Sharing Center on a workgroup/HomeGroup computer. If password protection is enabled, a person accessing a shared folder from a remote location must have a user account and password on the computer that holds the network share.

Permissions

Monitoring users and groups as well as the devices, data, and applications they have access to is important. Permissions control what can or cannot be done (permit or deny access) to files, folders, and devices from a remote connection. (This is similar to file attributes, covered in Chapter 15, "Introduction to Scripting.") A security best practice is to **restrict user permissions**, but permissions can cause havoc. Network administrators and end users can set permissions on folders, and these permissions may affect another user's access to files and folders. Technicians need to be familiar with permissions.

Two types of permissions can be assigned in Windows: share permissions and NTFS permissions. **Share permissions** provide and/or limit access to data across a network. Using share permissions is the only way to secure network resources on FAT16 or FAT32 drives. **NTFS permissions** provide tighter control than shared folder permissions. NTFS permissions can be used only on NTFS drives.

If file permissions change

If you ever notice that file permissions change (for example, you can no longer access an application or file that you once could), check for a virus. Note that in the case of some viruses that change file permissions, you may need to repartition the hard drive and reinstall the operating system to remove the virus.

Share Permissions

To share a folder other than the Public folder, use *Windows Explorer* (Windows 7)/*File Explorer* (Windows 8/10) > right-click or tap and briefly hold on the folder name > *Share With (Windows 7/8)/Give Access To (Windows 10)* > type the name of the person > *Add*. You can do one of the following at this point:

> If the computer is attached to a network domain, select the arrow to the right of the textbox > *Find* > type the name of the person with whom you want to share the folder > *Check Names* > *OK*.

> If the computer is on a workgroup, click the arrow to the right of the textbox, select the appropriate name, and click *Add*. If the name does not appear, click the arrow to the right of the textbox and click *Create a New User to Create the User Account*.

> If the computer is part of a HomeGroup, select *Homegroup (Read)* or *Homegroup (Read/ Write)* to share the folder, using the appropriate permissions. In Windows Home and Starter editions, you can only join a HomeGroup; you cannot create one.

> An alternative method is to locate the folder using *Windows Explorer* (Windows 7)/*File Explorer* (Windows 8/10) > right-click or tap and briefly hold on the folder icon > *Properties* > *Sharing* tab > click the *Share* button. Figure 18.27 shows this window in Windows 7.

FIGURE 18.27   Using the Sharing tab to share a folder

Share permissions are only applicable across a network

Notice that shared folder permissions are applicable only across a network. This type of share does not prevent someone sitting at the computer from accessing files and folders. For best protection across a network and at the computer, use NTFS file and folder permissions.

Permissions are set by clicking the *Advanced Sharing* button (see Figure 18.28). Notice that you can limit the number of simultaneous users who can connect to this folder from a remote location. Select the *Permissions* button. Notice in Figure 18.29 that you can select the Allow or Deny checkboxes for the individual permissions.

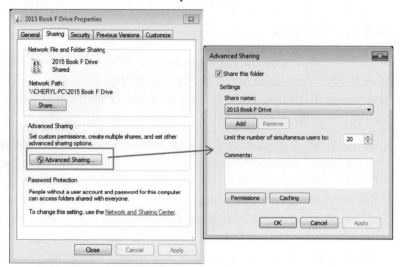

FIGURE 18.28   Folder Sharing tab > Advanced Sharing options

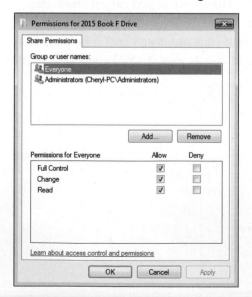

FIGURE 18.29   Folder Sharing tab > Advanced Sharing > setting Permissions

What is the maximum number of concurrent users?

A maximum of 20 users can simultaneously use the same shared folder.

Notice in Figure 18.29 that you can select Allow or Deny for specific types of permissions (Full Control, Change, and Read). Table 18.9 shows the effects of setting each of these permissions to Allow.

TABLE 18.9   Share permissions

Permission	Description
Full Control	Users can do everything, such as change the file permissions, take ownership of files, and perform everything that can be done with the *Change* permission.
Change	Users can add new subfolders, add files to a folder, change the data in a file, add data to files, change file attributes, delete folders and files, and do all the tasks that are possible with the *Read* permission.
Read	Users can look at file and folder names and attributes and can open files and execute scripts.

TECH TIP

Principle of least privilege

When determining access to a folder or to a server room, you should give access to only what is needed and only to the people that need access (and no more). Giving people access to an entire drive or building when they just need access to a particular folder or room puts the entire hard drive or company at risk. The **principle of least privilege** as it relates to computer and network security is that the maximum rights you give people are limited to only the rights they need to do their job.

File and folder security protection is a concern. A subfolder and any files created within that subfolder all inherit security permissions from the parent folder or the folder that contains the subfolder. This feature can be disabled when necessary.

Local and Administrative Shares

Files and folders can be shared in a network workgroup, a HomeGroup, or a domain. A **local share** is something—a printer, folder, or media device—that is shared on a specific computer. **Administrative shares** are shares created by Microsoft for drive volumes and the folder that contains the majority of Window files. An example of an administrative share is a drive volume letter (such as C) followed by the dollar sign ($) symbol (C$). The admin$ administrative share is used to provide access to the folder that contains the Windows operating system files.

Windows automatically creates administrative shares, but by default Windows prevents local accounts from accessing administrative shares through the network. If this feature is desired, a registry edit must be made. The `net share share_name$ /delete` command can disable a particular administrative share. However, the administrative share is back available when the computer is restarted. A better solution is to disable a particular administrative share through a group policy.

Any local share can be made a **hidden share**, which is a share that is not seen by default throughout the network. To make a share a hidden share, add the dollar sign ($) to the share name. This might be beneficial for computer users who want to access something from their remote computer without making it visible to other network users.

> **TECH TIP**

> **Access denied message**
>
> If a user or technician ever receives an access denied message on a shared folder or hidden share, ensure that the user login is one that has administrative privileges or check the assigned permissions on the shared folder.

Public Folder

Another way that Windows supports sharing is through using the Public folder. The default path for the Public folder is C:\Users\Public. You can copy or move any file to the Public folder. This makes it easier to share files with someone, but when files are copied into this folder, twice as much hard drive space is used because there are copies of the same material in two folders.

If sharing is enabled for the Public folder, anyone who has a user account and password on the computer can access the data. In addition, any user on the network can see all files and folders in the Public folder by selecting *Network* from Windows Explorer/File Explorer, accessing the appropriate computer, browsing to the *Users* folder, and opening the *Public* folder. You can set permissions so that this folder is inaccessible or can restrict anyone from changing files or creating new files. However, you cannot pick and choose what files can be seen by individuals.

The Public folder is not shown by default in Windows 7 (but it is shown by default in Windows 8 and 10). In Windows 7, you can create a shortcut on the desktop for it. To enable the use of the Public folder, the steps are a little different in Windows 7 than in Windows 8 and 10:

> Windows 7: Access the *Network and Sharing Center* Control Panel > *Change Advanced Sharing Settings* > expand the *Public* section by selecting the down arrow if it is not showing any information below it > locate the *Public Folder Sharing* area > select the *Turn on Sharing so Anyone with Network Access Can Read and Write Files in the Public Folders* radio button. Note that you must also turn on network discovery and file and print sharing to see shared files across the network. See Figure 18.30.

> Windows 8/10: Access the *Network and Sharing Center* Control Panel > *Change Advanced Sharing Settings* > expand the *All Networks* section by selecting the down arrow if it is not showing any information below it > locate the *Public Folder Sharing* area > select the *Turn on Sharing so Anyone with Network Access Can Read and Write Files in the Public Folders* radio button. Note that you must also turn on network discovery and file and print sharing to see shared files across the network.

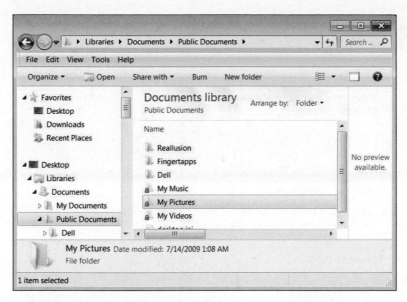

FIGURE 18.30   Windows 7 Public Documents folder

Libraries

Windows uses libraries. A library is similar to a folder, but a library contains files that are automatically indexed for faster searching, viewing, and access. For example, a teacher might store training video clips in a library and share them from the library. This library could contain files from different folders, an external drive, or even a network share.

Windows is configured to have four default libraries: Documents, Music, Pictures, and Videos. Windows Explorer and File Explorer automatically show the libraries. If you right-click the *Documents* library and select *Properties*, you can see that a particular user's Documents folder is shown and so is a public Documents folder. As shown in Figure 18.31. there is an *Include a Folder* button in this window. This button allows more folders to be included in the Documents library. No matter the source of the files, the files are all controlled through a single library as if the contents were stored in a single location. Each default library has two default locations configured (My Documents and Public Documents), as shown in Figure 18.31. It may also contain other locations if **cloud storage** is enabled. (Cloud storage involves storing data at a remote location that may be managed by the company or by a cloud storage service provider.) The public location is used by any user logged on to the computer. Only one location can be configured as the default save location for files that are moved, copied, or saved to the library.

FIGURE 18.31 Windows 7 libraries

NTFS Permissions

On an NTFS partition, additional security protection is available through Windows. To share a folder using NTFS permissions, locate the folder in Windows Explorer (Windows 7) or File Explorer (Windows 8/10). Right-click or tap and briefly hold on the folder name and select *Properties* (7/8/10) > select the *Security* tab (see Figure 18.32). Notice that more permissions can be administered on an NTFS partition using NTFS permissions rather than share permissions. Table 18.10 defines these permissions.

FIGURE 18.32 Windows 7 NTFS permissions—using the *Security* tab

TABLE 18.10 NTFS permissions

Permission	Description
Full Control	Users can do anything in the files and folder, including delete, add, modify, and create files and folders.
Modify	Users can list items in a folder, read data, and write data, but they cannot delete subfolders and files and cannot take ownership.
Read & Execute	Users can list items in a folder and read a file, but they cannot change or delete the file or create new files. Users can execute applications contained within the folder.
List Folder Contents	Users can only look inside a folder.
Read	Users can display folder and subfolder attributes and permissions as well as look at a particular file.
Write	Users can add files or folders, change attributes for the folder, and add or append data in a file.

Inherited permissions are permissions that are propagated from what Microsoft calls a *parent object*. For example, if a folder is given the Read permission, then all files within that folder cannot be changed (they are read-only). If a subfolder is created, it inherits that permission. If the Allow or Deny checkboxes for any object are selected, the current permissions have been inherited.

There may also be issues when copying or moving is performed on objects that have NTFS permissions set. Consider these guidelines for copying and moving:

> When you copy a file/folder on the same or different NTFS drive letter, the copy inherits the destination folder's permissions.
> When you move a file/folder on the same NTFS drive letter, the original permissions of the object are retained.
> When you move a file/folder to a different NTFS drive letter, the moved object inherits the destination folder permissions.
> When you copy or move a file/folder to a drive that uses a different file system (like FAT), the object loses all its permissions.
> If you change permissions on a folder that has content, only the new content inherits the changed permissions.

Effective permissions are the final permissions granted to a person for a particular resource. Effective permissions are important when you combine shared folder permissions given to an individual, shared folder permissions given to a group, and individual permissions. The following are some helpful tips when sharing folders and files across a network:

> Folder permissions are cumulative: When you grant folder permission to a group and then grant an individual permission to that same folder, the effective permission for that person is the combination of what the group gets and what the person gets. For example, if the group gets the Write permission and the person gets only the Read permission (and the person is a member of the group that has the Write permission), the person can both read and write files to the folder.
> Deny overrides any allowed permissions that have been set for a user or a group. For example, if a group is denied access to a folder, but a person is specifically allowed access to the folder, the person is not allowed to access the folder.
> When NTFS and shared folder permissions are both used, the most restrictive of the two is the effective permissions.

Windows provides help in determining effective permissions. In Windows 7, right-click a file or folder > *Properties* > *Security* tab > *Advanced* button > *Effective Permissions* tab (see Figure 18.33). In Windows 8 and 10, right-click or tap and hold on a file or folder > *Properties* > *Security* tab > *Advanced* button > *Effective Access*. Note that what is shown is only for NTFS permissions. Share permissions are not part of the Windows calculation for this window. Permissions-related issues are a common problem. A technician must be familiar with the results of misconfiguring them. If users have files stored in a mapped drive share and those files are moved to a different server, then the mapped drive will need to be redone and point to the new server and permssions will need to be reapplied on the new server.

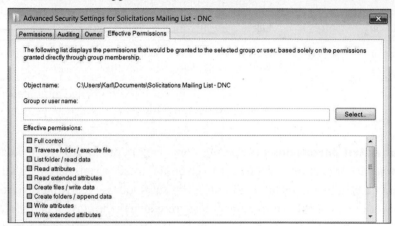

FIGURE 18.33   Windows 7 effective permissions

TECH TIP

All subfolders are shared when a folder is shared

When you share a folder, all subfolders are automatically shared unless you make the subfolders private.

File Attributes

File attributes are covered in Chapter 15 but need to be reviewed here as well. When a folder is shared across the network, the permissions given specify what a user is allowed to do with a particular folder. By default, all subfolders and files contained within a shared folder or subfolder inherit the same permissions. For example, if you select read-only as the shared folder permission, then someone can open a file but not modify and save it. If you right-click or tap and briefly hold on the name of a file within a shared folder that has read-only permissions assigned, you can then select *Properties* in order to access attributes, and you will see that the file has the read-only attribute already marked.

Getting the Job Done with the Correct Permissions

When working on a staff member's computer, remember that when you are logged on as that user, you may not be able to use specific utilities. Commonly used utilities or commands executed from a command prompt may not be available to you unless you operate from the administrator level. Search for `command prompt`. In the resulting list, right-click or tap and briefly hold on the *Command Prompt* option > select *Run as Administrator*.

To see some problems, you may need the user to be logged in. Logging in with an account that has administrator access may not allow you to see the same issues the user sees. Always ensure that users log on and test whatever you fix to ensure that it works for their own account and permissions.

Folder Options

Because of quarantined files or the need to check system files, a technician is required to be familiar with Windows Explorer/File Explorer display options. Use the following directions, based on the operating system used:

> Windows 7: Open *Windows Explorer*. Use the *Organize > Folder and search options > View* tab. Use the *Organize > Layout* option or the *Folder Options* Control Panel to configure how folders/files display and what information is included with that display.

> Windows 8 and 10: Open *File Explorer*. Access the *View* menu option > *Options* > *Change folder and search options* > *View* tab. Use the *Layout* section or *File Explorer Options* (Windows 10) Control Panel to configure how folders/files display and what information is in included with that display.

A technician often has to work with system files and folders that are not seen by default. Table 18.11 summarizes the security-related *View* tab options. A technician must remember to set the settings to the way they were previously so that users do not see them by default. The *View* tab has a *Restore Defaults* button that resets all settings.

TABLE 18.11   View tab options

Function	Description
View hidden files	*Hidden Files and Folders* section > enable *Show Hidden Files, Folders, and Drives*
View file extensions	*Files and Folders* section > uncheck *Hide Extensions for Known File Types*
View system files	*Files and Folders* section > uncheck *Hide Protected Operating System Files (Recommended)*
Sharing menu/options	*Files and Folders* section > enable *Use Sharing Wizard (Recommended)*

Protecting the Operating System and Data

Several chapters have contained important security-related tips, steps, and information related to protecting the operating system and data. In this section, let's review some tips that pertain specifically to the security of the operating system and data:

> Use the NTFS file system.

> Conduct good **patch/update management**. Ensure that operating system and application service packs and updates are applied regularly. If a Windows Update fails, a message usually appears when the machine reboots. Try the update again; sometimes an update might fail when being installed with other updates. Successfully install as many as you can and then reinstall the failed updates one by one. Note that in Windows 8 and 10, updates come as a package, but they can be uninstalled individually by update number. Note that mobile devices also need **patching/OS updates**, including updates to the phone's radio firmware.

> Have on hand an alternative boot source (such as an optical disc, a flash drive, another hard drive, or an operating system disc).

> Install antivirus/anti-malware software with the latest updates.

> Encrypt data that needs to be protected.
> Optionally, place operating system files and data files on separate hard drive partitions.
> Some firmware or driver versions may cause security issues. Keep the versions updated.
> Virtual machines need the same security software as host machines.
> If the computer you use does not need to share files or a printer with others on the network, use the *Network and Sharing Center* Control Panel and disable *File and Print Sharing*.
> To create a shared folder that is not seen by any others across the network, add a $ (dollar sign) to end of the share name. An example of a hidden shared folder is Book$.
> Use the System Restore program to control restore points before installing new software or hardware. Use the *System* Control Panel > *System Protection* link to access the restore points.
> Disable ports through the system BIOS/UEFI settings. Password protect the BIOS to prevent use of external devices that might be infected with viruses.

Backup/Restore

One hard drive preventive maintenance procedure that is commonly overlooked is performing a backup of the data and operating system as well as the restoration. Backup and restoration should be part of any disaster prevention plan. Most people do not realize that the most important part of any computer is the data that resides within it. Data cannot be replaced as easily as hardware can be.

Back up data routinely. Also make a backup of **critical applications**—applications that are critical to the family or business. Have a routine maintenance plan that you recommend to users. Important data should be backed up daily or frequently, but routine data is usually backed up monthly. The sensitivity and importance of the data determine how frequently backups are performed.

TECH TIP

Backup testing

Ensure that you test a backup to ensure that your method works and the time required to restore is as expected. **Backup testing** should be part of an implementation plan as well as a disaster prevention/recovery plan.

Traditionally, backups were saved to magnetic tape—quarter-inch cartridge, linear tape-open (LTO), or digital linear tape (DLT) being the most common types—but CDs, DVDs, BDs, thumb drives, external hard drives, and cloud storage (shown in Figure 18.34) are viable **local storage** alternatives today. Some people use optical discs or thumb drives to back up important data and periodically do a full backup to an external hard drive.

Advantages of local storage include the ability to control the security of that data and the cost of the media used. A disadvantage is that you have to store and maintain that media. Cloud storage can be free or for a charge, but security is a concern. In addition, restoration requires connectivity to the cloud storage.

TECH TIP

A second hard drive makes an excellent backup device

Hard drives are inexpensive and easy to install. Install a second one to back up your data. Another alternative is to put your operating system and applications on an SSD and use a mechanical drive for your data for easier backups.

FIGURE 18.34   Cloud storage for backups

Backups use the file archive bit. A **full backup** backs up all selected files and sets the archive bit to off. An **incremental backup** backs up all files that have changed since the last backup. The files selected are the ones that have the archive bit set to on. The backup software resets those archive bits to off. A **differential backup** backs up files that have changed since the last full backup (files that have the archive bit set to on), but the backup software does not reset the archive bit, as an incremental backup does.

Each of these types of backups are known as **file-level backups**. Another type of backup is an **image level backup**, which backs up an entire drive to one file (called an image). The drawbacks to this type of backup are the size of the image and the time involved. A company may have a computer image of an operating system and standard applications that is pushed onto the machine, and then users back up their data by using a file-level backup technique.

Windows 7 and 10 come with a backup utility, but many external hard drives come with their own software that is easier to use, has more features, and allows easy and selective data backup scheduling. Windows 8 and 10 have the File History utility. Many vendors have a **backup and recovery** option that is part of BIOS/UEFI, part of the Windows System Recovery Options, or accessed in another manner. No matter what method of backup you use, test your backup for restoration. Install it to a different drive, if necessary.

TECH TIP

Don't use the same hard drive as a backup device

Backing up data to a different partition on a hard drive is *not* a good idea. Even though there is some chance that your data might be saved, it is more likely the drive will fail. The drive is a physical device that may have moving parts—motor, heads, and so on. Mechanical failure is always a possibility.

Probably the most asked question of those with hard drive failures or failing/failed sectors is regarding file recovery. Windows does not have file recovery software beyond being able to locate and repair lost clusters. However, there are third-party file recovery utilities that you can use. Many times files cannot be recovered unless the file recovery utility was installed prior to the loss. Many companies also provide data recovery services.

Even though much data is stored locally, many companies favor centralized storage, even for individual users. This protects the company's interest and also ensures that backups are done on a regular and reliable basis. Another option in business is a thin-client environment, in which no hard drives are included with the systems. Storage is provided across the network to a central location. This reduces hardware and software costs and PC maintenance staffing costs, and it makes data security easier to manage as well.

Account Recovery Options

Whenever disaster occurs and backups/restores have to be done, there may also be a need to recover accounts from various vendors, including Microsoft, to aid in local account password recovery. This can be very time-consuming. Document critical information such as the following *before* disaster occurs:

> Computer/laptop/device make, model, year purchased, and warranty length
> Names, IP addresses, and backup configurations of network infrastructure devices
> Firewall rules
> Domain settings
> Account names and passwords for network infrastructure devices, network administrators, email, and Internet provider settings
> BIOS passwords
> Software license keys, information, applications, versions, and purchasing agreements

BitLocker

BitLocker encrypts an entire disk volume, including the operating system, user files, page files (also known as paging files or swap files), and hibernation files. It is available on Windows 7 Enterprise and Ultimate, Windows 8 Pro and Enterprise, and Windows 10 Pro, Enterprise, Education, Mobile, and Mobile Enterprise. BitLocker requires two NTFS disk partitions. **BitLocker To Go** is used to encrypt and password protect external drives and removable media 128 MB and larger. BitLocker can optionally use Trusted Platform Module (TPM), which is a chip that stores security information such as encryption keys.

Full Device Encryption

Mobile devices support **full device encryption**, which involves scrambling or encoding all user data. Once full device encryption is enabled, any new data created is automatically encrypted. A drawback to full device encryption is slower performance; in addition, disabling the option might require resetting the option back to factory defaults, which means you would lose any data and customization. On an Android device, use the *Security* or *Lock Screen and Security* settings option. Apple iPhones have encryption enabled by default, and the option cannot be disabled.

EFS

NTFS volumes can have files, folders, and subfolders encrypted using Encrypting File System (**EFS**). The EFS algorithm originally used Data Encryption Standard (DES), which used 56- or 128-bit encryption, but now the EFS algorithm uses Advanced Encryption Standard (AES), Secure Hash Algorithm (SHA), smart card–based encryption, and in Windows 7, 8, and 10, Elliptical Curve Cryptography (ECC). **AES** is an encryption standard with key sizes of 128, 192, or 256 bits. AES has been used in wireless government networks for some time and is now common in almost all wireless network implementations that use WPA2 (covered later in the chapter).

When a folder or subfolder is encrypted, all newly created files within the folder or subfolder are automatically encrypted. If any files are copied or moved into an encrypted folder or subfolder, those files are automatically encrypted. System files cannot be encrypted. EFS can use a certificate authority (CA) such as one issued from a server or use a self-signed certificate.

> **TECH TIP**
>
> **Can you encrypt someone else's files?**
>
> The answer is "yes" if you have the write attribute, create files/write data, and list folder/read data permissions for the file.

AutoRun and AutoPlay

Disable AutoRun to prevent software or programs from automatically starting from an optical disc, flash drive, or external drive. As an example of AutoPlay, when you insert a music CD, the music may automatically start playing or you may be prompted for the default action. To change what happens when you insert each type of media device, use the *Hardware and Sound* section of the Control Panel > *Auto Play* link. Use the following steps to disable AutoPlay and AutoRun so that the action will not occur and the user will not be prompted:

Step 1. At a command prompt or in the *Search* textbox, type **gpedit.msc** and press Enter.

Step 2. Expand *Administrative Templates* > expand *Windows Components*.

Step 3. Select *Autoplay Policies* > double-click or double-tap *Turn Off Autoplay* > select *Enabled* > select *All Drives* > restart the computer.

Note that specific Windows security updates are also required; see http://support.microsoft.com for more details.

Dealing with Mechanical Hard Drives

When donating a computer or replacing a hard drive, data on the drive needs to be removed after the data has been transferred to the new drive or is not needed any longer. Furthermore, the hard drive partitions need to be deleted and re-created. Some hard drive manufacturers offer utilities that rewrite (sometimes called **drive overwrite**) the drive with all 1s or all 0s to prevent data remnants from being recovered. Another utility is a **drive wipe**, which may use a number of techniques (not all guaranteed to be 100% effective on highly sensitive data) to remove data from the drive. A hard drive manufacturer may have a **low-level format** utility that is different than the format done through the drive installation/preparation process. You can use the SDelete utility, which can be downloaded from Microsoft (see http://technet.microsoft.com/en-us/sysinternals/bb897443.aspx).

Another option is to use the `format` and `cipher` commands. First use `format x: /p:n` (where `x:` is the drive letter and `n` is the number of passes) to format a disk volume with a zero in every sector. Then use the `cipher /w x:` command, where `x:` is the hard drive volume letter. The `cipher` command writes all unused sectors with 0s, then 1s, and then a random number. Because this command is performed on unused sectors, it is important to remember to use the `format` command first.

A company that has extremely sensitive data stored on a hard drive should destroy the hard drive by (1) securely erasing, which requires special software, (2) degaussing (using electromagnets to change the drive's magnetic fields, or 1s and 0s, which can be expensive and requires drive disassembly), (3) drilling through drive platters (see Figure 18.35) and then destroying the pieces with a hammer, or (4) using a machine designed for this purpose (see Figure 18.36). Specific requirements such as the HIPAA Privacy and Security Rules might need to be examined. For example, if non-sensitive protected health information (PHI) is on a drive, then securely erasing the data is fine, but if sensitive information is on there, the drive has to be degaussed.

FIGURE 18.35   Drilled hard drive platter

 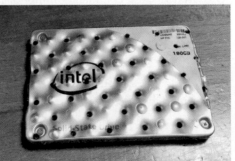

FIGURE 18.36   Hard drive/SSD destroying machine with destroyed drive

Data Execution Prevention (DEP)

Data execution prevention (**DEP**) is a security measure implemented in both hardware and software to prevent malicious software from running on a Windows-based computer. DEP is always on and enabled for 64-bit versions of Windows, but the setting can be customized. With hardware-based DEP, the CPU supports enforcing no execute (NX), sometimes called the NX bit (on AMD processors) or **execute disable** (on Intel processors). The processor marks memory with an attribute indicating that data inside that memory location should not be executable. (It should just be another type of data or code.) Different processors have different capabilities, but at a minimum, the processor can display a message if code tries to execute from those memory locations marked as no execute or execute disable. This option is simply a bit and is either turned on or off as an option.

With software-enforced DEP, if a program tries to run from a memory location that should not have executable code, the application is closed, and a message appears. To see this feature, access the *System* Control Panel > *Advanced System Settings* link > select the *Settings* button in the *Performance* area > select the *Data Execution Prevention* tab. Figure 18.37 shows the two options. The Data Execution Prevention tab also shows at the bottom of the window whether the processor is capable of DEP.

FIGURE 18.37   Windows 7 with DEP turned on

Internet Security

Internet security basics are covered in Chapter 12, "Internet Connectivity, Virtualization, and Cloud Technologies," in the "Basic Web Browser Issues" section. This section goes into more technical detail. First, no system should connect to the Internet without antivirus and anti-malware software installed. These applications are your first line of defense for Internet security, but they are not foolproof.

Second, pay attention to the security alerts provided by antivirus and anti-malware software, browser applications, and the operating system! If you see a message that you haven't seen before, write it down, take a screenshot of it, and research it. Even if you have seen it before, it's a good idea to research and ensure that nothing new is the problem.

Lack of money is not an excuse for not having antivirus software. Microsoft Security Essentials for Windows 7 can be downloaded from Microsoft for free, Windows Defender is included in Windows 8.1/10 and has virus scanning, or another free antivirus program can be downloaded. Ensure that any free antivirus program you obtain is from a reputable download site. Beware of **rogue antivirus** applications that pretend to be legitimate software to help you with a computer problem that are actually viruses.

For anti-malware, Microsoft provides the Malicious Software Removal Tool for free. Other vendors provide free anti-malware software, too. It is easier to deal with such issues with security software installed than without it.

Microsoft 8 and 10 come with **Windows Defender**, which works with Internet Explorer/Edge to warn for spyware. The Microsoft Baseline Security Analyzer (MBSA) identifies security misconfigurations on computers. Configure your browser to display a security warning or that you are asked or warned of potential security threats. Windows Defender can be customized as to when updates are downloaded and how often it scans the computer. It shows detailed information about software that is installed on the computer.

Malware Removal

Malware symptoms are numerous. A device may run slowly, crash, or lock; applications might behave abnormally or not at all; you might experience missing or **disappearing files**; you might see file attribute or **file permission changes**; there might be constant storage device activity or constant (greater-than-normal) network activity; your email might be hijacked (in which case you should change your password to something totally different as soon as you notice); you might get access denied messages or security messages; and you might experience removed, corrupted, or **renamed system files**. (Note that access denied messages are sometimes normal if a user account does not have administrative permissions to do a particular task.)

The following steps are best practice procedures for malware removal:

Step 1. Identify malware symptoms. Do not take a customer's word that he has a virus or malware. An application could be the culprit, or something else entirely might be happening. Be sure to log all actions performed.

Step 2. Quarantine the infected system. Disconnect the system from the network or disable the wireless NIC. Do not power the computer off or reboot it.

Step 3. Notify the appropriate personnel as dictated in the security policy.

Step 4. For Windows machines, disable *System Restore* by accessing the *System* Control Panel > select *Properties* > in the left pane, select *System Protection* > select the appropriate disk > select *Configure* > select *Turn Off System Protection* (Windows 7) or *Disable System Protection* (Windows 8/10) > *OK* > *OK*.

Step 5. Remediate the infected system. You might need to update the anti-malware software or might have to use another system to research your support options from your antivirus/anti-malware software vendor. Rescan the system for security issues using the updated software. Some antivirus software vendors have images that can be downloaded and used to create bootable antivirus discs or flash drives.

If the system still performs strangely, boot into Safe Mode and run the virus checker from there. Use the `msconfig` utility to isolate a startup application or service that might be causing the issue. If you purchased an antivirus disc, run the software from the optical disc. Boot from an alternative boot source (flash drive, external hard drive, or operating system disc).

With some worms and trojan horse viruses, files must be manually deleted because they cannot be repaired, but the antivirus software will "quarantine" such files so they cannot be dangerous and affect other files. If it an executable file is quarantined, you may have to reinstall one or more apps. A hijacked web browser, such as when the requested web page is redirected to a different web page, may require browser configuration, different DNS settings, or a new or updated HOSTS file applied after removal.

You might be required to use the `SFC /scannow` command to replace/repair operating system files after removing a virus. Test all applications to ensure that they operate. Then manually delete any files that are quarantined (see Figure 18.38).

Step 6. Schedule antivirus/anti-malware scans and run updates.

Step 7. For Windows-based computers, re-enable *System Restore*. Create a new restore point.

Step 8. Educate the user on security best practices.

FIGURE 18.38 Quarantined files

TECH TIP

Manually delete files, if necessary

If antivirus software or other preventive software applications state that a particular file cannot be deleted, make a note of the file and its location. Windows Explorer/File Explorer *View* options may have to be adjusted before viewing/deletion can occur.

DNS Issues

DNS is used to translate a URL to an IP address. Homes and small businesses almost always use the DNS server of the Internet provider. Medium to large companies may have their own server, might use the Internet provider's, or might pay for another company to host the DNS server. DNS is a common security target because the attacker can redirect the web browser to another website under control of the attacker.

If you suspect that the DNS server has been compromised because your browser is redirecting you to unusual websites or URLs that don't look quite right, you can change your **DNS configuration** setting to another DNS server just to see if the symptoms change. In a router, the setting is commonly found in the Setup or Basic Settings section. In Windows use the *Network Connections* Control Panel to access the network card > right-click to access *Properties* > double-click on *Internet Protocol Version 4 (TPC/IPv4)* > select *Use the Following DNS Server Addresses* to manually assign one or two DNS server IP addresses, as shown in Figure 18.39.

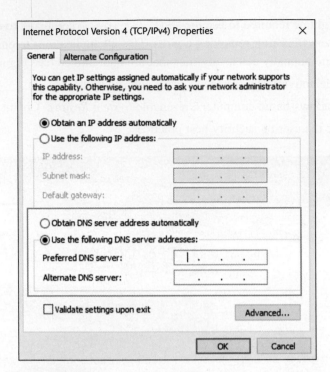

FIGURE 18.39 Manual DNS IP address configuration

On a Mac, access *System Preferences > Network Preference* pane > select the adapter you want to change > *Advanced > DNS* tab > + (plus sign) > enter the IP address of the DNS server.

OpenDNS offers free and fee-based configurations. The following IPv4 and IPv6 addresses can be used, and two of them are used to automatically prevent adult websites from being accessed (called FamilyShield).

IPv4 OpenDNS addresses:

> 208.67.222.222
> 208.67.220.220
> 208.67.222.220
> 208.67.220.222

IPv6 OpenDNS addresses:

> 2620:119:35::35
> 2620:119:53::53

OpenDNS FamilyShield addresses:

> 208.67.222.123
> 208.67.220.123

If you suspect DNS server issues, clear the browser history/cache using the directions below or by researching the browser being used:

> Edge: *Settings* (gear) icon > *Internet Options > General* tab *Browsing history* section > *Delete* button
> Firefox: *Open menu* icon in top-right corner > *Options > Privacy & Security* in the *History* section > *Clear History*
> Chrome: *Customize* (three vertical dots in the top-right corner) > *Settings > Settings* menu on left > *Privacy and Security > Clear Browsing Data* link > *Clear Data*

You should also clear the DNS cache on the computer. On a PC, access a command prompt and, as an administrator, type `ipconfig /flushdns`. On a Mac version 10.9 or higher, access *Terminal* and type the following two commands:

```
sudo dscacheutil -flushcache
sudo killall -HUP mDNSResponder
```

Email Issues

Email has its own section in this chapter because it is something most people deal with on a daily basis. Avoid checking email on a public computer or an unsecure network as it may lead to your email account being hijacked; if this happens, so will not being able to log in using normal procedures, you may get an automated message from an unknown person as if it were an automated response to your own email, people in your contacts might send you a note about constant emails or spam from the hijacked account, or your account might have a lot of undeliverable emails. For an account that has been hijacked, perform the following steps:

Step 1. Contact the email account company to report the problem.

Step 2. Ensure that Windows, antivirus, and anti-malware updates have been applied.

Step 3. Ensure that you have an alternative email account available for when you have to register with sites, such as for online shopping.

Step 4. Try logging in to the account from a different computer to see if the email settings have been changed. *Note:* If you can get to the account, change the password.

Step 5. Create rules in your email account to delete files from specific nontrusted sources.

Spam is unsolicited email from a company or person previously unknown. People who send this type of email are known as spammers. Most email applications have spam filters, but they do not catch all spam. Most email applications also enable you to create a rule to block messages from particular sources or with specific subject lines. Figure 18.40 demonstrates the concept of a spam filter.

Other problems include email messages sent in clear text. If such a message is intercepted, it is easy to read. Pretty Good Privacy (PGP) and Secure Multipurpose Internet Mail Extensions (S/MIME) are frequently used to provide encryption and authentication for email messages.

FIGURE 18.40 Spam filtering

Digital Security Certificates

A digital certificate authenticates and secures information. The certificate authority (CA) is the sender (the device or person who originated the communication). A digital certificate typically contains a public key (a key used with a private key so that messages can be unencrypted), sender information, and the length of time the certificate is to be considered valid. Browsers sometimes present security messages related to certificates. The following are sample messages:

> The security certificate presented by this website was not issued by a trusted certificate authority.
> www.hacker.com uses an invalid security certificate. The certificate is not trusted because the issuer certificate is unknown.
> The security certificate has expired or is not yet valid. The certificate for the particular website has expired, the time/date on the server is incorrect, or the time/date on the client computer is incorrect.
> www.watchout.com uses an invalid security certificate. The certificate is not trusted because it is self-signed.

If you visit a site you should avoid, close the browser. If you want to trust a self-signed certificate, then in Internet Explorer/Edge, use *Tools* (the gear icon in the upper-right corner) > *Internet Options* > *Security* tab > select *Trusted Sites* > *Sites* button > ensure URL is correct > *Add* > *Close* > *OK*. Refresh the web page in the browser. A message appears. Select *Continue to This Website (Not Recommended)* > *Certificate Error* > *View Certificates* > *Install Certificate* > *Next* > *Place All Certificates in the Following Store* > *Browse* > *Trusted Root Certification Authorities* > *OK* > *Next* > *Finish*. Return to the *Internet Options Security* tab > *Trusted Sites* > *Sites* > remove the URL. Close the browser, reopen the browser, and go to the URL. No certificate error appears.

Proxy Servers

A company may use a **proxy server** to protect its network. This server acts as an agent (a go-between) between an application such as a web browser and a remote server. A proxy server can also cache frequently accessed web pages and provide them when requested from a client instead of accessing the web server. A proxy server is commonly located with other network servers in a corporate network design, as shown in Figure 18.41.

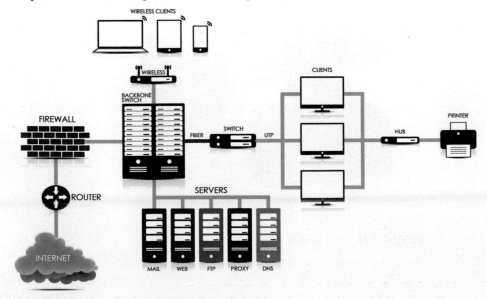

FIGURE 18.41 Proxy server

All traffic from corporate wired and wireless devices that is being sent to the Internet will be directed to the proxy server. The proxy server will then change the source IP address to its own address and send that traffic to the Internet. When the traffic returns from the Internet, the traffic will be sent to the proxy server (not the original device); the proxy server then forwards the traffic to the original network device. A symptom that the proxy server configuration is the issue is that the device can reach internal network resources but not external ones (especially if the Internet connection works).

To configure any device or application for a proxy server, obtain the following information:

> IP address of the proxy server
> Port number of the proxy server
> Optionally a username and password, but some organizations use server-based authentication

To configure Internet Explorer/Edge to use a proxy server, use the *Internet Options* from the *Tools* menu bar option > *Connections* tab > *LAN Settings* button > select the *Use a Proxy Server for Your LAN* checkbox > in the *Address* textbox, type the proxy server IP address > type the proxy server port number in the *Port* textbox. This information can be obtained from the company's network administrator or through the Web Proxy Auto-Discovery (**WPAD**) protocol. Click the *Advanced* button to set individual IP addresses and port numbers for different protocols. If you don't want the proxy server to be used when accessing resources in the local domain (and speed up this type of access), select the *Bypass Proxy Server for Local Addresses* Checkbox. Improperly configured proxy settings may cause a computer to be redirected to an invalid website with no Internet connectivity.

Firewalls

If a computer connects to the Internet, it should be connected behind a firewall. A firewall protects one or more computers from outside attacks and is used to implement security policies. The concept of a firewall is similar to the concept of a moat with a drawbridge protecting a castle. The castle is the inside network, the moat with the drawbridge is the firewall, and everyone outside the castle is an "attacker." The drawbridge controls access to and from the castle.

TECH TIP

Antivirus and anti-malware applications are needed even when a firewall is installed

A computer protected by a firewall still needs antivirus and anti-malware applications for protection. Having a firewall on each computer as well as on a router or modem that connects to the Internet (or a device dedicated to providing firewall services) is common in both home and business environments.

A firewall can be either a software application or hardware, and it should be implemented for any computer that connects to another network, especially a computer that connects to the Internet. A firewall keeps hackers from accessing a computer that connects to the Internet. A software firewall is a Windows tool or software application that is a good security solution for individual computers. A hardware firewall is a good solution for home and business networks. Both can be used concurrently. Look back at Figure 18.41 to see the concept of a firewall.

Whitelists and Blacklists

A security concept related to firewalls is whitelists and blacklists. Security measures are commonly implemented based on one of these two methods. A **whitelist** implementation is based on a list of who is allowed in (through the firewall to use a VPN, use an application, enter a secured network closet, and so on). An easy way to remember the whitelist method is to think of your front door at home. Anyone who has a key to the door is allowed in; each person with a key is on the whitelist.

Alternatively, a **blacklist** details what users or websites are not allowed. Anyone or any site that is not on the blacklist is allowed in. To remember the blacklist method, think of a college's list of people not allowed on campus or the list of blocked calls (your blacklist) on your cell phone.

DMZ

In a corporate environment, a firewall, router, or wireless router can be used to create an area called a demilitarized zone (**DMZ**). Servers such as web servers or application servers can reside in the DMZ. Customers can use a server within the DMZ without having to be let into the part of the network where the sensitive corporate data resides. A DMZ might also be used to separate IoT devices from the rest of the network.

A DMZ can also be created by using two firewalls, with one firewall connected to the router, as shown in Figure 18.41, and the DMZ connected to that firewall and to a second firewall. The second firewall also connects to the internal corporate network (see Figure 18.42), so the setup looks like this: Internet | firewall | DMZ | firewall | internal corporate network.

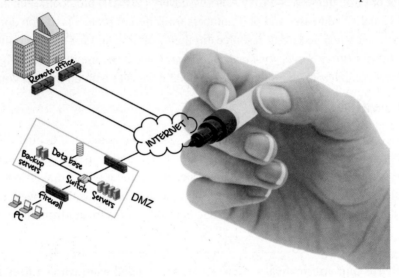

FIGURE 18.42   DMZ

Universal Plug and Play

Universal plug and play (**UPnP**) is used to set up a network with very little configuration such as in a home network. Devices such as a home router, printers, PCs, and mobile devices can all be configured for UPnP, and the devices discover each other. Note that this setting is commonly found in an Administration or Advanced tab or section and might be enabled by default. On a Windows computer, when you enable *Turn on Network Discovery* in the Network and Sharing Center Control Panel > *Change Advanced Sharing Settings* option, you are enabling UPnP.

Windows Firewall and Advanced Security

Windows 7 and 8 have an *Action Center* Control Panel that displays messages and warnings related to security and maintenance. Windows 10 has action center alerts, but not the *Action Center* Control Panel. For Windows 10, to control the types of messages seen, access *Settings* > *System* > *Notifications & Actions*.

The Windows Firewall application examines packets traveling to and from the computer and filters them (that is, denies or allows them) based on a configured access control list (ACL). Options chosen through the *Action Center* section of the Control Panel affect this ACL. **Port forwarding** is a term used for a packet allowed through the firewall based on a particular port number/protocol. Port triggering is a similar concept. **Port triggering** allows data into a computer temporarily, based on a configured situation.

TECH TIP

Allowing a program through Windows Firewall

In Windows 7, open the *Windows Firewall* section of the Control Panel > select the *Allow a Program or Feature Through Windows Firewall* > select *Change Settings* > enable the checkbox beside the program you want to allow > *OK*. In Windows 8 or 10, open the *Windows Firewall* section of the Control Panel > select the *Allow an App or Feature Through Windows Firewall* > *Change Settings* > enable the checkbox beside the app you want to allow and select the network types this applies to > *OK*.

To verify whether Windows Firewall is enabled, access the *Windows Firewall* section of the Control Panel > *Turn Windows Firewall On or Off* link. Use the `wf.msc` command to access the *Windows Firewall with Advanced Security* configuration page. To see open firewall ports, use the `netsh firewall show state` command from an elevated command prompt using the *Run as administrator* option.

Figure 18.43 shows a Windows 7 Firewall section of the Control Panel window. The *Block All Incoming Connections* checkbox should be selected when the computer is used in public places like a restaurant or bookstore, so outside users cannot access the computer.

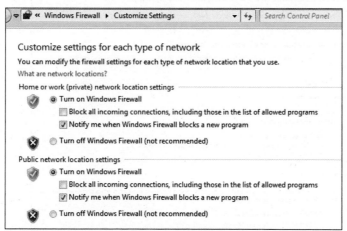

FIGURE 18.43 Windows 7 firewall settings

When Windows Firewall is installed and enabled on a Windows computer and another computer or application tries to connect, Windows Firewall blocks the connection and prompts with a security alert to allow a choice of *Unblock*, *Keep Blocking*, or *Ask Me Later*. Table 18.12 describes these options.

TABLE 18.12 Windows firewall security alert options

Option	Description
Unblock This Program	The program is allowed to execute, and the program is automatically added to the Windows Firewall exceptions list (whitelist).
Keep Blocking This Program	The program is not allowed to execute or listen. Use this option whenever you do not know the source of the alert.
Keep Blocking This Program, but Ask Me Again Later	Does not allow the program to execute or listen, but the next time you access the site, the security alert prompts you again.

Windows 7 has up to three possible network location settings, called profiles (depending on the Windows version), that configure the Windows Firewall differently. The profile that is active is shown as the current profile. Use the *Network and Sharing Center* Control Panel > *Change Advanced Sharing Settings* link to view this profile. Note that you may have to select a down arrow to view the contents of each profile or select the up arrow to collapse a section.

Following are the types of profiles you see in Windows 7:

> The *Private (Home or Work)* network location setting turns on file sharing and network discovery through the firewall, so communication will be easier at work or in a private home network.
> The *Public* setting configures these settings to be off through the firewall to help protect your computer when on a public network such as when you are in an airport.
> The *Domain* setting is when the computer participates in a Windows Active Directory domain environment.

Windows 8 and 10 have similar options (see Figure 18.44 for the Windows 10 options):

> The *Private* network location setting turns on file sharing and network discovery through the firewall, so communication will be easier at work or in a private home network.
> The *Guest or Public* setting protects the computer by turning off file sharing and network discovery and is used when connected to a public network such as in a restaurant or cafe.
> The *All Networks* setting includes private folder sharing, media streaming, file sharing, and password-protected sharing options that can apply to all types of network connections.

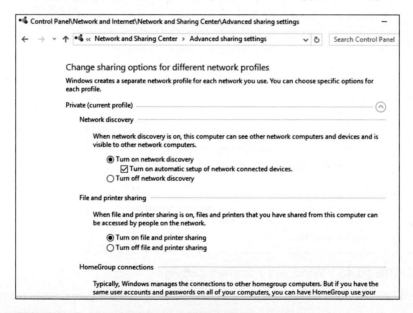

FIGURE 18.44   Windows 10 network profiles

TECH TIP

Be sure you work with the correct profile

If you cannot access devices and resources that are normally available through the wireless NIC, ensure that the correct location profile is used. Access the *Advanced Sharing Settings* link from the *Network and Sharing Center* Control Panel. The profile used will have the following words after the profile name: *(current profile)*.

Table 18.13 shows Windows Firewall issues and solutions to help with troubleshooting.

TABLE 18.13   Windows Firewall and advanced security troubleshooting

Windows firewall issue	Resolutions
The firewall is blocking all connections.	Access Windows Firewall and disable the *Block All Incoming Connections* checkbox.
The firewall is blocking a specific application.	If a dialog box appears, select the *Unblock* option to allow it through. If the dialog box does not appear, access Windows Firewall and use the *Exceptions* tab to create a rule that allows the application through the firewall.
No one can ping a Windows computer.	Ensure that *File and Print Sharing* is enabled through the *Network and Sharing Center* Control Panel. Access the *Administrative Tools* link and select *Windows Firewall with Advanced Security*. Select *Inbound Rules* in the left pane. Select *New Rule* in the *Actions* column. Select the *Custom* radio button and *Next*. Select the *All Programs* radio button and click *Next*. Select *ICMPv4* from the *Protocol Type* drop-down box. Select the IP addresses to which this rule will apply and name the rule.
Windows Firewall is turned off every time the computer restarts.	Another security firewall is installed.
No one can access local files and/or a shared printer.	File and Print Sharing has not been enabled.

Freeware programs are available as well as full security suites such as the ones from McAfee or Symantec that include software firewalls and components to prevent malicious types of software applications from executing.

Parental Controls

Special programs have been specifically created for managing devices used by children, but there are **parental control** options within Windows that can also help. On a Windows 7/8 computer, the *Internet Options* Control Panel > *Content* tab can be used to access the Family Safety button and parental controls.

On a Windows 10 computer, you need to create a child account in order to set up parental controls. Follow these steps to do so:

Step 1. Access *Windows Settings > Accounts*.

Step 2. Select *Family & Other People* from the left menu. Note that you have to sign in with a Microsoft account in order to create a child account. Once you do, the *Add a Family Member* option appears in the *Your Family* section. Select *Add a Family Member*.

Step 3. Enable the *Add a Child* radio button > enter an email address and a password > *Confirm* button.

Once a child account has been created and confirmed through the child's email, set up the parental control options by accessing Windows Settings again > *Family & Other People*. In the *Your Family* section, use the *Manage Family Settings Online* link to open the Microsoft Family parental control page. You can also sign in to the Microsoft account and use the *Family* tab. There you can block inappropriate websites, enter websites that are allowed, enter websites that are not allowed, create a schedule for when the child can use the device or limit by the number of hours allowed. From the *Activity* page you can log how much time has been spent on the device or get a weekly email report.

NAT/PAT

Companies use private IP addresses (192.168.x.x, 172.16.x.x through 172.31.x.x, 10.x.x.x) on devices inside the company, but these addresses cannot be routed on the Internet. A network device such as a router or firewall performs network address translation (**NAT**), which means it translates private IP addresses to public addresses that can be routed over the Internet.

One public address can be used for multiple internal company connections due to port mapping. **Port mapping** allows the combination of one public address and a specific port number to represent one internal company host. The same public address and a different port number represent a second internal company host. Some people also call this concept port forwarding or port address translation (PAT). Figure 18.45 shows this concept.

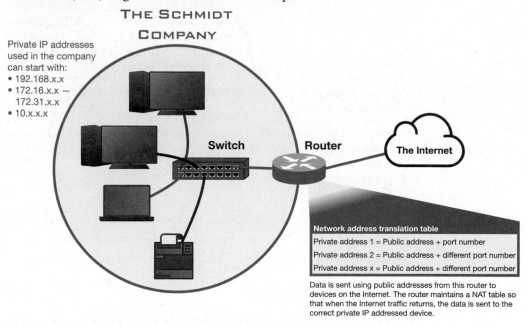

FIGURE 18.45 Network/port address translation

VPN Configuration

A popular business solution for security is a VPN. A virtual private network (VPN) is a special type of secure network created over the Internet from one network device to another. One example is a home PC that connects to a corporate server and has access to company resources that cannot otherwise be accessed except by being on a computer on the inside network. The VPN connection makes it appear as if the home computer is on the inside corporate network. Another example is a branch office network device connecting to a corporate server, VPN concentrator, firewall, or other network device. When connected, the branch office network device connects as if it were directly connected to the network.

TECH TIP

Both sides of the VPN tunnel must match

The two devices used to create a VPN tunnel must have identical VPN settings, or the VPN tunnel will not be formed.

To configure a VPN in Windows, open the *Network and Sharing Center* Control Panel > select the *Set Up a New Connection or Network* link > *Connect to a Workplace* > *Next* > *Use My Internet Connection (VPN)* > enter the IP address or fully qualified domain name of the network device on the other end of the VPN connection > *Next* > enter the required credentials > click *Connect*. Figure 18.46 illustrates the concept of a VPN.

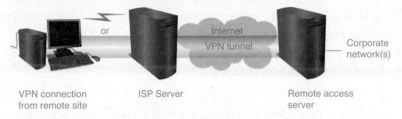

FIGURE 18.46 VPN connectivity

Remote Access to Network Devices

Corporate users commonly work from home or travel as part of the job and need to access printers, servers, and other devices within the company. Technicians commonly use the remote desktop or third-party tools in order to perform troubleshooting and repairs. Let's explore the protocols used to do remote access, the methods used, and how security is handled.

Remote Access Protocols

Three common protocols are used to remotely access devices. They are described in Table 18.14, along with security concerns.

TABLE 18.14 Remote access protocols and security concerns

Remote access protocol	Description	Security concerns
RDP (Remote Desktop Protocol)	Creates a peer-to-peer remote desktop connection from one computer to a remote computer. You might have to enable port forwarding (see Chapter 13, "Networking") and allow port 3389 in order to connect to the remote device.	Reported security issues should be taken into consideration before using RDP.
SSH (Secure Shell)	Uses port 22 to securely log in to a remote network device.	An alternative to Telnet that includes strong encryption within the secure channel created between devices.
Telnet	Uses port 23 to access a remote device on the network, such as a router, a server, an access point, or a switch.	Telnet uses clear text to send data and passwords. Telnet should not be used unless the network device supports no other remote access protocol.

Because of the security shortcomings of RDP, companies use third-party tools to share a screen with a user in order to troubleshoot a specific problem or share files. Examples of such software include LogMeIn Rescue, TeamViewer, AnyPlace Control, ConnectWise Control, GoToMyPC, AnyDesk, Bomgar, ShowMyPC, LiteManager, Splashtop, Radmin, BeamYourScreen, RealVNC, join.me, and Highfive.

CHAPTER 18

Internet Appliances

Other security devices similar to firewalls that an IT staff member should be familiar with include the end-point management server, UTM, IDS, and IPS. An **end-point management server** is used to discover and manage devices on the network. This could include the following:

> Providing an image to a new computer or re-imaging a computer that has a corrupt operating system or security issue
> Updating applications with patches that might include security updates
> Security and profile management
> Inventory management

A unified threat management (**UTM**) system is a single device that commonly provides multiple security functions such as content filtering, antivirus, antispyware, anti-malware, firewall, and intrusion detection and prevention. The device might also have the capability to route, accept VPN connections, and provide NAT.

Content filtering involves using a device or security software to screen data for specific web addresses, email, or files that are defined as being suspect. This is similar to applying parental controls on a home Windows computer.

An intrusion detection system (**IDS**) can be hardware or software that constantly monitors and scans network traffic for malicious traffic or violations of defined security policies. An IDS is considered a passive system; it doesn't take action, it just detects and sends data, reports, and alerts to the network management team (see Figure 18.47). It is like a babysitter whose job is to just tend to the kids (the network data). If there is a fight (a security threat), the babysitter notifies the parents (the network personnel), who deal with the problem.

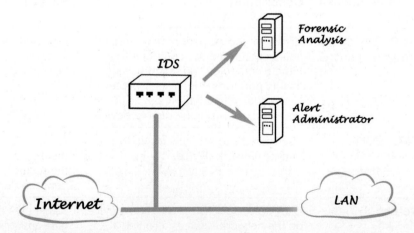

FIGURE 18.47   IDS

A device that is similar to an IDS is an intrusion prevention system (**IPS**). An IPS is an active system; it constantly monitors and scans network traffic for malicious traffic and violations of security policies, and it takes appropriate action. An IPS can send an alarm, reset connections, block traffic, disable ports, and drop packets. An IPS is like a teacher hall monitor that can issue detentions, break up fights, and restore order to the hallway. Sometimes, an IDS and an IPS are both used in a network design, with the IDS inspecting the network traffic and reporting the information and the IPS taking preventive action.

Wireless Network Security Overview

Traditionally security has been a concern when installing wireless networks because originally security was disabled by default and there was lack of knowledge about default passwords and misconfigured wireless settings. Wireless LANs (WLANs) are much more secure today than when they first came out and WLANs are abundant. Wireless LANs may use a security protocol or may be unsecure.

Wireless access points (APs) are an integral part of a wireless LAN and are normally mounted in the ceiling or on a wall where they are inconspicuous. Sometimes, they are mounted in or above the ceiling tile in a special enclosure. Networking equipment such as hubs, switches, routers, and servers are locked in a cabinet or behind a locked door in a wiring closet. Customized cabinets can be purchased to secure APs indoors and outdoors.

Data transmitted over air can be in clear text, which means that with special frame capturing software (packet sniffers or analyzers) on a computer with a wireless NIC installed, the data can be captured and viewed. Negotiation between the wireless devices and the AP can be in clear text so that information can be captured. Every frame includes a source MAC address. Someone with a wireless device and free hacking software can capture the frame to use the MAC address to gain access to other resources. (But note that the hackers are not this obvious!) (This is known as session hijacking or MAC spoofing.) By default, most APs transmit their SSIDs in clear text. All these issues must be considered when installing a wireless network.

TECH TIP

How a firewall helps a wireless computer

A firewall can protect a computer connected to a wireless network; however, the firewall cannot prevent the outgoing wireless data from being hijacked. The firewall simply protects a hacker from accessing the computer.

Mobile Device Management

Mobile device management (MDM) can help with security by enabling a technician to view and manage mobile devices, as shown in Figure 18.48. MDM software can be used to push application updates, enforce security policies, track, or remotely wipe data or the operating system from the device. A tracking module is available on some mobile devices and is used to track the device and provide recovery/wiping options if the device is lost or stolen. **MDM policies** vary from one company to another, but they commonly define operating systems supported as well as password and security requirements. Optional policies might include the following:

> Password storage
> Software/firmware installation
> System updates
> Backup process
> VPN connectivity
> How to report lost or stolen devices
> Steps involved when a security breach occurs
> Data storage

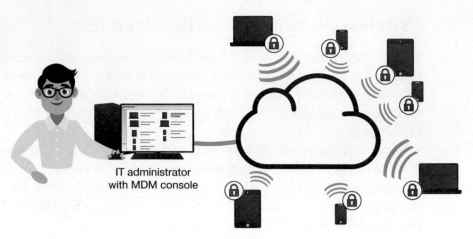

IT administrator
with MDM console

FIGURE 18.48   Mobile Device Management (MDM)

Wireless Security

Security on wireless devices has always been a concern, and several options can be used. Here are the most common ones:

> WEP
> WPA
> WPA2
> TKIP
> AES

TECH TIP

Mobile device security options must match AP settings

Whatever security is configured on an access point must be used on any mobile device that uses the wireless network.

The original 802.11 standard defined two mechanisms for wireless security: authentication and data confidentiality. The two types of authentication are open and shared key. **Open authentication** allows a wireless network device to send a frame to the access point with the sender's identity (MAC address). Open authentication is used when no authentication is required. **Shared key authentication** requires the use of a shared key, which is a group of characters that the wireless network device and access point must have in common. Shared key authentication does not scale well with larger wireless networks because each device must be configured with the shared key authentication (which is time-consuming), the users must be told of the shared key, and their individual stations must be configured for this. Optionally, a server may provide the shared key automatically. Also, when a manually input shared key is used, the key is not often changed, which leads to security issues. Figure 18.49 shows this concept.

A better solution for authentication is to use APs that support 802.1x authentication and use some form of Extensible Authentication Protocol (EAP). When any type of EAP is used, the user or client to be authenticated is called a *supplicant*. An authentication server holds valid usernames and passwords. The device that is in the middle that takes the client request and passes it on to the server is known as the *authenticator*. An AP can be an authenticator.

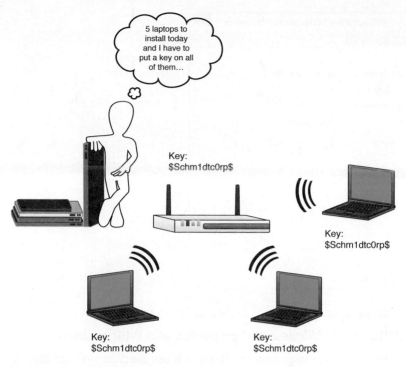

FIGURE 18.49   Wireless security keys

When shared key authentication is used, WEP must be enabled. Wired Equivalent Privacy (**WEP**) encrypts data being transmitted. WEP commonly has two versions: 64-bit and 128-bit. Some vendors may have 256-bit; 64- and 128-bit WEP may also be seen as 40- and 104-bit. This is because each of the two versions uses a 24-bit initialization vector (40 plus 24 equals 64, and 104 plus 24 equals 128). Sometimes, you might even see documentation or website wording where the author mixes the two types of numbers, such as 40-bit and 128-bit, so it can be confusing.

TECH TIP

How many characters do you type with WEP?

If 64-bit WEP is used, five characters are entered (5 times 8 bits—1 bit for each ASCII character—equals 40 bits) or 10 hexadecimal characters (10 times 4 bits—1 bit for each hexadecimal character—equals 40 bits). When using 128-bit WEP and entering the key with ASCII, 13 characters are entered. And if hexadecimal is used with 128-bit WEP, 26 characters are typed.

With WEP enabled, the shared "secret" key is normally entered into the wireless NIC configuration window. Vendors have a variety of ways of inputting this alphanumeric key, but normally it is input in either hexadecimal or ASCII characters.

Some wireless NIC manufacturers allow you to enter multiple WEP keys; however, only one key is used at a time. The multiple WEP keys are for multiple environments, such as a WEP key for the business environment and a WEP key for the home wireless network using the same wireless NIC. Figure 18.50 shows the configuration dialog box for a wireless NIC and where WEP is enabled on a Windows computer.

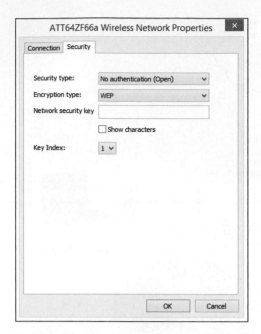

FIGURE 18.50 Wireless NIC properties with WEP enabled

To access this configuration in Windows, use the *Network and Sharing Center* Control Panel > *Change Adapter Settings* link > select the wireless NIC > *View Status of This Connection* link > *Wireless Properties* button > *Security* tab. Notice in Figure 18.50 that there is a drop-down menu for selecting WEP as an encryption type. Most installations require that the WEP key be entered manually. This adapter does not enable you to specify the length of the WEP key, so it is probably the 64-bit version. Some vendors have configuration utilities that allow wireless NIC configuration instead of the normal method of right-clicking the wireless NIC and selecting *Properties*.

WEP can be hacked. With special software on a laptop that has a wireless NIC installed, WEP can be compromised. Enabling WEP is better than using no encryption whatsoever. However, an improvement on WEP is **WiFi Protected Access** (**WPA**). WPA uses Temporal Key Integrity Protocol (**TKIP**) or Advanced Encryption Standard (AES) to improve security. TKIP is an improvement on WEP in that the encryption keys change, and AES is even better than TKIP.

WiFi Protected Access 2 (**WPA2**) is an improvement that includes dynamic negotiation between the AP and the client for authentication and encryption algorithms (see Figure 18.51). WPA2 is a common choice for securing wireless networks. The 802.11i standard includes Robust Security Network (RSN), which has some features of WPA2. Third-party products can be used with some vendors' wireless solutions, and some vendors provide extra security with their NICs and access points. The drawback to this is that other vendors' products are normally incompatible.

To manually configure wireless settings in Windows 7, use the *Network and Internet* section of the Control Panel link > *Manage Wireless Networks* > *Add* link > *Manually Create a Network Profile* link. The *Security Type* drop-down menu has the following options: No Authentication (Open), WEP, WPA2-Personal, WPA-Personal, WPA2-Enterprise, WPA-Enterprise, and 802.1x. If you select *WPA/WPA2*, then *TKIP* or *AES* is available from the *Encryption Type* drop-down menu.

In Windows 8 and 10, use the *Network and Sharing Center* Control Panel > select the *Set Up a New Connection or Network* link > *Manually Connect to a Wireless Network* > *Next* > type the SSID and appropriate security settings > *Next*. Figure 18.52 shows this window for Windows 10.

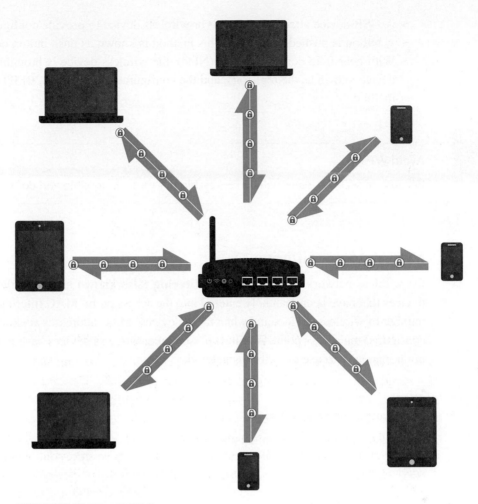

FIGURE 18.51   WPA2

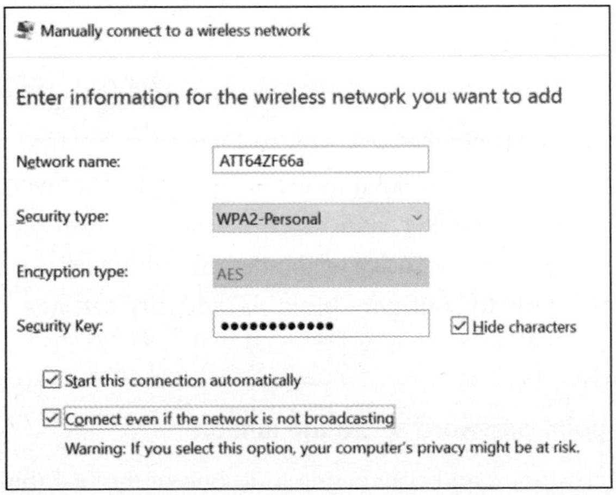

```
🖳 Manually connect to a wireless network

Enter information for the wireless network you want to add

Network name:        ATT64ZF66a

Security type:       WPA2-Personal        ∨

Encryption type:     AES

Security Key:        ●●●●●●●●●●●●        ☑ Hide characters

☑ Start this connection automatically
☑ Connect even if the network is not broadcasting
   Warning: If you select this option, your computer's privacy might be at risk.
```

FIGURE 18.52   Windows 10 wireless security window

WPS

WiFi Protected Setup (**WPS**) configures the SSID and WPA2 wireless security key for an AP or a client's devices. It supports 802.11a, b, g, n, and ac devices, including computers, access points, consumer electronics, and phones. The standard allows four ways to configure a wireless network:

> A personal identification number (PIN) is entered. This PIN is sometimes found on a sticker or display on the wireless product.

> A USB device attaches to the AP or wireless device to provide configuration information.
> A button is pushed or clicked. This method is known as push button configuration (PBC).
> With near field communication (NFC), the wireless device is brought close to the AP (or a device known as the registrar), and the configuration is applied. RFID tags are suited for this method.

> **TECH TIP**
>
> **Avoid WPS**
>
> Because of security issues with WPS, disable this mode if possible and do not use it.

MAC Address Filtering

On wireless networks, **MAC address filtering** (also known as MAC filtering) allows only the devices that have been manually entered into the access point. MAC filtering is used with a limited number of wireless devices and when those devices' MAC addresses are known by the person who configured the access point. Any new personnel or wireless devices have to be added to the access point manually to use the wireless network.

> **TECH TIP**
>
> **Who would use MAC filtering?**
>
> Most access points have a limited number of MAC addresses (20 to 50), so MAC address filtering tends to be used only by small companies that want to have strict control of who gets onto the wireless network.

AP Default Settings

All wireless networks have security features. A SOHO AP/router can come with a default password and SSID, but many such devices ask you to change it the first time you access the AP/router. Change both of these settings as soon as the access point is powered on. Default passwords are posted on the Internet, and a hacker could lock out access from the access point. Be careful using older APs that might have no security or the default administrator user ID and password. It is important that you know how to configure basic AP security settings.

> **TECH TIP**
>
> **Never leave an access point password set to the default**
>
> After powering up an access point and connecting to it, one of the first things to do is change the default password.

Change the access point's default password during installation. Do not leave it set to the default. Make the password a strong one. Use as many characters as feasible. Use uppercase and lowercase letters. Include non-alphanumeric characters, such as #, %, &, or @.

Firmware

Firmware is software that is embedded into a piece of hardware. Firmware can be upgraded in network routers, switches, access points, firewalls, and so on. Companies update firmware as security issues become known, when enhancements become available, or to support new technology. In a corporate environment, it is critical that firmware updates be applied. The process for obtaining and applying firmware updates varies per vendor but is commonly done through a web browser window used to access the network device.

SSID Broadcasting

As mentioned in Chapter 13, the service set identifier (SSID) announces to wireless devices that a particular wireless network is in the area. Most access points are configured for SSID broadcasting. With **SSID broadcasting**, the access point periodically sends out a beacon frame that includes the SSID. Wireless NICs can detect this SSID automatically and attach to the access point (see Figure 18.53). SSID broadcasting can be disabled as a preventive measure so that the wireless network is not announced in the area.

FIGURE 18.53   SSID broadcasting

TECH TIP

Reduce transmit power

If adjacent companies or people nearby are using the guest wireless network, reduce the signal power to reduce the size of the wireless network.

Wireless AP Installation Checklist

Many wireless access points have the capability to route. A router, whether standalone or integrated with a wireless point, connects wired and wireless networks together. A router also enables DHCP to service both wired and wireless networks and provides a firewall for network security.

Many of the parameters needed for wireless NIC configuration are also needed for access point installation. However, installing an access point is more involved because the access point is the central device of the wireless network. Answer the following questions *before* the access point is installed to help with the installation:

> What SSID is to be used?
> What static IP address will be assigned to the device?
> Is WEP, WPA, WPA-PSK, WPA2-PSK, TKIP, AES, or any other security option enabled?
> What security key lengths, security keys, or passphrases are used?
> Is MAC filtering enabled?
> Is there power available for the access point? Note that some access points can receive power through a Power over Ethernet (PoE) switch.
> How will the access point be mounted? Is mounting hardware provided with the access point, or does extra equipment have to be purchased?
> Where should the access point be mounted for best coverage of the wireless network area? Where should the antenna be placed, or how should it be angled? Perform a site survey to determine how to achieve the best performance. Temporarily mount the access point. With a laptop that has a wireless NIC and site survey software, walk around the wireless network area to see the coverage range. The site survey can also be conducted by double-clicking the network icon on the taskbar; the signal strength is shown in the window that appears. Move the access point as necessary to avoid attenuation and obtain the largest possible area coverage.
> What channel ID will be used?
> Will the access point connect to the wired network and, if so, is there connectivity available where the access point will be mounted?

Wireless networking is an important and popular technology. Technicians today must be familiar with wireless devices as corporations and home users install these types of products.

Wireless Security Conclusion

Wireless security is an important issue. The following list recaps some of the important issues and provides recommendations along with a few suggestions for a more secure wireless network:

> Change the default SSID and password. Make the password as long as possible and include non-alphanumeric characters.
> Enable encryption on the access point to the highest level possible while still allowing wireless NIC access. Use authentication when possible.
> Put the wireless network on its own subnetwork and place it behind a firewall, if possible.
> In a small company, consider enabling MAC authentication (MAC filtering) for company devices.
> If supported, authenticate using an authentication server.
> If the SSID is manually configured, periodically change the SSID.
> Assign a static IP address to the access point rather than use DHCP for it.
> Disable remote management on the access point.
> Place the access point in the center of the wireless network and not next to an outside window.
> Use wireless network scanning software to test the network security.
> Require that wireless clients use a virtual private network (VPN) tunnel to access the access point.
> When using a wireless network such as a hotspot, use a VPN to access a corporate network. When viewing private or financial data, make sure the website uses the HTTPS protocol so that it encrypts the data using Transport Layer Security (TLS) or the older Security Socket Layer (SSL) protocol.

> If a rogue access point (an unauthorized AP) is found on the network, disconnect the device and confiscate it. Try to determine who owns the device and report the owner to IT security personnel.

Wireless networks have a strong presence today and will continue to do so in the future. The 802.1x and 802.11 standards are constantly being improved to tighten security for wireless networks so that they rival wired solutions.

Wireless Network Troubleshooting

Troubleshooting wireless networks is sometimes easier than troubleshooting wired networks because of the mobility factor. A laptop with a wireless NIC installed can be used to troubleshoot connectivity, configuration, security, and so on. Most wireless network problems stem from inconsistent configuration. The standards deployed must be for the lowest common denominator. For example, if a wireless NIC supports only 64-bit WEP encryption, then that is what you must use, even if 128-bit WEP, WPA, or WPA2 is available on some of the cards.

The following list includes general wireless networking tips designed to steer a technician in the right direction. Most of these tips have been discussed in previous sections, but it is nice to have the following troubleshooting list in one spot:

> Is the SSID correct?
> Is the wireless NIC seen by the operating system? (Use Device Manager to check.) Check the mobile device for a wireless disable button or use a key to disable/enable the wireless NIC.
> Is the correct security level enabled?
> Can any devices attach to the access point? If not, check the access point.
> Is anything causing interference or attenuation? Check antenna placement.
> Is there a channel ID overlap problem?
> If a wireless printer is to be shared across the network, ensure the printer attaches to the company protected wireless network and not the open (guest) wireless network unless you want customers to use the printer.
> A program from the wireless NIC manufacturer can be installed and used instead of using Windows to control the wireless NIC. If the customer wants to use Windows instead of the software provided, access a command prompt with elevated privileges. At the prompt, type **netsh wlan show settings**. From the output, determine whether the Windows automatic wireless configuration is disabled. You may have to disable the wireless NIC and uninstall the vendor software to use Windows to control the NIC.

Security Incident Reporting

Many companies define what to do when a security incident has occurred. However, in some businesses or for an incident that occurs on a home network, people are not always sure what to do. Following are the steps to take:

Step 1. Identify the issue. (See Table 18.15 for issues and best practices.)

Step 2. Report the issue through the proper channels (refer to Table 18.15).

Step 3. Preserve the data/device by documenting the incident. Ensure that your documentation includes everything, including any changes or moves. Use a chain-of-custody form that travels with the data/device as more people get involved. Chain-of-custody forms commonly include the following information:

> What is the issue (with data, a device, or something else)?
> How did you get involved with the evidence?
> When did you see the issue?

> What did you do to handle the issue?
> To what person did you turn over the issue, data, device, and so on?

TABLE 18.15   Incident reporting and actions

Type of event	Description
Virus	Disconnect the computer from the Internet and log all actions. Do not power the computer off or reboot it. Run a full antivirus scan. Notify the appropriate personnel as outlined in the security policy. Do not forget that other IT personnel may need to be notified such as network personnel who may need to block connections to contain the spread of the virus, or personnel responsible for corporate messaging, for example. You may also need to contact legal or public relations personnel. You can also notify your Internet provider and file a complaint with the FBI Internet Crime Complaint Center.
Spyware or grayware	Use a freeware or other software application to remove the application. Many of the security suites have a method of reporting found incidents. Submit a report using the FTC Consumer Complaint Form.
Phishing	Notify the agency from which the contact was received. Report the incident to the U.S. Computer Emergency Readiness Team (CERT).
Child exploitation	Use parental control software to prevent this. Log off immediately and notify your local police department and/or the nearest FBI field office. You can also report the event to the National Center for Exploited and Missing Children.
Software piracy	Report incidents of organized software piracy to the Software and Information Industry Association (SIIA) and the Business Software Alliance (BSA).

If a security incident occurs and you do not know what to do, talk to your supervisor (see Figure 18.54). She should have the experience to guide you or know to whom she should go to resolve the issue. If you feel uncomfortable talking to your supervisor about this, consider going to the human resources department or a higher administrator. The BSA and other organizations allow anonymous reporting. Reporting and documenting security violations is important, especially in the business environment. It is every person's responsibility to be security aware and responsible.

FIGURE 18.54   Report security violations

A Final Word About Security

Whether a wired or wireless connection, standalone PC or networked PC, or full desktop computer, laptop, tablet, or smartphone, data and device security are important. Security measures must always be taken. Technicians must be aware of the latest threats, take proactive measures to implement security, and share their knowledge with users so the users can take proactive steps. Security risks and threats cause technicians a lot of work and time. These threats and attacks cost billions in lost data and time to businesses. Because most technicians do not see themselves as a dollar figure on a spreadsheet, they don't realize that if the business loses money as a result of security threats, the business has to cut costs, and one of those costs could be the technical position. Think about it and be proactive in guarding against security threats.

TECH TIP

Follow all policies and security best practices

It is very important for technicians to follow corporate policies and security best practices. If in doubt, ask your supervisor or ask for a copy of them.

SOFT SKILLS: BUILDING CUSTOMER TRUST

It is fitting in the security chapter to discuss building a trust relationship with the customer. Trust begins with professionalism. Be professional in your attire, attitude, written communication, and oral communication. Trust also includes being honest with the customer. If you are going to be late, let the customer know that. If you need to do more research, explain the situation. No one can be expected to know all technical information.

Trust also involves being honest if you find confidential material. Do not use or discuss any material you see while in a customer area. If you see confidential material, let the customers know you have seen the material. If the material is a password, let the customer know and recommend that he or she change the password immediately.

Do not touch or move things or papers in a customer's area. Always ask the customer to move or put things away to clear the area you need. Do not try to work around a mess. Simply explain that you need space to determine and/or repair the problem.

Trust involves giving customers documentation related to the product just installed or replaced. Trust involves doing what you say you will do. If you say you will call back to check on the situation in the next 24 hours, do so. If you say you will drop off the documentation the following week, do that. Be true to your word.

Trust also involves being honest about billing. Do not overcharge customers. When presenting customers with an invoice or a work order, explain details with patience. Do not allow customers to argue with you over facts or time. Your time is valuable, too.

You never know where you are going to meet your next boss. Every time you step into a customer's area or talk to a customer, it might lead to a professional reference, a job recommendation, a job lead, or a promotion. Part of building the customer relationship is building trust. Be professional in all that you do. See Figure 18.55.

FIGURE 18.55   Building customer trust

Chapter Summary

> A security policy guides a company in security matters. The policy defines things such as physical access, antivirus, acceptable usage of devices and data, password policies, email usage guidelines, remote access strategies, and emergency procedures.

> Physical security can include door access, key control, authentication methods including the use of smart cards, key fobs, RFID, biometric devices, physical protection of network devices such as servers, APs, switches, and routers, as well as privacy filters.

> BIOS/UEFI security options include configuring a supervisor/user password, disabling unused ports, disabling USB ports, and disabling device options.

> To protect the operating system, use NTFS and have a plan for updating the operating system, web browser, antivirus, anti-malware, and antispyware. Encrypt files and folders as necessary. Use BitLocker and TPM technologies, implement a firewall, and disable AutoRun and AutoPlay.

> If a computer with sensitive data on the hard drive is to be donated, moved, or sold, perform the following: (1) secure erasing, (2) degaussing, and (3) drilling through drive platters and then destroying the pieces with a hammer.

> If virtualization is used, ensure that each virtual machine has adequate protection (firewall, antivirus, anti-malware, and antispyware).

> After a security scan, some virus or malware files are quarantined and must be manually deleted.

> The Windows Guest account should be disabled; the administrator account should be renamed and have a strong password. User accounts should limit rights to only the rights the person requires to do his or her job; this is known as the principle of least privilege.

> Permissions should be assigned appropriately to remotely accessed files and folders. Use either share permissions or NTFS permissions (for more control) but not both on the same network share. If a file is placed in a folder that has permissions, the file inherits the folder permissions. Effective permissions are the bottom-line permissions someone has when group permissions and individual permissions have been granted.

> A hijacked browser can cause a different home page to appear, a particular web page to be displayed, a rootkit or other malware to be installed, different DNS settings to be applied, or a new or updated HOSTS file to be applied.

> Email applications now protect against spam, but you can also create rules to block messages from a particular source or subject line.

> On a wireless network, implement encryption and authentication. Change default SSIDs and passwords.

> When a security incident occurs, identify the issue, report it through the proper channels and to the appropriate authorities, and preserve the data by using a chain-of-custody form.

> When dealing with a customer, a coworker, or your boss, maintain your professionalism and do everything you can to build trust.

A+ CERTIFICATION EXAM TIPS

✓ This chapter includes information related to both the CompTIA A+ Core 1 (220-1001) and CompTIA A+ Core 2 (220-1002) exams. It is the most complex chapter in the book because many security issues need to be experienced to know exactly what things to try when problems arise.

✓ Be familiar with wireless security techniques and how to configure them: default usernames, firmware updates, SSIDs, frequency channels, encryption, SSID broadcasting, MAC filtering, radio power levels, and static IP addressing.

✓ Know the purpose of single sign-on, single factor authentication using a username/password, TPM, a VPN, an ACL, a firewall, a UTM, an IDS, an IPS, and an end-point management server and when to use each of them.

✓ Know what to do if you find prohibited content/data and what PII is.

✓ Review hard drive security, including BitLocker and what to do with a hard drive when moving it to another device or simply removing it. Know that PHI material requires special handling of hard drives.

✓ Practice security measures that a technician must implement, such as viewing hidden files, using an administrator account/rights, assigning Windows user roles, or adjusting Internet Explorer *Internet Options* tabs.

✓ Practice manually configuring a wireless router/AP with security settings and a wireless NIC.

✓ Review what to do with security problems such as computer slowdowns, lockups, pop-ups, viruses, botnets, zombies, malware, and spam. Know the steps to remove malware.

✓ Know the symptoms of a virus and malware.

✓ Compare and contrast cloud storage and local storage as well as image-level vs. file-level backups as part of an installation plan as well as a disaster prevention and recovery plan. Remember that backing up critical applications and testing the backup are also part of these plans.

✓ Configure basic firewall settings, including DMZ, port forwarding, NAT, UPnP, whitelists/blacklists, and MAC filtering.

✓ Explain the purpose of a VPN, NAT, MDM policies, port security, and the following Active Directory concepts: login script, domain, group policy/updates, home folder, and folder redirection. Know how to create and delete an Active Directory account, how to and reasons for disabling an account, as well as how to reset the password or unlock an account.

✓ Configure BIOS/UEFI security settings including passwords, drive encryption, TPM, LoJack, and Secure boot.

✓ Configure a screen lock that requires reauthentication if someone walks away from the computer or is on a private computer in a public area.

✓ Configure a Windows workstation for a VPN, DNS, a proxy server, and a firewall.

✓ Describe Windows users and groups, including administrator, power user, guest, and standard user. Review NTFS permissions, administrative shares vs. local shares, permission propagation, and inheritance factors.

Key Terms

acceptable use policy 960	anti malware 968	backup testing 998
account creation 984	antivirus 968	badge reader 962
account deletion 986	auditing 988	biometric lock 963
ACL 969	authentication 961	biometrics 966
Active Directory 983	authenticator app 966	BitLocker 1000
administrative share 991	authorization 981	BitLocker To Go 1000
AES 1001	backup and recovery 999	blacklist 1010

Review Questions

1. Match these security policy components with a definition from the following list.

    ____ Physical access

    ____ Acceptable use

    ____ Remote access

    ____ Password

    a. The specific web browser that is allowed to be installed

    b. Defines whether you can send the code used to access an account (such as shared network storage) via email

    c. The type of security required for a remote VPN connection

    d. The time, day, and year someone entered a network server room

2. Describe two-factor authentication.

    _____

    _____

3. List two BIOS/UEFI options associated with PC access.

    _____

    _____

4. What wireless security feature would be most likely to be used in a small company where the staff are the only individuals using the wireless network?

    a. VPN

    b. IDS

    c. MAC filtering

    d. WPA2

5. List five recommendations for protecting the operating system.

    _____

    _____

    _____

    _____

    _____

6. What is BitLocker?

    a. A wireless security setting

    b. A method used to secure passwords for websites, users, and files using TPM

    c. Online secure storage

    d. A utility that encrypts an entire disk volume, including operating system files, user files, and page files

7. [T | F] A new file is created and stored in an encrypted folder. The file must be manually encrypted because it was added after the folder was encrypted.

8. Describe the security rights for a subfolder when the parent folder is shared.

    _____

    _____

9.   List three password guidelines you would recommend that a company use.

_____

_____

_____

10. Where are domain user passwords stored?

[local database | registry | network server | the cloud]

11. A network administrator in a large corporation goes to a popular network vendor site to research security settings, but a message appears saying that this particular site cannot be accessed and is blocked. What security measure most likely caused this message?

   a. Antivirus software

   b. Anti-malware software

   c. Windows Defender

   d. Content filtering

12. Describe the difference between a local security policy and a domain policy.

_____

_____

_____

13. What two things are needed to configure a computer for a proxy server? (Choose two.)

[IP address of the proxy server | MAC address of the proxy server | administrator name on the proxy server | IP address of the local computer | MAC address of the local computer | port number on the proxy server | administrator password on the local computer]

14. What is the purpose of a DMZ?

_____

_____

_____

15. [T | F] A virtual machine should have anti-malware installed.

16. What Internet Explorer *Tools* menu option allows active scripting sites to be added for sites you trust?

[General | Security | Privacy | Content | Connections | Programs]

17. No one can ping a specific Windows computer. What administrative tool can change this default behavior?

[Windows Firewall | Local Security Policy | Internet Explorer > Internet options | Windows Defender]

18. What type of unsolicited Internet message records the URLs visited and keystrokes used?

[virus | grayware | spam | spyware]

19. An unofficial email is sent from your bank, asking you to click a link to verify your account information. What type of social engineering is this?

[phishing | grayware | spyware | VPN]

20. Match the incident on the left with the action on the right. Even though some of the incidents might have multiple answers, each answer is used only once.

   _____ virus   **a.** BSA

   _____ child exploitation   **b.** police department

   _____ software piracy   **c.** CERT

   _____ phishing   **d.** FBI Internet crime center

Exercises

Exercise 18.1

Objective: To become familiar with security incident response

Procedure: Answer the following questions.

1. Place the security incident response task in the appropriate order.

    ____ First

    ____ Second

    ____ Third

    a. Report the incident through the proper channels.

    b. Preserve the data/device(s) involved.

    c. Identify the threat.

2. A college requires that each employee use the last four digits of his or her Social Security number to access the copier. (A) Which type of security threat is this? (B) How would you respond to the incident if you were an IT security person for this college?

    a. Malware

    b. Sensitive PII

    c. Security policy

    d. Licensing

    2B. _____

    _____

3. Your neighbor asks if he can borrow your application DVD and code. He promises he will not register the application. How will you respond to this, given that it is a personal request and not a professional one? To whom would you report this, if anyone?

    _____

    _____

4. You work as an IT support person for a company. The user complains of slowness when opening files. No virus or malware is evident after complete scans have been completed. You open files to test this and find child pornography. What are your next three steps?

    Step 1: _____

    _____

    Step 2: _____

    _____

    Step 3: _____

    _____

Exercise 18.2

Objective: To become familiar with wireless security options

Procedure: Match the scenario to the term. Each answer is used only once.

Scenario:

a. Manually type Layer 2 addresses into a table.

b. Commonly used channels are 1, 6, and 11.

c. The most common corporate wireless security protocol is used.

d. Don't broadcast the name of the network.

e. Nearby companies get a stronger wireless signal than employees.

f. Only has 64- and 128-bit encryption.

g. Someone can get easily into the AP settings.

h. Easy to configure but has security risks.

i. Someone can get into the AP settings using hacking tools.

Task:

_____ WPA2

_____ WEP

_____ MAC filtering

_____ Move AP and/or antenna

_____ 2.4 GHz

_____ WPS

_____ Disable SSID broadcasting

_____ Default settings

_____ Update firmware

Exercise 18.3

Objective: To become familiar with regulated data

Procedure: Answer the questions.

1.   Match the type of regulated data with a characteristic.

a. U.S. companies are subject to this rule when engaging in trade in the European economic area.

b. This sensitive data should be encrypted when in storage or in transit.

c. The 1996 HIPAA law prompted this set of regulations.

d. Banks, businesses, colleges, airlines, and railroads are subject to these standards if credit cards are accepted as a payment method.

_____ PHI

_____ PCI

_____ GDPR

_____ PII

2.   [T | F] Personally identifiable information must be encrypted.

3.   [T | F] A U.S. citizen who retires to Italy is not subject to the GDPR but is only subject to U.S. federal laws.

4. Which information would be considered nonsensitive PII? (Choose all that apply.)
    [name | user ID | password | email address | passport number | Social Security number]

5. Of the four types of regulated data, which two are most likely to be encountered by a PC technician who works at a college? (Choose two.)
    [PII | PCI | GDPR | PHI]

Activities

Internet Discovery

Objective: To become familiar with researching computer security concepts using the Internet

Parts: A computer with Internet access

Questions: Use the Internet to answer the following questions.

1. Access the Internet Crime Complaint Center to answer the following questions. At the time of writing, the URL is https://www.ic3.gov.

    What are three recommendations for dealing with spam?

    _____

    _____

    _____

    _____

    What is Internet crime, according to this website? Write the answer and the URL at which you found the answer.

    _____

    _____

2. Access the U.S. Computer Emergency Readiness Team website and access the technical user link to answer the following questions. At this writing, the URL is https://www.us-cert.gov.

    What are the three highest-rated vulnerabilities for the past week?

    _____

    _____

    List three recommendations made by this site for a new computer being connected to a network.

    _____

    _____

    _____

3. Access the National Institute of Standards and Technology Computer Security Resource Center (CSRC) website to answer the following questions.

    Access the glossary of security terms. Windows allows programming of ACLs (access control lists). What are ACLs, and how do they relate to computer security?

    _____

    _____

    _____

    Select the CSRC site map link. List one security section that you find interesting and define one term from that section that is not in this chapter.

    _____

    _____

4. Access the Business Software Alliance website or use a search engine to answer the following questions.

    According to the website, what percentage of software installed is pirated?

    _____

    What is the current maximum fine for software pirated in the United States?

    _____

Soft Skills

Objective: To enhance and fine-tune a future technician's ability to listen, communicate in both written and oral form, and support people who use computers in a professional manner

Activities:

1. Prepare a presentation on any topic related to network security. The topic can relate to wired or wireless security. Share your presentation with the class.

2. In small groups, find a security policy on the Internet or use any of your school's computer policies. Critique the policy and make recommendations for how the policy can provide for stronger security.

Critical Thinking Skills

Objective: To analyze and evaluate information as well as apply learned information to new or different situations

Activities:

1. Create a wired workgroup network. Before users are created, determine what security policies will be enforced. Document the security policy. Also determine what activities are logged. Share folders between the computers with security implemented. Document the shares and policies. View and capture activities logged and include those captures with the documentation. Present your design, implementation, and monitoring to the class.

2. In teams, build a wired and wireless network with security in place. Document the security as if you were presenting it to a home network customer who hired you to build and implement it.

19 Operational Procedures

In this chapter you will learn:

> Proper personal safety precautions and equipment

> Workplace safety precautions, procedures, and equipment

> How to protect computer equipment from airborne pollutants

> How to dispose of waste (computers, mobile devices, batteries, laser printer toner cartridges, monitors)

> Types of IT documentation

> Change management processes

> Proper communication skills

CompTIA Exam Objectives:

What CompTIA A+ exam objectives are covered in this chapter?

✓ 1002-4.1   Compare and contrast best practices associated with types of documentation.

✓ 1002-4.2   Given a scenario, implement basic change management best practices.

✓ 1002-4.3   Given a scenario, implement basic disaster prevention and recovery methods.

✓ 1002-4.4   Explain common safety procedures.

✓ 1002-4.5   Explain environmental impacts and appropriate controls.

✓ 1002-4.7   Given a scenario, use proper communication techniques and professionalism.

Operational Procedures Overview

Being up-to-date on the latest safety precautions and procedures regarding both personal and workplace safety is beneficial to all involved. This chapter reviews the role that federal, state, and local governments play in protecting human health and the environment by operating regulated recycling and disposal sites for electronics. Also covered are the dangers of damaged batteries that leak acid and how to handle those situations. We review why and how:

> Electronics need to be protected from moisture, dust, extreme temperature fluctuations, and weight-bearing loads.
> Toxic fumes can cause degradation of components.
> Electronic waste (computers, mobile devices, batteries, laser printer toner cartridges, and monitors) is considered toxic waste.
> To protect computer equipment with surge (power) suppressors, personal enclosures, and clean rooms.
> Personal protective equipment and personal safety techniques are necessary.
> To properly handle and store electronics using antistatic bags, ESD straps, and ESD mats.
> Equipment grounding, self-grounding, and fire safety knowledge is important.

Paperwork is a part of any job, but it is especially critical in IT, where systems cross all parts of the business. Technicians use IT documentation as reference material and as a historical record of IT devices. Change is also a constant in IT, and change management is therefore important. This chapter covers the type of documentation commonly used and created within the IT department as well as the change management process. Finally, we discuss why looking, acting, and *thinking* like a professional, along with having good communications skills, are necessary for an IT professional.

Workplace Safety Precautions and Procedures

All companies are required to have workplace safety precautions and procedures posted and in effect, as mandated by the federal government. Most employers provide education and training on those procedures. Some precautions and procedures are a matter of common sense. Be sure to remove the power cord and/or battery before working on a PC or mobile device. Most people will not walk on a slippery floor if a "Wet Floor" sign is posted. As a technician, you will want to keep your work area relatively neat so as not to hamper other workers or potentially cause an accident. You want to make sure to practice good **cable management**, ensuring that no cables cause a trip hazard. (Chapter 13, "Networking," further discusses good network cable management techniques.) If an accident does occur, do the following:

> Immediately notify medical personnel, if needed.
> Report the incident to a supervisor.

The supervisor must then complete an incident report (see Figure 19.1).

TECH TIP

Always comply with local government regulations

There are many government regulations regarding workplace safety, and there are also local government regulations related to disposal requirements. Check with your supervisor if you are unsure about an unsafe environment or have questions about processes.

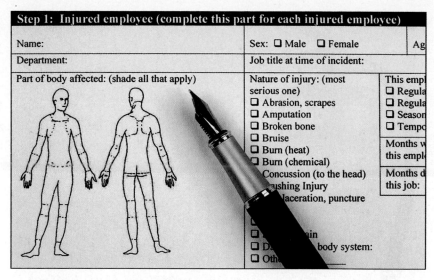

FIGURE 19.1   Incident report

OSHA

The Occupational Safety and Health Administration (**OSHA**) is a division of the U.S. Department of Labor. OSHA promotes safe and healthy working conditions by enforcing standards and providing workplace safety training. In addition, Environmental Protection Agency (EPA) standards and local government regulations specify that workplace environments should be free of harmful and/ or hazardous chemicals or situations. If harmful or hazardous agents are essential to a manufacturer's productivity, then appropriate precautions should be in place to work with those substances.

An important form required by OSHA is the material safety data sheet (**MSDS**), which outlines handling, storage procedures, disposal, and first aid on all potentially harmful or hazardous substances that you may come in contact with while working. Because MSDSs are available to employees, anyone working with these substances should review this important information. A similar form is the safety data sheet (**SDS**), which outlines similar information regarding chemicals.

Fire Safety

It is rare for electrical fires to occur in computers, but it is important to have **electrical fire safety** knowledge in case a fire does happen. If a fire occurs inside a computer or peripheral, unplug the equipment, if possible, but do not put yourself in harm's way in attempting to do this. A Type C or Type A-B-C fire extinguisher can be used to put out the fire. **Type C fire extinguishers** are made specifically for electrical (Type C) fires. **Type A-B-C fire extinguishers** can be used for Class A, Class B, and Class C fires. Here's some quick information about classes of fires:

> Class A fires involve paper, wood, cloth, or other normal combustibles.
> Class B fires involve flammable liquids and gases.
> Class C fires involve electrical or electronic equipment.

It is a good idea to have a dry chemical 20-pound A-B-C fire extinguisher in a home for the electronics (including computers) located there. Home computer equipment should be listed on the home insurance policy. Figure 19.2 shows a Type A-B-C fire extinguisher.

FIGURE 19.2   Fire extinguisher

Remember, though, that with an electrical fire, smoke is a breathing hazard. Burning plastics produce lethal toxic fumes. Always evacuate the people in the building and call the fire department.

In order to use a Type A-B-C or a Type C fire extinguisher, follow these steps:

Step 1. Pull out the fire extinguisher pin (see Figure 19.3).

Step 2. Aim the fire extinguisher nozzle at the base (bottom) of the fire.

Step 3. Squeeze the fire extinguisher handle and move the nozzle back and forth in a slow sweeping motion.

FIGURE 19.3   Pull the fire extinguisher pin

A Review of Safety Equipment in the Technical Field Kit

Let us examine three simple and inexpensive products that are essential parts of a technical field kit. Your **personal protective equipment** (PPE) should consist of safety goggles or glasses, latex or non-latex (neoprene) or nitrile powder-free gloves, and a dust mask/air filter mask. All of these items can be purchased at most hardware, drug, and grocery stores.

Safety goggles or glasses (see Figure 19.4) protect precious eyes from injury or irritation due to metal chips, wires, sparks, dust, airborne particles, debris, or any liquids or contaminants that might be in the working environment. Even though prescription eyeglasses provide some protection, it is wise to have a pair of safety glasses or goggles that fit over prescription eyeglasses.

FIGURE 19.4   Safety goggles

Wearing powder-free **gloves** (see Figure 19.5) while working on electronic equipment is recommended for the following reasons:

> To prevent the transfer of oils, grime, dirt, and food residue from your hands onto the component parts
> To prevent fingerprints on electronic parts that can hamper connectivity
> To keep your hands safe from particulates that may come from any task performed
> To present a professional image and show that you care enough about the client's equipment to take precautions

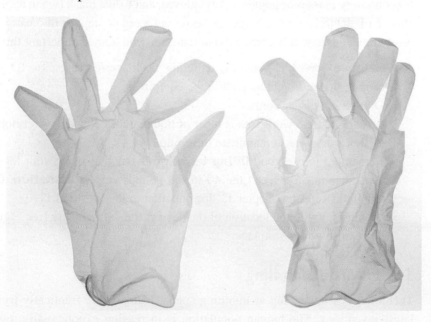

FIGURE 19.5   Gloves

Most technicians wear disposable gloves. Always remember to dispose of the gloves after your task is completed. Some people are allergic to latex or may have a skin reaction to latex or to the powder used to coat the inside of the gloves. The common symptoms include itching, dryness, burning, and scaling of the skin. More serious reactions include hives and hay fever–like symptoms. If in doubt, wear powder-free non-latex (neoprene) or nitrile gloves.

For some situations, such as when working with laser toner, it is important to wear a dust **mask** or an **air filter mask** to prevent inhalation of harmful airborne particulates, smoke, perfumes, odors, and fumes. When you use **compressed air**, dust and debris are an issue. Simply removing the cover from something that needs to be vacuumed poses a hazard. Use a **vacuum**, when possible, to remove dust and debris, but if in doubt, wear a mask. Dust masks like the one shown in Figure 19.6 are available in many hardware, grocery, drug, and discount stores.

FIGURE 19.6 Dust mask

Personal Safety

Personal and equipment safety is paramount in IT. Having proper personal safety precautions and equipment will facilitate a smoother repair task by getting you into a routine of automatically putting on safety glasses or goggles, vinyl gloves, and a dust mask (when applicable). It will lessen the chance of electrostatic discharge, of forgetting a repair step, or of a careless mishap because your safety procedures will become second nature to you. Other important things to remember follow:

> **Remove jewelry**, watches, dangling necklaces/earrings, or ID lanyards that could get caught, hooked, or entangled in the equipment.
> Disconnect power cords.
> Be sure that the work area is clear of liquids (coffee, soda, water bottles) and foods that may spill or otherwise contaminate the equipment.
> Remember to use good **lifting techniques** (such as using your legs, not your back) and be conscious not to exceed the 40- to 50-pound **weight limitation**. Get help when over this amount. (Refer to Chapter 1, "Introduction to the World of IT.")
> Be familiar with the location of the nearest fire extinguisher (see Figure 19.2) and the nearest fire exit in your workplace.

Toxic Waste Handling

Technology is advancing at lightning speed. Humans are frantically trying to keep up with the latest inventions. The human population is increasing exponentially, our landfills are growing, and our resources are decreasing. Much awareness has been raised in the past few decades about "going green," and the "reduce, reuse, recycle" movement is practiced in many communities. Collectively, as a society, we can make a huge impact. Individually, we can make a difference by being good stewards of our resources. Toxic waste handling does not apply only to oil spills, manufacturing plant chemical spills, pesticides, and other contaminants that pollute our land and waters; it also applies to electronic devices. **Toxic waste handling** involves dealing with things that can harm you and/or the environment. The physical parts, pieces, and batteries of computers, laser printers, and mobile devices must be handled carefully—especially the battery—if a unit suffers damage.

Environmental Impacts

Every state and many cities have specific guidelines about how to dispose of electronics or e-waste (see Figure 19.7). These rules must be followed by technicians who replace broken computer equipment. If you are unsure about how to get rid of any piece of broken electronic equipment, contact your direct supervisor for instructions.

PLEASE ⊠ ♻ RECYCLE

FIGURE 19.7   E-waste

The following list provides alternatives and suggestions for being environmentally conscious about discarding electronics:

> Donate equipment that is operational to schools and charities so that those who do not have access to technology can get some exposure. If the operating system is not transferred to another system, leave the operating system on the machine and provide proof of purchase along with documentation. Also, do not forget to erase all data stored on the computer before donating it.

> Recycle outdated electronics. If devices are so outdated that a school or charity cannot use them, consider recycling. Many companies accept old electronics and have found ways to reuse some of their parts.

> Remove parts that do work and donate or recycle them.

> Buy electronics that are designed to save resources and are easy to upgrade. Extend their usefulness by ensuring that they are energy efficient. They will also be more useful if they contain fewer toxins, use recycled materials, and have leasing or recycling programs.

> Check with the computer or component manufacturer to see if they have a recycling program. Most of them do.

Electronic Disposal/Recycling

Computers and other electronic devices contain materials such as beryllium, chromium, cadmium, lead, mercury, nickel, and zinc. The levels of these materials in landfills increase dramatically every year and can pose a threat to our environment. Plastics that are part of computers are hard to isolate and recycle, but many electronic parts can be recycled. Important disposal and handling measures should be taken with CRTs, cell phones, tablets, batteries, and laser printer toner cartridges.

The cathode ray tubes (**CRTs**) (see Figure 19.8) found in older displays and TVs usually contain enough lead and mercury to be considered hazardous waste. However, the EPA has been successful in obtaining exclusions from the federal hazardous waste standards for unbroken CRTs so that they can be recycled more effectively. In Florida and New York, steps have been taken to increase CRT recycling; however, other states regulate all CRTs as hazardous waste and ban them from being sent to landfills.

FIGURE 19.8   CRT monitor

Cell phones and **tablets** are now classified as toxic waste in the United States because of the lead they contain. Lead-free phones do not solve the problem because of the zinc, nickel, copper, and antimony within them. Manufacturers have not always been willing to take back old phones because extracting the gold, copper, silver, and other metals can be expensive.

Currently, the best advice is to follow local guidelines on disposal, look to see if the manufacturer of your new device has a trade-in program; donate to an organization that helps victims of violence, soldiers, or charities; or use a responsible recycler. The website e-stewards.org can help you find responsible e-waste recycling locations.

Don't forget to erase your data and remove the SIM card and any memory storage before donating or recycling a cell phone or tablet. If you have broken parts, wear a mask and gloves while handling. Place parts in a plastic bag and seal before disposing of it properly.

A **battery** produces DC voltage through a chemical reaction that occurs within the battery. Batteries contain acids that can potentially burn or hurt body parts. Batteries can introduce lead and acid into the environment; thus, they need to be recycled (see Figure 19.9). Heavy metals can leach into the ground and water sources. Use proper personal protective equipment such as safety goggles or gloves (see Figure 19.10) when handling batteries.

Lithium-ion batteries **(Li-ion batteries)** found in mobile devices and laptops may need to be replaced in the following cases:

> If the device has been subjected to extreme temperature changes
> If the device was dropped, crushed, or flooded with liquid
> If the device has sustained up to 500 cycles of discharge and recharge

The contents of a lithium-ion battery are under pressure; thus, Li-ion batteries can explode or catch on fire (see Figure 19.11) if subjected to high temperatures. If you see a bulging Li-ion battery, hear one hiss, or feel one that is overheated, immediately move the device away from anything that might catch on fire. If possible, remove the battery and put it in a safe fireproof place. If it catches on fire, use a foam or A-B-C fire extinguisher. If on a train or plane, you might see the attendant use water because a Li-ion battery has very little lithium metal that would react with water.

FIGURE 19.9   Battery recycling

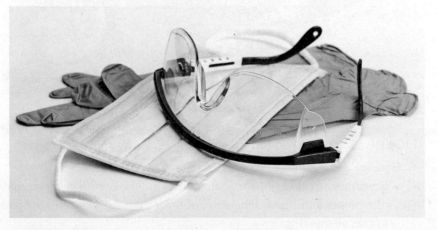

FIGURE 19.10   Personal protective equipment

FIGURE 19.11   Li-ion battery on fire

Recycling all batteries is important. The recommended method of disposal is to recycle batteries at regulated stations. Refer to your local municipality's regulations for recycling and disposing of Li-ion batteries.

Toner Safety and Disposal

The **toner** found in laser printer toner cartridges is not earth friendly. According to TonerRecycle. net, it is estimated that more than half of all toner cartridges go into the regular trash; it takes approximately 1,000 years for a print cartridge to fully decompose.

Toner is also not human friendly. If you accidently inhale toner, you could experience headaches, eye irritation, itching, and other side effects that are longer lasting. If you come in contact with it, toner can cause itchiness and skin irritation. Figure 19.12 shows some spilled toner.

FIGURE 19.12   Spilled toner

Here are some points to remember about toner safety:
> Remember to always wear some type of rubber or nitrile gloves and a dust mask when handling toner cartridges. Inhalation of toner particles can cause respiratory damage equivalent to that of smoking.

> Do not attempt to clean up any loose toner particles with a regular vacuum sweeper as the toner particles may seep into the vacuum's motor and melt. Always use a high-efficiency particulate air (HEPA) vacuum bag in the vacuum cleaner.
> Allow the printer (and cartridge) to cool before repairing or replacing the cartridge. The fusing assembly and heated toner can cause severe burns. You should wait after copying or printing before doing any service or removing a toner cartridge.

Component Handling and Storage

Proper handling and storage of electronic parts and equipment reduces the chance of electrostatic discharge (ESD). ESD is sneaky. It damages, weakens, and destroys electronic equipment—often without the technician being aware that it has happened. Atmospheric conditions play a part in ESD in that the potential for ESD is greater when the **humidity** (moisture in the air) is low. Antistatic bags for storage, ESD straps and mats for repair jobs, and self-grounding knowledge and techniques are all discussed in Chapter 5, "Disassembly and Power." The following is a brief review:

> Remember to use **antistatic bags** (see Figure 19.13) for storing adapters and motherboards when not in use for an extended period of time. Date the bags as a reminder to change them out after a few years as their protective quality diminishes.
> When repairing a computer, wear an antistatic strap, **ESD strap**, and/or heel strap to prevent ESD (see Chapter 5). Caution: The voltages are very high on a CRT monitor (even unplugged) and within a high-voltage power supply of a laser printer. Do not attempt to work on either one unless you have special training.
> Place a computer that is being repaired on an **ESD mat**. Some mats have a snap to which you can fasten an antistatic wrist strap.
> If an antistatic wrist strap or antistatic heel strap is not available, it is recommended that, after removing the external case, you rest your non-dominant arm on an unpainted metal part, leaving your dominant hand free to work the component parts. This **self-grounding** method is an effective way of keeping the technician and the computer at the same voltage potential. You will have, of course, previously disconnected the power supply to the computer.

FIGURE 19.13 Antistatic bag

Electronic Safety: Equipment Grounding

Equipment grounding is important with any piece of electronic equipment. **Equipment grounding** means that the components in a device such as a computer are at the same voltage potential. This is important to personal safety because consistent grounding minimizes the potential for voltage to be applied to places where it shouldn't be applied, such as the case. If a piece of equipment is not grounded, someone could receive a shock or be electrocuted simply by touching it (see Figure 19.14). You might see a grounding wire connect to a network rack or battery backup system. Review Chapter 5 for more information about power and grounding.

FIGURE 19.14 Electrical shock

Adverse Power Conditions

There are two adverse AC power conditions that can damage or adversely affect a computer: overvoltage and undervoltage. **Overvoltage** occurs when the output voltage from the wall outlet (the AC voltage) is over the rated amount. Normally, the output of a wall outlet is 110 to 130 volts AC. When the voltage rises above 130 volts, an overvoltage condition exists. The power supply converts the AC voltage to DC. An overvoltage condition is harmful to components because too much DC voltage destroys electronic circuits. An overvoltage condition can be a surge or a spike.

When the voltage falls below 110 volts AC, an **undervoltage** condition exists. If the voltage is too low, a computer power supply cannot provide enough power to all the components. Under such conditions, the power supply draws too much current, causing it to overheat and weakening or damaging the components. An undervoltage condition may be a brownout or sag. Table 19.1 explains these power terms.

TABLE 19.1 Adverse power conditions

Major type	Subtype	Explanation
Overvoltage	**Spike**	A spike lasts 1 to 2 nanoseconds. A nanosecond is one-billionth of a second. A spike is harder to guard against than a surge because it has such short duration and high intensity.
	Surge	A **power surge** lasts longer (3 or more nanoseconds) than a spike. Also called transient voltage. Causes of surges include lightning, poorly regulated electricity, faulty wiring, and devices that turn on periodically, such as elevators, air conditioners, and refrigerators.

Major type	Subtype	Explanation
Undervoltage	**Brownout**	In a brownout, power circuits become overloaded. Occasionally, an electric company intentionally causes a brownout to reduce the power drawn by customers during peak periods.
	Sag	A sag occurs when the voltage from the wall outlet drops momentarily.
	Blackout	A blackout is a total loss of power.

Surge Protectors

A **surge suppressor**, also known as a surge strip or surge protector, is commonly a multi-outlet strip that offers built-in protection against overvoltage. Surge protectors do not protect against undervoltage; they protect against voltage increases. Figure 19.15 shows a surge suppressor.

FIGURE 19.15   Surge suppressor

A surge protector commonly has an electronic component called a metal oxide varistor (**MOV**), which protects the computer or device that plugs into one of the outlets on the surge strip. An MOV is positioned between the AC coming in and the outlet into which devices are plugged. When a surge occurs, the MOV prevents the extra voltage from passing to the outlets. An MOV has some drawbacks, however. If a large surge occurs, the MOV will take the hit and be destroyed, which is better than damaging the computer. However, with small overvoltages, each small surge weakens the MOV. A weakened MOV might not give the proper protection to the computer in the event of a bigger surge. Also, there is no simple check for an MOV's condition. Some MOVs have indicator lamps attached, but they indicate only when the MOV has been destroyed, not when it is weakened. Still, having an indicator lamp is better than having nothing at all. Some surge protectors also have replaceable fuses and/or indicator lamps for the fuse. A fuse works only once and then is destroyed during a surge in order to protect devices plugged into surge protector outlets. Figure 19.16 shows a surge protector that has done its job.

FIGURE 19.16   Blown surge protector

TECH TIP

Do not create a trip hazard with a surge strip

When installing a surge protector, install it in such a manner that it does not cause a trip hazard due to the cord lying in an area where people walk.

Several surge protector features deserve consideration. Table 19.2 outlines some of them.

TABLE 19.2   Surge protector features

Feature	Explanation
Clamping voltage	The level at which a surge protector starts protecting the computer. The lower the value, the better the protection.
Clamping speed	The amount of time that elapses before protection begins. The lower the value, the better the protection. Surge protectors cannot normally protect against power spikes (overvoltages of short duration) because of their rated clamping speed.
Energy absorption/ dissipation	The ability of a surge protector to absorb or dissipate energy. The greater the number of joules (a unit of energy) that can be dissipated, the more effective and durable a surge protector is. A surge protector rating of 630 joules is more effective than a rating of 210 joules.
TVS (transient voltage suppressing) rating	This is also known as response time. The lower the rating, the better. For example, a 330 TVS-rated surge protector is better than a 400 TVS-rated one.
UL rating	UL (Underwriters Laboratories) developed the **UL 1449 VPR** (voltage protection rating) standard to measure the maximum amount of voltage a surge protector will let through to the attached devices. The UL 497A standard is for phone line protection, and the UL 1283 standard is for EMI/RFI.

The federal government designates surge suppressor grades—A, B, and C. Suppressors are evaluated on the basis of 1,000 surges at a specific number of volts and amps. A Class A rating is the best and indicates tolerance up to 6,000 volts and 3,000 amps.

Electric companies offer surge protection for homes. Frequently, there are two choices. A basic package protects large appliances, such as refrigerators, air conditioners, washers, and dryers. It allows no more than 800 volts to enter the electrical system. A premium package protects more sensitive devices (TVs, stereos, and computers) and reduces the amount of voltage allowed to 323 volts or less. Some suppressors handle surges up to 20,000 volts. The exterior surge arrestor does not protect against voltage increases that originate inside the building, such as those caused by faulty wiring.

TECH TIP

Which surge strip to buy?

When purchasing or recommending a surge protector, be sure it conforms to the UL 1449 standard and has an MOV status lamp. Also, check to see if the vendor offers to repair or replace any surge-protected equipment that is damaged during a surge.

Common criteria used when buying a surge suppressor include the following:

> Cable length
> Number of outlets
> Room to connect peripheral power connectors that may take additional space
> Diagnostic LED(s)
> Integrated circuit breaker
> Outlets that power off when not in use for nonessential electronics such as lamps, speakers, or printers
> Outlets that are always on for devices such as cordless phone handset cradles, modems, and external hard drives
> Insurance
> UL 1449 compliance

Surge protectors do not provide the best protection for a computer system because most provide very little protection against other adverse power conditions. Even the good ones protect only against overvoltage conditions. Those with the UL 1449 rating and an MOV status lamp are usually more expensive. Unfortunately, people tend to put their money into their computer parts but not into the protection of those parts.

Line Conditioners

An alternative for computer protection is a line conditioner. **Line conditioners**, sometimes known as power conditioners, are more expensive than surge protectors, but they protect a computer from overvoltages, undervoltages, and adverse noise conditions over electrical lines. A line conditioner monitors AC electricity. If the voltage is too low, the line conditioner boosts voltage to the proper range. If the voltage level is too high, the line conditioner clamps down the voltage and sends the proper amount to the computer.

Battery Backup

A **battery backup** provides AC power when power from the wall outlet fails such as during a brownout or blackout. The power is provided by a battery within a unit. Two different types of battery backups are available for home and business computers and devices: uninterruptible power supplies (UPSs) and standby power supplies (SPSs). Let's look at the differences between the two types.

UPS

A **UPS**, sometimes called an online (or true) UPS or a line-interactive UPS, provides power to a computer or other device for a limited amount of time when there is a power outage. A UPS provides enough time to save work and safely shut down the computer. Some operating systems do not operate properly if power abruptly cuts off and the computer is not brought to a logical stopping place. A network server, the main computer for a network, is a great candidate for a UPS. Network operating systems are particularly susceptible to problems during a power outage. A UPS might have a connection for a cable and special software that automatically maintains voltages to the computer, quits all applications, and powers off the computer. Some UPS units have USB and/ or network connections as well. Figure 19.17 shows the front and back of a UPS.

FIGURE 19.17   Front and back of a UPS

A UPS also provides power conditioning for the devices attached to it. The AC power is used to charge a battery inside the UPS. The battery inside the UPS supplies power to an inverter. The inverter makes AC for the computer. When AC power from the outlet fails, the battery inside the UPS continues to supply power to the computer. The battery inside the UPS outputs DC power, and the computer accepts (and expects) AC power. Therefore, the DC power from the battery must be converted to AC voltage. AC voltage looks like a sine wave when it is in its correct form, but cheaper UPSs produce a square wave (especially when power comes from the battery) that is not as effective. Some computer servers, systems, and peripherals do not work well on a 120 VAC square wave, modified sine wave, simulated sine wave, or quasi-sine wave. Figure 19.18 illustrates a sine wave and a square wave.

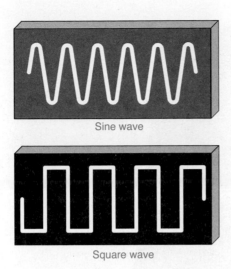

FIGURE 19.18 Sine wave and square wave

Do not plug a laser printer into a UPS unless it has a rating less than 1400 VA

Most UPSs cannot handle the very high current requirements of a laser printer. Other devices to avoid attaching to a UPS include space heaters, vacuums, curling irons, paper shredders, and copiers.

A UPS can provide the best protection against adverse power conditions because it protects against overvoltage and undervoltage conditions, and it provides power so a system can be shut down properly. When purchasing a UPS, be sure that (1) the amount of battery time is sufficient to protect all devices; (2) the amount of current the UPS produces is sufficient to protect all devices; and (3) the output waveform is a sine wave.

A UPS has a battery inside that is similar to a car battery (except that the UPS battery is sealed). Because this battery contains acid, you should never drop a UPS or throw it in the trash. Research your state's requirements for recycling batteries. All batteries fail after some time, and most UPSs have replaceable batteries.

Standby Power Supply (SPS)

A device similar to a UPS is a standby power supply (SPS). Much like a UPS, an **SPS** contains a battery, but an SPS battery provides power to the computer only when it loses AC power. It might not provide constant power, as a UPS does. It might use a simulated sine wave. An SPS is not as effective as a UPS because the SPS must detect a power-out condition first and then switch over to the battery to supply power to the computer. As a result, SPS switching time is important. Any time under 5 milliseconds is fine for most systems. Figure 19.19 shows a CyberPower UPS that produces a simulated sine wave (which would be fine for a home system).

FIGURE 19.19 CyberPower UPS (simulated sine wave output)

Comparison of UPSs and SPSs

Sometimes it is difficult to discern between UPS and SPS products. When providing protection and battery backup for a home computer, an SPS or simulated sine wave output might be fine for the supplied power time and the reduced cost. Figures 19.20 and 19.21 show the differences between how some SPSs and UPSs work.

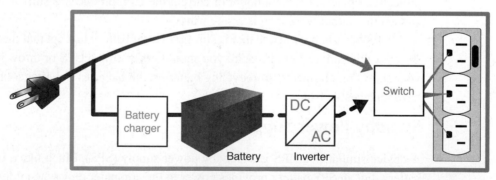

SPS/Line interactive UPS normal operation (solid line)
1. AC power is brought through the UPS.
2. The battery is charged simultaneously.
3. With some units, small over- or undervoltages are evened out before sending through the UPS.

SPS/Line interactive UPS abnormal power operation (dashed line)
1. When high voltage or large undervoltage for some units and with loss of power is present in all units, DC power from the battery is sent to the inverter for as long as the battery lasts.
2. The DC power is converted to AC and provided to the attached devices.

FIGURE 19.20 SPS/line-interactive UPS operation

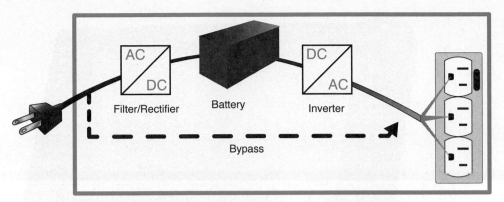

Online UPS normal operation (solid line)
1. AC power is brought into the UPS and cleaned up by the filter and converted to DC by the rectifier.
2. The battery is charged and outputs DC to the inverter.
3. The DC is converted to AC and provided to the attached devices.

Online UPS abnormal power operation (dashed line)
1. When the battery has died, the attached devices still receive power through the bypass circuit.

FIGURE 19.21   Online UPS operation

Protection from Airborne Particles

The EPA's Clean Air Act sets National Ambient Air Quality Standards (NAAQS) for pollutants. Particulate matter (PM)—or **airborne particle** pollution—is among these. The EPA works with regional partners in state and local air quality agencies to ensure that the required safety standards are met. PM can be extremely detrimental to humans, causing respiratory problems, and to environmental health, causing loss of visibility due to haze or smog. Make sure you always wear an air filter or mask when working in any environment where harmful airborne particles such as **dust and debris** are present. Use a vacuum to remove these particles where possible.

PM is also detrimental to computer equipment. Humidity, sea-spray, fog, dust, smoke from brush fires, motorized vehicles and machinery, incinerators, and various industrial processes are all harmful to sensitive computer equipment. Some companies utilize an enclosure assembly (**environmental enclosure**) for desktops or laptops to protect parts from PM. Such a case is constructed to house a computer while allowing access to operate keyboards, mice, flash drives, and so on, without PM contaminating the equipment. Vendors that supply the military might frequently be required to provide a model that has extra protection for the screen or the entire device. Some vendors target the civilian market with similar "rugged" models or enclosures designed for youngsters. Figure 19.22 shows a computer case designed for a rugged environment.

Computer enclosures can also be purchased to protect equipment against impact or weather conditions. One or more air filters may be needed for a non-traditional computer area such as at a construction site. A kiosk (see Figure 19.23) is likely to contain a lockable area for the computer contained within.

FIGURE 19.22 Rugged industrial computer enclosure

FIGURE 19.23 Kiosk

Some companies employ an environmental enclosure known as a clean room. A **clean room** (see Figure 19.24) is a climate-controlled (cool temperature and humidity of 45% to 60%) closed area with special air vents/filters, vacuums, blowers, and a circulation system that are specifically constructed to capture harmful/hazardous particulate matter, scrub and diffuse the PM, and safely eliminate it while allowing the sensitive computer equipment to run.

FIGURE 19.24 Clean room

Temperature and Humidity Control

Computers generate heat. When many units are being used in the same space—whether in a clean room or in a classroom—it may be necessary to provide a cooler ambient room temperature. Computers operate best in **temperatures** between 60 and 75 degrees.

TECH TIP

A temperature that is comfortable for you is good for a computer, too

A good rule of thumb related to computer temperatures is that if you are comfortable in the room, the room is probably an appropriate temperature for the computer.

High levels of humidity can cause computer equipment to short-circuit because the moisture corrodes the contact points and interrupts connectivity. Low humidity increases the chance of a technician causing ESD and causing damage to electronics when handling them. Dust and debris abrade, plug, and smother connection points and retard or interrupt flow of electricity.

Temperature and humidity are both important in the care and operation of computers and other electronic devices. For example, if a laptop is left outside in a car overnight in the winter and brought inside to a warm area in the morning, condensation will most likely form inside the case. Over time, this would reduce the effectiveness of the connectivity points. It could also prevent the computer from booting properly when first turned on.

Proper **ventilation** is important for any electronic device. Check to make sure that the unit's fan is not blocked. Heat generated from an electronic device, if not properly ventilated, can cause overheating and damage to the unit. Refer to Chapter 5 for more information on temperature and humidity control.

IT Documentation

For IT personnel, technical skills are important, but written and oral communications skills are just as important. A negative trend in recent years in those entering the technical arena is the decline in the ability to write clearly. Although being able to write clearly is important when documenting what has been done in the IT department, it is not everyone's favorite thing to do (see Figure 19.25).

"Know what I call a technician that doesn't document? ......unemployed"

FIGURE 19.25   Documentation is required of IT personnel

Every IT job requires documentation:

> Help desk personnel must log initial problems.
> PC repair technicians must document what was done for billing and historical purposes.
> Technicians of any type are required to close help desk problems with a written explanation of what was done.
> Updates to departmental documentation must be done in some instances.
> If an incident occurs, regulations or corporate policies may require some documentation.

In order to understand common operational procedures related to documentation, let's look at the practices associated with several types of documentation:

> Network topology diagrams
> Knowledge base/articles
> Incident documentation
> Regulatory and compliance policy
> Acceptable use policy
> Password policy
> Inventory management

Network Topology Diagrams

In addition to creating documentation, IT personnel must often update documentation. This might include using and updating **network topology diagrams** when moves, adds, or changes (MACs) are done, such as when someone changes cubicles or new personnel are due to arrive. You might have to refer to a network topology diagram to get an IP address of a printer being installed or update the diagram to document what IP address you assigned to the printer. A network topology diagram might be a high level one, as shown in Figure 19.26, or a more granular drawing, as shown in Figure 19.27. Some network drawings are even more detailed and include port numbers, IP addresses, VLAN numbers, rooms and location of access points, and so on. These are known as **physical network diagrams**.

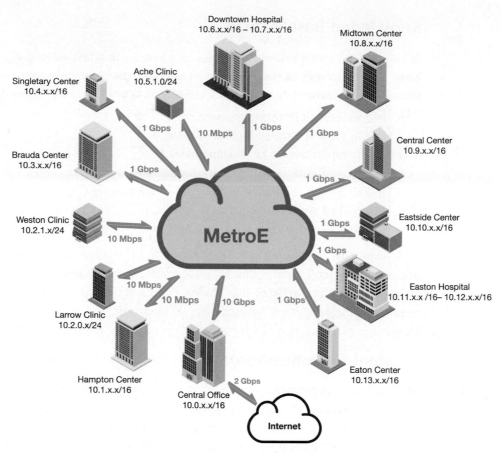

FIGURE 19.26   High-level network topology diagram example

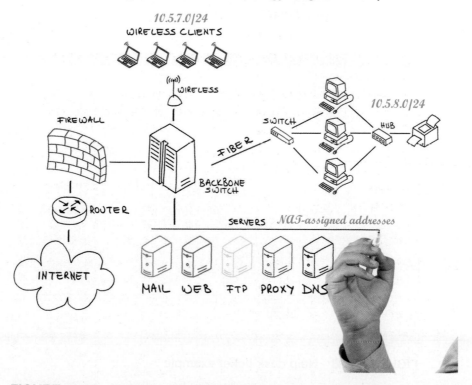

FIGURE 19.27   Detailed network topology diagram example

Knowledge Base/Articles

A knowledge base is extremely helpful to a technician when solving a problem. A **knowledge base** is a collection of documents with solutions to commonly asked questions or problems. Examples of documents included in a knowledge base include the following:

> How to reset an IP phone password
> How to request a wireless guest account
> How to report a spam or phishing incident
> How to configure a mobile device for email
> How to configure email with an out-of-office message
> How to do a web conference
> How to find and print to a network printer

A technician might copy information from a knowledge base document to send to a user or might directly send them a link to a document. Some companies or technicians might have a collection of online **articles** that answer commonly asked questions that are used to help the technicians themselves and/or users. Apple, Microsoft, and other IT vendors also have their own knowledge base to support their hardware, operating systems, or applications.

Incident Documentation

Incident documentation is used when an IT problem is solved. Most companies use an incident management system, a help desk, or some type of ticketing software for this. It is critical for technicians to clearly and succinctly document what was done to solve a particular problem for historical purposes, billing, to keep track of how much support each department receives, and in case another technician has to deal with the same or similar problem at a later date. Common information contained in incident documentation is shown in Figure 19.28.

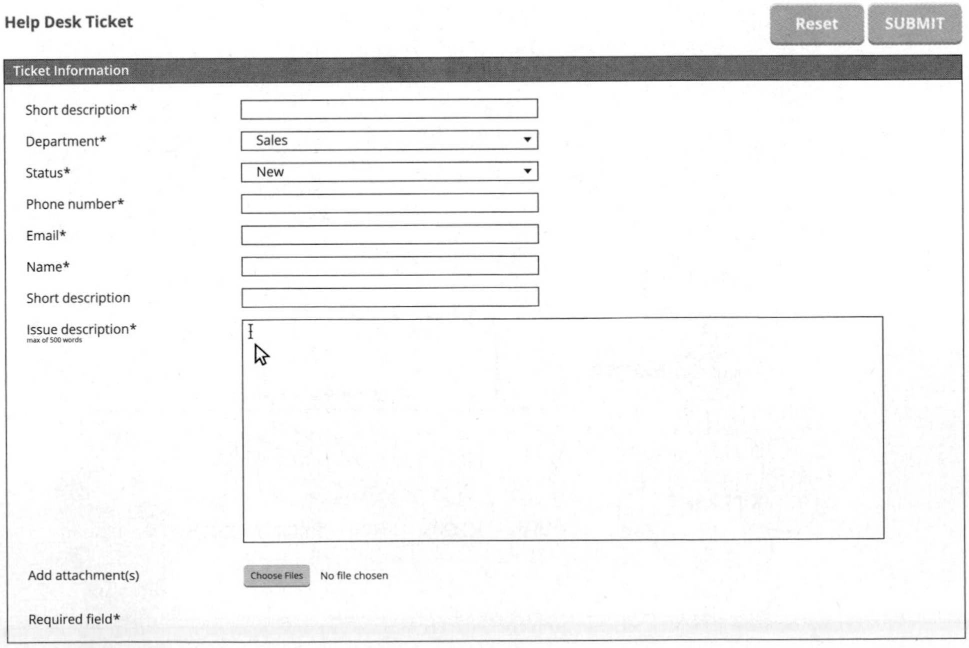

FIGURE 19.28   Help desk ticket example

At the end of a service call, a technician should provide the proper documentation on the services provided. This could include the following:

> Manuals
> Software or hardware boxes and materials that include proof of purchase, UPC codes, activation codes, registration numbers, and warranty information
> Invoice
> Research or information used in the repair that might benefit the customer
> Service ticket with details of work performed

Inventory Management

Many technicians do not like dealing with inventory management, but it is a fact of life in the IT department. Whenever any piece of hardware is moved, the move is commonly documented through an **inventory management** system. Some help desk software includes inventory management. Whenever a technician moves or installs a new piece of gear, the technician must commonly enter an **asset tag** number, which is a unique ID or an asset ID, and the relevant technical details, such as a model number, serial number, and possibly a MAC address on a wireless device. Inventory must be done regularly, typically once a year. Technicians are commonly asked to use a scanner to scan the **barcode** located on any item over a specified dollar amount, as shown in Figure 19.29. Items that cannot be found during the inventory period must be searched for and accounted for. Unfound items are placed on a report given to the executive leaders and board of directors; the report affects assets shown on the company balance sheet as well as net income on the income statement, and these write-offs can negatively affect both current employee bonuses and future capital budgets.

FIGURE 19.29 Technician doing inventory

Policies

Technicians may have to refer to specific policies in the normal course of their job or when issues arise. Four policies commonly relate to computer technicians. A technician does not need to know these policies verbatim but does need to know the main gist of them and where to find them easily (see also Chapter 18, "Computer and Network Security"):

> **Password policy**—Even though users are presented with the information regarding the password policy when resetting a password, they commonly request technical assistance with the process.

> **Acceptable use policy** (AUP)—Any service or app used today will have an AUP, but businesses also have their own AUPs that define what is allowed to be used or done when connected to the corporate network or using company-owned hardware/software. Technicians need to be familiar with the AUP and should refer users to it when necessary.

> **Regulatory and compliance policy**—Every industry (for example, healthcare, manufacturing) has unique regulations and compliance policies. A technician must be familiar with such policies because IT systems cross all departments within a company.

> **Security policy**—A security policy should outline what to do when a breach or an incident occurs, and it may include the AUP and password policy. Security policies are constantly being updated, and technicians should review them on a regular basis.

Change Management

The IT department, whether in house or outsourced, is a key part of any business because IT systems cross all departments. It is very important that an IT department use **documented business processes** and continue to update the documentation related to those processes. The IT department is a constant source of change—moves, adds, and changes (MACs) of PCs, printers, IP phones, monitors, servers, apps, and so on. The IT department should always **plan for change** instead of being reactive to situations. For example, servers that are on old hardware or that have outdated network operating systems are vulnerable to attacks and/or failure. Planning and executing their replacements is better than waiting for each piece of equipment to die.

Change management is the formal process of systematically choosing and implementing IT changes. A large company is likely to have a formal board that is known as a **change board**, change advisory board, software change control board, or change control board (CCB); whatever its name, this group makes decisions about which proposed changes are approved and implemented. The management cycle of any IT project commonly involves four steps (see Figure 19.30):

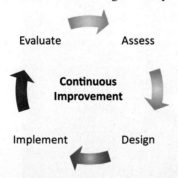

FIGURE 19.30   Management cycle

1. *Assess*—Determine the **purpose of the change**. Why is the change needed? Which corporate strategic goal(s) does the plan align with? Do a **risk analysis** to determine the risks involved and whether the benefits outweigh the risks.

2. *Design*—Make a plan for the change and share that plan. What is the timeline? What resources are needed? Who will do what? Are parts needed? What is the **scope of the change**? Defining limits of a project prevents project creep (that is, the tendency of a project to increase in complexity and depth). Project scopes include time, resources, money, deliverables, and acceptance criteria. Are other departments involved? If so, who is the contact person? What is the **backout plan**, or at what step do things get reversed if the changes are not working? A backout plan might be part of a document called a statement of work (SOW) that outlines all activities, deliverables, timelines, reporting structure, and quality checks.

3. *Implement*—Execute the plan. Have meetings or establish an online method to share progress. **Document changes**. Correct any issues that are discovered. Have an **end-user acceptance** process in which the person who will be using the IT system verifies that it works appropriately.

4. *Evaluate*—Ensure that each part of the plan was done properly. Document findings.

IT projects tend to be repetitive in nature in that a project that has been finished will have to be done again in the future; documentation and lessons learned are therefore very important.

SOFT SKILLS: COMMUNICATION SKILLS

The importance of proper communication cannot be stressed enough, no matter where you are or what situation you are in. Good communication skills are priceless. Throughout history, battles have begun because of miscommunication and feuds have been sparked by careless comments. Many good relationships falter and/or disintegrate because people don't communicate with one another well. A poorly worded communication, an off-hand remark, a facial or hand gesture—any of these may be misinterpreted by the receiver without the sender even realizing that he or she has just offended someone. Let's explore some areas in which your job as a computer technician will involve good communication skills.

Customer Service

What comes to mind when you hear the two words *customer service*? A feeling of security and confidence? A rising panic accompanied by a fervent search for antacids and aspirin? Being of service to others is very rewarding, educational, and fun! Be the best customer service representative that you envision a customer service person to be. You have the skills and training to be tops! Let Figure 19.31 inspire you as a computer technician.

FIGURE 19.31   Customer service inspiration

You can set the tone and instill assurance by being the confident, caring professional that you've trained to become. You are the expert. You know more about computer problems than the customers, and they are looking to you to solve their problems. You have many avenues of tracking down solutions. Don't be shy about tackling new things. Stretch yourself. Allow new situations to be learning opportunities. Step out of your comfort zone, as illustrated in Figure 19.32.

When you have been called in to fix a company's computer, have your ID badge visible. Introduce yourself and state your business. Ask to speak to the person in charge of the device and wait until you are invited or escorted to the work area. Some customers like to hover—out of curiosity, safety concerns, boredom, insecurity, or for some other reason. Don't let that bother you. Reassure your customers that you are working diligently on their problem and are taking care of them. Other clients will disappear, and you won't have any interaction with them the entire time you're working. As long as you have their contact information, no problem. Focus on the task at hand.

FIGURE 19.32 Comfort zone/opportunity

Proper Language

Always address customers by their title: Dr. Schmidt, Mr. Schmidt, Director Durrence, Miss Hannah, Your Honor, Officer Young, Professor Brauda, and so on. Most dictionaries have a section in the back that lists titles and proper forms of address. Mind your manners.

Grooming

Be neat, clean, and well groomed. Wear clean clothes and good shoes. Wear properly fitting attire because you might have to get in hard-to-reach places at times (see Figure 19.33). Employ good hygiene. Wash your hands and brush your teeth at least twice daily. Carry breath mints. Do you have dandruff? Do you smoke? Did you just enjoy a spicy lunch? Do a self-check before meeting a customer to avoid offending anyone or embarrassing yourself or the customer (see Figure 19.34).

FIGURE 19.33 Dress appropriately

FIGURE 19.34 Bad breath

You are your most valuable asset. Take care of your body, mind, and spirit. Your inner self will be reflected outward. Dress like the professional that you are. Always have clean hands when handling someone else's property. Never pick up or handle anything if you've been eating, drinking, or have just applied hand cream (which can leave a residue that might not come off). If you use cologne, hair spray, perfume, or scented lotion or cosmetics, avoid using too much as some people have reactions to the smells (for example, migraines, coughing episodes, breathing problems).

Be Organized

Be able to flip open your case and pull out exactly the tool or paperwork that you need. Not only does being organized save time, frustration and, ultimately, money, it instills confidence in both your client and you. Rate yourself on organization skills (see Figure 19.35) and make organization a goal. Keep in mind that a messy, fumbling technician would not make a very good impression. Before going on a service call or calling a customer, have all the relevant parts, paperwork, tools, and so on organized and easy to locate.

Pick up after yourself and leave the area at least as clean as it was before you arrived. Reassure your customers that you are working diligently and systematically on their problems and are taking care of them. Focus on the task at hand.

FIGURE 19.35   Organization measure

Use Proper Language

Use no slang, no profanity, and no jargon. Avoid acronyms. (An acronym is a group of words describing something, such as SATA.) Every profession/industry has its own vernacular, and you need to be conscious of using "geek speak" (see Figure 19.36). Be careful not to confuse or intimidate your customers.

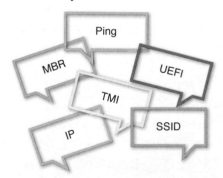

FIGURE 19.36   Avoid "geek speak"

Polish up your grammar skills. Rather than saying "Don't them look good?" or "I seen it doing this," say, "Don't they look good?" or "I saw it doing this." Do not use double negatives, such as "I don't got no paper with me." Brush up on your spelling and punctuation skills. Understand and properly use words such as too, two, and to; there, they're, and their; lie versus lay; and so on. Write your reports in complete sentences. Type in a word processing application to get grammar suggestions. Then, paste the text into an email message or technical support problem logging application.

Maintain a Positive Attitude: Project Confidence

Walk through the door with a purpose and a smile! Stand up straight, shoulders back, with your head held high. Offer your hand in friendship. Emphasize your customer's value with kindness, respect, and gratitude. Project confidence. The customer will be relieved to see you.

In many IT jobs, there is more work than time. Technicians must constantly juggle to keep up with it all. Make sure you take allowed breaks and do non-technical things. If you are sitting in an office, greet and acknowledge a visitor as soon as possible. Use a phone or a tablet to keep reminders for the day. If you are going to be late, call and let the customer know. Customers are often happy to rearrange their schedule and tasks to be available when the technician is coming. Courteous promptness will be rewarded.

Actively Listen

Listen attentively and maintain good eye contact. The customer will tell you what he or she wants. Take notes. If using an electronic tablet, explain to your customer that you are entering information about the problem to help you speculate on a solution. Be up front and let the customer see what you are doing.

Avoid interrupting the customer. Don't assume anything. Avoid finishing your customer's sentences to avoid seeming like you are rushing the customer (see Figure 19.37). Ask open-ended questions, such as "How long has this message been popping up?" or "Have you been to any new/different websites lately?" or "Who else has access to your computer?" After the customer has explained the problem, repeat it back to him or her to make it clear that you both understand the situation. Ask the customer what he or she would like to see happen.

FIGURE 19.37 Hatchet in monitor

Be Culturally Sensitive

Take the time to know your customers. Understand and accept that there will be differences among all people (see Figure 19.38) and it is not your place to judge. Be aware of things that you do that might be offensive to others. Always try to put yourself in your customers' shoes. Be aware of any facial expressions, hand gestures, or body movements you tend to make that may be deemed offensive or insulting. If the customer is doing something that you find offensive, you can politely ask her to stop. For example, if someone feels compelled to tell you a joke or an anecdote that is degrading, belittling, or humiliating to another person, immediately and politely ask that person to stop. If the behavior continues, you could say, "I'm trying to do a professional job here, and I am offended by that."

FIGURE 19.38 Diversity

Be on Time

It is better to be 10 minutes early than 5 minutes late. If something causes you to be late in reaching your next appointment at the agreed time, call that customer as soon as possible. Customers commonly get angry when techs are late (see Figure 19.39), so by calling ahead you can give them time to adjust. If you have kept your customer waiting—whether on the phone or in person—apologize, ask if you may go ahead with the work, and thank the customer. Be gracious.

FIGURE 19.39 Lateness can lead to angry customers

Time Management

Time management is how much time you budget and then actually spend on doing each task throughout the workday. IT personnel tend to have busy schedules (see Figure 19.40). Be aware of how you might improve your time management and the things that contribute to time management.

FIGURE 19.40   Time management

Always remember that you are a paid employee, and time is money to the company. If you encounter a chatty person, politely explain that you are on your company's billable hours. Emphasize that you like to stay on schedule for all of your customers, and it's best for you to stay on task. Steer the customer toward talking about the problem at hand in a constructive way. For example, if the person is frustrated and is just blowing off steam, politely suggest that perhaps a break or a drink of water might help. This would allow some cooling-off time for the client and time for you to work alone. If the person becomes confrontational, it may be a good time for you to take a break.

Avoid Distractions

Give your customer your undivided attention. Be in the moment. Here are some best practices:

> Turn off your cell phone or switch to vibrate mode so that you are not interrupted with personal or professional calls.
> Avoid looking at social media sites and doing any texting until you have finished with your customer.
> Avoid talking to coworkers while interacting with a client.
> Avoid gossiping.
> Avoid personal interruptions.
> Avoid checking your watch, drumming your fingers, yawning, rolling your eyes, sighing, and so on.

The most common customer complaints are that they feel ignored, not listened to or taken seriously, passed over or put aside, or kept waiting. Do what you can to ensure that you don't have any of these effects on your customers. Smile with your eyes as well as your mouth. Be pleasant and avoid being condescending. Avoid regaling your customers with stories of your personal life. This doesn't mean that small talk is off-limits. Just remember to keep it appropriate and professional. Remember that the customer is concerned about the immediate problem.

Don't Make Commitments You Can't Keep

Part of being professional is having integrity. Be business-like with clients and ensure that the subjects you talk about are relevant to the job. Even though the tone is light in Figure 19.41, the point is to be professional and take your job seriously. Do not be flippant.

"The computer repair people take their job very seriously."

FIGURE 19.41   Be professional

Do not make off-handed promises in hopes of appeasing your client and don't make commitments you can't keep. It is much better to say, "I am not sure how long this will take [or cost]" or "I am not qualified in that particular area, but I can check on that for you and get back to you." Don't be afraid to call someone else for help. For example, if the problem you see is out of your area of expertise, call up someone who is more experienced. If you do not have time to fix a particular problem but have committed to doing so, ask another technician for help. Many companies have tiers of technical support. There is probably someone senior or a manager that can offer you some advice after you have done all the research you can and exhausted your resources.

Dealing with a Difficult Customer or Situation

When you are faced with an uncomfortable situation, above all remember to breathe deeply and slowly. Not only will this provide your brain with oxygen-enriched blood, it will give you a moment to think and compose yourself before you answer. Here are some suggestions for dealing with difficult customers:

> Let the customer talk.
> Make good eye contact and give physical affirmation cues (for example, nodding your head "yes").
> Do not ever tell someone to "calm down." That is akin to scoffing and saying, "You don't have a legitimate complaint." Telling someone to "calm down" is likely to increase the person's anger.

> Do not argue with a customer or be defensive. Remember that the customer has been stewing and fuming about this particular problem and wants to tell you every last detail about it. Listen to him or her and don't interrupt or try to finish sentences.

> Remind yourself that you have been trained in this field and are the expert. Don't dismiss the customer's problems. Acknowledge that he is understandably upset, frustrated, angry, and so on, and reassure him in a calm, steady voice that you are there to help.

> Avoid being judgmental.

> Be personable yet professional. Replies such as "I'll do my absolute best to help you" or "I'm sorry that this glitch has been so upsetting to you" or "Let's see what I can do for you" can go a long way toward diffusing the situation. Let the client know that you have a hearty interest in her well-being—that you are genuinely concerned with helping.

> Be careful not to giggle or laugh inappropriately, or the customer may mistakenly think you are making fun of, belittling, or dismissing the problem.

> Avoid laughing constantly while talking. Some people do this—whether out of nervousness or habit—when engaged in conversation. Constant laughing could cause the other person to wonder what is so humorous about the situation.

> Always keep in mind what your customers want, need, and/or expect from you (or your company).

> Utilize resources that are available to you from which you can pull answers to solve the problem.

> Don't post work-related frustrations or experiences to social media sites.

> Go over and above the expected service.

> Pay attention to detail.

In order to keep the customer focused on the problem at hand, clarify customer statements by asking open-ended questions to narrow the scope of the problem; if necessary, restate the issue or ask questions to verify your understanding of the problem. Gently guide the customer by restating the problem and expanding a bit on the description. Do not frustrate a customer that seems to have some technical skills. Ask more open-ended questions to speed up the troubleshooting process if possible. After the job is complete, be sure to follow up with the customer by allowing time for questions and then thanking him or her for the opportunity to serve. Feedback keeps the lines of communication open and flowing between you and nurtures the active work relationship that is so vital to good customer service (see Figure 19.42).

FIGURE 19.42 Feedback

If someone is invading your space (getting too close for comfort), try stepping back a step. If she steps in, raise a palm to give the indication for her to stop (see Figure 19.43).

FIGURE 19.43   Stop what you are doing; stay back

If this does not work, stop what you are doing, look the person in the eyes, and politely ask him or her to give you more room. If someone is verbally abusive to you or even physically abusive, step back and raise a palm (refer to Figure 19.43). Prevent the situation from escalating by keeping your voice in an even, professional tone. You can always ask the person to take a short break or excuse yourself to give her a moment. You have the right to a safe work environment.

Set and Meet Expectations

A customer usually wants to know when his computer will be fixed. If you must give an estimated repair time, estimate a little longer than you anticipate. That way, if you finish earlier than you expected, you'll both be happy! Discuss and offer different repair or replacement options, if applicable. Keep your customer informed of your progress. A small morsel of information from time to time helps quell the anxiety about an unknown situation ("Here's where we're at now…" or "Just checking in to let you know that…"). This type of response reassures the customer that you are actively working to fix the problem. No one likes wondering or waiting. Think back to when you first encountered problems and frustrations when working with a computer. Treat others as you would like to be treated.

Deal Appropriately with Confidential and Private Materials

Discretion is another integral part of professionalism. Remember to be cognizant of all who may be in the area. Keep information private; for example, hard copies and faxed materials should be secured in folders—not spread around on a table for any passerby to read. Speak in a manner such that no one else can hear. Keep your laptop and mobile devices password protected. Keep your own personal information private. You wouldn't want a third party to expose your private information, would you?

When working for a client, if you notice what seems to be sensitive information (for example, passwords taped somewhere, documents left in a printer, employee evaluations), it is best practice to ask the client to remove that information. Also, it is prudent to notify the client if you might have inadvertently seen sensitive information so that the client can take any necessary measures (for example, change the password). If you spot a bad security practice such as a password taped somewhere, take the opportunity to talk about security in today's environment.

Never discuss a customer's business or your professional matters with anyone—while sitting in a restaurant, at a public venue, on social media, or even in off-hand conversation (see Figure 19.44). A 1942 American World War II poster by Designer Seymour R. Goff exclaimed, "Loose lips might sink ships," meaning it's important to beware of frivolous or unguarded talk as you never know who may be listening.

FIGURE 19.44 Social network

Closing Remarks

No IT person is perfect. All you can do is strive to be the best professional possible. Try to do the right thing, be professional, be honest, and apologize if you are in the wrong, and people will recognize that you are doing the best you can. Keep learning. Even if you remain in the same job for some time, there will be new technologies and areas that you can improve upon.

Good luck to you in your IT profession! It is a wonderful field, and there are always opportunities to slide into something new. An inspiring quotation to leave you with comes from Vincent van Gogh: "Your profession is not what brings home your weekly paycheck. Your profession is what you're put here on earth to do with such passion and such intensity that it becomes spiritual in calling."

Chapter Summary

> Three of the most important items you should have in your technician kit are safety goggles, vinyl or nitrile gloves, and a dust mask/air filter mask. These are your PPE.

> Power issues include overvoltage conditions such as a surge or spike that can be managed with surge protectors, power conditioners, and UPSs. Power conditioners and UPSs help with undervoltage conditions such as sags. A UPS is the only device that powers a computer when a blackout occurs.

> Ensure that a surge protector has a Class A rating and adheres to the UL 1449 standard.

> Two types of battery backup are UPS and SPS.

> You have the right to expect a safe working environment. Federal government agencies such as OSHA and the EPA work hand in hand with state and local governments to regulate, enforce, and promote safe work practices—both for individuals and for the environment.

> A good computer technician knows how to recycle and/or dispose of electronic waste (specifically how to handle batteries, toner cartridges, CRT monitors, PCs, cell phones, and tablets) and understands the importance this makes to the health of humans and to the environment.

> Federal government agencies, such as OSHA and the EPA, work in tandem with state municipalities and local governments to monitor environmental impacts of toxic waste. Batteries, mobile devices, computers, and printers all contain toxic heavy metals (for example, cadmium, lead, mercury) that, when tossed into landfills, can leach out into the surrounding soil and water. Most municipalities have electronic waste recycling/disposal toxic waste handling sites. Never attempt to dispose of any toxic electronic waste by burning it (such as in a bonfire or a burning barrel). Never lay heavy items on top of electronic equipment. Never crush or puncture any device that contains a battery as doing so can cause leakage of heavy metals or chemicals.

> IT documentation is an important part of any IT staff member's job and is used for reference and sometimes requires updating.

> Change management is a requirement for documented business processes within IT. A risk analysis should be done as part of the change management process to determine if the change is worth the risk of implementation. A backout plan should also be part of any IT plan.

> Proper communication and positive interaction with customers are required of IT professionals. Use no profanity, street-talk, or slang. Address customers by using their title and surname.

> Attentiveness to customers means making good eye-contact, listening actively, avoiding interrupting or finishing the customer's sentences, and taking detailed notes.

> Keep personal business and activities out of the workplace.

> Hygiene, appearance, manners, and confidence are important traits to possess.

> Look, act, dress, and think like a professional, and you will be a professional.

A+ CERTIFICATION EXAM TIPS

✓ Be cognizant of personal safety techniques and issues, including removing power before working on a PC, removing jewelry, being careful while lifting and minding weight limitations, taking measures to promote electrical fire safety, managing cables, and using an air filter mask and safety goggles when appropriate. Be sure to comply with all local government regulations.

✓ Know the purpose of MSDS as well as the temperature, humidity, and ventilation requirements for electronic equipment.

✓ Compare equipment needed for power surges, brownouts, and blackouts, including battery backup options and surge suppressors. Enclosures and air filters or a mask provide protection from airborne particles, including dust and debris. Compressed air and vacuuming can help, too.

✓ Explain equipment grounding and be familiar with proper component handling and storage, including the use of self-grounding techniques, antistatic bags, ESD straps, and ESD mats. A network rack that holds servers, routers, switches, and so on or a UPS might have a grounding strap attached.

✓ Describe how to handle toxic waste, including batteries, toner, CRTs, cell phones, and tablets.

✓ Know when to use the following types of documentation: network topology diagrams, knowledge base articles, incident documentation, regulatory and compliance policy, acceptable use policy, and password policy.

✓ Describe how asset tags and barcodes are used in inventory management.

✓ Be able to describe best practices related to documentation and change management. As part of the change management process, describe the purpose of the change, the scope of the change, and a plan for the change. Include a risk analysis to determine whether the change is worth the business risk. Include end-user acceptance testing as part of the plan. Documentation should include a backout plan and information on the changes implemented.

✓ The change management process may include a change board that determines whether an IT change is approved. A document that might be created in the change management process might include a SOW, which outlines the plan, responsibilities, due dates, and a backout plan.

✓ Communication techniques and key areas of professionalism include the following: use proper language; maintain a positive attitude; project confidence; actively listen; avoid interrupting the customer; be culturally sensitive; use appropriate titles; be on time; avoid distractions; be able to deal with a difficult customer or situation (don't argue or be defensive, don't be dismissive regarding the problem, avoid being judgmental); clarify customer statements with open-ended questions; set and meet expectations; communicate the status with the customer; and deal appropriately with customers' confidential and private information.

✓ At this point you've learned every topic that is covered on the CompTIA A+ exams. Now you should take time to specifically prepare for the certification exams and get the professional credentials you have earned. Refer to the Introduction of this book for details on the 220-1001 and 220-1002 CompTIA A+ exams, including how to sign up for them. And note that Pearson, the publisher of this book, is offering you an exclusive deep discount on several types of certification exam preparation resources. See the Introduction to this book and the advertisement inserts in the back for more details. Take a look at what Pearson has to offer and figure out which resource(s) would work best for your study style. Good luck!

Key Terms

acceptable use policy   1064
air filter mask   1044
airborne particle   1057
antistatic bag   1049
article   1062
asset tag   1063
backout plan   1065
barcode   1063
battery   1046
battery backup   1054
blackout   1051
brownout   1051
cable management   1040
cell phone   1046
change board   1064
change management   1064
clean room   1058
compressed air   1044
CRT   1046
document changes   1065
documented business
processes   1064
dust and debris   1057
electrical fire safety   1041
end-user acceptance   1065
environmental enclosure   1057

equipment grounding   1050
ESD mat   1049
ESD strap   1049
gloves   1043
humidity   1049
incident documentation   1062
inventory management   1063
knowledge base   1062
li-ion battery   1047
lifting technique   1044
line conditioner   1053
mask   1044
MOV   1051
MSDS   1041
network topology diagram   1060
OSHA   1041
overvoltage   1050
password policy   1064
personal protective
equipment   1043
physical network diagram   1060
plan for change   1064
power surge   1050
purpose of the change   1064
regulatory and compliance
policy   1064

remove jewelry   1044
risk analysis   1064
safety goggles   1043
SAG   1051
scope of the change   1065
SDS   1041
security policy   1064
self-grounding   1049
spike   1050
SPS   1055
surge   1050
surge suppressor   1051
tablet   1046
temperature   1059
time management   1072
toner   1048
toxic waste handling   1045
Type A-B-C fire
extinguisher   1041
Type C fire extinguisher   1041
UL 1449 VPR   1052
undervoltage   1050
UPS   1054
vacuum   1059
ventilation   1059
weight limitation   1044

Review Questions

1. Professionalism involves _____.

    [skill | training | integrity | discretion | two of the above | all of these]

2. Which IT documentation would a technician need to refer to when connecting a new PC and IP phone to a switch?

    [incident documentation | regulatory and compliance policy | security policy | physical network drawing]

3. On which piece of device would a PC technician most likely see a grounding strap?

    [patch panel | air vent | wiring rack | laser printer]

4. A company is implementing new payroll software. The project manager has outlined the scope of the project, responsibilities, due dates, and quality assurance checkpoints. What is missing from this plan?

    [end-user acceptance | network topology diagrams | backup testing | backout plan]

5. A computer technician's repair kit should always include which of the following?

    a. Pen, paper, ID badge

    b. Soap, toothbrush, toothpaste

    c. Surge suppressor, laptop enclosure case, resealable antistatic bags

    d. Safety glasses/goggles, gloves, dust mask/air filter mask

6. Which UL rating and surge suppressor grade would be best when ordering new surge strips for a small business? (Choose two answers.)

    [UL 497 | UL 1283 | UL 1449 | Class A | Class B | Class C]

7. Which part of the change management cycle would include an evaluation of whether a particular IT change is worth implementing?

    a. Plan scope

    b. Risk analysis

    c. Backup plan

    d. Plan purpose

8. What is a safety risk related to old or damaged batteries?

    a. They can leak acid.

    b. They can contain lead.

    c. They can contain water.

    d. All sizes are interchangeable.

9. Equipment grounding means which of the following?

    a. The equipment is tethered to a desk.

    b. The components in a computer are all the same potential.

    c. The technician wears a tether device.

    d. Someone could receive a shock or be electrocuted from simply touching the case.

10. Which method is best for cleaning up scattered laser toner particles?

    a. Use a hair dryer to blow away the residue.

    b. Use moist paper towels to wipe up particles.

    c. Use your shirt sleeve to make them disappear.

    d. Use a vacuum cleaner equipped with a HEPA filter while wearing your PPE.

11. In what two situations might a Li-ion battery need to be replaced even if it is new? (Choose two.)

     a. It is subjected to extreme temperature changes.

     b. It is stored in a plastic bin filled with white rice.

     c. It is submerged in water.

     d. It is used near high-voltage equipment.

     e. It is used near an approved regulated waste receptacle.

12. What is the best way to dispose of mobile devices, PCs, monitors, toner, and batteries?

     a. Burn them in bonfires.

     b. Dump them in landfills.

     c. Deposit them into local municipality-approved receptacle.

     d. Call 911.

13. In the event of an electrical fire, which two fire extinguishers would be best? (Choose two.)

     a. Type A fire extinguisher

     b. Type B fire extinguisher

     c. Type C fire extinguisher

     d. Type D fire extinguisher

     e. Type A-B-C fire extinguisher

14. A device that protects electronic equipment from an increase in power but not a decrease or outage is a _____.

     [battery backup | surge suppressor | CRT | UPS]

15. When encountering a difficult or confrontational customer, the best thing to do initially is which of the following?

     a. Step back and breathe deeply a few times before responding.

     b. Call a supervisor.

     c. Suggest a short break.

     d. Reschedule the appointment.

16. [T | F] Federal, state, and local governments do not interact with one another concerning toxic waste issues.

17. Particulate matter (PM), such as airborne pollutants, is _____.

     a. harmful only to humans

     b. common in computer components

     c. easily cleaned up

     d. potentially toxic to humans, animals, and environment

18. Laser toner cartridges _____.

     a. are easily recycled anywhere

     b. can be donated to charities

     c. can be refilled many times

     d. must be disposed of in an approved regulated receptacle

19. A user has requested help converting a Word document to PDF. Which of the following IT documentation types would a technician use in this case?

     [security policy | inventory management | article | network topology diagram | acceptable use policy]

20. Which two items would be used as part of inventory management? (Choose two.)

     [asset tag | flatbed scanner | incident documentation | barcode | AUP]

Exercises

Exercise 19.1 Determining a Power Solution

Objective: To be able to determine the proper power solution for a particular situation

Procedure: Match one of the power solutions to each situation. Note that a particular solution may be the answer for more than one situation.

Power solutions

a. Surge suppressor

b. Power conditioner

c. UPS

d. SPS

_____ A company has a very old building that has one corporate division. The company suspects a power issue in the lowest room because the three PCs located there continually reset.

_____ A particular network rack has a switch that is used to connect to every executive on a single floor. The president of the company has requested that these executives' computers remain powered as long as possible, even when power to the building is lost.

_____ A home tower computer has two monitors, powered speakers, and a printer attached, and it needs to be protected from an overvoltage condition.

_____ A cubicle in a company has only two outlets. The cubicle contains a thin client computer, a monitor, and an IP phone.

_____ An entrepreneur has a home office with a server that stores all company data, a PC, three monitors, and a printer. The owner wants to be protected in over- and undervoltage situations with clean power to all devices.

_____ A gamer would like to have power provided even when power to the house is lost but does not want the cost of a UPS.

Exercise 19.2 Determining the Type of Documentation Needed

Objective: To be able to determine which type of documentation is needed in a particular situation

Procedure: Match one of the documentation types to each situation. Note that a particular scenario is the answer for only one documentation type.

Documentation types

a. Network topology diagram

b. Knowledge base/articles

c. Incident documentation

d. Regulatory and compliance policy

e. Security policy

f. Inventory management

_____ A technician has solved a problem that required reloading a computer due to a virus infection.

_____ A technician has moved a barcoded network printer to a newly created divisional copy room.

_____ A technician is responding to a complaint about wireless connectivity in a particular area. The technician needs to know how many access points are in the area and the coverage area.

_____ A technician working in a hospital notices that a computer is displaying private patient health information.

_____ A person calls the help desk because of a problem with changing the domain password. The technician needs to know the company's exact password requirements.

_____ A technician needs to connect an IP phone and needs to know which switch port has been programmed for the appropriate phone VLAN.

Activities

Internet Discovery

Objective: To obtain specific information on the Internet regarding administrative procedures

Parts: Computer with Internet access

Questions: Use the Internet to answer the following questions.

1. Research how to dress professionally for your job. Write three things that impressed you the most about the advice given and whether you found the website helpful or confusing. Write the URL where the information was found.

    _____

    _____

2. Locate at least two videos of poor technician interaction/service with customers. Compare with the lessons in this book and write how the techs in the videos could improve their skills.

    _____

    _____

3. Research at least two local municipalities that have approved regulated sites for recycling and disposal of computer and electronic equipment. List what they advise for their communities. Describe differences in their regulations. List the URL for each municipality.

    _____

    _____

    _____

    _____

4. Research electrical fire safety videos. Combine the information from this book with what you learn from the fire safety videos. Document what new things were shown. How confident are you that you could extinguish an electrical fire? List the URL where your information was found.

    _____

    _____

    _____

5. Research at least five healthy things to do for yourself every day. Decide which ones you'd like to implement. List the URLs where your information was found.

    _____

    _____

Soft Skills

Objective: To enhance and fine-tune a future technician's ability to listen, communicate in both written and oral form, and support people who use computers in a professional manner.

Activities:

1. Refine your customer skills by play-acting situations with another student. One student should take the role of the technician and the other should take the role of the customer. Instead of asking "Did you do _____?" ask "When did you do _____?" "What happened when you did _____?" or "When did you first notice _____?" Rate each other, using positive words. You can give negative feedback but do it in a positive manner. For example, if the person spoke in a low tone, but the words were good, you might give the following feedback: "Your explanation was very good, but I had a hard time hearing you. You might want to speak up just a bit louder."

2. Hone your job interviewing skills by practicing with another student. Be prepared with questions about the company with which you are seeking employment. Think ahead to what questions a prospective employer might ask you.

3. In a group with other students, inspect the fire extinguisher in the room and then research electrical fire safety. After becoming familiar with fire safety signs and exit routes for the classroom, create a scenario to demonstrate fire safety. Produce an escape route, act out the scenario, and present an escape route drawing to the rest of the class.

4. Build a virtual wardrobe appropriate for your future job. Research websites and record in a professionally formatted document descriptions of the garments you would choose. Don't forget accessories such as shoes, hats, purses/briefcases, computer bags, and so on. Share and discuss with other students why you chose specific items. Provide feedback to other students on their choices. Optionally place your findings in a presentation to be shared with others.

Critical Thinking Skills

Objective: To analyze and evaluate information as well as apply learned information to new and different situations.

Activities:

1. Break into groups of three students. Each group receives a box containing a laser toner, a CRT monitor, and a battery. Research local municipality regulations regarding recycling and/or disposal of electronic waste. Present findings to the class. Aggregate all groups' findings in table form. Offer to share with the school.

2. Engage in conversation the number of friends/acquaintances specified by your instructor. Ask about and record specific problems they encounter with their mobile devices and laptops. What problem occurs most? What new problem(s) are presented that were unfamiliar to you? What solutions would you offer to these people? Record all your data in table form and present it to the class.

3. Divide into groups of three or four students. As a group, consider the following information: A local veteran's home has 100 computers and 10 printers; 96 computers and 8 printers are used by the staff, 4 computers and 2 printers are used by the veterans. The computers and printers used by the veterans experience a high rate of downtime. Think of different reasons the veterans' computers and printers might be frequently nonfunctional. Offer at least three solutions to improve the situation.

4. Prepare a change management plan for any of the solutions proposed in Question 3.

5. Use the Internet to locate a video that features a technician using poor communication skills. List things that were recommended in this chapter that were not addressed in the video or that the technician could have handled differently.

6. Find current news stories that feature safety issues related to technology.

A Subnetting Basics

In business, the subnet mask assigned to a device commonly is not the default mask based on the class of IP address being used. For example, at a college, the IP address 10.104.10.88 and subnet mask 255.255.255.0 are assigned to a computer. The 10 in the first octet shows that this is a class A IP address. A class A IP address has a default mask of 255.0.0.0. The 255 in the subnet mask is made up of eight 1s in binary in the first octet (11111111) followed by all 0s in the remaining octets (00000000.00000000.00000000).

The purpose of a subnet mask is to tell you (and the network devices) which portion of the IP address is the network part. The rest of the address is the host portion of the address. The network part of any IP address is the same 1s and 0s for all computers on the network. The rest of the 1s and 0s can change and be unique addresses for the network devices on the same network. The following important rules relate to subnetting:

> The network number *cannot* be assigned to any device on the network.
> The network number contains all 0s in the host portion of the address. Note that this does not mean that the number will be 0 in decimal (as explained next).
> The broadcast address (the number used to send a message to all devices on the network) *cannot* be assigned to any device on the network.
> The broadcast address contains all 1s in the host portion of the address. Note that this does not mean that the number will be 255 in decimal.

Consider the IP address and mask used in the earlier example: 10.104.10.88 and 255.255.255.0. Put these numbers in binary, one number on top of the other, to see the effects of the subnet mask:

```
    10              104           10             88
00001010.01101000.00001010.01011000
11111111.11111111.11111111.00000000
```

The 1s in the subnet mask show which bits in the top row are the network part of the address. The subnet mask is always a row of consecutive 1s. Where the 1s stop is where the network portion of the address stops. Keep in mind that this does not have to be where an octet stops, as in this example. A good technique is to draw a line where the 1s in the subnet mask stop, as shown in the example that follows:

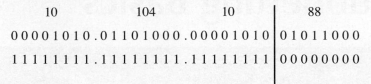

```
        10              104              10      |    88
  0 0 0 0 1 0 1 0 . 0 1 1 0 1 0 0 0 . 0 0 0 0 1 0 1 0 | 0 1 0 1 1 0 0 0
  1 1 1 1 1 1 1 1 . 1 1 1 1 1 1 1 1 . 1 1 1 1 1 1 1 1 | 0 0 0 0 0 0 0 0
```

At this point, there is no other purpose for the subnet mask. You can get rid of it, as shown in the example that follows:

```
        10              104              10      |    88
  0 0 0 0 1 0 1 0 . 0 1 1 0 1 0 0 0 . 0 0 0 0 1 0 1 0 | 0 1 0 1 1 0 0 0
```

All 1s and 0s to the left of the drawn line are the network portion of the IP address. All devices on the same network will have this same combination of 1s and 0s up to the line. All 1s and 0s to the right of the drawn line are in the host portion of the IP address:

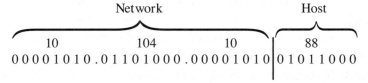

The network number—the IP address used to represent an entire single network—is found by setting all host bits to 0. The resulting number is the network number:

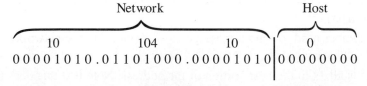

The network number for the network device that has the IP address 10.104.10.88 is 10.104.10.0. To find the broadcast address, the IP address used to send a message to all devices on the 10.104.10.0 network, set all the host bits to 1:

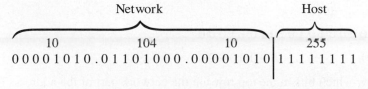

The broadcast IP address is 10.104.10.255 for the 10.104.10.0 network. This means that hosts can be assigned any addresses between the network number 10.104.10.0 and the broadcast address 10.104.10.255. Another way of stating this is that IP addresses 10.104.10.1 through 10.104.10.254 are usable IP addresses on the 10.104.10.0 network.

Consider the IP address 192.168.10.213 and the subnet mask 255.255.255.224 assigned to a computer in a college. What would be the network number and broadcast address for this computer? To find the answer, write 192.168.10.213 in binary octets. Write the subnet mask in binary under the IP address:

```
     192              168             10              213
1 1 0 0 0 0 0 0 . 1 0 1 0 1 0 0 0 . 0 0 0 0 1 0 1 0 . 1 1 0 1 0 1 0 1

1 1 1 1 1 1 1 1 . 1 1 1 1 1 1 1 1 . 1 1 1 1 1 1 1 1 . 1 1 1 0 0 0 0 0
```

Now draw a line where the 1s in the subnet mask stop:

```
     192              168             10              213
1 1 0 0 0 0 0 0 . 1 0 1 0 1 0 0 0 . 0 0 0 0 1 0 1 0 . 1 1 0|1 0 1 0 1

1 1 1 1 1 1 1 1 . 1 1 1 1 1 1 1 1 . 1 1 1 1 1 1 1 1 . 1 1 1|0 0 0 0 0
```

Remove the subnet mask because it is not needed anymore:

```
     192              168             10              213
1 1 0 0 0 0 0 0 . 1 0 1 0 1 0 0 0 . 0 0 0 0 1 0 1 0 . 1 1 0|1 0 1 0 1
```

Set all host bits to 0 to find the network number:

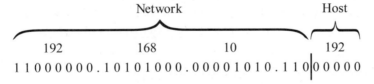

```
     192              168             10              192
1 1 0 0 0 0 0 0 . 1 0 1 0 1 0 0 0 . 0 0 0 0 1 0 1 0 . 1 1 0|0 0 0 0 0
```

The network number for the network device that has IP address 192.168.10.213 is 192.168.10.192. To find the broadcast address, set all host bits to 1:

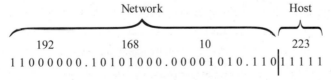

```
     192              168             10              223
1 1 0 0 0 0 0 0 . 1 0 1 0 1 0 0 0 . 0 0 0 0 1 0 1 0 . 1 1 0|1 1 1 1 1
```

The broadcast address for the network device that has the IP address 192.168.10.213 is 192.168.10.223. Notice how all eight bits are used to calculate the number 223 in the last octet. Valid IP addresses are any numbers between the network number 192.168.10.192 and the broadcast IP address 192.168.10.223. In other words, the range of usable IP addresses is from 192.168.10.193 (one number larger than the network address) through 192.168.10.222 (one number less than the broadcast address). Practice problems in the following exercise help you explore this concept.

Exercises

Exercise A.1 Subnet Practice Exercise

Objective: To be able to determine the subnet number, broadcast address, and IP addresses that can be assigned to network devices

Procedure: Complete the following procedures and answer the accompanying questions.

1.   Determine the network address for each of the following IP address and subnet mask combinations.

210.141.254.122 255.255.255.192

_____

206.240.195.38 255.255.255.224

_____

104.130.188.213 255.255.192.0

_____

69.89.5.224 255.240.0.0

_____

10.113.71.66 255.128.0.0

_____

2.   Determine the broadcast address for the following IP address and subnet mask combinations.

166.215.207.182 255.255.255.240

_____

198.94.140.121 255.255.255.224

_____

97.57.210.192 255.255.224.0

_____

133.98.227.36 255.255.192.0

_____

14.89.203.133 255.128.0.0

_____

3.   Determine the valid IP addresses on the networks that contain the following IP address and subnet mask combinations.

131.107.200.34 255.255.248.0

_____

146.197.221.238 255.255.255.192

_____

52.15.111.33 255.255.248.0

_____

192.168.10.245/30

_____

209.218.235.117 255.255.255.128

_____

Glossary

Numerals and Symbols

.. (navigation command) From a Windows command prompt, the two dots (. .) represent the parent directory.

+12 V A voltage level from the power supply that is used for drive motors, CPU, internal cooling fans, and the graphics card.

+5 V A voltage level from the power supply that is used for electronics, the motherboard, adapters, ports, and peripherals.

1.8-inch A storage device form factor.

115 V vs. 220 V input voltage Some power supplies accept 120 V (listed as 115 V on the certification) or 220 V power from an electrical outlet.

10,000 RPM A hard drive speed. The faster the drive RPM, the faster the transfer rate.

15,000 RPM A hard drive speed. The faster the drive RPM, the faster the transfer rate.

2.4 GHz A common frequency used for 802.11 wireless networks.

2.5-inch A storage device form factor.

2.5-inch drive A storage device form factor.

24-pin motherboard connector Main ATX motherboard power connector.

3.5-inch drive A storage device form factor.

32-bit architecture A device that has a processor that can handle 32 bits at one time.

3D printer A type of printer used to create 3D solid objects out of various materials, including plastic, metal, clay, and ceramics.

3G Third generation of wireless cellular technology that allowed mobile devices to have faster Internet connectivity.

4G Fourth generation of cellular network that supports IP telephony, gaming services, mobile TV, and video conferencing at speeds up to 1 Gb/s.

5 GHz A common frequency used for 802.11 wireless networks.

56 Kb/s modem A modem that produces higher transmission speeds and uses traditional phone lines. Actual modem speed is determined by the number of analog-to-digital conversions that occur through the phone system.

5,400 RPM A hard drive speed. The faster the drive RPM, the faster the transfer rate.

568A/B An ANSI/TIA/EIA Ethernet network cabling standard.

5G Fifth generation of cellular networks that does not have formal standards yet; supports speeds up to 10 Gb/s.

64-bit architecture A device that has a processor that can handle 64bits at one time.

7,200 RPM A hard drive speed. The faster the drive RPM, the faster the transfer rate.

802.11a An IEEE wireless standard that used the 5 GHz range and had speeds up to 54 Mb/s.

802.11ac An IEEE wireless standard that uses the 5 GHz range and supports speeds up to 4.9 Gb/s.

802.11b The first IEEE wireless standard to hit the market; used the 2.4 GHz range and supported speeds up to 11 Mb/s.

802.11g An IEEE wireless standard that was an upgrade to 802.11b and was backward compatible with it; used the 2.4 GHz range and had speeds up to 54 Mb/s.

802.11n An IEEE wireless standard that uses both the 2.4 and 5 GHz ranges and that supports speeds up to 600 Mb/s.

A

A/V (audio/video) A reference to sound and visual data, such as movies or stills.

AC (alternating current) The type of electrical power from a wall outlet.

AC circuit tester A device that checks a wall outlet's wiring.

accelerometer A technology in mobile devices to detect screen orientation and adapt what is shown onscreen for that viewing mode. A gyroscope measures and maintains that orientation.

acceptable use policy (AUP) A policy that defines rules regarding using a company network, data, and a specific application.

access control entity (ACE)   Changes made to a monitored file or folder cannot be changed even by an administrator unless the administrator takes ownership and adds the appropriate access control entities.

access control list (ACL)   An access control list relates to the permissions for a specific object such as what is allowed to be done to the object (such as a file or directory) by particular users or operating system processes. A means of providing a security filter where traffic is allowed or denied based on configured parameters.

access denied   Notifies the user that he or she must have specific security rights or be logged on as an administrator.

access point   A component of a wireless network that accepts associations from wireless network cards.

account creation   In Active Directory, select the group you want to create the account in and use the *Action > New* menu option.

account deletion   In Active Directory, locate the user name you want to delete, right-click on it, and select *Delete*.

account settings   Settings required when putting a thick client or thin client onto a network.

ACL   See *access control list*.

ACPI (Advanced Configuration and Power Interface)   Technology that allows the motherboard and operating system to control the power needs and operation modes of various devices.

activation clock   A timer for the Windows operating system. When creating an image, a technician must reset or re-arm the activation clock if a single activation key is used. This gives a 30-day (Windows 7) or 90-day (Windows 8/10) grace period before having to re-enter the product key.

Active Directory (AD)   A service used on Microsoft Windows Server to manage network accounts and devices.

active listening   An effective communication technique that ensures what the speaker says is accurately received.

Activity Monitor   A troubleshooting tool in a macOS system that sees what processes and services are running, as well as what system resources are used.

ad hoc mode   A type of wireless configuration in which two 802.11 wireless devices can make a wireless network without the use of an access point.

ad hoc wireless printing   Enables two 802.11 wireless devices to communicate directly without the use of a wireless access point or a wireless router.

adapter   An electronic circuit card that inserts into an expansion slot. Also called a controller, card, controller card, circuit card, circuit board, and adapter board.

add-on   An extension or plug-in that provides to a browser additional features such as a toolbar or the capability to dim everything on the screen except for a running video. Add-ons can also cause security risks.

add-on video card   A video adapter added even if the motherboard has onboard video and integrated video ports.

adding array (Disk Management)   Right-click inside unallocated space of a drive > *New Spanned Volume* or *New Striped Volume* > select another drive to be added> select a drive letter and file system.

adding drive (Disk Management)   Ensure that the drive is recognized by the BIOS and create a partition and format for a particular file system.

ADF (automatic document feeder)   A feature found on some scanners and printers that is used to feed multiple pages into the device.

ADF scanner   A scanner that has the added feature of having an automatic document feeder (ADF) to allow multiple pages to be fed or input into the scanner.

ADK   See *Windows Assessment and Deployment Kit*.

administrative privileges   A security function in Windows that requires elevated security rights in order to execute specific commands. Use the *Run as administrator* option if blocked.

administrative share   A share created by Microsoft for drive volumes and the folder that contains the majority of Windows files. An administrative share has a dollar sign at the end of its name.

administrator   A person responsible for setting up and maintaining a system, such as a Windows computer. Logging in as an administrator allows settings to be changed that may not be allowed for other users.

ADSL (Asymmetrical DSL)   A type of digital subscriber line (DSL) that provides speeds up to 150 Mb/s; it provides faster downloads than uploads.

Advanced Boot Options   A Windows boot menu used to access tools used for troubleshooting. Press [F8] when the computer is booting (and before Windows loads) to access the Advanced Boot Options menu.

Aero   A look and feel for the computing environment in Windows 7 that includes transparent icons, animations, and customized desktop gadgets.

AES (Advanced Encryption Standard) Used in wireless networks and offers encryption with 128-bit, 192-bit, and 256-bit encryption keys.

AFP (Apple Filing Protocol) A set of rules for file services on an Apple device that uses macOS. AFP uses port 548.

AGP (accelerated graphics port) An extension of the PCI bus (a port) that provides a dedicated communication path between the expansion slot and the processor. AGP is used for video adapters.

AHCI (Advanced Host Controller Interface) One mode of operation for SATA drives, which enables SATA devices to be inserted or removed when power is applied and communication exists between the host controller and attached SATA devices.

air filter/mask The air filter or mask should be used whenever dust, airborne particles, or debris could cause personal issues. An air filter might also be used in an area where the air quality is not appropriate for a computer or networking equipment.

airborne particle Something in the air, such as dust, that could potentially be a problem for a technician.

Airplane Mode Enables users to disable all wireless communication but still view a movie or play a game that does not require Internet connectivity.

AirPrint An Apple print server.

alphanumeric character A character that can be a letter of the alphabet (uppercase or lowercase), a digit from 0 through 9, or a punctuation mark or symbol, such as @, #, or !.

alternative configuration A method of configuring IPv4 parameters that will be used if the main IPv4 parameters (such as DHCP) cannot be used or are impractical to use. A good use of an alternative configuration is when a laptop is used both at work and at home. At work, DHCP could be configured, but at home, the alternative configuration might contain a statically assigned IP address.

alternative IP address A method of assigning an IP address used when the DHCP server is down or the server could not assign an IP address, such as when there are network problems.

ALU (arithmetic logic unit) The part of a processor that does mathematical manipulations.

AMD (Advanced Micro Devices) A company that makes processors, graphics processors, and chipsets. AMD is the largest rival of Intel for PC processors.

amp Short for ampere, a measurement of electrical current.

amplification Increasing the strength of a sound. Amplification output is measured in watts. Sound cards usually have built-in amplification to drive the speakers. Many speakers have built-in amplifiers to boost the audio signal for a fuller sound.

analog signal Used mainly by older video ports, modems, and sound devices; its signal strength varies in amplitude.

AND operator Used with two or more conditions and returns true only if all expressions are true.

Android A mobile device operating system.

Android OS A mobile device operating system.

antenna A component that attaches to a wireless device or is integrated into it. An antenna radiates or receives radio waves.

anti-glare filter Helps in certain lighting environments and when outside light affects the display.

anti-malware Software used to protect the operating system and applications.

antistatic bag A plastic enclosure that protects electronic gear from being affected by static charges if the equipment is left exposed.

antistatic wrist strap A strap that connects a technician to a computer that equalizes the voltage potential between the two to prevent electrostatic discharge (ESD).

antivirus Software that protects the operating system and applications from malware.

AP (access point) See *wireless access point*.

APIPA (automatic private IP addressing) A Windows option that enables a computer to automatically receive an IP address from the range 169.254.0.1 to 169.254.255.254.

APK A file format that can be used to distribute and install Android apps.

app log errors An application may create a log of any error that occurs when the application crashes. Use the operating system tools like Event Viewer, Console, and Finder (Diagnostic Reports folder) to retrieve.

app scanner An online tool in which you can type the name of an app to see if any of your data is at risk and the seriousness of any risk.

App Store An Apple tool that enables a user to shop for various applications to download on a device.

Apple Configurator A free mobile device management (MDM) tool that enables you to view and manage multiple mobile devices. Can also wipe the device.

Apple Macintosh OS Any operating system on an Apple device, including OS X, iOS, and macOS.

application crash   A situation in which a specific program quits working. In the Windows environment, use Task Manager to quit a crashed application.

application incompatibility   An application is written for a specific operating system and may not work on a previous or future version or on a different operating system.

application layer (OSI)   Layer 7 of the OSI model, which defines how applications and the computer interact with a network.

application layer (TCP/IP)   The top layer of the TCP/IP model. It formats data specific to a particular application. It is equivalent to the OSI model's application, presentation, and session layers. Common application layer protocols include Telnet, HTTP, HTML, DNS, POP, IMAP, and FTP.

application log   Whenever an application is crashing or not operating properly, the operating system logs that issue. In Windows, use Event Viewer to see such information.

application log error   When troubleshooting a particular Windows program, the application log provides detailed error information.

apply button   An option within the Windows OS that makes any changes take effect immediately.

apply update   After an operating system installation, do not forget to download and install the operating system and application updates as well as check for newer device drivers.

apps not loading   In this situation, see if the app is running already. Restart the device. Delete the app and reload it.

apt-get   The Linux command line interface tool that is the equivalent of Ubuntu Software Center; a utility to manage software.

APU (accelerated processing unit)   A processor that combines a central processing unit (CPU) with a graphics processing unit (GPU).

AR (augmented reality) headset   A device used in gaming and in educational or training settings to allow users to interact in a simulated environment.

archive attribute   A designation that can be attached to a file that marks whether the file has changed since it was last backed up by a software program.

ARP (Address Resolution Protocol)   A protocol that can discover the destination MAC address when the destination IP address is known.

article   Information contained in a magazine or online that might be used to answer a question or provide technical guidance on a particular procedure.

artifact   An unusual pattern or distortion that appears on a screen, such as green dotted or vertical lines, colored lines on one side of the screen, or tiny glitters, which could indicate problems such as an overheated GPU or insufficient air flow, or with a video driver.

ASR (Automated System Recovery)   An older Microsoft operating system recovery method used just for the operating system and not user data.

asset tag   A method of IT inventory used on hardware and network items.

assigning/changing drive letter   In Disk Management, right-click on a drive volume > *Change Drive Letter and Paths.*

asynchronous   Transmissions that do not require a clock signal but instead use extra bits to track the beginning and end of the data.

ATA standard (Advanced Technology Attachment standard)   The original IDE interface that supported two drives. Now in two types: PATA and SATA.

ATAPI (AT Attachment Packet Interface)   The hardware side of the IDE specification that supports devices such as optical drives and tape drives.

attrib   A command that designates a file as hidden, archived, read-only, or a system file.

attribute   An operating system condition used to hide, archive, make a file read-only, or designate a file as a system file.

attitude   A person's behavior and/or mindset toward another person or a thing.

ATX (Advanced Technology Extended)   A form factor for motherboards, cases, and power supplies.

audio/video editing workstation   A computer used to create and modify sound or video files. The computer commonly has multiple powerful multicore processors, maximum system RAM, specialized video and audio cards, one or more fast and large-capacity hard drives, good speakers, a high-quality mouse, dual displays, and possibly a digital tablet and scanner.

auditing   Tracking network events such as logging onto the network domain. Auditing is sometimes called event logging or simply logging.

AUP   See *acceptable use policy.*

authentication   The process of determining whether a network device or person has permission to access a network.

authentication server   A server used in a corporate environment that is used to verify credentials such as a username and password.

authenticator app   An app that can be downloaded and, if a site is configured to use it, provides an additional level of security for mobile devices.

authorization   Controls what network resources—such as files, folders, printers, video conferencing equipment, fax machines, scanners, and so on—can be accessed and used by a legitimate network user or device.

auto-switching   A type of power supply that monitors the incoming voltage from the wall outlet and automatically switches itself accordingly. Auto-switching power supplies accept voltages from 100 VAC to 240 VAC at 50 Hz to 60 Hz. They are popular in desktops, laptops, and mobile device power adapters.

Automatic Updates   A method for getting newer Windows operating system files.

B

`.bat`   A file extension used with a batch file (a file that has multiple commands that, when executed, run one after another). See also *batch file*.

b/s (bits per second)   The number of 1s and 0s transmitted per second.

back side bus   Connection between a CPU and the L2 cache.

Back to My Mac   A feature in the *System Preferences* iCloud menu that enables you to browse that Mac from another macOS device. The remote Mac appears as a shared device in Finder, enabling you to browse the file system.

backed up print queue   A situation in which one or more documents have been queued up for printing, and the printer does not execute the `print` command, causing a logjam effect.

backlight   A fluorescent lamp or LEDs that are always on for an LCD.

backup   A precautionary technique used to have a secondary piece of hardware or backup software/files.

backup and recovery   A process that should be performed as part of an implementation plan as well as a disaster prevention/recovery plan.

backup testing   A process that involves making a backup and then verifying that the backup works.

backward compatibility   In software, the ability of an application to run on older operating systems.

badge reader   A security device to allow entry into a space.

bandwidth   The width of a communications channel, which defines the channel's capacity for carrying data.

barcode   A series of lines used to uniquely identify items. In IT, a barcode is commonly used on an asset tag for PC hardware and network items.

barcode scanner   A handheld device that reads barcodes in checkout lanes and in retail establishments.

baseband   A networking technology in which the entire cable bandwidth transmits a digital signal.

baseband update   An update applied to a phone's radio firmware (a low-level software that manages items related to the phone's radio).

baseline   A snapshot of a computer's performance (memory, CPU usage, and so on) during normal operations (before a problem or slowdown is apparent).

basic disk   A Windows term for a drive that has been partitioned and formatted.

basic storage   A Windows term for a partition. Contrast with *dynamic storage*.

batch file   A Windows-based script that can only be interpreted by the Windows operating system. A batch file has the extension `.bat`.

battery   A small self-contained unit used to power a device without using an AC outlet.

battery backup   A device that provides power to the computer when a brownout or a blackout occurs.

battery charger   A portable battery pack that can be charged and carried to charge a mobile device in lieu of plugging the mobile device into an outlet.

battery not charging   In this situation, inspect the battery compartment. Try to charge with a different connector, such as a car adapter.

battery pack   A portable battery device that can be charged and carried to charge a mobile device in lieu of plugging that device into an outlet.

baud   The number of times an analog signal changes in 1 second. If a signal that is sent changes 600 times in 1 second, the device communicates at 600 baud. Today's signaling methods (modulation techniques, to be technically accurate) allow modems to send several bits in one cycle, so it is more accurate to speak of bits per second than baud.

`bcdedit`   A command that can modify the Windows boot settings.

BD (Blu-ray disc)   An optical medium with a higher data capacity than a CD or DVD.

BD-R (Blu-ray disc recordable)   A Blu-ray drive or disc to which information can be written to one time.

BD-RE (Blu-ray disc recordable erasable)   A Blu-ray drive or disc to which information can be written, erased, or rewritten.

be on time   A good work habit to have. If you are going to be late for work, contact your supervisor. If you are going to be late for a customer appointment, notify the customer.

belt   In an inkjet printer, the belt connects to the stepper motor and print head assembly to move the print head and ink cartridge from one side of the printer to the other side.

biometric device   A device used to authenticate someone based on one or more physical traits, such as a fingerprint, an eyeball (retina), or a hand, or a behavioral trait such as voice or signature.

biometric lock   A device that uses a physical trait such as a fingerprint, handprint, retina characteristics, or facial data points to allow access to a resource or location.

biometrics   The use of one or more devices that can authenticate someone based on one or more physical traits such as a fingerprint, an eyeball (retina), or a hand, or a behavioral trait such as voice or signature.

BIOS (basic input/output system)   A chip that contains computer software that locates the operating system, POST, and important hardware configuration parameters. Also called ROM BIOS, Flash BIOS, or system BIOS. Replaced with UEFI BIOS.

bit   An electrically charged 1 or 0.

BitLocker   A Microsoft utility that encrypts an entire disk volume, including operating system files, user files, and paging files. The utility requires two disk partitions at a minimum.

BitLocker To Go   A Microsoft application that can encrypt and password protect external drives and removable media that are 128 MB or larger.

black screen   In this situation, check the video cable, power to the display, and the video card, if installed. Use the *Safe Mode* or *Last Known Good Configuration* boot option.

blacklist   A method of denying access to a user, an app, a website, protocols, or devices into a company or particular network device.

blackout   A total loss of AC power.

blank screen on bootup   In this situation, check the video cable, power, motherboard, and CPU.

Blu-ray   A type of optical disc technology that uses a blue laser instead of a red laser (like the kind used in CD/DVD drives) to achieve higher disc capacities.

blue screen *or* blue screen of death   See *BSOD*.

Bluetooth   A wireless technology for personal area networks (PANs).

BNC connector (Bayonet Neill–Concelman connector)   A connector used on coaxial cable.

Bonjour   An Apple printer server that enables Apple and Windows devices to share printers without any configuration required.

boot   The process of a computer coming to a usable condition.

Boot Camp   A boot loading utility designed to assist with partitioning, installation, and support in running Windows on a Mac.

boot options   In the BIOS configuration settings, boot options prioritizes devices in the order in which the computer looks for boot files. Also known as boot drive order, boot sequence, or boot menu.

boot order   A setting within BIOS/UEFI to control the order in which the computer looks to devices for an operating system.

boot partition   A type of partition found in Windows that contains the operating system. The boot partition can be in the same partition as the system partition, which is the part of the hard drive that holds hardware-specific files.

boot process   The specific order a device goes through to power up, locate an operating system, and automatically load services and applications.

boot sector   Previously called DBR or DOS boot record, a section of a disk that contains information about the system files (the files used to boot the operating system).

boot sector virus   A virus program placed in a computer's boot sector code, which can then load into memory. When in RAM, the virus takes control of computer operations. The virus can spread to installed drives and drives located on a network.

boot volume   Holds the majority of the Windows operating system files. Can be the same volume as the system volume (which holds the Windows boot files.

bootrec   A Windows command used to repair and recover from hard drive problems.

botnet   A security attack in which software spreads from device to device because a hacker has control of computers called zombies.

bps (bits per second)   A measurement of speed.

BranchCache   A wide area network (WAN) bandwidth optimization technology.

bridge   A physical network device or software that connects two or more networks. It could connect a wireless network to a wired network. Bridges are part of the data link layer of the OSI model and part of the network access layer in the TCIP/IP model.

brightness   A measure of light output coming out of video equipment.

broadband   A networking technology in which the cable bandwidth is divided into multiple channels; thus, the cable can carry simultaneous voice, video, and data.

broadcast   See *broadcast address*.

broadcast address   An IP address that communicates with all devices on a particular network.

brownout   A loss of AC power due to overloaded electrical circuits.

browser   A program that views web pages across the Internet. Common web browsers are Internet Explorer, Microsoft Edge, Firefox, Chrome, and Safari.

browser redirect   An instance in which a hijacked browser sends a browser to a different web page. A browser redirect can also be malware or may install a rootkit that can act as a backdoor to the operating system.

brute force   A type of attack in which repeated attempts are made to try to gain access to a network device or stored material.

BSOD (blue screen of death)   In Windows, the monitor screen displays all blue, and the computer locks or is nonfunctional.

buffer memory   Memory installed in optical drives and hard drives that reduces transfer time when writing data to the drive by securing more data than requested and placing the data in the buffer. It holds the extra data in the drive and constantly sends data to the processor instead of waiting on the drive.

buffered memory   A type of memory in which the modules have extra chips (registers) that delay data transfers to ensure accuracy.

burn-in   An image imprint, or ghost image seen on a display screen when an LCD or plasma display has been left on too long.

burning smell   A symptom that there is something wrong with the power supply.

bus   Electronic lines that enable 1s and 0s to move from one place to another.

bus speed   The rate at which a computer pathway used for transmitting 1s and 0s operates.

BYOD (bring your own device)   A situation in which personal mobile devices are brought to the work environment and used on the wired or wireless network.

byte   8 bits grouped together as a basic unit.

C

c   A Linux command used to list the contents of the current working directory.

cable   Wired media used in networking or a type of Internet connection that could also be used to deliver video channels.

cable lock   A security device to prevent theft of a laptop.

cable management system   A system that helps keep network cables neat and organized. Ladder racks are a type of a cable management system.

cable modem   A modem that connects to the cable TV network.

cable select   A setting used on PATA IDE devices when a special cable determines which device is the master and which one is the slave.

cable stripper   A tool used to cut away the sheathing over a cable's copper wire. Also called a wire stripper.

cable tester   A tester that checks coaxial and UTP cable ends (depending on the model) to determine if cable terminals are suitable for use.

cache memory   Fast memory designed to increase processor operations.

CAD (computer-aided design)   A technology that uses software on a PC in order to create a plan for something.

calibrate (inkjet print head)   A print head alignment process that must be performed when installing the printer and when replacing the print head.

camera   A peripheral used to capture video.

cannot display to external monitor   In this situation, check the cable, use the proper Fn key, and ensure that the external monitor or projector is turned on.

CAPTCHA (completely automated public Turing test to tell computers and humans apart)   A technology used on web-based forms to prevent an attack where the form is filled out automatically and submitted multiple times to overwhelm the network device that hosts the form. The user is presented with randomized text or graphic and then required to input a response.

carriage   An internal inkjet printer part that carries the printhead.

Cat 5   Another name for Category 5 twisted pair cable that has a bandwidth maximum of 100 MHz, a maximum transmission speed of 100 Mb/s, and a 100-meter (328-foot) maximum cable distance.

Cat 5e   Another name for Category 5e twisted pair cable that has a bandwidth maximum of 100 MHz, a maximum transmission speed of 1,000 Mb/s, and a 100-meter (328-foot) maximum cable distance. This type of cable reduces crosstalk found in Cat 5 cable.

Cat 6   Another name for Category 6 twisted pair cable that with the Cat 6a specification has a bandwidth maximum of 500 MHz, a maximum transmission speed of 10,000 Mb/s, and a 100-meter (328-foot) maximum cable distance.

CCFL (cold cathode fluorescent lamp)   The older flat-panel backlight technology used before LED backlights were used.

cd   The same as the chdir command in Windows. Used from a Windows or a Linux/macOS command prompt to move into a different directory.

CD (compact disc)   A storage medium that holds up to 700 MB of data, such as audio, video, and software applications.

CD-ROM (compact disk read-only memory)   A type of drive that cannot write to a disc.

CD-RW (compact disc rewritable)   A CD drive that can write data multiple times to a particular disc.

CDFS (Compact Disc File System)   A file system for optical media.

cell phone   A mobile device used to make calls using the cellular network (or wireless network, if enabled) and optionally to run apps.

cell tower analyzer   Also called a cell signal analyzer, software that shows information about the cellular network and sometimes 802.11 wireless networks as well.

cellular   A type of network connection provided by a cell phone carrier that can also provide access to the Internet.

cellular card   Used to connect a laptop to a cell phone network.

CERT (Computer Emergency Response Team)   A group of people that are called in to handle a security incident.

certificate-based credential   An alternative to a user ID/password credential that can be provided by smart cards and other security devices that allows someone to access a website or an application and that is used in the corporate environment.

certificate of destruction   A security measure that provides proof that printed material or stored data has been destroyed.

change board   A group of individuals who approve IT projects within an organization.

change default admin user account password   A security best practice is to change the default admin user account password or create an account that has Administrator access and disable the default account.

change management   The formal process of systematically choosing and implementing business changes.

channel   A specific number that signifies the frequency used by a wireless device to transmit and receive. Also called a channel ID.

channel ID   Used in wireless networks to define the frequency used to transmit and receive.

charging   A laser printing imaging process that can also be known as conditioning. This process gets the drum ready for use by applying a uniform voltage on the drum surface by using a primary/main corona or a conditioning roller.

charging USB port   A port that can provide power to charge and run an unpowered attached device such as a flash drive.

Charms   A Windows 8/8.1 sidebar item that, when displayed, provides quick access to a particular function, such as Search, Share Content, Start Screen, Devices, and Settings.

checkpoint   In a virtualization environment, a copy or backup of the virtual machine (VM) at a particular point in time used to revert the VM to that point in time.

chip reader   A device that accepts cards that are inserted into the device in order to read data from the card or the chip on the card.

chipset   One or more motherboard chips that work with the processor to allow certain computer features, such as motherboard memory and capacity.

chkdsk   A program that locates clusters that are disassociated from the appropriate data file.

chmod   A Linux command that gives the file owner read, write, and execute permissions.

chown   A Linux command that changes ownership.

Chrome (OS) An operating system supported by Google and Google partners that is used on laptops.

CIDR (classless interdomain routing) A type of subnet mask that does not have a classful boundary. CIDR is a method of allocating IP addresses based on the number of host addresses needed for a particular network.

CIFS (Common Internet File System) A version of Server Message Block (SMB) that can provide access to shared network devices, files, and printers, especially in a mixed environment of MAC and Windows computers. SMB/CIFS use port 445.

cipher A Windows command used to decrypt, modify, or copy an encrypted file.

CL rating (column address strobe [CAS] latency rating) The amount of time (number of clock cycles) that passes before the processor moves on to the next memory address. Chips with lower access times (CL rating) are faster than those with higher access times (larger numbers).

clamping speed The time that elapses from an overvoltage condition to when surge protection begins.

clamping voltage The voltage level at which a surge protector begins to protect a computer.

clean install Loading of an operating system on a computer that does not already have one installed.

clean room A specifically constructed, climate-controlled (cool temperature and humidity of 45% to 60%) closed area with special air vents/filters, vacuums, blowers, and a circulation system that captures harmful/hazardous particulate matter, scrubs and diffuses the PM, and safely eliminates it while allowing the sensitive computer equipment to run.

cleaning A laser printing imaging process that describes removing residual toner from the drum by using a wiper blade or brush.

Cleanup tool A Windows utility that scans the drive volume to see what files might possibly be deleted. To run this tool, use cleanmgr from a prompt.

client-side DHCP The configuration required on a PC, printer, mobile device, or other device to enable that device to receive IP addressing information from a DHCP server.

client-side DNS A situation in which individuals or businesses configure their computer to use one or more Domain Name System (DNS) servers to translate uniform resource locators (URLs) into IP addresses.

clock An electronic component that provides timing signals to all motherboard components. A PC's clock is normally measured in MHz.

clock speed The rate at which timing signals are sent to motherboard components (normally measured in MHz).

closed source operating system A vendor-specific operating system, such as macOS for Apple devices only.

cloud-based application An application that loads some of the code needed to run so the application does not have to be installed locally. Also called virtual application streaming.

cloud-based network controller A device that controls network infrastructure devices such as switches or access points that is not housed within the company's network operation center but in the cloud.

cloud file storage service A remote storage option that might include synchronization of files and/or folders.

cloud printing Enables users to print in a remote location or from a wireless printer.

cloud storage Storage of data on a server that is located somewhere other than the home or company, usually a data center or cloud storage service provider.

cluster The minimum amount of space that one saved file occupies.

cmdlet A function used and associated with a particular operation when creating tasks within PowerShell.

CMOS (complementary metal oxide semiconductor) A special type of memory on a motherboard in which Setup configuration is saved.

CMOS battery A small, coin-shaped lithium battery that provides power to CMOS memory.

CNR (communications and networking riser) An older slot that allowed a network, analog modem, or audio card to be inserted.

coaxial A type of cabling used in video connections that has a copper core surrounded by insulation and shielding to protect against EMI.

cold boot The process that occurs when a computer is turned on with the power switch and executes POST.

collate In printing, complete copies of documents in numerical order one set at a time.

color depth The number of bits that control color and determine the maximum number of colors that can be displayed.

`command`   A command issued from the Run utility in Windows to bring up a command prompt window.

`command /?`   A command issued from the Run utility in Windows to list commands and options that are available for that particular command. Replace *command* with a particular command, such as `dir /?`.

command line interface   An operating environment that is not graphical and in which only typed commands are available.

command prompt   Otherwise known as a prompt, or command line interface (CLI) a text-based environment in which commands are entered.

command switch   An option used when working from a command prompt that allows a command to be controlled or operated on differently.

comment   In a script, a comment is used to explain what some part of the code does, but it is ignored by the computer when running the script.

commercial license   Software purchased for a specific number or users and machines.

community cloud   A type of cloud deployment model that is a combination of a private cloud and a public cloud.

CompactFlash (CF)   A type of removable flash memory storage that can be inserted into many devices, such as disk drives, cameras, mobile phones, and tablet PCs.

comparison operator   A function used in scripting to evaluate two values.

compatibility   A feature of hardware or software that allows functionality on multiple models.

Compatibility Mode   A Microsoft Windows tool used to emulate older operating systems so that older applications or hardware can be used on a newer operating system.

compiled program   Software that must be turned into machine language before it can execute.

component/RGB video   Three RCA jacks commonly found on TVs, DVD players, and projectors. One connection is for luminescence (or brightness), and two jacks are for color difference signals.

Component Services   A Microsoft Management Console snap-in that can configure and administer Component Object Model (COM) components, COM+ applications, and the Distributed Transaction Coordinator (DTC).

composite video   A yellow RCA port normally found on projectors, TVs, gaming consoles, stereos, and optical disc players.

compound condition   A situation in scripting in which two test conditions are contained in a single statement.

compressed air   A can of air whose top can be pressed to direct high-powered air that removes dust from hard-to-reach places such as under keys, under motherboards, and inside power supplies and devices.

compression   Compaction of a file or folder to take up less disk drive space.

Computer Management   A Windows tool that displays a large group of tools on one screen.

computer reboots   A symptom that something is wrong with the power supply, CPU, or motherboard.

COM*x*   A designation for a communications port, where the *x* represents a COM port number, such as COM1 or COM2.

conditioning roller   Used in a laser printer to generate a large uniform negative voltage to be applied to the drum.

Console   In macOS, a centralized place to find system and application logs and messages. It allows parsing manually or by searching for something specific.

construct   In the 1960s, scientists proved that all programming code can be done using three constructs: sequence, selection (or decision), and repetition (or loops).

content filtering   A device or software that screens data for suspect security risks.

context menu   A menu of options usually available from the main menu that is brought up by right-clicking an item.

continuity   An electrical resistance measurement to see if a wire is good or broken.

continuous ink system   A method of providing extra ink in an inkjet printer for heavily used printers.

continuous reboot   A symptom of a CPU, motherboard, or power supply problem.

Control Panel   A Windows utility that allows computer configuration such as adding or removing software, adding or removing hardware, configuring a screen saver, adjusting a monitor, configuring a mouse, installing networking components, and so on.

convergence   The use of the traditional data network for other type of traffic, like voice and video traffic (which used to have a network of their own).

`convert`   A command issued from a command prompt that changes an older file system into NTFS.

cookie   A program that collects information that is stored on a hard drive. This information could include your preferences when visiting a website, banner ads that change, or what websites you have visited lately.

`copy`   A command used from a command prompt to transfer one or more files from one place to another.

core   A central processing unit. CPUs are compared by the number of cores they contain.

Cortana   The name of the Windows 10 virtual assistant.

counter   A specific measurement for an object in the Windows System Monitor tool.

`cp`   A Linux command to copy a file. Short for copy.

cps (characters per second)   The number of characters a printer prints in 1 second.

CPU (central processing unit)   See *processor*.

CPU speed   The rate at which the CPU operates. It is the speed of the front side bus multiplied by the multiplier. Normally measured in GHz.

CPU throttling   Reducing the clock frequency to reduce power consumption.

CRC (cyclic redundancy check)   An advanced method of data error checking.

creased paper   Paper that does not feed properly through a printer; check paper size, fit, and manufacturer's specifications.

Credential Manager   Where Windows stores login credentials such as usernames, passwords, and addresses.

credit card reader   A small wired or wireless device that attaches to a mobile device to record point of sale transactions; some allow printed receipts, others allow an email input instead.

crimper   A tool that permanently attaches an RJ-45 or RJ-11 connector to a copper core cable.

critical application   Any application that is important to a family or to the success of a business that should be backed up as part of a disaster prevention/recovery plan.

crossover cable   Cabling that connects two like devices (for example, two computers, two switches, two routers).

crosstalk   A type of EMI in which signals from one wire interfere with the data on an adjacent wire.

CRT (cathode ray tube)   The main part of an older type of CRT monitor; the picture tube.

CSMA/CA (Carrier Sense Multiple Access/Collision Avoidance)   A common access method (set of communication rules governing networked devices) used in wireless and older Apple networks.

CSMA/CD (Carrier Sense Multiple Access/Collision Detection)   A common access method (set of communication rules governing all network devices) used by Ethernet.

CTS (clear to send)   Part of the RTS/CTS hardware handshaking communication method. Specific wires on the serial connector are used to send a signal to the other device to stop or start sending data. The CTS and RTS (request to send) signals indicate when it is okay to send data.

D

D-shell connector   A connector with more pins or holes on the top side than the bottom so that a cable inserts in only one direction. Examples include older parallel, serial, and video ports.

DaaS (Data as a Service)   A type of cloud service that provides data to a company.

DAC (Discretionary Access Control)   A security measure that applies security based on the group to which an object belongs.

Dash   The universal search tool built in the macOS Launcher bar. It searches local content as well as Internet sources, all of which can be enabled or disabled simply by opening up Dash.

data bits   A serial device setting for how many bits make up a data word.

data link layer   Layer 2 of the OSI model, which accurately transfers bits across the network by encapsulating (grouping) them into frames (usable sections).

data privacy   A security concern about whether measures are implemented that protect data being transmitted or stored.

Data Sources   Also called Data Sources ODBC (open database connectivity), a programming interface that allows applications to access data from a database.

data type   The value of a variable is stored in the computer's memory as a specific type of data. The number of data types vary from language to language but are normally some variation of numeric or alphanumeric value. The data type of a variable determines how much space is allotted in memory for the variable's value and determines what operations can be done with that data.

DB-25   A male port on very old motherboards and some networking equipment. Also known as a serial or RS-232 port.

DB-9   A male port on older motherboards, networking equipment, and projectors. Also known as a serial or RS-232 port.

DBaaS (Database as a Service)   A cloud-based service that allows a provider to host, organize, and manage stored data for a company (not strictly data storage, but handling one or more databases).

DBR (DOS boot record)   An area of a disk that contains system files.

DC (direct current)   The type of power a computer needs to operate.

DC jack   A part on a laptop where the external power brick attaches.

dd   In Linux, an advanced command line interface command that copies and converts files.

DDoS (distributed denial of service)   A type of security attack in which several computer systems are used to attack a network or device with the intent of preventing access such as to a web server.

DDR (Double Data Rate)   A memory technology in which the data was clocked on both the rising and falling edges of a clock signal to double the amount of data that could be transferred.

DDR RAM (Double Data Rate random-access memory)   A type of volatile memory that used DDR technology.

DDR2 (Double Data Rate 2)   An upgrade to the DDR SDRAM standard that sometimes is called DDR2 RAM. It includes the following modules: DDR2-400, DDR2-533, DDR2-667, DDR2-800, and DDR2-1000. DDR2 uses 240-pin DIMMs and is not compatible with DDR; however, the higher-end (faster) DDR2 modules are backward compatible with the slower DDR2 modules.

DDR3 (Double Data Rate 3)   An upgrade from DDR2 for speeds up to 1,600 MHz that better supports dual-core and quad-core processor-based systems.

DDR4 (Double Data Rate 4)   Operates at a lower voltage and faster speeds than DDR3 and lower modules.

dead pixel   A pixel on an LCD monitor that does not illuminate. Displays commonly have one or more of these.

decision structure   A decision (or selection) structure consisting of a test condition together with one

or more groups (or blocks) of statements. The result of the test condition determines which block of statements will be executed.

declaration   To create a variable in a script, it must be declared. The exact syntax of how to do this is known as a variable declaration.

decoder   In DVD drives, hardware or software that converts MPEG-2 video to readable images.

default gateway   The IP address of a Layer 3 device, such as a router, that is directly connected to its immediate network. It tells a device on its network where to send a packet destined for a remote network.

default printer   When a computer can use multiple printers, the one printer that all applications use by default. A computer user can change the printer to a different one through the Print dialog window. To mark a printer as default, right-click the printer icon and click the *Set as Default* option.

defrag   The Windows command line command that starts the defragmentation process of reordering and placing files in contiguous sectors for better performance.

defragment   To reorder files in contiguous clusters on the hard drive.

defragment the hard drive   See *defragment*.

defragmentation   A process of reordering and placing files in contiguous sectors.

degausser   A device that demagnetizes monitors. Also called a degaussing coil.

del   A command issued from a command prompt that deletes a file or folder.

density control blade   A part inside a laser printer's toner cartridge that controls the amount of toner released to the drum.

DEP (data execution prevention)   Software-based and hardware-based security measures to prevent malicious software from executing in specific memory locations.

desktop   The interface between the user and the applications, files, and hardware, which is part of the graphical user interface environment. It is the area in which all work is performed.

developing   A laser printer process in which toner is attracted to the laser printer drum.

developing cylinder   A component inside a laser printer's toner cartridge that applies a static charge to the toner so that it will be attracted to the drum. Sometimes called a developing roller.

device driver   Special software that allows an operating system to access a piece of hardware.

Device Manager   A Windows program that views and configures hardware.

Devices and Printers   A Windows Control Panel used to view, install, remove, and manage wired and wireless devices.

DFS (Distributed File System)   A Microsoft-provided set of network services that allow easy access to network shares.

DHCP (Dynamic Host Configuration Protocol)   A method to automatically assign IP addresses to network devices from a pool of IP addresses. DHCP uses ports 67 and 68.

DHCP reservation   One or more IP addresses set aside for specific network devices like routers, switches, and printers that need an IP address that does not change.

DHCP server   Software configured on a network server or router that issues IP addresses from its pool of numbers upon request to a network device.

dial-up   A type of connection in which one modem calls another modem.

dial-up network   A network formed by using a modem that connects to the traditional phone network. The modem connects to a remote network device.

dialog box   A window used by the operating system that allows user interaction to set preferences on various software parameters.

dictionary [attack]   A brute-force security attack that tries to determine a password by using words in a dictionary in order to gain access to data.

differential backup   A backup that backs up files that have changed since the last full backup (files that have the archive bit set to on) but in which the backup software does not reset the archive bit, as an incremental backup does.

digital assistant   A voice-activated device that answers questions or responds to commands.

digital signal   A signal using 1s and 0s to represent data.

digital signature   Confirms that the hardware or updated driver being installed is compatible with Windows; sometimes called driver signing.

digitizer   Provides input into documents such as architectural drawings, technical plans, and photos. It can also be used to draw electronic pictures.

dim display   In this situation, check display settings and the battery level. The display could require calibration.

dim image   A video condition in which little to no image displays on a laptop, but you can hear the hard drive. Reset the display to the factory default. May require replacing the inverter.

DIMM (dual inline memory module)   A style of 168-pin, 184-pin, 240-pin, or 288-pin memory chip normally used for RAM chips on Pentium and higher motherboards.

DIN (Deutsches Institut fur Normung)   A German connector standard originally used on the IBM PC and later modified to be smaller and known as a PS/2 or mini-DIN connector.

dir   A command used from a command prompt that displays the contents of a directory.

directional antenna   A type of antenna that radiates energy in a specific direction.

directory   In older operating systems, an electronic container that holds files and even other directories. Today's operating systems use the term *folder*.

directory permissions   A logical security method used when data is shared across a network or stored in one or more folders on a server.

DirectX   A Microsoft technology that integrates multimedia drivers, application code, and 3D support for audio and video.

disable a service   In Windows, use the *Services* option from within the Computer Management console in order to disable a service that might be causing issues.

disable account   In Active Directory, an alternative to deleting an account is to disable it and move it into a group of other disabled accounts.

Disable Autorun   A setting that dictates whether software or programs start automatically from discs, USB, or other drives.

Disable Execute Bit   When enabled in BIOS/UEFI, prevents executable code such as that found in viruses or other malware from loading into memory locations where operating system code resides.

disable guest account   A Windows security best practice.

disable unused ports   A security measure performed on network devices to protect ports in case the room where the device is located is compromised.

disable Windows application   Use the System Configuration utility *Startup* tab to disable applications that start automatically.

disappearing files   A symptom of malware.

disc   Optical media such as CDs, DVDs, and BDs.

disk   Media such as mechanical hard disk drives (HDDs) used to store data.

Disk Administrator   A Windows program that allows testing, configuration, and preventive maintenance on hard disks.

disk cache   A portion of RAM set aside for hard drive data that speeds up hard drive operations. A cache on a hard drive controller is also known as a data buffer.

Disk Cleanup   A Windows utility that helps free up hard drive space by emptying the Recycle Bin, removing temporary files, removing temporary Internet files, removing offline files, and so on.

disk duplexing   A technique that uses two disk controllers and allows the system to continue functioning if one hard drive fails. Data is written to both sets of hard drive systems through the two controllers. Disk duplexing is considered to be RAID level 1.

Disk Management   A Windows tool used to partition and manage hard drives.

disk mirroring   A process that protects against hard drive failure by using two or more hard drives and one disk controller. The same data is written to both drives. If one hard drive fails, the other hard drive continues to function. Disk mirroring is considered to be RAID level 1.

disk striping   Another name for RAID 0, in which data is alternately written on two or more hard drives, thus providing increased system performance.

Disk Utility   A powerful application that manages disks and images in macOS. The utility can rename, reformat, erase, repair, and restore disks. It should be approached with caution because the wrong usage could delete all data on the system or on an attached external disk.

diskpart   A command-based utility used in preparing hard disk partitions and volumes for use.

dism (Deployment Image Servicing and Management)   A Window utility used to repair and prepare Windows images.

display   A device that shows computer output. Also called a monitor.

DisplayPort   A port, developed by Video Electronics Standards Association (VESA), that can send and receive audio and video signals. Used primarily for display devices and can connect to a single-link DVI or HDMI port with the use of a converter.

distended capacitor   A bulging end or top of this small component indicates that it is time to change it or the component of which it is a part, including the motherboard.

distorted geometry   A video issue in which the screen looks unusual and is not centered correctly. Check video cables or set the display to factory defaults.

distorted image   Caused by broken or bent video pins on a display cable.

DLP (data loss prevention)   Software that protects corporate data from being sent outside the corporate network.

DLP (Digital Light Processing)   A technology used in projectors and rear-projection TVs that is an array of miniature mirrors that create pixels on a projection surface.

DLT (digital linear tape)   A type of magnetic tape storage used for data backup.

DMA (direct memory access)   A computer resource viewed through Device Manager that allows a particular device to access RAM without requesting permission from the CPU.

DMZ (demilitarized zone)   A network area that is separate from the corporate network but contains servers that are accessible to outside devices.

DNAT (destination network address translation)   A method of mapping a public IP address to a specific private IP address used in a home or small business network.

DNS (Domain Name System)   Translates Internet names into IP addresses. DNS uses port 53.

DNS configuration   A DHCP-provided or manual setting for the IP address of the DNS server that provides domain name translation, such as for web browsing.

DNS server   Application on network server that translates Internet names into IP addresses.

Dock   The shortcut organizational bar used for launching, switching, and managing applications in the macOS graphical user interface (usually the bar at bottom of screen).

docking station   A part that has connections for a monitor, printer, keyboard, and mouse that allows a laptop computer to be more like a desktop system. Sometimes called a mobile docking station or a laptop docking station.

document changes   The part of change management that creates a historical record of what changes occurred.

documented business processes   A set of business documents that relate to how things are supposed to be done or have been done in the past.

domain   A term used in Windows server-based networks where users are required to have logins, and file storage, email, and web-based services are commonly provided. A way of organizing user accounts and network devices in Microsoft's Active Directory service.

domain access   Allowing an account or a device onto a Microsoft corporate network.

door lock   A keyless entry option for a smart home that allows keyless entry. It is also important to have a door lock of any type on the room(s) that hold network infrastructure equipment such as routers and switches.

DoS (denial of service)   A type of security attack in which the intent is to make a machine or a network unusable.

dot matrix printer   See *impact printer*.

double-sided memory   A single memory module that contains two memory modules in one container (two banks). Data is still sent to the CPU 64 bits at a time. Some use the terms single-sided and double-sided to describe memory modules that have chips on one side (single-sided) or both sides (double-sided). Another name is double-ranked memory.

downstream   Describes information pulled from the Internet, such as when viewing web pages or downloading a file.

DPI (dots per inch)   A printer measurement used with inkjet and laser printers that refers to how many dots are produced in an inch.

DRAM (dynamic random-access memory)   One of two major RAM types, which is less expensive but also slower than SRAM. DRAM requires periodic refreshing of the stored 1s and 0s.

drive array   The use of two or more hard drives configured for speed, redundancy, or both.

drive encryption (BIOS)   A BIOS/UEFI setting that scrambles all the data on the hard drive as a security measure.

drive not recognized   A storage device error condition that indicates something is wrong with the physical settings, BIOS/UEFI settings, or cabling, or that there is a lack of power.

drive overwrite   A utility that rewrites the drive with all 1s or all 0s to prevent data from being recovered.

drive partition   A method of allocating space on a hard drive that is recognizable by the operating system.

drive status   A storage device state that can be viewed in Windows Disk Management.

drive wipe   A technique that can be used to eradicate personal or corporate data from a hard drive before donating or reusing a computer.

driver   See *device driver*.

driver rollback   A feature in Windows Device Manager that allows an older driver to be reinstalled when a new driver causes problems.

driver signing   A technology that verifies whether a driver has been digitally signed and approved to work with the specific Windows operating system environment.

DRM (digital rights management)   Technology used to implement controls placed on digital media.

DSL (digital subscriber line)   A type of Internet connection that uses a traditional phone line. A filter is needed on each phone outlet that has a normal analog device attached to separate the analog sound from the Internet data.

dual boot   Capability to boot from one of two installed operating systems.

dual-channel   A system in which the motherboard memory controller chip handles processing of memory requests more efficiently by handling two memory paths simultaneously.

dual-core   A type of processor that combines two CPUs in a single unit. Note there are now tri-core, quad-core, hexa-core, and even octa-core processors.

dual-link   A type of Digital Visual Interface (DVI) connector from the computer port to the display.

dual-rail power supply   Describes two +12-volt lines available in a power supply.

dual-voltage   A type of power supply that accepts either 115 V or 220 V input voltage.

dual-voltage memory   Motherboard memory modules that use less power and produce less heat if the motherboard supports this feature. Not all installed modules must support the lower voltage for the system to take advantage of the modules that do support the lower voltage.

dumpster diving   A social engineering type of threat in which someone digs through trash in or out of the office as a way to get information.

duplex   An assembly option that allows a printer to print on both sides of a paper without intervention. Duplex is also a NIC setting to choose between half (transmits in one direction at a time), full (transmits and receives simultaneously), or auto.

duplexing assembly   An option available on some printers to allow two-sided printing.

dust and debris   An unsafe condition for technicians to work in without an air filter or mask.

DVD (digital versatile disc *or* digital video disc)   A newer media technology than CDs but having less capacity than a Blu-ray disc.

DVD drive   A drive that supports CDs as well as music and video DVDs.

DVD-R   A technology created by Pioneer that allowed a disc to be written to once and read from repeatedly.

DVD-RAM (DVD random-access memory)   A technology that allows data to be written and rewritten. Contrast with DVD-RW and DVD+RW.

DVD-ROM   A technology that has a higher storage capacity than CDs and can only be read from (not written to).

DVD-RW (DVD-rewritable)   A type of read/write DVD format supported by the DVD Forum. Similar to DVD-R except you can erase and rewrite data. Uses 4.7 GB discs, and most DVD-ROM drives and DVD-video players support this format. Sometimes known as DVD-R/W or DVD-ER.

DVD-RW DL (DVD-rewritable dual layer)   A disc that has two physical layers on the same side of the disc.

DVD+RW (DVD-Rewritable)   A standard created by Phillips and Sony in an organization called the DVD+RW Alliance.

DVI (Digital Visual Interface)   A port on a digital video adapter that connects flat panel monitors to the computer.

DVI port   A port on a video adapter that connects flat panel monitors to the computer.

DVI-D   A type of video connector used with digital monitors.

DVI-I   The most common type of DVI video connector that is used with both analog and digital monitors.

DVI-to-HDMI adapter   A video connector with a DVI connector on one end and an HDMI connector on the other.

DVI-to-VGA adapter   A video connector with a DVI connector on one end and a VGA connector on the other.

dxdiag   A Windows command to access DirectX software that helps resolve DirectX display and sound driver problems.

dynamic disk   A Windows term for a volume that can be resized and managed without rebooting.

dynamic link library (DLL)   A type of file that contains reusable code used by multiple applications. A DLL must be registered with the Windows registry to function.

dynamic storage   A disk that has been configured for the Windows operating system that can be resized and managed without rebooting and contains primary partitions, extended partitions, logical drives, and dynamic volumes.

E

e-reader   An electronics device used to read digital media such as an e-book or e-mag.

Easy Transfer   A free application from Microsoft that copies files and operating system settings to another drive, removable media, over a network, or to another storage location.

ECC (error correcting code)   Uses a mathematical algorithm to verify data accuracy. ECC is more expensive than parity, and the motherboard or memory controllers must also have additional circuitry to process ECC.

echo off   A command used from a command prompt that prevents characters from displaying on the screen.

Edge   Windows 10 browser that is meant to replace Internet Explorer.

edit   A command that brings up a text editor. A text editor enables file creation and modification.

EEPROM (electrically erasable programmable read-only memory)   A non-volatile memory technology that can store a small amount of data. EEPROMs were previously used for computer BIOS. Flash memory is used today.

effective permissions   The final permissions granted for a particular resource. Folder permissions are cumulative—the combination of the group and the person's permissions. The deny permission overrides any allowed permission set for a user or a group. When

NTFS and shared folder permissions are both used, the more restrictive of the two becomes the effective permissions.

EFS (Encrypting File System) A Windows encryption feature in which only the authorized user may view or change a file encrypted with EFS.

EIDE (Enhanced Integrated Drive Electronics) Signifies two IDE connectors (four devices) and support of the ATAPI standard.

electrical fire safety Knowledge of how to extinguish an electrical fire using fire extinguisher Type A-B-C or fire extinguisher Type C.

electronic key card An alternative to a key for room or building access.

email filtering Security rules specific to email that process incoming messages before forwarding on to a specific user.

embedded system A computer that has a specific function within a larger system, such as in medical, manufacturing, or airport industries.

emergency notification Wireless emergency alert (WEA); a U.S. method of propagating an emergency announcement such as an amber alert, presidential announcement, or weather alert.

EMI (electromagnetic interference) Electronic noise generated by electrical devices.

EMP (electromagnetic pulse) A short burst of energy that can cause problems in electronic equipment.

emulator A technique used to make one operating system act like another operating system.

encryption A method of securing data from unauthorized users in which data is converted into an unreadable format.

end-user education A great security method to use because by educating users, security issues get reported and dealt with earlier with less damage to a company. Part of a technician's job might be to teach a user how to do something to avoid technical issues or to prevent security issues.

end-of-life A term used with hardware or software that typically means the vendor no longer supports the product.

end-point management server A centralized solution used for distributing software, configurations, security management, profile management, imaging/re-imaging computers, and inventory management.

end-user acceptance A part of change management in which the person who will use an IT system tests the changes to ensure that the deliverables or outcomes have been met.

end-user device configuration Every end-user device on a wired or wireless network must be configured with some basic settings, such as an IP address, default gateway, and subnet mask.

energy absorption/dissipation A surge protector feature. The greater number of joules that can be dissipated by the surge protector, the more effective and durable it is.

ENERGY STAR A set of energy efficiency standards including those related to total energy requirements and low power mode(s) and an efficiency standard that a product must meet to achieve this standard.

entry control roster A list of employees who are authorized in a particular area. Also called an access control roster.

environment variable A variable that describes the environment in which a program runs. It contains a name and a value, where the value is the path to the program identified by the variable name.

environmental enclosure A housing assembly that encloses a desktop or a laptop computer to protect it from particulate matter (PM) while allowing user access to a keyboard, a mouse, and other components.

EPEAT rating system A rating system that works with the Environmental Protection Agency (EPA) to identify products that have a green (and clean) design.

EPROM (erasable programmable read-only memory) A type of non-volatile memory (which means the contents remain when power is removed).

equality operator A method in scripting used to compare two values. Another name for comparison operator or equals operator.

equals operator A method in scripting used to compare two values. Another name for comparison operator or equality operator.

equipment grounding The components in a device such as a computer that are at the same voltage potential. Grounding is important to personal safety because consistent grounding minimizes the potential of voltages being applied to places it shouldn't be applied, such as the case. If a piece of equipment is not grounded, someone could receive a shock or be electrocuted simply by touching it.

GLOSSARY

erase lamp   A component inside a laser printer that neutralizes any charges left on the drum so that the next printed page receives no residuals from the previous page.

ERD (emergency repair disk)   A disk used with older Microsoft operating systems to start the computer and begin the operating system repair process.

Error Checking   A Windows tool that checks the drive for file system errors, bad hard drive sectors, and lost clusters.

error code   A code that may be displayed when a printer has inadequate memory or when a computer has a problem.

error correcting   A type of memory called error correcting code (ECC) memory that can correct memory errors on systems like servers and financial institution computers.

error message   An indication provided by a system or an application that should be noted to help in troubleshooting.

eSATA (External Serial ATA)   A port used to connect external SATA devices to a computer.

eSATA bracket   A part that installs into an empty expansion slot that has one or more eSATA ports. Each port on the bracket has a SATA cable that attaches to an available motherboard SATA port.

eSATA card   An adapter used to add external SATA ports so that external storage devices can be used. May include ports for internal SATA devices.

eSATA port   A nonpowered port used to connect external storage devices at a maximum of 2 meters (6 feet).

eSATAp port   A port that accepts both eSATA and USB connectors, which can provide power when necessary. Also known as eSATA/USB or power over eSATA.

ESCD (Extended System Configuration Data)   A specification that provides the BIOS and operating system a means for communicating with plug-and-play devices. As the computer boots, the BIOS records legacy device configuration information. Plug-and-play devices use this information to configure themselves and avoid conflicts. When an adapter has resources assigned and the resources are saved in ESCD, the resources do not have to be recalculated unless a new device is added to the computer.

ESD (electrostatic discharge)   Occurs when stored-up static electricity is discharged in an instantaneous surge of voltage. Cumulative effects of ESD weaken or destroy electronic components.

ESD mat   A pad that is placed on a surface to prevent electrostatic discharge events. Such a mat commonly has a place to attach an antistatic wrist strap.

ESD strap   An item that fits around a technician's wrist and connects to an electronic component so that the technician and the component are at the same voltage potential, thus preventing an electrostatic discharge event, which can cause damage to electronic components.

Ethernet   A network system that carries computer data along with audio and video information. Ethernet adapters are the most common network cards.

Ethernet over Power (EoP)   Also called powerline communication. Sends network data to EoP modules that are plugged into power outlets to extend Ethernet networks.

Ethernet port   An RJ-45 port that connects a device to the wired network.

EULA (end user license agreement)   Legal language that specifies what can and cannot be done with a particular software application or operating system.

Event Viewer   A Windows tool that monitors various events in the computer.

exabyte (EB)   1 billion times 1 billion bytes, or 2^{60} (1,152,921,504,606,800) bytes.

Exchange Online   An email option for mobile devices.

executable file   A file with a `.bat`, `.exe`, or `.com` extension that starts an application, a utility, or a command. A file on which the operating system can take action.

execute disable   An Intel feature that prevents malicious software from executing in specific memory locations.

exFAT   A file system type that improves upon FAT32 by having a theoretical maximum file size of 16 EB, maximum volume size of 64 ZB (but 512 TB is the current limit), smaller cluster sizes than FAT32, and an increased number of files allowed in a directory. Created for external storage media such as flash drives and hard drives for saving images/video.

exit   A command that closes the command prompt environment window.

expand   A command used to uncompress a file from a CAB file.

expansion slot   A motherboard socket into which adapters are connected.

Explorer A Windows-based application that details certain information for all folders and files on each drive. It is used most commonly to copy or move files and folders. Sometimes called Windows Explorer or, in recent versions of Windows, File Explorer.

exposing A laser printer imaging process that has also been called the writing phase. Light is directed toward the drum to put 1s and 0s on the drum surface. Everywhere the light hits the drum changes the drum surface voltage.

ext2 (Second Extended File System) An old file system used in Linux-based operating systems.

ext3 (Third Extended File System) A file system type used in Linux-based operating systems that introduced journaling.

ext4 (Fourth Extended File System) A file system type used in Linux-based operating systems that supports larger volumes and file sizes than ext3.

extend (partition) The act of making a partition larger.

extended partition A hard drive division.

extending partition (Disk Management) Increasing the size of a partition by right-clicking on the drive letter and selecting *Extend Volume*.

extensible software Software that is easily upgraded.

extension In operating systems, the three or more characters following the filename and a period (.). The extension associates the file with a particular application that executes the file.

external data bus The electronic lines that allow a processor to communicate with external devices. Also known as an external data path or external data lines. See also *bus*.

external data lines See *external data bus*.

external hard drive (boot option) An operating system boot option when a USB or eSATA drive is used.

external shared resources In cloud computing, resources such as servers, applications, hardware such as CPUs and RAM, data storage, and network infrastructure equipment that are shared between organizations through an external vendor.

external storage device A peripheral that attaches to a computer used for saving data.

extremely short battery life In this situation, possibly replace the battery and also close apps and services that are not being used.

F

F connector A type of coaxial cable terminal end that simply screws into the receiving connector.

facial recognition lock A type of security lock on a mobile device or computer that uses the integrated camera and stored data to determine whether someone is granted access to the computer.

factory recovery partition A drive partition that contains files and folders including the operating system, drivers, and preinstalled programs that is used when a system must be rebuilt, restored, or re-created or when troubleshooting Windows problems.

factory reset An option to reset a computing device back to original settings.

faded print A condition that arises due to inadequate ribbon, ink level, or toner. Check quality settings. In a thermal printer, reduce the print head energy or print head pressure setting.

fail to boot An error condition that occurs when a boot device such as a hard drive is not responding.

failed attempts lockout A Windows feature that locks out a user after a specific number of failed login attempts.

failure to boot A Windows condition that may require operating system repairs or reload.

fan A mechanical cooling device attached to or beside the processor or in the case.

FAT (File Allocation Table) A method of organizing a computer's file system.

FAT (file system type) A file system type also known as FAT16.

FAT12 An old file system that was originally designed for floppy disks.

FAT16 A file system supported by DOS and all Windows versions since DOS. DOS and Windows 9x have a 2 GB limit. Newer Windows operating systems have a 4 GB FAT16 partition size limit.

FAT32 A file system that supports hard drives up to 2 TB in size.

fault tolerance The capability to continue functioning after a hardware or software failure. An example of fault tolerance with hard drives is RAID configurations.

FCM (flash cache module) Predicts what data is used and puts that data on an SSD that is separate from the mechanical hard drive.

GLOSSARY

FDD (floppy disk drive)   A piece of hardware used to store data on a 3.5-inch magnetic disk (or wider for really, really old computers).

FDDI (Fiber Distributed Data Interface)   A high-speed fiber network that uses the ring topology and token passing access method.

feed assembly   The part of a computer responsible for taking the paper through the printer.

feeder   On a printer, a device that rolls the paper through the paper tray.

fiber   A type medium or Internet connection that carries data using light.

fiber cable   An expensive network cabling made of plastic or glass fibers that carry data in the form of light pulses. Handles the greatest amount of data with least amount of data loss. Comes in single mode and multi-mode.

fiber network   High-speed, high-capacity computer network composed of fiber-optic cables.

FIFO setting   A serial device setting that enables or disables the UART's buffer.

file   An electronic container holding data or computer code that serves as a basic unit of storage.

File History   A Windows tool that allows backing up a specific user's libraries instead of the entire system and supports scheduling these backups.

file permission change   A symptom of malware.

file recovery software   An application used to recover data from a storage device.

file server   A computer configured to store files that can be accessed and managed from a remote location.

file system   Defines how data is stored on a drive. Examples of file systems include FAT16, FAT32, exFAT, and NTFS.

file type   A specific type of file based on the application that created it. For example, a .txt file created in Word is a different file type than an Acrobat reader .pdf file.

file-level backup   A method of backup that involves backing up files one file at a time. Contrast with image-level backup.

filename   The name of a file. In older operating systems, the filename was limited to 8 characters plus a 3-character extension. Today's operating systems allow filenames up to 255 characters.

Finder   Finder is used for navigating and managing files or folders in the file system. It is similar to Microsoft's Windows Explorer/File Explorer.

fingerprint lock   A type of security lock on mobile devices and computers that requires a valid and stored fingerprint to be matched with the fingerprint of the person trying to gain access.

fingerprint reader   A biometric device used for user identification.

firewall   Software or a hardware device that protects one or more computers from being electronically attacked. It inspects data for security purposes and filters traffic based on network protocols and rules established by a network administrator. Firewalls operate at the application layer of the OSI model.

firmware   A combination of hardware and software attributes. An example is a BIOS chip that has instructions (software) written into it.

firmware updates   Also known as flashing the BIOS, obtaining and installing updates to the BIOS/UEFI so that the latest options or security patches are applied.

fitness monitor   A wearable mobile device.

flash BIOS   A type of motherboard memory that allows updates by disk or by downloading Internet files.

flash memory   A type of non-volatile memory that holds data when the power is off.

flatbed scanner   A peripheral used to digitize a photo or text.

flickering display   In this situation, check the resolution, refresh rate, and video cable. Move the display to see if the flicker is related to display movement.

flickering image   The display has something on it that appears and then disappears. In this situation, check the video cable.

floating-point number   Numbers that can be written in the form $x \div y$, which means they are numbers that include a decimal value, even if that value is 0. For example, the number 7 is an integer, but the number 7.0 is a floating-point number.

flow control   A serial device setting that determines the communication method.

folder   In Windows-based operating systems, an electronic container that holds files as well as other folders. It is also called a directory.

folder redirection   A feature of Microsoft Active Directory that maps a folder on the local machine to a network location such as a server so the user has access to the folder from any device on the network domain.

`for loop`   A shorthand way to write a `while` loop.

Force Quit   The macOS feature used to stop a program when it stops responding or working correctly.

form factor   The shape and size (height, width, and depth) of motherboards, adapters, memory chips, power supplies, and so on. Before building or upgrading, make sure the device's form factor fits the computer case.

`format`   A command that prepares a disk for use.

formatted (disk)   A disk that has been prepared to accept data.

forward compatibility   A design feature in software that means a system should be able to accept input intended for a later version.

FQDN (fully qualified domain name)   The full path for a specific device on a network that includes the domain name and the network device name (hostname). An example is `webmail.fscj.edu`, where `webmail` is the hostname for a mail server, and `fscj.edu` is a web domain for a college in Florida.

fragmentation   Occurs over time as files are saved on the hard drive in clusters not adjacent to each other, which slows hard disk access time.

frame   The encapsulated data found at Layer 2 of the OSI model.

frequency response   The number of samples taken by a sound card.

frequency response range   The range of sounds a speaker can reproduce.

front panel connector   A connector found on the motherboard that can have a cable that attaches from the motherboard to the front panel of the computer.

frozen system   On a frozen mobile device, check brightness, sleep mode, misbehaving app, lid close sensor, and battery. Also check for malware.

FRU (field replaceable unit)   Describes a computer part that can be replaced without having to send the entire computer to the manufacturer.

FSB (front side bus)   Part of the dual independent bus that connects the CPU to the motherboard components.

FTP (File Transfer Protocol)   A standard used when transferring files from one computer to another across a network.

full backup   A method of backing up a hard drive in which the archive attribute is used. The backup software backs up all selected files and sets the archive bit to off.

full device encryption   A security measure on mobile devices that supports encoding or scrambling all user data.

full duplex   A serial device setting that allows the sending and receiving devices to send data simultaneously. On a cable, the capability to transmit data in both directions simultaneously.

full format   During an installation process to partition a hard drive, this option identifies and marks bad sectors on the drive so they will not be used for data storage. Contrast with quick format.

function key   A function (Fn) key that, when used with another key, provides a specific function such as turning up speakers, connecting to an external monitor, or turning on the wireless adapter. This key is commonly found on laptops.

fuser assembly   Found in a laser printer; melts the toner onto the paper.

fusing   A laser printing process in which toner is melted into the paper.

G

game controller   A device used to play games and control items or characters within the game.

game pad   A device that attaches to a USB port and interacts with games.

gaming PC   A computer design that includes a powerful processor, high-end video or specialized GPU, an SSD, a good sound card, and high-end cooling due to the demands placed on hardware when playing computer-based games.

garbled characters   A printed output indication that the printer cable is not securely attached or a print driver problem exists.

gateway   An IP address assigned to a network device that tells the device where to send a packet that is going to a remote network. Also known as a default gateway or a gateway of last resort.

Gb   An abbreviation for gigabit.

GB   See *gigabyte*.

GDDR (graphics double data rate)   A type of memory used on video cards.

GDI (graphics device interface)   A part of Windows that allows graphics and text to be formatted so it can be output to different devices, such as a monitor or printer.

GDPR (General Data Protection Regulation)   A European Union (EU) security standard developed to protect individuals and firms within the EU.

generic credentials   Authorizations provided by applications such as OneDrive or Xbox Live to an operating system like Windows.

geotracking   The ability to track where a GPS-capable mobile device, such as a cell phone, is located. Companies can also use geotracking to locate lost or stolen mobile devices.

gestures   On a touch device, finger motions (swipe, pinch, tap, spread, and so on) used to manipulate applications or features.

ghost cursor   A situation in which the pointer moves across the screen even if no one is touching the input device. Commonly caused by improper touchpad sensitivity settings, outdated drivers, or malware.

ghost image   A burn-in; an image seen on a display screen when an LCD or a plasma display has been left on for too long.

gigabyte   Approximately 1 billion bytes of information (exactly 1,073,741,824 bytes); abbreviated GB.

gigahertz   1 billion cycles per second (1 GHz). Expresses the speed of a processor.

glasses   Wearable mobile device.

gloves   Latex, nonlatex, neoprene, or vinyl protection for hands when working on electronic equipment.

Google/Inbox   An email option for mobile devices.

Google Play   A feature on Android devices that enables users to purchase applications.

GParted   Bundled with Ubuntu, a disk management tool that allows the creation, deletion, and resizing of partitions on a physical disk.

gpresult   A command that displays Group Policy settings. A Group Policy determines how a computer is configured for both system and user (or a group of users) settings.

GPS (Global Positioning System)   A satellite-based navigation system that transmits location information to receivers in mobile devices. Most mobile devices have GPS capability.

GPS not functioning   In this situation, check reception, ensure GPS is on the device, ensure GPS is enabled, and try turning the device off and back on again.

GPT (GUID [globally unique identifier] partition table)   A type of partition table available in 64-bit Windows editions. GPTs can have up to 128 partitions and volumes up to 18EB.

GPU (graphics processing unit)   A video adapter processor that assists in video communication between the video adapter and the system processor. Also known as video processor, video coprocessor, or video accelerator.

gpupdate   A command used to refresh local and Active Directory–based Group Policy settings.

graphic/CAD/CAM design workstation   A powerful computer system utilized by design engineers or graphic designers. It usually has multicore processors, high-end video cards with maximum GPU and video RAM, large displays, a large-capacity hard drive and SSD, and maximum system RAM. Uses output devices such as scanner, plotter, or 3D printer.

graphical interface fails to load   A Windows startup problem in which startup files are missing or corrupt or there are hardware problems.

grep   A common Linux utility that searches output for a specified term.

grounding   Also called grounding out, occurs when the motherboard or adapter is not installed properly and has a trace touching the computer frame.

Group Policy   A type of security policy applied in a network domain environment. The policy dictates what a set of users can do.

GRUB (Grand Unified Boot Loader)   A Linux bootloader that generally replaces the earlier LILO bootloader. It contains all information about how a disk is organized, such as the size and layout of partitions. The latest version is called GRUB2.

GSM (Global System for Mobile Communications)   An older worldwide cellular network standard previously used in Europe and other places (and still used in some countries).

GUI (graphical user interface)   In operating systems, an interface in which the user selects files, programs, and commands by clicking pictorial representations (icons) rather than typing commands at a command prompt.

GUID (globally unique identifier)   A unique number used by a Windows operating system to keep track of specific items being used or controlled by the OS.

gyroscope   A technology used in mobile devices that measures and maintains screen orientation. Used with an accelerometer so that a mobile device can be turned and the screen orientation also turns.

H

HAL (hardware abstraction layer) A connection between hardware devices and parts of the operating system.

half duplex A serial device setting that enables either the sending or the receiving device to send data, one device at a time. On a cable, the capability to transmit in both directions but not at the same time.

handshaking The method by which two serial devices negotiate communications.

hard drive A sealed data storage medium on which information is stored. Also called a hard disk.

hard drive caching Data sent to and stored on a PC's hard drive.

hard reset Describes turning a device off and back on or a factory reset of a mobile device.

hardware A tangible, physical item, such as the keyboard or monitor.

hardware token A physical device used to gain access to a resource such as a file or company.

HAV (hardware-assisted virtualization) A required feature of Microsoft's Windows Virtual PC and Hyper-V. This feature is available on some computers and can be enabled or disabled through the system BIOS.

HCL (hardware compatibility list) A list of devices that is compatible with a particular operating system.

HDCP (High-bandwidth Digital Content Protection) A technology used to prevent copying of audio and video discs as the data travels through a video port such as a DP, DVI, or HDMI port.

HDD (hard disk drive) A mechanical drive with metal platters used to store data.

HDMI (high-definition multimedia interface) An upgraded digital interface that carries audio and video over the same cable.

head crash Occurs when a read/write head touches a platter in a mechanical hard drive, causing damage to the heads or the platter.

headset A mobile wearable device that commonly has a microphone and headphones.

heat sink A metal device for cooling the processor by conducting heat to its fins or bars. Convection then transfers the heat away by flowing air through the case.

heat spreader Aluminum or copper fittings on memory modules used to dissipate heat.

help A command used to list all of the available commands.

hertz A measurement of electrical frequency equal to 1 cycle per second. Abbreviated Hz.

hexa-core A six-core processor.

HFS (Hierarchical File System) A type of file system used with Apple computers that has been upgraded to HFS+ and then later upgraded to Apple File System (APFS).

hibernate mode A low-power state used in computing devices that saves information in RAM to nonvolatile memory such as a hard drive or flash media.

hidden share A share that has a dollar sign ($) added to the share name so that the share is not shown to a remote networked computer.

high-level format A process that sets up the file system for use by the computer. It is the third and last step in preparing a hard drive for use.

high resource utilization A situation in which a mobile device is slow to respond due to applications taking all the memory and processor power.

HIPS (host intrusion prevention system) Software on a device used to detect malicious activity.

HomeGroup A Windows 7 and higher feature to make home networking easier to configure and join. HomeGroups were removed from Windows 10 (Version 1803) and later versions.

home folder A network folder that allows users to store their files and have access to them from any device that they log onto within the same domain.

home server A server commonly used to act as a web server and print server, control home devices, manage backups, and be accessed from outside the home. A home server commonly includes the capability to stream sound or video, share files, have a Gigabit NIC, or have a RAID hard drive array.

horizontal streaking Occurs in a laser printer; may be due to insufficient toner levels in the cartridge.

host Another name for a network device. It also represents a part of an IP address. An IP address has a network portion and a host portion.

host address A portion of an IP address that represents the specific network device.

host machine In a virtualization environment, the real computer.

hot fix   Software that has one or more files that fix a particular software problem. Contrast this to a patch or a service pack.

hot swappable   Describes hardware that can be installed while power is applied.

hot swapping   Inserting adapters into a slot or attaching or unattaching devices while the computer is powered.

hotspot   A wireless network that has free Internet access. Security is a concern because no encryption or authentication is commonly required.

HPA (Host Protected Area)   A hidden part of the hard drive that is used to reinstall the operating system. It sometimes contains applications that installed when the computer was sold. Using an HPA reduces the amount of hard drive space available to the operating system.

HPFS (High Performance File System)   An old file system used with IBM OS/2 computers.

HT   See *Hyper-Threading*.

HTML (Hypertext Markup Language)   A programming language used to create Internet web pages.

HTPC (home theater PC)   A computer used to control devices contained in a home theater, such as the speaker system, TV, and video recorder.

HTTP (Hypertext Transfer Protocol)   A standard for Internet data communication.

HTTPS (HTTP over SSL)   HTTP communication encrypted through an SSL session. With HTTPS, web pages are encrypted and decrypted.

hub   A device used with the universal serial bus or in a star network topology that allows multiple device connections. A network hub cannot look at each data frame coming through its ports like a switch does. It forwards data frames (packets) to all ports.

humidity   The amount of moisture is in the air. The potential for an electrostatic discharge (ESD) event is higher when the humidity is low.

hybrid cloud   A type of cloud technology in which the company has some cloud services maintained by internal staff (private cloud) and some cloud services that are outsourced (public cloud).

hybrid drive   A storage device that uses two technologies: a mechanical hard drive and flash memory used as an SSD.

hybrid SSD   A drive that has two parts: a mechanical hard drive as well as flash memory used as an SSD.

Hyper-V   A hypervisor for running virtual machines inside Windows.

Hyper-Threading (HT)   A technology created by Intel that is an alternative to using two processors. HT allows a single processor to handle two separate sets of instructions simultaneously.

HyperTransport   AMD's I/O architecture in which a serial-link design allows devices to communicate in daisy-chain fashion without interfering with any other communication. Thus, I/O bottleneck is mitigated.

hypervisor   In a virtualization environment, the software that creates the virtual machine (VM) and allocates resources to the VM. Also called a virtual machine monitor or virtual machine manager (VMM).

I

I/O (input/output)   A way to describe data flow going into and out of a computing device.

I/O address (input/output address)   A port address that allows an external device to communicate with the microprocessor. It is analogous to a mailbox number.

I/O shield   A part that allows for optimum air flow and grounding for the motherboard ports.

IaaS (Infrastructure as a Service)   A type of cloud technology service that describes routers, switches, servers, virtual machines, load balancers, access points, storage, and any other infrastructure device that is provided through the online environment.

iCloud (offsite data storage and email option)   An Apple cloud-based service that comes with macOS, offering storage, application support, and syncing of contacts, photos, email, bookmarks, documents, and more between multiple macOS, iOS, and even Windows devices.

ICMP (Internet Control Message Protocol)   A Layer 3 protocol used for troubleshooting network connectivity. Commands that use ICMP include `ping`, `pathping`, and `tracert`.

icon   An operating system graphic that represents a file, an application, hardware, and shared network resources.

ICR (intelligent character recognition)   A technology that allows text and handwriting to be identified, processed, and input into a computer.

IDE (Integrated Drive Electronics)   An interface that evolved into the ATA (now PATA) standard that supports internal storage devices.

IDE cable   Another name for a PATA cable, an older 40-pin parallel cable that could have two devices attached to the same cable that connects to the motherboard.

IDE connector   A motherboard connector used to attach a cable between the connector and a PATA IDE drive.

IDS (intrusion detection system)   Software or hardware that is designed to detect potential security issues that could allow an illegal entry to the computer or network. The IDS could log the incident and contact someone in order to prevent invasion.

IEEE (Institute of Electrical and Electronics Engineers)   An organization that provides a framework for defining standards related to computers and networks.

ifconfig   In Linux/Unix environments, a command that shows network interface information for Ethernet ports.

IGP (integrated graphics processor)   Sometimes called an iGPU, speeds up video processing.

iGPU (integrated graphics processing unit)   See *integrated graphics processing unit*.

IIS (Internet Information Services *or* Internet Information Server)   An older type of server software used to host web pages.

image deployment   An operating system installation method in which a system image is taken from an external drive, disc, or server and put on a computer.

image management software   Software used for creating, storing, modifying, and deploying one file that could include the operating system as well as applications.

image-level backup   A method of backup that backs up the entire computer, including the operating system, applications, and data. Contrast with file-level backup.

imaging drum   A photosensitive drum located inside a toner cartridge; attracts laser toner particles.

IMAP (Internet Mail Access Protocol)   A protocol used to receive email through the Internet. Uses port 143 by default.

IMEI (International Mobile Equipment Identity)   A unique serial number given to a cell phone or possibly a satellite phone that is used to identify the device.

impact paper   Special paper designed to withstand the pressure of images struck upon it.

impact print head   Holds tiny wires called print wires; found in impact printers.

impact printer   Sometimes called a dot matrix printer. A type of printer that physically impacts a ribbon that places an image on the paper.

impersonation   A social engineering security threat in which someone pretends to be from your bank or a company such as Microsoft to get you to divulge information or gain access.

IMSI (International Mobile Subscriber Identity)   A unique number that is stored in a smartphone's subscriber identification module (SIM) card. It is used to identify the subscriber of the device.

in-place upgrade   A method of upgrading Windows when an older Windows version is already installed.

incident documentation   The part of a technician's job to provide details on what has been done about a particular problem.

incineration   Destruction by fire.

incorrect color pattern   A problem caused by bent or broken video pins on a monitor's cable ends.

incremental backup   A method used with a full backup. The incremental backup goes faster because it backs up only files that have changed since the last backup.

indexing   A Microsoft Windows configurable feature that allows quick searches for files and folders.

indicator lights   Used for troubleshooting a computer and controlled by the POST.

infrared   A technology utilizing infrared light that allows devices to communicate across a wireless network. Examples are laptop computers, printers, and handheld computing devices.

infrastructure mode   A type of wireless network that contains an access point for wireless devices to be connected together.

inherited permissions   A Windows NTFS permission type that is propagated from what Microsoft calls a parent object. For example, if a folder is given the permission Read, then all files within that folder inherit the read-only attribute.

initialization   The process in which a variable in a script is given an initial value.

initialize disk   A disk option available through the Windows Disk Management tool that enables a disk so that data may be stored on it.

initializing (Disk Management) Making a drive available to be used by right-clicking on a drive > *Initialize Disk.*

ink cartridge A container that holds the ink and the nozzles for an inkjet printer. Also known as a print cartridge.

inkjet print head Holds the ink reservoir and the spray nozzles; easily replaced.

inkjet printer A type of printer that squirts ink through tiny nozzles to produce print. Inkjet printers produce high-quality, high-resolution, color output.

input A method used to put data into a device or program.

integer A whole number, including zero and negative numbers.

integrated GPU (graphics processing unit) Speeds up video processing with reduced power consumption.

Intel Corporation The largest processor manufacturer in the world. Intel also makes chipsets, motherboards, network cards, microcontrollers, and other electronic chips and components.

interface A go-between, such as an operating system between the user and the computer or an interface between a specific application and the hardware.

interface configuration A BIOS/UEFI configuration category. May also be shown as an individual interface and listed separately (for example, IDE, SATA, PCI, or PCIe configuration).

intermittent connectivity A symptom of poor or faulty connections with devices on the same network. Use the `ping` command to check connections all around the network.

intermittent device failure A symptom of a faulty device when sporadic or irregular problems occur with that device.

intermittent wireless In this situation, turn off WiFi and turn it back on again. Move the device to see if you get a higher signal strength (display on a laptop).

internal data bus The electronic lines inside a processor. See also *bus.*

internal fixed disk (boot option) An operating system boot option that boots from a partition on an internal hard drive.

internal hard drive partition (boot option) An operating system boot option that boots from a bootable partition.

internal shared resources In cloud computing, resources such as servers, applications, hardware such as CPUs and RAM, data storage, and network infrastructure equipment that are shared among people within an organization.

internal USB connector One or more connectors on a motherboard that allows a cable to connect from the motherboard to the front panel or from the motherboard to a piece that has one or more USB ports on a plate that fits into an expansion slot place, but do not have an adapter that fits into the expansion slot.

Internet appliance Any device that can connect to the Internet through a wired or wireless network.

Internet calling Communicating using the Internet and an app such as Skype, Google Hangouts, or WhatsApp.

interpreted program Code that is carried out one line at a time.

interrupt See *IRQ.*

intrusion detection/notification Also known as chassis intrusion, this option provides notification when the computer cover is removed. It is enabled/disabled through the BIOS/UEFI.

inventory management A system sometimes included as part of a help desk software application or network management application that is used to keep track of hardware and network devices.

inverter Converts low DC voltage to high AC voltage for the backlight bulb in an LED display.

IOPS (input/output operations per second) A measurement of hard drive speed for both magnetic drives and SSDs that takes into account sequential reads/writes and random reads/writes.

iOS An Apple operating system for mobile devices.

IoT (Internet of Things) A phrase to describe the technology wave that includes sensors and smart devices to provide data, information, warnings, and control of things like lights, cameras, appliances, thermostats, and locks.

IP (Internet Protocol) A Layer 3 protocol that is part of the TCP/IP protocol suite.

IP address A type of network adapter address used when multiple networks are linked. Known as a Layer 3 address, in IPv4 it is a 32-bit binary number with groups of 8 bits separated by a dot. This numbering scheme is also known as dotted-decimal notation. Each 8-bit group represents numbers from 0 to 255. An example of an IPv4 IP address is 113.19.12.102. Also see *IPv4* and *IPv6.*

IP address conflict A situation in which two devices have been manually assigned the same IP address. Check any device that has a manually configured IP address for any duplicate IP address.

ipconfig A command used from a command prompt in Windows to view the current IP configuration settings.

IPP (Internet Printing Protocol) A protocol used for network-connected printers that can include remote print job management and print configuration such as media size or print resolution.

IPS (intrusion prevention system) A security device that actively monitors and scans network traffic for malicious traffic and violations of security policies as well as takes appropriate action.

IPsec (Internet Protocol Security) A suite of protocols for securing a communication session such as a VPN tunnel.

IPv4 (Internet Protocol version 4) A type of IP address that uses 32 bits (four groups of 8 bits each) shown as decimal numbers in dotted-decimal format. An example of an IPv4 address is 192.168.10.1.

IPv6 (Internet Protocol version 6) A type of IP address that uses 128 bits represented by hexadecimal numbers. An example of an IPv6 IP address is fe80::13e:4586:5807:95f7. Each set of four digits represents 16 bits.

IR (infrared) A technology used for wireless input/output that is useful only over short distances.

IrDA (Infrared Data Association) An industry group that creates standards related to wireless infrared communications.

IRP (incident response plan) A documented method of what is to be done if a security event occurs.

IRQ (interrupt request) A microprocessor priority system that assigns a number to each expansion adapter or port to facilitate orderly communication.

ISA (Industry Standard Architecture) An old type of expansion slot used in the original IBM PC.

ISDN (Integrated Services Digital Network) A digital phone line that has three separate channels: two B channels, and a D channel. The B channel allows 64 Kb/s transmission speeds. The D channel allows 16 Kb/s transmissions.

ISO (Industry Standards Organization or International Organization for Standardization) An international group that provides technical specifications related to computers, networks, and telecommunication.

isotropic antenna A type of antenna used as a reference for other antennas. It is not a real antenna. An isotropic antenna theoretically transmits an equal amount of power in all directions.

ISP (Internet service provider) A vendor that provides a connection to the Internet.

iteration A programming loop that consists of a block of statements that are executed repeatedly for a specific number of times or until a specific condition is met.

iTunes An Apple program that allows users to play and manage music, books, movies, and lectures.

ITX A motherboard form factor size that is smaller than ATX, the most common form factor. Comes in mini-ITX, nano-ITX, and pico-ITX sizes.

iwconfig In Linux/Unix systems, a command that shows network interface information for wireless adapters.

iWork A macOS office productivity suite containing a word processor, a spreadsheet, and presentation applications.

J

.js A file extension used with JavaScript files.

jailbreaking Compromising the operating system so the user has an increased level of privilege on an iOS mobile device.

JavaScript A programming language that can be run on any operating system. Creating and running command line JavaScript requires installing Node.js. The extension that identifies a JavaScript file is .js.

JBOD (just a bunch of disks or just a bunch of drives) A term given to combining more than one drive that is recognized as a single drive letter or a single virtual disk. This is similar in concept to RAID but is not one of the RAID levels.

joule dissipation capacity A measure of a surge protector's capability to absorb overvoltage power surges. The higher the capacity, the better the protection.

joystick A device that attaches to a USB port and is used to interact with games.

jumper A plastic cover for two metal pins on a jumper block.

K

Kb   Abbreviation for kilobit.

KB   See *kilobyte*.

KB (knowledge base)   A collection of documents related to a particular subject. In IT, these documents provide step-by-step procedures for technicians and/or users in support of specific hardware, operating systems, or apps.

kernel   The heart of an operating system, which acts as the controller and interpreter for nearly everything in a system so that hardware and software can interface and work together. It controls memory management, peripherals, and allocating other system resources to processes.

kernel panic   A critical system error that the operating system cannot recover from. When this happens in macOS, the Mac reboots to return to a stable state.

key fob   Used for keyless entry.

Key Management Service (KMS)   See *KMS*.

keyboard   Allows users to provide input into the computer.

keyboard port   A DIN connector on the motherboard into which only the keyboard cable must connect.

Keychain Access   A macOS utility for managing saved passwords securely.

keylogger   Software designed to capture keystrokes in an effort to collect user IDs and passwords.

keyword   A set of characters that is an instruction in a particular programming or scripting language.

kibibyte   A binary prefix term that is used to describe 2^{10} or 1,024 and is abbreviated KiB. Instead of saying that it is 1 kilobyte, which people tend to think of as approximately 1,000 bytes, the term kibibyte is used.

kill   A command used through the Terminal application on a Mac or in Linux to halt a program that has frozen or is not responding: `kill -9` (where 9 is the `process_id`).

kill task   A step to take if an application has frozen or quit responding.

kilobyte   Approximately 1,000 bytes of information (exactly 1,024 bytes).

KMS (Key Management Service)   A service used in companies that have 25 or more Windows computers to deploy. KMS is a software application installed on a computer. All newly installed computers register with the computer that has KMS installed. Every 180 days, the computer is re-activated for the license. Each KMS

key can be used on two computers up to 10 times. Contrast with *MAK*.

knowledge base   A collection of documents used to answer commonly asked IT questions or contain IT procedures.

KVM (kernel-based virtual machine)   A Linux technology that allows the Linux kernel to function as a hypervisor.

KVM (keyboard, video, mouse)   A component that allows multiple computers to be connected to a single keyboard, monitor, and mouse.

L

L1 cache   Fast memory located inside the processor.

L2 cache   Fast memory located inside the processor housing but not inside the processor.

L3 cache   Any fast cache memory installed on the motherboard when both L1 and L2 cache are on the processor. Could also be located inside the processor housing.

LAN (local area network)   A group of devices sharing resources in a single area, such as a room or a building.

laptop docking station   A device used to provide increased connectivity such as one or more displays, wired network connectivity, full-sized keyboard, mouse, and so on.

laser lens   A component of the optical drive that reads the data from the optical disc; susceptible to dust accumulation. Also known as an objective lens.

laser printer   A type of printer that produces output using an imaging process similar to a copier. Laser printers are the most expensive type of printer.

laser printer maintenance kit   A kit that may include a separation pad, pickup roller, transfer roller, charge roller, and fuser assembly, depending on the vendor.

Last Known Good Configuration   Used when the Windows 7 configuration has been changed by adding hardware or software that is incompatible with the operating system or when an important service has been accidentally disabled.

latency   In networking, the amount of delay experienced as a packet travels from source to destination.

launcher   A dock-like shortcut bar that allows manipulation of the graphical user interface (GUI) so that multiple apps and/or commands are easily deployed. It has the functionality of being an application launcher shortcut as well as having a universal search feature built-in to it.

Launchpad   A macOS application launcher shortcut.

LBA (logical block addressing)   A technology used with hard drives so that chunks of data can be stored and then located.

LC (Lucent Connector)   A type of connector used with fiber optic cable.

LC fiber connector   A connector commonly used with fiber-optic cable, often manufactured by Lucent.

LCD (liquid crystal display)   A video technology used with laptops and flat screen monitors. The two basic types of LCD are passive matrix and active matrix.

LDAP (Lightweight Directory Access Protocol)   A networking protocol that is used to access, maintain, and distribute directory and database-type information. LDAP uses port 389.

LED (light-emitting diode)   A video output technology that is a low-power, low-heat, long-lasting electronic device using liquid crystals.

legacy system   An outdated computer system or piece of network equipment that needs to be replaced or updated.

less   A common macOS and Linux command that shows the contents of a file.

Li-ion battery   A lithium battery, which is light and can hold a charge for a long period of time; found in cell phones and portable devices such as cameras.

library   Windows storage that is similar to a folder but that is automatically indexed for faster searching.

lifting technique   When lifting equipment, remember to use your legs and not your back.

light switch   A smart IoT device that can be programmed, motion-activated, and controlled by voice or an app.

Lightning port   An Apple port/cable used to connect displays and external drives. Commonly used to connect Apple mobile devices like iPhones and iPads to host computers and USB battery chargers.

limited connectivity   An error condition in which Internet connectivity is lost.

line conditioner   A device that protects a computer from overvoltage and undervoltage conditions as well as adverse noise conditions. Also known as a power conditioner.

line-of-sight wireless Internet service   In WiMAX wireless networks, the between-towers connection that travels from WiMAX tower to WiMAX tower to provide Internet connectivity in remote areas. Also called line-of-sight backhaul.

link-local address   A type of IPv6 address assigned to a NIC. It is used to communicate on a particular network and cannot be used to communicate with devices on a different network.

Linux   Released in 1991 by developer Linus Torvalds, a widely used operating system platform that is similar to Unix. It is a free open source operating system that anyone can use, contribute to, and modify. It is widely used in many different areas of technology, such as servers, desktops, embedded systems, and smartphones.

liquid cooling   An alternative to a fan or sink for processor cooling. Liquid is circulated through the system, and heat from the processor is transferred to the cooler liquid.

live tile   A Windows 8/8.1/10 feature that allows the content within to change, such as a news headline feed.

load alternate third-party driver   Part of the Windows installation process that a technician must download drivers for hardware such as a RAID controller before starting the installation process.

local administrator   A user account that has full power over a Windows-based computer. A local administrator can install hardware and software; uses all the administrative tools; creates and deletes hard drive partitions or volumes; and creates, deletes, and manages local user accounts.

local connectivity   Describes devices on the same network, including the default gateway. Pinging devices on the same network is a good check of local connectivity.

local resources   Can refer to network devices on the same network or resources within a company such as network shares, printers, and email.

local security policy   Security rules that can be applied to a computer.

local share   Something such as a printer, folder, or disc that has been made available across a network.

local storage   Saving data locally on a DVD, CD, flash drive, or internal/external hard drive.

Local Users and Groups A Windows tool used to create and manage accounts for those who use the computer or computer resources from a remote network computer. These accounts are considered local users or local groups and are managed from the computer being worked on. In contrast, domain or global users and groups are administered by a network administrator on a network server.

`locate` A macOS command that searches for a file in a database of paths. Commonly used subsequently to `update`, which is a command used to update a local database on the system that contains the full pathname of each file.

locator app Software used to pinpoint where a mobile device can be found.

log entries and error messages When troubleshooting problems related to motherboards, RAM, CPUs, and power, pay attention to any error messages displayed. Use the Windows Advanced Boot Options window to select *Enable Boot Logging* and examine the `ntbtlog.txt` file. Also consider viewing logs in the Windows Event Viewer Application and System logs.

logical drive A division of an extended partition into separate units, which appear as separate drive letters.

logical operator Used in scripting to allow for two or more conditions to be tested in one statement. Examples of logical operators include `AND`, `NOT`, and `OR`.

logical partition A division of an extended partition. A logical partition can be assigned a drive letter, formatted, and used for storage.

login script A set of tasks that run when a user logs in when the device is part of a Windows domain.

logon script See *login script*.

logon time restriction A network setting that restricts when the network user can log in to the domain.

LoJack (BIOS option) A BIOS setting option that controls locating the device, remotely locking the device, remotely deleting data, and displaying an "if lost" message.

loop In scripting, a method of repeating something.

loop structure In a loop (or repetition) structure, a loop contains a block of statements that is executed repeatedly.

loopback address A private IP address of 127.0.0.1 (IPv4) or ::1 (IPv6) that can test a NIC's basic network setup and the TCP/IP stack.

loopback plug A troubleshooting device that allows port testing.

lost cluster A sector on a disk that the file allocation table cannot associate with any file or directory.

loud clicking noise A symptom that a mechanical hard drive is failing.

loud noise A symptom that the power supply has a problem.

low memory error Caused by a printer not having enough memory or by insufficient hard drive space.

low RF signal Caused by a wireless device being too far away from a wireless access point/router or obstructions such as walls.

low-level format A utility that formats a drive; note that this is different from the high-level format done on a newly installed drive or during an operating system installation.

LPD/LPR (line printer daemon/line printer remote) protocol A protocol used with network printers.

LPT (line printer terminal) A name given to a specific printer port such as LPT1 or LPT2 by the operating system.

`ls` A Linux command that lists the contents of a currently working directory.

LTE (Long Term Evolution) A version of 4G that optimized the network for video streaming and online games.

LTI (Lite Touch Installation) A corporate image deployment method. Windows software, drivers, and updates are added to a network share, and configuration files are created. The resulting boot image is burned to optical media and used to boot in a computer. Then the installation files are transmitted across the network and installed without further intervention from a technician.

lumens A measure of light output or brightness; how much visible light is coming out of equipment such as lamps, lighting equipment, or projectors.

LVD (low voltage differential) A type of connector used with SCSI.

M

M.2 A type of connector that allows attachment of modules of varying size. First found in mobile devices and used for SSDs but now found on desktop motherboards.

M.2 slot A BIOS/UEFI setting that might need to be enabled in order for an SSD installed in the slot to be recognized.

MAC (mandatory access control)   A secure security strategy in which the operating system requires credentials to be provided before access is given to any resource. Contrast with discretionary access control, in which the resource owner determines who can have access.

MAC (Media Access Control)   A Layer 2 technology used to describe the way a device gets data onto a network.

MAC address (Media Access Control address)   One of two types of addresses assigned to network adapters, used when two devices on the same network communicate. Known as a Layer 2 address.

MAC address filtering   A security feature on an access point that allows MAC addresses to be entered to limit the number of wireless devices allowed on the wireless network.

macOS   A Unix-based operating system that was developed by Apple, Inc., for its Macintosh line of computers, called Mac for short. macOS is the second-most-commonly used desktop operating system behind Windows and is the most-used type of Unix/Linux-based desktop operating systems.

magnetic card reader   A device that accepts input from a card or chip on a card such as an ID card, magnetic room key, or credit card.

magnetic reader   A device that accepts cards that are inserted into the device in order to read data from the card or the chip on the card.

mail server   Also known as an email server. Used to maintain a database of email accounts, store email that has been sent and received, and communicate with other mail servers.

maintain a positive attitude   A great idea for professionalism and good rapport with customers.

maintenance counter   Reset through the laser printer menu to count the number of pages until the message to apply the maintenance kit appears again.

maintenance kit   A collection of items commonly used for technical support. Includes a portable vacuum, toner vacuum, compressed air, swaps, monitor wipes, lint-free cloths, general-purpose cloths, general-purpose cleanser, denatured alcohol, antistatic brush, optical drive cleaning kit, gold contact cleaner, safety goggles, and an air filter or mask.

MAK (Multiple Activation Key)   A method in which the Internet or a phone call must be made to register one or more Windows computers with

Microsoft. This software license method has a limited number of activations.

malware   Software code designed to damage an electronic device (cause lockups, slowness, crash an app, cause the device to not run or boot, and more).

man   A Linux command, short for *manual*, that can be used with another command to bring up an instruction manual for using the other command.

MAN (metropolitan area network)   In a networking environment, a networks that spans a city or town.

man-in-the-middle (MITM)   A security attack in which a hacker inserts a device between a sender and a receiver so that this device can receive the intended traffic. APs, DHCP servers, and default gateways (routers or Layer 3 devices) are common devices simulated.

managed switch   A type of switched used in a corporate network that has an IP address assigned that can be remotely accessed, configured, and monitored by an administrator.

mantrap   A method of separating a nonsecure area from a secure area to prevent unauthorized access and tailgating.

MAP (Microsoft Assessment and Planning Toolkit)   Used for planning a Windows deployment in a corporate environment.

MAPI (Messaging Application Programming Interface)   A Microsoft-proprietary protocol used with email.

Marketplace   A Microsoft platform for obtaining apps. Replaced by the Microsoft Store.

mask   An article of personal protective equipment that is to be used to prevent inhalation of harmful airborne particulates and fumes when working in dusty environments such as when working on a computer or laser printer or inside a network wiring closet.

master   A jumper setting used to configure a PATA IDE device; the controlling device on the interface.

mATX   See *micro-ATX*.

MAU (media attachment unit)   An older device used to connect an Ethernet cable to an attachment unit interface (AUI) connector.

Mb   An abbreviation for megabit.

MB   See *megabyte*.

MBR (master boot record)   A program that reads the partition table to find the primary partition used to boot the system.

MBSA (Microsoft Baseline Security Analyzer)   A tool that can identify security misconfigurations.

MCBF (mean cycles between failures)   A performance comparison measurement that is found by dividing the mean time between failures (MTBF) by the duration time of a cycle (operations per hour). The lower the number, the better the performance.

md   A command issued from a command prompt that creates a directory (folder) or subdirectory.

MDM (mobile device management)   The capability to view and manage multiple mobile devices.

MDM policy (mobile device management policy)   A set of rules or recommendations related to mobile device security that might include password requirements, security requirements, procedures for a lost or stolen device, security breach process, or data storage recommendations.

MDT (Microsoft Deployment Toolkit)   A GUI shell used to make Windows image deployment easier. Tools such as USMT, Application Compatibility Toolkit (ACT), Microsoft Assessment and Planning Toolkit (MAP), and the volume licensing application are inside the MDT shell.

measured service   The capability to track cloud consumer usage and apply resources as needed, based on usage.

mebibyte   A binary prefix value that describes a value 2^{20} or 1,048,576 and is abbreviated MiB.

mechanical drive   A traditional hard drive that has moving parts.

Media Center   Can be used to turn a Windows computer into a home entertainment hub but is no longer supported.

megabyte   Approximately 1 million bytes of data (exactly 1,048,576 bytes). Abbreviated MB.

memory   The part of a computer that temporarily stores applications, user documents, and system operating information.

memory address   A unique address for memory chips.

Memory Diagnostic Tool   A tool accessed by booting from the Advanced Boot Options menu in Windows to thoroughly test RAM.

menu bar   A component of the macOS GUI that is anchored to the top of a screen and is a dynamically changing bar that presents contextual drop-down menu options on the left side, depending on which window is active. On the right side, it provides shortcuts such as connecting to a WiFi network or changing volume.

It is also informative, displaying information such as battery life on laptops and the time.

metered service   In cloud computing, a company pays an amount based on how much of the service is used on an hourly or monthly basis.

metro UI   A Windows graphical user interface in which tiles are used on the desktop.

MFA (multifactor authentication)   A security measure in which more than one security method of access is required, such as a bank card and a personal identification number (PIN).

MFD (multifunction device)   A device such as an all-in-one printer that includes a printer, scanner, copier, and fax machine. The term might also describe a network device that commonly includes a router, an access point, a and switch.

MFP (multifunction product, printer, or peripheral)   Also known as an all-in-one printer. See also *MFD*.

micro-ATX   A smaller version of a standard ATX-sized motherboard form factor.

micro-USB   A standard interface port on mobile devices and smartphones.

microDIMM (micro dual inline memory module)   A smaller memory module.

microphone   An audio input device that can be integrated into a mobile device or that can be added externally, as with a wireless Bluetooth device; controlled with an app.

microprocessor   See *processor*.

microSD   A storage device with non-volatile flash memory that is used for mobile devices.

Microsoft Management Console   Holds snap-ins or tools used to maintain the computer. Also known as the Computer Management console.

Microsoft Security Essentials   A free antivirus program for Windows Vista and 7 (but not Windows 8 or 10 because it is integrated into Windows Defender).

Microsoft Store   Computer software and mobile device apps can be purchased and downloaded or downloaded for free through this online website.

MIDI (Musical Instrument Digital Interface)   An interface built in to a sound card to create synthesized music.

MIME (Multipurpose Internet Mail Extensions)   When used with SNMP, allows non-ASCII character sets and other rich media content to be included with email.

MIMO (multiple input/multiple output)   Describes 802.11n wireless technology in which multiple antennas operate cooperatively to increase throughput on a wireless network.

mini PCIe   A 52-pin expansion slot or card used in mobile devices.

mini-DIN   A motherboard connector, sometimes called a PS/2 connector, that connects keyboards and mice.

mini-DIN connector   A 6-pin connector that is round with small holes keyed to prevent incorrect cable insertion. Mouse and keyboard connectors are examples of this type of connector.

mini-HDMI   A type of connector that is an upgrade to DVI and is used with mobile devices. Carries audio and video over the same cable.

mini-ITX   A smaller version of the ITX motherboard form factor size.

miniSD   A storage device with non-volatile flash memory that is used for mobile devices.

mini-USB   A port found on mobile devices that is a miniaturized version of the Universal Serial Bus (USB) interface created for connecting smartphones, GPS devices, printers, and digital cameras.

Mission Control   A macOS utility that gives an overview for managing all application windows and virtual desktops.

mITX   See *mini-ITX*.

mkdir   A Linux (and Windows) command used to make a directory.

MLC (multi-level cell)   A cell that stores more than 1 bit in a memory cell that is used in a SSD (solid-state drive). Contrast with *SLC*.

mmc (Microsoft Management Console)   A Windows container for management tools. The one already built is known as the Computer Management console. Holds tools such as Device Manager, Disk Management, Local Users and Groups, Event Viewer, Task Scheduler, Performance, Shared Folders, and Services. mmc is also the command used from a command prompt to open the Microsoft Management Console.

mobile docking station   A recharging station that provides a stable environment for mobile devices. Some mobile docking stations can charge more than one device at a time.

mobile hotspot   A place where wireless Internet connectivity is available.

mobile payment service   A service that enables payment for goods or services through a mobile device instead of with cash or a credit card.

modem (modulator/demodulator)   A device that connects a computer to a phone line or connects computers and mobile devices to broadband, wireless, WiFi, Bluetooth, or satellite networks.

modem card   Allows PCs to connect to a remote modem using an analog phone line.

Molex   A type of power connector that extends from a computer's power supply to various devices.

monitor   Displays information from the computer to the user.

motherboard   The main circuit board of a computer. Also known as the mainboard, planar, or system board.

motion sensor   A device used to detect movement.

mount   To make a drive available and recognizable to the operating system through the diskpart command utility.

mounting (Disk Management)   An options that maps an empty folder on an NTFS volume by right-clicking on a partition or volume > *Change Drive Letter and Paths* > *Add* > *Mount in the Following Empty NTFS Folder* and either type the path or browse to an empty folder > *OK* > *OK*.

mouse   A data input device that moves the cursor or selects menus and options.

mouse port   A DIN connector on the motherboard that should accept only a mouse cable.

MOV (metal oxide varistor)   An electronic component built in to some surge protectors to absorb over-voltage spikes or surges.

MP3 (Moving Picture Experts Group Layer 3)   Also known as MPEG Audio Layer 3, a standard for audio compression.

MP4 (Moving Picture Experts Group Layer 4)   A storage format used for files that contain images, video, audio, and/or subtitles.

MPEG (Moving Pictures Experts Group)   An organization that sets standards for audio and video compression.

msconfig   A system configuration utility command that allows an administrator to enable or disable services, access control panel links, and control applications.

MSDS (material safety data sheet)   A safety-related document that contains information about a product, including its toxicity, storage, and disposal.

GLOSSARY

MSI (message-signaled interrupts)   A type of interrupt method that delivers up to 32 interrupts to the CPU using software and memory space on behalf of a single device. A PCIe card is required to support MSI.

`msinfo32`   A Windows command used to bring up the System Information window from a command prompt. The System Information window contains details about hardware and hardware configurations as well as software and software drivers.

MSI-X (message-signaled interrupts)   A type of interrupt method that allows a device to allocate up to 2,048 interrupts. Note that most devices do not use this many. A PCIe card is required to support MSI-X.

`mstsc`   A Windows command used to control and use a remote computer; brings up the Remote Desktop Connection utility.

MT-RJ (mechanical transfer registered jack)   A type of fiber connector.

MTBF (mean time between failures)   The average number of hours before a device fails.

MU-MIMO (multi-user multiple input/multiple output)   A wireless technology used with the 802.11ac that allows up to eight simultaneous streams from multiple devices.

MUI (multilingual user interface)   A technology used with software like Microsoft Windows or Microsoft Office that allows the user to select a language preference and supports multiple language options.

multi-mode fiber   A type of fiber-optic cabling that allows multiple light signals to be sent along the same cable.

multi-monitor taskbar   A Windows option in which the taskbar can display on all displays or across them.

multiboot   A situation in which a computer can boot from two or more operating systems.

multicore   A term used to indicate multiple processor cores in the same housing.

multifactor authentication   Use of two or more factors to provide access. The factors can be something you possess, such as a card, current location, security token–provided code, PIN, fingerprint, facial recognition, palm print, or password.

multimeter   A tool used to test voltage, current, resistance, and continuity.

Multiple Activation Key (MAK)   See *MAK*.

multiple failed print jobs   A printer issue in which something is usually wrong with the printer like lack of paper, low ink or toner, or paper jam. The print queue should be checked and possibly cleared, and jobs should be resent after resolving the issue.

multiplier   A motherboard setting used to determine CPU speed. (Multiplier times bus speed equals CPU speed.)

mutual authentication for multiple services   Sometimes called single sign-on (SSO), allows one authentication to provide access to multiple services like apps or websites.

`mv`   A Linux command that moves a file.

N

.NET Core   Used for the cross-platform version of Windows PowerShell.

NaaS (Network as a Service)   A cloud technology in which a provider can provide specific infrastructure devices, applications, servers, a place to test code, and so on.

NAC (network access control)   A security strategy in which a network device is checked for certain parameters, such as operating system type, operating system revision number, and/or security software installed, before being allowed onto the network.

NAND flash memory   An SSD storage technique in which data is retained even when the device is not powered.

`nano`   An easy-to-use Linux text editor.

nanometer (nm)   A measurement of processor technology length equal to .000000001 meter (1 times 10^{-9}). For example, chipsets created using 22 nm technology have more transistors in the same amount of space as chipsets created using 32 nm or 45 nm technology.

nanosecond   One-billionth of a second.

NAS (network-attached storage)   See *network-attached storage device*.

NAS drive   A drive used in a network-attached storage device that costs more than a drive of the same capacity used in a PC, for example, because a NAS drive is built to run 24/7.

NAT (network address translation)   A method of conserving public IP addresses. NAT uses private IP addresses that become translated to public IP addresses.

native resolution   The number of pixels going across and down a flat panel monitor. This resolution is the specification for which the monitor was made and is the optimum resolution.

Nautilus   The default file manager for the GNOME desktop in Linux systems.

NBT (NetBIOS over TCP/IP)   Uses TCP ports 137–139 to support outdated applications that rely on the NetBIOS API to use a TCP/IP-based network. Also known as NetBT.

nbtstat   A command to view other network devices by their assigned names and display statistics relevant to current TCP/IP connections on the local computer or a remote computer using NBT.

net   From a prompt, the net command manages almost everything on a network. It is followed by other options, each of which has different parameters.

net use   From a prompt, the net use command is used to map a network share to a drive letter or view mapped drives on a Microsoft-based machine.

net user   From a prompt, the net user command is used to create, delete, or make changes to user accounts from a command prompt on a Microsoft-based machine.

NetBEUI (NetBIOS Extended User Interface)   An update to NetBIOS standard to allow communication on a network. A nonroutable network protocol found on peer-to-peer networks. Can work only on simple networks, not on linked networks.

NetBIOS (Network Basic Input/Output System)   An older method of providing name resolution and connectivity methods for both connectionless and connection-oriented communication sessions.

NetBT (NetBIOS over TCP/IP)   Uses TCP ports 137–139 to support outdated applications that rely on the NetBIOS API to use a TCP/IP-based network. Also known as NBT.

netdom   From a prompt, a command that can manage workstations in a domain environment.

netstat   A command that can view current network connections and the local routing table for a PC.

network   Two or more devices that can communicate and share resources between them.

network boot   Sometimes called a Preboot Execution Environment (PXE) boot, where the system boots from a server that deploys an operating system image to a computer.

network interface card   See *NIC*.

network layer   Layer 3 of the OSI model, which coordinates data movement between two devices on separate networks.

network number   The portion of an IP address that represents which network the computer is on.

network port   A port that connects a computer to a wired network.

network printer mapping   Enables network users to add the printer to their computer using the domain printer name or IP address.

network protocol   A data communication language.

network share   A folder or network device that has been shared and is accessible from a remote computer.

network topology diagram   A type of IT documentation that shows how wired and wireless devices connect.

network-attached storage device   A special hardware component of virtualization to increase storage space that can be shared with other devices. Also see *NAS drive*.

NFC (near field communication)   A technology that connects nearby devices without a cord.

NFC device   A wireless device used to securely authorize payment for a transaction.

NFS (Network File System)   An open standard protocol used for sharing files across a network.

NIC (network interface card)   A port on a device that allows connectivity to a network. A NIC can connect to a wired or wireless network.

NiCd (nickel cadmium)   A type of battery used in small devices such as mobile devices, tools, and video recorders.

NiMH (nickel metal hydride)   A rechargeable type of battery.

NLX (new low-profile extended)   A computer case form factor.

NNTP (Network News Transfer Protocol)   A protocol used to deliver news to network clients. Uses TCP port 119. If TLS (Transport Layer Security) is used, then the port number is commonly 563.

no Bluetooth connectivity   An issue that could be helped by turning the device off and back on, check for interference, ensure that Bluetooth is enabled, and enter passkeys/PINs.

no connectivity   An error condition that exists if the self-test issued from a computer fails.

no display   With this problem on a mobile device, attach an external display if possible. If attached to a projector, check the output port chosen. Check the lid close detector. Turn the device off and back on. Charge the device fully.

no image on the printer display   In this situation, check that the printer is powered on, check the power outlet, and check the power brick.

no image on the screen   In this situation, check power to the display, power to the computer, power to the video card, and power from the power supply, driver, and video cable.

no OS found   A situation where the operating system is corrupt, there is a problem with the boot device such as the hard drive, or the BIOS/UEFI settings are incorrect.

no power   In this situation, check that power cord is attached, the power button pushed, the surge strip turned on, and the monitor is turned on; could be an indication of a faulty power supply. On a mobile device, check brightness, lid close sensor, and battery. Check for malware.

no sound from speakers   In this situation, check for muted or low volume, correct sound output device, cabling, and speaker power.

no wireless connectivity   In this situation, check whether WiFi is enabled and ensure that the device is not in Airplane Mode. Turn off WiFi and turn it back on again. Move the device to see if you have a higher signal strength (display on a laptop). Ensure that the correct wireless network is chosen.

non-ECC   A type of memory that does not do error correction. Most workstation memory is non-ECC memory.

non-metered service   In cloud computing, a service that has a fixed charge for fixed resources or configurations.

non-parity   A less expensive type of memory chip that does not perform error checking.

non-volatile memory   Memory that remains even when the computer is powered off. ROM and flash memory are examples of non-volatile memory.

noncompliant system   A system that does not meet security policy guidelines and could be a potential security threat.

NOT operator   Flips the result of an expression so that if an expression is true, it will return false and vice versa; if the expression is false, it will return true.

Notepad   An accessory text editor program in Windows.

notification area (mobile)   A place on mobile devices that contains information such as battery life, wireless signal strength, time, or external media

connectivity. Usually in the lower-right corner on a tablet and at the top of the display on a smartphone.

notification area (Windows)   The far-right area of the taskbar, which contains information about an application or a tool, such as security, network access, speaker control, or date and time.

nslookup   A Windows troubleshooting command that displays network domain names and their associated IP addresses.

NTFS (New Technology File System)   The file system used with Microsoft operating systems today (starting with Windows NT). Offers encryption, compression, larger file sizes, and longer filenames.

NTFS permissions   A security measure that can dictate what a specific user or group can do with a file or folder.

NTLDR (New Technology Loader)   A file used during the Windows XP boot process. In Windows Vista and higher, this function is performed by the Windows Boot Manager, which calls the winload. exe executable file to handle the boot process.

NTLDR is missing   A Windows 7 boot error condition in which the operating system needs to be reinstalled.

NTP (Network Time Protocol)   A protocol that synchronizes time between network devices.

NTSC (National Transmission or Television Standards Committee)   A committee dedicated to standards for transmitting and receiving video signals.

Num Lock indicator light   The light above the Num Lock key that glows when the key is pressed and the function is activated.

NVMe (non-volatile memory express)   A technology used with SSDs that provides fast performance when accessing NAND flash memory.

O

OCR (optical character recognition)   A technology used to convert an image into text. It is commonly used with scanners.

octa-core   An eight-core processor.

ODD (optical disc drive)   A collective term for CD, DVD, and BD because they use optical discs that are read from, written to, or both.

OEM (original equipment manufacturer)   The original producer of a product. That product is bought by a company that rebrands or sells the part or computer under its own name.

off-site email application A common cloud-based technology in which the company email server is located in a remote site or provided by a cloud-hosted email provider.

ohm A measurement of electrical resistance.

OLED (organic LED) Display screen technology used in many monitors, TV's, and mobile devices today. It does not require a backlight like LCDs but has a film of organic compounds placed in rows and columns that can emit light. Ii is lightweight and has a fast response time, low power usage, and a wide viewing angle.

omnidirectional antenna A type of antenna that has a radiation pattern in all directions.

on-demand 24/7 access from anywhere and possibly any device.

onboard NIC (BIOS/UEFI) An option in the BIOS, UEFI, or settings used to configure the network interface, whether it be wired or wireless.

onboard video card Video circuits built into the motherboard that support the video port.

OneDrive Microsoft's cloud storage solution.

open authentication Used in wireless networks; allows a wireless device to send a frame to the access point with the sender's identity (MAC address).

open source Software that allow vendors to use the core source code and the ability to customize the software, such as, Google Android or Linux.

operating system (OS) A piece of software that loads a computer and makes it operational.

optical disc (boot option) A boot method that uses a CD, DVD, or Blu-ray disc that has an operating system on it.

optical drive A storage device that accepts optical discs such as CDs, DVDs, or BDs that have data, music, video, or software applications.

Optimize and Defragment A Windows tool accessed with the Defragment button or through the defrag command. It is used to put files in contiguous clusters on the hard drive for better performance.

OR operator Returns false if and only if both sides of the expression are false.

orientation The way in which a document or screen is presented: portrait versus landscape.

OS See *operating system*.

OS not found An issue when the boot order in the BIOS/UEFI is incorrect, the hard drive does not contain an operating system, or there is an issue with the drive that contains the operating system being recognized by the computer.

OS X An older Apple operating system family replaced by macOS.

OSHA (Occupational Safety and Health Administration) A division of the U.S. Department of Labor that promotes safe and healthy working conditions by enforcing standards and providing workplace safety training.

OSI model (Open Systems Interconnect model) A standard for information transfer across a network that was developed by the International Standards Organization. The model has seven layers; each layer uses the layer below it, and each layer provides some function to the one above it.

output In programming or scripting, the result, which could be a screen, a value, a computation, a printed document, and so on.

overclocking Manually changing the front side bus speed and/or multiplier to increase CPU and system speed, but at a cost of increasing the CPU operating temperature. Overclocking a CPU may void the manufacturer's warranty.

overheat shutdown Causes artifacts on the display screen and/or the system to power off. In this situation, check the GPU or video adapter for overheating; check the power supply for adequate power output; and check the CPU fan, case fans, and motherboard.

overheating On a mobile device, power off the device and let it cool. See if you can determine if a specific spot is getting hotter than other places. Check the battery and replace it, if necessary.

oversized images and icons This situation may indicate an issue with the video driver or the resolution.

overvoltage A condition when the AC voltage is over the rated amount of voltage.

ozone filter A part of a laser printer that filters out the ozone produced by the printer.

P

.ps1 A file extension used for a PowerShell script.

.py A file extension used with Python scripts.

PaaS (Platform as a Service) A type of cloud service that describes servers, databases, operating system, storage, and development tools provided in an outside environment to relieve the support burden on companies that need an environment to perform high-level programming and develop applications.

packet   Encapsulated data found at Layer 3 of the OSI model.

PAE (physical address extension)   A feature provided by Intel that allows up to 64 GB of physical memory to be used for motherboards that support it.

page   In Windows hard disk caching, a 4 KB block of memory space. The operating system swaps or pages the application to and from the temporary swap file (paging file) as needed if RAM is not large enough to handle the application.

page file   A single block of memory space, 4 KB in size, used to store files that may also retrieve a file located on a disk.

paging file   A temporary file in hard disk space used by Windows that varies in size depending on the amount of RAM installed, available hard drive space, and the amount of memory needed to run the application. Also known as a swap file.

PAL (phase alternating line)   A method of encoding color for video systems.

PAN (personal area network)   A network of personal devices such as cell phones, laptop computers, and other mobile devices that can communicate in close proximity through a wired network or wirelessly. A Bluetooth wireless keyboard and mouse form a PAN.

Panel   A part of a Linux GUI and similar to macOS, Panel is a menu bar at the top of the screen containing contextual information on the left side with static information on the right side.

paper jam   A problem that occurs when paper gets stuck along the printer paper pathway.

paper not feeding   A problem that may be due to poor paper quality or to the inefficiency of the rubber rollers that move the paper.

parallel ATA   See *PATA*.

parental control   A Windows security option for controlling websites that children can access or limiting the amount of time they can use a computer or the Internet.

parity   A method of checking data accuracy.

partition   A process that can divide a hard drive so that the computer sees more than one drive.

partition table   A table that holds information about the types and locations of partitions created. In mechanical hard drives, it occupies the outermost track on the platter (Cylinder 0, Head 0, Sector 1) and is part of the master boot record.

passcode lock   Security configuration on a mobile device.

passwd   A Linux/Unix command to set or change a user password.

passwords (BIOS)   A BIOS/UEFI settings that provide protection of the BIOS menu option by configuring one or more passwords to access the Setup program.

password policy   A policy that may be contained within the security policy that defines password requirements (length and types of characters) as well as the password change process.

password reset   In Active Directory, locate the user account, right-click on it, and select *Reset Password*.

password security   The act of being conscientious about where passwords are written and stored.

PAT (port address translation)   PAT is used to allow one public IP address for thousands of private IP addresses by the device performing network address translation also tracking port numbers so that traffic streams can be identified and sent to the device that originally requested the data from inside a company to a device on a network outside the company. Some technical articles and technicians refer to PAT as network address translation (NAT).

PATA (parallel ATA)   A technology used with IDE devices that allows two devices per channel.

patch   A piece of software that fixes a specific problem in an application or operating system.

patch panel   Used with twisted pair cable as a central location to which network cables terminate. It mounts in a network wiring rack, has network ports on the front, and has wiring connected to the back to provide network connectivity.

patch/update management   A security best practice in which the operating system, drivers, and BIOS/UEFI are kept up to date so that known security issues are addressed.

patching/OS updates   A security best practice for mobile devices in which the operating system (OS) and radio firmware for devices such as cell phones are updated.

path   A reference that tells where a file is located among drives and folders (directories).

PATH variable   Used in programming and scripting to tell a program where to find the files that it may need.

PC (personal computer) A common name for a computer, derived from the IBM PC brand.

PCI (Payment Card Industry) A generic term for the entities surrounding business using payment cards, such as debit and credit cards, for transactions.

PCI (payment card information) A type of regulated data related to a credit card, debit card, and the finance industry.

PCI (Peripheral Component Interconnect) An older 32-bit and 64-bit, 66 MHz local bus standard found in computers.

PCI bus speed The speed at which data is delivered when the PCI main bus is used on the motherboard. Commonly operates at 33 MHz and 66 MHz.

PCIe A point-to-point serial bus used for motherboard adapters. Each bit can travel over a lane, and each lane allows transfers up to 250 MB/s, with a maximum of 32 lanes (which gives a total of an 8 GB/s transfer rate).

PCIe bus speed (Peripheral Component Interconnect Express) The main high-speed serial motherboard bus, designed to replace the PCI, PCI-X, and AGP bus standards.

PCIX (Peripheral Component Interconnect Extended) An expansion slot mostly found on servers that provided 32- or 64-bit data transfers.

PCL (Printer Command Language) A set of codes that allow any application to send output to a specific printer.

PCMCIA (Personal Computer Memory Card Industry Association) A local bus architecture used in older laptops.

PD (Power Delivery) A USB standard that allows up to 20 V at 5 A for 100 watts of power. The standard has five levels of power: 10 W, 18 W, 36 W, 60 W, and 100 W.

PE (preinstallation environment) Part of the operating system installation process that is used to get the operating system installed or reinstalled when the OS is corrupt or has issues.

performance (virtual memory) A computer's performance is affected by the virtual memory settings, which allocate a specific amount of hard drive space that can be used when more applications and data are loaded than the amount of RAM installed.

Performance Monitor A Windows tool that monitors resources such as memory and CPU usage and that allows creation of graphs, bar charts, and text reports.

Performance utility A utility that monitors memory and other hardware parameters usage aspects.

personal protection equipment (PPE) Part of a computer technician's work kit: safety glasses/goggles, latex or nonlatex/vinyl gloves, and an air filter/dust mask.

petabyte (PB) 1 thousand terabytes, or 2^{50} (1,125,899,906,842,600) bytes.

PGA (pin grid array) A type of processor housing.

PGA2 (pin grid array 2) A type of processor housing used in mobile devices.

PGP (Pretty Good Privacy) A type of encryption used to protect emails and data.

PHI (protected health information) The Health Insurance Portability and Accountability Act (HIPAA) developed a U.S. government standard to protect certain types of private health-related information.

phishing (pronounced "fishing") A type of social engineering that attempts to get personal information through email from a company that appears legitimate. Targets obtaining ATM/debit or credit card numbers and PINs, Social Security numbers, bank account numbers, an Internet banking login ID and password, an email address, security information such as a mother's maiden name, full name, home address, or phone number.

phone communication skills An important skill set for technicians when talking to users and supporting them over the phone.

phone filter A part used with DSL Internet connectivity that must be attached to every phone outlet. The traditional analog device connects to this part. The filter allows the DSL signal to be separated from the normal analog traffic.

physical laptop lock Also called a laptop locking station, a security measure to attach a laptop to a location such as a desk.

physical layer Layer 1 of the OSI model, which defines how bits are sent and received across the network without regard to their structure.

pickup rollers Printer feed rollers.

picosecond One-trillionth of a second.

PII (personally identifiable information) Any personal data or method of identifying, locating, or contacting a particular person.

PIN (personal identification number) A unique identifier used to access an account or a device such as a mobile tablet.

pin 1   A designated pin on every cable and connector that must be mated when attaching the two. Usually designated by a stenciled or etched number, a color stripe, and so on.

pin firing   The act of a print wire coming out of a dot matrix printer's print head and impacting the paper.

ping   A network troubleshooting command used to test TCP/IP communications and determine whether a network path is available, whether any delays exist along the path, and whether a remote network device is reachable. Use `ping` with the private IP address 127.0.0.1 (IPv4) or ::1 (IPv6) to test a NIC's basic network setup.

pinning   The act of placing favorite applications in either the Start button, on the taskbar, or on a tile on the Windows desktop.

pinwheel   A spinning wheel, often seen in macOS, generated by the operating system to indicate possible problems such as a nonresponsive application.

pipe symbol   A character (|) used at the command prompt that allows control of where or how the output of the command is processed. For example, a command can be "piped" to display only one screen at a time.

pipeline   Separate internal data buses that operate simultaneously inside the processor.

piracy   The act of copying or distributing copyrighted software.

PKI (Public Key Infrastructure)   A method of managing digital security certificates.

plan for change   A good IT department should always be getting ready for change rather than being reactive when something fails or is attacked.

plastic filament   A supply that a 3D printer needs for printing instead of using ink or toner.

platter   A metal disk of a hard drive on which binary data is recorded.

plenum cable   A type of cable that is treated with fire-retardant materials so that it is less of a fire risk.

PnP (plug and play)   A bus specification that allows automatic configuration of an adapter or a device.

PoE (Power over Ethernet)   A method of powering a remote device through an Ethernet switch or a patch panel.

PoE injector   A method of providing power to a remote device using an injector when a PoE switch or patch panel is not available.

PoE switch   A switch that has the ability to provide power to devices such as access points or IP phones through the Power over Ethernet standard.

pointer drift   A situation in which the mouse pointer moves across the screen even if no one is touching the input device. Commonly caused by improper touchpad sensitivity settings, outdated drivers, or malware.

POP (Point of Presence)   An Internet access point.

POP3 (Post Office Protocol)   A protocol used to retrieve email from a mail server. Uses port 110.

pop-up   A small window that appears (pops up) to display a message, warning, or advice. Pop-ups often are a nuisance but can be managed through the browser's pop-up blocker feature.

port   A connector located on the motherboard or on a separate adapter.

port forwarding   The process of sending data through a firewall, based on a particular port number or protocol.

port mapping   The combination of one public address and a port number that represents one internal company host; also called port address translation (PAT).

port replicator   A part that is similar to a docking station that attaches to a laptop computer and allows more devices, such as a monitor, keyboard, and mouse, to be connected.

port security   A security feature on a corporate switch that detects whether someone has swapped one corporate device for another one.

port triggering   Temporarily sending data through a firewall, based on a preconfigured condition.

PoS (point of sale)   A terminal, computer, or printer used in retail.

POSIX (Portable Operating System Interface)   A designation that meets the specifications of a standardized operating system outlined by the IEEE Computer Society, containing a Bourne shell and other standard programs and services that are found in all POSIX-compliant operating systems. macOS is POSIX compliant.

POST (power-on self-test)   Startup software contained in the BIOS/UEFI that tests individual hardware components.

POST card   A PCI/PCIe adapter or a USB attached card that performs hardware diagnostics and displays the results as a series of codes on an LED display or in LED lights.

POST code beep   An indication that a hardware error exists, such as an error in the CPU, motherboard, or RAM or a stuck key. Look up the code for more information.

POTS (plain old telephone service)   The traditional analog phone network used to connect homes and small businesses.

power   A measurement, expressed in watts, that represents how much work is being done.

power rating   A measurement, expressed in watts per channel, that represents how loud the speaker volume can go without distorting the sound.

PowerShell   A Windows technology that helps technicians and network administrators automate support functions through the use of scripts and snippets.

power supply   A device that converts AC voltage into DC voltage that the computer can use to power all internal and some external devices.

power supply fan spins but no power   In this situation, check the power supply output voltages.

power supply tester   A tool that checks DC voltages sourced from the power supply.

power surge   An overvoltage condition that is like a spike but has a longer duration.

ppm (pages per minute)   A measurement of printer speed that indicates how many pages can be printed in 60 seconds.

PPP (Point-to-Point Protocol)   A connection-oriented Layer 2 protocol that encapsulates data for transmission over remote networks.

PPTP (Point-to-Point Tunneling Protocol)   A method/protocol used to create a VPN.

prefix notation   A method used to describe a subnet mask. It includes a forward slash followed by a number, such as /24. The number is how many consecutive bits are set in the subnet mask.

presentation layer   Layer 6 of the OSI model, which defines how data is formatted, encoded, converted, and presented from the sender to the receiver, even though a different computer language is used.

preventive maintenance   Something that is done to prolong the life of a device.

PRI (Primary Rate Interface)   The 24 64 Kbps channels used with ISDN.

PRI (Product Release Instructions)   A configuration file in a smartphone that specifies what frequency bands can be used and the default preferred roaming list (PRL) to use.

PRI update (Product Release Instructions update)   A configuration file updated by a cellular service provider.

primary corona   A wire in a laser printer that is responsible for generating a large negative voltage to be applied uniformly to the laser's drum.

primary partition   The first detected drive partition on a hard drive that has been configured with a basic disk.

principle of least privilege   A security measure in which a user receives only enough security permissions (on devices, files, network resources, and so on) to do his or her job.

print cartridge   A container that holds the ink and the nozzles for an inkjet printer. Also known as an ink cartridge.

print driver   A piece of software that coordinates between the operating system and the printer.

print head   The part of the impact printer that holds the print wires and impacts the ribbon.

print log   A listing of print jobs sent to a printer. Could include error conditions.

Print Management   A Windows administrative tool used to manage printers. Use the Print Management administrative tool from the System and Security Control Panel or use the printmanagement.msc command.

print ribbon   A ribbon that is struck by the print head to leave images on paper in an impact printer.

print server   A device (a computer or a separate device) that connects to a printer used by multiple people through a network.

print spooler   Also known as a print manager, a software program that intercepts a request to print and sends print information to the hard drive, from which it is then sent to the printer whenever the processor is not busy with other tasks. A print spooler allows multiple print jobs to be queued inside the computer so that other work can be performed.

print to file   An option that saves a print job as a .pm file to be printed later.

print to image   Virtual printing; printing to a location other than to the directly connected printer and to a specific file so that the information can be viewed, saved, or emailed.

print to PDF   A print job that is saved to a Portable Document Format (.pdf) file and can be printed later on any printer.

GLOSSARY

print to XPS A Microsoft file that allows a document to be printed on any printer but not modified.

print wire A component of an impact printer's print head that is a single wire that connects to a spring and impacts a ribbon to make a single dot on the paper.

printer A peripheral used to output text and/or graphics onto paper.

printer sharing Commonly used in a home or small business environment to allow multiple users on the same printer. Contrast with a printer server, used in corporate environments.

printer will not print This situation might arise for a variety of reasons, such as paper not being inserted correctly, power cord being dislodged or not plugged in, or printer not reading the computer command.

printing blank pages In this situation, ensure that the print driver is working properly; check the ribbon (impact and thermal), ink levels (inkjet), or toner (laser). Check quality settings.

printing issue A problem when trying to send output to the printer. In Windows, try to print a test page from the printer's *Properties > General* tab. Use the Windows Troubleshooting tool.

prints in wrong color In this situation, check ink levels and check the computer `printer` command.

privacy screen A physical filter added to a monitor to distort the display output for anyone except for the person looking directly at the screen. Also known as a privacy filter.

private cloud Part of a company's network infrastructure located outside the business in a remote location, but the company has responsibility for managing the software and hardware.

private IP address An IP address used inside a home or business that is not allowed to be transmitted across the Internet. Contrast to a public IP address.

PRL (preferred roaming list) The default roaming list created by a cell network provider.

PRL update A software configuration changed pushed out to a smartphone by a service provider.

proactive A good trait to have as a technician by implementing measure to avoid problems rather than just wait for a problem to occur before implementing the measure.

probe Used with a tone generator to identify cables when they are unlabeled or incorrectly labeled.

processing A laser printing process in which the data is converted from the printer language into a bitmap image. This process is also known as raster image processing.

processor The central 32-bit or 64-bit electronic chip that determines the processing power of a computer. Also known as a microprocessor or central processing unit (CPU).

Program Compatibility Wizard A program that can check for software application compatibility with a newer Windows version.

projector A device that takes input from a device such as a computer, laptop, camera, and so on and sends that image to a screen or wall.

PROM (programmable read-only memory) A type of memory chip that stores data that cannot be changed and is used to boot a system such as firmware.

prompt A command that changes how the command prompt appears. See also *command prompt*.

proprietary crash screen An error condition on a particular computer or application that is unique to the manufacturer.

proprietary system A type of computer that only allows a particular operating system or has hardware that is incompatible with other vendors. macOS is used only on Apple devices and is a proprietary system.

proprietary vendor-specific ports Ports primarily for power connections or as a communication option(s).

protective cover On mobile devices, a cover that provides protection for either the screen or for the entire whole unit.

proxy server A server that acts as a go-between for an application and another server.

ps A Linux/Unix command that lists all current processes.

PS/2 (Personal System/2 connector) An IBM-created port that uses a 6-pin miniDIN connector to connect a mouse or keyboard.

PS/2 port Common name for keyboard and mouse connectors, which are examples of miniDIN-6 connectors.

PSTN (public switched telephone network) The traditional phone network, including satellite, cellular, wired, and wireless worldwide connectivity.

PSU (power supply unit) See *power supply*.

public cloud   A service or an environment operated by an external vendor to provide a service or an application to a company.

public IP address   A private IP address that a service provider or company translates to a public IP address that is seen on the Internet.

punch-down tool   An implement that terminates cable on a patch panel.

purpose of the change   In change management, the part of the planning process that documents why a change is needed.

PVA (patterned vertical alignment)   A type of thin-film-transistor (TFT) liquid crystal display (LCD).

PVC (polyvinyl chloride)   Cable that has a plastic insulation or jacket that is cheaper and easier to install than plenum cable. It can have flame-retardant added.

pwd   In the Linux environment, a command that identifies the current working path you are in.

PXE (Preboot Execution Environment) boot   An option some computers have that can be modified to search for the network device that holds the computer image.

Python   A good language for writing scripts because it is easy to learn and Python scripts can be run on most operating systems. The extension.py is used with Python files.

Q

QoS (quality of service)   A collection of techniques that ensure that the most important corporate data, voice, and/or video is sent before other noncritical data that may get dropped as a result.

QR scanner   A peripheral or an app used to scan a QR code that contains a URL or other embedded information.

quad-core   Four processors on a single motherboard achieved by having either two dual-core CPUs installed on the same motherboard or two dual-core CPUs installed in a single socket.

quadruple-channel   A memory type in which a motherboard can access four memory modules simultaneously.

quality   A printing option that dictates how much ink/toner/DPI is used.

quick format   During an installation process, a function used to prepare a hard drive partition but not identify and mark bad sectors so that they will not be used for data storage. A full format, in contrast, does evaluate the drive for bad sectors but takes quite a bit longer to prepare the partition for use.

Quick Launch bar   Located immediately to the right of the *Start* button on the taskbar, a section of the Windows taskbar that contains icons used for opening applications.

R

radiation pattern   Sometimes called a propagation pattern, the direction(s) a radio frequency is sent or received.

radio   A wireless input/output technology that has a longer range than infrared.

radio firmware   Low-level software that manages a cell phone's radio connection to a network. A baseband signal sends updates to both the phone's operating system and its radio firmware. Without the same updates, the cell phone experiences problems.

RADIUS (Remote Authentication Dial-in User Service)   A secure method of authentication using a server.

RAID (redundant array of independent [or inexpensive] disks)   Allows writing to multiple hard drives for larger storage areas, better performance, and fault tolerance.

RAID 0   Also called disk striping without parity, a type of RAID that enables data to be alternatively written on two or more hard drives but be seen by the system as one logical drive. RAID level 0 does not protect data if a hard drive fails; it increases only system performance.

RAID 1   Also called disk mirroring or disk duplexing, a type of RAID that protects against hard drive failure. See also *disk mirroring* and *disk duplexing*. Requires two drives at a minimum.

RAID 10   A RAID condition in which a mirrored set and a striped set are combined. Takes four hard drives as a minimum.

RAID 5   Describes putting data on three or more hard drives, with one of the three drives used for parity. See also *RAID*.

RAID not found   An error condition that sometimes occurs with a power failure or surge, misconfiguration in BIOS/UEFI, system upgrade, application upgrade, or new application installation.

RAID stops working   An error condition that requires using the Windows Disk Management tool to verify the status of the drives used in the RAID.

GLOSSARY

rainbow table A security attack method used to obtain a password in a shorter amount of time because the attacker has a table that contains previously discovered hash values.

RAM (random-access memory) A volatile type of memory that loses its data when power to the computer is shut off.

RAM limitation The maximum amount of memory that an operating system can recognize. Even if a system has more installed, the operating system will not be able to use that extra memory.

random-access time A performance comparison measurement; it is the amount of time a drive requires to find the appropriate place on the disc and retrieve information.

ransomware A security situation in which a hacker has restricted access to a device until the user is pressured to pay money to regain access.

rapid elasticity The ability for a provider to expand software and hardware quickly in response to a customer's needs.

RAS (remote access service) Software that allows one network device to connect to another network device.

RAW volume A part of a hard drive that has been set aside as a volume but has never been high-level formatted and does not contain a specific type of file system.

RCA A type of connector used with coaxial cable.

rd A Windows command used to remove a directory (folder).

RDP (Remote Desktop Protocol) A Microsoft protocol used for accessing and controlling networked computers and mobile devices. RDP uses port 3389.

read/write failure An error condition that indicates a hard drive has a defective area.

read/write head The part of a floppy or hard drive that electronically writes binary data on disks.

ReadyBoost A utility that can speed up the Windows boot process by caching some startup files to a 256 MB+ flash drive, SD card, or CF card.

reboot A restart of an operating system, also known as a warm start.

rebuild a Windows profile If a message appears that the user profile cannot be loaded, make a copy of the user profile folder, rename the registry key, and have the user log in again.

recover OS The process of repairing, replacing, uninstalling, and reinstalling the operating system.

recovery disc A disc used to boot a system when you don't have an original operating system disc and then restore the computer from a previously saved system image. Sometimes called a system repair disc.

recovery partition An optional partition provided by some vendors that contains the operating system, files, and applications installed on the system when purchased.

Recycle Bin A location in Windows-based operating systems in which user-deleted files and folders are held. This data is not discarded from the computer. The user must empty the Recycle Bin to erase the data completely.

refresh (installation method) A Windows 8/8.1 tool that reinstalls the operating system but keeps user data and settings. Windows 10 uses Reset This PC for this purpose.

refresh (process) A rewrite of the information inside memory chips.

refresh rate Measured in hertz (Hz) or milliseconds (ms), the amount of time it takes a screen to be drawn in one second. In LCDs, it is also called temporal resolution. LCD refresh rates are traditionally 60 Hz.

Refresh Your PC A Windows 8/8.1 tool that reinstalls the operating system but keeps user data and settings. Windows 10 uses Reset This PC for this purpose.

ReFS (Resilient File System) The Microsoft replacement file system for NTFS.

regedit A Windows utility that can modify and back up the registry.

regedt32 One of two Windows registry editors. See also *registry* and regedit.

region code A setting on a DVD or Blu-ray drive or disc that specifies a geographic region. The drive's region code must match the disc's region code.

registered memory Memory modules that have extra chips (registers) near the bottom of the module that delay all data transfers by one clock tick to ensure accuracy.

registry A central Windows database file that holds hardware and software configuration information.

regsvr32.exe A command used to register .dll files in the Windows registry.

regulatory and compliance policy   A policy that is specific to an industry such as health care or manufacturing.

re-image   A process of putting a new image (operating system, applications, and settings) on a corporate computer.

relational operator   An operator that compares one side of an expression to another and is used in scripts.

Reliability Monitor   A tool that provides a visual graph in Windows Vista or 7 of how stable the system is and shows details on events that might have affected system reliability.

reload OS   A repair option that installs a new copy of the operating system when other repair options haven't been successful in fixing the problem.

Remote Assistance   A Windows tool used to remotely access a Windows device. The remote computer displays a prompt requesting permission for remote access. Contrast with Remote Desktop, which does not request permission.

remote backup   An option on a mobile device to allow the device or specific data like personal contacts, videos, pictures, and/or music to be backed up to remote storage.

Remote Desktop Connection   A Windows tool used to remotely access a Windows-based device that does not require someone to be at that computer and does not prompt for permission. Contrast with Remote Assistance, which does prompt for permission.

Remote Desktop Services   Previously known as Terminal Services, software on a server that can be used to deploy images to computers and to access, control, and manage remote computers and servers.

Remote Disc   A feature that allows the use of a Mac computer's optical drive (even from a Windows computer).

remote network   A different network. A term used to describe the situation where a server or network share that contains a created image is accessed and the image is deployed to a computer on a different network.

remote network installation   Pulling an image from a server or network share in order to load an operating system.

Remote Settings (link)   A link used from the *System* Control Panel utility to configure Remote Desktop and Remote Assistance.

remote wipe   The process of using software to send a command to a mobile device to delete data, perform a factory reset, remove everything from the device so that it cannot be used, and overwrite data storage to prevent forensic data recovery.

removable screen   Some devices that serve as laptops have screens that can be detached.

remove jewelry   Before working on equipment, remove all jewelry, watches, dangling necklaces/earrings, and ID lanyards.

renamed system files   A symptom of malware.

repair an application   Select the application in the *Windows Programs and Features* section of the Control Panel and select *Repair*.

repair installation   Used when you have to reload the Windows operating system. Sometimes called an in-place upgrade or a reinstallation.

repeater   A network device that boosts the network signal. Network switches are repeaters. Wireless repeaters boost the wireless signal to extend the wireless network.

repetition   In a repetition (or loop) structure, a loop contains a block of statements that is executed repeatedly.

Reset This PC   A recovery option that reinstalls Windows and deletes users' files, apps, and settings.

Resilient File System   See *ReFS*.

resistance   A measurement, in ohms, of how much opposition is applied to an electrical circuit.

resolution   The number of pixels shown on a monitor or the output of a printer.

Resource Monitor   A Windows graphic tool that shows performance for the main system components.

resource pooling   Using an outside vendor to pool cloud-based resources (servers, storage space, and more) with other companies.

restart service   In Windows, use the *Services* Computer Management tool to restart a service that has stopped responding.

restore (installation method)   A Windows installation method that takes the operating system back to a previous point in time.

restore point   A snapshot image of the registry and some of the dynamic system files that have been saved previously by the System Restore utility. This is used when a Windows computer has a problem.

restrict user permissions   A security best practice in which shared network resources such as files and folders have the appropriate permissions assigned.

return   The center (round) AC outlet plug. Other terms used are common or neutral.

review system and application logs   When a system is behaving abnormally, review logs to help identify the problem.

RF (radio frequency)   A specific range of frequencies used for transmitting data of some type, including audio.

RFI (radio frequency interference)   A specific type of EMI noise that occurs in the radio frequency range. Often results from operation of nearby electrical appliances or devices.

RFID (radio frequency identification)   A technology that allows automatic identification of people, objects, or animals.

RFID badge (radio frequency identification badge)   A card that can be used to access to a locked area and a record of that entry logged.

RG-59   A type of coax cable used in video networks.

RG-6   A type of coax cable that can connect to cable TV, satellite disc, or a rooftop antenna.

RGB (red, green, blue)   A technique used in video devices such as TVs, monitors, scanners, and cameras to produce colors.

RGB/component video   Red, green, and blue RCA jacks for connecting a scanner or camera.

rights   Permissions granted or denied to files, folders, and network resources.

RIP (Routing Information Protocol)   A protocol used between Layer 3 devices such as routers to exchange network information in an effort to send data from one network device to a remote network.

RIS (remote installation service)   A service that allows PXE-enabled devices to execute specific variables used to remotely control and even reload a remote device.

RISC (reduced instruction set computer)   A type of processor used for smaller computers. Contrast with CISC (complex instruction set computer), in which the processor has a full set of programmed instructions.

riser card   A board that connects to the motherboard that holds adapters.

risk analysis   A part of change management in which the risks of the proposed changes are weighed against the company benefits.

RJ-11   A type of connector used with analog modems and traditional phone jacks.

RJ-45   A type of connector used on Ethernet network cards and ports. Used to connect a device to the wired network.

rm   Short for remove, a Linux command that deletes a file or directory.

RMA (return materials authorization)   A number used to track and return defective parts (normally under warranty).

robocopy   A command used to copy files. It has more parameters than COPY or XCOPY.

rogue antivirus   A downloaded application that appears to help someone with a problem, but that is, in reality, a virus.

roll back device driver   Use *Device Manager* and right-click on a particular piece of hardware > *Properties* > *Driver* tab > *Roll Back Driver* button to take a device driver back to a previous version.

roll back Windows update   If a Windows update causes a system to have issues, roll back the update to at least one previous version and then apply the updates one at a time.

roller   A printer part that is part of the system used to move paper through a printer.

ROM (read-only memory)   Non-volatile memory that can be read from but not changed.

root   In Unix/Linux, the administrator account. The root user has absolute power on a system, including within macOS.

root directory   The starting place for all files on a disk. A hard drive is limited to 512 entries. The designation for a hard drive's root directory is C:\.

rooting   A term used to describe accessing or having an operating system on a mobile device in such a way that the user has an increased level of privilege on the device. It is often associated with attaining privileged control on Android devices. Compare with jailbreaking iOS-based devices such as iPhones.

rootkit   Malicious software that hackers install to gain administrator access to an operating system. It can also be downloaded and installed to a flash drive.

rotating/removable screen   A display that can be turned 180 to 360 degrees and that commonly allows a laptop display to be used as a tablet.

router   A network device that determines the best path to send a packet. Works at OSI model Layer 3.

router/switch functionality   A common wireless device in a small office home office (SOHO) environment that connects multiple networks such as the home network to the Internet (the routing function) and also allows multiple integrated switch ports for fast wired connectivity (the switch function).

RPO (recovery point objective) Part of a disaster recovery plan for the amount of time from a failure to when files can be recovered from a backup.

RS-232 An older port/connector standard used for serial data transfer.

RS-232C An older updated RS-232 port/connector standard used for serial data transfer.

RSA security token (Rivest–Shamir–Adleman security token) A security algorithm used with a security token, hardware token, DES card, and authentication card serial interface standard.

RTC (real-time clock) A chip used to keep track of time in a PC or computing device.

RTO (recovery time objective) The estimated time it takes to return a particular business process to normal operation after an outage, a disaster, or a failure.

RTOS (real-time operating system) An operating system that processes data from a real-time application as the data comes into the system.

RTS (request to send) Part of the RTS/CTS hardware handshaking communication method. Specific wires on the serial connector send a signal to the other device to stop or start sending data. The CTS (clear to send) and RTS signals indicate when it is okay to send data.

RTS/CTS (request to send/clear to send) A method of serial device handshaking that uses signals on specific pins of the connector to signal the other device when to stop or send data.

S

.sh An extension used with a shell script or a text file that has a sequence of commands for a Unix-based system.

S/MIME (Secure Multipurpose Internet Mail Extensions) Allows encryption and signing of MIME data; used along with SMTP to send emails that can have pictures and attachments.

S/PDIF (Sony/Phillips Digital Interface Format) Defines how audio signals are carried between audio devices and stereo components. It can also be used to connect the output of a DVD player in a PC to a home theater or some other external device.

S-video port A composite video port, coded yellow, that uses a 7-pin mini-DIN connector.

SaaS (Software as a Service) A type of cloud service that describes hosted applications such as a learning management system, enterprise resource planning (ERP), human resources management (HRM), payroll, antivirus, and inventory management that are hosted by another company and accessible from anywhere.

Safe boot A Windows System Configuration option found on the Boot tab.

safe mode (Mac) A way to start a Mac so that the startup disk is checked and repaired if possible. Hold down ⇧Shift while starting the computer.

Safe Mode (Windows) A Windows option used when the computer stalls, slows down, does not work properly, or has improper video settings or intermittent errors or when a new hardware/software installation causes problems. In Safe Mode, Windows starts with minimum device drivers and services.

safety goggles A personal protection device that should be worn when working on equipment to protect the eyes from debris, chemicals, and liquids.

SAN (storage area network) A collection of storage media that is centrally managed and available to a multitude of network devices, such as servers, network-based applications, virtual machines, and users.

SAS (Serial Attached SCSI) SAS devices connect in a point-to-point bus. Used in the enterprise environment in which high reliability and high mean time between failures is important.

SATA (Serial ATA) A point-to-point architecture for IDE devices that provides faster access for attached devices.

SATA 1 (Serial ATA 1) A SATA device that has a maximum transfer rate of 1.5 Gb/s.

SATA 2 (Serial ATA 2) A SATA device that has a maximum transfer rate of 3 Gb/s.

SATA 3 (Serial ATA 3) A SATA device that has a maximum transfer rate of 6 Gb/s.

SATA cable A cable used to connect one SATA device to a motherboard SATA port.

SATA connector A motherboard connector used to attach a cable between the motherboard and a SATA device. This connector can also be used to connect an adapter that contains one or more additional external SATA ports.

SATA-PM (Serial ATA Port Multiplier) A device that connects multiple eSATA devices to a single eSATA port.

satellite A type of Internet connection that has slower speeds than the other methods but allows connectivity in remote locations.

GLOSSARY

satellite modem   A type of modem that can provide Internet access at speeds faster than an analog modem but slower than cable or DSL access.

SC (subscriber connector)   An older type of fiber-optic connector.

scanner   An input device that allows printed documents to be brought into the computer and from there digitally displayed, printed, saved, or emailed.

scope of the change   As part of the change management planning phase, an IT change plan should include the scope of the project.

SCP (Secure Copy Protocol)   A means of using SSH to securely transfer one or more files across a network.

screen lock   A feature on a mobile device that requires something (a PIN, fingerprint, facial features, security pattern, voice, and so on) to access the device and unlock the screen of the device.

screen saver   An operating system feature that puts a specific graphic or pattern or lock when the device is not being used.

screen sharing   A macOS feature that allows one user to view and even control the display of another Apple computer that is on the network.

screwdriver   A tool that removes screws. Common types of screwdrivers used in IT support are flat-tipped and Phillips.

scribe   A plastic tool that helps with prying plastic parts or covers off laptop and mobile devices.

script   A small program written in one of several scripting languages that is designed to do a specific task.

scripting   The act of using a specific scripting language to create a script (a program) that can automate administrative tasks.

SCSI (Small Computer System Interface)   A standard that allows multiple devices to be connected to the same adapter.

SCSI cable   A Serial Attached SCSI (SAS) drive cable that attaches from the SAS drive to a SATA controller that is capable of supporting a SAS drive.

SCSI connector   A Serial Attached SCSI (SAS) drive connector is like the SATA data and power connector combined into one connector.

SCSI ID   A unique number assigned to a device connected to a SCSI chain.

SD (Secure Digital)   A storage device with non-volatile flash memory used for mobile devices.

SDK (Software Development Kit)   Contains a set of tools, such as application programming interfaces, programming tools, analytic tools, and sample code that develop an app for a specific mobile OS or platform.

SDS (safety data sheet)   A document that describes a product, including its toxicity, storage, and disposal procedures. Also contains information regarding health or safety concerns.

sector   The smallest amount of storage space on a disk or platter, holding 512 bytes of data.

secure boot   A BIOS/UEFI setting option that prevents unauthorized software from loading during the boot process.

Secure Sockets Layer   See *SSL*.

security camera   A device used for monitoring that can be wired or wireless.

security guard   A human who provides physical security into a controlled space.

security identifier   See *SID*.

security policy   One or more documents that provide rules and guidelines related to computer and network security.

security settings   A section of BIOS/UEFI Setup options that allows configuration of specific security such as power on password, chassis Intrusion detection, TPM, LoJack, and so on.

security threat   An operating system that is no longer supported by a vendor can present a problem in that it becomes a risk to the business due to lack of security updates.

selection   A selection (or decision) structure consists of a test condition together with one or more groups (or blocks) of statements. The result of the test condition determines which block of statements will be executed.

self-grounding   The act of placing a part of your body in contact with an electronic device to prevent an electrostatic discharge (ESD) event.

self-powered hub   A hub that has an external power supply.

separate pad   A bar or pad in a laser printer that can have a rubber or cork surface that rubs against the paper as it is picked up.

sequence   One of the three basic programming constructs. It means that code executes one instruction at a time, in the sequence the code is written.

Serial ATA   See *SATA*.

serial cable   A type of cable that connects to an RS-232 or DB-9 port.

server lock   A type of physical security provided for the cabinets where servers are kept. A server lock can also be electronic and can provide monitoring and security for individual server cabinet doors.

server-based network   A basic type of LAN in which users log in to a controlling computer, called a server, that knows who is authorized to connect to the LAN and what resources the user is authorized to access. Usually found in businesses that have 10 or more computers.

service   A Windows process that provides a specific function to the computer.

service fails to start   In this situation, use the *Services* Computer Management tool to investigate and possibly manually start the service.

service pack   A group of upgrades or patches provided by Microsoft for an operating system.

service release   Software available from a manufacturer to fix a known problem (bug) in its applications program.

Services   A tool that can be accessed through Windows Computer Management console or by typing `services.msc` from a command prompt. You can also control it from System Configuration utility > Services tab.

services.msc   A command that brings up the *Services* snap-in Computer Management tool so that you can start and stop services.

session layer   Layer 5 of the OSI model, which manages communication and administrative functions between two network devices.

sessions   A list of network users currently connected to the user as well as the network users' computer names, network connection type, the number of resources opened by a user, how long a user has been connected, and whether a user connects using the Guest user account.

Setup   Software that tells a computer about itself and the hardware it supports, such as the amount of RAM memory, type of hard drive installed, current date and time, and so on.

sfc   A command used to start the System File Checker utility, which verifies operating system files.

sfc /scannow   The most common `sfc` option, used to check and replace any Windows files and

.dll files that might have issues. This is especially important after removing some viruses.

SFF (small form factor)   Sometimes called an SFX case, a small type of computer case that has no official dimensions.

SFTP (Secure File Transfer Protocol)   A set of communication rules for safely transferring files from one network device to another network device.

Shadow Copy   A Windows technology used with the System Restore program that uses a block-level image instead of monitoring certain files for file changes.

share   A folder that has been set so that others can use it. This can be on a computer, printer, or network resource such as a scanner.

share permissions   A security measure that can dictate what a specific user or group can do with a file or folder that can be accessed across a network.

share screen feature   The ability for a technician to remotely access a computer and share a screen in order to educate a user or solve a problem.

Shared Folders   A Windows tool used to view shares, sessions, and open files.

shared key authentication   A method of authentication used in wireless networks that involves a group of characters that the wireless device and the access point have in common.

shared resources   In cloud computing, resources such as servers, applications, hardware such as CPUs and RAM, data storage, and network infrastructure equipment shared among people within an organization or between organizations.

shared system memory   The amount of motherboard RAM used for video because the amount of video memory on the video adapter or built in to the motherboard is not enough for the applications used.

shell   A standardized user interface to interact with the operating system.

shell script   A text file that contains a sequence of commands for a Linux/Unix-based system. Shell scripts may not run correctly on a Windows system. A shell script file extension is .sh.

shielded twisted pair (STP)   See *STP*.

shielding   Cancels out and keeps magnetic interference from devices.

shortcut   An icon with a bent arrow in the lower-left corner. It is a link to a file, a folder, or a program on a disk. If the file is a document, it opens the application used to create the document.

shoulder surfing   Someone behind you looking at what you type or what is on the screen to glean unauthorized information.

shrink (partition)   The act of making a hard drive section smaller. In the *Disk Management* tool, right-click the drive letter > *Shrink Volume*.

shutdown   A Linux/Unix and Windows command to shut down or restart the system, depending on the options used.

SID (security identifier)   A unique number assigned to a Microsoft-based computer.

side-by-side apps   A feature in Windows 7 and higher that allows you to drag a window to one side of the screen and another window to the other side and then snap in equal distance from the sides of the screen.

sidebar   In Windows 7, a collection of customizable desktop gadgets.

signature pad   A peripheral used to accept signatures, such as when someone pays with a credit card.

sigverif.exe   A command used to view signed device drivers.

SIM (subscriber identification module)   A small card in mobile devices and phones that stores personal contacts, numbers, and phone services.

SIM (System Image Manager)   Used in Windows to deploy an image of one computer to multiple computers.

SIMM (single in-line memory module)   A memory module used in aged computers but that can sometimes be found as a type of memory in printers.

simple volume   A Windows term for the storage unit that contains the files needed to load the operating system. The system volume and the boot volume can be the same unit.

single link   A type of DVI video connection that allows resolutions up to 1920×1080.

single-core processor   A processor that has only one core CPU.

single-factor authentication   A method of proving who a person or a device is by the use of just one control, such as a password.

single-mode fiber   A type of fiber-optic cabling that sends one light beam down the cable.

single-sided memory   A memory module that the CPU accesses at one time. The module has one "bank" of memory, and 64 bits are transferred out of the memory module to the CPU. More appropriately called

single-banked memory. Note that the memory module may or may not have all its "chips" on one side.

single sign-on   An authentication technique that allows a user to authenticate to multiple systems, servers, printers, and other network devices with a minimum of a user ID and password.

site survey   Used in wireless network design to determine the best wireless hardware placement for the optimum coverage area.

slave   An IDE setting for the second device added to a cable. The device should be a slower device than the master.

SLC (single-level memory cell)   A cell that stores 1 bit in a memory cell and is more expensive and longer lasting than an MLC.

sleep mode   A low power state that allows a device to be "woken up" and resumed faster than with a cold start.

sleep-and-charge USB port   A computer port that provides power to an attached device (power to charge the device) even when the computer is powered off.

SLI (Scalable Link Interface)   A technology used with video cards that allows two cards to work together.

SLI (Scan-Line Interleave) mode   A technology that allows two video cards to work together as a means of combining processing power.

SLI (system-level integration)   A term used to describe how systems connect to one another.

slmgr   A command used to reset and rearm the number of times the Windows activation clock has been reset and to see how many times the computer has been rearmed. There is no limit to the number of times a computer can be reimaged, but there is a limit on how many times a computer can be rearmed.

slow boot   A situation that could be caused by the operating system, startup applications, services, or too many startup login scripts.

slow performance   An indication that a computer system is operating in a less-than-efficient manner. Could be caused by lack of hard drive space, not enough memory, a poorly performing application, malware, or insufficient CPU cores/speed. For mobile devices, check battery power level, close apps that aren't being used, close services that aren't being used, connect to a WiFi network, and move closer to the AP.

slow profile load   The company may make use of local or domain policies including user and group profiles. Too many profiles that are required at startup slows the startup/login process.

slow transfer speed   The results of network latency, the time measured to transmit data from source to destination.

SLP (Service Location Protocol)   A TCP/IP protocol that announces and discovers services in a LAN. SLP uses port 427.

S.M.A.R.T. (Self-Monitoring, Analysis, and Reporting Technology)   A feature that allows a storage device to send messages about possible failures or data loss. Configuration setting located in the BIOS/UEFI.

smart card   A small ID-size card that can store data, be encrypted, and swiped through and/or interact wirelessly with a smart card reader. Examples of smart cards are identification, medical, credit, and access card.

smart card reader   A device that can read flash media. Also called a multi-card reader. It can also be a device used to read the embedded chips in smart cards.

smart watch   Wrist watch capable of limited functions, such as syncing with a smartphone, downloading apps, or GPS tracking.

smartphone   A device that has more capabilities than a cell phone, such as Internet connectivity, GPS tracking, running apps, taking pictures, playing music, or connecting wirelessly to other devices.

SMB (Server Message Block)   A means of providing access to shared network devices and files. SMB uses port 445.

smoke   An indication of a power supply problem.

SMTP (Simple Mail Transfer Protocol)   A standard used for email or for transferring messages across a network from one device to another. SMTP uses port 25.

snapshot   In a virtualization environment, a copy or backup of the virtual machine (VM) at a particular point in time that is used to revert the VM to that point in time. It is similar in concept to a restore point.

SNMP (Simple Network Management Protocol)   A standard that supports network monitoring and management. SNMP uses ports 161/162.

social engineering   A technique used to trick people into divulging information, including their own personal information or corporate knowledge.

SODIMM (small outline DIMM)   A special small DIMM used in laptops and printers.

soft reset   Simply restarting a device. Contrast this to a hard reset, which is also called a factory reset.

software   An application or operating system consisting of a set of instructions that makes the hardware work.

software compatibility   Before installing an app, ensure it will work with the operating system.

software firewall   A software application or tool provided with a computer or device like an access point that can be configured to permit or block specific types of traffic.

software token   A security technique in which a code is delivered via text, phone call, or email, and this code is required in addition to the user ID and password.

Software Updater   An Ubuntu tool used to update Linux operating systems and applications.

SOHO (small office/home office)   A description given to a small network that might consist of wired and wireless devices, Internet connectivity, VoIP, and even a VPN connection to the corporate network.

sound card   An adapter, also known as an audio card, that has several ports that convert digital signals to audible sound and also the reverse. Common devices that connect to the ports include microphones and speakers.

SP   See *service pack*.

spam   Email that is unsolicited and comes from unknown people or businesses.

spanned volume   A Windows term that describes hard drive space created from multiple hard drives.

SPD (serial presence detect)   An extra EEPROM feature that allows the system BIOS to read the EEPROM (which contains memory information such as capacity, voltage, error detection, refresh rates, and data width) and adjusts motherboard timings for best CPU-to-RAM performance.

SPDIF (Sony-Phillips Digital Interface Format)   See *S/PDIF*.

speaker   A mechanical device that produces acoustic sound and that may be internal or external to a computer or mobile device.

spear phishing   A targeted type of social engineering in which the attackers know some information about someone that lulls them into thinking an email or other electronic message is safe.

special function key   One of the uppermost keys on a keyboard, which activate specific functions. Labeled ⒡1, ⒡2, and so on, these keys control things like sound on/off, screen brightness dimmer/brighter, and more.

special thermal paper   Paper sensitive to heat that is used with thermal printers in retail establishments.

speed (NIC property)   A network card configuration property. It is normally configured automatically, but manual options include 10 Gb/s, 1 Gb/s, 100 Mb/s, and 10 Mb/s.

SPGA (staggered pin grid array)   A type of processor slot or package.

spinning pinwheel   An error indication that can indicate a lack of response from the hard drive and/or a particular application. Commonly seen in macOS.

split (partition)   The act of dividing a particular space on a storage device.

splitter   A convenient device used with twisted pair and coaxial cables that allows two inputs and one output. Splitters degrade signal quality so should be avoided, if possible.

splitting partition (Disk Management)   A way of dividing space on a hard drive or making one partition smaller (right-click the drive > *Shrink Volume*) and then creating a new partition with the relinquished drive space.

spoofing   Sending an Ethernet frame with a fake source MAC address to trick other devices into sending traffic to a rogue device.

Spotlight   A macOS universal search tool that can locate every file and directory and also search email, contacts, music, and even the web.

SPS (standby power supply)   A device that provides power to the computer only after it first detects an AC voltage power-out condition.

spyware   Software that collects information without user consent, using keystroke logging, gaining access to saved documents, and recording Internet activity. Results in unsolicited pop-ups and identity theft.

SRAM (static random-access memory)   Memory that is faster but more expensive than DRAM. SRAM is also known as cache memory, or L1, L2, or L3 cache.

SSD (solid-state drive)   A drive that uses non-volatile flash memory and no moving parts to store data. It is faster but more expensive than a mechanical hard drive.

SSH (Secure Shell)   A means of securing data communication including remote connectivity of devices and file transfers. SSH uses port 22.

SSHD (solid-state hybrid drive)   A drive that contains both a mechanical hard drive and flash memory used as an SSD.

SSID (service set identifier)   A set of up to 32 alphanumeric characters used in wireless networks to differentiate between networks.

SSID broadcasting   Used with wireless network access points to periodically send out a beacon frame that includes the SSID. Wireless devices can automatically detect the SSID from this beacon.

SSID not found   If a particular SSID is not found in the list of wireless networks, it could be that the wireless router/AP has been configured to not broadcast the SSID, and it has to be entered. Otherwise, the device might be out of range of the wireless network.

SSL (Secure Sockets Layer)   A protocol used to transmit Internet messages securely.

SSO (single sign-on)   A method of authentication or proving who you are by signing on once and gaining access to several services.

ST (straight tip)   A type of fiber connector.

ST fiber connector   A (straight tip) common type of fiber-optic connector.

standard thick client   A business computer that has applications loaded on the local hard drive and that meets recommended requirements for the selected OS. Contrast with thin client.

standard privileges   A security function in Windows that allows people using a Standard user account execute specific commands from a CLI.

Standard user   One of the two basic types of Windows user accounts that, by default, cannot install most applications or change system settings. Contrast with an Administrator account that has full control over a system.

standby mode   A low-power Windows power option mode that allows a computer to be used again faster than if it were powered on as a cold start.

standby power   Power that is always provided, even when a computer is powered off. It is why you have to unplug a computer when working inside it.

standoff   A plastic connector on the bottom side of a motherboard.

star topology   The most common Ethernet network topology, in which each device connects to a central hub or switch. If an individual device or a cable fails, the rest of the network keeps working. But if the hub or switch fails, the entire network goes down.

start bit A bit used in asynchronous communications that signals the beginning of each data byte.

Start button Located in the lower-left corner of the Windows desktop, a button that is used to access and launch applications, files, utilities, and help, as well as to add/remove hardware and software.

Start screen The standard look of Windows 8 that has tiles instead of icons, like the traditional Windows desktop. Windows 8.1 has both the traditional desktop and a Start screen.

sticking key In this situation, shake out keyboard dirt, spray with compressed air, or remove a key to clean it.

stop bit A bit used in asynchronous communications that signals the end of each data byte.

storage card A removable data storage device frequently used in mobile devices and laptops. Also known as a flash memory card.

storage pool A Microsoft Windows 8/10 technology that allows the creation of a storage area that is made from two or more physical drives that can be different types, such as an internal SATA drive and an external USB drive.

Storage Spaces A Windows 8/10 technology that allows combining different types of storage devices into one writable space.

STP (shielded twisted pair) Network cable with extra foil to prevent outside noise from interfering with data on the cable.

straight-through cable A network cable that uses twisted pair copper wires and RJ-45 connectors at each end. The cable uses the same pinout and is also known as a patch cable.

streak A paper issue in a printer caused by the drum, toner cartridge, dirty or damaged fusing assembly, or the paper.

string A basic data type that is simply a string of characters.

striped volume A Windows term describing how data is written across 2 to 32 hard drives. It is different from a spanned volume in that each drive is used alternately instead of filling the first hard drive before going to the second hard drive. Other names include striping and RAID 0.

su A Linux command that switches from one user account to another.

subdirectory A directory contained within another directory. Subdirectories are also called subfolders.

subfolder A folder contained within another folder that might also be called a subdirectory.

subnet A portion of a network number that has been subdivided so that multiple networks can use separate parts of a single network number. Subnets allow more efficient use of IP addresses. Also called a subnetwork or a subnetwork number.

subnet mask A number a computer uses to determine which part of an IP address represents the network and which portion represents the host.

sudo A Linux command that allows a user temporary root privileges.

surge suppressor/protector A device that helps protect power supplies from overvoltage conditions. Also known as a surge strip.

suspend mode Another name for sleep mode, used to conserve power in a computing device.

swap partition Also known as a paging file, acts as a memory overflow and allows secondary storage to let programs exceed the size of available physical memory by using hard drive space as memory.

swipe lock Ability to lock out a mobile device or its screen with a finger sweep movement.

switch In star networks, a Layer 2 central controlling device that looks at each data frame as it comes through each port.

swollen battery A bulging battery requires immediate replacement as it may not hold a charge and could soon leak.

Sync Center A Windows 7 Control Panel area used to synchronize files between computers.

synchronization app An option sometimes available with cloud file storage or a program that you can download that allows you to access files that have been placed in a special folder.

synchronize to the automobile Mobile devices can synchronize data such as address books to a vehicle. Some vehicles support text-to-speech and can read text messages.

synchronize to the cloud Storing data in a remote location in which it can be viewed, retrieved, saved, shared, and/or forwarded based on the cloud vendor used and user preferences.

synchronize to the desktop A mobile device exchanging and storing data with one or more desktop computers using an app, software, the operating system, or a combination of these.

synchronous   Describing transmissions that require the use of a clock signal.

syntax   A set of symbols and rules used to create instructions. Every scripting language has its own syntax.

syslog server   A device used to receive information from multiple network devices and used as a historical record of events such as devices losing power, a particular interface going down, or access (login/logout) to the device.

Sysprep   A tool used to deploy Windows in a corporate environment. Also known as Windows System Preparation.

system attempts to boot to an incorrect device   In this situation, change the boot order in BIOS/UEFI.

system attribute   A file designation to mark a file as a system file. By default, files with this attribute set do not appear in directory listings.

system bar   On a mobile tablet, the bottom area, containing a back button, home button, recent applications opened, and the notification area.

system board   Sometimes spelled systemboard or called a motherboard, a mobile device part that holds the majority of the electronics.

System Configuration utility   A Windows utility that allows boot files and settings to be enabled/disabled for troubleshooting purposes. The command that brings up this utility is `msconfig.exe`.

system file   A file that is needed to allow a computer to boot. A file type that is also known as a startup file.

System File Checker (SFC)   A Windows tool used to verify operating system files.

system image   Contains a saved copy of the operating system and all user files that can be used to restore a damaged or corrupted computer.

System Image Manager   See *SIM*.

System Information   A macOS utility that provides an overview of the Mac, including basic diagnostic information such as installed hardware, software, and network settings.

system lockout   A configuration setting to prevent unauthorized access when a security method is not successful. For example, incorrectly entering a password three times.

system lockup   A symptom of a motherboard, CPU, RAM, or power supply problem.

system log   Each operating system has logs that can be viewed when things go wrong. In Windows, Event Viewer is used.

system log error   An error that provides detailed information about Windows-controlled events.

System Monitor   A Windows utility that monitors specific computer components and allows creation of graphs, bar charts, and text reports.

system partition   A type of active hard drive partition that contains the hardware-specific files needed to load the operating system.

System Preferences   A macOS basic management and troubleshooting tool, equivalent to Control Panel utilities in Windows. It contains most of the system settings, such as desktop backgrounds and screen savers, as well as more advanced settings, such as user accounts and file sharing. Third-party applications can also insert their own preferences menu into the System Preferences menu.

system protection   The *System* section of the Control Panel > *System Protection* tab is used to set up and configure System Restore, manage restore points, and manage the amount of disk space used by System Restore.

system requirements (application)   The hardware and software required for an application to be installed.

system resources   The collective set of interrupt, I/O address, and DMA configuration parameters.

System Restore   A utility that makes a snapshot of the registry and backs up certain dynamic system files. When a problem occurs, use this utility to take your system back to a time before the error started.

system volume   A Windows term describing the storage space that holds Windows operating system files used to boot the computer.

systemboard   Synonymous with motherboard and sometimes also spelled system board. In a computer, holds the majority of the electronics, contains a processor, has memory, and supports having ports attached.

T

T568A   An ANSI/TIA/EIA Ethernet network cabling standard.

T568B   An ANSI/TIA/EIA Ethernet network cabling standard.

tablet   A mobile device with a touchscreen, camera(s), microphone, and possibly one or more ports, such as sound, USB, miniDisplayPort, or miniThunderbolt. Tablets connect to the Internet; take, send, receive, and store pictures and video; and are often a good choice for people who travel. Trade in, donate, or recycle broken or old tablets responsibly.

TACACS (Terminal Access Controller Access-Control System)   A secure method of authentication using a server.

tailgating   A breach of physical security that occurs when an unauthorized person enters a secure space behind an authorized person. Training and diligence by all employees are the only ways to stop tailgating.

tap-to-pay device   A wireless device used to securely authorize payment for a transaction.

tape drive   A means of backup used with servers.

taskbar   On a Windows program, the bar that runs across the bottom of the desktop. It holds buttons that represent files and applications currently loaded into RAM. It also holds icons representing direct access to system tools.

taskkill   A command used to halt a process or task.

tasklist   A command used to list process IDs for active applications and services. This command should be used before the `taskkill` command.

Task Manager   A Windows-based utility that displays memory and processor usage data and also displays currently loaded applications as well as currently running processes.

Task Scheduler   A Windows-based utility that allows applications or tasks to be executed periodically or at a specific date and time. This can include a systemwide message.

Task View   A Windows icon that allows the user to create multiple desktops and switch between them.

TCP (Transmission Control Protocol)   An OSI model Layer 4 standard that ensures reliable communication between two devices.

TCP printing   Also known as TCP/IP printing, the ability to connect to and print to a printer that has been assigned an IP address.

TCP/IP (Transmission Control Protocol/Internet Protocol)   The most widely used network protocol stack for connecting to the Internet. Developed by the Defense Advanced Research Projects Agency in the 1970s, it is the basis of the Internet.

TDR (time domain reflectometer)   A device used to check fiber connectivity.

teamwork   The ability to work with others toward a common goal.

Telnet   A nonsecure application protocol that allows connection to a remote network device. Telnet uses port 23. Commonly replaced by the more secure SSH.

temperature   Computers should operate in temperatures between 60 and 75 degrees.

terabyte (TB)   Approximately 1 trillion bytes of information, or 2^{40} (1,099,511,627,776) bytes.

Terminal   The terminal emulator for macOS and Linux that allows the command line interface (CLI) access to the operating system. Certain tasks or functions are not GUI-friendly, and CLI commands are required.

terminal services   Software on a server that allows multiple simultaneous client sessions.

tethering   Allows sharing of Internet connectivity among mobile devices in the area. It is a form of hotspot.

text file   A file where each byte represents one character of ASCII code. Scripts are all text files.

TFTP (Trivial File Transfer Protocol)   A nonsecure means of quickly transferring files from one device to another device.

thermal paste   Applied between the processor and its heat sink to provide a thermal pad that disperses heat more evenly.

thermal printer   A printer commonly used in retail that uses heat and special thermal paper to create the printed image.

thermal sensor   A feature found on memory modules that is used by the BIOS/UEFI to read and adjust settings for optimum performance.

thermal wax transfer   A type of printer that uses wax-based inks similar to the solid ink printer, but it prints at lower resolutions.

thermostat   A smart IoT device that is programmable and can be remotely controlled through a phone or tablet. It provides real-time data.

thick client   See *standard thick client*.

thin client   A type of computer that does not have all the ports and components (such as a hard drive) of a traditional PC. It includes basic applications, meets minimum requirements for the selected OS, and has network connectivity.

thread   A unit of programming code that receives a slice of time from Windows, so it can run concurrently with other units of code or threads.

throttle management   The ability to control processor speed by slowing the processor down when it is not used heavily or is running too hot.

Thunderbolt card   An adapter that allows the addition of a Thunderbolt port to a computer that does not have one. A Thunderbolt port is an updated port that uses some of the DisplayPort technology developed by Intel and Apple.

Thunderbolt port   A type of video port on PCIe adapters or on Apple computers.

tile   A square block on a Windows 8/10 Start screen with a picture of the function it performs when activated.

Time Machine   A bundled application in macOS that performs full and incremental system backups to an external hard drive. It gets its clever naming from the capability to navigate past backups as if traveling backward through time.

time management   How much time you budget and then actually spend on doing each task throughout the workday.

time/date/region/language settings   Part of the operating system installation process is to set the regional time, date, and language preferences.

timeout/screen lock   A security feature in which, after a period of nonuse, the computer requires a username and password to again access the computer.

TKIP (Temporal Key Integrity Protocol)   A method of encryption that is an improvement over WEP because the encryption keys periodically change.

TLS (Transport Layer Security)   A set of rules that provide secure transmissions over a network.

TN (twisted nematic)   A technology used with LCDs.

tone generator   A tool used with a toner probe to identify cables when they are unlabeled or incorrectly labeled.

toner   The combined particles in a laser toner cartridge that produce an image when fused onto paper. Harmful if inhaled. Messy if spilled.

toner is not fused   In this situation, determine if the problem is in the fuser assembly or elsewhere in the printer; send output to the printer. When the printer finishes the writing stage and before the toner fuses to the paper, open the laser cover and remove the paper. If the paper is error free, then the problem is most likely in the transfer corona or fusing assembly.

toner vacuum   A vacuum used inside a laser printer that will not damage the vacuum as a result.

TOSLINK   A type of fiber S/PDIF connection.

touch   A Linux command used to create a file.

touchpad   A part of a laptop or keyboard that allows cursor control.

touchscreen   An way to input information into a computer by using a finger or stylus; used in kiosks.

touchscreen non-responsive   When this occurs, close apps. See if the problem is app specific. Restart the device. Turn off the device, remove the battery, allow the device to dry or cool, reinstall the battery, and turn on the device. Remove the screen protector, calibrate the screen, and do a factory reset.

tower   A computer model with a motherboard that mounts perpendicular to the floor.

toxic waste handling   The regulated removal and disposal of anything harmful to people and the environment. Some physical parts, pieces, and batteries of computers, laser printers, and mobile devices are considered toxic e-waste because of the heavy metals and chemicals they contain.

TPM (Trusted Platform Module)   A motherboard chip used for hardware and software authentication. TPM can authenticate hardware devices. Applications can use TPM for file and folder encryption, local passwords, email, VPN/PKI authentication, and wireless authentication.

TPM (BIOS)   Trusted Platform Module (TPM) is a BIOS/UEFI option that allows initialization and setting a password for the TPM motherboard chip that generates and stores cryptographic keys.

tracert   A Windows command line network troubleshooting command that displays the path a data packet takes through a network, thus allowing you to see where a fault occurs in larger networks. Compare with **traceroute**, used in macOS and Linux.

transfer belt   Located at the bottom of the printer.

transfer corona   A wire inside a laser printer that applies a positive charge to the back of the paper so that the toner is attracted to the paper as it moves through the printer.

transfer roller   A roller inside a laser printer that replaces the transfer corona. The roller applies a positive charge to the back of the paper so that the toner is attracted to the paper as it moves through the printer.

transferring A laser printer imaging process in which the toner (image) moves from the drum to the paper.

transport layer Layer 4 of the OSI model, which determines the details of how data is sent, supervises the validity of the transmission, and defines the protocol for structuring messages.

`tree` A structure used to represent files and folders where the root directory is the top-level directory and all directories and subdirectories with their specific files are shown as branches of the tree.

tree A Windows command that shows a directory and file structure, depending on the option used.

triple-channel A type of memory execution in which motherboards access three memory modules simultaneously.

trojan A virus program that appears to be a normal application but that, when executed, changes something. It does not replicate but could gather information that could later be used to hack into someone's computer.

trusted source A security measure that is built in to some browsers and security software that indicates whether a website or downloaded file is a trusted or untrusted software source.

TVS rating (transient voltage suppressor rating) A measure of a surge protector's capability to guard against overvoltage conditions. The lower the TVS rating, the better.

twisted pair cable Network cable made of eight copper wires twisted into four pairs. Can be shielded or unshielded.

`type` A command that displays a file's contents on the screen.

Type 1 hypervisor In a virtualization environment, a hypervisor that has the operating system running on top of the hypervisor. Also known as a native hypervisor.

Type 2 hypervisor In a virtualization environment, a hypervisor that runs on top of a host operating system to manage and oversee the virtual machine. Also known as a hosted hypervisor.

Type A-B-C fire extinguisher A fire extinguisher that can be used on either Type A, Type B, or Type C fires.

Type C fire extinguisher A fire extinguisher that can be used only on electrical fires.

U

UAC (User Account Control) A Windows dialog box that appears and asks permission to do something that might be harmful or change the operating system environment. Some changes require an administrator password to continue.

Ubuntu Software Center A software manager to access Ubuntu's repositories of open source software. It can install new applications and uninstall existing ones, many of which are available for free.

UDF (Universal Disk Format) A file system used for DVDs so data can be read and acted upon through the operating system, as for other devices, such as a flash drive.

UDF (user-defined function) Something built into a program that allows a specific function to be provided by the person using the program.

UDP (User Datagram Protocol) A Layer 4 connectionless standard that applications use to communicate with a remote device.

UEFI (Unified Extensible Firmware Interface) The replacement for the traditional BIOS that has a boot manager instead of the BIOS controlling the boot process. The UEFI environment allows for a graphic interface, the use of a mouse, antivirus software to be used before the operating system loads, and Internet access.

UL 1449 VPR A voltage protection rating standard developed by Underwriters Laboratories to measure the maximum amount of voltage a surge protector allows through to attached devices.

unable to install printer In this situation, check cabling and power; follow the manufacturer's instructions; delete the print driver and try installation again; download a different print driver and try installation again; research the error on the manufacturer's website; and document.

unable to decrypt email In this situation, use S/MIME, use a web browser add-on, or obtain the security certificate.

unattended installation A method of installing Windows in which the remote computer does not have to be touched. Use Microsoft Deployment Toolkit with Configuration Manager or another imaging product.

unavailable resources   A symptom of a network problem in which the network device cannot access the Internet, a network printer, a network share, a particular server, email, and/or other resources.

unbuffered memory   Memory that does not delay all data transfers by one clock tick to ensure accuracy as registered memory does. Used in low- to medium-powered computers.

UNC (universal naming convention)   Used at the command prompt to obtain network shares.

undervoltage   A condition that occurs when AC power drops below 100 volts, which may cause the computer's power supply to draw too much current and overheat.

unexpected shutdowns   A symptom of an issue with the processor, motherboard, or power supply.

unique identifier   An item that must be removed during the Windows image creation process before deploying an image to computers. Unique identifiers include the computer name, security identifier (SID), network domain.

Unity   The graphical user interface in Ubuntu. It has some similarities to the user interface of macOS, but it is drastically different from Windows.

unlock account   In Active Directory, locate the user account and right-click on it > select *Reset Password* > use the *Unlock the User's Account* checkbox.

unmanaged switch   A type of switch that cannot be remotely accessed and is commonly found in home and small business wired networks.

unshielded twisted pair   See *UTP* and see also *twisted pair cable*.

untrusted source   A security measure that is built in to some browsers and security software that indicates whether a website or downloaded file is a trusted or untrusted software source.

updatedb   A Linux command that updates the file database.

update boot order   One thing that can cause a Windows computer to not boot is the boot order in the BIOS/UEFI settings.

update network settings   A device might need the network settings updated in order to get onto the wired or wireless network. This could involve using the `ipconfig /release` and `ipconfig /renew` commands or changing the IP address to a manually assigned one.

upgrade   To install a newer or more powerful operating system where one already exists. An upgrade can also involve installing newer hardware.

UPnP (universal plug and play)   An alternative to port forwarding that allows peer-to-peer (P2P) gaming applications to function without further configuration.

UPS (uninterruptible power supply)   A device that provides power for a limited time to a computer or device during a power outage.

upstream   Describes information that is sent to the Internet, such as transmitting email or uploading a file to a server.

upward compatibility   A technique used by a software manufacturer when a product is designed in such a way that it can accept input intended for a future version. Another name for forward compatibility.

URL (uniform resource locator)   A method of accessing Internet resources.

usable host numbers   The number of host bits (and associated IP addresses) that can be used by network devices residing in a subnetwork.

usable subnets   The number of subnetworks that can be used when an IP network number is subdivided to allow more efficient use of IP addresses.

USB (universal serial bus)   A bus that allows 127 devices to be connected to a single computer port.

USB 2.0   A standardized port that supported speeds up to 480 Mb/s, a maximum of 0.5 amps, 5 VDC, as well as Type A and Type B connectors.

USB 3.0   A standardized port that supports speeds up to 5 Gb/s, a maximum of .9 amps, and 5 VDC.

USB 3.1   A standardized port that supports speeds up to 10 Gb/s and supports the Type C connector.

USB A-to-USB B converter   Connector cable with a USB A plug and a USB B plug.

USB expansion card   A metal plate that has one or more USB ports and a cable that connects to the motherboard. The metal plate fits in a slot that a normal card in an expansion slot would take.

USB flash drive   Sometimes called a flash drive or a memory stick, a drive that allows storage via a USB port.

USB C   See *USB Type-C*.

USB lock   A security device that prevents USB storage devices from being inserted into a USB port.

USB port   A port on a motherboard or on an adapter that allows the connection of up to 127 devices.

USB to Bluetooth   An adapter that connects Bluetooth to a laptop or mobile device that has a USB port.

USB to RJ-45 dongle   An adapter that connects Ethernet to a laptop or mobile device that has a USB port.

USB to WiFi dongle   An adapter that connects WiFi to a laptop or mobile device that has a USB port.

USB-to-Ethernet converter   A connector cable with a USB plug and an Ethernet end.

USB Type-A   An upstream male connector on a USB cable that connects to an upstream Type-A port on a host computer or other hub.

USB Type-B   A downstream male connector on a USB cable that connects to a Type-B connector on the downstream device.

USB Type-C   A reversible plug connector for USB devices and hosts and that will eventually replace USB Type-A/Type-B plugs.

USB-PD   A USB power delivery standard that allows up to 20 V at 5 A for 100 watts of power. The standard has five levels of power: 10 W, 18 W, 36 W, 60 W, and 100 W.

use appropriate titles   IT personnel should use appropriate titles, such as Dr., Mr., Professor, and Ms.

User Account Control   See *UAC*.

user account management   The process of creating a user, adding that user to a group, and managing those functions.

user authentication/strong passwords   A security method used to ensure that a person accessing a device, network, or resource is allowed to do so.

user profile   All settings associated with a specific user, including desktop settings, network configurations, and applications that the user has access to. It is part of the registry.

User State Migration Tool   See *USMT*.

USMT (User State Migration Tool)   A Windows tool used when deploying a large number of Windows computers.

UTM (unified threat management)   A security device that provides multiple functions, such as content filtering, antivirus, antispyware, anti-malware, firewall, and intrusion detection and prevention.

UTP (unshielded twisted pair)   The most common network cable. Comes in different categories for different uses. See also *twisted pair cable*.

V

.vbs   A file extension for VBScript files.

VA (vertical alignment)   An LCD panel technology that provides wide viewing angles, good color, and high contrast.

vacuum   A device used to suction dust and debris from computers and wiring closets.

variable   In scripting, the name of a storage location in the computer's internal memory. The value of the variable is the contents at that memory location. It Is called a variable because the value can change (vary) as the program runs.

VBScript   A scripting language designed specifically for use with Microsoft Internet Explorer. A VBScript file has the extension .vbs.

VDC (volts direct current)   The type of voltage used inside computers, printers, laptops, and displays.

VDI (virtual desktop infrastructure)   An environment in which the PC's operating system resides on a server.

vendor-specific operating system   A closed source operating system that is not allowed to be modified or distributed unless authorized by the developer, such as Apple's iOS.

ventilation   Computers require good ventilation. Never block air vents, especially on a laptop.

vertical lines   Lines that appear on printer paper that may be caused by debris on the corona wires or in the developer unit in the cartridge. Replace cartridge.

vertical streaking   Streaking that can occur on printer paper because of toner cartridge. Remove the toner cartridge, hold the toner cartridge in front of you with both hands, and rock it gently back and forth, reinsert the cartridge into the printer, and test the printer.

VFAT (Virtual File Allocation Table)   An extension of the FAT file system that allowed filenames to be up to 255 characters starting with Windows 95.

VGA (Video Graphics Array)   A type of monitor that displays at least a 640×480 resolution or greater and connects to a 15-pin D-shell connector.

VGA mode   A mode used when a computer boots into Safe Mode.

VGA port   A type of 15-pin three-row video port that normally has a CRT monitor attached.

vi   A command line text editor used by macOS and Linux.

video card An adapter used to output video to a display. Contrast with onboard video card.

virtual application streaming A situation in which an application does not have to be installed on an individual device, and just some of the code needed to run the application is loaded. Also called cloud-based application.

virtual assistant A mobile operating feature that uses voice commands to obtain information such as directions and current sports scores and to dictate emails or texts.

virtual desktop An environment in which the client computer operating system and applications are hosted remotely in a cloud environment.

virtual machine A way for an operating system to appear as a separate computer to each application. One computer that has two or more operating systems installed that are unaware of each other due to virtualization software.

virtual memory A method of simulating extra memory by using the hard disk space as if it were RAM.

virtual NIC A network interface card used in a virtual environment. Each virtual NIC has its own MAC address and can have an IP address assigned.

virtual printing Printing to somewhere other than to the directly connected printer and to a specific file so that the information can be viewed, saved, emailed, or sent to another printer.

virtual technology Another name for virtualization, which is a process that allows multiple operating systems to be installed and share hardware resources.

Virtual XP mode A Windows 7 tool that was previously known as Windows XP Mode that can be downloaded and used in Windows 7 Professional and higher versions to allow older applications to run.

virtualization A process that allows a computer to run multiple operating systems without affecting each other, share hardware, and provide a test environment for software that may not be compatible on a specific platform.

virtualization support A BIOS/UEFI option to enable or disable the capability of the computer to be used in a virtualization environment where more than one operating system can share the same hardware resources.

virtualization workstation A computer that has multiple operating systems in a virtual environment in which one operating system has no interaction with the other operating system; they are independent of one another. A virtualization PC has multiple powerful multicore processors, maximum RAM, multiple fast large-capacity hard drives, 1 Gb/s network connection, virtualization software, and a possible NAS.

virus A program designed to change the way a computer originally operated.

VIS (viewable image size) The actual area of a monitor seen by a user.

VLAN (virtual local area network) A switch technology that allows assignment of ports to a specific VLAN number, thus creating separate networks so that the devices that connect to ports assigned to one VLAN number cannot see devices that connect to switch ports assigned to a different VLAN number.

VLK (volume license key) Used when deploying Windows in the enterprise environment.

VM (virtual machine) See *virtual machine*.

VNC (virtual network computing) A situation in which one computer can be controlled from a remote network, device such as when a computer technician needs to install a network printer onto a remote computer.

voice-enabled smart speaker A wireless device that originally was designed to respond to voice commands for music control but now may contain a digital assistant and/or control other smart devices.

VoIP (Voice over IP) A way of sending phone calls over the Internet or over networks that traditionally transmitted only data.

volt The measurement for voltage.

voltage An electronic measurement of the pressure pushing electrons through a circuit. Voltage is measured in volts.

volume A section of a storage device that receives a drive letter and to which data can be written.

volume license key See *VLK*.

VPN (virtual private network) A remote computer connecting to a remote network by "tunneling" over an intermediate network, such as the Internet or a LAN.

VR (virtual reality) headset A peripheral similar to goggles used to see high-definition images in a simulated environment.

VRAM (video random-access memory) A type of memory that was used on older video cards.

W

Wake on LAN   A BIOS and adapter feature that allows a network administrator to remotely control power to a workstation and allows a computer to come out of the sleep mode.

Wake on Ring   A BIOS and adapter feature that allows a computer to come out of sleep mode when the telephone rings, so the computer can accept faxes, emails, and so on when the user is absent.

wallpaper   In an operating system, a background picture, pattern, or color located behind desktop icons.

WAN (wide area network)   Two or more LANs communicating, often across large distances. The most famous WAN is the Internet.

WAP (wireless access point)   See *wireless access point*.

warm boot   Restarting a computer by pressing Ctrl+Alt+Del, using the restart function, or by clicking the Windows Restart option. Puts less strain on a computer than a cold boot.

waterproofing   A mobile device accessory that protects against liquid damage. Waterproofing options provides different levels of protection.

watt   The electrical measure in which computer power supplies are rated.

wattage rating   A measure used to determine whether a power supply is powerful enough to power the devices within a computer.

WDS (Windows Deployment Services)   Uses the corporate network to deploy Windows-based operating systems, drivers, updates, and applications using a network-based installation.

wearable devices   Mobile devices worn on one's person, such as smart watches, fitness monitors, headsets, and even glasses.

wear leveling   The process of writing and erasing data in different memory blocks of SSDs (solid-state drives) to prolong the life of a drive.

web credentials   Logon information for specific websites stored by Skype, Edge, and other Microsoft apps in Windows 8 and 10.

web server   A computer configured to provide web-based content that is accessed through a web browser.

webcam   Short for web camera, a small camera used for communicating via video across the Internet.

weight limitation   Do not lift anything that weighs over 40 pounds by yourself.

WEP (Wired Equivalent Privacy)   A type of encryption that is sometimes used in wireless networks.

while loop   In scripting, a type of loop that begins with the keyword `while` along with a test condition. If the condition is true, the loop begins, and the block of statements in the loop repeats until the condition is no longer true.

whitelist   A method of controlling access by permitting devices, access, services, people, apps, protocols, or websites through to a site or network device.

WiBro (mobile Wireless Broadband)   Also known as mobile WiMAX, allows wireless connectivity for moving devices, such as those on a bus or train.

WiFi (Wireless Fidelity)   A type of network in which no wires are needed to connect to the network.

WiFi analyzer   A tool used to identify what wireless networks are in the area, determine what frequencies (channels) are used, and find a less crowded channel for any wireless installations, hotspot, or tethering that may be needed in a particular area. Also known as a wireless locator.

WiFi antenna   Attaches to a WLAN card to receive or transmit wireless signals.

WiFi calling   A common mobile device app used to make phone calls using a WiFi connection rather than a cell phone network.

wildcard   A special character used at the command prompt when typing commands. The ? character is used to designate "any" for a single character place, whereas the * character denotes any characters from that place forward.

WiMAX   A wireless technology that could be used to connect the Internet with a large-scale coverage area and access speeds up to 1 Gb/s. Also used for connectivity as part of a cellular network.

window   A specific area of the screen that has contains information.

Windows Assessment and Deployment Kit (ADK)   A set of Microsoft tools used to deploy system images in the corporate environment.

Windows Automated Installation Kit (AIK)   An older set of Microsoft tools used to deploy system images in the corporate environment that has been replaced by the Windows Assessment and Deployment Kit.

Windows credentials   Information used only by Windows and its services. Can be used to automatically log someone into shared folders of another network.

Windows Defender   A Windows application that detects spyware.

Windows domain   A type of computer network in which all user accounts, computers, printers, and other network devices are registered with a central database located on one or more clusters of central computers known as domain controllers.

Windows Explorer   See *Explorer*.

Windows Memory Diagnostic tool   A tool used to thoroughly test RAM. Accessed from a command prompt using the mdsched command or using the *Administrative Tools* section of the Control Panel > *Diagnose Your Computer's Memory Problems* link.

Windows Mobile   A Microsoft operating system for phones that has been discontinued.

Windows Recovery Environment   See *WinRE*.

Windows Resource Protection   See *WRP*.

Windows Storage Spaces   A Windows 8/10 technology that allows the combination of different types of storage devices into one writable space.

Windows Update   Modified files provided for the current operating system.

Windows Upgrade Advisor   A Microsoft tool that can be downloaded and executed to determine if a computer can function well with a higher version of Windows installed.

Windows XP mode   See *Virtual XP mode*.

WinRE (Windows Recovery Environment)   A tool found on the Windows installation disc and also in Windows that includes multiple tools used to troubleshoot Windows when it does not work properly.

wire stripper   A tool used when adding a connector to a network cable.

wireless access point   A device that receives and transmits data from multiple computers that have wireless NICs installed. The access point can be a standalone unit or can be integrated into an ADSL router.

wireless broadband   A feature available from service providers that allows PC Cards, USB modems, mobile data cards, or integrated laptop connectivity to have the capability to receive, create, and communicate Internet information within a specific coverage area.

wireless card   Also known as a wireless NIC, an electronic device that allows wireless network connectivity.

wireless extender   Another name for a wireless repeater that increases the size of a wireless network.

wireless locator   Also called a WiFi analyzer, which is used to identify wireless networks in the area (frequencies or channels used), range, SSIDs, and so on.

wireless network   A type of network that uses air as the medium to connect devices.

WLAN (wireless LAN)   A wireless network that consists of an access point and some wireless devices, including laptops, tablets, and smartphones.

WMN (wireless mesh network)   A type of wireless network that does not require access points. Peer radio devices allow connectivity over distances, which is especially good in emergency situations. Data is passed from one device to another to reach its final destination.

workgroup   A term given to a peer-to-peer Windows network. A workgroup does not use a server to authenticate users during the login process.

workstation   A computer used by a user in a business or other professional work.

worm   A virus program that replicates from one drive to another. The most common worm virus today is an email message that, when opened, sends the virus to every address in the user's address book.

WPA (WiFi Protected Access)   A data encryption program that uses Temporal Key Integrity Protocol (TKIP) or Advanced Encryption Standard (AES) to improve security.

WPA2   An improvement over WPA that includes dynamic negotiation between the AP and the client for authentication and encryption algorithms. It is a common choice for securing wireless networks.

WPAD (Web Proxy Autodiscovery)   A method of discovering the proxy server IP address and port number.

WPS (WiFi Protected Settings)   A method used to easily configure a wireless device for the SSID and WPA2 security.

write amplification   The minimum amount of storage space affected by a request to write data on a solid-state drive. For example, if the SSD has a 128 KB erase block with a 4 KB file to be saved, 128 KB of memory is erased before the 4 KB file is written.

written communication   An important skill for a person in IT to have, especially when communicating with others and documenting IT issues/processes.

WRP (Windows Resource Protection)   A tool that protects system files and registry keys in Windows.

WWAN (wireless wide area network)   A wireless network that extends across more than one county, such as when WiMAX is used.

X-Y

xcopy   A command that transfers files from one place to another in the command prompt environment.

xD (extreme digital)   A storage device with non-volatile flash memory used for mobile devices.

xDSL   Used to describe the various types of digital subscriber lines (DSLs) available for connecting to the Internet. Examples include ADSL, CDSL, DSL Lite, HDSL, RADSL, SDSL, VDSL, and x2/DSL.

Yahoo   An email provider.

Z

Z-Wave   A wireless standard used in smart homes that allows a wireless mesh topology where each device can talk to another device until the controller is reached.

zero day   A vulnerability in a particular software application that is found by hackers before it is known or fixed by the developer of the application.

ZIF socket (zero insertion force socket)   A common CPU socket that has a lever that provides easy access for CPU removal.

Zigbee   A wireless standard managed by the Zigbee alliance used in low-power, low-distance devices such as sensors and devices found in smart homes, like lights, thermostats, security, cameras, door locks, garage doors, and digital assistants.

zombie   A device that has been hacked and is controlled by someone else or that carries out malicious tasks.

GLOSSARY

Index

INDEX

INDEX

INDEX

INDEX

INDEX

INDEX

INDEX

W

INDEX

INDEX

To receive your 10% off
Exam Voucher, register
your product at:

www.pearsonitcertification.com/register

and follow the instructions.